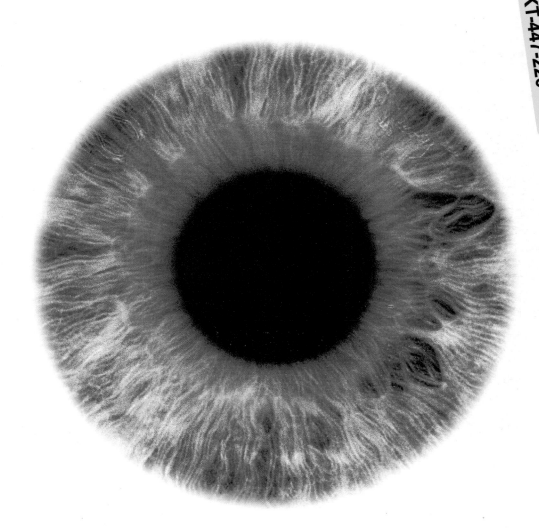

Collins

PSYCHOLOGY
A2 FOR AQA A

CARDWELLCLARKMELDRUMWADELEY

FOURTH EDITION

William Collins' dream of knowledge for all began with the publication of his first book in 1819. A self-educated mill worker, he not only enriched millions of lives, but also founded a flourishing publishing house. Today, staying true to this spirit, Collins books are packed with inspiration, innovation and practical expertise. They place you at the centre of a world of possibility and give you exactly what you need to explore it.

Collins. Do more.

Published by HarperCollinsPublishers Limited
77–85 Fulham Palace Road
Hammersmith
London W6 8JB

Browse the complete Collins catalogue at **www.collinseducation.com**

© HarperCollinsPublishers Limited 2009

Psychology for A Level first published 1996
First A2 edition published 2000
Fourth edition published 2009

Reprint 10 9 8 7 6 5 4 3 2 1

ISBN 978-0-00-725504-7

British Cataloguing in Publication Data.

A cataloguing record for this publication is available from the British Library.

Commissioned by Emma Woolf
Edited by Margaret Levin
Project managed by Jo Kemp
Cover design by Oculus
Typesetting by Ken Vail Graphic Design, Cambridge
Picture research by Jill Thraves
Index compiled by Christine Boylan
Production by Simon Moore
Printed and bound by xxx

Acknowledgements

Claire Meldrum, as always, wishes to thank Stuart for his patience and steadfast support throughout the months spent editing this latest edition. Thanks also go to Claire's past students and colleagues for their insights and constructive comments over many years.

Once again, **Liz Clark** would like to thank Charley for his unwavering, loving support, encouragement and patience over the past year. A writing/editing project of this magnitude and complexity inevitably takes longer than planned and this new edition was no exception! My parents and all the rest of my family also deserve a special mention for being so understanding about the impact of the gestation of this book on family time that can never be regained. Finally, I would like to acknowledge the input of those young people studying A2 psychology – as always, their robust feedback has helped us to improve this latest edition.

Mike Cardwell would like to apologize to his long-suffering wife Denise, who once again has had to put up with his Jekyll and Hyde transformation from attentive husband to the grumpy old man who has spent long hours staring at (and occasionally cursing) a computer screen, while at the same time battling an abysinnian cat for ownership rights of the comfy chair in front of it.

Alison Wadeley would like to thank her husband and daughters for understanding her need for time during the preparation of this book and for mutual support through possibly the busiest 12 months of all our lives. Holly overcame so much to achieve great A-level grades and sail into university, Imogen passed a large number of GCSEs while simultaneously engaging in impressive amounts of extra-curricular drama and Ian's working life was more demanding than ever, but he still managed to be our head chef. We also owe a debt of gratitude to The Funkehmunkehsistaz for keeping us all laughing.

The editors would like to thank Emma Woolf whose commitment and drive have seen this huge project through to completion. Despite the many difficulties and complications involved in producing a book of this size, Emma's focus and determination have never faltered. Our thanks also go to Margaret Levin for copy editing, to the proof readers Jo Kemp, Karen Seymour and Mark Walsh, to Hugh Hillyard-Parker for the chapter summaries, to Ken Vail Graphic Design, and to Christine Boylan, Ros Connolly and Laura Pass.

150 CAR

3 wk Main

Contents

Mike Cardwell has taught psychology for 35 years and is currently Senior Lecturer in social psychology at Bath Spa University. Mike was an A level psychology examiner for over 25 years, including 10 years as Chief Examiner. He has written numerous textbooks for psychology and is an editor of the journal *Psychology Review*.

Currently working at The Open University and previously at the Royal College of Nursing as Head of Distance Learning, **Liz Clark** has always been passionate about flexible education. She is particularly interested in pushing the boundaries of educational innovation and creating learning resources that help to make learning enjoyable and fun, so that future generations can share some of the excitement that she felt when learning about psychology. Her experience of creating highly accessible, interactive learning materials influenced the original ideas and vision behind the first edition of this book back in 1996.

Claire Meldrum has over 25 years experience of teaching A level psychology in both colleges and schools. She has written support materials for A level teachers, revision and study guides for students and has been a consultant and author for the National Extension College's A level course. Now that she has retired from teaching, Claire has more time to spend on developing her interests in art history, theatre and gardening.

Alison Wadeley is Senior Lecturer in Psychology at Bath Spa University. She taught GCSE, AS and A level for 20 years and has many years experience as an examiner for a major awarding body. Alison has published a number of textbooks and revision guides ranging from GCSE to undergraduate level psychology. She is commissioning co-editor for *Psychology Review* to which she also contributes regular articles.

Chris French is Professor of Psychology and Head of the Anomalistic Psychology Research Unit in the Psychology Department at Goldsmiths. He has published over 100 articles and chapters covering a wide range of topics within psychology. His main current area of research is the psychology of paranormal beliefs and anomalous experiences. He frequently appears on radio and television casting a sceptical eye over paranormal claims. He is the editor of *The Skeptic* magazine (UK version).

Dr Mark Griffiths is a Chartered Psychologist and Professor of Gambling Studies at the Nottingham Trent University. He is internationally known for his work into gambling and gaming addictions and has won many awards for his research, including the *John Rosecrance Prize* (1994), *Joseph Lister Prize* (2004) and the *Excellence in the Teaching of Psychology Award* (2006). He has published over 215 refereed research papers, three books, 60 book chapters, and over 550 other articles.

Dr Guy Cumberbatch is a Chartered Psychologist and Director of the Communications Research Group. He has specialized in media psychology for over three decades, particularly the effects of media violence and the representation of minority groups. Guy is proud that half of his work has been commissioned by regulators (such as Ofcom, the Council of Europe, BBFC) and half by broadcasters and production companies (such as the BBC and Warner).

Jane Ogden is Professor in Health Psychology at the University of Surrey. She is involved in research exploring different aspects of eating behaviour, including the control and loss of control over eating, medical and surgical management of obesity and how parents manage their children's diets. She also studies aspects of women's health and coordinates studies into communication in the consultation. She is author of over 100 papers and five books, including *The psychology of eating* and *Health psychology: a textbook*.

Sandie Taylor is Senior Lecturer at Bath Spa University. She has experience of teaching at both A level and university. Her interests in teaching and research span both developmental and criminological psychology: cerebral lateralization and its relationship to human emotion and facial expression; offender profiling; mock juror deliberation; the influence of defendant extra-legal characteristics and social cognition on determining guilt. She has collaborated in the past on projects for the Welsh Office and Probation Service.

Jane Willson has taught psychology for over 20 years at degree and A level and has been a senior examiner with a leading examining board for many years.

Lance Workman is Head of Psychology at Bath Spa University. His research interests include the evolution of cerebral lateralization and its relationship to human emotion and language and development in animals. He is also interested in clinical issues and supervises postgraduate research on autism. Lance regularly works in the media, appearing on radio, television and in national newspapers explaining and discussing psychological principles. He co-authored *Evolutionary Psychology* (2008) with Will Reader.

Credits and permissions

The publishers gratefully acknowledge the following for permission to reproduce material. Every effort has been made to trace copyright holders but if any material has been inadvertently overlooked, the publishers will be pleased to correct this at the earliest opportunity.

Fig 1.1, 1.2 (p.52) Breedlove, S. M., Rosenzweig, M. R. and Watson, N. V.(2007). *Biological Psychology*, Mass: Sinauer.
Fig 1.3 (p.60) – Kalat, *Biological Psychology* (8th Ed), 2004, Belmont, CA: Wadsworth.
Fig. 2.6 (p.72) – Palmer (1975)
Fig. 2.7 (p.73) – Gibson (1950)
Fig 2.10 (p.75) – Palmer (1975b)
Key Research (77) – Harcourt Brace and Co Ltd
Fig 2.22 (p.84) – Scientific American Inc
Fig 2.26 (p.88) – Deregowski (1972)
Source: Tuzin 1982, cited in Sosis 2006 (p155) Herdt, Gilbert H., *Ritualized Homosexuality in Melanesia*, 1984, University of California
Fig 5.6, 5.7, 5.8 (p.183) – Prentice and Jebb (1995)
Fig 8.6 (p.262) – Hughes (1975)
Table 8.5 (p.267) – Vygotsky (1987)
Table 8.6 (p.268) – Bruner et al (1966)
Table 8.8 (p.276) – Kohlberg (1976)
Table 8.9 (p.283) – Adapted from Eisenberg (1986)
Case study (p.332) – Reprinted with permission of John Wiley and Son Inc
Fig 9.1 (p.315) – Zimbardo et al (1995)
Appendix 2 (p.581) – With permission of the McGraw-Hill Companies
Appendix 3 (p.583) – Reprinted with permission from the *Journal of the American Statistical Association* © 1965 by the American Statistical Association. All rights reserved
Appendix 4 (p.584) – Reprinted with permission from the *Journal of the American Statistical Association* © 1972 by the American Statistical Association. All rights reserved

Photographs

The publishers would like to thank the following for permission to reproduce photographs. Page numbers are in brackets and are followed, where necessary, by t (top), b (bottom), l (left) or r (right).

Advertising Archives: 167b, 416, 417, 423
Alamy:8, 39l, 63, 114, 116, 119, 156, 265, 349t, 365t, 366, 377, 378, 401, 501tl, 518c
Ardea: 242
Susan Blackmore: 479
CartoonStock.com: 425, 428
Christopher Brown: 353
Corbis: 15, 30c, bl, br, 43br, 53, 334, 336, 380, 407
Mary Evans Picture Library: 473, 487, 501tr
FLPA: 246
Getty Images:12c, 13, 31, 37l, 39r, 46, 64, 94, 102, 104, 111, 112, 119, 124, 125, 135t, 148, 167t,199, 248, 266, 272, 322, 323t, 339b, 352, 396br, 398, 445, 507, 512, 514, 516, 518t, 519
Ronald Grant Archive: 309
David King Collection: 302b
iStockphoto: 5, 7, 14r, 38, 69, 92, 122, 125, 132, 136, 142, 143b, 144, 147, 150, 151, 161, 164, 174, 176, 179, 192, 197, 203, 215, 227, 232, 237, 241, 255, 284, 285, 287, 312, 325, 339t, 342, 349b, 364, 367, 369, 381, 388, 396bl, 422t, 446, 448, 450, 474, 486, 513, 588
PA Photos:101, 331, 391, 422b,
Mary Evans Picture Library:
Alexander Milgram: 24
Oxford Scientific Films: 239
Rex Features: 6, 9, 12b, 19, 72, 81, 86, 103, 121, 131, 135b, 137, 143c, 154, 155, 288, 307, 365b, 373, 379, 389, 390, 412, 414, 455, 457, 484
Jeffrey A. Schaler, permission granted, www.szasz.com: 302t
Science Photo Library: 30t, 57, 351
Times Newspapers: 71
Philip Zimbardo: 28

This book provides detailed coverage of all aspects of Specification A of the A2 psychology course offered by the Assessment and Qualifications Alliance (AQA).

What's new in A-level psychology?

The most important change is that the Qualifications Curriculum Authority (QCA) has classified psychology as a science and this is reflected in the new AQA specification.

How has this affected the new specification?

Since psychology is a science, students will now study psychological research and scientific methodology. This has been incorporated into the specification as *How Science Works*, which is a set of core concepts that enable the student to understand and contextualize science for themselves, and also to appreciate how scientists investigate scientific phenomena in order to explain the world about us. These concepts are shown in detail in the subject specification published by AQA (www.aqa.org.uk).

We like to think of *How Science Works* as a thread of principles that run throughout your entire psychology course and that hold all the key elements together. Thus, *How Science Works* isn't something that can be studied in isolation, but rather is intrinsic to all aspects of the study of psychology.

The other significant change in the new specification is that research methods are now studied in the context of specific areas of psychology rather than in isolation.

How are these changes reflected in this book?

How Science Works

We have woven *How Science Works* into the main text and into the key features of the book and we flag up its presence by using an icon (shown above), so that you can see exactly when you are practising these skills.

Stretch and Challenge

Stretch and Challenge features encourage you to extend your skills of critical thinking, to undertake independent research and to think like a psychologist.

What are the benefits of using this book?

- **A full coverage of the new AQA specification at exactly the right depth** – delivering all the content and up-to-date research to ensure complete coverage

- **Bringing psychology to life** with our 'Psychology in context' feature that looks at psychology in your everyday world

- **Even more student support and exam preparation** with exam-style practice and in-depth guidance from experienced examiners

- **A strong focus on *How Science Works*** to develop essential evaluation and analysis skills

- **A student-friendly approach with topic maps, engaging activities and visual features** – written by teachers and examiners who understand the needs of psychology students.

Key features

Psychology in context
Membership of the 'human club'

Celebrities and gossip seem to go hand in hand, with part of the attraction of celebrities being the opportunity they offer the rest of us to analyse their lives in fine detail with our friends. Do you have a tendency to gossip? Try the following items from the 'Tendency to Gossip Questionnaire' (Nevo *et al.* 1993).

- I like analysing with a friend the compatibility of celebrity couples.
- I like talking with friends about the personal appearance of celebrities.
- I enjoy analysing with my friends the motives and reasons for the behaviour of celebrities.
- I tend to talk with friends about the love affairs of celebrities.
- I like reading biographies of famous people.

Did you mostly agree with the above statements? No need to worry, Medini and Rosenberg (1976) coined the term 'same-boat phenomenon' to explain how gossiping about famous people serves to confirm our membership of the 'human club'. Hearing about famous people's lives, particularly when they engage in behaviour that is frowned upon (such as getting drunk in public) or that would cause conflict (such as having an affair), tells us that we are not the only person on this planet who engages in such behaviour or who experiences that conflict. Gossip breaks down inhibitions, lifts the 'public mask' and illuminates the 'private face', to find that the private face is not that bad after all (Medini and Rosenberg 1976).

See at a glance how this book delivers the specification content by the **Explaining the specification** table at the start of each chapter.

Immediately engage with new ideas through **Psychology in context** at the start of each topic.

Practise as you learn, using the **Activities** throughout the book.

Activity — Rewarding behaviour

Can you think of examples in your own life when:

1 an aspect of your behaviour is rewarded so much that you cease to feel motivated to do it
2 an aspect of your behaviour is reinforced regularly so you keep it up
3 an aspect of your behaviour is reinforced irregularly and unpredictably so you keep it up?

Some suggestions are given in the Answers to activities on p.603. ▶

Get to grips with **key research studies**, which are clearly broken down into aims, procedures, findings, conclusions and evaluations of the research. Many of the key studies feature a further analysis section, which enables you to further develop important analytical skills.

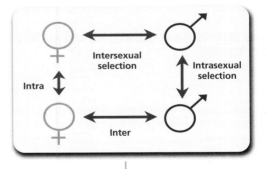

'Lads mags' condemned for their possible influence on parenting

HOW SCIENCE WORKS

Key research: Geher *et al.* (2007)

According to Conservative spokesman, Michael Gove, some modern men's magazines (the so-called 'lads mags' such as *Nuts* and *Zoo*) may be influencing young males and creating a generation of feckless fathers with little or no respect for traditional family values (September 2008). Gove (2008) believes that it is important to see parenting 'as a shared responsibility, with fathers playing an equal and complementary role, to mothers'.

The relatively low level of male parental investment in the UK and other Westernized cultures may, therefore, be attributed to cultural forces which 'corrupt' what would otherwise be a greater share of parental responsibility. We have already seen that men demonstrate a greater interest than women in pursuing several short-term mates, and they also show less commitment to the offspring produced by these mate pairings (Buss and Schmitt 1993). Parental investment theory also suggests that females are better prepared (both physically and psychologically) than males for dealing with infants. But are these differences a product of evolutionary or cultural forces? Geher *et al.* (2007) asked 91 undergraduates (who were not parents) from the State University of New York to complete a parental investment perception scale, which measured how prepared they perceived themselves to be for parenting. This part of the study found no real difference in the perceptions of males and females in their perceived readiness for parenting.

However, this was not the only measure used in the study. Male and female participants were then exposed to a series of statements that illustrated typical scenarios where parenting might be seen as costly (e.g. it would be necessary to cancel a work appointment to look after a sick child) in terms of the investment of time and effort needed. As participants viewed these scenarios, their **autonomic nervous system** (ANS) arousal was measured. Males showed significantly higher ANS arousal compared to females when presented with scenarios that emphasized the psychological costs of parenting. This finding is consistent with previous research, which suggests that males are less prepared to confront issues associated with parenting than females.

Evaluation

The differences between *perceived* parental readiness and *actual* parental readiness (as measured by ANS arousal) can be explained in terms of the **social desirability bias** associated with self-reports of attitudes towards parenting. Males may well recognize the importance of coming across as having parenting potential when courting females; heterosexual males are, therefore, more likely to be motivated to see themselves as being capable of parenting (Geher *et al.* 2007).

Psychological material is made even more accessible through the frequent use of **diagrams**, **tables** and **pictures**.

	Intra	Intersexual selection	Intrasexual selection	Inter

1	**Sampling**	The couple explores the rewards and costs in a variety of relationships.
2	**Bargaining**	The couple 'costs out' the relationship and identifies the sources of profit and loss.
3	**Commitment**	The couple settles into a relationship; the exchange of rewards becomes relatively predictable.
4	**Institutionalization**	The interactions are established; the couple have 'settled down'.

Source: Adapted from Thibaut and Kelley (1959)

IDA boxes are designed to help you use issues, debates and approaches as tools of analysis, essential if you are to earn high marks in your exams. The Introduction to issues, debates and approaches (see p.2) also provides helpful background and context here.

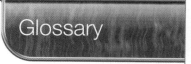

IDA Cultural bias in research

There is a real danger of making cross-cultural psychology just 'doing psychology in exotic places', i.e. taking issues and phenomena that are of interest to (dominant) Western psychology and seeing if they replicate in other cultures. This takes no account of what is important in that 'other' culture. Kim and Berry (1993) address this issue with a call for *indigenous* psychologies, which study phenomena that have developed within particular cultures and are seen as important and functional to those cultures (rather than risking a psychology of North American self-interest).

Understand key concepts and terms by using the **Glossary** of key terms at the back of the book.

Glossary

Ablation: surgical removal of brain tissue.

Absolute zero: a quality of a measurement scale such that zero signifies absolutely nothing and below which it is impossible to go. This is in contrast to other scales, such as degrees centigrade on which zero signifies a temperature below which there are minus values.

Accommodation: the process of modifying an existing schema by expanding it or creating a new one when new information, a new object or a new situation cannot be assimilated into the original schema.

Aggression: the delivery of an aversive stimulus from one person to another, with intent to harm and with an expectation of causing such harm, when the other person is motivated to escape or avoid the stimulus (Geen, 1990).

Agoraphobia: a fear and avoidance of public places.

Adaptive response (or characteristic): an evolved behaviour (or trait) that increases the likelihood of the individual's survival and successful reproduction.

Addictive personality: a concept that some (usually lay people) use to explain why some people are more prone to addiction than others. It also suggests nthat some people will inevitably become dependent on drug taking or some other activity because of a personality fault.

Alien abduction: alleged phenomenon of individuals being taken against their will by extraterrestrial beings, often involving them being taken on board spaceships and subjected to medical examination.

variation has determined the results obtained. In a well-designed experiment, this should be due to the effect of the independent variable.

Altruistic: helping another person with no personal gain and some cost to the person doing the helping.

Androcentric: refers to the tendency of some theories to offer an interpretation of women, based on an understanding of the lives of men (i.e. a male perspective).

Androcentrism: a view of human behaviour that is based on and concerning males only.

Androgyny: the tendency in a female body to approximate to that of a male and vice versa.

Anomalistic psychology: sub-discipline of psychology primarily concerned with developing and testing non-paranormal explanations for ostensibly paranormal experiences and related beliefs.

Anorexia nervosa: a form of eating disorder that involves under-eating and weight loss (see also **restricting anorexia** and **binge eating/purging anorexia**).

Antagonists: a drug which 'acts against' or blocks the action of a naturally occurring substance in the body. For example, antipsychotic drugs work by blocking receptors for the neurotransmitter dopamine, thus preventing it from stimulating post-synaptic nerve cells.

Anti-anxiety drugs: minor tranquillizers designed to reduce levels of anxiety.

Anxiety disorders: the most common of adult mental disorders, characterized by such severe anxiety and fear that the sufferer cannot lead a normal life. Phobic disorder is the most

A **Check your understanding** feature at the end of each topic will help you review what you have just read and help you pinpoint any areas you need to revisit.

CHECK YOUR UNDERSTANDING

Check your understanding of eating behaviour by answering the following questions. Try to do this from memory. You can check your answers by looking back through Topic 1, Eating behaviour.

1. List at least five different cognitions that people may hold about food.

2. Describe one social cognition model that has been used to predict eating behaviour.

3. What are the main strengths and limitations of a social cognitive approach to eating behaviour?

4. Outline the three mechanisms that illustrate a developmental approach to eating behaviour.

5. Explain how parental control can influence children's food preferences.

6. How can mood influence eating behaviour?

7. Explain how stress can affect what people eat.

8. What is the preload/taste-test method and how has it been used to investigate eating behaviour?

9. What key factors may influence successful weight loss and maintenance?

10. Explain why people on a diet sometimes overeat when trying to lose weight.

A visual overview of the key points in the chapter content is provided by the **Chapter summary** – ideal for revision.

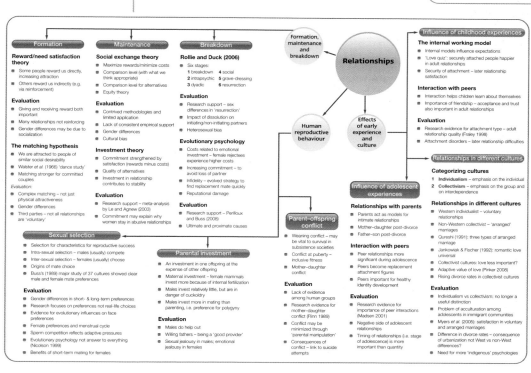

Introduction to approaches, issues and debates in psychology

This introductory chapter differs from the other chapters in the book, as it provides background that will be helpful when you study the later chapters. You will encounter these approaches, issues and debates in the context of the main areas of Units 3 and 4 of the A2 specification for AQA (Specification A).

You will already have discovered, through your AS studies, that psychology is a fascinating subject focusing on many topics of real human interest that can affect our daily lives. There are also a number of different approaches in psychology, and some key issues and debates that occupy the minds of psychologists. This chapter introduces these in three sections:

- Section 1 provides an overview of five different approaches: two biological approaches (the physiological approach and the evolutionary approach), the psychodynamic approach, the behavioural approach and the cognitive approach.

- Section 2 focuses on three key issues: gender bias and cultural bias in psychological research, and ethical challenges faced by psychologists when undertaking research with human participants and non-human animals.

- Section 3 introduces some of the debates that are currently being discussed in psychology, including arguments for and against free will, determinism and reductionism; the nature–nurture debate, and arguments about whether or not psychology can be regarded as a science.

Section 1: Approaches in psychology

Introduction

Psychologists offer many different explanations for human behaviour and experience. The type of explanation depends on the **approach** (perspective) adopted by the psychologist. Inevitably, you will encounter different explanations for the same event. This does not mean that only one explanation is right and all the rest are wrong, but rather that explanations are influenced by the approach used.

Like these three women, psychologists have characteristic ways of looking at behaviour and investigate the same thing in different ways.

The different approaches in psychology influence how we view people and what methods are used to study specific phenomena. Each approach adds to our overall understanding of what makes people behave and experience the world in the way they do, but no single approach is able to provide the whole story. These approaches are sometimes referred to as 'perspectives', but whatever we choose to call them, each approach is made up of the same components:

- a *set of assumptions* (or key concepts) about the basic influences on behaviour and experience

- *specific methods of investigating* particular aspects of behaviour and experience (**methodology**)

- *evidence* that adds to our overall understanding of people.

The approaches outlined in this first section of the chapter differ quite considerably, and you may wonder how such different approaches can co-exist within the same discipline. However, two things unite them:

1 their focus on the behaviour and experience of individual people

2 their attempts to collect evidence systematically in order to enhance our understanding of human and non-human animals.

We will consider four of the traditional approaches used by psychologists. They focus on different aspects of behaviour and experience:

1 what we *are made of* and *how we evolved* (the biological approach)
2 what we *feel* (the psychodynamic approach)
3 what we *do* (the behavioural approach)
4 what we *think* (the cognitive approach).

The biological approach

The biological approach includes both **physiological** and **evolutionary** explanations of behaviour, each of which can be regarded as an approach in its own right because it has a set of core assumptions and a unique way of investigating behaviour. These two approaches will therefore be discussed separately.

The physiological approach

The main assumption of the physiological approach is that all behaviour can be explained in terms of bodily activity.

Key concepts of the physiological approach

Bodily activity can be described using two of the major systems of the body:

1 the central nervous system (CNS), which consists of the brain and spinal cord
2 the autonomic nervous system (ANS), which controls the release of hormones.

Both of these systems help to explain how people behave. The CNS provides rapid responses; the ANS is slightly slower and governs behaviours that are largely outside conscious control (they are automatic).

The central nervous system (CNS)

A summary of the central nervous system is given below.

Brain organization

The brain is divided into two hemispheres. Research has suggested that the two hemispheres have different characteristics. For example, the left hemisphere, which usually contains the language centres, is generally more verbal, whereas the right hemisphere is more involved with visuo-spatial processing and emotion (see Fig. 1).

The brain is also divided into lobes, each associated with different activities. For example, the frontal lobe contains the motor cortex (responsible for fine movement) and the pre-frontal cortex (responsible for forward planning and goal-directed behaviour, as well as working memory).

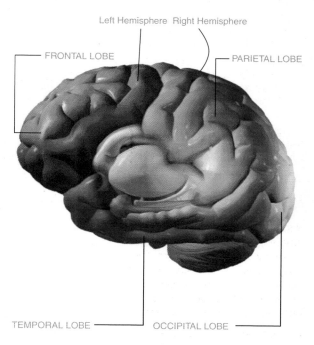

Left Hemisphere Right Hemisphere

FRONTAL LOBE   PARIETAL LOBE

TEMPORAL LOBE   OCCIPITAL LOBE

Figure 1 *The brain*

Deeper inside the brain are many important sub-cortical structures such as the limbic system (the centre for emotions) and the hypothalamus (which regulates the autonomic nervous system). Olds and Milner (1954) identified a specific region in the hypothalamus (the pleasure centre) which may be used to explain reinforcement: when an animal's behaviour is reinforced this part of the brain is activated producing a sensation of pleasure. The same sensation can be created by directly stimulating this part of the brain.

Many aspects of human behaviour can be explained in terms of localized areas of the brain (see panel, London taxi drivers). When certain regions of the brain are damaged, they lead to characteristic behaviours. For example, Wernicke and Broca studied patients with localized brain damage which permitted them to demonstrate the function of specific language centres.

London taxi drivers

A study of London taxi drivers by Maguire *et al.* (2000) showed that an area of the hippocampus was active when the drivers recalled their routes around the capital, and that this area was bigger than in other adults. This is not because taxi drivers were born this way but because their hippocampi had responded to increased use.

Brain chemistry: neurotransmitters

The last 30 years have seen a dramatic growth in our knowledge about the way chemicals affect our behaviour and experience. The centre of the action is the synapse – the gap between nerve cells that is bridged by the release and uptake of neurotransmitters (see Fig. 2). It has been found, for example, that morphine and other opium-based drugs attach themselves to specific receptor sites at some synapses. They are able to do this because they resemble the class of neurotransmitters called 'endorphins' (Snyder 1984). Opiates and endorphins block pain pathways.

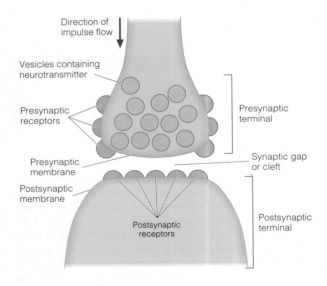

Figure 2 *The synapse*

Other important neurotransmitters include *serotonin*, *dopamine* and *noradrenaline* (norepinephrine).

Neurotransmitters have a wide range of effects, depending on the neuron they are acting on. For example:

- low levels of serotonin in the brain lead to abnormal behaviours such as depression, suicide, impulsive aggression, alcoholism, sexual deviance and explosive rage

- high levels of serotonin have been associated with obsessive compulsion, fearfulness, lack of self-confidence and shyness

- dopamine affects brain processes that control movement, emotional responses and the ability to experience pleasure and pain. It may be that this link with pleasure explains the role of dopamine in addictions to things such as drugs, sex and chocolate. According to Volkow *et al.* (1997), dopamine may be 'the master molecule of addiction' which creates intense feelings from any enjoyable activity. High levels of dopamine have also been linked to hallucinations and schizophrenia (see Chapter 9, p.300).

The autonomic nervous system (ANS)

The autonomic nervous system has two branches:

1 the *parasympathetic division* which governs the resting state

2 the *sympathetic division* which is associated with bodily arousal; when heart rate and blood pressure increase, fats and carbohydrates are mobilized, and activity in the digestive system slows down. This bodily arousal – 'fight or flight' – takes place when adrenaline and noradrenaline are produced by the adrenal medulla when activated by the hypothalamus. *Adrenaline* and *noradrenaline* are hormones, as well as neurotransmitters.

Hormones

The ANS produces its effects either through direct neural stimulation or by stimulating the release of hormones from endocrine glands (such as the adrenal and pineal glands). Hormones are biochemical substances released into the bloodstream; they are present in very small quantities and individual molecules have a very short life, so their effects disappear quickly if they are not secreted continuously.

There are a large number of other hormones. For example:

- *melatonin* is released by the pineal gland and acts on the brainstem sleep mechanisms to help synchronize the phases of sleep and activity

- *testosterone* is released in the testicles and may influence aggressiveness

- *oxytocin* is released by the pituitary gland and affects milk production and female orgasms.

Some hormones are released as a response to external stimuli, such as the pineal gland responding to reduced daylight. Other hormones follow a circadian rhythm, with one peak and one trough every 24 hours. For example, levels of *cortisol* rise about an hour before you wake up and contribute to feelings of wakefulness or arousal.

Pheromones

Pheromones are similar to hormones and when released by one individual can affect the behaviour of another individual of the same species. Russell *et al.* (1980) reported that women's menstrual cycles became synchronized if sweat (which contains pheromones) from one woman was transferred to another.

Methods used by the physiological approach

Physiological psychologists use a variety of methods, including laboratory and natural experiments (see Chapter 2, p.96), and case studies of brain-damaged individuals (see Chapter 2, pp.96–7). Such methods may involve the use of techniques to measure hormone levels or brain activity. Methods used to investigate brain function can be broadly divided into invasive and non-invasive techniques.

Invasive techniques of studying the brain

Invasive techniques involve direct interference with the brain:

- *Electrical stimulation* is one of the oldest techniques: thin wire electrodes can be implanted in the brain and used to stimulate brain neurons artificially to investigate their effects on behaviour. For example, Penfield (1958) stimulated the temporal lobe in humans and some people reported experiencing vivid memories from their childhood.

- *Chemical stimulation* involves administering drugs that either stimulate a post-synaptic receptor (stimulants or agonists) or, by combining with the receptor, inactivate it (blockers or antagonists). For example, to investigate the role of dopamine synapses in behaviour, researchers give animals drugs that stimulate or block dopamine receptors. Conclusions can be drawn about the effect of the dopamine system by observing the behavioural effects.

- *Ablation and lesioning* involve the physical destruction of brain tissue. Thousands of experiments have been done using these techniques with non-human animals. Early experiments involved rather primitive needle points or knife cuts. Today, localized areas of damage, or 'lesions', are usually produced using thin wire electrodes. A current is passed through which heats the tip of the electrode and the heat creates a small sphere of destruction around the tip. Psychosurgery, which still continues on a small scale (see Chapter 10, p.353), also involves making lesions.

As well as systematic damage in non-human animals, researchers also study accidental damage in humans. Brain tumours, strokes, car crashes and other accidents can damage brain tissue and produce effects on behaviour that can be systematically studied.

Non-invasive techniques of studying the brain

Non-invasive techniques do not involve direct interference with the brain; rather, they record electrical activity from the skull surface, or create images of the brain using a variety of scanners:

- *Recording electrical activity* – The electroencephalograph (EEG) records the electrical activity of billions of cortical neurons, using a number of small metal electrodes on the surface of the skull. Certain patterns of electrical activity correlate highly with behavioural states (see Chapter 1, p.56).

- *Scanning and imaging* – Brain scanning and imaging have become the main sources of information on human brain function since the technology was developed in the early 1970s. *Functional magnetic resonance imaging (fMRI scanning)* involves placing the head in a powerful magnetic field and bombarding the brain with radio waves. Molecules in the brain

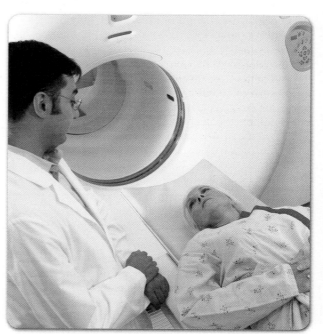

An fMRI scanning machine

vibrate in response to the radio waves and emit radio waves of their own which are used to create an accurate, three-dimensional picture of brain structures. *Positron emission tomography (PET scanning)* involves injecting radioactive glucose into the bloodstream. The more active parts of the brain take up more glucose and emit more radioactivity; a computer is used to generate an activity map of the brain. This procedure can be used to identify, for instance, those parts of the brain that are most active during speech or problem-solving or recognizing faces, etc. This ability to correlate activity in different brain areas with psychological functions makes PET scanning a very useful computer-based technique.

Evaluation of the physiological approach

- *Determinist* – An entirely physiological view of human behaviour suggests that we are not capable of self-determination (free will) and are ruled by predictable bodily functions. On the positive side, the physiological approach lends itself to scientific investigation, as it assumes determinist relationships between variables (i.e. that everything has a cause and an effect).

- *Reductionist* – One way to understand complex behaviours is to break them down into smaller units in order to discover causal relationships. Rose (1997) suggests that there are many different levels of explanation, with the physiological level located at the opposite end to the sociological (explaining behaviour in terms of social groups). There are advantages associated with each level of explanation. However, the challenge is in knowing which kind of explanation to select. Selecting the wrong level may overlook a better understanding of a behaviour. For example, the use of an antidepressant to treat depression may miss the *real* causes of a person's depression (e.g. a family problem). Thus **reductionism** has both advantages and disadvantages.

- The **mind–body** challenge – One of the main challenges with the 'lower' levels of explanation is that they suggest all behaviour can be reduced to physical activity (the body) and deny the existence of separate mental states (the mind). Ryle (1949) described the mind as nothing more than a 'ghost in the machine'. Others, such as 'dualists', believe in separate mental states and the possibility that such mental states can control physical states (and vice versa).

- Individual and cultural differences – Physiological explanations can explain individual differences such as differences between men and women. However, they don't explain why people respond differently to the same drugs, nor why they react differently to stressful situations. Nor can they explain cultural differences. In fact, much of the research has been carried out with male undergraduates and mistakenly generalized to all people. For instance, the human stress response was initially assumed to be universal, whereas it is now recognized that not all people respond in the same way.

- Useful applications – Understanding how the body works has led to many therapeutic interventions, such as treating mental illness with drugs. However, some of these treatments have not been entirely successful (see Chapter 10, pp.350–53).

(see Chapter 10, pp.350–53).

> **Activity** **Explaining your behaviour in physiological terms**
>
> At this very moment what aspects of your behaviour can you explain using physiological concepts?

The evolutionary approach

If you had to select one scientific idea that has had the greatest effect on modern thought, you might well choose the theory of evolution. This has transformed the way we look at ourselves and has influenced psychology, particularly the growing interest in genetic explanations of behaviour. In 1859, Darwin published his well-known book entitled *On the Origin of Species*, which presented an argument for the development of species over time through the process of natural selection.

Darwin (1809–1882)

Key concepts of the evolutionary approach

Natural selection

According to Darwin's (1859) account of evolution, natural selection influences the way that species change over time and become increasingly better adapted to their environment (i.e. possess characteristics that enhance their survival and reproduction). These are the key features of natural selection:

- Individuals have unique genetic characteristics, including the way they behave.
- Some individuals survive and breed, while others do not.
- The genetic characteristics of the survivors are retained.
- The genetic characteristics of those who do not breed are lost.

What this means is that the characteristics that enable some individuals to survive and reproduce are likely to be passed to the next generation. The species then develops through a process of selective breeding, responding to selective pressures exerted by the social and physical environment. Characteristics which do not 'fit' the environment are not selected, while those that do fit are passively selected. Note that *characteristics* are selected, not individuals or species.

Sexual selection

Darwin recognized that the principle of natural selection could not explain all behaviour. For example, it cannot explain why some animals possess characteristics that appear to threaten their survival, such as the peacock's bright and lengthy tail, which does not help the bird to fly faster or better and, in fact, would actually appear to threaten an individual's survival rather than enhance it.

According to the principles of natural selection, such a characteristic should not continue. Darwin (1871) proposed that the force of natural selection is complemented by the force of sexual selection: individuals possess features that make them attractive to the opposite sex or help them compete with members of the same sex for access to mates. These features mean

The peacock's tail

that the possessor breeds successfully, whereas those individuals without the features are less successful. Thus, traits solely concerned with increasing reproductive success are naturally selected and retained.

In general, it is the males of any species that possess sexually selected traits. This is because females are generally the selectors and so males that possess attractive traits are more successful in reproduction. The reason why females are selectors is because they produce relatively few eggs at a greater physiological cost compared with sperm. Those females who take the greatest care with each reproduction are the most successful in the long term, whereas males, who produce thousands of sperm, do best by mating as often as possible (see Chapter 3, p.115).

Kin selection

The issue of altruism also presents a major problem for the theory of natural selection. Any behaviour that is selfless should not be naturally selected because it does not promote the possessor's survival. Darwin could not explain this, but sociobiologists (who seek to explain the evolution of social behaviours such as altruism in terms of adaptiveness) have provided an answer. Hamilton (1963) argued that natural selection does not operate directly on individuals but on their genetic make-up. This means that an individual may pass on their genes to future generations not just by means of their own reproductive success, but also by facilitating the reproductive success of genetic relatives, such as caring for the offspring of close relatives, since they share a significant number of genes. The phrase the 'selfish gene' was used by Dawkins (1976) to describe the fact that it is genes that are the driving force behind evolution. Hamilton used the phrase 'inclusive fitness' to describe an individual's own fitness, together with their effect on the fitness of any relative.

Mental modules

Cosmides and Tooby (1987) took the argument a step further. They proposed that human behaviour was not directly related to genes, but that underlying psychological mechanisms (or mental modules) were.

These genetically determined modules evolved in our ancestral past in response to the selective pressures operating at that time. Mental modules evolved in the same way that complex physical structures (such as the eye) evolved. This 'ancestral past' of behavioural evolution is called the 'environment of evolutionary adaptation' (EEA), which occurred some 35 000 to three million years ago. This approach to understanding human behaviour has been called 'evolutionary psychology' – the view that in order to understand a particular behaviour you need to appreciate what natural selection designed it to do.

The rank theory of depression

An example of the evolutionary approach is the rank theory of depression, which proposes that depression is an adaptive response to losing rank in a status conflict. Loss triggers a 'yielding sub-routine'. This response is adaptive because it helps the individual adjust to the fact that they must now adopt a subordinate position in the dominance hierarchy. It also shows the winner that they have really won and should cease conflict, with no further damage to the loser. When this mental module is activated in situations of loss today, the response may not be adaptive. This evolutionary explanation can help us understand the ultimate cause of the behaviour, i.e. the underlying reason for the response, rather than the proximate (immediate) cause (e.g. loss of rank).

Methods used by the evolutionary approach

Demonstrating genetic causes

The basis of any evolutionary explanation is that the target behaviour is inherited. The process of natural selection (and sexual selection and kin selection) applies only to behaviours that have a genetic basis. Therefore, one way to investigate such explanations is to demonstrate whether the behaviour has a genetic cause.

Kinship studies

The most common way to do this is through the use of kinship studies (sometimes called 'concordance studies'), which investigate twins, adopted children and their biological and non-biological relatives, or simply study individuals who are related. For example, the genetic basis of IQ has been investigated by comparing the IQs of identical twins (which should be the same if caused entirely by genes, even when the twins are reared apart). Identical and non-identical twins can also be compared. Identical twins should have a greater concordance for IQ than non-identical twins, who share only 50 per cent of their genes (see Chapter 7, p.247).

Studies have also been carried out with adopted children, comparing their IQs with those of their biological parents and adopted parents and/or siblings. Finally, research has considered whether there is increasing similarity in IQ the more closely related two individuals are (for example, siblings share 25 per cent of their genes, parents and children share 50 per cent of their genes).

Gene mapping

Gene mapping is a different approach to studying genetic causes. Analysis of chromosomes from different individuals allows researchers to discover the genes certain individuals share in common. So, if one looked at the chromosomes from highly intelligent children and compared these with the genes of less intelligent children, it may be possible to find out whether certain genes were present in one group rather than another.

Experiments

It is also possible to conduct *natural experiments*, where environmental conditions vary naturally, such as degree of relatedness (the independent variable), to observe the effect this has on characteristics that may be inherited, such as IQ (the dependent variable). There have also been attempts to conduct *field experiments* to test the predictions of evolutionary theory, although these invariably involve non-human animals (see panel, Male widow birds).

> ### Male widow birds
>
> Andersson (1982) cut the tails of male widow birds and replaced them with tails of varying lengths to see which birds were preferred by females – the females preferred those with longer tails, thus supporting the hypothesis that females prefer males with exaggerated characteristics.
>
>

Observation and survey research

Psychologists working within the evolutionary approach sometimes use observational methods. For example, Dunbar (1995) investigated the prediction arising from evolutionary theory that women should seek men with resources, but advertise their own physical attractiveness, and vice versa for men. An analysis of 'lonely hearts' advertisements supported this hypothesis. Survey

methods are also employed: Buss (1989) carried out a survey of men and women's preferences in 37 different cultures and found that the predictions arising from evolutionary theory were supported (see Chapter 3, p.113).

Cross-cultural studies

Human behaviours that have evolved through selective pressure should be the same all over the world. Therefore, if people in different cultures are studied, significant differences should not be found. This type of research has been used to support, for example, *attachment theory* – parents and infants in different cultures were studied and attachment behaviours were reported to be relatively similar all over the world, which suggests that this is an innate and adaptive behaviour (Van Ijzendoorn and Kroonenberg 1988).

> **Activity** **Explaining behaviour in evolutionary terms**
>
> Try to use the evolutionary approach to explain some aspect of human behaviour. For example, you might have observed that newborn babies have a very strong grip – if they ever get hold of your hair, you certainly know about it! This gripping behaviour might well have had some advantage when mothers carried their young around – those who managed to hold on to her body hair were more likely to survive than those who did not manage to do so.
>
> What about our anxiety/fear responses, enjoyment of dancing, or pleasure associated with good food? How might the evolutionary approach attempt to explain why older men marry younger women more often than older women marry younger men? Indeed, could the evolutionary approach also explain why people are more disapproving of the latter kind of relationships?

Evaluation of the evolutionary approach

- *Reductionist and determinist* – Like physiological explanations, evolutionary explanations may be regarded as an oversimplification. They suggest that adaptiveness is the single guiding principle for complex behaviours. Such explanations are also determinist because they propose that behaviour is genetically determined by past environments and that current behaviour is not subject to free will.

- *Difficult to falsify* – The concept of adaptiveness can be applied to many behaviours but is difficult to disprove. Popper (1959) argued that it should be possible to disprove any explanation, otherwise there is no way of establishing its validity (see panel, Post-industrial moths).

Post-industrial moths

There is some experimental evidence to support the process of natural selection, such as Kettlewell's (1955) study of how moths adapted to the new, post-industrial environment in England. Within a short period of time, a species that had been light-coloured became darker in colour, presumably because they were less likely to be eaten on trees blackened by smoke from the new industries. However, causal conclusions are not justified because this is a natural experiment.

- *Based on research with non-human animals* – Darwinians and sociobiologists present a range of examples from the animal world to support their argument, although it is difficult to see the similarity between, for example, wasp society and human society. It is also worth noting that they offer relatively few examples of mammal behaviour to support their theory. Human behaviour is affected by many other factors, such as emotion and thought.

- *Advantages of the evolutionary approach* –This approach considers ultimate, rather than proximate, causes and may, therefore, lead to more valid ways of treating apparently maladaptive behaviours by understanding their adaptive significance. For example, evolutionary psychiatrists propose that it is necessary to understand the ultimate problem (the individual's yielding behaviour) in order to treat depression, rather than focus on the proximate problem (the feeling of being depressed).

The psychodynamic approach

Freud's approach to understanding human behaviour – psychoanalysis – has had a profound effect in psychology. His approach is one of many that share some common assumptions, while differing fundamentally in others. Contemporaries of Freud, such as Carl Jung and Alfred Adler, were inspired by Freudian theory, but emphasized different issues in human development and experience. Collectively these theories are described as '**psychodynamic**' because they emphasize the factors that *motivate* behaviour (i.e. the 'dynamics' of behaviour).

The Freudian iceberg

Freud's ideas about the mind have been likened to an iceberg, with the area above the water being the conscious mind, and that under the water, the unconscious mind. In this image, the *id* lies below the surface of conscious awareness and cannot be seen (so we are unaware of its influence). As with an iceberg, the majority of the mass of the mind, and therefore its greatest potential influence, is

Freud (1856–1939)

under the surface. This analogy should not be overworked, but it does help to illustrate the relationship between consciousness and Freud's three aspects of the mind.

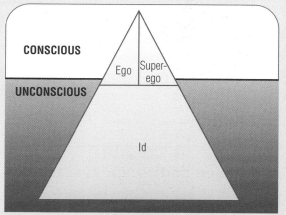

Figure 3 *The iceberg representation of the human mind*

At this point it might be helpful to re-read the material on Freud's psychoanalytic theory in your AS textbook (*Psychology AS for AQA A,* pp.228–230).

Key concepts of the psychodynamic approach

The structure of the mind

Freud believed that the human mind had conscious and unconscious areas. The unconscious part of the mind was seen as being dominated by the '*id*' – a primitive part of the personality that pursues pleasure and gratification. The id is not concerned with social rules, but only with self-gratification and is driven by the pleasure principle. This disregard for the consequences of behaviour is referred to as 'primary process thinking'.

The second area is the '*ego*', which dominates the conscious mind. This part of our mind is in contact with the outside world and considers the consequences of an action. Thus the ego carries out 'secondary process thinking' and is driven by the reality principle.

The third part of the mind is the '*superego*' which develops around the age of 4, as we become more aware of the rules and conventions of society and, specifically, of our parents. It contains our social conscience and guides us towards socially acceptable behaviour through the experience of guilt and anxiety when we do something wrong. According to Freud, the ego and the superego are located largely in the conscious mind, while the id is in the unconscious area of our mind.

Drives and ego defences

According to Freud, we have two drives or instincts – sex and aggression. Everything we do is motivated by one of these two drives:

- *Sex* represents our drive to live, prosper and produce offspring.
- *Aggression* represents our need to stay alive and stave off threats to our existence, power and prosperity.

When the sexual instinct is high, the id demands gratification and triggers behaviours that will result in sexual (or sensual) gratification. In most civilized societies, however, sexual gratification is not something that can be achieved without considering social morality. The superego may, therefore, *oppose* gratification, with the result that the ego is caught between

Stage in development	Description	Personality structure	Fixations	Effects on adult personality
The oral stage (0–18 months)	The infant's main source of pleasure is the mouth.	The id	Fixations may be caused by insufficient breastfeeding or too much pleasure at the breast.	The oral receptive personality is very trusting and dependent on others whereas the oral aggressive personality is dominating. Orally fixated individuals may seek gratification through smoking, thumb-sucking and pencil chewing.
The anal stage (18–36 months)	Pleasure is derived from expelling and/or withholding faeces.	The ego	Fixations may be caused by strict toilet training, or by intense pleasure associated with, for example, smearing faeces on the wall.	The anal-retentive character wants to make a terrible mess and therefore builds up defences against this, such as being very orderly, rigid and hating waste. Other associated traits include stinginess, punctuality, possessiveness. The anal-expulsive character is very generous and may also be creative and productive.
The phallic stage (3–6 years)	Children focus on their genitals and on the opposite-gender parent. Resolution is by identifying with the same-gender parent.	The superego	Fixations are caused by a lack of identification with an adult.	A fixation at this stage results in the phallic personality type who is self-assured, vain and impulsive. Conflicts may result in homosexuality, authority problems, and rejection of appropriate gender roles.
Latency stage	Little development takes place. Boys and girls do not interact much.			
The genital stage (Puberty)	The main source of pleasure is again the genitals. Focus is also on the development of independence.		If some issues remain unresolved, the individual can't shift focus from their immediate needs to larger responsibilities involving others.	

Table 1 *Freud's psychosexual stages and their consequences*

two conflicting demands – the id demands immediate gratification, while the superego demands conformity to the moral conventions of society. The ego struggles to maintain a balance between these conflicting demands and is helped by ego defences. Such defences deal with the anxiety created by conflict – for example, repression shifts anxieties into the unconscious, while regression deals with anxiety by returning to an earlier, safer stage of development (see *Psychology AS for AQA A*, pp.229–30).

Ego defences are not necessarily unhealthy – in fact, the lack of such defences may lead to problems. However, we sometimes employ these defences inappropriately or overuse them, which can be destructive.

Psychosexual stages of development

Another of the key aspects of Freud's theory is the claim that people move through a series of developmental stages. Each of the stages in Table 1 is characterized by a focus on a different region of the body. Freud believed that an individual's libido (or sexual drive) is fixated on a part of the body during particular periods of a child's life. The focus on particular body regions is related to phases of development: the mouth is important in the early months, the anal region becomes important during toilet training, and the genitals are the focus during gender identity development.

If we receive either too much or too little gratification, we become fixated in a particular stage, i.e. we continue to have the same demand for gratification at that stage throughout the rest of our life. This condition is thought to produce a variety of neurotic behaviours, depending on the type of fixation. Freud believed that to deal with fixation at any particular stage, we must regress (go back) to that stage and resolve the issues that led to the fixation.

Methods used by the psychodynamic approach

Case studies

Freud supported his theory of personality by providing case histories of patients, indicating how the patient's behaviour and experience could be explained using psychoanalytic concepts. Freud used several techniques to enable unconscious thoughts to be revealed, including free association and dream analysis:

- *Free association* – A client is asked to lie on a couch with the therapist out of sight, and to allow the free flow of feelings, thoughts and images. The client expresses these without any censorship while the therapist listens carefully. The therapist may request further elaboration or ask the client to comment on the personal significance of any associations. It is assumed that associations arise from, and therefore reflect, internal dynamic conflicts.

- *Dream analysis* – Since Freud believed that unconscious thoughts are expressed uncensored in a person's dreams, discussions of dream content may offer a way to access the unconscious mind. However, the true meaning (the actual or latent content) is disguised in dreams to protect the conscious mind, so the therapist has to try to understand the symbolic form (the manifest content) of the dream.

Case studies are likely to draw on the unique experiences of only a few individuals because they are concerned with unusual behaviours (and therefore ones that are less usually encountered) and/or because of the in-depth nature of the method. It is difficult, therefore, to make generalizations about other people on the basis of individual cases, each with a unique set of circumstances.

Experiments

Several experiments have investigated Freud's explanations, such as those that investigated repression (e.g. McGinnies 1949 and Myers and Brewin 1994). So although Freud tended to rely on case studies as the main method to study aspects of psychodynamic theory, experiments are sometimes used.

Evaluation of the psychodynamic approach

- *The theory of psychoanalysis lacks empirical support* – This is largely because the concepts are not falsifiable (i.e. cannot be demonstrated to be wrong – they can be made to fit most sets of data). There is, however, empirical support for some of the concepts, such as repression, and a limited amount of support for personality types.

- *Determinist and reductionist* – The objection to determinist accounts is they suggest that individuals have no ability to be self-determining. Reductionism tends to oversimplify complex behaviours, which may prevent us from investigating more complex and possibly more useful explanations, such as social and cultural influences.

- *Overemphasis on sexual influences* – Such factors may have been important in 19th century society, but are less applicable today. Subsequent psychodynamic theories (such as Erikson's) have emphasized social influences more.

- *Recognition of influences of which we are unaware* – Psychoanalysis has made a significant contribution to our understanding of unconscious motivations and the importance of childhood experiences in adult behaviour. The British Psychological Society recognized Freud's contribution to the advancement of psychology when it awarded him honorary membership in 1926.

- *Accounts for rationality and irrationality* – Jarvis (2000) identifies the most significant feature of Freudian theory as the notion that the human personality has more than one aspect: '...we reveal this when we say things like "part of me wants to do it, but part of me is afraid to"'. Freud's introduction of the concept of the unconscious helps to explain how someone can be both rational and irrational; it can account for several aspects of behaviour, such as people predicting they will behave in one way and actually doing something quite different.

Activity **Explaining behaviour in psychodynamic terms**

Consider the following psychoanalytic explanation of behaviour:

Sarah is very shy and also has a severe stutter. This means that she tends to avoid social occasions because of the anxiety triggered when she even thinks about talking to others.

According to Freud, adult stuttering develops in childhood as a result of a conflict between the wish to defecate symbolically on one's parents (and authority figures more generally) by using hostile words, and a simultaneous fear of retaliation that causes the stutterer to hold the faecal-orientated words inside.

Other psychoanalysts have proposed that stuttering could be a conflict developed at the same time as speech is developing, around the age of 2. A child wants to be independent, while also wishing to remain completely dependent. Stuttering develops as a conflict between wanting to talk (and grow up) and not wanting to talk and thus remain a baby (Knapp 1997).

● How might a psychologist investigate whether either explanation is valid?

The focus of this activity is not on how to treat Sarah, but on how to test an explanation to find out if it is correct.

This certificate awarding Freud his honorary membership of the BPS can be seen in the Freud Museum in Vienna.

The behavioural approach

Behaviourism was a central approach during the 20th century and it continues to have a far-reaching effect on the way we see ourselves and on how we deal with people. The term 'behaviourism' was first used by John B. Watson in a paper written in 1913, in which he outlined a plan for the conduct of psychology that was to dominate the discipline for the following 50 years. The **behavioural approach** is concerned with behaviour that can be observed, and explains all behaviour in terms of learning and the environment (i.e. **nurture** not **nature**, see p.94). It has led to a number of effective applications, including therapies for treating mental disorders, classroom management techniques and teaching strategies.

Key concepts of the behavioural approach

Learning theory

The basic principles of learning theory are described in Chapter 7, p.235. A brief summary of the essential concepts is provided below. A classic study by Watson and Rayner (1920) illustrates how humans can acquire emotional responses through conditioning (see the case of 'Little Albert' on p.232 of *Psychology AS for AQA A*).

Classical conditioning

Classical conditioning describes how we learn through association (Pavlov 1927). This association of two things (one 'old' and one 'new') that occur together results in the new stimulus acquiring the properties of the old one. For example, an 'old' stimulus, such as the smell of bacon frying, produces a reflex response of salivation. The response occurs with no thought and cannot be controlled; it is automatic. If a 'new' stimulus occurs at the same time as the 'old' one on a number of occasions, an association between the two will be formed. For example, every time bacon is fried, you hear certain sizzling sounds (the sound of bacon frying); these two stimuli become associated so that the neutral stimulus (the sizzling sound) takes on the properties of the unconditioned stimulus (the smell). The neutral stimulus now becomes a conditioned stimulus and will produce

Pavlov (1849–1936)

the unconditioned response (the salivation) if heard at another time when no bacon is being fried. The sizzling sound is now a conditioned stimulus.

Operant conditioning

Operant conditioning describes how we learn through reinforcement. The likelihood of behaviour being repeated is increased or decreased through experience. Once again, this change of behaviour is produced without thought or control. An animal operates in its environment. From time to time, a particular behaviour results in a reward – for example, hunger is satisfied by eating a piece of fruit, which is also tasty. The fact that this is rewarding means the behaviour is likely to be repeated. Each time the same action is repeated and rewarded, the behaviour becomes increasingly likely. If, however, you take a bite of fruit that tastes nasty, this will decrease the probability of repetition. Through reward and punishment, behaviours are learned or unlearned. Skinner (1938) described this as the ABC of behaviour:

Antecedent ➡ **B**ehaviour ➡ **C**onsequence

It is the *consequences* of any particular behaviour that determine the likelihood that it will be repeated.

Skinner (1904–1990)

Reinforcers

Rewards are also called 'reinforcers'. Positive reinforcement occurs when the reward is pleasant. Negative reinforcement is also pleasant, but as a consequence of escaping from something unpleasant. The frequency of rewards affects the success of conditioning. Schedules of reinforcement include partial and continuous schedules, each of which is effective in particular circumstances. For example, continuous reinforcement schedules induce rapid initial learning and rapid extinction, whereas the opposite is true of partial reinforcement schedules (see Chapter 7, p.239).

Shaping

Although it is difficult to see how complex behaviours might be learned through this process, animal trainers use the principles of operant conditioning to teach complex activities (see panel, Targeting pigeons).

Targeting pigeons

Skinner demonstrated that he could train pigeons to operate a missile guidance system. He achieved this using the process of shaping. The animal is initially rewarded for quite simple behaviours, but gradually the rewards are reserved for behaviours that are closer and closer to the target behaviour.

Generalization, discrimination and extinction

Things that are learned may be generalized to other similar situations. This applies to both classical conditioning and operant conditioning. For example, having learned a conditioned response to the sound of frying, one might salivate to similar sounds. However, if subsequent experience produces no further association (sound of frying but no smell of bacon), then the learned response will become extinguished *unless* the sizzling sound continues to be linked to the smell of bacon while other frying sounds have no associated smell. In this case, an individual learns to *discriminate* between different stimuli.

Social learning theory

Direct and indirect reinforcement

Bandura (1965) recognized that learning theory could only explain a limited amount of what we learn, because classical and operant conditioning rely on *direct experience*. Animals, however, also learn *indirectly* by observing the behaviours of others and imitating them. Social learning theorists emphasize that for behaviour to be imitated, it must be rewarding in some way, i.e. *reinforced.* The term 'vicarious reinforcement' describes how we experience reinforcement indirectly by observing others being reinforced. The likelihood of a person imitating another person's behaviour is determined by:

- previous experiences of that behaviour – both their own and that of others

- the degree to which their own similar behaviour was successful in the past

- the current likelihood of whether the behaviour will be rewarded or punished.

This means that memory is involved – a concept that was alien to learning theorists. Social learning theory is sometimes referred to as 'neo-behaviourism' because it is a new kind of behaviourism, which includes mental concepts. According to social learning theory, we observe others and store representations of behaviour. If a

Albert Bandura (b. 1925)

behaviour is imitated, then it may or may not receive *direct* reinforcement. This determines the extent to which the behaviour becomes part of an individual's repertoire.

Reciprocal determinism

Bandura introduced the concept of reciprocal determinism to convey how individuals can exert some control over their development. As the individual acts, this changes the environment, which can affect subsequent behaviour. For example, if a child watches someone baking a cake and that person then slows down the process to make it clearer, the child has then modified the adult's behaviour, giving the child some control.

Self-efficacy

Bandura (1977) also claimed that people's behaviour and what they ultimately achieve may be influenced by their sense of their own effectiveness (or efficacy). If you believe that you can jump over a two-metre bar, this will affect the way you approach the task and, therefore, what you achieve. Your sense of self-efficacy is an important personality trait based on both direct and indirect experience. In the case of direct experience, your own successes and failures alter future expectations of success. You may also learn indirectly by watching others' successes and failures and apply this knowledge to your self-expectations.

Methods used by the behavioural approach

Laboratory experiments

Behaviourists use laboratory experiments as the main method to investigate their explanations. This fits with their view that behaviour can be reduced to simple units. Experimental design is covered as part of your AS studies (see *Psychology AS for AQA A*, Chapter 1, pp.13–15). It involves identifying one or more independent variables (the variables manipulated by the experimenter) and dependent variable(s) (the behaviours to be measured). For example, if a researcher wanted to investigate whether helping behaviour was caused by reinforcement, the independent variable would be the reinforcement and the dependent variable would be the helping behaviour.

The next step would be to operationalize these variables. For example, reinforcement could be operationalized as spoken praise, a smile or some physical reward.

Helping behaviour could be operationalized in terms of how much litter some school children collected (with or without reward).

A hypothesis could then be written based on these variables and an experimental design chosen to test the hypothesis (e.g. repeated measures or independent groups). It might also be necessary to identify and control any possible extraneous variables. Other decisions include what sampling technique to use, how to address any ethical issues and how to analyse the quantitative data.

Research with non-human animals

A fundamental belief in behaviourism is that all organisms learn and behave in essentially the same way, and so the processes of learning and conditioning must be the same in all species. Behaviourists argue that it is justifiable to investigate human behaviour by studying simpler species in order to understand more about these processes in a more basic form.

Behaviourists have used rats to investigate the processes of learning

Evaluation of the behavioural approach

- *Learning theory is based on research with non-human animals and is reductionist* – Learning theory suggests that all behaviour can be reduced to stimulus–response units. This may be true for the behaviour of non-human animals, and learning theory may account for some complex animal behaviours. However, it cannot provide a complete explanation of human behaviour, which often has multiple influences, such as emotion and thought. Social learning theory provides a richer explanation of behaviour, but still ignores influences such as emotion.

- *Research is conducted in contrived laboratory environments* – Consequently, the research is not seen as representing the complexities of real life. Laboratory-based studies also typically focus on short-term effects and may not explain how longer-term behaviours are learned.

- *Learning theory is determinist and suggests that people have no free will* – This has implications for moral responsibility and self-responsibility in general. Learning theory is also focused on environmental determinism, suggesting that only nurture and not nature can explain the development of behaviour. This

Anna is 12 years old and loves sending and receiving text messages. At first she did this a couple of times a day and thought it was fun, particularly if she did it while in class. She now sends lots of texts every day and becomes miserable and distracted if she doesn't receive answers almost immediately. She is constantly watching or listening to see if she has a new text message and feels neglected if she doesn't receive as many messages as she sends. This is affecting her concentration and her schoolwork.

1 Describe how the behavioural approach might explain why Anna has become preoccupied with sending and receiving text messages.

2 What are the strengths and limitations of this approach?

3 How might behaviourists investigate excessive use of text messaging in young people?

Discuss your answers with other students in your psychology class.

---

assumption ignores the fact that learning itself is inherited and varies from species to species. For example, there is evidence that animals are born with a predisposition to learn certain fears more rapidly (see biological preparedness, Chapter 7, p.237).

- *Learning theory can explain individual differences* – On the positive side, environmental determinism can explain why people are different (due to different reinforcement experiences).

- *It is a scientific approach* – The reductionism of the behavioural approach can also be regarded as a strength because it permits variables to be operationalized and explanations to be tested using experimental research.

- *Social learning theory includes social influences* – As a result, it is able to explain the influence of cultural, as well as individual, differences.

The cognitive approach

The **cognitive approach** is probably the dominant approach in modern psychology today. It looks at how mental processes, such as perception, memory, problem-solving and language, affect our behaviour. This approach became popular when the problems associated with the behavioural approach could no longer be ignored. Behaviourists viewed the mind of people as a 'black box', studying what went into the box (stimuli) and what came out (responses), but not investigating what went on inside. We all know that a lot goes on inside our heads and much of our behaviour can be affected by mental events. The cognitive approach may be viewed as a reworking of the ideas of Watson and Skinner, but with a twist. The cognitive approach views people as being like machines, or computers, looking at the inputs (the stimuli) to the machine, the outputs (what it does), as well as the various processes that occur between input and output.

What are the similarities and differences between people and computers?

Make a list of some cognitive activities and consider how they are similar and different in people and computers. For example, how might a person's culture or mood affect their ability to think or remember something?

You might find it helpful to re-read Chapter 3, the memory chapter, in your AS textbook.

Key concepts of the cognitive approach

Mental and perceptual set

Problem-solving

Behaviourists focused on trial-and-error learning as a way of explaining problem-solving. During the first half of the 20th century, Gestalt psychologists recognized that there was more to problem-solving than this. They suggested that problem-solving requires structural understanding, i.e. the ability to understand how all the parts of the problem fit together to achieve the goal. A key requirement is the reorganization of the different elements of the problem in such a way that the problem can be solved. However, people often get stuck when they try to solve problems because they cannot change their problem-solving or mental set (also called 'functional fixedness'). When given a clue, most people can solve the problem quite quickly because they break free of their usual way of thinking about it.

Gestalt psychology

The Gestalt school of psychology, which emerged in Germany in the 1920s and 1930s, focused on the organization of cognitive processes, especially perceptual processes. Gestalt is a German word that means 'form' or 'overall pattern'. Gestalt psychologists were not interested in breaking down behaviour and experience into its constituent parts in the way that behaviourists advocated. Instead, they claimed that the brain creates coherent perceptual experiences, based on innate organizational principles, and that 'the whole is greater than the sum of its parts'.

Gestalt psychologists were particularly interested in the, then, recent invention of motion pictures and how motion appeared as a unified process, even though the motion picture comprised a series of individual still photographs presented in quick succession through a projector. This perception of motion is more than the sum of the information provided in the individual frames. Studying how the human mind actively organizes such information into unified wholes (gestalts) was central to the work of Gestalt psychologists, such as Wertheimer, Köhler and Koffka, who created perceptual demonstrations which supported the Gestalt view of perception.

Max Wertheimer (1880-1943)

Perception

The concept of perceptual set is similar to mental set. According to constructivist theories, successful perception involves combining sensory information with knowledge based on previous experience. This intelligent perception applies, for example, to how we learn to see depth, as well as how we interpret the words we read (for example, knowing that 'read' is an English word). We have expectations about what we are likely to encounter and this sometimes leads us to make mistakes. When shown the symbols TAI3LE, we tend to read this as 'table' because the digits are interpreted as letters, due to expectations created by the context – a perceptual set. See Chapter 2, p.76 for further examples of perceptual set.

Schema, stereotypes and social representations

Memory

Schemas are knowledge packages which are built up through experience with the world and which also embody cultural expectations. Bartlett's (1932) famous 'War of the Ghosts' research (see panel below) showed how participants' recall of unfamiliar information was affected by cultural knowledge. Other research has explored the effects of stereotypes on memory. Stereotypes are mental short cuts that help us process information more quickly, but which also lead to errors and prejudices. For example, Cohen (1981) showed how people recalled different information about a woman in a video, depending on whether they were told beforehand that the woman was a librarian or a waitress. These labels conjure up expectations about a person and they influence what we 'see' and later recall. People tend to remember information that is consistent with their stereotypes.

Bartlett's 'War of the Ghosts' research

Bartlett (1932) carried out the pioneering work on reconstructive memory, arguing that we do not record memories passively as we would if we were taking a photo. In a now famous study, he investigated the effects of unfamiliarity on the recall of a folk story over time. English participants heard an unfamiliar North American folk tale called 'The War of the Ghosts', which contained words and ideas that would not have appeared in a conventional Western story. After 20 hours, participants were asked to recall as much of the story as possible and thereafter were asked to retell the story many more times. Bartlett found many distortions in their recall. Participants retold the story, using language and narrative techniques of their own cultural and literary background. The story was often reordered and also became shorter as participants omitted details. Over time, distortions became more pronounced and the reproductions increasingly resembled an ordinary English story. Bartlett concluded that, when given an unfamiliar tale to remember, people remembered the gist, but used their own experiences and schemas to provide the detail and to make the story coherent.

Language

Stereotypes are often communicated through the words we use. For example, using the term 'chairperson' instead of 'chairman' can affect our stereotypes about the person in that position. It is questionable whether language merely shapes our thinking or actually determines it (for example, whether people who speak in different languages actually think in different ways because of the

INTRODUCTION

language they use). There is evidence to suggest there are some differences. For example, the Chinese have fewer words for numbers, which may mean that they can count more quickly.

Thinking may affect language, as well as language affecting thinking. Learning new concepts enables learners to acquire new vocabularies because they become capable of making the finer discriminations necessary (thought affects language).

The 'Great Eskimo Vocabulary Hoax'

This is the claim that Inuit people (Eskimos) have a large vocabulary of words for snow, which enables them to make finer distinctions (language affecting thought). However, the same could be argued in reverse – it is their wider experience of snow that leads them to develop and use the wider vocabulary (thought affecting language). Interestingly, Pinker (1994) claims there are as many words for snow in English.

Social cognition

Social cognition refers to the area of social psychology concerned with how people think about other people or groups of people. This field shares many similarities with cognitive psychology (e.g. studying stereotyping), but assumes that the way in which we think about other people (i.e. our social world) differs in important ways to how we think about the physical world. One area of particular interest is the attribution of causality – how we explain our own and others' behaviour. Different theorists have attempted to understand the rules we use to make causal attributions about each other's behaviour. This is not as clear-cut as it might at first appear, because much of our attributional thinking is biased (e.g. the **self-serving bias**; or the **fundamental attribution bias**, which is the tendency to hold other people personally responsible for the outcomes of their behaviour).

Maladaptive thinking

Cognitive-behavioural therapies suggest that psychological problems arise because individuals have developed maladaptive ways of thinking – the problem only exists because of the inappropriate way that a person thinks about their problem. In order to treat such disorders, therefore, clients need to be challenged about their maladaptive and irrational thoughts. See Chapter 10, p.357 for more information on cognitive-behavioural therapies.

Methods used by the cognitive approach

Research in cognitive psychology tends to involve laboratory experiments. Case studies of brain-damaged individuals are also used to enhance our understanding

of how the physiology of the brain relates to cognitive behaviours. For example, the case study of H.M. showed that the hippocampus was implicated in short-term memory, which supported the idea of separate memory stores (Milner 1966).

More recently, imaging techniques, such as PET scans, have been used to study brain activity. For example, Squire *et al.* (1992) used PET scans to show that blood flow in the right hippocampus was higher when participants were engaged in a cued recall task compared with a word-completion task. This suggests that different areas of the brain may govern different kinds of memory, linking aspects of cognitive processing to a physical brain state.

Brain damage and memory

Using the case study method, Milner (1966) reported on a young man referred to as H.M., who was left with severe memory impairment after brain surgery. He was able to talk normally and to recall accurately events and people from his life before surgery and his immediate digit span was within normal limits. He was, however, unable to retain any new information and could not lay down new memories in long term memory (LTM). When told of the death of his favourite uncle, he reacted with considerable distress. Later, he often asked about his uncle and, on each occasion, reacted again with the level of grief appropriate to hearing the news for the first time.

Evaluation of the cognitive approach

- *Lack of evidence for abstract concepts such as memory* – Although we are able to record information, store it and subsequently recall it, there is no physical evidence of this 'thing' we call memory. The same critique applies to all cognitive concepts which may merely be attempts to make abstract concepts into something. The danger is that this 'something' becomes real (e.g. the 'id' in psychoanalytic theory) and prevents a better understanding of the underlying processes.

- *It is a scientific approach* – Although many concepts in cognitive psychology are abstract, the approach lends itself to testable theories and hypotheses. This is both a strength and a limitation. It is a strength because it permits theories to be tested, falsified and adapted in the light of new evidence. However, it is also a limiting factor because it reduces behaviour to something quite different to real life and, therefore, the findings cannot always be generalized.

- *Social and cultural factors are often ignored* – Social and cultural factors do not form part of the general debate in cognitive psychology. A review of mainstream psychology journals in the UK found that very few articles considered issues of culture, social class or sexual orientation (Banyard and Hunt 2000). This is not to say that these variables will affect all research issues in cognitive psychology, but it is not reasonable to assume they will affect none of them.

- *Is the brain really like a computer?* – If the brain can be legitimately conceived of as a computer, it should be possible eventually to build a computer that does what a human brain can do (see panel, 'The Turing test'). To date, the computer analogy remains an inadequate way of modeling (representing) human cognitive processes.

'The Turing test'

Turing (1950) suggested that it was possible to test whether a computer could think like a person by asking a person to communicate with two 'people' hidden from view: one a real person and the other a computer program. If participants cannot reliably differentiate between the computer and the person, then the computer program has passed the test and it can be claimed to be able to think and understand like a person. Tests have shown that under certain circumstances computers can pass the so-called 'Turing test', but it is clear that their use of rather unintelligent pattern-matching strategies is not the same as understanding (Searle 1980).

CHECK YOUR UNDERSTANDING

Check your understanding of approaches in psychology by answering the following questions. Try to do this from memory. You can check your answers by looking back through Section 1.

1. List the five approaches discussed in Section 1 and outline one strength and one weakness of each approach.

2. Identify one method/technique used to investigate physiological explanations and outline two criticisms of this method.

3. Identify each of the bulleted items in the section 'Evaluation of the physiological approach' on pages 5 and 6 – determinist, reductionist, mind–body challenge, individual and cultural differences, and useful applications – as either a strength or a weakness or both.

4. Explain one strength of the evolutionary explanation of behaviour.

5. Why are kinship studies useful in investigating possible genetic causes of behaviour?

6. How do cross-cultural studies help psychologists to investigate evolutionary explanations of human behaviour?

7. Identify and explain one criticism that can be made of psychodynamic explanations of behaviour.

8. What is the main assumption of the behavioural approach and what implications does this have for the study of human behaviour?

9. Why are laboratory experiments particularly suitable for research by behaviourists?

10. How do behaviourists justify the use of non-human animals to learn about human behaviour?

11. What do cognitive psychologists today model the human mind on? How successful is this analogy?

12. What research methods are typically used by cognitive psychologists? What are the strengths and the limitations of the cognitive approach?

Section 2: Issues in psychology

Introduction

This section explores some key issues relating to psychological research that concern psychologists:

- gender bias
- cultural bias
- ethical challenges in research with human participants and non-human animals.

Some of these issues should already be familiar from your AS studies – for example, ethical issues arising from the requirement to balance participants' rights against the needs of researchers to design and execute scientifically robust studies. As we shall see, **socially sensitive research** poses its own special ethical challenges for

researchers. Psychologists need to be mindful that research findings can be manipulated and exploited for bad purposes, as well as good ones.

The constraints on the use of non-human animals in psychological investigations will be considered, as there are strong moves to recognize equal rights for some non-human animals and human beings. Ethical and scientific arguments for and against the use of non-human animals in psychological research will be examined.

The term '**bias**' implies some systematic form of distortion that can affect how particular individuals or groups are perceived. A survey of psychology studies in the 1980s found that the majority used psychology students as their participants – mainly North American, male undergraduates (Sears 1986). This would not be an issue if we believed that males and females were similar in their beliefs, attitudes and motivations. Equally, there would be no problem if we assumed that students were similar to the general population or that Americans were the same as people from other cultural groups. However, what is clear is that psychology is largely a record of American, undergraduate, male behaviour.

Gender bias

Gender bias is certainly not new: for centuries, people have held biased views about the differences between the sexes. The ancient Greek philosopher, Aristotle, suggested that women's inferiority was biologically based ('We should look upon the female as being a deformity'). In Aristotle's writings, women are portrayed as not possessing fully developed rationality. It was, therefore, assumed that men must rule women and be responsible for them!

What is new is an understanding of the effects of such biases on our perceptions of reality. We may believe there are differences between men and women – for example, that women are kinder than men or men are more intelligent than women – but such gender differences may not be based on reliable research evidence. Rather, they may be a

Aristotle (384–322 BC)

product of the way we construct theories. This means that what we perceive as differences may not actually exist.

Alpha bias

Alpha-biased theories assume there are real and enduring differences between males and females. Alpha-biased theories sometimes heighten the value of women, as in Chodorow's (1978) conception of women as more relational and caring, and are sometimes used to devalue women. Within sociobiology, for example, differences in male and female behaviour may be attributed to genetic determinism. Thus, male social dominance or sexual promiscuity might be regarded as a product of their evolutionary history.

Beta bias

Beta-biased theories ignore or minimize sex differences. They do this either by disregarding questions about the lives of women or by assuming that research findings from studies of men apply equally to women. Such approaches, which are at best misguided and at worst arrogant, have resulted in what is essentially an **androcentric** view of human behaviour (i.e. one based on and concerning males), rather than offering insights into what is essentially one half of the human race. There are also a few examples of **estrocentrism** in psychology, which is a bias towards females.

Hare-Mustin and Marecek (1988) suggested that our stereotypes of gender (and culture, age, class, etc.) are social constructions of reality and these constructions lead to two types of bias in psychological research: theories that exaggerate the differences between men and women, and those that ignore them. Hare-Mustin and Marecek describe these as **alpha-biased** and **beta-biased** theories respectively (see alpha bias/beta bias panel).

Gender bias in psychological theories

Alpha-biased theories

Alpha-biased theories may exaggerate the differences between men and women from either an androcentric (male-centred) or estrocentric (female-centred) view. An example of each is described below:

- *Androcentrism* – Freud's theory of psychoanalysis took male behaviour as the standard for all human behaviour and described female behaviour as a deviation from the male standard. This is particularly evident in Freud's description of the genital stage of development.

- *Estrocentrism* – Gilligan's (1982) theory of moral development was developed in response to Kohlberg's (1969) theory of moral understanding (see Chapter 8, p.276 Cognition and development). She argued that women have a different moral voice from men; they discuss the world and make judgements using different criteria, such as interpersonal concerns and caring, rather than justice and logic, which are male principles.

Beta-biased theories

Beta-biased theories minimize gender differences. There are two kinds of beta-biased theories: the unisex view of human behaviour; the universal theory of human behaviour, based on research with one gender only.

- *Unisex theories* – For example, Bem's (1976) theory of psychological androgyny proposes that androgyny is a healthy psychological state, where both men and women are free to select whatever personality traits they wish. They can integrate masculine and feminine qualities according to their individual temperament rather than being constrained by stereotypes. However, Hare-Mustin and Maracek (1988) point out that this assumes that masculine and feminine qualities are equivalent, whereas even Bem acknowledges that masculine qualities are often regarded as more adaptive and thus more highly valued. The theory of androgyny, therefore, overlooks the social context in which choices are made.

- *Theories based on research with one gender* – Hare-Mustin and Maracek (1988) suggest that prior to the 1970s, psychologists based most of their generalizations on observations of male behaviour, which was assumed to represent *all* experience. A classic example is Kohlberg's (1969) theory of the development of moral understanding. Kohlberg used moral dilemmas to find out about how people made moral decisions, and then, based on the answers given, classified the stage or level of moral reasoning that a person had reached. This led him to develop an age-related theory of moral development, which he claimed was universal. However, the sample he used to develop this stage theory was based entirely on American boys. Not surprisingly, females were found to be inferior when Kohlberg assessed them using his moral dilemmas (which were androcentric) and classified them with his stage theory (based on male responses).

Consequences of gender bias in psychological theories

- *Positive consequences of alpha bias* – Alpha bias has led some theorists, such as Gilligan, to assert the worth of certain feminine qualities (they may not be truly feminine, but are possessed by the majority of women), which counters the devaluation of women (Hare-Mustin and Maracek 1988).

- *Negative consequences of alpha bias* – A focus on differences between genders, even when the differences favour women, implies similarity *within* each gender. Saying that women value interpersonal relationships and men value abstract justice ignores the many ways in which women differ from each other and men differ from each other.

- *Positive consequences of beta bias* – Beta bias encourages people to see men and women as the same, which has led to their equal treatment in legal terms and also in terms of equal access to, for example, education and employment. However, a focus on similarities between genders has had the disadvantage of drawing attention away from women's special needs and the power differences between men and women.

- *Negative consequences of beta bias* – Some theories *appear* to be gender neutral while really being gender biased. Beta bias is an apparently egalitarian position, but it results in major misrepresentations of one or both genders and, more importantly, it can create and/or sustain prejudices.

Feminist psychology

The strong androcentric bias of much psychological research, reflecting the power of males in our society, has led some psychologists to develop an alternative force – feminist psychology. Its main aims are to:

- *challenge androcentric generalizations* by highlighting instances where statements are made about human behaviour which are really only relevant to male behaviour (and probably Western, middle-class, male behaviour)

- *challenge the pathologization of female behaviour* by avoiding the situation where female behaviours are regarded as abnormal or pathological (i.e. as a form of illness); for example, pre-menstrual syndrome is regarded by some as an unhealthy and undesirable state rather than simply as a facet of 'normal' behaviour

■ *challenge biological explanations of differences* by avoiding explanations which suggest that gender differences are biological and, consequently, inevitable and universal. It may be that gender differences are partly biological, but they are also socially constructed. A psychology that highlights biological differences is perpetuating stereotypes.

Bias-free theories

There are a number of ways that psychological theories can avoid biases. Worell and Remer (1992) suggest four criteria by which theories might be evaluated in order to overcome the often detrimental models of women that develop from more traditional, non-feminist models.

1 *Gender-free* – Theories should view males and females as similar in their psychological make-up and avoid sexist and stereotyped concepts.

2 *Flexible* – Theories should emphasize within-sex differences in behaviour, as well as between-sex differences. This will avoid devaluing one or the other as being less mature, incomplete or unhealthy, due to some preconceived notions of what might be considered 'normal' or healthy.

3 *Interactionist* – Theories should recognize the interaction between a range of individual factors (including affective, cognitive and behavioural factors) and those which are more environmental (such as other people, institutions, etc.). Interactionist theories recognize multiple influences on a person's behaviour and accept that an individual cannot be fully understood without consideration of all the relevant factors. Gender is only one factor contributing to a person's behaviour.

4 *Lifespan* – This assumes that behaviour changes throughout an individual's lifetime. When applied to gender-related behaviours, lifespan theories propose that these are not fixed in people, but may always be open to change.

Gender bias in psychological studies

Bias in the research process

Denmark *et al.* (1988) state that gender bias is found at all stages of the research process, including the following:

■ *Question formation* – Gross (2003) points out that topics studied in psychological research often reflect the prevalent cultural gender stereotypes. For example, leadership is often defined in terms of dominance, aggression and other characteristics that are stereotyped as being typically 'male'.

■ *Research design* – Experimental research can be viewed as a 'masculine' approach based on logic and rationality, rather than the 'feminine' characteristics of caring and relatedness.

■ *Research methods* – Rosenthal (1966) reported that male researchers were more pleasant, friendly, honest and encouraging with female participants than with male participants, leading him to conclude that 'male and female subjects may, psychologically, simply not be in the same experiment at all'. This might explain why some studies discover gender differences that are not really there.

■ *Selection of research participants and inappropriate conclusions* – Findings based on one sex are inappropriately applied to both. Psychologists have typically developed theories about *human* behaviour based only on white, male undergraduates (Fine and Gordon 1989).

■ *Publication bias* – There is a definite trend in all areas of science for journals to publish only those studies that produce positive findings. In gender research, this means that studies that find gender *differences* are more likely to be published than those that find no such differences. This can exaggerate the difference, producing an alpha bias (Tavris 1993).

Alpha-biased studies

Evolutionary psychology has been accused of alpha bias and the studies used to support this theory can also be criticized on the same grounds. The basis of the argument is that males and females face different problems in order to ensure reproductive success. See Chapter 3, pp.112–115 for more detail about the evolutionary approach.

Derived from this argument is a range of expectations about male and female human behaviour. For example, we would expect men to seek physical attractiveness and youth as signs of fertility, and for women to seek men with resources who would be good providers. We would also expect men and women to advertise themselves differently. Research analysing personal advertisements supported this hypothesis (e.g. Dunbar 1995). Such research is, however, an example of gender bias because of the way the research question was asked and the research designed.

Beta-biased studies

Did you know that several of the classic studies of social influence that were part of your AS studies (e.g. those by Asch, Zimbardo, Milgram) did not involve any women? This was not because the researchers wished to find out about how *men* behaved: they wanted to find out how *people* behaved and *assumed* that the findings from studies conducted with males could be generalized to men *and* women.

Some social influence research has involved women. For example, Hofling *et al.* (1966) studied female nurses, but this is still an example of beta bias because, once again, the findings were generalized to both men and women.

Milgram did investigate obedience in women in some later studies and found that obedience rates were as high as those for men, just as Hofling and colleagues had found. However, an Australian study found that women were much less obedient than men (16 per cent rather than 40 per cent). These contradictory findings may be due to the fact that, in Milgram's study, females gave males electric shocks, whereas in the Australian study, females were required to administer shocks to other females.

Consequences of gender bias in psychological studies

- *Gender bias in action* – Many of the issues raised in relation to gender bias in psychological theories apply also to gender bias in psychological studies. Traditional psychological research has often presented women in an unfavourable and unrealistic way because of both alpha and beta bias.

- *More constructive approaches* – Psychologists and society in general now think more constructively about gender roles. Although we may never be able to differentiate fully the real effects of sex (based on biological factors) from those of gender (based on social factors), we can be aware of biases that distort what we think of as reality.

Cultural bias

What is cultural bias?

According to Hofstede (1980), 'culture refers to the collective programming of the mind which distinguishes members of one group from another'. The term '**culture**' does not refer to a group of people, but the beliefs, attitudes, practices and so on that a group of people share. Cultural bias can affect psychological theories and studies in a similar way to the effect of gender bias. Hare-Mustin and Maracek (1988) proposed that the same alpha and beta biases apply to culture as to gender.

Gender as a subcultural group

It can be argued that gender is an example of culture insofar as males and females display different beliefs, attitudes and practices. More accurately, gender should be seen as a 'subcultural' group – a group of people within a dominant culture who share many of the cultural characteristics of that culture, but also have some distinctive characteristics of their own.

Types of cultural bias

Ethnocentrism and Eurocentrism

Probably the most significant cultural bias is **ethnocentrism** – the effect that one's own cultural perspective has on perceptions of other cultures. Our own cultural perspective (beliefs, attitudes, etc.) is taken as the standard by which we judge other cultures, which inevitably leads us to regard our own cultural practices as superior.

Eurocentrism is the most dominant form of ethnocentric bias in psychology because most psychologists are European/North American. Their theories are therefore taken to be universal descriptions of human behaviour although they are clearly culturally biased.

Individualism versus collectivism

Individualist cultures are those where an individual's identity is more defined by personal achievement and independence. In a collectivist culture, identity is defined by collective achievement and interdependence. Many psychological explanations are individualist because of their Eurocentric bias. Individualism also tends to be associated with urban, post-industrial societies, whereas collectivism relates to rural, non-industrialized societies.

The emic–etic distinction

Another type of cultural bias that affects psychology can be described in terms of emics and etics:

- *Etic analyses* of behaviour focus on the universals of human behaviour; for example, phonetics is the general study of vocal sounds.

- *Emic analyses* of behaviour focus on the ways in which activities and development are observed in a specific cultural setting; for example, phonemics is the study of sounds used in a specific language.

In summary, the etic approach ignores the cultural context of any behaviour and observes it from a position outside the culture. Since observers are inevitably influenced by their own culture, they often make biased judgements of behaviour in other cultures. In an emic approach, the researcher attempts to understand a culture by learning its rules and beliefs from within the culture's own logic system.

Historical bias

The concept of culture can apply to historical comparisons, as well as national or ethnic ones. The culture of Britain in the early 21st century is considerably different from that of the 1950s. Theories developed 50 years ago may well not apply to human behaviour today.

Commentary on cultural biases

Howitt and Owusu-Bempah (1994) argue that 'we have a moral obligation to challenge cultural bias, otherwise we are "guilty of complicity"'. The biases outlined above can be addressed in various ways, including:

- *cultural relativism* – the recognition that there are no universal standards for behaviour, but that all behaviours are relative to the cultural context in which they originate

- *abandoning the etic approach* because it is inevitably biased; all research should be conducted from an emic perspective.

Smith and Bond (1998) highlight the dangers in attempting to distinguish one culture from another. In doing so, psychologists are attempting to draw definitive lines in terms of what is generally a characteristic in one culture but not, perhaps, a characteristic of another. There are two major problems associated with this:

- Behaviour differences between any two countries may also be found between different subcultures within the same country.

- It assumes that cultures are free from conflict and dissent in the behaviour of their members; yet it is clear that within any culture there will be considerable divergence in the experiences of individuals that make up that culture.

Cultural bias in psychological theories

Before reading further, try the activity 'Noticing cultural bias'.

Activity   Noticing cultural bias

Think about the theories that you have studied so far in your psychology course.

1. Try to identify at least two theories that are culturally biased and describe:
   - in what way they are biased
   - how this affects the way they explain human behaviour.
2. Are there other, less biased theories that can explain the target behaviours of these theories?

Discuss your answers with other students in your psychology class.

A selection of theories is described below as examples of different forms of bias. However, most of the theories could equally well be placed in several other categories – for example, Kohlberg's theory of the development of moral reasoning is beta biased, but is also an example of an individualist and an etic approach.

Beta bias

Any theory based on research conducted with one cultural group that is then presented as a theory of *all* human behaviour is beta biased, as it minimizes or ignores cultural differences. Kohlberg's (1969) theory of the development of moral reasoning is beta biased in terms of culture, as well as gender. Kohlberg proposed that his developmental stages are driven by biological changes in cognitive maturity which must be universal. That is, all individuals, regardless of culture, experience the same developmental processes at about the same ages.

Ethnocentric and Eurocentric bias

One explanation of the formation and maintenance of relationships is the so-called 'economic theories' of interpersonal attraction, such as social exchange theory and equity theory (see Chapter 3, p.105). Economic theories of relationships are mainly based on the study of North American students – a fairly narrow part of one particular culture. Such theories probably only apply to North American middle-class individuals in short-term relationships – a very specific subculture. Moghaddam *et al.* (1993) suggest that North American relationships are predominantly individualist, voluntary and temporary (i.e. they can be ended if desired), whereas non-Western relationships are typically collective, obligatory and permanent.

Bias in the etic approach

Mental illness is diagnosed using the Diagnostic Statistical Manual or the International Classification of Diseases. Both are used with individuals, regardless of their cultural background, assuming that the behaviours of the dominant white culture should be applied to all people. For example, hearing voices is regarded as a symptom of schizophrenia in some cultures, whereas it is regarded as normal behaviour in others. This misapplication of norms from one culture to another may explain why African–Caribbean immigrants in the UK are seven times more likely than white people to be diagnosed as schizophrenic (Cochrane and Sashidharan 1995).

Historical bias

Psychodynamic theories have been criticized for their historical bias. Freud's overemphasis on sex may be partly due to the fact that he was working in an era of great sexual repression, which may not apply now or to other cultures. Later, theorists played down the role of sexual motivation, although even then they have been accused of historical bias. For example, Erikson (1978) proposed that identity formation is related to role decisions, but this may also be related to a historical period when people sought a 'job for life'; this may be less true today than it was 40 years ago.

Commentary on cultural bias in psychological theories

Various comments have already been made about individual psychological theories. Many of these points are relevant to all the theories discussed (e.g. the issue that differentiation between cultures in terms of individualism and collectivism masks differences *within* cultures). Two further points are important:

1 *How is culture operationalized?* – Using country of origin as an indication of culture assumes that all the people within a country share the same culture. Using race or ethnicity as a representation of an individual's belief system may be equally inappropriate.

2 *Does ethnocentricity imply superiority?* – An ethnocentric position does not have to be one of superiority/inferiority. It is possible to acknowledge differences as differences. Other forms of bias, such as Afrocentrism (centred on individuals of Black–African descent), can redress the balance by providing alternative perspectives that remind us that biases may go unrecognized.

Cultural bias in psychological studies

Cross-cultural research

Research is conducted to test universal theories by repeating the same studies in different cultural contexts (for example, replications of Milgram's obedience studies). Findings have ranged from 16 per cent obedience in female students in Australia (Kilham and Mann 1974), to 92 per cent in Holland (Meeus and Raaijmakers 1986). Differences may be attributed to different cultural behaviours, but it is also possible that differences are due to a lack of equivalence in the procedures. Smith and Bond (1998) highlight the following problems:

▪ *Translation* – Participants are instructed by spoken or written word, and their verbal or written responses often constitute the main findings of the research. These instructions and responses must therefore be carefully translated to allow a proper comparison.

▪ *Manipulation of variables* – The operationalization of variables and the impact of any manipulation must be the same in each cultural group studied. For example, the expression of happiness might be different in different groups, and the impact of a specific independent variable (such as an insult) might be dramatically different, depending on the way it is interpreted by those involved in the study.

▪ *Participants* – Although participants may be selected from similar social groups (university students, schoolchildren, etc.), they may have quite different social backgrounds and belong to different cultural groups. To gain access to a university education in some cultures, for example, does not involve the same criteria as it does in the West.

Sampling biases

Another potential source of bias is associated with the researcher's choice of participants. Almost all American and British research is carried out on members of the researcher's own culture. This bias is clearly seen in an analysis of introductory psychology textbooks by Smith and Bond (1993). They found that in one standard American textbook (Baron and Byrne 1997), 94 per cent

of the studies referred to were American, and in one British textbook (Hewstone *et al.* 1988), 68 per cent of the cited studies were also American.

Research populations may be even more restricted than this. Sears (1986) reported that 82 per cent of research studies used undergraduates as the participants in psychology studies, and 51 per cent were psychology students. This suggests that a considerable amount of psychology is based on young, male, middle-class, academic adults. Psychology findings are not only unrepresentative on a global scale, but also within Western culture.

Imposed etics

One way of overcoming the problem of restricted sampling is to encourage research which uses participants from other cultures. However, this may lead to another source of bias. For example, a researcher using a method or technique that has been developed by Western psychology, such as using an American IQ test to assess intelligence, is adopting an emic perspective (based on their own culture) and using it as the basis for a comparison between the two cultures – an imposed etic. This imposed etic makes the assumption that whatever measures have been used in one cultural context (in this case the USA) will have the same meaning when applied in a different cultural context. This is unlikely to be true (see panel 'The Strange Situation' in Japan).

'The Strange Situation' in Japan

Takahashi (1990) conducted a study of Japanese infants and found that the infants responded quite differently in the 'Strange Situation' from how American infants behave (see *Psychology AS for AQA A*, pp.123–128). The Japanese infants were much more disturbed when left alone. This may be due to the fact that Japanese infants experience less separation – they are almost never left alone. The behaviours observed were therefore reactions to extreme stress, which was not the original aim of the Strange Situation. Thus, using the Strange Situation (an imposed etic) with Japanese infants was not comparable to using it with American infants.

Commentary on cultural bias in psychological studies

There are some possible solutions to the problems identified above:

▪ *A derived etic approach* – Participants could be observed in their natural environment in order to learn about any culture-specific traditions before the research is carried out. This would enable researchers to adopt more of an emic viewpoint and design their research appropriately.

- *Ethnography* – This research approach, typically used by anthropologists, involves gathering data in different cultural contexts, including patterns of behaviour, dynamics, institutions, etc. The data can then be used to prepare a broader picture of human behaviour.

- *Indigenous psychologies* – The growth of psychology and psychological research in many different countries means that we will become more enlightened about how people in different cultures behave. According to Yamagishi (2002), there are now more social psychologists working in Asia than in Europe.

Activity **Ethical issues**

1 Think back to your AS course. List all the ethical issues you remember studying. To help you begin, look at the photograph below from Milgram's obedience study (see *Psychology AS for AQA A*, pp.192–198).

Milgram's 'learner' confederate

- What issues does it raise?
- What made Milgram's experiments so controversial?

2 Make a list of some of the other key research studies you studied in your AS course.

- Give each study a rating on a scale of 1 to 10, where 1 is not at all ethical and 10 is highly ethical.
- Discuss your ratings with other students in your psychology class. What criteria did you use to make your judgements?

Ethical issues with human participants

Morals concern what is acceptable or right in terms of human behaviour, and **ethics** are a set of moral principles used by professionals to promote the long-term welfare of their work. Ethical issues arise in psychological research when there are conflicts between the rights of participants and the needs of researchers when conducting valid

investigations. Ethical guidelines have been developed as a way of dealing with ethical issues. Other ways of addressing ethical issues that arise when planning and conducting research include:

- the use of ethics committees to scrutinize research proposals
- the decision to stop a study earlier than planned.

At this point, refresh your memory of the British Psychological Society's *Code of Ethics and Conduct* (2006) by looking at Table 16.6 in Chapter 16.

The main ethical issues that concern psychologists are considered below.

Deception

Deception involves withholding information or misleading research participants. Psychologists use deception in research because participants' behaviour may be altered by their expectations about how they should behave in a study and this would invalidate the findings. The issue is one of weighing the need for deception against the potential harm to a participant. The potential harm to participants ranges from the distrust that such practices create in participants (and thus their unwillingness to participate in future studies), to actual physical or psychological harm experienced without having had the chance to decline to participate.

Resolving the issue of deception

- *Deception is acceptable* in certain situations, such as when the deception is minor or where there is no potential for harm (for example, in memory experiments).
- *Deception is not acceptable* in certain situations, such as when an investigation is trivial in nature or when the potential harm to participants is large.
- *Debriefing* and the *right to withhold their data* may be offered to participants.
- *Passive deception* may be more acceptable than active deception. There is a difference between withholding certain research details and deliberately misleading participants about the true purpose of a study.

Commentary on deception

- *Informed consent* – Perhaps the most serious consequence of deception is that it removes the ability of participants to give their fully informed consent to take part in an investigation. If participants are not told about everything that is going on, how can they make a fully informed decision about whether to take part?
- *Other consequences of deception* – Baumrind (1985) suggests the use of deception may decrease the number of naive participants available for future research, and may reduce support for psychological research in general (e.g. via the media).
- *An alternative to deception* – Tell participants about the nature of the study and ask them to *role play* the

procedure as though they were naive participants. More often that not, however, the findings from studies using role play procedures are different from those where investigators have concealed the true purpose of the study.

- *Does deception actually work*? – Kimmel (1996) suggests that for deception to be effective, the level of naivety among participants should be high. The experimental procedure should not produce cues that might be interpreted by participants as indicating that deception is taking place, and participants' suspiciousness of deception should not alter the experimental effect. Some participants may not fully believe the deception used by a researcher.

Informed consent

The essence of informed consent is that participants can agree or refuse to participate in the light of comprehensive information about the nature and purpose of the research. Homan (1991) suggests there are two issues implied in the 'informed' element of informed consent and two involved in the 'consent' part.

'Informed'
To be informed means that:

1 all pertinent aspects of what is to happen and what might happen are disclosed to the participants

2 the participants should also be able to understand this information.

Epstein and Lasagna (1969) reported that only one third of participants volunteering for an experiment really understood what was involved. Even if researchers have sought and obtained informed consent, this does not guarantee that participants really understand what they have agreed to. Another problem is the requirement for the researcher to highlight any risks of participation or possible benefits. Researchers are not always able to predict accurately the risks of taking part in a study.

'Consent'
To give consent means that:

1 participants must be competent to make a rational and mature judgement

2 the agreement to participate should be voluntary and entirely free from coercion or any undue influence.

Some participants may initially give their consent to take part in a study, but if they later realize they want to withdraw that consent (for whatever reason), they should be free to do so, even if they have previously accepted payment for participation.

Issues surrounding informed consent

Researchers should be open and honest in their research because this is more likely to generate public respect. Even researchers who claim to have obtained informed consent may sometimes be selective in how much they tell participants. The issue is not between telling the truth and telling lies, but about where one draws the line in deciding how much information is sufficient. A general rule is that the greater the risk, the more meticulous the researcher must be in informing potential participants (Homan 1991).

The issue of informed consent is slightly different when considering research that takes place in more naturalistic settings (field research). The major obstacle to obtaining informed consent here is that it is often not feasible to do so (Kimmel 1996). In situations where behaviour is public (such as in shopping centres and at football matches) and where the procedures used do not significantly affect participants' lives or pose any risk for them, then informed consent may be deemed to be cumbersome and unnecessary (Kimmel 1996). In such situations, obtaining informed consent may be seen as ethically and methodologically undesirable, provided other measures have been taken to safeguard the interests of the participants (e.g. to ensure anonymity and to minimize invasions of privacy).

Alternatives to fully informed consent

If it is not feasible to obtain fully informed consent, one alternative is not to conduct the research. Other alternatives include:

- *debriefing* – fully informing participants after the study has taken place and giving them the option to withhold their data; however, this cannot eradicate any bad experiences

- *presumptive consent and prior general consent* – for *presumptive consent*, a random sample of the target population to be studied is introduced to the proposed research design, including the deception to be used. If, knowing the true aim of the investigation, the sample agree that they would still have given their voluntary informed consent, the researcher presumes they represent the views of the rest of their population group. For *prior general consent*, prospective participants are informed that participants are sometimes misinformed about the true purpose of the study and asked to give consent without knowing whether their study will involve deception.

Privacy

Privacy is an important issue in field research, where people are frequently unaware they are acting as research participants. Four dimensions are used to determine where a particular piece of research lies on the privacy continuum, and therefore how acceptable observation is under such circumstances:

1 *How public the setting is* – People can less reasonably expect privacy in shopping malls or football grounds than in their own homes.

2 *The public profile of the person* – Public personalities are regularly subject to the kind of public scrutiny and reports that would be considered to be an invasion of privacy for less public individuals.

3 *The degree of anonymity provided* – Privacy is maintained when there is no possible link between an individual and the information obtained.

4 *The nature of the information disclosed* – Certain information (e.g. about sexual practices or benefit fraud) is considered more sensitive and poses a greater risk to participants than other information.

Psychological and physical harm

In some ways deception is an example of psychological harm. No research participant should leave a research study in a different state from the one at the beginning of the study. No participant should feel humiliated, embarrassed or with a lowered sense of self-esteem. However, such outcomes are possible if not inevitable in many studies. The key issue is to balance the researcher's needs against the participants' rights not to be harmed. A certain degree of potential harm or risk is considered to be acceptable if it is no greater than the risks participants might be expected to face in their everyday lives. Therefore, some stress may be deemed to be reasonable, as in the case of the Strange Situation study by Ainsworth and Bell (1970).

One of the problems with risk assessment is that it is difficult to assess risks or harm *before* conducting a study. In some studies, the amount of distress displayed by participants was not anticipated. In such situations, researchers may respond to unexpected levels of distress by stopping a study early (see Zimbardo *et al.*'s 1973 prison simulation study, p.137).

Evaluation of ways of dealing with ethical issues

The 'commentary' sections of the preceding pages outline some of the ways that ethical issues may be resolved. Other general comments include the following:

▧ *Costs and benefits* – Ethical issues are usually resolved by weighing costs against benefits; for example, the costs to participants or costs to research validity against the importance of the research. However, there are many problems associated with this. It is not always possible to calculate costs beforehand. It is also difficult to decide which costs to consider – there are costs to the participant, costs to the research process and costs to society more generally.

▧ *Hidden ethical issues* – Techniques, such as prior general consent and presumptive consent, may not be real alternatives because they raise further ethical issues (passive dishonesty to participants, invalidating the research process by alerting participants to possible deception).

▧ *Debriefing by itself may not be sufficient* – The use of debriefing does not address all issues: for example, participants may not listen to the debriefing because they are keen to go home or they may not believe that the researcher is *now* telling the truth.

▧ *Ethical guidelines can have problems* – Ethical guidelines may lead individual researchers to feel absolved of responsibility for ethical decisions. Guidelines can remove the need for individuals to think through ethical issues for themselves.

▧ *Other ways to deal with ethical issues* – Institutions involved in research are required to have an ethics committee composed of lay and professional members to assess the costs and benefits of proposed research and safeguard the rights of research participants. Research that is deemed to be unethical is not permitted to proceed.

Ethical issues in psychological investigations with human participants

Milgram's (1963) obedience research

Deception and lack of informed consent

Milgram's studies of obedience are discussed in detail on pp.192–198 of *Psychology AS for AQA A*. For Milgram, deception was a necessary part of his research design: without it, participants would have behaved differently. There is support for and against this belief. Prior to the study, Milgram asked a group of students how they thought participants would respond. They estimated that less than three per cent would go to the maximum level. This suggests that if participants knew it was fake, they would behave as the students predicted; this prediction was borne out in a study by Mixon (1972) who replicated Milgram's research. However, Orne and Holland (1968) claimed that Milgram's participants knew the shocks could not be real because it would not make sense for such an extreme amount of harm to be inflicted on the learner in an experiment.

Commentary on justifications for Milgram's research

Milgram's use of deception may be further justified by looking at the circumstances when deception is considered to be acceptable:

▧ *If the effects of deception were unanticipated* – Milgram (1974) argued that he could not predict how the participants would behave, as previous information suggested that most people would not obey.

▧ *Where the potential for harm is minimal* – As he believed that most participants would not obey, Milgram expected that any psychological harm would be minimal. In any case, it is unclear how much harm the participants did experience (see below).

▧ *If the research is non-trivial* – Many psychologists regard Milgram's study as extremely important. Elms (1972) called it the 'most morally significant research in psychology'. Milgram started from the viewpoint that more crimes are committed against humanity in the name of obedience than in the name of rebellion.

▧ *If there is adequate debriefing* – After the study was completed, Milgram's participants were debriefed.

They were introduced to the 'learner' so they could see that all was well; they were also interviewed about their experiences and sent documents about the findings of the study. In addition, some were interviewed one year later.

Harm

Baumrind (1964) accused Milgram of showing insufficient respect for his participants. The participants trembled, stuttered and sweated; one even reportedly had a full blown seizure. As well as such short-term effects, Darley (1992) suggested there are possible harmful long-term effects. The evil that is latent in all of us might have been activated by participation in this investigation and, therefore, participants' future behaviour might have been altered in an undesirable way. Milgram (1974) acknowledges that once the investigation was underway it became clear that some participants would go all the way and experience stress. At that point he did wonder whether he should abandon the study, but he thought there was no indication of any injury and that 'momentary excitement was not the same as harm'.

It is difficult to produce evidence to counter Darley's criticism, but Milgram did argue that there were actually benefits from his research for the participants. When sent a questionnaire, 74 per cent of the participants said they had learned something of personal importance from taking part. One participant wrote to Milgram later, saying that the experiment had provided an insight into *why* he had behaved in this way, and that he was later able to apply this understanding to his decision to register as a conscientious objector (he did not want to be placed in a position where he might have to obey orders with which he disagreed).

In summary, Milgram's research has been both harshly criticized and highly praised. Milgram (1974) suggested that the ethical disapproval was related to the findings, not the procedures, that is, the horror was that people could behave like that, but this was turned into a horror about the way he had treated the participants.

Other investigations

Table 2 summarizes two key studies from the AS specification. You might like to create your own table for some of the key research studies you read about in Chapters 2 to 14 of this book.

Activity **Justifying deception**

Consider whether:
- Milgram's findings could be produced without the deception.
- Milgram's findings are sufficiently important to justify any of the short- and long-term psychological effects?

Interestingly, psychologists remain divided in their answers to this second question.

Research study	Ethical issues	Attempts to deal with issues
Curtiss (1977) Genie was isolated throughout her childhood and then studied intensively by psychologists interested in the effects of privation on development.	(See p.135 of *Psychology AS for AQA A.*) In 1979, Genie's mother filed a case against the psychologists, claiming they had subjected Genie to 'extreme, unreasonable and outrageous intensive testing, experimentation, and observation ... under conditions of duress and servitude'. In short, performing unethical human experimentation (Rymer 1993).	The case was settled by Curtiss giving the proceeds from a book to Genie ($8,000). One of the psychologists commented: 'It turned out that Genie, who had been so terribly abused, was exploited all over again, just by a different set of characters, of which I'm sorry to say I was one' (Rymer 1993).
Zimbardo et al. (1973) Stanford prison study. Students were given a role as either a guard or a prisoner in a mock prison at Stanford University.	(See pp.187–190 of *Psychology AS for AQA A.*) The 'guards' became brutal, harassing the prisoners by making them perform offensive tasks such as cleaning toilets with their bare hands. The 'prisoners' felt humiliated and some of them became anxious and depressed, requesting early release.	The importance of this study has been challenged because it did little to change prison environments (the aim of the study). The study was designed with special attention to ethical issues. Fully informed consent was obtained, except for 'prisoners' arrested at home. However, Zimbardo thought that withholding this kind of procedural detail was justifiable, given the nature of the study. The study was ended prematurely. Participants were thoroughly debriefed both after the study and one year later.

Table 2 *Ethical issues in psychological investigations (from AS studies)*

The ethics of socially sensitive research

Social psychologists, such as the late Stanley Milgram, have an ethical responsibility to society as a whole, and we might argue they would not be fulfilling that responsibility if they did not carry out socially important (often referred to as 'socially sensitive') research to the best of their ability. This idea of socially sensitive research and the particular ethical issues that arise from it will be considered next.

'Prisoners' and 'guard' in the Stanford prison study, 1973

What is socially sensitive research?

Sieber and Stanley (1988) offer the following definition of socially sensitive research: '...studies in which there are potential social consequences or implications, either directly for the participants in research or the class of individuals represented by the research'. Much of what is studied in psychology has a social impact, but the potential for that is greater with some investigations than others. For example, it is difficult to imagine any social impact of research into perceptual illusions. Investigations of the genetic basis of criminality, on the other hand, can have profound social consequences (such as compulsory genetic testing). One of the problems of any research that is deemed to be socially sensitive is that it is likely to attract a lot of attention from the media and the general public, as well as other psychologists (Wadeley et al. 1997).

Controversies associated with this kind of research could be avoided by restricting research interests to areas that attract little attention from the media or from colleagues working outside of the particular field. Ignoring these important areas of research, however, would amount to an abdication of what Aronson (1999) refers to as the 'social responsibilities' of the psychological researcher.

Ethical issues in socially sensitive research

The kind of research that would come under the heading of socially sensitive research includes research into sexual orientation, racial differences, gender-related abilities and mental illness. Some of the ethical issues that arise in such research are outlined below:

- *Privacy* – During the research process, a skilled investigator may extract more information from participants than they intended to give. Some research (e.g. into AIDS) may lead to social policies that are an invasion of people's private lives (e.g. through compulsory antibody testing).

- *Confidentiality* – In some areas of research, questions may reveal information of a sensitive nature (such as sexual habits or drug use). Confidentiality is paramount in such situations. Otherwise, participants would be less willing to divulge this information in the future and further research would be compromised.

- *Sound and valid methodology* – Some of the controversies that arise from socially sensitive research can be attributed to poorly designed or poorly executed studies or inappropriate interpretations of the findings. Although other scientists may be aware of these problems, the media and the general public may not, and therefore there is a danger that poor studies might shape social policy.

- *Justice and equitable treatment* – All participants must be treated in an equitable manner and resources that are vital to the participants' wellbeing (e.g. educational opportunities) must not be withheld from one group while being available to another. Likewise, ideas that create prejudicial treatment of one sector of society are seen as unfair and, therefore, unacceptable. Freud's ideas of the 'deficient' nature of women were instrumental in the treatment of women as second-class citizens in the early part of the 20th century.

- *Scientific freedom* – The role of a researcher is to carry out scientific research. This freedom to pursue scientific research is balanced against the obligation to protect those who take part and those they represent. Censorship of scientific activity is generally regarded as unacceptable, but some careful monitoring of the research process is necessary.

Commentary on ethical issues in socially sensitive research

- *The psychologist's dilemma* – Are the needs of society more important than the needs of the individual? Aronson (1999) suggests that psychologists face a particularly difficult dilemma when their wider responsibility to society conflicts with their more specific responsibilities to each individual research participant. This conflict is greatest when the issues under investigation are of great social importance. The more important the issue and the more potential benefit a study might have for society, the more likely it is that the individual participant may experience some degree of anxiety or discomfort. Longer-term social issues should be carefully weighed against concern about shorter-term individual rights.

- *Use of ethical guidelines* – Ethical guidelines are essential, but they tend to focus on the immediate needs of research participants and may not deal with all the possible ways in which research may inflict harm on a group of people or section of society.

The use of non-human animals in psychological investigations

Non-human animals have been used in many different kinds of psychological investigation. We begin with a few well-known examples with which you will be able to supplement other examples that you encounter in this textbook.

Experimental research

Harlow's monkeys
Harlow's original interest lay in research about learning. He needed monkeys for these experiments and wanted to reduce disease in the monkeys by raising them in his own laboratory away from their mothers. He noticed that the motherless monkeys formed strong attachments to pieces of cloth in their cages, leading him to wonder whether contact comfort rather than feeding was critical for attachment to develop. To test this, Harlow and Harlow (1962) isolated young monkeys with surrogate wire mothers. In one study the wire mothers blasted the monkeys with strong jets of air, and metal spikes pushed the monkeys away in order to test the effects of abusive mothering. However, the most significant ethical issue raised by this research was the lasting effect on all the monkeys. They became maladjusted adults, had difficulties in reproductive relationships and were poor parents (see also p.119 of *Psychology AS for AQA A*).

Harlow's monkey with the cloth-covered 'mother'

Animal language
The experimental nature of some field studies may not be immediately apparent (i.e. the study may appear to be observational, whereas in fact some manipulation of the environment was undertaken). For example, Seyfarth and Cheney (1992) recorded the use of different alarm calls in vervet monkeys. They tested the monkeys' understanding of these alarm calls by using playback and were able to demonstrate a causal link between the vocalization and a monkey's response. It is possible that monkeys may habituate (become used) to hearing these calls in the absence of a predator, which may put the animals in danger should they fail to respond to alarm calls involving real predators.

A vervet monkey

Teaching human language to non-human animals
Studies by Gardner and Gardner (1969) and Savage-Rumbaugh (1988) attempted to teach human language (sign language and lexigrams) to primates, such as Washoe and Kanzi, while immersing them in human culture. Some of the primates in these studies have continued to be cared for by research foundations, but this has not been true of all primates in such research programmes.

Naturalistic observation

Social learning and sweet potatoes
One of the most famous examples of imitation in non-human animals is the incidence of sweet potato washing in Japanese macaque monkeys. Researchers studying the monkeys tried to bring them into the open by placing sweet potatoes along the beach. One monkey, named Imo by the researchers, began to wash the sand off her sweet potatoes in the water instead of brushing it off with her hand like the other macaques did. Over time, this behaviour spread to other members of the troop and was passed on from generation to generation (Kawai 1965).

A macaque monkey

Dance of honey bees

Von Frisch (1967) recorded the remarkable dance used by honeybees to communicate the location of a source of nectar to other bees in the hive. The 'waggle dance' communicates the direction and distance of the source. Wenner (1964) also studied communication in bees, recording their dance with a camera and a tape recorder. He found that the duration of the sounds made by the bees was equivalent to the distance to the source.

Dance is demonstrated within the hive

Commentary on the use of non-human animals in psychological investigations

▪ *Physical or psychological harm* – It is worth remembering that laboratory experiments involving non-human animals do not always involve harm. Although field experiments may appear to be potentially less harmful, they may actually cause as much harm to animal participants as laboratory experiments. By their very nature, field experiments alter the natural environment of the animal in some way. This tampering with nature in order to understand it places great responsibilities on the researcher to ensure that the disruptive effects of any manipulation are minimized. In an analysis of over 930 research papers published in the journal *Animal Behaviour* between the years 1986 and 1990, Cuthill (1991) calculated that 46 per cent were field studies, of which one third involved experimental manipulations.

▪ *The importance of research findings* – As with research with human participants, it is important to weigh any harm to non-human animals against the benefits for humans (and possibly non-human participants also).

Harlow's research with monkeys has made a significant contribution to our understanding of behaviour. Prior to this research, no one believed that comfort alone might be so important. The long-term effects of the experiment were surprising.

▪ *Humane treatment of non-human animal participants* – Humane treatment is most importantly to do with their care during and after an experiment. Careless and insensitive handling usually causes more harm than the experimental procedures themselves. The legislation that regulates animal research focuses on this aspect of the research as much as on the procedures used in the experiment.

Guidelines for working with animals

The British Psychological Society, like other professional organizations around the world, has prepared guidelines for psychologists working with animals (BPS 2007). Any psychologists contravening the principles may be struck off the professional register.

The main points of the BPS guidelines in relation to working with animals in psychology include the following:

▪ *Legislation* – Psychologists must familiarize themselves with the laws regarding animal welfare and conform to relevant legislation.

▪ *Replacing the use of animals* – Alternatives, such as video recordings or computer simulations, should be used where possible.

▪ *Choice of species and strain* – Psychologists should choose a species that is scientifically and ethically suited to the research purpose. This requires knowledge about the species' natural history and their level of sentience. The researcher should also be aware of an individual animal's previous experience (e.g. whether it was bred in captivity).

▪ *Numbers of animals* – Researchers are legally required to use the smallest numbers of animals needed to achieve the research goals.

▪ *Procedures* – Any procedure that might cause pain, suffering, injury, lasting harm, physiological or psychological stress, or significant discomfort or disturbance should be carefully evaluated and alternatives considered. Regulation of food intake (e.g. for conditioning experiments) may be harmful and researchers should consider an animal's normal food intake and metabolic requirements. Investigators studying animals in the field should minimize interference.

▪ *Procurement of animals* – Common laboratory species must come from Home Office Designated Breeding and Supply Establishments.

▪ *Animal care* – Researchers are also responsible for the conditions under which animals are kept when they are not being studied. This should include a minimum of freedom of movement, food, water and care appropriate to the animals' health and wellbeing.

- *Disposing of animals* – The reuse of animals after a research study has been completed requires approval from the Home Office. Appropriate measures must be taken to ensure that they continue to receive a high standard of care. If animals have to be killed during or after a study, this must be done as humanely and painlessly as possible, using acceptable methods and following specific guidelines.

- *Other issues* – Researchers should also be concerned with the use of animals in psychology training, the use of animals for therapeutic purposes and the clinical assessment and treatment of animal behaviour.

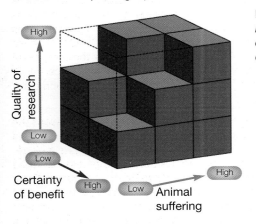

A 'lab rat'

Criteria for assessing research on animals

If animals are to be used in research, then additional criteria to those covered by the Animals (Scientific Procedures) Act 1986 are important. Bateson (1986) proposed a system based on three criteria – quality of the research, degree of animal suffering and certainty of benefits – which enables researchers to evaluate research with non-human animals. It is referred to as Bateson's decision cube (see Fig. 4).

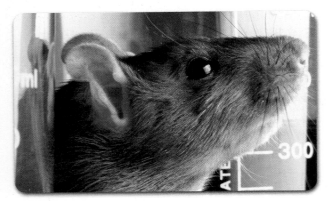

Figure 4
Bateson's decision cube

Quality of the research

The high costs of carrying out animal research, together with difficulties in obtaining research funding, means that research grants are only awarded to animal research of the highest quality in terms of design and procedures.

Degree of animal suffering

It is difficult to assess the degree to which a particular animal is or is not suffering as a result of specific research procedures. When threatened by danger, some animals remain rigid and silent because that is the safest thing to do, but we may not recognize such behaviour as being a state of stress. As our knowledge of how animals behave increases, psychologists will become more aware of what is likely to be stressful for a particular species.

Certainty of benefit

Some people may believe that great human suffering is far worse than the possibility of moderate levels of discomfort inflicted on animals in the course of research. However, the funding of high-quality psychological research may not be viewed in that light by its critics. It is difficult to predict exactly what the likely benefits of such research might be to the lives of humans and other animals. An example of this is research conducted on Alzheimer's disease (see following panel on Alzheimer's disease). There is no known cure, but investigations using rats and monkeys allow us to begin to understand how certain brain circuits may function. In such cases, do you think that the ends really do justify the means? Try the Activity on the use of non-human animals in psychological research.

One of the major social problems of the 21st century will be the increasing numbers of old people. A proportion of these will suffer from senile dementia, including Alzheimer's disease. In its severest form, Alzheimer's produces severe memory loss, confusion, loss of the sense of self-identity and double incontinence. Caring for sufferers is usually a family affair, 24 hours a day every day of the year, and involves watching a husband or wife, father or mother, steadily degenerating.

As yet, there is no cure for Alzheimer's disease ... We know from the brain changes seen at postmortem that there is a particular pattern of damage to brain circuits, and we know from animal studies that these circuits are also involved in memory in rats and monkeys ... this model of Alzheimer's disease is being used to develop possible treatments. These include new drugs to restore brain function, and the use of grafts of brain cells to replace cells that have died. ... Animal research is also helping to reveal the biochemical abnormalities responsible for producing the brain damage.

There are encouraging signs that a treatment for Alzheimer's disease may emerge, which will have depended absolutely on the use of animal testing for its development. If successful, it would have a dramatic impact, improving the quality of life for both those with Alzheimer's and those who would otherwise sacrifice their lives in caring for them. Is this potential benefit sufficient to justify the use of animals in psychological research?

Source: Green (1994)

Evaluation of the Bateson decision cube

This model provides an indication of when animal research may be tolerated and when it cannot. It is also clear that certain levels of animal suffering cannot be tolerated, regardless of the quality of the research or the probability of benefit. The model would, however, permit research of no direct benefit, if it was of high scientific quality and involved little animal suffering. The effectiveness of any model, such as that proposed by Bateson, depends on an accurate assessment of issues, including quality, benefit and suffering. This is not as straightforward as it might appear:

- *Evaluating the quality of proposed research* – Scientists use peer review to assess the quality of research. All research proposals are routinely assessed by experts in the relevant field.

- *Measuring animal suffering* – Three factors are commonly used to assess animal suffering: an animal's state of physical health, signs of stress and the animal's behaviour.

- *Evaluating the potential benefits of the research* – This can be a difficult judgement to make. The aim of the research should always go beyond curiosity and have the potential to contribute real understanding.

Arguments *for* and *against* the use of non-human animals

Arguments for and against the use of non-human animals can be separated into ethical and scientific arguments. Ethical arguments concern what is right or wrong, whereas scientific arguments concern usefulness (i.e. how much can we find out from using non-human animals in research).

Ethical arguments

Ethical arguments in favour of using animals are summarized in the left-hand column of Table 3 below, and some counter arguments are outlined in the right-hand column.

Scientific arguments

Scientific arguments in favour of using animals in psychological research are listed in the left-hand column of Table 4 and some counter arguments are summarized in the right-hand column.

Commentary on the animal rights position

- *In defence of the use of animals in research*, the British Association for the Advancement of Science produced a Declaration on Animals in Research (1990), which includes the following statements: 'Experiments on animals have made an important contribution to advances in medicine and surgery, which have brought major improvements in the health of human beings and animals' and 'Continued research involving animals is essential for the conquest of many unsolved medical problems, such as cancer, AIDS, other infectious diseases, and genetic, developmental, neurological and psychiatric conditions'.

- *The utilitarian argument* is that whatever produces the greatest pleasure and happiness (relative to pain and suffering) for the greatest number of people is ethically acceptable; no one person's happiness is more important than any other's. In *Animal Liberation*, Peter Singer (1990) extends this to include all creatures that are capable of sensation (sentient creatures). Singer's 'principle of equality' claims that all sentient creatures have an equal interest in avoiding pain and suffering, therefore there is no moral basis for elevating the interests of one species (e.g. humans) over those of

Arguments for	Arguments against
Easing human suffering *We are morally obliged to use animals to ease human suffering* Evolution has placed human beings on top of the phylogenetic tree, so it is natural to make use of 'lower' animals for our own ends. If, by using animals, we can ease human suffering, then we are morally obliged to do so.	**An obligation to ease human suffering?** The argument opposite is known as the 'naturalistic fallacy'. If our moral reasoning is the result of evolution, then not using other species for our own ends may be seen as the next step in that evolution. Those who argue for using animals to ease human suffering have a tendency to overemphasize the benefits and play down the suffering that produced those benefits.
Human, not animal, rights *Animals do not have any rights* Rights arise as a result of implicit contracts between members of society, and imply duties. Animals have no such responsibilities, cannot reciprocate and, therefore, have no rights.	**Animal rights?** Animals have rights by virtue of their 'inherent value' (Regan 2004). These rights include the right to be treated with respect and not to be harmed. The traditional scientific position on animal research treats animals as 'renewable resources' rather than as organisms of value whose rights must be respected. Furthermore, some humans, such as infants and people who are mentally ill, might not be able to fulfil their obligations to society, but they are not denied rights within it.
Human, not animal, feelings *Animals do not have the same feelings as humans* The traditional defence of the use of non-human animals has focused on the philosophical view that humans and non-humans can be differentiated: non-humans do not possess a soul and so are not capable of moral choice or any other feelings or emotions that are peculiarly human.	**Animals' feelings and emotions?** Research evidence is accumulating that suggests animals are capable of experiencing a range of emotions and feelings. For example, a recent study found that fish can feel pain (Sneddon *et al.* 2003). Despite such research, the view of animals as 'mechanical systems' or 'renewable resources' is a hard one to shake off.
Protection through legislation *Animal welfare is protected by legislation* There are strict laws (e.g. the Animals (Scientific Procedures) Act 1986) and codes of conduct (e.g. guidance published by the British Psychological Society) that protect animals used in research.	**Legislative protection** Ethical guidelines tend to be based on a cost–benefit model, where the recipients of costs (i.e. the animals) and of benefits (i.e. humans) tend to be different, ignoring the substantive rights of animals in favour of practical, utilitarian considerations (Regan 2004)
Using less invasive methods *Modern methods are less invasive* A number of less invasive procedures have been developed in animal research. This minimizes animal suffering and provides a moral justification for animal research.	**Using less invasive methods** If researchers were not allowed to use animals in research, they would have to develop other techniques (such as clinical and epidemiological studies) to take the place of animal research. CT, PET and MRI scans are among the modern alternatives to animal research. If we were to adopt a model based on animal rights, then animals would have the right not to be used by humans for research regardless of how non-invasive the research procedures, or how potentially beneficial the consequences for human beings.

Table 3 *Ethical arguments* for *and against the use of animals in psychological research*

another species. To do so would be to commit *speciesism* – logically parallel to other forms of discrimination such as racism and sexism. Research on animals would, therefore, only be permitted when the potential benefits of the research are high and the research could not be carried out using human participants.

CHECK YOUR UNDERSTANDING

Check your understanding of issues in psychology by answering the following questions. Try to do this from memory. You can check your answers by looking back through Section 2.

Arguments for	Arguments against
Usefulness of the research *Non-human animal research is useful* The use of animals in research is usually justified to the public because it contributes directly to the relief of human suffering. In developing a cure for a disease, such as cancer or Alzheimer's, the animal's suffering is offset by the relief from much of the physical, social and economic suffering that inevitably accompanies such conditions.	**Useful research?** Those who calculate the benefits to humankind, rather than the costs to animals, could be accused of 'speciesism' (see the utilitarian argument below).
Greater control and objectivity *Animals offer the opportunity for greater control and objectivity in research procedures* Much behavioural theory was established using animal studies for just this reason. Objectivity is more easily achieved with non-human animals than humans, simply because it is difficult to remain completely objective when studying our own species.	**Greater control and objectivity** The BPS *Guidelines for psychologists working with animals* highlights the possibility that even rewards given to animals may be considered harmful. Deprivation and aversive stimulation can cause distress to animals and alternatives should be used wherever possible (BPS 2007).
When research on humans is not possible *We may use animals when we can't use humans* Animals have been exposed to various procedures and events that would not be possible with humans. Harlow's deprivation studies with rhesus monkeys could not have been carried out on humans. Often the need to establish cause-and-effect relationships in psychological research involves participants in procedures that they would not consent to take part in.	**When research on humans is not possible** This raises the moral question of why psychologists might expose animals to research procedures that could not be justified with human participants.
Similar physiologies *Use animals because they resemble humans* Human and non-human animals share sufficient of their physiology and evolutionary past to justify conclusions drawn from the one being applied to the other. Behaviourists, such as Skinner, saw sufficient similarity between rats and humans to warrant a special interest in rats as research subjects. Green (1994) argues that the basic physiology of mammalian brains and nervous systems is essentially the same, although the human brain might be more highly developed.	**Not similar enough** Critics of animal research assert that the physiologies of humans and non-humans are not similar enough to justify generalizing conclusions from animal research to humans. They argue that the only way to understand human physiology or behaviour (e.g. pathologies such as drug abuse or dependency) is to study human beings.

Table 4 *Scientific arguments for and against using animals in psychological research*

Bias in psychological research

1. What term is used to describe a theory that minimizes differences between men and women?

2. Give one example of an alpha-biased theory.

3. Give one positive and one negative consequence of beta-biased theories.

4. Describe the four criteria that Worell and Remer (1992) suggest could lead to bias-free theory.

5. Describe four ways in which the research process can be gender-biased.

6. What is the difference between the emic and etic approaches in psychology?

7. In addition to the emic–etic distinction, describe two further kinds of cultural bias in psychology.

8. Give an example of a psychological theory that represents an individualist perspective, and explain in what way it is individualist.

9. Outline two reasons why cross-cultural research may lack validity.

10. What is an 'imposed etic'?

Ethical issues in psychological research

11. In what way is 'informed consent' an ethical issue, whereas debriefing is not?

12. Psychologists resolve ethical issues by using ethical guidelines; describe two additional ways of resolving ethical issues.

13. Under what circumstances might psychological harm be acceptable in a research study?

14. Briefly explain what is meant by 'socially sensitive research'.

15. Summarize the scientific arguments in favour of using non-human animals in psychological research.

Introduction

People participate in public debates to help crystallize their own views on topics (e.g. whether capital punishment should be reintroduced in the UK). We can usually think of arguments to support our own opinion, but it is also important to be aware of possible counter arguments.

In many debates there are no 'right' answers; rather the aim is to arrive at a better understanding of the issues involved, in order to hold a more informed opinion. Three of the four debates we shall examine in this section have a long history in psychology and philosophy:

- free will versus determinism
- reductionist explanations – arguments for and against
- nature versus nurture.

Few psychologists today adhere rigidly to only one side of such debates. Increasingly, psychologists appear to be resolving some of these issues by adopting a more **interactionist** approach.

The debate over whether psychology is – or should even strive to be – a science is the final debate we shall consider. It remains a highly contentious issue, which gets to the very heart of what psychology is about, and how psychologists should conduct their investigations. Exploring differing views on these debates should help you make up your own mind about what *you* think about these key issues.

The free will/determinism debate in psychology

Activity Exercising your own free will?

List various things you have done today (e.g. behaviours and activities):

- For each one, try to identify how the particular behaviour might have been determined by some internal or external factor (e.g. hormones, genes, another person, past experience).
- Are there any things that you freely chose to do? If so, were they truly free choices or were they selected from a limited range of possibilities?

Free will

The idea that we have some choice in how we act is fundamental to most common-sense theories of psychology. The notion of '**free will**' allows us to separate out what is clearly the intention of an individual from what has been caused by some internal or external event beyond the person's control. It assumes we are free to choose our behaviour, i.e. we are self-determining. The term 'free will' does not imply that behaviour is random (caused by chance), but rather that we are freed from the causal influences of past events (such as instinct or our past reinforcement history).

Determinism

The determinist approach, on the other hand, proposes that all behaviour is determined and is, therefore, predictable. Some approaches in psychology see the source of this **determinism** as being outside the individual – a position known as **environmental determinism**. Others see it as coming from inside the organism (e.g. in the form of unconscious motivation or genetically determined); this position is known as **biological determinism**. The position psychologists take on this issue can have an important effect on the way they explain human nature.

Reconciling free will and determinism

The idea of free will seems incompatible with the idea of determinism because determinism assumes that all behaviours are the result of some prior cause. Part of the scientific perspective in psychology is a belief in causal determinism. Free will would, therefore, appear to be incompatible with the goals of scientific psychology. However, this is not necessarily the case, as indicated by the potential resolutions below.

- *Proximate and ultimate goals* – The concept of 'will' refers to the idea that people make decisions about the goals they are seeking to achieve. These goals, such as passing your A-level exam, are then translated into current (or proximate) thoughts and actions. For example, if I decide that I want to learn to play the piano (my ultimate goal), I might buy a piano, find a piano teacher and start practising. All these actions are the product of conscious planning (i.e. my free will), but are *determined* by my final (ultimate) goal of being able to play the piano. Anyone who knew of my intention to learn the piano could probably predict my proximate actions. Therefore, the concept of free will is compatible with a wider view of determinism.

- *Soft determinism* – In the 19th century, William James coined the phrase 'soft determinism' to indicate that behaviour can be separated into mental activities and physical states. Mental activities are subject to free will, whereas physical states are determined. If one accepts this dualist position (i.e. that mental and physical events are separate) then both free will and determinism are possible.

Liberal determinism – Others have also attempted to define a softer kind of determinism. Heather (1976) suggested a version known as liberal determinism – the view that behaviour is determined to the extent that people act consistently with their character. It is easier to reconcile this view of determinism with the idea of free will because the liberal version allows for choice (free will) within a limited range of options (that are determined).

- *Free from coercion* – Others take the view that free will implies freedom from coercion. Handing over money to someone who is collecting for charity is seen as an example of free will, whereas the same act is seen as determined if it is carried out at gunpoint. In fact, these psychologists would argue that both acts are determined, but the latter is not 'free' because the behaviour is the result of coercion.

Arguments *for* free will and *against* determinism

The psychological argument
People have a subjective sense of free will. Most people feel that they possess free will and are able, at any time, to make free choices. However, simply *feeling* that you are free does not mean this is true. Skinner (1971), for example, claimed that free will was an illusion – we think we are free because we are not aware of how our behaviour is determined by reinforcement. Freud also believed that free will was an illusion. He argued that although we may think we are acting freely, our behaviour is, in fact, determined by unconscious forces.

Valentine (1991), on the other hand, claims that this subjective sense of free will is a tenable proposition. It is something that can be studied and demonstrated to be true. For example, the acceptance of free will has been found to increase with age and also is more common in individualist cultures where personal responsibility is emphasized.

The ethical argument
It is often argued that if we expect people to be morally responsible, we must accept the concept of free will. If an individual's behaviour is determined by forces beyond their control, then the individual cannot be held responsible for their actions. Behaviourists, for example, suggest that moral behaviour is learned largely through the processes of conditioning. Therefore, there is no individual responsibility because good or bad behaviour is determined by external forces. In other words, it may be possible to behave in a moral fashion without having moral responsibility. However, our laws insist that adults do have individual responsibility for their actions and so have free will. We can be held responsible, as long as we have a range of choices to choose from, even if those choices are largely predetermined. Free will only requires that choices exist.

Determinism is not falsifiable
Scientific theories should generate hypotheses that can be tested to see if they are true or false (see Chapter 15, p.514). If this is not possible, then the validity of the theory cannot be tested. It is not possible to test the statement 'All behaviour can be explained within a determinist framework'. Even if, one day, it might be possible to explain all human behaviour in terms of causal relationships, it is simply a matter of faith at present that, theoretically at least, all behaviour could be determined and so is predictable. Therefore, the argument for determinism is not falsifiable.

Valentine (1991), who supports the concept of free will, suggests that determinism *is* falsifiable because it *has been falsified* by the uncertainty principle (see below). The proof that determinism is not true demonstrates that at least it can be falsified!

Arguments *against* free will and *for* determinism

Difficulty in specifying free will
The notion of free will implies there is something doing the 'willing', i.e. something that is mental rather than physical. Besides trying to establish what might do the willing, there is a further important question of how mental states might interact with physical states.

We may gain insights into this interaction by considering mental illnesses, such as schizophrenia, where patients lack voluntary control or the ability to initiate activity. Such deficits have been associated with the limbic system; this association is also supported by research with non-human animals where the removal of the limbic system prevents the animal from being able to initiate activity (Ridley 2003).

If the 'will' has a physical basis then it is also determined – an outcome of brain activity (as suggested above) and subject to the same influences as all other physical activities (e.g. hormones and genes). In other words, so-called free will can be located within a deterministic framework.

Free will is inconsistent with science
The notion of current events being determined by something in the past is fundamental to scientific psychology. It could be argued that discovering the determinants of behaviour is the ultimate goal of psychology. Indeed, the essence of experimental research is that we measure behaviour before and after an experimental intervention in order to investigate the relationship between cause and effect. If, however, human behaviour is governed by free will, there is no causality to be discovered.

Psychological research has been accused of oversimplifying complex behaviours, so its findings do not relate to real life. Later in this section, arguments against reductionism and against psychology as a science will be examined, both of which suggest that scientific research may not always be an appropriate way to understand human behaviour.

Furthermore, modern science no longer upholds the view that the world is predictable. Heisenberg's 'uncertainty principle' (Heisenberg 1927) suggests that the behaviour of subatomic particles cannot be systematically predicted, so it is not possible to make statements about causal relationships that will always be true. However, O'Connor (1971) concludes that 'the findings of quantum mechanics do not offer any clear and indisputable evidence in favour of free will'. So, the fact that indeterminism has been found in physics does not mean that there is free will.

Predictability of people's behaviour

The same argument that was presented for free will can also be made for determinism – we have a subjective sense that the psychological world, like the physical world, is predictable. For example, if we know ourselves to be generous or mean with money we expect to behave in a similar way in the future. Similarly, we expect that a person who has previously been generous will continue to behave that way in the future.

Mischel's theory of personality (1968), however, proposed that people do not have a consistent personality, which would appear to challenge the claim that personality is predictable. He argued that people are only consistent in the same situations, and their behaviour varies from one situation to another. You might, for example, be shy in class, but quite different when with your friends. However, other research (e.g. Fleeson 2001) has found that people are actually highly consistent (and therefore predictable) even across different situations, and if people are predictable, then their behaviour must be caused in a lawful way (i.e. it is determined).

Free will and determinism in psychological research

Another way to present arguments for determinism is to consider whether determinist approaches have been successful in psychology. The three examples below can therefore be used to argue for determinism, although, in some cases, the limitations of such approaches can be viewed as arguments against determinism (or arguments for free will). Similarly, the success of free will approaches can be used as an argument for free will.

The psychodynamic approach

An essential part of psychoanalytic theory is a belief in psychic determinism, that is, events do not occur by chance, but are purposefully related to unconscious, internal processes. Because of this control by internal forces, and the belief that any perceived freedom of choice is in fact illusory, psychodynamic theory is an example of biological determinism (see Section 1 of this chapter for more detail about the psychodynamic approach).

Commentary on the psychodynamic approach

- *Successful therapeutic application* – The assumptions of psychoanalysis have been applied to the treatment of abnormal behaviour, using psychoanalysis. This method has been widely used and found to be successful with certain types of people and with certain types of disorder. Some older reviews presented a rather unfavourable view of psychoanalysis (e.g. Eysenck 1952), whereas others (e.g. Bergin 1971) have reported that some patients undergoing psychoanalysis have benefited from it. Such success supports the determinist explanation of the development of human behaviour. However, the fact that psychoanalysis is successful may be due to factors other than the correctness of the explanation (e.g. it may be the warmth of the therapist–patient interaction that enables a patient to become more self-accepting).

The psychoanalytic therapist and patient

- *The theory lacks falsifiability* – Freud's account of personality permitted him to place interpretations on behaviour that could not be shown to be wrong. For example, he would argue that a person behaved in a certain way because of something that had happened in infancy. If the person agreed, this showed that Freud was right. If the person disagreed, Freud could argue that this showed that the patient was repressing certain experiences.

- *Overemphasis on sexual influences as determinants of behaviour* – Subsequent psychologists (sometimes referred to as 'neo-Freudians') have adapted Freud's theory to incorporate social influences and address the rather unreasonable way that Freud viewed women.

The behavioural approach

Behaviourists believe that behaviour is a product of the reinforcement provided by the environment. Although many people accept that such conditioning takes place, they may still cling to the belief that they are free to plan their actions. For behaviourists, the position is much clearer: actions are determined by factors in the environment which, either directly or indirectly, mould behaviour. This approach is an example of 'environmental determinism'.

Commentary on the behavioural approach

- *Successful therapeutic application* – Behavioural assumptions have been applied to the treatment of abnormal behaviour (e.g. systematic desensitization, discussed on p.380). One ethical criticism made of such therapies is that they are manipulative – the therapist determines suitable goals for the patient and manipulates the patient's behaviour through conditioning to achieve these goals. Such manipulation is based on a determinist view of behaviour.

- *Behavioural explanations are reductionist* – They reduce complex behaviour to a series of stimulus–response units that respond to reinforcement. This explanation may be suitable for non-human animal behaviour, but is less relevant to many human behaviours, which have multiple determinants and where the ability to think about choices (free will) matters. Therefore, the behaviourist approach in psychology has limited application to real-world behaviour.

Behavioural experiment in a laboratory

- *Bandura's notion of reciprocal determinism* – Both learning theory and social learning theory portray the individual as being controlled by their environment. However, Bandura (1977) suggested that individuals are controlled by – but are also in control of – their environment. As the individual acts, this changes the environment, which in turn influences subsequent behaviour. Individuals are capable of making their own choices and this ultimately affects what they imitate.

The cognitive approach

The cognitive approach might appear to be an approach that exemplifies free will because of its emphasis on thinking. For example, the cognitive explanation of mental illness suggests that maladaptive and irrational thinking, which takes place without full awareness, can lead to a distorted view of reality. Treatment, therefore, involves learning to think in a different and more rational way, and learning to be self-determining – a feature of free will.

Commentary on the cognitive approach

- *Successful therapeutic application* – The assumptions of the cognitive approach have also led to successful therapies (see cognitive-behavioural therapies described on p.357). Despite such therapies being ultimately related to self-determination, they are also quite directive. The therapist challenges the patient's current thinking and trains the patient to think more rationally. In this way, the therapy is not related to free will.

- *The cognitive approach is also deterministic* – Another example of the cognitive approach is the use of the concept of 'schema'. A schema is a set of interrelated concepts, i.e. a representation of previous experiences. These schema create expectations about the world which determine our perceptions and behaviours. In this way, the cognitive approach is also deterministic.

Conquering irrational fears?

Reductionism as a form of explanation

One of the major developments in scientific thinking in the behavioural sciences has been the notion that the simplest explanations of events are usually the best. C. Lloyd Morgan (1852–1936) supported this view. Morgan's *law of parsimony* states that we have no need to explain behaviour in terms of complex psychological processes when it can be explained adequately in terms of much simpler processes. This logical principle underlies scientific explanations, models and theory building.

This tendency to simplify an explanation is one form of reductionism – reduction in explanations. Another kind of reductionism is 'methodological reductionism': reductionism as a method of investigating phenomena. In order to demonstrate causal links, a researcher reduces behaviour to a set of variables (the independent and dependent variables) that can be controlled and measured.

Arguments *for* reductionist explanations

- *Reductionism as a scientific approach* – Reductionism has worked well in other sciences. Scientific research is reductionist and has led to many important discoveries which have enabled people to understand, control and predict the world better. For example, knowledge about how various metals respond to stress has enabled people to build bridges. Reductionism creates the possibility of a fully scientific psychology, where we might be able to understand completely the causes of behaviour. As we have already noted, breaking complex behaviours into smaller units enables us to discover causal relationships.

- *Appropriate for certain levels of explanation* – We can explain any particular behaviour at each of Rose's different levels of explanation (see below). For example, mental illness can be explained in physiological terms (the activity of neurotransmitters at a synapse), in terms of the psyche (e.g. unconscious motivations) or in terms of social systems (e.g. family relationships).

Rose's five levels of explanation

Rose (1997) distinguishes between different levels of explanation, each with a valid contribution to make. Starting at the lowest level they are:

- the molecular level (physics)
- the intra-cellular level (biochemistry)
- parts of individuals (physiology)
- behaviour of individuals (psychology)
- the behaviour of groups (sociology).

- *Reductionist explanations are successful* – Later in this section, some reductionist explanations in psychology will be outlined, together with their criticisms. These explanations can also contribute towards an argument for reductionism.

Activity **Levels of explanation**

Using Rose's idea of different levels of explanation, how would you explain eating disorders (or any other example of human or animal behaviour) in:

- physiological terms
- psychological terms
- social terms?

1 Which of these do you think is most appropriate for explaining the chosen behaviour?

2 Why do you think it is difficult to link the different levels of explanation?

Discuss your ideas with other students in your psychology class.

Commentary on arguments *for* reductionism

- *Reductionism as a scientific approach* – Methodological reductionism may be appropriate for the physical sciences, but less appropriate when explaining behaviour that is more complex. Complex systems may not be a simple summation of their constituent parts. Gestalt psychologists argued that the whole is more than the sum of its parts. This *holist approach* can also be seen in connectionist (or neural) networks, which is a more current model of memory than the rather linear and reductionist multi-store model (which you studied as part of your AS course). The connectionist memory model is based on the fact that the brain consists of an interconnected network of neurons, with each neuron connected on average to 10,000 other neurons. The behaviour of such an interconnected network is not a simple sum of the individual links. Networking permits new properties to emerge, so that the entire system has properties that do not belong to the individual parts.

- *Levels of explanation* – Rose (1997) suggests that biologists need all five levels of explanation and no one explanation is correct; it all depends on the kind of explanation that is required. The challenge is knowing which kind of explanation to select. For example, the use of antidepressants to treat depression may miss the *real* causes of a person's depression (e.g. a family problem). If it were possible to link the different levels of explanation, there would be less of a problem when choosing one explanation rather than another. There are some examples in psychology where links between levels of explanation have been found, such as understanding that learning through conditioning can be equated to certain neurochemical changes in the brain (Kandel 1979), linking the psychological and physiological levels. In general, however, such links are not possible because of the essential conflict between mental and physical state (this is sometimes referred to as the mind–body problem).

Arguments *against* reductionist explanations

- *Erroneous explanations of behaviour* – Methodological reductionism aims to make the study of behaviour more accessible by reducing the variables. The findings of experimental research may not apply to other settings because key variables have been oversimplified. For example, memory research often involves learning nonsense syllables or word lists, which are a gross simplification of real-world memory tasks. They are easy to use, but the results do not generalize to memory in general. Memory studied in the real world can generate quite different findings (see *Psychology AS for AQA A* p.87 for a description of Bahrick *et al.'s* (1975) research in memory for names of old high-school colleagues).

- *Reductionist goals are inappropriate* – Another argument against reductionism is that reductionist goals are inappropriate for psychology. Within psychopathology, some psychologists argue that it is entirely inappropriate to view schizophrenia as a physical–chemical system that has gone wrong. The disorder, they claim, only makes sense when studied at the level of the experience, and treatment should therefore target this level of explanation.

- *Appropriate only for certain kinds of question* – Reductionist explanations may only be appropriate for certain kinds of question. Valentine (1992) suggests that physiological explanations focus on structures, whereas holist explanations are more concerned with process. For example, when studying stress, it might be appropriate to consider physiological systems because one is studying structures; stress management, on the other hand, is more concerned with process and so holist approaches are more appropriate.

Commentary on arguments *against* reductionism

- *The value of different explanations* – It would be wrong to dismiss all studies conducted under artificial circumstances as being ungeneralizable; such research may contribute to a greater understanding. However, it is also essential to acknowledge the limitations of such studies.

- *Inappropriate for psychology* – A holist view would appear to be supported by the modest success achieved by drug therapies in the treatments of mental illness (see Chapter 10, pp.349–50). If physical–chemical explanations were appropriate, we ought to find far fewer individual differences and higher success rates. However, a humanistic view would lead to the use of more psychological treatments, which are also not universally successful.

Reductionism in psychological research

Two examples of reductionism in psychological theory and research – physiological and evolutionary – are discussed next.

Physiological reductionism

Since human beings are biological organisms, it should be possible to reduce even complex behaviours to their constituent neurophysiological components. The clear advantage of this is that it leads to the application of concise and concrete concepts, which are then susceptible to scientific methods of research (Wadeley *et al.* 1997). For example, scientists interested in the causes of schizophrenia have found evidence that excess activity of the biochemical neurotransmitter dopamine is a characteristic of schizophrenia (see Chapter 9, p.315). This discovery has led to the hope that schizophrenia might be eradicated by controlling the brain chemistry of people with schizophrenia by the administration of antipsychotic drugs that reduce dopamine activity. This biochemical theory of schizophrenia reduces the importance of environmental factors in the development of the disorder.

Evaluation of physiological reductionism

Most theorists agree that schizophrenia is probably caused by a combination of factors:

- Genetic and biological factors may establish a predisposition to develop the disorder.

- Psychological factors, such as stress, may trigger its onset or recurrence.

- Other psychological and socio-cultural factors, such as individual misinterpretations or societal labelling, may help to maintain or worsen the symptoms.

Thus we see that complex phenomena cannot easily be explained solely in terms of physiological imbalance.

Evolutionary reductionism

Darwin's theory of evolution offers a reductionist explanation of the complex living phenomena in our world, based on the principles of natural selection (see p.6). Together with Mendelian genetics (unknown to Darwin), which explained how dominant and recessive genes were passed from parent to offspring, it provides a way of explaining how species change and how variety is possible within the natural world. Some human behaviours may also have evolved because of their survival value or their ability to increase an individual's opportunities for passing on their genes (see Chapter 3, p.112).

Evolutionary theory also claims that differences between species are *quantitative* and not *qualitative* (i.e. implying differences in kind). In other words, some species have evolved further than others along the evolutionary path. Based on this idea of evolutionary continuity, behaviourists have chosen to study simpler species in order to understand more about these processes. Slife and Williams (1995) suggest that this argument provides the justification for studying non-human species and then generalizing the findings to human beings.

Evaluation of evolutionary reductionism

- *Drawing unwarranted conclusions about cause and effect* – We sometimes think that our biology affects the way we experience the world, but the opposite may also be true. There are many studies that have shown how a stimulating environment can change the structure of an animal's brain (this is known as 'neural plasticity') (see margin panel below on Improving brain performance).

Improving brain performance

The suggestion that an efficient brain is the result of superior performance rather than the cause of it is supported in research by Haier *et al.* (1992). In this study, participants who played a computer game for several weeks showed a slower glucose metabolism rate (i.e. they were more neurologically efficient) than a control group who did not play the computer game.

- *Exaggerating the power of genes* – When we read about the role of genetics in a particular behaviour, we might assume that genes are the cause and the only cause. Even the words that we use to describe genetic influence, such as 'control' and 'determine' imply an inevitability that may not actually exist (Tavris and Wade 1995).

The nature–nurture debate

The nature–nurture debate is one of the standard debates in psychology and is particularly important in developmental psychology. What is it that has made each of us into what we are today? What elements of our physical and mental being can be explained purely in terms of our nature? And what elements are due to nurture, i.e. our social and physical environment?

- *Nature* – This refers to the influence of our genes on all our characteristics and abilities. This is not the same as the characteristics you are born with, because these may have been determined by your pre-natal environment. In addition, some genetic characteristics only appear later in development as a result of the process of maturation. Supporters of the nature view have also been called 'nativists'.

Nurture – This refers to the influences of experience, i.e. what is learned through interacting with both the physical and social environment. Supporters of the nurture view are 'empiricists' who believe that all knowledge is gained through experience. You may have already encountered the term *empirical research*, where data are collected through sensory experience rather than a reliance on thoughts and ideas.

The nature–nurture debate used to be described as nature *versus* nurture, as if either one or the other could provide the full explanation for human development. However, it has been evident for some time that neither nature nor nurture on their own can provide complete explanations. All characteristics are a product of nature *and* nurture. The psychologist, Donald Hebb (1958), used the analogy of the length and width of a rectangle – neither can be said to contribute more to the area of the rectangle; they are both important. The same is true of nature and nurture.

Activity: Nature and nurture in psychology

- Prepare three lists – one headed 'nature', one 'nurture' and the third 'nature and nurture'.
- Under each heading, record all the theories or explanations that you have studied so far which would fit. For example, any genetic explanations belong in the 'nature' list; behaviourism is an example of the 'nurture' approach; the transactional model of stress emphasizes the role of both nature and nurture.

Assumptions made about nature and nurture in psychological research

Nature

Evolutionary explanations of human behaviour exemplify the nature approach in psychology. The main assumption underlying this approach is that any particular behaviour has evolved because of:

- its survival value, or
- its ability to increase an individual's opportunities to pass on their genes.

An example of this is Bowlby's (1969) theory of attachment (see panel on p.43).

Another example from your AS studies concerning the role of evolution is the explanation of stress as an adaptive response to environmental pressures. Animals born without such responses quickly die.

Nurture

The behavioural approach, and radical behaviourism in particular, is the clearest example of the nurture position in psychology. Watson, the 'father' of behaviourism famously said: 'Give me a dozen healthy infants and my own specified world to bring them up in, and I'll guarantee to take anyone at random and train him to become any kind of specialist I might select: doctor, lawyer, artist, merchant-chief, and yes, beggar and thief, regardless of his talents, penchants, tendencies, abilities, vocations and race of his ancestors' (Watson 1913). Behaviourists believe that all behaviour is the result of learning through classical or operant conditioning. Neo-behaviourists also include social learning. Perhaps the best-known social learning explanation is of aggression, based on Bandura's studies using the Bobo doll (see Chapter 4, p.133). Social learning theory proposes that much of what we learn is through observation and indirect reinforcement. However, behaviour only becomes part of an individual's behavioural repertoire when it is directly reinforced.

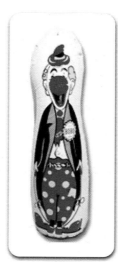

Bandura's Bobo doll

Although behavioural accounts focus on learning, even learning has a genetic basis: the ability to learn relies on appropriate neural mechanisms. For example, research has shown that mutant fruit flies with one crucial gene missing cannot be conditioned (Quinn *et al.* 1979). It can also be argued that Skinner's concept of reinforcement depends on an instinctive propensity to be reinforced by the pleasure that results from having a drive met.

Nature *and* nurture in psychological research

There are many areas in psychology where you can find examples of the nature–nurture debate (i.e. biological versus environmental explanations). We outline just two examples below; other possibilities you will encounter during your A2 studies include interpersonal attraction, aggression, mental illness and intelligence.

Perception

The extreme nativist view claims that we are born with certain perceptual abilities which develop through a genetically programmed process of maturation and which owe nothing to learning. Empiricists, on the other hand, believe that we are born with only the most basic sensory capacity and that our perceptual abilities develop through experience and interaction with our environment. It is unlikely that the acquisition of perceptual skills can be fully explained by either of these extreme views. It seems more likely that perceptual skills develop as a result of an interaction between innate and environmental factors, as supported by studies of infant perceptual development and also cross-cultural research (see Chapter 2, p.90).

Piaget's theory of cognitive development

Piaget's (1926) theory is significant in two respects:

1 It bridges the gap between nature and nurture by arguing that biologically given structures unfold when placed in a nurturing environment.

2 In Piaget's theory, the individual is the main focus, whereas the role of the environment is merely to facilitate the automatic unfolding of biological, cognitive structures. What is particularly interesting about this theory, in terms of its position in the nature–nurture debate, is that it emphasizes the potential available to all children with the right environmental events to bring it about. See Chapter 8, p.254 for further details about cognition and development.

Jean Piaget (1896–1980)

Commentary on nature *and* nurture in psychological research

- *Perception* – The work of Blakemore and Cooper (1970) illustrates neural plasticity, which is the ability of the nervous system to adapt to the environment. Such plasticity combined with neural specialization makes good evolutionary sense. At birth it is advantageous for an animal's brain to have certain hardwired capacities, such as the ability to respond to lines of certain orientations. However, it is also advantageous for the brain to be able to adapt to environmental conditions and specialize in the areas required by the environment, so that the nervous system can be used efficiently.

- *Vygotsky: a contrast to Piaget* – Vygotsky (1934, reprinted 1964) presented an account of cognitive development that contrasts with Piaget's theory. According to Vygotsky, cognitive development occurs largely as a consequence of social influences (nurture). A child is born with innate elementary mental functions (attention and sensation), which are transformed into higher mental functions through cultural influences, such as language and the influence of people with greater knowledge. Vygotsky's account combines elements of nature and nurture, but places more emphasis on nurture (see Chapter 8, p.264 for more details).

Methodological challenges associated with the nature–nurture debate

- *Manipulation of variables* – There is no agreement about how we might define or measure the environment in which a person grows up. There are no standard units that can be used to compare one environment with another. At best, efforts to manipulate environmental variables have focused on general dimensions and, at worst, they are associated with value judgements about 'good' and 'bad' environments, with minimal empirical support (Horowitz 1993).

- *Animal research and human behaviour* – Researchers using animals have been much more successful in defining and manipulating environmental variables. This kind of research emphasizes that much of behavioural development that was assumed to be innate (and, therefore, effectively unalterable) is subject to environmental influence. Trying to understand how such environmental variables would affect human behavioural development is a more complex issue. This difficulty becomes most pronounced at the cultural level, yet it is probably at the level of cultural influences that the most powerful and subtle environmental variables may operate (Horowitz 1993).

Different views of the relationship between nature and nurture

Gene–environment interactions

Genes may not only influence behaviour, they may also influence the environment itself. In other words, our experiences may be partly influenced by our genetic make-up; for instance, people may react differently to us because of some inherited aspect of our personality. Likewise, we may choose certain experiences because they fit best with our innate preferences.

Three types of gene-environment relationships

Research by Azar (1997) has suggested three types of gene–environment relationships:

- *A passive relationship* may occur between genes and environment because parents transmit genes that promote a certain trait and also construct the rearing environment. For example, if we assume that musical ability is genetic, then musically gifted children may be assumed to have parents who are musically inclined and who provide both the genes and the environment that promote the development of musical talent.

- *An evocative relationship* between genes and environment may occur because genetically distinct individuals may evoke different reactions in those around them. For example, a musically gifted child may be chosen for special training and opportunities by teachers or may trigger reactions of awe from their peers.

- *An active relationship* between genes and environment may occur because individuals actively select experiences that fit in with their genetically influenced preferences. For example, musically gifted children may seek out musical friends and new musical opportunities.

Reaction range

An alternative view of gene–environment interactions was put forward by Gottesman (1963). He argued that, although experience can affect the development of any particular skill or ability, this is inevitably limited by our biological endowment. For example, adult height is affected by the quality of food eaten through childhood. However, even with the best possible diet, a person would never grow beyond the height laid down by their genes. Genes do not determine development precisely, but establish a **reaction range** within which development occurs. The same 'genotype' (i.e. the genes an individual possesses) determines different 'phenotypes' (an individual's observable characteristics as an expression of their genes), depending on life experiences.

Nature *via* nurture

Ridley (2003) proposed nature via nurture as a further way of conceptualizing gene–environment interaction. Our understanding of how genes behave has led scientists to realize that genes do not simply interact with the environment, but are activated by it. This occurs through tiny stretches of DNA called 'promoters'. Our bodies have hundreds of these, which both switch genes on and turn them off. Some promoters are affected by our environment. This process helps explain how nurture has such a profound impact on the individual – nurture influences living organisms via their genes.

An interesting extension of the nature via nurture understanding is that genetic explanations, which have always been regarded as determinist explanations, can now be reframed as examples of free will. Genes are not our hardwired masters, but rather 'the means by which creatures can be flexible, the very servants of experience' (Ridley 2003).

Psychology as a science

Definitions and varieties of science

Most people assume that they know what **science** is, but what does it really mean to describe something as 'scientific'? Can psychology really be considered scientific in the same way that the natural sciences, such as biology, are considered to be scientific? Try the activity in the margin now.

> **Activity**
> ### How do you know what you know?
>
> Pause to consider various things that you know, for example the following:
>
> - How do you know that you can (or cannot) drive a car, know that snow is cold to touch, know that a particular person is a very good friend?
> - How did you come to gain your knowledge about the physical and social world?
> - How do you decide whether or not something is true?

The Latin root of the word 'science' literally means 'knowledge'. Science is concerned with what we *know* to be true, rather than what we merely *believe* to be true. Science is, therefore, an important way of distinguishing what is true and real from what is not.

Science as knowledge or as method

Science can be characterized in the following ways:

1. *A body of knowledge that explains the nature of the world* – Viewed from this perspective, scientific knowledge has two main characteristics:

   - Scientific explanations are preferred to, and may challenge, other explanations of naturally occurring phenomena (e.g. supernatural explanations).

   - Scientific explanations are often stated as laws or general principles about the relationship between different events. The regularity of the way in which specific events occur together means that it becomes possible to control and predict them.

2. *A method of studying phenomena* – Scientific investigation involves empirical observation and the development of theories, which, in turn, are rigorously tested and, where necessary, refined in the light of new evidence.

Key characteristics of science

Probably the most fundamental characteristic of science is its reliance on the empirical methods of observation and investigation, i.e. observation through sensory experience rather than a reliance on thoughts and ideas. All scientific ideas must, at some point, be subjected to empirical investigation through careful observation of perceivable events or phenomena. Science has emerged as a trusted approach to the acquisition of knowledge because of its reliance on empirical methods. This does not mean, however, that science is purely empirical in nature. For science to 'make sense', it is necessary to explain the results of empirical observation. That means constructing theories, which, in turn, can be tested and refined through further empirical observation.

Slife and Williams (1995) identify a number of further attributes that characterize science:

- Scientific observation is made under *objective conditions*, i.e. observation is not influenced by factors such as bias or expectation or the particular cultural values of the researcher.

- Scientific observation takes place under *controlled conditions*, often in the context of an experiment.

- Science involves making *predictions* about what is expected to happen under specified conditions.

- Scientific investigations are open to *public scrutiny*, i.e. the methods and results of scientific investigations are there for all to see and to check.

See Chapter 15 for a more detailed discussion of these important issues.

'Hard' and 'soft' science

'Hard' sciences, such as physics and chemistry, lend themselves to reductionist approaches and experiments. People involved in 'soft' sciences, such as psychology and sociology, attempt to use the determinist and reductionist approaches of the 'hard' sciences but, because of the subject matter, cannot conduct research with the same degree of rigour as in the 'hard' sciences. This lack of rigour may make 'soft' sciences appear less scientific, but this does not mean they are unscientific because they embrace the aims of scientific research, including objectivity and replicability.

The development of psychology as a separate discipline

Psychology as a scientific discipline has a fairly short history of around 130 years. Before that, psychology had been classified as a branch of philosophy. Wilhelm Wundt, a German physiologist and psychologist, founded the first laboratory for experimental psychology in Leipzig in 1879. Wundt stressed the use of scientific methods in psychology, particularly introspection (a process by which a person looks inwards at their own mental processes to gain insights into how they operate). Although the value of introspective reports was questionable, this approach highlighted the need for systematic observations.

Wilhelm Wundt (1832–1920)

Some psychologists felt that psychology would never be accepted as a science unless it employed more objective methods than introspection. Such views led to the development of behaviourism by Watson (1913) in America. About the same time as behaviourism was becoming established in America, Gestalt psychology was developing in Germany (see 'Gestalt psychology' box on p.16 above). This approach had relatively little influence on psychology until the 1950s, when the behavioural movement was in decline.

Activity   **Searching the internet**

Using your favourite search engine, do an internet search for ideas about key events, people and theories in the development of psychology as a separate discipline. Depending on the key words that you use, you are likely to uncover a lot of information, so you will need to be highly selective!

When you have completed your search and summarized some of the information you discovered, pool your findings with those of one or two other students in your psychology class.

Does your pooled information provide evidence to support the view that psychology can be regarded as a scientific discipline?

Arguments *for* and *against* psychology as a science

Arguments *for* the claim that psychology is a science

- *Psychologists use scientific methods* – When viewed from this perspective, it seems clear that psychology does qualify as a science because scientific methods are the preferred methods of investigation for most psychologists. Indeed, the laboratory experiment is widely used in psychology, providing psychologists with opportunities for control and prediction that are absent in less 'scientific' methods.

- *Some levels of psychology are scientific* – As highlighted in the section on reductionism above (see p.39–42), psychology embraces explanations at different levels, ranging from the physical to the sociological. It could therefore be argued that at least some levels of psychology are scientific, such as research into the neurobiology of dreaming or mental illness.

Commentary on arguments *for* psychology as a science

- *Low validity of psychology's scientific methods* – Psychologists may use scientific techniques, such as the laboratory experiment, but such research has been criticized for lacking internal and **external validity**. As regards **internal validity**, **demand characteristics** may invite predictable responses from participants, so they do not behave as they normally would, but are cued to behave in a particular way by the experimental conditions. Examples from your AS studies include Asch's studies of conformity (1956), see *Psychology AS for AQA A*, p.184. These studies have also been criticized for low external validity. Asch's study involved conformity on a relatively trivial topic (length of lines) and this may not tell us much about conformity in other settings (i.e. ecological validity was low). It could be argued, therefore, that although psychologists use scientific methods, the validity of the results from these scientific methods can be low.

- *Many levels, no paradigm?* – If psychology consists of different levels or kinds of explanation, some of which are more scientific than others, then it cannot claim to have an overarching paradigm (i.e. a shared set of assumptions and a shared methodology) which Kuhn (1962) claimed was a key feature of any science. So, although some levels of psychology are scientific, psychology as a whole cannot claim to be a science.

Arguments *against* psychology as a science

- *Science is determinist* – The basis of the scientific approach is that cause-and-effect relationships can be discovered and these explain human behaviour. However, as we have seen, the determinist view raises difficulties for the concepts of free will and moral responsibility, which might lead us to reject the scientific approach as the best way of investigating human behaviour.

- *Science is reductionist* – In order to carry out a scientific test, psychologists must be able to observe whatever it is they are investigating. Although this may seem a straightforward requirement, it is not always so. For example, there are many psychological concepts (such as motivation or fear) that cannot be directly observed. Instead, researchers reduce the concept to observe something else that is assumed to represent the thing they are really interested in. For example, a psychologist may use reductionism to operationalize (define) fear in terms of a physiological change such as pupil dilation. However, in their efforts to be 'scientific', psychologists may end up measuring something different from their intended phenomena and draw inappropriate conclusions.

- *Objectivity is not possible* – Earlier, it was suggested that objectivity was an important characteristic of all scientific enquiry. This would mean that the results are not distorted by the subjectivity of the investigator. There are many difficulties with objectivity in psychology; for example, observer bias – when a researcher observes behaviour, these observations are inevitably affected by the observer's expectations. Interviewer bias and experimenter bias can lead to changes in participants' behaviour as a consequence of the researcher's expectations.

- *Psychology does not have a paradigm* – Scientists working within a particular discipline think about a problem in their own particular way. It is debatable whether psychology has a paradigm or even whether it is actually possible ever to establish a paradigm in psychology (see the activity on p.520).

Commentary on arguments *against* psychology as a science

- *Science is not necessarily determinist* – The discussion above on determinism highlights ways to incorporate the concept of free will within a determinist framework (see p.36) and also that there is regularity in human behaviour. In addition, the physical sciences no longer subscribe to a purely determinist framework, so psychology is in line with thinking in other sciences.

- *Is science always reductionist?* – Reductionism in science has been very successful in gaining useful information and is deeply embedded in our Western scientific culture. Nevertheless, according to Gallagher and Appenzeller (1999), shortfalls in reductionism are becoming apparent owing to (a) the recognition that scientists 'know more and more about less and less' as specialisms within disciplines increase and hinder the flow of information, and (b) the tendency to oversimplify complex phenomena, e.g. by searching for a gene to explain behaviours or abilities (such as the 'gene for intelligence'). Robert Laughlin (2005), who won the Nobel Prize for physics in 1998, has argued that if we are to understand the way complex systems (e.g. tornadoes) emerge, it is better to study the whole phenomenon – the tornado – rather than how individual streams of air combine to form a tornado. In other words, if we try to understand certain things (like tornadoes and tsunamis) by reducing them to their constituent parts, we may fail to understand them at a macro level because the 'whole is more than the sum of its parts'. Therefore, the limitation of reductionist techniques to explain fully complex psychological phenomena (such as fear or motivation) does not necessarily exclude psychologists from scientific enquiry, as a growing body of scientists now reject a purely reductionist approach.

- *Objectivity is not possible in any science* – The same challenges associated with objectivity occur even in the physical sciences, not just psychology. Heisenberg's uncertainty principle is derived from the observation that the simple act of measuring a subatomic particle changes the behaviour of that particle. Thus, true objectivity can only be an ideal for scientific research. The concept of science as being objective is also challenged by those who point out that science is as much a social activity as a mechanical application of correct procedures (Jones and Elcock 2001). The work of scientists is influenced by prevailing social attitudes (which influence the shape and structure of knowledge), and the day-to-day activities of scientists are affected by everyday human concerns (being liked by colleagues, getting promotion, and so on). This is discussed further in Chapter 15, p.509.

- *Paradigms in psychology* – It could be argued that psychology has a number of mini-paradigms, such as behaviourism, psychoanalysis and the cognitive approach. As we saw in Section 1 of this chapter, each of these approaches has a common set of assumptions and specific forms of methodology. We could also argue that psychology has always had a dominant paradigm through its history – behaviourism was dominant in the first half of the 20th century and was then superseded by the cognitive approach during the 1960s. Kuhn's concept of paradigms in science is also subject to criticism. Some philosophers of science regard his position as being too extreme. For example, Lakatos (1970) proposed that science is an evolving body of knowledge that pursues thematic lines of enquiry. There is a succession of theories that are linked by core assumptions. These theories are tested and revised in the light of new discoveries and science is viewed as essentially a rational process. This description of science fits psychology.

Alternative views on the science–psychology relationship

The issue of whether psychology might be considered a science has been examined, but there is an equally important question: *should* psychology be scientific? Some aspects of human behaviour might be more accessible than others to this type of empirical evidence. For example, it may be fairly straightforward to use scientific methods to investigate issues such as short-term memory span. However, psychology is concerned with human behaviour in all its richness and complexity, and scientific methods may not be the best route to investigate all areas of interest, such as human emotions.

Slife and Williams (1995) present three positions on whether a science of human behaviour is possible or even desirable:

1   *The need for empirical validation* – All theories about human behaviour should be subject to rigorous testing to find out whether they can explain a range of events consistent with the predictions of the theory. It is also important that the claims of a particular theory can be demonstrated through actual, observable behaviour.

2   *The value of qualitative methods* – The study of human experience requires the use of different methods from those used in the study of the natural world. Scientists studying humans should place a great deal of importance on the experience of their participants as a way of understanding their behaviour. Qualitative research methods are not concerned with measurement or the quantification of behaviour. Instead, they allow participants to describe their experiences in their own words. The role of the researcher should be to describe and interpret this experience. Examples of qualitative techniques include discourse analysis and ethnographic methods.

3   *The need for a variety of research methods* – The study of human behaviour and experience requires methodological pluralism. Researchers must select the most appropriate research method for the problem they are investigating. Therefore, no one method can be considered superior to any other – they all have a contribution to make to our overall understanding of human experience and the behaviour of human and non-human animals.

CHECK YOUR UNDERSTANDING

Check your understanding of debates in psychology by answering the following questions. Try to do this from memory. You can check your answers by looking back through Section 3.

Free will and determinism

1   Briefly explain why free will is seen as the opposite to determinism.

2   How can moral responsibility be explained within a determinist framework?

3   What is the difference between 'proximate' and 'ultimate' causes?

4   Outline two arguments *for* determinism.

5   Explain what is meant by the term 'environmental determinism'?

Reductionism

6   Explain what is meant by the term 'methodological reductionism'.

7   Describe two arguments *for* reductionism. For each of these arguments, briefly describe a counter-argument.

8   Explain why everything cannot be reduced to physiological influences.

9   In what way is the evolutionary approach reductionist?

Nature and nurture

10   What is meant by the terms 'nature' and 'nurture'?

11   Identify two developments in the history of the nature–nurture debate.

12   Outline the three types of gene–environment interaction proposed by Gottesman (1963), Azar (1997), and Ridley (2003).

13   Use the example of Piaget's theory to explain how nature and nurture each contribute to behaviour.

Psychology and science

14   Write a brief definition of science (about 100 words).

15   What is meant by 'empirical investigation'?

16   Summarize the key arguments for and against psychology being considered to be a science.

Further resources

Dennett, D. (2003) *Freedom Evolves*, London: Allen Lane.
Dennett argues that free will is not incompatible with determinism, but has evolved as a special characteristic of humans.

Eysenck, M.W. (1994) *Perspectives on Psychology*, Hove, Sussex: Lawrence Erlbaum Associates.
Part of the 'Principles of Psychology' series written for A-level students and undergraduates. Brief coverage of the major approaches, plus chapters on controversies such as reductionism.

Glassman, W.E. and Hadad, M. (2008) *Approaches to Psychology* (5th edn), Buckingham: Open University Press.
An account of five major approaches (biological, behaviourist, cognitive, psychodynamic and humanistic) and the assumptions, methods and theories associated with each.

Jones, D. and Elcock, J. (2001) *History and Theories of Psychology: A critical perspective*, London: Hodder.
A comprehensive text that explores how psychology has been shaped by ideas from different disciplines.

Ridley, M. (2003) *Nature via Nurture: Genes, Experience and What Makes Us Human*, London: Fourth Estate.
A wide-ranging and accessible look at research on nature and nurture.

Slife, B.D. and Williams, R.N. (1995) *What's Behind the Research? Discovering hidden assumptions in the behavioural sciences*, Thousand Oaks, CA: Sage.
A clearly written text that discusses many aspects of scientific enquiry.

Valentine, E.R. (1992) *Conceptual Issues in Psychology* (2nd edn), London: Routledge.
A summary of the major approaches and controversies in psychology.

Wadeley, A., Malim, T. and Birch, A. (1997) *Perspectives in Psychology* (2nd edn), Basingstoke: Macmillan.
This book discusses approaches, debates and methods at a level appropriate for A-level students.

Websites:
www.psych.ucsb.edu/research/cep/
Centre for evolutionary psychology with a primer on evolutionary psychology and an interview with Leda Cosmides.

www.anth.ucsb.edu/projects/human/evpsychfaq.html
Frequently asked questions about evolutionary psychology.

www.freud.org.uk/
The Freud museum site with some background theory and useful links.

http://psych.athabascau.ca/html/Behaviorism/
A tutorial on behaviourism with questions on the text (these are checked).

http://dannyreviews.com/h/Lifelines.html
A précis and book review of Steven Rose's book Lifelines: Biology, freedom and determinism.

http://www.rigb.org/contentControl?action=displayContent&id=00000001106
Gives simple explanations of heredity, nature versus nurture and includes a brief account of Mendelian genetics.

CHAPTER 1 Biological rhythms and sleep

Lance Workman

EXPLAINING THE SPECIFICATION

Specification content	The specification explained
Biological rhythms (Topic 1)	In this part of the specification you are required to know about different types of biological rhythm (specifically circadian, infradian and ultradian rhythms) and how they impact on our lives. To do this, you need to be able to:
Circadian, infradian, and ultradian rhythms, including the role of endogenous pacemakers and of exogenous zeitgebers	■ Describe each of the three types of rhythm, and evaluate research evidence and commentary relating to them. ■ Describe the nature of endogenous pacemakers and exogenous zeitgebers and comment on their significance to humans and on research evidence supporting each.
Consequences of disrupting biological rhythms, for example shift work, jet lag	■ Describe and evaluate research relating to at least two consequences of any of the three rhythms previously covered. Shift work and jet lag are the most obvious examples of such consequences.
Sleep states (Topic 2)	In this part of the specification you are asked to consider both the nature of sleep (that is, what happens during sleep) and its possible functions. To do this, you need to be able to:
The nature of sleep including REM sleep and the four stages of slow wave sleep	■ Describe the stages of sleep and the distinction between different types of sleep. ■ Describe the different stages of sleep and comment on research that has explored these stages.
Functions of sleep, including evolutionary explanations and restoration theory	■ Describe and evaluate at least two theories of the functions of sleep including the evolutionary explanation of sleep (the word functions applies here to different evolutionary functions such as safety from predators). ■ Describe and evaluate different perspectives of restoration theory.
Lifespan changes in sleep	■ Describe and evaluate research that has examined how and why sleep patterns change with age.
Disorders of sleep (Topic 3)	In this final part of the specification you will study different disorders of sleep, how they have been studied and how they impact on our lives.
Explanations for insomnia, including primary and secondary insomnia and factors influencing insomnia, for example, apnoea, personality	■ Describe and evaluate explanations for both primary and secondary insomnia. ■ Describe and evaluate research into the factors influencing each of these (sleep apnoea and personality are given as examples).
Explanations for other sleep disorders, including sleep walking and narcolepsy	■ Describe and evaluate explanations for both sleep walking and narcolepsy.

A **biological rhythm** can be defined as any change in a biological activity (such as sleep and waking) that repeats periodically. These biological rhythms are most often synchronized with daily, monthly, or annual cyclical changes in the environment.

By the time you reach the age of 60 you will have spent 20 years of your life asleep. To some this might seem an enormous waste of time, but to psychologists who study sleep it is clear that without it we would be unable to function. This daily pattern of sleeping for eight hours in every 24 is the most obvious of our biological cycles and is known as a **circadian** (from the Latin words *circa* 'about' and *dies*, 'day') rhythm. In addition to 24-hour circadian rhythms, organisms also exhibit cycles of periods longer than a day – **infradian** (*infra* is Latin for 'below') and those that take less than a day – **ultradian** (*ultra* is Latin for 'beyond'). An example of an ultradian cycle would be the feeding patterns of many animals and an example of an infradian cycle would be the human 28-day menstrual cycle or the hibernating behaviour of squirrels and hedgehogs.

The control of circadian rhythms

Animals kept under constant light conditions still maintain a daily rhythmical cycle of roughly 24 hours. That is, they sleep for broadly normal amounts of time in each day and eat and conduct other activities at normal regular intervals. (Note that in experiments where this is studied it is also important to maintain a constant temperature and likewise control for air-pressure and external noises.) This finding suggests that circadian (and other) rhythmic activities can be 'endogenous' (i.e. in-built) and so persist even when the environmental stimuli are absent. However, such '**endogenous pacemakers**' (or 'biological clocks') are not perfect and normally require some sort of environmental input in order to correct them each day. Where exogenous (external) events have a role in rhythmic activities, they are called '**exogenous zeitgebers**' (meaning literally, 'external time-givers'). Much of the research into biological rhythms has focused on understanding the relationship between endogenous (internal) pacemakers and exogenous (external) zeitgebers.

Endogenous pacemakers and exogenous zeitgebers

Endogenous pacemakers (or biological clocks) probably represent an inherited genetic mechanism. For example, regular rhythms of activity and rest can be measured in the unborn human embryo that has never been exposed to the outside world. But, as pointed out earlier, these rhythms have to respond to exogenous zeitgebers if the behaviour they control is to be fully coordinated with the external world. One of the most influential zeitgebers is light, and its role in fine-tuning bodily rhythms has been reasonably well mapped out.

Role of the pineal gland

For many birds and mammals the most important endogenous pacemaker in the brain is probably the **pineal gland** (a small pea-shaped gland in the brain). This structure contains receptors that respond to external light, penetrating the thin layer of skull that lies above the pineal gland. In turn, these light receptors influence the activity of neurons in the pineal gland. These neurons have a natural rhythmic activity and also convert the neurotransmitter serotonin into the hormone melatonin. Melatonin is then released into the general circulation, which acts on many of the body's organs and glands, and seems to be responsible for the rhythmic nature of many activities. For instance, it acts on brainstem sleep mechanisms to help synchronize the phases of sleep and waking, and it has been shown that injections of melatonin can produce sleep in sparrows (Abraham *et al.* 2000). The manufacture and release of melatonin is regulated by the amount of light falling on the pineal gland, decreasing as light increases. Research has shown, for instance, that chickens wake and become active as dawn breaks and melatonin secretion falls (Binkley 1979). This means that although their waking is controlled by the biological clock in the pineal gland, it is adjusted to the actual time that morning begins, which varies throughout the year. This is a good example of how endogenous pacemakers interact with exogenous zeitgebers.

Role of the suprachiasmatic nucleus (SCN)

In mammals, including humans, the pathways are more complicated. The main biological clock seems to be a small area in the **hypothalamus** (an area of the brain involved in motivation and lying a little behind the eyes) – the **suprachiasmatic nucleus (SCN)** – whose neurons have an in-built circadian rhythmic firing pattern. When the SCN of a rat is **lesioned** (damaged by cutting) the circadian rhythm including sleeping and feeding patterns is totally disrupted for the animal (Stephan and Zucker 1972, see below). In intact animals the SCN regulates the manufacture and secretion of melatonin in the pineal gland via an interconnecting pathway. Another pathway connects the retina of each eye to the SCN. This allows the amount of light falling on the retina to influence the activity of SCN neurons and, indirectly, the release of melatonin from the pineal gland. So the link between light and melatonin production is maintained. An interesting recent discovery is that light can reach the brain without passing through the eyes. Campbell and Murphy (1998) applied light to the back of the knees of human participants and were able to shift the circadian rhythm in body temperature and melatonin secretion.

The pineal gland and the SCN function jointly as endogenous pacemakers (or biological clocks) in the brain. There are many bodily rhythms, and it is likely that there are other structures involved in maintaining their regularity. Research has shown, for example, that animals fed on a regular basis soon become active just before their feeding time. This happens even in the absence of other environmental cues and must therefore rely on some sort of internal clock. Rosenwasser *et al.* (1981) found that rats still showed this anticipation after their SCN was destroyed, so another biological clock must also be able to perform this function.

The SCN and infradian cycles

Although the SCN has a vital role in 24-hour biological rhythms, it also has important functions in infradian biological rhythms much longer than 24 hours. Male hamsters show annual rhythms of testosterone secretion,

and these appear to be based on the amount of light that occurs each day. The breeding season of hamsters begins as the days lengthen and ends when the days draw in again. Lesions of the SCN destroy these annual-breeding cycles, and male hamsters secrete testosterone all year round (Rusak and Zucker 1975). These lesions probably disrupt the annual cycles because they destroy the 24-hour clock against which daily light levels are measured to determine the season. If the period of light is less than 12 hours, it must be winter; if it is more than 12 hours, it must be summer (Carlson 2002).

Psychology in context

The hamster on the wheel – how scientists measure rhythmical activity in animals.

One of the most commonly used animals to study rhythmical activity in the lab is the golden hamster. Just as with pet hamsters, those reared in labs are often provided with a wheel to play in, but in this case sleep scientists are interested in recording wheel running as an example of general activity levels. In the traditional set up each revolution is recorded as the wheel causes a pen to deflect briefly on a roll of paper that is moving very slowly. The roll can later be arranged into strips to represent the activity of each 24-hour circadian cycle. In a modern day set up computers have largely superseded the paper roll, but the pattern of recording remains the same. As can be seen in Figure 1.1 below, under normal light/dark conditions, hamsters begin to be active around dusk and continue to wheel run intermittently throughout the night. Quite often in order to study which parts of the brain are involved in the control of circadian rhythms, a hamster may have a part of its brain damaged to see how this alters the cyclical pattern of behaviour. In the case of the trace, see Figure 1.2 below, the **optic tract** (the nerve fibres from the eyes to the back of the brain where visual processing occurs) is cut but fibres from the eyes to part of the brain – the **hypothalamus** – are not severed. Subsequently, the hamster becomes active earlier on in

the day; the synchrony is still there but the phase has shifted a little. When the same hamster is placed under constant dim light it begins to be active a few minutes later each day (Zucker 1976). This slight daily increase in the hamster's circadian cycle suggests that its endogenous clock has a period that is slightly longer than 24 hours. This is generally found to be the case with rodents and other species. Such experiments clearly have ethical issues as parts of the brain are purposely damaged in these animals. Scientists that do this sort of work would argue that they have helped in our understanding of sleep-related disorders in humans and in the development of treatments for such problems.

1 In research such as this, scientists must balance out the costs and possible benefits of the study. What do you consider are the main costs and benefits of *this* study?

2 Using books and the Internet, try to find out what other studies of circadian rhythms have contributed to the development of treatments for sleep related disorders.

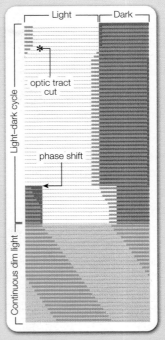

Figure 1.2 *A hamster's free-running activity rhythm indicating a hamster has an endogenous clock once the optic tract has been severed but the fibres from the eye to the hypothalamus have been spared*

Figure 1.1 *A running wheel in a hamster's cage is monitored by an event recorder*

Removing exogenous zeitgebers

The sensitivity to light of the pineal gland and the SCN, and the role of melatonin in controlling sleep and other activity, mean that despite the endogenous nature of biological clocks, their activity is synchronized with the light/dark rhythm of the world outside. Occasionally, slightly bizarre studies have allowed us to look at the effects of removing light as an exogenous zeitgeber, allowing these biological clocks to run free, that is, without the influence of zeitgebers. Studies such as these show that humans with free-running biological clocks settle into a rhythmic sleeping/waking pattern of between 25 and 27 hours, that is, slightly longer than under normal conditions. So we can draw two conclusions:

- Endogenous mechanisms can control sleep/waking cycles in the absence of light.

- Light as an exogenous zeitgeber is necessary to reset the clock every day so that the biological rhythm is coordinated with the external world.

Evaluation of research studies into biological rhythms

- *Positive research findings* – A number of studies undertaken with both humans and non-human animals have established the existence of endogenous pacemakers regulated by exogenous zeitgebers. They have also shown how these processes play a vital part in regulating behaviour.

- *Generalizability of research* – Much of the work, especially on the brain mechanisms of pacemakers, has been carried out on non-human animals, so it is important to be careful about generalizing the findings to humans. Also we need to bear in mind that these studies were conducted under lab conditions. This means that, although there is a greater degree of control, it is difficult to relate such finings to the animal's natural habitat. Hence there may be a lack of **ecological validity**.

- *Individual differences* – Studies of free-running biological rhythms in humans also show that there are significant individual differences in these mechanisms, i.e. that they may not operate in exactly the same way in all people. Hence to talk about 'the human endogenous pacemaker' might be to simplify the real situation.

- *How do zeitgebers interact?* – Although studies into the nature of various exogenous zeitgebers (such as temperature, light, humidity, noise and the availability

Research into free-running biological rhythms in humans

Key research: Siffre (2002)

Michel Siffre takes up residence in another trip underground in 1999.

The most famous study of free-running biological rhythms involved a French cave explorer called Michel Siffre who, in 1972, spent six months in an underground cave in Texas, separated from natural light/dark cycles. He was wired up so that various bodily functions could be recorded. When he was awake, the researchers put the lights on; when he went to bed, they turned the lights off. He ate and slept whenever he wanted. At first his sleep/waking cycle was very erratic, but settled down to a fairly regular pattern of between 25 and 30 hours, that is, slightly longer than a 24-hour cycle. When he finally emerged, it was the 179th day, but by his 'days' it was only the 151st day since he went underground!

In a similar study, Aschoff and Weber (reported in Kleitman 1963) used an underground bunker. Student participants therefore had no cues to light and dark, and could select their own light-on active or light-off sleep periods. As with Siffre, the participants settled into regular sleep/waking cycles and again, like Siffre, the normal circadian rhythm extended slightly to between 25 and 27 hours. Such studies suggest that the human endogenous pacemaker has a tendency to run a little slower than 24 hours and needs to be corrected a little each day through exogenous zeitgebers.

Evaluation

The case of Michel Siffre may be dismissed as the study of just one unusual individual (after all, what *normal* person would spend six months in an underground cave?) However, before dismissing studies such as this as atypical, we should consider the important role that they play in helping us understand the nature of circadian rhythms. Although unusual, such studies offer an extremely rare insight into what happens when rhythms are left to 'free-run', and therefore play an important role in confirming what experimental studies with larger groups have already suggested.

of food) has established their existence, the relative importance of each is still unclear as is the nature of their interaction.

- *Numbers of participants* – Some research, such as Siffre's cave study, has used very few or even single participants. This means that we can only generalize the findings with great care (see earlier comments in 'How Science Works' feature).

Consequences of disrupting biological rhythms

The studies on free-running rhythms in humans indicate how we use stimuli around us to coordinate our biological clocks. The gradual lengthening and shortening of the days is reflected in gradual shifts in rhythms of activity and sleep/waking cycles. These biological processes are also influenced by other stimuli, such as outside temperature and social patterns. Inuit Eskimos have regular sleep/waking cycles, even though they have continuous daylight in summer and continuous darkness in winter, showing that for them the social rhythms of life are the dominant zeitgebers.

Usually, exogenous zeitgebers, such as light or social behaviour patterns, change very slowly, if at all. However, there are times when they change radically and quickly, and the usual coordination between our internally controlled biological rhythms and the outside world (the exogenous zeitgebers) breaks down. Modern living has led to two common examples – jet travel and shift work – which we will consider next.

Jet lag

If you travel by plane from East to West – for example, from the UK to the east coast of the USA, leaving the UK at noon – you arrive at about 7 p.m. UK-time, but it would be 2 p.m. USA-time. All your biological rhythms are working to UK-time, so that by 7 p.m. USA-time your internal clock is telling you that it is midnight and you are feeling ready to sleep with a falling body temperature and decreasing bodily arousal. This dislocation of our physiological rhythms from the outside world produces the sensation of jet lag that many people experience and which lasts as long as it takes for the body to resynchronize. Studies have shown that the quickest way to achieve this adjustment is to follow the local exogenous zeitgebers rather than your body, so in the example above you should force yourself to stay awake until 11 p.m. USA-time and also adjust your meal times and socializing patterns. If you follow your biological clocks, adjustment takes much longer.

Strangely, jet lag is more severe travelling from West to East (from the USA to the UK, for example) than from East to West. This may be because it is easier to adjust our body clocks when they are ahead of local time (called 'phase delay') than when they are behind (a situation when they have to 'phase advance'). Because of its role in controlling body rhythms, melatonin has been studied as a possible treatment for jet lag and other desynchronization problems and, although nothing very

systematic has emerged yet, the research may eventually lead to an effective therapy. Recently, for instance, Takahashi *et al.* (2002) reported that melatonin speeded up the resynchronization of biological rhythms after an 11-hour flight and reduced the symptoms of jet lag.

Activity | **Melatonin and jet lag**

1 Ask yourself (or someone else) - Why would melatonin help to resynchronize biological rhythms and so reduce jet lag?

2 What evidence is there that melatonin is effective at doing this?

Answers are given on p.603. ▶

Shift work

Organizations and industries that work around the clock require their employees to do shift work. This means that employees are required to work when they would normally sleep and to sleep when they would normally be awake. A classic pattern is to divide the day into three eight-hour shifts fom midnight to 8 a.m., 8 a.m. to 4 p.m. and 4 p.m. to midnight. Switching shifts obviously disrupts links between external zeitgebers (light/dark, meals, social life, etc.) and biological rhythms, and, as with jet lag, some time is necessary for readjustment. Many shift patterns require a change every week, with workers moving back one shift every time. Studies of jet lag suggest that one week is barely enough time to allow for such a major resynchronization, so that the workers are in a permanent state of 'jet lag', impairing performance and increasing stress. The backward movement is the same as West to East jet travel, leading to the more difficult phase-advance situation. There is anecdotal evidence that performance, especially vigilance, is lowered at times when biological rhythms are pushing for sleep. For example, it is interesting to note that both the near-nuclear accident at Three Mile Island nuclear power station in Pennsylvania in 1979, and the actual nuclear disaster at Chernobyl (in the north east of Ukraine in the former Soviet Union) in 1986, occurred because of decision failures during the early hours of the morning.

Experimental support comes from a study of a chemical plant in Utah by Czeisler and colleagues in 1982. High incidence of health problems, sleep difficulties and work-related stress was noted in staff employed on short rotation shifts. Czeisler persuaded the company to change to a phase-delay system (moving a shift forwards every time) and to increase the shift rotation from seven to 21 days, allowing more time for adjustment. After nine months of the new system, worker satisfaction was significantly increased and factory output was higher. Alternative approaches to reducing the negative effects of shift work include the use of melatonin. Sharkey (2001) found that the hormone could speed up biological adjustment to shift patterns and increased sleep time during non-work periods.

The problems of jet lag and shift work are due to the way we have artificially dislocated the normal coordination between our biological clocks and the external world. We are the result of a long evolutionary history, in which the alternation of day and night has shaped the lives of all organisms. It is no surprise that we should still be under the same influence and suffer consequences when we interfere with things. Coren (1996) has pointed out that a culture shift occurred at the beginning of the 20th century when electric lighting became widely available. Factories and offices could operate around the clock, introducing widespread shift work and longer working hours. Social life also could extend late into the night. Coren estimates that on average we sleep for around one-and-a-half hours less than we did a century ago, so that many of us are in a constant state of mild sleep deprivation.

Activity — Shift worker experiences

Try interviewing someone who works shift work about their experiences. Do their answers confirm what research suggests? What, according to your interviewee are the main difficulties that they face trying to adjust their biological rhythms?

Evaluation of research on disrupting biological rhythms

- *Research findings* – A strength of this research is the consistent evidence for the idea that disrupting biological rhythms can have cognitive and emotional effects on people, sometimes leading to drastic consequences. For example, Czeisler *et al.* (1982) found that on short-rotation shifts (where the effects of shift-lag are most dramatic) there was a high incidence of health problems, sleep difficulties and work-related stress.

- *Methodological issues* – Much of the research evidence is generated by field studies that have high ecological validity. However, many confounding variables, such as personality and other individual differences in biological rhythms, are not controlled. This makes it more difficult to reach firm conclusions about the causal influences in any resulting behaviour.

- *Real-life significance?* – Although there are examples where disrupting rhythms has had drastic effects, many thousands of people carry out shift work without any obvious effects on their cognitive abilities, such as attention and concentration, or their emotional well-being. This demonstrates an impressive ability of our biological rhythms to adapt to changing environmental circumstances.

CHECK YOUR UNDERSTANDING

Check your understanding of circadian, infradian and ultradian rhythms, including the role of endogenous pacemakers and of exogenous zeitgebers by answering these questions. Try to do this from memory. You can check your answers by looking back through Topic 1.

1. What does the term 'circadian rhythm' mean?

2. How do circadian, infradian and ultradian cycles differ?

3. Provide an example of an infradian and an ultradian cycle.

4. What does the term zeitgeber mean? Give examples of two different zeitgebers.

5. In what sense can the pineal gland be considered to be an endogenous pacemaker?

6. What does the term SCN mean and where is it found?

7. Why is jet lag more severe when travelling West to East than travelling East to West?

8. In what ways are jet lag and shift work similar in their effects on human performance?

9. Why might shift work cause problems with sleep patterns and what can be done to improve this?

10. Present two criticisms of research into disrupting biological rhythms.

Psychology in context

Siamese twins – do they have the same sleep patterns?

'Siamese' (or co-joined) twins are rare, and ones that are unfortunate enough to be co-joined at the head are rarer still. When such twins are born and survive (the mortality rate is very high) psychologists are keen to determine to what extent they are able to live separate lives and to what extent they share the same physiology and life style. In the early 1970s Lenard and Schulte were able to study the sleep EEG patterns of a pair of German Siamese twins co-joined at the head. Despite being joined in this very intimate way and having extensive connections between their blood supplies, separate EEG recordings demonstrated that the pair had quite different patterns of EEG and indeed sleep/wake cycles (Lenard and Schulte 1972). Interestingly, the pair also demonstrated quite different personalities. The more psychologists learn about co-joined twins the more it becomes clear that they can

be very different and are, in a very psychological sense, complete individuals. Sadly the pair died at the age of only 21 whilst undergoing separation surgery.

1 What are your sleep patterns, for example are you a morning or evening person? One way of finding out is by completing the Horne-Östberg morningness, eveningness questionnaire. An adapted version of this test is available at http://news.bbc.co.uk/1/hi/programmes/breakfast/3703940.stm

2 Research suggests that sleep patterns may be determined by our genes. You could try a simple study to test this by asking members of your family to complete the test as well.

3 If you do this, what do your findings suggest about the genetics of sleep?

The nature of sleep

IDA   The relevance of animal studies

Have you ever wondered why most naturalists are 'birders' rather than 'mammalers'? (In fact there isn't even such a word as 'mammalers!'). To put it another way, why is there this bias towards bird watching over mammal watching? The answer is quite simple, most avian species are **diurnal** (active during the day) whereas, unlike our own species, most mammals are **nocturnal** (active at night). This is almost certainly due to the fact that birds are able to escape predators through flight and by living (in many cases) a relatively safe **arboreal** (tree-living – see chapter 7) life style. Interestingly, the reason we share this diurnal habit with birds is almost certainly due to our own ancient arboreal past (most present living primates are arboreal and nearly all are diurnal). Despite this, much of what we know about the circadian sleep and waking cycle has been gained from observing and conducting experiments on nocturnal mammals in the lab (mainly rodents such as rats, mice and hamsters) but we need to bear in mind that we differ from most other mammals in our diurnal life style when considering such research findings.

Stages of sleep

Despite much speculation, very little was known about the nature of sleep until the 1930s when scientists began to study it in the lab by use of **electroencephalography (EEG)**. In electroencephalography electrodes attached to the scalp record the gross electrical activity of the brain and allow researchers to classify different levels of arousal (Breedlove *et al.* 2007). EEG produces brain waves (either on paper or on a computer screen) that vary in terms of frequency and amplitude (the number of waves per second and the height of the waves respectively). Frequency is measured in Hertz (Hz) which consists of the number of waves per second. In the early 1950s, based on EEG recordings, Aserinsky and Kleitman (1953) divided sleep into two main classes: **slow-wave sleep (SWS)** and **rapid-eye-movement sleep (REM)**. Further investigations led to SWS being sub-divided into four stages (Breedlove *et al.* 2007).

The four stages of slow-wave sleep

- *Stage 1* – heart beat slows down, muscle tension is reduced, eyes may roll a little, alpha waves are replaced by slower, smaller desynchronized activity.

- *Stage 2* – EEG pattern becomes synchronized with larger slower waves interrupted by periodic bursts of fast spiking activity called sleep spindles (12 to 14 Hz) that last one or two seconds.

- *Stage 3* – large amplitude very slow waves (delta waves – 1–3 Hz) dominate the EEG pattern and sleep spindles become less common. Heart rate continues to fall as does body temperature.

- *Stage 4* – EEG recordings consist purely of delta waves and metabolic rate reaches its lowest. Arousal threshold (i.e. a measure of how hard it is to wake someone up) is very high.

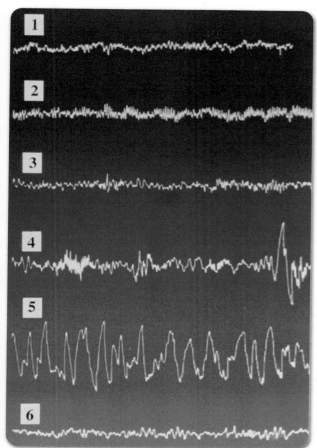

Brain waves showing different patterns of sleep. Electroencephalogram (EEG) recording of brain waves in various states of sleep. Trace 1 is of a brain when awake. Trace 2 shows the alpha-waves of a person still awake, but with eyes closed, receiving no external stimuli. Trace 3 shows theta-waves, as the person falls asleep. Trace 4 shows more complex patterns and trace 5 shows the standard delta-wave pattern usually associated with sleeping. At certain times during normal sleep, the brain becomes unusually active, and the EEG records traces similar to that of a brain when awake (trace 6). This is called rapid eye movement (REM) sleep, and is the period when dreaming occurs.

Stages 1 – 4 are often seen as 'deeper' stages of sleep. Although a simplification of the nature of sleep, since people become increasing difficult to wake up as they move through these stages, it is broadly correct. On average it takes people about one hour to pass through the 4 stages and then enter a quite different state – REM sleep. When a person enters REM sleep the EEG pattern suddenly changes to high-frequency, small-amplitude activities. This pattern is similar to when a person is awake, but unlike someone who is awake, the skeletal muscles become completely relaxed and, paradoxically, in this state a person is more difficult to wake up (that is, the arousal threshold is high). For this reason REM sleep is also called **paradoxical** sleep. One of the most apparent features of REM sleep is the fact that the eyeballs move rapidly in their sockets (which is how the term rapid eye motion sleep was originally derived). Interestingly, if people are woken up during REM sleep they nearly always report they were dreaming, whereas this is less common during SWS stages 1–4. At one point it was widely considered that dreaming only took place during REM sleep but today it is known that dreams can also happen during SWS (although they are invariably less vivid and closer to meandering thoughts, Breedlove *et al.* 2007). In contrast to SWS dreams, REM dreams usually involve visual imagery, and other sensory modalities such as sounds and smells are often apparent. Also REM dreams normally involve a form of a story in which the dreamer plays a central role.

Contrasting characteristics of SWS and REM sleep

During slow wave sleep, sensory information is largely inhibited from entering consciousness by a lower brain area called the **thalamus** (an evolutionary ancient area sitting on top of the brain stem that largely determines how much sensory information reaches higher centres). This may serve to maintain sleep by stopping external distractions. Also during SWS there is a move towards conserving energy as heart rate, blood pressure and respiratory rates decrease.

During REM sleep motor regions of the **cortex** (the outer covering of the brain) are activated, which begs the question why don't we get up and walk around (Jouvet 1975)? The reason is that despite the excitation of the motor cortex, the motor neurones (that control the skeletal muscles) are normally inhibited. Hence the instructions to move parts of the body that may occur during REM are countermanded by other parts of the brain, leading to a state of temporary paralysis although this does not apply to the eyeballs. I say 'normally inhibited' because, as we will see when we consider sleep disorders, for some people this does not always work properly. Unlike SWS, during REM sleep information does sometimes seep in from the external world and this may lead to things like rainfall being incorporated into our dreams.

What is the function of sleep?

From the earliest recorded history people have wondered why it is that we and other species enter into this strange dormant stage that we call sleep for lengthy periods each day (Horne 1988). You might be surprised to learn that psychologists still do not know why we sleep. But, as in many areas of psychology, they have developed a number of competing theories for the function of sleep. Broadly speaking there are three theories to explain the function of sleep (Toates 2007):

- Restoration
- Evolution
- Maintaining brain plasticity.

Restorative theories of sleep

Restorative theories of sleep are also known as homeostatic theories since they are concerned with maintaining **homeostasis** (the notion that the body is constantly striving to achieve an optimal physiological state). Restorative theories are the most intuitive ones since they suggest that the function of sleep is rest and recuperation in order to restore the body to its full waking capacity (Horne 1988). Although having intuitive appeal, does it stand up to scrutiny? During SWS (and in particular stages three and four) growth hormone is released into the blood in large quantities. Growth hormone serves an important role in protein synthesis which thereby helps to restore bodily tissues. This suggests that sleep serves a restorative function. Even amongst those that consider sleep to be restorative, however, there are debates as to the precise nature this might take. Two influential restorative theories are those of Horne (1988) and of Oswald (1980).

Oswald's (1980) restoration model

Oswald suggests that the high level of brain activity seen during REM sleep reflects brain recovery, while an increase in the body's hormone activities (especially growth hormone) during SWS reflects restoration and recovery in the body. Oswald views REM sleep as essential for brain repair and restoration. This is supported by the high proportion of REM sleep seen in the newborn baby, where it makes up 50 to 60 per cent of sleep time, gradually falling to the normal proportion of about 25 per cent as the child grows.

The months before and after birth are a time of rapid brain growth and development, so if REM sleep is a time when such processes occur, it is logical that a baby should show increased amounts of REM sleep (see Lifespan changes of sleep).

Horne's (1988) core sleep/optional sleep model

This account is similar to the restoration model put forward by Oswald (1980). In a review of the effects of sleep deprivation, Horne (1988) concluded from a number of controlled laboratory studies that sleep deprivation in normal participants produces only mild effects such as those seen in Randy Gardner (see sleep deprivation record below), together with some sleep recovery concentrated mainly in Stage 4 SWS and in REM sleep. Although the effects of sleep deprivation were not dramatic, they did involve some problems with cognitive

Sleep deprivation record

Key research: Gulevich et al. (1966)

Early sleep researchers suggested that a lack of sleep can lead to serious bizarre behaviour including hallucinatory states (Breedlove et al. 2007). One deprivation study, however, suggests that although these effects can be seen they are transitory, provided the participant is able to have a good night's sleep afterwards. Gulevich et al. (1966) report the case of a 17-year-old schoolboy, called Randy Gardner, who stayed awake for 264 hours (11 days) in 1964 and at the time held the record for total sleep deprivation. He developed blurred vision and incoherent speech, some perceptual disturbances, such as imagining objects were people, and a mild degree of paranoia, imagining that others thought him to be stupid because of his cognitive problems. The effects, however, seemed mild compared to the degree of sleep deprivation and he recovered quickly when he eventually slept. The first night he slept for 15 hours and only recovered about a quarter of his overall lost sleeping time during the nights that followed. Recovery was specific to particular stages – two-thirds of Stage 4 SWS and a half of REM sleep were recovered, but little of the other stages of SWS (Gulevich et al. 1966). This was an uncontrolled single case study, which raises methodological issues. Due to the lack of control it is difficult to determine whether-or-not microsleeps (sleep periods that last a matter of seconds and are difficult to spot without an EEG) had occurred.

Since Gardner's record of 1964, a number of claims have been made that this record has been broken including an astonishing 449 hours without sleep achieved by Maureen Weston during a 1977 'rocking chair marathon' (Pinel 2003). That is 18 days and 17 hours – a full week longer than Gardner! Hence it is difficult to determine whether or not there is an absolute upper limit to how long people can go without sleep.

Evaluation

Studies such as the one involving Randy Gardner are problematic because they lack the control of extraneous variables necessary to draw confident conclusions about the ill effects of sleep deprivation. For example, Gardner's sleep deprivation produced somewhat unexpectedly mild effects, so we might question whether 'total' sleep deprivation in an uncontrolled study is possible (i.e. a sleep deprived participant may experience 'microsleeps' of which they are not aware).

Studies such as the one carried out with Gardner raise serious ethical issues because of the potential for harm associated with total sleep deprivation. We cannot be sure of the health risks associated with total sleep deprivation, nor in fact whether such deprivation might cause irreversible physiological damage.

abilities, such as perception, attention and memory, while the recovery of Stage 4 SWS and REM sleep suggests that these are the critical phases. Horne therefore proposes that 'core sleep', consisting of Stage 4 SWS and REM sleep, is essential in humans for the normal brain functioning essential for our cognitive abilities, while the lighter stages of SWS are not essential, and he refers to these as 'optional sleep'. During core sleep the brain recovers and restores itself after the activities of the day.

The main difference between the accounts of Horne and of Oswald concerns the proposed functions of slow-wave sleep. As total sleep deprivation produces few obvious effects on the body, Horne (1988) believes that body restoration is not the purpose of sleep. He suggests that this occurs during periods of relaxed wakefulness, leaving core sleep to provide for the restoration of brain systems. However, Horne is specifically discussing studies carried out with human participants and it is quite possible that the sort of division between brain restoration and body restoration put forward by Oswald could apply to non-human animals. As there are significant differences between species in the precise details of their sleep/waking cycle, it is possible that no single hypothesis could cover them all.

Evaluation of restoration theories of sleep

- *Effect of energy expenditure* – It is perhaps surprising that the view that sleep has a vital restorative function is only weakly supported by research. One way of testing this hypothesis is by looking at the effects of pre-sleep activities on the duration of sleep. According to the restorative perspective, intense energy expenditure during the day should increase the duration of sleep in order to restore the resources used. For most people, intense exercise may cause them to fall asleep more quickly, but it does not cause them to sleep for longer (Breedlove *et al.* 2007). Also it is known that the giant sloth sleeps for about 20 hours a day even though its energy expenditure is small.

- *Body function and sleep deprivation* – Sleep deprivation studies have also failed to provide conclusive evidence that sleep is necessary to keep the body functioning normally. Horne (1988) reviewed 50 studies in which humans had been deprived of sleep. He found that very few of these studies reported that sleep deprivation had interfered with the participants' ability to perform physical exercise. Neither was there any evidence of a physiological stress response to the sleep deprivation.

- *Growth hormone and sleep* – As we have seen, one of the most important claims for the restorative function of sleep was that growth hormone is released during SWS and that this has an important role in protein synthesis. However, Horne (1988) points out that as amino acids (the constituents of proteins) are only freely available for five hours after a meal, and most people eat several hours before going to bed, then the supply of available amino acids is low for most of the

night. This implies that not much protein synthesis would go on during sleep.

- *Animal studies* – Some support for restoration accounts comes from animal studies. Prolonged sleep deprivation in rats appears to cause them to increase their metabolic rate, lose weight and die within an average of 19 days (Everson *et al.* 1989). Allowing these animals to sleep within that time prevents their death. However, animal studies such as this do not allow us to separate the effects of sleep deprivation from the methods used to keep the animals awake. In order to keep animals awake they must be constantly stimulated, and hence stressed. Studies to isolate which organs are most affected by chronic sleep deprivation have failed to isolate one specific system that is affected to the exclusion of others. It is most likely that sleep deprivation in animal studies interferes with the immune system, which then leads to death. It is possible that sleep provides the only opportunity for tissue restoration in some species. For example, when rats are awake, they generally spend all their time foraging for food, seeking mates or avoiding predators. Humans, on the other hand, are capable of resting during the day. In fact, our metabolic activity when we are in a state of quiet restfulness is only nine per cent higher than it is when we are asleep.

- *Fatal familial insomnia* – Some humans have a rare inherited defect that prevents them sleeping normally. People with this disorder, called 'fatal familial insomnia', sleep normally until middle age when they simply stop sleeping, leading to death within two years. Autopsies have revealed a degeneration of the thalamus, which may well be responsible for the onset of the insomnia. Although these cases support restoration accounts, they are very rare and such patients clearly have brain damage, making it difficult to generalize the findings.

- *REM sleep and restoration of brain neurotransmitters* – Stern and Morgane (1974) propose that REM sleep is specifically for the restoration of brain **neurotransmitters**. Neurotransmitters are chemicals that allow the transmission of a nerve impulse from one nerve cell across the gap between it and an adjacent nerve cell, where it activates a receptor in the membrane of the receiving cell. Stern and Morgane (1974) observed that after REM sleep deprivation, participants show 'REM rebound', that is, an increase in REM sleep when they are allowed to sleep normally. It is as if REM rebound is necessary for restoring something lost during REM sleep deprivation. They noted that antidepressant drugs also reduce REM sleep, but that there is no REM rebound when people stop their drug treatment. They argue that the drugs increase the levels of brain neurotransmitters such as serotonin and dopamine that are normally a function of REM sleep. However, since people taking anti-depressant drugs have increased levels anyway, they do not need REM sleep and do not therefore show REM rebound when they stop taking the drugs.

Evolutionary theories of sleep

Evolutionary theories of the function of sleep suggest that it evolved to aid survival in the evolutionary past. The main idea here is that sleep forces us to conserve energy at times when it would be inefficient for us to be awake (Kleitman 1963; Webb 1974). It is certainly the case that mammalian bodies fall by one or two degrees Celsius when asleep, saving a little energy and that when food is scarce many animals increase their sleeping time (Berger and Phillips 1995). These two facts may be taken as some support for the evolutionary theory of sleep; but they are by no means persuasive. The evolutionary-based theories have another card up their sleeve, however. As Meddis (1975) pointed out, mammalian physiology does not vary a great deal and yet the time that animals of each species spend asleep does. Horses, for example, sleep just under four hours in every 24 whereas, foxes sleep for nearly nine hours. Cats spend 14.5 of their 24 daily hours asleep and the giant sloth (as mentioned earlier) and some species of bats come close to 20 hours. In an attempt to extend previous evolutionary theories of sleep, Meddis suggested the amount of time animals spend asleep depends on the safety of their sleeping habits and on how much time they need to spend gathering food. Herbivores, for example, such as horses, spend a large part of the day grazing on low quality grass and cannot afford to spend much time asleep since they have to spend so much time feeding. In addition, large carnivores such as wolves would have proved a threat when asleep. We can think of the diet and the existence of large predators as the evolutionary pressures that led to this relatively brief period of sleep. In the case of a carnivore such as a fox, the opposite is the case. There is little to disturb their sleep and feeding involves nutrient rich meat. Hence they sleep long and deep. Bats may not be large carnivores, but many species sleep high up in caves where they are protected by their surroundings and through safety in numbers. Because it relates directly to an animal's ecology, Meddis' evolutionary-based theory has also been called an ecological theory of the function of sleep.

Evaluation of evolutionary theories of sleep

- *Animals do vary in sleeping habits* – It is difficult to explain Meddis' finding of such a wide range of sleeping habits, with some animals sleeping six times as long as others, in terms of restoration. Surely if restoration were the main function of sleep, then the various species should sleep for a similar amount of time. Hence the ecological theory appears strong on this finding alone.

- *Is sleep the most adaptive approach?* – Although the ecological theory seems to be a very plausible explanation, it is not clear why such a complex physiological mechanism as sleep would evolve, simply to keep vulnerable animals out of harm's way, when a state of behavioural inactivity would serve much the same purpose. Many animals do, indeed, 'play possum' by freezing when threatened by predators and you could argue that the safest state would be to remain inconspicuous but alert.

- *Why hasn't sleep been 'selected out'?* – A persuasive argument against the view that sleep serves an important adaptive function is the fact that sleep is found in species that would seem to be better off without it (Carlson 2002). For example, the Indus dolphin lives in the muddy waters of the Indus River in Pakistan. Over the years, this animal has become blind because good eyesight is unnecessary, given the extremely poor visibility of its environment. It does, however, have an excellent sonar system that it uses to navigate. Despite the dangers of falling asleep (potential injury from floating debris and passing river traffic), sleep has not disappeared. Although the Indus dolphin never stops swimming, it sleeps in short naps of between four and 60 seconds for a total of around seven hours each day. If sleep merely served an adaptive function, then surely it would have been eliminated through the process of natural selection in the same way that vision was (Carlson 2002).

Maintaining brain plasticity theories of sleep

When asked to make a big decision such as whether to buy a new car or take up a job offer people often state that they would like to 'sleep on it'. Such a statement suggests that we feel we make better decisions following a period of sleep. The question is, is this just folklore or are we better decision makers following a good night's sleep? Adherents of the brain plasticity theory of sleep consider the latter to be the case (Benington and Frank 2003; Toates 2007). According to brain plasticity theories, sleep aids processes such as memory consolidation that rely on long term changes in the brain. Plasticity refers to the fact that neurons in the brain are constantly rearranging themselves, either by the production of new neurons or by altering the connections between pre-existing ones. Hence this theory sees sleep as a period when some **synaptic connections** (the areas where neurons make contact with each other) are selectively strengthened whilst others are eliminated (Benington and Frank 2003).

Much sleep per day
bat
armadillo
cat

Moderate amount of sleep per day
fox
rhesus monkey
rabbit
human

Little sleep, easily aroused
cow
sheep
goat
horse

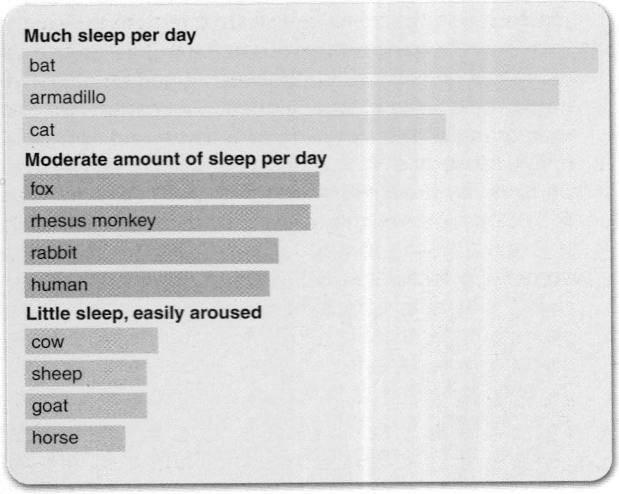

Figure 1.3 *The number of hours of sleep per day for a range of animal species* Kalat, J.W. (2004), Biological Psychology (8th Edition)

Brain plasticity theories suggest learning and long term memory formation are related to changes in neurons that occur during sleep. One simple idea is that an organism can best assimilate new experiences into **long term memory (LTM)** during sleep since the animal is not controlling any behaviour or attending to external stimuli (Cohen 1979). Note that we can make direct predictions from the brain plasticity function of sleep theory.

1 At least some forms of LTM should improve following sleep.

2 LTM should be impaired in the sleep deprived.

Evaluation of maintaining brain plasticity theories of sleep

- *Animals do sleep longer following learning* – when a lab animal such as a rat is presented with a new enriched environment or when it is given problems to solve it will tend to sleep for longer (Benington and Frank 2003). This suggests that sleep is related to LTM.

- *Animals demonstrate disrupted learning following sleep deprivation* – lab rats that have been sleep deprived show poorer learning than those that are allowed to sleep after learning new information (Benington and Frank 2003). Again this suggests sleep is necessary for LTM formation.

- *The same brain regions are activated* – when humans were given a reaction-time task that activated specific brain areas and were then allowed to sleep, the same areas are active during (REM) sleep (Maquet *et al.* 2000). This might be taken as evidence that people were 'practicing' the task during sleep and hence consolidating LTM traces. This evidence suggests REM sleep in particular is involved in LTM formation.

- *Some people sleep very little yet still maintain good LTM* – Dement (1974) described a University professor who slept only three to four hours each night and lived to be 80, and Meddis (1977) described a lady of 70 who slept only one hour in every 24 without any cognitive problems. If sleep is needed to maintain brain plasticity and hence boost LTM storage, then surely these people would find it difficult to operate on such a small amount of sleep?

Lifespan changes in sleep

People often ask: Am I getting enough sleep? It is not easy to provide an adequate answer to this question, because how much sleep we can expect to have depends in part on our age. Most people are aware that babies sleep more than adults and that older adults sleep less than younger adults. What is often not appreciated is that not only does the amount of time spent asleep change with age but also the ratio of time spent in slow wave sleep (non REM sleep) and REM sleep changes. As we saw when discussing Oswald's restorative theory of sleep, in the newborn baby REM sleep accounts for 50 to 60 per cent of total sleep, whereas for older children this falls to 25 per cent. This reduction in the proportion of time spent in REM continues

Activity **Explore your own experience of sleep deprivation**

Think back to a time when you experienced significant sleep deprivation, perhaps during a hectic period of clubbing and partying, or a series of late-night revision sessions before important exams.

1 What was your experience? Did you feel tired? Did you notice any loss of concentration or any problems with your memory?

2 What does this suggest about the function of sleep? Does it support a restoration, evolutionary or brain plasticity account of the function of sleep?

3 When you returned to your usual sleep routine, did you sleep for longer and recover all the sleep you had lost?

Often excitement or stress can override our biological clocks and keep us awake when the body wants to sleep, and the arousal of examinations, for instance, can minimize the effects of sleep deprivation on concentration and memory, at least for a while.

so that for young adults it makes up 20 per cent of total sleep whereas for those in their 70s and 80s it might only account for 10 per cent. Interestingly, premature babies spend even more of their sleep time in REM with those born a month premature spending 80 per cent of their sleep in this state. This begs the question, why do they spend so much of their time in REM sleep? We saw earlier how Stern and Morgane (1974) suggested that REM sleep functions for the restoration of neurotransmitters in the brain. It has been suggested that the high level of REM during both prenatal and early post natal life serve the purpose of stimulating the brain to help it grow and become more organised (Breedlove *et al.* 2007). If this is the case, then the reason we have less of it as we age might be because we learn less as we age. This might suggest we need to sleep less as we grow older. This is a possibility but there are other possibilities. It might be that as with other parts of the body, sleep mechanisms just do not work as well as we age. Interestingly, in humans and other mammals the reduction in amount of time spent sleeping is largely due to a dramatic decline in Stages 3 and 4 SWS. By the age of 60 we spend half as much time in this state than we did at the age of 20. Remarkably people who reach 90 lose these stages of sleep completely (Breedlove *et al.* 2007).

This is also true of people a little younger that are suffering from senile dementia. Hence it is possible that the loss of these stages rather than the loss of sleep overall is related to a reduction in the ability to store new memories. The only problem with this hypothesis is that there are many people in their 90s that lack Stages 3 and 4 but are still cognitively unimpaired and intellectually 'sprightly!' In relation to a reduction in sleep in the elderly we should also bear in mind that McCrae *et al.* (2005) have uncovered evidence that elderly people actually sleep longer hours than they report, and that part of this is because they frequently cat nap during the day!

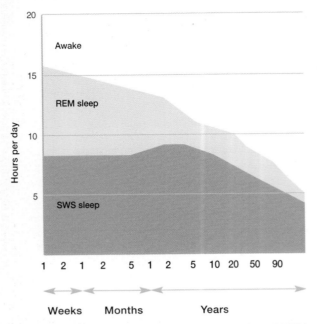

Figure 1.4 *Changes in proportions of SWS and REM sleep with age*

CHECK YOUR UNDERSTANDING

Check your understanding of sleep states by answering these questions. Try to do this from memory. You can check your answers by looking back through Topic 2.

1 In relation to EEG patterns what do the terms frequency and amplitude mean?

2 Outline the four stages of Slow Wave Sleep (SWS).

3 Suggest two ways in which REM sleep differs from SWS.

4 How do Horne's (1988) and Oswald's (1980) restorative theories of sleep differ?

5 In what ways are Horne and Oswald's theories similar?

6 Outline two supportive pieces of evidence for the restorative theory of sleep.

7 What is the evolutionary theory of sleep? Why is it sometimes also called the ecological theory of sleep?

8 What is the brain plasticity theory of sleep?

9 How do sleep patterns alter over a lifespan?

10 Present two possible explanations for why we sleep fewer hours as we grow older.

Topic 3: Disorders of sleep

People vary greatly in their sleep patterns, but rare (and lucky) are those who sleep well every night. We may feel tired and irritable following a poor night's sleep but unsatisfactory sleep can lead to far more serious problems than mild irritation. On Friday 2 March 2001, following a sleepless night, Gary Hart fell asleep at the wheel of his Land Rover, ran off the M62, careered down an embankment and into the path of an oncoming express train. Although Hart was able to get out of his vehicle in time, he could do nothing to stop the train crashing into it. This would have been bad enough, but the deflected train then ran into a freight train travelling in the opposite direction. Gary Hart's lack of sleep the night before led to the death of 10 people and serious injury for dozens of others. It also led to Hart being sentenced to five years in prison. This is not an isolated incident, and according to Kalat 'unsatisfactory sleep is a major cause of accidents...comparable to the effects of drugs and alcohol' (Kalat p.279, 2004). Here we explore the major sleep disorders including various forms of insomnia, sleep walking and narcolepsy.

Insomnia

Insomnia can be defined as problems with sleep patterns and in particular difficulties falling asleep or maintaining sleep. Given that we vary so much in what is considered a normal amount of sleep each night, we might ask what constitutes insomnia? A diagnosis of insomnia is not based on the number of hours slept but on how a person feels and operates the following day. Some people operate comfortably on five to six hours sleep a night whereas others require 10. Hence it is not the number of hours sleep that a person has each night but whether-or-not they feel refreshed following a night's sleep that determines the diagnosis of insomnia. Insomnia is believed to affect 25 per cent of the population intermittently and 9 per cent regularly (Ancoli-Israel and Roth 1999).

There are many causes of insomnia from external factors such as excessive noise or uncomfortable temperatures, to medications and substance abuse and psychological problems such as depression or anxiety. Additionally, certain neurological disorders such as epilepsy, brain tumours or Parkinson's disease can be the causes of insomnia.

Primary and secondary insomnia

In terms of the causes of insomnia, it is important to distinguish between **primary** and **secondary insomnia**. In the case of primary insomnia there is no apparent medical (or psychological) reason for the lack of sleep. This means that the disrupted sleep pattern is not a secondary consequence of, for example, medication or a medical problem such as Parkinson's disease or a brain tumour. An example of primary insomnia might be shift work insomnia where a person may well be attempting to sleep at times when their body clock tells them they should be awake (see shift work on p.54). In secondary insomnia, the disrupted sleep pattern is a secondary consequence of another problem including emotional disorders such as depression, anxiety or more specifically **post-traumatic stress disorder**. Other examples of secondary insomnia might be a result of neurological disorders such as the aforementioned Parkinson's disease or of other health problems such as chronic pain or coronary heart disease. Secondary insomnia can also be due to over-indulgence in alcohol, caffeine or nicotine and counter-intuitively long term use of sedatives (Webb 1992).

A good way to recall the difference between the two types of insomnia is to think of secondary insomnia being a secondary consequence of another diagnosed problem, whereas for primary it is the primary problem. Although secondary insomnia may be frustrating for many sufferers, at least, since the cause has been established it can sometimes be more easily treated (in particular where the cause is related to life-style habits such as smoking or drinking).

Sleep apnoea

One particular form of secondary insomnia occurs when a person experiences difficulties breathing whilst asleep. This is known as **sleep apnoea** and in severe cases can lead to the inability to breathe for anything from a matter of seconds to a matter of minutes (Kales and Kales 1984). One major cause of sleep apnoea is obesity due to the narrowing of airways but it can also occur in the elderly due to the brain mechanisms for respiration ceasing to function properly during sleep (Mezzanotte *et al.* 1992). Occasional, mild bouts of sleep apnoea are very common especially for people who snore, but for the chronic

sufferer it can make life very difficult. During a bout of apnoea carbon dioxide builds up in the bloodstream to a point where it stimulates **chemoreceptors** (specialised neurons that detect specific chemicals in the blood) and these cause the sufferer to wake up gasping for air. Once carbon dioxide is removed from the lungs and sufficient oxygen is taken in, sleep usually returns, but soon after the apnoea returns and the cycle repeats itself often leading to a very disturbed sleep pattern. In chronic cases of sleep apnoea the sufferer can use a machine that provides **continuous positive airway pressure** (CPAP) that pumps air under pressure into the nose and/or mouth cavity in order to keep the air passages open.

Photo of a person with continuous positive airway pressure

Sleep walking

Sleep walking or **somnambulism** occurs when an individual leaves their bed and walks around as if awake. Most episodes are quite short varying from a few seconds to a matter of minutes. Sleep walking is known to run in families and, although it is more common in childhood than in adulthood, in some cases it may persist into maturity. Episodes typically occur during SWS Stages 3 and 4 and tend to happen during the first half of the night. Contrary to popular belief it is not harmful to wake someone up who is sleepwalking; it is not psychologically damaging but can lead to a degree of confusion (Moorcroft 1993). Also contrary to popular belief somnambulists are not normally acting out a dream, but on occasions this can happen (Parkes 1985). When this does occur it usually takes place during REM sleep in which case it is labelled a special form of sleep walking known as **REM behaviour disorder (RBD)**. Unlike simple sleep walking, cases of RBD are relatively rare and involve quite organised behaviour patterns such as eating food or imaginary fighting (Schenck and Mahowald 2002). One reason for its rarity is the fact that the skeletal muscles are normally paralysed during REM sleep so people do not act out their dreams in this state. Interestingly, RBD frequently follows the onset of Parkinson's disease, which suggests that it is related to damage to the motor systems of the brain (Parkinson's disease is known to involve degeneration of motor responses). Again unlike simple sleep walking RBD tends to occur later in life, most frequently beginning after the age of 50 and more commonly affects men than women (Breedlove *et al.* 2007). In some cases a dream may be recalled in which the behaviour acted out occurs and in exceptional cases violence or sexual assault takes place during the episode (Broughton *et al.* 1994). In one case a young male student entered a women's dormitory and attempted to remove one woman's underwear and cut off another's shirt. He was acquitted on the grounds that he had been sleepwalking (Broughton *et al.* 1994). In another remarkable case a man pleaded not guilty to murder on the grounds that he was sleepwalking and the jury acquitted him. Clearly in such cases it is difficult to determine whether the accused was really sleepwalking (and in particular the special form of sleep walking called RBD) or whether they were 'faking it'. It really depends on how convincing they appear in front of the jury.

Narcolepsy

Narcolepsy is a general term used to describe the frequent occurrence of periods of sleepiness throughout the day. Like sleepwalking, it tends to run in families and is believed to affect one in a thousand people (Aldrich 1993). Four general symptoms are associated with narcolepsy (Mahowald and Schenck 1992), but not all suffers will show all of them:

- Bouts of extreme sleepiness during the day. These may begin either suddenly or gradually.

- In some cases **cataplexy** occurs, where the skeletal muscles suddenly give way and a person collapses. Cataplexy most frequently follows strong emotions such as laughter, excitement or rage.

- **Sleep paralysis**, where there is an inability to move just prior to falling asleep or waking. This may occur regularly.

- Dreamlike experiences may also occur when still awake. These are called **hypnagogic hallucinations**

and are often difficult to distinguish from reality. Hypnagogic hallucinations most frequently occur around the onset of sleep.

In terms of causes, specifically in relation to cataplexy, it is known that various neurons in the **medulla** (a part of the brain stem) that are normally active during REM sleep, become active when such a collapse occurs. These neurons normally send messages to the spinal cord to suppress skeletal muscle movements during REM sleep; hence they are inappropriately active during normal waking hours.

IDA

Comparative Psychology: Narcolepsy in dogs might provide a clue to the cause in humans

A number of strains of dogs exhibit narcolepsy, where following excitement (such as the appearance of food or another dog) they suddenly keel over and pass directly into REM sleep (Aldrich 1993). Interestingly, the same drugs that are used to treat the cataplexy part of narcolepsy in humans also work to suppress this condition in dogs. A mutant gene was identified in these animals which was found to affect a **receptor** (the area on the surface of a neuron where chemicals called **neurotransmitters** can excite the neuron causing it to fire, Lin *et al.* 1999). This gene affects specialised brain cells called **hypocretin** neurons (i.e. neurons that secrete hypocretin, a chemical involved in sleep regulation).

Interestingly, since uncovering this gene in dogs it has been found that humans with narcolepsy have lost around 90% of their hypocretin neurones (Thannicakal *et al.* 2000). Such neurones are found in the hypothalamus in both dogs and humans (as mentioned earlier, the hypothalamus is an important part of the brain when it comes to the control of sleep).

It should be pointed out that narcoleptic dogs are bred by scientists in order to study this problem in humans and hopefully produce treatments. As with the hamsters that were purposely brain injured in order to understand the biological bases of sleep, the breeding of dogs with specific problems is often an emotive topic. Once again scientists have to weigh up the cost and benefits of such breeding programs.

A dog going into narcolepsy

Does personality affect how much sleep we have?

Key research: Soehner et al. (2007)

Is there a relationship between personality and sleep patterns? Adriane Soehner and co-workers (2007) decided to find out by measuring sleep quality and sleep duration and then correlating these with scores on two personality questionnaires. For this purpose they asked 54 adults (32 per cent male, 68 per cent female with a mean age of 23 to 48 years) a number of questions relating to how long they took to fall asleep and how long they habitually slept by using both the Pittsburgh Sleep Quality Index (PSQI) and the Sleep Timing Questionnaire (STQ). In terms of personality tests they measured extraversion and neuroticism via the Eysenck Personality Inventory (EPI), and the level of potential manic-type symptoms by use of the Attitude to Life Questionnaire (ATLQ).

Their findings suggest that manic-type symptoms were significantly associated with those that went to bed later and had later times of waking and that neuroticism was associated with poorer quality of sleep as indicated by higher PSQI scores. Despite these associations there were no significant correlations between any of the **personality variables** and sleep duration. Hence, according to Soehner *et al.* (2007)

although there may be a relationship between manic-type behaviour and staying up late, and people who score highly on neuroticism reporting a lower quality of sleep, personality in itself does not appear to affect sleep duration.

Evaluation

Tests and questionnaires used in research such as this must be both reliable and valid. One way of testing reliability is to assess consistency over time through *test-retest* reliability, producing a correlation for the same people tested on the same measure on two separate occasions (e.g. after three months). Buysse *et al.* (2000) assessed the test-retest reliability of the PSQI and found that they were positively correlated at .85, indicating a high level of reliability (or consistency) between the two sets of scores. For a test to be *valid*, it should test what it claims to test. As the PSQI claims to assess sleep quality, then patients with sleep disorders should score significantly differently compared to healthy individuals. Again, Buysse *et al.* (2000) tested this and found a significant difference between the two groups on the PSQI as predicted.

CHECK YOUR UNDERSTANDING

Check your understanding of sleep disorders by answering these questions. Try to do this from memory. You can check your answers by looking back through Topic 3.

1. Explain the difference between primary and secondary insomnia.

2. List three causes of insomnia.

3. What problems might be encountered in the diagnosis of insomnia?

4. Define the term sleep apnoea?

5. What do the terms somnambulism and REM behaviour disorder (RBD) mean?

6. List the four general symptoms associated with narcolepsy.

7. What is the relationship between narcolepsy and cataplexy?

8. What is a hypnagogic hallucination?

9. Do you feel that the breeding of dogs specifically to have narcolepsy is justified by the knowledge this gains?

10. Is there any evidence of a link between personality and sleep?

Three types of rhythmic activity

Three types of rhythmic activity
1 Circadian – about a day
2 Infradian – less frequent
3 Ultradian – more frequent

Control of circadian rhythms

- **Endogenous pacemakers** – 'biological clocks'
- **Exogenous zeitgebers** correct biological clock

Role of pineal gland

- Receptors respond to external light
- Manufactures and releases melatonin
- Acts on brainstem sleep mechanisms

Role of suprachiasmatic nucleus (SCN)

- Neurons have an in-built circadian firing pattern
- Regulates manufacture of melatonin in pineal gland
- Pineal gland & SCN jointly act as pacemakers

How Science Works

- Hamsters regularly used to study control of sleep
- Have to weigh use of animals with benefit gained

Biological Rhythms

Biological rhythms

Consequences of disrupting biological clock

Jet lag

- More severe travelling from West to East
- Melatonin used to help

Shift work

- Backward movement – same as West to East jet travel
- Increasing shift rotation to 21 days – more time for adjustment

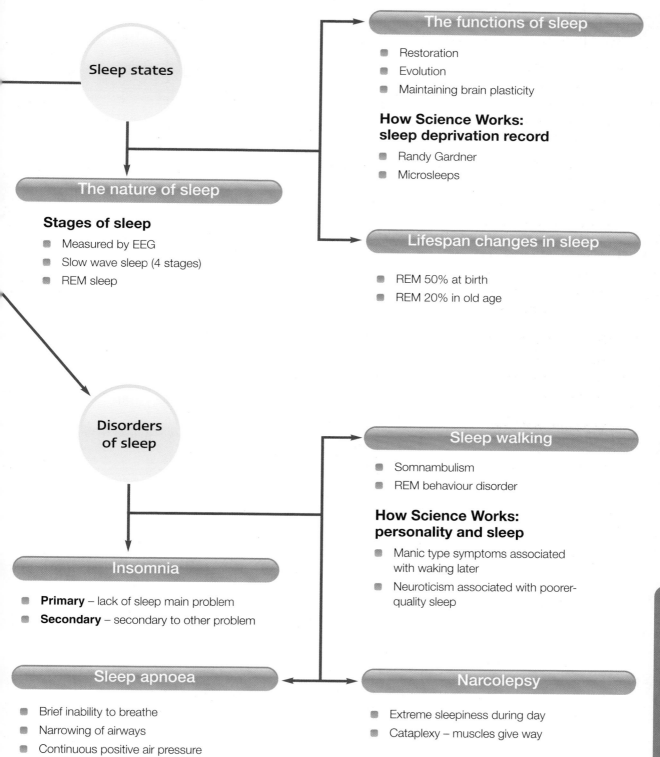

Sleep states

The functions of sleep

- Restoration
- Evolution
- Maintaining brain plasticity

How Science Works: sleep deprivation record

- Randy Gardner
- Microsleeps

The nature of sleep

Stages of sleep

- Measured by EEG
- Slow wave sleep (4 stages)
- REM sleep

Lifespan changes in sleep

- REM 50% at birth
- REM 20% in old age

Disorders of sleep

Sleep walking

- Somnambulism
- REM behaviour disorder

How Science Works: personality and sleep

- Manic type symptoms associated with waking later
- Neuroticism associated with poorer-quality sleep

Insomnia

- **Primary** – lack of sleep main problem
- **Secondary** – secondary to other problem

Sleep apnoea

- Brief inability to breathe
- Narrowing of airways
- Continuous positive air pressure

Narcolepsy

- Extreme sleepiness during day
- Cataplexy – muscles give way

Perception

EXPLAINING THE SPECIFICATION

Specification content	The specification explained
Theories of perceptual organization (Topic 1)	**The specification focuses on visual perception. In this part of the specification you are required to know about two theories concerned with how we organize and interpret sensory stimuli to form our perceptions (inner representations) of the external world. To do this, you need to be able to:**
Gregory's top-down/indirect theory of perception	■ Describe and evaluate Gregory's top-down theory of perception. Gregory's theory claims that we use our past experience and stored knowledge to search for the best interpretation of the available sensory data.
Gibson's bottom-up/direct theory of perception	■ Describe and evaluate Gibson's bottom-up theory of perception. Gibson's theory claims that our perceptual experience can be explained in terms of the array of visual information provided by the environment alone without need for further information processing.
Development of perception (Topic 2)	**In this part of the specification you are required to know about how perception develops over time. To do this, you need to be able to:**
The development of perceptual abilities, for example depth/distance, visual constancies. Infant and cross-cultural studies of the development of perceptual abilities	■ Describe and evaluate research findings in at least two areas of perceptual development. In this chapter, we focus on depth perception and visual constancies. ■ Describe and evaluate research using infants and also research carried out in different cultures (cross-cultural studies).
The nature–nurture debate in relation to explanations of perceptual development	■ Demonstrate an understanding of the nature–nurture debate in psychology. ■ Outline and critically comment on how explanations of perceptual development contribute to the nature–nurture debate.
Face recognition and visual agnosias (Topic 3)	**In this part of the specification you need to know about the processes involved in recognizing faces and why some people are unable to recognize objects presented visually to them. To do this, you need to be able to:**
Bruce and Young's theory of face recognition, including case studies and explanations of prosopagnosia.	■ Describe and evaluate Bruce and Young's theory of face recognition. ■ Describe what is meant by visual agnosias, including prosopagnosia. ■ Describe and evaluate case studies of prosopagnosia and discuss them in relation to two explanations of prosopagnosia.

Perception is an important area of study for psychologists. The world around us is filled with people and objects, which we can see, hear, touch, smell or taste. We receive this information as sensations arriving at sense organs in the body, such as the eyes, ears and nose. These sense organs contain sensory receptors that detect the physical properties of the world around us, such as light and sound, and pass this information to the brain and the central nervous system (CNS). This information is then converted through a number of processes into our perceptual experience of the world. Cognitive psychologists are interested in explaining the mental activity required in order to convert physical information from the environment into the psychological experience of perception. There has been a lot of research into perceptual processing. Most of this research has concentrated on **visual perception** – the process by which we transform (organize and interpret) incoming sensory information from the eyes to produce an experience of depth or distance, for example. Visual perception will be the focus of this chapter.

Although perception occurs within the brain, our first contact with the external visual world is through our sense organs. It is, therefore, important to know something about the physical make-up of the eye and visual pathways in the brain, so we will look briefly at the structure and function of the visual system before embarking on Topic 1.

In Topic 1, we consider two different theories of perceptual organization. We start by examining Gibson's bottom-up (direct) theory of perception, which claims that we pick up sufficient information from the visual environment to be able to form our perceptions. We will then explore Gregory's top-down (indirect) theory of perception, which states that we often need to go beyond the information contained in the visual stimulus and use stored memories based on our previous experience to help us build or construct our conscious experience of the world.

In Topic 2, we focus on perceptual development and how this relates to the nature–nurture debate, i.e. the question of whether perceptual skills are innate or develop as a result of learning through experience. In Topic 3, we turn our attention to face recognition and the clinical condition known as prosopagnosia, which is the inability to recognize faces.

The structure and function of the visual system

Light is the starting point for visual perception. The reason that we are able to see is that light is reflected from the various objects and people around us into our eyes. This reflected light is focused to create an image in the eye which, in turn, causes electrical signals to trigger a sequence of events in the brain, leading to conscious perception. Light falls on the back of the eyes as two, small, upside-down, two-dimensional images, but what we actually 'see' is a coherent, colourful, three-dimensional world that is the right way up. How does this transformation occur?

The eye

Look at the cross-section of the eye in Fig. 2.1 before reading any further.

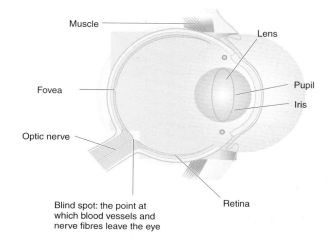

Figure 2.1 *Cross-section through the eye*

Light enters the eye through the pupil, which is controlled by a ring of coloured muscles called the iris, which regulates the size of the pupil in response to external stimuli. Bright light will cause the pupil to constrict to as little as 2 mm in diameter, but, under dim light conditions, the pupil can dilate to up to 8 mm. This process of contraction and dilation occurs automatically and is not under conscious control.

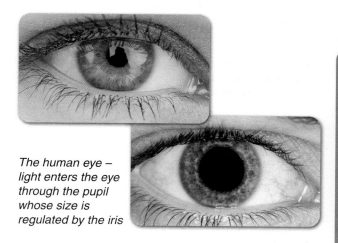

The human eye – light enters the eye through the pupil whose size is regulated by the iris

The lens is situated directly behind the pupil and its function is to complete the process of bringing light into focus on the retina at the back of the eye. Through a process called 'accommodation', the lens can change its shape to bring objects at various distances into focus. The retina at the back of the eye consists of three main layers of cells – photoreceptors (light sensitive cells), bipolar cells and ganglion cells (see Fig. 2.2). Photoreceptors consist of two different types of cell – cones and rods – which allow humans to see over a wide range of light intensities.

- *Cones* – responsible for vision under bright conditions (photopic vision) and also for the experience of colour vision. There are about 5 million cones in each retina and about 50,000 are packed into the small central area called the fovea (Tyler 1997). The fovea is a small depression at the centre of the retina that is no bigger than the size of this 'o'. It is responsible for our most detailed and accurate vision (see Fig. 2.2).

- *Rods* – responsible for vision under dim light conditions (scotopic vision). All 120 million rods are in the peripheral retina.

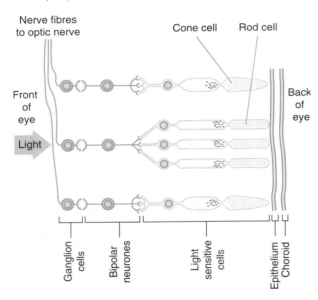

Figure 2.2 *Schematic diagram of the retina*

Once light has been focused on the retina by the lens, it is changed into neural impulses and sent along the optic nerve to the brain for processing and integration. The optic nerve leaves the eye at what is commonly known as the blind spot – an area at the back of the retina that is completely free of photoreceptors. We are not usually aware of the blind spot. This is partly because we have two eyes and so, if the image falls on the blind spot of one eye, it will be picked up by receptors in the other eye. We also seem to compensate for the blind spot by 'filling in' the area from which the information has disappeared.

The visual pathways

The optic nerves from each eye come together at the base of the brain to form the optic chiasma (see Fig. 2.3). The optic nerve fibres from the nasal retinas (the parts of the retina closest to the nose) cross to the opposite side of the brain at this point, while the fibres from the temporal retinas (the parts of the retina closest to the temples) continue on the same side of the brain. After they pass through the optic chiasma, most of the nerve fibres lead to the lateral geniculate nucleus (LGN) in the thalamus. From here they lead to the primary visual cortex, where additional processing is carried out.

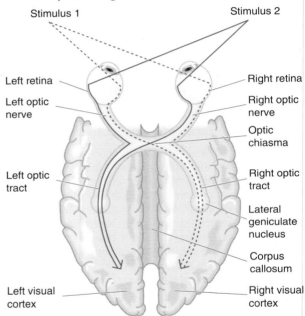

Figure 2.3 *Visual pathways showing the optic nerves coming together at the base of the brain to form the optic chiasma*

Topic 1: Theories of perceptual organization

The term **perceptual organization** refers to 'the structure of experiences based on sensory activity and the underlying processes that produce that perceived structure' (Palmer 2003). Theories of perceptual organization tend to fall into two categories:

- **Bottom-up (direct) theories** are based on the assumption that the process of visual perception begins with the physical properties of visual stimuli, e.g. patterns of light reflected from objects in the environment. It is thought that there is sufficient information in the sensory stimulus to allow the individual to make sense of their environment without the involvement of stored knowledge or problem-solving skills. The incoming information triggers a response in the retina, which in turn triggers a response higher up in the visual pathways and so on. Bottom-up processing, then, is concerned with physiological processing from the senses, processed upward in the direction of the cognitive system. These theories are sometimes known as 'data-driven' because the data (the sensory input) received by the sensory receptors determines or 'drives' perception.

Psychology in context   The slimming effect of stripes

Fashion 'experts' have long suggested that outfits with vertical stripes make us look taller and slimmer. However, they are wrong. Many of us were surprised to read in newspapers and magazines in September 2008 that this commonly held belief is mistaken. The person responsible for exploding this myth is Dr Peter Thompson of York University whose research findings (presented at the British Association Festival of Science in Liverpool) were widely reported in the broadcast and print media.

As part of his research, Dr Thompson asked 20 volunteers to look at pairs of pictures. In each pair, one woman wore a dress with horizontal stripes and the other wore a dress with vertical stripes. The women in each pair of pictures were exactly the same size. The participants judged which woman in each pair looked slimmer. Participants tended to think that the women wearing the horizontal stripes were slimmer.

Dr Thompson is puzzled as to why we should ever have thought that vertical stripes have a slimming effect, as psychologists have known for well over 100 years that this was not the case. The slimming illusion of horizontal stripes was first reported by Helmholtz, a 19th century scientist, in his squares illusion which consists of two sets of parallel lines, one horizontal and the other vertical. Each set of lines forms a square of exactly the same size (see Fig. 2.4), but the square with horizontal lines appears taller and thinner than the square with vertical lines. Helmholtz even advised women to wear horizontal stripes to make them look taller!

Not all fashion advice lacks research evidence: black does make you look slimmer. As Thompson reported: 'A black circle on a white background looks smaller than a white circle on a black background.'

Now try your own experiment, using:

1 pictures of people wearing vertical or horizontal stripes

2 the Helmholtz squares illusion.

Look at the squares below. What do you think causes this illusion?

Figure 2.4 *Helmholtz squares*

Some suggestions are given in the Answers to activities on p.603. ▶

Cognitive approach

The terms 'top-down' and 'bottom-up' derive from the information processing approach – a theoretical perspective within cognitive psychology in which the human mind is compared to a computer. According to this view, the human mind manipulates and transforms information through a series of processing stages. These can be represented schematically in flow diagrams that show the direction of the flow of information through the system (see Fig. 2.5).

Input processes → Translation/storage processes → Output processes

Bottom-up theories focus on the input processes (e.g. in the retina) and top-down theories concentrate on the role of knowledge and experience, that is, the translation and storage processes. An advantage of the cognitive approach is that it permits theories to be tested experimentally. It does, however, have its critics – see the panel below, 'Reductionism'.

Figure 2.5 *A simple flow diagram to represent processing stages*

Reductionism

The use of terms from information processing by cognitive psychologists has led to accusations of reductionism – the tendency to oversimplify explanations of complex phenomena. It is reductionist to represent the process of perception in terms of a simple flow diagram (see the panel, 'Cognitive approach') because this implies that an important aspect of human cognition functions in the same way as a machine.

- **Top-down (indirect or constructivist) theories**, on the other hand, emphasize the involvement of context and prior knowledge in interpreting information derived from the sensory system. This approach stresses the importance of higher cognitive processing right from the beginning of the perceptual process. This kind of processing is also called 'concept-driven' processing because prior knowledge (stored mental concepts) determines (drives) the interpretation of the sensory data.

HOW SCIENCE WORKS

Interaction of bottom-up and top-down processing

Key research: Palmer (1975a)

Palmer (1975a) carried out a study that demonstrates the way in which bottom-up and top-down processes interact. Look at Fig. 2.6(a). In themselves these drawings consist of little more than lines on the page. Palmer found that participants in his study were usually unable to recognize the objects depicted in them.

However, when he showed the participants the drawing shown in Fig. 2.6(b), they were easily able to identify the same 'squiggles' as facial features because they were embedded in a face. In Fig. 2.6(a), there is very little information available to us in the actual stimulus and there is no context to help us – we have to rely completely on bottom-up processing. In Fig. 2.6(b), however, we can use both bottom-up and top-down processing – the facial features remain exactly the same (bottom-up), but we now have the context of a surrounding face (top-down) and so have no difficulty in identifying the whole face and its constituent parts.

(a)

(b)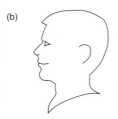

Figure 2.6 Recognizing shapes in context (source: Palmer 1975a)

Perception is an important area of study within the cognitive approach in psychology – see the bottom panel on p.71, 'Cognitive approach'.

Bottom-up and top-down processing are not mutually exclusive and we probably use both simultaneously in our everyday life. The particular kind of processing used is likely to depend on the nature of the visual stimulus. See the panel, 'Interaction of bottom-up and top-down processing' on the left.

Gibson's theory of direct (bottom-up) perception

According to direct theories of perception, the array of information in our sensory receptors is all we need to perceive anything. We do not need to call upon stored knowledge or past experience to mediate between sensory experience and perception (Sternberg 1996).

J.J. Gibson (1979) is the best-known champion of direct perception. He felt strongly that it was important to study perception in real-world environments instead of in the artificial surroundings of a laboratory. For this reason he sometimes referred to his theory as an 'ecological approach'. For example, during World War II he was concerned with developing training films for pilots. One of the most difficult tasks for pilots is to land the plane: they require good depth perception to accomplish this successfully. However, Gibson found that traditional training measures designed to help pilots make use of depth information were of little use. This finding led him to review contemporary ideas of perception and to formulate his own theory. He saw real movement as a vital part of perception and one that had been overlooked in many laboratory studies of visual perception. Gibson's theory is complex and was developed over a period of more than 30 years, so we provide a simplified version here.

According to Goldstein (1999), Gibson's theory is based on four major assumptions:

1 The pattern of light reaching the eye can be thought of as an optic array (unambiguous information about the layout of objects in space) which contains all the information necessary for perception.

2 Important information is provided by the movement of the observer.

3 The optic array contains invariant information (i.e. information that remains constant as the observer moves).

4 This invariant information leads directly to perception.

The optic array

The optic array contains all the visual information from the environment that strikes the eye. Gibson believed that the starting point for perception is the structure of the light that reaches the observer. To perceive objects, the light has to be structured by the presence of objects, surfaces and textures (the optic array). The structure is immensely complex because there are rays of light converging on the observer from every part of the surrounding environment and, also, this structure will change every time the observer moves.

According to Gibson, the optic array contains unambiguous, invariant information about how and where objects are situated in space. This invariant information comes in a number of forms, four of which we consider below.

The optic flow
The optic flow is the name given to the changes in the light patterns that reach an observer when the person moves, or when the visual environment moves. If you think about it, most of our perception occurs as we move relative to our environment. Even if we are not actually walking, running, driving, etc., we move our eyes and our heads in order to observe things going on around us. Gibson was particularly interested in describing elements in the optic array that convey information to the observer who is moving.

Flow patterns are created when objects in the visual environment flow past a moving observer. The nature of the flow provides information to the observer about position and depth. Consider how it feels to be the driver or front passenger in a car travelling along a straight road such as a motorway. You are faced with an expanding visual field in which elements that begin in the middle of your visual field pass around you as you move forward. For example, a motorway sign, first seen as a distant feature on the horizon, eventually passes to the left of you as you drive forward.

If you sit in the back seat of the car and look out of the rear window, the situation will be reversed and you will be faced with a contracting flow field. So, the nature of the flow field (i.e. expanding or contracting) will provide information to the observer about whether they are moving forward or backwards. Looking out of the side window of a car will produce yet another type of optic flow pattern. Objects close to the observer, such as fence posts, appear to be moving very fast in a backwards direction, while objects further away (e.g. trees on the horizon) appear to be moving much more slowly and in a forwards direction (motion parallax). Gibson was particularly interested in the role of optic flow patterns (OFPs) for pilots when landing aircraft. He believed that they provided unambiguous information about the direction, speed and altitude of the plane.

Figure 2.7 illustrates the optic flow field for a pilot coming into land. The object or pole (the landing strip) towards which the pilot is aiming appears stationary while the rest of the visual environment appears to move away from that point, that is, towards the pilot. This optic flow provides information about speed, direction and altitude.

Texture gradient
Texture gradient is of fundamental importance in Gibson's theory. According to Gibson, our perceptual world is made up of surfaces of different textures, and these

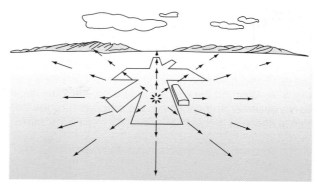

Figure 2.7 *The flow pattern for a pilot landing a plane (source: Gibson 1950)*

textures can be used to assist the perception of depth and orientation. A visual texture can be broadly defined as a collection of objects in the visual field, and the gradient refers to the change in the relative size and compactness of these elements.

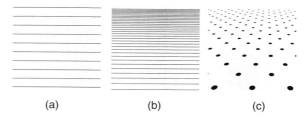

(a)   (b)   (c)

Figure 2.8 *Texture gradient*

Look at Fig. 2.8. Figure 2.8(a) has a uniform texture and so appears like a representation of something flat like, for example, an upright garage door. In Fig. 2.8(b), however, the compacted lines at the top of the picture give the impression of depth, perhaps of some decking stretching out in front of us. There is an even stronger impression of depth when the gradient appears in both the horizontal and vertical placing of the object elements as shown in Fig. 2.8(c).

In addition to providing information about depth and distance, texture gradient also indicates the orientations of surfaces. Sudden changes in the texture often signal a change in the direction of a surface, e.g. a shift from floor to upright wall.

Horizon ratio

Figure 2.9 *The horizon ratio – a perceptual invariant*

Horizon ratio is another perceptual invariant and refers to the fact that all objects of the same height, whatever their distance from the observer, are cut by the horizon in the same ratio of one-third above and two-thirds below. Objects of different sizes, but at the same distance from the observer, however, have different horizon ratios (see Fig. 2.9). Although the size of the tree may become larger as an observer approaches it, the proportion of the tree that is above or below the horizon will remain the same.

Affordances: recognizing the meanings of objects

How do we know that the object we are looking at is something to eat, sit on, grasp, etc.? Gibson suggested that the uses of objects are perceived directly. That is, all offer (afford) certain responses to be made, so a door handle affords turning, a chair affords sitting, a bed affords lying down. The affordance of an object depends on the particular circumstances in which it is encountered. So, for example, a chair affords 'sitting down' if you are tired, but 'stepping on' if you want to reach an item on a high shelf. The same object can also offer different affordances for different species: a washing line affords hanging out clothes for a human, but perching for a bird.

According to McGrenere and Ho (2000), Gibson used the term affordance to mean 'an action possibility available in the environment to an individual, independent of the individual's ability to perceive this possibility'. Direct perception occurs, therefore, when there is an affordance (e.g. the 'openability' of a door) plus enough information in the environment is present to specify the affordance (e.g. the door and its handle are clearly visible).

Evaluation of Gibson's direct theory of perception

- *Research rooted in the real world* – Gibson has shown that traditional laboratory methods have underestimated the richness of information available in the visual stimulus input. In particular, he has shown how important it is to take into account the movement of the observer and how this affects the optic flow. Gibson was unable to explain visual illusions – situations where an observer's perception of a stimulus does not correspond to the physical properties of the stimulus, demonstrating that perception can sometimes be inaccurate. However, Gibson stressed the importance of studying perception in real-life situations where movement and the passage of time are important. Gibson believed that studies based on the perception of illusions carried out in highly artificial laboratory conditions where participants were stationary had little or no relevance to real-life situations.

- (HOW SCIENCE WORKS) *Practical applications* – Gibson's work on training programmes for pilots has already been mentioned, and airports are now constructed with the best possible lighting and markings to enhance optical flow patterns for incoming pilots. Another practical application can be seen on approach roads to busy roundabouts where a set of parallel lines is painted on the road surface. The lines are painted closer and closer together as the road approaches the roundabout, so the driver gets the erroneous impression that they are accelerating. Without being given explicit instructions to do so, drivers tend to slow down automatically. As Hampson and Morris (1996) have pointed out, this traffic control technique changes perception by changing the structure of the perceived world, not by appealing to internal perceptual or cognitive mechanisms with a 'Reduce Speed' sign. These applications illustrate the importance of Gibson's work in helping people act more safely in their everyday lives in low-key yet important ways.

- *Affordances* – The idea of affordance is seen as a weakness in Gibson's theory. Bruce and Green (1990) have suggested that the concept of affordance may be able to explain the visually guided behaviour of insects, which have no need for a conceptual representation of the environment, but is an inadequate explanation of human perception. Humans function in an environment where knowledge about objects and their uses is influenced by cultural expectations and values. For example, Gibson claimed that all the potential uses of objects were directly perceivable. But how might someone from a culture where there is no postal service and, therefore, no post boxes perceive the affordances of a post box? According to Eysenck and Keane (2005): 'If he had not proposed the notion of affordances, then Gibson would have been forced to admit that the meaning of objects is stored in long-term memory.'

Gregory's top-down (indirect) theory of perception

A much older, but still current, approach to perception is found in the top-down (constructivist) theories. Top-down theories emphasize the combination of several sources of information required to build or construct our conscious perception of the visual world. They originated with the German psychologist, Helmholtz (1821–1894), and survive in the work of researchers such as Gregory (1997). This approach states that we need to use higher cognitive processes to interpret the information available in the sensory stimulus appropriately. According to Helmholtz, past experience and knowledge influence our perception. He called this the likelihood principle – i.e. we will perceive the object that is most likely to occur in that particular situation.

Palmer (1975b) demonstrated this by showing a picture of a scene and then briefly presenting a picture of an object. If the object was appropriate to the scene, it was identified more accurately than if it was inappropriate. See the Key Research panel.

The effect of context on identification of objects

Key research: Palmer (1975b)

The experiment investigated whether the prior presentation of visual scenes would affect how accurately participants would identify briefly presented drawings of real objects. Seventy-one undergraduates participated in the study.

Palmer presented participants with a familiar contextual scene such as a kitchen (see Figure 2.10). He then very briefly flashed a drawing of an individual object onto the screen and asked participants to identify it. The projected object was either appropriate to the scene (a loaf of bread), inappropriate (a drum), or misleading in the sense that it was visually similar to an appropriate object (a mailbox).

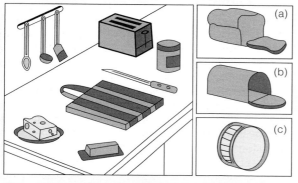

Figure 2.10 *Stimuli used by Palmer (1975b) in his experiment on the effect of context on object identification*

The rate of correct identification was 84 per cent for objects that might be expected from the context (e.g. a loaf of bread). However, performance fell to below 50 per cent for unexpected objects, such as a letterbox or a drum. Performance was worst in the 'misleading' condition.

Palmer concluded that an appropriate context can facilitate identification of objects; for example, exposure to a kitchen scene primes recognition of associated objects.

Evaluation

- *Top-down theory* – The findings from this experiment support the top-down theory of perception. The fact that participants often confused the mailbox with the loaf shows that their expectations (based on experience and memory) about what would be appropriate in a kitchen influenced their ability to make correct identifications. Palmer (2003) acknowledged that obviously people can identify objects correctly in bizarre contexts, but that an appropriate context makes identification quicker and more accurate.

- *Methodology* – This study has the advantage of being a well-controlled laboratory experiment, which means that we can make a causal link between the independent variable (the pairings of the object and the familiar scene) and the dependent variable (how accurately objects were identified). However, there is a degree of artificiality in the study that might lead to accusations of poor ecological validity: do the findings represent what happens in situations outside the research setting? Furthermore, the participants were university undergraduates (which is often the case in psychological research) and so questions about population validity also arise: to what extent can the results be generalized to other groups of people? It is important, nevertheless, not to overstate possible problems with laboratory experiments. What might be lost in ecological validity is compensated for in terms of the precision, control and replicability of the study.

Hypothesis testing

A more recent formulation of the likelihood principle is to be found in Gregory's (1997) idea that perception is governed by *hypothesis testing*. Although a constructivist, Gregory acknowledges the contribution made by Gibson to our understanding of perception. In particular, he acknowledges the importance of sensory cues such as texture gradient (see p.73) and motion parallax (see p.79). However, he is not able to accept Gibson's key assertion that perception occurs directly without any intervention from higher cognitive processes. Gregory believes that human perceivers act like intuitive scientists, i.e. they formulate and test hypotheses about the world. These hypotheses are sometimes wrong and this can lead us to experience visual illusions (see pp.76–78), but they can often help us to identify stimuli that are ambiguous or incomplete. A good example is when we are able to decipher poor handwriting.

Unfortunately the 5.00pm class is cancelled today.

Figure 2.11 *Handwriting sample*

Look at Fig. 2.11. You should have no difficulty in reading what it says: 'Unfortunately the 5.00 pm class is cancelled today'. However, if you look closely, you will notice that the '5' and the 's' at the end of 'class' are written in exactly the same way. Also, the 'U' of 'Unfortunately' is the same as the 'll' of 'cancelled', and the 'cl' of 'class' is the same as the 'd' at the end of 'cancelled'. It is only the context that allows us to differentiate between them.

In practice, we can see that perception involves a combination of top-down (conceptually driven) and bottom-up (data-driven) processing. You were not conscious of having to solve a problem when you read this sentence, but at some level, you were applying problem-solving strategies to this ambiguous handwriting. So, you know that 'class' is an English word and, moreover, that it fits appropriately into the sentence context. You also know that there is no such word as 'dass', so you read the word correctly. According to constructivist theories, successful perception requires intelligence and reasoning in combining sensory information with knowledge based on previous experience. For this reason, it is sometimes referred to as 'intelligent perception'.

Perceptual set

One aspect of intelligent perception is the concept of perceptual set identified by Allport (1955). This is a top-down activity involving the expectancies or predispositions that an observer brings to a perceptual situation that results in their seeing what they expect to see. Look at Fig. 2.12 below.

$$A$$
$$12 \quad 13 \quad 14$$
$$C$$

Figure 2.12 *The effect of perceptual set in interpreting ambiguous stimuli*

The symbol in the centre is read as a '13' if the horizontal set of symbols is scanned first. However, the same symbol is read as a 'B' if the vertical set is looked at first (Bruner and Minturn 1955). These effects depend on the reader being familiar with this system of numbering and the shape of English letters. Now try the activity opposite.

STRETCH AND CHALLENGE How could you use the concept of perceptual set to explain how labels, such as 'mental patient' or 'hoodie', might lead to dangerous forms of prejudice?

Ambiguous perceptions

Gregory (1997) maintains that our perceptual representation of the world around us is much richer and more detailed than might be expected if we were simply relying on the information contained in the visual stimulus. We are often presented with incomplete and ambiguous stimuli that lack detailed information, and yet we usually manage to make sense of them.

Gregory suggests that we use visual stimuli as a starting point for making informed guesses about their meaning. To illustrate this approach, look at the figure called the Necker cube in Fig. 2.13. You will have no difficulty in identifying a cube, but, if you stare at it for long enough, you will find that the cube seems to pop in and out and you cannot stop this happening.

Activity **Perceptual set**

What do you see in this picture? Study the picture carefully before reading on.

Now show this picture to some of your friends (individually) and ask them to tell you what they see. If they don't spot the Dalmatian dog after about 20 seconds, give them a clue by telling them, 'there's a dog'.

1 Why do you think it is sometimes difficult for people to detect the dog in the picture?

2 Why is it so much easier for them to detect the dog after they have been given the clue?

3 How would you design an experiment to test the effect of perceptual set using the 'Dalmatian' picture? What design would you use, how many participants, etc.

Answers to questions 1 and 2 are given on p.603. ▶

Gregory explains this in terms of hypothesis testing. The figure is ambiguous because the small circle could be on the inside back wall of the cube or the bottom left-hand corner of the front face of the cube. Gregory believes that we test first one hypothesis and then the other and, because there is no surrounding context to tell us which interpretation is correct, we switch between the two. In the real visual world, Gregory believes that there are usually enough contextual clues to remove ambiguity and allow us to confirm a single hypothesis.

However, if perception involves hypothesis testing, we will sometimes make errors. Visual illusions are examples of perceptual errors.

Visual illusions

Most of the illusions that have been studied by psychologists are artificial ones that have been devised specifically for experimental purposes so that investigators can uncover some of the reasons why we might misperceive in real-life situations. Gregory (1997) has taken a particular interest in perceptual illusions and has identified four major categories:

- *Ambiguous figures* can be interpreted in two equally plausible ways, e.g. the Necker cube (see Fig. 2.13). In the absence of any contextual information to reduce the ambiguity, the brain switches backwards and forwards between the two. In other words, the same input results in two different perceptions. Now try the activity 'Ambiguous figures' below.

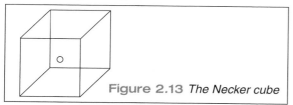

Figure 2.13 *The Necker cube*

- *Paradoxical figures* look perfectly normal at first glance, but would be impossible to reproduce as a three-dimensional object, e.g. the Penrose triangle in Fig. 2.15. It usually takes a few seconds to scan such a figure before we realize that it is impossible.

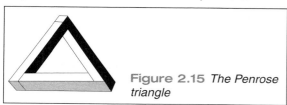

Figure 2.15 *The Penrose triangle*

- *Fictitious figures* are illusory figures that do not actually exist. In other words, we perceive a shape in the absence of appropriate sensory data. An example is the Kanizsa triangle in Fig. 2.16, where we 'see' a white triangle with its apex pointing upwards

superimposed on another triangle with its apex pointing downwards. Each point of this illusory triangle appears to be obscuring a segment from each of three green 'circles'. This is an example of how illusory contours (experiencing edges that are not present) help organize our visual perception so that what we 'see' makes sense, but actually leads to perceptual error (Mendola 2003).

Figure 2.16 *The Kanizsa triangle*

- *Distortions* appear to elicit a genuine misperception; for example, the Müller-Lyer illusion in Figure 2.17 where the two identical vertical lines appear to differ in length.

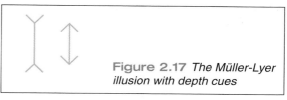

Figure 2.17 *The Müller-Lyer illusion with depth cues*

Top-down explanation of the Müller-Lyer illusion

The perceptual illusion that has probably attracted the most attention from researchers is the Müller-Lyer illusion. Gregory (1997) has explained the Müller-Lyer illusion in terms of 'misapplied size constancy' (the tendency for objects to provide the same perceptual experience despite

Look at the three pictures below and note what you see at first glance. Then look again at each one: you should eventually be able to see each picture in two different ways.

Figure 2.14 *Ambiguous figures*

changes in viewing conditions; see pp.79–80 for more information on constancies. In other words, we try to apply constancy mechanisms, which usually serve us well, in circumstances where it is not appropriate to do so.

Gregory has suggested that, in Western cultures at least, we are used to interpreting two-dimensional drawings as three-dimensional objects and that we attempt to do this when presented with the Müller-Lyer lines. He thinks that we 'see' the left-hand drawing as the inside corner of a room and the right-hand drawing as the outside corner of a building (see Fig. 2.18).

Figure 2.18 *The Müller-Lyer illusion*

Our retinal image of the two vertical lines is identical but, because the inside corner appears to be more distant than the outside corner, we assume that the left-hand line is longer. Gregory believes that this constancy scaling occurs unconsciously because of our ingrained, past experience in interpreting drawings. There is some evidence to support his view from cross-cultural studies (see pp.87–90). However, not all psychologists agree with him.

Day (1990) rejected the idea that we use depth information and proposed an alternative explanation, which he has called 'conflicting cues theory'. He suggests that we use two separate cues when judging the length of lines like those in the Müller-Lyer illusion:

1 the actual length of the line

2 the overall length of the figure.

In the Müller-Lyer illusion, the actual length of both the lines is the same, but the left-hand one is part of a considerably longer figure (i.e. the outward pointing fins make the overall length greater). Day believes that we try to integrate these two pieces of conflicting information by forming a compromise perception of length and deciding that the left-hand line is longer than the right-hand line.

Evaluation of top-down theories of perception

- *Intuitive appeal and experimental support* – It seems clear that we often use top-down processes to help us make perceptual sense of our visual environment, particularly in ambiguous circumstances. The intuitive appeal of the constructivist approach is supported by a number of experimental studies that have demonstrated the role of perceptual set and the role of participants' expectations and motivations. For example, Leeper (1935) found that when people were shown the famous

reversible figure of the young/old woman (see the Activity on p.77), the figure they were most likely to see first was the one they had been led ('set') to expect. Solley and Haig (1958) also found that as Christmas approached, children drew larger and more detailed pictures of Santas. However, despite its intuitive appeal, the top-down approach is criticized for overemphasizing the importance of expectations and underestimating the wealth of information in the retinal image.

- *Visual illusion* – Constructivist theories can account for perceptual errors more satisfactorily than direct theories. However, there is perhaps an emphasis in constructivist theories on perceptual errors whereas, in fact, most people see the world accurately most of the time. Furthermore, certain illusions (e.g. the Müller-Lyer) persist even when we know that our eyes are being 'tricked' (see Fig. 2.19). It is difficult for constructivists to explain this.

Figure 2.19 *The Müller-Lyer illusion without depth cues*

- *Artificiality* – Gibson criticized the constructivist view because he felt that the laboratory studies that appear to support the top-down approach were artificial and did not reflect real-world perception, where movement provides important visual cues. It is true that many of the studies that appear to support the constructivist position involve the presentation of ambiguous and fragmented information and presentations are extremely brief. Under these circumstances, it would be very difficult to rely on bottom-up processing. It could be, then, that the effects of context and experience are magnified in constructivist studies because of the nature of the stimulus material, and that they may not be so important in our normal, rich, visual environment. We are remarkably accurate and consistent in our perceptions. If perception relies so heavily on hypothesis testing and making 'best guesses', we would be likely to make more mistakes than we actually do.

It seems likely, therefore, that the process of perception uses a combination of information from sensory input and from our past experience and knowledge. The first part of visual processing may be bottom-up, but the top-down process begins an instant later (Matlin 2005).

Bottom-up and top-down explanations of perceptual organization

Clearly, perception is not a straightforward activity. In order to make sense of the complex visual information around us, we need to impose some form of organization on incoming stimuli. Both direct and constructivist theorists acknowledge the importance of organization, but they explain it in different ways. We will now look at two aspects of perceptual organization: depth perception and visual constancies.

Depth perception

Imagine that you are looking out of the window at a busy road. You will have no difficulty in seeing one lamp-post as nearby and another one on the other side of the road as being further away, or of understanding that the space between the two has depth. How do we achieve this three-dimensional experience when the image falling on our retina is flat and two-dimensional?

- *Bottom-up explanation* – Gibson explained depth perception in terms of visual cues, such as texture gradient, picked up from the optic flow. He believed that these cues are picked up directly from the visual array.

- *Top-down explanation* – Constructivists, on the other hand, suggest that visual cues are sometimes learned through past experience with the objects around us.

It is likely that both views are reasonable. It is possible, for example, that we have an innate ability to make use of depth cues, but that we learn through experience to use them more efficiently and rapidly. Some depth cues are based on the fact that each eye receives a slightly different view of the scene in front of us. These are called 'binocular depth cues' because both eyes are working together. Other cues seem to be effective, even when one eye is closed and these are called 'monocular cues'.

Binocular depth cues
Binocular depth cues include:

- *Binocular convergence* – When you rotate your eyes so that the image of an object straight in front of you falls directly on the fovea, each eye has to turn inwards slightly. The closer the object, the more the eyes have to turn. Feedback from the eye muscles helps us to determine the distance of objects.

- *Retinal (binocular) disparity* – This refers to the slight discrepancy in the viewpoint of each eye. The process by which these disparate views are merged into a single internal representation is called 'fusion'. The closer the object is to the viewer, the greater the disparity between the two images presented to each eye.

Activity   The process of fusion

With both eyes open, line up your index finger with a vertical line on a nearby wall. Now close each eye in turn and you'll find that your finger seems to jump. With both eyes open, the image is fused and you see your finger straight ahead of you.

Monocular cues
There are several monocular cues that refer to features of the visual field itself. Artists frequently use these to imply depth in paintings, so they are also called 'pictorial cues'. These are listed below:

- *Overlap* – When one object partially blocks the view of another, the blocked object is perceived to be further away.

- *Linear perspective* – Parallel lines, such as those at the side of a road or a railway, appear to converge in the distance.

- *Relative height* – Objects with their bases below the horizon are seen as more distant if they are higher in the visual plane (see, for example, the trees in Fig. 2.9); objects above the horizon are seen as more distant if they are lower in the visual field.

- *Relative size* – As an object moves further away, its retinal image diminishes in size. Smaller objects are, therefore, perceived to be further away.

- *Aerial perspective* – The image of a very distant object, such as a mountain in the distance, will appear slightly bluer in colour and less distinct than closer objects.

- *Shadowing* – Light usually travels in straight lines. This means that surfaces facing a light source will be relatively bright and surfaces away from the light source will be in shadow.

- *Texture gradient* – A change in the relative size and density of objects when viewed from different distances; for example, pebbles on the beach look smaller and more closely packed the further away they are.

There is one further monocular depth cue, but since this cannot be conveyed in pictures it is not called a pictorial cue. **Motion parallax** is a cue that depends on movement. If you are sitting on a train looking out of the window, you will have the feeling that objects close to the track are moving very swiftly in the opposite direction, and that objects in the distance are moving much more slowly and in the same direction as you.

None of these cues is particularly strong on its own, but, in combination, they can provide powerful cues to depth and distance.

Visual constancies

One remarkable aspect of perception is that our world remains stable in spite of the constantly changing image on our retinas as we move around, or dart our eyes about. If we took our retinal image at face value, objects and people would appear to shrink and grow as they moved towards or away from us; objects would change shape if we viewed them from different angles, and colours would alter in response to different levels of illumination. The fact that we do not experience such wild fluctuations depends on the **visual constancies**, that is, the tendency for objects to provide the same perceptual experience despite changes in the viewing conditions.

Size constancy

Size constancy is the perception that an object remains the same size regardless of the size of the image on the retina. The same object will provide differently sized retinal images, depending on the distance of that object from the observer. If you are talking to a friend, for example, and she then walks away from you down the road, her image will become smaller and smaller on your retina as she moves further away. You do not, however, believe that she is shrinking.

- *Constructivist explanation* – Size constancy depends on past experience and stored knowledge. We know from experience that people do not grow and shrink rapidly in the real world so, when our retinal image of a familiar person is very small, we infer that she is standing at a distance from us. If the image starts to grow, we infer that she must be walking towards us. The cue of familiarity is obviously important, but it cannot be the only explanation because size constancy also seems to operate with unfamiliar objects.

- *Direct theory explanation* – We also make use of the cue of relative size. In other words, we always judge the size of an object in the context of its surroundings. If you look at the telephone as you go to answer it, you will find its retinal image gets larger as you walk towards it. However, the table on which it stands will also get larger, as will the phone book lying next to it, so the ratio of the various objects remains constant. Thus, objects appear to stay the same as we walk around because they maintain the same size relative to other objects around them. This fits in with Gibson's view that all the information necessary for size constancy is located within the stimulus.

Shape constancy

Shape constancy is the ability to perceive objects as having a stable shape in spite of changes in orientation. Imagine looking at a door as someone opens it and comes into the room. The retinal image of the door will change from being a rectangle to a trapezoid as it swings open, and yet you will not think that the door is changing shape (see Fig. 2.20).

Figure 2.20 *Shape constancy*

- *Constructivist explanation* – We depend on our past experience of doors opening and infer that it remains the same shape.

- *Direct theory explanation* – There is sufficient information in the background and in the unchanging texture elements on the door (wood-grain, panels, etc.) to recognize directly that we are looking at the same door. As usual, however, the direct theory has difficulty in accounting for perceptual errors (see the 'Size constancy and shape constancy' panel below).

Size constancy and shape constancy

Coren et al. (2004) give the following example of the close relationship between size and shape constancy, which is hard to explain in terms of direct perception. Look at the two shapes in Fig. 2.21 and consider the two box tops. Do you think they are the same shape? Now look at the two sides labelled (a) and (b). Which side is longer?

Now take a ruler and measure the two sides. You will probably be surprised to discover that they are exactly the same length. If you were to trace the top of the box on the left and, after rotating it, place it on the top of the other box, you would also find that the shapes of the two tops are exactly the same.

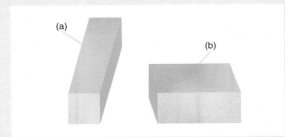

Figure 2.21 *Shape constancy*

STRETCH AND CHALLENGE

Activity ## Psychology as a science

Think about the extent to which research in perception (including specific studies and the development of theory over time) can be used to support the argument that psychology is a science. Turn to pp.46–48 to find out more about the issue of psychology as a science.

Check your understanding of perceptual organization by answering these questions. Try to do this from memory. You can check your answers by looking back through Topic 1.

1 What is meant by the terms 'bottom-up' and 'top-down' processing?

2 List the assumptions of Gibson's theory of direct perception.

3 Explain why Gibson believed that texture gradient was important for perception.

4 Outline two strengths and two weaknesses of direct theories of perception.

5 Prepare a descriptive 150-word précis of Gregory's constructivist theory of perception.

6 List five monocular cues to depth perception and give a brief description of each.

7 Summarize Gibson's ideas about how we perceive movement.

8 Briefly outline what is meant by size constancy and explain how direct theory and constructivist theory differ in their explanation of this.

9 Describe one example of perceptual set and explain how it supports the concept of top-down perception.

10 'Top-down theories provide a satisfactory explanation of visual illusions.' Construct a 300-word précis that considers this statement, giving equal weight to descriptive and evaluative material.

Topic 2: Development of perception

Psychology in context   Hard work or natural talent?

Roger Federer

Rafael Nadal

If you are a tennis fan, you will have admired the skills of Rafael Nadal and Roger Federer, who have both reached the top of their sport through a combination of talent and hard work. They possess superb hand–eye coordination, agility and strength. Although the perceptual abilities of Nadal and Federer may be less striking than their powerful serves and speed on the court, they could not perform as they do without high levels of visual acuity (ability to see details) and excellent ability to judge distance (depth perception).

1 Identify some aspects of tennis playing (or any other sport that interests you) where visual acuity and depth perception are particularly important.

2 To what extent do you think the achievements of sportspeople like Nadal and Federer are the result of inherited natural ability as opposed to sheer hard work?

In Topic 2, we will examine the so-called **nature–nurture debate** in the context of **perceptual development**.

Psychologists have long been interested in finding out about how our perceptual abilities develop and to what extent these abilities are innate or are learned through experience. In this topic, we shall discuss the results of research from two areas – infant studies and cross-cultural studies – and consider how these findings relate to the nature–nurture debate.

The nature–nurture question reflects a long-standing debate about the relative importance of innate and environmental factors in the acquisition of psychological abilities. If you have not already done so, look at the Introduction for a discussion of the nature–nurture debate in psychology.

As far as perception is concerned:

- The *extreme nativist* view asserts that we are born with certain perceptual abilities that develop through a genetically programmed process of maturation and owe nothing to learning.

- *Empiricists*, on the other hand, believe that we are born with only the most basic sensory capacity and that our perceptual abilities develop through experience and interaction with our environment.

In the following sections we will look at the research evidence concerning which abilities are innate and which are more dependent on experience.

Infant studies of perceptual development

The most direct method of investigating the nature–nurture debate is to observe human neonates (newborn infants). If perceptual abilities are inborn, you might expect that they should be apparent in neonates. If perceptual skills are developed through learning and experience with the environment, they would be absent in young babies. However, this is not as easy to establish as it might at first seem. Some of the difficulties of neonate research are outlined in the panel on the right.

As a result of using some of the techniques outlined in Table 2.1, psychologists now know that babies have considerably more sophisticated perceptual skills than was previously thought. We will consider some of these abilities.

IDA   Ethics in infant studies

Any research on human behaviour raises some ethical issues and psychological ethical guidelines stress the importance of:

- gaining participants' informed consent
- ensuring the privacy of participants
- protecting participants from physical or psychological harm.

Researchers who involve very young children in their studies must gain informed consent from parents or guardians and must protect the privacy of children by maintaining their anonymity. A child who resists participating must not be coerced and any child who becomes distressed must be comforted. Research involving infants, especially neonates, requires special skill and sensitivity on the part of the investigators.

Difficulties of neonate research

- *Ethical and practical difficulties* exist in obtaining permission from parents to run experiments with human neonates. See the panel 'Ethics in infant studies'.

- *Attracting young babies' attention* can be difficult and it is even more difficult to hold it.

- *Maturation versus experience* – Some abilities are not present at birth, but emerge during the first few weeks of life. It can be difficult to disentangle the effects of maturation (biological programming) of the visual system from the effects of experience with the visual environment.

- *Limited behaviour* – Due to physical and cognitive constraints, babies can only produce a limited range of observable behaviours. It seems relatively easy to show that a baby cannot do something, but it may simply be that babies do not have the behavioural repertoire to demonstrate all their abilities.

- *Limited cognitive ability* – Babies cannot understand instructions from the experimenter and cannot answer verbal questions.

Psychologists have therefore devised a number of experimental techniques to try to overcome some of the difficulties; these are outlined in Table 2.1 opposite.

Acuity and contrast

'Visual acuity' refers to the ability to perceive visual details, and it is poorly developed at birth (Courage and Adams 1996). The level of acuity found in newborns seems to vary slightly with the technique used to measure it. However, it is generally considered to be about 20/800 (i.e. the infant must view a stimulus from 20 feet in order to perceive it in the same detail as a normally sighted adult at 800 feet). Visual acuity seems to develop rapidly over the first few months and reaches the adult level of 20/20 shortly after the age of 12 months (Haith 1990). Low acuity in infancy seems to be accounted for by physiological factors. For example, it has been demonstrated that the rapid development of neurons in the visual cortex, which occurs between the age of three and six months, coincides with the parallel rapid development of visual acuity (Conel 1951).

Infants are unable to perceive contrast in the same way that adults do and it has been estimated that the vision of one-month-old infants is slightly worse than adult night vision (Pirchio *et al.* 1978). This can be explained in terms of the undeveloped fovea, which forces infants to rely mainly on their rod-dominant peripheral retina.

However, in spite of the low acuity and poor contrast sensitivity, four-day-old infants already show a preference for human faces (see the Fantz study on p.84), and a two-

Technique	Description	Explanation
Preferential looking (PL)	The experimenter presents two distinctive visual stimuli together on a screen and monitors how long the baby looks at each of them.	If the baby looks at one for longer than at the other, the experimenter assumes that the baby can distinguish between them and has a preference for one over the other.
Eye-movement monitoring	The experimenter photographs babies' eye movements while they are viewing patterns on a screen.	If the infant appears only to focus on certain features of the stimulus, it suggests that the whole stimulus cannot be perceived.
Habituation	A single stimulus is presented to the infant, who will normally spend time looking at it. As time passes, the infant becomes familiar with it (habituates to it), loses interest and looks away. At this point, a new stimulus is presented.	If there is renewed interest in this novel stimulus, the experimenter infers that the infant has recognized that something has changed.
Sucking rate	The infant is given a dummy to suck and the intensity of sucking is measured. Infants tend to suck at a faster rate if they are interested in something. Once the infant habituates to a stimulus, sucking rate declines.	If the sucking rate increases again when a novel stimulus is presented, it can be assumed that the infant is able to distinguish between the old and the new stimulus.
Conditioning	The baby is rewarded every time the baby's head turns towards a specific visual stimulus. The infant usually learns rapidly to respond to the visual stimulus.	If the baby continues to show a preference for this particular stimulus, even when it is embedded in an array of other visual stimuli, it is assumed that the baby can distinguish it.
Heart and breathing rate	Heart and/or breathing rate is/are measured for changes when various visual stimuli are presented.	If there are changes in rate when novel stimuli are presented, it is assumed that the baby can distinguish between them.
Positron-emission tomography (PET)	Electrodes that detect electrical activity in the brain are attached to the baby's scalp. Certain patterns, known as visually evoked potentials (VEPs), occur in response to visual stimuli.	The experimenter can assume that the baby differentiates between two stimuli if each stimulus provokes a different pattern of VEPs.
Visually evoked potentials (VEPs) and functional magnetic resonance imaging (fMRI)	These are advanced techniques that allow brain function to be mapped.	If different patterns of infant brain activity are recorded in response to different visual stimuli, it is assumed that the infant can distinguish between them.

Table 2.1: *Techniques used in neonate research*

day-old infant can recognize its mother's face at close range (see the study by Walton *et al.* 1992 on p.84). Before reading on, read Fantz' key study and think about the two questions in the activity on the right.

Evaluation of face preference research

- *Nature of stimuli* – Other researchers have criticized Fantz's conclusions, saying that the stimuli were artificial and bore little resemblance to the real, animated and mobile faces that infants would encounter in the real world. Flavell (1985) found that babies, presented with faces and other stimuli with similar amounts of movement and contour, showed no preference for faces. Bremner (2003) has suggested that infants looked longer at the 'face' stimulus because it contained more information around its

Activity Research into face recognition

Read the key research 'Preference for human faces' and then answer the following two questions:

1 What difficulties might Fantz have encountered when using the visual preference technique in this study?

2 Try to think of an explanation, other than 'innate preference', for the infants in this study preferring the human face. How would you investigate this possible, alternative explanation?

Answers are given on p.603.

Preference for human faces

Fantz (1961) conducted studies that seemed to demonstrate that face recognition was an innate ability. He presented four-day to six-month-old infants with stimuli similar to those in Fig. 2.22. All possible pairings of the stimuli were shown.

(a)

- Stimulus (a) is a representation of a human face.

(b)

- Stimulus (b) depicts exactly the same black features, but not configured to look like a face.

(c)

- Stimulus (c) has the same amount of black shading, but presented as one solid block of colour.

Babies of all ages showed a slight, but distinctive preference for (a) over (b), and most of them paid little attention to stimulus (c). This suggested to Fantz that human babies possess an innate preference for human faces over other visual objects.

Figure 2.22 *Fantz's face stimuli*

edge and infants are known to scan the edges of complex figures.

- *Mother's face* – Whether or not babies have an innate preference for faces, it now seems that they are able to distinguish their mother's face from a very early age. Walton and her colleagues (1992) filmed the faces of 12 new mothers and then filmed the faces of 12 other women who were matched in terms of hair colour, eye colour, complexion and hairstyle. Neonates were then showed pairs of videos – one was of their mother and the other was of the woman who was matched with their mother. By sucking on a dummy, babies as young as one-day-old were able to maintain the preferred image (of their mother) on the screen.

It seems that many perceptual abilities are present in the newborn baby or appear in the first weeks of life. It is highly likely that most of the abilities discussed above arise from maturational changes in the visual system and owe little to experience and learning. As we shall see, the distinction between innate and environmental factors is rather less clear-cut in the area of depth perception and the acquisition of the visual constancies.

Depth and distance perception

Depth perception is a complex skill. Babies need it from an early age in order to carry out what appear, on the surface, to be quite simple tasks such as reaching out for a toy. Babies seem to be able to start making these kinds

The visual cliff study

Gibson and Walk constructed a glass-topped table with two halves. One half of the table had glass covering a checkerboard design immediately below the glass, and the other half had the same design four feet below the glass. The depth cues from the apparatus therefore gave the impression of a deep 'drop' (visual cliff) on one side of the table, even though the glass top continued, in reality, to provide a solid continuous surface.

Gibson and Walk used babies between the ages of six and 14 months. They were unable to use infants under the age of six months because they needed to have babies who were independently mobile. They tested 36 babies by placing them individually on the 'shallow' side of the apparatus and encouraged them to crawl over the 'cliff' to the 'deep' side by having their mothers call to them. In spite of this encouragement from their mothers, most of the babies would not crawl over the perceived drop (see Fig. 2.23). Gibson and Walk concluded that depth perception is an innate ability (see activity opposite).

Figure 2.23 *Gibson and Walk's (1960) 'visual cliff' study*

of judgements from about three-months-old and are often quite skilled by about six to seven months. This coincides with the time when many babies learn to crawl (Bornstein *et al.* 1992). The interesting question for psychologists is whether depth perception is innate or learned.

A classic experiment investigating this question was carried out by Gibson and Walk in 1960 (see the key study above). Read the account of this study and then answer the questions in the activity below before you read on.

Conclusions from the 'visual cliff' study

Read the account of Gibson and Walk's (1960) 'visual cliff' study and then answer the following questions:

1 Why do you think that some psychologists have disagreed with the conclusion drawn by Gibson and Walk? What alternative conclusion might you draw?

2 How might researcher bias have affected the results of this study?

Evaluation of infant studies of the development of depth perception

- *Role of experience* – Critics argued that babies aged six months could have learned this ability through experience. Gibson and Walk responded to these criticisms by repeating the experiment using newborn, non-human animals (including goat kids and lambs), which are independently mobile from birth. These animals refused to cross over the cliff and, if placed on the 'deep' side, showed signs of distress. This suggests that depth perception in such animal species is innate, but there are too many differences between humans and animals for us to be able to generalize this finding to humans.

- *Heart rate and the visual cliff* – More convincing evidence came from a study by Campos and colleagues in 1970. They compared the heart rates of two-month-old babies when placed on the 'shallow' and the 'deep' side of the apparatus. Heart rates decreased slightly on the deep side, suggesting that babies were able to make a distinction between the two sides. However, older babies (approximately nine months) showed an increased heart rate (an indicator of anxiety) when placed on the deep side. It may be that depth perception is innate since it can be demonstrated in such young babies, but that avoidance behaviour (i.e. recognizing the danger associated with certain situations) can only be learned through experience.

- *Infants' avoidance behaviour* – Babies as young as two months have shown avoidance behaviour when a different technique is used to test depth perception. Babies were shown a film of an object that appeared to be moving towards them on a direct collision course. If depth perception is present, the babies should flinch, blink or move their head to one side. Such avoidance behaviour has been demonstrated in babies between two and three months (Yonas and Owsley 1987), suggesting that some awareness of depth perception is present in these very young babies.

- *Post-term babies* – An earlier study by Yonas (1981) supports the nativist argument. He compared two groups of six-week-old infants – one group of infants had been born on time, but the other group had been born four weeks late. The post-term babies were significantly more likely to respond to looming objects with an avoidance reaction than the normal-term babies, even though both groups had been exposed to environmental influences for the same time (i.e. six weeks).

- *Monocular (pictorial) cues: learned or innate?* – The use of pictorial cues discussed on p.79 appears to emerge rather later and probably means that they depend on experience with the environment rather than on physiological maturation. Granrud and Yonas (1985), for example, investigated infants' ability to perceive depth using the cue of overlap. They showed babies two-dimensional cardboard cutouts like the ones in Fig. 2.24. Infants have a tendency to reach out for objects that seem nearer to them, so Granrud and Yonas reasoned that they were more likely to reach out for picture (a), which has the impression of depth provided by overlap cues, than for either (b) or (c). This was found to be the case for seven-month-old babies, but not for five-month-old babies, which suggests that the ability to use the pictorial cue of overlap emerges around the seventh month. Later research by Yonas *et al.* (2001) investigated infants' depth perception, using shadow as a cue to depth. In line with earlier research, they found that older infants made better use of the depth cues provided by shadows compared with young infants.

  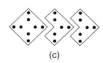

(a)   (b)   (c)

Figure 2.24 *Stimuli used in Granrud and Yonas' (1985) experiment*

Visual constancies

You may recall from Topic 1 that constancies are an important means of maintaining a stable visual environment. The important question for developmental psychologists again concerns the nature–nurture debate: are visual constancies inborn or learned through experience? We will look at size and shape constancy because these have attracted the most research interest.

Shape constancy

Bower (1966) found that two-month-old infants responded to a tilted rectangle as if it were the same as the original rectangle, even though a rectangle that is viewed from such an angle projects a trapezoid on to the retina.

Babies also seem to be able to match visual shapes to a shape that they have experienced through touch or feel. Kaye and Bower (1994) placed one of two different types of dummy in the mouths of one-day-old infants. Once the baby started sucking, an image of the dummy would appear on a computer screen in front of the baby. If the baby paused in sucking, the dummy would disappear from the screen and be replaced by an image of the other dummy (which the baby had not experienced sucking). Once the baby started to suck again, the first dummy would reappear on the screen. In this way, the baby was able to control which image appeared on the screen. Babies consistently controlled their sucking to keep the image of the dummy that was in their mouth on the screen. This suggests that newborn infants are capable of sensing the shape of a dummy in their mouth and then generalizing this perception from the tactile to the visual modality. It is not clear what mechanism underlies this ability, but it is likely that it is innate rather than learned.

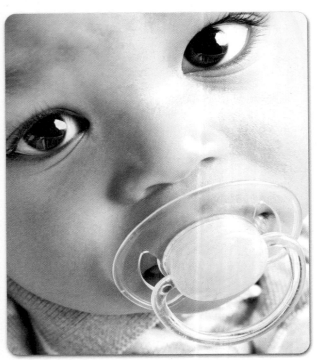

From the tactile experience of sucking a dummy, the baby can envisage how the dummy will look

Size constancy

Bower (1965) conducted the classic study into size constancy in infants.

HOW SCIENCE WORKS

Size constancy in infants

Key research: Bower (1965)

Bower conditioned nine infants aged between 40 and 60 days by rewarding them every time they turned their head in response to the presentation of a 30-centimetre (cm) cube that was placed 1 metre away. This is called a conditioned response. The reward was a peek-a-boo action by an adult who popped up in front of the baby, smiled and tickled the baby and then disappeared from view again (see Fig. 2.25).

Figure 2.25 *The set-up in Bower's (1965) study*

Once the baby had clearly learnt to respond to this particular cube, Bower introduced new stimuli:

- The original 30-cm cube was placed 3 metres away from the infant (i.e. a smaller retinal image than the original).
- A 90-cm cube placed 1 metre away from the infant (i.e. a larger retinal image than the original).
- A 90-cm cube placed 3 metres away (i.e. the same retinal image as the original).

Bower recorded the number of times the babies reacted with a conditioned response to the new stimuli. The results are shown in Table 2.2.

Bower found, as he had predicted, that retinal size was not the crucial factor and that babies responded to the actual size of the cube, regardless of the retinal image. They looked least at the stimulus that had the same retinal image, but which differed from the original both in terms of size and distance. He concluded that babies have innate size constancy.

Bower was interested in finding out what cues the babies were using in order to judge the distance of the cubes. Several types of cue are known to assist in depth perception and these include

	Original stimulus	Test stimulus 1	Test stimulus 2	Test stimulus 3
Size	30 cms	Same (30 cm)	Different (90 cm)	Different (90 cm)
Distance	1 metre	Different (3 metres)	Same (1 metre)	Different (3 metres)
Retinal image		Different (smaller)	Different (smaller)	Same
Total number of conditioned responses	98	58	54	22

Table 2.2 *Results of Bower's tests*

texture gradient, motion parallax and retinal disparity (see pp.XX and XX). Using three ingenious variations of his original experimental technique, Bower (1965) again tested nine infants for size constancy:

- Condition 1: cues available = texture gradient and motion parallax
- Condition 2: cues available = texture gradient
- Condition 3: cues available = retinal disparity and texture gradient.

In condition 2, the infants no longer seemed able to judge distance or the real size of the cubes, suggesting that texture gradient was not being used as a guide to distance. Performance in condition 1, however, was at the same level as in the original experiment where babies seemed to understand distance and size constancy. Since texture gradient did not seem to be an important cue, Bower concluded that they were relying on motion parallax. Performance in condition 3 was intermediate between the two other conditions, suggesting that retinal disparity was being used to a limited extent to judge distance.

Evaluation

- *Infants possess size constancy* – On the basis of this series of experiments, Bower suggested that infants aged between six and eight weeks have some degree of depth perception and size constancy and that this ability depends mainly on the cue of motion parallax. Retinal disparity provides an additional but weaker cue and texture gradient is not yet being used.

- *Procedures* – It is not easy to obtain a conditioned response in babies as young as this, and their behaviour and body movements can often be misinterpreted. This means that experimenter bias may affect the results if those observing the infants' responses are aware of the hypothesis being tested. However, in Bower's study of size constancy, a recorder fitted to the baby's pillow detected the head movement (conditioned response), which would have reduced the potential for experimenter bias. This gives an indication of the care taken in designing this investigation.

- *Support for Bower's findings* – Slater et al. (1990) studied size constancy using preferential looking. Each infant became familiarized with either a small or a large cube and was then exposed to the same cube at different distances. The next step involved the infant being exposed to the two cubes, placed at different distances so they produced the same retinal images (i.e. the larger cube was placed further from the infant). All the infants looked longer at the unfamiliar cube, showing that they found it novel and different from the one with which they had been familiarized (even though both cubes produced the same sized retinal image). This is evidence of size constancy and supports the nativist viewpoint that size constancy is innate.

Cross-cultural studies of perceptual development

Cross-cultural studies involve comparing the behaviours or abilities of people from more than one cultural background. We have seen how perception is shaped by an interaction of biological and environmental factors. Given that there appears to be at least some requirement for experience with the visual environment in order for the visual system to develop normally, psychologists and anthropologists have been interested in finding out the role of cultural background in the development of

perceptual skills. People from different cultures may differ from one another in two important ways: biological and ecological.

- *Biological* differences depend on factors such as genetic inheritance, diet, disease patterns within the culture, etc. Although such factors could influence perceptual abilities, there has been little research interest in these areas.

- Researchers have been far more interested in *ecological factors*, such as local environment, cultural history and education. This raises a number of interesting questions. Do people who live in dense forest, for example, develop different perceptual skills from people who live in open plains? Do people from cultural backgrounds with no tradition of drawing find it difficult to understand the pictorial cues found in paintings and drawings from other cultures?

Research on size constancy

Much of the research in this area has focused on the experience of visual illusions (see pp.76–78). Now read the key research on p.86.

Further research on size constancy

Further evidence demonstrating that lack of experience with certain environmental depth cues can impair perceptual abilities, such as size constancy, was reported by Turnbull (1961). He observed the behaviour of a group of Bambuti Pygmies who lived in dense forest. They had little opportunity to look far into the distance because trees and vegetation enclosed their environment. Turnbull reported on a particular occasion when he accompanied his guide, Kenge, out of the forest for the first time in his life. On their journey, they crossed a broad, open plain and could see a herd of grazing buffalo a few miles away in the distance. The guide was puzzled and asked what kind of insects they were and laughed when he was told that they were buffalo. As they drove towards the herd in the car, Kenge seemed alarmed, although his anxiety disappeared once they had got very close and he could verify that they were indeed buffalo. However, he continued to be confused about what had happened and wondered how the buffalo had grown larger as they approached and whether some kind of witchcraft or trickery was involved. This suggests that the environment we grow up in can influence the way in which we perceive new stimuli.

Research on two-dimensional drawings

Another area of cross-cultural research into perception has focused on the interpretation of two-dimensional drawings, pictures and photographs. In Western cultures, we are inundated with pictorial images in books, newspapers, television, etc., from a very early age. We usually have no difficulty in recognizing objects and in understanding the spatial relations between objects depicted in pictures and yet, pictures rarely reflect an accurate representation of the real-world scene – for example, they are flat and often in black and white, whereas the real world is three-dimensional and coloured. Some people (e.g. Gombrich 1972) have suggested that we can only understand and interpret pictures drawn according to Western artistic tradition because we are aware of a set of conventions agreed within that culture. If this were true, it would follow that people from other cultures would not readily be able to understand Western pictorial convention.

Hochberg and Brooks (1962) carried out a rather bold study on one of their own children. They shielded their son from any sort of pictures for the first 19 months of his life. They made sure that there were no pictures, magazines, newspapers or television in the child's vicinity.

They even removed all the labels from tins and food packages. At the end of this period, they showed him some simple line drawings of everyday objects such as shoes. In spite of his restricted upbringing, the child had no difficulty in identifying all the objects. If we can generalize this finding, we can assume that the recognition of objects in pictures is not a learned convention. There is evidence from cross-cultural studies that individuals are able to recognize objects in pictures, even if they have never seen examples of Western pictures before. Hagen and Jones (1978) found that people who had never experienced pictures readily understood coloured photographs. It seems, however, that less realistic pictures, such as black and white photographs or line drawings, present more problems.

Deregowski (1980) has collected a number of reports from anthropologists and missionaries, suggesting that spontaneous object identification can be difficult under these circumstances. It should be noted that these findings derive from anecdotal evidence rather than from rigorously conducted scientific study. One report from a missionary working in Malawi tells of the initial puzzlement of local people when shown a line drawing of an ox and a dog. However, after carefully pointing out individual features, such as the nose and ear of the dog and the horns and tail of the ox, recognition dawned. This suggests that object recognition can occur very quickly if attention is directed appropriately and so supports the idea that learning via prolonged exposure is unnecessary. Hudson (1960, 1962) showed pictures containing various pictorial depth cues to groups of people in South Africa. Figure 2.26 shows an example of the type of picture he used.

Figure 2.26 *A picture used in Hudson's studies (source: Deregowski 1972)*

In this picture, there are two depth cues:

1 The *cue of overlap* tells us that the hunter and the antelope are standing in front of the rocks and are, therefore, closer to us.

2 The *cue of familiar size* tells us that the elephant must be furthest away from us because, even though it is casting a smaller image on our retina, we know it is actually larger than either a man or an antelope.

Hudson's technique was to ask observers firstly to name all the objects in the picture. Observers were then asked questions such as 'What is the man doing?' and 'What is closer to the man?' Results from Hudson's own study and from subsequent studies conducted in various parts of Africa, reported by Deregowski (1980), indicated that non-Western observers had difficulty seeing pictorial depth. However, as Rock (1995) has commented, the cues are quite weak in this picture and there is likely to be some ambiguity, even for Westerners.

There is some evidence that formal education, using picture books and drawings, can increase the ability to perceive depth in two-dimensional pictures (Pick 1987). Hagen and Jones (1978) have also demonstrated that certain cues, such as aerial perspective and texture gradient, seem to enhance the ability to perceive depth in pictures. It may be the case that some pictorial cues are more helpful and familiar to non-Westerners than others. Non-Western cultures with no experience of pictures seem to find particular difficulty in perceiving implied movement in drawings. Look at the pictures in Fig. 2.27.

Figure 2.27
Illustrations implying movement

The carpentered world hypothesis

Key research: Segall *et al.* (1963, 1966)

In a classic study, Segall *et al.* (1963, 1966) showed various straight-line illusions, including the Müller-Lyer illusion, to nearly 2,000 adult and child participants. There were 14 non-European groups, mostly from Africa, but also from the Philippines and three so-called European groups (actually they were from South Africa and North America).

The researchers found clear cultural differences: the European groups were considerably more susceptible to the Müller-Lyer illusion than the non-European groups. Segall and colleagues explained their findings in terms of the 'carpentered world hypothesis'. According to this hypothesis, many people live in an environment that is full of lines and angles and rectangular objects. Unless these objects are viewed from exactly the right angle, they will project a non-rectangular image onto the retina and yet we continue to perceive them as rectangular.

Segall and colleagues believed that this tendency to interpret trapezoid shapes on the retina is so pervasively reinforced in people who live in carpentered environments that it becomes automatic and unconscious from a very early age. People who live in environments with few straight lines and angles are less used to interpreting acute and obtuse angles on the retina as representations of right angles in the real world. When presented with a drawing of the Müller-Lyer illusion, the Europeans were likely to try to perceive it as a two-dimensional representation of a three-dimensional object. In other words, they would interpret the drawings as, for example, the outside corner of a building and the inside corner of a room. Using misapplied size constancy, they would then perceive the apparently closer line to be shorter than the line that was apparently further away. The non-Europeans from non-carpentered environments were much more likely to take the drawing at face value.

Evaluation

- A *biological explanation* – Pollack (1963) suggested that there might be a biological rather than environmental explanation for these findings. He had noted findings from several studies that susceptibility to the Müller-Lyer illusion declines with age. Since older people also experience increasing difficulty in detecting contours, Pollack hypothesized that there might be a functional relationship between these two abilities. Pollack and Silvar (1967) demonstrated that there was such a relationship – the harder people found it to detect contours, the less susceptible they were to the Müller-Lyer illusion.

Pollack and Silvar (1967) then took this idea a stage further and demonstrated in a second study that there is a relationship between contour detection and retinal pigmentation – the denser the pigmentation, the poorer the contour detection. Pollack suggested that retinal pigmentation, which may be denser in people with dark skins, might have been responsible for the reduced susceptibility to the Müller-Lyer illusion found among the non-European samples in the study by Segall and colleagues. In other words, biological rather than cultural differences might be responsible for the different responses to visual illusions. There was some support for the Pollack explanation from Berry (1971) and Jahoda (1971), but both these studies have been criticized on methodological grounds.

Cultural bias

Cross-cultural research is important in trying to uncover either differences in development that are attributable to differences in experience or universal patterns of development, regardless of different experiences.

However, cross-cultural comparisons are difficult to do well. Ways of assessing in one culture may be inappropriate in another. Misunderstanding can arise if investigators from a different culture assume that their questions are understood in the same way as they would be within their own culture (this is called an 'imposed etic'). Cross-cultural studies to investigate the effects of physical environment and cultural background on perceptual abilities often result in ambiguous findings that are difficult to interpret. Some conclusions, based on early observations by missionaries and anthropologists, were not conducted under controlled conditions, and the more rigorous studies can often still be criticized for experimenter bias and for underestimating perceptual abilities.

In these pictures, the artist has used a technique to imply movement that is familiar to Western observers from as young as four years of age. Duncan *et al.* (1973) showed a cartoon picture to a group of rural African children in which a boy's head was shown in three different positions to imply rapid movement of the head. The children did not understand the implied motion and several of them reported that the boy must be deformed. However, the ability to understand implied motion in line drawings is another skill that can be acquired through education, urbanization and exposure to pictures (Friedman and Stevenson 1980).

Summing up the nature–nurture debate in relation to perceptual development

We have already discussed aspects of the nature–nurture debate in relation to specific studies. In the last part of this topic, we summarize the debate in relation to infant and cross-cultural studies of perceptual development in general. It is unlikely that our acquisition of perceptual skills can be fully explained by either the extreme nativist or the extreme empiricist view. It seems much more likely that perceptual skills develop as a result of an interaction between innate and environmental factors. What conclusions can we draw from infant and cross-cultural studies about how perception develops and how this relates to the nature–nurture debate?

Infant studies and the nature–nurture debate

- *Many skills are present in infancy* – It seems that both innate and learned factors have a role to play in the development of perceptual skills. With the development of ingenious experimental techniques, psychologists have been able to show that human infants possess remarkable perceptual abilities, including size and shape constancy, the ability to recognize faces and even cross-modal transfer of perceptual information. Research comparing post-term with normal term babies has added to the already strong evidence that infants possess depth perception. Many of these abilities are present at birth or appear in the first few weeks of life as the nervous system matures, i.e. they are the product of an innate maturational process.

- *Role of experience* – However, there is also evidence that we need at least some minimal level of experience of the environment to develop our perceptual abilities to their full potential. Much of this evidence comes from studies carried out on non-human animals, where animals are deprived of certain environmental stimuli (see Chimpanzees panel opposite). It is difficult to generalize findings to humans, and it would clearly be unethical to carry out such studies on human neonates, but it does suggest that perceptual abilities depend, to some extent, on interacting with the environment. This conclusion is supported by studies of children who have suffered deprivation for some reason or another. Dennis (1960) studied babies in Iranian orphanages who had been kept in highly impoverished environments with no stimulation or opportunity to move around. He found that these children showed major deficits in their perceptual and motor skills.

Cross-cultural studies and the nature–nurture debate

- *Illusions* – There has been very little empirical research in this area in recent years. However, as Segall *et al.* (1990) comment in their review of cross-cultural susceptibility to illusions: 'People perceive in ways that are shaped by the inferences they have learned to make in order to function most effectively in the particular ecological settings where they live … we learn to perceive in the ways we need to perceive.'

- *Pictorial art* – The issue of pictorial art is rather more complex. It is possible that the difficulties people from other cultures experience with Western art reflect aesthetic rather than perceptual factors. Hudson (1962), reported in Deregowski (1972), asked groups of African adults and children who had not been exposed to Western culture to choose their preferred picture of an elephant from the two shown in Fig. 2.28. Picture (b) shows a realistic, aerial view of an elephant, as it would appear in a photograph taken from above. However, (a) was overwhelmingly the preferred choice in spite of its unnatural pose. Deregowski maintains that children from all cultures prefer split drawings, but that such preferences are suppressed in Western societies. This is because drawings using perspective cues convey more information than split drawings and so are thought to have more practical use. However, certain societies, where this preference has not been suppressed, have developed the split drawing technique to a high artistic level. It is possible, therefore, that initial puzzlement with Western-style drawings reflects unfamiliarity with the artistic convention rather than lack of perceptual ability.

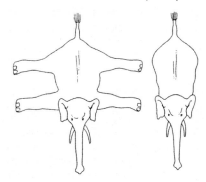

Figure 2.28 *Drawings of elephants used in Hudson's studies*

- In conclusion, it seems that the ability to identify objects does not depend on learning or cultural background. There may be more of a problem, however, in interpreting spatial relationships within two-dimensional pictures and this ability may well reflect different cultural conventions. Western artists have long made use of monocular pictorial cues (see p.79) to imply three dimensions in their paintings. However, there is no binocular disparity between elements in the picture, and all objects require the same degree of accommodation and convergence. As Pick (1987) points out, this means that in order to perceive a flat, two-dimensional picture as a scene in three dimensions, we need to pay attention to some depth cues and ignore the absence of others. Perhaps people who have no experience of Western art find it difficult to use pictorial cues in this way.

Other research findings and the nature–nurture debate

Animal studies

In addition to infant and cross-cultural studies, investigations using non-human animals have contributed to the nature–nurture debate in perception. Look at the next panel on 'chimpanzees' for findings in this area. Findings from animal studies generally support the empiricist standpoint.

Studies of patients with cataracts

A famous case study by Gregory and Wallace (1963) is often cited as evidence of the effect of nurture on the development of perception.

Chimpanzees raised in the dark

1 *Chimpanzees raised in the dark* – Riesen (1965) reared chimpanzees in the dark and found that nerve cells in the retina and visual cortex began to atrophy (waste away). In order to avoid this destruction of nerve cells, Riesen conducted further studies in which he allowed chimpanzees and monkeys to experience some light stimulation by wearing translucent goggles from birth. At about three months, the animals could distinguish brightness and size like 'normal' members of their species, but could not follow a moving object with their eyes or discriminate between shapes. This suggests that the animals needed to experience patterned light (i.e. a more enriched visual environment) for normal perceptual development.

S.B. had been blind from birth. At the age of 52, his cataracts were removed and he was able to see for the first time. He could judge size and recognize objects, but only if he was already familiar with them through touch. He had difficulty in estimating distance, which meant he was afraid to cross roads although he had done so when he was blind, and he never learned to interpret facial expressions. S.B. preferred to sit in the dark rather than put on a light. He suffered from depression and died three years after gaining his sight.

Other case studies (e.g. Von Senden 1960) of patients whose cataracts have been removed after a lifetime of blindness found even more serious impairments in perception than those experienced by S.B. However, it is important to remember the inherent weakness of the case study method when considering these findings. Try the activity below now.

Activity **Case study of S.B.**

Why is it difficult to be confident that the case of S.B. provides unambiguous evidence for the nurture side of the nature–nurture debate? Think about:

1 the physical effects on the visual system of being blind for 52 years

2 the weaknesses of the case study method (look at your AS psychology book if you need a reminder)

3 how the confusion and distress after the operation might have affected S.B.'s ability to 'see' his new world.

Nature and nurture combined

It seems, then, that both innate and learned factors are involved in perceptual development, and psychologists have therefore started to look beyond the nature–nurture debate. They are now beginning to ask how such factors are combined to produce a whole perceptual experience and what patterns of systematic change occur over time in the development of perceptual skills.

CHECK YOUR UNDERSTANDING

Check your understanding of perceptual development by answering these questions. Try to do this from memory. You can check your answers by looking back through Topic 2.

1. Explain what you understand by the term 'nature–nurture debate'.

2. Outline four difficulties involved in using human infants to investigate the development of perception.

3. Prepare a brief description of three experimental techniques that have been used in research with human neonates.

4. Explain why newborn babies do not have adult levels of visual acuity.

5. Outline one study that has investigated depth perception in infants and evaluate its findings and conclusions.

6. Describe research by Bower that has investigated size and shape constancy in infants.

7. Summarize and evaluate the findings and conclusions of infant research in relation to the nature–nurture debate.

8. What is the main purpose of carrying out cross-cultural studies in psychology, including the study of perceptual development?

9. Summarize the findings and conclusions of cross-cultural research into visual illusions.

10. Evaluate the contribution of cross-cultural research to the nature–nurture debate in perception.

Topic 3: Face recognition and visual agnosias

Psychology in context — Photo identity cards

We are increasingly expected to carry photo identity cards if we want to borrow books from a library, join a gym, benefit from reduced bus or train fares or, in some cases, even use a credit card. The belief is that having a photo on a card will reduce its fraudulent use. Do you agree? This is an area where psychologists can contribute some useful, applied research.

Three psychologists (Kemp et al. 1997) worked with a credit card company to create four different credit cards for each of 46 undergraduate students. The photographs on the cards varied as follows:

- Card A: actual photo of the student

- Card B: photo of the student but with slightly altered appearance (e.g. no glasses)
- Card C: photo of another individual who looked similar
- Card D: photo of another individual who looked different (but same gender and ethnic background).

The students used their cards to buy goods at a supermarket where the staff had been told the study would be taking place.

The findings might surprise you:

- Card A was correctly accepted 93% of the time
- Card B was correctly accepted 86% of the time
- Card C was wrongly accepted 64% of the time
- Card D was wrongly accepted 34% of the time.

1 What conclusions do you draw about people's accuracy in judging whether a photo on a credit card matches the face of the cardholder?

2 Try to design your own, less elaborate, study to test whether people can match accurately the face of a cardholder and the photo on the card.

Face recognition

Face recognition is an area of psychological research concerned with pattern recognition, which investigates how we process and recognize faces. Recognizing faces is very important for human social functioning. It can help us to form relationships, recognize a friend in a crowd and provide some non-verbal cues about what a person is thinking and feeling.

One of the most active, current research areas in pattern recognition concerns the perception of faces. All faces have eyes, a nose and a mouth placed in the same relative locations and yet we are able to identify thousands of different faces. Furthermore, we are able to recognize a particular face, such as the face of a best friend, regardless of the expression – angry, sad, amused, etc.

Feature analysis versus holistic processing

Some psychologists have suggested that we might recognize faces using a feature-detection approach, i.e. we might use information about individual features, such as eye colour or mouth shape, to build up a representation of the face. This bottom-up approach is the basis of Identikit – a system used by some police forces to build up the face of a criminal on a feature-by-feature basis.

Bradshaw and Wallace (1971) used Identikit to construct pairs of faces that shared a number of features, but differed in others (see Fig. 2.29). Participants were asked to decide as quickly as possible whether pairs of faces were the same or different. The more differences there were between the two faces, the faster the judgments were made. They concluded that participants were processing facial features independently and in serial fashion. Using sequential comparison of features, participants would encounter differences between the two faces sooner if there were several features that differed. However, these data can be interpreted differently.

Sergent (1984) pointed out that the faces that differed in several features were also very different in terms of their overall configuration and that it may have been this factor which allowed participants to make speedy judgements. Sergent conducted her own study based on Identikit pictures and found that the faces were being processed in a holistic form, rather than as a set of independent features. **Holistic processing** refers to recognition based on overall shape and structure, rather than on individual elements.

In another study, Young *et al.* (1987) supported the idea that we recognize faces by processing information about the overall configuration of the face, rather than by analysing individual features. For example, we analyse the spatial relationships between individual features and the way the shape of one feature might interact with another (e.g. the nose and mouth). They combined photos of the top half of one celebrity face with the bottom half of another. When the two halves were closely aligned to create a single face, participants experienced great difficulty in identifying the top half. This task became much easier when the two halves

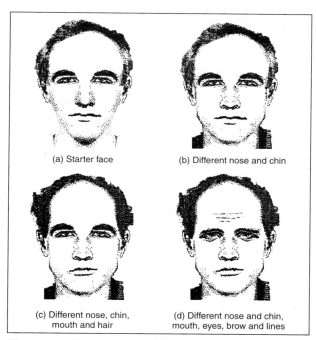

(a) Starter face

(b) Different nose and chin

(c) Different nose, chin, mouth and hair

(d) Different nose and chin, mouth, eyes, brow and lines

Figure 2.29 *Examples of faces similar to those used by Bradshaw and Wallace (1971). Face pairs were constructed showing differences in two, four or seven facial features (source: Roth and Bruce 1995)*

were misaligned, or when the top half was presented in isolation. This seems to suggest that the close alignment in the first condition produced a novel configuration that interfered with recognition.

Recognizing faces versus recognizing other objects

It seems likely that we process faces rather differently from other visual stimuli. Tanaka and Farah (1993) showed participants a set of six visual stimuli, including pictures of houses and pictures of faces. Once participants had become familiar with the items, they were given various recognition tests. On some trials, they were asked to choose which of two face parts they had seen before, e.g. two noses. On other trials, they were asked to select which of two whole faces they had seen before, where one feature only had been changed. On these trials, the faces usually differed only by one feature – for example, they had a different nose. Similar trials were carried out, showing pictures of whole houses or individual features such as windows.

Tanaka and Farah found that participants were far more accurate at recognizing facial features when they appeared in the context of a whole face, rather than in isolation. However, in the house trials, they were just as accurate when the house features were presented in isolation as they were when the house features appeared in the context of the whole house.

Yin (1969) found that recognition for faces is far superior to recognition for buildings, but that this superiority is reversed when the pictures are turned upside down. The explanation for such findings seems to be that normal recognition of upright faces depends on holistic processing, but that this configuration of facial features is lost when the face is turned upside down. Look at the photos in the Activity below, which illustrate what is called the 'Thatcher illusion' (Thompson 1980), but recreated using pictures of Tony Blair.

Then try the activities below that demonstrates the loss of holistic processing when trying to recognize people from inverted photographs.

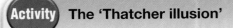

Activity The 'Thatcher illusion'

A   B

Look at these pictures for a few seconds. Do you notice any differences?

Now turn the book upside down and look at these same pictures the right way up. What difference do you see now?

Answers are given on p.603. ▶

Activity Upside-down facial recognition

Find a magazine that contains lots of photos of famous people. Turn the magazine upside down and look through it.

How many celebrities are you able to identify? Did you find that people who would be instantly recognizable in the upright position became much harder to identify?

Bruce and Young's theory of face recognition

As we saw above, some psychologists (e.g. Bradshaw and Wallace 1971) proposed a feature-detection approach to explain how we recognize faces. However, most psychologists now accept that face recognition involves a more holistic approach, involving the inter-relationships between features.

Bruce and Young (1986) have put forward an influential model of face recognition. Their model incorporates aspects of earlier formulations by Hay and Young (1982) and Ellis (1986) (see Fig. 2.30).

The model includes a number of different processing modules that are linked in sequence and in parallel:

▪ *Structural encoding* – produces representations of faces.

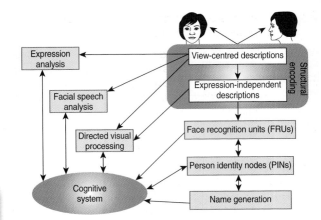

Figure 2.30 *A functional model for face recognition (source: Bruce and Young 1986)*

▪ *Expression analysis* – drawing inferences about a person's emotional state from their facial features.

▪ *Facial speech analysis* – making use of visual information from the face while deciphering speech. Bruce and Young (1986) sometimes refer to this as lip-reading.

▪ *Directed visual processing* – allows for certain kinds of face processing to occur without necessarily recognizing the identity of the person; for example, seeing whether or not the individual has a moustache.

▪ *Face recognition units (FRUs)* – stored descriptions of familiar faces. There is a unit for every face you know.

▪ *Person identity nodes (PINs)* – provide personal details about an individual who is already known to the observer (e.g. their occupation or interests).

▪ *Name generation* – the name of the individual is stored separately from their other details.

▪ *Cognitive system* – this seems to hold additional information that might be of use in face recognition. For example, imagine you see someone in a local shop who looks like the Queen. The cognitive system would evaluate the likelihood of seeing her in such a context and save you from the potential embarrassment of misidentification. It also seems to play a part in determining which components of the system need to be attended to.

According to this model, recognizing familiar faces involves structural encoding, FRUs, PINs and name generation. Processing unfamiliar faces involves structural encoding, expression analysis and directed visual processing.

Modifications to the Bruce and Young model

Burton *et al.* (1990) and Burton and Bruce (1993) have revised the original model and implemented aspects of it, using an artificial intelligence model. The major differences in the new formulation are as follows:

▪ There is no separate store for names.

▪ Decisions about the familiarity of a particular face are made at the person identity nodes, instead of at the face recognition units.

- The model has been made more precise and has been demonstrated in a computer simulation.

This model is being extended and updated and seems to provide plausible accounts of many aspects of face recognition. It cannot, however, account adequately for the processes that allow new faces to be learned and for new identities to be stored in memory.

Evaluation of Bruce and Young's theory of face recognition

- *Empirical evidence* – There is considerable empirical evidence to support Bruce and Young's model that there are independent routes involved in processing facial expressions, facial speech and the identification of specific individuals. Much of this evidence comes from clinical studies of people with neurological defects that disrupt normal perception. For example, Young *et al.* (1993) investigated face perception in 34 ex-servicemen who had received missile wounds to the back (posterior) regions of the brain. Some were selectively poor at familiar face recognition, whereas others only experienced difficulties in matching unfamiliar faces. Others found it difficult to decipher facial expressions accurately. These findings suggest that independent routes operate for the different aspects of face recognition, as proposed by Bruce and Young's model. This type of evidence is called 'double dissociation', where some individuals do well at task A but poorly at task B, whereas others show the opposite pattern.

Sergent and Signoret (1992) conducted a study in which healthy individuals were given similar tasks to do while undergoing a PET scan. The three different activities were found to activate slightly different locations in the brain. These findings provide compelling evidence for the independence of these three functions.

- *Name generation* – According to the model, we should only be able to generate a name for a face after we have accessed the appropriate personal identity node (i.e. have some details about the person). In a diary study, Young *et al.* (1985) asked 22 participants to record over an eight-week period any difficulties they had in recognizing people. None of the participants reported putting a name to a face without first knowing some details about the person they were trying to recognize.

- *Role of the cognitive system* – The model has been influential and seems to account successfully for certain aspects of face recognition. However, some of the components of the model have been less well explained than others. In particular, the role of the cognitive system is not clearly specified. Bruce and Young (1986) have recognized this weakness and admitted that the cognitive system 'serves to catch all those aspects of processing not reflected in other components of our model'.

Activity **Face recognition**

A number of research studies have demonstrated that people find it easier to recognize human faces than non-face objects such as buildings (e.g. Yin 1969). Try to think of an evolutionary explanation for the superiority of face recognition. See pp.6–9 if you need to refresh your memory about the evolutionary approach.

Visual agnosias

Visual agnosia is the inability to recognize familiar objects presented visually. Most neuropsychologists distinguish between 'apperceptive agnosia' and 'associative agnosia':

- *Apperceptive agnosia* – a perceptual deficit, i.e. a failure of recognition due to impaired visual perception. An example of this would be a failure to distinguish between a square and a circle. See the case study of Mr S. in the panel below (p.96).

- *Associative agnosia* – intact perceptual ability but a failure of recognition because of difficulty in accessing the relevant knowledge from memory – a 'normal percept stripped of its meaning' (Teuber 1968). An example of this would be having the ability to copy a line drawing of an object accurately, but not being able to name the object. See the case study by Rubens and Benson (1971) in the panel below (p.96).

Prosopagnosia

One of the most fascinating examples of associative agnosia is **Prosopagnosia**. This is the inability to recognize faces despite intact intellectual functioning and even apparently intact visual recognition of most other stimuli (Farah 2004). Prosopagnosia appears to be a failure of visual and associative memories to come together to produce recognition. For example, a woman with prosopagnosia might be able to describe the facial features of a person standing in front of her, but not recognize that this person is her daughter until she speaks (Palmer 1999). The clinical study undertaken by Young et al. (1993) that investigated face perception in 34 ex-servicemen is outlined above. Another well-known case study of prosopagnosia is described in the panel below (p.96).

Two explanations of prosopagnosia
A unique face-specific problem
With the development of sophisticated non-invasive brain-imaging techniques (such as PET and fMRI – see the panel, 'Physiological approach'), it is now possible to study how the brain functions during a range of cognitive activities. A number of such studies (e.g. Farah and Aguirre 1999) show that the right fusiform gyrus (often called the fusiform face area or FFA) is activated during face recognition, but much less so during object recognition.

Case studies of visual agnosia

Case study of apperceptive agnosia (based on Benson and Greenberg 1969)

Mr S. was a young man who sustained brain damage after accidental carbon monoxide poisoning. His memory, spontaneous speech and comprehension of spoken language were intact. He could name colours, but was unable to name objects (or pictures of objects) if they were presented visually. He was unable to copy letters or simple figures and could neither describe nor trace the outline of common objects.

Case study of associative agnosia (based on Rubens and Benson 1971)

The subject of this case was a middle-aged man who had suffered brain damage, following a sudden (acute) drop in blood pressure. His mental and language abilities were normal, but he was unable to identify objects without touching them. When shown a stethoscope he could not name it, describing it as 'a long cord with a round thing at the end'. He was never able to describe or demonstrate the use of an object if he could not name it. He found it difficult to recognize pictures of objects but, remarkably, he could copy line drawings accurately.

Case study of prosopagnosia (McNeil and Warrington 1993)

W.J. was a middle-aged professional man who developed prosopagnosia, following a series of strokes. When he was shown the photograph of a famous person, together with the pictures of two unknown people, he was unable to select the famous one. After developing prosopagnosia, W.J. changed his career and went into sheep farming. Although he was unable to recognize most humans he was able to recognize most of his sheep. This suggests that W.J.'s recognition impairment did not affect the recognition of all groups of visually similar patterns, but was selective for human faces.

(Source: Farah 2004).

IDA   Physiological approach

Brain functioning techniques, such as fMRI, used to identify the areas of the brain that are involved in various behaviours, such as face or object recognition, form part of the physiological approach to explaining psychological functioning.

The physiological approach has provided explanations for many behaviours, but it is criticized for being overly reductionist. See pp.39–42 for more information on reductionism.

Studies by Barton *et al.* (2002) and Hadjikhani and de Gelder (2003) found that the FFA was damaged in people with prosopagnosia. This suggests that there are specific processing mechanisms that are used only for face recognition (see the key research by Barton *et al.* 2002). Farah (2004) has undertaken extensive research in this area and concludes that 'studies of prosopagnosics ... show that faces are "special" and that they depend on neural systems, which can be selectively damaged'.

Not a face-specific problem

Research by Gauthier *et al.* (1999), using brain-imaging techniques, showed that:

- Some people with prosopagnosia have problems that extend beyond face recognition; for example, they are inferior to 'normal' controls in recognizing complex objects, as well as faces.

- Holistic processing and activation of the FFA are associated with recognizing objects with which we are familiar or have particular expertise. While this includes face recognition, it is not exclusive to it.

Evaluation of research on visual agnosias

- HOW SCIENCE WORKS *Research methods* – Case studies, which dominated research in this area before the advent of brain-imaging techniques, have provided much rich and interesting data about people with prosopagnosia. However, as you will know from your AS studies, case studies have their drawbacks. One of the difficulties can be that other researchers cannot produce corroborative findings by studying the same patient, who will tend to work with one individual researcher; Farah (2004) refers to this as a lack of 'inter-laboratory verification'.

  The emergence of PET and fMRI scanning has made it possible to investigate brain activity in living participants and has led to significant advances in our knowledge about which areas of the brain are activated during cognitive activities. Imaging has helped clarify how object versus face recognition systems might be segregated. Most neuroscientists agree that the functional imaging of those with visual agnosias will play an increasingly dominant role.

- *Faces are special* – According to this point of view, people with prosopagnosia are unable to recognize faces, even though they can recognize familiar objects, because they have sustained damage to the specific mechanism that is used only for face recognition. In addition to the evidence already described, further support for this argument comes from Farah *et al.* (1995), who studied L.H., a patient with prosopagnosia. Using a recognition test, they found that he could discriminate between familiar objects (e.g. spectacles, chairs), but not between faces. Not all evidence supports this position.

- *Faces are not special* – Gradually evidence is accumulating to support this viewpoint. Gauthier and Tarr

Impaired perception of facial configuration in prosopagnosia

Key research: Barton *et al.* (2002)

The researchers tried to determine whether lesions of (damage to) the fusiform gyrus (the FFA) are associated with impaired face perception in people with prosopagnosia. Five patients suffering from brain injuries were asked to discriminate faces in which the configuration of the features had been altered (e.g. distance between the eyes, vertical position of mouth).

The researchers' findings were as follows:

- The four patients whose brain damage included the FFA performed poorly.
- The remaining patient, whose FFA was not damaged, performed normally.
- When told that only changes in the position of the mouth would be shown, two of the four patients, who had initially performed poorly, improved markedly.

The researchers' conclusions were as follows:

- The ability to perceive changes to facial configurations is impaired in people with prosopagnosia whose FFA is damaged. The impairment is stronger when patients had to attend to more than one feature.
- This impaired ability to perceive changes to facial configurations may contribute to the failure to recognize faces that people with prosopagnosia experience.

Evaluation:

- *Research support* – The small number of participants might make one cautious about generalizing the findings. However, the findings have received support from Hadjikhani and de Gelder (2003). Using fMRI, they found that people with prosopagnosia showed no activation of the FFA when viewing faces, compared to those without prosopagnosia.

- *Role of FFA* – The findings add to the considerable body of research that identifies the FFA as playing a key role in face recognition. This particular study, however, does not demonstrate that the FFA is *solely* concerned with face recognition; other researchers (e.g. Gauthier *et al.* 1999 – see above) claim the FFA is involved in the perception of other familiar objects, besides faces.

- *Applying findings* – It has been suggested that the findings could be used to develop techniques to help those with prosopagnosia – for example, by encouraging them to pay attention to individual facial features.

(Based on Hewstone *et al.* 2005)

(2002) claimed that the apparent differences between face and object processing can best be explained in terms of expertise. The mechanisms used to identify faces are also used to identify objects about which we know a lot. For example, they found that the FFA in bird watchers was activated when they were viewing birds, but not when they were viewing cars! Looking at cars, however, activated the FFA in car enthusiasts, whereas watching birds produced no FFA activation.

HOW SCIENCE WORKS Currently, there is evidence for both explanations of prosopagnosia. What we have seen over recent years is a shift from accepting that face recognition and prosopagnosia involve different mechanisms from other forms of recognition or object agnosias. According to Eysenck and Keane (2005), the most recent evidence is pointing towards the view that faces are not as special as we once thought!

CHECK YOUR UNDERSTANDING

Check your understanding of face recognition and visual agnosias by answering these questions. Try to do this from memory. You can check your answers by looking back through Topic 3.

1. What is meant by the term 'holistic processing' in relation to face recognition?

2. Describe and evaluate the findings and conclusions of two studies of face recognition.

3. Outline the face recognition model developed by Bruce and Young, including its eight components.

4. What are the main modifications made to the model by Burton and Bruce?

5. Identify one strength and one weakness of Bruce and Young's model.

6. What is visual agnosia? Explain how apperceptive agnosia and associative agnosia differ.

7. Define prosopagnosia and describe a case study that illustrates this condition.

8. Identify at least one strength and one weakness of the case study method as used in the study of prosopagnosia.

9. Outline two explanations for prosopagnosia.

10. With reference to research findings, evaluate the claim that prosopagnosia is different from other object agnosias.

Gregory's top down/indirect theory

- Perception constructed using higher cognitive processes – e.g. depth perception and visual constancies learned through past experiences
- Process of hypothesis testing – e.g. ambiguous figures
- Role of expectations – e.g. perceptual set

Evaluation

- Explains visual illusions
- Experimental support
- Artificiality of laboratory studies
- Overemphasis on expectations and perceptual errors

Gibson's bottom-up/direct theory

- Ecological theory
- Visual array provides all the necessary information to permit perception
  - Optic flow for movement
  - Texture gradient and horizon ratio for depth and orientation
  - Affordances for meaning (uses) of objects.

Evaluation

- Real-world practical applications (e.g. for pilots)
- Affordances – a weak concept

Face recognition

Feature analysis

- Information from individual features leads to representation of whole face
- Explanation now rejected in favour of holistic processing

Holistic processing

- Recognition based on overall configuration of the face
- Face recognition different from and superior to object recognition (Tanaka and Farah 1993)

Bruce and Young's theory (1986)

- Eight processing modules
- For familiar faces: FRUs, PINs and name generation
- For unfamiliar faces: structural encoding, expression analysis and directed visual processing

Evaluation:

- Model modified by Burton and Bruce (1993)
- Support from clinical studies, including PET scan studies and name generation studies
- Cognitive system is not well explained
- Does not account for learning new faces

Visual agnosias

Inability to recognize familiar objects presented visually

- **Apperceptive agnosia**: perceptual deficit
- **Associative agnosia**: memory deficit

Prosopagnosia (type of associative agnosia)

- Inability to recognize familiar faces despite visual recognition of other stimuli (Farah 2004)
- Case studies and clinical studies:
  - W.J. (McNeil and Warrington 1993)
  - L.H. (Farah *et al.* 1995)
  - 34 ex-service men (Young *et al.* 1993)

Explanations of prosopagnosia

- **Face-specific problem** caused by damage to part of fusiform gyrus (fusiform face area – FFA)
  Evaluation:
  - Support from some case studies (e.g. Farah *et al.* 1995) but not all
  - Support from clinical study of five patients with brain damage (Barton *et al.* 2002)
- **Not face-specific problem** but form of object agnosia
  Evaluation:
  - Gauthier *et al.* (1999): some people with prosopagnosia have other recognition problems
  - Gauthier and Tarr (2002): so-called FFA is not used exclusively for face recognition

Theories of perceptual organization

Development of perception

Perception
The process of interpreting information using the senses

Face recognition and visual agnosias

Nature–nurture debate

Perceptual ability innate
Nativist view

Perceptual ability learned through experience
Empiricist view

Infant studies

- **Acuity** develops rapidly between 3 and 6 months
  - Human faces preferred
  - Mother's face identified by one-day-old infant
- **Depth perception**: found in 6-month-old infants (Gibson and Walk 1960: visual cliff study)
  Evaluation:
  - Babies had experience of depth already
  - Support from avoidance and heart rate studies
  - Monocular depth cues require experience
- **Visual constancies**: shape and size innate
  Evaluation:
  - Role of motion parallax uncovered
  - Research procedures are challenging
  - Research supports (Slater *et al.* 1990)

Conclusions

- Many skills present in infancy (support nativist view)
- Studies of deprived children show that experience is needed for some abilities to develop fully (supports empiricist view).

Cross-cultural studies

- Research on **'carpentered world' hypothesis**
  - Segall *et al.* (1963): Europeans misapply size constancy and experience Müller-Lyer illusion; those from non-carpentered environments do not
    Evaluation: differences in retinal pigmentation may provide biological explanation
  - Turnbull (1961): environment influenced way new objects seen by Bambuti pygmies
    Evaluation: lack of control in studies
- **Two-dimensional drawings**
  - Hudson (1960): without experience, difficult to see pictorial depth
    Evaluation: possible cultural bias

Evaluation

- Ability to identify objects not dependent on learning
- Experience influences perception of illusions and interpretations of pictorial art

Other research findings

Animal studies

Tend to support nurture/empiricist view

- Riesen (1965): chimps raised with goggles
- Blakemore and Cooper (1970): kittens raised in vertical world

Case studies of cataract patients

Tend to support nurture/empiricist view

- Gregory and Wallace (1963): SB could only recognize objects if he could touch them; difficulty in estimating distance

EXPLAINING THE SPECIFICATION

Specification content	The specification explained
The formation, maintenance and breakdown of romantic relationships (Topic 1)	**In this part of the specification you are required to know about theories of the formation, maintenance and breakdown of romantic relationships. To do this, you need to be able to:**
Theories of the formation, maintenance and breakdown of romantic relationships: for example, reward/need satisfaction, social exchange theory.	■ Describe and evaluate two theories for each of these three phases of romantic relationships. (It is important to note that formation and maintenance are often examined together in one question, but breakdown tends to be questioned on its own.)
Human reproductive behaviour (Topic 2)	**In this part of the specification you are asked to consider the relationship between evolutionary forces and human reproductive behaviour. To do this, you need to be able to:**
The relationship between sexual selection and human reproductive behaviour.	■ Explain what is meant by sexual selection in the context of human reproductive behaviour.
	■ Describe and evaluate this relationship, using research studies relevant to human mating behaviour.
Evolutionary explanations of parental investment: for example, sex differences, parent–offspring conflict.	■ Explain what is meant by parental investment and how this is linked to at least two areas of human reproductive behaviour. As sex differences and parent–offspring conflict are given only as examples (although both are covered in this chapter), you might wish to consider other areas to illustrate parental investment.
Effects of early experience and culture on adult relationships (Topic 3)	**In this final part of the specification you will study how the experiences of childhood and adolescence shape our adult relationships. To do this, you need to be able to:**
The influence of childhood and adolescent experiences on adult relationships, including parent–child relationships and interaction with peers.	■ Describe and evaluate material for different question combinations, i.e. both childhood *and* adolescent experiences on both parent–child relationships *and* interaction with peers. (It is worth noting that 'parent–child relationships' and 'interaction with peers' are preceded by the word including, which means that these can specifically be asked for in an exam question.)
The nature of relationships in different cultures.	■ Describe and evaluate how relationships differ between different cultures. Although not explicitly stated in the specification, it is implied that 'different' in this context means a comparison between Western and non-Western cultures.

Introduction

We may define a relationship as 'an encounter with another person or with other people that endures through time'. A relationship is likely to be characterized by many features such as expectations, responsibilities, rules, roles, and giving and taking. It may be institutionalized (as in the case of marriage), permanent or impermanent, formal or informal. At least some of our relationships with others will constitute the most important aspects of our social lives.

So why do we engage in relationships? What do we get out of relationships for ourselves and what do we give to others? Why do we begin some relationships and end others? What determines which relationships we derive the most, or the least, satisfaction from? These are just some of the questions that psychologists have considered in their attempts to build general explanatory models of relationships and which you will consider in this chapter.

If we think about the times in our lives that we associate with great happiness or great sadness, it is highly likely that the majority of them have involved other people. They might include falling in love, the loss of a loved one, the birth of a child, the pain of a divorce, or being told that our parents were splitting up. It follows from this that one of the most important aspects of psychology – and social psychology in particular – is the study of the relationships that we have with other people.

Psychology in context   Fake relationships

Brad Pitt

Penelope Cruz

Have you ever bonded with Brad or pined for Penelope? The beneficial effects of romantic relationships are well established, but for many people, the admiration of celebrities, such as Brad Pitt or Penelope Cruz, can have important benefits for their self-esteem. Derrick *et al.* (2008) discovered how these 'fake' relationships (called **parasocial relationships**) could provide a safe route for people who have a difficult time with real interpersonal relationships. People with low self-esteem can use parasocial relationships to feel closer to their ideal selves (i.e. the person they would *like* to be rather than the person they actually are). Derrick and colleagues studied 300 university students to examine the relationship between self-esteem, parasocial relationships and discrepancies between actual and ideal selves. Participants identified their favourite celebrity and described that celebrity in an essay. Results showed that students who had low self-esteem saw their favourite celebrities as very similar to their ideal selves. When primed with images or stories about their favourite celebrity, these students could escape the reality of their actual selves and felt closer to their ideal selves. This research shows that even fake relationships, which have a very low risk of rejection, can have self-enhancing benefits for people with low self-esteem that they do not receive in actual relationships.

The research by Derrick *et al.* suggests that many people 'escape the reality of their actual selves and felt closer to their ideal selves' by associating with a celebrity. How might you test this amongst your own friends? For example, you might ask each of your friends to list three things about themselves and three things about the person they would like to be (i.e. their ideal self). You might then ask them to name a particular celebrity they admire and list three things about that person that they admire. Is there a link between your friends' *ideal selves* and their description of their chosen celebrities?

Relationships have three distinct phases: they begin, they are maintained, and (sometimes) they end. Psychologists have tried to explain why each of these three phases occurs. Under what circumstances do we move beyond mere attraction to the development of a romantic relationship with someone else? Later we will look at how these relationships develop (or fail to develop) and why they sometimes break down, but first we will focus on the formation of relationships.

The formation of romantic relationships

A number of theories have been put forward to explain how romantic relationships are formed. In this section we will consider two: the reward/need satisfaction model and the matching hypothesis.

The reward/need satisfaction model (Byrne and Clore 1970)

According to Byrne and Clore (1970), a possible reason why we spend so much of our time in social relationships is that we find them rewarding, or that we find life alone unpleasant and unrewarding. Some people may reward us directly (**operant conditioning**), perhaps by meeting our psychological needs such as the need for friendship, love and sex, etc. Alternatively, they may reward us indirectly, in that they are associated with pleasant circumstances (**classical conditioning**). Since some individuals are directly associated with reinforcement (i.e. they provide it), we like them more and are more likely to enter into a relationship with them.

Direct reinforcement

Argyle (1992) points out that individuals who are rewarding (because they are friendly, helpful and cheerful) tend to be liked the most. Positive, non-verbal signals, such as smiling, are signs of liking and are particularly important because they provide positive reinforcement. If we meet someone when we are in a negative emotional state (e.g. when we are sad) and they help us to escape that state (e.g. by offering some comfort), they provide us with negative reinforcement. This increases both our liking for them and the likelihood that we would form a relationship with them. A different way of looking at how relationships may be reinforcing is to consider how they may satisfy our social needs.

Argyle (1994) has identified motivational systems which he claims are at the roots of social behaviour (see Table 3.1). Read through the table and think carefully about the extent to which you agree with Argyle.

Needs/motives	How relationships help meet needs
Biological needs	e.g. collective eating and drinking behaviours
Dependency	e.g. being comforted or nurtured
Affiliation	e.g. seeking the company and approval of others
Dominance	e.g. making decisions for other people, being 'bossy'
Sex	e.g. flirting, making love
Aggression	e.g. engaging in football violence
Self-esteem and ego identity	e.g. being valued by others

Source: Adapted from Argyle (1994)

Liking through association

Some research has suggested that people may be liked because they happen to be associated with something pleasant. If we meet someone when we are in a good mood, we may associate that person with our good mood and consequently find him or her more attractive. For example, May and Hamilton (1980) asked female students to say how much they liked the look of male strangers whose photographs they were given. Some students looked at the photographs while pleasant music was being played. Others looked at the same photographs while unpleasant music was being played. A comparison (control) group viewed the same pictures, but no music was played. As predicted, the students who had heard the pleasant music while looking at the photographs liked the men best and rated them as better looking. This and many other experiments (e.g. Cunningham 1988) have shown that positive affect (feeling/emotion) can lead to attraction.

Evaluation of the reward/need satisfaction model

■ *Giving and receiving reward* – Hays (1985) found when examining student friendships that as much value was given to rewarding the other person as being rewarded oneself. The key factor was the totality of both giving and receiving, not merely the latter in isolation. Participants in relationships are often more concerned with equity and fairness in rewards and demands than with the desire to maximize their own benefits (see section on equity theory, p.105).

■ *Limitations* – Many social relationships that are more commonly found in non-Western collectivist cultures show little concern for the receipt of reinforcements. For example, Hill (1972) showed that kinship bonds are very influential, resilient and are not dependent on reinforcement.

■ *Gender differences* – There is evidence of gender differences, as well as cultural differences. It has been shown that in many cultures, women are socialized into being more attentive to the needs of others (such as husbands and children), rather than being oriented towards the gratification of their own needs (Lott 1994). It could, of course, be argued that this 'meeting the needs of others' might be reinforcing in itself.

The matching hypothesis

If you take a quick look at couples you know who are romantically committed to each other, you may notice that most people tend to pair up with those who are similar in terms of their physical attractiveness. The handsome man and the beautiful woman date and marry each other, while their plainer counterparts also seem to pair up. Walster *et al.* (1966) proposed a 'matching hypothesis' of attraction that would explain why people who are similar in many ways end up together. This includes two specific hypotheses:

1 The more socially desirable a person is (in terms of physical attractiveness, social standing, intelligence, etc.), the more desirable they would expect a dating or marriage partner to be.

2 Couples who are matched (i.e. both partners are equally desirable) are more likely to have happy, enduring relationships than couples who are mismatched in terms of social desirability.

Individuals looking for a partner will be influenced by both the desirability of the potential match (what they want) and the probability of the other person saying yes (what they think they can get). Walster and colleagues referred to this notion as *realistic choices* because each individual is influenced by the chances of having their affection reciprocated.

What makes a person socially desirable?

Murstein (1972) argues that individuals' initial attraction towards each other in the formative stages of a relationship formation depends on available cues that indicate their social desirability (e.g. physical attractiveness). Physical attractiveness becomes the major determinant of courtship desirability because it is an accessible way for each partner to rate the other as a possible mate. An individual's initial attraction toward a particular target, therefore, should be determined largely by the comparison between the attractiveness level of the target individual and the individual's own level of attractiveness.

The dance study

Key research: Walster *et al.* (1966)

Walster *et al.* (1966) tested the matching hypothesis in a dance study. In this study, 752 first-year undergraduates at the University of Minnesota were invited to attend a 'get-acquainted' dance. They believed they had been matched with their 'date', although they were, in fact, randomly matched with their partners. The success of these random matches was assessed, using a questionnaire distributed in an interval during the dance and in a six-month follow-up.

Before the dance, the more attractive the student, the more attractive they assumed their date would be. However, once participants had met their matches, and regardless of their own level of physical attractiveness, they reacted more positively to physically attractive dates, and were more likely to try to arrange subsequent dates with them. Other factors, such as intelligence and personality, did not affect liking for the dates or subsequent attempts to see them again. Even when researchers manipulated the physical attractiveness of a date and presented false information about how likely the date would be to enter a relationship with the participant, the physical attractiveness effect (i.e. liking someone more the more attractive he or she was) predominated over a matching effect or any concern about rejection.

Disco dancing

Matching in the real world

Data collected in the real world, however, tells another story. Stronger evidence for the matching effect has been found in correlational studies conducted with actual couples (e.g. Murstein 1972, Silverman 1971). In these studies, psychologists measured the attractiveness level of each partner of actual couples. More than one 'judge' provided the ratings and the ratings of one member of a couple were carried out independently of the ratings of the other member (often through photographs). These studies provide strong evidence for the matching hypothesis, showing significant similarity between partners' levels of physical attractiveness. Research (e.g. Cavior and Boblett 1972) has also consistently found a stronger matching effect among more committed couples (i.e. those going steady, engaged or married) than for less committed couples (i.e. casual daters).

STRETCH AND CHALLENGE

Activity

Preferences, realistic choices and reality

One explanation for the different findings across contexts is that they involve different phenomena. Kalick and Hamilton (1986) suggest that we must make a distinction between preferences, realistic choices and what actually occurs (i.e. what people will settle for).

- *Preferences* – If issues of competition or rejection are not relevant, then most people prefer someone who is physically attractive. For those who are physically attractive, what they desire and what they can get is the same. For those who are physically unattractive, however, desire conflicts with reality.

- *Realistic choices* – In more realistic social situations, where an individual must approach someone, rejection is a real possibility for some people. Under these conditions, although they might *prefer* a more desirable partner, they would be likely to approach someone of a similar level of attractiveness to their own.

- *Reality* – In real life, however, anything can influence our choice – what we desire, whether the other person wants us in return, market considerations (e.g. the availability of more desirable alternatives) and so on. In the competitive marketplace, where less desirable people risk being rejected by more desirable males and females, most people must settle for 'attainable' relationships.

Evaluation of the matching hypothesis

- *Complex matching* – Although the original matching hypothesis proposed that people would pair up with someone of similar '**social desirability**' (in all its different forms), over time it has come to be associated specifically with matching in terms of *physical attractiveness* alone. However, people come to a relationship offering many desirable characteristics, perhaps compensating for a lack of physical attractiveness with an attractive personality, status, money and so forth. The idea that individuals can sometimes compensate for their lack of attractiveness by offering other desirable traits has been termed 'complex matching' (Hatfield and Sprecher 2009). A traditional type of complex matching occurs when an older, wealthy and successful man pairs up with a younger, attractive woman.

- *Gender differences* – Although more attractive individuals are preferred in heterosexual courtship and marriage, Takeuchi (2006) has shown that a gender difference exists in the degree to which physical attractiveness is valued by an opposite-sex partner. Physical attractiveness of women is valued more heavily by men, but physical attractiveness of men is valued less by women, and so has less of an impact on the perception of men's social desirability. This gender difference implies that men can compensate for any deficit in physical attractiveness with other desirable qualities, such as high social status, e.g. money or power, and certain personality traits such as kindness and generosity.

- *The role of a third party* – Although nowadays most people make their own dating and mating choices, matching is sometimes influenced by third parties such as friends, family or even Internet dating sites. Hatfield and Sprecher (2009) suggest it is likely that these third parties would consider compatibility because they determine who will make suitable matches. For example, in traditional 'arranged marriages', parents may be in a better position to judge compatibility in the long term than are their children, whose decisions may be swayed by emotions or hormones (Xiaohe and Whyte 1990).

The maintenance of romantic relationships

Although the matching hypothesis helps to explain why two people would choose each other initially, other theories have been used to explain why a couple would maintain their relationship beyond its formative stages. Two of the most influential theories that have been used to help us understand why we maintain certain relationships and close others down are 'social exchange' theory (and its refinement as 'equity theory') and the investment model. These are generally referred to as 'economic theories' because they assume a view of social relationships analogous to economic activity such as cost/benefit analysis: What do I gain? What do I lose? What do I give? What do I receive?

Economic theorists argue that we run our relationships according to a balance sheet principle, i.e. we aim to maximize our rewards and minimize our costs. Rewards are exchanged for resources that are pleasurable and gratifying (e.g. security, companionship and sex). Costs are exchanges that result in a loss or punishment (e.g. abuse, boredom and missed opportunities for other relationships). Blau (1964) argued that our social interactions are 'expensive' (because they take energy, time, commitment and other 'valuable', finite personal resources) and so what we get out of the relationships must at least pay us back in equal amount (and preferably give us a profit).

Social exchange theory

Social behaviour is viewed as a series of exchanges between individuals. Each person attempts to maximize their rewards and minimize their costs. The *exchange* part of this process is that when individuals receive rewards from others, they feel obliged to reciprocate. Rewards, as we have seen, are those exchanged resources that are pleasurable and gratifying. These might include company, security and sexual favours. Costs are those exchanges that result in a loss or punishment, e.g. physical or psychological abuse and loss of other opportunities. The rewards minus the costs equal the outcomes (or profits).

Comparison levels

On the basis of this general model of **social exchange**, Thibaut and Kelley (1959) proposed a four-stage model of long-term relationships (see Table 3.2). They recognized the importance of influences beyond an analysis of the relationship itself (called the 'reference relationship'). They introduced two 'reference' levels: **comparison level** and **comparison level for alternatives**:

- The comparison level is concerned with the past and the present; that is, the comparison between the rewards and costs of the reference (current) relationship and what we have been used to in the past or believe is appropriate given the nature of the relationship. If the reference relationship compares favourably, we are motivated to stay in the relationship. A person may also use the experiences of others (e.g. by discussing relationships with friends) as a yardstick to evaluate their own relationship.

- The comparison level for alternatives, on the other hand, is concerned with the benefits of possible alternative relationships. We compare the outcomes of the reference relationship with others that we could

be in (e.g. the more positive outcomes offered by an alternative partner). If we feel that we could do better in another relationship, we may be motivated to finish the current one. This process may also involve a consideration of what might be available to them from their social network (e.g. more time to spend with friends) if they were not in a steady relationship.

Although many of the central assumptions of exchange theory were supported by research, it soon became clear that for most people, profit is less important than *fairness* in relationships. The social exchange model was modified in several respects, which eventually resulted in the equity theory.

Equity theory

Equity theory (Walster *et al.* 1978) offers an explanation of how social exchange works in real-life romantic relationships. It assumes that people strive to achieve fairness in their relationships and feel distressed if they perceive unfairness. Unlike social exchange theory, where individuals are seen as trying to maximize their rewards and minimize their costs, in equity theory it is *inequity* in relationships that is seen as having the potential to create dissatisfaction. People who contribute a great deal in a relationship and receive little in return would perceive inequity, as would those who *receive* a great deal and give little in return. Both of these relationships would be perceived as inequitable, resulting in dissatisfaction for both partners. Note that equity does not necessarily mean equality; rather it refers to balance and stability. Furthermore, equity may be defined differently by each member of the social relationship or by outsiders. Walster and colleagues (1978) suggested four principles of equity theory:

1 People try to maximize their rewards and minimize negative experiences within any relationship.

2 The distribution of rewards is negotiated to ensure fairness. This may be achieved through trade-offs or compensations (i.e. a 'favour' or 'privilege' for one person is paid back by an equivalent favour/privilege).

3 Unfair (or inequitable) relationships produce dissatisfaction. Not surprisingly, the 'loser' feels the dissatisfaction more acutely; the greater the degree of perceived unfairness, the greater the sense of dissatisfaction.

Table 3.2 *Thibaut and Kelley's four-stage model of long-term relationships*

1 **Sampling**	The couple explores the rewards and costs in a variety of relationships.
2 **Bargaining**	The couple 'costs out' the relationship and identifies the sources of profit and loss.
3 **Commitment**	The couple settles into a relationship; the exchange of rewards becomes relatively predictable.
4 **Institutionalization**	The interactions are established; the couple have 'settled down'.

Source: Adapted from Thibaut and Kelley (1959)

4 As long as the 'loser' feels there is a chance of restoring fairness and is motivated to save the relationship, he or she will endeavour to re-establish equity. Furthermore, the greater the degree of inequity that the loser perceives, the greater will be the effort at realignment.

Evaluation of equity theory

- *Contrived methodologies and limited application* – Many of the studies associated with social exchange theories have been characterized by rather contrived methodologies, which have little ecological (real-world) validity. Ragsdale and Brandau-Brown (2007) reject the claim that equity is a key determinant of relationship satisfaction. They claim that this does not reflect the way that partners in long-term relationships behave with respect to each other. For example, Feeney et al. (1994) found that equity theory failed to predict relationship satisfaction because it fails to take into account the considerable variance in the contexts of modern-day relationships.

- *Lack of consistent empirical support* – Clark and Mills (1979) identified two different styles of couples: the 'communal couple' and the 'exchange couple'. In the communal couple, concern and positive regard for the other motivates giving; only in the exchange couple is there the kind of 'score-keeping' that is predicted by exchange theory. People in communal relationships do have some concerns over equity, but they are more relaxed over what it comprises. They tend to think that in a relationship, rewards and costs eventually balance out and equity is achieved.

- *Gender differences* – Prins et al. (1993) found that among Dutch couples, inequity in a relationship had different consequences for males and females. Males who perceived inequity in their relationship did not express the desire to have an affair and nor did they report that they had done so. Women, however, were more likely to respond to perceived inequity in their relationships by considering an extra-marital affair and more reported that they had already had an extra-marital affair for just this reason. Other research (e.g.

Kahn *et al.* 1980) has found that men are more likely to focus on the norm of equity in relationships, i.e. what you get out of a relationship should be more or less equal to what you put in. Women, on the other hand, were more likely to focus on the norm of equality (i.e. both partners should receive equal amounts of benefits, regardless of how much they put into the relationship).

The investment model of relationships (Rusbult 1983)

Research into relationship breakdown has focused on those factors that influence a decision to remain in a relationship and those which influence the decision to leave. In this context, the term 'commitment' is used to describe the likelihood that the relationship will persist. Commitment is strengthened by the amount of *satisfaction* derived from a relationship and is weakened by the presence of possible *alternatives* to the relationship. Rusbult introduced a third concept, *investment*, which further increases commitment.

Satisfaction

As with social exchange theory, satisfaction is a product of the outcomes of a relationship (i.e. the rewards minus the costs). The outcomes are compared to a personal standard of what constitutes acceptable outcomes (i.e. the 'comparison level'). If outcomes surpass the comparison level then the individual is satisfied with the relationship. If they fall short, then they are dissatisfied.

Quality of alternatives

If an individual perceives that an attractive alternative to their current relationship exists, they may be led towards that relationship and away from the current relationship. If no such alternatives exist, an individual may persist in a relationship due to a lack of better options. Attractive alternatives are not necessarily other people because for some individuals, having *no* relationship is a more attractive option than being in an unsatisfactory one.

Investment

Rusbult also proposed that the level of investment contributed to the stability of a relationship. Investment is 'anything a person puts into a relationship that will be lost if they leave it'. Investments can be those things that are put directly into the relationship, such as time or emotional energy, or those things that are indirectly related to it such as shared friends or material possessions.

Rusbult (1983) tested her investment model of relationships by asking college students in heterosexual relationships to complete questionnaires over a seven-month period. They kept notes about how satisfactory their relationships were, how they compared with possible alternatives and how much they had invested in it. Students also noted how committed they felt to the relationship. The results are summarized in Figure 3.1. We can see that satisfaction, comparison and investment each contributed to commitment and to break-up. High satisfaction and investment seem to be important in committed relationships. The existence of an attractive alternative appears to feature large in deciding to end a relationship.

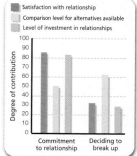

Figure 3.1 *Factors that contribute to a committed relationship versus a relationship breakdown*

Evaluation of Rusbult's investment model of relationships

Research support – The investment model has been supported by numerous studies. The **meta-analysis** by Le and Agnew (2003) (see below) also highlighted its

A meta-analysis of research into Rusbult's investment model

Key research: Le and Agnew (2003)

Le and Agnew (2003) conducted a meta-analysis of 52 studies and over 11 000 participants (54 per cent females and 46 per cent males) carried out between the late 1970s and 1999 in order to investigate whether research supported the major claims of Rusbult's investment model of relationships. Studies were included from five countries (in the US, UK, Netherlands, Israel and Taiwan) and involved both heterosexual and homosexual participants. Measures of relationship satisfaction, quality of alternatives and investments were correlated to see which, if any, of these correlated with commitment to a romantic relationship.

The results showed that across all studies, satisfaction level, quality of alternatives and investment were highly positively correlated with commitment. However, the strongest correlation was between *satisfaction* and commitment. Commitment was also found to be a significant predictor of subsequent 'stay or leave' behaviour, i.e. whether the person leaves the relationship. No sex differences were found in these trends, although a comparison of heterosexual and gay men showed that the relationship between *investment* and commitment was stronger for heterosexual men, even though the satisfaction–commitment relationship did not differ according to sexual orientation. In a comparison of heterosexual females and lesbians, the relationship between

alternatives and commitment was stronger for lesbians than it was for heterosexual women.

Evaluation

These findings suggest that external influences, such as alternatives and investments, are individually less predictive of commitment to a relationship than internal factors such as satisfaction. However, the research also demonstrates the important role of these influences because both alternatives and investments in conjunction with satisfaction predict commitment better than satisfaction alone. When looking at correlation size alone, satisfaction is the winner in terms of predicting commitment to a relationship (and ultimately whether the relationship will survive), but it clearly provides an incomplete explanation when used on its own.

A strength of a meta-analysis, such as the one undertaken by Le and Agnew, is that the reliance on single studies is reduced by combining the results of several studies investigating similar research hypotheses; it allows researchers to gain an important overview of research in a specific area. However, a weakness of meta-analysis is that it relies on published studies, which, given the publication bias towards publishing only studies that show positive results, may show an overall effect that is not really indicative of relationships in real life.

relevance for participants from different ethnic groups and both homosexual and heterosexual relationships. However, the relative importance of the three proposed components of commitment (and therefore the likelihood of remaining in a relationship) differed for different participant groups.

Commitment in abusive relationships – Rusbult and Martz (1995) applied this model to abusive relationships. They asked women who were living in refuges why they had stayed with abusive partners instead of leaving as soon as the abuse began. As predicted by the model, women had felt the greatest commitment to their relationship when their economic alternatives were poor and when their investment was great.

The breakdown of romantic relationships

The ending of a relationship can be one of the most emotionally demanding times of our lives. We must, however, be mindful of the different needs of the people within the relationship. The end of a relationship may be a catastrophe for some, but for others it may provide a liberating opportunity for a new start. A relationship may end even though both partners wish it to continue or even develop (e.g. lovers thwarted by parental prohibition, geographical separation or the death of one of the partners).

A model of relationship breakdown (Rollie and Duck 2006)

Stephanie Rollie and Steve Duck (2006) have developed a model of the termination of close or intimate relationships (see Figure 3.2). Unlike Duck's earlier four-phase model, this model focuses on the *processes* that typify relationship breakdown, rather than being tied to distinct phases that people pass through. These processes may overlap or have common features, but also have different purposes and, ultimately, different consequences.

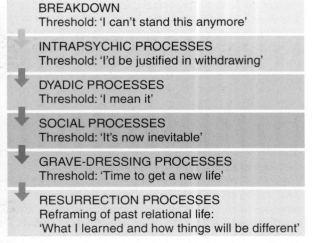

Figure 3.2 *A model of relationship breakdown (Rollie and Duck 2006)*

1 *Breakdown* – One partner becomes increasingly dissatisfied with the relationship. If the dissatisfaction is sufficiently great, there is 'progression' to the next set of processes.

2 *Intrapsychic processes* – These are characterized by social withdrawal and resentment, with the dissatisfied partner focusing on their partner's 'faults' and a sense of being 'underbenefited' (i.e. getting little satisfaction from the relationship). Research suggests that when people are depressed (e.g. as the result of an unhappy relationship), they have a tendency to withdraw from social interaction with others (Segrin 2000). The result of these processes may cause them to re-evaluate the relationship and consider possible alternatives.

3 *Dyadic processes* – These occur when partners begin talking to each other about the problems or perceived inequities that at least one of them is unhappy with. This may result in reconciliation, as the other partner accepts the validity of the dissatisfied partner's views. The ability to talk about issues in a constructive way (e.g. by problem solving) rather than a destructive manner (such as scapegoating) is critical if the relationship is to be saved. Partners may make promises to change and may form an agreement to try and make things work. These dyadic processes may bring up many reasons for staying in the relationship (e.g. for the good of the children) but also reasons to go (e.g. a belief that things cannot change).

4 *Social processes* – The break-up is 'aired' and made public (e.g. to friends and family). Advice and support are sought from people outside the relationship and alliances are created. These processes often include denigration of the partner ('I never liked him', 'You could do so much better') and scapegoating ('It's all her fault'). It is also where the social implications (such as care of children) are negotiated. Break-up becomes increasingly inevitable. For young adults, relationships might be expected to form and end quite frequently as they 'test the market', but with older adults there are likely to be lower expectations of finding (or even a desire to find) a replacement partner (Rollie and Duck 2006).

5 *Grave-dressing processes* – This is so-called because as a relationship dies, we must create an account of how it came into being, what it was like and why it died, much as we would create an inscription on a tombstone for a deceased relative. Ex-partners must begin to organize their post-relationship lives and begin to publicize their own accounts of the breakdown. What might be communicated as part of the grave-dressing processes could be stories of betrayal (by the other partner) or perhaps of two people who tried hard but were unable to save the relationship. It is likely that different stories are offered to different listeners (e.g. parents, friends) rather than one version for all.

6 *Resurrection processes* – This final process addresses how each partner prepares themselves for relationships afterwards. They must recreate a sense of their own social value, defining what they want to get out of a future relationship and what they must avoid as they prepare for a new relationship. Particularly for young adults, the end of one relationship usually means the beginning of a new one; therefore, the newly single partners may believe that 'this time everything will be different'.

Evaluation of Rollie and Duck's model of relationship breakdown

■ *Research support* – Traditional models of relationship breakdown have focused primarily on the distress caused by break-ups, rather than on the potential for growth, as indicated by the Rollie and Duck model. This type of growth, referred to as 'resurrection' in the model, allows people to grow beyond their previous level of psychological functioning, as a direct result of a highly stressful life event such as a relationship breakdown. However, there appear to be sex differences in the degree to which people report personal growth as a result of break-up, with women reporting more post-relationship growth than men. The reason for this is not yet clear. It is possible that it is due to the greater social support available to women, although research has shown that increased social support is not associated with growth, nor do women report more social support than men.

■ *The impact of relationship dissolution* – Akert (1998) found that the role people played in the decision to end the relationship was the single most powerful predictor of the impact of the dissolution experience. Akert discovered that the partners who did not initiate the break-up tended to be the most miserable, reporting high levels of loneliness, depression, unhappiness and anger in the weeks after the end of the relationship. Those who initiated the break-up of the relationship found the end of the relationship the least upsetting, the least painful and the least stressful. Although they reported feeling guilty and unhappy, they had fewer negative symptoms compared to partners who were less responsible for the break-up of the relationship.

IDA **Heterosexual bias**

A limitation of most of the models of relationship breakdown is that they have been developed from the experiences of White, middle-class, heterosexual participants. They may not, therefore, represent the experiences of other groups such as gay and lesbian partnerships. Similarly, even within heterosexual relationships, there are many different types of relationship, including married, cohabiting and dating couples. Given the differences between these types of relationship, it is doubtful that the processes experienced within these relationships will be exactly the same.

An evolutionary explanation of relationship breakdown

The breakdown of romantic relationships is not a modern phenomenon. Evidence supports the view that this has been a recurrent theme throughout our evolutionary history. Among the hunter-gathering culture of the !Kung San in Botswana, for example, the average tribe member experiences numerous romantic relationships before settling down with a long-term partner. Among the Ache of Paraguay, a typical adult has had 12 marriages and experienced 11 break-ups by the age of 40 (Hill and Hurtado 1996)! As a long-term relationship has historically been the context that allows for successful reproduction and child-rearing, we might, therefore, expect evolution to have shaped, to some extent, the behaviour of the rejectors (those who initiate the split) and of the rejectees (i.e. the rejected partner).

Predictions from evolutionary psychology

As we shall see in Topic 2, there are significant sex differences in what males and females look for in a potential mate. These are largely determined by the different levels of investment that males and females typically make in the child-rearing process. These two basic assumptions about human relationships inform what we might expect to find when such relationships fail.

■ *Costs related to emotional investment* – Women more than men prefer mates with resources or the potential to acquire resources (Buss 1989). However, this assumes that men are willing to share their resources with their female partners. Willingness to share can be gauged by the level of emotional commitment by the man towards the woman – for example, through expressions of love or public displays of commitment. Because of the importance of these resources to the female, female rejectees (more than male rejectees) would experience higher costs associated with losing the emotional investment of their partner.

■ *Increasing commitment* – Since women value emotional commitment so highly in their mates, males threatened with the breakdown of a romantic relationship may employ strategies to exploit this fact (Perilloux and Buss 2008). They may attempt to maintain sexual access to their female partners by signalling an increase in their emotional investment in the relationship (for instance, they may suggest cohabitation, getting married or even having children).

■ *Infidelity* – According to evolutionary theory, males have an evolved desire for sexual variety (Buss and Schmitt 1993). Infidelity, therefore, can serve this desire by obtaining sexual access to females outside the relationship. Alternatively, it can be used as a tactic to end the relationship and may help the rejector to find a replacement mate quickly, following an anticipated break-up. Based on these assumptions, males are more likely than females to engage in sexual activities with new potential mates prior to break-up.

• *Reputational damage* – Those responsible for ending a relationship (the rejectors) may be perceived as cruel and heartless by their peers, whereas the rejectee tends to be perceived as the victim (Perilloux and Buss 2008). Any damage to their reputation may adversely affect the chances of the rejector obtaining a long-term mate in the future. As a result, rejectors may be motivated to reduce consequent reputational damage by behaving sympathetically towards their partner during the break-up.

Evaluation of the evolutionary explanation of relationship breakdown

• *Research support* – Although relationship breakdown has only recently been explained in adaptive terms, there is some research evidence to support these claims. The study by Perilloux and Buss (2008), outlined below, provides clear support for the adaptive nature of coping behaviours when faced with, or following, relationship breakdown. A particularly interesting finding of their study is that the largest reported sex difference in coping strategies was in terms of the act of shopping. Women were far more likely than men to use shopping as a coping strategy, following the breakdown of a relationship, regardless of whether they were the person who had initiated the breakdown or were the victim of it. Presumably such behaviour may function as a strategy of appearance enhancement prior to re-entering the mating 'marketplace'.

• *Ultimate and proximate causes* – Evolutionary psychologists argue that much of human behaviour is a product of psychological adaptations that evolved to solve the problems that are typically faced by our ancestors (i.e. an ultimate explanation). However,

Breaking up romantic relationships, costs and coping strategies

Key research: Perilloux and Buss (2008)

The aim of this study was to test evolutionary predictions relating to the breakdown of relationships. Participants were 98 males and 101 females drawn from the university population of a US university (mean age 20.6 years). All had experienced at least one break-up of a romantic relationship. All participants were heterosexual, and 69 per cent were White Caucasian and the rest were from other ethnic backgrounds (e.g. Hispanic, African–American and East Asian). Of these participants, 80 per cent had experienced a break-up as a rejector (i.e. had initiated the break-up) and 71 per cent as a rejectee.

Participants either completed a questionnaire online or in person in a psychology office at the university. The survey asked participants about their most recent break-up. It included questions about the emotions experienced immediately following the break-up, the costs associated with the break-up, and any strategies used after the break-up. Selected results were as follows:

■ Females more than males reported higher levels of cost associated with losing their partner's emotional commitment.

■ More males than females reported success at preventing a break-up by increasing their level of commitment.

■ Male rejectors more than female rejectors reported engaging in sex with other potential mates prior to the break-up.

■ Rejectors indicated a higher cost of being seen as cruel and heartless compared to the rejectees.

As predicted by evolutionary theory, there were significant differences in the post-break-up experiences of rejectors and rejectees, and also significant sex differences in the costs of break-up and the strategies used. The major conclusions that can be drawn from this study are:

1 Men and women experience a wide range of costs from a break-up.

2 Men and women employ many diverse strategies to deal with these costs.

3 The costs experienced and the strategies used depend largely on whether the individual does the rejecting or is the recipient of the rejection.

4 Men and women differ in the costs they experience and the strategies they employ.

5 The strategies used tend to be specific to the costs experienced.

This study lends support to the claim that breaking-up poses critical adaptive problems for individuals, and that humans have developed specific strategies to solve these problems.

Evaluation

■ This study was limited as a test of evolutionary theory because of the narrow age range of participants used, i.e. students. Although this is not necessarily an inappropriate sample (given that this is probably the age where relationships form and end with considerable frequency), the adaptive problems faced as a consequence of break-up may well differ with age (for example, older individuals are more likely to have children).

■ Another limitation of the study is the reliance on self-report data. Self-reporting is notoriously unreliable, particularly because of the tendency of individuals to try to present themselves in a favourable light when participating in a survey and responding to a questionnaire or an interview (**social desirability bias**).

Nichols (1985) argues that such explanations place too much emphasis on ultimate causes and neglects important proximate (or contemporary) causes. For example, research (see p.124) has demonstrated important cultural differences in the way relationships are viewed and enacted, and also in the way that men and women deal with the loss of a mate in these cultures. These differences can be attributed to local forces and traditions rather than to the adaptive problems faced by early humans.

CHECK YOUR UNDERSTANDING

Check your understanding of the formation, maintenance and breakdown of romantic relationships by answering the following questions. Try to do this from memory. You can check your answers by looking back through Topic 1.

1 What are the main assumptions of reward/need satisfaction theory?

2 According to reward/need satisfaction theory, what are the main rewards offered by relationships?

3 What are the main assumptions of the matching hypothesis?

4 What are the main assumptions of social exchange theory and equity theory?

5 What is the essential difference between social exchange theory and equity theory?

6 What are the main assumptions of Rusbult's investment model?

7 What are the six 'processes' that make up Rollie and Duck's model of relationship breakdown?

8 What are the four predictions from evolutionary psychology concerning relationship breakdown?

Topic 2: Human reproductive behaviour

Psychology in context   Investigating sexual selection theory

Photo of a woman in a lapdancing club

One of the key assumptions of sexual selection theory is that men are attracted to women who are fertile, healthy and so on. However, even when women are of fertile age and physical health, they must be 'in oestrus' (i.e. ovulating and able to become pregnant) for mating to be successful. In many species, such as chimpanzees, there are obvious signs when the female is in oestrus, whereas in human beings ovulation is hidden. It makes sense that women must have evolved a way of advertising when they are in oestrus, and that males must be able to recognize these signs.

Miller *et al*. (2007) compared the earnings of lap dancers who were menstruating naturally with those of dancers who were taking the contraceptive pill (which prevents oestrus). During the non-fertile periods of their menstrual cycle, both sets of dancers earned similar tips. However, when dancers who were not on the pill entered their fertile period, they earned significantly more in tips than dancers who were on the pill. This suggests that somehow dancers advertise their fertility to men, who then consider them more attractive during

this fertile phase (as reflected in the tips they receive). It is unclear how they advertise this and whether they do it consciously. Previous research (e.g. Roberts *et al*. 2004) has shown that women's faces and scent become more attractive in oestrus, and Haselton *et al*. (2007) found that women were judged to dress more attractively during their fertile periods. Other studies have shown that women become more confident during oestrus which may subtly change the dancers' behaviour and make them more appealing to their clients.

1 Very few studies have investigated the attractiveness effects linked to human oestrus outside the laboratory. What do you think are the specific advantages and disadvantages of this type of study?

2 The researchers were able to use a repeated measures design, as all the dancers were assessed for tip earning at different stages of their ovulatory cycle. Why is this preferable to using different dancers?

3 The authors acknowledge that an important limitation of this study is that they did not take the 'precise proximal mechanisms that influence tip earnings' into consideration. What do you think that this psychological terminology means in this context and what might some of these 'proximal mechanisms' have been?

4 If you are really interested in this study you can access the paper at: http://www.unm.edu/~gfmiller/cycle_effects_on_tips.pdf

The relationship between sexual selection and human reproductive behaviour

In addition to natural selection (see p.6), Darwin also suggested that species evolve through 'sexual selection' – a view that competition for mates between individuals of the same sex affects the evolution of certain traits. An example of sexual selection operating over time is the relative hairlessness of human beings compared with the other great apes. The accepted explanation for this phenomenon has been that hairlessness enabled our ancestors to keep cool through sweating (an adaptation that would have occurred through 'natural selection'). However, more recently, Pagel and Bodmer (2003) have put forward the theory that hairlessness would have allowed humans to 'advertise' their reduced susceptibility to parasitic infection (hairless skin is much easier to keep clean). This trait therefore became desirable in a mate (i.e. hairless skin would have been a consequence of sexual selection). The greater loss of body hair in women would have resulted from stronger sexual selection pressures from men to women.

The nature of sexual selection

The strange case of the peacock's tail
Darwin's idea of natural selection was that animals should end up with physical and behavioural characteristics that allow them to perform well in competition with their rivals. Therefore, most features of plants and animals should have some adaptive function in their struggle for existence. Nature should allow no extravagance or waste. So how does this explain the peacock's tail? It does not help a peacock to fly any faster or better. Also, the elaborate plumage of the male peacock makes him more conspicuous to predators, and the piercing calls that he makes to attract females informs predators of his whereabouts. Since one of the principles of natural selection is to promote anti-predator adaptations, the peacock's tail should have been eliminated by natural selection long ago. In contrast, the tail of the peahen is far more modest and sensible, and her overall colouration is less gaudy and ostentatious than that of the male.

The peacock's tail

Sexual selection and reproductive success
Darwin provided the answer to the apparent paradox of the peacock's tail in his book *Descent of Man and Selection in Relation to Sex*, first published in 1871. Here he explained that the force of sexual selection complements the force of natural selection. Therefore, individuals possess features that make them attractive to members of the opposite sex or help them to compete with members of the same sex for mates. Viewed from this perspective, we are better able to explain the gaudy and cumbersome tail of the peacock: it is a consequence of female choice. If a particular characteristic becomes established as a universal preference among females, then males who possess the best examples of that characteristic will have greater reproductive success. As a result, there is selective pressure on males to produce brighter and more dramatic tails. If natural selection involves the survival of the fittest, then sexual selection could be described as 'survival of the sexiest'. This is as true for humans as it is for other species.

Studies of human mate preference (e.g. Buss 1989) have shown how men from a wide range of cultures find the classic hourglass shape of young women particularly attractive. This makes sense when applying sexual selection theory because this shape is an indicator of fertility in women (Workman and Reader 2008). This is the basic premise of the theory of sexual selection – any trait that increases the reproductive success of an individual will become increasingly exaggerated over evolutionary time.

Intrasexual and intersexual selection

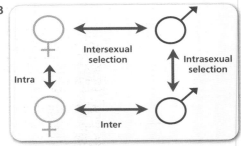

Figure 3.3
Inter- and intrasexual selection

There are two important types of sexual selection – intrasexual and intersexual (see Fig. 3.3). Where conditions favour 'polygyny' (more than one partner), males must compete with other males, and this leads to 'intrasexual' selection (meaning selection *within* the same sex). On the other hand, females who invest heavily in their offspring, for example, those who are only capable of raising a few offspring in their lifetime (such as humans), need to make sure that they have made the right choice. There will probably be no shortage of males, but the implications of a wrong choice for the female are more serious than for the male, who may be seeking access to a number of partners. Under these conditions, females can afford to be choosy. This leads to 'intersexual' selection (meaning selection *between* the sexes). The usual arrangement, therefore, is for males to compete with other males for access to females (intrasexual selection) and for females to choose males they consider worthy as mates (intersexual selection). There are exceptions to this for some species but for humans, males compete and females choose.

The origins of mate choice

Mate choice is a product of mate preferences formed in the **'environment of evolutionary adaptiveness'** (EEA). Our ancestors evolved neural adaptations that favoured mating with those individuals possessing particular traits (such as relative hairlessness). Mate choice among modern-day humans operates by females rejecting some potential mates and accepting or soliciting others. The fundamental principle of mate choice is that it pays to be choosy because the genetic quality of your mate will determine half the genetic quality of your offspring. By forming a joint genetic venture with a high-quality mate, one's genes are much more likely to be passed on (Miller 1998). Some of the main criteria of mate selection are described below.

Selection for indicators
These can take many forms because almost any perceivable bodily or behavioural trait can serve as an indicator of mate quality, revealing information about age, health, strength, disease resistance, etc. These indicators reveal traits that might be passed on to offspring (selection for 'good genes'), as well as the likelihood that the mate will survive to provide for, protect and support their offspring (selection for 'good parents'). Indicators are also subject to the 'handicap principle', i.e. they must be costly to produce in order to be reliable because if not, they can be faked too easily (Zahavi 1991).

Selection for provisioning
Females can gain benefits from mate choice if they favour those males that offer gifts. Evidence of the importance of male provisioning in sexual selection can be seen in male insects giving nuptial gifts such as caught prey, male birds building nests, and sex-for-meat exchanges in some human cultures (Fisher 1992). Male provisioning is useful to females because it increases their resource budget and so eases the burden (in terms of nutrition and energy expenditure) of producing eggs, pregnancy and feeding the young (Workman and Reader 2008). In modern-day, polygynous, hunter-gatherer societies, the best hunters have the most wives and are also more likely to have extra-marital affairs (Hill and Kaplan 1988).

Selection for mental characteristics
Human brain size has tripled over the last two million years, resulting in the evolution of phenomenal mental capacities, many of which might be attributable to sexual selection. A particular characteristic of human beings is our love of novelty (which is known as 'neophilia'). Before the arrival of television and computers, our ancestors would have had to amuse each other and neophilia would have led to ever-more creative displays from potential mates. This would explain many of the characteristics that are universally and uniquely developed in humans, such as music, art and humour, all of which are highly valued during mate choice (Miller 1998). The gradual evolution of language was also important in the process of selecting a mate because it gave potential mates a unique window into each other's minds.

HOW SCIENCE WORKS

Sex differences in human mate preferences

Key research: Buss (1989)

David Buss explored whether there were universals of human mate preference. According to evolutionary theory, men should look for indicators of fertility (e.g. youth, attractiveness and health) whereas women should look for indicators of resources (e.g. wealth or ambition). The study spanned 37 cultures in six continents and five islands and involved over 10 000 people of many different religious, ethnic and economic groups. Sampling procedures varied by country; for example, the West German sample was obtained using newspaper advertisements and participants completed postal questionnaires, whereas in the South African Zulu sample, questions were read aloud to the predominantly rural participants. Data were collected by local residents in each country and sent to the US for analysis. The main results were:

- Women of all cultures showed a preference for men with resources, or possessing characteristics that would translate into resources in the future (e.g. ambition and intelligence).

- Men universally placed more emphasis on physical attractiveness – an indication of a woman's health and therefore her fertility and reproductive value.

- Men of all cultures desired a partner who was younger than they were; this is an indication that men universally value fertility in potential mates. As the male preference was for females of just under age 25, this suggests that other factors (such as similarity) may also be important in mate choice.

- Some characteristics were universally desired by both sexes. Both men and women wanted partners who were intelligent (more skilful at parenting), kind (more likely to be committed to a long-term relationship) and dependable (willing to help their mate in times of trouble).

Evaluation

- One of the interesting findings of this study was that, contrary to what might be expected from evolutionary predictions, males preferred women who were already well into adulthood. However, research (e.g. Anderson 1986) has shown that fertility may peak earlier in females than previously thought, perhaps as early as the mid-twenties, suggesting that when choosing a mate, men value fertility in a mate more than reproductive value (i.e. potential child-bearing years).

- Any large-scale survey, such as this, relies on representative sampling across the target populations studied. However, in this study, rural and less well-educated individuals were under-represented, and the sampling method used varied widely across the different cultures. An additional problem is that in many cultures, arranged marriages are the norm, which poses the question that if these arrangements stretch back to our ancestral environment, how could mate preferences have evolved in the first place?

Facial preferences

The human face plays an important role when choosing a mate, but why are some types of face considered more attractive than others? The evolutionary view is that human facial attractiveness is linked to the advertisement of 'good genes'. Individuals who possess attractive facial features are preferred as mates, partly because of the potential benefits from passing on these attractive characteristics to offspring.

Research has shown that females are attracted to male faces with 'masculine' facial characteristics such as a large jaw and prominent cheekbones (Grammer and Thornhill 1994). These characteristics arise as a result of the actions of male sex hormones, such as testosterone, but may also be a handicap because testosterone is also known to suppress the immune system. As a result, only 'healthy' individuals can afford to produce these masculine traits, indicating their dominance and the strength of their immune system to females who are then more likely to select them as possible mates (Thornhill and Gangestad 1999).

Males also have clear facial preferences, preferring females with more child-like faces, including large eyes, small noses and full lips. These characteristics indicate youth and fertility, making them more attractive as potential mates (Thornhill and Gangestad 1993).

Activity: What do the personal ads tell us?

One of the easiest (and most accessible) ways of testing the influence of sexual selection on mate choice is by examining the personal advertisements that appear in most local newspapers (men seeking women, women seeking men, men seeking men and women seeking women). Although people may have to settle for less, this could be an indication of what they ideally want in a partner, and what they offer in return.

1 Look at some personal ads.

2 In the 'males seeking females' category, make a list of common characteristics *offered* by males (e.g. resources, intelligence).

3 In the 'females seeking males' category, make a list of common characteristics *offered* by females (e.g. age, attractiveness).

4 In the 'males seeking females' category, make a list of common characteristics *sought* by males (e.g. age, attractiveness).

5 In the 'females seeking males' category, make a list of common characteristics *sought* by males (e.g. resources, intelligence).

6 Do your findings support the predictions of sexual selection theory?

Personal ads

The consequences of sexual selection

Short-term mating preferences

An interesting consequence of sexual selection is that human beings have evolved a considerable menu of mating strategies, some of which are used for 'short-term' mating (e.g. casual sex). The logic of sexual selection dictates that the more females a male manages to impregnate, the greater his reproductive success. However, the consequences of random, casual sex are greater for a woman (mating with a poor-quality male leads to poor-quality offspring, possible reputational damage, etc.) than they are for a man. We might, therefore, expect significant sex differences in males' and females' motivation for casual sex. This does appear to be the case. In a study by Clark and Hatfield (1989), attractive male and female experimenters approached total strangers on a university campus and, among other requests, asked them whether they would come back to their apartment and have sex. None of the female students who were approached agreed to sex, although a staggering 75 per cent of the males did. Since this was a psychology experiment, no sex actually took place! This finding, which has been replicated in other studies, provides evidence that men have evolved psychological mechanisms to ensure success in short-term mating. One of these is the tendency for men to show a marked decrease in attraction for their 'casual partner' following copulation (the act of sexual reproduction); this is an evolved adaptation which ensures they do not spend too long with one woman, and can move on to the next (Buss and Schmitt 1993).

Sperm competition

The mate selection process does not end when copulation begins. In many species, females mate with more than one male during a breeding season, so 'sperm competition' is an important factor in determining which male is successful in fertilizing her egg. Seen from this perspective, males do not compete for females, but rather they compete for fertilizations. As a result of this competition, males have evolved larger penises and larger testicles, larger ejaculates and faster-swimming sperm.

Among primates, testicle size tends to increase with the intensity of sperm competition across different species (Harvey and Harcourt 1984). For example, female chimpanzees are highly promiscuous and so male chimpanzees have evolved large testicles in an effort to increase their chances in the 'reproductive lottery'. When a female chimpanzee is sexually receptive, she is attended by a number of males, many of whom she will mate with. The male with the biggest testicles is more likely to be successful in fertilizing the female because he will produce the most sperm. Gorillas, on the other hand, live in groups, which usually consist of one adult male and two to three adult females. When a female is ready to mate, just one male mates with her. The male gorilla can, therefore, afford to have tiny testes (relative to body size) because the only sperm attempting to fertilize the female's egg are his own. By comparison, male humans have medium-sized testicles, suggesting that females in the EEA were moderately promiscuous (Baker and Bellis 1995).

Activity Choosing a mate

Why do these mechanisms of mate choice evolve in the first place? There is logic behind sexual selection that makes these sex differences entirely predictable. Random mating is essentially stupid mating. As the genetic contribution of a mate is 50 per cent towards any offspring, it pays to be choosy when picking a long-term partner. Low-quality mates produce low-quality offspring. Mating with a high-quality partner, on the other hand, produces high-quality offspring and a greater chance of an individual's genes being passed on beyond the next generation.

Evaluation of the relationship between sexual selection and human reproductive behaviour

- *From preferences to real-life choices* – Much of the research documenting sex differences in mate choice has focused on *preferences* rather than on real-life choices. For example, people may express a preference for an ideal partner (e.g. intelligent, kind, ambitious), but may have to settle for less. However, a study of real-life marriages (Buss 1989) has confirmed many of these predictions: for example, men *do* choose younger women, and when they divorce and remarry, they marry women who are increasingly younger than they are.

- *Evidence for evolutionary influences on facial preferences* – Differential interest in attractive adult female faces emerges early in the first year of infancy; this implies that the preference for attractive faces is more likely to be an evolved response than a learned behaviour (Langlois *et al.* 1987). There is also a significant degree of cross-cultural agreement in ratings of facial attractiveness (Perrett *et al.* 1994). Taken together, this evidence disproves the argument that the criteria of facial attractiveness are determined by cultural conventions.

- *Facial preferences and women's menstrual cycles* – Women's preferences for attractive faces are not static, but change according to their position in the menstrual cycle. Penton-Voak *et al.* (1999) found evidence that women are attracted to more masculine-looking men during the most fertile time of their menstrual cycle, and showed a preference for more feminine-looking faces during their less fertile times. This may indicate that a less masculine-looking man may make a better long-term partner (being seen as kinder and more cooperative), but that women benefit from being unfaithful in order to produce the strongest, healthiest children as a result of a quick 'fling' with a more masculine-looking man.

- *Sperm competition* – Harvey and May (1989) suggested that ethnic differences in testicle size may reflect adaptive differences in mating strategies within different ancestral populations. Measurements made during autopsy showed that testicle size in two Chinese samples was approximately half the size of testicles in a Danish sample, whereas differences in body size only made a small contribution to these values.

- *Evolutionary psychology is not the answer to everything* – Nicolson (1999) argues that the relevance of evolutionary factors has been overemphasized. She argues that this is not actually how people really live and choose partners and that decisions are more likely to be made on a whole range of issues. She suggests, therefore, that evolutionary influences on human reproductive behaviour are most probably lost in today's social context.

IDA Gender bias

As described earlier, sexual selection has shaped different mating strategies for males and females. It is claimed that males in particular are more predisposed to short-term mating opportunities, and would be willing to have casual sex with a stranger because for them, reproductive success is determined solely by the number of fertilizations achieved (which, theoretically, are limited only by opportunity). Females, on the other hand, are less disposed towards casual sex because the costs of inappropriate mating are much higher. Of course, men often do commit to one relationship and invest a great deal in the care of their children. Similarly, women sometimes pursue short-term mates under certain conditions. Greiling and Buss (2000) suggest that blind acceptance of sexual selection theory ignores the possible benefits of short-term mating to the female. These include the possibility of producing more genetically diverse or better-quality offspring, or even using short-term mating as a way of exiting a poor-quality relationship. In other words, both males and females include short- and long-term strategies in their mating repertoires (i.e. 'strategic pluralism' exists for both sexes).

Evolutionary explanations of parental investment

Parental investment theory

More than 100 years after Darwin first proposed the mechanism of sexual selection, Robert Trivers suggested that choosiness in females is a direct result of the fact that they invest more in their offspring than males do. Trivers (1972) defined **parental investment** as 'any investment by the parent in an individual offspring that increases the offspring's chance of surviving (and hence reproductive success) at the cost of the parent's ability to invest in other offspring'. In most species, males and females do not invest equally. Female investment tends to be far greater because female gametes (eggs) are less numerous and more costly to produce than male gametes (sperm). A female can only have a limited number of offspring, whereas a male can potentially have a virtually unlimited number. As a result of this asymmetry, the sex that invests least will compete over access to the sex that invests most, and the sex that invests most will have more to lose by a poor match and so will be choosier over their choice of partner.

Sex differences in parental investment

Maternal investment

Females usually invest more time and effort in the rearing process. The human mother must carry the developing embryo and foetus to full term (nine months), and even after birth, the infants of early humans would have been completely dependent on their mother's milk for up to two years. In addition, the gradual increase in brain size over the last two million years has resulted in a more difficult childbirth (due to the enlargement of the skull). To compensate for this difficulty, childbirth occurred earlier in development, and human infants were born relatively immature compared to other animals. Whereas the young of most other species became independent in a matter of months, humans remained dependent on their parents until at least their teenage years. But why was the majority of postnatal care carried out by the mother rather than the father? As women breast-fed their babies, they were obliged to care for small children, but evolutionists also suggest that part of the greater parental investment of females could be explained because they were more certain that they were the mothers as a result of internal fertilization in mammals.

Paternal investment

Human males can opt out of parental investment in a way that females cannot. By expending a relatively large part of their reproductive effort on courtship and mating, males of most species can afford to devote comparatively little time to parental care (Daly and Wilson 1978). Males do not have the same degree of certainty concerning the paternity of offspring, and determining fatherhood may be tricky in promiscuous-mating arrangements (see 'Sperm competition' above). The great vulnerability for men is that they may use up valuable resources raising children who are not their own (this is known as 'cuckoldry'). The possibility of sexual infidelity posed different adaptive problems for males and females. For a man, an unfaithful mate meant that he risked investing in offspring that were not his own. For a woman, an unfaithful mate may have led to the diversion of resources away from her and the family. Buss (1995) suggested that sexual jealousy might have evolved as a solution to these problems. Due to the risk of cuckoldry, men are more jealous of the sexual act itself, whereas women are more concerned about the shift in emotional focus (and consequent loss of resources) towards another woman.

HOW SCIENCE WORKS

'Lads mags' condemned for their possible influence on parenting

Key research: Geher et al. (2007)

According to Conservative spokesman, Michael Gove, some modern men's magazines (the so-called 'lads mags' such as *Nuts* and *Zoo*) may be influencing young males and creating a generation of feckless fathers with little or no respect for traditional family values (September 2008). Gove (2008) believes that it is important to see parenting 'as a shared responsibility, with fathers playing an equal and complementary role, to mothers'.

The relatively low level of male parental investment in the UK and other Westernized cultures may, therefore, be attributed to cultural forces which 'corrupt' what would otherwise be a greater share of parental responsibility. We have already seen that men demonstrate a greater interest than women in pursuing several short-term mates, and they also show less commitment to the offspring produced by these mate pairings (Buss and Schmitt 1993). Parental investment theory also suggests that females are better prepared (both physically and psychologically) than males for dealing with infants. But are these differences a product of evolutionary or cultural forces? Geher et al. (2007) asked 91 undergraduates (who were not parents) from the State University of New York to complete a parental investment perception scale, which measured how prepared they perceived themselves to be for parenting. This part of the study found no real difference in the perceptions of males and females in their perceived readiness for parenting.

However, this was not the only measure used in the study. Male and female participants were then exposed to a series of statements that illustrated typical scenarios where parenting might be seen as costly (e.g. it would be necessary to cancel a work appointment to look after a sick child) in terms of the investment of time and effort needed. As participants viewed these scenarios, their **autonomic nervous system** (ANS) arousal was measured. Males showed significantly higher ANS arousal compared to females when presented with scenarios that emphasized the psychological costs of parenting. This finding is consistent with previous research, which suggests that males are less prepared to confront issues associated with parenting than females.

Evaluation

The differences between *perceived* parental readiness and *actual* parental readiness (as measured by ANS arousal) can be explained in terms of the **social desirability bias** associated with self-reports of attitudes towards parenting. Males may well recognize the importance of coming across as having parenting potential when courting females; heterosexual males are, therefore, more likely to be motivated to see themselves as being capable of parenting (Geher et al. 2007).

An evolutionary perspective

In the study by Geher *et al.* reported above, the tendency for males to overestimate their attitudes toward investing in offspring suggests that this is *adaptive* in nature. An evolutionary explanation suggests that males who are prone towards this error should reap mating-relevant benefits, i.e. they may be rated by females as being more desirable as a potential mate, when compared with other males.

Sex differences in investment in stepchildren

Key research: Anderson *et al.* (1999)

Anderson *et al.* (1999) looked at the willingness of men to pay for their children's college education as a means of assessing paternal investment strategies. Men were most willing to pay for their own child when they were still living with the child's mother. A surprising finding was that men did not discriminate financially between a child who was born to a current partner from a previous relationship and their own child from a previous relationship. This is puzzling because a man is genetically related to the latter child, but is only the stepfather of the former child. How can we explain this, using parental investment theory?

A man may invest less in his children from previous failed relationships because he may not be sure that he is the true father. However, he may invest in a stepchild of his current partner in order to convince the mother that he is a 'good provider' and so promote future mating possibilities.

Evaluation of sex differences in parental investment

- *Males do help out* – The fact that human infants are born in a relatively immature and helpless state means that they need almost constant attention for a large part of their development. One way that females can reduce the burden of prolonged maternal care is by forming long-lasting pair bonds with male partners who are prepared to help provide for the offspring. It is, therefore, in the interest of the male to impress females with their potential skills as carers and show their value as a potential mate.

- *Willing fathers* – According to parental investment theory, males are more likely to share resources with children who they know are their own, and are less likely to share with those with whom they do not share a blood relationship. However, a study by Anderson *et al.* (1999) suggests that this is an oversimplification of paternal investment (see research study above).

Activity: Parental investment and mating behaviour

Trivers concluded that because of the differential investment of males and females, the optimum number of offspring for each parent would be different. In the case of many mammals, a low-investing male will have the potential to sire more offspring than a single female could produce. A male will therefore increase his reproductive success by increasing the number of his copulations.

Clutton-Brock and Vincent (1991) suggested that a fruitful way of understanding mating behaviours is to focus on the potential offspring production rate of males and females. They argued that it is important to identify whether it is men or women who are acting as a 'reproductive bottleneck' for the other. It is the female mammal's involvement in gestation and nurturing that places limitations on their reproductive output.

Humans are a special case in point. Although the range of possible parental investment by a male ranges from near zero (if the male deserts) to equal or more than that of the female, a male is capable of siring more offspring than a single female could bear. With this in mind, it is probably true to say that among humans, the limiting factor in reproduction is marginally with the female. This by itself would predict competition between males over access to females – one of the defining features of sexual selection in humans.

Therefore, the male's best strategy to optimize his reproductive success would be to divert more effort into mating than to parenting; in other words, to pursue polygyny. A female, on the other hand, will be more disposed towards monogamy (just one partner) since success, as she sees it, is not the number of times she is impregnated, but the level of resources she is able to access to support gestation and to nurture her offspring. The law in Western countries prescribes monogamy, but this may not be the ancestral system to which we are adapted.

Polyandry (i.e. having more than one male partner at a time) among humans is very rare. It seems that males and females that are linked polyandrously would appear to gain little. From the female's perspective, sperm from one male is sufficient to fertilize all her eggs, so why bother to mate with more than one male? From the male perspective, it is even worse; if a male is forced to supply some parental care, then the last thing he should want is to share his mate with another male and face the prospect of rearing offspring that are not his own.

- *Sexual jealousy* – Research by Buss *et al.* (1992) found that male students showed more distress (measured by the galvanic skin response, which is an objective measure of emotional arousal) when asked to imagine sexual infidelity of their partner, whereas female students showed more concern about emotional infidelity. Although this supports parental investment predictions about male and female concerns, Harris (2003) questions whether such gender differences are an adaptive response. She has discovered that men respond with greater arousal to any sexual imagery, regardless of its context. This suggests that such gender differences are more likely to be a product of social learning than of evolutionary history.

Parent–offspring conflict

Although we might expect families to be characterized by cooperation and harmony, this is clearly not always the case. Kin selection theory (Hamilton 1964) proposes that individuals are more likely to act altruistically towards genetic relatives, so why is family conflict so common? Conflict within a family can sometimes be put down to dysfunctional family processes such as poor parenting, inadequate role models or ways of resolving conflict. Why then, in the absence of these factors, does conflict persist?

Parent–offspring conflict and psychoanalysis

Freud's theory of psychoanalysis places great emphasis on the importance of the oral stage of development, but why is this stage so vital in human development? Freud would not have known it, but in many subsistence societies, the birth of a subsequent child within the first four to five years of a child's life is the biggest single threat to that child's continued existence (Badcock 2000). In such societies, where breastfeeding is universally the norm, it is very difficult for a mother to maintain two closely spaced babies at the same time. In Africa, the 'balloon belly' and general emaciation that is characteristic of gross underfeeding is sometimes referred to as 'the disease of the displaced child' (Thapa et al. 1988). In these difficult conditions, persistent sucking of the mother's nipples by a baby inhibits the re-establishment of her sexual cycles for up to three years after birth. This also triggers a reflex that inhibits oestrogen production by the ovaries, reducing the likelihood of ovulation (Short 1987). Freud argued that sucking occurs independently of hunger and is, therefore, unlikely to be triggered solely by the need for food or drink. When we take into account that the need to suck a mother's nipples compulsively can save a child's life in subsistence conditions, it is easier to understand why such behaviour has become instinctive, and why natural selection would have played a part in forming it. In primal conditions, children who sucked compulsively would have postponed the birth of new siblings and would, therefore, have been more likely to survive and pass on this characteristic to future generations.

Workman and Reader (2008) suggest that the answer lies in Trivers' theory of parental investment, and nowhere is this more clearly demonstrated than in weaning conflict.

Weaning conflict

Why is there a conflict?
Because a mother shares 50 per cent of her genes with her biological offspring, it makes sense that she should devote considerable resources to their care. The problem arises, however, when we reach weaning, which is the point at which the mother is ready to breed again. Her child is now better able to fend for itself and so in reproductive terms, it benefits the mother more to produce another offspring and transfer the majority of her resources to the new child. However, the point at which it is beneficial for the mother to switch investment to another child comes much earlier for her than it does for the current child. Therefore, we predict increased attempts by the child to hold onto parental investment and competition (sibling rivalry) with any new brother or sister who threatens their current exclusive access to parental resources.

How do children deal with decreased parental investment?
Trivers (1974) argued that offspring use psychological weapons, such as temper tantrums, to obtain parental investment. This tendency has been observed in both non-human and human primates; for example, young orangutans often 'whine' at their mothers day and night while being weaned (Horr 1977). Also, according to Hill and Hurtado (1996), weaning is an '… extremely unpleasant experience for mothers, with children screaming, hitting, and throwing tantrums for several weeks' among the Ache of South America. Children appear universally not to want to be weaned, even in societies where breastfeeding continues for several years.

A child's attitude to a new sibling is frequently hostile, involving sibling–sibling competition because mothers often reduce their investment in older offspring in order to redirect it towards new (i.e. younger) offspring. Children for their part resist reductions by engaging in 'psychological warfare' in an attempt to convince parents that *they* need the parents' investment more than the new sibling. Daly and Wilson (1988) also describe strategies, such as **regression**, in which children exaggerate their dependency through baby talk and increased demands for their parents' time and attention.

Mum breastfeeding her newborn baby while her toddler looks on

Weaning conflict in the children of Bofi farmers and foragers

Key research: Fouts *et al.* (2005)

Parent–offspring conflict theory suggests that the reproductive interests of parents and children may conflict when parents want to have another child and an existing child wants continued parental attention and resources. This conflict leads their existing child to throw temper tantrums and use other psychological weapons to maintain parental investment. In one of the only studies to test these predications in a non-Western culture, Fouts *et al.* (2005) studied Bofi farmers and foragers living in the Northern Congo Basin area of central Africa. The foragers spend part of the year living on the outskirts of the farmer villages and the rest of the year living in the forest. Twenty-two forager children and 21 farmer children were studied. Children were selected for inclusion in this study if they were between the ages of 18 and 59 months and had two living parents. Researchers observed one child at a time, recording their behaviours and interactions with caregivers, in order to gather quantitative data. The behaviours recorded included the child's emotional state, attachment behaviours, social behaviours and care-giving responses to temper tantrums and crying. Three four-hour observation sessions were conducted for each child over two to three days. With the assistance of a farmer who translated the responses from Bofi to French, semi-structured interviews were conducted with the parents to find out about cultural practices regarding weaning. Parents were also asked to describe the experience of weaning their most recently weaned children. The children of Bofi farmers exhibited high levels of fussing and crying at weaning while Bofi forager children showed no marked signs of distress. Children of farmers are weaned earlier and more abruptly than are forager children and this may partly explain why they exhibited marked distress. Breastfeeding gradually declined for forager children and this may account for the lower levels of distress observed among these children.

Evaluation

- Studies in other cultures always create special problems for researchers. One such problem is translation. The use of a Bofi farmer as the translator for the semi-structured interviews introduces some challenges. It is possible that the translator's own 'cultural schema' as a Bofi farmer may have interfered with the objectivity of interviews with Bofi foragers.

- A second weakness lies with the small sample size used in this study. Given the difficulties of gaining access to such a widespread group of individuals, the observation of 43 children of weaning age is an impressive achievement, but this sample size may not be sufficient to generalize the findings to the wider target population.

Conflict at puberty

Mothers and daughters and the role of inclusive fitness

Conflict between parent and child is not restricted to weaning, but may re-emerge when the child, particularly the daughter, reaches sexual maturity. Flinn (1989) has suggested an extension of Trivers' parental investment theory that takes account of this problem, one that revolves around the concept of **inclusive fitness**. Although evolutionary theory predicts that women would want to become grandmothers, the problem is that they share only 25 per cent of their genes with any potential grandchildren, whereas with their own children, they share 50 per cent of their genes. From a purely biological perspective then, if there is a choice, it is more beneficial (in reproductive fitness terms) for a mother to have another child than a grandchild, particularly if any resultant offspring will be a drain on the family's limited resources.

Mother–daughter conflict

According to this perspective, women in this position will be in conflict with their daughters over the 'right' to reproduce. Workman and Reader (2008) suggest that a 'reproduction suppression mechanism' may exist (e.g. operating through maternal pheromones) that somehow controls the likelihood of daughters becoming pregnant while the mother is still of reproductive age. They suggest that since daughters share the same proportion of genes with a new sibling as they do with their own child (i.e. 50 per cent), it does not benefit them to reproduce themselves while they are still inexperienced and lack the necessary resources for successful child-rearing. This might explain why the conflict is felt more intensely by the mother, and also why daughters have not evolved a counter-mechanism to overcome this 'maternal suppression' of their own reproduction.

Evaluation of parent–offspring conflict

- *Lack of evidence among human groups* – Although well established among many non-human species, the debate about parent–offspring conflict in humans has remained largely theoretical rather than evidence-based. There are a number of reasons why the theory has remained largely untested among humans. Although there are many anthropological descriptions of breastfeeding and weaning practices, the majority are based on data that have been collected unsystematically from small samples over short time periods of time, using non-standardized and indirect procedures (Sellen 2001).

- *Conflict at puberty: research evidence* – Flinn (1989) provides evidence to support his views on mother–daughter conflict. This study, carried out in Trinidad, found that conflict encounters between mothers and their daughters were significantly more likely if the mother was still of reproductive age compared to situations with similar-aged daughters and a mother who was beyond reproductive age. Flinn also found that, in Trinidad, girls rarely if ever became pregnant while living with their mother until the mother's last-born child was at least four years old. This finding supports the hypothetical suggestion of a pheromone-based reproduction suppression mechanism operating while the mother is of reproductive age.

- *Dealing with conflict* – Alexander (1974) suggested that parents can respond to this 'battleground' of conflict, and increase their own inclusive fitness by teaching moral codes to their children. In particular, parents tend to teach their offspring to behave benevolently to each other. Alexander calls this 'parental manipulation' because it is the parents' genes that will benefit from increased cooperative behaviour among siblings.

- *The consequences of parent–offspring conflict* – Under some circumstances, offspring may go to extreme lengths to maintain parental investment. A startling illustration of this comes from Andrews (2006), who analysed responses from a survey of 1600 adolescents in the US. He found that severe suicide attempts were much more common among middle-born children rather than first- or last-born children. Andrews claimed that middle-born children would need to make increasingly risky attempts to extort increased investment (e.g. parental love) from their parents. This study supports the view that even extremely risky behaviours, such as suicide attempts, may be an adaptive response to the perception of decreased parental investment.

Topic 3: Effects of early experience and culture on adult relationships

The influence of childhood experiences on adult relationships

The internal working model

Bowlby (1982) described the development and functioning of internal models of relationships in the child. He proposed that individuals develop an internal working model of the self in relationship to the primary attachment figure, based on early experiences with (usually) the mother. These internal working models of attachment are thought to contain information about how available and reliable the other person is likely to be, what sorts of emotional experience can be expected, and how disappointment and emotional discomfort are likely to be handled (Sroufe and Fleeson 1986). Thus the internal models influence the child's expectations about future relationships. Adult relationships are likely to reflect early attachment styles (i.e. secure or insecure), as experiences with the primary attachment figure influence the child's expectation of similar experiences in later relationships.

Attachment and adult relationships

The importance of the issues addressed by **attachment theory** for sustaining satisfactory intimate relationships has led to considerable interest in the role of attachment in adult romantic relationships. For example, Hazan and Shaver (1987) published a 'love quiz' in an American newspaper, collecting information from people about their early attachment experiences and their current romantic attitudes and experiences. They found that people who were securely attached, as infants, tended to have happy and lasting love relationships in adulthood. These people also believed that love was both enduring and based on mutual trust. Insecure types, on the other hand, found adult relationships more difficult, were more likely to be divorced and felt that true love was rare.

Feeney *et al.* (1994) reviewed studies that investigated the association between attachment, interpersonal communication and satisfaction in close relationships. They found that security of attachment was associated with greater and more responsive self-disclosure and with less rejecting and more supportive interpersonal interaction. They also found evidence that security of attachment was associated with relationship satisfaction.

Psychology in context — Arranged marriages in the movies

A widespread practice in many cultures is the arranged marriage, where the bride and groom are brought together more to satisfy the wishes of their respective families than the wishes of the individuals themselves. The real-life issues surrounding arranged marriages in Asian communities in the UK are reflected in the prominence given to the subject by British-Asian film makers. For example, in the comedy *Bride and Prejudice* (a thinly disguised homage to Jane Austen's novel *Pride and Prejudice*), Mrs Bakshi is keen to find suitable husbands for her four unmarried daughters.

A Hindu bride

The film tells the story of an attractive, intelligent Asian girl 'dumped' by her White boyfriend – itself a commentary on the fickleness of young White men, whose cultural background allows them to 'use' their Asian girlfriends without being interested in developing a long-term relationship. But, as in Jane Austen's version of the same story, the outcome is also predictable. Marriage, it appears, is all about finding an *appropriate* partner – who turns out to be handsome, of similar or higher caste or class and, perhaps most importantly, financially secure.

Romantic comedies can also deal with some of the more tricky aspects of marriage – for example, where one or both of the central characters deviate from the norm by breaking ethnic or religious boundaries. In the play, *Strictly Dandia*, the heroine is a Hindu, yet the hero (who eventually gets his girl) is Muslim. However, in this case, the bride's family accepts the hero because he shows many redeeming features. He is respectful towards the girl and her family and is equally respectful towards his own religion, and, of course, he is financially secure. Plays, such as *Strictly Dandia*, ultimately demonstrate that when it comes to arranged marriages, different cultural groups may share values that make them suitable marriage partners (Griffin 2007).

There are many other representations of 'arranged marriages' in film and other media. From your experiences of such media representations, do you feel they:

1 Show a number of different 'types' of arranged marriage as detailed on p.124–5 of this chapter?

2 Present an accurate representation of arranged marriages in the UK?

3 Represent arranged marriages in a positive or negative light?

Feeney and colleagues concluded that anxiety about attachment issues was the 'driving force behind a range of destructive patterns of communication' in intimate relationships. They reported that anxiety was negatively related to relationship satisfaction for both men *and* women: the more anxious they were about a relationship, the less satisfied they were with it.

Interactions with peers

Research suggests that early relationships with peers are also important in shaping young people's attitudes to adult relationships. Qualter and Munn (2005) found that children learn about themselves as a direct result of their experiences with other children. These experiences are internalized in the form of expectations about future relationships. For example, a child develops a sense of their own value (e.g. their popularity, their ability to satisfy others and so on) through their interactions with other children. These internalized expectations influence how they approach adult relationships in much the same way as the internal working model outlined earlier. Nangle et al. (2003) highlight the importance of friendship in this process. The experience of having a close friend to trust and confide in creates feelings of acceptance and of being understood by another person; these characteristics are important in later romantic relationships.

Evaluating the effect of early experiences on adult relationships

- *Research evidence for the association between attachment and adult relationships* – Morrison et al. (1997) asked college students in the United States (151 men, 217 women) to complete questionnaires, describing their current or most recent intimate relationship. They also completed an attachment style inventory to assess their attachment style (i.e. secure, avoidant, ambivalent, etc.). Students with avoidant or ambivalent attachment styles described more hostility in their intimate relationships than did students with a secure style. Those with greater attachment security also described more interdependence in their relationships. In a meta-analysis of studies in this area, Fraley (1998) found significant positive correlations for the relationship between early attachment style and quality of adult relationships.

- *Attachment disorders* – In some cases, children who fail to bond with a caregiver in infancy may develop an **attachment disorder**. Reactive attachment disorder is characterized by the non-development of a child's social abilities, and can be caused by a number of factors, including child neglect or frequent changes in caregivers (such as in children's homes). Children who are adopted from children's homes/orphanages outside the UK are frequently affected, particularly if they had been removed from their parents in the first weeks of life. Children with reactive attachment disorder may display either indiscriminate social relationships (e.g. treating everybody as if they were their best friend) or show a lack of responsiveness towards, and a complete mistrust of, almost everyone. The pervasive nature of this disorder means that it can interfere with the development of subsequent relationships, including intimate relationships in adulthood.

The influence of adolescent experiences on adult relationships

Relationships with parents

Attachment in adolescence is distinctive from attachment in childhood. For example, emotional ties to parents may be indicated in quite subtle and private ways, such as through friendly teasing, as well as through more obvious displays such as shared activities and self-disclosure to one or both parents (Lerner and Sternberg 2004). Whereas young children typically view attachment solely in terms of the parent–child relationship, adolescents are aware of the similarities and differences between relationships with their parents and those with their peers and (eventually) their romantic partners.

Secure attachments with parents, however, function in a similar way in both childhood and adolescence. In the young child, security allows them to explore their immediate environment, whereas the existence of a secure relationship gives the adolescent confidence in their explorations outside the family, including the formation of intimate relationships with other adolescents.

Parents as models of intimate relationships

According to Erikson's theory of psychosocial development (Erikson 1968), a major task of adolescence is working through intimacy issues. Middle to late adolescence is an important time in this respect because adolescents are beginning the transition to adulthood and are making intimate relationships. According to **social learning theory**, parents may transmit ideas about opposite-sex relationships to their children through the process of modelling. Although adolescents may learn about intimacy from peers and the media, their exposure to intimacy is often through observing how their parents relate to each other, and also to them. Gray and Steinberg (1999) report how adolescents who are raised in an environment where their parents treat them with warmth and are emotionally available, may be better prepared for relationships and intimacy in their own adult relationships.

Post-divorce parental relationships

The high rates of divorce, remarriage and single-parenting typical of individualist societies expose large numbers of children and adolescents to significant family transitions. Because children are likely to live with their mothers in the majority of divorce cases, most research has focused on the mother–daughter relationship following divorce. Relatively few studies have examined how the quality of the relationship with a noncustodial father can shape adolescents' attitudes toward intimacy and divorce.

Mother–daughter relationships

Some post-divorce mother–daughter relationships can take the form of allegiances, based in part on negativity towards the father. These allegiances can, in some cases, lead to a relationship built on mutual disappointment in men (Beal and Hochman 1991). Research also suggests that during the first two years after divorce, most mothers with teenage daughters disclose sensitive information to their daughters about a number of divorce-related topics, including their feelings towards the ex-husband (Koerner et al. 2002). This inclusion of daughters in their parents' relationship can lead to 'parentification' of the daughter. Parentified daughters act as emotional caretakers for their mothers and can contribute significantly to daughters' poor adjustment in adulthood (Jurkovic et al. 2001), including their attitudes about marriage and divorce.

Father–son relationships

Studies that have compared post-divorce relationships between the father and adolescent girls and boys have generally found that father–son relationships are more strongly associated with the quality of later adult relationships than are father–daughter relationships. For example, Moeller and Stattin (2001) found that boys who shared an affectionate and trustful relationship with their fathers in adolescence felt greater satisfaction with their romantic partners in adulthood, but the same was not true for girls. As with mother–daughter relationships, fathers also socialize their sons to think and behave in ways that may later influence their expectations about intimacy and marriage.

Father and son bonding

Interactions with peers

Peer relationships assume a more significant role during adolescence. Frey and Rothlisberger (1996) found that adolescents had twice as many relationships with peers than with family. During childhood, friendships are important but these become deeper in adolescence and take on additional importance in relation to the 'psychological tasks' facing adolescents such as establishing autonomy, independence and more intimate relationships. Blos (1967) offered an explanation of the importance of the peer group. He suggested that peers provide a 'way-station' on the route to achieving separation and individuation because they help the adolescent avoid feelings of loneliness, without having to make any commitment to a long-term partner. Kirchler et al. (1993) pointed out that adolescents who do not develop

Importance of early attachment experiences for shaping adult relationships

Key research: Simpson *et al.* (2007)

Recent research by Simpson *et al.* (2007) provides further support for the importance of early attachment experiences for shaping adult relationships. They studied 78 participants at four key points in their life:

- At age one, the caregivers reported on the child's attachment behaviours.
- At six to eight years old, teachers rated the children on how well they interacted with their peers.
- At age 16, the children (now adolescents) were asked to describe their close friendships.
- As young adults, the participants' romantic partners were asked to describe their experiences during their relationship.

The researchers found that participants who were securely attached as infants were rated as having higher levels of social competence as children, were closer to their friends as 16 year olds, and were more expressive and more emotionally attached to their romantic partners in early adulthood.

Evaluation

- This is an example of a **longitudinal study** in psychology. Longitudinal studies collect data about the same individuals at multiple points over time. Such an approach is essential when the phenomenon of interest is directly concerned with change at an individual level – for example, when studying the effect of childhood experiences on later development. The main advantage of a longitudinal study is that it allows the researcher(s) to infer causation from temporal ordering, i.e. they can assess whether an experience at one point in time is likely to influence behaviour at subsequent time points.

- In the study by Simpson and colleagues, the longitudinal approach is particularly appropriate because the researchers wanted to know whether the attachment experiences of individual children influenced their later romantic relationships. Although this cannot determine causality as such, it does allow a researcher to predict, with reasonable confidence, what a likely outcome would be in specified circumstances. In this case, children with more secure attachment experiences appeared to enjoy better quality romantic relationships in adulthood.

---

peer relationships and who remain closely attached to their families may have difficulty in establishing their autonomy and engaging in adult relationships.

Peer friendships provide warmth and support, i.e. peers become attachment figures who provide a secure base for independent exploration in the adult world. In later adolescence, attachments change again – this time from peer attachments, which require little commitment, to more intimate 'romantic' relationships. Romantic relationships during adolescence allow the adolescent to develop a type of emotional and physical intimacy, which is quite different to that experienced with their parents. Erikson (1968) claimed that romantic relationships were only possible if the individual had successfully resolved their identity crisis. Peers are important for healthy identity development because they allow adolescents to explore different identities, test their ability to form intimate relationships with others, and relinquish their psychological dependence on parents.

Evaluating the effect of adolescent experiences on adult relationships

- *Research evidence for the importance of peer interactions* – Madsen (2001) investigated the effects of dating behaviour in adolescence on the quality of early adult relationships (aged 20/21). She found that individuals who engaged in low or moderate levels of dating between the ages of 15 and 17 tended to experience more satisfying and higher-quality relationships when aged 20/21, whereas individuals described as 'heavy daters' during adolescence tended to experience poorer-quality relationships as young adults. Madsen concluded that although adolescent-dating experiences *did* have a positive influence on the quality of later relationships, it was evident that too much dating could have a deleterious effect. The reasons for this are not clear, but in the activity below (p.124) you might like to speculate on the possible reasons.

- *The negative side of adolescent relationships* – Although research appears to indicate that adolescent relationships are an important influence on later adult relationships, there appear to be some unfortunate by-products. Haynie (2003) found that there was a significant association between romantic involvement and deviant behaviour, with increases in deviant behaviour (sometimes by as much as 35 per cent) found among those adolescents who were regularly involved in romantic relationships. Neeman *et al.* (1995) found that romantic involvement in adolescence was also associated with a *decrease* in academic achievement and an *increase* in behaviour problems. This was only evident in early and middle adolescence, however; in later adolescence, this was no longer the case, suggesting that it is the *timing* of adolescent relationships that is more important in determining what outcomes, if any, are likely to occur.

Thinking about dating experiences

Madsen's research on the effects of dating experiences in adolescence on the quality of later adult relationships found that light to moderate dating when aged 15 to 17 had a positive influence on the quality of later relationships, whereas heavy dating had the opposite effect (Madsen 2001).

1 Why do you think light to moderate dating had a *positive* effect?

2 Why do you think heavy dating had a *negative* effect?

The nature of relationships in different cultures

Categorizing cultures

In one of the largest studies ever carried out in the social sciences, Hofstede (1980) analysed data on the work experiences of over 100 000 employees in 50 different countries. On the basis of this analysis, he was able to classify the different countries on a continuum from extremely **individualist** to extremely **collectivist**. These terms are employed a great deal in the social sciences, and are frequently used to explain cultural differences in particular types of behaviour (such as relationships), so what do they mean?

Individualism

In individualistic cultures (such as the US and the UK), the emphasis is on the individual person, and his or her rights, goals, aspirations and so on. Individual performance and achievement are praised, while reliance on others is not regarded as being particularly desirable. People in individualist cultures strive for autonomy, and there is greater emphasis on 'I' rather than 'we' in interpersonal relationships. Where there is a conflict between the goals of the individual and the goals of the collective (e.g. group or society), personal needs are considered to be more important. We have already discussed this idea earlier in the context of so-called 'economic' theories of relationships, where individuals expect a 'profit' proportional to the amount of effort they invest in a relationship (see pp.104–8).

Collectivism

In contrast, collectivist cultures, such as China and Pakistan, value the 'we' more than the 'I' in social encounters. Ties between, and responsibilities to, collective units (such as family or community) are regarded as more important than the desires of particular individuals. Members of collectivist cultures, therefore, are encouraged to be *interdependent* rather than independent in their dealings with others. For example, Shkodriani and Gibbons (1995) investigated relationship differences between Mexican (collectivist) and US (individualist) students. Results revealed that students in Mexico were significantly more interdependent in terms of their relationships with friends, neighbours and co-workers compared with students in the United States. It follows therefore, that in collectivist cultures, a marriage is often seen more as a union between *families* than a union between individuals (Moghaddam *et al.* 1993).

Large extended family from a non-Western 'collectivist' culture

Relationships in different cultures

Voluntary or involuntary relationships?

People in many Western, industrialized societies have considerable geographical and social mobility and are, therefore, free to interact with a relatively large number of people on a daily basis. When it comes to the formation of relationships, there is a greater choice of potential partners and fewer restrictions on choice. More traditional, non-Western cultures, on the other hand, have less geographical and social mobility and so less choice in who they interact with and who might be deemed a 'suitable choice' as a potential partner.

Arranged marriages

Where mate selection is voluntary, which tends to be the case in Western individualist societies, romantic love is considered to be the primary basis for marriage. In countries with a collectivist orientation, the criteria for selecting individuals to be joined as a couple include family alliances, economic arrangements between families and health (Udry 1974). In the Western world, young men and women are expected to date, fall in love and then decide whether or not to get married, with or without parental consent. In contrast, in many collectivist societies, the traditional system of mate selection is characterized by a marriage that is *arranged* by families of the two individuals.

Qureshi (1991) identifies three main types of arranged marriage:

- *The planned type* – Parents plan the entire process, based on family and community factors. The bride and groom may not meet until the day of the wedding.

Chaperoned interaction – Children, usually males, tell their parents about their desires, and the parents try to find someone who matches them.

- *The joint-venture type* – Both parents *and* children are involved in selecting a mate; open dating may well be involved.

Cultural differences in romantic love

The universality of romantic love

Consistent with our understanding of the nature of relationships in Western and non-Western cultures, we might expect that romantic love would be common only in Western, industrialized cultures and less important in traditional cultures where family ties are more important. However, this appears not to be the case. Two anthropologists searched for evidence of romantic love in a sample of 166 hunting and gathering societies (Jankowiak and Fischer 1992). They found clear evidence of passionate, romantic love in most of the societies they studied. In only one society was there no compelling evidence of romantic love. In almost all these societies, young lovers talked about passionate, romantic love; they recounted tales of love and spoke of the anguish of infatuation. Jankowiak and Fischer concluded that romantic attraction is a distinct emotional motivational system present in all human beings. All human beings, regardless of cultural background, appear to crave romantic love and experience the same highs and lows when they find it.

Marrying for love?

As we have seen, marrying for love is considered the norm, although there are exceptions in the West. Allgeiert and Wiederman (1991) asked US college students 'If a boy (girl) had all the other qualities you desired, would you marry this person if you were not in love with him (her)?'. Only 14 per cent of the males and nine per cent of the females said they would consider marrying someone they did not love. Research such as this suggests that, in the West, romantic love is a prerequisite for marriage, but what about in other cultures?

Sprecher *et al.* (1994) asked American, Japanese and Russian students the same question. Surprisingly (to the American researchers!), the Japanese were as romantic as the Americans and expressed a reluctance to marry in the absence of love. The Russian students, on the other hand, were far more practical about marriage and, particularly the women, were far more likely to settle for a loveless marriage, provided all the other 'requirements' were met. Similarly, Levine *et al.* (1995) found that only in traditional, collectivist cultures, such as Thailand, India and Pakistan, were students willing to compromise and marry someone they did not love. In such societies, the extended family continues to be of primary importance, and romantic love is considered to be a luxury.

The adaptive value of love

Pinker (2008) offers an evolutionary perspective on the universality of romantic love. He suggests that love is a species-specific adaptation that has evolved to promote survival and reproduction among human beings. Research appears to support Pinker's claim because being in a long-term committed relationship is associated with lower mortality rates, increased happiness and decreased levels of stress. As a result, there is a clear adaptive value of being in a long-term relationship. For love to be an essential ingredient of such relationships, it should be found in all human societies, regardless of whether they are traditional or industrialized. This is precisely what Jankowiak and Fischer (1992) found in their study of traditional societies. What we now call 'romantic love' would have kept our distant ancestors alive long enough to reproduce and pass on their genes, so that nowadays our uniquely human predisposition for romantic love is still alive and well.

Cultural differences in online relationships

Increasingly, people are using the Internet to meet other people and even to build long-term, stable relationships. By engaging in frequent verbal exchanges through email, chat rooms or other person-to-person interfaces, partners interacting via the Internet may come to feel close to, and bond with, each other. In the early stages of typical face-to-face interactions, people tend to exchange relatively non-intimate details (e.g. taste in music, what they do for a living), gradually opening up and sharing more intimate types of information as they begin to trust their partner and find the relationship rewarding. Research has suggested that greater self-disclosure is linked to greater emotional involvement in dating relationships (Rubin *et al.* 1980).

Self-disclosure in online relationships may reflect cultural differences

Yum and Hara (2005) studied the role of self-disclosure in relationship development on the Internet in three different cultures: Korea, Japan and the US. For all three cultures, self-disclosure was directly associated with online relationship development. However, increased self-disclosure was related to increased levels of trust in the other person only for the Americans. Research suggests that self-disclosure is not always gradual and can sometimes take the form of a 'quick revelation' without any form of relational commitment to another person (the 'stranger-on-the-train' phenomenon). The Internet provides an ideal context for quick self-disclosure in which people may break the rules that typically govern self-disclosure (e.g. that it should be a gradual process based on developing trust). Ma (1996) studied Internet relationships in East Asian and North American college students and found that both groups of students tended towards more rapid self-disclosure on the Internet, compared with face-to-face interactions. However, in relationships between American and East Asian students, the American students did not regard East Asian students to be as self-disclosing as they perceived themselves to be.

Permanent or impermanent relationships? The issue of divorce

Almost all cultures have provision for divorce, although there is greater stigma attached to divorce in cultures with traditional arranged marriages. Betzig (1989) studied divorce in 160 countries and found that the most common grounds for divorce (in descending order) were: infidelity (particularly women's rather than men's), sterility, cruelty and/or maltreatment (usually the husband towards the wife).

The rising divorce rates in many Asian countries reflect changing influences on marriage and divorce in those countries. Huang (2005) outlines some of the key influences on divorce in these countries:

- *Rapid urbanization and changing cultural norms in Asian societies* – The stress of modern work life appears to have spilled over into marital relationships.

- *Enhanced choice through educational/employment opportunities for Asian women* – As Asian women have become better educated and more economically independent, they have more choice about whether to leave abusive or unacceptable relationships.

- *The loosening of social control over marriage* – In many Asian countries, the traditional community and extended families are gradually losing their influence over couples.

- *Increased leniency in divorce laws* – There appears to be a positive correlation between reduced legal restrictions on obtaining divorce in many Asian countries and rising divorce rates in these countries.

- *The importance of 'romantic love'* – In many communities this has led to a gradual decline in arranged marriages. Western media also influences many young Asian people to adopt a Western-style conceptualization of love.

- *Growth of individualism* – Traditionally, Asian marriages are not the union of two individuals, but rather of two families. Through modernization, however, many economically prosperous Asian countries are moving in the direction of individualism, and so young people are less willing to sacrifice personal desires and ambitions for their family. Simmel (1971) argues that individualism is associated with higher divorce levels because it encourages individuals constantly to seek their ideal partner.

Evaluation of research into Western and non-Western relationships

- *Individualism versus collectivism* – Hofstede's (1980) original distinction between individualist and collectivist cultures has provided the explanatory background for much of the research into cultural differences in relationships. However, research over the last 10 years or so has begun to cast doubt on the usefulness of this distinction. For example, Li *et al.* (2006) compared attitudes towards various types of relationship for people from Canada (individualist) and China and India (both collectivist societies). The study produced several unexpected findings, particularly as it showed very few differences between the Canadians and the Chinese, but it *did* show differences between the Chinese and Indian samples. Other researchers have attributed the lack of expected cultural differences in such studies to methodological issues. For example, Heine *et al.* (2002) suggest a 'reference-group effect', in that people tend to evaluate themselves by comparison with members of their reference group. Therefore individual members of a collectivist culture may think of themselves as not particularly interdependent when comparing themselves to other more 'collectivist' members of their culture.

- *Voluntary or involuntary relationships?* – In those societies where geographical and occupational mobility is limited, 'non-voluntary' (arranged) marriages seem to be the accepted alternative to Western voluntary relationships. However, among many immigrant communities there appears to have been a gradual transition from the traditional patterns of mate selection towards a more Westernized approach of choosing one's own partner, although still with parental consent. Furthermore, many Asian children living in the US insist on their prospective partner having had some exposure to the ways of the West (Kurian 1991). For example, in a study of 70 Hindu Gujarati couples living in Leicester, only 8 per cent had completely 'arranged' marriages. Three-quarters had been introduced by a third party and were given the option of refusing their partner. They had often met each other at large social events (but had been given little opportunity for close interaction). According to Goodwin *et al.* (1997), Hindu Gujaratis had considerable choice about the timing of their marriage. Research therefore suggests hat many Asian immigrant families have undergone substantial changes in their attitude to marriage, compared with families in their country of origin. For many, this process appears inevitable, as the children involved are often more acculturated in the Western way of life than their parents and grandparents.

- *Is choice related to satisfaction?* – Despite the widespread occurrence of arranged marriages – for example, the majority of marriages in India, Pakistan, Bangladesh and Sri Lanka are arranged (Kurian 1991) – few studies have compared satisfaction in arranged marriages compared to marriages of choice. Myers *et al.* (2005) asked 45 individuals (22 couples and one widowed person) living in India in arranged marriages to complete a questionnaire measuring marital satisfaction, as well as the characteristics they considered to be important in a marriage. Their responses were then compared with those from individuals living in marriages of choice in the US. The most significant finding of this study was that there were no differences in marital satisfaction between people living in arranged marriages and marriages of choice. There were, however, some cultural differences in the factors considered important for a successful marriage. For example, those living in the US placed a high priority on love as a precursor to marriage, whereas in India, love was regarded as less important. These results suggest that, regardless of the different factors considered important in the two cultures, satisfaction with one's marital relationship is not affected.

- *Permanent or impermanent relationships?* – The shift to more non-permanent relationships in the West is relatively recent. Divorce was relatively rare in the West 50 years ago, but with greater urbanization and mobility, the impermanence of relationships has become a feature of urban societies. The collectivist/individualist dimension in this area is well illustrated in a study of over 4000 Jewish households in New York undertaken by Brodbar-Nemzer (1986). He asked participants about their denomination (orthodox or liberal), their behaviour (e.g. attending synagogue) and their friendship networks (the proportion of their closest friends who were Jewish). He found a strong link between Jewish commitment and disinclination to divorce, attributing this to a stronger sense of social integration and more favourable attitudes towards the family found in the more 'committed' members of the Jewish community. Research suggests that the relationship differences found in a range of cultures may not be a product of Western versus non-Western differences, or even individualist versus collectivist features, but rather these differences may be a product of increasing urbanization in societies around the world.

IDA Cultural bias in research

There is a real danger of making cross-cultural psychology just 'doing psychology in exotic places', i.e. taking issues and phenomena that are of interest to (dominant) Western psychology and seeing if they replicate in other cultures. This takes no account of what is important in that 'other' culture. Kim and Berry (1993) address this issue with a call for *indigenous* psychologies, which study factors that have developed within particular cultures and are seen as important and functional to those cultures (rather than risking a psychology of North American self-interest).

CHECK YOUR UNDERSTANDING

Check your understanding of the effects of early experience and culture on adult relationships by answering these questions. Try to do this from memory. You can check your answers by looking back through Topic 3.

1. What is meant by the 'internal working model' and how does this influence the development of adult relationships?

2. How are different attachment styles linked to later adult relationships?

3. Does research support the link between attachment styles in infancy and the quality of adult romantic relationships? Explain your answer.

4. In what ways do adolescent relationships influence the quality of adult relationships?

5. How do post-divorce mother–daughter relationships and father–son relationships influence future attitudes to intimacy and marriage for the adolescent?

6. Does research support the link between adolescent romantic experiences and the quality of adult romantic relationships? Give reasons for your answer.

7. What are the negative aspects of adolescent romantic relationships?

8. Distinguish between individualism and collectivism – how are these claimed to influence interpersonal relationships?

9. Are individualism and collectivism still useful concepts for understanding cultural differences in relationships?

10. What are the main differences between relationships in Western and non-Western cultures?

11. What is an arranged marriage? What, according to Qureshi (1991), are the three different *types* of arranged marriage?

12. Does research support the claim that relationships characterized by freedom of choice are happier than relationships that are 'arranged'? Cite some research evidence to support your answer.

Formation

Reward/need satisfaction theory

- Some people reward us directly, increasing attraction
- Others reward us indirectly (e.g. via reinforcement)

Evaluation

- Giving and receiving reward both important
- Many relationships not reinforcing
- Gender differences may be due to socialization

The matching hypothesis

- We are attracted to people of similar social desirability
- Walster *et al.* (1966) 'dance study'
- Matching stronger for committed couples

Evaluation:

- Complex matching – not just physical attractiveness
- Gender differences
- Third parties – not all relationships are 'voluntary'

Maintenance

Social exchange theory

- Maximize rewards/minimize costs
- Comparison level (with what we think appropriate)
- Comparison level for alternatives
- Equity theory

Evaluation

- Contrived methodologies and limited application
- Lack of consistent empirical support
- Gender differences
- Cultural bias

Investment theory

- Commitment strengthened by satisfaction (rewards minus costs)
- Quality of alternatives
- Investment in relationship contributes to stability

Evaluation

- Research support – meta-analysis by Le and Agnew (2003)
- Commitment may explain why women stay in abusive relationships

Breakdown

Rollie and Duck (2006)

- Six stages:
  1 breakdown 4 social
  2 intrapsychic 5 grave-dressing
  3 dyadic 6 resurrection

Evaluation

- Research support – sex differences in 'resurrection'
- Impact of dissolution on initiating/non-initiating partners
- Heterosexual bias

Evolutionary psychology

- Costs related to emotional investment – female rejectees experience higher costs
- Increasing commitment – to avoid loss of partner
- Infidelity – evolved strategy to find replacement mate quickly
- Reputational damage

Evaluation

- Research support – Perilloux and Buss (2008)
- Ultimate and proximate causes

Sexual selection

- Selection for characteristics for reproductive success
- Intra-sexual selection – males (usually) compete
- Inter-sexual selection – females (usually) choose
- Origins of mate choice
- Buss's (1989) major study of 37 cultures showed clear male and female mate preferences

Evaluation

- Gender differences in short- & long-term preferences
- Research focuses on preferences not real-life choices
- Evidence for evolutionary influences on face preferences
- Female preferences and menstrual cycle
- Sperm competition reflects adaptive pressures
- Evolutionary psychology not answer to everything (Nicolson 1999)
- Benefits of short-term mating for females

Parental investment

- An investment in one offspring at the expense of other offspring
- Maternal investment – female mammals invest more because of internal fertilization
- Males invest relatively little, but are in danger of cuckoldry
- Males invest more in mating than parenting, i.e. preference for polygyny

Evaluation

- Males do help out
- Willing fathers – being a 'good provider'
- Sexual jealousy in males; emotional jealousy in females

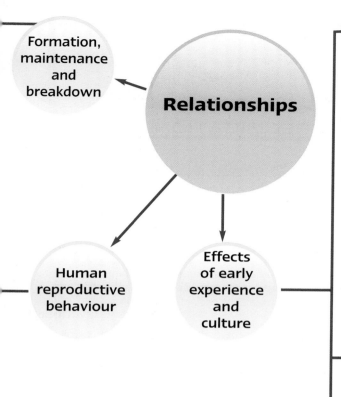

Formation, maintenance and breakdown

Relationships

Human reproductive behaviour

Effects of early experience and culture

The internal working model

- Internal models influence expectations
- 'Love quiz': securely attached people happier in adult relationships
- Security of attachment – later relationship satisfaction

Interaction with peers

- Interaction helps children learn about themselves
- Importance of friendship – acceptance and trust also important in adult relationships

Evaluation

- Research evidence for attachment type – adult relationship quality (Fraley 1998)
- Attachment disorders – later relationship difficulties

Relationships in different cultures

Categorizing cultures

1 **Individualism** – emphasis on the individual
2 **Collectivism** – emphasis on the group and on interdependence

Relationships in different cultures

- Western individualist – voluntary relationships
- Non-Western collectivist – 'arranged' marriages
- Qureshi (1991): three types of arranged marriage
- Jankowiak & Fischer (1992): romantic love universal
- Collectivist cultures: love less important?
- Adaptive value of love (Pinker 2008)
- Rising divorce rates in collectivist cultures

Evaluation

- Individualism vs collectivism: no longer a useful distinction
- Problem of acculturation among adolescents in immigrant communities
- Myers et al. (2005): satisfaction in voluntary and arranged marriages
- Difference in divorce rates – consequence of urbanization not West vs non-West differences?
- Need for more 'indigenous' psychologies

Influence of adolescent experiences

Relationships with parents

- Parents act as models for intimate relationships
- Mother–daughter post-divorce
- Father–son post-divorce

Interaction with peers

- Peer relationships more significant during adolescence
- Peers become replacement attachment figures
- Peers important for healthy identity development

Evaluation

- Research evidence for importance of peer interactions (Madsen 2001)
- Negative side of adolescent relationships
- Timing of relationships (i.e. stage of adolescence) is more important than quantity

Parent–offspring conflict

- Weaning conflict – may be vital to survival in subsistence societies
- Conflict at puberty – inclusive fitness
- Mother–daughter conflict

Evaluation

- Lack of evidence among human groups
- Research evidence for mother–daughter conflict (Flinn 1989)
- Conflict may be minimized through 'parental manipulation'
- Consequences of conflict – link to suicide attempts

Aggression

EXPLAINING THE SPECIFICATION

Specification content	The specification explained
Social psychological approaches to explaining aggression (Topic 1)	**This part of the specification requires a consideration of social psychological (as distinct from biological or evolutionary) explanations of aggressive behaviour. To do this you need to be able to:**
Social psychological theories of aggression, for example, social learning theory, deindividuation	■ Describe and evaluate *at least two* theories of aggression. Social learning theory and deindividuation are *examples* of appropriate theories. Both these theories apply to a number of different behaviours, but you need to be able to discuss how they explain aggression.
Explanations of institutional aggression	■ Discuss *at least two* explanations of institutional aggression. Institutional aggression refers to 'collective violence', for example, violence *within* institutions, such as prisons, and violence *between* different collectives, such as religious or tribal groups.
Biological explanations of aggression (Topic 2)	**This part of the specification requires a consideration of biological explanations of aggressive behaviour. To do this you need to be able to:**
The role of neural and hormonal mechanisms in aggression	■ Describe and evaluate how neural (e.g. neurotransmitters) and hormonal (e.g. testosterone) 'mechanisms' influence aggressive behaviour. It is not necessary to understand the detailed biology of these influences, but rather the evidence for their influence.
The role of genetic factors in aggressive behaviour ·	■ Describe and evaluate how genes may be involved in aggressive behaviour – e.g. does aggressive behaviour run in families and is there a 'gene for aggression'?
Aggression as an adaptive response (Topic 3)	**This part of the specification requires a consideration of evolutionary explanations of aggressive behaviour. To do this you need to be able to:**
Evolutionary explanations of human aggression, including infidelity and jealousy ·	■ Describe and evaluate *at least two* evolutionary explanations of human aggression. Infidelity and jealousy are specified and, therefore, must be covered. They are, however, linked, and could count as *one* explanation. The evolution of murder is discussed in this chapter as another evolutionary explanation of aggression.
Explanations of group display in humans, for example sports events and lynch mobs	■ Describe and evaluate *at least two* evolutionary reasons for displays of aggressive group behaviour. Sports events (e.g. football crowds) and lynch mobs are given, but only as examples. It is important to maintain an *evolutionary* level of explanation for both of these if used. *Note:* Lynch mobs and religious displays are discussed in this chapter but sports events are not.

Introduction

Geen (1990) defines **aggression** as:

> '…the delivery of an aversive stimulus from one person to another, with intent to harm and with an expectation of causing such harm, when the other person is motivated to escape or avoid the stimulus.' (Geen 1990)

The 'aversive stimulus' referred to by Geen can come in many different forms, including physical aggression (e.g. a slap) and verbal aggression (e.g. vicious gossip). There are other forms of aggression that fall outside Geen's definition, including self-directed aggression (e.g. self-harm and suicide). It is also common to distinguish between:

- aggression that is *affective* in nature (i.e. intended to harm another person), and

- aggression that is *instrumental* in nature (i.e. used as a means to an end, such as assaulting a person during a robbery).

There is considerable controversy over the causes of aggression. For example, is aggressive behaviour the result of inherited biological drives or is it acquired as a result of learning and experience? In this chapter, we begin by looking at the latter, the *psychological* origins of aggressive behaviour. In Topic 2, we will discuss biological explanations, and in Topic 3 we will consider the evolutionary perspective and discuss aggression as an adaptive response.

Psychology in context   Bullying

School provides opportunities for young people to mix with other young people, often independently of adults' influence. Validation from friends is important and individuals face pressure to fit in with the norms of their friendship groups, which may sometimes include involvement in bullying behaviours.

Research suggests that a 'hot spot' for bullying is during the first year after moving from junior to secondary school (Espelage 2002). In the 1960s, Albert Bandura pioneered social learning theory to explain the phenomenon that people (and especially children) are more likely to imitate behaviour where the 'model' is seen as powerful and one who tends to be rewarded, rather than punished, for their behaviour. In the context of bullying, bullies are seen as powerful and, more often than not, suffer no negative consequences for their actions. Bullying behaviour tends to be rewarded by the bully's peers, who either join in the bullying or condone and encourage it. A child who has successfully bullied other children will come to believe this is a good way to gain rewards, enhancing the value of aggression for the bully and also for those watching.

1 Discuss incidents of bullying that you may have experienced or witnessed when at school. How closely did these incidents fit the social learning theory of bullying described above?

2 Imagine you were a school counsellor trained in social learning theory. How might you use this training to reduce the incidence of bullying in your school?

3 Before embarking on this chapter, discuss with your classmates whether you think aggression is primarily a product of *biology* or of *learning*.

Topic 1: Social psychological approaches to explaining aggression

Social psychological explanations of aggression

Social psychological theories, such as social learning theory and deindividuation, propose that the causes of aggressive behaviour arise out of our interactions with others in our social world.

Social learning theory

According to social learning theorists such as Bandura (1965), aggressive behaviour is learned either through direct experience or by vicarious experience, that is, by observing others and learning from their experiences.

Direct and vicarious experience

- *Learning by direct experience* is derived from Skinner's principles of operant conditioning; e.g. if a child pushes another child and, as a result, gets something they want, the action is *reinforced* and is more likely to occur in similar situations in the future.

- *Learning by vicarious experience (observational learning)* occurs, for example, when a child sees a role model behaving in a particular way and imitates the behaviour of the model. Children witness many examples of aggressive behaviour (e.g. at home, at school and on television). **Social learning theory** claims that we learn to be aggressive primarily by observing the aggressive behaviour of those around us, particularly the behaviour of significant others in our life. From these 'models' we learn about the nature of aggressive behaviour, the situations in which it is appropriate, and its likely consequences.

Reinforcement

Social learning theorists emphasize that for behaviour to be imitated, it must be seen to be rewarding in some way, i.e. it must be *reinforced.* The likelihood of a person behaving aggressively in a particular situation is determined by:

1 their previous experiences of aggressive behaviour – both their own and that of others

2 the degree to which their aggressive behaviour was successful in the past

3 the current likelihood of their aggressive behaviour being rewarded or punished

4 cognitive, social and environmental factors that are operating at the same time; for example, aggressive behaviour may increase under hostile environmental conditions (e.g. very noisy situations), but fear of retaliation from the 'victim' may inhibit the expression of aggression.

In a later development of social learning theory, Bandura (1986) claimed that for social learning to take place, individuals must be able to form a mental representation of the aggressive behaviour and any anticipated rewards or punishments that might be associated with it. If an appropriate opportunity should arise in the future, individuals will display the aggressive behaviour, *provided*

the expectation of reward is greater than the expectation of punishment. For example, Huesmann (1988) suggests that children may use television models as a source of 'scripts' that act as guides for their own behaviour. These scripts are stored in memory, and are strengthened and elaborated through repetition and rehearsal.

Research into social learning theory

In order to demonstrate the importance of modelling in the acquisition of aggressive behaviour, Bandura and colleagues carried out a series of experiments involving children exposed to the aggressive behaviour of an adult model. These have become known as the 'Bobo doll' experiments because they used an inflatable clown doll (Bobo) with a weighted base so that it bounced back when punched (see Key research: Bandura *et al.* 1963). A major aim of the experiments was to demonstrate that there were two distinct effects of exposing young children to aggressive models:

1 a *teaching* effect – in which the child acquired the behaviour

2 a *motivating* effect – which made the reproduction of the behaviour more or less likely.

Evaluation of social learning theory

- *Explaining inconsistencies in aggressive behaviour* – Social learning explanations can account for the lack of consistency in people's aggressive behaviour. If someone is aggressive and domineering at home but meek and submissive at work, it means they have *learned* to behave differently in the two situations because aggression brings rewards in one context but not in the other.

- *Explaining cultural differences in aggressive behaviour* – A particular strength of social learning theory is its ability to explain differences in levels of aggression in different cultures. The 'culture of violence' theory (Wolfgang and Ferracuti 1967) proposes that some cultures (and subcultures) emphasize and model aggressive behaviour. Other cultures emphasize and model *non*-aggressive behaviour, and so are more likely to produce individuals with low levels of aggression. For example, among the !Kung San people of the Kalahari Desert, aggression is comparatively rare. !Kung San parents do not use physical punishment, and aggression is devalued by the society as a whole. The absence of aggressive models means there is little opportunity for !Kung San children to learn aggressive behaviour.

- *Social learning or biology as primary causal agent?* – Biological explanations of aggression have stressed factors unrelated to social learning. High levels of the male hormone testosterone have been cited as a primary causal agent in aggressive behaviour, and premenstrual syndrome has even been cited in criminal trials as a reason for aggressive behaviour (Benedek 1985). These cases, together with other biological explanations, cast doubt on aggression

Television models may provide scripts that guide children's behaviour

Social learning and aggression

Bandura and colleagues divided 66 nursery school children into three groups. All three groups watched a film where an adult model kicked and punched a Bobo doll, accompanying this with aggressive comments.

Figure 4.1

For example, the model laid the Bobo doll on its side, sat on it and punched it on the nose while shouting *"Pow, right on the nose, boom, boom"*. For one group of children, the film ended after watching the model behaving aggressively towards the doll, but for another group of children there was an additional scene showing the consequences of the model's aggressive actions. This 'consequences' group was further subdivided into model-*rewarded* condition (e.g. another adult rewarded the model for being aggressive towards the doll with 7–Up and sweets) and model-*punished* condition (e.g. another adult punished the model by telling the model off for their aggression towards the Bobo doll).

To summarize:

- *Condition 1:* Aggressive model was neither rewarded nor punished
- *Condition 2:* Aggressive model was rewarded by a second adult
- *Condition 3:* Aggressive model was punished by a second adult.

After watching the film, each child was watched at play with the doll and other toys, and any imitative aggressive acts were recorded by observers. The results were as follows:

- In Condition 1 *and* Condition 2, there was a marked tendency for the children to show spontaneous, imitative aggressive acts.
- Children in Condition 2 behaved most aggressively
- Children in Condition 3 behaved least aggressively.

Social learning theory also predicts that the consequences of behaviour have a controlling (motivating) effect on its performance. Therefore, although the aggressive acts were not *spontaneously* demonstrated in the punished condition, they would nevertheless have been acquired (learned). To test this, the researchers offered incentives (e.g. sweets) for each repetition of the model's aggressive behaviour. This led to high levels of imitative aggression in all three groups, showing that the children in Condition 3 had *learned* as many aggressive behaviours as the children in Condition 2 but initially they had not displayed them because they were not motivated to do so.

Evaluation

- *Methodological problems with the Bobo doll studies* – Social learning theories of aggression rely heavily on experimental evidence such as this study. There are, however, some methodological problems in the experiments described by Bandura and colleagues. A Bobo doll, after all, is not a living person and does not retaliate when hit, which raises questions as to whether this study tells us much about the imitation of aggression towards other human beings.

- *Other findings* – Other investigators have cast doubt on the conclusion that Bandura's child participants had learned their aggressive behaviour merely from watching a filmed model. In one study, nursery school children who behaved most violently towards the doll were also rated by their teachers and peers as being most violent generally (Johnston *et al.* 1977).

Deindividuation

Deindividuation is another social psychological explanation for aggression. Hogg and Vaughan (2008) define deindividuation as: 'a process whereby people lose their sense of socialized individual identity and engage in unsocialized, often antisocial behaviours'.

People normally refrain from acting in an aggressive and antisocial manner, in part because they are easily identifiable and in part because they belong to societies that have strong norms against such 'uncivilized' behaviour. In certain situations, such as in crowds, restraints on aggressive behaviour may become relaxed, so that we may engage in 'an orgy of aggressive, selfish

being purely a *learned* behaviour. Social learning theorists, however, point to societies that exhibit no aggressive behaviour (such as the Amish in the US) as powerful evidence of the dominant role played by learning. Interestingly, in most societies where non-aggressive behaviour is more prevalent than aggressive behaviour (such as the Arapesh of New Guinea and the Pygmies of central Africa), there are few distinctions made between males and females. Although differences between the roles of males and females do exist in these societies, no attempt is made to project an image of brave, aggressive masculinity (Deaux *et al.* 1993).

and antisocial behaviour' (Hogg and Vaughan 1998). In his study of the situational determinants of destructive obedience, Milgram (1964;1965) found that participants were more likely to give higher levels of shock when they could not see (or be seen by) their victim. When the 'victim' was in the same room, the participants were more reluctant to deliver high levels of shock to someone they could see (and who could see them).

Individuated and deindividuated behaviour

Zimbardo (1969) distinguished between *individuated* behaviour, which is rational and conforms to acceptable social standards, and *deindividuated* behaviour, which is based on primitive urges and does not conform to society's norms. According to Zimbardo, being part of a large crowd can diminish awareness of individuality because individuals are faceless and anonymous. There is less fear of retribution and a diluted sense of guilt. Conditions that increase anonymity serve to minimize concerns about evaluation by others and thus weaken the normal controls on behaviour that are based on guilt, shame or fear. The larger the group, the greater the anonymity and the greater the difficulty in identifying a single individual. Malamuth and Check (1981) questioned male students at an American university and found that almost one-third of them admitted that there was a chance they might commit rape if there was no chance of their being identified.

Public and private self-awareness

The concept of deindividuation has been refined to distinguish between the effects of reduced *public self-awareness* (being anonymous to others) and reduced *private self-awareness*. A person who is self-focused tends to act according to internalized attitudes and moral standards. If, however, individuals become submerged within a group, they may lose their self-focus and become less privately self-aware. According to Prentice-Dunn and Rogers (1989), it is this reduction in private self-awareness that is associated with increased antisocial behaviour rather than reduced public self-awareness (feeling anonymous).

Research related to deindividuation

Many research studies have investigated deindividuation and how it affects behaviour. One of the most famous studies is the Stanford Prison experiment.

The Stanford Prison experiment (Zimbardo et al. 1973)

Zimbardo was interested in finding out whether the brutality reported among guards in American prisons was due to the sadistic personalities of the guards or had more to do with the prison environment (Zimbardo *et al.* 1973). The 'prison' was recreated in Stanford University, with students acting as guards and prisoners. The prison environment, in which 'prisoners' were dressed in smocks and nylon caps, and addressed only by their number, appeared to be an important factor in creating the brutal behaviour of the 'guards'. The dehumanization of the

prisoners by the guards, together with the relative anonymity of each group (leading to a reduction in self-awareness in the guards), made it easier for the guards to treat the prisoners in a brutal manner so that the study had to be stopped after just six days. See *Psychology AS for AQA* (pp.187–189) for more information about the Stanford Prison experiment.

Deindividuation in mobs

- *The baiting crowd* - Mann (1981) used the concept of deindividuation to explain a particular form of collective behaviour: the 'baiting crowd'. Study of the 'baiting' or taunting crowd lends support to the notion of the crowd as a mob. Mann analysed 21 incidents of suicides reported in American newspapers in the 1960s and 1970s. He found that in 10 of the 21 cases where a crowd had gathered to watch, baiting had occurred (i.e. the crowd urged the potential suicide to jump). These incidents tended to occur at night, when the crowd was large and when the crowd was some distance from the person being taunted (particularly when the 'jumper' was high above them). Mann claimed that these features – darkness, size of crowd and distance – were likely to produce a state of deindividuation in the individual members of the crowd.

- *The faceless crowd* – In a similar vein to Mann, Mullen (1986) analysed newspaper cuttings of sixty lynchings that took place in the United States between 1899 and 1946. As with the baiting crowd described above, the more people there were in the mob, the greater the deindividuation that occurred and the greater the savagery with which members of the crowd killed their victims.

Now read the Key research: 'Deindividuation and intergroup aggression'.

Evaluation of deindividuation

- *Deindividuation and prosocial behaviour* – Much of the early evidence linked deindividuation and antisocial behaviour. However, there is other evidence showing that deindividuation may sometimes produce increases in *prosocial* behaviour (e.g. expressions of collective good will at religious rallies) rather than antisocial behaviour (Diener *et al.* 1980).

- *The role of anonymity* – Researchers have often failed to distinguish between the effects of the anonymity of those being aggressed against, (e.g. a 'faceless' enemy or victim), as opposed to the anonymity of those doing the aggressing, (e.g. hooded terrorists). Another issue that needs to be addressed is whether the likelihood of aggression is increased if our *in-group* (the group to which we belong) cannot recognize us, or only if our *out-group* cannot. Manstead and Hewstone (1995) argue that anonymity among the in-group does not really reflect the reality of most crowd situations, where many in-group members will recognize each other.

Deindividuation and intergroup aggression

The real-world relevance of deindividuation theory was dramatically demonstrated in a study by Harvard anthropologist Robert Watson in 1973. Watson tested the hypothesis that warriors who significantly changed their appearance when going to war would be more likely to torture, mutilate and kill their victims than would warriors from societies that did not change their appearance when going to war.

To test this hypothesis, Watson found data from the 'Human Relations Area Files' (HRAF – an anthropological database) relating to 23 societies, together with evidence of whether they changed their appearance significantly before going to war and how they treated their victims.

The results were remarkable:

- Of the 13 societies that killed, tortured and mutilated their victims, all but one changed their appearance (through the use of war paint or other deindividuating features) prior to battle.

- Of the 10 societies that were less brutal towards their victims, seven of the ten did *not* change their appearance prior to battle, and thus were not deindividuated.

Evaluation

- *Researcher bias* – The HRAF is an important anthropological database consisting of books, articles and dissertations relating to over 400 cultures. A problem with databases such as this, however, is that the reports they contain were typically produced by researchers with cultural practices and expectations different from those of the people studied. Consequently, while the reports may include important information, they may also reveal more about the biases and values of the researchers who created them. Often, these studies fail to represent accurately the culture being studied.

- *Support from Zimbardo* – Zimbardo has concluded, from his own studies and from research such as this by Watson, that when we want '...usually peaceful young men to harm and kill other young men...it is easier [for them] to do so if they first change their appearance to alter their usual external façade by putting on military uniforms or masks or painting their faces' (Zimbardo 2007).

- *Social norms and behaviour* – According to the deindividuation perspective, when we are submerged in a group, this undermines the influence of social norms. This is in sharp contrast to social psychological research that has demonstrated the strong normative hold that groups have on individual members. Rather than individuals pursuing behaviour 'based on primitive urges and not conforming to society's norms', they might be seen as conforming to a 'local' group norm (Manstead and Hewstone 1995). This norm need not necessarily be antisocial, and could thus account for some apparently contradictory findings that show an increase in prosocial behaviour when people are deindividuated (e.g. Diener *et al.* 1980).

- *The Zimbardo et al. 1973 prison study* – It is sometimes concluded that the brutality of the guards in Zimbardo's study indicates the power of deindividuation to produce aggressive behaviour. However, the guards' brutality, together with the relative submission of the prisoners, suggests that

Violence at a football match

they were acting in terms of *perceived* social roles rather than losing 'their sense of socialized individual identity'. The study failed to tell us much about how *real* guards behave, but rather how people behave when they are asked to *act* like guards.

- *Deindividuation and football crowd violence* – It is tempting to apply the concept of deindividuation to crowd violence in British football. Stereotypical images of football fans on the rampage (see the photo on the previous page) make all too familiar reading in the press and suggest a faceless crowd engaged in an 'orgy of aggressive, selfish and antisocial behaviour' (Mann 1981). A study of football hooliganism by Marsh *et al.* (1978) tells quite a different story. Marsh and colleagues found that what might appear to be an undisciplined mob on match days can actually consist of several different groups, each with their place in a status hierarchy. They also found that much of the aggression displayed was highly ritualized rather than physically violent.

Explanations of institutional aggression

Institutional aggression refers to violent behaviour that exists *within*, and may be a defining feature of, certain institutions and groups. It can also refer to other forms of collective violence *between* social groups (such as the violent behaviour observed in riots and intergroup conflicts). It is not surprising, therefore, that institutional aggression can take many different forms. 'Institutions' may be distinct entities (e.g. a school or prison), larger bodies (e.g. the police or armed forces), or may represent a whole society. Acts of institutional aggression range from physical abuse of individuals during initiation 'rituals', to acts designed to destroy a national, racial or religious group (genocide). As a result, institutional aggression involves more complex psychological processes than interpersonal aggression and may have more traumatic consequences for its victims.

In this section we shall look at institutional aggression in prisons and in student initiation rituals.

Institutional aggression in prisons

Across England and Wales in 2006, there were 11 476 violent incidents between prisoners, a 541 per cent rise on the 1791 violent incidents recorded a decade earlier. These statistics clearly show that prisons can be violent places for both the inmates and for those individuals who work in prisons. To understand why interpersonal violence occurs so frequently in prisons, two major models (theories) have been proposed – importation and deprivation. The work of Zimbardo (2007) has also contributed to our understanding of institutional aggression.

The importation model

The importation model (Irwin and Cressey 1962) claims that inmates who enter prison with particular characteristics (e.g. values, attitudes and experiences) are more likely to engage in interpersonal violence than other inmates. According to this theory, interpersonal violence in prisons is not a product of the institution itself but rather of the characteristics of individuals who enter such institutions. Younger rather than older inmates are thought to have a more difficult time adjusting to prison and thus are more likely to have confrontations with other inmates and with prison staff. They are also more likely to view

Prisons can be violent places for inmates and for those who work in them.

violence as an appropriate response to conflicts. This assumption has been confirmed in a number of studies (e.g. Adams 1981). Research in the US has shown that Black inmates, when compared to Whites, are more likely to be associated with interpersonal violence. The explanation offered for this is that Black prisoners often enter prison from more impoverished communities with higher rates of violent crime. Thus, they bring (import) into prison the cultural norms that condone violent behaviour.

The deprivation model

The deprivation model claims that it is the characteristics of the prison itself rather than the prison population that accounts for prison violence. Proponents of this model do not deny the possibility that inmates enter prisons with certain cultural norms that are more or less permissive of violence. They argue, however, that it is primarily the experience of imprisonment that causes inmates extreme stress and frustration and which, in turn, leads to violence or aggression against other inmates and staff. Harer and Steffensmeier (1996) describe how inmate behaviour is a response to the 'problems of adjustment posed by the deprivations or pains of imprisonment'. These 'pains' include, according to Sykes (1958), the loss of freedom and of heterosexual relationships, isolation from the free community, boredom, discomfort and loneliness. As imprisoned inmates experience these 'pains', they engage in interpersonal violence as a reaction to the hurt that they feel. For example, the overcrowding crisis in UK prisons has forced many more inmates to share cells and is linked to an increase in interpersonal violence, self-harming and suicides. Violence is relatively commonplace in crowded prisons as the conditions exacerbate tensions among inmates, as well as between inmates and staff.

The power of the situation and the effect of dehumanizing labels

In his book *The Lucifer Effect*, Zimbardo (2007) emphasizes the powerful influence that the situation can have on people's willingness to inflict harm on others. In his Stanford Prison Experiment (Zimbardo *et al.* 1973), he first noticed that when psychologically well-adjusted college students played the roles of guards, they became brutal and abusive towards prisoners. This study showed how institutional factors, such as the lack of external constraints and peer pressure, led the 'guards' to disregard the potential harm of their actions towards the 'prisoners'. In the absence of external constraints, people are at greater risk of deviating from societal norms of conduct. This was true in the Stanford Prison Experiment, but is also true in real-life cases of institutional aggression, such as in initiation rituals among students (see p.138) and the abuse of prisoners in Iraq (see right). Zimbardo argues that people are also more likely to be aggressive when they dehumanize or label others. For example, in an experiment by Bandura *et al.* (1975), student participants were told they were to work with students from another school on a group task. In one condition, the participants overheard an assistant refer to the students from the other school as 'animals', while, in another condition, these students were referred to as 'nice'. When later required to deliver what they thought were real electric shocks to the other students, higher shocks were delivered in the first ('animals') condition.

Evaluation of the explanations of institutional aggression in prisons

- *Research support for the importation model* – Harer and Steffensmeier (1996) analysed data from 58 US prisons and found that Black inmates displayed significantly higher levels of violent behaviour but *lower* rates of alcohol and drug misconduct compared to White inmates. They concluded that these differences reflected racial differences in these behaviours within US society generally, providing support for the claim that such characteristics are *imported* into the prison environment. Keller and Wang (2005) found that prison violence is more likely to occur in facilities that hold the most troublesome inmates. For example, they found that prisons holding maximum-security inmates had higher levels of assaults on staff by inmates, than prisons with lower-security inmates.

- *Limitations of the importation model* – McCorkle *et al.* (1995) claim that this model fails to provide suggestions for how best to *manage* violent offenders or how to reduce prison violence in general. The importation model also predicts that membership of a violent gang prior to confinement will result in increased levels of violence and misconduct in prison, as gang members import their gang involvement into the prison setting. However, a study of over 800 male inmates by DeLisi *et al.* (2004) found no evidence that gang membership prior to prison had any bearing on violence or misconduct within prison.

- *Research support for the deprivation model* – Although some studies have provided support for the deprivation model of prison violence, one of the largest studies in this area (McCorkle *et al.* 1995) failed to support its major assumptions. The sample in this study included 371 state prisons in the US and found little evidence to support the connection between violence and measures such as overcrowding and living conditions.

- *Limitations of the deprivation model* – McCorkle and colleagues also point out that levels of stress associated with imprisonment (e.g. loss of freedom, overcrowding) are generally constant, whereas serious outbreaks of violence, such as found in prison riots, are not. They claim that serious violence is more a consequence of the *management* of prisons rather than the general deprivation that all prisoners endure. The deprivation model is also challenged by the finding that among juvenile offenders in four different institutions, pre-institutional violence was the best predictor of inmate aggression, *regardless* of the particular features of the institution (Poole and Regoli, 1983). This supports the importation model.

- **HOW SCIENCE WORKS** *Real-life relevance* – Zimbardo (2007) claims that the same social psychological processes that were found in the Stanford Prison Experiment were also apparent during the abuse of Iraqi prisoners at Abu Ghraib prison in Iraq. These included deindividuation, dehumanization, group conformity and lack of supervision, which led to a

A dehumanized prisoner in the Abu Ghraib prison in Iraq

diminished sense of accountability from the guards responsible for the abuse. The power of dehumanization was also evident in the 1994 genocide in Rwanda. The Tutsi minority were routinely referred to by the Hutu majority as *inyenzi* (meaning cockroaches) that must be 'stamped out'. This was instrumental in the chilling statistic of 800 000 Tutsi and moderate Hutu being killed in just 100 days.

Activity

Limitations of Zimbardo's explanation

Reicher and Haslam (2006) argue that the institutional aggression observed in prisons such as Abu Ghraib was not simply a product of the situational factors identified by Zimbardo, but more to do with one group's way of thinking about another. Although Iraqi prisoners in Abu Ghraib were subjected to physical abuse, there have been other similar situations where prisoners of war have been treated with compassion by their captors. During World War II, for example, German captors treated their prisoners of war differently, depending on their nationality. British prisoners of war were regarded as equal and were treated in a relatively civilized way. Russian and Slav prisoners, on the other hand, were regarded as subhumans and treated barbarically. Similarly, Iraqi prisoners at Abu Ghraib were labelled as vermin and evildoers by their captors, and so physical abuse was made more likely.

1 Read what Reicher and Haslam have to say about institutional aggression at: http://www.bbcprisonstudy.org/pdfs/BJSP(2006)Tyrannny.pdf

2 Try Googling 'war' and 'dehumanizing language' to find other examples of the ways that language has been used to dehumanize an enemy.

Institutional aggression in initiation rituals

Initiation rituals

Initiation rituals are special rituals and requirements for new members of a group. Such rituals may be fairly innocuous, such as having to drink excessive amounts of alcohol. They may, however, be painful and psychologically stressful. One function of intense initiation rituals is to create a common bond among members of a group. Having endured extreme initiation, the new recruit will feel part of a select group, all of whose members have endured the same initiation rituals. In the US, 'hazing', as painful initiation rituals are called, is deemed unlawful in forty-three states. The major reason for this type of initiation in males is symbolically to take away the weakness of childhood and replace it with the confidence of adulthood (Raphael 1988). If initiates can tackle the

extremes of initiation, suggests Raphael, they know they can handle the rest. Inherent in this belief is a culturally constructed notion of what it takes to be a 'real man', with an emphasis on physical and mental toughness and obedience to superiors. As a result, 'hazing' is evident in many branches of the military. Winslow (2004) quotes a Canadian Air Force soldier on the topic of initiation on the airborne assault course:

'For the young guy, it's a question of gaining confidence and showing the others that they can do it. For the older guys, it's like they check out the younger guys to see who they feel they can trust. You have to be able to trust the guys you're jumping with.' (Winslow 2004)

In the Russian military, such initiation is called 'dedovshchina' and can be extreme and very violent. The *dedovschina* ritual involves nightly beatings from drill sergeants, and is approved by many of the top generals. Recently, however, a high-profile incident in which a private was forced to sit on a block of ice for four hours, ending with the amputation of his leg, prompted a national outcry on the matter and an investigation into this practice in the Russian military.

Evaluation of explanations of initiation rituals

- *Research support* – A number of studies have found evidence for the use of initiation rituals to establish dominance and to initiate newcomers in institutions such as colleges, the police and the military. McCorkle (1993) found that in prisons, the domination of the weak during initiation rituals was seen by inmates as essential to maintaining status.

- *Why is hazing effective?* – Probably the most important explanation for the effectiveness of 'hazing' in the initiation process is provided by **cognitive dissonance theory** (Festinger 1957). This states that when a person behaves in a way that does not fit with an existing attitude or belief, they will experience an unpleasant state of dissonance because the action conflicts (is dissonant) with the belief. In the context of hazing, those who voluntarily endure a demeaning or painful ritual, while at the same time believing the ritual is pointless or wrong, will experience psychologically uncomfortable cognitive dissonance. One way to reduce this dissonance is to change their attitude towards the behaviour. Once the initiation process is complete, the initiate is able to reflect on the experience. It is at this point that an attitude change to reduce dissonance is likely to occur, and the initiate will come to value the experience no matter how seemingly pointless and degrading it may have seemed at the time. In this way, the 'value' of the initiation experience becomes an important part of group membership, and the degree of suffering endured during the initiation ritual becomes directly related to the value they place on it and on being a group member (Davis 1997).

Check your understanding of social psychological approaches to explaining aggression. Try to do this from memory. You can check your answers by looking back through Topic 1, Social psychological approaches to explaining aggression.

1 What is the difference between direct and vicarious reinforcement?

2 According to social learning theory, the likelihood of a person behaving aggressively is determined by what four factors?

3 What conclusions can be drawn from the Bobo doll study concerning the imitation of aggression?

4 Explain two evaluative points concerning the social learning theory of aggression.

5 What is meant by 'deindividuation' in the context of aggression? What is the difference between 'individuated' and 'deindividuated' behaviour?

6 What conclusions can be drawn from Zimbardo's Stanford Prison Experiment concerning the causes of aggressive behaviour?

7 Explain two evaluative points concerning the deindividuation explanation of aggression.

8 Explain the difference between the importation and deprivation models of institutional aggression.

9 Explain two evaluative points concerning each of the importation and deprivation models of institutional aggression.

10 Outline what is meant by initiation rituals (including 'hazing') and provide one explanation for this phenomenon.

11 Explain two evaluative points concerning initiation rituals as a form of institutional aggression.

Topic 2: Biological explanations of aggression

Psychology in context
The role of genes in aggression

Jeff Landrigan was adopted at the age of six months. As a teenager he committed a series of crimes, progressively becoming more and more violent until he finally committed a murder in Oklahoma. He escaped from jail, fled to Arizona and committed another murder there, for which he was sentenced to death. While on death row he found out that he had a whole family history of violent crime. He was adopted at a very young age but while on death row a prison guard pointed out that someone who looked almost identical to him but 20 years older was on death row in Arkansas. Landrigan subsequently discovered that this person was his biological father, who hadn't seen him since he was six months old. Since making this discovery, Landrigan has argued that he has a genetic predisposition to violence based on his family history and, therefore, could not be held responsible for his actions.

1 What, if anything, does this tell you about the origins of extreme violence?

2 If scans and other biological evidence became admissible evidence, what *moral* issues would this raise concerning guilt and responsibility?

3 Check out other cases of murder reported on the internet. Do any of these suggest that *biological* factors (such as genetics or brain dysfunction) may have contributed to the person's behaviour?

Neural and hormonal mechanisms in aggression

In 2007, over 65 000 people, both male and female, were sentenced by courts in England and Wales for actual or grievous bodily harm or for common assault (British Crime Survey 2007 – see www.homeoffice.gov.uk/rds/crimeew 0708.html). This worrying statistic has led some researchers to investigate whether there is an underlying biological cause of aggression. For example, many studies over the last 30 years have reported high levels of the hormone testosterone in violent criminals. More recently, advances in neuroscience have resulted in attention switching to the influence of neural mechanisms, such as the role of neurotransmitters (e.g. serotonin and dopamine). As we will see, however, the relationship between biology and aggression is far from straightforward.

Neurotransmitters

Neurotransmitters are chemicals that allow impulses in one area of the brain to be transmitted to another area. Therefore, all behaviours are influenced by the action of neurotransmitters. Two neurotransmitters are believed to be particularly important in the control of aggressive behaviour. Aggression in both animals and humans has been associated with:

- *low* levels of **serotonin**, and
- *high* levels of **dopamine**

Serotonin and aggression

Studies have shown that serotonin, in normal levels, exerts a calming, inhibitory effect on neuronal firing in the brain (Cases 1995). It is claimed, therefore, that low levels of serotonin, particularly in the prefrontal cortex, remove this inhibitory effect with the consequence that individuals are less able to control their impulsive and aggressive responses. Support for this claim comes from research that shows that the major metabolite (waste product) of serotonin tends to be low in the cerebrospinal fluid of people who display impulsive or aggressive behaviour (Brown *et al.* 1982). Further evidence for the role of low levels of serotonin in aggressive behaviour comes from studies where levels of serotonin are manipulated. Mann *et al.* (1990) administered the drug dexfenfluramine (developed to help with weight loss but now withdrawn) to 35 healthy adults. The drug is known to deplete serotonin levels in the brain. The researchers used a questionnaire to assess hostility and aggression levels, and found that among males (but not females) hostility and aggression levels increased after treatment with the drug.

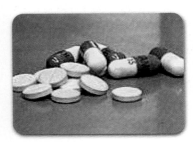

When dexfenfluramine was administered, serotonin levels were reduced, and aggressive behaviour increased in males.

Dopamine and aggression

The link between dopamine and aggressive behaviour is not as well established as the link between serotonin and aggression. However, there is some evidence to suggest that *increases* in dopamine activity (e.g. via the use of amphetamines) are associated with increases in aggressive behaviour (Lavine 1997). Similarly, the use of dopamine **antagonists** (which reduce dopamine activity in the brain), have been used successfully as a way of reducing aggressive behaviour in violent delinquents (Buitelaar 2003).

Recent research suggests a slightly different role for dopamine in its relationship with aggression. It is well established that dopamine is produced in response to rewarding stimuli such as food, sex and recreational drugs. Couppis *et al.* (2008) have now found evidence that dopamine also plays an important reinforcing role in aggression. Their research suggests that some individuals intentionally seek out aggressive encounters because of the rewarding sensations, caused by the increase in dopamine, which these encounters provide.

Evaluation of neural mechanisms in aggression

- *Serotonin: alternative explanations* – It is possible that aggression is not caused by low levels of serotonin in the brain, but by low serotonin metabolism which

leads to increased numbers of receptors. Serotonin receptor density has an inverse relation to serotonin levels in the brain, such that an increase in the number of receptors is likely to occur under conditions of chronic serotonin depletion. For example, Arora and Meltzer (1989) found a relationship between violent suicide and elevated serotonin receptor density in the pre-frontal cortex. Similarly, Mann *et al.* (1996) found that among suicide 'completers', those with increased numbers of pre-frontal cortex serotonin receptors had chosen more violent methods of suicide.

- *Alcohol, serotonin and aggressive behaviour* – Badawy (2006) claims that the influence of serotonin on aggressive behaviour may be important in explaining the well-established relationship between alcohol and aggressive behaviour. He found that alcohol consumption caused major disturbances in the metabolism of brain serotonin; in particular, acute alcohol intake depleted serotonin levels in normal individuals. In susceptible individuals, this depletion may induce aggressive behaviour.

- *Research support* – Ferrari *et al.* (2003) provide support for the influence of both serotonin and dopamine in aggressive behaviour. They allowed a rat to fight every day for 10 days at precisely the same time. On the eleventh day, the animal was not allowed to fight, but the researchers measured the levels of serotonin and dopamine in its brain. They found that in anticipation of an imminent fight, the rat's dopamine levels had increased and serotonin levels decreased, despite the fact that the animal did not actually fight. This shows that experience had changed the animal's brain chemistry, gearing it up for a fight by altering levels of serotonin and dopamine in ways consistent with the onset of aggressive behaviour.

- *Why is it difficult to establish a link between dopamine and aggression?* – Although researchers have long suspected a relationship between dopamine and aggression, this has been difficult to demonstrate experimentally. Studies with mice (e.g. Couppis *et al.* 2008) demonstrate the problem. Effectively 'turning off' dopamine in the animal's brain also makes it difficult for the animal to move, because of dopamine's important role in the coordination of movement. Consequently, it is difficult to explain any subsequent drop in aggressive behaviour, which could be due *either* to a lack of motivation to be aggressive *or* simply to the fact that the mice find it difficult to move, and hence difficult to respond aggressively.

Hormones

Hormones (e.g. testosterone, cortisol) are chemicals that regulate and control bodily functions. The endocrine system produces several hundred hormones which interact with each other and with the nervous system to regulate short-term processes, such as responses to an external threat, and longer-term processes, such as sex differentiation, maturation and reproduction.

Testosterone and aggression

Males produce testosterone in the testes. Women also produce testosterone, but in smaller amounts by converting dehydroepiandrosterone (DHEA) produced in the adrenal glands. Testosterone is one of the androgen hormones, so called because they produce male characteristics. Levels of testosterone reach a peak in young adult males and typically, in Western societies, levels of testosterone gradually decline with age.

The nature of the link between testosterone and aggressive behaviour is not a simple biological 'cause-and-effect' mechanism. Rather, testosterone makes it *more likely* that a particular behaviour will be expressed. Whether or not increased levels of testosterone lead to increased levels of aggressive behaviour, it is important to remember that aggression is also influenced by factors such as previous experience.

Findings of research studies into testosterone and aggression include the following:

- Archer (1991) carried out a meta-analysis of five studies and found a low positive correlation between testosterone and aggression.

- A larger meta-analysis of 45 studies (Book *et al.* 2001) found a mean correlation of 0.14 between testosterone and aggression.

- Olweus *et al.* (1980, 1988) compared samples of institutionalized delinquent boys and non-delinquent male students. They found that although testosterone

The challenge hypothesis

The challenge hypothesis, originally formulated to explain aggression in birds, proposes that, in monogamous species, testosterone levels should only rise above the baseline level in response to social challenges (Wingfield *et al.* 1990). As humans are essentially monogamous, we might expect male testosterone levels to rise sharply in response to social challenges such as male–male aggression or threats to reproductive success. The challenges might be direct, such as a dispute over a woman, or indirect, e.g. a dispute over resources or status, both of which are linked to reproductive success in humans. One would expect, therefore, that competitive encounters between young men would lead to an increase in levels of testosterone.

was slightly higher in the delinquent sample, the difference was not statistically significant. Delinquents with a history of violent crimes had slightly higher testosterone levels than those with a history of non-violent offences, but again the difference was not statistically significant. The researchers did, however, find that adolescents with higher levels of testosterone were likely to respond more vigorously in response to challenges from teachers and peers.

Testosterone and aggression: experimental research

Key research: Kouri et al. (1995) and Pope *et al.* (2000)

A problem with many studies of the relationship between testosterone and dominant or aggressive behaviour is that they merely provide a correlation between the two variables, and of course, correlation does not prove causation. However, if the administration of testosterone were followed by an increase in dominant behaviour, then there would be a stronger case for proposing a causal relationship between the two variables. Two experiments have done just that.

- In one study, using a double-blind procedure, young men were given doses of either testosterone or a placebo. They were then paired with a fictitious participant and told that each member of the pair could, by pushing a button, reduce the amount of cash received by the other person. The participant was also told that the other individual was reducing the cash that the participant was receiving. Participants who received testosterone rather than the placebo pushed the button significantly more times (Kouri *et al.* 1995).

- A second study with the same design was carried out with men aged 20 to 50 years (Pope *et al.* 2000). This time, however, testosterone was administered over a six-week period; in all other ways, the experimental design was the same. Results indicated that those who had received the testosterone pushed the button many more times than those who had received the placebo over the same time period.

Evaluation

- *Experimental method* – Because these studies used the experimental method, they enable us to claim more confidently that testosterone can *cause* aggressively dominant behaviour.

1 Check what is meant by a 'double-blind' procedure and explain why it is important in the studies by Kouri *et al.* (1995) and Pope *et al.* (2000).

2 What ethical issues are raised by these studies? How might they be dealt with?

Although much research (particularly research with non-human animals) has concentrated on the relationship between testosterone and aggression, in humans (and other primates) higher testosterone is more associated with the type of dominance that *sometimes* entails aggression. Whereas aggression is behaviour that is intended to inflict physical injury on another individual, dominance is behaviour intended to gain or maintain status (Booth *et al.* 2006). The majority of dominance behaviours are not aggressive, that is, they are not intended to cause physical harm.

Now read the Key research panel 'Testosterone and aggression: experimental research'.

Cortisol and aggression

Van Goozen *et al.* (2007) claim that that there is a link between aggression and the hormone cortisol. Cortisol is produced by the adrenal medulla and is an important part of the body's reaction to stress. The relationship between cortisol and aggression is an inverse correlation, as *lower* levels of cortisol are associated with *higher* levels of aggressive behaviour. Studies have reported low levels of cortisol in habitually violent offenders (Virkkunen 1985) and also aggressive schoolchildren (Tennes and Kreye 1985).

Why would people with lower levels of cortisol be more aggressive? The possibilities include:

1 having low autonomic nervous system (ANS) arousal (and therefore low cortisol levels) is aversive, or unpleasant; aggressive behaviour is then an attempt to create stressful situations which provoke ANS activation and cortisol release

2 cortisol plays an important mediating role in aggression by inhibiting the likelihood of aggressive behaviour. A study by Popma *et al.* (2006) revealed a significant interaction between cortisol and testosterone in relation to overt aggression; they found a significant positive relationship between testosterone and overt aggression in participants with low cortisol levels but not in those with high cortisol levels.

Evaluation of hormonal mechanisms in aggression

- *Inconsistent evidence on testosterone and aggression* – The relationship between testosterone and aggression is far from clear cut. A number of studies have found that high testosterone levels correlate positively with high levels of aggression, but other studies have found no such relationship. For example, Bain *et al.* (1987) found no significant differences in testosterone levels between men who had been charged with murder or violent assault, and men who had been charged with nonviolent crimes such as burglary. Kreuz and Rose (1972) also found no difference in testosterone levels in a group of 21 young prisoners who had been classified, according to their prison records, as either 'fighting' or 'non-fighting' while in prison. However, the 10 prisoners with

histories of more violent crimes in their adolescence did have significantly higher levels of testosterone than the 11 prisoners without such a history. The researchers concluded that 'within a population that is predisposed by virtue of social factors to develop antisocial behaviours, levels of testosterone may be an important additional factor in placing individuals at risk to commit more aggressive crimes in adolescence'. This suggests that within a population predisposed to violent behaviour, testosterone may be an important additional factor that places individuals at risk for violent or criminal behaviour.

- *The positive influence of testosterone* – Zitzmann (2006) argues that the link between testosterone and aggression is most probably only relevant in strength athletes (such as weightlifters) who may supplement their testosterone to excessively high levels. However, among many older males, testosterone supplements have been positive and found to enhance vigour and energy. In addition, reduced testosterone in older males is associated with depressive disorders. Barrett-Connor *et al.* (1999) found that depression increased with age (in the range 50 to 89 years), and this increase in depression was also clearly associated with lower testosterone levels, independent of other factors, such as weight change and levels of physical activity. Increases in positive mood and decreases in negative mood with testosterone replacement therapy were confirmed in a study of 208 men with testosterone deficiency (McNicholas *et al.* 2003).

Strength athletes may risk becoming more aggressive if they supplement their testosterone levels excessively.

- *Research support for cortisol link* – Support for the inverse correlation between cortisol and aggression is evident in a number of longitudinal studies. For example, McBurnett *et al.* (2000) evaluated 38 boys, aged 7 to 12, who had been referred to a clinic, for problem behaviours. The children's behaviours were evaluated annually for four years. Salivary cortisol level measurements were taken during the second and fourth years of the study. The researchers found that boys with lower cortisol concentrations exhibited three times the number of aggressive symptoms compared with boys with fluctuating or higher cortisol levels. The boys with low cortisol levels were also consistently named as the most aggressive and the 'meanest' by peers, that is three times as often as the boys who had higher cortisol concentrations at either sampling time.

- *Lack of consistent research evidence* – Although a number of studies have found evidence of lower cortisol levels in aggressive samples, many other studies have found no significant differences between aggressive samples and controls. Some studies (e.g. Gerra *et al.* 1997) have even reported *higher* cortisol concentrations in participants with higher levels of aggression.

IDA **The issue of gender bias in research**

... minant females high in testosterone? ...r Prime Minister Margaret Thatcher was ...ed as an aggressive male in the 1980s TV ...show 'Spitting Image'

...what we know about the relationship ...testosterone and aggression is based on ...males, because they produce far more ...e than females. As a result, the hormone ...measure, and its effects are clearer in ...n females. Currently, there is too little ...testosterone-behaviour associations to ...ossible link between testosterone, ...d aggression in females. Some ...Grant and France 2001) has found ...high testosterone' women *are* more ...dominating behaviour, but other ...und no such relationship. Archer and ...ggest that some women may ...nging situations with increased ...so display characteristics such as ...d dominance. What is clear, ...h so many conflicting results, the ...n testosterone and aggression in ...stablished than it is for males.

The role of genetic factors in aggressive behaviour

The relationship be... complex one. A subs... genome is devoted to *enes and behaviou...* expressed in the brain th...*portion of the hu...* 2002). Research into beha...*and more genes a...* that most aspects of behaviou...*er organ (Hamer...* to some degree. Our increasing...*s has shown* factors in behaviours such as aggr...*by heredity* the good (e.g. by improving psyc... forms of intervention). However, the...*genetic* could be used to discriminate against p...*for* 'quick fixes' for the social problems that w... create in our society.

Researchers have approached the investigatio... factors in aggressive behaviour in a number of ways to try and establish whether aggression is ... product of inherited characteristics (nature) or environmental influences (nurture). These methods include twin and adoption studies as well as a search for individual genes that may influence the development of aggressive behaviour. Read the 'Twin studies' panel before reading further.

Twin and adoption studies

Twin studies

In humans, aggressive behaviour is more highly correlated in identical twins than in fraternal twins. For example, McGuffin and Gottesman (1985) found a **concordance rate** of 87 per cent for aggressive and antisocial behaviour for MZ twin pairs, compared with 72 per cent for DZ twin pairs. What is notable about this finding, however, is that it indicates that family environment, shared across siblings (DZ twins in this case), exerts an important

Twin studies

...g twins raised in the ...nozygotic (MZ or ...heir genes, while dizygotic ...are only 50 per cent of their ...ompares the similarity between ...the similarity between sets of DZ ...ch as aggression, and finds that MZ ...alike in terms of this trait, then this 'extra' ...uld be due to genetic rather than ...ntal factors. This method is used to estimate ...tability of traits such as aggression, i.e. the ...entage of variance in a population that can be ...tributable to genes.

Most twin studies rely...
same family envi...
identical) tw...
(DZ or f...
ge...

Twin studies are based on a number of assumptions. As we shall see, however, these assumptions are not always met (Winerman, 2004):

1 *Random mating* – Twin study researchers assume that individuals are as likely to choose partners who are different from themselves as they are to choose partners who are similar for a particular trait. If, instead, as research on relationship formation suggests, people tend to choose mates who are *like* themselves, then DZ twins could share more than 50 per cent of their genes and hence more similarities on genetically influenced traits because they would receive similar genes from their mothers and fathers.

2 *Equal environments* – Twin researchers also assume that MZ and DZ twins raised in the same homes experience the same environments. However, research suggests that parents, teachers, peers and others may treat MZ twins more similarly than they do DZ twins.

3 *Gene–environment interaction* – Some researchers believe that *interactions* between genes and environment, rather than genes and environment separately, may influence many traits, including aggression. Many twin study designs do not take this complication into account.

---

influence on juvenile delinquency. Such studies support the importance of genetic factors in aggression, but also highlight the significance of environmental factors, particularly among young people. A problem for researchers, therefore, is to disentangle the relative effects of each.

- *Meta-analysis* – A meta-analysis by Mason and Frick (1994) of 12 twin studies (and three adoption studies) involving 3795 twin pairs concluded that approximately 50 per cent of the difference between antisocial and non-antisocial behaviours could be attributed to genetic factors, with larger estimates of genetic influence found for more violent behaviours than for less violent behaviours.

- Coccaro *et al.* (1997) – In one of the few twin studies specifically to investigate aggressive behaviour rather than more general antisocial or criminal behaviour, Coccaro and colleagues assessed the degree of genetic and environmental influences on aggression in male participants. Data from 182 MZ twin pairs and 118 DZ twin pairs were analysed. From the data they estimated that:

  – genes accounted for more than 40 per cent of the individual differences in aggression

  – environmental influences accounted for around 50 per cent of individual differences in *physical* aggression, and about 70 per cent of individual differences in *verbal* aggression.

Adoption studies

A second way of studying genetic factors in ... behaviour is by studying children who have b... up by adults who are not their biologic... researchers find a greater similarity in level... between adopted children and their *bi*... than between adopted children and... parents, then this suggests an importan... is at work. If, however, the children... their adoptive parents (with whom t... than their biological parents, the... environmental influences are m... development of aggressive beha...

- *Danish study* – In one of... studies, Hutchings and... over 14 000 adoptions... significant positive corre... convictions for crimina... parents (particularly...

Destined for a li...
crime? Adoptic...
studies sugge...
children who...
adopted ma...
more simi...
their biol...
parents...
adopti...

Are d...
Forme...
portray...
puppet...

Much of...
between...
studies of...
testostero...
is easier to...
males than...
research on...
explain any p...
dominance a...
research (e.g...
likely to report...
studies have fo...
Coyne (2005) su...
respond to challe...
testosterone, and...
aggressivenes a...
however, is that w...
relationship betwee...
females is far less e...

consistently named as the most aggressive and the 'meanest' by peers, that is three times as often as the boys who had higher cortisol concentrations at either sampling time.

- *Lack of consistent research evidence* – Although a number of studies have found evidence of lower cortisol levels in aggressive samples, many other studies have found no significant differences between aggressive samples and controls. Some studies (e.g. Gerra *et al.* 1997) have even reported *higher* cortisol concentrations in participants with higher levels of aggression.

IDA

The issue of gender bias in research

Are dominant females high in testosterone? Former Prime Minister Margaret Thatcher was portrayed as an aggressive male in the 1980s TV puppet show 'Spitting Image'

Much of what we know about the relationship between testosterone and aggression is based on studies of males, because they produce far more testosterone than females. As a result, the hormone is easier to measure, and its effects are clearer in males than in females. Currently, there is too little research on testosterone-behaviour associations to explain any possible link between testosterone, dominance and aggression in females. Some research (e.g. Grant and France 2001) has found evidence that 'high testosterone' women *are* more likely to report dominating behaviour, but other studies have found no such relationship. Archer and Coyne (2005) suggest that some women may respond to challenging situations with increased testosterone, and so display characteristics such as aggressiveness and dominance. What is clear, however, is that with so many conflicting results, the relationship between testosterone and aggression in females is far less established than it is for males.

The role of genetic factors in aggressive behaviour

The relationship between genes and behaviour is a complex one. A substantial proportion of the human genome is devoted to behaviour, and more genes are expressed in the brain than in any other organ (Hamer 2002). Research into behavioural **genetics** has shown that most aspects of behaviour are influenced by heredity to some degree. Our increasing knowledge about genetic factors in behaviours such as aggression can be used for the good (e.g. by improving psychiatric diagnoses or forms of intervention). However, the same information could be used to discriminate against people or to provide 'quick fixes' for the social problems that violent individuals create in our society.

Researchers have approached the investigation of genetic factors in aggressive behaviour in a number of different ways to try and establish whether aggression is more a product of inherited characteristics (nature) or environmental influences (nurture). These methods include twin and adoption studies as well as a search for individual genes that may influence the development of aggressive behaviour. Read the 'Twin studies' panel before reading further.

Twin and adoption studies

Twin studies

In humans, aggressive behaviour is more highly correlated in identical twins than in fraternal twins. For example, McGuffin and Gottesman (1985) found a **concordance rate** of 87 per cent for aggressive and antisocial behaviour for MZ twin pairs, compared with 72 per cent for DZ twin pairs. What is notable about this finding, however, is that it indicates that family environment, shared across siblings (DZ twins in this case), exerts an important

Twin studies

Most twin studies rely on studying twins raised in the same family environments. Monozygotic (MZ or identical) twins share all of their genes, while dizygotic (DZ or fraternal) twins share only 50 per cent of their genes. If a researcher compares the similarity between sets of MZ twins to the similarity between sets of DZ twins for a trait such as aggression, and finds that MZ twins are more alike in terms of this trait, then this 'extra' likeness should be due to genetic rather than environmental factors. This method is used to estimate the heritability of traits such as aggression, i.e. the percentage of variance in a population that can be attributable to genes.

Twin studies are based on a number of assumptions. As we shall see, however, these assumptions are not always met (Winerman, 2004):

1 *Random mating* – Twin study researchers assume that individuals are as likely to choose partners who are different from themselves as they are to choose partners who are similar for a particular trait. If, instead, as research on relationship formation suggests, people tend to choose mates who are *like* themselves, then DZ twins could share more than 50 per cent of their genes and hence more similarities on genetically influenced traits because they would receive similar genes from their mothers and fathers.

2 *Equal environments* – Twin researchers also assume that MZ and DZ twins raised in the same homes experience the same environments. However, research suggests that parents, teachers, peers and others may treat MZ twins more similarly than they do DZ twins.

3 *Gene–environment interaction* – Some researchers believe that *interactions* between genes and environment, rather than genes and environment separately, may influence many traits, including aggression. Many twin study designs do not take this complication into account.

influence on juvenile delinquency. Such studies support the importance of genetic factors in aggression, but also highlight the significance of environmental factors, particularly among young people. A problem for researchers, therefore, is to disentangle the relative effects of each.

- *Meta-analysis* – A meta-analysis by Mason and Frick (1994) of 12 twin studies (and three adoption studies) involving 3795 twin pairs concluded that approximately 50 per cent of the difference between antisocial and non-antisocial behaviours could be attributed to genetic factors, with larger estimates of genetic influence found for more violent behaviours than for less violent behaviours.

- Coccaro *et al.* (1997) – In one of the few twin studies specifically to investigate aggressive behaviour rather than more general antisocial or criminal behaviour, Coccaro and colleagues assessed the degree of genetic and environmental influences on aggression in male participants. Data from 182 MZ twin pairs and 118 DZ twin pairs were analysed. From the data they estimated that:

  – genes accounted for more than 40 per cent of the individual differences in aggression

  – environmental influences accounted for around 50 per cent of individual differences in *physical* aggression, and about 70 per cent of individual differences in *verbal* aggression.

Adoption studies

A second way of studying genetic factors in aggressive behaviour is by studying children who have been brought up by adults who are not their biological parents. If researchers find a greater similarity in levels of aggression between adopted children and their *biological* parents than between adopted children and their adoptive parents, then this suggests an important genetic influence is at work. If, however, the children are more similar to their adoptive parents (with whom they share no genes) than their biological parents, then this suggests that environmental influences are more important in the development of aggressive behaviour.

- *Danish study* – In one of the largest-ever adoption studies, Hutchings and Mednick (1973) reviewed over 14 000 adoptions in Denmark. They found a significant positive correlation between the number of convictions for criminal violence among the biological parents (particularly the fathers), and the number

Destined for a life of crime? Adoption studies suggest that children who are adopted may show more similarities to their biological parents than to their adoptive parents

of convictions for criminal violence among their adopted sons.

- *Meta-analysis* – In a meta-analysis of 24 twin and adoption studies concerned with the genetic basis of aggression, Miles and Carey (1997) found a strong genetic influence, which accounted for as much as 50 per cent of the variance in aggression. Although they found that both genes *and* family environment were influential in determining aggression in young people, at later ages the influence of the rearing environment decreased and the influence of genes increased.

Read the Key research panel 'Meta-analysis of twin and adoption studies' below.

Meta-analysis of twin and adoption studies

Key research: Rhee and Waldman (2002)

Rhee and Waldman carried out a meta-analysis of 51 twin and adoption studies comprising over 87 000 individuals. Antisocial behaviour was operationalized in terms of:

- psychiatric diagnoses, such as antisocial personality disorder
- delinquency
- behavioural aggression.

They calculated that the genetic component of antisocial behaviour across these 51 studies was approximately 40 per cent, and the environmental contribution around 60 per cent. They found little evidence of gender differences in the data (i.e. little evidence that genetic factors affected boys and girls differently).

Evaluation of research method

- *Reporting aggression* – The studies included in this meta-analysis used either self-report (where the participants assessed their own levels of aggression), or reports by others of the participants' levels of aggression. Significant differences were found between these two different methods, with a genetic component assessed at 39 per cent for studies where a self-report had been used, and 53 per cent where the assessment was done by another person. This suggests that the *method* of assessing aggression plays an important moderating role in estimates of genetic influences.

1 Why was it important to operationalize antisocial behaviour?

2 Why do you think that the two methods used to assess aggression led to different estimates of the genetic component in antisocial behaviour?

Evaluation of twin and adoption studies

- *The imperfect nature of twin studies* – The evidence for the role of genes from twin studies is compelling, but all such studies share an important common flaw. Finding large numbers of MZ twins who are reared apart is extremely rare and, therefore, in a classic twin study, researchers must compare MZ and DZ twins in order to assess which type of twin pair is more similar on a given trait (thus demonstrating the importance of genetic influences on that trait). However, not only do MZ twins share genes, they also share an environment that frequently treats them more similarly than it treats DZ twins. Because they look so much alike, society tends to treat MZ twins as one person or as two 'versions' of the same person. Consequently, twin studies are not the perfect genetics versus environment experiment that we would like to imagine they are.

- *Gender differences in heritability* – Button et al. (2004), in a study of 258 twin pairs aged 11 to 18, found that both aggressive and non-aggressive antisocial behaviour are subject to significant genetic influences. The heritability of *aggressive* antisocial behaviour, however, was significantly higher in girls than in boys (this was not the case for non-aggressive antisocial behaviour, such as truancy and lying). These results suggest a stronger genetic effect on aggression in females than in males.

- *Problems with the interpretation of adoption studies* – Adoption studies have a number of methodological problems which limit the conclusions that can be drawn from them. One problem is that in some countries, such as New Zealand and the US, children given up for adoption display a higher rate of antisocial behaviour (including aggression) *at the time of their adoption* compared with the general population (Fergusson et al. 1995; Sharma et al. 1998). Tremblay (2003) maintains that the *parents* who give up their children for adoption also display higher levels of antisocial behaviour compared with the general population and with potential adoptive parents. Consequently, correlations between adoptees and their biological parents may be due to *either* the transmission of antisocial genes from the biological parents *or* to environmental influences, such as the biological parents' antisocial behaviour (before the adoption), or from feelings of abandonment.

Genes for aggression

Finding a 'gene' that triggers aggression in humans seems fairly unlikely, but researchers have identified a number of 'candidate genes' that are thought to contribute to an increased risk of engaging in antisocial behaviour. Studies in this area typically examine whether one particular variant of a candidate gene occurs more often in people who display aggressive behaviour than in a comparison group.

Candidate genes: DRD4 and DRD3

As we have already seen, dysfunctions of serotonin and dopamine are thought to increase aggressiveness. Associations have been found between genes associated with both serotonin and dopamine pathways. The dopamine receptor D4 has been the most heavily researched. A meta-analysis of studies of the gene for this receptor (DRD4) found a modest association between DRD4 and a tendency to attention deficit hyperactivity disorder or ADHD (Faraone *et al.* 2001). Another study (Retz *et al.* 2003) found an association between a DRD3 variant (the gene for dopamine receptor D3) and both impulsivity and ADHD-related symptoms in violent offenders.

Candidate gene for MAOA

Researchers have discovered that the gene responsible for producing the enzyme monoamine oxidase A (MAOA) may also be associated with aggressive behaviour. MAOA's job is to break down three neurotransmitters (noradrenaline, serotonin and dopamine) in the brain after they have carried nerve impulses from one cell to another. Noradrenaline is a neurotransmitter that raises blood pressure and increases alertness and is a part of the body's fight or flight response. The other two neurotransmitters are serotonin and dopamine, imbalances of which are often found in patients with high levels of aggression.

The breakthrough for the role of MAOA in aggressive behaviour came with the study of a family in the Netherlands, many of whose male members behaved in a particularly violent and aggressive manner (see Key research panel: Brunner *et al.* 1993). These men were subsequently found to have abnormally low levels of MAOA in their bodies, resulting in extremely high levels of all three neurotransmitters – a finding that casts further doubt on the claim that low levels of serotonin are *always* associated with a rise in aggressive behaviour. A defect in the gene for MAOA was later identified in the violent members of this family; this was absent in its nonviolent members. Before reading further, read the Key research panel 'Aggression and the gene for MAOA'.

Evaluation of genes for aggression

■ *Genes for aggression do not predict aggressive behaviour* – Morley and Hall (2003) argue that genes associated with aggression are not deterministic and only poorly predict the likelihood that an individual will display higher levels of aggressive behaviour than the general population. Additionally, the presence or absence of environmental risk factors cannot be identified by a genetic test, thus making the accurate prediction of specific behaviours even less likely.

Aggression and the gene for MAOA

Key research: Brunner et al. (1993)

In the late 1970s, scientists discovered a family in Nijmegen, in the Netherlands, with a particularly worrying problem – many of the men in the family had a history of extreme violence. One had tried to rape his sister; another had tried to run his boss down with a car. One of the family members had traced this 'condition' back as far as 1870, identifying nine other males with similar behavioural characteristics. The first clue as to the origins of this behaviour was that all the violent family members were men. Brunner and colleagues discovered that the violent men in this family all suffered from a genetic defect on their X chromosome, a defect that cripples an enzyme which regulates aggressive behaviour. Brunner and colleagues analysed the X chromosomes of 28 members of the Dutch family and found a marker on the X chromosome which was present in all the violent men in the family but not in the nonviolent men. One particular gene for MAOA lay in the vicinity of this marker. Brunner and colleagues reasoned that if the violent men were suffering from defective MAOA, excess levels of the neurotransmitters that are normally broken down by MAOA would accumulate in their bodies and in their urine. When they tested the men's urine, they found

excess levels of all three neurotransmitters, and extraordinarily low levels of the substances normally left over after MAOA has done its work. Brunner and colleagues believe that the excess neurotransmitters may in some way predispose the men to violence when they are under stress.

Evaluation

● *Limited influence of gene* – Although this study is informative, the assumption that the gene responsible for MAOA is *the* gene for aggressive behaviour has not been widely endorsed, not even by Brunner himself. Brunner contended that it was unlikely that there was a direct causal relationship between a single gene and a specific behaviour. Rather, genetic deficiencies may exert *some* influence on an individual's behaviour, but they are not the *sole* cause of the behaviour.

● *Role of environmental factors* – The kind of behaviour found in the family studied by Brunner and colleagues may be more widespread than in 'normal' families not because of any inherited genetic disorders but because of shared environmental factors, such as bad parenting and inappropriate role modelling.

■ *Positive implications of genetic research* – Findings from genetic research on antisocial and violent behaviour may have some valuable uses in offender treatment and rehabilitation. Morley and Hall (2003) suggest that information obtained from genetic studies may be used to help develop new treatments for personality disorders that have been identified as risk factors for criminal behaviour. What is less certain, however, is what the consequences of such genetic tests might be for criminal cases, where the findings may be cited as evidence of a defendant's diminished responsibility. (See the panel: 'The genetics of aggression and the question of free will'.)

■ *Gene–environment interaction* – Rather than either genetics or environment alone being responsible for the development of a particular trait, some researchers believe that *interactions* between genes and environment influence many traits, including aggression. For example, Caspi *et al.* (2002) found that male children who had been maltreated *and* possessed a variant of the gene that resulted in an *increased* expression of MAOA were less likely to express antisocial (including violent) behaviour. Under normal circumstances, an increase in MAOA would be expected to result in a decrease in serotonin (and therefore *increased* aggressive behaviour). Although the reasons for this disparity are not known, Caspi and colleagues believe that it is possible that early abuse alters serotonin in some way or that decreases in serotonin affect some types of antisocial behaviour but not others.

IDA — The genetics of aggression and the question of free will

Can we hold people responsible for their genetic makeup or their early experiences? How much responsibility should people bear for their actions if they possess a genotype which predisposes them to violent criminal behaviour?

Some legal experts now question the assumption that a violent offender can still exercise free will *despite* possessing a genetic predisposition to violent crime (see 'Psychology in Context', p.139). Such a change may force us to revise our notions of moral and legal responsibility. However, future research may also provide the tools to help identify potential offenders sooner and intervene before it is too late.

CHECK YOUR UNDERSTANDING

Check your understanding of biological approaches to explaining aggression. Try to do this from memory. You can check your answers by looking back through Topic 2, Biological explanations of aggression.

1. Explain the main difference between the serotonin and dopamine explanations of aggression.

2. Explain two critical points concerning the serotonin and dopamine explanations of aggression.

3. Outline, in 50 words, the relationship between testosterone and aggression.

4. What was the main conclusion of Archer's meta-analysis of the relationship between testosterone and aggression?

5. What is meant by the 'challenge hypothesis' in the context of aggression?

6. Outline, in 50 words, the relationship between cortisol and aggression.

7. Explain three critical points concerning the relationship between hormones and aggression.

8. Outline the main conclusions that can be drawn from twin and adoption studies of aggression.

9. Explain three critical points concerning twin and adoption studies of aggression.

10. In about 50 words, outline the relationship between aggression and the gene for MAOA.

Evolutionary explanations of human aggression

In this final topic, we take a different approach to the origins of aggression. As we can see from Carrier's research (Psychology in context), it is possible that at least some aspects of human aggression have their origins in the challenges faced by our ancestors millions of years ago. Some physical characteristics (such as a squat physique and stance) and some behaviour (such as aggression to deter other males from approaching a female partner) would have made it more likely that our ancestors survived and passed on their genes. How successful they were at this has been defined as a measure of their **reproductive fitness**. The very fact that they *are* our ancestors means that they were successful; early humans with different characteristics were not successful and consequently failed to pass on *their* characteristics.

Natural selection effectively weeds out characteristics that confer no advantage for survival and reproduction, and 'selects' those characteristics that are advantageous. Such characteristics help the individuals who possess them to survive, and so are referred to as '**adaptive**'. A major concern for our male ancestors was to find a mate, and then having found one, to hold on to her. This need to find and retain a mate brings males into competition with other males and, according to Carrier (2007), is the root of much male aggressive behaviour. Among early humans, males lived in fear of losing their mate to another male, something that would have devastating consequences for them in terms of being able to pass on their genes to the next generation. This may well have led to the development of male sexual **jealousy**, a state of fear caused by a real or imagined threat to their status as an exclusive sexual partner. Male sexual jealousy was caused by the female's suspected sexual **infidelity** (having sexual relations with other men). Because female sexual infidelity may result in her leaving for a new partner,

---

Psychology in context — Aggression and leg length

Recent research (Carrier 2007) suggests that ape-like human ancestors known as *australopiths* maintained short legs for two million years because a squat physique and stance helped males fight over access to females. For example, short legs make you more stable and less easy to knock over. All modern great apes – humans, chimps, orangutans, gorillas and bonobos – engage in at least some aggressive behaviour as males compete for females.

To find out how aggression related to leg length, Carrier compared Australian aborigines with eight primate species, including gorillas, chimpanzees, bonobos and orangutans. He used the scientific literature to obtain typical hind limb lengths, and data on two physical features that previously have been shown to correlate with male–male competition and aggressiveness in primates: male–female body size ratio and male–female canine tooth-size ratio. Research has shown that males fight more in the species where there is a greater difference between the body and canine tooth size of males and females.

The study found that hind limb length correlated inversely with both indicators of aggressiveness: primate species with greater male–female differences in body weight and length of the canine teeth had shorter legs, and displayed more male–male aggression.

Carrier argues that if we want to prevent violence we have to understand *why* we are violent, and that means looking at:

- the conditions under which aggressive behaviour evolved in the first place
- the adaptive problems it was designed to solve.

He concludes that our evolutionary past may help us to understand the circumstances in which humans behave violently. However, Carrier acknowledges that male–male competition doesn't fully explain human violence.

1 In what *other* circumstances faced by our distant ancestors might aggression have been particularly useful?

2 If the short legs of the *australopiths* did not evolve because of male–male aggression among our ancestors, for what other reasons might they have evolved?

3 To find out more about this research, read Carrier's paper at: http://www.anthro.utah.edu/PDFs/carrier-e-61-596.pdf

or bearing the child of another man, it had to be deterred at all costs. For our early ancestors, therefore, sexual jealousy was an adaptive response leading to a number of adaptive mate-retention behaviours (some of which are discussed in the next section).To find out more about the evolutionary approach to behaviour, look at pp.6–9 in the Introduction to this book.

Infidelity and jealousy

Daly and Wilson (1988) claim that men, in particular, have evolved a number of mate-retention strategies to deter their mate from either leaving them or committing adultery (infidelity) with another man. Retaining a mate is of great importance to a male as, without a mate to bear and raise his children, the chance of passing on his genes to the next generation is reduced. Mate-retention strategies, therefore, are ways of enhancing reproductive fitness. These strategies range from vigilance (e.g. mate 'guarding') to violence as ways of deterring infidelity. One strategy is

'direct guarding', whereby males attempt to restrict their partner's sexual autonomy to prevent other males from gaining access. This can take the form of prohibiting their partners from speaking to or interacting with other men. Other forms of guarding might include snooping through personal belongings to look for signs of infidelity.

Cuckoldry and sexual jealousy

Cuckoldry occurs when a woman deceives her male partner into investing in offspring conceived with another man. Although the risks of cuckoldry are high for women (e.g. retaliation, loss of partner leading to loss of resources for offspring), the risks are even higher for males. Cuckolded men lose both invested resources and reproductive opportunity (Platek and Shackelford 2006). Males have evolved a number of strategies to stop their mates from straying and thus prevent themselves from being cuckolded. According to the evolutionary approach, all such mate-retention strategies are driven by sexual

 HOW SCIENCE WORKS

Mate retention and violence against women

Key research: Shackelford et al. (2005)

Shackelford and colleagues studied a sample of 461 men and 560 women from US universities or their surrounding communities. All participants were in committed, heterosexual relationships.

- Study 1: The mean age of the 461 male participants was 24.2 years; the mean age of their partners was 23.2 years; and the mean length of their relationships was 37.3 months.
- Study 2: The mean age of the 560 female participants was 21.5 years; the mean age of their partners was 23.7 years; and the mean length of their relationships was 28.8 months.

Note: None of the men in Study 1 were married to any of the women in Study 2. Therefore the two studies were independent of each other.

- In Study 1 – the male participants completed the MRI (Mate Retention Inventory) concerning their use of 104 different mate-retention strategies in the previous month, ranging from 0 (never) to 3 (often). Males were also asked how often they performed each of 26 violent acts against their partners, and how often their partners sustained each of 20 different injuries as a result of their violence.
- In Study 2 – the female participants answered questions about their partner's use of mate-retention strategies with them, and the degree to which their partner had been violent towards them.

Shackelford and colleagues found in Study 1 that:

- men's use of two broad types of mate-retention strategy was positively correlated with their

violence scores. The two mate-retention strategies were:
  – 'intersexual negative inducements' (e.g. shouting at her for looking at another man)
  – 'direct guarding' (e.g. monopolizing her time at a party).
- men who consistently used emotional manipulation (e.g. making her feel guilty or saying they would kill themselves if she left) were more prone to use violence in their relationship.

In Study 2, they found that:

- the results confirmed the validity of the findings from Study 1, with reports of 'intersexual negative inducements' and 'direct guarding' being associated with female-directed violence.
- women also stated that male partners who used emotional manipulation were also more likely to have used violence against them.

Evaluation

- *Limitation of correlations* – Shackelford and colleagues recognize the major limitation of this research: as the data were correlational, they were not able to establish a causal relationship between the use of mate-retention strategies and violence against women.
- *Lack of information* – Another limitation of the research is that it does not control for *actual* relationship threats (a man's suspicion or knowledge of his partner's infidelities).

jealousy: an adaptation that evolved in males as a way of dealing with paternal uncertainty. Because fertilization in humans is internal, males, until recently, could never be 100 per cent certain that offspring were their own. One consequence of cuckoldry is that the male may unwittingly invest his resources in offspring that are not his own. Sexual jealousy, therefore, serves to help prevent the female mating with other males outside the pair bond, and so it can be seen as an adaptive response. Sexual coercion (i.e. forcing an unwilling partner to have sex) is a tactic used by some males to reduce the risk of cuckoldry. The 'cuckoldry risk hypothesis' (Camilleri 2004) predicts that males will be more willing to use sexually coercive tactics such as partner rape when the risk of cuckoldry is high, for example when they suspect infidelity or where there have been previous instances of infidelity. According to Lalumière et al. (2005) some men carry out partner rape in order to decrease paternity uncertainty. Thornhill and Thornhill (1992) argue that a woman who resists having sex with her partner might be signalling to him that she has been sexually unfaithful, thus increasing the male's sexual jealousy and fear of cuckoldry.

Mate retention and violence

Buss and Shackelford (1997) examined mate-retention tactics in married couples. They studied 214 individuals and found that, compared to women, men reported a significantly higher use of debasement (e.g. giving in to her every wish) and intra-sexual threats (e.g. threatening to beat up the other man). Women, on the other hand, reported a greater use of verbal possession signals (e.g. indicating to other women that 'he was taken') and threats of punishing infidelity (e.g. by leaving her man if he was ever unfaithful). They also found that, compared to men married to older women, men married to younger women reported devoting greater effort to mate-retention tactics, including commitment manipulation (e.g. professing love and commitment to the relationship), violence against rival men and threats against the female partner. Now read the Key research panel 'Mate retention and violence against women'.

Sexual jealousy may lead to violence against women

Evaluation of infidelity and jealousy as explanations for aggression

- *Use of mate-retention tactics* – The claim that sexual jealousy is a major cause of violence against women is supported by studies of battered women, where victims frequently cite extreme sexual jealousy on the part of male partners as the major cause of violence against them (Dobash and Dobash 1984). The use of direct guarding as a mate-retention tactic is also evident in a study by Wilson et al. (1995), who found that among women who reported the use of this tactic by their male partners (e.g. not allowing her to talk to other men) 72 per cent had required medical attention following an assault by their male partner.

- *Research on sexual coercion* – Research tends to support the idea that sexual coercion of females by their male partners is an adaptive response to the threat of infidelity. Camilleri (2004) found that the risk of a partner's infidelity predicted the likelihood of sexual coercion in men but not women. This is important for an adaptive explanation, as it is men who are at risk of being cuckolded, not women. Goetz and Shackelford (2006) also found that men who had sexually coerced their partners were more likely to report that they thought their partners were being unfaithful. Women who reported that their partners had sexually coerced them were more likely to admit to having been unfaithful.

- **HOW SCIENCE WORKS** *Practical applications of research* – An important implication of research in this area is that mate-retention tactics may be seen as early indicators of potential violence against a female partner. The use of mate-retention tactics can alert friends and family members to the danger signs that might lead to future violence in relationships. Relationship counselling may then be used before the situation escalates into the type of violence reported in the Dobash and Dobash (1984) study described above.

The evolution of murder

UK law defines murder as taking a life with 'the intention to kill or do very serious harm'. Roughly one in 15 000 people is murdered in the United States each year (Stolinsky and Stolinsky 2000). When computed over a 75-year lifespan, however, this equates to approximately a one in 200 chance of any one individual being murdered at some point in their lifetime. Fortunately, the risk is considerably less than this in the UK (about one in every 100 000 loses their life to murder), but in other countries the risk is much greater. In Colombia and South Africa, for example, the lifetime risk of being a victim of murder is close to one in 20, and among the Yanomamo of South America this figure rises to a staggering one in three (Chagnon 1988).

Before reading on, look at the activity 'Killing by conspecifics'.

Murder as an adaptive response

Buss and Duntley (2006) propose that humans possess adaptations (i.e. characteristics that make it more likely they will survive, given the typical challenges they will face during their lifetime) that have evolved specifically through the process of natural selection to produce what we now refer to as murder. The activation of these evolved adaptations is determined by factors such as:

1 the degree of genetic relatedness between killer and victim

2 the relative status of the killer and victim

3 the sex of killer and victim

4 the size and strength of the killers' and victims' families and social allies.

According to the evolutionary perspective, murder could not have evolved as a strategy unless it was associated with greater reproductive success than competing strategies. In most circumstances, the extremely high costs of committing murder would have outweighed the benefits of adopting it as a strategy. Buss and Duntley propose, however, that rare circumstances would have occurred sufficiently often in our evolutionary history where the benefits of murder would have outweighed the costs. In certain sets of recurrent circumstances, therefore, murder would have been the best of available strategies. Before reading further, try the activity below.

Buss and Duntley (2006) claim that for our ancestors, murder was functional in solving adaptive problems such as:

- *preventing harm* – e.g. the exploitation, injury, rape, or killing of the individual, their family, mates and allies by other members of the same species

- *reputation management* - e.g. avoiding being perceived as easily exploited, injured, raped, or killed by others

- *protecting resources* – e.g. territory, shelter, and food.

Predisposing factors for murder

Daly and Wilson (1988) noted that although men commit the vast majority of murders, this form of aggression is not restricted to males alone (see Figure 4.1). They observed that males and females commit murder for different reasons. Men are more likely to kill other men whom they perceive to be sexual rivals or those who challenge their position in the dominance hierarchy. Women, on the other hand, are more likely to kill in self-defence, e.g. murdering male sexual partners who have been physically abusing them (see Table 4.1).

Nature of murder	Frequency
Male offender/Male victim	65.3%
Male offender/Female victim	22.7%
Female offender/Male victim	9.6%
Female offender/Female victim	2.4%
Source: FBI, Supplementary Homicide Reports, 1976-2005.	

Table 4.1 *Most victims and perpetrators in homicides (murders) are male*

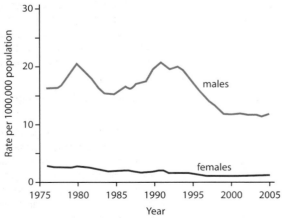

Figure 4.1 *Homicide offending by gender, 1976–2005*

Wilson and Daly (1985) also observed that murders tended to be age related, peaking for males around their early 20s, a time when males are in the peak years of their reproductive competition. Research suggests the

following are common predisposing factors in the competition for reproductive status:

- *Sexual jealousy* – This appears to be an important cause of same-sex aggression and murder. Because of the association between infidelity and cuckoldry, men are predominantly both the perpetrators (i.e. the person doing the killing) and also the victims. Daly and Wilson (1988) summarized data from eight studies of same-sex killings that involved 'love triangles' (i.e. a male-female pair bond plus an outsider sexually involved with one of the pair). They found that 92 per cent of these murders involved males killing males and only eight per cent involved females killing another female.

- *Lack of resources* – Research on sexual selection in humans has shown that females are attracted to males who possess resources. Wilson and Daly (1985) suggest that a lack of resources increases male–male competition and the risk of murder. They cite murder statistics in Detroit, US, which showed that 43 per cent of the male victims and 41 per cent of the male perpetrators were unemployed, although the overall unemployment rate for adult males in Detroit at that time was just 11 per cent.

- *Threats to male status* – The biggest single factor related to murder is maleness, the second is youth. In addition to sexual jealousy and lack of resources, threats to status appear to be an important determinant of murder among young men. Daly and Wilson (1988) argue that females are attracted to males who are dominant over other males and, therefore, men are shaped by evolution to seek status. When there is intense competition for scarce resources (e.g. territory, mates) this status is more likely to be threatened than when these resources are in generous supply. Daly and Wilson cite a strong correlation between degree of income inequality and murder rates – countries with more income inequality tend to have higher murder rates. According to the evolutionary perspective, loss of male status would have been catastrophic for the survival and reproduction of our ancestors, and mechanisms to prevent loss of status still operate today when triggered by threatening events.

Evaluation of the evolutionary explanation of murder

- *Comparative evidence* – the 'murder as adaptation' hypothesis is supported by comparative studies of other species. Among mammals, for example, there are many well-documented cases of conspecific (members of the same species) killing. Male lions and cheetahs have been observed killing the offspring of rival males (Ghiglieri 1999). In such cases, the advantage to the killer's reproductive fitness is clear, as the mothers of the killed infants will go into oestrus sooner, allowing the killer to impregnate them with offspring of his own. Among primates, the killing of rival adult males has also been well documented among mountain gorillas (Fossey 1984) and chimpanzees (Wrangham and Peterson 1996).

- *An alternative explanation – the Evolved Goal Hypothesis* – this alternative evolutionary explanation of murder argues that humans have evolved motivations for specific goals (such as 'strive for status' or 'acquire a mate') that were, among our ancestors, associated with greater reproductive success. Goals could be reached by using evolved problem-solving mechanisms. According to this view, there need be no evolved mechanism to engage in a specific behaviour such as murder, only a mechanism to work out how best to achieve a specific goal. Hrdy (1999) claims that our early ancestors would consciously calculate the costs and benefits, as well as any future consequences, of different actions. These calculations might, on occasion, conclude that murder was the best solution to achieve a particular goal.

STRETCH AND CHALLENGE

Activity

Implications of an evolved adaptation for murder

The impact of a murder victim's death goes well beyond the loss of the victim's individual genes. Murder has a series of adverse effects on the victim's inclusive fitness. **Inclusive fitness** is a measure of how successful individuals are in passing on a high proportion of their genes to succeeding generations. Inclusive fitness may be achieved *directly* (through their own offspring) or *indirectly* (by helping close genetic relatives with whom they share a proportion of their genes). The total number of their genes passed on in these ways determines the individual's *inclusive* fitness. The costs to an individual's inclusive fitness as a result of their being killed include:

- *the loss of all future reproduction* – the reproductive costs, therefore, are greater for those killed at younger ages
- *damage to existing children* – they receive fewer resources and are more vulnerable to exploitation or injury by others
- *damage to the extended kin group* – the murder victim can no longer protect or invest in them.

Consequently, it seems likely that humans will have evolved anti-murder defences (such as killing in self-defence) to make murder an increasingly costly strategy to pursue. This creates an 'evolutionary arms race', with the development of deceptive murder strategies (e.g. the use of poison rather than more overt killing) to avoid activating the potential victim's defences against being murdered.

To find out more about this topic go to http://loki.stockton.edu/~duntleyj/pdfs/Duntley-

Evaluation of evolutionary explanations of aggression

- *Limitations* – An evolutionary approach to the understanding of aggression fails to explain why individuals might react in such different ways when faced with the same adaptive problem. Buss and Shackelford (1997) offer an example which highlights this shortcoming. Different men, when confronted with their wife's infidelity, react in very different ways, such as violence (i.e. inter-sexual aggression), or debasement (e.g. giving in to her every whim in an attempt to keep her), or simply avoiding the issue by getting drunk.

- *Cultural differences* – An evolutionary perspective also fails to explain why some cultures (e.g. the Yanomamo of South America) seem to *require* male violence to attain social status, whereas in other cultures (such as the peaceful !Kung San of the Kalahari) aggression leads to irreparable damage to the reputation of the aggressor (Buss and Shackelford 1997).

Evolutionary explanations of group display in humans

There is a widespread belief that people behave differently when in groups compared to how they behave as individuals. For example, people in groups may sometimes behave more antisocially (see discussion of deindividuation, p.133), but in different circumstances they become more cooperative and selfless in the presence of other group members. Group behaviour frequently confers advantages on the individuals who make up a particular group. Some behaviours only occur when a collection of like-minded individuals come together for the same purpose. When they join forces and act together, people's behaviour might be regarded as a group display. We are more familiar with the idea of **group display** in the behaviour of non-human animals, e.g. a group of meerkats adopting a threat display to scare away a predator. However, some group-based human displays may well serve an important adaptive purpose for the individuals within those groups.

In this section we look at two very different types of group display:

- *The behaviour of **lynch mobs*** – where a group of people, without legal authority, kill a person for some presumed offence. The word 'mob' suggests that such behaviour is without planning or direction, yet a display of such extreme violence may serve an important purpose for the members of the mob that goes way beyond the killing of one individual.

- *Self-directed aggression during religious and cultural displays* – As we shall see, such self-directed aggression serves the important function of signalling commitment to a group.

Adaptive explanations for lynch mobs

At least 2805 people were lynched between the years 1882 and 1930 in the southern states of the US.

History tells us that there were 2805 (documented) victims of lynch mobs killed between the years 1882 and 1930 in ten southern states in the US. The vast majority of the victims were African-American males. The scale of this carnage was such that, on average, a black man, woman or child was murdered nearly once a week, every week, between 1882 and 1930 by a hate-driven white mob (Tolnay and Beck 1995). The reasons given for Black lynchings were numerous, but included justifications as obscure as 'being improper with a white woman', 'demanding respect' and 'being disreputable'. Among the evolutionary explanations offered for the behaviour of lynch mobs are:

- the power-threat hypothesis
- dehumanization of the victim.

The power-threat hypothesis

Blalock (1967) suggests that as minority group membership grows, majority group members will intensify their efforts to maintain dominance. According to Blalock, the concept of 'power-threat' represents a fear of political power in the hands of the minority. For example, among the reasons given by Tolnay and Beck for Black lynchings are: 'trying to vote' and 'voting for the wrong party'. Blalock suggests that as the minority group percentage *increases*, so the majority group's discriminatory behaviour also increases. This fear of 'Negro' power meant that White mobs frequently turned to 'lynch law' as a means of social control. This was particularly the case in the period after the abolition of slavery, when the ensuing social transition left the White community feeling particularly at risk. Ridley (1997) suggests that group displays of solidarity and discrimination against outsiders become more likely when groups feel at risk.

Now read the panel 'Dehumanization of the victim' before moving on to the section 'Lynch mobs and dehumanization'.

Dehumanization of the victim

The following extract from the *New York Tribune* of 24 April 1899, describes the ritualistic killing and bodily degradation of a 19-year-old Negro, Sam Hose, burned at the stake in a public road in Coweta County, Georgia for the alleged murder of his White employer.

'Before the torch was applied to the pyre, the Negro was deprived of his ears, fingers and other portions of his body with surprising fortitude. Before the body was cool, it was cut into pieces, the bones were crushed into small bits, and even the tree upon which the wretch met his fate was torn up and disposed of as souvenirs. The Negro's heart was cut into several pieces as was also his liver. Those unable to obtain ghastly relics directly paid more fortunate possessors extravagant sums for them. Small pieces of bone went for 25 cents and bits of liver, crisply cooked, for 10 cents.'

Lynch mobs and dehumanization

Hyatt (1999) argues that through the 'hysterical desecration' of the Black body in lynching burnings and other forms of ritual killing, the mob attempted to reduce the body to bits of bone and dead flesh, to a form that was unrecognizable as a human being (see panel above). Tolnay and Beck (1995) suggested that years of racist propaganda had, in the minds of many Whites, reduced Blacks to simplistic and often animalistic stereotypes. These debasing stereotypes further dehumanized the victim, reducing him to a hated object devoid of worth. By defining victims such as Sam Hose in this way, the lynch mob's actions were reassuring because they were 'defending their community from Black brutality'. In other words, lynching could be seen as an evolved adaptation to perceived threats. However, social psychology offers a different explanation (see the panel, 'Social psychology approach: lynch mobs and deindividuation').

Evaluation of adaptive explanations for lynch mobs

- *The power-threat hypothesis* – Clark (2006) studied murders by lynch mobs in Sao Paulo, Brazil and concluded that evidence contradicted the power-threat hypothesis. Afro-Brazilians, although they were the main victims of lynch mobs were not considered to pose any particular threat, political or economic, to the dominant community. Consequently 'fear of the minority' was *not* a major causal factor in these ritual murders.

- *Evidence for dehumanization* – In Guatemala, as with some other South American countries, lynch mob violence has become commonplace in recent years. Rothenberg (1998) observes that although most cases are in response to serious crimes such as murder,

Social psychology approach: lynch mobs and deindividuation

Earlier in this chapter, we met the concept of deindividuation (see p.133) defined by Hogg and Vaughan (2008) as 'a process whereby people lose their sense of socialized individual identity and engage in unsocialized, often antisocial behaviours'. This concept can be usefully applied to the actions of lynch mobs *without* the need to see such behaviour as an evolved adaptation to threat. Mullen (1986) carried out an archival analysis to see whether the actions of lynch mobs could be explained in terms of deindividuation processes. He analysed 60 newspaper reports of lynching, looking for information about the number of people in the crowd and the level of violence against the victim (e.g. whether it involved hanging, burning, dismembering, etc.). He found that as the size of the mob increased, the lynchers became more violent. Consistent with the predictions of deindividuation theory, the increase in the size of the mob had led to a breakdown in normal self-regulation processes, which in turn led to an increase in the level of violence against the victim.

Now, try the activity 'Explaining the behaviour of lynch mobs'.

Activity — Explaining the behaviour of lynch mobs

Use the Internet to read further about individual cases of lynch mobs (for example at http://www.nationmaster.com/encyclopedia/Lynch-mob).

1 Can you explain any of the cases you read about in terms of the explanations given above?

2 What characteristics do the mobs in the different cases have in common?

others are for minor offences, such as stealing chickens or pickpocketing. Consistent with the idea of dehumanization, enraged crowds frequently douse the bloodied corpses with gasoline and burn them, violating a victim already killed, as if seeking some further degradation of the victim. Dehumanization makes it easier to kill by removing any moral constraints associated with killing other human beings. By reducing their victims to the status of animals, the elimination of rivals becomes easier, which is ultimately beneficial to group members.

■ *The role of deindividuation* – There is some support for the claim that lynching may be a group display of extreme discrimination made more likely through the processes of deindividuation (see Social psychology approach panel above). As Rothenberg (1998) points out, however, although some lynchings took place at night, where violence was obscured by darkness, most occurred during the day. In some cases, only a handful of angry citizens were actually party to the violence, whereas in others there may have been thousands of witnesses. Although some aspects of deindividuation (e.g. large numbers of group members) were present in the majority of cases, there appears to be no clear relationship between deindividuating factors and the ferocity of the violence.

Adaptive explanations for religious/cultural displays

'Among the Ilahita Arapesh, boys as young as three years old are pinned down by adult males dressed as frightening boars and their genitals are forcefully rubbed with stinging nettles. Having just seen slightly older boys attacked by these 'boars' and suffer lacerations to their penises, the watching toddlers have something to look forward to in a few years when it is their turn. Later in childhood the boys' penises are abused again with bamboo razors and pig incisors, this time in a wooden structure built over a stream. Following the assault, the boys insert their penises through the floor boards to let the blood drip into the water below.' (Tuzin 1982, cited in Sosis 2006).

The example above is not an anthropological oddity; ritual practices throughout the world are often torturous and terrifying (Glucklich 2001). Furthermore, *self-inflicted* violence is not uncommon during rituals. This is demonstrated in the Shia Muslim practice of self-flagellation during *Ashura*, a major religious festival which commemorates the martyrdom at Karbala of Hussein, a grandson of the Prophet Mohammad. Some Shia men symbolically recreate the suffering of Hussein by flagellating themselves with chains and knives or cutting their foreheads until blood streams from their bodies.

Shia Muslims self-flagellate in Dhaka, Bangladesh, during the religious festival of Ashura

Extreme displays such as this appear to *contradict* the principles of natural selection. If such displays represent an adaptive strategy that has evolved through natural selection, then they must have solved some common problem that all societies face. One such problem that has been posed is how to achieve cooperation among group members while discouraging outsiders who may wish to enjoy the benefits of group membership with none of the commitments.

Religious displays and cooperative gains

Irons (2001) suggests that a universal dilemma faced by all groups is how to promote cooperation. He argues that in human history, the adaptive advantage of group living was the benefits that individuals gained through cooperating with each other, e.g. in activities such as hunting, food sharing, defence and warfare. By engaging in painful rituals such as self-flagellation, an individual is signalling their commitment to a group and all that it stands for. A committed group member is likely to be a cooperative group member. Therefore, because painful rituals promote cooperation within the group, natural selection would have *favoured* their development rather than militated against them.

Costly signalling to deter free riders

A problem for all groups is how to deal with the 'free rider', that is, the individual who takes all the advantages of group membership yet fails to cooperate and contributes nothing in return. The significant costs (e.g. to physical health) of many cultural and religious displays act as a deterrent for anyone who wants to join a group in order to take selfish advantage of the benefits available to group members. Zahavi (1975) refers to such 'costly signalling' rituals as handicaps (comparable to the bright plumage of the peacock which attracts females but also makes the male conspicuous to predators). Handicaps are reliable indicators of such things as status and breeding potential because they are too costly to be displayed or performed by 'low quality' individuals. Sosis (2006) uses the example of Israeli, Ultra-Orthodox Jews, known as *Haredim*. One of the most notable features of the Haredim, in the heat of an Israeli summer, is how overdressed they are for the season. In their thick beards, long black coats and heavy hats, Haredi men spend their days sweating as they sing praises to God in the desert sun. Thus, the 'quality' that these men are signalling is their level of commitment to their religious group.

The adaptive benefit of religious displays, therefore, appears ultimately to be the promotion and maintenance of cooperation within a group, as well as deterring potential 'free riders' who might be tempted to exploit group membership.

Evaluation of the adaptive explanations of religious/cultural displays

A number of research studies have provided support for the adaptive value of costly religious displays and other cultural rituals:

■ *Religious displays* – Ruffle and Sosis (2005) studied Israeli communes (called kibbutzim). They found that religious males in the kibbutzim were significantly more cooperative towards members of their own kibbutz than were religious females. This result is understandable if we consider the types of rituals and demands imposed on religious Jews. Males engage in highly visible ritual requirements, most notably public prayer which occurs three times daily. Ruffle and Sosis found synagogue attendance to be positively correlated with cooperative behaviour in males. Ruffle and Sosis found no correlation between synagogue attendance and cooperative behaviour among females, as attendance is not a requirement for women and so does not serve as a signal of commitment to the group. (The requirements made of females in the kibbutzim do not involve public displays and are generally carried out privately or in the home, e.g. baking bread and lighting Shabbat candles). These results are consistent with the predictions of costly signalling theory: more conspicuous displays of commitment are related to (positively correlate with) higher levels of cooperation within the group.

■ *Cultural rituals* – Sosis *et al.* (2005) collected data from 60 geographically dispersed societies on the costs of group rituals and the frequency of warfare. They found that the frequency of warfare was the strongest predictor of the costliness of that society's male ritual displays. They also found that the *type* of displays favoured within a particular society as a signal of commitment, depended on the nature of warfare common in that society. In societies where *external*

Haredi men dressed for prayer, Jerusalem, 1999

warfare was more common (i.e. war against other societies), groups were concerned with uniting unrelated males into as large a combat group as possible. For these societies, permanent, costly displays of group commitment (such as scars, tattoos and incisions) would serve to minimize the likelihood of males absconding to another group. In societies where *internal* warfare was the norm, communities continually break up and fuse, so someone who is an ally one day may well be an enemy the next. Males will, therefore, be less willing to commit to permanent displays of group allegiance but instead will engage in temporary displays, such as body painting or ingesting toxic substances (e.g. hallucinogenic drugs and emetics). Sosis and colleagues' results showed a positive correlation between external warfare and permanent 'badges' of group membership, which supports the hypothesis that costly male ritualistic displays have evolved to signal commitment and promote solidarity among males who must cooperate in warfare.

■ *The evolutionary approach* – Understanding the adaptive value of religious displays allows us to explain the success of some religions from a purely evolutionary perspective. By making membership 'costly', they increase intragroup solidarity and deter outsiders from taking advantage of the benefits of membership without contributing to the group. However, this perspective would also suggest that, although *intragroup* solidarity is a significant adaptive advantage, a disadvantage is that this accentuates *intergroup* conflict. Sosis (2004) claims that the major benefit of intragroup solidarity is the ability of unified groups to defend and compete against other groups. This certainly appears to be the case, in that societies with stricter religious displays tend to experience higher levels of intergroup conflict (Roes and Raymond 2003).

CHECK YOUR UNDERSTANDING

Check your understanding of aggression as an adaptive response. Try to do this from memory. You can check your answers by looking back through Topic 3, Aggression as an adaptive response.

1 Give three examples of mate-retention strategies commonly used by human males.

2 Explain the relationship between cuckoldry, infidelity and sexual jealousy.

3 Explain two critical points concerning the infidelity/sexual jealousy explanation of aggression.

4 Give two reasons why murder might be an evolutionary adaptation.

5 Outline two situations in which murder has been shown to be an adaptive behaviour.

6 Explain two critical points concerning the 'murder as an adaptive behaviour' explanation.

7 Outline two explanations of the behaviour of lynch mobs being an adaptive response.

8 Explain two critical points concerning the behaviour of lynch mobs.

9 What is meant by 'costly signalling theory' in the context of religious displays?

10 Explain two evaluative points concerning the 'costly signalling theory' of religious displays.

Social learning theory (SLT)

- Learning by direct experience
- Learning by vicarious experience
- Reinforcement determines likelihood of behaviour recurring
- Bandura *et al.* (1963) – children imitated aggressive models

Evaluation

- Explains inconsistencies in aggressive behaviour
- Explains cultural differences
- Social learning may not be only causal agent

Deindividuation

- Loss of socialized individual identity through group membership
- Reduction in private self-awareness associated with antisocial behaviour
- Demonstrated in SPE (Zimbardo)
- Deindividuation in cultures who change appearance when at war

Evaluation

- Role of anonymity not clear from research
- Deindividuation can also lead to prosocial behaviour
- Does not fully explain violent football crowd behaviour

Explanations of institutional aggression

- Importation model – prisons violent because of inmates
- Deprivation model – prisons violent because of situation
- Zimbardo's 'Lucifer Effect' – bad situations corrupt people
- Other contexts – initiation rituals (e.g. in military)

Evaluation

- Research support for importation model, some types of prison inmate more violent
- Importation model does not offer ways of reducing violence
- Mixed support for deprivation model
- Abu Ghraib prison – real life relevance of Zimbardo's model
- Initiation rituals explained by cognitive dissonance theory

Neural mechanisms

Serotonin

- Low levels of serotonin = high levels of aggression
- Dexfenfluramine depletes serotonin and increases aggression

Evaluation:

- Serotonin metabolism rather than levels may be responsible for aggression
- Can explain link between alcohol and aggression

Dopamine

- Increased levels may be linked with aggression
- Aggression may be rewarding (through dopamine pathway)

Evaluation:

- Methodological difficulties in establishing link between dopamine and aggression

Hormonal mechanisms

Testosterone

- Testosterone makes it 'more likely' that aggression happens
- Research suggests link is with dominance rather than aggression
- Challenge hypothesis – testosterone rises in social challenges

Evaluation:

- Evidence for link is inconsistent
- Increased testosterone in older people may have positive effects
- Gender bias in researcher

Cortisol

- Lower levels of cortisol = higher levels of aggressive behaviour
- Low levels of cortisol may be aversive hence person becomes aggressive
- Cortisol might normally inhibit aggressive behaviour

Evaluation:

- Some research support (e.g. in longitudinal studies), but research inconsistent on link

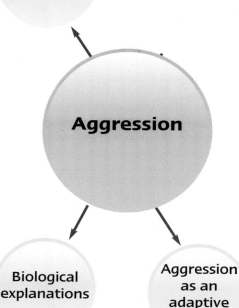

Social psychological explanations

Aggression

Biological explanations

Aggression as an adaptive response

- Males have evolved mate retention strategies to deter infidelity
- Sexual jealousy evolved to meet problem of cuckoldry
- Evidence from Buss and Shackelford (1997)

Evaluation

- Support from studies of battered women
- Research support – risk of infidelity predicted sexual coercion
- Practical applications include intervention before violence

Murder as an evolved adaptation

- Murder evolved as an adaptation in specific circumstances
- Predisposing factors include sexual jealousy and lack of resources
- Research support from animal studies (Ferris *et al.* 2003)

Evaluation

- Evidence of killing of conspecifics in many species
- An alternative explanation – the 'evolved goal hypothesis'
- Murder 'defences' also evolve so murder becomes more risky

Genetic factors in aggression

- Twin and adoption studies suggests important role for genetic factors
- Rhee and Waldman (2002) genetic component of aggression to be 40%
- Some evidence for role of 'candidate genes' such as DRD4 and gene for MAOA

Evaluation

- Difficult to disentangle genetic and environmental effects in twin studies because MZ twins have more similar environmental experiences
- Research suggests genetic factors are more important in females
- Specific problems with adoption studies
- Genes are not deterministic
- Gene–environmental interaction effects

Group displays

- Lynch mobs explained by power-threat (fear of minority) and the need to dehumanize victim
- Religious displays are 'costly signals' – indicate commitment to a group and so deter free-riders

Evaluation

- Power-threat hypothesis challenged by evidence that many lynchings are of those not considered a threat
- Evidence of dehumanization
- Some lynchings match conditions of deindividuation but many do not
- Ruffle and Sosis (2005) – More conspicuous displays of commitment related to higher levels of cooperation within the group
- Type of displays matched type of warfare, permanent costly displays (e.g. scars) only common where external warfare is more common than internal warfare

EXPLAINING THE SPECIFICATION

Specification content	The specification explained
Eating behaviour (Topic 1)	In this part of the specification you are required to know about factors influencing attitudes to food and eating behaviour, and the reasons why dieting succeeds and why it fails. To do this, you need to be able to:
Factors influencing attitudes to food and eating behaviour: for example, cultural influences, mood, health concerns	■ Describe people's attitudes to food and eating behaviour and discuss at least two factors that affect people's attitudes to food and eating behaviour; we focus on cultural influences, mood and health concerns. ■ Describe and evaluate research that has investigated how these factors influence attitudes to food and eating behaviour.
Explanations for the success or failure of dieting	■ Describe and evaluate the key reasons why dieting succeeds and why it fails, with reference to relevant research.
Biological explanations of eating behaviour (Topic 2)	In this part of the specification you are required to explain eating behaviour from a biological perspective. To do this, you need to be able to:
The role of neural mechanisms involved in controlling eating and satiation	■ Explain the ways in which neural mechanisms control eating behaviour and satiation, including reference to relevant research. ■ Evaluate biological explanations of eating behaviour and satiation.
Evolutionary explanations of food preference	■ Explain food preferences from an evolutionary perspective, including reference to relevant research. ■ Evaluate evolutionary explanations of food preference.
Eating disorders (Topic 3)	In this part of the specification you are required to describe and explain one eating disorder from a psychological, a biological and an evolutionary perspective. To do this, you need to be able to:
Psychological explanations of one eating disorder: for example, anorexia nervosa, bulimia nervosa, obesity	■ Explain one eating disorder from at least two psychological perspectives; in this chapter we focus on obesity. ■ Describe and evaluate psychological research into obesity. ■ Evaluate the usefulness of at least two psychological explanations of obesity.
Biological explanations, including neural and evolutionary explanations, for one eating disorder: for example, anorexia nervosa, bulimia nervosa, obesity	■ Describe and evaluate at least two biological explanations of obesity – these must include a neural and an evolutionary explanation. ■ Describe and evaluate research into neural and evolutionary explanations of obesity.

Introduction

You only have to look at any women's magazine to see that eating, dieting, obesity and eating disorders are frequently discussed. It is clear that what we eat can affect our health in a number of different ways. Overeating, undereating or eating the wrong foods can influence our weight and may lead to eating disorders or obesity. Eating disorders are linked to physical problems such as stunted growth, heart attacks, osteoporosis and reproductive difficulties, while obesity is linked to diabetes, heart disease and some forms of cancer. Research suggests a direct link between diet and illnesses such as heart disease, cancer and diabetes, and that certain foods, such as fruit, vegetables, oily fish and oat fibre, can be protective, while others, such as salt and saturated fats, may contribute to poor health.

Diet is also important in terms of treating a person once an illness has been diagnosed. For example, obese patients are mainly managed through dietary-based interventions, while patients diagnosed with angina, heart disease or following a heart attack are recommended to change their lifestyle, with particular emphasis on stopping smoking, increasing their physical activity and eating a healthy diet. Diet is also central to the management of both Type 1 and Type 2 diabetes. Eating behaviour is therefore central to our health. The eatwell plate, shown in Figure 5.1, is a pictorial guide showing the proportion and types of foods that make up a healthy balanced diet. It is consistent with the Government's eight tips for eating well published in October 2005.

Figure 5.1 *The eatwell plate (British Nutrition Foundation 2007)*

In Topic 1, we explore three key factors – cultural influences, mood and health concerns – that can affect our attitudes to food, our eating behaviour and what we eat. The various factors that determine whether or not diets succeed are also examined. The biological basis of eating behaviour is discussed in Topic 2, including the neural mechanisms that control hunger, eating and satiation, and evolutionary explanations of food preferences. In the final topic, we focus on obesity which is increasingly prevalent in the western world, and explore what biological and psychological perspectives have contributed to our current understanding of obesity.

Topic 1: Eating behaviour

Psychology in context   Children's eating habits

Jamie Oliver campaigned for better food in schools and he shocked many of us by revealing what was in some of the fast-food versions of chicken pieces. However, many children in the UK enjoy foods such as chicken nuggets, turkey twizlers, pizza and chips.

Jamie Oliver would argue that if children are given healthier foods, they may start to prefer them. After all, children in Japan and India enjoy foods that many children in England might find unappetizing, and 50 years ago, children did not eat chicken pieces shaped like a chicken because they were not available.

- Do you think that children's food preferences result from nature, nurture or both?

- Are high-fat, high-salt foods possibly tastier than healthier options?

- Do some children prefer unhealthy foods because that is all they know?

There has recently been a great deal of media coverage about unhealthy eating. As we shall see, much of this debate could be informed by psychological and biological theories of eating behaviour.

Factors influencing attitudes to food and eating behaviour

The importance of diet for health raises the question 'Why do we eat what we eat?' There are many theories of eating behaviour. This topic focuses on attitudes to food and the role of attitudes, cultural influences, mood and health concerns on the choices we make about what we eat.

Attitudes to food

People hold many different *attitudes* to specific aspects of their life – friends, work, school or family may be regarded as 'good', 'fun', 'boring', 'safe', 'exciting', 'dull' and so on. In the same way, people also hold different attitudes towards eating, and food is associated with a multitude of meanings. For example, food can represent comfort when you are feeling unhappy; it can be used as distraction when you are bored, or a way of showing someone they are special. This complex array of meanings is summarized by Todhunter (1973): 'Food is prestige, status and wealth ... It is a means of communication and interpersonal relations, such as an 'apple for the teacher' or an expression of hospitality, friendship, affection, neighbourliness, comfort and sympathy in time of sadness or danger. It symbolizes strength, athleticism, health and success. It is a means of pleasure and self-gratification and a relief from stress. It is feasts, ceremonies, rituals, special days and nostalgia for home, family and the 'good old days'. It is an expression of individuality and sophistication, a means of self expression and a way of revolt. Most of all it is tradition, custom and security. ... There are Sunday foods and weekday foods, family foods and guest foods; foods with magical properties and health and disease foods.'

One approach to the study of eating behaviour focuses on an individual's attitudes to food. This research tends to concentrate on a number of core *cognitions* about food, including the following:

- self-efficacy (e.g. 'I am confident I eat healthily')
- costs (e.g. 'Eating makes me fat')
- benefits (e.g. 'Eating well enables me to stay healthy')
- subjective norms (e.g. 'My friends are all on a diet')
- attitudes (e.g. 'Salad is not very filling')
- perceptions of risk (e.g. 'Eating too much meat may be bad for me')
- perceptions of severity (e.g. 'Being overweight is a serious health problem').

Social cognition models

Much of the research on attitudes has drawn on *social cognition models*, which describe how a fixed set of

cognitions may relate to any given behaviour. Several models and theories have been developed, including the:

- *health belief model* developed by Becker and Rosenstock (1984)
- *protection motivation theory* by Rogers (1985)
- *theory of reasoned action (TRA)* by Fishbein and Ajzen (1975)
- *theory of planned behaviour* by Ajzen (1985).

These models vary in terms of whether they use behavioural intentions (e.g. 'I intend to eat healthily') or actual behaviour (e.g. 'I always eat healthily') as an outcome variable and the combination of cognitions they include. Figure 5.2 illustrates how Ajzen's (1985) theory of planned behaviour can predict someone's behaviour, such as eating vegetables, on the basis of their behavioural intention ('I intend to eat vegetables'), which would be influenced by their attitude ('Vegetables are nice to eat'), their subjective norms ('My family eats lots of vegetables') and their behavioural control ('I am confident I will eat vegetables'). See Ogden (2007) or Conner and Norman (2005) for further detail of these models.

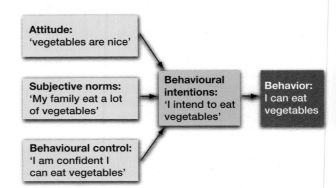

Figure 5.2 *Applying the theory of planned behaviour (TPB) to healthy eating*

A social cognitive approach can also be used to develop an intervention to try to change a person's behaviour. For example, if the aim was to encourage people to eat more vegetables, a suitable intervention might be to promote a more positive attitude ('Vegetables taste nice'), change someone's subjective norms ('People all around you are eating vegetables') and improve perceptions of behavioural control ('I can teach you how to buy and cook vegetables and once you start eating them you are likely to feel more confident about eating them in the future').

Focusing on attitudes in order to understand eating behaviour raises the question 'What cognitions do we have about food and how do they affect what we eat?' We consider this question next.

Use of social cognition models to predict eating behaviour

Social cognition models are used to predict behaviours ranging from the highly specific, such as 'adding salt to my food', to more general ones, such as 'healthy eating'. Some research has focused on predicting people's intentions to consume particular foods or types of food, for example, examining the extent to which cognitions relate to the intention to eat biscuits and wholemeal bread (Sparks *et al.* 1992), to drink skimmed milk (Raats *et al.* 1995) and to eat organic vegetables (Sparks and Shepherd 1992).

The research evidence suggests that behavioural intentions are not particularly good predictors of actual behaviour and this has stimulated work exploring the intention–behaviour gap (Sutton 1998). Therefore, some studies have explored the cognitive predictors of actual behaviour. For example, Shepherd and Stockley (1985) used the TRA to predict fat intake and found that attitudes were a better predictor than subjective norms. Similarly, attitudes have been found to be the best predictor of the use of table salt (Shepherd and Farleigh 1986), eating in fast-food restaurants (Axelson *et al.* 1983), frequency of consuming low-fat milk (Shepherd 1988) and of healthy eating, conceptualized as a high intake of fibre, fruit and vegetables and low levels of fat (Povey *et al.* 2000).

Evaluation of the social cognitive approach to eating behaviour

- *Emphasis on cognitions* – By emphasizing a person's cognitions about food and examining the extent to which these relate to eating behaviour, social cognition models/theories provide:
  - a framework for designing research to investigate people's cognitions about food
  - a means of thinking in a structured way about the many types of cognitions people may have about food
  - a useful basis for developing interventions to change how people think about food; an intervention could be designed to target and change each of the cognitions included in a particular model.

- *Use of quantitative research methods* – Much of the research that has been carried out using a social cognitive approach uses quantitative methods, particularly structured questionnaires based on existing models. This means that the cognitions investigated are chosen by the researcher rather than suggested by the participants. It is possible that important cognitions which are central to understanding eating behaviour may be missed.

- *Overly simple use of cognitions associated with food* – Although focusing on cognitions, those that have been incorporated into the various models/theories are limited and ignore the multiplicity of meanings associated with food.

- *Ignoring the role of emotions* – Research undertaken from a social cognitive perspective assumes that behaviour is a consequence of rational thought and ignores the role of emotions, such as fear (e.g. of weight gain or illness), pleasure (associated with success that deserves a treat) and guilt (about overeating), which might also contribute towards eating behaviour.

- *The views of others* – Although some social cognitive models incorporate the views of others in the form of a 'subjective norm' construct, this does not adequately address the central role that others play in a social behaviour such as eating.

The role of cultural influences

Children in the UK may develop positive attitudes to food, such as pizza, chips, chicken nuggets and fish fingers, believing them to be 'tasty', 'a treat' and so on. However, children in India grow up believing that spicier foods taste better, while children from Japan may prefer a fish-based diet. There is also considerable variation in food preferences within a culture, with some families preferring a meat-based diet and others a vegetarian diet. Rozin (1982) stated that 'there is no doubt that the best predictor of the food preferences, habits and attitudes of any particular human would be information about his ethnic group ... rather than any biological measure that one might imagine'.

The developmental approach

Much research has therefore focused on the learning processes that are associated with eating behaviour and has asked questions such as 'Where do our beliefs about food come from?' and 'How do we learn what to eat?' These questions are usually investigated from a developmental perspective, which focuses on the importance of childhood and families. Eating behaviour has been studied extensively using a developmental approach and three main mechanisms have been highlighted (Birch 1999):

- exposure to food
- social learning
- associative learning.

Activity **Thinking about food preferences**

The literature investigating exposure suggests that food preferences are influenced by familiarity. Think of some foods that you really like and those you really do not like.

- List the reasons why you like or do not like each of these foods.
- Are your preferences a result of exposure/lack of exposure or some other reason(s)?
- Do you think that you could ever come to like any of the foods you currently dislike?

Discuss your answers with some other students in your psychology class, then list all the different types of reasons you identified for either liking or disliking particular foods.

Some suggestions are given in the Answers to activities on p.603. ▶

Exposure to food

People need to eat a variety of foods in order to have a balanced diet and yet some show fear and avoidance of new foods; this fear is known as neophobia. Young children may show *neophobic* responses to food, but usually come to accept and eat foods that may originally have appeared threatening. Research has shown that mere exposure to new foods can change children's preferences. For example, Birch and Marlin (1982) introduced two-year-old children to novel foods over a six-week period. One food was presented 20 times, one 10 times, one five times and one remained novel. The results showed a direct relationship between exposure and food preference, and found that eight to 10 exposures were usually necessary before preferences began to shift significantly. The mechanism of exposure simply suggests that we like foods that we are most familiar with. Therefore, if children are given chicken nuggets for their tea, they will prefer these to other foods; if children are given curry, sushi or noodles, then these will become their favourite foods.

Social learning

Social learning describes the impact of observing other people's behaviour on one's own behaviour and is sometimes referred to as 'modelling' or 'observational learning'. Research has investigated the extent to which watching other people eat influences children's eating behaviour. A study by Birch *et al.* (1980) used peer modelling to change children's preference for vegetables. On four consecutive days, the children participating in the study were seated at lunch next to children who preferred a different vegetable to themselves (peas versus carrots). By the end of the study, the children showed a definite shift in their vegetable preference, which was still evident at a follow-up assessment several weeks later. Those who initially did not like peas at the outset did like them by the end of the study, and those who initially did not like carrots also showed a shift in their food preferences.

The impact of social learning has also been demonstrated in an intervention designed to change children's eating behaviour (Lowe *et al.* 1998). Children were shown videos of 'food dudes', who were older children enthusiastically consuming food that the younger children with a history of food refusal would not eat. The results showed that exposure to the 'food dudes' significantly changed the children's food preferences and specifically increased their consumption of fruit and vegetables. Food preferences can, therefore, change through watching others eat.

Parental attitudes to food and eating behaviours are also central to the process of social learning. For example, Olivera *et al.* (1992) reported a clear relationship between mothers' food intake for most nutrients and their pre-school children, and suggested that parents could be targeted to try to improve children's diets. Similarly, Brown and Ogden (2004) reported consistent correlations between parents and their children in terms of reported snack-food intake and eating motivations. Parental behaviour and attitudes are therefore central to the process of social learning, with research highlighting a positive correlation between the diets of parents and their children.

Associative learning

Associative learning (also known as classical conditioning) refers to the impact of contingent factors on behaviour, i.e. the impact of pairing one factor with another. On occasions, these contingent factors are reinforcers, in the context of operant conditioning, or they may be aspects of the environment, specific behaviours or even food. In terms of eating behaviour, research has investigated the impact of pairing food cues with aspects of the environment. In particular, food has been:

1 paired with a reward

2 used as a reward

3 paired with physiological consequences, such as feeling sick.

Pairing food with a reward

Some research has examined the effect of rewarding eating behaviour ('If you eat your vegetables I will be pleased with you'). For example, Birch *et al.* (1980) gave children food in association with positive adult attention, which was found to increase food preference. Similarly, a study using video to change eating behaviour reported that rewarding vegetable consumption increased the eating of vegetables (Lowe *et al.* 1998). Rewarding eating behaviour can change food preferences.

Using food as a reward

Other research has examined the impact of using food as a reward. In these studies, gaining access to the food is contingent on another behaviour (e.g. 'If you are well behaved you can have a biscuit'). Birch *et al.* (1980) presented children with foods either as a reward, as a snack or in a non-social situation (the control group). The results showed that food acceptance increased if the foods were presented as a reward, but that the other two conditions had no effect. This suggests that the use of food as a reward can increase preference for that food.

The relationship between food and reward, however, is more complex than this, as illustrated by a study by Lepper *et al.* (1982) involving imaginary foods (see Key Research by Lepper *et al.* 1982).

The relationship between food and rewards

Key research: Lepper *et al.* (1982)

In a classic study, Lepper and colleagues used imaginary foods, which they called 'hupe' and 'hule', to investigate the relationship between food and rewards. Twenty-eight pre-school children were told a short story about either a little boy or a little girl (depending on the sex of the participant) who were given two new foods called 'hupe' and hule'. Half the participants were told that the mother in the story offered first one of the foods and then the other to the child in the story (for example, they were told you can have hupe then hule OR hule then hupe). This was the non-contingent condition, as having one kind of food was NOT contingent on eating the other. For the other half of the participants, the mother in the story explained to the child in the story that he/she could only have one of the foods (the hupe or the hule) IF they ate the other food. For example, they were told you can have hupe IF you eat hule OR you can have hule IF you eat hupe. This was the contingency condition, as having one food WAS contingent on eating the other food.

All the children were asked which food they would prefer to have. The order of presentation of the two foods was always counterbalanced to eliminate any possible order effect. The results showed that there were no preferences in the non-contingent condition. However, in the contingency condition, children preferred the food that had been used as the reward for eating the other food. So, if the mother had said eat hupe then you can have hule, the children preferred the hule and rated it as tasting better. Many parents say to their children 'If you eat your vegetables you can have your pudding'. However, the evidence indicates that this may be increasing the child's preference for pudding even further, as pairing two foods in this way can result in the 'reward' food being viewed more positively than the food that provides the access to the reward food. Other research has also demonstrated that rewarding an activity can reduce children's interest in it. For example, Fabes *et al.* (1989) reported that children, aged between seven and 11, who were accustomed to being rewarded for good behaviour were less likely to help others than those who were not accustomed to receiving rewards.

Food and physiological consequences

Studies have also investigated the association between food cues and physiological responses to food intake. There is a wealth of literature illustrating the acquisition of food aversions following unpleasant gastrointestinal consequences (e.g. Garcia *et al.* 1974). For example, an aversion to shellfish can be triggered by just one case of a stomach upset after eating mussels. Therefore, a single physiological consequence can alter a person's food preferences.

Food and control

The association between food and rewards suggests a possible role for parental control over eating behaviour. Some research has examined the impact of control, as studies indicate that parents often believe that restricting access to food or forbidding children to eat certain foods are effective as a way of improving food preferences. Birch (1999) reviewed the evidence of the impact of imposing any form of parental control over food intake and reported that it is not only the use of foods as rewards which can have a negative effect on children's food preferences, but also any attempts to limit a child's access to foods. She concluded that 'child feeding strategies that restrict children's access to snack foods actually make the restricted foods more attractive' (Birch 1999, p.52). For example, when a range of foods is made freely available, children will choose more of the restricted than the unrestricted foods, particularly when their mother is not present. From this perspective, parental control would seem to have a detrimental impact on children's eating behaviour.

However, other studies have suggested that parental control can lead to reduced weight and improved eating behaviour. For example, Wardle *et al.* (2002) argue that 'lack of control of food intake [rather than higher control] might contribute to the emergence of differences in weight' (p.453). Similarly, Brown and Ogden (2004) report that greater parental control is associated with higher intakes of healthy snack foods. Ogden *et al.* (2006) suggest that these contradictions in the literature may have arisen because control is not made up of one dimension only, but is far more complex than previously thought. To assess this, Ogden and colleagues examined the effect of differentiating between 'overt control' which can be detected by the child (e.g. being firm about how much your child should eat) and 'covert control' which cannot be detected as easily by the child (e.g. not buying unhealthy foods so they are not available in the home). The results showed that these different forms of control predicted snack food intake differently – higher covert control was related to decreased intake of unhealthy snacks and higher overt control predicted an increased intake of healthy snacks.

IDA — Different approaches to the study of eating behaviour

Research investigating eating behaviour illustrates two psychological approaches:

1 Research focusing on cognitions draws on a cognitive perspective.

2 The developmental approach draws on a behaviourist perspective.

However, these two perspectives are now rarely considered as separate and discrete. For example, it is assumed that the cognitions described by a cognitive model have been learned, and although a developmental approach may focus on behaviour, it assumes that these behaviours are linked to cognitions.

IDA — Debates associated with the study of eating behaviour

Research into eating behaviour highlights two core debates in psychology.

1 The nature–nurture debate – This raises the question of whether we are born with a preference for specific tastes or whether these are learned.

2 The debate around free will and determinism – If eating behaviour is determined by inherent taste and food preferences, then we have no free will over what, and how much, we eat. If, on the other hand, our food preferences are learned during childhood, do adults have much choice over what they eat? In which case, where does the freedom to make healthier choices and change the way we eat come from?

Evaluation of the developmental approach to eating behaviour

■ *Role of learning* – A developmental approach emphasizes the role of learning, provides evidence of how food preferences are learned during childhood and places the individual in an environment that is rich in cues and reinforcers.

■ *Controlled research environment* – Research undertaken from a developmental perspective is often carried out in a controlled environment, enabling alternative explanations to be excluded, and the impact of specific variables to be investigated while other variables are held constant.

■ *Generalization of the findings* – On the other hand, as much of this research has been carried out in a tightly controlled laboratory setting, the extent to which the results can be generalized to real-life settings remains unclear.

■ *A limited set of meanings associated with food* – A developmental approach has been used to explore the meaning of food in terms of food as a reward, food as a means to gain a reward, food as status, food as something pleasant and also as something aversive. However, food has an even more diverse set of meanings which have not been incorporated into the model.

■ *Role of cognitions* – A developmental model includes a role for cognitions, as some of the meanings of food, including reward and aversion, are considered to motivate behaviour. These cognitions remain implicit, however, and are not explicitly described.

The role of mood

Our mood and whether we are feeling bored, upset or anxious has been shown to influence what, and how much, we eat. Early research on obesity suggested that people became obese because they ate for emotional reasons, whereas thin people ate because they were hungry. This was known as the emotionality theory of obesity (Schachter 1968). In a similar vein, research on anorexia nervosa and bulimia suggested that undereating and overeating in the context of an eating disorder was an individual's way of managing their emotions. This was investigated using a psychosomatic perspective (Bruch 1965).

Nowadays, however, it is generally recognized that most people eat in response to their mood, regardless of their weight and also in the absence of an eating disorder. For example, people may eat more when they are in a more negative mood state as a means of improving their mood, or they may eat more when their mood is positive because of the role of food in celebration and social interaction (Ogden 2003). One form of mood that has been widely studied is stress, and researchers have asked 'Do people eat more or less when feeling stressed?'

Stress and eating

Some research has indicated that stress causes a reduction in food intake. For example, laboratory studies on humans found that research participants ate less when they felt stressed (Willenbring *et al.* 1986); a similar decrease in eating has been reported in marines during combat situations (Popper *et al.* 1989). A longitudinal study carried out by Stone and Brownell (1994) recorded daily records of stress and eating patterns of 158 students for 84 days and reported that eating less was the predominant response to stress. Other studies, however, have found the reverse relationship. For example, in a study of students' perceptions of the relationship between stress and snacking, 73 per cent of respondents stated that stress increased their snacking and decreased their consumption of 'meal-type' foods (Oliver and Wardle

1999). In addition, a naturalistic study of stress at work concluded that periods of high workload were associated with greater intakes of energy, particularly saturated fats and sugar (Wardle *et al.* 2000). Stress may elicit eating as a coping response (Spillman 1990); it may be a possible trigger for binge eating (Herman and Polivy 1975) and cause weight gain in adults and children (Mellbin and Vuille 1989).

Stress, therefore, can sometimes decrease food intake and at other times it increases food consumption. Stone and Brownell (1994) have called this contradictory relationship between stress and eating the 'stress eating paradox'. Greeno and Wing (1994) proposed two hypotheses to explain this paradox:

1   The general effect model which predicts that stress changes food intake generally.

2   The individual difference model which predicts that stress only causes changes in eating behaviour in vulnerable groups of individuals.

More recent research has focused on the individual difference model and has examined whether the variability in the response to stress relates to aspects of the individual. For example, Cools *et al.* (1992) reported that stress only triggered increased eating in people who were already dieting. Similar results have also been reported by Wardle *et al.* (2000), based on a naturalistic study of work-related stress.

However, not all research findings are consistent with this suggestion. Conner *et al.* (1999), for example, examined the link between daily hassles and snacking in 60 students who completed food diaries for seven consecutive days. The results showed a direct association between increased daily hassles and increased snacking, with no differences in relation to either gender or dieting. Similarly, Oliver *et al.* (2000) reported no impact of dietary

restraint on stress-induced eating, but indicated a role for emotional eating, with emotional eaters eating more, following experimentally induced stress.

To sum up, our mood influences what, and also how much, we eat. Research investigating the link between stress and eating behaviour has highlighted individual differences which appear to relate to levels of dieting (see p.168 for further details on dieting).

The impact of health concerns

Health-education campaigns currently advise us to eat a diet that is low in fat and salt, high in complex carbohydrates and includes at least five portions of fruit and vegetables a day. This approach emphasizes health as a motivation for eating behaviour. There is also a significant increase in the number of foods available that are marketed as being healthy. These include 'healthy options' with low-fat and/or low-salt content and specific food products designed to lower cholesterol, and protect against cancer or heart disease. Some television programmes also focus on healthy eating and how to cook healthy foods.

The research evidence indicates that people are motivated by health in contradictory ways. For example, the existence of such products and TV programmes suggests there is a growing interest in, and market for, healthy foods, so health must be a motivation for some people (Rapoport 2003). However, at the same time, the population is becoming heavier, more people are eating out rather than cooking at home, and the consumption of processed foods shows no sign of declining. In a large-scale survey, Steptoe *et al.* (1995) found that health was a motivation for food choice but that it was only one of many other factors. Other factors included sensory appeal, price, convenience of purchasing and preparation, weight control, familiarity of the food, mood regulation, the natural content of the food and ethical concerns about manufacture and the country of origin. Eating behaviour is, therefore, motivated by many factors and health is probably not a particularly high priority for many people.

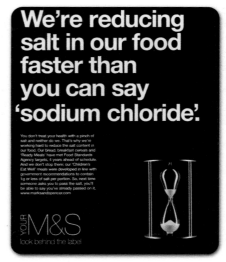

Explanations for the success or failure of dieting

So far, this topic has explored cognitive and developmental models of eating behaviour. Cognitive models emphasize the role of attitudes and beliefs, while developmental models emphasize the role of learning and association. However, food is associated with many meanings, such as treats, celebrations, family get-togethers, being a good mother and being a good child (Ogden 2003). Moreover, once eaten, food can change a person's shape and body weight which, in turn, are associated with meaning about attractiveness, success and control (Ogden 2003). As a result, many people are concerned about their weight and dissatisfied with their bodies, which often results in dieting. How dieting influences eating behaviour will be examined next.

What is dieting?

Dieting involves trying to eat less than usual. It means placing a cognitive limit on food intake and attempting to eat up to a limit that is less than the person would normally want and eat. Research shows that dieting is extremely common, and that up to 70 per cent of women diet at some time in their lives. Restraint theory (Herman and Mack 1975, Herman and Polivy 1984) was developed to investigate the causes and consequences of dieting (sometimes referred to as 'restrained eating') and suggests that dieting can be either successful, resulting in undereating and subsequent weight loss, or unsuccessful, resulting in overeating and weight gain.

When dieting is successful

Restrained eating aims to reduce food intake and several studies have found that this aim can be successful. For example, Kirkley et al. (1988) assessed the eating style of 50 women, using dietary self-monitoring forms for four days, and reported that the restrained eaters consumed fewer calories than the unrestrained eaters. Similarly, studies which investigated the effectiveness of dietary interventions have shown that interventions involving strategies, such as calorie-controlled diets, cognitive-behavioural therapy or healthy eating, can result in substantial changes in eating behaviour and weight change in the first few months (Wadden 1993, Glenny et al. 1997).

Factors that increase the success of dieting

Research has also investigated the factors that increase the success of dieting and has highlighted a role for a number of psychological variables. For example, Rodin et al. (1977) carried out a study to assess the baseline psychological predictors of successful weight loss. The results indicated a role for an individual's beliefs about the causes of obesity and their motivation for weight loss. Williams et al. (1996) also reported that motivational style was predictive of weight loss and weight maintenance. Likewise, Kiernan et al. (1998) found that individuals who were more dissatisfied with their body shape at baseline were more successful, suggesting that motivation for weight loss, underpinned by a high value placed on attractiveness, may be important.

Ogden (2000) investigated differences in psychological factors between weight-loss regainers, people who are stable obese and weight-loss maintainers (i.e. those individuals who had previously been obese, **body mass index** (BMI) > 29.9, and had lost sufficient weight to be considered non-obese, BMI < 29.9, and had maintained this weight loss for a minimum of three years). The results showed that the weight-loss maintainers were more likely to endorse a psychological model of obesity in terms of its consequences, such as depression and low self-esteem. They were also motivated to lose weight for psychological reasons, such as wanting to boost their self-esteem and feel better about themselves. Furthermore, they were less inclined to endorse a medical model of causality, including the contribution of genetics and hormone imbalance. In a similar way, Ogden and Hills (2008) interviewed people who had successfully lost weight and maintained their weight loss, and reported that much weight loss was triggered by a key life event, such as divorce or illness, or a salient milestone, such as a significant birthday. This initial behaviour was translated into longer-term behaviour change if a number of sustaining conditions were met, including:

- a belief in a behavioural model of obesity
- a reduction in choice over what and when they eat
- a reduction in the benefits and function of eating
- a process of reinvention, whereby the person no longer saw themselves as an overweight person, but rather they created a new identity for themselves as a thinner, healthier person.

Overall, these results suggested that it is not only what individuals *do* that is predictive of success, but also what they *believe*. For dieting to be successful, a person needs to:

1 hold a model of obesity that focuses on behaviour as central to their weight problem
2 avoid a state of denial whereby they want to eat but do not
3 create a situation where food is no longer regarded as rewarding
4 establish a new identity as a thinner person.

When dieting is not successful

In contrast, several research studies have found that dieting is sometimes unsuccessful and can result in overeating. For example, Ruderman and Wilson (1979) used the preload/taste-test procedure to explore eating behaviour in a laboratory setting. This procedure involved giving participants either a high-calorie preload (e.g. a high-calorie milk shake or chocolate bar) or a low-calorie preload (e.g. a cracker). After eating/drinking the preload, participants were asked to participate in a taste test in which participants were asked to rate a series of different foods (such as biscuits, snacks and ice cream) for a variety of qualities, including saltiness, sweetness and preference. The participants were then left alone for a fixed amount of time to rate the foods and the amount they ate was recorded (participants were not told that this would happen). The aim of the preload/taste-test method is to measure food intake in a controlled environment (the laboratory) and to examine the effect of preloading on eating behaviour.

Using this approach, Ruderman and Wilson (1979) reported that restrained eaters consumed significantly more food than the unrestrained eaters, irrespective of the size of the preload. In particular, restraint theory has identified the disinhibition of restraint (or the 'what-the-hell' effect) as characteristic of overeating in restrained eaters. Disinhibition has been defined as 'eating more as a result of loosening restraints in response to emotional distress, intoxication or preloading' (Herman and Polivy 1988, p.342).

Herman and Mack (1975) carried out the original study demonstrating disinhibition (see Key research on p.170).

HOW SCIENCE WORKS

Activity Developing and testing health education advice

If you were told before a lecture 'Whatever happens you mustn't think that your lecturer looks a bit like a hobbit', then probably all through the lecture you would be thinking 'Doesn't he look like a hobbit?' It is the same with food. If you wake up in the morning and decide 'I'm not going to think about chocolate today', the chances are you will think about chocolate a lot. This is the dilemma that faces health professionals who are trying to help people to eat less.

1 Think about how you would phrase some health education advice designed to encourage people to eat healthily and that does not make them become preoccupied with food.

2 Then consider how you would design a study to evaluate the success of your health education intervention. Make some notes and discuss these with your teacher and/or other members of your psychology class.

Some suggestions are given in the Answers to activities on p.603. ▶

Possible causes of overeating

Research has investigated possible mechanisms for the overeating shown by restrained eaters. These include the causal model of overeating, mood modification and denial.

Causal analysis of overeating

Herman and Polivy (1980) presented a causal analysis of eating behaviour. They suggested that dieting and bingeing were causally linked and that 'restraint not only precedes over-eating but contributes to it causally' (Polivy and Herman 1985). It would appear that attempting not to eat can, paradoxically, increase the probability of overeating. This causal analysis of restraint represented a new approach to eating behaviour, and the prediction that restraint can actually cause overeating was an interesting reappraisal of the situation. Wardle (1980) developed this analysis further and in 1988 Wardle and Beales tested the causal analysis of overeating experimentally, using people who were dieting. Their results indicated that trying to diet could result in overeating (see Key research study on p.171).

Mood modification

Dieters tend to overeat in response to lowered mood. Researchers have argued that disinhibitory behaviour enables the individual to mask their negative mood with the temporary heightened mood caused by eating. This is known as the 'masking hypothesis' and has been empirically tested. For example, Polivy and Herman (1999) informed female participants that they had either passed or failed a cognitive task and then either gave them as

Using the preload/taste-test method to study eating behaviour

Key research: Herman and Mack (1975)

Using the preload/taste-test method, Herman and Mack gave a group of dieters and a group of non-dieters either a high- or low-calorie preload. The results indicated that whereas the non-dieters showed compensatory regulatory behaviour, and ate less during the taste test after the high-calorie preload, the dieters consumed more in the taste test if they had had the high-calorie preload than the low-calorie preload (see Figure 5.3). This form of disinhibition involves overeating in response to a high-calorie preload. A number of research studies have since examined the role of restraint in predicting overeating behaviour (e.g. Ruderman 1986, Herman *et al.* 1987 and Polivy *et al.* 1988).

Although Herman and Mack (1975) only studied a fairly small sample, the report of their research was published in a peer-reviewed journal (but not the one widely regarded as the most prestigious journal in the field at that time). This paper has, however, been cited widely across the English-speaking world and triggered a new way of thinking about eating behaviour. The impact of this research is probably due to three factors:

- The approach they used was novel, interesting and the findings challenged some of the contemporary ways of thinking about eating behaviour.

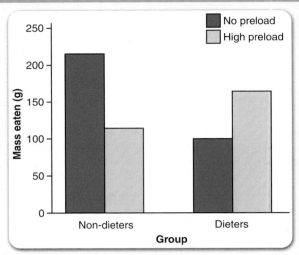

Figure 5.3 *Overeating in dieters in the laboratory (after Herman and Mack 1975)*

- The results demonstrated that trying not to eat could result in overeating – a finding that probably resonated with the personal experience of many researchers, clinicians and lay people alike.
- The study was undertaken in a controlled laboratory setting, giving it some scientific credibility.

much food as they wanted, or small, controlled amounts of food. The results partly supported the masking hypothesis because the dieters who ate as much as they liked attributed more of their distress to their eating behaviour than to failure on the task. Polivy and Herman argued that dieters may overeat as a means of shifting responsibility for their negative mood from uncontrollable aspects of their lives onto their eating behaviour.

The role of denial

Cognitive research has shown that thought suppression and thought control can have the paradoxical effect of making the thoughts that an individual is trying to suppress more salient (Wenzlaff and Wegner 2000). This has been called the 'theory of ironic processes of mental control' (Wegner 1994). For example, in an early study, participants were asked to try not to think about a white bear, but to ring a bell if they did (Wegner *et al.* 1987). The results showed that those trying not to think about the bear actually thought about the bear more frequently than those who were told to think about it. A decision to eat less, or not to eat specific foods, is central to the dieter's cognitive set and may set up a similar process of denial. Therefore, as soon as food is denied, it simultaneously becomes forbidden and is, eventually, translated into eating. Soetens *et al.* (2006) undertook an experiment to investigate the impact of trying to suppress eating-related thoughts on

subsequent thoughts about eating. Their sample was divided into restrained and unrestrained eaters; the restrained eaters were then divided into those who were either high or low on disinhibition. The results showed that the disinhibited, restrained eaters (i.e. those who try to eat less but often overeat) used more thought suppression than the other groups. This group also demonstrated a rebound effect following the thought-suppression task. This means that restrained eaters who tend to overeat try to suppress thoughts about food more often, but if they do, they usually think about food more often afterwards.

Dieting and weight loss

As we have seen, dieting can be associated with periods of overeating, and research has shown that this can result in weight fluctuations. Although dieters aim to lose weight by attempting to restrict their food intake, this is not always achieved. Heatherton *et al.* (1991) reported that restrained eaters show both undereating and overeating, and that this behaviour resulted in weight fluctuations, but not actual weight loss. Thus, actual weight loss is limited by compensatory overeating. Heatherton *et al.* (1988, p.20) argued that 'the restrained eater who is exclusively restrained ... is not representative of restrained eaters in general, whereas the restrained eater who occasionally splurges is'. Ogden (1993) examined the concept of restraint, as assessed by a variety of measures, and found

An experimental investigation of the causal analysis of overeating

Key research: Wardle and Beales (1988)

Wardle and Beales carried out an experiment to investigate whether dieting resulted in overeating. They randomly assigned 27 obese women either to a diet group, an exercise group or a control group (no intervention) for seven weeks.

All participants took part in a laboratory procedure to assess their food intake at weeks four and six. The results indicated that participants in the diet condition ate more than those in the exercise group and also those in the control group, supporting a causal link between dieting and overeating. From this analysis, the overeating shown by dieters appears to be caused by attempts at dieting.

Evaluation

Wardle and Beales' study has several strengths:

- *An experimental design* – The researchers were able to manipulate whether people dieted, exercised or did neither. Comparisons could therefore be made across the different groups.

- *Random allocation* – Participants were randomly allocated to the different conditions, so they should have been similar in all other ways, except the type of experimental intervention.

- *Laboratory conditions* – These enabled eating behaviour to be assessed while other factors were controlled.

- *A non-student sample* – Results could then be generalized to a wider population.

The main weaknesses of this study include:

- *Small sample size* – The numbers in each condition of the independent groups design were therefore even smaller, limiting the representativeness of the sample, so any generalizations must be tentative.

- *Participants' alternative agenda* – Although the women were randomly allocated to the three conditions, they may not have complied with what they were asked to do because they all wanted to lose weight. It is likely that they will have continued with whatever attempts they had been making to lose weight prior to the study.

- *A non-natural setting* – Measuring eating behaviour in a laboratory setting is associated with a number of challenges, and participants are aware they are being assessed, which may cause their behaviour to change (this is known as the Hawthorne effect).

In spite of its limitations, this study has been influential in several ways. It highlighted the possible detrimental impact of dieting in the context of restraint theory. The results were disseminated in the non-scientific community and have influenced beliefs such as 'dieting can make you fat' and 'dieting doesn't work'. Although this may actually be the case, it is possible that there may be a self-fulfilling prophecy element: believing that dieting is not effective means that diets become less successful because people assumed they would not work before they had even started to try to lose weight. Wardle and Beales' study also paved the way for further research.

that high scorers on measures of restraint were characterized by both successful and failed restriction, suggesting that restrained eating is best characterized as an intention which is only sporadically realized. Research evidence suggests that dieting is probably best understood as 'attempting to lose weight but not doing so' and 'attempting to eat less but which may result in eating more'.

Evaluation of the research evidence on dieting

- *Emphasis on bodily dissatisfaction* – The research focuses on bodily dissatisfaction, which is a common determinant of the ways in which people eat.

- *Use of experimental research* – Much of the research has used an experimental approach, enabling key variables to be manipulated in a controlled way.

- *The findings reflect people's experiences* – The research findings reflect the experiences of many

Activity Changing eating behaviour

As we have seen, some research suggests that trying to eat less can result in overeating.

- Think about people who successfully manage to change the way they eat, e.g. vegetarians who stop eating meat but do not crave it, or those who change their diet for religious reasons.

- Note down some possible reasons why they can successfully change their eating behaviour and discuss these with other students in your psychology class.

Some suggestions are given in the Answers to activities on p.603. ▶

people who have tried to lose weight by limiting what they eat (see the discussion of obesity, p.179).

- *Limitations of restraint as an explanatory theory* – Restraint theory relies on the belief of an association between food restriction and overeating. Although dieters, people with bulimia and those with anorexia nervosa who binge report episodes of overeating, restricting anorexia cannot be accounted for by restraint theory. If attempting not to eat results in overeating, how do people with **restricting anorexia** manage to starve themselves? Also, if attempting not to eat something can result in eating it, how can the fact that vegetarians never eat meat be explained?

CHECK YOUR UNDERSTANDING

Check your understanding of eating behaviour by answering the following questions. Try to do this from memory. You can check your answers by looking back through Topic 1, Eating behaviour.

1 List at least five different cognitions that people may hold about food.

2 Describe one social cognition model that has been used to predict eating behaviour.

3 What are the main strengths and limitations of a social cognitive approach to eating behaviour?

4 Outline the three mechanisms that illustrate a developmental approach to eating behaviour.

5 Explain how parental control can influence children's food preferences.

6 How can mood influence eating behaviour?

7 Explain how stress can affect what people eat.

8 What is the preload/taste-test method and how has it been used to investigate eating behaviour?

9 What key factors may influence successful weight loss and maintenance?

10 Explain why people on a diet sometimes overeat when trying to lose weight.

Topic 2: Biological explanations of eating behaviour

Psychology in context

Cravings

Women often report that their food preferences change during pregnancy – some suddenly dislike coffee but crave strong-tasting foods such as curry; others develop a craving for unusual foods such as pickled onions, radishes or liquorice. It has also been observed that many children seem to have a sweet tooth which often disappears in adulthood, only to reappear in old age. Some women also crave sweet foods around the time of their period. Furthermore, drugs used for the treatment of a number of different illnesses can have a side-effect of either increasing or decreasing a person's appetite and weight.

1 What do these observations suggest about the possible basis of eating behaviour?

2 How might this help to explain the reasons why we choose certain foods and avoid others?

3 How might changes in food preference help us understand what drives us to start or stop eating?

4 Think about any biological reasons behind what you eat. Compare and contrast your ideas with those identified by other students in your psychology class. Did you identify any factors beyond the psychological mechanisms discussed in Topic 1?

Eating behaviour seems to have a strong biological basis. Feeling hungry is one of the basic biological drives that cause us to eat in order to stay alive. A biological model of eating behaviour focuses on hunger, satiety and the role of neurochemicals in determining when and how much we eat. Hunger is generally regarded as a state that follows food deprivation and reflects a motivation (or drive) to eat. It also reflects a more conscious state, reflecting a feeling or desire to eat (Blundell *et al.* 1989). Satiety is considered to be the opposite to hunger – the motivation to stop eating and the conscious feeling that enough food has been consumed. This topic will focus on metabolic models of eating, including the role of the hypothalamus, the impact of neurochemicals on hunger and satiety, and an evolutionary approach to eating in terms of some research evidence for innate food preferences.

Neural mechanisms and eating behaviour

From a biological perspective, eating behaviour is generally referred to as ingestive behaviour. The dominant model for understanding why and when we eat emphasizes homeostasis and focuses on the role of negative feedback. At the beginning of the 19th century, Walter Cannon coined the term **homeostasis** to refer to the mechanisms by which biological variables, including eating, are regulated within defined limits. For example, when we get hot we sweat, which cools us; when we become dehydrated we experience thirst, which makes us drink more; and likewise when we need food we experience hunger, which makes us eat. Homeostasis is maintained via a negative feedback loop which assumes that any given bodily variable has a set point (or range) and that the actual value of this variable is compared by the body to where it should be and adjusted accordingly.

In terms of body weight, it has been suggested that each person has a set point and their weight is regulated around this point. In relation to hunger, the body has a sense of what is acceptable and regulates eating around this. Several different mechanisms have been proposed as the basis for this negative feedback loop, including our fat stores (the lipostatic hypothesis) and our glucose levels (the glucostatic hypothesis), which suggests that when either our fat stores are depleted or when our blood glucose levels are low, we feel hungry, which makes us eat.

More recently, researchers have emphasized the importance of cellular energy in the regulation of food intake. In particular, research has highlighted a role for adenosine trisophate (ATP), which is a product of the breakdown of macronutrients. It is suggested that fats, carbohydrates and proteins are initially broken down into small molecules and then eventually into cellular energy and waste via a metabolic chain, called the citric acid cycle. ATP is a form of cellular energy and is considered important for the regulation and maintenance of homeostasis.

Although these biological models of eating behaviour have been the basis of much research, most approaches to eating behaviour today regard biological factors as only the starting point to an understanding of food intake, given what we know about the role of learning and cognitions (described in Topic 1).

The hypothalamus

Researchers working within a biological approach have attempted to locate areas of the brain associated with feeding. Early clues to the role of the brain came from patients with tumours of the basal hypothalamus who became obese. Research has since been carried out, using a number of methods, including:

- experimentally induced lesions to the hypothalamus in animals

- investigations of changes in feeding after damage to specific sites in the brain

- the effects of neurotransmitters introduced into discrete parts of the brain

- the impact of drugs (recreational and medicinal) on feeding

- the use of **functional magnetic resonance imaging (fMRI)**.

Early studies proposed a simple model of feeding and indicated that the hypothalamus was central to food intake, with the medial hypothalamus being the 'satiety centre' and the lateral hypothalamus being the 'feeding centre'. More recently, researchers have proposed a more complex approach to understanding feeding and have developed a hierarchical model which emphasizes the

hypothalamus as important, but also highlights a role for numerous other brain regions. From this perspective, the regions of the brain most closely linked with feeding are the paraventrial hypothalamus and the perifornical area. Central to both the simple and more complex models, however, are a number of neurotransmitters which are regarded as key to our understanding of the neurobiological basis of eating behaviour.

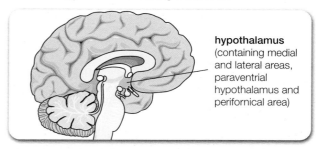

hypothalamus (containing medial and lateral areas, paraventrial hypothalamus and perifornical area)

Figure 5.4 *The hypothalamus*

The psychophysiology of food intake highlights the role of three main neurotransmitter pathways that influence appetite and are situated either in the central nervous system or the peripheral nervous system. These are:

- the catecholamines

- serotonin

- peptides.

These will now be considered in terms of those that increase food intake and those that decrease it.

Neurotransmitters that increase food intake

A number of neurotransmitters are associated with an increase in eating behaviour:

- *Norepinephrine (NE)* – This catecholamine was the first neurotransmitter to be linked with eating behaviour. Research indicates that injections of NE into the hypothalamus can stimulate feeding if injected into the paraventricular nucleus and can reduce feeding if injected into the perfornical area of the hypothalamus. Studies also show that the injection of NE is most effective if given at mealtimes. Leibowitz (1986) has carried out a lot of research in this area and suggests that NE may not only increase calorie intake, but may also trigger a specific desire for carbohydrate intake.

- *Neuropeptide Y* – This is a 33 amino acid peptide and high concentrations of it are found in the paraventricular hypothalamus and the perifornical hypothalamus. Research has found that if injected with neuropeptide Y, rats who are already full will still consume large amounts of food. It also appears to cause a preference for carbohydrates (Leibowitz 1986).

- *Galanin* – This is a 29 amino acid peptide that is widespread in the brain but is particularly found in the paraventricular hypothalamus. Injections of galanin into rats cause an increase in food intake and a preference for fats rather than carbohydrates (Leibowitz 1986).

Neurotransmitters and modulators that decrease food intake

A number of neurotransmitters decrease food intake (Rowland *et al.* 1996):

- *Cholecystokinin (CCK)* – This endogenous 33 amino acid peptide is released into the bloodstream during meals and is widespread in the brain. If injected into rats, CCK causes a reduction in appetite and satiation. It also suppresses weight gain.

- *Bombesin* – This peptide has been shown to reduce food intake in rats.

- *Corticotropin-releasing hormone (CRH)* – This is a 41 amino acid peptide produced in the paraventricular hypothalamus and a number of other brain sites. It has been shown to reduce food intake.

- *Serotonin (5HT)* – Serotonin or 5HT is a neurotransmitter which has also been shown to decrease food intake.

Neurotransmitters, therefore, seem to function by either increasing or decreasing food intake. The role of neurotransmitters has also been investigated through research on the impact of drugs on eating behaviour.

The impact of drugs on eating behaviour

Studying the impact of drugs on eating behaviour provides another means of understanding the neurochemical basis of hunger and satiation (Blundell *et al.* 1989). Much of this research has been carried out on animals in the laboratory; only a few studies have been carried out on humans. The effects of these drugs are relevant to our understanding of the psychophysiology of hunger and satiety because they provide a window into the chemical and metabolic processes involved and so have been described as 'pharmacological scalpels which may be used to dissect the structure of eating behaviour' (Blundell *et al.* 1989, p.85). If we understand the ways in which particular drugs make us want to eat more or less, and also how these drugs affect our brains, we can begin to comprehend how the chemicals in our brains influence what, how and when we eat and stop eating. We will now consider the effects of drugs on hunger, and how these drug effects are linked to the neurotransmitters:

- *Nicotine* – decreases food intake; smokers generally weigh about three kilograms (seven pounds) less than non-smokers (US Department of Health and Human Services 1990). According to Ogden and Fox (1994), some dieters use smoking as a weight-loss strategy, and smoking cessation may result in increased consumption of calories, particularly from sweet foods (Ogden 1994).

- *Amphetamines* – also closely linked with food intake. In particular, they have been shown to have a dramatic suppressant impact on both subjective hunger and food intake (Silverstone and Kyriakides 1982), and have been given both legally and illegally to dieters for many years.

- *Marijuana* – has been shown to increase hunger and food intake (e.g. Hollister 1971).

- *Alcohol* – seems to influence food intake in contradictory ways: some studies indicate that it can have a weak inhibitory effect and others have reported that alcohol can stimulate hunger (Hollister 1971).

- *Anti-psychotic drugs* – given to those suffering from psychosis, usually schizophrenia or manic depression. Studies of these drugs show that both lithium and chlorpromazine cause considerable weight gain (Vendsborg *et al.* 1976, Robinson *et al.* 1975).

- *Tricyclic anti-depressants* – until recently, the main medical treatment for depression. Studies show that amitryptiline has a slight effect on hunger and is associated with a craving for sweet food and weight gain (Blundell *et al.* 1989).

- *Selective serotonin reuptake inhibitors (SSRIs)* – now more commonly used for patients with depression. These anti-depressants do not appear to induce either weight gain or an increased desire for sweet foods and may even promote weight loss (Blundell *et al.* 1989).

- *Analgesics* – drugs that are used for pain relief and have been shown to influence hunger and satiety. For example, Naloxone can trigger decreased food intake (Trenchard and Silverstone 1983) and morphine has also been found to have a weak depressant effect on hunger (Beecher 1959).

- *Appetite-suppressant drugs* – e.g. Fenfluoramine and Dexfenfluoramine, have been shown to have a consistent depressant effect on hunger and to reduce food intake (Blundell and Hill 1988). These have now been removed from the market because they were linked with heart problems. Likewise, Tryptophan and Sibutramine can also reduce eating behaviour (Kopelman 1999). In addition, hormones of the small intestine, such as cholecystokinin (CCK), have also been shown to inhibit food intake (Kissileff *et al.* 1981), although it is not currently available as a prescribed drug.

In summary, drugs appear to have differential effects on hunger. Studying these effects has highlighted the ways in which these drugs influence the chemical activity of our brain and how this chemical activity in turn relates to eating behaviour. It has been suggested that the catecholamine, serotonin and peptide pathways influence eating behaviour in the following ways:

- The serotonin pathways influence the feelings of fullness (known as satiety) during a meal, thereby causing the person to stop eating.

-

Catecholamines influence satiety between meals, thereby triggering hunger and determining the intervals between eating.

- Peptides appear to influence the reward and pleasurable (sometimes referred to as 'hedonic') properties of food (Blundell *et al.* 1989).

The drugs mentioned on p.174 influence these pathways in the following ways:

- Amphetamine, amitryptiline and other tricyclics influence the catecholamine pathway.

- SSRIs, Fenfluoramine and Tryptophan influence the serotonin pathway.

- CCK, Naloxone and morphine are peptides and influence the pleasure associated with eating food.

Some drugs have non-specific effects, including chlorpromazine and lithium, which influence both the catecholamine and serotonin pathways, and others, such as nicotine and marijuana, appear to have more generalized effects.

Therefore, the drugs which have been shown to influence hunger and weight gain provide insights into the physiology of hunger and satiety. They illustrate the extent to which the neurotransmitters affected by these drugs influence the commencement of eating, the end of eating and the pleasure associated with food intake. Further details about the physiology of food intake can be found in Mela and Rogers (1998).

> ### IDA Is a biological approach reductionist?
>
> As we have seen, there are several different approaches to understanding eating behaviour, including social, cognitive and developmental perspectives. A focus on the biological mechanisms associated with eating reflects a reductionist approach, as it takes a complex human behaviour and reduces it to brain chemicals. However, researchers who endorse such an approach do not necessarily regard it as being reductionist, but rather they believe that all behaviour will ultimately be understood in terms of brain activity.

Evaluation of neural mechanisms and eating behaviour

- *Reflection of people's experience* – Biological explanations emphasize the importance of hunger and satiety and reflect how people experience their eating behaviour: they feel hungry and eat; during eating, they begin to feel full and so stop eating.

- *Insight into brain chemicals* – Investigations into the brain chemicals behind eating behaviour could be used to develop medical interventions to help change what we eat.

- *Explanation of some differences* – This approach can help explain why some people with certain medical conditions (e.g. brain lesions, diabetes, cancer) may eat differently.

- *Laboratory-based research sometimes involving non-human animals* – Much psychobiological research has been undertaken in laboratories and some has used non-human animals to provide models of food choice by humans. The extent to which the research findings from highly controlled studies, particularly animal studies, can enhance our understanding of eating behaviour in humans remains unclear.

- *Influence of social factors and social drives* – Although food choice may relate to neurochemicals and brain pathways, eating is an inherently social behaviour and often takes place in the presence of others. Food has, therefore, acquired and represents a range of important social meanings. Our biological drives are often moderated and modified by social drives. A biological explanation of food choice does not explicitly acknowledge social learning or social meanings.

- *Physiological drives can be overridden* – A biological approach assumes that an individual will respond to hunger by eating, and to satiety by stopping eating. However, many individuals override their physiological drive to eat, due to factors such as a desire to be thin, a dislike of food or a fear of losing control. They can also override the drive to stop eating because of social cues to continue eating or the availability of more food.

> ### IDA Studying non-human animals to understand human eating behaviour
>
> Much of the research on eating behaviour undertaken from a biological perspective involves the study of non-human animals. This either involves research on non-human animals that are deemed to have similar feeding mechanisms to humans, or explores the ways in which non-human animals eat to inform our understanding of how human beings eat. This approach raises two important issues:
>
> 1 Is it ethical to undertake research with non-human animals as a means of understanding human beings (see pp.33–34 of the Introductory chapter)?
>
> 2 Do human beings still behave in similar ways to non-human animals, or have they become so socialized that any prior animal-like behaviours have become submerged or eliminated by the social processes of learning and culture?

Evolutionary explanations of food preference

According to an evolutionary approach, current human behaviour can be understood in terms of how it may have been adaptive in our ancestral past. Evolutionary psychologists refer to this as the 'ultimate explanation'. So, although current behaviours may appear to be maladaptive or dysfunctional, evolutionary psychologists argue that they can be analysed and understood as having been adaptive and functional in some way in the past. To undertake this type of analysis, they draw on the theory of natural selection and suggest that all species, including humans, evolve through a process of natural selection and that only those characteristics that confer advantage, or at least do not confer disadvantage, survive as the species evolves. This is an interactionist approach, as an individual's genetic predisposition is assumed to interact with their environment.

In terms of eating behaviour, an evolutionary psychologist is interested in the following questions: 'Are there innate preferences for certain foods?', 'How would these preferences have been adaptive in the past?' and 'How do these preferences function now?' We will examine each of these issues in turn.

Innate preferences for food

Early research by Davis (1928, 1939) investigated the eating behaviour of infants and young children. Davis observed the kinds of choices children living in a paediatric unit made in relation to their diet. Based on her data, Davis concluded that young children have an innate, regulatory mechanism and are able to select a healthy diet. However, she emphasized that they could only do this if healthy food was available, and suggested that the children's food preferences changed over time and were modified by experience (see Key research by Davis 1928).

Subsequent research has provided further support for some form of innate regulatory mechanisms. For example, there is consistent evidence that newborn babies demonstrate innate food preferences. Using facial expressions and sucking behaviour as an index of preference, babies have been shown to prefer sweet-tasting substances (Desor *et al.* 1973) and to reject bitter tastes (Geldard 1972). There is also some evidence for an innate preference for salt, based on animal research, although this has been controversial (Denton 1982). Taken together, these studies suggest that some food preferences are innate. Beauchamp and Moran (1982) reported, however, that six-month-old babies who were accustomed to drinking sweetened water drank more sweetened water than those babies who were not. So, although innate food preferences may exist, these may be modified very quickly by learning and familiarity.

Food preferences of young children

Key research: Davis (1928)

In an early study, Davis investigated the kinds of choices that children make about their diet. This research was conducted at a time when feeding policies typically imposed a highly restricted feeding regime. Davis was interested to examine young children's responses to a self-selected diet and whether there was an 'instinctive means of handling ... the problem of optimal nutrition' (Davis 1928).

The children, who were living in a paediatric unit in the USA for several months, were offered a predetermined range of 10 to 12 healthy foods prepared without sugar, salt or seasoning and were free to eat whatever they liked. Davis observed and recorded which foods they chose. The findings indicated that the children were able to select a diet that was consistent with growth and health and no feeding problems were observed. These findings formed the basis of a 'wisdom of the body' theory which highlighted innate food preferences.

Since observation was used in a naturalistic, yet controlled, environment, Davis was able to assess eating behaviour in a relatively natural environment, which means it could be assumed that the children's food intake and choices would, to some extent, reflect those they would make in their daily lives.

Davis' research represented a novel and interesting study and was published in a prestigious, peer-reviewed medical journal. It has since been widely cited by researchers and clinicians from both medicine and other allied disciplines, including psychology, nutrition and sociology. It was published at a time when children's diets were highly prescribed and the findings were therefore considered to be controversial. The research findings have been used to support different sides of the same argument:

1 They highlight the wisdom of the body and the existence of biological drives.

2 They can also be used to demonstrate the importance of the environment, since the types of foods offered to the children were restricted and healthy.

Research methods for measuring eating behaviour

Assessing eating behaviour in any research context is problematic and all methods of measurement have their strengths and weaknesses:

- *Laboratory observation* – Assessing eating in a laboratory provides an environment in which other variables can be controlled and assessed, but this artificial approach may not reflect eating in the real world.

- *Questionnaires and food diaries* – These provide insights into what people eat in their daily lives, but are reliant on self-report data which may not be accurate, as people often forget what they have eaten, particularly if it is not part of a meal. Furthermore, the act of recording what is eaten may change what is eaten because people become more aware of their food intake.

- *Naturalistic observation* – These methods may capture real-life eating, but if the participants know they are being observed this may change their behaviour (see the **Hawthorne effect**). Even if they do not know they are being observed, eating in a public place where they can be observed may not accurately reflect how and what they eat in private.

How might innate food preferences have been adaptive?

Our early human ancestors lived in hunter-gatherer communities in which the men were responsible for hunting and the women were responsible for gathering. Their diets consisted mainly of fruits, berries, vegetables and some meat. Our innate food preferences can be explained as follows:

- An innate preference for sweet foods would have encouraged people to eat fruit with its natural fructose content. Sweet foods in nature provide important calories which are needed for energy.

- Natural avoidance of bitter foods would have helped to protect people from eating food that was poisonous. This would also have been helped by neophobia (the fear of eating novel foods).

- A preference for salt is less easy to explain, although we do know that salt is essential for the sodium balance in our bodies. Sheep manage their sodium levels by licking naturally occurring minerals that contain salt because grass has very low sodium content. Human beings, on the other hand, have very little need for additional salt, particularly if they eat meat. The innate preference for salt may, therefore, have originally functioned by encouraging people to eat meat.

Activity · Design a study to investigate the influence of social and biological drives on eating behaviour

Although we are social beings, some research into eating behaviour suggests that we may still eat in response to some innate biological drives. Design a research study to investigate whether biological drives are modified by learning.

Discuss your ideas with other students in your psychology class, focusing on any possible problems with the research method you are proposing to use and whether it is possible to disentangle the contribution of social and biological drives to eating behaviour in humans.

Some suggestions are given in the Answers to activities on p.603. ▶

Innate food preferences in the modern world

In our ancestral past, the main challenge facing people would have been avoiding malnutrition by eating enough food to support a physically active lifestyle. Our innate food preferences may have helped us to survive. For much of the modern world, however, food is no longer scarce and our lives are no longer as physically active (see Topic 3 on obesity, pp.179–187). Nowadays, a preference for sweet foods may no longer encourage a person to eat berries, but rather to eat highly calorific, energy-dense foods, such as chocolate bars. Furthermore, a preference for salty foods may facilitate the consumption of high-fat foods flavoured with salt, such as chips and processed foods.

An evolutionary explanation for obesity has been put forward, based on biological preferences for foods which cause overeating and problems with weight in our modern world, which has been called an '**obesogenic environment**'. There are many factors in our environment, such as fast-food outlets and cars, which encourage an unhealthy lifestyle and may contribute to higher levels of obesity.

Activity · Looking at your environment

On your way to school or college in the morning, look about you and note down any aspects of the environment that could be considered to be 'obesogenic'. Think about how our environment has changed over the past 50 years or more.

1 Do you think that these changes have made it more difficult to be thin and easier to be overweight? Give reasons for your answer.

2 Discuss your answers with your teacher and/or other students in your psychology class.

Some suggestions are given in the Answers to activities on p.603. ▶

IDA — Biological models of eating behaviour

Several different theoretical perspectives have informed our current understanding of eating behaviour. The biological models described in Topic 2 draw on physiological and evolutionary perspectives. Both these approaches locate human beings within their biological past and make connections between us as social beings and also as animals.

Evaluation of evolutionary explanations of food preference

- *Reductionist and determinist* – Like biological explanations, evolutionary explanations of eating might be regarded as an oversimplification by suggesting that adaptiveness is the single, guiding principle. Such explanations are also determinist, as they propose that eating behaviour is determined by past environments, thereby overlooking the notion of free will and the fact that human behaviour is affected by many other factors such as thoughts, emotions and social factors. Evolutionary drives are moderated and modified by social drives.

- *Evolutionary accounts can explain innate food preferences* – evolutionary approaches can explain innate food preferences that were important for our ancestors' survival. An innate preference for sweet foods may lead us to consume energy-dense foods, such as chocolate bars, which are no longer needed in the current obesogenic environment of the Western world, and can help to explain the recent upsurge in obesity.

- *Observed food preferences can support nature and nurture* – Innate preferences for food can be used to demonstrate the wisdom of the body, the existence of biological drives and also the importance of the environment. It is also difficult to measure eating behaviour accurately in a research context.

- *Difficult to falsify* – The central concept of adaptiveness can be applied to many behaviours, including eating, and is difficult to demonstrate empirically or disprove. This means that we have no means of establishing the validity of the explanation.

-

Focus on ultimate rather than proximate causes – A strength of evolutionary explanations is that they consider ultimate causes and so may lead to more valid ways of treating seemingly maladaptive behaviours by taking account of their adaptive significance and not merely focusing on the proximate problem (such as overeating).

- *Has human evolution stopped?* – Evolutionary explanations appear to suggest that we are no longer adapting to changing environmental conditions. Some scientists believe that humans are continuing to evolve both physically and psychologically and are doing so at a faster rate than any other close species (Wills 1999).

CHECK YOUR UNDERSTANDING

Check your understanding of biological explanations of eating behaviour by answering the following questions. Try to do this from memory. You can check your answers by looking back through Topic 2, Biological explanations of eating behaviour.

1. How can homeostasis and negative feedback explain why and when we eat?

2. Which part of the brain is most associated with feeding?

3. How can the impact of drugs help us understand eating behaviour?

4. Which neurotransmitters influence what we eat and how do these neurotransmitters influence eating behaviour?

5. Outline three different ways in which eating behaviour can be measured. Why is it difficult to measure eating behaviour accurately?

6. Describe an evolutionary approach to eating behaviour.

7. What evidence is there for innate food preferences? What are the limitations of this evidence?

8. What is an obesogenic environment? Give three examples of obesogenic elements of our environment today?

9. What are the main strengths and the limitations of a biological approach to eating behaviour?

Psychology in context Eating disorders and obesity

Two important, health-related issues in society today could seem contradictory. On the one hand, there is an epidemic of obesity in Western society and, on the other hand, we have an apparent dramatic increase in eating disorders such as anorexia nervosa. The media is full of stories about eating disorders in young women and, increasingly, in young men, and the fast-food culture is often blamed for the recent upsurge in obesity. Magazines include photos of people who are grossly overweight and also of stick-thin celebrities, accompanied by headlines questioning whether this is an indication of an eating disorder.

As we have seen in Topics 1 and 2, there are psychological and biological explanations of eating behaviour. However, a key test of any theory of eating behaviour is how well it explains both the life-threatening weight loss associated with anorexia nervosa and increasing levels of obesity.

1 Can obesity and eating disorders be explained entirely by biological problems in, say, hormone levels or brain mechanisms of weight regulation? Or, do they involve more complex interactions between biology and psychology?

2 Does a person who is obese simply lack will power? Do you think that people with anorexia suffer from deep-seated psychological problems? Or are they both victims of their biological constitution?

3 Find a recent copy of a celebrity magazine and think about the images of physical attractiveness that are being promoted. What images are used to indicate a problem with food? What contradictions are we bombarded with when we read this type of magazine?

This topic focuses on obesity and examines its prevalence, causes and how it has been explained from psychological and biological perspectives.

Obesity

According to Tataranni (2000), one out of two adult Americans in the US were either overweight or obese in the late 1990s. In the UK, there is an upward trend in obesity, with over half of women and about two-thirds of men either overweight or obese. It has been estimated that deaths linked to obesity shorten life by an average (mean) of nine years (National Audit Office 2001). It is little wonder, therefore, that Mokdad *et al.* (1999) refer to the 'obesity epidemic'.

Moreover, the World Health Organization has identified obesity as one of the major chronic diseases that increases the risk of a number of non-communicable diseases (such as **Type 2 diabetes** and high blood pressure) and reduces life expectancy (Must *et al.* 1999). A recent study by Massó-González (2009) estimated the incidence and prevalence of diabetes in the UK general population (aged between 10 and 79) between 1996 and 2005. While the incidence of **Type 1 diabetes** remained relatively constant throughout the study period, the proportion of individuals newly diagnosed with Type 2 diabetes increased from 46 per cent to 56 per cent. This

marked increase over a decade is probably largely explained by the rise in obesity in the UK.

What is obesity?

Obesity can be defined in a number of ways – the two most common and useful ways involve **body mass index (BMI)** and waist circumference:

▪ BMI is calculated by dividing a person's weight (in kilograms) by their height (in metres) squared (i.e. weight in kilograms/height in metres^2. This produces a figure which has been categorized as normal weight (20–24.9), overweight (grade 1, 25–29.9), clinical obesity (grade 2, 30–39.9) and severe obesity (grade 3, >40). Although this is the most frequently used definition of obesity, it does not allow for differences in weight between muscle and fat (for example, a bodybuilder would be classified as obese!), nor does it account for the location of fat.

- Waist circumference – An analysis of the location of fat is important because abdominal fat, rather than lower body fat, can predict the incidence of health problems such as diabetes. Researchers initially used waist–hip ratios to assess obesity although, more recently, waist circumference on its own has become the preferred approach. According to Lean *et al.* (1998), weight reduction is recommended when waist circumference is greater than 102 centimetres (40 inches) in men and greater than 88 cms (35 inches) in women.

How common is obesity?

Obesity rates are increasing in the UK. If obesity is defined as a BMI greater than 30, reports indicate that in 1980, six per cent of men and eight per cent of women were obese. This had increased to 17 per cent and 21 per cent respectively by 1998, with no sign that this upward trend is reducing (National Audit Office 2001). Chinn and Rona (2001) analysed data for English children and reported that nine per cent of boys and 13.5 per cent of girls were overweight in 1994, and that 1.7 per cent of boys and 2.6 per cent of girls were obese; these figures were more than 50 per cent higher than 10 years earlier. Estimates for the US suggest that roughly half of American adults are overweight, that a third are obese, that women in particular have become heavier in recent years, and that the prevalence of overweight children has doubled in the past 20 years (Ogden *et al.* 1997, National Institute of Health 1998).

Across the world, the highest rates of obesity are found in Tunisia, the USA, Saudi Arabia and Canada, and the lowest in China, Mali, Japan, Sweden and Brazil. The UK, Australia and New Zealand are all placed in the middle of the range. Across Europe the highest rates are in Lithuania, Malta, Russia and Serbia and the lowest are in Sweden, Ireland, Denmark and the UK. Overall, people in Northern and Western Europe are thinner than in Eastern and Southern Europe, and women are more likely to be obese than men (www.who.int/mediacentre/factsheets/fs311/en/index.html).

The consequences of obesity

Obesity is associated with a range of physical and psychological problems.

Physical health problems

Obesity has been associated with cardiovascular disease, diabetes, joint trauma, back pain, cancer, high blood pressure and mortality. The effects of obesity are related to where the excess weight is located. Weight stored in the upper body, particularly the abdomen, is more detrimental to health than weight carried on the lower body. It is interesting to note that although men are more likely than women to store fat on their upper bodies, and are therefore more at risk if obese, women are more concerned about weight than men, and most treatment studies involve women. In terms of the link between obesity and mortality, a study of 14077 women found a direct linear relationship between BMI and risk factors for heart disease, including blood pressure, cholesterol and blood glucose (Ashton *et al.* 2001). Similar studies have

also reported a relationship between BMI increases in the lower range of the spectrum and high blood pressure, diabetes and heart attack (Romero-Corral 2006).

Psychological problems

Research has examined the relationship between obesity and psychological problems. The current cultural obsession with thinness and an aversion to fatness in both adults and children, and the attribution of blame to people who are obese may promote low self-esteem and poor self-image in those individuals who do not conform to the stereotypically attractive thin image. Studies investigating levels of depression in those waiting for surgical treatment for obesity have consistently found that such patients report more depressive symptoms than individuals of average weight (e.g. Wadden *et al.* 2006). In addition, Rand and McGregor (1991) reported that individuals who had lost weight following gastric bypass surgery stated that they would rather be deaf, suffer from dyslexia, diabetes, heart disease or acne, than return to their former weight and size. More recently, Simon *et al.* (2006) carried out a large survey on over 9000 adults in the US and concluded that obesity was associated with increased lifetime diagnosis of major depression, bipolar disorder, panic disorder or agoraphobia.

However, it is possible that obese individuals who are depressed are more likely to seek treatment for their obesity than those who are not depressed, and that there may be many obese individuals who are quite happy and do not, therefore, come into contact with health professionals. Ross (1994) investigated this possibility and conducted telephone interviews with a random sample of over 2000 adults. These were individuals who varied in weight and were not necessarily seeking help for any weight-related issues. The results from this large-scale study indicated that being overweight was not related to depression. Ross identified a small subgroup who were both overweight and depressed, and who tended to be better educated. Since they were also dieting to lose weight, Ross suggested that it might be the attempt to lose weight rather than the weight per se which was the cause of their distress. Although many obese people may experience their obesity in negative ways, there is no consistent empirical support for a simple relationship between body size and psychological problems.

Psychological explanations of obesity

Psychological theories of obesity have examined the role of behaviour, with a particular emphasis on physical activity and on eating behaviour.

Obesity and physical activity

Increases in the prevalence of obesity have coincided with decreases in daily energy expenditure due to improvements in transport systems and a shift from an agricultural society to an industrial and, increasingly, an information-based society. Most people spend their days sitting at a desk and their evenings watching TV. They drive to school, college or work rather than walk or cycle, and many towns are built in such a way that the only way to get to shops or restaurants is by car. A telephone company in the USA has reported that in the course of one year an extension phone saves an individual approximately one mile of walking, which could be the equivalent of 2–3 pounds of fat or up to 10 500 kcals (Stern 1984). And with widespread use of mobile phones this would be even more!

Although data on changes in activity levels are problematic, there is a useful database on television viewing. This shows that the average viewer in England in the 1960s watched 13 hours of television per week and that this has now doubled to 26 hours per week. This is further exacerbated by increased use of computer games and DVDs. It has therefore been suggested that obesity may be caused by inactivity. To examine the role of physical activity in obesity, researchers have asked 'Are changes in obesity related to changes in activity?' and 'Do people who are obese exercise less?' These two questions will now be examined.

Are changes in obesity related to changes in activity?

This question can be answered in two ways: using **epidemiological** data on a population, and **prospective data** from individuals.

In 1995, Prentice and Jebb presented epidemiological data on changes in physical activity between 1950 and 1990, as measured by car ownership and television viewing, and compared these with changes in the prevalence of obesity (see Key research below).

An alternative approach to assessing the relationship between activity and obesity was used in a large Finnish study by Rissanen *et al.* (1991) which examined the association between levels of physical activity and excess weight gain of 12 000 adults over a five-year, follow-up period. The results showed that lower levels of activity were a greater risk factor for weight gain than any other baseline measure. However, although these data are prospective, it is still possible that a third factor may explain the relationship (e.g. those with lower levels of activity at baseline were women with children, who may therefore have put on more weight). No firm conclusions can be drawn about causality unless experimental studies are carried out.

Relationship between car ownership, television viewing and obesity levels

Key research: Prentice and Jebb (1995)

This study investigated the association between reports of car ownership and TV viewing and population changes in obesity. The results suggest a strong positive correlation between an increase in both car ownership and television viewing and an increase in obesity (see Figure 5.5).

Prentice and Jebb (1995) claim that low levels of physical activity in Britain and reduced energy needs must have played an important role and, possibly even a dominant role, in the development of obesity.

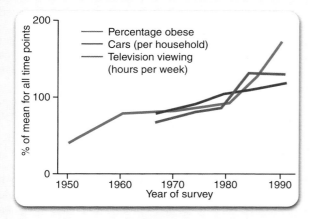

Figure 5.5 *Changes in physical activity and obesity*

Evaluation

The strengths of this research are that:

■ it used a large population, which means that the results are generalizable

■ it also included an objective measure of activity in the form of car ownership, which is less contaminated by the problems of self-report than other measures used in questionnaires

■ population data of obesity were used rather than using people's self-reported height and weight, which are known to be inaccurate.

However, the main weaknesses are that:

■ the data are correlational; therefore, it remains unclear whether decreases in activity cause increases in obesity or whether, in fact, increases in obesity actually cause decreases in activity. Moreover, it is possible that obesity and physical activity are not directly related and that some third, as yet unidentified, factor may determine both obesity and activity

■ the data are at the population level and may, therefore, overlook important individual differences (i.e. some people who are obese and active and some who are thin and inactive).

Activity levels past and present

Consider how people's lives have changed over the past 50 years and how active you are in comparison to previous generations.

1 Ask your parents and/or grandparents about how active they were as children. Did they watch TV? Did they have a car? How did they get to school or work?

2 Keep a record for at least a day, and preferably for one week, of how active you are. Write down all the structured exercise you take, such as swimming, running or playing football, but also record other behaviours such as walking up stairs, using the lift, walking up escalators, walking or cycling to school or college.

3 Based on the data you collect, how physically active do you consider yourself to be? How do your data compare with those recorded by other students in your psychology class?

How could you make your day-to-day life a bit more physically active, assuming of course that you want to!

Some suggestions are given in the Answers to activities on p.603.

Do people who are obese exercise less?

Research has also examined the relationship between activity and obesity using **cross-sectional designs** to examine differences between people who are obese and those who are not. In particular, several studies in the 1960s and 1970s examined whether obese individuals exercised less than those who were not obese. Using time-lapse photography, Bullen *et al.* (1964) observed girls considered to be obese and those of normal weight on a summer camp. They reported that during swimming, the girls who were obese spent less time swimming and more time floating. Similarly, the obese girls were inactive for 77 per cent of the time when playing tennis, compared with 56 per cent for the girls of normal weight. In addition, people who are obese walk less on a daily basis than those who are not and are also less likely to use stairs or walk up escalators.

However, it is unclear whether reduced exercise is a cause or a consequence of obesity. It is possible that people who are obese take less exercise, due to factors such as embarrassment, stigma or discomfort when exercising. Lack of exercise may play a part in the maintenance of obesity but may not be the original cause.

In summary, the role of exercise in obesity remains unclear. There appears to be a positive correlation between population decreases in activity and increases in obesity. Prospective data support this association and indicate that lower levels of activity are an important risk

factor. Moreover, cross-sectional data indicate that people who are obese appear to exercise less than those who are not. However, whether inactivity is a cause or a consequence of obesity is unclear. It is possible that an unidentified third factor may be responsible for this observed association.

The influence of stereotypes

It is generally assumed that those who are obese overeat and underexercise, and this has resulted in a widely held stereotype of obese people as gluttonous and lazy. This stereotype, held by lay people and researchers alike, could influence research in several ways. Imagine a researcher choosing to observe whether overweight children exercise as much as those who are thinner, rather than less than children who are thin. Such a bias could influence the research question asked and the ways in which the data are recorded and interpreted because researchers may be motivated to present evidence to support their existing beliefs. Finally, it may even influence whether the research is submitted, and accepted, for publication.

Obesity and eating behaviour

An alternative approach to understanding the causes of obesity has focused on eating behaviour. Earlier in this chapter, the different explanatory theories of eating behaviour were outlined (pp.162–167). It is possible that these can also help explain obesity. Those who are obese may have different beliefs about food; they could have been brought up in a family in which they were often exposed to unhealthy food, or where unhealthy food was used as a reward and restricted in ways that made food forbidden and, therefore, more desirable; or early weight gain may have resulted in dieting which, over time, led to further weight gain and obesity.

The psychological literature which has specifically looked at obesity in the context of eating behaviour has asked 'Are changes in food intake associated with changes in obesity?', 'Do people who are obese eat for different reasons than those who are not obese?' and 'Do obese people eat more than non-obese people?' Each of these questions will be examined in turn.

Are changes in food intake associated with changes in obesity?

The UK National Food Survey collects data on food intake in the home which can be analysed to assess changes in food intake over the past 50 years. The information from this database illustrates that, although overall calorie consumption increased between 1950 and 1970, there has been a distinct decrease in the amount we eat since 1970 (see Figure 5.6).

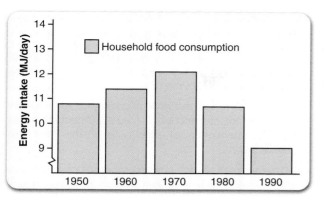

Figure 5.6 *Changes in food intake from the 1950s to the 1990s (Prentice and Jebb 1995)*

Prentice and Jebb (1995) also examined the association between changes in food intake in terms of energy intake, fat intake and changes in obesity. Their results indicated no obvious association between the increase in obesity and changes in food intake (see Figure 5.7).

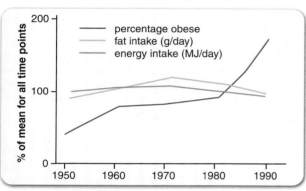

Figure 5.7 *Changes in calorie consumption and obesity (Prentice and Jebb 1995)*

Therefore, population data appear to indicate that there is no relationship between changes in food intake and changes in obesity. Population data, however, do show that the ratio between carbohydrate consumption and fat consumption has changed – we now eat less carbohydrate and proportionally more fat (as indicated in Figure 5.8).

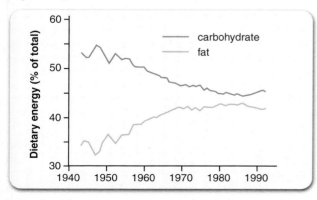

Figure 5.8 *Fat/carbohydrate ratio 1940–1995 (Prentice and Jebb 1995)*

Do people who are obese eat for different reasons than those who are not obese?

Schachter's externality theory suggested that although all people were responsive to environmental stimuli, such as the sight, taste and smell of food, and that such stimuli might cause overeating, people who are obese are highly and, sometimes, uncontrollably responsive to such external cues. It was argued that individuals who were a normal weight mainly ate as a response to internal cues (e.g. hunger, satiety) and that obese individuals tended to be underresponsive to internal cues and overresponsive to external cues (Schachter 1968).

Research therefore examined the eating behaviour and eating style of people who were obese and those who were not obese, in response to external cues such as the time of day, the sight of food, the taste of food and the number and salience of food cues (e.g. Schachter 1968, Schachter and Gross 1968, Schachter and Rodin 1974). The results from these studies were inconsistent, probably because the simple distinction between obese people and those who are not obese overlooked a number of other relevant variables, such as whether or not they were fit or trying to lose weight. Also, the research did not take into account how long they had been obese or whether they were in a stable or dynamic phase of obesity.

Schachter developed an emotionality theory of obesity which claimed that although many people eat for emotional reasons (eating more when they are upset, in need of comfort or bored), this is particularly the case for people who are obese. Since the research generated contradictory results, further research examined whether obese people ate more than non-obese people.

Do obese people eat more than non-obese people?

Research has investigated the food intake in restaurants and at home of people who are obese, and has also examined the food they buy. For example, Coates *et al.* (1978) went into the homes of 60 middle-class families to examine the contents of their food cupboards. They weighed all members of the families and found no relationship between body size and the mass and type of food they consumed at home. In an attempt to clarify the issue of whether obese people eat more than those who are not obese, Spitzer and Rodin (1981) examined previous research into eating behaviour. They suggested that 'of 29 studies examining the effects of body weight on amount eaten in laboratory studies … only nine reported that overweight subjects ate significantly more than their lean counterparts'. However, it is recognized that measuring food intake is highly problematic, as people change their food intake when they are being monitored by others in observation studies or laboratory studies, or when they are monitoring their own food intake, using food-frequency questionnaires or food diaries. It is difficult, therefore, to assess precisely how much people are actually eating. However, if overeating is defined as 'compared with what the body needs', it could be argued that all obese people overeat because they have excess body fat. Recent research has focused on the eating behaviour of people who are obese, not in terms of the calories consumed or amount eaten, but more specifically in terms of the type of food eaten.

One theory that has been put forward is that although obese people may not eat more overall than those who are not obese, they eat proportionally more fat. Moreover, it has been argued that not all calories are equal and that calories from fat may lead to greater weight gain than calories from carbohydrates (Prentice 1995). To explore this theory, a study of 11500 people in Scotland showed that men consuming the lowest proportion of carbohydrate in their diets were four times more likely to be obese compared with those consuming the highest proportion of carbohydrate (Bolton-Smith and Woodward 1994). A similar relationship was also found for women, although it was only a two- to three-fold difference. It was, therefore, concluded that relatively lower carbohydrate consumption is related to higher levels of obesity (Bolton-Smith and Woodward 1994). A similar study in Leeds also provided support for the fat proportion theory of obesity (Blundell and Macdiarmid 1997). This study reported that high-fat eaters (i.e. those who derived more than 45 per cent of their total energy from fat) were 19 times more likely to be obese than those who derived less than 35 per cent of their energy from fat. Taken together, these studies suggest that people who are obese may not consistently eat more overall than those who are not obese, but eat more fat compared with the amount of carbohydrate (i.e. the overall proportion of fat in their diet is higher).

So how might a relative increase in fat consumption relate to obesity? Blundell and colleagues suggest that the relatively higher consumption of fat to carbohydrate may result in obesity because carbohydrates are burned while fat is stored, and complex carbohydrates (such as bread, pasta and rice) are better than fat at switching off hunger (Blundell *et al.* 1996, Blundell and Macdiarmid 1997).

Evaluation of psychological explanations of obesity

◼ *Role of behaviour* – Psychological explanations of obesity emphasize the role of behaviour and highlight underactivity and overeating.

◼ *Increases in the prevalence of obesity* – Psychological explanations can account for the significant increases in the prevalence of obesity over the past few decades.

◼ *Differences in obesity rates by country* – Psychological theories also help to explain differences in the rates of obesity between different countries.

◼ *Interventions* – They provide a theoretical framework for developing interventions to help people lose weight.

◼ *Use of cross-sectional studies* – Much of the research on physical activity and eating behaviour uses cross-sectional designs (i.e. behaviour and weight are measured at the same time), so it is unclear which comes first – does obesity cause inactivity or does inactivity cause obesity?

◼ *Food-intake measurement* – Measuring food intake is difficult because eating may change according to the situation and the way it is assessed. It is problematic, therefore, to assess accurately how much people who are obese are actually eating.

◼ *Genetic predisposition to obesity* – There is sound evidence of a genetic predisposition to obesity (discussed on pp.185–186). How this influences eating behaviour and physical activity is, however, unclear.

Activity — Patterns of eating then and now

1 Ask your parents and/or grandparents to tell you what they used to eat on an average weekday when they were your age.

2 Compare this to what you eat now. Make sure you remember everything you eat and not just food you think of as meals.

3 Talk about your findings with other students in your class and discuss whether what you eat could become more healthy by making small changes to your diet (e.g. changing your latte to one made with skimmed milk).

Some suggestions are given in the Answers to activities on p.603. ▶

Activity — HOW SCIENCE WORKS — Developing a treatment intervention for obesity

Imagine that you have been asked to try to help someone who is obese to lose weight successfully.

Consider how you would tackle this task, drawing on the different psychological theories introduced in this chapter to ensure that your approach is research based. Think about the factors relating to eating behaviour in Topic 1, including the role of learning, the impact of the meaning of food, the influence of denial, restraint theory and the possible negative effects of dieting (including weight gain). How might you avoid denial and the person becoming preoccupied with food, making it even more difficult for them to change their behaviour and eat less?

Make notes about your ideas and then discuss with other students in your psychology class.

Some suggestions are given in the Answers to activities on p.603. ▶

Biological explanations of obesity

A number of theories of obesity focus on biological factors. This section will explore genetic models, neural models and an evolutionary approach to obesity.

Genetic theories

Theories focusing on genetics have examined family clusters or have used data from studies involving twins or individuals who have been adopted.

Family clusters

Body size appears to run in families and the probability that a child will be overweight is related to the parents' weight. For example, if one parent is classified as obese this results in a 40 per cent chance of the child also being obese, and having two parents who are classified as obese results in an 80 per cent chance. On the other hand, the probability that thin parents will produce overweight children is only about seven per cent (Garn *et al.* 1981). This observation has been replicated in studies exploring populations living in different environments in various parts of the world (Maes *et al.* 1997). However, since parents and children usually have a shared genetic makeup, as well as a similar environment, these findings could be explained by either factor. To address this issue, research has examined twins and individuals who have been adopted (adoptees).

Twin studies

Twin studies have examined the weights of identical twins living apart, who have identical genes but have been raised in different environments. Studies have also examined the weights of non-identical twins reared together, who have different genes but live in similar environments. The results show that the identical twins reared apart are more similar in weight than non-identical twins reared together. For example, Stunkard *et al.* (1990) examined the BMI of 93 pairs of identical twins reared apart and reported that genetic factors accounted for 66–70 per cent of the variance in their body weight, suggesting a strong genetic component in determining obesity. However, the role of genetics appears to be greater in lighter twin pairs than in heavier pairs of twins.

Studies of people who have been adopted

Research has also examined the role of genetics in obesity using adoptees. Studies have compared the adoptees' weight with that of their adoptive parents and biological parents. In a Danish study, Stunkard *et al.* (1986) gathered information about 540 adult adoptees, their adopted parents and their biological parents. The results showed a strong relationship between the weight category (thin, median weight, overweight or obese) of the adoptee and their biological parents' weight category, but no relationship with their adoptee parents' weight category. This relationship again suggests a major role for genetics and was also observed across the entire range of body weight. Interestingly, the relationship to biological mother's weight was greater than the relationship with the biological father's weight.

Research therefore suggests a strong role for genetics in predicting obesity. Research also indicates that the primary distribution of weight (upper versus lower body) is inherited (Bouchard *et al.* 1990). However, how this genetic predisposition expresses itself remains unclear. Metabolic rate and appetite regulation may be influenced by genetics and these two factors are examined next.

Metabolic rate theory

The body uses energy for exercise and physical activity and to carry out all the chemical and biological processes that are essential to being alive (e.g. respiration, heart rate, blood pressure). The rate of this energy use is called the 'resting metabolic rate', which has been found to be highly inheritable (Bouchard *et al.* 1990). It has been argued that lower metabolic rates may be associated with obesity, as people with lower metabolic rates burn up fewer calories when they are resting and therefore require less food intake. Research has investigated the relationship between metabolic rate and weight gain (see Key research).

Body weight gain in Pima Indians

Key research: Tataranni *et al.* (2003)

According to Knowler *et al.* (1991), the Pima Indians living in southwest Arizona have one of the highest reported prevalence rates of obesity in the world. Tataranni *et al.* (2003) used state-of-the art methods to assess energy intake and energy expenditure in 92 free-living, adult Pima Indians in Arizona. These methods allowed the researchers to measure energy intake and total energy expenditure accurately outside the laboratory in order to test their role in the aetiology of obesity prospectively.

The results demonstrate, for the first time, that baseline total energy intake is a key determinant of long-term changes in body weight in Pima Indians, and also confirm that a low resting metabolic rate is a risk factor for weight gain in this population. In addition, baseline energy expenditure, due to physical activity, was not found to be associated with changes in body weight.

Tataranni and colleagues' results (see Key research) indicate a possible relationship between metabolic rate and the tendency for weight gain. If this is the case, then it may be that some individuals are predisposed to become obese because they require fewer calories to survive than thinner individuals. Therefore, a genetic tendency to be obese may express itself in lowered metabolic rates. However, there is no evidence to suggest that obese people generally have lower metabolic rates than thin people. In fact, research suggests that overweight people tend to have slightly higher metabolic rates than thin people of similar height. To explain these apparently contradictory findings, it has been suggested that obese people may have lower metabolic rates to start with, which results in weight gain and this weight gain results in an increase in metabolic rate (Ravussin and Bogardus 1989).

Appetite regulation

A genetic predisposition may also be related to appetite control. Over recent years, researchers have attempted to identify the gene or collection of genes responsible for obesity. Although some work using small animals has identified a single gene associated with profound obesity, the evidence is unclear for humans. Two children have been identified with a defect in their 'ob gene', which produces leptin that is responsible for telling the brain to stop eating (Montague *et al.* 1997). It has been argued that obese people may not produce leptin and may, therefore, overeat. To test this, the two children were given daily injections of leptin, which resulted in a decrease in food intake and weight loss at a rate of 1–2 kg per month (Farooqi *et al.* 1999). However, research investigating the role of genetics on appetite control in humans is still at a very early stage.

The paper by Montague and colleagues identifying the 'ob gene' and proposing a genetic basis for obesity was published in a highly respected, peer-reviewed scientific journal. The media subsequently picked up the study, with many newspapers and magazines publishing articles on the existence of a gene for obesity. There are several possible reasons for the widespread interest in this paper:

1 It provided a fairly simple model of obesity, which is usually preferred to a more complex model that highlights the importance of a number of different factors.

2 Genetics is often regarded as 'proper' science, whereas behavioural research may be viewed as 'soft' science, so explanations based on 'hard' scientific evidence are sometimes assumed to have greater validity than other forms of explanation.

A neural model of obesity

The role of neurotransmitters in understanding food intake was outlined in Topic 2. In terms of obesity, it could be argued that people overeat and gain weight because they have too many neurochemicals that trigger food intake and too few that cause satiation. Recent developments in this area suggest that body fat may be an active organ rather than a benign structure and may trigger hunger and subsequent eating behaviour. It may, therefore, be the case that even if the stage of becoming obese is not directly linked to overactive neurochemicals, once individuals have gained surplus body fat, they then feel more hunger and are less sensitive to the normal signals of satiation.

An evolutionary model of obesity

An evolutionary model of obesity is interested in whether the tendency to be overweight and store excess body fat could have been adaptive in our ancestral past. Since much of our past has been characterized by a relative lack of food, compared with conditions in the western world today, it would be reasonable to assume that the tendency to store fat would have been functional in a world where food was often in short supply.

Some researchers have argued for the 'thrifty gene' hypothesis of obesity to support this approach. This hypothesis, first proposed by James Neel argues that, over thousands of years, those individuals who were most

---

IDA   Free will versus genetic inheritance

Biological theories of eating disorders and obesity might seem to challenge the concept of free will, as people are viewed as a product of their genetic inheritance, which is regarded as being beyond their control.

Scientists have been searching for an obesity gene and have analysed the DNA in blood samples from nearly 39000 white people in the UK and Finland and have recently discovered evidence of a genetic link to obesity (Frayling *et al.* 2007). Of the participants in the study, about 25 per cent were categorized as 'obese' (a BMI of 30 or more). Frayling and colleagues found that small variations in the FTO gene, which sits on chromosome 16, were more common among the obese participants. People with two altered copies of the gene were, on average, three kilograms heavier than those with normal copies. This study is of particular interest because this is the first time a gene that is common in the human population has been identified (around 45 per cent in the western/central European population compared

with 14 per cent in a Chinese/Japanese population). This gene is also associated with increased risk of Type 2 diabetes (Zeggini *et al.* 2007).

The function of the FTO gene remains unclear – people with the gene may burn calories less efficiently or may eat more food. This evidence may make it tempting to claim that 'It's the fault of my genes' as the excuse for being overweight or obese. However, these researchers suggest that it is changes in diet and lifestyle that are mainly responsible for the recent upsurge in obesity because, as the gene pool has not changed in 20 or 30 years, it would not be reasonable to claim that the FTO gene variant has caused the obesity problem. People who are overweight need to eat less and exercise more, although some may find it more difficult to lose weight because of their genes. This research may help to explain why one person may be significantly fatter than another even though they eat the same and do similar amounts of exercise.

energy efficient in terms of burning off excess energy and remaining thin would have been less successful, although this is now highly prized in the 21st century (Neel 1962). Evolutionary mechanisms would therefore have selected against such people in favour of those who stored excess body fat and were less efficient at burning it off (such as the Pima Indians discussed on p.185). According to this analysis, what we have left in today's world are those who were best adapted to surviving harsh winters and floods, which resulted in food shortages and periods of famine. However, now that food is plentiful and our lives are far more sedentary, these are the people who overeat, become obese and develop health problems, such as Type 2 diabetes, because the environment no longer requires their thrifty genes.

HOW SCIENCE WORKS

The diet of our early ancestors

At the 2009 annual meeting of the American Association for the Advancement of Science in Chicago, William Leonard, an expert in nutritional anthropology at Northwestern University in Illinois, USA, presented a paper claiming that eating large portions of high-energy food became necessary to support the rapid evolutionary increases in the size of the human brain and body of our early ancestors around two million years ago. We know that about one-quarter of the energy we burn while resting is used by our brains, while other primates use far less (about eight to 10 per cent). Hunter-gatherers, therefore, required energy-rich diets and had to search for food over large areas, burning up a lot of calories in the process: 'Think about our ancestors. Human hunter-gatherers typically moved eight miles per day in the search for food. In contrast, we can simply pick up the phone to get a meal delivered to our door' (Sample in *The Guardian*, 12 February 2009). This significant imbalance between energy intake and energy expenditure is likely to be the root cause of obesity in the industrialized world.

Evaluation of biological explanations of obesity

Biological explanations of obesity focus on genetics and how a genetic predisposition may translate into obesity; they also emphasize neural and evolutionary mechanisms.

▪ *Explains family links* – A genetic model of obesity explains why obesity tends to run in families.

▪ *Relatively simple explanations* – Biological theories offer relatively simple explanations of the causes of obesity that may be welcomed by those who are obese and believe they have little or no control over their weight.

▪ *Changes over time* – The prevalence of obesity has increased dramatically over the past 40 years. Our gene pool, however, has remained constant over the same period. A biological approach cannot, therefore, explain this change. However, the thrifty gene hypothesis, an evolutionary approach, would suggest that our genes are no longer suited to this new environment.

▪ *Geographical relocation* – Research shows that when people move from a country that has a low rate of obesity (such as India) to a country with a high rate (such as the USA), their weight typically changes in line with the new country. This cannot be the result of their genes.

▪ *Genetic predisposition* – Although there is some evidence for a genetic predisposition to obesity, the way in which this is expressed remains unclear.

Check your understanding of eating disorders by answering the following questions. Try to do this from memory. You can check your answers by looking back through Topic 3, Eating disorders.

1 How is obesity defined?

2 What are the main physical and psychological consequences of being obese?

3 What evidence is there to support the suggestion that obesity is related to activity levels? What are the limitations of this evidence?

4 What evidence is there to support the suggestion that obesity is related to eating behaviour? What are the limitations of this evidence?

5 What are the strengths and limitations of psychological explanations of intimacy?

6 Explain how studies of family clusters, twins and adoptees have helped psychologists to understand the role of genetics in obesity.

7 What is meant by the term 'resting metabolic rate'? Is there any evidence to suggest that a low resting metabolic rate may influence weight gain?

8 What are the strengths and limitations of biological explanations of obesity?

Eating behaviour

Factors influencing attitudes to food and eating behaviour

Social cognition models

- Used to predict eating behaviour, including the theory of reasoned action (Ajzen 1985)

  Evaluation of a social cognition approach:
  - highlights the many types of cognitions associated with food
  - useful framework for research
  - useful basis for developing interventions
  - use of quantitative research methods could mean that important cognitions are overlooked (e.g. emotions such as fear, pleasure, guilt)
  - some research disregards the multiplicity of meanings associated with food
  - key role of others is not adequately addressed

Cultural influences

Emphasis on food preferences and learning processes (i.e. a developmental approach):

- Exposure to food
- Social learning
- Associative learning (pairing food with a reward; using food as a reward; physiological consequences of food)
- Food and control (e.g. parental control)

  Evaluation of a developmental approach:
  - explains how food preferences are learned
  - highlights the role of learning – our environment is rich in cues and reinforcers
  - research is usually undertaken in a tightly controlled environment – may limit the generalizability of findings
  - diverse set of meanings associated with food not reflected in this approach
  - role of cognitions is implicit rather than explicit

Role of mood

- Stress eating paradox: evidence suggests that stress can trigger either a decrease or an increase in food consumption
- Individual differences important in explaining this

Impact of health concerns

- Health can be a motivation for food choice but is only one of many factors (Steptoe *et al.* 1995)
- Health is probably not a high priority for many people

Explanations for the success or failure of dieting

Restraint theory (Herman and Mack 1975): dieting can result in eating less and weight loss (successful), or can result in overeating and weight gain (unsuccessful)

Successful dieting

Psychological factors that increase success:

- Beliefs are key, including beliefs about the causes of obesity and motivation for weight loss
- Behaviour is recognized as fundamental to a weight problem
- Avoid denial
- Boost self-esteem
- Create a situation whereby food is no longer viewed as rewarding
- Role of life events (e.g. divorce, illness or a significant age milestone)
- Establish new identity as a thinner, healthier person

Unsuccessful dieting

- Disinhibition of restraint can result in overeating in those dieting – Herman and Mack (1975) preload/taste-test method
- Attempting not to eat can paradoxically increase the probability of overeating (Polivy and Herman 1985)
- Wardle and Beales (1988) – possible negative effect of dieting
- Mood modification – overeating in response to lowered mood (Polivy and Herman 1999)
- Role of denial – thought suppression/thought control can increase the saliency of the very thoughts that an individual is trying to suppress

  Evaluation
  - emphasis on bodily dissatisfaction
  - research findings reflect many people's experiences
  - limitations of restraint theory as an explanatory model
  - gender bias – much of the research has been carried out with women

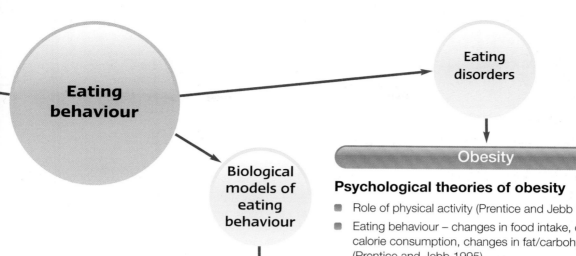

Eating behaviour

Eating disorders

Obesity

Psychological theories of obesity

- Role of physical activity (Prentice and Jebb 1995)
- Eating behaviour – changes in food intake, changes in calorie consumption, changes in fat/carbohydrate ratio (Prentice and Jebb 1995)

Evaluation
- role of behaviour (eating and activity) emphasized
- can explain increases in the prevalence of obesity
- can explain differences in obesity rates between different countries
- provides a theoretical framework for developing interventions to help people lose weight
- issue of causality unclear in cross-sectional research
- difficult to assess food intake accurately
- there is sound evidence of a genetic predisposition to obesity, but unclear how this influences eating behaviour and physical activity

Biological explanations of obesity

- **Genetic theory** – studies of family clusters, twins and adoptees; metabolic rate theory (study of Pima Indians); appetite control (search for gene(s) responsible for obesity)
- A **neural model** of obesity – suggests that people overeat and gain weight because they have too many neurochemicals that promote food intake and too few that indicate satiation; also suggests that body fat may promote hunger and subsequent eating behaviour
- **Evolutionary model** of obesity – thrifty gene hypothesis

Evaluation
- genetic model of obesity can explain family links
- biological theories offer relatively simple explanations of the causes of obesity
- thrifty gene hypothesis can help to explain why obesity is increasing as the environment changes
- prevalence of obesity has increased drastically while our gene pool has remained relatively constant
- significant weight changes when living in a different country cannot be explained by a genetic model
- still unclear how a genetic predisposition to obesity is expressed

Biological models of eating behaviour

Emphasis on the importance of hunger and satiety

Metabolic models of eating behaviour

- Homeostasis and the role of negative feedback as a means of regulating eating
- Hypothalamus is a key area of the brain
- Neurotransmitters that *increase* food intake: norepinephrine, neuropeptide Y and galanin
- Neurotransmitters that *decrease* food intake: cholecystokinin, bombesin, corticotropin-releasing hormone, serotonin
- Studying the effects of drugs (such as nicotine, amphetamines) has highlighted the ways in which certain drugs influence the chemical activity of the brain and hence eating behaviour

Evolutionary approach to eating behaviour

- Innate food preferences (Davis 1928) and their possible adaptive function
- Effects of an obesogenic environment

Evaluation
- biological explanations only provide the starting point of our understanding of eating behaviour
- a biological approach helps to explain some of the observed differences in eating behaviour (e.g. people with certain medical conditions may eat differently)
- much of the research on eating behaviour has been carried out in the laboratory on animals; the generalizability of the findings to humans is therefore unclear
- the role of social learning and social meaning is not adequately acknowledged
- biological drives either to eat or stop eating can be overridden

Gender

EXPLAINING THE SPECIFICATION

Specification content	The specification explained
Psychological explanations of gender development (Topic 1)	The specification focuses on gender. In this part of the specification you are required to know about theory and research studies concerning psychological explanations of gender development. To do this, you need to be able to:
Cognitive developmental theory, including Kohlberg, and gender schema theory	■ Describe **cognitive developmental theories** of gender development including both Kohlberg's gender consistency theory, and gender schema theory. ■ Evaluate cognitive developmental theories of gender including both Kohlberg's theory and gender schema theory.
Explanations for psychological androgyny and gender dysphoria including relevant research	■ Describe two or more explanations of psychological androgyny and gender dysphoria including relevant research. ■ Evaluate two or more explanations of psychological androgyny and gender dysphoria including relevant research.
Biological influences on gender (Topic 2)	In this part of the specification you are required to know about theory and research studies concerning biological influences on gender development. To do this, you need to be able to:
The role of hormones and genes in gender development	■ Describe the role of both hormones and genes in gender development. ■ Evaluate the role of both hormones and genes in gender development.
Evolutionary explanations of gender roles	■ Describe two or more aspects of gender role from an evolutionary perspective. ■ Evaluate explanations of two or more aspects of gender role from an evolutionary perspective.
The biosocial approach to gender development	■ Describe the biosocial approach to gender development. ■ Evaluate the biosocial approach to gender development.
Social contexts of gender role (Topic 3)	In this part of the specification you are required to know about theory and research studies concerning social influences on gender role. To do this, you need to be able to:
Social influences on gender role: for example, the influence of parents, peers and schools, media	■ Describe two or more social influences on gender role using examples such as the influence of parents, peers, schools and the media. ■ Evaluate two or more social influences on gender role using examples such as the influence of parents, peers, schools and the media.
Cross-cultural studies of gender role	■ Describe two or more cross-cultural studies of gender role. ■ Evaluate two or more cross-cultural studies of gender role.

Introduction

If there is an interaction between nature and nurture in determining gender, how does this operate? This is a very interesting question but before attempting an answer, it is necessary to clarify some important concepts. Firstly, the term sex is used to refer to biological differences between male and female (Unger 1979, cited in Archer and Lloyd 1992) which are chiefly determined by the influence of genetics and hormones. Secondly, gender refers to **masculine** and **feminine**, which are psychological types consisting of ascribed traits and behaviours defined by the cultural context. The importance of separating **gender differences** from **sex differences** is illustrated by Archer and Lloyd (1992) in a study of abnormal **sexual differentiation** in cultures such as the Omani, in which it was found that there are more than two genders. Cases such as this show that the terms sex and gender must not be used interchangeably.

In the next section, the concept of gender will be considered in the light of psychosocial research. The constitution of the gender concept and how children come to understand what it is to be a boy or a girl will be considered in the light of cognitive-developmental theory: **gender consistency theory** (Kohlberg 1966) and **gender schema theory** (Martin and Halverson 1983). This will be followed by explanations of **androgyny** and **gender dysphoria**. The following section will consider the impact of biological influences on gender by addressing the question of whether innate sex differences drive gender differences. Next, we consider whether gender differences prevalent in our society today are related to our evolutionary past. Finally, the impact of the social environment will also be considered including other cross-cultural contexts.

Topic 1: Psychological explanations of gender development

The concept of gender

Gender refers to culturally constructed distinctions between femininity and masculinity. Individuals are born female or male but they become feminine or masculine through complex developmental processes that take many years to unfold. In order to understand this complex process, psychologists have defined what it takes to realise that 'he is a boy' or 'she is a girl.'

The development of the gender concept

Slaby and Frey (1975) found that there are three distinct stages that children must go through in order to develop an understanding of their gender. This happens in the following order:

1 *Gender identity* – Children can correctly label themselves as a boy or girl.

2 *Gender stability* – Children understand that they always have been and always will be a boy or a girl (then a man or a woman).

3 *Gender consistency* – Children realise that their gender will not change even if they change appearance e.g. dress as the opposite sex.

Slaby and Frey (1975) also discovered the ages at which these concepts developed: three-year olds didn't understand any of these concepts; 4-year olds understood gender identity and 4½ – to 5-year olds understood all three concepts. Other studies give different ages for the comprehension of these concepts but agree with the order of their acquisition (Thompson 1975; Kuhn *et al.* 1978; Marcus and Overton 1978).

Slaby and Frey's (1975) evidence comes from questioning and observing young children. When children over the age of 2 are shown a picture of a young boy and girl and asked 'Which one are you?' they can give an appropriate response by pointing at the appropriate picture. Children with gender stability can give correct answers to, 'Were you a little boy or a little girl when you were a baby?' and 'When you grow up, will you be a mummy or a daddy?' To test for gender consistency, pre-school children were shown a film with men on one side and women on the other. Those children who had previously been rated as having greater gender consistency watched more same-gender models. This shows that children at this stage of development are more focused on same-gender models that will provide them with information about gender-appropriate behaviour.

There are genuine differences between males and females in areas of cognition, social behaviour and personality which may underlie **gender stereotypes**. Taking cognitive skills first, Halpern (2000) found that females tend to exhibit slightly better verbal skills than males. They tend to start speaking earlier and have larger vocabularies and higher reading scores during the school years. They are superior at tasks requiring rapid access to semantic and other information stored in long term memory (Halpern 1997). On the other hand males show an advantage on tests of mathematical ability. At the high end of the ability distribution there is a large gender gap (Stumpf and Stanley 1996). Males tend to score higher on visual spatial skills (Voyer *et al.* 1995). These findings relate to some of our more pervasive gender stereotypes: 'Why can't you read the map?' (male to female) 'Don't you know where you're going?' (male to female) 'Why can't you do two things at once?' (female to male) 'Oh I give up arguing with you I can't get a word in edgeways' (male to female) 'I'm listening, you're just too slow' (female to male).

With regard to social behaviour and personality there are robust differences here too. Males tend to be more verbally and physically aggressive (Coie and Dodge 1997). Females engage more in covert and relational aggression such as ignoring and undermining others' reputation and status (Crick and Rose 2000). Females are more sensitive than males to subtle nonverbal cues (McClure 2000). Males score higher than females on various assessments of risk-taking (Byrnes *et al.* 1999) and tend to have more permissive attitudes about casual, pre-marital and extra-marital sex (Baumeister 2001). Males score higher on assertiveness and global self-esteem whereas females score higher on measures of anxiety and agreeableness (Costa *et al.* 2001). Again there are popular stereotypes that confirm these behavioural differences.

The actual behavioural differences between males and females are nevertheless fewer and smaller than popular stereotypes suggest. In fact Tavris (1992) has suggested that many gender differences founded in gender stereotyping have turned out to be more mythical than real.

Activity Gender stereotypes in the media

To demonstrate gender stereotypes operating within the context of our society, carry out a content analysis (see pp.73–5 in *Psychology AS for AQA A*, as well as Chapter 17 in this book) on news articles addressing the way men and women are portrayed in the media and consider the language used when referring to men and women.

1 Is there a difference?

2 What explanations are given for their behaviour – say if there is a car accident?

3 In what way are the sexes accountable for their behaviour and is there a difference?

4 If so what are the differences in the way this is documented?

---

asking them to verbalise a response could be an unfair test of their understanding. The children were also of an age where they would have seen other boys and girls and men and women. They were therefore familiar with different faces so the use of pictures of people as stimulus material has face and ecological validity, in other words it appears to be highly appropriate to children's everyday experience. As children's cognitive competence improved, more searching questions were asked which were still very simple and child-friendly, requiring a 'yes' or 'no' answer.

The procedure of using films in order to measure how much children watched same or opposite sex characters is another simple and unobtrusive way to tell us which gender they identified with more in a way which is ethically acceptable because it is harmless to the children involved. Greater gender consistency was positively related to more observation of the same gender model whereas lowered gender consistency means looking at same and opposite gender models equally. While this suggests that gender consistency is the cause of identification, rather than the effect, caution is needed in making this interpretation: the analysis is correlational rather than experimental so does not allow us to conclude that consistency has caused model preference. Finally,

Slaby and Frey's method is appropriate for the age group considered. Pointing at pictures is a good technique for testing young children because their understanding of speech may be greater than their ability to produce it so even very young children are aware of trying to make a good impression and give the responses they think adults expect. This could have been an unwanted source of bias in the questioning stages of the study but is unlikely to have affected the stage using films thus giving more trustworthy results.

Cognitive developmental theories of gender development

There are two main theories of gender development which emphasise the importance of cognitive (internal thought) processes in the development of gender. They are gender consistency theory and gender schema theory.

Kohlberg's gender consistency theory

Kohlberg (1966) is the main proponent of this view. According to him, children are active agents and the masters of their own gender-role **socialization**. He proposed a stage theory of gender development: gender identity (acquired at 2 to 3 years), gender stability (acquired at 3 to 7 years) and gender consistency (acquired at 7 to12 years) see Table 6.1.

Gender concepts develop in a sequence which parallels cognitive changes taking place alongside the maturing brain (see Slaby and Frey 1975). In his influential theory of cognitive development, Piaget described how, during the concrete operational stage which occurs between about 7 and 11 years of age, children grow to understand the concept of conservation and are no longer fooled by appearances. For instance, before children can conserve, they may tell you that a glass of water changes in volume if it is poured into a differently shaped glass. Children who can conserve do not make this error because they can tell whether something is truly different or just appears different. This has implications for the development of understanding of the gender concept which also becomes more sophisticated as the brain develops. Once children understand conservation in inanimate objects, they are also capable of understanding that a change in a person's appearance does not change their sex, thus they acquire gender consistency. Furthermore, as a child matures

cognitively, so does the ability to classify objects and concepts and understanding others' gender in this way is no exception to the rule. (For more detail on Piaget's theory refer to Chapter X). Once a child has an established gender identity, it follows that more attention is paid to same sex individuals and the behaviour they model. This preferential observation makes it possible for children to internalise gender-stereotypical behaviour (Geis 1993). Children's sense of gender identity is thus crucial for sex-role identification. Once it is established, children imitate same-sex models and follow sex-appropriate models/activities because they think this is what a child of their sex does. This is called **self-socialization** because it is independent of external reinforcement from others such as parents (Maccoby and Jacklin 1974).

Evaluation of gender consistency theory

- *Supporting evidence* – In addition to the evidence provided by Piaget, Kohlberg, and Slaby and Frey, there are many studies that concur with the gender constancy theory, for example, once gender identity, stability and consistency are acquired we should see a preference for gender-typed behaviour and activity. An observational study of 2- to 3-year old children by Weinraub *et al.* (1984) supports this. It showed that children who had mastered gender identity made more sex-stereotyped toy preferences than children who had not acquired gender identity. Once children viewed themselves as a boy or a girl they behaved in ways that they thought individuals of that sex should behave.

- *Universal sequence of development* – Cross-cultural research provides us with an opportunity to determine aspects of human development and behaviour that are unique to cultures or are universal. According to research by Munroe *et al.* (1984) the sequence of development of the gender concept is similar in other cultures (Kenya, Nepal, Belize and Samoa). Cross-culturally biological development (especially brain maturity) is similar, lending credibility to claims that cognitive maturation is more important than different social experiences in gender concept development.

Approx. age	Stage of understanding of gender	Description
2-3 years	**Gender identity**	The child recognizes that he/she is a boy or a girl.
3-7 years	**Gender stability**	Awareness that gender is fixed. The child accepts that males remain male and females remain female. Little boys no longer think they might grow up to be a mummy and little girls give up their hopes of becoming Batman.
7-12 years	**Gender consistency**	Children recognize that superficial changes in appearance or activities do not alter gender. Even when a girl wears jeans or plays football, or when a boy has long hair or a burning interest in needlepoint, the child's gender remains constant.

Source: Kohlberg (1966), cited in Hetherington and Parke (1993) p.547

Table 6.1 *Kohlberg's stages in the development of gender identity*

- *Conflicting evidence* – Evidence from Martin and Little (1990) suggests that Kohlberg was wrong in suggesting that children do not begin collecting information about appropriate **gender role** behaviour before they achieve consistency. Martin and Little (1990) measured gender concepts, sex-typed preferences and stereotyped knowledge in children aged 3 to 5. Gender concept measures included the ability to identify and to discriminate the sexes, understand gender group membership, temporal stability of gender, and gender consistency over situational changes. Martin and Little found that pre-school children had only very basic gender understanding, yet they had strong gender stereotypes about what boys and girls were permitted to do, i.e. they had already collected information about gender-appropriate behaviour. Thus, only rudimentary gender understanding is needed before children learn about sex stereotypes and show strong sex-type preferences for peers or toys.

- *Ages and stages* – As with all stage theories, there is some disagreement about the actual age when these changes take place, although the sequence is not contested. Age discrepancies may be due to the methods used to test the children's understanding. For example, when pre-school children were shown *drawings* where gender-inappropriate changes in hairstyle or dress have been made, very few of them were able to recognize that gender remains the same despite the changes (Emmerlich *et al.* 1977). However, if they were shown *photographs* of real children, first in the nude with their sexual anatomy visible, and then dressed in gender-inappropriate clothing, almost half the 3- to 5-year olds knew that the child's gender had not changed (Bem 1989). An additional finding is that when pre-schoolers are asked whether they themselves would change gender if they wore gender-inappropriate dress, almost all of them realized that they would remain the same (Martin and Halverson 1983). It seems that children grasp this concept earlier when applied to themselves, than when applied to others (Wehren and DeLisi 1983).

Gender schema theory

Gender schema theory is Martin and Halverson's (1983) alternative to the cognitive-developmental approach proposed by Kohlberg (1966). It is different insofar as they suggest that children are motivated to begin to acquire knowledge about their gender at a much younger age. In Kohlberg's theory, children must recognize the permanence of gender before they can begin to imitate same-gender models. In gender schema theory, rigid early gender identity acquired at about the age of three is the starting point for gender development. Children then begin searching for rules or '**schemas**' which will help them make sense of the world around them. The term 'schema' refers to clusters of concepts that a child acquires about the world. Another way to view schemas is as if they are 'theories' (or cognitive structures or frameworks) concerning how males and females should behave. They help children both to organize and to interpret their experiences and to process new, incoming information. It is thus the *readiness* to categorize gender information that drives the development of gender. An example of how this operates has been demonstrated in the study by Martin *et al.* (1995) described in How Science Works 'Gender and toy preference'. This provides support for the importance of schemas and how they affect the processing of information, particularly in terms of what is attended to and internalised.

The concept of schemas can be tricky to grasp. Picture a child in an old fashioned sorting office with a pile of papers to organise into pigeon-holes. Each paper has a piece of information on it. The first attempt to organise might result in just two categories: masculine and feminine. After a while this becomes too simple and more categories (pigeon-holes) are needed e.g. things males do/things females do, things males say/things females say, things males wear/things females wear. There may also be categories for things that apply equally to both genders. Eventually, a system (schema) will be in place which allows the child to store any new piece of incoming information.

HOW SCIENCE WORKS

Gender and toy preference

Key research: Martin, Eisenbud and Rose (1995)

Martin *et al.* (1995) showed toys to children aged 4 to 5 years of age. Children were informed, before choosing a toy to play with, that it was a girl or boy toy. They were then asked whether they and other boys or girls would like to play with the toys. They found that if a toy, such as a magnet, was given the label of being a 'boy toy' then boys, and not girls, would play with these toys at a later time. However, if boys were told it was a 'girl toy' then they didn't want to play with it. Similarly, girls would not play with toys labelled for boys. The label given at the start consistently affected children's subsequent toy preference.

This study supports research which demonstrates the pervasiveness of gender schemas and the stronghold that perceived gender stereotypes have over behaviour (e.g. Fagot 1985; Liben and Signorella 1993). It is an important finding in that it highlights the labelling and the categorisation of objects that children are subjected to from a young age, in particular how objects close to a child's heart – their play things – can be labelled in the same way as appropriate gender behaviour and gender stereotypes.

Evaluation

What we cannot be entirely sure of in studies such as these is the extent to which children try to please adults by making what they think will be an acceptable response. It is possible that they might think they would be punished for choosing to play with a toy which is not meant for them, rather than understanding gender in a more complex way.

The age of appearance of gender schemas

Bauer (1993) set out to study the way in which children call upon gender schemas when processing information. Pre-school-age and older children have been found to process gender-consistent and gender-inconsistent information differently so the question of interest to Bauer was whether this occurs in very young children too. In the past it had been difficult to address this question due to a lack of appropriate testing methods, but Bauer devised a way to test girls and boys as young as 25 months of age. Children observed the experimenter carry out short sequences of stereotypically female, male or gender neutral activities e.g. changing a nappy, shaving a teddy bear or going on a treasure hunt. Bauer tested children by 'elicited imitation' both immediately and after a delay of 24 hours, to see if they would copy what they had seen. Girls showed equivalent quality of recall for all three types of sequence. Boys, on the other hand, showed superior recall of male stereotyped activities at the expense of female stereotyped activities and their recall for gender neutral activities was the same as for male stereotyped activities. These results indicate that boys more than girls tend to make use of gender schemas by the age of 25 months. Boys appear to remember more accurately event sequences consistent with their own gender, whereas girls show no difference in recall of gender-consistent and gender-inconsistent information.

This difference could have something to do with the fact that boys are more likely to be penalised by their parents, especially fathers, for adopting or aspiring to traditionally female pursuits. It might also have something to do with the fact that Bauer, who modelled the sequences, is female.

argued that these beliefs are like lenses through which we view males and females and it is important to make these lenses visible so that we are looking at them and not through them. In this way we will be better able to understand how they might bias or distort our views of gender. Bem expanded on the three lenses under these headings:

1 *Androcentrism* – This is used to describe a male-centred society that is structured around the male as the norm and females as not the norm.

2 *Gender polarization* – Society is structured around perceived differences between the genders usually with the male way of doing things given the greater value.

3 *Biological essentialism* – Points one and two are seen as natural – men and women are biologically different, especially sexually, and therefore play different roles.

One repercussion of viewing things through these three lenses is that society is structured in a way that empowers men but not women. Another is that our acceptance of the view through the lenses shapes the way in which we socialise our children so the gender divide is self-perpetuating.

In contrast to this, Bem takes an interactionist viewpoint whereby the similarities between the sexes outweigh the differences. Society should be gender depolarized through the redefinition of our gender traits and the perception of what it is to be human rather than what it is to be male or female.

Activity — HOW SCIENCE WORKS

The appearance of gender schemas (Bauer 1993)

Read the account of Bauer's research into the appearance of gender schemas:

1 Is this method a reliable way of ascertaining whether children have gender schema and apply them to what is perceived as traditionally male or female activity?

2 What other explanations of the results can we offer?

Answers are given on p.605. ▶

Lenses of Gender (Bem 1993)

With regard to Bem's ideas about 'lenses of gender':

1 Is there an important analogy to be drawn here with the Gender Schema Theory?

2 Consider the mechanisms underlying the Gender Schema Theory. What is happening here? In what way is socialisation involved and how does it operate?

3 Who determines what activity is for a boy or girl?

4 What parallels can you draw between Bem's 'Lenses of Gender' and Gender Schema Theory?

Answers are given on p.605. ▶

Lenses of gender

In 'Lenses of Gender' Bem (1993) further addressed the way in which Western culture defines gender role and perceives masculinity and **femininity**. Gender schemas become the lenses through which we view the world. She addressed three main beliefs held in Western society that influence that view: men and women differ psychologically and sexually, men are the dominant and superior sex and these differences are natural. Bem

Evaluation of gender schema theory

■ *Empirical support for stereotypes* – Liben and Signorella (1993) showed young children pictures of adults engaging in stereotypical activities normally attributed to the opposite sex (for example a male nurse). They found that children later insisted that the nurse was female. This suggests children register information consistent with their existing stereotypes which then shapes further knowledge about gender. Such gender stereotypes are persistent and robust. Their very existence and continuation can be accounted for by gender schema theory because research shows people remember gender schema-consistent information and ignore, forget or distort gender schema-inconsistent information.

- *Reinforcement selectivity* – Children are receptive to same-gender reinforcement but will not be persuaded by gender-contradictory reinforcement, so adults reinforcing feminine behaviours will not encourage a boy to adopt feminine ways. Fagot (1985) observed the behaviour of 40 children aged 21 to 25 months who attended a playgroup. She observed what was **reinforced** by the children and teachers, how they did it, whether it was effective and whether the effects were lasting. Reinforcement varied with what activity was being reinforced and by whom. The findings showed that boys were influenced by other boys, and girls were influenced by teachers and other girls. In particular, boys were not influenced by teachers or girls during typical boy play such as rough and tumble or playing with masculine toys such as cars and trucks. In addition, Fagot showed that, despite teachers reinforcing traits typifying femininity in a classroom situation, boys and girls still behave differently, suggesting that the boys' gender schemas prevail over the cross-gender reinforcement.

- *Gender awareness and gender-typed behaviour* – Gender schema theory predicts a close relationship between gender awareness and gender-typed behaviour, but research has failed to find a robust connection e.g. girls tend to have more flexible gender concepts than boys and have more of a tendency to engage in gender activities and behaviours normally reserved for boys (Archer 1989). If gender awareness drives gender behaviour, this should not happen.

- *The appearance of gender schemas* – The age at which gender schema appears could be earlier than the theory suggests. The study by Bauer (1993) suggested it could be as young as 25 months. A more recent study has compared 18- and 24-month-old children with respect to how long they looked at male and female actors portraying masculine and feminine-stereotyped activities and found that 24-month-old children showed gender consistent preferences but 18-month olds did not (Hill and Flom 2006) lending support to the earlier appearance of gender schemas.

Explanations of psychological androgyny

Exaggeration of the differences between men and women is just one perspective on understanding gender development and this is characteristic of **alpha-biased** theories such as Freud's (1920) androcentric (male-centred) and Gilligan's (1982) estrocentric (female-centred) approach. It is the other perspective encompassed in **beta-biased** theories which is relevant to **psychological androgyny**. The most eminent beta-biased theory is Bem's (1974) unisex theory of psychological androgyny; men and women can adopt similar personality and behavioural traits and only differ because they choose to do so.

Bem's theory of psychological androgyny

According to Bem's (1974) theory of psychological **androgyny,** optimal health and wellbeing is achieved when a person can freely select and enact whatever personality traits they want, regardless of their male or female orientation. By doing this people can integrate both masculine and feminine qualities that are suited to their individual temperament. Bem also considers that it is possible for people to have both feminine and masculine traits in abundance – a state referred to as psychological androgyny. This means that people no longer need be constrained by cultural stereotypes representing their own sex.

The Bem Sex Role Inventory (BSRI) was developed by Bem (1974) to measure an individual's gender type. The details of how this was done appear in the Key research box opposite and the four key gender types appear in Figure 6.1. Androgynous individuals score high on both femininity and masculinity, unlike others who score high on either femininity or masculinity (sex-typed) and typically accept traditional gender stereotypes. Those scoring low on both masculinity and femininity are classified as undifferentiated.

Bem went on to compare responses of androgynous people and sex-typed people when given the opportunity to perform either a stereotypical or a non-stereotypical activity. She found that sex-typed individuals tended to favour a stereotypical activity, even when it cost them money to do so. Compared to androgynous types, sex-

		Femininity	
		High	Low
Masculinity	High	Androgynous	Masculine
	Low	Feminine	Undifferentiated

Figure 6.1 *Gender types measured using the BSRI*

typed individuals were also more likely to express discomfort about performing non-stereotypical activities. In further studies, Bem tested the ability of individuals to present a minority opinion, which might be considered a masculine behaviour. Masculine and androgynous types out-performed feminine types on this task.

Findings such as these led Bem to suggest that androgynous types have the greatest flexibility when faced with different situations. This is psychologically healthy for them, therefore the encouragement of androgynous characteristics in anyone is desirable.

Bem's Sex Role Inventory

Key research: Bem (1974)

Bem developed the BSRI by presenting 200 personality traits for two separate dimensions of masculinity (e.g. assertive) and femininity (e.g. loyal) to a sample of 100 students. A further 200 personality traits perceived as socially desirable (e.g. happy) or undesirable (e.g. jealous), and equally applicable to males and females, were considered. Bem (1974) asked students to rate all traits using a specific question format. For example: "In American society, how desirable is it for a man to be truthful?" The procedure was carefully designed so that males and females were able to respond equally in number to male and female questions. A seven-point Likert scale was used ranging from one (not at all desirable) to seven (extremely desirable). Traits judged by both males and females as more desirable for one gender than the other were thus identified. Traits rated as neither masculine nor feminine were labelled as neutral items. In this way, the original 400 traits were reduced to 20 traits for masculinity and 20 for femininity. The final BSRI contained these 40 traits mixed in with a further 10 desirable and 10 undesirable neutral 'filler' traits. To test for gender type, individuals rate themselves on each of the 60 items from one (never or almost never true) to seven (almost always true). Ratings for the masculine and feminine items are separately summed and divided by 20 and the balance between masculinity and femininity determines gender type. A score on both of these above the median of 4.9 indicates androgyny.

Evaluation

Measurement of psychological androgyny in this way has been challenged. The BSRI was developed in America in the 1970s and some critics have questioned its temporal and context validity. The terms used to devise the scale sound a little out-dated when used to describe today's males and females and it may be inappropriate to use it outside American culture which has a particular view on desirable qualities in males and females.

STRETCH AND CHALLENGE

Designer personalities

Archer (1989) claims that girls tend to have more flexible gender concepts than boys and, as a result, engage in cross-gender activity. We know that women's roles have become more diverse which may in part be due to a changing world where equal rights have allowed women to work and participate in society in different ways. It can only be expected then that their gender concepts will be more flexible and perhaps intrude in what was traditionally the male domain.

1 Can we draw a connection between flexible gender concepts and Bem's theory? For example, can we say that girls (and boys) are being selective about the personality and behavioural traits that they want to portray?

2 Can the next step from designer houses be designer personality?

Answers are given on p.605.

Activity — Investigating gender traits

Devise a list of masculine and feminine traits and ask your male and female friends to select the traits that they feel apply to them. Now compare the traits selected by your friends and score the number of masculine traits that your male friends have selected and the number of feminine traits that your female friends have selected and test to see if there is a significant difference.

Androgyny in cross-sex behaviour

Androgyny can be considered from a different perspective to that of Bem. It concerns cross-sex preferences where boys would rather be girls and girls would rather be boys. Often this means preferring to play with children of the opposite sex or to play with toys typical of the opposite sex. It could be that such children have been guided to behave like the opposite sex through parents reinforcing aspects of behaviour socially ascribed to the opposite sex e.g. a boy bought dolls to play with might want to become a girl.

Roberts *et al.* (1987) studied boys who had a strong preference for female toys and playing with girls but found no evidence that these boys were being reinforced for cross-sex behaviours by their parents. If anything the contrary was found where the father was concerned: he provided a masculine role model. Roberts *et al.* also found that in comparison to masculine looking boys, boys who looked feminine from birth tended to be ill during their early life and had less daily contact with their parents. This is difficult to account for using a social learning model and can be more easily explained biologically.

Activity — Androgyny in cross-sex behaviour

Considering the results of Roberts *et al.'s* study of cross gender children:

1 How could we account for feminised boys' poorer health and reduced contact with their parents?

2 What biological influence might feminise a boy's appearance?

3 Could a similar but opposite mechanism 'masculinise' girls?

Answers are given on p.605.

Activity — An ideal personality

Write a list of desirable traits that you would choose in order to design your ideal personality. Then get your friends to do the same thing. Compare notes to see how similar you are to your friends. It is claimed that we tend to mix with people who are similar to ourselves and have common interests.

Evaluation of explanations of psychological androgyny

■ *The role of pre-natal hormones* – While there is some evidence that exposure to pre-natal hormones can be related to later cross-sex behaviour, there are some studies that contradict this. Money and Norman (1987) has claimed that children born with ambiguous genitalia can adopt the gender label assigned them even if this contradicts their genetic make-up. In these cases, the environmental influences appear to be more powerful than biological ones. (But see 'A case of penectomy' on p.204.)

■ *Androgyny and psychological health* – Bem (1975) and Spence and Helmreich (1978) have argued that an androgynous person, who has both masculine and feminine strengths, is more likely to be psychologically healthy and have higher self esteem. Some researchers have shown that androgynous adolescents tend to be more psychologically balanced, popular with peers, are more self confident and know themselves well (Dusek 1987; Ziegler *et al.* 1984). However others, such as Taylor and Hall (1982), have argued that it is the masculine dimension alone which is responsible for the link with both psychological wellbeing and self esteem. This could be because masculine characteristics are more highly valued by both individuals and others.

■ *Androgynous societies* – Bem argued that if we, as a society, ignore the gender of the person whose behaviour we are trying to attribute meaning to, we would no longer need to use concepts of masculinity or femininity. Archer (1992) disagrees. He argued that it is difficult to have a completely androgynous society because it seems to be a natural developmental pathway to perceive oneself as being male or female. Very young children develop a sense of gender identity and this helps to construct an understanding of self. Once this is established other facets of gender concept develop which are reinforced and shaped by socialisation. It is possible to customize personality at a later date by choosing desired masculine or feminine traits, but this can only be achieved first through the successful acquisition of gender identity.

Gender dysphoria

While Bem's concept of psychological androgyny can be regarded as a sign of health and well-being, **gender dysphoria** is considered to be a disorder. Occasionally, boys and girls and men and women feel that there is a mismatch between their anatomy and gender identity so they identify more with the opposite sex. Neave (2007) says that there are a number of conditions in which '…there appear to be no underlying hormonal, metabolic, physiological or physical abnormalities, yet the individuals display atypical gender role/sexual orientation'. For some individuals, this causes psychological discomfort known as gender dysphoria.

The feeling that there is a mismatch between anatomy and gender identity, and wanting to be the opposite sex, is referred to as gender dysphoria. This is currently categorised in the American Psychiatric Association's (APA) *Diagnostic and Statistical Manual of Mental Disorders (DSM-IV-TR*, APA, 2000), as a 'gender identity disorder'. The most extreme case is **transsexualism** which may result in opting for sex reassignment to change the external genitalia and secondary sexual characteristics to match the desired sex. Transsexualism should not be confused with transvestitism. **Transvestites** cross-dress and are sexually aroused by doing so, but at no point do they consider themselves to be, or want to be, the opposite sex. The opposite is very true of transsexuals who do not gain any sexual satisfaction by cross-dressing but instead do it to feel more comfortable about themselves.

The most commonly agreed upon diagnostic criteria stipulated in DSM-IV-TR (APA, 2000) are as follows:

- Confusion between sex, gender identity and gender role such that there is a mismatch between gender identity and the sex one is born with

- Presence of strong and on-going cross-gender identification

- Desire to live and be accepted as a member of the opposite sex

- Persistent discomfort with one's anatomical sex

- A sense of inappropriateness in the gender role of that sex

- A wish to have hormonal treatment and surgery to change one's body to the desired sex and consistent with one's psychological type

- The experience of gender dysphoria has to be present for at least two years

- Demonstration that the distress caused by gender dysphoria is alleviated through cross-gender identification

- Absence of physical intersex conditions (known as hermaphroditism) such as androgen insensitivity syndrome (AIS) or congenital adrenal hyperphasia (CAH)

- Absence of genetic abnormality such as Klinefelter Syndrome (XXY chromosomal type) and Turner Syndrome (X chromosomal type)

- Absence of a coexistent mental disorder such as schizophrenia.

A list of symptoms in children with gender dysphoria has also been generated:

- Insistence that they are of the opposite sex

- Dislike of and refusal to wear clothes typical of their sex

- Dislike of and refusal to participate in activities specific of their sex

Measuring the prevalence of gender dysphoria

Basing their estimate on figures from the Netherlands, the APA (2007) placed the incidence of gender dysphoria at one in 30400 for biological females and one in 11900 biological males. NHS Direct estimate that men are diagnosed with gender dysphoria five times more often than women and that 1:4000 individuals in the UK are actually receiving some kind of medical attention for it. These figures underline the importance of clarifying what we are actually describing: is it the total estimated incidence, the number who seek treatment, the number who seek treatment and are diagnosed or the number who have sought treatment, been diagnosed and succeeded in getting treatment? Furthermore they tell us nothing about the level of gender dysphoria experienced which could range from mild to severe.

Figures concerning transsexualism – the most extreme form of gender dysphoria – are possibly less ambiguous. Eklund *et al.* (1988) looked at the prevalence of transsexualism in the Netherlands over a period of time.

They found that in 1980 transsexualism was 1:45000 rising to 1:26000 in 1983 and to 1:18000 in 1986. This suggests that this form of gender dysphoria is on the increase but again this is misleading as this could merely be a reflection of increased tolerance towards transsexuals, such that they feel more confident about disclosing their condition, and advances in medicine such that they feel that solutions are available. Both of these advances help to clarify the actual numbers involved.

The Gender Recognition Act (2004), which permits transsexuals to marry as their new gender and have it recognised in their passport and other legal documents, provides another source of statistical data which can be cross-checked against medical records. Furthermore, with this Act, more transsexuals might consider sex reassignment, so there may be a further increase in the figures. Statistical data can therefore only be used as a guide to the true figure of transsexualism.

- Playmate preference of the opposite sex
- Dislike of or refusal to pass urine in a way typical of their sex
- A hope that their genitalia will change to the opposite sex
- Distress at the physical body changes during puberty.

(Source: NHS Direct)

Gender dysphoria as a psychological condition

The psychiatric model of gender dysphoria comprises more than one point of view. A minority, and somewhat extreme, view held by only a few psychiatrists is that transsexualism is caused by delusional psychosis and hence should be treated with electric shock therapy or antipsychotic drugs. While not discounting that such conditions could exist, there are at least three alternative schools of thought. Psychoanalytic approaches, founded on Freudian concepts, state that problems can result from difficulties with establishing gender identity in toddlerhood, from incomplete resolution of the Oedipal and Electra conflicts during the phallic stage of personality development and/or from identification with an inappropriate role model. Lothstein (1979), for example, claimed that some female-to-male transsexuals had mothers who lacked a cohesive self with which it was difficult for girls to identify.

An explanation that combines evolutionary and behaviourist ideas is that gender identity develops through imprinting and conditioning. Imprinting occurs first – the young animal forms an attachment bond with its parent during a biologically determined window of opportunity known as a critical period. Once imprinted, the individual preferentially observes and learns from, and is conditioned by, its own species. Furthermore, if imprinting fails, problems relating to the opposite sex when mature can occur. If parallel processes occur in humans, failure to imprint could then lead to conditioning incongruous with the individual's sex and difficulties relating to the opposite sex such that gender dysphoria may follow. Otherwise, cross gender conditioning and/or inappropriate role modelling might be an underlying cause, although the research that exists on this is inconclusive. If anything, it shows that parents are generally tolerant of early **cross-gender behaviour** (Zucker and Bradley 1995) but less so in boys (Fagot 1974) and this is also true of parents, teachers and peers (Fagot 1985).

Cognitive approaches, such as Piaget's, claim that gender identity is a result of maturation. By the age of three, children have developed gender identity (Slaby and Frey 1975) but it is during the adolescent years that they consolidate their understanding of gender. Adolescents are in the formal operational stage of cognitive development so their thinking and reasoning skills become more abstract and sophisticated. This enables them to deal with hypothetical situations with a number of different outcomes, including their own gender concept. It is at this point that they may become aware of gender dysphoria and the possibilities open to them.

STRETCH AND CHALLENGE

Activity Gender dysphoria as a psychological condition

1 These three approaches appear at surface level to be different but can you make any connections between them?

2 How might you test for these approaches using ethical methodology?

Answers are given on p.606. ▶

Evaluation of psychological explanations of gender dysphoria

- *Pathologising gender identity* – The existence of gender identity disorder as a psychiatric condition is contentious because it appears to pathologise particular forms of gender identity. This arguably increases the psychological distress and risk of mental health problems in people who, in an intolerant society, feel discriminated against, and possibly isolated, because of their gender orientation. (See 'One tribe, three genders' on p.220 for an example of a more tolerant society.) However, supporters of the classification argue that, if it were disposed of, there would be no formal grounds for diagnosis and therefore no reason to find the resources to support people who wish to express their gender in a particular way. Also, there is no doubt that gender dysphoria can be so distressing that it does constitute a mental disorder that would benefit from a wide range of treatments.

- *Difficulty in testing psychoanalytic explanations* – There is little evidence to suggest that some boys identify with their mothers and girls with their fathers and so go on to experience gender dysphoria. Studies considering intra-familial relationships, divorce, dominance of parents and other socio-emotional factors produce a mix of findings that also fail to account for gender dysphoria. Transsexuals come from all types of familial backgrounds and their sexual orientation, even after reassignment, could be heterosexual, gay, lesbian or bisexual. These mixed findings illustrate how difficult it can be to test, support or falsify psychoanalytic concepts.

- *Problems with imprinting and conditioning explanations* – There is evidence that animals and humans imprint on the first caregiver they observe, usually the mother, but this is more to do with ensuring a bond forms with the caregiver and with one's species for survival purposes. Children are subjected to many human models and are generally socialised to adopt appropriate gender schemas (Martin and Little 1990), so to assume that imprinting on the mother causes gender dysphoria would be rigid and over-simplified. In any case, it would only account for male-to-female transsexualism.

- *Gender identity, maturation and cognition* – Cognitive psychologists claim that gender identity is established by three years of age (Slaby and Frey 1975) and that it is during the adolescent years that they consolidate their gender understanding and deal with any associated issues. However, transsexuals tend to report that they were aware of how they felt about their gender long before adolescence so the timing proposed by cognitive psychologists, and the role of maturation in adolescence, is called into question.

Gender dysphoria as a biological condition

Alternative explanations of the origins of gender dysphoria are mainly biological and have been informed by individuals with **hermaphroditism**. While these conditions may provide useful insights into gender dysphoria, the DSM-IV-TR criteria for gender dysphoria specifically exclude them. Nevertheless, a biological basis to gender dysphoria seems plausible and one such explanation, brain sex theory, has recently emerged from the Netherlands Institute for Brain Research.

Brain sex theory

Brain-sex theory is based on the difference in size of certain brain structures in men and women. There has been particular interest in those that are sexually dimorphic i.e. taking a different form in males and females. In 1995, Zhou, Hofman and Gooren studied an area of the brain, which is also located in the hypothalamus, and is known as the bed nucleus of the stria terminalis central subdivision (BSTc). This is believed to be fully developed by five years and influences sexual behaviour. In post-mortems of six male-to-female transsexuals who had received feminising hormones, it was found to be the same size as in heterosexual women. Additional post-mortem comparisons, this time with non-transsexual clients with abnormal hormone levels, concluded that the small size of the BSTc in the male-female transsexuals could not wholly be accounted for by their sex hormone exposure in adulthood.

In further studies the number of neurons in the BSTc was assessed and this was found to be even more sexually dimorphic than the volume. Using the same tissue from the six male-female transsexuals, Kruijver *et al.* (2000) found that the number of neurons in the BSTc showed a similar pattern to that in heterosexual women. The BSTc neuron number was the same in an untreated gender dysphoric male as in the heterosexual women and for a female-male transsexual it was in the heterosexual male range. Further examination of the non-transsexual clients with abnormal hormone levels led Kruijver *et al.* to conclude that the hormone exposure in adulthood did not show a definitive relationship with the neuron number in the BSTc.

IDA   Reductionism and gender dysphoria

It is generally difficult to tease out any behavioural effects influenced by nature and nurture but this becomes even more so in the sensitive area of gender dysphoria where a strictly biological reductionist explanation could be inadequate. If researchers resort to reductionist measures, the fMRI scan is most informative as it shows the brain in action. Other scanning techniques give an indication of brain structure differences but will not inform scientists about how these differences were derived. The brain develops pre-natally and continues to mature post-natally when exposed to the environment. It is therefore impossible to gauge any predetermined differences during pre-natal development when the brain is still immature.

Evaluation of biological explanations of gender dysphoria

- *The complex interaction of nature and nurture* – The human brain undergoes considerable development pre-natally and continues to develop after birth. By the time it is fully developed, the child has also been subjected to numerous environmental influences, including gender socialisation. It then becomes impossible to disentangle the effects of nature and nurture on both the brain and gender-related behaviour. It appears that whilst researchers are prepared to accept a biological element to gender dysphoria, they are uncertain of the extent to which it can be explained this way.

- *A challenge to brain sex theory* – A study by Chung *et al.* (2002) challenged the time at which dimorphism in the BSTc appears claiming that differences in volume and neuron number did not develop until adulthood. This is inconsistent with the fact that individuals with gender dysphoria are often aware of it from an early age. Chung *et al.* have argued that pre-natal hormonal influences might remain dormant until adulthood and then trigger the change. Alternatively failure to develop gender identity congruent with one's sex might affect the BSTc in an as yet unknown way.

- *The role of hormones* – Contrary to Zhou *et al.* (1995) and Kruijver *et al.* (2000), Hulshoff Pol *et al.* (2006) found that transgender hormone therapy does influence the size of the BSTc. This has important implications because it suggests that hormones can have an effect on the BSTc even in adulthood – hence even after the BSTc is supposedly fully developed at five years. This means that the tissue examined at post-mortem could have been changed due to hormone therapy and not shaped during pre-natal development. In other words the findings by the Zhou *et al.* and Kruijver *et al.* studies could have been a side effect of cross-sex hormone therapy.

- *Lessons from transsexualism* – Transsexualism is described by Gooren (2006) as an extreme form of gender dysphoria and a better understanding of its underlying causes could throw light on less pronounced conditions. Gooren distinguishes between early and late transsexualism. In the former, the individual asserts from an early age that they are not the gender they appear to be. Reassignment to the opposite gender, most commonly male to female, is often successful. In the latter, the onset of dysphoria is more gradual, the direction of change is more often from female to male and the success rate is lower. Neave (2007) argues that it is difficult to explain this without recourse to pre-natal hormonal influences, as yet not fully understood.

- *Frequency of transsexualism* – Neave (2007) notes that the human foetus is female by default until, in the case of normal males, masculinising hormones set it on a male course of development. If this process does not happen as it should, it follows that there should be a greater proportion of male to female than female to male transsexuals and this does appear to be true, (1.5 to 3 times more) especially in the early onset group. Neave argues that this must be due to different levels of exposure to pre-natal androgens which could be either environmentally or genetically caused, but again, the exact mechanism is not understood. However, it may also be true that females have more flexibility over how they express their gender role so the pressure on them to change to male is not so great.

- *Complexity of the issue* – Researchers in this area advise that gender dysphoria is very complex and at the moment there is no adequate explanation of the cause. The only thing known for certain is that individuals with gender dysphoria should be listened to, taken seriously, their distress understood and their treatment considered in an empathic manner.

CHECK YOUR UNDERSTANDING

Check your understanding of psychological explanations of gender development by answering the following questions. Try to do this from memory. Check your answers by looking back through Topic 1.

1. Complete the following sentence. A fully developed gender concept comprises the following three elements ...

2. What is meant by alpha and beta bias in psychological research?

3. What are the main differences between different cognitive-developmental theories explaining how the gender concept is formed?

4. How do children self reinforce or refuse to process information that is incongruent with their own gender schema?

5. What do we mean by psychological androgyny?

6. How have psychologists attempted to account for psychological androgyny?

7. What are the main criticisms of these explanations?

8. What are the main features of gender dysphoria?

9. Outline some psychological explanations of gender dysphoria.

10. What are the main criticisms of these explanations?

11. Outline biological explanations of gender dysphoria?

12. What problems are there with biological explanations of gender dysphoria?

Topic 2: Biological influences on gender

Introduction

In psychology there is the constant debate surrounding nature and nurture. Nurture explanations of gender identity cannot easily account for everything. They struggle to explain why sex hormones have a profound effect on sexual development, including subjection to sex hormones that are incongruent with one's genetic make-up and why some individuals experience gender dysphoria. Clearly there is a place for a biological interpretation of how we develop gender identity. What happens during pre-natal development? When do crucial windows of sexual development occur? And can evolutionary theory enlighten the debate?

IDA Reductionist methods in gender research

Methods of investigation that reduce gender typical behaviour to the action of hormones have been criticised for leaving out the greater picture i.e. the context in which the behaviour occurs and cross-cultural gender differences. Therefore such reductionism can be misleading and too singular a dimension for explaining something as complicated as differences of behaviour between men and women. Without knowledge of the context the behaviour occurs in, the triggering of hormone production, required to make the behaviour possible doesn't inform us of anything except that the presence of a particular hormone will make one feel a certain way.

Psychology in context — Gender and risky behaviour

Males feature in crime statistics far more than females and this applies across the board for the type of crime committed and the age of the perpetrator. Antisocial behaviour is on the rise especially amongst young boys who, at the age of 10, are more likely to receive an antisocial behaviour order known as 'ASBO' than girls of the same age. Nigel Morris, the Home Affairs Correspondent (2006) reported that 3500 ASBOs were handed out in England and Wales in 2004-05, a rise of 60 per cent on the previous year, but over half were ignored. Furthermore Goodchild (2006) reported that court records in Liverpool showed that more than 97 boys and 18 girls under the age of 10, and more than 500 boys and about 100 girls between 10 and 14 were given ASBOs for drunken behaviour.

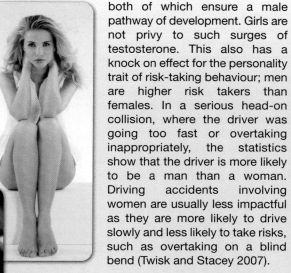

What is behind this difference between boys and girls? Testosterone is one of a group of male hormones called androgens and it is known to increase aggressive and sexual behaviour in males. During males' pre-natal development, there is a surge of foetal testosterone with another during pubescence,

both of which ensure a male pathway of development. Girls are not privy to such surges of testosterone. This also has a knock on effect for the personality trait of risk-taking behaviour; men are higher risk takers than females. In a serious head-on collision, where the driver was going too fast or overtaking inappropriately, the statistics show that the driver is more likely to be a man than a woman. Driving accidents involving women are usually less impactful as they are more likely to drive slowly and less likely to take risks, such as overtaking on a blind bend (Twisk and Stacey 2007).

If we consider Darwin's evolutionary account of why there are differences between the sexes, it is plain to see that men are more aggressive and higher-risk takers than women for good reason. In our evolutionary past, men had to compete with other men for a mate and to be successful at this they had to show strength and might which would have had a risk element. A woman, on the other hand, could pick and choose which male she preferred. Competitiveness could be another reason why males feature more in the crime statistics.

The role of genes and hormones in gender development

Genes and gender development

As outlined at the beginning of this chapter, when we refer to the term 'sex' we are identifying a person chromosomally as male (XY) or female (XX). When we consider 'gender' we are referring to masculine and feminine traits and behaviours. Although pre-natal development follows an obvious pathway, which for the most part is similar for males and females, having the male chromosome combination or the female chromosome combination will result in differences in male and female pre-natal hormone levels. These have different impacts on the developing male and female sex organs and the brain. For the first six weeks after conception there are no structural differences between genetically male and genetically female embryos. Both males and females have two ridges of tissue, called gonadal ridges, from which the male and female sex organs will develop. Six weeks after conception, the crucial window for **sexual differentiation** opens and the genes inherited determine

whether the gonadal ridges become testes or ovaries. It is important that specific foetal hormones, consistent with being either genetically male or female, are produced at this time. At six weeks the Y–chromosome of the male triggers the synthesis of H–Y antigen, a protein which causes the gonadal ridges to grow into testes. If H–Y antigen is injected into a genetically female foetus at six weeks of pre-natal development, the result is a genetic female with testes. Likewise if drugs blocking H–Y antigen are injected into a genetic male at six weeks, the result is a genetic male with ovaries. This demonstrates the interrelationship between genes and hormones.

Hormones and gender development

Another crucial event takes place during the early pre-natal period involving the internal reproductive ducts. Prior to six weeks both males and females have two sets of reproductive ducts. The male Wolffian system has the capacity to develop into the male reproductive ducts: this includes the seminal vesicles and vas deferens. The female Mullerian system has the capacity to develop into the female ducts: this includes the uterus, upper vagina and fallopian tubes. During the third month of male foetal development, the testes produce testosterone and a Mullerian–inhibiting substance. Testosterone, which is a male hormone, stimulates the Wolffian system to develop further whilst the Mullerian–inhibiting substance causes the Mullerian ducts to shrivel away and the testes to descend into the scrotum. The study by Imperato-McGinley et al. (1974) illustrates what happens if this process is delayed. See 'The Batista family' on p.205.

Interestingly, the development of sex differences in the brain, which ultimately influence us throughout the lifespan, happen to coincide with sexual differentiation. Male genes promote the production of testosterone at certain times of development. This has an impact on how the brain develops structurally and on behavioural patterns, especially sexual behaviour, that separates men from women. For instance, testosterone slows down the development of certain parts of the brain whilst at the same time speeding growth of other parts. This masculinisation of the foetal brain effectively primes it for male sexual behaviour and a host of other differences relating to function. In the absence of male foetal hormones during pregnancy, the brain of a baby boy is likely to follow a more female pathway. Levels of testosterone also account for differences in behaviour across the sexes e.g. men are innately more aggressive and prone to taking risks and women are more gentle and conservative.

Geschwind and Galaburda (1987) have observed in males that during pre-natal development the right side of the brain develops earlier than the left side. They suggest that development of the left hemisphere is slowed down, especially near the Wernicke's area (concerned with language processing) so that the right hemisphere and other parts of the left can develop more quickly. Testosterone is believed to be the key influence here and it is therefore not surprising to find that the right hemisphere of the male brain is actually thicker than that of the female brain. Geschwind and Galaburda (1987) further suggest that the role of testosterone in slowing the development of parts of the left hemisphere might explain why males are not as good as females in verbal abilities but are superior at spatial abilities. Men have been shown time and time again to be superior at tasks involving visual-spatial skills such as map reading, navigation, rotating images mentally and mathematical reasoning (Maccoby and Jacklin 1974).

 HOW SCIENCE WORKS

A case of penectomy

Key research: Money and Ehrhardt (1972)

David Reimer was born an identical twin. Both twin boys had problems urinating and it was suggested that they be circumcised to relieve the pressure around the penis. At 8 months, David was circumcised but it went wrong and his penis was burnt off. This created a dilemma for his parents who were unsure what to do next. They consulted specialist John Money, who had many years of experience with intersex clients who had undergone gender realignment surgery, and he advised them to raise their son as a girl. David's testicles were removed, and a rudimentary vulva created. His parents were told to nurture their son as a girl while continuing to nurture the other twin as a boy. David's life was followed closely by Money and they met for the occasional interview.

Money reported his findings in a positive light, making claims that this natural experiment was a success and that gender identity is undifferentiated at birth. He claimed further that, as long as children are assigned a gender identity before 18 months, they can be nurtured to live as the opposite sex therefore showing that gender identity is largely socially determined (Money, Hampson and Hampson 1955a, 1956, 1957).

However, Money's reports did not tell the whole story. Initially, raising David as a girl called Brenda went well. Brenda was encouraged to do feminine things and participate in feminine activities. However, the reality was that she was unhappy, had no friends and liked to play with her brother's toys. When she reached 12, Brenda reluctantly took female sex hormones to facilitate puberty. At school she was teased and called 'cave woman' by the other girls, because of her masculine gait. The problems experienced by Brenda escalated to a point whereby at, the age of 14, she was relieved to hear the full story of what had happened to her. She started taking masculinising hormones and underwent a mastectomy and phalloplasty. Brenda became David and married a woman who had three children from a previous relationship. The struggle David had experienced (which culminated in his suicide, aged 38) was only revealed 30 years later.

Milton Diamond, a biologist, challenged Money's assumptions and argued that research shows the importance of pre- and peri-natal sex hormones on gender identity and gender role via sexual differentiation of the brain. What mattered in David's case was that he shared the same pre-natal environment as his brother. Money chose to ignore the biological approach. In David's case it would appear that Diamond's theory is supported (Diamond and Sigmundson 1997) and Money's theory rejected (Money 1995; Money and Ehrhardt 1972).

Other research has shown that the corpus callosum (which is a bundle of neural fibres interconnecting the left and right hemispheres) is larger in females than in males (Driesen and Raz 1995). This finding is controversial but, if true, might go some way towards explaining why women are superior at processing verbal information. Communication involves not just processing language but all the pragmatics of language such as emotional expression, gesticulation, emphasis, context and anticipation and women are far better at this than men. Having a larger and richer collection of neural fibres in the corpus callosum in women could explain the superior speed of processing and integrating information. It could mean quicker access to information from both hemispheres of the brain, and faster processing of that information and being able to integrate this information proficiently – all things that women are generally good at doing.

In spite of research such as this, we should be aware that, although small and consistent differences may be found in the abilities of males and females, there is also substantial common ground which makes them more alike than different. The key question to ask is whether the differences are large enough to be important in any practical sense such that males and females should be treated differently.

Sex hormones in animals and humans

There are many examples from the animal kingdom demonstrating the impact of male and female hormones during pre-natal development on future behaviour. Young *et al.* (1964) showed that female monkeys, exposed to male hormones during pre-natal development, tended to engage in rough and tumble play in their early years in comparison to their female counterparts who were not thus exposed. Animal studies such as this one can be contrived as monkeys are injected with male or female androgens or they can be naturally occurring events. For instance it has been shown in rats that if there is more than one foetal rat in the womb, conditions can get crowded. Vandenbergh (2003) says that foetuses line up like peas in a pod. Females next to males are exposed to more testosterone than their more distant sisters and, as a consequence, show more masculine behaviour.

Similar findings to Young *et al.*'s were obtained in human mothers who took male sex hormones to cease uterine bleeding during pregnancy and consequently had girls who behaved in a tomboyish manner (Ehrhardt and Money 1967). The reverse occurs in boys whose mothers were injected with female hormones during pregnancy. They were less athletic and engaged in less rough and tumble play (Yalom *et al.* 1973). Studies such as these show that the children involved did not necessarily have abnormal gender identity but exhibited higher than usual levels of cross-gender behaviour. This is exactly what has been found in animal studies. In the case of the monkeys, the offspring just engaged in cross-gender behaviour; they were not intersex or transsexuals.

HOW SCIENCE WORKS

Activity **Sex hormones in animals and humans**

Look again at the findings of the sex hormone studies by Young *et al.* (1964) and Ehrhardt and Money (1967).

1 How accurate do you think these findings are?

2 How valid are the contrived and naturally occurring experiments?

Answers are given on p.606. ▶

HOW SCIENCE WORKS

The Batista family

Key research: Imperato-McGinley *et al.* (1974)

Imperato-McGinley's *et al.*'s (1974) study concerned cases of **pseudohermaphroditism** in the Batista family of the Dominican Republic. Ten children in this family were born with an exceptionally small penis and scrotum which resembled female anatomy. They were raised as girls despite being XY. Once puberty began, testosterone levels increased and a normal-sized penis grew and testicles descended into the scrotum. This had resulted from the inability to produce hormones responsible for shaping the penis and scrotum during foetal development. Twenty two other families in the region are similarly affected and their condition can be traced to a common ancestor whose defective gene has to be carried by both parents to be manifested in their sons. What is remarkable about the findings is the relative ease with which the boys adapted to their new gender as if nothing unusual was happening to them.

This naturally occurring event offers scientists the opportunity to study the impact that nature has over nurture on gender development. It is a natural experiment that has none of the ethical problems associated with injecting animals with androgens during gestation or extrapolating findings from animal research to humans. Although laboratory-based research does offer an understanding of how hormones impact on animal and human anatomical development, a naturally occurring event such as that seen in the Dominican Republic strengthens findings from the laboratory by offering method triangulation. In other words evidence from laboratory-based research is supported by evidence gathered from a naturally occurring phenomenon.

An experiment in child-rearing

Imagine that a baby could survive on an island by him or herself (you need to dispense with practicalities).

1 If the baby grows in to a healthy male or female child, would they show typical gender-role behaviour for instance in the strategy used for obtaining food and for building a shelter?

2 Let's assume that this individual was taken from the island and brought back to 'civilisation' how would you differentiate between the contribution of nature and nurture for their behaviour?

3 What kind of tests would you run and how would you look at the brain?

Answers are given on p.606. ▶

Evaluation of the role of hormones and genes in gender development

■ *Biological determinism* – An over-emphasis on biological influences in determining behaviour could be a problem for several reasons. Firstly it is a reductionist approach which does not take sufficient account of the whole human functioning in a complex social and cultural environment in that the whole may be greater than the sum of its parts. There is also a tendency to assume that biologically determined characteristics are hard-wired and cannot easily be changed which research into hormonal influences in particular has shown is not necessarily true.

■ *Selectivity in research reporting* – In the world of academic publishing there is a tendency to publish research findings that show significant effects. In the case of gender research, this tends to consist of studies in which sex differences have been found. This can give a false impression that differences are robust. Maccoby and Jacklin (1974) reviewed research into sex differences and found some support for the idea that boys were more aggressive and had better mathematical and spatial ability than girls but that girls' verbal ability was greater. In other respects Maccoby and Jacklin concluded that research showed far more similarities than differences between males and females (and this was at a time far less egalitarian than now). The tendency to look for differences could lead researchers to overlook this.

■ *Socially sensitive research* – Researching questions about biologically based sex differences is politically sensitive. The tendency to emphasise differences in the expected direction, reinforces gender stereotypes and is potentially limiting for both males and females e.g. in choice of career. These limits might be self-imposed or imposed by others because 'science' tells us they are so. This also helps to maintain a status quo in which women are over-represented in less valued and less well-paid occupations, thus maintaining gender inequality.

■ *The use of animal research* – The debate about whether we should extrapolate findings from animal research to humans has split the field. Some researchers claim that the biological processes of anatomical functioning are similar across species. Therefore, when examining universal principles about the effects of stimulating various parts of the brain known to be responsible for basic motivational activity, or the effects of hormones for stimulus-response behaviour, then the findings from animal research is valid and reliable. Others claim that regardless of the simplicity of the behaviour researched, animals are different and humans are unique and so should be regarded as such.

Evolutionary explanations of gender roles

In the previous section, the connection between our genes, hormonal effects on brain structuring and the specific strengths of the ability of men and women was considered. Gender socialization then continues, reinforcing these differences through the use of gender stereotypes and role modelling. But why have these pre-natal differences arisen? What is the driving force that pushes sex differences of behaviour, ability and personality? These questions can be more readily understood by taking an evolutionary perspective.

Natural selection, fitness and sexual selection

In his book, *On the Origin of Species by Natural Selection*, Charles Darwin (1859) defined and explained the process of evolution. He spoke of **natural selection** and **fitness** and supported these concepts with evidence from the natural environment.

Natural selection is the primary force behind evolutionary change. It refers to the process by which certain physical and psychological traits of animals, including humans, have been passed down from one generation to another due to their advantages in terms of survival and reproduction. To illustrate this, take the example of the giraffe. The giraffe has not always had a long neck. In its evolutionary past, there must have been some giraffes with slightly longer necks than the rest – a genetic mutation occurring at random. In adverse environmental conditions (e.g. drought), giraffes with longer necks would be at an advantage. They could reach higher branches and would therefore be able to compete successfully for food resources leading to 'survival of the fittest'.

This giraffe's enhanced ability to survive increases its chances of being able to achieve the prime objective of reproducing, so fitness, according to Darwin, refers to the potential to pass on one's genes by having as many offspring as possible. Fitness is 'A measure of the number of offspring produced, or, in the view of some evolutionists, the proportion of genes passed on to future generations' (Workman and Reader, 2008).

In his book, *The Descent of Man and Selection in Relation to Sex* (1871) Darwin also spoke of a second mechanism of evolutionary change called **sexual selection**. 'Sexual selection 'selects for' characteristics that help an individual gain access to mates' Workman and Reader (2008). Characteristics are chiefly selected by two so-called selection pressures; competition between males for females and the selection of preferred male characteristics by females.

Sexual selection and sexual dimorphism

Differences in physiology, anatomy and behaviour across the sexes are referred to as **sexual dimorphism** (from the Greek di meaning two and morph meaning form). As stated in the previous section, this is a likely consequence of male versus male competition and female choice which leads to sexual selection and the different forms that males and females take. To impress a female, a male had to demonstrate his fitness, i.e. that he was worthy of her attentions and would make a good mate. He had to show her that he could survive and ensure that she and their offspring did too. This would entail not only being fit and healthy, and therefore being of good stock with good genes, but also being a successful and resourceful provider and protector. If men were to compete against other men for a female mate then they had to win. In some

The runaway selection hypothesis

A good illustration of sexual selection is the story of the peacock's tail. The peacock is an exotically coloured male bird with a huge tail that it puts on display when attracting a female peahen (who is nothing to look at – plain, brown and boring). The more elaborate and huge the male's tail display is the more impressed is the peahen hence, the bigger the tail display, the more likely the peacock is to find a mate. But what if sexual selection is taken to a dangerous extreme? Fisher (1930) proposed the runaway selection hypothesis where the feature (in this case the tail) becomes exaggerated with each generation, as this is what the peahen wants, until it reaches a stage where the peacock can no longer outrun its predators. This has happened in India where peacocks are falling prey to tigers.

1 What will become of the peacock if they continue to be killed by tigers?

2 How would this affect their fitness?

3 Is the impact on sexual selection for the peacock likely to continue?

4 Can it be stopped; is human intervention necessary?

Answers are given on p.606. ▶

The hunting hypothesis (Morris 1866)

Researching into the influence of evolutionary forces on human characteristics, behaviour and abilities is challenging so innovative studies have to be devised. For instance it is possible to devise a means of investigating the impact of sexual selection in humans by looking at differences in abilities of males and females. The hunting hypothesis, first applied in the context of Darwinian evolution by Morris (1866), is one example of how differences between men and women (even today) can be explained in evolutionary terms of sexual selection and adaptation to the environment. In our evolutionary past, a good hunter was a male who was strong enough to throw a spear with intent and speed and, most importantly, accuracy so it is argued that he adapted to environmental pressure to become good at hunting. Accurate spear throwing involves strength, good visual spatial skills and good hand-eye coordination, skills in which, even today, men are superior over women. In modern tests involving visual spatial skills such as map reading, navigation, mentally rotating images and mathematical reasoning, men do better on average than women.

If the male physique and temperament were being shaped by processes of sexual selection leading to competitiveness with other males and environmental adaptations, then what was happening to females? One point of view is that, with the onset of humans' bipedal gait, the angle of the pelvis meant that during pregnancy the foetus' growth and development was compromised, so much so that it was delivered while still relatively immature. So why give birth to an offspring that couldn't fend for itself or do anything? The answer is simple – it is a matter of getting the baby out before it is too big to get out. Given these disadvantages, it was pertinent that the mother would look after her offspring – hence the bonding process of attachment.

Often females in our evolutionary past were pregnant or lactating or looking after children. They would find it difficult to join their male counterparts in hunting because of their offspring who needed much of their attention. It was important for females to be the caregivers of their offspring and this meant that they had to interpret any subtle signals given off like cries, smiles and indicators of wanting to be held. To this day women are the better communicators; verbally, non-verbally and emotionally. By considering the differences in performance at school or in the workplace between human males and females, evolutionary psychologists can indirectly test the repercussions of sexual selection.

cases, this might involve being larger, stronger, more muscular and more aggressive than one's rivals. Effectively, by trying to impress a potential female mate of his fitness, he is succumbing to female choice thus females determine males' traits. Females are the driving force here and it makes perfect sense that they are. They are the ones left holding the baby so they want to get it right.

Two aspects of gender role from an evolutionary perspective

It is clear that the evolutionary forces that Darwin speaks of have influenced human behaviour. Differences in anatomy are seen as central to gender role differences. Sexual selection shapes both physiological (anatomical) and behavioural differences between the sexes and this

has a knock-on effect for mate selection and parental investment.

Evolutionary forces in mate selection

In the previous section, the process of sexual selection by male-male competition and female choice, and how this results in sexual dimorphism, was described. Since males generally compete for females they not only have to impress the female but have to ward off any other males who might also be interested in her. This also has a knock on effect on male behaviour in terms of them being more aggressive and dominant which are male traits encompassed in the masculine stereotype and male-role. The enlarged body size of men and the lowered threshold for aggression have been sexually selected in the past but also play a major role in male-male competition. Nevertheless, men do not compete indiscriminately. Daly

Sex differences in jealousy

Key research: Buss et al. (1992)

In humans and 4000 other species, internal fertilisation and gestation occurs so females can usually be 100 per cent certain of the identity of the father, unlike males who rely on the word of the mother. There are cases where men have been duped into believing that they are the fathers of the offspring when in fact they are not – in other words they have been cuckolded. Under these circumstances males could end up parentally investing in someone else's offspring hence there are strong pressures on males to ensure paternity. It has been argued by Daly, Wilson and Weghorst (1982) that male sexual jealousy has evolved to solve this problem. Men who don't pay attention to cues of infidelity or choose to ignore them are more likely to be at risk of lower paternity certainty. Buss et al. (1992) designed a study to test which form of infidelity (sexual or emotional) will trigger more distress in men and women. They presented the following dilemma to 202 undergraduate students:

Please think of a serious committed romantic relationship that you have had in the past, that you currently have, or that you would like to have. Imagine that you discover that the person with whom you've been seriously involved became interested in someone else. What would distress or upset you more (please circle only one):

1 Imagining your partner forming a deep emotional attachment to that person.

2 Imagining your partner enjoying passionate sexual intercourse with that other person.

Students were then given another dilemma, but this time the following choices applied:

1 Imagining your partner trying different sexual positions with that other person.

2 Imagining your partner falling in love with that other person.

A large sex difference in the reporting of distress was found. 60 per cent of men reported greater distress over their partner's sexual infidelity compared with 17 per cent of women while 83 per cent of women reported greater distress over a partner's emotional attachment. About 44 per cent of men and 12 per cent of women reported greater distress over a partner's sexual involvement with someone else (a 32 per cent difference). In the case of a partner falling in love with a rival, the majority of women reported greater distress.

This study, however, is limited in that findings pertain to undergraduate students of a particular age and culture so to test for the second evolutionary prediction would involve the participation of different age groups and people in different levels of involvement. It would be interesting to see if similar findings occur cross-culturally and with people of different occupations. This study has a further flaw in that participants answering the questions could be relating to a current relationship that they have or could be imagining what it is like to be in a committed relationship. These two types of groups should be separated as their feelings are based on different sources: the real thing or imagined. As we know it is difficult to simulate feelings and decisions based on an imagined relationship: one doesn't know how one will react and feel unless there is a sense of truly experiencing what it is to be involved in a relationship. The extent that findings can be generalised is limited due to sampling procedure and face validity.

and Wilson (1988) believe they weigh the fighting ability of the opponent relative to their own against the benefit of winning the fight before they engage in combat. The more successful men will get the women.

Most combat is against same-sex rivals because they are competing for the same resources. Daly and Wilson (1994) found that same-sex homicides, concerning unrelated individuals tended to involve men (97.2% of 13 680). Male fighting in the name of reproductive competition can be direct or indirect. If direct it involves overtly fighting over women. Indirect fighting takes a number of forms, for example:

- for resources which are necessary for reproduction or acceptable to women
- for reputation which is necessary for obtaining and keeping resources
- for defending women and children in their care from other men.

In the case of sexual conflict (i.e. male-female), men assault wives (the very resource for which they competed) in order to deter them from pursuing other interests, particularly other men.

Parental investment theory

According to Trivers (1973) differences between the sexes, in both anatomy and behaviour, may be traced back to differences in the degree of parental investment. Female anatomy enables women to be the bearers of offspring. It is designed for the fertilisation of ova and to provide a safe and nourishing haven for the developing foetus in the uterus until it is ready to be born. In humans, gestation lasts for nine months which, in mammalian species, is a relatively long time to be carrying a growing foetus. The female body undergoes many changes during this period. The birth process itself takes its toll on the mother who experiences hormonal surges to help enlarge the birth canal and encourage uterine contraction. Post birth, the provision of nourishment from the mother continues through the production of milk. The baby is at a vulnerable developmental stage so bonding between mother and baby forms quickly and lasts a lifetime. Compared to the father, mothers' parental investment in their offspring is far greater, ranging from conception to gestation to giving birth and post-natal care. It is for this reason that females give careful consideration to the health, fitness and resources of a potential father.

Male anatomy, on the other hand, is designed for ensuring fertilisation. Men do not experience the menstrual cycle and the associated changing levels of hormones on a monthly basis and obviously cannot become pregnant and give birth. Males can therefore afford to take more risks with sexual involvements and be more promiscuous than women. They have less to lose and can choose whether or not to invest in their offspring. All these behaviours can be predicted from Darwin's account of evolution and other evolutionists such as Trivers (1972) and Workman and Reader (2008).

Activity **Universal and species-specific maternal behaviour**

Make a list of behaviours you wish to observe. For instance how a mother cares and looks after her offspring or defends her offspring against a potential threat. Observe these behaviours in humans and other animals such as a pet dog or cat or birds in a park. Look for universal similarities of behaviour and species-specific behaviour.

Activity **Pre-natal hormones and looking preferences.** Lutchmaya et al. (2002)

It has been suggested that male and female brains are different as soon as they are born. Why should this be and did sexual selection have a hand in this? A study by Lutchmaya et al. (2002) showed that girls made far more eye contact than boys. They filmed 29 girls and 41 boys at one year of age and measured how often they looked at the mother's face. Amniocentesis tests during the first three months of pregnancy enabled the researchers to measure testosterone levels present in the amniotic fluid. As expected, it was found that the foetal testosterone level was higher for the boys than girls. A correlation between higher levels of testosterone in boys and less eye contact at the age of one was found. Could nurture have had a hand in these findings? Connellan et al. (2000) gave 102 24-hour-old babies a choice between looking at the researcher's face or a mechanical mobile about the same size as the face. Boys preferred to look at the mobile and the girls at the face. There appears to be an early distinction between girls who prefer the social world and boys who prefer the physical world.

1 To what extent do you think these studies have validity in furthering our evolutionary understanding of gender-role differences?

2 Is a valid connection being made between observing stimuli post-natally and pre-natal hormone levels?

Answers are given on p.606. ▶

Evaluation of evolutionary explanations of gender development

- *Extrapolation between species* – Much evolutionary evidence involves comparison between humans and animal species. Some researchers would say we should not do this because animals are qualitatively different from humans. Others, such as behaviourists, argue that Darwin's theory has demonstrated that there is evolutionary continuity between species and it follows from this that there is also physical and behavioural continuity. It follows that it makes sense to compare humans with closely related animal species. Furthermore, there are universal principles that apply to every living thing: the differences between males and females are universal. All female animals have anatomy for bearing offspring and all male animals have the means for fertilisation, therefore the pressure of male-male competition for females applies regardless of species.

- *The only universal theory* – Evolutionary theory is the only complete theory that explains animal and human behaviour. Evolution can explain the diversity of life forms and differences between the sexes and has evidence to demonstrate how the evolutionary pressures impacted on us in the past make us what we are today. Furthermore, evidence arises from many different subject areas such as palaeontology, anthropology and geology. Multiple sources of evidence help to corroborate evolutionary ideas.

- *Supportive empirical evidence* – We cannot research evolution directly because it is an on-going process but we can look at the impact of proposed evolutionary processes on many aspects of behaviour. In the case of mate choice and parental investment, for example, the evidence is strongly in support of sexual selection forces at work. We can see the differences between men and women in how jealousy is manifested: men find the sexual element more worrying and women find the attachment element more worrying (Buss *et al.* 1992). Sexual selection provides a parsimonious explanation for this sex difference which is difficult to explain in other terms.

- *The chicken and the egg dilemma* – Is gender role driven by biologically occurring sex differences or is it the other way round? This is a chicken and the egg argument – which comes first? Differences in anatomy of the male and female body, especially with regard to reproduction, are indisputable but their relationship to gender role is less certain. If biological forces come first, there is a tendency to believe that there is little we can do to address inequality between the genders. If gender role comes first, it could be argued that change is possible because, child-bearing apart, both sexes have a wide range of abilities. Just like the chicken and egg question this is difficult to resolve.

- *Cultural influences* – Biological characteristics and culture interact with each other in a myriad of different ways. This is reflected in the wide variety of ways in which gender is expressed both within and between cultures making it difficult to disentangle their influences. The most likely explanation of gender differences is one that combines the two: a biosocial approach.

The biosocial approach to gender development

Biosocial theory
The biosocial theory approach to gender development sees gender differences as emerging from a complex interaction between:

- biologically-based sex differences which are chiefly due to women's child-bearing capacity and men's greater size, strength, and speed

- developmental processes which determine what individuals are capable of at different ages

- culture which provides an environmental context including social, ecological and economic aspects.

Wood and Eagly (2002, 2007) distinguish this approach from the evolutionary one:

'Our biosocial model does not assume that any sexual selection pressures that contributed to physical dimorphism between the sexes are major influences on sex-typed psychological attributes such as men's aggressiveness and competitive dominance'. (Wood and Eagly 2002).

Thus there is a shift in emphasis away from purely biological influences to the view that social environment also has an important role to play in bringing about psychological sex differences. Sexually dimorphic characteristics tend to determine what males and females do in order for their society to function efficiently but how this is manifested depends on their circumstances. It follows from this that we would expect gender to be expressed differently across cultures.

To illustrate further, Wood and Eagly (2002) explain the consequences of reproduction for women in the following quote:

'…the sex that can more readily perform the activities that yield status and power is advantaged in a gender hierarchy. Thus, patriarchy is not a uniform feature of human societies but instead emerges to the extent that, for example, women's reproductive activities conflict with the behaviours that yield status in a society.'

Wood and Eagly are alerting us to the fact that the extent to which women's reproductive activities conflict with their everyday activities will ultimately be the cause of lost status within a society. It is not patriarchy *per se* that influences status and power but rather the extent that women's reproductive activities prevent them from engaging in activities giving status and power. So if there is provision available to alleviate women from child care, leaving them free to engage in other activities, then those activities are more likely to have status and power like that available to men.

Wood and Eagly (2002) further say:

'…given the cross-cultural variability in sex differences that is anticipated by our **biosocial model**, it is likely that extensive socialisation is required to orient boys and girls to function differently insofar as they are expected to occupy different social roles within their society.'

This is a contentious point. Studies have shown that there are distinct gender differences in preference for certain activities, such as being drawn to play with certain types of toys and also eye gaze preferences in newborns. Baby girls gaze more often and longer at faces and baby boys at mechanical mobiles. These differences do not rely entirely on socialization.

STRETCH AND CHALLENGE

Patriarchy and power

1 How can Wood and Eagly's statement about the emergence of patriarchy be tested?

2 In what way would a psychologist interested in gender-role differences link this to which sex has the power in society?

3 What behaviours would support the statement?

Answers are given on p.607. ▶

The behaviour of women and men across cultures

Empirical support for the biosocial approach comes primarily from cross-cultural studies. Wood and Eagly (2002) considered several non-industrialised societies using the Ethnographic Atlas of 1264 societies (Murdock 1967) and the Atlas of World Cultures of 563 societies (Murdock 1981). They also had access to the Standard Cross-cultural Sample which holds a set of 186 societies considered to be a representative sample from around the world (Murdock and White 1969). Thus the data consisted of secondary source, written, ethnographic records of observations which were recoded so that they could be subjected to content analysis. The codings which Wood and Eagly considered related to the nature of and uniformity and variability of gender-role activities performed by men and women. Similarities that arise across cultures, despite socioeconomic differences, suggest a biological basis to gender role while differences suggest a dependence on factors that vary across the societies. For instance, across non-industrialised cultures men generally contributed more than women to providing food although this difference was greatest in societies dependent on hunting large animals and less in societies whose ecology meant dependence on gathering food. Women contributed much more to child-care, especially in infancy, but fathers' involvement did increase in later childhood. In other respects, divisions of labour by gender were found everywhere but there was great variability in the activities concerned. Activities such as making fire, milking, weaving and harvesting were referred to as 'swing activities' because they could be performed predominantly by either men or women depending on the society involved.

With any **ethnographic approach** there are problems associated with the accuracy of observation and the authenticity of the behaviour observed. Recoding behaviour into simple traits loses the context of the behaviour and this can be criticised for being reductionist. In addition the decision about what coding categories to include could be open to distortion by biases the researchers bring from their own culture. Nevertheless, archival data is a permanent record which makes it accessible to other researchers who can check the reliability of each other's claims.

Gender and food-getting

Ember (1978) analysed 181 foraging societies finding that in about 60 per cent of the societies in Sub-Saharan Africa and 50 per cent of the societies in the Insular Pacific, gathering food was the major form of foraging undertaken primarily by women. Hunting and fishing however, was more common in East Eurasia, North America and South and Central America where only one per cent of women contributed to the foraging process. Another study of similar approach was that of Aronoff and Crano (1975) who looked at 862 societies including intensive agriculture and animal husbandry and foraging. Women contributed to about 44 per cent of food produced. The conclusion was that contribution towards subsistence varied between the sexes as a result of the different strategies of acquiring food.

HOW SCIENCE WORKS

Activity

Gender and food-getting (Ember 1978)

Think about Ember's findings about men and women and food getting.

1 Why do you think there were noticeable differences of women's contribution towards subsistence?

2 Which study shows more validity and offers a more accurate representation and why?

Answers are given on p.607. ▶

Activity

Lifestyle and division of labour

Think of some heterosexual, two-parent families in your own culture that you know well. Select two or three whose lifestyles are very different. What do the mother and father do to provide for their families? What is their pattern of food-getting? How do they divide the domestic labour? Are any of these things affected by the age of the children?

Fertility decision-making

Key research: Foster (2000)

Foster (2000) has looked at limits to low fertility by adopting a biosocial approach. Population and motherhood statistical data going back to the 1960s suggest that industrialised countries are now experiencing their lowest levels of fertility. Foster claims that total fertility rates (TFRs) are dropping below the replacement level of 2.1 children per woman and have been below this level for the past two decades. She believes that there is a strong genetic predisposition for maternal or nurturing behaviour in women which, in most, influences their fertility motivation. Additionally, there are environmental factors which influence fertility motivation. How can a biosocial approach account for this?

The biological influence is the genetic predisposition to nurture and the societal one is normative pressure i.e. from the family to bear more children or to stop bearing children. For instance, under Ceauçescu in Romania, women with a low genetic predisposition for nurturing would have had no choice but to bear children because of the governmental policies of the day, they were denied contraception and abortion. In China there is the opposite problem. Women may have a high fertility motivation but can only have one child as decreed by law: exceed this and there will be sanctions. The third factor is the number of children already born: a good experience of pregnancy and giving birth and the post-natal hormone surge will encourage the need for further nurturing but a bad experience might deter any decision to have more children. Lastly there are factors such as being in a relationship or not, maternal age and financial considerations. The biosocial approach thus offers a causal explanation of fertility decision making.

Activity   Images of gender in the media

Gather as many pictures from magazines and newspapers depicting women and men performing subsistence tasks such as hunting or picking tea-leaves and see if the nature of the subsistence activities can be divided into two camps and if these reflect being male or female.

Evaluation of the biosocial approach to gender development

- *Cross-cultural similarity for male and female behaviour* – One major prediction made by the biosocial theory is that there should be similarity across cultures for behaviours and activities strongly linked to sex-typed physical attributes and reproduction. So for instance activities that involve being away from the home would cause conflict for women with children as they are needed to be in close proximity to their children to take care of them. But for men, who have greater speed and upper body strength, activities requiring intense energy bursts would be more suited to them. Cross-cultural research is widely supportive of this as division of labour in non-industrialised societies does reflect women's reproductive function and men's physical strength.

- *Impact of different social environments* – The social aspects of any society also influence these sex-role activities. For instance in societies where there is supplementary feeding available to women, they are more likely to be free from breastfeeding and therefore not as bound to their offspring. This means that they could potentially get involved with other activities normally reserved for men and this is evident in wealthy industrialised societies in which gender equality is greater and even legislated for. The social environment therefore can be shown to influence behavioural sex differences.

- *The role of pre-natal hormones* – Whilst the biosocial theory does offer adequate levels of explanation, especially for cross-cultural similarity and incongruence of behaviour across the sexes, it does not easily account for the existence of pre-natal hormones circulating during foetal development that relate to psychological and behavioural sex differences. The fact that hormones precede gender-typed behaviour is a thorn in the side for the biosocial approach (Luxen 2007). In their defence, biosocial theorists might point to evidence, e.g. of swing activities, that illustrates the great flexibility of gender role regardless of the influence of pre-natal hormones.

- *An alternative evolutionary account* – This is based on Darwin's thesis which maintains that physical and psychological differences have evolved between men and women through the processes of natural and sexual selection. Hormones circulating during pre-natal development can explain psychological differences between the sexes and can account for differences in the structuring of the neuro-cognitive systems between men and women. This can further explain why there are sex-dependent differences in cognitive ability. This is a parsimonious (economical) account but is still too biologically determinist for sociobiologists who can, once again, call on evidence of flexibility in gender behaviour and of continuing patriarchy in some societies which institutionalises gender roles and makes them difficult to break down.

CHECK YOUR UNDERSTANDING

Check your understanding of biological influences on gender by answering these questions. Try to do this from memory. You can check your answers by looking back through Topic 2.

1 What happens biologically at six weeks of foetal development?

2 Why is it that from six weeks onwards the pre-natal developmental pathways of males and females differ?

3 Give four ways in which males and females differ in terms of cognition, personality and behavioural traits.

4 How would you trace differences in male and female cognitive strengths back to pre-natal development?

5 Complete the sentence. Sexual selection is...

6 What drives sexual selection?

7 In what way does jealousy in males and females differ?

8 What do the findings from studies by Lutchmaya *et al.* and Connellan *et al.* tell us about gender differences in babies?

9 In what ways does Wood and Eagly's biosocial account differ from Darwin's evolutionary account of sexual dimorphism?

10 How did Wood and Eagly conduct their research?

11 What were Wood and Eagly's key findings?

12 Explain one strength and one weakness of biosocial theory.

Topic 3: Social contexts of gender role

Introduction

Clearly there is room for both social-psychological and biological explanations of gender differences. A purely social account would certainly struggle to explain how gender differences arose in the first place, but it does have particular strengths which are most obvious when explaining how gender differences are perpetuated.

There are socializing forces within any society that shape how we should behave. Two major types are at work. **Informal socializing agents** are people we come into close contact with like our parents, siblings, extended family and peers. **Formal socializing agents** are more distant but nevertheless exert a strong influence on what

is regarded as appropriate and acceptable. Such agents include the educational system (teachers, curriculum and school), law enforcement (police, courts and government) and all forms of media. The next section explores the impact of social contexts on gender-role.

Social influences on gender role

Social learning theory and social cognitive theory

Social learning theory, or SLT, (Bandura and Walters 1963) is a precursor to **social cognitive theory** (Bussey and Bandura 1999). Both emphasise the importance of our social environment in shaping all kinds of behaviour. Mischel (1966, 1970) adopted two principles from learning theory to help understand how children acquire gender concept. The first is that behaviour which is **reinforced** is likely to be altered in frequency. Positive reinforcement of behaviour (e.g. praise or attention) for doing something regarded as gender appropriate is likely to lead to an increase in frequency of that behaviour. Negative reinforcement is also rewarding but in the sense that we behave in order to escape an unpleasant situation e.g. boys may quickly decrease the frequency of their own girlish behaviour to escape disapproval from peers. In addition, gender inappropriate behaviour which is punished or just ignored, is extinguished fairly rapidly. The second principle is **observational learning.** Children observe role

Psychology in context   Gender in the classroom

An important question to ask regarding gender differences in performance at school is to what extent are there differences? In 2006, Key Stage Two statistics from the Department for Education and Skills showed relatively poor performance in English for boys: 59 per cent of boys attained the expected Level Four for writing compared with 75 per cent of girls. With reading this was 79 per cent for boys and 87 per cent for girls. Translated into figures, 77 100 boys and 44 700 girls failed to reach the expected level for their age in English. At Key Stage Three, the gender differences in English remained but in Maths and Science had all but disappeared. In Maths the girls were just one per cent ahead of boys, while in Science the difference was two per cent.

Why has the difference remained in English but closed in Maths and Science? This is a difficult question to address empirically because of the complex interaction between all kinds of forces including innate differences, teacher expectations and the nature of school processes. Perhaps schools should be in a position to identify and compare the number of boys and girls who

are generally highly competent at school and who are highly competent in certain subjects. They should have mechanisms in place to monitor and compare progress in different subjects across different ages. Schools should be able to identify underachievers and the subjects they are taking and to have access to the attitudes of boys and girls towards achievement across the curriculum. Additionally, school audits should include: careers' advice (is there a **gender bias**?); gender role models (such as teachers teaching **contra-gender** subjects); awareness raising of the influences of gender stereotyping (e.g. publicity that all subjects are open to boys and girls); and the influence of single-sex and mixed-sex grouping methods for different subjects. Finally, what goes on at a classroom level can be monitored for simple types of interaction between the teachers, boys and girls e.g. are boys chosen to answer questions more regularly than girls? Are boys allowed to interrupt during the classroom session more often than girls? These are part and parcel of school processes that could be changed to be more fairly suited to both girls and boys.

models and, under the right circumstances, might internalise the behaviour and later imitate it themselves. It is not always necessary to reinforce, punish or be ignored by someone else in order for learning to take place.

Social cognitive theory (Bussey and Bandura 1999) combines ideas from SLT, cognitive developmental theory and gender schema theory. Early gender concept is shaped mainly by external influences which begin immediately in the form of such things as how children are dressed, decoration of their bedroom, the toys they are given and the role models which surround them. Parental and peer reactions to behaviour such as 'gender inappropriate' toy choice are also influential. Up to this point, mechanisms of SLT which include reinforcement and modelling seem to matter most.

As the child's cognitive abilities develop, internal cognitive mediating variables play an increasing part in enabling the child to decide how to behave, thus gender-related behaviour becomes increasingly internalised or self regulated. As gender schema theory predicts, they begin to attend selectively to gender-related aspects of the environment, organising and storing information about gender. Social cognitive theory, however, takes this a step further. Children mentally rehearse the behaviour they see around them and decide whether to enact it themselves. What they finally decide to do is driven by both what they think the outcome of the behaviour will be and, most importantly, how they will then evaluate themselves. Their primary motivation, then, is to behave in a way which makes them feel positive about themselves.

Bussey and Bandura (1992) tested the importance of self-evaluation by asking 3 to 4 year old boys and girls whether they would 'feel great' or 'really awful' about themselves if they played with same sex or cross-sex toys. They found that feelings were strongly predictive of toy choice which was consistent (good feelings or not bad feelings) with their gender. By combining aspects of different approaches to gender, Bandura and Bussey have been able to account for the choice and flexibility individuals have in expressing gender-related behaviour.

Influence of parents and peers on gender role: Informal socialization

Social cognitive theory predicts that behaviour comes before self-perceptions. In other words, children acquire gender-type responses through modelling and then they organise these behaviours into gender-linked ideas about themselves: they copy first and ask questions later. Our parents are our first socializing influence and role models, therefore it is not surprising that their expectations and stereotypes of how a boy or girl should behave will have a lasting impact on our own gender schemas.

Parents' own gender schemas include information about what toys are appropriate for a boy or girl and many studies have addressed parental influence over children's play. Fagot (1974) and Picariello et al. (1990) showed that children already have toy preferences by 2 to 4 years of age. Masters et al. (1979) found that 4- to 5-year-old girls would play with toys labelled 'for girls' even though a man played with them beforehand. Play choice was dominated by the label and not by the sex of the role model adult. It would appear that both the label provided and the behaviour modelled by adults is already shaped by their own gender schemas. In 'Baby X' studies, Smith and Lloyd (1978) found that when adults were asked to play with babies who were arbitrarily given either a boy or girl name, they typically stimulated boys more through physical activity like bouncing and jiggling them up and down. The toys they offered were typically stereotyped: boys were given a toy hammer and girls a soft cuddly toy. Culp *et al.* (1983) also showed that adults engaged more in active play with babies they thought were boys, and engaged in more gentle play and were more verbal towards babies they thought were girls.

Activity Boys' (and girls') toys

What kind of play behaviour do you expect in boys and girls? What toy choices would you expect boys and girls to make? Make a list of these behaviours and observe your young male and female relatives. See if they conform to your list of play behaviours.

Fagot and Leinbach (1989) looked at the relationship between children's **gender labelling** ability and sex-typed behaviour in relation to parental behaviour in a longitudinal study. Forty-eight children aged 16 to 18 months and their parents were visited monthly over a year and again when the children were four.

- Children were shown head and shoulder pictures of boys and girls, matched for size of face and age and asked to point to the boy or girl.

- Family members were observed at home on five separate one-hour sessions using the Fagot Interactive Behaviour Code (Fagot 1983) to record children's activities including play and parental reactions.

- Parents were given a Child Rearing Practices Report.

- The Attitudes toward Women Scale was used to measure parents' views towards women.

- The Personal Attributes Questionnaire considered parent choice of socially desirable traits in men and women.

- The Sex Role Learning Index was applied to the children.

At 18 months none of the children passed the gender-labelling task nor did they differ in play activity. The mean age for successful gender-labelling task was 28 months and, at about this age, early gender-labellers showed greater gender type behaviour. Both mothers and fathers of children who began gender-labelling at an early age responded more (both positively and negatively) to gender-related play. Fathers had more traditional attitudes towards women. At 4 children who gender-labelled at an early age scored higher on sex-role discrimination.

Activity The young child's gender schema

HOW SCIENCE WORKS

Look at the methods and conclusions in the study by Fagot and Leinbach (1989).

1. What did they want to show by asking additional questions of parents?

2. Was it good practice to use so many measures?

3. In what ways did the findings from these questionnaires link with the purpose of the study?

4. Did it actually help Fagot and Leinbach to make dependable interpretations about the parent-child behaviour they observed?

5. Was this a well designed study or unnecessarily fussy?

Answers are given on p.607. ▶

HOW SCIENCE WORKS

Reinforcing toy preference

Langlois and Downs (1980) studied reactions of both parents and peers to children's play with stereotypically opposite gender toys. Mothers showed equal warmth towards sons' or daughters' play regardless of the activity involved whereas fathers were more openly disapproving of cross-gender play, especially if it involved sons playing with girls' toys. If Fagot and Leinbach (1989) are correct in that children show gender-typed play as young as 28 months, by the time they are old enough to engage in play with their peers, they will already have similar toy preferences to children of their gender. Indeed, pre-schoolers, at the age of three, show a marked preference for stereotypically gender-appropriate toys. Langlois and Downs' (1980) study also showed that children were very alert to and reacted negatively towards peers playing with opposite sex toys. Boys, like fathers, were particularly disapproving if boys did this, resorting to ridicule and even physical aggression. Thus, early toy preference is not only shaped by social reinforcement from peers of both genders, it also draws children into same sex groups where they will continue to socialize with each other.

Activity   Sex change

Write a brief account, no more than a side of A4, describing how you would spend 24 hours as a member of the opposite sex. On reflection, would you prefer to be that sex? What are your reasons?

Influence of schools on gender role: Formal socialization

Teachers' beliefs may be important social influences in shaping children's gender. Teachers have their own gender schemas and stereotypes and these may play a role in the nature of expectations teachers have of boys' and girls' behaviour and academic abilities. Girls, for example, tend to spend more time on their homework and are more committed to their school work than boys, which is likely to be thought typical by most teachers. Research by Pankhurst (1994) showed that there is an expectation that boys will misbehave in the classroom, belittle female peers and dominate the situation. On the other hand, more boys than girls are identified as being gifted even though the school achievement records for both boys and girls are just as good (Freeman 1996). Furthermore, when girls achieved highly in mathematics teachers perceived them to be using inferior skills compared to their male counterparts.

IDA   Nature nurture and school performance

Recently, attention has been drawn towards the differences in areas of achievement between girls and boys in that, generally, girls have greater verbal ability than boys. This disparity has been explained by a combination of inborn differences, self perception and the education system. This amounts to a nature-nurture issue and the challenge to the education system is how to respond to it when determining the curriculum and how to teach boys and girls.

Gender bias in school staffing

To understand further why teacher expectations of academic success for boys and girls differ, it is important to consider their role models. There is a definite gender bias amongst teachers. National Statistics (2004) for England recorded that 69 per cent of teachers were female and 31 per cent male. There were twice as many women infant and junior school head teachers compared to men, but this pattern reversed at secondary level where head teachers' salaries are generally higher. There is also more chance of being taught a science subject by a man. In 1996, 40 per cent of female teachers taught science at primary school level which decreased to 15 per cent at 'A' Level. More female teachers at secondary school

teach English and languages (Freeman 1996) a pattern which remains similar today.

What signals are such biases sending out to pupils? Furthermore, why is it the case that fewer female teachers teach traditionally male dominated subjects? To answer this we need to take account of the skills that males and females are generally better at as there does seem to be a possible biological explanation to do with brain anatomy as discussed earlier. However, Delamont (1990) p.3 says, 'Schools develop and reinforce sex segregations, stereotypes and even discriminations which exaggerate the negative aspects of sex roles in the outside world when they could be trying to alleviate them.' A practical response to this disagreement, and one which recognises both the different rates at which boys and girls mature (nature) and the environment (nurture), is to adopt a Diamond Model so that boys and girls are taught separately from age 11 to 16 but together before and after that. The Equal Opportunities Commission in Britain is even more environmentalist and, in April 2007, brought the Gender Equality Duty into effect in public organisations which includes everyone learning or working in schools. This consists of guidance, rather than legal requirements but still indicates a growing belief that it is possible to address inequalities.

The portrayal of gender in school books

Cross-cultural studies have shown that schools may foster gender inequality through the use of gender biased textbooks. During the Turkish Republic (1920s) men and women were represented in texts equally until the 1950s when women were depicted as housewives (Gümüşçüoğlu 1995 cited in Özdoğru et al. 2002). These findings were supported by Helvacıoğlu (1996) who studied textbooks published from 1928 – 1995. Textbooks published from the 1950s targeted males and portrayed women as mothers or wives (Arslan 2000). Özdoğru, et al. (2002) analysed textbooks for differences in the way males and females were depicted and found that there were discrepancies in the portrayal of occupational and familial roles. These differences reflected the values of Turkish society, where males and females had traditional roles.

The data in this study are archival in that examples of textbooks throughout the years were analysed for gender content. Researchers would be looking specifically for content information related to such things as gender role, behaviour, activity, ability, personality and occupation. This kind of analysis is a tallying such that the amount of times a boy is depicted as playing rough and tumble games and being aggressive as opposed to playing with dolls and crying is noted.

The influence of media on gender role: Formal socialization

There has been an explosion in mass media communication in recent decades. Through television in particular it is now possible for children to be exposed for hours, on a daily basis, to both recreational and

Activity — The evolution of school books

Look back at the study by Gümüşçüoğlu (1995) into the content of school books.

1 What method is being used?

2 Can you think of any major problems with this approach?

Answers are given on p.607. ▶

educational programmes. Expectations of boys and girls and men and women and what is considered to be 'normal' for them are both explicit and implicit in these.

Durkin (1995) provided a developmental outline of the factors influential for gender development. During the pre-school years, children learn to discriminate between people using gender so their time is taken interacting with family and peers rather than television. At 4 to 7 years, gender concept becomes understood and stereotyped, so children pay attention to same-sex models and this would come not only from television but from many other sources such as school, teachers and friends. At 7 to 12 years children use television to adjust their understanding of gender. Durkin believes that television is at its most influential during adolescence but only in a reinforcing capacity.

A survey by Ofcom in 2003 claimed that 'Children [across the UK] aged 8 to15 watch a (self-reported) average of 13.9 hours of TV per week. Children in Scotland (15.2 hours), Northern Ireland (16.1), those from minority ethnic groups (15.2), and those living in low income households (15.5) watch significantly more.' Furthermore, 73 per cent of children had a TV in their bedroom and 35 per cent of 8 to 11 year olds and 49 per cent of 12 to15 year olds said they watched TV mostly on their own.

Lauer and Lauer (1994) looked at what children watch on television. They showed that when watching footage involving male to female interaction, men were portrayed as dominant, rational, ambitious, competitive, powerful, stable, violent and tolerant. Females were depicted as sensitive, happy, romantic, attractive, sociable, submissive and timid. The emphasis for males on strength, performance and skill and for females on attractiveness and desirability reflects gender stereotypes that are already prevalent in society and further reinforce and perpetuate these stereotypes. In the UK children aged 5 to 12 years of age were asked about the nature of jobs they had seen characters on the television have. The typical male jobs were rooted in occupational roles unlike female jobs that were orientated towards the service industry or were clearly related to childcare (Wober *et al.* 1987). It was found further that these job characterisations informed children of what they wanted to do when they grew up.

A study which examined the effect of the introduction of television into a community was carried out by Williams (1986). You can read about it in 'Introducing television'. This study uncovered some negative changes in attitudes to gender and gender-related behaviour but researchers could not be sure about their cause. A strength of social influences' approaches to gender lies in its ability to bring about change for the better. Bianchi and Bakeman (1978) found that the early signs of gender typing disappeared

Introducing television

Key research: Williams (1986)

Williams (1986) conducted a series of surveys into the effect of television in three logging, farming, and mining-based communities in Canada. The three communities were named:

- *Notel* – no television channels because of being in a reception 'blind spot' but about to be connected to the Canadian Broadcasting Company, CBC.
- *Unitel* – had received CBC only for seven years.
- *Multitel* – had received CBC and three further channels for 15 years.

After Notel had been receiving CBC for two years, and Unitel had gained a second channel, Williams returned to carry out further surveys. She measured many variables, including gender stereotyping and aggression levels. For gender she found that exposure to television increased children's perceived differences between boys and girls but not between men and women. In Notel aggression levels rose with the introduction of TV but, even though this is stereotypically higher in boys, there was no gender effect and, in any case, the rise was due to a small number of children. Aggression levels also rose in Unitel and Multitel but not by as much. Furthermore, the differences between these two communities were not as great as between the two of them together and Notel, suggesting that it is the presence of TV rather than the number of channels that is important.

The link between the presence of TV and behaviour is correlational so Williams cannot claim that it causes changes in behaviour. Its introduction may have had other effects, such as reducing face to face socialization, which were partly responsible for changes in behaviour. Research using experimental designs would give a clearer idea of cause.

when children were enrolled in an open school where both male and female teachers encouraged equality of roles. In another study, several thousand 9–12 year-old children watched the television series, *Freestyle*, (a programme designed to reduce sex-role stereotypes) once a week for 13 weeks (Johnston and Ettema 1982). They found substantial reductions in the stereotypical attitudes and beliefs about gender roles following exposure to these programmes. Overall, there were moderate positive effects in studies featuring counter-stereotypical themes, with children becoming less stereotyped or prejudiced in their attitudes or beliefs. Such research counters the claim of biological determinists that gender differences are unchangeable at least at a cognitive, if not behavioural level.

Activity **Your socializing influences**

The evidence suggests that we are influenced by a variety of social factors. Who and what do you believe has made the most impact on our behaviour, specifically behaviour relating to gender role? If you were in a position to influence someone to behave in a male or female oriented manner how might you alter their behaviour without using constraints, punishment or force?

STRETCH AND CHALLENGE

Activity **A thought experiment on gender**

A thought experiment is a way of thinking outside the box without any consideration of ethical issues and plausibility. Try to apply it to this example:

It is difficult to separate nurture from nature as far as deciding how children acquire appropriate gender behaviour.

1 What comes first: do parents socialize children to adopt their appropriate gender or are they merely reinforcing a natural event?

2 If you had to design an experiment as a way of answering this question what would you do?

3 Is there anything that can be manipulated such that it doesn't contravene any ethical issues?

Answers are given on p.608. ▶

Evaluation of research into social influences on gender development

▪ *Inconsistent evidence* – According to social influences' approaches, sex-stereotyped behaviour should be reinforced differently in girls and boys but there is conflicting evidence about this. For example, Jacklin and Maccoby (1978) found that boys and girls are not treated differently in terms of the kinds of gender reinforcements they receive. Also, Smith and Daglish (1977) found that parents who exhibited more gender-stereotypical behaviour (i.e. behaved in a particularly masculine or feminine fashion) did not necessarily have children who were equally gender-stereotyped. However, Bianchi and Bakeman (1978) found that neither parents nor teachers encourage aggressive behaviour in boys yet boys, including those who did not have a father role model, were found to be more aggressive than girls. This suggests that there is a range of flexibility in gender-related behaviour such that some aspects of behaviour are more easily changed by social influences than others. The sociobiological approach is better placed to explain variability in such findings.

▪ *Research design issues* – Social influences on gender are many and complex, making them particularly challenging to research. Studies in naturalistic settings such as communities (Williams 1986) and homes (Jacklin and Maccoby 1978) may appear to have good external validity but there are so many uncontrolled variables that it is not necessarily possible to generalise the findings more widely. Highly controlled research, such as toy labelling and Baby X studies, narrows the range of responses participants can give and this could lead to overly stereotyped behaviour that even very young participants may feel is demanded of them. For these reasons conclusions about social influences on gender need to be made with caution as research findings could be the result of design aspects that have been over-looked.

▪ *Alternative explanations* – A social influences approach might argue that peers', parents' and teachers' gender stereotypes shape their expectations about boys' and girls' behaviour and that this, in turn shapes it in predictable ways. On the other hand, there could be a biological grain of truth in the stereotypes. Baron-Cohen (2008) has proposed that there are male/female differences in the brain, such that boys tend to be 'systematisers' and girls 'empathisers'. Boys prefer to deal with rule-based mechanical and theoretical systems and girls with relationships and feelings. This is reflected in girls performing better in literacy. However, girls equal boys in numeracy. One possible reason for this is that education has become feminised such that the naturally energetic behaviour of many boys is seen as disruptive in the classroom and this interferes with both their learning in literacy, which already challenges them, and in their numeracy. Social influences cannot, therefore, offer a complete account of gender differences but could be used in harmony with biological ones to bring out the best in both genders.

Cross-cultural studies of gender role

Culture and gender

What does the term 'culture' really mean? Moghaddam *et al.* (1993) say it is the 'human-made part of the environment' and that it can be both objective and physical (e.g. everyday objects, structures, and works of art). It can also be subjective and psychological (e.g. beliefs, identities and values). Psychologists usually concentrate on the latter.

Research findings in relation to social influences on gender have consistently referred to the importance of the cultural setting. It therefore makes sense to compare different cultures and consider how their gender socialization practices differ or not and how this is reflected in adulthood.

Anthropological research consistently favours the view that men everywhere are similar and that they are more aggressive, violent, competitive and dominant and less empathic and sensitive than women (e.g. Segall *et al.* 1990; Ghiglieri 1999) but the way in which their behaviour is expressed is interwoven with many other factors including cultural ones. This puts the emphasis on there being a biological or nature explanation of why men and women are different. However, it is society that perpetuates these gender role differences. Mead's (1935) classic study of three New Guinea tribes (see 'Sex and Temperament in Three Primitive Societies' below) shows that, in spite of living in a similar geographical area, the three tribes expressed their gender roles in different ways.

The six cultures study

An extensive cross-cultural study started in the 1950s by Whiting and Whiting (1975) supported Mead's observations about flexibility in gender role. They studied child-rearing practices in six cultures drawn from North America, the Philippines, India, Mexico, Kenya and Japan. Researchers integrated themselves with the communities so that they could identify individuals and were known to them. Systematic observations of the children's daily lives were made by watching each of them for five minutes per day, and recording what happened. Twenty-four 3- to 10-year-old children from each group were each observed 15 times. Whiting and Pope Edwards (1988) later extended this work to a further six groups so that, eventually, 500 families were observed by 17 researchers.

In all the cultures, the parents' basic goals were the same. They wanted their children to survive, to be attached to the family, to be healthy and to learn survival skills. In addition, they were all concerned that the children learned appropriate social behaviour which included gender role. Parents achieved this through a combination of nurturing and supporting, direct training, control and praise.

In the cultures studied by Whiting and Whiting, children's socialization was strongly influenced by how much work

Sex and temperament in three primitive societies

Key research: Mead (1935)

Margaret Mead was an American anthropologist who adopted an ethnographic approach to studying different cultures. This involved immersing herself in a culture and conducting participant observation and interviews. Her most famous descriptions came from three different pre-industrialised societies of New Guinea: the Arapesh, Mundugumor (now called the Biwat) and Tchambuli (now called the Chambri). She described these societies as having differing gender roles. In the Arapesh, the gender roles of men and women were similar, both being unaggressive and sensitive and of a peaceful temperament. The opposite was true of the Mundugumor where men and women were uncooperative, aggressive, insensitive and warlike. The women of the Tchambuli were described as dominant with economic and political influence, unlike their submissive male counterparts. Here the men stayed at home taking care of the children while the women engaged in work and were more practical. The Arapesh according to Mead adopt feminine qualities, the Mundugumor masculine qualities and the Tchambuli men adopt feminine qualities whilst the women adopt masculine qualities. Mead (1935), claimed:

'We are forced to conclude that human nature is almost unbelievably malleable, responding accurately and contrastingly to contrasting cultural conditions.' (p.280)

Mead's work has been questioned in a number of ways:

- *The reliability of her findings* – Gewertz (1981) observed the Tchambuli in the 1970s and found males to be more aggressive than females. He argued that Mead studied these tribes when they were facing a transitory phase in their lifestyle e.g. Australian laws on violence forced them to behave differently from normal. (Mead herself noted contradictions in her field diaries.) Mead's work shows how important it is to consider the influence of a culture's historical context.

- *Cultural determinism* – Mead may have over-emphasised the role of culture at the expense of biological influences. In later years, she questioned this belief herself and became more open to biological and evolutionary based arguments. In 1949 she wrote 'Male and Female' acknowledging motherhood as a biological inclination and fatherhood as a social invention thus developing biosocial-cultural anthropology.

they were expected to do and what it consisted of. North American children did the least spending only two per cent of their time working compared with Kenyan children for whom it was 41 per cent. This can be accounted for by the degree of complexity there is in people's lives and how much control they have over their environment. In the Kenyan group, for example, tending animals, farming for food, food preparation and obtaining water is demanding of everyone including children but in North America where food is bought and water is on tap, the demands are less. The North American children did little work so gender differences were negligible. Where demands are high, both boys and girls work from a young age, sharing some tasks but mainly doing work ascribed by gender. In cultures such as the Kenyan one, where sharp distinctions are made between males and females, girls start typically feminine tasks from a very young age. By the time they are in their teens, they work most of the time in the company of women doing 'women's work' such as subsistence activities, food preparation and child-rearing while males do more typically masculine tasks depending on the cultural setting.

HOW SCIENCE WORKS

Activity The six cultures study

From the information provided about Whiting and Whiting's (1975) six cultures study:

1 How can we account for gender differences in the type of work done by males and females in the Kenyan culture?

2 What effect do you predict that working patterns will have on gender role in American and Kenyan children?

3 Whiting and Whiting were limited to studying fixed cultures in agricultural, herding or industrial settings. Compare this to nomadic people who possess little and move around regularly. How might the expression of gender roles differ between fixed and nomadic people?

Answers are given on p.608. ▶

Location and environmental conditions are strongly associated with expression of gender role. For people to survive in their ecological niche, they need to be socialized to behave in particular ways. Whether gender role is driven by socialization practices that strengthen biological differences between the sexes or are merely influenced by them is uncertain but the result is often division of labour that is rarely equal for males and females. See the six cultures study (Whiting and Whiting 1975).

The contribution of women to subsistence, particularly food-getting, that we encountered in the sociobiological approach, has far-reaching effects, not just on work, but also on many other culturally prescribed aspects of gender role (Barry and Schlegel 1986). In cultures where the contribution of women is high there is also a tendency to find:

- exogamy (seeking partners from outside the community)
- bride price (gifts from the male's family to the female's family)
- birth control (contraception or long gaps between pregnancies)
- polygyny (men taking more than one wife)
- work training for females (not just for domestic roles)
- higher status for females
- greater tolerance of pre-marital sex
- less risk of rape.

Cross-cultural research shows us that, while males and females might have fairly consistent tendencies to behave in particular ways because of biological differences, they are also capable of adapting their behaviour to different circumstances and relating to each other in many different ways. How gender role is ultimately expressed is the result of a complex interaction between biological, social, ecological and cultural influences.

HOW SCIENCE WORKS

One tribe, three genders

Key research: Medicine (1997)

The blurring of gender role can be clearly seen in the Lakota tribe where they have a word, 'winkte' meaning 'wants to be like a woman' (Medicine 1997). In Lakota society some males did not want to be warriors but not all were labelled the third gender of winkte. Those labelled winkte excelled in women's crafts and preferred to take care of the children. It was regarded as lucky to be bestowed a name by a winkte. Some of the winkte went with warriors serving them as personal domestics and some as sexual partners. So in Lakota society there is an additional gender whose role is not quite male or female. Furthermore, the word for children is wakan ye(c)a (wakan = sacred and ye(c)a = "to be"). Children were seen as sacred beings and were regarded as autonomous individuals. If they wanted to become winkte then it was seen as acceptable by the parents.

Activity Comparing cultures

A variety of different cultures have been described here, in what ways do they differ from your own culture? Comprise a list of some of the differences and similarities so that you can see more clearly culturally relative and universal behaviours.

Emics and etics in cross-cultural research

Anthropologists have introduced the emic-etic distinction as a means of reducing cultural bias when members of one culture observe another. Emic constructs are considered to be descriptions and analyses of the concepts and categorisations used by members of the culture under observation. Etic constructs are descriptions and analyses expressed using concepts and categories which are considered appropriate in the observers' culture. An etic inappropriately applied to another culture is an imposed etic (e.g. a particular view of what is appropriate male or female behaviour) but one which emerges from adapting the measure to the culture concerned is a derived etic. Cross-cultural researchers try to work with emics and derived etics.

1 Taking Mead's research on three tribes as an example, how would you reduce cultural bias due to etics?

2 What measures would you take to ensure that what the people were saying is supported in emic fact?

3 What measures would you take before assuming that the participants' attitudes towards gender were representative of a particular culture and could be considered a derived etic?

Answers are given on p.608.

Evaluation of cross-cultural studies of gender role

- *Cross-cultural studies as natural experiments* – Cross-cultural research allows psychologists to study a range of influences on gender that could not, ethically speaking, be manipulated in a laboratory e.g. it would not be acceptable to move people into different locations or manipulate how they obtain their food in order to observe the effects on gender role. Although extraneous variables are many and there is no direct control over independent variables it is still possible to view some cross-cultural studies as natural experiments which allow us to unravel cause and effect, thus providing a good scientific basis to our knowledge about gender.

- *Understanding cultural universality and relativity* – If certain characteristics of gender role remain similar irrespective of people's cultural context they might be considered as universal amongst humans and therefore, more likely to be biologically based. More flexible aspects of gender role which change relative to cultural context are more likely to be environmentally based. Comparing cultures allows us to gain a better understanding of nature and nurture in determining gender and how they might interact and what we may be able to change (or not) for the greater good.

- *Challenges of participant observation* – Cross-cultural researchers are often in direct contact with the people they are studying even to the extent that they will live among them as a participant observer. The idea behind this is that, as the novelty of being studied wears off, people behave as they normally would and research findings are more trustworthy. Nevertheless, the presence of the observer, even when it becomes unremarkable, changes the dynamics of a social group and has an effect on behaviour. There is no way of controlling for this and no way of knowing the extent of its effect. A researcher could resort to covert observational techniques and measures of behaviour and that is unethical because there is no consent between the researcher and participant.

- *Challenges of ethnography* – Ethnography involves interviewing people, listening to folklore, attitudes and beliefs and sifting through archival information. Often, translation will be necessary and, even if the researcher knows the language, it can be difficult to interpret information. At some point, the researcher has to speculate on what the data potentially mean and acknowledge that their own cultural biases will probably affect their interpretation. This is a potential source of 'noise' in qualitative research such as this, although some would argue that a degree of subjectivity is inevitable in all kinds of research and that it is important to acknowledge it and find ways of managing it.

CHECK YOUR UNDERSTANDING

Check your understanding of social influences on gender role by answering the following questions. Try to do this from memory. You can check your answers by looking back through Topic 3.

1 How do children learn gender role according to social learning theory (SLT)?

2 What has social cognitive theory added to SLT?

3 What is the relationship between gender labelling and gender behaviour?

4 How do parents and peers shape gender behaviour through play?

5 Describe two ways in which the school environment might shape gender role.

6 Outline research showing that TV exposure can be linked to changes in behaviour for better and for worse.

7 What reasons are there for doing cross-cultural research?

8 How does occupying a particular ecological niche affect male and female behaviour?

9 What knock-on effects do responses to an ecological niche have for the ways in which males and females lead their lives and relate to each other?

Further resources

Archer, J. and Lloyd, B. (1992) *Sex and Gender*, Cambridge: Cambridge University Press Cambridge.
   This provides useful material on gender differences within a biosocial cognitive approach.

Halpern, D. F. (2000) *Sex Differences in Cognitive Abilities*, Mahwah, NJ: Erlbaum.
   This provides useful material on cognitive differences of ability across the sexes.

Maccoby, E. E. and Jacklin, C. N. (1974) *The Psychology of Sex Differences*, Stanford, CA: Stanford University Press.
   This provides useful material on behavioural differences across the sexes.

Smith, P. K., Cowie, H. and Blades, M. (2003) *Children's Development*, (4th ed.) Oxford: Blackwell.
   This clearly written text provides useful material on gender development.

Tavris, C. B. (1992) *The Mismeasure of Woman: Why Women are not the Better Sex, the Inferior Sex or the Opposite Sex*, New York: Touchstone.
   This accessible text provides useful material on gender development.

Websites:

All theses websites are worth visiting as they provide up-to-date information regarding definitions, gender differences and cross-cultural differences.

http://www.webster.edu/~woolflm/sandrabem.html#gender

http://www.psychology.sbc.edu/moon.htm

http://www.nhsdirect.nhs.uk/articles/article.aspx?articleid=435

http://www.garysturt.free-online.co.uk/bem.htm

http://www.wwu.edu/~culture

http://www.statistics.gov.uk

http://www.ofcom.org.uk/

Cognitive developmental theory

Kohlberg's gender consistency theory (1966)

- Stage theory: gender identity, stability and consistency
- Preferential observation of own gender
- Gender behaviour internalized

Evaluation:

- Support: toy preference studies
- Universal sequence of development
- Conflicting evidence
- Disagreement over ages of stages

Gender schema theory (Martin & Halverson 1983)

- Gender identity begins process
- Children develop gender schemas
- Links with Bem's 'Lenses of gender'

Evaluation:

- Support for stereotypes
- Reinforcement selectivity
- Link between gender awareness and gender-typed behaviour?
- Timing of gender schemas

Explanations of psychological androgyny

Bem's theory of psychological androgyny (1974)

- High masculinity and femininity on BSRI indicates androgyny
- Attitude to contra-gender activities
- Cross-sex studies

Evaluation:

- BSRI: temporal/contextual validity?
- Pre-natal hormone influences
- Psychological health
- Androgynous societies unlikely

Concept of gender

Definitions

- Sex
- Gender
- Gender identity
- Gender constancy

Explanations of gender dysphoria

- Mismatch between sex and gender identity
- DSM-IV-TR (2000) – GID
- Transsexualism = extreme type

Psychological explanations

- Psychiatric: delusional psychosis
- Psychoanalytic: Oedipal conflict
- Evolutionary/behaviourist: failed or inappropriate imprinting
- Cognitive: abstract and hypothetical thinking

Evaluation:

- Pathologizing gender identity
- Difficulty in testing psychoanalytic explanations
- Problems with imprinting and conditioning explanations
- Gender dysphoria occurs before adolescent cognition develops

Biological expanations

- Hermaphroditism studies
- Brain sex theory: the sexually dimorphic BSTc
- Sex hormone therapy in transsexuals

Evaluation:

- Reductionist explanations
- Early awareness of dysphoria
- Sex hormones in adulthood
- Hormonal influences on transsexualism

Gender development: Psychological explanations

Gender development: Biological influences

Role of genes and hormones

Genes and gender development

- Males chromosomally XY; females XX
- Critical prenatal sexual differentiation at 6 weeks
- H-Y antigen triggered by Y chromosome

Hormones and gender development

- Female form is the default
- Effects of testosterone
- Prenatal hormones link predictably with masculine or feminine behaviour
- Socialization cannot easily overcome accidental penectomy

Evaluation

- Biological determinism over-stated?
- Research may selectively report sex differences
- Emphasis on differences may have socially sensitive consequences
- Relevance of animal research to humans?

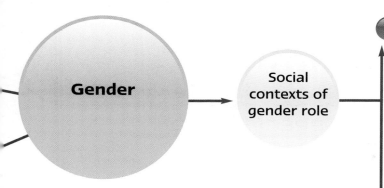

Gender

Social contexts of gender role

Social learning theory (SLT; Bandura and Walters 1963)
- Role of social agents
- Observation of role-models

Social cognitive theory (Bussey and Bandura 1999)
- Internalized gender-related behaviour
- Positive self-evaluation as primary motivation

Parents and peers
- Parents influence toy choice
- Parents' responses to gender-related play

Schools
- Teachers' expectations and responses
- Gender stereotyping in school books
- Diamond Model and Gender Equality Duty

Media
- TV viewing ubiquitous and unsupervised
- Gender stereotypes on TV

Evaluation
- 'Freestyle': gender-stereotype reduction
- Research: balance between realism and precision
- Effect of altering the social environment

Evolutionary explanations of gender roles

Natural selection, fitness & sexual selection
- Natural selection (Darwin 1859)
- Fitness
- Runaway selection hypothesis (Fisher 1930)
- The hunting hypothesis (Morris 1866)

Gender role from evolutionary perspective
- Greater male aggression – sexual selection pressure?
- Male same-sex homicide figures – sexual jealousy?
- Parental investment theory
- Sexual jealousy in males; commitment jealousy in females
- Mechanical world (male) or social world (female)

Evaluation
- Extrapolation between species
- Only universal explanation of human form and behaviour?
- Supportive empirical evidence, e.g. of mate choice
- Which came first: gender role or biological differences?
- Cultural differences cannot be ignored

Biosocial approach to gender development

The biosocial approach (Wood & Eagly 2002)
- Interaction between biological, developmental and cultural influences
- Sexual selection played down
- Influence of sexually dimorphic characteristics
- Extensive socialization of boys and girls is necessary
- Ecological differences between cultures

Evaluation
- Cross-cultural similarity in division of labour
- Influence of social environment
- Influence of prenatal hormones on behaviour

Cross-cultural studies

Culture and gender
- Anthropological research supports universal, biologically-based sex differences
- Research concerned with how biological, social and cultural influences interact
- Flexibility in expression of gender role
- Flexible adaptation to ecological niche
- Female contribution to subsistence

Evaluation
- Natural experiments
- Cultural universality and relativity helps to address the nature–nurture question
- Challenges of participant observation
- Challenges of ethnography

Intelligence and learning

EXPLAINING THE SPECIFICATION

Specification content	The specification explained
Theories of intelligence (Topic 1)	The specification focuses on intelligence and learning in humans and non-human animals. In this part of the specification you are required to know about theories of human intelligence. To do this, you need to be able to:
Theories of intelligence, including psychometric and information processing approaches **Gardner's theory of multiple intelligences**	■ Describe and evaluate two approaches to intelligence. Note that 'psychometric' and 'information processing' approaches are preceded by the word *including*, which means that these can be specifically asked for in an exam question. ■ Describe and evaluate Gardner's theory of multiple intelligences.
Animal learning and intelligence (Topic 2)	In this part of the specification you are asked to consider explanations of how animals learn and whether animals have intelligence. To do this, you need to be able to:
The nature of simple learning (classical and operant conditioning) and its role in the behaviour of non-human animals.	■ Explain both classical and operant conditioning and how these might explain at least two aspects of animal behaviour. ■ Describe and evaluate these explanations using research studies relevant to classical and operant conditioning.
Evidence for intelligence in non-human animals, for example, self-recognition, social learning, Machiavellian intelligence.	■ Review evidence for intelligence in non-human animals. Self-recognition, social learning and Machiavellian intelligence are given only as examples (although all are covered in this chapter). You might consider other areas to illustrate non-human intelligence.
Evolution of intelligence (Topic 3)	In this part of the specification you will study factors involved in the evolution of human intelligence. To do this, you need to be able to:
Evolutionary factors in the development of human intelligence, for example, ecological demands, social complexity, brain size. **The role of genetic and environmental factors associated with intelligence test performance, including the influence of culture.**	■ Cover the role of at least two evolutionary factors in the development of human intelligence. Ecological demands, social complexity and brain size are just examples of these factors. ■ Remember four distinct factors. First, you need to consider both genetic *and* environmental factors. Second, these must be linked to performance on intelligence tests. Third, you must, as part of the environmental factors, include the role of culture. Fourth, you must be able to describe *and* evaluate this material. ■ Evaluate your material to gain the all important AO2 and AO3 marks in any question on this topic.

Introduction

Psychologists have long struggled to agree upon a generally accepted definition of intelligence. Surely defining a concept that is so central to psychology should not be difficult? Why is there a problem? There are probably two reasons for this:

1 By its very nature, the notion of intelligence is somewhat 'fuzzy'. We all have ideas of who is bright and who is less so, but pinning down exactly how we came to this conclusion is not easy.

Psychologists have been devising intelligence tests for over 100 years but have yet to agree on what exactly intelligence is

2 The definition that is accepted by one psychologist is likely to be directly related to their particular approach to intelligence. As we will see below, there are different approaches to the notion of intelligence (and in some cases 'intelligences'). Hence, if different psychologists *use* the term 'intelligence' differently, then they are likely to *define* it differently.

The renowned Yale psychologist, Robert Sternberg described a symposium where 24 experts met up to agree upon a definition (Sternberg 2002). Following lengthy discussions, it became clear that even these experts could not agree on one definition. They did, however, manage to develop definitions with 'overlapping themes'. The most common overlapping theme was 'adaptation to the environment'. This is reflected in the definition put forward by Smith *et al.* (2003) that will serve our purpose well. They define intelligence as:

'The ability to learn from experience, think in abstract terms, and deal effectively with one's environment' (Smith *et al.* 2003).

Topic 1: Theories of intelligence

Psychology in context   The Flynn effect: are we getting brighter?

In 1984, a New Zealand academic provided the scientific community with a bit of a conundrum. Professor James Flynn of the University of Otago pointed out that during the years 1932 to 1978, IQ scores rose by 14 points for successive cohort groups. His finding was based on 73 studies and involved 7500 people ranging in age from two to 48 during this 46-year period. When first reported, this sharp rise in apparent intelligence caused a major furore in academic circles and continues to do so today (Flynn 2007). Flynn has maintained his interest in this area since the mid-1980s and has observed that IQ scores continue to rise throughout the developed world. On average, American children today achieve an IQ score that is 18 points higher than their grandparents would have achieved at that age.

There are two key questions to be answered here:

1 How did this come about?

2 What does it mean? Are we really getting smarter with every generation?

Interestingly, when other measures of how smart each generation is are examined, it does not appear that we are improving at all. The SATS (Scholastic Aptitude Test) scores in the USA today are no better than they were two generations ago. To return to the two questions above, there appears to be no easy answer

to either. It is possible that students are tested more often and have developed better strategies towards these tests. But Flynn does not believe this is the answer. Whilst admitting that he does not have the complete answer, he suggests that our ways of thinking have changed over the last century such that we have developed a more abstract way of dealing with problems and this is borne out by the IQ data. In Flynn's words, earlier generations relied very much on **pre-scientific** rather than current **post-scientific operational** thinking. To illustrate this, Flynn (2007) uses the following similarities-type question: 'What do rabbits and dogs have in common?' Before reading on, try answering this question yourself.

Most people living in the early years of the 20th century would answer along the lines of 'You use dogs to hunt rabbits'. The correct answer in terms of an IQ test is that they are both mammals. The second answer is very much a post-scientific way of thinking and would be considered the correct answer on an IQ test but, interestingly, the first answer may well have helped your great-grandparents to survive. Hence, our way of thinking about the world has changed in ways that help us to score more highly on these tests, rather than because people are 'getting smarter'. The Flynn effect illustrates that what we consider to be intelligence may have changed over time and is not as fixed as we like to think.

Activity | **The Flynn effect**

What has caused the Flynn effect?

1 List three possible reasons for the rise in IQ scores over the last 50 years (i.e. what has caused the Flynn Effect?).

2 How would you determine which of these is the most likely explanation?

The psychometric approach

Psychometrics literally means 'mental measurement'. Hence, the psychometric approach to intelligence is concerned with the design and use of intelligence tests (Blades 1998). The goal of a psychometrician (someone who works in psychometrics) is not to construct an abstract theory of what constitutes intelligence but simply to find the best way of measuring it. This might sound an odd state of affairs and has led to criticism of psychometrics from many quarters. One recent author did not sit on the fence as the title of his book was *IQ: The Brilliant Idea that Failed* (Murdoch 2007). Cambridge psychologist Nick Mackintosh (Mackintosh 1998) considers such criticism to be misplaced. To him the important point of psychometrics is not whether we have a perfect definition of intelligence, but how good the tests are at measuring it. He identified four criteria that support the use of IQ to test ability:

1 An individual's score does not fluctuate from day to day with other changes such as mood.

2 IQ tests do require abstract reasoning – a concept that 99 per cent of people questioned consider central to intelligence.

3 There are a wide variety of IQ tests: some ask for definitions of words, some require arithmetic problem solving, some require detection of hidden patterns. Despite the variability of content, these IQ tests show a great deal of agreement, i.e. an individual's scores are very similar between the various tests.

4 Success on IQ tests is a good predictor of other academic measures, such as school or university grades.

The origins of intelligence testing

In order to understand psychometrics, it is necessary to trace the origins of intelligence testing. The earliest records of testing individuals in order to assess their mental abilities date back 4000 years to a time when the Chinese used various 'intelligence' tasks to select their civil servants (Cooper 2002). However, the first recognizable intelligence test was devised by French psychologists Alfred Binet and Theophile Simon in 1905. They had been asked by the French government to find a way of measuring the cognitive abilities of children who were slow learners in order to help their teachers understand their degree of learning difficulty. They reasoned that slow learners were just that – children who lagged behind their peers. Hence by providing a child with a series of tasks of increasing difficulty they were able to plot where that child fell in relation to others. An eight-year-old child that could only solve the tasks of a typical six-year-old would have a mental age of six. Conversely, a six-year-old that could perform to the typical level of an eight-year-old would have a mental age of eight.

The Simon-Binet test of intelligence was developed further at Stanford University where it became known as the Stanford-Binet test. By using Binet's notion of mental age, dividing this by **chronological** (actual) age and then multiplying by 100, the Stanford-Binet test allowed an intelligence quotient (IQ) to be derived:

$$IQ = \frac{\text{mental age}}{\text{chronological age}} \times 100$$

Hence, an individual with a mental age *above* their chronological age will have an IQ of over 100, whereas an individual with a mental age *below* their chronological age will be below 100 (e.g. 6 divided by 8 x 100 = IQ of 75, but 8 divided by 6 x100 = IQ of 133). Since this form of intelligence is based on the ratio of mental age to chronological age, it is known as ratio IQ. In recent years, ratio IQ has been replaced by deviation IQ, which is a measurement of how far an individual deviates from the mean of 100. Note that this overcomes the problem of testing adults in relation to mental and chronological age because, under ratio IQ, an adult with a score of 50 would have to score twice as highly as an adult with a score of 25 in order to achieve the same IQ.

Although the original Simon-Binet test was devised in order to identify children that needed special attention, it quickly become the preferred method of ranking and selecting people for a wide variety of purposes. This included university, entrance to the job market and even the army. During the First World War, a single test score could decide who was suitable for officer material and who was destined for other ranks (Gould 1981).

Modern-day intelligence testing

Modern-day intelligence tests include a wide range of abilities. An example of this is the Wechsler Adult Intelligence Scale, which is currently in its third form (WAIS-III) and covers 13 different mental tasks (Deary 2001) – see the panel on the right.

The WAIS-III was tested and **normed** using 2450 men and women between the ages of 16 and 89. The sample used for this process included a wide range of educational attainment and ethnic groups in the USA, where it was developed. Although the 13 different tests appear to tap into a wide range of abilities, when each one was correlated with all of the others (that is 78 correlations), every single **correlation coefficient** was positive (varying from 0.33 to 0.81). This may be taken as evidence that these various abilities are all related to an overall **general intelligence** or 'g'. The term 'g' was first coined in 1923 by the British

Tasks used in the Wechsler Adult Intelligence Scale

- *Vocabulary* – defining specific words
- *Similarities* – identifying what two words have in common
- *Information* – general knowledge
- *Comprehension* – solving problems of everyday life
- *Picture completion* – spotting a missing part of a picture
- *Block design* – representing two-dimensional patterns using three-dimensional blocks
- *Picture arrangement* – placing a series of cartoon pictures in the correct order to complete a story
- *Matrix reasoning* – finding a missing element from an array of patterns
- *Arithmetic* – solving mental arithmetic problems
- *Digit span* – repeating back a sequence of numbers (varying in length from one to nine digits)
- *Letter-number sequencing* – repeating back series of numbers and letters (similar to a car number plate)
- *Digit-symbol coding* – writing down a number that corresponds to a particular symbol (as many as can be achieved in 90 seconds)
- *Symbol search* – identifying abstract symbols from an array of symbols, e.g. which one of a pair of symbols is in a list provided.

Thurstone's seven primary mental abilities

- *Verbal comprehension* – ability to read, write, level of vocabulary and general understanding of language
- *Word fluency* – ability to generate and manipulate words quickly
- *Number* – ability to carry out mathematical operations accurately
- *Space* – ability to make spatial visualizations and mentally transform spatial figures
- *Associative memory* – rote memory
- *Perceptual speed* – speed in perceiving visual details such as similarities and differences
- *Reasoning* – ability to induce and deduce facts.

Although Thurstone was able to differentiate between these seven mental abilities, subsequent investigators uncovered small but significant positive correlations between these measures, suggesting that there is a 'g'. Thurstone eventually came to accept 'g', but saw it as a secondary factor that was made up of his seven primary ones (Thurstone 1938; Myers 2001).

Factor analysis

One way to gather information about how closely separate mental abilities are related is via a statistical process called **factor analysis**. This consists of taking a large number of measures (e.g. scores on a number of tests items) and conducting a series of correlations on them. The higher the correlation coefficient, the more likely it is that two items are tapping into the same mental ability and, by clustering them together in this way, a much smaller number of variables is produced. For example, we might test for 'mental rotation' (the ability to rotate two-dimensional drawings in the mind's eye) and for 'pattern recognition' (the ability to match a portion of a pattern to another one when given a choice of similar patterns) and then discover that scores on these two measures correlate positively to a high degree. This would suggest that we are really tapping into just one mental faculty, which we might then label 'visuospatial ability' (i.e. the overall ability to recognize and manipulate patterns and designs). Today, many psychologists who work in psychometrics agree that intelligence involves several distinct abilities but that they cluster together to a sufficient degree to allow a small underlying 'g'.

psychologist Charles Spearman (Spearman 1923), who, having conducted a large number of correlations between separate test items, suggested that each of these skills is related to an underlying core intelligence.

Thurstone's primary mental abilities

Although many psychologists agreed with Spearman that there is an underlying general capacity for intelligence, others have argued that we have a range of separate and independent 'intelligences', rather than a single 'g'. One major figure who took issue with Spearman was Louis Thurstone, who, having given 56 different tests to a large number of people, argued that we each have seven **'primary mental abilities'** (Thurstone 1924; Myers 2001) – see the panel on the right.

The stability of intelligence over a life span

Key research: Deary *et al.* (2000)

One intriguing question that we might ask about intelligence is: does it remain stable over a life span? One study that seems to have helped to answer this question was published by psychometrician Ian Deary and his co-workers at the turn of the century (Deary *et al.* 2000). In 1998, Deary and his co-workers gained access to the data from a cohort of 11- year-old Scottish children who had been tested in 1932. They then managed to contact 66 of the original sample and arranged for them to be given the same test 66 years on (to the day) at the ripe old age of 77. Two findings emerged from the study:

1   Most participants achieved a higher score at the age of 77 than they did at the age of 11.

2   There was a great deal of consistency of scores between the test and re-test with those gaining high scores in 1932 also achieving high ones in 1998. The same applied to those who gained a low score, and those in the middle of the distribution.

Evaluation

This is an example of a longitudinal study where correlations between measures are taken at at least two different points in time for the same sample. Few longitudinal studies involve such a lengthy time span as 66 years. Note how well the scores from 1932 correlate with the scores from 1998. The researchers were able to conduct such a lengthy longitudinal study because all Scottish children born in 1921 (87 498) undertook a well-developed and widely used intelligence test known as the Moray House Test. Overall, the correlation coefficient between the two points of testing on the Moray House was + 0.73. It is good methodological practice using a subset of the same sample rather than comparing two different groups at these very different times as correlating two different groups of people would not allow researchers to study the stability of intelligence with ageing.

Figure 7.1

Moray House Intelligence Test

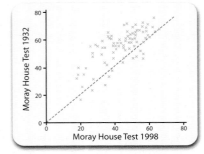

Overall evaluation of the psychometric approach

- *The self fulfilling prophecy of IQ scores* – The originators of intelligence testing, Binet and Simon, saw their tests as being useful for helping children with learning difficulties rather than being applied to the public in general. Despite this, according to some critics, psychometricians appear to be keen to provide all schoolchildren with a number (IQ). This number might then alter the way that teachers treat their pupils, leading to self-fulfilling prophecies about levels of achievement (Murdoch 2007).

- *IQ as a 'sticky' number* – Critics have argued that the psychometric approach supports a nativistic theory of intelligence, whereby the ability is largely fixed and biologically determined   (Schlinger 2003). If, for example, a person achieves a score of 100 on an IQ test, it would be difficult for them later to claim that their IQ is now 115, despite real improvements, since such numbers are 'sticky' (Murdoch 2007).

- *IQ scores are misleading* – One particularly severe critic of the psychometric approach, Steven Jay Gould (1981) has argued that intelligence is not truly measurable and to suggest that a single number (as in an IQ score) describes how clever a person is is highly misleading, if not meaningless.

- *A restricted account of intelligence* – According to Gardner (2006, see p.232), the psychometric approach to intelligence only taps into a small subset of the actual abilities people possess. If Gardner is right, then a score achieved on a current IQ test misses a great deal of human abilities such as 'interpersonal intelligence'.

- *Predictive power* – In support of the psychometric approach, however, as stated above, Mackintosh (1981) suggests that the wide variety of intelligence tests that have been developed do correlate with future scholastic achievement. This suggests that they are tapping into real abilities and potential.

The information-processing approach

The psychometric approach to intelligence was – and remains – a very useful one since, as Binet and Simon first anticipated, it has helped to identify those in need of special attention. Moreover, it has saved innumerable companies vast sums of money by speeding up selection processes. It is, however, largely descriptive in its aims (Blades 1998) in that the psychometric approach concerns IQ scores that describe, in a quick and easy way, some aspect of a person's abilities. It also examines how these scores are derived. It does not, however, really explore what intelligence is in terms of the underlying processes. Since the advent of the cognitive revolution in the 1960s, as in many other areas of performance, the information-processing approach has been used to explore the underlying cognitive processes involved in intelligence.

According to Sternberg and Kaufman (1998), the information-processing approach asks three important questions:

1 What mental processes are involved when we test intelligence?

2 How rapid and accurate are these mental processes?

3 What form do the mental representations of information take that these processes act on?

The psychometric approach describes how people differ on various aspects of intelligence, whereas the information-processing approach asks about the nature of the cognitive processes that underlie intelligence.

The triarchic theory of intelligence

The most notable figure in the information-processing approach to intelligence is Robert Sternberg. Sternberg (1985; 1988) developed the **triarchic theory of intelligence**, which means there are three parts (subtheories) to his theory:

1 **The contextual subtheory** – i.e. the context in which the intelligent behaviour takes place. According to Sternberg, Westernized ideas about intelligence as measured by psychometric tests are limited and should be expanded to take into account what is considered 'smart' in other cultures.

2 **The experiential subtheory** – i.e. the role that experience, novelty and automaticity (smooth performance of complex operations that follows a great deal of experience) play in problem solving. In an IQ test, for example, some of the items are likely to be familiar and others unfamiliar. If individuals are unfamiliar with test items, they are less likely to succeed on the test.

3 **The componential subtheory** – i.e. the underlying cognitive processes of intelligent behaviour (the actual components of thought). Sternberg identified three types of components under the componential subtheory:

■ *Metacomponents* – are involved in planning, controlling and evaluating a task. These are higher-order processes such as producing hypotheses or running a simulation.

■ *Performance components* – consist of the actual mental processes involved in performance. An example of this might be a plumber fixing a central heating system.

■ *Knowledge-acquisition* – components encode information in memory and allow us to combine and compare information. An example of this might be learning how to drive a car based, in part, from riding a push bike.

Evaluation of the triarchic theory of intelligence

■ *Real-world validity* – Both the contextual and the experiential subtheories highlight the importance of

experience. In this way, the triarchic theory can be said to have high real-world validity. This is important since, despite their abstract nature, tests on for example pattern-matching are likely to be influenced by an individual's previous experience of factors, such as the features of their home environment.

■ *Too broad a definition* – Cooper (2002) has criticized the triarchic theory on the grounds that it is so broad it appears to overlap with personality. In particular the experiential subtheory appears to broaden intelligence to the point where it includes highly automatized skills such as driving or even walking. To Cooper, there are good reasons to keep the definition of intelligence relatively narrow so that tasks used to test people should reduce the role of individual differences. In contrast, the triarchic theory of intelligences appears to increase individual differences.

■ *An incoherent theory?* – Richardson (1986) argues that the theory has too many components making it incoherent and difficult to see how the various subcomponents interact, both in terms of the three subtheories and the components of the componential subtheory.

The bio-ecological theory of Ceci

Another information-processing theory is the **bio-ecological theory** of Stephen Ceci (1990). The bio-ecological theory has certain similarities to Sternberg's triarchic theory in as much as it focuses on cognitive processes, but it differs in that Ceci suggests we have biologically based potentials that place limitations on our mental abilities. According to Ceci, the development of these mental abilities is contingent on the opportunities and challenges that arise from an individual's environment. This means that the form of intelligence that a person develops depends on the learning that is available in a given environment within broad biological constraints. The bio-ecological theory might be considered as a **knowledge-based** theory of intelligence since the form that intelligence takes depends in part on the local knowledge structure (hence the use of the term 'ecological'). Ceci is particularly critical of the way that traditional notions of intelligence underplay both the role of society and of biology. Hence, context – which includes the mental, social and physical aspects – is of great importance in this theory.

Evaluation of the bio-ecological theory of intelligence

■ *Real-world validity* – As with the triarchic theory, the bio-ecological theory may be seen as having high real-world validity in that it also considers contextual, experiential and componential factors in intelligence. In fact, it can be argued that it has even greater validity than Sternberg's theory since culture and physical surroundings are given central importance.

■ *A flexible theory* – Ceci's view of intelligence has a high degree of flexibility. This may be seen as both a strength and a weakness in that, on the one hand, it suggests that children may problem solve in different ways due to their culture but, on the other, it is difficult to devise ways of testing it. To illustrate, if children from different cultures solve the same problem, how can we be certain that they used different methods?

- *Too broad* – In a similar fashion, the bio-ecological theory can also be criticized for being so broad as to overlap with personality. Hence we might ask what are the boundaries of what constitutes 'intelligence'?

Gardner's theory of multiple intelligences

Sternberg and Ceci's assertion of the 1980s and 1990s that we need to broaden our concept of what constitutes intelligence was taken to its logical conclusion by Harvard's Howard Gardner. Whereas Sternberg and Ceci had both suggested that we should consider the social and cultural context of intelligence, Gardner went further, suggesting that IQ tests actually measure only a very small proportion of a person's intellectual abilities and that we should consider abilities as 'intelligences' that might include 'interpersonal intelligence' and 'bodily-kinesthetic intelligence' as well as traditional academic abilities. Beginning in the early 1980s with a list of six, Gardner (1983; 2006) has subsequently expanded this to eight

intelligences, each of which is independent of the other (i.e. the level of performance on one of these intelligences in no way predicts performance on any of the others) – see Table 7.1.

Looking at Table 7.1, it is clear that the first three 'intelligences' would fit well into a conventional IQ test, but the remaining five are well beyond our typical view of intelligence. It is important to realize that Gardner sees these eight 'intelligences' as quite distinct from one another – being strong on one does not predict strength on the others. We might ask on what basis does he make this claim? Gardner suggested that if these abilities are unrelated, then individuals should exist who are particularly well endowed with one 'intelligence' while being merely average or even below average on the others. Can we identify individuals that fulfil this requirement?

Do premier league football players have a high level of 'bodily-kinesthetic' intelligence?

Table 7.1 *The eight intelligences of Howard Gardner*

Form of intelligence	Mental abilities covered
Linguistic intelligence	The ability to make use of the spoken language and the mechanisms underlying it, such as syntax (e.g. placing words in the correct order) and semantics (the meaning of words). This is similar to the sort of things that traditional tests measure (as are the next two).
Spatial intelligence	The ability to perceive and manipulate visual or spatial information, including mental rotation of images. Although this overlaps with traditional views of intelligence, Gardner emphasized how much this is a 'real-world' ability, as demonstrated in the navigational skills of Polynesian Islanders.
Logical–mathematical intelligence	The ability to reason mathematically and use abstract thought. Again this is similar to the performance on traditional IQ tests, but in this case, problem solving involves that 'Aha! Now I get it!' type of answer without necessarily knowing why. (This is supported by the findings with autistic savants – see p.233.)
Musical intelligence	Musical ability, including the creation and appreciation of music and the underlying components, such as rhythm and pitch. This would apply to talented musicians and composers.
Bodily-kinesthetic intelligence	The ability to control body movements, including both gross and fine motor actions, which is exemplified by sporting prowess.
Interpersonal intelligence	The ability to understand other people's feelings, beliefs and intentions, e.g. by picking up on vocal intonation and body language, which reveal how a person really feels rather than what they say.
Intrapersonal intelligence	The ability to understand one's own feelings and motivations. Intrapersonal intelligence involves a clear sense of self and the strengths and weaknesses that an individual possesses.
Naturalistic intelligence	The ability to read, understand and act on the natural world, such as the ability to recognize different species of animal and how they are likely to react. According to Gardner, this specific ability to understand plants and animals may have helped our ancestors to survive.

Autistic savants

One interesting area that offers some support for Gardner is the existence of **autistic savants**. These are individuals who have been diagnosed with autistic spectrum disorder and, as such, show deficits in social and cognitive performance but, in contrast to this lack of general ability, demonstrate one or two areas where they may outperform the vast majority of non-autistic individuals. Examples of such special abilities include exceptional artistic and mathematical prowess, such as being able to draw complex buildings in great detail or being able to multiply large numbers without the aid of a calculator.

Autistic savants – islands of exceptional ability in a sea of deficits

Key research: Oliver Sacks (1985; 1995)

Most individuals diagnosed with autism lack cognitive and emotional skills. Despite a great deal of variability, the average IQ for these individuals is around 70 and most autistic individuals are unable to lead independent lives. In a relatively small proportion of cases, however, there are specific skills that are not only preserved but appear to be developed above and beyond the normal population. Such cases are called autistic savants (literal translation 'wise fools').

Professor of neurology Oliver Sacks described a number of these in his book *An Anthropologist on Mars* (Sacks 1995). One particular case, Stephen Wiltshire, despite suffering from autism, was able, by the age of eight, to draw from memory monumental buildings of London such as the Albert Hall and the National History Museum in great detail with perfect perspective. Despite this exceptional artistic prowess, Stephen rarely made eye contact or engaged in play with other children, and his IQ was assessed to be just 52. In addition to artistic skill, Sacks also documents cases of astonishing mathematical ability, such as in the identical adult twins Charles and George. Since they lacked social skills, Charles and George were looked after in a residential home where they demonstrated an obsession with prime numbers (Sacks 1985; 1995). Sacks found that they regularly took turns in exchanging six-figure prime numbers (i.e. numbers that cannot be divided by another number). This is mathematically a very impressive feat, but astonishingly when Sacks challenged them to find larger prime numbers within a matter of minutes they were able to exchange primes of up to 20 digits!

As yet, nobody knows how autistic savants are able to perform at this level in very specific areas whilst demonstrating such deficits elsewhere (Blades 1998). For our purposes, the important point is that individuals exist with very low-measured IQ scores who are exceptional in very specific areas of cognition. Clearly, this supports Gardner's position that we have a range of quite separate 'intelligences'.

Evaluation of Gardner's multiple intelligences

- *Multiple intelligences or just one?* – Whilst the notion of multiple intelligences is an attractive one in many ways, there are problems with it. For example, while the case of autistic savants would appear to offer support for Gardner's view of separate and independent forms of intelligence, it is known that the first three of his intelligences – namely linguistic, visuospatial and logical-mathematical – *do* correlate positively with each other for the population at large (Cooper 2002). This suggests that they are by no means fully independent.

- *Difficult to test* – A second problem is that the remaining five intelligences are rather difficult to test accurately. Perhaps some test of naturalistic intelligence will emerge in the future. Such a test might involve, for example, the ability to demonstrate a good working knowledge of the classification of plants and animals. At first this might sound reasonable, but we have to ask whether such a task really taps into the concept of naturalistic intelligence and would a strong performance on such a task really be independent from good general linguistic skills?

- *Modularity theory supports multiple intelligences* – A theory that has gained a large number of supporters in recent years is **Modularity** theory. This theory holds that different tasks require separate analytical devices (or mental modules), which could be taken as support for Gardner's theory as it might suggest a series of different forms of intelligence (Fodor 1983). The problem with this argument is that there are debates about whether such modules are peripheral or central in processing. The originator of the modern-day modular mind theory, Fodor (1983), sees them largely as serving a peripheral purpose, whereas for Gardner's thesis to be correct, they would have to play a more central role.

- *Brain damage can lead to quite specific deficits* – In the 2006 edition of his book *Multiple Intelligences*, Gardner describes how damage to the frontal lobes often leads to a reduction specifically in interpersonal skills but leaves other abilities intact. This suggests that specific parts of the brain might be devoted to different skills.

In summary, whilst an exciting idea, the jury is still out on Gardner's multiple intelligences.

Activity — How do you test Gardner's forms of intelligence?

Gardner suggests we have eight types of intelligence including interpersonal, naturalistic and musical intelligences. One problem that his theory faces is how do you test for such forms of intelligence?

Devise a way of testing for each of these three types of intelligence. Note that this might involve tests that are quite different from traditional IQ tests and might involve an expert making a judgement and scoring participants.

CHECK YOUR UNDERSTANDING

Check your understanding of the theories of intelligence by answering these questions. Try to do this from memory. You can check your answers by looking back through Topic 1, Theories of intelligence.

1. Why do psychologists find it difficult to define intelligence?

2. What does the Flynn effect mean? How does Flynn explain the Flynn effect?

3. How does the psychometric approach to intelligence differ from the information-processing approach?

4. What are the three main subtheories of Sternberg's triarchic theory of intelligence?

5. List two similarities and two differences between Sternberg's triarchic theory of intelligence and Ceci's bio-ecological theory.

6. List Gardner's eight intelligences. Which of these would fit in with a 'traditional' view of intelligence?

7. Devise a test of either 'interpersonal intelligence' or 'bodily-kinesthetic' intelligence.

8. What evidence might be presented to support Gardner's theory of multiple intelligences?

9. Outline the possible weaknesses of Gardner's theory.

10. Explain what is meant by the term 'autistic savant'?

Topic 2: Animal learning and intelligence

A recent psychology textbook defines learning as 'a process by which experience produces a relatively enduring and adaptive change in an organism's capacity for behaviour' (Passer *et al.* 2008, p.281). Note that this definition uses the term 'organism' rather than 'human' for the entity that is doing the learning. Psychologists have long sought to understand the nature of learning and many have turned their attention to animals to help them in this pursuit. The use of non-human animals in studies of learning begs a number of questions (quite apart from ethical ones). We might, for example, ask do other species learn in similar ways to ourselves? We might also ask can they be taught some of the skills that humans naturally pick up such as an awareness of self and the ability to understand the mental states of others. We will explore some of these questions, but first we need to have a clear understanding of the main types of learning that both humans and other species are capable of.

Psychology in context — How do people rate animal intelligence?

In 2002, three researchers asked students in Japan and the USA to rank the level of intelligence of 56 species of animals on a scale of 0 to 100 points (Nakajima *et al.* 2002). Of all 56 species, chimpanzees were seen as the most intelligent with an average score of 77, followed by orangutans and dolphins in equal second place with 72 points, and gorillas next with 68. In the middle of the rankings were parrots with 48, rats with 35 and octopus with 24. The last four were jellyfish with 15, earthworms and slugs each with 10 and amoeba with eight points. Two interesting points can be made from these findings:

1. The students did not have a problem placing the animals in rank order (nobody refused to do this on the grounds that it was impossible), suggesting that people have some sort of view that animals can be sequenced in a terms of intelligence from lowest to highest.

2. Despite a high level of general agreement on the rank order, the students were unable to explain how they reached this distribution. It is interesting to speculate as to how the students reached their rank order. Was it based on brain size or perhaps through watching wildlife programmes featuring animals showing various clever responses? Unfortunately, we don't know this question as the study did not tell us. This next topic may well answer this and other questions about intelligence in our non-human relatives.

Ethology and behaviourism – nature and nurture

During the 20th century, two different approaches to the study of animal behaviour emerged – **ethology** and **behaviourism**. Whereas **behaviourists** focused on what animals were capable of learning under very controlled laboratory conditions, ethologists were more concerned with instinctive behaviour observed in the field. Behaviourists considered that animals were born as blank slates (*tabula rasa*) and that all species obeyed the same set of learning principles. In contrast, ethologists were more interested in the function or **adaptive significance** of each species' behavioural repertoire. If we consider this in the light of the nature/nurture debate, it is clear that the ethologists were on the nature (genes and evolution) side of the equation and the behaviourists on the nurture side (learning via reward and punishment from the environment) as primary determinants of behaviour. Today, most animal behaviourists see some middle ground as it has become increasingly clear that all behaviours are a product of both innate factors and learning – the only question is what is the relative importance of nature and nurture in a given behavioural response (Hinde 1970; Pearce 2008).

The nature of simple learning

Psychologists have identified and studied two main types of simple learning in animals: **classical** and **operant** (or instrumental) conditioning.

Classical conditioning

Classical conditioning involves learning to make an association between two events. An example of this might be putting your foot on the brake when you see a red traffic light. You have learned to associate the red light with stopping the car. This notion of associative learning was discovered quite by accident by the Russian physiologist Ivan Pavlov during the 1860s. Pavlov was interested in the process of digestion and, in order to learn more about this, set about measuring the amount of saliva that dogs produce when food is presented to them. In doing so, he noticed that the dogs would often began to salivate before the food appeared – when they heard the footsteps of the approaching experimenter, for example. Pavlov realized that the dogs had made an association between the meat and the sound of the experimenter's steps, and this led them to salivate in anticipation of the food. He then began to see if he could associate the salivation response to other stimuli such as a light or a specific tone. By pairing, for example, a light with the appearance of the meat powder he found that, once the association had been made, the dog would salivate to the appearance of the light alone (in absence of the powder). He called the salivation response to the meat powder the **unconditioned response** or **UCR** (a reflex action that did not need to be 'conditioned') and the meat powder the **unconditioned stimulus** or **UCS** (i.e. a stimulus that automatically leads to the response). In the case of the light, this is initially termed a **neutral stimulus** (**NS**), which, following training, is called a **conditioned stimulus** or **CS** (as it is a learned stimulus) and the salivation response to the light the **conditioned response** or **CR** (since dogs do not naturally salivate to lights). Note that the unconditioned response and conditioned response are the same response (in this case salivation), but that they are given different labels because they are the result of different stimuli (the 'innate' meat powder response and the learned response to the light). This form of learning became known as classical conditioning but in honour of Pavlov is also referred to as **Pavlovian conditioning** (see Fig. 7.2).

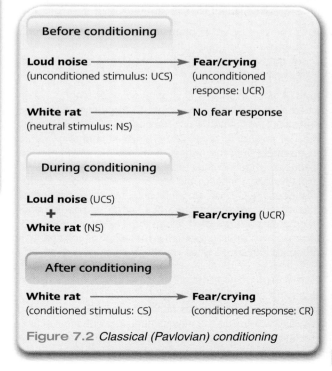

Figure 7.2 *Classical (Pavlovian) conditioning*

Timing

In order for an initially neutral stimulus (such as a light) to become a reliable CS, it has to be paired at the correct time and in the correct sequential order in relation to the UCS.

Acquisition and extinction

Pavlov called the pairing of the UCS and CS **acquisition** as the animal acquires knowledge of the association. He also noted, however, that acquisition of a CS does not mean that the response will last forever. If the CS stops predicting the UCS for a number of trials then **extinction** occurs (see Fig. 7.3), that is the animals appear to have 'unlearned' the association between say the light and the meat powder. The response has been extinguished. This means that although the original behaviour remains in the presence of the UCS (salivating in this case), it is not entirely 'fixed' with regard to the CS.

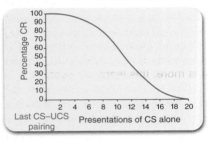

Figure 7.3
Extinction of CR when UCS is no longer paired with CS

Spontaneous recovery

Interestingly, although the CS can be extinguished, Pavlov discovered that extinction is not a process of forgetting. Under the right conditions, the extinguished CR can suddenly reappear. This is known as **spontaneous recovery**, and there are two main situations that can bring this about:

1 A time lapse between one extinction trial and another may be sufficient to reinstate the CR.

2 If the participant is startled (e.g. by a sudden event, such as a loud noise, that occurs during the process of extinction training), this may bring back the CR, however briefly.

Both of these examples of spontaneous recovery question whether extinction is analogous to forgetting. When the participant is retrained, using the original CS+UCS pairings, the CR is quickly reinstated. This reinstatement occurs much faster than the original conditioning, which may be taken as evidence that the CR was not really 'lost'. To explain this process of response extinction, Pavlov described the CR as being 'inhibited', much like the energy that may be maintained in a coil spring by keeping your hand pressed down on it. When the inhibition is removed, the response returns (using the metaphor of coil spring, it rebounds into shape when your hand pressure is removed).

Stimulus generalization and discrimination

If, having undergone classical conditioning, an animal is presented with a stimulus similar to the CS, it may also respond likewise to the new stimulus provided it is similar enough. We might, for example, train a dog to salivate to a specific tone. If we present another tone that is not too dissimilar, it is likely also to salivate to this new tone. This is called **generalization**, as the dog generalizes its response to similar stimuli. In the case of a tone that is very different to the original CS, however, there will be **discrimination**, that is, the dog will not salivate as it has discriminated this tone from the CS. You might wonder why generalization occurs – why aren't organisms built to be very specific in what they will respond to? It makes evolutionary sense not to discriminate to an extreme extent since generalizing is a good way to learn about your environment. If, for example, you are frightened by a snake, it may well pay you to avoid other snakes in future rather than having to learn this fear response anew for each species. However, it would not make sense to generalize to the extent that earthworms or the branches of trees lead you to run away every time you encounter them. Hence we also need to have a degree of discrimination.

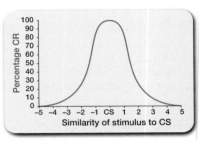

Figure 7.4
Generalization of CR to stimuli similar to CS

The role of classical conditioning in the behaviour of non-human animals

The importance of classical conditioning in animals lies primarily in their ability to learn that one thing (the CS) predicts the occurrence of something else (the UCS). In Topic 1, we discussed how animal behaviour might be influenced by evolutionary factors. It makes sense, therefore, to examine classical conditioning from this perspective. One possibility is that the display of conditional responses (CRs) in some way gives animals a selective advantage – for example, in the following ways:

- *Foraging and hunting behaviour* – In their foraging behaviour, animals may learn that certain tastes will be followed by illness, whereas others have more beneficial consequences. The importance of the relationship between the CS and CR in feeding was demonstrated dramatically in a conditioned taste-aversion study by Garcia *et al.* (1977). In a taste-aversion study, an animal is conditioned to avoid a particular food that has been associated with some painful outcome or toxic reaction. The animal learns to avoid that food because of a conditioned-aversion response to its smell or taste (Reber 1995). In the study by Garcia and colleagues, coyotes and wolves were made ill by feeding them mutton wrapped in raw sheep hide and laced with a toxic substance, lithium chloride. By allowing the animals to approach live sheep the effects of this conditioning episode were tested. Rather than attacking the sheep, as they would normally, the coyotes sniffed their quarry and turned away, some of them retching. The wolves initially charged the sheep and made oral contact on their flanks, but then immediately released their prey. During the next half hour, the sheep became increasingly dominant and the wolves withdrew like submissive pups (Garcia *et al.* 1977). These responses are evidence that the CS (the taste and smell of sheep) paired with illness was sufficient to change the behaviour (CR) of the predators towards their prey. In the natural world, learning to avoid food that makes you ill is a valuable lesson.

◼ *Behaviour towards conspecifics* – Research with male blue gourami fish lends some support to the prediction that animals that change their behaviour in response to CS have a selective advantage. In one study by Hollis (1984), male gouramis were trained to expect an aggressive encounter with another male following the lighting of a red panel on the side of their tank. The fish showed evidence of having learned the relationship between the CS (red light) and the UCS (rival male's arrival) by beginning their aggressive display during the CS. When control males (who had not been conditioned to the CS) and conditioned males were allowed to fight each other, the conditioned males directed more bites, showed more aggressive displays and invariably won. In many species, males who hold territories behave aggressively towards any animal approaching their territory, even females. Mating would be facilitated if males could anticipate the approach of a female and inhibit aggression towards her (Shettleworth 1998). Using techniques similar to the experiment described earlier, Hollis (1990) found that conditioned males directed fewer bites and more courtship behaviour towards a test female than did the controls. More importantly, this behaviour translates into greatly enhanced reproductive success. Conditioned males fathered, on average, over 1000 young, whereas the control males (where the CS had not been paired with a female) fathered, on average, less than 100 young (Hollis *et al.* 1997).

By wrapping mutton in a sheep's hide and lacing it with a toxic substance wolves can be taught through classical conditioning to avoid eating sheep

Evaluation of classical conditioning

Insights from classical conditioning research have led to striking discoveries about animal behaviour. The appealing simplicity of Pavlov's views has come under attack as psychologists have discovered certain limitations of the generality of findings relating to classical conditioning (Zimbardo *et al.* 1995):

◼ *Biological preparedness* – Different animals face different challenges in order to survive in their particular ecological niche. As a result, different species may well have different capabilities for learning in a given situation. Therefore, we might expect some relationships between CS and UCS to be more difficult for some species to learn than for others. To accommodate this possibility, Seligman (1970) proposed the concept of 'preparedness':

Animals are *'prepared'* to learn associations that are significant in terms of their survival needs.

Animals are *'unprepared'* to learn associations that are not significant in this respect.

Animals are *'contraprepared'* to learn any association that in some way runs contrary to any naturally-occurring behavioural predisposition.

◼ *Taste-aversion learning* – This is an example of an association for which animals might be biologically prepared. As discussed earlier, research on taste-aversion learning poses particular problems for Pavlovian conditioning. You may recall that an animal may eat poisoned food, and later become ill (but survive). After just one experience, and despite a long interval between the CS (tasting the food) and UCS (becoming ill), the animal learns to avoid all foods with that taste. What is more, this learned association is remarkably resistant to extinction. This form of learning challenges the assumptions of Pavlov's view of classical conditioning in three ways:

1 *Number of trials* – Classical conditioning is a gradual process, requiring many associations between the neutral stimulus (NS) and the UCS. In taste aversion, learning takes place after just one trial; this phenomenon is known as 'one-trial learning'.

2 *Delay between NS and UCS* – The longer the delay between the NS and the UCS, the less likely a learned association will develop between the two. In taste-aversion, conditioning takes place despite several hours between the two.

3 *Extinction* – In classical conditioning, the withdrawal of the UCS means that extinction sets in rapidly. Yet in taste-aversion, the time period before extinction is prolonged way beyond what we would normally expect.

◼ *How universal is classical conditioning?* – It is clear that species differ in terms of their motives, motor and cognitive capacities, and certainly in the degree to which their natural style of life depends on learning. We must, therefore, be cautious about generalizing from one species to another. Each species' genetic make-up places limitations on their learning abilities. These biological constraints suggest that the principles of classical conditioning cannot be universally applied across all species or all situations. Some aspects of classical conditioning clearly depend on the way an animal is genetically predisposed towards stimuli in its environment. What any organism can and cannot readily learn appears to be as much a product of its evolutionary history as its learning opportunities.

Although classical conditioning helps to explain how a great deal of learning takes place and how a neutral stimulus comes to take on importance, it is not possible to use it to teach an animal to do something novel. Try to think, for example, of an unconditioned stimulus that can be used to make your dog 'shake paws' with you. Simply presenting it with a treat of patting it on the back won't lead it to offer you its paw – it is more likely to respond by wagging its tail or licking your face (unconditioned responses). The problem is that in classical conditioning the 'conditioned response' is invariably part of the animal's natural repertoire and it is not part of that repertoire to shake paws with you. The only way to do this is to reward the dog for doing something approximate to this new response (such as allowing you to pick its paw up with your hand). If you then reward it for allowing you to do this a number if times it will eventually do it spontaneously to gain a reward. (Technically, you might also teach your dog to do this by punishment – i.e. doing something unpleasant to it until it does the trick, but most pet owners would find this unacceptable.) It has now associated a response that was previously not in its repertoire with the reward. This alterative form of learning to classical conditioning is the way that both we and other animals learn to solve many problems that the environment throws at us. It was first studied by a contemporary of Pavlov in America, Edward Thorndike.

Operant conditioning

At the same time that Pavlov was studying classical conditioning in Russia, Thorndike (1898) was exploring problem solving in animals via a new piece of equipment that he built to test their ability to learn to solve problems. He called this a **puzzle box** – the puzzle that his animals had to solve was how to escape from it. An example of the type of experiment Thorndike designed is shown in Fig. 7.5. Here, a cat is placed in the box and a bowl containing fish is placed outside (to ensure that the cat wants to get out). In order to reach the food, the cat has to learn how to pull a lever to open the hatch. Typically, when first placed in the box, the cat would scratch around for some time before stumbling on the lever. Once the cat had made the correct response and gained its fishy reward, it was placed back in the box for a second trial (again with a food reward outside). Typically, over successive trials, the cats escaped from the box more quickly, demonstrating that they were learning the task (see Fig. 7.5). Note that the learning takes some time, with the cats' performance gradually improving over trials. Thorndike argued that the fact that the period it takes for cats to escape was gradually decreasing tells us about the nature of this learning. To him, if animals were learning via reason or thought, then once the task was solved, the time taken to escape would come right down and stay down from then on. The actual shape of the graphs suggested to Thorndike that the problem was solved via trial and error learning rather than by reason. An example of this is the graph on the right – notice how this cat appears to have learned to solve the task on the second trial – but then takes a lot longer on the third trial and gradually improves on subsequent trials. This suggests that the animal is learning by trial and error rather than solving the problem very quickly on trial two (when it probably stumbled on the solution quickly).

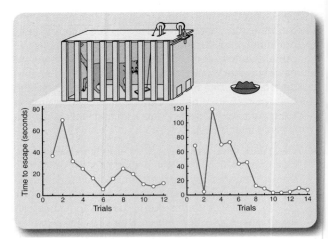

Figure 7.5 *Trial and error learning*

Following a large number of these experiments, Thorndike (1911) began to refer to this type of problem solving as **instrumental learning** since the animal's behaviour is instrumental in achieving a satisfying outcome.

A modern-day definition of instrumental learning would be 'the process by which responses are learned because they operate on, or affect, the environment'.

Skinner's behaviourism
Thorndike's work became very influential during the early years of the 20th century amongst the new breed of psychologists emerging in the USA who called themselves behaviourists. The most influential behaviourist of the 20th century was B. F. Skinner. Skinner, who worked at Harvard University, built on the work of Thorndike by expanding the terminology of instrumental learning. He did this by reducing the complexity of the tasks that an animal had to learn. Rather than giving animals a task to solve that might involve a number of responses (the cat in the box had to learn about the box and the way that it opened), Skinner simplified this by giving them just one response at a time.

The Skinner box
Like Thorndike before him, in order to study an animal's problem solving abilities, Skinner built a special box. In this case, however, Skinner kept his design very simple; in his box an animal (invariably a hungry rat or pigeon) had to make the single response of pressing a lever in order to receive a food reward. This box become known as a **Skinner box** and very quickly became the preferred instrument of behaviourists to help them understand instrumental learning. Typically, when a hungry rat is placed in a Skinner box, it will move around until it happens to press a bar that is conveniently attached to one of the walls. Immediately the bar has been pressed, a food pellet is released into a little cup below and the animal consumes it. Quite rapidly, the rat comes to associate the food with the single response of pressing the bar (i.e. it is rewarded or **reinforced** by pressing the bar). Skinner called this learning **operant conditioning** and he defined it as 'a type of learning where behaviour is influenced by the consequences that follow it' (Skinner

1938). This is really just another name for instrumental conditioning. In the Skinner box, instrumental learning occurs where one action (pressing the bar) is related to one change in the environment (the food appears). In a sense, the animal 'operates' on the environment, which is how Skinner came up with the term operant conditioning.

Skinner box

Reinforcement

Following Thorndike's lead, Skinner focused on the notion that operant learning takes place via reinforcement, i.e. behaviours that bring about successful outcomes for the animal are likely to be repeated. Many interesting insights have been gained about how reinforcement takes place by use of the Skinner box, some of them surprising. For instance, the delivery of one food item for every bar press might seem to be the optimal way of ensuring the response is learned and maintained. But this is not what Skinner discovered. He demonstrated that reinforcement exerts subtle (but nonetheless predictable) effects on behaviour depending on how the reinforcer is made dependent upon the response. As in classical conditioning, the time of the interval between two elements of the conditioning process (in this case the response and the reinforcer) is crucial. If the reinforcer follows immediately after the response, conditioning is more effective than if they are separated by a delay (Pearce 2008).

Schedules of reinforcement

If a food reinforcer is not dispensed for every single response (bar press), but is arranged according to a predetermined 'schedule', such as one food pellet for every fifth bar press, then different response patterns arise, depending on the exact relationship between response and reinforcement.

There are four ways in which reinforcement may be scheduled. It may occur by either a time-based or *response-based* criterion (1 and 2 below); it may also be applied in either a *fixed* or a *variable schedule* (3 and 4):

1 As a **ratio of the number of responses** such as the 1:5 example above.

2 As a result of the **time-base** or **time-interval** criterion – for instance, this might mean the delay of a food pellet at the end of, say, one minute *provided that the subject has responded to that interval* (and not otherwise).

3 A fixed schedule dispenses reinforcement on a reliable basis, e.g. in a 1:5 fixed-ratio (FR5) schedule, the reinforcer is delivered after every fifth bar press. Similarly, a fixed-interval schedule of one minute (FI1) will deliver reinforcement at the end of the required response (e.g. bar pressing) in that time.

4 Variable schedules dispense food on an erratic basis, e.g. a variable ratio schedule of 1:5 (VR5) will deliver

food *on average* once every five responses, but during any one trial that number may vary from 5. Only over a large number of trials will the schedule be seen to have averaged one reinforcer per five responses. On a variable interval schedule of one minute (VI1), the interval is varied around the period of one minute, although this interval alters from trial to trial, so that only over the long run does the one minute average become apparent.

Punishment and negative reinforcement

As well as reinforcement, where the positive consequences of a response lead an animal to make the response more often, Skinner also dealt with its opposite – **punishment** – where the unpleasant consequences of a response lead to an animal making the response *less often*. For example, rats in a Skinner box receiving an electric shock after pressing a bar will become less likely to repeat the action. This also happens in everyday life for humans. If you are given 'the cold shoulder' by your partner for turning up very late for a date, then this form of punishment should (in theory) make you less likely to repeat the offence.

Often confused with punishment is **negative reinforcement**, where a response is used to stop an aversive stimulus. Returning to the Skinner box, a rat may be able to *stop* a shock from occurring by pressing a bar. Note the difference here – punishment is used to stop an organism doing something, whereas negative reinforcement is used to make it do something.

The role of operant conditioning in animal behaviour

Unpredictable environmental changes during an animal's lifetime cannot be anticipated by pre-programmed forms of behaviour. The individual animal must rely upon its own resources in adapting to any such changes. The ability to modify behaviour in the light of unpredictable environmental changes is clearly a sign of intelligence, and gives such animals a clear selective advantage. Although most of the work on operant conditioning has taken place in the laboratory, there are also examples of natural behaviours that utilize the principles of operant conditioning.

An example of operant conditioning 'in action' comes from a study of the mating behaviour of cowbirds. Cowbirds are brood parasites (i.e. like cuckoos the chicks are parasitic in that they take the food that was meant for the chicks of another species) and so young males do not hear the songs of adults of their species during the early part of their life. West and King (1988) studied the origins of two geographical 'accents' in cowbirds in the USA. They discovered that rather than being less complex, the songs of males reared in isolation were more complex than males reared normally. Male cowbirds appear to have the elements of both dialects, but through the process of operant conditioning, narrow down their song pattern so that it matches the 'preference' of the local females. When the male sings particular elements from his repertoire, the female responds with a brief 'wing-stroking' display, similar to the copulation invitation found in many types of nesting birds. The male responds by increasing the frequency with which he produces the rewarded elements of his song, eliminating those that have no effect on the female.

Evaluation of operant conditioning

- *Instinctive drift* – The principles of operant conditioning have been used in many different experimental settings and in many different applications, often with spectacular success. But how universal is operant conditioning, and can we truly teach anything to anyone using these techniques? Breland and Breland (1951) used operant conditioning techniques to train animals of many different species to perform a diverse range of behaviours. The Brelands believed that the principles of operant conditioning derived from laboratory research could be applied successfully to the control of animal behaviour outside the laboratory. After their training, however, some of the Brelands' animals no longer performed the 'tricks' they had learned using operant conditioning techniques. For example, a racoon was trained to pick up coins and put them in a 'piggy' bank for food reinforcement. The racoon eventually refused to give up the coins, rubbing them together in its paws, and 'dipping' them into the piggy bank before taking them out again. This is not surprising if we consider the fact that this is how racoons behave naturally, rubbing crayfish together to remove their shells and then washing them. The Brelands believed that even after conditioning, behaviours drift back towards instinct after a time. They called this process '**instinctive drift**' (Breland and Breland 1951). The racoon's behaviour could not be explained by the simple relationship between stimulus–behaviour–consequence, but was understandable if we consider the species–specific behaviour tendencies of racoons. These tendencies override the temporary changes that are brought about by operant conditioning, i.e. the animals' inherited behaviour pattern was incompatible with the operant conditioning task (Zimbardo *et al.*1995).

- *The incompatibility of responses* – Attempts to teach totally arbitrary responses in the laboratory (such as bar-pressing in rats or disc-pecking in pigeons) may fail because these arbitrary responses are incompatible with the responses related to the animals' motivational state (e.g. the hungry racoon 'washing' the coins). In this case, the required operant response of releasing the coins (to obtain food as reinforcement) is incompatible with the classically conditioned response of rubbing them together as if they were food.

- *Operant or classical conditioning?* – One of the main assumptions of operant conditioning is that the consequences of a behaviour determine the likelihood of it occurring in the future. In one experiment pigeons were trained to peck a small illuminated disc on the wall of a Skinner box to obtain the reward of food. Hence the delivery of food depended on the response of pecking the illuminated disc. However, if the disc was merely illuminated for a few seconds prior to the delivery of food, regardless of the pigeons' behaviour (i.e. whether they pecked or not) the birds would end up pecking the disc as vigorously as if their pecking behaviour had previously been reinforced. Hence, in this case the relationship is simply one between the stimulus and the reinforcer, with the response of the pigeon being irrelevant to the delivery of the food. The classically conditioned association between light and food is sufficient to generate the high rate of pecking behaviour. This has led some people to conclude that classical conditioning is responsible for much of what researchers have been recording as operant behaviour (Mackintosh 1981).

Evidence for intelligence in non-human animals

When asking my students to discuss whether they consider animals capable of thought, I have noticed that, almost invariably, two opposing 'camps' emerge. Broadly speaking, one camp will argue that animals are capable of thought, whereas the opposing camp takes issue with this, suggesting that thinking is a purely human phenomenon. Interestingly, these two camps reflect a dichotomy amongst academic psychologists who work with animals. We can think of these two camps as 'advocates' (i.e. those who advocate that animals are intelligent entities capable, at some level, of human-like cognitive processes) and 'sceptics' (i.e. those who view animals and humans as discontinuous, with humans having far superior cognitive abilities).

Issues: The internal mental states of animals

The debate concerning the cognitive and emotional abilities of animals is not a new one. The 16th-century philosopher Rene Descartes argued that animals were machines rather like complex clocks and, since they did not have internal mental states, they were incapable of feeling pain. To Descartes, when damaged, the 'machine' acts as though it is in pain simply to protect itself from being damaged (Rachels 1990). So the **Cartesian** view of animals was one of automatons. This allowed people for the next 200 years to treat animals with indifference. Samuel Pepys, for example, described in his famous diary an after-dinner treat of watching a live, un-anaesthetized dog being dissected. Darwin's *Origin of Species* (1859) outlining his theory of evolution by **natural selection** led to a reappraisal of the internal state of animals since acceptance of evolution means that other species are related to us. This has opened the door to the notion that they may also have internal states and be capable of suffering.

The question is who is right – the advocates of animal intelligence or the sceptics? It is far from certain that we can give a definitive answer yet, but we can at least be more precise about what the questions are and then explore the evidence that might help to answer them. Important questions that are seen by academic advocates and sceptics include evidence of problem-solving, self-recognition, social learning and the ability to manipulate others.

Intelligence in non-human species

You may recall that psychologists find it difficult to agree on a definition of intelligence for humans. So how much harder is it to explore intelligence in non-human species, given that we can't talk to animals let alone give them an IQ test. Hence, most of the evidence for animal intelligence has been gathered indirectly (this is also true of babies and very young toddlers). To recap we began with a definition of intelligence of 'The ability to learn from experience, think in abstract terms, and deal effectively with one's environment'. Most people would agree that animals can both learn from experience and deal effectively with the environment, but what of thinking in abstract terms? We'll return to this last question later, but first we consider learning from experience – how do other species compare with humans?

Angermeier (1984) suggested that we might understand the relative levels of intelligence in different animal species better by comparing the speed with which each learns to solve a task. In Angermeier's study, animals from a range of species had to decide which of two stimuli led to a food reward. The animals used included bees, fish, various species of birds and mammals, and a human baby. Mammals had to press the correct lever; birds had to peck a disc; fish push a rod; bees had to discriminate between two colours; and five-month-old human infants had to turn their heads in the right direction to a puff of air. Angermeier recorded the number of rewards delivered to hungry subjects until they had reached a criterion of responding correctly at a constant rate. The results are shown in Table 7.2.

Animal	No. rewards
Bees	2
Triggerfish	4
Koi carp	4
Silverbarb	4
Quail	8
Hybrid chickens	10
Pigeons	10
Rats	22
Raccoons	24
Rabbits	24
Human infants	28

Table 7.2 *Number of rewards delivered before criterion was reached in a simple learning task from 11 animals arranged in ascending order (redrawn from Pearce 2008)*

The remarkable finding of this study is that the pattern is precisely the reverse of what we might have intuitively expected. The smaller the brain of the animal, the more rapidly it learned from experience. As Table 7.2 shows, bees learn the task after two trials, whilst three species of fishes learn it after four trials. The birds vary from eight to 10, and the mammals from 22 to 28 (for a human!). So we either have to accept that bees are the most intelligent of animals studied so far or we have to jettison the idea of speed of learning as an accurate index of relative intelligence.

Evaluation of Angermeier's study

- *Is the information retained?* – Although the small-brained animals demonstrate more rapid learning than larger-brained ones, no attempt was made to see if any of the animals retained this information, i.e. how well would the various animals have performed a day or a week later?

- *Use of an infant to represent humans?* – Was it really fair of Angermeier to compare an infant human with 'adults' of other species? Perhaps an adult human would have performed as well as the bees?

- *Use of the same task* – On a more positive note, Angermeier did at least use the same task for each species. Very few studies have been able to compare between species in this way.

Perhaps animals with a small brain can learn simple tasks more quickly than those with larger brains because their nervous systems are built to process simple information rapidly. Perhaps we need to consider more demanding tasks if we are to determine how the cognitive processes of other species compare with those of our own. One area that demands a high degree of cognitive processing is that of self-recognition.

Are honey bees the most intelligent of animals?

Theory of mind and self-recognition

Today, we tend to think of consciousness and intelligence as social phenomena (Pearce 2008). One area where psychologists have become particularly excited in recent years is the notion that children come to develop a **theory of mind** (see p.287). This is the idea that, by around four years of age, children begin to realize that people have mental states that include beliefs and desires. From this point on, they begin to 'mind read' or 'mentalize', i.e. work out the mental state of others and to act on this information. The sophistication of this theory of mind develops as does the child, so that by late childhood we begin to consider what other individuals might think about other individuals. By adulthood, we explain the behaviour of others continually on the basis of their thoughts and feelings. Evolutionary psychologists suggest that the theory of mind developed as a **social module**, i.e. a part of the brain/mind that has evolved to deal with social stimuli and social behaviour (Baron-Cohen 1995). The first indication of the development of a theory of mind is the ability to pass a test of self-recognition. If children are to work out the mental state of others, they must first be aware of themselves as having a 'self'. Toddlers appear to recognize themselves as individuals around the age of 15 months (see p.286). Given that we split from the great apes only around 5 000 000 years ago (Workman and Reader 2008), we might ask, do apes also have the ability of self-recognition?

The mirror-test

This question has been studied using a simple technique called the **mirror-test**. With children, this involves placing a coloured spot on the head of a young baby and presenting it with a mirror. Initially, the baby touches the spot on the mirror. But when it is a little older, it looks at the mirror and touches the spot on its own head (Keenan et al. 2003). This is taken as evidence that the child has begun to develop the ability of self-recognition.

Since the 1970s, a number of psychologists have used the mirror test to assess a wide range of animal species (Povinelli 2000; Pearce 2008). Pearce reviewed the findings in this area recently and concluded that 'at least some species can behave as if they recognize themselves in mirrors' (Pearce 2008, p.321). Interestingly, chimpanzees are unable to recognize themselves in mirrors until they are more than four years old. Prior to this age, they typically touch the spot on the mirror; after this age, they begin to touch the spot on themselves when looking in the mirror. This does not tell us whether, prior to this age, they lack the capacity of self-recognition or just the ability to understand how mirrors work (or both).

Female orangutan making use of a mirror to examine herself

Evaluation of self-recognition research

- *Many or few species?* – Although there is general agreement that some species have the capacity to use mirrors for self-recognition, there is great debate about which ones can do so. Povinelli (2000) suggests that only the great apes (gorillas, chimpanzees, bonobos and orangutans) have this ability. Others claim that quite a wide range of species including sea-lions, cats, dogs and even fishes do attend to images of themselves in mirrors in ways that suggest self-recognition (Gallup 1975).

- *Supporting evidence* – As Pearce points out, however, whilst the evidence for the apes stands up well (such studies have been well controlled and replicated), for most non-ape species, it is very much the researchers' view that their animals use mirrors in convincing ways. For one non-ape, however, there is now clear evidence that they are able to use mirrors in ways that suggest self-recognition. Plotnik *et al.* (2006) demonstrated that elephants could use mirrors to observe marks on their bodies, which they touch with their trunks.

> **Activity** **Do elephants recognize themselves in mirrors?**
>
> Judge for yourself how well this stands up to scrutiny by viewing a video clip of elephants using mirrors at: www.pnas.org/content/103/45/17053/suppl/DC1

Tactical deception

The mirror test suggests self-recognition does occur in non-human animals, at least for apes and elephants. But is self-recognition sufficient evidence of an ability to infer the state of 'mind' of another individual? One way of testing this would be to see whether animals can use planned **tactical deception**. Arguably, planned tactical deception can only be achieved if you have some notion of the mental state of another; – to tell the truth, all you have to do is report what you have seen, but to deceive, you first have to know something about the mental state of the one you are deceiving.

Deception and Machiavellian intelligence in animals

Psychologists have long wondered why it is that the primates (including humans) appear to be more intelligent than other species. One theory, which has been around since the 1980s, has come to be known as the **Machiavellian intelligence hypothesis** (Humphrey 1982; Whiten and Byrne 1988; Pearce 2008). This is a social theory of animal intelligence and consciousness and it is rather a dark one. The idea is that we, and possibly other highly social primates, developed a theory of mind in order to manipulate each other. By being able, to some small degree, to look into another's 'mind', our primate ancestors may have been able to predict how others are likely to respond and therefore to manipulate their responses. This would have had a huge selective advantage over those who did not have this ability (no matter how slight). This hypothesis suggests that highly intelligent, social animals may have developed this ability in order to deceive and manipulate others.

The original theory of mind (TOM)

Key research: Woodruff and Premack (1979)

The original theory of mind (TOM) test was developed for use with chimpanzees in a classic study by Woodruff and Premack (1979) before it was used to test young children. In order to examine the notion that chimps might have a theory of mind, Woodruff and Premack allowed a chimpanzee to observe a man hiding food under one of two possible containers that were out of reach of the chimp. The man then left the room. One of two other men would then enter the room. One of the men was a 'cooperator' (the chimp had previously seen him acting in a friendly way) and the other a 'competitor' (the chimp had previously seen him acting in a hostile manner). To ensure that the chimp could distinguish between the men, the cooperator was dressed in 'normal' clothes, whereas the competitor was dressed as a bandit. Remember only the chimp saw where the food was hidden. In order to gain the food, the chimp had to guide the cooperator to the correct container by pointing or staring. If the chimp was able to do this, then this man would open the container and give the food to the chimp. When, however, the competitor entered the room, the chimp would still be able to earn the food reward provided he directed this man to the container that did not contain the food.

Woodruff and Premack ran the test with four different chimpanzees and observed that all four were able to guide the cooperator to the food and two were able to guide the competitor away from the food, suggesting that they had an understanding of the intentions of each man. For the successful chimps, Woodruff and Premack suggested that they guided the cooperator to the food 'knowing' that he would hand it over, whereas they guided the competitor away from the food 'knowing' that he

would not give it to them had they guided him to it. This might be taken as impressive evidence that chimpanzees can use intentional communication and tactical deception. This, in turn, might suggest they do possess a theory of mind. In today's language we might call it an example of Machiavellian intelligence.

Evaluation

- It might, however, be open to another, simpler interpretation. Methodologically, the chimps needed a large number of training trials before they were able to guide the cooperator towards, and the competitor away from, the food. With this degree of training, it might be suggested that they were associating certain responses with specific men and that this led to an association with specific outcomes (as in classical conditioning discussed earlier). It might be the equivalent of, say, salivating to meat powder but not to wood shavings, rather than actually understanding the intentions of the two men.

- In terms of strengths, the design made use of two conditions (cooperative trainer condition and competitive trainer condition) that might be compared, and the chimps were unable to touch the containers themselves and hence had to guide the men to them. Also four chimps were used rather than reporting the behaviour of just one.

- We should bear in mind, however, that two of the chimps were unable to guide the competitor away from the food. Also, the lab-based set up was quite artificial compared to the natural habitat of chimpanzees. Hence the jury is still out on how we might interpret the findings of Woodruff and Premack.

Tactical deception in the field

While Woodruff and Premack's lab-based study is open to more than one interpretation, there are now well-documented field observations of primate social behaviour that suggest they are able to deceive in a way that necessitates an awareness of the mental state of others. Richard Byrne (1994) has described the sexual behaviour of males in gorilla troops, where normally only the dominant male silverback has access to the mature females for mating purposes. Sometimes, subordinate male gorillas will sneak off and mate with a female in **oestrus** (i.e. during her fertile period) in a hidden place. Moreover, both gorillas will inhibit the calls that gorillas normally make during mating. Similarly, in a troop of captive chimpanzees, Frans de Waal (1989) described 'sneaky' copulations. Dominant alpha male chimps constantly keep an eye on the lower ranking males and on the fertile females, but one particular low-ranking male

called 'Dandy' would often meet up with a particular female in oestrus behind rocks and bushes. They would copulate behind a large rock with their top half showing, but both would act as if eating, and, again, Dandy would inhibit the normal shrieks that chimps make during mating.

Since the females were willing parties to the deception, it could be asked why don't they just go for the biggest, most dominant male? To speculate, female apes might find clever males 'sexy' since it would pay them to have clever offspring. Whether or not this is the case, females may at least increase the variability of their offspring by mating with a range of different males. Such behaviour patterns are difficult to explain in terms of classical or operant conditioning, and today, many animal behaviourists consider that the internal states of at least some non-human animals might be more similar to our own than the old, behaviourist tradition would have us believe.

Evaluation of tactical deception in the field

- *Helps to pass on genes* – These behaviour patterns suggest to both Byrne and de Waal that these apes have developed a theory of mind and that this is evidence that they were making use of knowledge of the internal states of other individuals in order to achieve their Machiavellian aims. Note that in relation to evolution, one strength of these observations is that the observed behaviour patterns may well have helped these individuals to pass on their genes and, since genes are the ultimate currency of natural selection, they fit in well with the approach of evolutionary psychology.

- *High ecological validity* – Observing the behaviour of chimps in their natural environment means that ecological validity is high. In comparison to the relatively artificial context of the **Sally Anne test** (see p.289), these observations took place without human intervention and training.

- *Lack of control and the need for interpretation* – As with all field observations, there is no control group and the researchers' conclusions are very much based on their impressions of each animal's behaviour. In de Waal's observations of chimpanzees, for example, Dandy might just have happened to have been behind a large rock when copulating with a female (Pearce 2008).

Topic 3: Evolution of intelligence

Evolutionary factors in the development of human intelligence

You sit here reading this with a brain approximately the size of a grapefruit (around 1500 cubic centimetres), yet your ancient ancestors from four million years ago (the *Australopithecines*) had to make do with a satsuma-sized brain (about a quarter of the size at 450 cubic centimetres). The brain of these **hominids** (early human ancestors) is comparable to modern-day chimps (*Pan troglodytes*), the species we shared a common ancestor with around some five million years ago. These facts beg two questions:

1. 450 cubic centimetres is a very large brain by vertebrate standards and requires explanation (i.e. compared to its body size, this is almost twice the size predicted).

2. 1500 is enormous by any standards and also needs explaining (i.e. compared to body size this is almost four times what would be predicted).

So why do primates have large brains and why has our brain quadrupled in size in a mere four million years?

Activity — How many people receive your Christmas cards?

Dunbar claims that on average we send Christmas cards to around 150 people (this figure includes all members of the family that receive each card). If some in your family keep a 'Christmas card list' then get hold of this and try to work out how many individuals will receive these cards (again you would need to work out how many are in each family group). Is this figure close to Dunbar's?

The role of ecological factors

Currently, there are two competing theories to explain the evolution of human intelligence. The first of these considers the role of *ecological factors*, i.e. a large intelligent brain arose as a result of the pressures of foraging within their **arboreal** (tree living) environment.

Psychology in context — One hundred and fifty people is just enough

Professor Robin Dunbar of Oxford University claims that the human brain has evolved to deal with 150 social contacts (Dunbar 1992). 'Dunbar's number', as it has become known, is based on the ratio of our **neocortex** ('new cortex' – the recently evolved part of the outer covering of a mammal's brain) to the rest of the brain. By plotting the correlation between social group size and neocortex size for a series of primates, he was able to work out how large a human social group 'should be'.

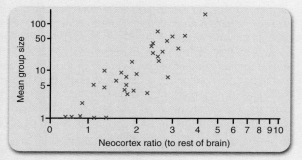

Figure 7.6 *Dunbar's number*

Dunbar considers that humans have evolved to a position where we can maintain stable relationships with approximately 150 individuals. The question is does this figure stand up to scrutiny? Dunbar suggests that on average the following all add up to around 150 people each:

- christmas card lists (including named family members)
- ideal size for church congregations
- the maximum number of members for online games
- the average village size recorded in the Doomsday Book in 1086 AD.

All of this appears to support the notion of Dunbar's number, but we might ask has he selected groupings that fit his number best? How meaningful are our relationships with 150 people? I might send Christmas cards to 50 people and they may have an average of three named people on each card, but in many cases I don't really know the other two named family members to the extent that I can consider them a part of my social network.

Arboreal foraging and savannah hunting

A large proportion of herbivores spend a great deal of their time grazing grass on the open savannah or prairie. Gaining access to this source of nutrients does not pose much in the way of an intellectual challenge, and grazing herbivores have small brains relative to body size. Carnivores, by way of contrast, have to locate, capture, kill and consume their prey. Hence, carnivores tend to have relatively larger brains to support their greater problem solving capabilities. This, of course, gives them a greater range of behavioural responses (and is almost certainly why most of us have the carnivorous cats and dogs as pets rather than grazing animals).

So, how do primates fit into this pattern? The vast majority of primates are arboreal and many of these are **frugivorous** (fruit eaters) (Leakey and Lewin 1992). It is known that such primates require quite high-powered perceptual and cognitive skills for successful foraging. Unlike grass, fruit has to be searched for, as a limited number of trees will have ripe fruit at any given time within the forest – hence a selective pressure to improve both memory and navigational skills. Such fruits have to be identified by their colours and gathered efficiently within a three-dimensional setting. For those primates that do not rely on fruit but consume nuts or leaves, there may also be problems to solve. Nuts have to be opened and many leaves have prickles or develop toxins if eaten when they are too old. Such feeding is known as **extractive foraging** since the food has to be dealt with rather then just grazed. So, even for non-frugivorous primates, arboreal feeding leads to cognitive demands. Such demands, so the argument goes, led to the increase in brain size for primates.

Tool use during foraging

In the case of our closest relative, the chimpanzee, the diet has become more varied and includes insects, meat and nuts. Gathering all of these extra sources of food require extra intellectual skills. Termites, for example, are extracted from crevices by placing a stripped grass stem inside and waiting for the insects to attack this probe, before retrieving it and licking them off (Goldsmith and Zimmerman 2001). Eating nuts may require the ability of learning how to break their shells open with a heavy piece of wood or a stone (i.e. primitive tool use), and meat requires hunting skills.

Whilst we humans were never chimps, we did share a common ancestor with them. Hence, some experts have argued that the road to the modern-day human brain began with chimpanzee-like ancestors expanding their range of diet and that this may have predated the *Homo/Pan* split. Having come out of the forests and onto the open savannah, the potential to exploit 'game' was vastly increased for hominids and this required cooperative hunting that further increased brain size and intelligence. In particular during the period between two million and 200 000 years ago, our ancestors began to develop complex stone tools that were clearly used for hunting and butchering of prey (Goldsmith and Zimmerman 2001). Hence indirectly, the brain increased in size through developments first in gathering and then in hunting (which collectively we can call foraging).

Chimpanzees breaking open nuts

Evaluation of ecological explanations of intelligence

- *Cause or effect?* – Although many mammalian species forage extractively (see Photo above), there is no clear evidence of a relationship between this form of feeding and overall intelligence (Parker and Gibson 1979). It may be argued that more complex forms of feeding follow the evolution of a larger brain rather than vice versa.

- *The cost of having a large brain* – The change from eating vegetation and fruit to meat may have led to improvements in brain function, but the development of meat eating may also have had a costly side effect – the increasing incidence of schizophrenia. Horrobin (1998) proposes that the biochemical changes resulting from these dietary changes increased brain size, improved neural connectivity and led to creative intelligence, but also produced a series of disordered behaviour patterns such as paranoia and mild **sociopathy**. These were kept in check by sufficient dietary levels of the essential fatty acids, which modern diets tend to replace with saturated fatty acids. As levels of essential fatty acids have dropped in the modern diet, the very behaviours that led to the development of human intelligence are expressed in the more extreme behaviours of schizophrenia and manic depression.

The social complexity hypothesis

Explanations based on social complexity argue that the complexity of social pressures faced by our ancestors led to the evolution of a large brain. We have already considered the notion of the development a theory of mind and the Machiavellian theory of intelligence in primates that relies on this. Both ideas suggest that, for primates, the driving evolutionary force was dealing with *social* factors rather than foraging activities. This 'social theory of intelligence' suggests that our ancestors developed intelligence further by building upon pre-existing primate intellectual abilities (i.e. the relatively large brains needed to deal with complex extractive foraging), to develop skills of social cognition.

Why should this be the case? Dunbar (1992) has suggested that as group size increases, so does brain size for primates (see earlier). Dunbar noted that social primates spend a great deal of their time grooming each other and that, in addition to removing parasites, this serves to maintain social bonds in the group. When early hominids came out onto the open savannah, they became more likely to encounter the large carnivores such as the big cats. For safety reasons, this led to the formation of larger groups but this, in turn, led to problems of social complexity. Since grooming appears to be the main way in which primates maintain social bonds, the larger the group the more time they have to spend grooming. Human ancestors dealt with this problem of greater social complexity by evolving language (and a large brain to support this), which was used very much for gossip in order to groom socially more than one individual at a time. Having formed larger social groups, humans could then use these to engage in hunting coalitions and the sharing of meat. At this point the social brain hypothesis overlaps with the foraging explanations of intelligence.

HOW SCIENCE WORKS

Can apes use language?

Key research: Rumbaugh (1977)

Psychologists have long argued over whether or not apes can learn to use language. One advocate of animal language, Duane Rumbaugh (1977) considers that chimpanzees are capable of simple language – but since their vocal tract does not allow for the production of many of the human-like sounds, he has made use of a keyboard with special symbols to examine this possibility. In Rumbaugh's research, both common chimps and pygmy chimps (also known as bonobos) were trained to press keys (linked to a high-powered computer) that symbolize specific words ('lexigrams'). Pressing one of these lexigrams leads to a specific symbol being projected onto a screen above the keyboard. In order to create a sentence each chimp has to press the keys in a sequence that then leads to a string of lexigrams appearing on the screen. Such sentences have to obey the grammatical rules of an artificial language called '**Yerkish**' (broadly

similar to English). In an early study, Rumbaugh (1977) described a number of sentences produced by a chimpanzee called Lana including 'Please machine give juice'. In addition to 'writing sentences' the computer was also programmed to instruct the chimps to carry out various tasks via Yerkish. Typically, instructions might include 'Lana give Sue Apple', which typically Lana obeyed. Through this set-up Rumbaugh claims that different types of chimp are able both to produce and to understand a form of language at a level similar to a young child (Rumbaugh 1977). There are a number of reasons for this claim. First, four-word sentences are regularly put together with correct syntax. Second, when presented with four-word instructions, Lana and others were able to comply. These facts may be taken as evidence that chimps *can* learn to understand language.

Evaluation

Methodologically, such studies have both strengths and weaknesses allowing for other interpretations. As with the study of Woodruff and Premack discussed earlier, in Rumbaugh's studies chimps require a great deal of training in order to learn the lexigrams; in contrast, children appear to soak up the meaning of new words very rapidly (Pearce 2008). Also, Yerkish is not a naturally occurring language but one that was devised to aid these apes in their communications and as such has a simplified grammar compared to other languages (Hayes 1994).

In their favour (of both Rumbaugh and his 'participants'), the chimps did often record strings of four lexigrams that made grammatical sense. Later studies conducted by Duane Rumbaugh's wife Sue Savage-Rumbaugh, using mainly bonobos, suggests that these apes are able to follow instructions that contain subclauses such as 'Show me the ball that's on TV,' 'Put on the monster mask and scare Linda,' (Savage-Rumbaugh and Lewin 1994). Despite these impressive feats, many sceptics such as Pinker (1994) remain unconvinced, considering that apes such as the bonobos do not really understand the symbols, but are merely reacting in ways that they have learned to associate with gaining food and other rewards such as attention (the initial training generally involves the rewards of food or attention).

Evaluation of the social brain hypothesis of intelligence

- *Social complexity does correlate with neocortex size* – A number of measures of social complexity of primates correlate well with the size of neocortex tissue. Such measures include the size of the social group (Dunbar 1992), the numbers involved in grooming cliques (Kudo and Dunbar 2001) and the time spent engaged in social play (Lewis 2001).

- *Language is used mostly to gossip* – Specifically in relation to gossip, cross-culturally 60 to 70 per cent of all conversations consist of gossip (this is true for both men and women, Dunbar *et al.* 1995). This might be taken as evidence that gossip is an essential part of human nature.

- *Cause or effect?* – The problems of dealing with a large group size might have led to a larger brain, but evolving a larger brain (for some other purpose) might then have led to an expansion of the group's size (Workman and Reader 2008).

The role of genetic and environmental factors associated with intelligence test performance

Although evolutionists debate the nature of the pressures that led to our intellectual prowess, they do at least agree that it came about due to the advantages that this gives us over other species. This being the case, we might ask why do we vary so much in intelligence? In order to explore this question, it is necessary to gain an understanding of the biological and environmental causes of this variability.

The role of genetic factors – do genes 'determine' intelligence?

Psychologists have long debated the extent to which intelligence is determined by inheritance (nature) on the one hand and by the environment (nurture) on the other. This nature/nurture debate is not a question of either/or, but concerns the relative contributions of each to differences between people. One way of answering this question is to estimate the extent to which individuals differ from each other for a specific feature because of genetic differences between them. This is known as the **heritability** of a trait and may be thought of as the proportion of the **trait** (characteristic) that is due to genes rather than to the environment. Heritability can vary from 0 to 1.0 (i.e. no genetic influence to total genetic influence). A series of studies examining the correlations between various relatives (and in particular twins) under different rearing conditions by Plomin *et. al.* (2001) suggested a heritability of 0.68 for IQ test results. Hence, according to Plomin *et al.*, around two-thirds of the variance in IQ scores is accounted for by genetic factors. It is important to realize that heritability studies are attempts to understand the sources of differences between members of a population not attempts to determine how much of an individual's intelligence (or any other trait) is due to genes (Mackintosh, 1998).

> ### Approaches: behavioural genetics
>
> **Behavioural genetics** is an approach that attempts to partition out the relative contributions of genes and environment to behaviour. By giving personality or IQ tests to **monozygotic (MZ)** twins (identical twins who share all genes by common descent) and **dizygotic (DZ)** twins (non-identical identical twins who share half of their genes by common descent) and then examining the correlation between scores, behavioural geneticists can estimate to what extent genes are involved in a given trait. The rationale underlying this is that, since MZ twins share all of their genes and DZ ones share only half of theirs (by common descent), then if genes are important determinants of IQ, the former will have a much higher positive correlation between their scores than the latter. In fact when reared together, IQ correlations for MZ twins average 0.87 in contrast to the correlation of 0.53 for DZ twins. Interestingly, when reared apart the correlation between scores for MZ twins is still very high at 0.74 (Plomin 1988). Behavioural genetics traces its theoretical approach back to the evolutionary approach, in that it assumes genes selected by evolutionary processes underlie intelligence.

The Minnesota Twin study

Key research: Bouchard *et al.* (1990)

The study of twins has helped us to understand better the heritability of intelligence. The biggest study of this kind was conducted by Tom Bouchard and his co-workers (Bouchard *et al.* 1990) and is known as the 'Minnesota Study of Twins Reared Apart' (MISTRA). The research involved tracing pairs of identical and non-identical twins who were separated either at birth or during early childhood and giving each member of the pair 50 hours of psychological and medical tests. In this way, Bouchard has been able to look at the correlation coefficients between scores on physical ability, personality and, importantly for our purpose, intelligence.

This study has found similar correlation coefficients to the work of Plomin and colleagues outlined above, with correlations of 0.69 for MZ twins reared apart and correlations of 0.88 for those reared together. In addition to the overall trends in the data, however, are some remarkable individual cases. An example of this is the case of Gerald Levy and Mark Newman, identical twins separated shortly after birth who,

when they met up as adults, had both become firemen, had both grown sideburns and moustaches and both wore metal-rimmed aviator style glasses. Additionally, the twins had voices that were indistinguishable and had identical mannerisms. While such similarities are uncanny, most cases do not reveal quite this level of similarity and it is the overall data we need to concentrate on.

Evaluation

In terms of methodology, the MISTRA had two parts, medical and psychological. Once twins (both MZ and DZ) reared apart had been detected and had agreed to take part, they were then given a week-long medical (including the wearing of a 24-hour heart monitor and a psychiatric interview). Additionally, spouses of each pair were interviewed with a view to determining how similar or dissimilar they were. Finally, a series of psychological assessments (including measures of personality, reading and spelling ability) were carried out on each twin pair and correlations performed on the data. MISTRA was arguably methodologically sound and extremely thorough. It might be argued, of course, that only people who were, say, extrovert might come forward and that this, in turn, might have reduced the variability of the participants. It should be noted that the non-identical twins were acting as controls for the identical ones (i.e. even though the tendency to volunteer might have screened out the more introvert participants, the important point is how similar were the identical twins to each other in comparison to the non-identical ones).

Identical twins

Evaluation of behavioural genetics twin studies

Although the twin studies of both Plomin *et al.* (2001) and of Bouchard *et al.* (1990) have generally been well designed, heritability studies of intelligence are not without their criticisms. Criticisms include the following:

- *Identical twins are expected to act the same* – MZ twins are likely to be treated more similarly than DZ ones even to the point of being dressed identically. Cooper (2002) claims that this might lead to them developing greater cognitive similarities.

- *Not randomly assigned to households* – Unlike a controlled experiment, twins reared apart are not assigned randomly to adoptive homes, but rather these are selected for them (Haugaard and Hazan 2003). Hence, they might be adopted by similar families, which might lead to a greater degree of similarity. An example of this was a pair called Oskar and Jack, who demonstrated very similar habits and preferences for clothes. It was later discovered,

however, that they were raised by relatives, that they had met briefly as young adults and that their wives regularly wrote to each other. This might increase positive correlations between IQ and other measures.

- *Birth trauma* – Twin studies may not be entirely representative of the population as a whole, since twins are more susceptible to birth trauma, such as the reduction of oxygen to the brain. This might then affect development of both individuals (Littlefield *et al.* 1999). Since birth trauma can lead to damage at this early stage in development then, if more MZ than DZ twins suffer from trauma, their IQ scores are likely to be affected.

- *Counter evidence* – When Devlin *et al.* (1997) conducted a **meta-analysis** of nine family studies, they uncovered a figure for heritability of 0.48, which is clearly lower than those produced by Plomin and Bouchard. Hence, conveniently, we can think of genes and environment as contributing around 50 per cent each to differences between individuals in IQ scores.

Have specific genes been identified for intelligence?

Despite the criticisms of heritability studies, it is clear that genes *do* have an influence on intelligence. Until the last decade or so, using correlational data from different family members was the only way to estimate the influence of genes on intelligence. But this is only scratching the surface when it comes to understanding the role that genes play in intelligence. We might ask which genes are involved and just how do they influence intelligence? Genes are found on specific locations on a chromosome called **loci** (the singular is **locus**). At each locus there will be one of a range of possible alternative genes. Genes are labelled by letters and numbers rather like a car number plate, so that no two genes (or number plates) are the same. One gene on chromosome six, known as IGF2R ('insulin-like growth factor 2 receptor'), was discovered in the late 1990s to be associated with intelligence. Different versions of this gene (**alleles**) are associated with different degrees of intelligence (Plomin *et al.* 1997). For some time this was the only gene discovered that appeared to affect IQ test performance. Recently, however, another gene has been uncovered that appears to have quite specific effects on a person's ability to organize things logically, such as placing items in the correct sequence. This gene has been found on chromosome seven and has been labelled CHMR2 (Dick *et al.* in press). Once again, different versions of this gene seem to boost (or depress

if you have the 'wrong' allele) test performance by around 4 to 5 IQ points. Interestingly, whether or not you have the 'best' version of this gene has no effect on performance on other aspects of IQ such as verbal acumen. Such a finding might be taken as supportive evidence for Gardner's view of multiple intelligences.

How do genes for intelligence work?

Finding out that genes are involved in intelligence might be taken as some support for the nature side of the intelligence debate, but we also need to understand how such genes work. In the case of IGF2R, versions of the gene are believed to alter brain growth, whereas for CHMR2, it appears that different versions of the gene activate a large number of signalling pathways in the brain that are involved to different degrees in memory, learning and attention. This demonstrates that genes may affect intelligence in a number of different ways.

With the uncovering of IGF2R and CHMR2, it may seem as if researchers are suggesting genetic determinism of intelligence, but it should be pointed out that these specific genes account for small changes in IQ points. Currently, behavioural geneticists think that there may be as many as 100 different genes involved in intelligence and that each of these in turn may be affected by the environment (both internal and external).

Environmental factors in intelligence test performance

Having established that genes account for around 50 per cent or 0.5 of the variation in intelligence, we now have to account for the 0.5 contributed by environmental factors. What sort of environmental factors affect intelligence?

In terms of the effects of the environment on the development of an individual's intelligence (or indeed personality), there are two separate influences – the **shared environment** (i.e. influences common to all siblings) and the **non-shared environment** (experiences specific to that child such as interactions with peers and teachers). These two influences together with the genes should explain 100 per cent of the variability in intelligence. Hence:

Genes + shared environment + non-shared environment = 1.0

If the genes account for 0.5 of this, then the next obvious question is what proportion does each of the shared and non-shared environment account for? You might guess at 0.25 each. You would be wrong. Research since the 1990s suggests that the shared environment accounts for very little of the variation, whereas the non-shared environment accounts for the vast majority of the 0.5 left to explain (Harris 1998; 2006). How do we know this? As we saw above, by comparing pairs of MZ twins reared apart with those reared together it has been shown that

there is very little difference in correlations between IQ scores between these pairs (0.74 and 0.87 see above; Plomin *et al.* 1994). Given they share all of their genes, MZ twins reared apart will have different non-shared environments, so if this accounts for much of the variability, then we would expect them to have a much lower correlation that those twins reared together. Moreover, unrelated individuals that are reared as siblings in the same home are only slightly more similar in IQ scores than children living apart and chosen at random (Plomin and Daniels 1987). In this case, no genes are shared by common descent but there is a shared environment. Overall the strongest estimate of the effects of the shared environment on IQ is 0.1 (Turkheimer 2000).

There is evidence, then, that the most important thing that parents provide for their children in terms of intelligence is their genes. The non-shared environment (largely outside the home) appears to be of greater importance than the shared one. We are concerned here of course with the *average effect* of the shared (largely home) environment. When we look at impoverished families, then the home environment might have a more profound (and negative) influence on IQ. Whether this is due to a lack of opportunities to study, lack of resources such as books and computers or a poor diet is yet to be determined.

Socioeconomic status and IQ

Social psychologists and sociologists have often claimed that IQ is determined by opportunity, and that many opportunities are the preserve of those of high socioeconomic status (SES) (Mackintosh 1998). One study that considered SES in relation to IQ uncovered a surprising finding. Turkheimer *et al.* (2003) measured the IQs of twins of families of both low and high SES. Among the poorest families, most of the variability was explained by the shared environment, whereas for the wealthiest families almost none of the variability was determined by the shared environment. What might this tell us? Turkheimer and colleagues concluded that, whilst genes are involved in determining IQ, when an environment is impoverished below a certain level, it may be sufficient to stop an individual from attaining their potential level of intelligence. In contrast for those in high SES families, the environment has reached a 'ceiling' (i.e. the home environment is so conducive to educational attainment that any further improvements are likely to have negligible affects).

Why do we vary in intelligence?

Having examined the relative contribution of nature and nurture to intelligence, we are now in a better position to answer the question why, as a species, we vary so much in measured intelligence. There are at least seven reasons for this variability:

- Since intelligence is due in part to a variety of genes, new combinations due to the mixing-up of genes that occurs every time we reproduce (conception brings half of each partner's genes together) leads to variability.
- The uterine (womb) environment and the environment following birth are likely to have quite a significant effect. Examples of this include the diet of the mother during gestation – alcohol, for example, is known to depress brain development in embryos and there is some evidence that breast feeding boosts IQ a little (Anderson *et al.* 1999).
- It is well known that parental income has a strong positive correlation with IQ, which may be due to features such as the availability of books, computers and room to study.

- For some individuals congenital genetic factors such as Downs' syndrome depress intelligence.
- What we perceive as large differences are actually quite small. IQ test scores for 90 per cent of the population vary from 90 to 110. This appears to suggest that for the majority of the population, there is a 20 percent range in how clever people are but, in reality, compared to our closest relatives, chimps, these are very small differences amplified by IQ tests.
- IQ tests may have a built-in bias as they have been written largely by middle-class, White, Western men. This means that socioeconomic class, ethnicity and even gender might not be taken into account in test construction (but note Mackintosh 1998 below).
- If Gardner (1983; 2006) is correct, then when we use traditional measures we might only be measuring a small proportion of what actually constitutes *intelligent* behaviour.

Intelligence, ethnicity and cultural factors

The study of cultural and ethnic differences between groups has a long and not very illustrious history. Debates about the differences between various ethnic groups and their source was hotly contested throughout the 20th century (Ridley 2003) and was rekindled by the publication of *The Bell Curve* by Herrnstein and Murray in 1994. Herrnstein and Murray presented evidence that White Americans outperformed their Black African-American counterparts on IQ tests and went on to suggest that this difference was due to genetic differences between these ethnic groups.

Clearly, we need to tread carefully with such claims, as they have both scientific and political repercussions. It has often been argued that, since IQ tests have been constructed by White, middle-class academics, they are biased against people of other ethnicities since they make use of White, middle-class language. There may well be some truth in this argument, but Mackintosh (1998), having studied the evidence, concludes that even 'culture-fair' tests (i.e. where the ability to answer questions should not depend on cultural background) demonstrate this difference. In tests such as **digit span** or block design (where a pattern has to be duplicated using blocks), where cultural factors due to language are unlikely to vary, White Americans still outperform Black ones to a significant degree. Does this suggest that this difference is due to genetic differences between these two groups, as Herrnstein and Murray propose? Mackintosh suggests that because a test is non-verbal and 'culturally fair', then we should not assume that this provides a more direct measure of innate intelligence than verbal tests. The reason is that, although they do not involve language, they are no less learned than linguistic tasks. In fact, there is clear evidence that schooling influences the ability to solve block design and mental arithmetic tasks just as much as it does for solving linguistic-based tasks (Mackintosh 1998). Hence the ethnic background, which may affect the school and the home environment, might, in turn, affect the ability to solve almost any type of test item, even those that are culture fair.

The big question remains whether Herrnstein and Murray were correct in their assertion that there are genetically based reasons for the differences between Black and White

Americans' scores on IQ tests? In fact, there is a strong likelihood that they were mixing up ethnicity with socioeconomic class. Twenty years prior to the publication of *The Bell Curve*, Scarr and Weinberg (1976) had already demonstrated that, when Black children from low-**SES** families are adopted by White high-SES parents, they then perform on IQ tests at the same level as their White counterparts.

As we saw earlier, the form of intelligence that IQ tests 'reveal' is very much a product of the European and North American educational systems and culture. Other cultures have quite different views of what it means to be intelligent. Many African cultures, for example, place more emphasis on cooperation and obedience (especially within the family context) in what is considered to be intelligent behaviour (Sternberg 2000). Likewise, Chinese and Taiwanese people view self-knowledge and the ability to act in a socially appropriate manner as signs of intelligence (Yang and Sternberg 1997). Hence, it is entirely possible that individuals from non-Western cultures might have developed other aspects of intelligence rather than aspects measured by IQ tests. It is also possible that the motivation to perform well on such tests varies between cultures, which might lead to a reduction in performance for people of non-Western cultures.

Debates: Targeting educational resources

Compensatory education projects attempt to boost the educational attainment of children from low socioeconomic class by funnelling educational resources to poorer households (Mackintosh 1998). The 'Milwaukee Project' that took place in the 1960s spent $14 million to boost the IQs of 20 children by providing them with extra education from the age of three months to five or six years of age. Tuition was provided by trained professionals five days a week for 12 months each year. After five years, when compared with 20 control children, the IQ scores were raised by around 10 points for this small group (Spitz 1986). The Milwaukee Project opens debates about the cost of such initiatives and the lack of resources for control groups.

Gene/environment interactions and 'interactionism'

No doubt, when it comes to human intelligence, the nature vs. nurture debate will long continue. In a sense, however, this debate is redundant as it really is not a question of nature versus nurture but rather what is the nature of the interaction between the two in determining a person's level of intelligence. In his book *Nature via Nurture*, Ridley has pointed out that 'Genes are designed to take their cues from nurture' (Ridley 2003), demonstrating the interactionist nature of intellectual development by suggesting that genes can only fulfil their potential given the right environmental conditions. Such environmental factors include everything from the quality of the air we breathe to our diet, the friends we decide to make, the influences of our parents and teachers, and microorganisms and toxins that invade our bodies

throughout life. We should also bear in mind that a person's inherited abilities and motivations might make them more likely to seek out certain specific stimuli, which then boost their abilities in that area. In this sense, the environment is partly selected by the genes, which then increase the effects of those genes. Ultimately, completely disentangling nature from nurture may be a futile activity.

Activity: Using the internet to explore debates surrounding the relationship between genes and environment

Using the internet, try to find further information regarding the interactive relationship between genes and environment. In particular, try to find ways in which the environment might affect how an animal's genes work and how the genes might affect the environment of the animal.

Tip: a good starting point might be to consider the activity of beavers!

CHECK YOUR UNDERSTANDING

Check your understanding of the evolution of intelligence by answering these questions. Try to do this from memory. You can check your answers by looking back through Topic 3, Evolution of intelligence.

1. What is Dunbar's number? List three pieces of evidence that support Dunbar's number.

2. What is the arboreal foraging hypothesis that has been put forward to explain the evolution of primate intelligence?

3. What is the social brain hypothesis that has been put forward to explain the evolution of primate intelligence?

4. What does it mean to state that intelligence shows a heritability of 0.68?

5. How do behavioural geneticists partition out the relative contributions of genes and environment to behaviour?

6. Outline three criticisms of the studies of twins by Plomin and Bouchard in relation to the heritability of intelligence.

7. Name two genes that have been implicated in the development of intelligence. If each of these contributes up to five points in IQ, what would it mean if 20 genes were uncovered that contribute to intelligence?

8. Outline four reasons why people vary in their degree of intelligence.

9. What central claims did *The Bell Curve* make?

10. Do these claims stand up to scrutiny?

The psychometric approach

Psychometric approach deals with:

1 Design of tests to measure intelligence
2 Measurement of intelligence

Evaluation:

- Labelling with IQ leads to self-fulfilling prophecies
- Supports biological determinism of intelligence
- Intelligence not measurable by a single number
- Only taps into a small subset of the actual abilities
- Variety of tests do correlate with future achievement

The information-processing approach

Sternberg's Triarchic theory

1 Contextual subtheory
2 Experiential subtheory
3 Computational subtheory

Evaluation:

- Highlights importance of experience – leads to high ecological validity
- So broad it appears to overlap with personality (Cooper 2002)
- Too many components – incoherent and hard to see how they interact

Ceci's bio-ecological theory

1 Biologically based potentials
2 Contingent on opportunities and challenges of environment

Evaluation:

- High ecological validity
- Differences may be due to culture, but hard to test this
- So broad as to overlap with personality

Gardner's theory of multiple intelligences

Eight different and independent 'intelligences'

1 Linguistic
2 Spatial
3 Logical-mathematical
4 Musical
5 Bodily-kinesthetic
6 Interpersonal
7 Intrapersonal
8 Naturalistic

Evaluation:

- Autistic savants offer support
- But linguistic, visuospatial and logical-mathematical do correlate positively with each other (Cooper 2002)
- Difficult to test intelligences 4–8
- Modularity theory (Fodor 1983) supports theory of multiple intelligences
- Brain damage can lead to specific deficits

Classical conditioning

Learning to make an association between two events (Pavlov)

1 Naturally occurring reflex (the UCS-UCR reflex) is associated with another stimulus (the CS)
2 After consistent association with the UCS, the new stimulus then triggers the response (the CR)

Evaluation:

- Biological preparedness (Seligman 1970)
- How universal is classical conditioning? Species differ in terms of motives, capacities and need to learn

Operant conditioning

Involves an animal operating on the environment:

1 Learning dependent on outcome of a response
2 Positively reinforcing a response makes it more likely to happen; negatively reinforcing it makes it less likely to happen

Evaluation:

- Instinctive drift back to inherited patterns (Breland & Breland 1951)
- Incompatibility of responses
- Operant or classical behaviour? Often hard to tell which is responsible (Mackintosh 1981)

Evidence for intelligence in non-human animals

1 Comparing speed of learning helps us understand relative levels of intelligence in animal species (Angermeier 1984)
2 Smaller brained animals learned a simple discrimination task faster than larger brained ones

Evaluation:

- Is the information retained?
- Fair to use infants to represent humans?
- Use of same task allows for comparison

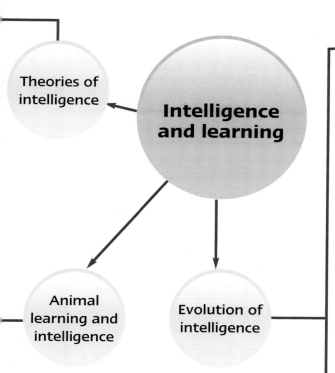

Theories of intelligence

Intelligence and learning

Animal learning and intelligence

Evolution of intelligence

1 Primates have large brains
2 Humans have large brains even by primate standards

Role of ecological factors

1 Arboreal foraging requires large brain
2 Savannah foraging lead to larger brain still
3 Tool use increased brain size further still

Evaluation:

◼ Cause or effect?
◼ Mental illnesses = cost of having a large brain?

Social complexity hypothesis

1 Complexity of social pressures led to large brain
2 Overlaps with Machiavellian intelligence hypothesis
3 Social complexity on savannah for hunting/protection

Evaluation:

◼ Social complexity correlates with brain size (Dunbar 1992)
◼ Language used mostly to gossip (Dunbar *et al.* 1995)

Theory of mind and self-recognition in animals

Theory of mind

1 Ability to impute states of mind to others
2 Self-recognition – prerequisite for theory of mind
3 Mirror test used – passed by some animals

Evaluation:

◼ Povinelli (2000): only great apes have this ability
◼ Plotnik *et al.* (2006): elephants also pass mirror test

Tactical deception

1 Use by animals = strong support
2 Machiavellian intelligence hypothesis (Whiten and Byrne 1988)
3 Deception used in both lab experiments and observations

Evaluation:

◼ Level of training suggests classical conditioning involved
◼ Deception aids passing on genes (natural selection)
◼ Field observations have high ecological validity
◼ Field observations have lack of control and open to field worker's interpretation

Role of genetic and environmental factors in intelligence test performance

Heritability and behavioural genetics

1 Heritability is an estimate of proportion of differences between individuals that is due to genetic differences
2 Behavioural geneticists attempt to partition out contribution of genes to a trait
3 Twin studies important – suggest genes contribute strongly to intelligence (Plomin 1988)
4 MISTRA – MZ twins very similar in IQ (& personality)

Evaluation:

◼ Self-fulfilling prophecy of expectations (Cooper 2002)
◼ Twins assigned to similar households (not random)
◼ Birth trauma? Twin studies not entirely representative of population (Littlefield *et al.* 1999)

Environmental factors in test performance

1 Genes account for 0.5 of variability in intelligence
2 Non-shared environment accounts for 0.4 and shared environment accounts for 0.1 (Harris 1998)

Evaluation:

◼ 'The Bell Curve' (Herrnstein and Murray 1994)
◼ Socio-cultural differences rather than 'racial' ones
◼ Genes and environment interact throughout life

Cognition and development

EXPLAINING THE SPECIFICATION

Specification content	The specification explained
Development of thinking (Topic 1)	**In this part of the specification you are required to know about three explanations (theories) of how our thought processes develop and discuss how these ideas can be applied to education. To do this, you need to be able to:**
Theories of cognitive development, including Piaget, Vygotsky and Bruner	■ Describe and evaluate Piaget's, Vygotsky's and Bruner's theories of cognitive development. ■ Describe and evaluate research that underpins each of these theories.
Applications of these theories to education	■ Discuss how the theoretical ideas of Piaget, Vygotsky and Bruner have been applied to educational practice.
Development of moral understanding (Topic 2)	**In this part of the specification you are required to know about at least one theory of moral understanding: Kohlberg's theory and/or Eisenberg's theory of prosocial reasoning. To do this, you need to be able to:**
Theories of moral understanding (Kohlberg) and/or prosocial reasoning (Eisenberg)	■ Describe and evaluate Kohlberg's theory of moral understanding, including relevant research. and/or ■ Describe and evaluate Eisenberg's theory of prosocial reasoning, including relevant research.
Development of social cognition (Topic 3)	**In this part of the specification you are required to explain how children develop (a) a sense of self, and (b) an understanding of others, and know how social understanding is explained from a biological perspective. To do this, you need to be able to:**
Development of the child's sense of self, including Theory of Mind (Baron-Cohen)	■ Explain how children develop their sense of self – this should include Baron-Cohen's Theory of Mind. ■ Describe and evaluate research that has investigated children's development of their sense of self.
Development of children's understanding of others, including perspective-taking (Selman)	■ Explain how children's understanding of other people develops over time – this should include Selman's work on perspective taking. ■ Describe and evaluate research that has investigated children's perspective-taking and understanding of others.
Biological explanations of social cognition, including the role of the mirror neuron system	■ Explain the development of social understanding (social cognition) from a biological perspective, including the role of the mirror neuron system. ■ Describe and evaluate research investigating the role of the mirror neuron system on the development of social cognition.

Cognition is the term psychologists use to refer to mental activities. The study of cognitive development focuses on the development of our mental abilities, including thinking, problem-solving, mathematical skills and also the way we think about right and wrong (moral development).

Although Piaget is one of the best known theorists in this field, he is not the only psychologist to have studied the development of cognitive competency in children – Vygotsky and Bruner have also made important contributions in this area. However, many years before the work of any of these psychologists, the issue of how children learn and become competent adult thinkers was addressed by philosophers such as John Locke. Locke was particularly interested in whether we are born equipped with some knowledge or start life with a blank slate (a *tabula rasa*) on which knowledge gained through experience is imprinted. Locke believed that children learn everything through physical and social interactions with their immediate environment which is a key issue in any discussion of cognitive development (see pp.42–45 of the Introductory chapter for a discussion of the nature–nurture debate in psychology).

Piaget's theory of cognitive development is based on detailed observations of children, including his own, and their performance on a number of standardized tests in the 1920s. At about the same time, Vygotsky was doing similar work in Russia, but his work was less known until it was translated into English in the 1960s and 1970s. The work of the American psychologist, Bruner, was initially influenced by Piagetian ideas and then he subsequently built on Vygostky's work.

In Topic 1 we focus on the work of Piaget, Vygotsky and Bruner and consider how their theories have been applied in education. Kohlberg's theory of moral understanding and Eisenberg's theory of prosocial reasoning are discussed in Topic 2. In the final topic on the development of social cognition, Baron-Cohen's theory of mind and Selman's work on perspective-taking and the role of mirror neurons in social cognition are explored. Links are made to Piaget's theory, especially his work on perspective-taking which he undertook long before the theory of mind was conceptualized in relation to human development.

Since the mental processes studied by psychologists working in this field are largely invisible, they have had to devise some quite ingenious tasks to assess the cognitive abilities of infants and young children. As you work through this chapter, you might like to make a note of each new test procedure you read about and jot down a few ideas about whether you think it is meaningful, child-friendly, reliable and valid. At the end of the chapter you could have a class discussion about the effectiveness of the various methods that have been used by Piaget, Vygotsky, Bruner, Kolhlberg, Eisenberg, Baron-Cohen and Selman.

Psychology in context

Real-life examples may not be best for teaching maths

What do you think are the attributes of a good teacher when they are introducing complex abstract ideas? Note down your own ideas and then discuss these with other students in your psychology class in order to arrive at a consensus. Now compare your notes with some recent research findings published in *Science* (a very prestigious scientific journal).

You may have assumed that a good teacher is someone who provides engaging, real-life examples when teaching abstract concepts. However, a new study by Kaminski and colleagues (2008) suggests that when teaching maths, it may be best to keep things abstract. Students were taught the rules governing mathematical relations between three items. All students were able to learn these rules, but only those taught using abstract symbols were able to transfer their learning to a new, real-life situation. Students who had been taught with the aid of water jugs, slices of pizza or tennis balls in a container were less able to transfer their learning.

The effectiveness of a purely abstract teaching approach and an approach that provided concrete examples first, followed by an abstract illustration, were compared in a second experiment. Students in the purely abstract condition performed better than those who were given the concrete/abstract mix. The researchers conclude that although concrete examples may be more engaging, they may also constrain students' ability to apply their knowledge to new situations.

Theories of cognitive development

People used to believe that the main difference between the thinking of children and of adults was that children knew less than adults. However, psychologists have since shown that the way children think is different to the way adults think, and the way younger children think differs from the way that older children think. So how does children's thought develop into more adult-like thought?

Piaget's theory of cognitive development

Jean Piaget (1896–1980) was born in Switzerland and trained initially as a zoologist; he was particularly interested in how animals adapt to their environment. Piaget subsequently applied the concept of adaptation to his study of cognitive development. Early in his career, working alongside Alfred Binet, who was well known for his work on intelligence testing, Piaget became fascinated with how knowledge is acquired. Piaget regarded intelligence as a process that developed over time as a result of biological maturation, enabling a child to adapt to its environment.

Piaget's theory of cognitive development was based on detailed observations of children and their performance on standardized tasks designed to assess mental abilities. He noticed that children of the same age tended to make similar kinds of errors on specific test questions and wanted to find out whether younger and older children were using different rules of logic. Many of the children's errors were predictable and could be explained in terms of a universal, stage-like progression. In other words, the errors made at certain ages indicated a stage of development, and these stages formed a sequence. Piaget suggested that children's thinking changes qualitatively as they pass through the different stages and this formed the basis of his theory of cognitive development.

In this theory, first developed in the 1920s, Piaget (1952, 1970, 1977) claims that children pass through four stages, as their brain, intellect and ability to perceive relationships between variables in their immediate environment mature (see Table 8.1). These stages occur in a fixed order of progression and all children, regardless of their nationality, develop according to these ordered stages. Since a stage cannot be skipped, his theory is described as a universal theory of cognitive development. Piaget's theory focuses on the development of thinking patterns from birth to adulthood, although most of the research has been carried out with children up to the age of 12. You will notice that three of the four stages in Table 8.1 include the term 'operation' and may be wondering what it means in this context. Piaget used this word to refer to logical mental actions/manipulations on objects (such as addition, subtraction, reversibility and serial ordering) and dealing with the relationships between schema.

The sensorimotor stage	
(0 to 2 years)	Infants are born with a set of reflexes which they use to explore and manipulate objects; knowledge of the world develops through their sensory and motor abilities. Between 12 and 18 months, the young child begins to understand the properties and permanence of objects. Piaget identified six sub-stages within the sensorimotor stage.
The pre-operational stage	
(2 to 6 years)	Children use language to represent objects, although their understanding of concepts is general (e.g. a toddler knows the word 'ball' and uses the same word to refer to many other round objects). Although they can perform simple classification tasks, their understanding of the world is limited to their own perspective (**egocentrism**).
The concrete operational stage	
(7 to 11 years)	Children now use logical mental rules and can understand ordering and class inclusion, but only in the context of concrete information and not in relation to abstract ideas. For example, they can only solve the problem 'Mary is taller than Susan, Susan is taller than Ann, who is the tallest?' when it is presented in concrete form (e.g. using dolls).
The formal operational stage	
(from around 12 years of age and continuing into adulthood)	This final stage is characterized by the ability to think in abstract terms, reason logically and draw conclusions from available information. Hypothetical thinking becomes possible rather than more random methods of problem-solving such as trial and error.
Note: the age ranges in this table are only guides and are not fixed; it is the sequence that is important.	

Table 8.1 *Piaget's stages of cognitive development (Piaget 1952)*

Mechanisms underlying Piaget's developmental stages

According to Piaget (1952, 1977), cognitive development is biologically driven, occurring as a result of the maturation of innate structures in the brain, including the senses and reflexes. He also acknowledged the role of experience – that nurture is intertwined with nature, with children constructing their knowledge in response to their experience. Development occurs when:

- the child's brain has matured to a point of 'readiness'

- some new information or experiences that cannot be assimilated into the child's existing understanding challenge the child's thinking.

When this happens, a new experience leads to a major reorganization of existing schema. Piaget used the term **schema** (sometimes referred to as 'scheme') to describe an internalized representation of a physical or mental action that enables an individual to interact with, and understand, the world in which they live. Infants are born with reflex action schema (such as sucking or gripping) and gradually develop simple sensory or motor schemas for tasting, looking and reaching for objects. Over time, ever more complex schemas are developed, enabling individuals to function effectively in their environment.

Piaget's training in zoology may explain why he used the analogy of a mollusc's adaptation to its environment as a metaphor for understanding intellectual development in humans. Bell-Gredler (1986) describes this as follows: 'He [Piaget] found that certain molluscs, transported from their calm-water habitat to turbulent wind-driven waters, developed shortened shells. This construction by the organism was essential for the molluscs to maintain a foothold on the rocks and thereby survive in rough water. Furthermore, these biological changes, which were constructed by the organism in response to an environmental change, were inherited by some descendents of the molluscs. The organism, in response to altered environmental conditions, constructs the specific biological structures that it needs.'

Piaget (1952, 1977) claimed that babies are born with a set of biological processes (which he called 'structures'), including reflexes (such as sucking and grasping) and a set of innate schema. An example of an innate schema is a mental representation of a human face and there is some evidence (e.g. Fantz 1961) which suggests that infants are born with an innate ability to recognize faces. From birth, an infant's schemas develop through interaction with their environment. New experiences lead to the development of new schemas (e.g. infants develop separate schemas for different people's faces).

Piaget proposed two cognitive processes by which schemas become more complex:

- **assimilation** – the process of fitting new information and experiences into existing schemas (i.e. into what a child already knows and understands)

- **accommodation** – the process of modifying an existing schema by expanding it or creating a new one

when new information, a new object or a new situation cannot be assimilated into the original schema.

For example, a young child's schema for a dog may initially be: 'four legs, fur and a wet nose'. Every new case of a creature possessing these characteristics is assimilated into this schema until the child is introduced to 'cat' for a broadly similar creature with four legs and fur; this challenges the existing schema. Since the new information cannot be assimilated into the existing schema, a new schema is formed to accommodate the new information.

The driving force behind these cognitive changes (which Piaget referred to as adaptation) is the biological principle of **equilibration** whereby the intellect strives to maintain a sense of balance (equilibrium). If an experience cannot be assimilated into existing schemas, a state of imbalance (disequilibrium) arises. Cognitive development is the result of adaptation between an individual's existing schema and environmental 'demands' for change, which arise when new experiences or situations do not fit existing schema. (See the box on p.258 for further detail about the important concepts of assimilation, accommodation and equilibration.) Piaget believes that cognitive structures develop through interaction with the environment: experience is important for the construction of new cognitive structures.

The four developmental stages

Each of the four stages is characterized by specific cognitive abilities that operate during a particular stage. Some empirical evidence related to each stage will be briefly examined.

Sensorimotor stage

Piaget's account of the sensorimotor stage is based on his detailed observation of infants, including his own three children. He noticed that early movements are unco-ordinated and that an infant gradually realizes that the

The three cognitive processes involved in the development and refinement of schema

Assimilation involves the integration of new information within existing internal mental structures (i.e. children translate all incoming information into a form they can understand). If a child is shown a coarse-grained rock and is told that it is granite, this new information is assimilated into the existing schema for rocks.

Accommodation, on the other hand, involves adjusting current cognitive structures to allow new information to be understood and appropriately categorized (i.e. current knowledge structures are adapted to accommodate new information). For example, a child who has already developed a cognitive structure (schema) for 'rocks', is introduced to a 'gold nugget' and realizes that although its structure and appearance is similar to a rock, it is not a rock. Since it would not be appropriate to classify a gold nugget as 'a rock', the child has to revise the existing schema to include a new, overarching concept, such as 'mineral', that will encompass both 'rock' and

'gold nugget' while acknowledging their key differences.

Equilibration has a biological origin – any organism must maintain a steady internal state and yet remain open to the environment to deal with new events. The process of equilibration enables a child to develop cognitively while maintaining stability by balancing assimilation and accommodation to create stable understanding. A child may, for example, know that Christmas dinner is likely to include Brussels sprouts and yet also believe that few people actually like Brussels sprouts. This contradiction may cause temporary confusion (disequilibration) in the child's understanding. To deal with this, the child might discover that Brussels sprouts are traditional vegetables for Christmas dinner, are a healthy food and should be eaten, even if they are not particularly liked. Equilibration is restored through the acquisition of this new information.

---

object waving back and forth in front of its eyes is its own hand. Over time, sensory and motor information become co-ordinated and a new schema is constructed.

At the start of the sensorimotor stage, an infant learns to manipulate objects but, according to Piaget, does not understand the permanency of these objects. In other words, once an object is removed from the infant's immediate visual field, he or she does not appear to understand that it still exists (out of sight is out of mind), so the infant will not try to search for the object. The infants' perceptual world is limited to what it sees, feels, hears, tastes and smells and is sensory and motor driven. Initially, infants rely on the reflexes they are born with to interact with the environment. Piaget used the term 'circular reactions' to describe the repetitious nature of infants' actions that result in learning new schemas. What is important about the sensorimotor stage and progression through the six sub-stages that Piaget identified, is that behaviour is initially dependent on what abilities babies are born with, but becomes more intentional and refined as their brain matures and develops through interaction with the environment. The main developmental achievement of the sensorimotor stage is the acquisition of **object permanence**, which is the realization that objects continue to exist even when they can no longer be seen. By 18 months, object permanence is securely developed and infants will search for an object where it was last seen, expressing surprise if it is not there.

Pre-operational stage
During this stage, children's thinking and reasoning is still dominated by the appearance of objects although knowledge is increasingly represented by language,

mental imagery and symbolic thought. The pre-operational stage is divided into two sub-stages:

- Preconceptual thinking (2–4 years) is characterized by a lack of ability to classify objects in an ordered way. Objects that are broadly similar are typically regarded as being the same – for instance, all four-legged animals are called 'doggies'. Young children also tend to assign living attributes to inanimate objects – a doll is assumed to feel pain when it is broken (Piaget refers to this as animism).

- Intuitive thinking (4–6 years): during the intuitive thinking sub-stage, children start to use mental operations to solve problems but cannot explain the underlying principles. If shown a picture of seven boys and four girls and asked 'Are there more boys than girls?' a child would usually respond by saying 'Yes'. However, if asked 'Are there more boys or more children?' a child in the intuitive thinking sub-stage would also be likely to respond positively. Although intuitive thinking is closer to adult logic than preconceptual thinking, there are limitations associated with their logic, as demonstrated by their performance on conservation tasks (see Activities on p.259 and p.260).

Language develops rapidly during the pre-operational stage and children use words and images to engage with their environment. However, their cognitive competence is affected by some key limitations summarized in Table 8.2. Interestingly, the pre-operational stage is mainly characterized by what children cannot do rather than what they can do.

Activity — Testing a child's understanding of conservation

Piaget used a number of conservation experiments to assess young children's ability to conserve number, mass and volume of liquid. **Conservation** is the ability to understand that key properties do *not* change, even if the physical appearance or arrangement of objects has changed. To test the conservation of number, Piaget presented a child with two rows of coloured counters and got the child to agree that there were the same number of counters in each row. Then he changed the way that one row of counters was displayed by spreading them out (see below) and asked the child again if each row had the same number of counters.

1 How would you test a young child's understanding of the conservation of volume?

2 Consider carefully how you would word the questions you would ask the child.

3 Compare your ideas with those of other students in your psychology class.

When you have completed this activity, turn to the box on p.260 to see how Piaget tested for the conservation of volume and also read the brief description of the study by Rose and Blank (1974) on p.261.

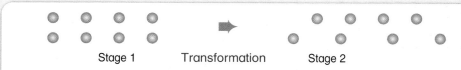

Stage 1   Transformation   Stage 2

Figure 8.2

Egocentric thought

This refers to the child's belief that everyone sees the world in the same way that they do – the child is unaware that others may have different ideas. Piaget used the three mountains task to demonstrate egocentrism (see the Key research by Piaget and Inhelder (1956) opposite) which dominates a pre-operational child's thinking.

Irreversible thinking

Reversible thinking requires a child to understand that something can be returned to its original state and that quantity does not change, even when a display is transformed. Piaget used a number of different conservation tasks to demonstrate this. For example, the counter task outlined in the activity above was used to assess the conservation of number. Children at the pre-operational stage typically claim there are more counters in the row where they had been spread out. They have not, therefore, grasped the principle of conservation.

Centration

A child focuses (centres) their attention on only one dimension of an object or event of a task and on static states rather than transformations.

Table 8.2 *Key limitations of pre-operational thinking*

Three mountains task

Key research: Piaget and Inhelder (1956)

Piaget and Inhelder (1956) used the three mountains task, which they developed during the 1940s, to investigate children's representation of the world. The three mountains in the three-dimensional model (see Figure 8.3) could be distinguished because there was a distinctive feature on the top of each (snow on top of one mountain, a cross on top of another and a house on top of the third).

Figure 8.3 *The set-up in Piaget's 'three mountains' task*

A toy doll was placed in a number of different viewing positions in turn and the child was invited to study the model carefully and work out what the doll would be able to see from each position. After each trial the child was shown a series of photographs of different scenes, including the correct one (i.e. the one the doll would be able to see), and asked to select which photo showed what the doll would be able to see.

Children under the age of seven (i.e. at the pre-operational stage) typically indicated that the doll's view would be the same as their own viewpoint, irrespective of where the doll was placed (i.e. they provided an egocentric response to the task).

Piaget's three mountains task

Piaget claimed that young children find it difficult to take another person's perspective (i.e. their thinking is egocentric) and used the three mountains task to demonstrate this. When you have read the account of the three mountains task on p.259, answer the following questions:

1 What are the main problems associated with investigating egocentrism in this way?

2 Think about how you would devise another task that would address the problems you identified above.

When you have completed this activity, read the key research study by Hughes (1975) on p.262 and note how his findings were different.

Concrete operational stage

At the concrete operational stage (7 to 11 years) the use of logical rules replaces intuition. However, children's understanding remains limited because it requires actual concrete examples and cannot deal with hypothetical problems or abstract concepts they have never encountered before. Children in the concrete operational stage have developed the ability to focus on more than one aspect of a stimulus, so are now able to complete conservation tasks successfully. In order to give the correct answer to the conservation of volume task, a child has to consider both the height and width of the glass (see the box opposite). They are able to decentre and are beginning to understand other perspectives, as well as their own. They also understand the concept of ordering and grouping (classification) and can apply this to concrete objects.

The abilities associated with the concrete operational stage of cognitive development are summarized in Table 8.3.

However, children in the concrete operational stage find it difficult to classify abstract objects because abstract thinking develops during the formal operational stage from around the age of 12 onwards.

Formal operational stage

Young people at the formal operational stage are capable of systematic, abstract reasoning and can now deal with hypothetical problems. They have a better understanding of the world, including cause-and-effect relationships, and are now able to develop their own theories about the world which they can test in an organized way. They can also understand and apply abstract concepts. When solving a real or hypothetical problem, formal operational thinkers typically attempt to explore all logical possibilities systematically. Piaget and Inhelder (1969) demonstrated this in the following way: participants were given four beakers of colourless liquids and asked to find out which combination produced a yellow liquid. The younger

Piaget's conservation tasks

Piaget conducted many conservation tests with children in the pre-operational and concrete operational stages of development. The task he used to investigate conservation of volume involved pouring a set volume of water from a glass that was short and wide to another glass that was tall and thin (see Figure 8.4). The researcher would pour the set volume of water into two identical small glasses in front of the child (Stage 1). The child would then watch as the researcher poured the water in one of the two identical glasses into the tall glass (Stage 2). There appears to be more water in the tall glass. The child was then asked which glass contained more water and since the volume of water remains the same, the child's answer should have been that there is no difference between the two glasses. However, Piaget consistently found that children in the pre-operational stage would indicate that the tall glass contained more water: over two-thirds (70 per cent) of the pre-operational children tested got the answer to this question wrong.

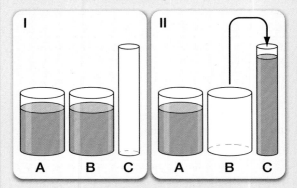

Figure 8.4 *Piaget's conservation of volume task*

Piaget reported similar findings for the conservation of mass when clay was remoulded from a round ball (Stage 1) into a long sausage shape (Stage 2). Children in the pre-operational stage indicated that the sausage shape was bigger (see Figure 8.5).

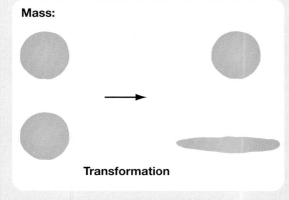

Mass:

Transformation

Figure 8.5 *Conservation of mass task*

Classification
The ability to identify and name sets of objects according to some specified characteristic such as appearance.
Seriation
This cognitive operation enables a child to sort (order) objects according to a dimension such as size, colour or other characteristic.
Transivity
This term refers to the ability to recognize logical relationships within a series (e.g. David is taller than John, and John is taller than Mike, then it follows logically that David is taller than Mike).
Decentring
The ability to take account of multiple aspects of a situation or problem in order to solve it (e.g. the height and width of a glass).
Reversibility
An understanding that objects can be changed and then returned to their original state.
Conservation
An understanding that mass, volume or quantity of items is unrelated to appearance or physical arrangement.
Ability to view thing things from another person's perspective
A child in the concrete operational stage is no longer egocentric.

Table 8.3 *Key mental processes during the concrete operational stage*

children tried random combinations and might or might not find the correct answer. Older children typically adopted a more logical approach and systematically excluded possibilities until they identified the correct solution. They used abstract reasoning to develop and test a hypothesis.

Empirical evidence against Piaget's claims

Although Piaget's methods for testing children were considered to be innovative when he initially devised them, it has since become apparent that his results can only be replicated if the researcher sticks exactly to the design of the standard Piagetian tests. If slightly modified to make them more meaningful and 'child friendly', children often complete the task successfully at an earlier age. For example, Bower and Wishart (1972) showed an object to infants, aged between 1 and 4 months, and just as the infant reached for it, the light was turned off. An infra-red camera was then used to observe the infant who continued to reach for the object, even though it could no longer see it. Bower (1977, 1982) also reported that one-month-old babies expressed surprise if an object

disappeared behind a screen and was not there when the screen was lifted, suggesting that they expected the object to continue to be there.

Hughes (1975) devised a similar test to the three mountains task but which differed in some important ways. It involved a boy doll hiding from a policeman doll (see Key research study on p.262).

Rose and Blank (1974) criticized the approach Piaget used in his conservation studies and suggested that asking the same question twice may have confused the younger children. In the original experiment, the children were shown the first display and asked 'Are the two displays the same?' and then asked the same question again after the transformation. A pre-operational child might think that if the same question is asked a second time, the adult must be expecting a different answer, even though nothing has changed. This **demand characteristic** may therefore lead the child to respond in a particular way in order to please the questioner. When Rose and Blank only asked the question once, after the transformation had take place, they found that pre-operational children performed better. There were, however, still age differences.

Donaldson and colleagues highlighted another limitation of Piaget's conservation tasks. They argued that another demand characteristic was the deliberate change of the display, suggesting to the child that the researcher was looking for a different response. Donaldson (1978) proposed that if the change was presented as accidental, the children would focus more on the actual transformation. This prediction was tested by McGarrigle and Donaldson (1974), using a 'naughty teddy' glove puppet that accidentally spread out one of the rows of counters in the standard Piagetian number conservation task. The children's ability to conserve was much improved, compared to performance on Piaget's original version of the task. However, more recent research indicated that the children may have became so absorbed by the 'naughty teddy' routine that they did not notice the transformation. Moore and Frye (1986) tested this by investigating how children would respond if a change occurred because the 'naughty teddy' actually removed or added a counter. The children still answered that no change had taken place, despite the fact that there had been a change, suggesting that the 'naughty teddy' had indeed been a distraction.

Samuel and Bryant (1984) carried out a large-scale study, involving four age groups (5, 6, 7 and 8 year olds), three conservation tasks (volume of liquid, number and mass) and three ways of presenting the tests: (i) the standard Piagetian method, (ii) the single question (used by Rose and Blank), and (iii) no visible transformation. Children performed significantly better when only one judgement was required, supporting the findings of Rose and Blank (1974). Overall, the older children performed significantly better than the younger ones, supporting Piaget's general theory about changes over time.

Hiding from a policeman

Key research: Hughes (1975)

Hughes' task involved a model with two intersecting walls that formed a cross and two dolls – one doll representing a policeman and the other a little boy. The policeman was positioned so he could see the two areas marked B and D but the areas A and C were hidden by the wall, as shown in Figure 8.6 below.

The task was introduced carefully to maximize the child's chances of understanding it and what was being asked. Firstly, Hughes placed the boy doll in area A and the child was asked if the policeman could see the boy there. The question was subsequently repeated for areas B, C and D. The policeman doll was then placed on the opposite side, facing the wall that divides A and C and the child was asked to hide the boy doll so that the policeman could not see him. The children made very few errors and when a child did make a mistake, the error was explained and the question was repeated until the correct answer was given.

Following this initial session, the actual test was introduced, involving two doll policemen (see Figure 8.7) and the child was asked to hide the boy doll so that he could not be seen by either of the two policemen. This required the child to understand two different perspectives and was repeated three more times so that a different area of the model was the only correct hiding place.

Hughes (1975) reported that 90 per cent of the responses were correct for a sample of 30 children aged between three-and-a half and five. Even the 10 youngest children (with a mean age of three years and nine months) achieved an 88 per cent success rate.

Hughes carried out further trials, using more intersecting walls to create five and six areas in the model and introduced a third policeman. Although the three-year-olds found these trials more difficult, they still responded correctly on about 60 per cent of the trials and the four-year-olds achieved a 90 per cent success rate.

Donaldson (1978) suggested that the egocentric responses reported by Piaget using his original 'three mountains' test may be explained by the fact that they did not fully understand what they were supposed to do (and it also involved left-right reversals which some adults find difficult). The 'policemen' task, on the other hand, was introduced very carefully, made sense to the child because they understood the concept of hiding from someone (although were unlikely to have personal experience of hiding from a policeman!) and the motives and intentions of both the policeman doll and the boy doll would have been understood, even by children as young as three, i.e. it made what Donaldson called 'human sense'. Moreover, the test merely required the child to work out what could be seen and not how it would appear and did not involve left-right reversals. When Hughes devised a simplified mountains task which he introduced carefully he recorded a high proportion of correct responses in pre-school children, which again suggested that the children may not have understood Piaget's original task.

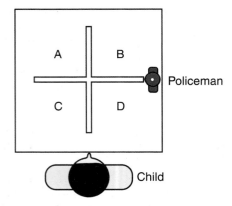

Figure 8.6 *The model used by Hughes (1975) seen from above before the boy doll is placed on the model*

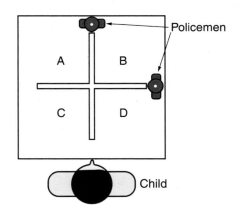

Figure 8.7 *The model when two policemen are used*

It would appear that Piaget underestimated what infants and young children can do at particular ages. However, Piaget would argue that the important issue is not so much the age at which specific changes occur, but the fact that the changes occur in a fixed order. When studying young children's cognitive abilities it is clearly important for psychologists to devise meaningful tasks that will provide an accurate indication of their capability.

The cognitive-developmental approach

A cognitive-developmental approach focuses on inner mental processes (as does the cognitive approach in general) and how these processes vary over time. It aims to explain any observed changes in mental processes. Although much of the research focuses on changes in mental abilities during childhood, it can also be applied across all ages, including old age.

Working within a cognitive-developmental approach, Piaget was concerned with how mental structures matured with age. Although he emphasized the importance of innate structures that enable children to learn how to think and reason, Piaget also acknowledged the role of experience and interaction with the environment in his theory of cognitive development.

Evaluation of Piaget's theory of cognitive development

- *Rich description of children's thinking* – Piaget's theory of cognitive development provides a detailed description of children's thinking, backed by some empirical evidence.

- *Sampling method* – Piaget has been criticized for studying restricted and biased samples of children: many of his studies were carried out with his own children and their friends. Piaget described the errors of reasoning that children made and then generalized his findings to all children at that developmental stage.

- *Focus on processes* – Piaget was better at describing the processes underpinning cognitive development than explaining how these processes operated.

- *Methods used to test infants and young children* – Although the tests Piaget devised were considered to be innovative, his results can only be replicated if the researcher sticks precisely to the detailed design of the standard Piagetian tasks. If they are modified to make them more meaningful, children can usually complete them successfully at an earlier age (e.g. Hughes' (1975) replication of the three mountains study, using a boy doll hiding from policeman dolls). Piaget clearly underestimated what infants and young children can do. However, the issue for Piaget is not so much the age at which specific changes occur, but the fact that they occur in a fixed sequence.

- *Piaget underestimated the age at which children could do things* – This may be because he failed to distinguish between competence (what a child is capable of doing) and performance (how a child performs on a particular task). Piaget's studies tested performance and he assumed that a child who failed a particular task lacked the underlying cognitive structures required to succeed on that task.

Subsequent research, such as Hughes (1975), suggests that a child may acquire these competences earlier than Piaget suggested.

- *Demand characteristics* – Rose and Blank (1974) criticized the test Piaget used in his conservation studies and suggested that asking the same question twice may have confused the younger children. This demand characteristic may have led the children to respond in a predictable way. Donaldson (1978) argued that another demand characteristic of Piaget's studies was the deliberate change of the display which may have suggested to the children that the experimenter was looking for a different response.

- *Focus on children's mistakes* – Piaget may have overlooked important mental abilities of children by focusing on the errors they made on specific tasks, or he may have misinterpreted the reasons behind their mistakes.

- *Individual differences* – Piaget's emphasis on universal stages may have deterred research on individual differences: his theory of cognitive development does not take account of variability of development between children.

- *Uneven development* – Piaget's theory assumes that cognitive development occurs concurrently across different domains of knowledge such as verbal understanding and numerical ability (i.e. it is domain general) and cannot account for uneven development (e.g. a developmental lag in numerical understanding or acceleration in verbal understanding). However, differences between the sexes in these domains should be anticipated (see Chapter 6 on Gender).

- *Universality* – The formal operational stage may not be universally achieved as claimed by Piaget: Dasen (1994) reported that only about a third of adults reach this stage. Piaget's assumption that everyone achieves this final abstract level of reasoning may reflect his own experience of studying intelligent individuals (i.e. the use of biased samples).

- *Piaget's timetable of development has been criticized for being overly prescriptive* – Although a valid criticism, Piaget's theory is not only concerned with age boundaries, but rather is about identifying universal cognitive changes that are biologically regulated during development. This is supported by cross-cultural research that has replicated Piaget's findings (Dasen 1977).

- *Practice should not improve performance* – If a person is not biologically ready to progress to the next stage, no amount of practice should enable them to get there. However, there is evidence to suggest that practice can make a difference (e.g. Bryant and Trabasso (1971) successfully taught children under the age of 7 to use logical mental rules).

- *Piaget underplayed the role of language and social factors in cognitive development* – Piaget's views on the lack of influence of language were supported by an experiment carried out by one of his co-workers, Sinclair-de-Zwart (1969). She reported that there was a difference in the language used by children who were unable to conserve and those who could conserve. Non-conservers mainly used absolute rather than comparative terms (e.g. 'big' rather than 'larger') and also tended to use a single word to describe different dimensions (e.g. 'small' to mean 'short', 'thin' and 'few'). These findings suggest that cognitive and linguistic developments are closely related, but which comes first? In a further experiment, Sinclair-de-Zwart tried to teach appropriate verbal skills to non-conservers, but 90 per cent of these children were still unable to conserve, which supports Piaget's view that cognitive maturity is a pre-requisite for linguistic development. Piaget is also accused of ignoring the impact of social influences on learning and understanding which is the focus of Vygotsky's theory of learning.

Despite a number of shortcomings, Piaget's contribution should not be underestimated, including the fact that he produced the first comprehensive theory of children's cognitive development. His theory has been more extensively tested than any other and has fundamentally changed our ideas about children and, as we shall see, has had a considerable influence on educational practice. Like all good theories, it has generated a lot of research which has enhanced our understanding of cognitive development, and several fundamental aspects of his theory are still accepted today.

Vygotsky's theory of cognitive development

Lev Vygotsky (1896–1934) was born in the USSR in the same year as Piaget, but they never met. In fact, very little was known about Vygotsky's work outside of Russia until it was translated into English from the 1960s onwards, by which time he was already dead (he died at the age of 38). You may notice that the date references for Vygotsky's work are usually after his death because this was when the work was published in English.

While Piaget proposed a biological approach to cognitive development, Vygotsky believed that culture and social interaction (i.e. the social environment) were fundamental to children's development. Children are not born with knowledge – rather it is gained as the child develops through social interactions with peers and adults. Knowledge is not, therefore, independent of the social context and we become ourselves through others. Vygotsky did not rule out the importance of biological processes, but proposed instead an interdependent relationship between biological development and the immediate social and cultural world of the child (primarily the family, peers and teachers).

The influence of culture

Vygotsky's socio-cultural approach asserts that culture and social interaction are key determinants of development and that in order to understand a child it is necessary to understand the child's background and surroundings. The cultural context affects the child's immediate social environment and leads to the development of higher mental functions which shape language and make thought possible.

Vygotsky (1962, 1966) suggested that the intellect consisted of elementary and higher mental functions. Vygotsky believed that cultural influences are required to transform the elementary mental functions of attention, sensation and perception into more sophisticated higher mental functions, such as understanding language, decision-making, reasoning and memory, and that an individual would not progress beyond the elementary functions without culture. When Vygotsky used the concept of 'culture', he was referring to the body of knowledge held by, for example, books and experts, and which is largely transmitted through language.

If higher mental functions depend on cultural influences, one would expect to find different higher mental functions in different cultures. Gredler (1992) provides empirical support for this: children in Papua New Guinea are taught a counting system which begins on the thumb of one hand and proceeds up the arm and down to the other fingers, ending at 29. This makes it difficult to add and subtract large numbers which limits mathematical calculations (a higher mental function) in that culture.

Further evidence of the influence of culture is provided by attempts to teach primates to use human language and other symbol systems (such as arithmetic). For example, bonobo chimpanzees have been taught to use human language, as well as to use number and quantity concepts, by immersing the chimpanzees in a human learning environment. In the wild the chimpanzees' elementary mental functions are not transformed to higher mental functions, but were able to develop some higher mental functions when given appropriate cultural input (Savage-Rumbaugh and Fields 2000).

A further source of evidence for the influence of culture comes from research on IQ, which shows that IQs in many countries have been steadily increasing in recent decades (Flynn 1994, 1999) and too rapidly to be explained in terms of genetic change. One possible explanation is the general increase in accessible knowledge: many more books and vast amounts of information, available via the internet, enhance the culture that surrounds today's children and may contribute to a general increase in IQ. Improved diet or the possibility that we may be getting better at doing timed activities of the kind used to measure intelligence are other possible explanations.

The process of cultural influence

In Piaget's theory the process of cognitive development was driven by the biological principles of maturation and disequilibrium. Vygotsky, on the other hand, argued that it is the influence of others that drives the process of cognitive development – knowledge is socially constructed and mediated by culturally derived symbol systems. The concepts that Vygotsky used to explain the process of social/cultural influence include the zone of proximal development, semiotic mediation, social and individual plans, and the role of language. Each of these is considered in turn.

The zone of proximal development

The zone of proximal development (ZPD) is the *'distance between the actual developmental level as determined by individual problem solving and the level of potential development as determined through problem solving under adult guidance or in collaboration with more capable peers'*. The zone of proximal development defines those functions that have not yet matured but are in the process of maturation, functions that will mature tomorrow but are currently in an embryonic state (Vygotsky 1978; use of italics as in the original text). According to Vygotsky, an individual's potential can only be achieved with the support and guidance of others. Assisted performance defines what a child can do with the support and guidance of a more knowledgeable other. Ideally, this person is sensitive to the learner's current capabilities and able to guide the learner through the ZPD (see the key research by McNaughton and Leyland (1990) in the box below).

McNaughton and Leyland's study shows how an instructor (in this case the child's mother) can use the ZPD to facilitate learning. Vygotsky predicted that the most effective teaching input occurs at the edge of the ZPD (i.e.

the point at which the child can still cope). Within the ZPD, skills that are too difficult for a child to master alone can be achieved with guidance and encouragement from a more knowledgeable other (MKO). This is someone who has a better understanding/higher level of ability than the learner who may be a peer, older sibling, parent, teacher or other adult. In the case of computer and technology skills, a child/young person may be the MKO for an adult!

Freund (1990) also studied the role of guided learning within the ZPD. Children were asked to place miniature items of furniture in particular rooms of a doll's house. Some of the children did something similar with their mothers before attempting the task on their own, while others worked on it alone. Those who had previously worked with their mother showed greater improvement compared with their first attempt at the task. This suggests that guided learning within the ZPD can lead to a better understanding than working alone (Piaget's discovery learning): 'What a child can do with assistance today she will be able to do by herself tomorrow' (Vygotsky 1978).

The concept of the ZPD implies that human potential is limited by the quality of social interaction and that virtually any problem can be solved, as long as we have access to a more knowledgeable other.

The ZPD at work

Key research: McNaughton and Leyland (1990)

McNaughton and Leyland used jigsaw puzzles of differing levels of difficulty to investigate the ZPD. Children were invited to complete a number of jigsaw puzzles that were progressively more difficult with the help of their mother. The highest level of jigsaw puzzle difficulty achieved by the children when working with their mothers was recorded. One week later the same children were invited back and worked by themselves on a new set of jigsaw puzzles. McNaughton and Leyland found that the level of difficulty of the puzzles successfully completed was lower for most of the children during the second session. The difference in performance between the two sessions enabled McNaughton and Leyland to define each child's ZPD. The child's performance when working alone demonstrated his/her current ability and aided performance indicated the potential capability.

The main variables were tightly controlled in this study, enabling the researchers to measure children's performance with and without their mother's help, which revealed the amount of progress that is possible through social interaction.

By observing the mothers working with their children, McNaughton and Leyland identified types of scaffolding provided by the mothers during the first session and these were directly linked to the level of task difficulty. **Scaffolding** is the metaphor first used by Wood *et al.* (1976) to describe the temporary support structure around a child's attempts to understand new ideas and complete new tasks, involving the provision of graduated assistance by withdrawing adult/peer support as the learner's mastery improves.

When working on jigsaw puzzles that were too easy for the child (i.e. below the child's ZPD), the mothers were mainly concerned with keeping the child's attention on the task. When the task was of medium difficulty (within the child's ZPD), mothers focused on helping their child to complete the puzzle by themselves; the mother's role was mainly one of guidance. When the puzzle was too difficult (beyond the child's ZPD), the mothers would try to complete the puzzle by whatever means possible which usually involved taking control when they realized the task was beyond their child's capabilities and that no further learning was likely to take place.

Parents' use of scaffolding in everyday play situations

What types of scaffolding support might the adult provide to help the child succeed in this construction task? For example, they might try to simplify the task by breaking it down into component parts.

Note down your answers and then discuss them with other students in your psychology class and compile one agreed list of the various types of support that would scaffold a young child's learning. When you have completed this activity, compare your ideas with the list on p.274.

Semiotic mediation

The process of cognitive development is mediated by language and other cultural symbols (**semiotics**). The symbols act as a medium through which knowledge can be transmitted from others to the child (e.g. the experts instructing the child or 'culture' more widely). Use of these symbols transforms the child's elementary abilities into more sophisticated, higher cognitive abilities. Semiotic mediation is a social process.

Social and individual planes

Learning begins as a shared, social activity. Over time, dialogues between the teacher and learner become internalized as the learner takes greater responsibility for his/her own learning. This marks the shift from other- to self-regulation and from the social to the individual plane. Research by Wertsch (1985) has shown how self-regulation increases with age. In one study, children under

the age of five were observed while working on jigsaw puzzles with their mothers. Self-regulation was assessed by analysing the children's gaze – looking towards their mother was taken to imply less self-regulation and this decreased with age. In another study, children were observed as they solved puzzles. As the session went on and the children became more proficient, regulation was transferred from the other to self.

The role of language

Language is a primary form of social interaction through which adults transmit the rich body of cultural knowledge to children. Vygotsky believed that the acquisition of language was crucial for cognitive development and was particularly interested in the relationship between language and thought; he identified a set of developmental stages (see Table 8.4). In Vygotsky's view, speech (language) and thought are separate functions in children under the age of two and it is only later that they influence each other. Vocal activity (or pre-intellectual language) is socially driven and enables social interaction and emotional expression. At the same time, children use prelinguistic thought – mental activities, such as problem-solving, which do not use verbal operations. This period of practical intelligence, during which elementary functions are developing, is assumed to be largely biologically determined (which is similar to Piagetian thinking).

Around the age of two, children begin to use external symbols or signs, such as language, to assist their problem-solving. A young child will use speech to communicate with others (social or communicative speech) and will often talk aloud when solving problems, using a kind of egocentric speech (sometimes referred to as 'self-talk'). Egocentric speech directs young children's thinking. Around the age of seven, egocentric speech becomes silent (known as 'inner speech') and differs in form from social speech. Inner dialogues are used as a means of self-regulation to control cognitive processes. Learning has therefore shifted to the individual plane but continues to be mediated by language. From then onwards, language serves a dual purpose: for thought and for social communication. Social processes shape both language and thought. Vygotsky regarded language and thought as instruments for higher cognitive activity such as planning and organizing conceptual thought.

Speech stage	Age (in years)	Function of language
Pre-intellectual, social speech	0–3	Language serves a social function only. At the same time thought is prelinguistic.
Egocentric speech	3–7	Language is used to control the child's behaviour, but is usually spoken out loud.
Inner speech	7+	Language becomes internalized as thought and is used to direct and control the child's thinking and behaviour, as well as for communicating thoughts and ideas to others. Inner speech vastly enhances a child's problem-solving ability.

Table 8.4 *The development of language and thought*

Thinking becomes increasingly sophisticated as language develops and as children experience more of the social world they live in.

Vygotsky's view of inner speech has been supported by a number of experimental studies. For example, he reported that inner speech increased dramatically when he deliberately introduced obstacles to a child's activity (Vygotsky 1962). Berk also conducted research on inner speech by observing children's behaviour in school. Berk (1994) reported that children talked to themselves more when faced with a difficult task, when working by themselves, or when a teacher was not available to help. Berk and Garvin (1984) studied inner speech in children from low-income Appalachian families, as well as middle-class children, and found that Appalachian children's private speech developed at a slower pace than those from middle-class families. One possible explanation of this finding is that middle-class parents typically talk to their children more than low-income Appalachian parents. This would also support Vygotsky's theory that inner speech stems from social communication.

IDA   Social constructivist approach

Like Piaget, Vygotsky studied cognitive development in children, but his approach is based on a **social constructivist** perspective. Although the role of biological processes and mechanisms is acknowledged, social interaction is considered to be crucial to the development of thinking skills in children and achieving their optimum potential. What is also important for Vygotsky is how children interpret their social environment and re-evaluate their experiences in their social world as a consequence of the guided assistance they receive from more knowledgeable others (peers or adults).

Stages in the development of thinking

Vygotsky does not refer to stages in the same way as Piaget, and although he identified stages in the development of language and thought (see Table 8.4), his theory is not a stage theory. Vygotsky (1987) proposed four stages in the process of concept formation based on research evidence. Children were given wooden blocks of varying height and shape and each block was labelled with a nonsense symbol (e.g. 'ZAT' was used to label tall

and square blocks). The child's task was to work out what these labels meant. Vygotsky observed that children went through three stages before achieving mature concepts (see Table 8.5). These four stages of concept formation steadily increase in terms of their level of difficulty.

Although narrower in focus than Piaget's theory of cognitive development, Vygotsky's work has also had a lasting impact on education practice which will be considered in the section on applications to education.

Activity   Comparing theories (Part 1)

Consider the similarities and differences between Piaget's and Vygotsky's theories of cognitive development. To help you organize your ideas, prepare a table, using the following headings to guide your thinking:

- Role of innate factors and biological processes
- Role of experience
- Social/cultural influence
- What drives (motivates) cognitive development?

Which approach to cognitive development do you find the more convincing? Give your reasons. You will be returning to this activity later in this topic when you have studied Bruner's theory.

Answers are given on p.609. ▶

Evaluation of Vygotsky's theory

- *Relationship between cognitive development and learning* – Vygotsky's account of the relationship between cognitive development and learning acknowledges individual differences within the same culture and also between people from different cultures.

- *Emphasis on the role of social/cultural factors* – Once his work was translated into English, Vygotsky's ideas became influential because they addressed the role of social factors in cognitive development which Piaget overlooked.

- *Vygotsky's theory can help explain unusual case studies* – Children living amongst wolves and other animals (known as feral children) behave and communicate using sounds and gestures similar to

Stage	Description of the stage
Vague syncretic stage	Largely trial and error without understanding (random strategies).
Complex stage	Some appropriate strategies are used but the main attributes are not identified.
Potential concept stage	Only one attribute (feature) can be dealt with at a time (e.g. tall).
Mature concept stage	The child is able to deal with several attributes simultaneously (e.g. tall and square).

Table 8.5 *Vygotsky's stages of concept formation (Vygostky 1987)*

those used by their 'surrogate family', highlighting the importance of the cultural context. Once these children were returned to a human culture, they adopted the social nuances of that culture and, provided this happened before the age of 12 years (which is when language becomes lateralized to the left hemisphere), their language skills usually developed well. To achieve their full developmental potential it is important for children to interact and engage with the social environment. Piaget's theory cannot account for these findings, but Vygotsky can explain the 'what?' and the 'why?' of feral children: without social interaction a child can only achieve a basic primitive form of knowledge enabling survival. However, with social interaction a child can achieve an understanding of general principles and abstract concepts.

- *Lack of empirical support* – For many years there was little empirical support for Vygotsky's theory, but this evidence base is now growing, as interest in his theory has increased (e.g. Tharp and Gallimore 1988). Part of the reason for the lack of research is that his theory focuses on the *process* of cognitive development that is more difficult to investigate than the outcome. Since empirical support for Vygotsky's theory has been fairly limited, there is also relatively little critique of his ideas.

- *Vygotsky's theory can explain why children successfully complete Piagetian tests at an earlier age when they are made more meaningful to the child* – Vygotsky argued that it was important to take account of social context. The ZPD is crucial in making Piagetian tasks understandable to the child, which was demonstrated when Hughes (1975) and Donaldson (1978) made the tasks more child friendly by providing a familiar social context (see p.262).

- *Vygotsky may have overemphasized the importance of social influence* – Vygotsky's theory may overemphasize the importance of social influences and underemphasize biological and individual factors in cognitive development. If social influences alone were necessary for cognitive development, we would expect learning to occur faster than it actually does. The fact that it does not might suggest there must be a biological element determining brain maturation.

- *Application to education* – Vygotsky's ideas have been successfully applied in education (see pp.273–274).

Bruner's theory of cognitive growth

Jerome Bruner (born in 1915) is regarded as one of the most influential American psychologists of the 20th century. For most of his life he has lived and worked in the USA, although he worked at the University of Oxford between 1972 and 1980. Bruner argued that cognitive-developmental approaches should focus on how children process information, how the environment affects that processing and how transitions occur between developmental stages.

His early research in the 1950s contributed to the shift from a behaviourist to a cognitive perspective in psychology and this, in turn, triggered his interest in cognitive growth. He is best known for his influence on education and some of his books, such as *The Process of Education* (1960, 1977) and *Toward a Theory of Instruction* (1966), have become widely read classics. His early work was influenced by Piagetian ideas but later, and to a far greater extent, Bruner built on Vygotsky's ideas and was largely responsible for introducing Vygotsky's ideas to researchers outside the former Soviet Union.

Vygotsky's influence on Bruner's thinking is reflected in his growing interest in the influence of the social and cultural context. In one of his more recent books, entitled *The Culture of Education*, Bruner (1996) claims that learning is a creative process, involving the making of meanings which exist 'in the mind' but 'have their origins and significance in the culture in which they are created'. Bruner considered language, which enables symbolic representations of the world, to be the most important cultural factor in children's learning and their cognitive growth. He was particularly interested in how knowledge is represented and organized through different modes of representation.

Three modes of internal representation

Bruner *et al.* (1966) were interested in how knowledge was represented and organized as a child develops and so he proposed different modes of internal representation (see Table 8.6) rather than formalized universal stages of development (as put forward by Piaget) or the stages in the development of language and thought and concept formation proposed by Vygotsky. Although the **three modes of representation** – enactive, iconic and symbolic – are not neat stages, they are broadly sequential, with one translating into another. They are different forms that human knowledge and understanding can take; Bruner's focus is therefore knowledge in general rather than cognitive growth *per se*.

Enactive (action-based)
Represents actions and objects via motor behaviours; information is stored in the form of 'muscle memories' (remembering the feel of actions); thinking is based entirely on physical actions.
Iconic (image-based)
Represents the world in terms of images (this explains why children using iconic representation are not successful on conservation tasks).
Symbolic (language-based)
Use of words, language and other symbols to categorize and summarize information makes the manipulation of increasingly complex ideas and reasoning possible.

Table 8.6 *Bruner's modes of representation (Bruner et al. 1966)*

The enactive mode

Infants initially represent the world through actions. This enactive mode involves encoding action-based information and storing it in memory (this is similar to Piaget's sensorimotor stage). This mode of representation is not only used by young children – older children and adults continue to use this mode of representation when it provides the quickest and easiest way to learn or explain something. For example, adults use enactive representation to carry out a range of physical activities (such as tying a knot, driving a car or skiing) that are more difficult to describe using other modes of representation. This rudimentary form of representation is not, therefore, entirely relinquished with age. Although there is a developmental shift in modes of representation over time and one mode of representation is dominant during a particular developmental phase, the main difference between this and a stage theory is that once a mode of representation has been acquired it is not lost and all three modes eventually coexist.

The iconic mode

The iconic mode uses mental images (icons), usually visual images, as a means of understanding and reasoning and this may explain why it is often helpful to have illustrations or diagrams, as well as verbal information, when learning something new. The mental images may also be based on hearing, smell or touch. This mode of representation corresponds to the end of Piaget's sensorimotor stage and the pre-operational stage when things are as they look. Bruner and Kenney (1966) demonstrated the use of iconic representation in an experiment that involved arranging glasses in a particular order (see Key research, Transition from the iconic to the symbolic mode of representation, below).

HOW SCIENCE WORKS

Transition from the iconic to the symbolic mode of representation

Key research: Bruner and Kenney (1966)

At the start of the session, children aged 3 to 7 were shown nine plastic beakers arranged by size and width on a board divided into nine squares, with the tallest positioned at the back and the widest beakers on the left (see Figure 8.8a). In the *reproduction task*, designed to use the iconic mode of representation, the arrangement of the beakers was scrambled and each child was asked to return the glasses to how they were at the outset.

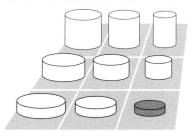

Figure 8.8a *The original layout for Bruner's plastic beaker task*

Participants were then given a *transposition task*, which requires the symbolic mode of representation. All the glasses were removed from the grid, except the one that had previously been placed in the bottom, right-hand corner of the 3 by 3 grid, which was now placed in the bottom, left-hand square of the grid.

The child was then asked to create a transposed (mirror image) arrangement (see Figure 8.8b).

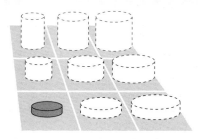

Figure 8.8b *The transposed layout for Bruner's plastic beaker task*

The children typically found the reproduction task easier than the transposition task and most seven-year-olds could successfully complete both tasks (see Table 8.7).

According to Bruner, this demonstrates that the older children were able to translate the visual information into the symbolic mode to perform the transposition task, and the restrictions associated with the iconic mode no longer dominated the children's cognitive activity. On the other hand, a child who was only able to use visual imagery (the iconic mode) could reproduce the arrangement but not restructure it.

	Five-year-olds	Six-year-olds	Seven-year-olds
Reproduction task	60%	72%	80%
Transposition task	0%	27%	79%

Table 8.7 *Percentage of 5-, 6- and 7-year-old children who successfully completed the two types of task*

The symbolic mode

The symbolic mode of representation develops last – information is stored using symbols (e.g. language or some other form of symbol system such as mathematical symbols) which facilitate abstract thinking. The use of symbols allows information to be classified and manipulated; the user is no longer constrained by actions or images and the immediate context, and can 'go beyond the information given' (Bruner 1957). Bruner (1983) has argued that the use of language is crucial, ensuring that thinking and knowledge are not restricted to what can be learned through actions (the enactive mode) and images (the iconic mode). It is only when children begin to use the symbolic mode can they handle abstract concepts (which are expressed symbolically through language or other symbol systems). An example of an important abstract concept in psychology is ethics. Would it be possible to communicate ethical issues effectively using only enactive or iconic modes of representation?

Bruner views symbolic representation as crucial for cognitive growth and attaches great importance to language in determining cognitive development. Children learn language through social exchanges within the family where the knowledge of the situation and its routines help the child to understand the accompanying language. However, when learning new material adult learners sometimes follow the progression from enactive to iconic to symbolic representation.

Activity — Using different modes of representation

Try to describe to another person:

(a) how to ride a bicycle and

(b) how to tie a shoelace.

How did you do it and how easy did you find it?

Now ask one or two of your friends to describe the same two things. Listen and observe carefully how they do this. How do your observations of their responses relate to Bruner's modes of representation? Which modes of representation did they use? Why do you think they used the modes of representation they did?

Some key differences between Bruner and Piaget

The main difference between the ideas of Piaget and Bruner is that Bruner's modes of representation coexist, rather than representing different and separate modes of thought at different points of development. He proposes a gradual development of cognitive skills into more integrated adult cognitive abilities and it is the environment that determines developmental progress rather than age – environments can slow down or speed up the process. Since language provides a key means of

symbolizing the world, Bruner emphasizes the role of language more than Piaget, regarding it as an important factor in cognitive development. While Piaget believed in learning readiness, based on brain maturation, which could constrain the age at which something can be learned, Bruner proposes that anything can be taught at any age, as long as it is presented appropriately in a way that corresponds to the child's development. What is important is *how* something is taught (i.e. the process of instruction) rather than *what* is taught.

Learning new concepts

Like Vygotsky, Bruner was also interested in concept formation. Based on the findings of a classic study by Bruner and colleagues (1956), Bruner suggested that people learn new concepts through a process of generating and refining hypotheses in the light of new evidence as it emerges (see the Key research study, Learning about new concepts, opposite).

The role of scaffolding

While working at the University of Oxford, Bruner and colleagues wrote a paper on the role of tutoring in problem-solving in which the concept of scaffolding is suggested as one of the key roles of a teacher (Wood *et al.* 1976). So although scaffolding has become closely associated with Vygotsky's concept of the ZPD, it was first proposed many years after his death by Wood, Bruner and Ross who built on Vygotsky's original ideas. Although use of the term 'scaffolding' might seem to imply a fixed, rigid structure, Bruner and colleagues saw it in terms of a temporary support structure, involving constant adjustments made in response to a child's progress. Support is gradually reduced as a child's mastery of a given task increases.

Activity — Comparing theories (Part 2)

Using the same headings as for the activity on p.267, add another column to your table headed 'Bruner' and complete it to capture Bruner's views on each of the four issues.

Answers are given on p.609. ▶

There are similarities between the ideas of Bruner and Vygotsky. Like Vygotsky, Bruner believed that the fundamental social agents for the development of cognition in children are mothers and other care-givers who provide much of the social interaction during the early years. During social interaction, children receive instruction and guidance (scaffolding) on how to understand, make sense of and test hypotheses about the world they see and experience.

Evaluation of Bruner's theory

■ *The flexibility of different modes of representation –* The flexibility of the different modes of representation

Learning about new concepts

Bruner believes that people understand their world in terms of similarities and differences between categories. In a classic study, which has been described by Eysenck and Keane (1995) as the first systematic attempt to investigate concept development in adults as well as children, using a cognitive perspective, Bruner and colleagues presented participants with a display of 81 rectangular cards. Each card was printed with a varying combination of four properties:

i   number (1, 2 or 3 images)

ii shape (circle, square or cross)

iii shading of the shapes (plain, black or striped)

iv number of borders around the card (1, 2 or 3) as illustrated in Figure 8.9.

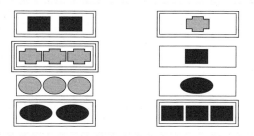

Figure 8.9 *Examples of some of the cards used by Bruner et al. (1956)*

The researchers pointed to one of the cards in the display and participants were told that it belonged to a particular category which was given a made-up name (such as JIF). Participants then had to point to other cards and ask whether they also belonged to the same category until they could identify the correct hypothesis that determined whether or not a particular card belonged to the category.

Bruner and colleagues recorded the number and type of questions that participants asked before arriving at the correct hypothesis. They identified a number of strategies that were used to identify the categories, including *successive scanning* (which involved testing one hypothesis at a time until it was found to be incorrect) and *conservative focusing* (which involved ruling out classes of hypotheses by choosing instances that differed by one attribute only). Participants using the conservative focusing strategy learned the categories faster than those using successive scanning.

Interestingly, when meaningful attributes were used instead (girl or boy, smiling or frowning), participants took longer to learn the categories. Possible reasons for this are that the children's prior knowledge of the relevance of the links between categories made it harder to test out all the logically possible categories, focusing instead on those that made sense based on their prior experience.

Evaluation

Bruner and colleagues deliberately used artificial stimuli to eliminate the effect of prior associations, in the hope that the results would accurately reflect the underlying processes of category learning. However, this meant that their research lacked ecological validity and the results may not generalise to more natural learning situations. Moreover, the artificial categories lacked any coherence between attributes that normally belong together in natural categories (e.g. fish have fins which enable them to swim).

---

has been confirmed in the classroom – all three modes can be used, alongside the learner's interests and life experiences.

■ *Building on Vygotsky's work* – Bruner was largely responsible for bringing Vygotsky's work to the attention of Western psychologists long after Vygotsky's premature death and extending some of his thinking. Scaffolding, which is widely used in teaching contexts, has enabled educators to apply Vygotsky's concept of the ZPD.

■ *Curriculum design* – Bruner believes that a sound education curriculum should build on learners' existing knowledge and understanding and enable the learner to achieve the required learning outcomes. His spiral curriculum is designed to do just that and has been widely and successfully used in schools, colleges and universities.

■ *Focus on the role of the mother* – Like many developmental theorists, Bruner refers almost exclusively to the role of the mother in development. However, his ideas could apply equally to any adult (or even an older child) with whom a young child spends a lot of time.

HOW SCIENCE WORKS **Application of the theories of Piaget, Vygotsky and Bruner to education**

The influence of Piaget's theory

During the 1950s in the USA, concerns were expressed about the IQ of the nation and whether this reflected the educational system of the time. New ideas for a better system of educating young children were therefore explored. The prevailing thinking favoured Piaget's theory of cognitive development. Using his stage approach to cognitive development, educationalists reconsidered and redeveloped the curriculum and the way in which it was delivered in the classroom. Piaget believed that children are curious, intrinsically motivated to learn and construct their own understanding of the world through discovery and active interaction with their environment, rather than being passive recipients of facts to be learned (rote learning). This influenced the way subjects were taught, especially mathematics. In the UK this led to the introduction of the Nuffield Mathematics Project (1967).

Piaget's views of cognitive development also had a significant influence on education in the UK. In the 1960s, the Plowden Report (1967) recommended that primary education should move from being teacher-led to being child-centred, based on Piaget's view that children have an inbuilt tendency to learn (through adaptation) about aspects of the real world that are waiting to be discovered. The role of the educator is not, therefore, to teach but to provide opportunities for children to explore and learn about their world for themselves through discovery; this is known as discovery learning.

Piaget's stage theory of cognitive development assumes that maturation is important, as well as actively engaging with the environment. Since the stages were age based and occurred progressively, the concept of readiness is important and it made no sense to try and speed up the process – the stages were assumed to be invariant and children would progress to the next stage when their brain had matured sufficiently to enable this to occur. If this is the case, what can teachers do to encourage learning? According to Piaget, cognitive growth can be encouraged through experience that children can become involved in and apply their own level of thinking abilities to make sense of it. Therefore educationalists should encourage the development of children's thinking skills specific to their stage of cognitive development (i.e. child-centred).

This also has implications for the curriculum. There is no point in presenting problem-solving tasks which require concrete operational thought to a pre-operational child. By drawing on Piaget's descriptions of what children of different ages and stages can do, educationalists can use these guidelines as an indication of the suitability of curriculum content. In this way, children can feel motivated to engage in tasks, knowing they are solvable and more specifically that they can solve them. Activities that are too challenging will inhibit their motivation to try and children will also lose interest and become bored if tasks are too simple. Classroom activities should enable the processes of assimilation and accommodation to occur through the play activities and the discovery learning and activity-based work used in nursery and primary schools. For older children this may take place through practical laboratory projects. The Nuffield Science programmes, for instance, enable children operating at the concrete and formal operational stages to practise their new-found cognitive skills. A Piagetian approach to education can be fun!

Some of the implications of Piaget's work for the role of the teacher:

■ Teachers should focus on the process of learning. Active interaction and engagement are important because children learn effectively by trying things out for themselves rather than being told how to do things and taught factual information, which may result in partial understanding.

■ The child's level of development is important – children should be encouraged to engage in activities that reflect their level of readiness and stage of development.

■ Children are usually more motivated to learn when the experience is novel and interesting. New understanding should be built on existing schemas and it is important to achieve a balance between accommodation (learning new concepts) and assimilation (practising and using concepts). There needs to be sufficient challenge to encourage some disequilibrium and the creation of new schemas through accommodation.

Activity **Piaget's discovery learning**

Three implications of Piaget's theory for educational practice are outlined below:

(a) Children learn by constructing their own knowledge when placed in novel situations.

(b) Logic is not an innate mental process but rather it is the outcome of cognitive development.

(c) Concrete materials should be used when teaching young children.

Which specific aspect of Piaget's theory of cognitive development supports each of these assertions? Discuss your ideas with other students in your psychology class.

- Children may sometimes prefer to work on their own because what one child will find interesting, another may not. Working in pairs/small groups, however, can also be useful when children can learn new ways of doing things from each other. A teacher should change learning strategy if a particular approach does not appear to be working.

- Abstract concepts should initially be introduced through the use of concrete examples, particularly with children at the concrete operational stage.

- Teachers can encourage intellectual development through open discussion of themes. However, Piaget did not agree with Bruner that language training can be used to speed up cognitive reasoning.

The influence of Vygotsky's theory

Vygotsky (1978) maintained that the main purpose of education is to transmit socially and culturally determined knowledge from adults to children. He also believed that 'humans learn best in co-operation with other humans' and children learn through interaction with others. The curriculum needs, therefore, to be designed to stretch and challenge, with an emphasis on learning through interaction between learners which requires careful grouping of learners to include different levels of ability. His ideas have influenced the current interest in collaborative learning in the classroom. Indeed, Tharp and Gallimore (1988) proposed a definition of teaching based on Vygotsky's concept of the ZPD: 'Teaching consists in assisting performance through the ZPD. Teaching can be said to occur when assistance is offered at points in the ZPD at which performance requires assistance'. According to Vygotsky, the teacher's role (i.e. the 'more knowledgeable other') is to lead by sharing their expertise and knowledge, clarifying any difficulties in understanding displayed by the learners and shaping children's thinking. He believed that the language the adult used was key in this important interactive process and also play, which 'creates its own zone of proximal development of the child. In play a child is always above his average age, above his daily behavior; in play it is as though he were a head taller than himself' (Vygotsky 1978).

The idea of peer tutoring (a form of collaborative learning) is based on Vygotsky's notion of assisting learning by focusing on tasks within a child's ZPD and involves a more competent learner (who takes on the role of 'tutor') being paired with a less competent learner to guide their learning. This method is used when young people/adult students share information about a topic they have studied with other students. The teacher merely listens but will step in to clarify any material that is difficult to comprehend or that is not explained clearly by the presenting student. Vygotsky believed that as long as a person has access to a more capable other, any problem can be solved. As we shall see on p.274, Vygotsky's ideas about supporting learners through the ZPD led Bruner and colleagues to develop the important concept of scaffolding (Wood *et al.* 1976).

Using a similar approach, reciprocal teaching has been used to develop children's reading skills. The teacher and a small group of children read the same text silently to themselves and at some point the teacher will ask questions to explore the children's understanding of the text. The content is then summarized and the group is encouraged to re-read the text, using the summary and then once again invited to clarify its meaning. And lastly children are asked to predict what is likely to follow the point at which they stopped reading. This approach focuses on the content, summarizing, clarifying and predicting and it enables children to engage with their social environment by hearing and seeing their teacher and the other children and modelling appropriate skills for comprehension.

Collaborative group work is another method of learning. Slavin (1987), for example, noted how important motivation and intergroup competition is in the learning process. As a group, students will delegate tasks, discuss concepts and share information. Different ideas may be suggested which others might not have thought of, so new information is shared, discussed and learned. All this takes place within the ZPD of the group members. This method can help weaker students whose understanding might be limited and who, through the group process of engagement, will be motivated to understand the views of other group members.

HOW SCIENCE WORKS

Working in pairs

Vygotsky (1978) believed that the capacity to teach and benefit from instruction was a fundamental attribute of all human beings. Working in pairs as a method of learning was investigated by Blaye *et al.* (1991). Eleven-year-olds were given the task of solving difficult problems in a computer adventure game. Children could either work in pairs or alone. When children tried to solve the problems alone, the success rate was low and only a few of the pairs performed any better. However, when they had a second session of working alone or with their pair, there was some improvement: 20 per cent for lone workers and 50 per cent for the pairs. During the final session, all children worked on their own, trying to solve the problems set. It was found that those children who had previously worked alone their performance had improved to 30 per cent but this figure was 70 per cent for the children who had previously worked in pairs. This demonstrated the advantages of working in a pair. Children managed to do better when they worked with their partner and the shared problem solving and learning that had taken place was evident when they worked individually. This method of learning has been used in education and is based on Vygotsky's concept of the ZPD and Bruner's concept of scaffolding.

Vygotsky also believed that children whose development has been impeded by a disability may develop differently from other children but should not be educated separately from 'normal' children and that their development would be likely to suffer if they were educated apart.

The influence of Bruner's theory

Bruner also views learning as an active process, involving the construction of new ideas and concepts, based on existing understanding. Children are regarded as active problem-solvers who are keen to learn and explore challenging subjects rather than passive recipients of adult instruction and guidance. Bruner (1983) refers to the 'handover principle' as the child becomes an increasingly active participant in the learning process which involves a shift from regulation by others to self-regulation.

Bruner's spiral curriculum is perhaps his most important contribution to education. His approach acknowledges that there are individual differences and not every child will learn and respond to different teaching styles in the same way. The curriculum needs, therefore, to be sufficiently flexible to allow teachers to accommodate the needs of different learners. If teachers are taught to monitor the learning progression of their pupils and identify those who are struggling to understand key concepts, they should be in a better position to use another form of explanation (mode of representation). Different teaching strategies can be used which make use of essentially different levels of explanation, including enactive, iconic and symbolic modes of representation. This is why Bruner claims that as adults we use whatever mode of representation is most appropriate.

The concept of scaffolding, first introduced by Bruner and colleagues (Wood et al. 1976), provides a framework to support a child's attempt to understand new ideas and complete new tasks, highlighting an active instructional role for teachers. Scaffolding involves a range of activities to assist the learner through the ZPD, illustrating how Bruner's work built on Vygotsky's ideas. These include:

- simplifying tasks

- providing direction

- helping to motivate and encourage the learner

- highlighting critical features of the task

- demonstration (modeling what needs to be done so that it can be imitated).

In a review of several studies on the scaffolding provided by mothers with their pre-school children, Moss (1992) also identified teaching new skills that the learner is unable to do alone; encouraging the learner to continue to use effective strategies that were initially used spontaneously; and discouraging the use of ineffective/inappropriate strategies.

Based on Tharp and Gallimore's idea of assisted performance when working within the ZPD, Bruner also developed the idea of contingency, i.e. responding flexibly and appropriately to the individual needs of the learner but only when required. Wood and Middleton (1975) investigated the idea of contingency by observing mothers as they helped their children do a puzzle. They found that mothers offered different amounts of support, depending on the level of difficulty that their child was having.

In his book entitled *The Process of Education*, Bruner (1960/1977) highlights a range of issues that are relevant to educational practice:

- *Readiness for learning* – Bruner argues against the concept of readiness and the notion of delaying teaching subjects because they are considered to be too difficult. He believes that children (even very young ones) are capable of learning any subject – 'any subject can be taught effectively in some intellectually honest form to any child at any stage of development' (Bruner 1960). For Bruner, the key to successful learning is the appropriateness of the instruction to the individual's learning needs, including coaching in an appropriate mode of representation. This assumption underpins the spiral curriculum which involves structuring material so that complex ideas are initially presented in a simplified form and then later revisited at more complex levels.

- *Motives for learning* – Bruner argues that interest in the material is the best stimulus for learning rather than the use of external goals (such as grades).

- *Intuitive versus analytical thinking* – Although the role of analytical thinking is emphasized in education, intuition can often be overlooked. Bruner believes intuition to be an essential aspect of thinking and reasoning that should be encouraged through schooling and the curriculum.

- *Knowing is a process rather than a product* – Education should focus on teaching children to participate in the process of learning rather than on learning lots of facts; the emphasis is more on the process of learning rather than on what is learned (the content). Teachers should help the learner think beyond the information that is presented to formulate new ideas and thoughts of their own.

> **Activity** **Comparing theories (Part 3)**
>
> Return to the table you created to compare the theories of Piaget, Vygotsky and Bruner (for the activities on p.267 and p.270 respectively) and add a new row entitled 'The role of teaching in cognitive development' and note down each of their views on this important issue.
>
> Answers are given on p.609. ▶

Check your understanding of the development of thinking by answering the following questions. Try to do this from memory. You can check your answers by looking back through Topic 1.

1 Explain briefly what Piaget meant by the following terms: schema, operations, circular reactions, assimilation, accommodation, adaptation and equilibration.

2 What, according to Piaget, is cognitive development driven by?

3 What led Piaget to conclude that children think differently from adults and younger children think differently from older ones?

4 What is meant by a universal stage theory of cognitive development?

5 In what ways does Piaget's theory of cognitive development acknowledge the role of both nature (innate factors) and nurture (environmental factors)?

6 Prepare a list of the main strengths and limitations of Piaget's theory of cognitive development.

7 In what ways are Piaget's and Vygotsky's ideas about cognitive development similar and in what ways do they differ?

8 According to Vygotsky, cognitive development occurs by means of: (a) discovery; (b) the influence of others; (c) cultural knowledge; (d) b and c. Which of these four options do you think is correct?

9 What, in Vygotsky's view, is the role of language in development?

10 What is meant by the following terms: the zone of proximal development; scaffolding?

11 What are the three modes of representation identified by Bruner? Under what circumstances might each be used?

12 Outline the key contributions to education practice made by Piaget, Vygotsky and Bruner.

Topic 2: Development of moral understanding

The rules that make social life possible are embodied in a society's morality. In addition to a society's written laws, there are also unwritten moral rules such as helping others. In order to behave morally it is necessary to distinguish between right and wrong. The study of **moral development** is concerned with the rules about the rightness and wrongness of certain behaviours and how people ought to behave towards each other. Psychologists have studied three aspects of moral development:

- how children *think* and *reason* about moral issues

- how children actually *behave* when required to exercise moral judgement

- how children *feel* about moral issues (e.g. feelings of guilt).

In Topic 2 we focus on the contribution of two key theorists – Kohlberg and Eisenberg – whose work has built on Piaget's early work on moral development.

Psychology in context   Wife killer, 100, spared prison

This was one of the headlines on the BBC News website on Thursday 8 July 2004, following the trial of Bernard Heginbotham at Preston Crown Court for the murder of his wife, Ida, by cutting her throat at the nursing home where she was being cared for (http://news.bbc.co.uk/1/hi/england/lancashire/2971819.stm).

Bernard Heginbotham, a retired butcher, was a devoted husband to Ida (aged 87) for 67 years and they had had six children. Ida had become dependent on her husband, following a series of falls and surgery, and was, finally, unable to continue living at their home. Bernard had become increasingly distressed by Ida's failing health and also because she had been moved between a number of nursing homes. He had been particularly distraught after a telephone call from his son, Neville, telling him that Ida was to be transferred to another care home some distance away. Bernard did not want his wife to be moved again and did not

think that she was going to receive the kind of care he wanted her to have. He went to the home with a knife and cut her throat.

In this topic we will be examining research about moral understanding, so to start you thinking about this important subject, consider the following questions and note down the reasons for each of your answers:

- Do you think that Bernard was right to kill his wife?

- Was it right for his case to be tried in court?

- Should Bernard have been sent to prison? What kind of punishment, if any, do you think was appropriate for Bernard?

- How do you think their son, Neville, and the other five children might have reacted to the news that their father had killed their mother?

Discuss your ideas with other students in your class. Are your answers and the reasons for your answers similar? If not, how do they differ?

Theories of moral understanding

Cognitive development influences children's understanding of their social, as well as their physical, world. In addition to studying cognitive development, Piaget (1932) was interested in how children come to understand the social conventions and moral rules of their society. He observed children playing the then popular game of marbles and asked questions about the rules they were using. He found that the youngest children did not use any rules. By the age of five, children were using rules in a fixed and unchangeable way – rules had to be obeyed and punishment followed if they were not (he called this the heteronomous stage of morality). Around the age of 10 or 11, children began to realize that rules are procedures that facilitate co-operation between humans and are not absolute but can be changed, as long as everyone agrees (the autonomous stage of morality).

Piaget also told stories to the children. In each pair of stories, there was one where the child had good intentions, but accidentally caused considerable damage, while in the other story there was less damage, but the child's intentions were also less good. After each pair of stories, Piaget asked which person was naughtier and should be punished more. Piaget focused on the reasons the children gave for their answers rather than the actual answers themselves. In particular, he was interested in whether it was the consequences of specific actions or the intentions that formed the basis of the child's moral judgements. Younger children focused on the consequences of an action (i.e. the outcome) rather than on the intention behind the action, whereas older children also considered the intention when deciding the morality of an action. In a story where a young boy breaks 15 cups while trying to help his mother and another story where a boy broke one cup when trying to steal some biscuits, the younger children tended to think that the first boy was worse than the second boy who only broke one cup. Older children, on the other hand, tended to think the opposite, based on the underlying motives (Piaget 1932/1965).

Kohlberg's theory of moral understanding

Lawrence Kohlberg (1927–1987) developed a more detailed stage theory of moral understanding during the late 1950s, building on Piaget's work and extending it to include adolescence and early adulthood. Like Piaget, Kohlberg believed it is necessary to focus on children's cognitive functioning to understand how they think about moral issues. He studied aspects of moral development for nearly 30 years, starting as a postgraduate student in the late 1950s. See the Key research feature opposite, Kohlberg's original study of moral understanding, for an outline of the early research he undertook for his doctorate.

Although Kohlberg's theory is more complex than Piaget's, consisting of three levels and six stages of moral reasoning, there are some similarities:

- Both Piaget and Kohlberg suggested that moral development proceeds through a sequence of innately determined stages that occur in an invariant sequence.

Level 1: Preconventional morality	
Stage 1: Punishment and obedience orientation	Children decide what is wrong, based on what is punished. Obedience is important and adults (and those in positions of authority) are obeyed because of their superior power.
Stage 2: Individualism, instrumental purpose and exchange	Rules are followed by children when it is in their personal interest to do so and produce pleasant results (self-interest).
Level 2: Conventional morality	
Stage 3: Mutual interpersonal expectations, relationships and interpersonal conformity	Moral behaviour is influenced by the expectations and approval of others (e.g. family, friends and significant others). It is important to be seen to 'be good'.
Stage 4: Social system and conscience	The rules and laws of society define morality in order to maintain social order (e.g. protecting life and respecting other people's property).
Level 3: Postconventional or principled morality	
Stage 5: Social contract or utility and individual rights	Young people/adults realize that some laws can be changed and some values are relative, while others (such as the sanctity of life) are not negotiable. Moral behaviour is guided by the principle of trying to achieve the greatest good for the greatest number.
Stage 6: Universal ethical principles	To determine what is right and wrong, an adult develops and follows an integrated set of ethical principles and values which are carefully selected and can be articulated to others.

Table 8.8 *Kohlberg's theory of moral understanding (Kohlberg 1976)*

Kohlberg's original study of moral understanding

Kohlberg carried out a cross-sectional research study using 10 moral dilemmas which he developed and presented to 72 boys, aged 10, 13 and 16, from Chicago to assess their moral reasoning. A moral dilemma always involves powerful arguments for and against a central issue. One of the best known of Kohlberg's dilemmas was about whether a man, called Heinz, was right to steal a drug in an attempt to save his wife's life (see the description in the box below).

During two-hour interviews, each participant was asked a series of questions to probe their reasons for recommending a particular course of action after reading each dilemma in turn. Cognitive developmental theories, such as Piaget's and Kohlberg's theory of moral development, are concerned with the reasons underlying moral judgements rather than the judgements themselves because the same answer could be given but for entirely different reasons. In addition to asking whether Heinz was right to steal the drug, he also asked other questions such as would a good husband steal in these circumstances; was the pharmacist right to charge so much for the drug; and what kind of sentence should the judge give Heinz? Based on these data, Kohlberg developed a system for classifying moral understanding, involving six qualitatively different stages spanning three levels (see Table 8.8). Although Kohlberg did not assert that everyone progresses through all six stages, he claimed that the order of the stages was fixed and universal.

- Both assumed that development occurs as a consequence of maturation and disequilibrium (i.e. current thinking is challenged by inconsistencies arising through experience).

- They were both interested in the reasoning behind the moral choices rather than the answers themselves: the focus is on how people think rather than what they think.

- They both assumed that moral principles and moral behaviour were linked.

Evaluation

1 Kohlberg has been criticized for using hypothetical dilemmas to test moral understanding. When a situation is artificial, participants may resort to using rules learned from significant adults (such as parents and teachers) to judge right and wrong rather than their own views, so their responses may not provide an accurate indication of moral reasoning ability.

2 All the participants in the study were boys and therefore the research is gender biased and the resulting theory is androcentric (i.e. it reflects a male approach to moral understanding).

3 Kohlberg's dilemmas may be more relevant to middle-class, Western Europeans living in individualistic cultures which promote achievement and personal rights. In collectivist cultures which place greater emphasis on social duties and obligations, meeting family needs and submitting to the authority of others would be regarded as indicating the highest moral principles, and yet would be scored at lower levels using Kohlberg's stages (Snarey et al. 1985).

4 Kohlberg focused on the development of reasoning about the moral values of justice and fairness, overlooking values such as empathy and the role of emotions such as shame and guilt. Kohlberg acknowledged this weakness in his later work (Kohlberg et al. 1983).

Heinz steals the drug

'In Europe, a woman was near death from a special kind of cancer. There was one drug that the doctors thought might save her. It was a form of radium that a druggist [pharmacist] in the same town had recently discovered. The drug was expensive to make, but the druggist was charging ten times what the drug cost him to make. He paid $200 for the radium and charged $2000 for a small dose of the drug. The sick woman's husband, Heinz, went to everyone he knew to borrow the money, but he could only get together about $1 000 which is half of what it cost. He told the druggist that his wife was dying, and asked him to sell it cheaper or let him pay later. But the druggist said 'No, I discovered the drug and I'm going to make money from it'. So Heinz got desperate and broke into the man's store to steal the drug for his wife. Should the husband have done that? Why?' (Kohlberg and Elfenbein 1975)

Activity   Is Heinz right to steal the drug?

1 Re-read the story about Heinz in the previous box above on p.277.

2 Do you think that Heinz was right to steal the drug to try and save his wife's life? Note down your answer and the reasons for your answer.

3 Work in a small group of up to 10 students from your psychology class and create a summary table to record: (i) each person's yes/no answer and (ii) the reasons for the answer.

4 Read the text on p.276 and then each person in the group individually analyse the reasons each individual gave for their answer (including their own) to identify which of the six stages it represents.

5 Finally, discuss any differences in your analysis of the stages; try to reach a consensus about the stage that each person's reasoning represents. Which of the six stages were represented in your group and how many people were operating in each of the stages?

The six stages of moral reasoning

Kohlberg (1976) found that individuals tended to use one dominant stage of reasoning across all the dilemmas. The six stages he identified are outlined below.

Preconventional morality (Level 1)

At Level 1 it is assumed that rules must be obeyed and these are defined by people in authority (parents, teachers and other adults). The standards used to distinguish right from wrong are external and determined by the likelihood of an action resulting in punishment rather than thinking through the moral issues.

Stage 1: Punishment and obedience orientation

For children at Stage 1, the rightness or wrongness of an action is judged on its consequences – behaviour that leads to punishment is wrong and good behaviour is associated with avoiding punishment. The rules used are defined by those in authority and should be obeyed unquestioningly in order to avoid punishment. They will usually indicate that Heinz was wrong to steal the drug (e.g. Heinz *should not* steal the drug because he might get caught and be sent to prison). Even if a child does not agree with Heinz's actions, the reasoning employed is still Stage 1 (e.g. Heinz *should* steal the drug because he must not let his wife die and if she does die he will be punished).

Stage 2: Individualism, instrumental purpose and exchange

Children start to do things that are rewarded or in their own best interests. By Stage 2, they begin to realize that there are usually different sides to any issue (and these may conflict): they are likely to see Heinz's viewpoint (stealing the drug is permitted because my wife is dying)

and the conflicting perspective of the pharmacist (it is wrong to steal from me). Since everything is relative, an individual may pursue their own needs and self-interest. Reasoning at this stage may involve exchanging favours (reciprocity) and doing deals ('you scratch my back and I'll scratch yours') and focuses on individuals in isolation rather than as part of a wider community or society. Possible Stage 2 answers are: Heinz *should* steal the drug, so his wife won't die and he won't be left alone and if he gets caught he can give the drug back to the pharmacist. Or Heinz *should not* steal the drug because if he gets caught and sent to prison, his wife will probably die before he is released from prison.

Conventional morality (Level 2)

At Level 2 individuals begin to understand that norms and conventions are necessary to uphold society. Moral reasoning involves a shift towards moral judgements based on conforming to the rules and conventions of a local reference group (e.g. family or peers) which become internalized but not questioned or challenged by the child. Decisions about the rightness or wrongness of specific actions are no longer based solely on external authority, but take account of others' views and needs, seeking approval, and the maintenance of positive relations with others and the rules of society.

Stage 3: Mutual interpersonal expectations, relationships and interpersonal conformity

Children/young people in the first stage of conventional morality (Stage 3) are usually entering their teenage years. As members of a society, local community and family, they conform by behaving in ways considered to be 'good', which please or help others and live up to their expectations (which is why this stage is sometimes described as the 'good boy/good girl' orientation). Good behaviour involves good intentions and empathy and concern for others. Individuals begin to take account of the intentions behind an action – if a bad outcome occurred by accident but the original intention was good, this is deemed to be less serious than an equally bad outcome that was deliberate. Heinz is often judged as right to steal the drug by those at Stage 3 because he wanted to be seen to be good by trying to save her life (e.g. Heinz *should* steal the drug for his wife because it shows that he loves his wife and is a good husband). An alternative Stage 3 response might be that Heinz *should not* steal the drug because his family will be ashamed of him. If his wife dies it will be the pharmacist's fault, not Heinz's fault. Responses are classified as Stage 3 reasoning if they imply wanting to be good, achieve group approval or impress others.

Stage 4: Social system and conscience

At Stage 4, individuals become more socially aware and community oriented, and they consider the possible effect of a particular behaviour on wider society. Reasoning tends to focus on doing one's duty, obeying laws and respecting authority so that social order is maintained. Those in Stage 4 typically suggested that Heinz was wrong to steal the drug by considering the importance of rules and laws for society as a whole (e.g. Heinz *should not* steal the drug because he must obey the law which is designed to protect everyone and ensure society can function in an orderly way. Without laws, our whole society would suffer). Alternatively, a person might argue that Heinz *should* steal the drug because it is not wrong to steal in this particular situation; the law cannot take account of every possible case.

Post-conventional or principled morality (Level 3)

At this highest level individuals realize that there are circumstances when society's rules and laws can legitimately be broken because what is morally right may conflict with what is legally right. A new authority emerges based on carefully chosen ethical ideals integrated into a personalized system of moral values and principles used to guide an individual's decision-making about what is right and wrong.

Stage 5: Social contract or utility and individual rights

At Stage 5, individuals become interested in the rights and values that a fair and egalitarian society *ought* to uphold so that everyone can benefit in the long term. However, the emphasis shifts from maintaining the *status quo* of society through rules and laws to consideration of important questions about what rights, justice and values a society should endorse, and recognizing that there may be occasions when rules and laws need to be ignored or changed. In response to Heinz's dilemma, individuals at Stage 5 responded by saying that although laws should be upheld, someone's right to life should also be protected. A typical response might be: Heinz *should* steal the drug because human life is more valuable and important than any property and although Heinz is wrong to steal, the moral perspective should transcend other considerations, including the rights of the pharmacist. Alternatively, a person at Stage 5 might argue that Heinz *should not* steal the drug because although it is understandable if he did steal it (and he could not be blamed for doing so), it is not appropriate to take the law into one's own hands; the end does not justify the means. Laws provide a framework that enables people to live together in society.

Stage 6: Universal ethical principles

In Stage 5, individual rights and justice and the right to live are typically achieved through a democratic process which protects the majority but not everyone – some people will always benefit at the expense of others. This is illustrated when a group of friends try to decide where they will go and what they will do for an evening out – at least one person is likely to be outvoted by the others in the group and a decision is usually based on the majority view (which is how democracy operates). For individuals at Stage 6, on the other hand, the principles of justice should be universal and apply to all. Laws should not only favour the majority. In relation to Heinz, everyone's perspective needs to be considered – Heinz, his wife and the pharmacist. The pharmacist should recognize that the right to life is more important than property and all concerned ought, therefore, to agree the fairest outcome is that the wife should be given the drug in an attempt to save her life. For example, Heinz should steal the drug

because the moral principle of respecting and preserving human life is sacrosanct and takes precedence over all other values; when there is a choice between obeying the law and saving a life, the latter is more important. Alternatively, Heinz should not steal the drug because his wife is not the only person who is sick and needs the treatment. He should not disregard the needs of others who also require the drug to save their lives.

Research evidence

According to Bee (2000), Kohlberg's theory is one of the most provocative in developmental psychology, with hundreds of studies investigating specific aspects of the theory. She concludes: 'The remarkable thing is how well Kohlberg's ideas have stood up to this barrage of research and commentary'. As noted earlier, Kohlberg's original study (1963) was based on cross-sectional research (i.e. he interviewed different children at various ages to see if their reasoning differed). However, the best way to investigate whether all children follow the same sequence of stages is to carry out longitudinal research (see the Key research by Colby *et al.* (1983) below).

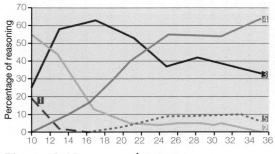

HOW SCIENCE WORKS

Longitudinal study of moral reasoning

Key research: Colby *et al.* (1983)

Colby *et al.* (1983) followed up 58 of Kohlberg's original sample of 72 boys for 20 years in a longitudinal study. They were tested six times, at three-yearly intervals, and the results, which are summarized in Figure 8.10, show that all the participants progressed through the stages in the predicted sequence. At age 10, the children mainly displayed Stage 2 reasoning, with some examples of Stages 1 and 3. By the age of 22, no one used Stage 1 reasoning, and Stages 3 and 4 were predominant. By the age of 36 and the end of the study, there was still little evidence of Stage 5 reasoning (only five per cent): Stages 3 and 4 were the most common form of moral reasoning in adulthood.

Figure 8.10 Age group

As a result of this longitudinal research, Kohlberg decided that the moral dilemmas and interviews could not distinguish effectively between thinking at Stages 5 and 6, so Stage 6 was dropped and all post-conventional responses were classified as Stage 5.

Kohlberg's findings have also been replicated by others, including a cross-sectional study by Walker and colleagues (1987) and a longitudinal study by Walker (1989). Similarly, Rest (1983) concludes that there is compelling empirical evidence to support Kohlberg's theory that moral reasoning changes over time in the sequence he identified, based on his 20-year longitudinal study of men from adolescence to their mid-30s. Gibson (1990) also studied men in their forties and fifties and found that only 13 per cent were using Stage 5.

To demonstrate the universality the sequence of six stages, Kohlberg (1969) studied the moral reasoning of children in a number of other countries – Britain, Mexico, Taiwan, Turkey, USA and Yucatan – and reported the same pattern of development. Colby and Kohlberg (1987) reported broadly similar findings from longitudinal studies in Turkey and Israel. In his critical review of many research studies, Snarey (1985) indicates that Kohlberg's dilemmas have been presented to children, young people and adults in 27 Western and non-Western, industrialized and non-industrialized countries and that the collective evidence is strong for the universality of Kohlberg's stages. Some differences have also been highlighted – for example, Stage 4 is usually the highest level reported in less complex societies (what Snarey refers to as 'folk' societies) whereas Stage 5 has been reported in both Western and non-Western urban societies.

The Heinz dilemma has also been presented to people living in Hindu villages in India and their moral reasoning analysed. Some people were found to be using high levels of moral reasoning which could not be scored on Kohlberg's scale because it was so different to Western reasoning. The idea of 'the divine' tended to be used rather than 'justice' (Shweder *et al.* 1987, 1997).

Iwasa (1992) used the Heinz dilemma to compare Japanese and American participants. Although no overall differences in levels of moral development were found, the reasons about why human life was highly valued differed. The Americans emphasized the importance of prolonging human life and most stated that Heinz should steal the drug, while the main concern of the Japanese participants was to make life purer, and the majority thought that Heinz should not steal the drug. Their answers reflected the cultural norms of their society.

Kohlberg applied his ideas to moral education. He suggested that children's moral reasoning might develop through participation in moral discussions rather than being taught new forms of thinking (Power, Higgins and Kohlberg 1989). The resulting 'Just Community' education programme aims to:

- facilitate moral development through discussion of moral issues
- develop a culture of moral norms through the democratic establishment of rules for the community
- provide an environment where everyone can act on their moral decisions.

 A cognitive-developmental versus social-cultural approach to moral development

Cultural factors have been identified as important in a number of studies of moral reasoning. For example, Nisan and Kohlberg (1982) carried out a cross-sectional and a longitudinal study of young people, aged between 10 and 28, in Turkey. Using Kohlberg's moral dilemmas and a new manual to score the responses which required criteria judgements, they found that the Turkish youngsters scored lower than Americans, and that those living in a rural environment scored lower than those living in cities. A social-cultural explanation would suggest that what develops over time is a person's ability to manage the moral expectations of the culture in which they live and that these expectations are expressed through language and other symbol systems. Kohlberg's cognitive-developmental approach, on the other hand, focuses on changes in mental processes occurring within an individual's head.

Activity **Acting on your moral beliefs**

Concern has been expressed about the assumed relationship between a person's moral beliefs and their actions. Do you always or usually act in accordance with your moral beliefs and principles?

If your actions do not usually/always reflect your moral beliefs, how can you explain any inconsistency? When is this inconsistency likely to occur? What implications do your answers have for the ability of Kohlberg's theory of moral development to predict moral behaviour?

Evaluation of Kohlberg's theory of moral development

- *Kohlberg's findings have been replicated* – Walker *et al.* (1987) reported broadly similar results, confirming Kohlberg's original findings, but highlighted nine stages (rather than six) because the reasoning often fell between two of Kohlberg's stages.

- *Cross-cultural support* – Snarey (1985) carried out a meta-analysis of 44 cross-cultural studies conducted in 27 countries and all 44 studies reported a progression from Stages 1 to 4 at similar ages. However, very few studies found evidence of Stage 5 reasoning and when it was reported it tended to be in urban areas. Eckensberger's (1983) review of over 50 studies also supported the invariant progression of stages.

- *The importance of social interaction* – Like Piaget, Kohlberg believed that moral understanding develops not from being told what is right or wrong, but through experiencing situations that demand moral responses. In support of this, Berkowitz and Gibbs (1983) claimed that the key to moral progression lay in 'transactive interactions' which involve discussion and asking questions such as 'Have you considered what would happen if…?' This supports Kohlberg's view that cognitive challenges to a person's current thinking promote moral growth, but only if the person is cognitively ready.

- *Not all the stages have been identified* – Colby and Kohlberg (1987) carried out a more careful analysis of Kohlberg's original data and found only 15 per cent of people reached Stage 5 and there was very little evidence of Stage 6 judgements. It would appear that judgements at Stage 6 may only be found in a very small number of exceptional individuals, such as Martin Luther King and Gandhi, and only in certain areas of their lives. The universal ethical principles associated with Stage 6 appear not to be universal (Eckensberger 1994); instead, they may represent an ideal moral disposition that is rarely achieved. There is, however, extensive empirical support for the first four stages of moral development.

- *Gender bias* – Based on his stage theory, Kohlberg reported that men were more morally developed than women (most women were at Stage 3 and most men at Stage 4). According to Gilligan (1982), one of Kohlberg's students, his theory is androcentric (male centred) and this difference may be explained because women were being judged using a male standard, due to **gender bias** in Kohlberg's original research. Kohlberg's early work was based solely on the study of men, so his theory reflects a male approach to moral understanding. Gilligan approached morality from a different angle – that of an 'ethic of care', rather than the 'ethic of justice' that Kohlberg used. She interviewed 20 women who were facing the real-life dilemma of whether to have an abortion and also presented her findings in a stage theory of moral development which is quite different to Kohlberg's theory. This difference may be explained by the fact that Gilligan's participants were women. Gilligan claims that women have a different moral voice from men and make judgements using different criteria, such as compassion and interpersonal issues, rather than justice and logic. Gilligan is therefore challenging some of the fundamental assumptions of Kohlberg's theory.

- *Responses to Kohlberg's moral dilemmas are difficult to score* – Rest and colleagues (1999) found it was difficult to score moral reasoning responses accurately and so they developed and revised their own test of moral development – the Defining Issues Test (DIT2).

- *Emphasis on justice and fairness* – Some of Kohlberg's critics, such as Gilligan (1982), have argued that Kohlberg studied the development of reasoning about the moral values of justice and fairness and ignored values such as empathy and the role of emotions such as shame and guilt. In fact, Kohlberg himself acknowledged this weakness in his later work (Kohlberg *et al.* 1983). Eisenberg's model of prosocial reasoning, which we consider next, focuses on moral reasoning influenced by a concern for relationships with others (Eisenberg 1986).

- *Reasoning versus actual behaviour* – Kohlberg has been criticized for his emphasis on moral thought rather than on moral behaviour (e.g. Walker 2004). So does moral reasoning lead to moral behaviour? Evidence suggests that the two may not be closely related. In a very early study, Hartshorne and May (1928) studied the moral knowledge of children, aged between six and 14, and also observed their behaviour in situations where there was an opportunity to be either honest or dishonest. They found that most children were honest in some situations and not in others; their behaviour appeared to depend on how attractive the reward was and how likely the children were to get caught. More recently, Santrock (1975) reported that children's level of moral reasoning did not predict whether they would cheat when given the opportunity to do so. As a result of this criticism, Kohlberg emphasized moral action in the 'Just Community' education programme (Power, Higgins and Kohlberg 1989).

- *Artificiality* – Kohlberg's dilemmas have been criticized for being artificial tests of moral understanding. Children have experience of sharing toys and food, but not of the kinds of issues in Kohlberg's dilemmas. Using simple, concrete tasks Damon (1977) found that children as young as eight were using the ideas of justice and fairness to others to make moral judgements and act on them. And yet when presented with Kohlberg's dilemmas, they scored at Stages 1 or 2 and appeared unable to apply the concept of justice and fairness. Hart *et al.* (2003) claim that children's moral understanding is more sophisticated and complex than suggested by Kohlberg's research.

- *Cultural bias* – Kohlberg's theory may apply to Western cultures only. Although the cross-cultural evidence cited earlier appears to indicate that Kohlberg's stages of moral reasoning are universal, some doubt remains about the extent to which individuals from other countries can fully understand and identify with the dilemmas Kohlberg used. It could be argued that his dilemmas were more relevant to middle-class, Western Europeans living in individualistic cultures that promote achievement and personal rights. In collectivist cultures (such as kibbutzim in Israel), which place greater emphasis on family and community obligations, meeting family needs and respecting the wisdom of elders would be regarded as reflecting the highest moral principles, and yet would be scored at lower Kohlbergian stages (Snarey *et al.* 1985). Research undertaken in India and the United States by Miller and colleagues (1990) has suggested that the moral code in India tended to emphasize social responsibilities compared with personal decisions in America. Eckensberger (1999), on the other hand, claims that Kohlberg's theory is not as western in its orientation as others have suggested, arguing that what is important is the degree of industrialization, as the highest stages have been reported in Israel, Taiwan and India. Cultural factors may therefore play a significant role in moral reasoning.

- *Kohlberg's thinking has evolved over the years* – Like many great theorists, Kohlberg has been able to accommodate new ideas and evidence gathered over nearly 30 years of research without fundamentally changing the core aspects of his original theory. Moreover, his theory has generated a lot of research which has enhanced our understanding of moral development.

- *Others have built on Kohlberg's work* – Kohlberg's ideas were used to develop the first edition of the Defining Issues Test (DIT) in 1979, which was subsequently revised in 1999 to become the DIT-2 (Rest *et al.* 1999). This test is used in areas, such as medicine, where it is important to assess moral thinking.

Eisenberg's theory of prosocial reasoning

Nancy Eisenberg claimed that Kohlberg placed too much emphasis on justice and fairness and overlooked the strong emotional dimension of moral decision making. Although her approach is broadly similar to that of Kohlberg in that she also used dilemmas to investigate children's prosocial reasoning, her underlying approach is different because she focuses on the emotional component of moral decisions. **prosocial reasoning** refers to an area of thinking that is concerned with helping or comforting others, sometimes at personal cost. Like Piaget and Kohlberg, Eisenberg (sometimes referred to as Eisenberg-Berg) believed that changes take place in prosocial reasoning in parallel with the maturation of cognitive abilities.

The role of empathy

According to Eisenberg (1986), empathy is a key feature in the development of prosocial reasoning. **Empathy** is a person's ability to understand someone else's emotions. Eisenberg places considerable importance on empathy and assumes that a child needs to be able to empathize with another person's situation in order to make a prosocial decision about a dilemma. One way to develop this is through adopting the role of others and seeing the world from another person's perspective. Children's games often involve practising these role-taking skills which may be vital for prosocial reasoning.

Eisenberg *et al.* (1983) reported that empathy develops during Level 4 (from about the age of 12 onwards), but other research has reported evidence of empathy at an earlier age. For example, Zahn-Waxler *et al.* (1979) reported that infants as young as two demonstrated concern when they witnessed others in distress, based on the results of an observational study. Mothers were trained in observational techniques and asked to record their child's reactions and also their own in relation to everyday situations involving the expression of distress (such as pain, sorrow, discomfort). Distress was also simulated by mothers and researchers. The mothers were also encouraged to highlight another child's feelings when their child had hurt that child (e.g. 'Stop doing that because you're hurting John and will make him cry').

As empathy develops, children become capable of experiencing 'sympathetic distress' and the ability to show compassion. However, experiencing distress at another person's suffering does not trigger a child's ability to respond appropriately. Although they may feel distressed when they see someone suffering, they also need cognitive awareness to guide their behaviour towards altruism. It is the child's level of cognitive maturity that provides an understanding of another person's condition and sufficient awareness to help someone in need intentionally either for altruistic or non-altruistic reasons (which is known as **prosocial behaviour**). There is, therefore, an important distinction between a younger child's more primitive empathetic distress displayed when they are with someone who is suffering (as reported by Zahn-Waxler and colleagues) and a cognitive understanding of another person's condition which results in sympathetic distress (compassion). Cognitive awareness is more likely to result in a child going to the assistance of others, whereas distress on its own does not.

Eisenberg's research

As we have seen, Kohlberg's studies of moral reasoning focused on behaviours that are normally considered to be unacceptable (such as stealing), so his approach was prohibition dominated. Eisenberg, on the other hand, argued that to assess children's prosocial reasoning ability it is important to focus on situations where there is a conflict between the child's own needs and those of others. Eisenberg also used dilemmas but these involved some kind of cost–benefit analysis and the hypothetical stories were set in a context where laws, rules, formal obligations or punishments were minimized. In each scenario the central character has to decide whether to help or comfort someone when this prosocial act would involve some personal cost (see the box on p.283 for an example of one of the stories Eisenberg used).

Eisenberg (1982, 1986) therefore undertook a series of research studies during the 1980s in which children and young people were presented with a series of hypothetical stories in which the main character has to make a choice between self-interest and helping another person at some personal cost to themselves.

Eisenberg-Berg and Hand (1979) found that pre-school children's responses to the stories tended to be 'hedonistic' and self-centred. For example, they might say that Mary shouldn't help the injured child because she would miss the party. Alternatively, they might argue that

One of the stories Eisenberg used to assess prosocial reasoning

One day a girl named Mary was going to a friend's birthday party. On her way she saw a girl who had fallen down and hurt her leg. The girl asked Mary to go to her house and get her parents so they could come and take her to a doctor. But if Mary did run and get the child's parents, she would be late for the birthday party and miss the ice cream, cake, and all the games. What should Mary do?

(Eisenberg 1982)

Mary should help the other child so that she would be helped by others when in need. Over time this shifts towards needs-oriented reasoning: older children appeared to take the other person's feelings and needs into account. By adolescence, some of those interviewed indicated that they would lose self-respect if they ignored the needs of the other person.

Based on the reasoning given, Eisenberg (1986) identified five main levels in her theory of prosocial reasoning; these demonstrate whether a person's actions are intended to help another individual and the reasons why (see Table 8.9). Eisenberg-Berg and Hand (1979) also reported some evidence that an individual's level of prosocial reasoning predicted actual prosocial behaviour. For example, more sharing behaviour was noted for individuals at Level 2 compared with those at Level 1.

Eisenberg and colleagues carried out a longitudinal study which followed a group of children from age four through to adolescence (Eisenberg et al. 1987, 1991, 1995). Every two years the same dilemmas were presented to the same group of individuals who were asked 'What should the person in the story do next?' Their reasoning was analysed using a scale with a minimum score of 4 and a maximum score of 16 and changes recorded over time. They found that moral understanding was not always entirely consistent when children were tested on different dilemmas. For example, some pre-school children mentioned their own feelings as well as the needs of others, displaying the characteristics of two different levels of prosocial moral reasoning. When subsequently tested, there was evidence of development with less hedonistic reasoning and an increase in altruistic justification. As children's cognitive understanding developed, so their reasoning tended to shift towards helping others.

Figure 8.11 on p.284 demonstrates the marked decrease in hedonistic reasoning during childhood and adolescence and a corresponding increase in needs-oriented reasoning. Eisenberg reports that similar patterns have been found in children in West Germany, Italy and Poland but that children raised on kibbutzim in Israel showed little needs-oriented reasoning and were more likely to use internalized values and norms (i.e. Level 4) as the basis of their reasoning (Eisenberg 1986). This suggests that culture may play a greater role in children's prosocial reasoning than in reasoning about justice (Kohlberg's theory). Similarly, Fiske (2004) argues that

Level	Brief description	Age range
1: Hedonistic (self-centred) reasoning	Main concern is the consequences for oneself; prosocial reasoning is only likely to occur when it helps to meet own needs.	Up to 7 years (Pre-school and infant school)
2: Needs-oriented reasoning	Considers the needs of others even if they conflict with own wishes or desires; responds to expressed needs but there is little or no evidence of sympathy for the other or any guilt if help is not given.	7–11 years (A few pre-school children but mostly infant and junior school)
3: Approval and interpersonal orientation	Child is most likely to help others in return for the reward of approval and praise; evidence of stereotyped understanding of what is good and bad behaviour (e.g. it's good to help others, especially if they're hurt).	11–14 years (Some junior school but mostly secondary school)
4a: Empathic orientation	Evidence of sympathetic responses and concern for others and feelings of guilt if help is not given.	12 years and above (Mostly secondary school)
4b: Transitional orientation	Internalized values, duties or norms relating to helping others are evident but are not usually explicitly articulated.	12 years and above (Mostly secondary school)
5: Strongly internalized	Meets obligations to others and society; helping behaviour is based on strongly internalized beliefs and values which are clearly articulated and important for self-respect.	16 years and above (A few school-aged young people and mostly adults)

Table 8.9 *The five main levels of prosocial reasoning (adapted from Eisenberg 1986)*

views about what is beneficial to another person are socially and culturally defined and may, for example, include things such as foot-binding, piercing and scarring.

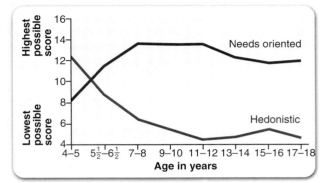

Figure 8.11 *Changes in hedonistic and needs-oriented reasoning during childhood and adolescence (Eisenberg et al. 1995)*

In further follow-up studies, Eisenberg *et al.* (1999, 2005) reported that those children who had displayed spontaneous prosocial behaviour in childhood continued to behave in this way in early adulthood, suggesting that there may be stable individual differences in prosocial behaviour which have their origins in childhood.

In a review of nearly 20 years of research, Eisenberg (1996) claims that, as predicted, children rarely indicated that they would help someone to avoid punishment or because they felt they had to obey authority figures such as parents and teachers. Although this is not unexpected because children are not punished for not responding in a prosocial way, it differs from Kohlberg's views of moral reasoning which are largely based on prohibition and punishment. Kohlberg claimed that other-oriented thinking emerges relatively late (Stage 3) whereas Eisenberg found that even pre-school children appeared to be aware of the needs of others and showed some basic indications of empathy. According to Eckensberger (1999), positive emotions (including empathy) are increasingly regarded as important in any explanation of moral understanding, suggesting a shift away from Kohlberg's theory. What is needed is a theory of moral development that combines the various patterns of moral reasoning identified by researchers, such as Piaget, Kohlberg and Eisenberg, with the motivational and social/cultural conditions under which moral behaviour (including altruism) occurs at different stages across the lifespan.

Evaluation of Eisenberg's approach

- *Primitive empathetic and sympathetic distress* – The distinction between primitive empathetic and sympathetic distress and the prediction that prosocial reasoning and behaviour is motivated by sympathetic distress but not by the more primitive empathetic distress (in which another individual's pain is felt as one's own pain) shown by younger children is supported by other research. For example, Caplan and Hay (1989) found that children, aged between three and five, often showed distress at another child's suffering, but rarely offered to help. The reason they gave for not helping was based on an assumption that adult intervention was needed. Older children realize that assistance does not always have to be provided by an adult and will usually offer to help.

- *Empathy and altruism* – Eisenberg believes that prosocial (altruistic) behaviour is possible when we understand the distress of another person. The empathy–altruism hypothesis (Batson 1991) supports Eisenberg's assertion that human altruism is motivated by experiencing the distress of another person. However, not everyone agrees: Cialdini *et al.* (1982), for example, have challenged this view, suggesting instead that we feel distressed when someone else is distressed but act in a way that helps to alleviate our own feelings of distress rather than for the good of the other person (the negative state relief hypothesis). This suggests a selfish angle to altruistic behaviour motivated by a need to reduce one's own feelings of distress.

- *A different perspective on moral understanding* – Eisenberg's theory offers a different perspective on the development of moral understanding to that of Piaget and Kohlberg. She emphasizes the importance of emotional factors and focuses on prosocial reasoning rather than on issues of wrongdoing and behaving badly. Nevertheless, there are strong parallels between Eisenberg's and Kohlberg's theories. Both endorse a stage approach based on cognitive maturity: individuals progress from one stage/level to another and although the stages/levels appear to be age-related, they are actually determined by underlying cognitive competence. Eisenberg's account broadens Kohlberg's original approach but without changing the fundamental tenets (Bee and Boyd 2007).

- *Practical relevance* – Eisenberg's work can provide useful guidance to parents, and others involved with children, about how to socialize children appropriately, especially on moral matters, including altruism. Examples include highlighting that the consequences of a behaviour matter, actively encouraging children to do helpful things, such as looking after pets and younger siblings, and giving their toys away, rather than just telling children what they ought to do and generally acting as role models of prosocial reasoning and behaviour (Bee and Boyd 2007).

CHAPTER 8 Cognition and development

Activity Alpha and beta bias

What is meant by the terms alpha bias and beta bias? If you cannot remember then turn to p.21 in the Introductory chapter to remind yourself.

To what extent is Gilligan's theory as guilty of alpha bias as Kohlberg's theory is of beta bias? Compare your views with those of other students in your psychology class.

CHECK YOUR UNDERSTANDING

Check your understanding of the development of moral understanding and behaviour by answering the following questions. Try to do this from memory. You can check your answers by looking back through Topic 2.

1 List the levels and stages of Kohlberg's theory of moral development and prepare a brief description of each of the six stages.

2 Kohlberg's theory has been accused of being androcentric. What is meant by the term 'androcentric' and is it a valid criticism of Kohlberg's research?

3 Outline the reasons why Kohlberg's research has been criticized by Gilligan (1982). Does Gilligan's research address all the concerns she raises?

4 Evaluate the key strengths and limitations of Kohlberg's theory of moral reasoning?

5 Prepare a brief summary (about 150 words) of the five levels proposed by Eisenberg.

6 Why might you expect there to be differences between individualist and collectivist societies in terms of their moral and prosocial reasoning?

7 In what ways does Eisenberg's theory of prosocial reasoning differ from Kohlberg's theory of moral development and in what ways is it similar?

8 Can children and young people be moral without being taught? Give reasons for your answer.

Topic 3: Development of social cognition

Social cognition is an area of theory and research that focuses on how people think about others and their understanding of social relationships. In this final topic we examine how social cognition develops in children, starting with some research evidence on visual self-recognition which suggests that an understanding of oneself occurs at an early age. We then go on to consider how children develop their understanding of others, including the role of perspective-taking which, as we saw in the previous topic, is a key aspect of our ability to empathize and is important for the development of prosocial reasoning.

Psychology in context   Feeling embarrassed at a very young age

As adults we experience a range of **self-conscious emotions**, such as guilt, shame and pride, but how early do these emotions develop?

Imagine the following scene: Anna, who is 18-months-old, has been playing happily in an entirely unselfconscious manner in a room where there are several adults and older children. Her aunt arrives and gives her a pretty dress and suggests she puts it on. When Anna returns to the room wearing her new dress, several people comment on how beautiful she looks. Anna lowers her eyes, fiddles with her dress and tries to hide behind her aunt. She has become the centre of attention and is feeling embarrassed. According to Lewis (2000), self-conscious emotions, such as

embarrassment, do not occur until self-recognition has developed.

For many years, psychologists have been interested in investigating the age at which infants can recognize themselves since this is important for the development of social cognition. Below are some questions for you to think about. You might wish to tackle these questions in a small group.

- How would you attempt to study self-recognition systematically in infants aged between nine and 18 months?
- What task(s) would you use?
- How would you assess self-recognition in a valid and reliable way?
- What would be the main challenges of designing and carrying out such a study?

Development of the child's sense of self

A person's self-concept consists of many facets, including self-recognition, self-awareness, self-identity and self-esteem. Understanding one's 'self' starts to develop at an early age and research has been carried out with children of various ages. Before reading on, try the activity below.

Self-recognition

Possibly one of the earliest indicators of an awareness of the existence of 'self' is through self-recognition. Early research by Lewis and Brooks-Gunn (1979) examined infants' understanding of their own existence, focusing on the ability to recognize oneself (self-recognition) which is particularly challenging to study in very young children because they cannot tell the researcher how they experience themselves.

A sense of self appears to develop at around 18 months, which is also the starting point for understanding others. Lewis and Brooks-Gunn (1979) argue that the two are inextricably linked and put forward three principles of social awareness:

- knowledge about another person must also be gained about the self

- what is known about the self can be known about the other and vice versa

- attributes (i.e. characteristics/qualities) of oneself and others can be used to describe other people.

The idea that knowledge about the self and others are related is also supported by Bischof-Kohler (1988), who used a mirror test with 16- to 24-month-olds. Additionally, level of empathy shown towards a researcher who shows sadness when the arm of a teddy bear falls off was noted. Level of self-recognition and empathy were found to be highly correlated, regardless of the infant's age. Bischof-Kohler concluded that empathic understanding of others and self-recognition is well developed by 20 months, and that both are necessary for self-conscious emotions (such as guilt, shame, embarrassment and pride) to develop. Such emotions are referred to as 'self-conscious' because they rely on some understanding of how others might perceive you and your situation.

Understanding emotions

Children's ability to understand emotions develops rapidly, so that by three to four years of age they can understand other people's emotions, desires and beliefs. Harris (1989) suggests that the reason this happens quickly is that children become aware of their own mind which they can then generalize to others. To be able to do this relies on children being:

- self-aware (which they are at about 18 months) and able to verbalize how they feel (which they can begin to do from the age of two)

- able to pretend, which they can do quite well by the age of two as shown during pretend play (e.g. teddy is hungry and needs to be fed)

- able to separate reality from pretence, which they can do without any ambiguity by the age of three or four as shown in play behaviour (e.g. you can be the daddy and I'll be the mummy).

Harris proposed that once a child is aware of his or her emotional state then this can be projected in a pretend way onto an inanimate object such as a toy or another person. This is done in such a way that the child is aware that the pretend emotional state is different to his or her own. To test this hypothesis, Harris (1989) designed a study to find out whether children were able to understand that another person's emotions in a given situation were founded on desires and wants. Children, aged between four and six, were told stories based on imaginary animal characters with their own particular likes and dislikes. For example, 'Ellie the elephant really liked drinking cola and when she got thirsty she looked forward to her favourite drink (cola). However, Mickey (a mischievous monkey) emptied a cola can and refilled it with milk (which Ellie did *not* like) and offered her the cola can'. The children were asked how Ellie would feel when she was given the can of cola and also when she had taken a drink and discovered it was milk. The younger children focused on Ellie being sad when she was first offered the can of cola (based on *their* knowledge) while the older children realized that Ellie would initially be happy until she discovered that the can contained milk (not cola) then she would become sad. By the age of six children can take account of another person's desires to work out their emotional state. They are also able to develop hypotheses about other people's emotions, desires and beliefs.

Piaget (1952) was also interested in this topic when he investigated children's egocentrism. Using the three mountains study, Piaget and Inhelder (1956)

Studying self-recognition

Key research: Lewis and Brooks-Gunn (1979)

Lewis and Brooks-Gunn conducted a series of studies to investigate infants' visual self-recognition. In the first study, infants were shown photos of themselves amongst photos of other babies of a similar age. They reported that infants were able to recognize themselves as early as 9–12 months; this was inferred because they smiled and looked longer at the photos of themselves than at the other photos. Older infants (15–18 months) said their own name when they saw a photo of themselves whereas photos of other babies were labelled as 'baby'.

Their most famous experiment was the 'mirror test'. Ninety-six infants aged 9, 12, 15, 18, 21 and 24 months participated in this large-scale study (there were 16 infants in each age group). The baby sat on its mother's lap in front of a large mirror and their behaviour was observed for 90 seconds. After this baseline measure of behaviour, rouge was dabbed onto the baby's nose by the mother during a routine nose wipe. As before, the mother and baby sat in front of the mirror for a further 90 seconds. The percentage of time the infants smiled and touched their own nose while viewing their reflection in the mirror is shown in Table 8.10.

Regardless of age, most of the infants smiled at their image, but very few touched their nose in the 'no rouge' condition. When rouge was applied to the nose, the older infants touched their nose and this increased with age – nearly three-quarters of those aged 21 and 24 months touched their nose while

only 25 per cent of the 18-month-old infants did so. The assumption is that increased touching of the nose indicates that the infant recognizes him/herself in the mirror and is surprised by the unusual red mark because this is not what he/she normally looks like. From these findings, it was concluded that infants have well-developed self-recognition by the age of two.

Povinelli *et al.* (1996) also found that three- and four-year-olds would remove a sticker that had been discretely placed on their forehead when they realized its presence by seeing themselves on video playback. Younger infants, aged two, on the other hand, did not remove the sticker. According to Povinelli and colleagues, this is because although the younger infants may recognize themselves on the video footage, they did not appear to understand that the recent video footage of them would continue to apply until they removed the sticker from their forehead.

Evaluation

The methods used in these studies of infants and young children were carefully chosen. The need for verbal communication was eliminated by using responses (dependent variables) that relied on a motor response to a stimulus (looking, smiling, touching one's nose or removing a sticker). The independent variable was kept simple – showing photos, using a mirror reflection or presenting video footage. The initial observation period in the 'mirror test' provided a useful baseline measure of behaviour before the introduction of the independent variable. The findings have ecological validity, as infants will naturally look at faces of others in real life.

Infant's behaviour	Condition	Age (in months)					
		9	12	15	18	21	24
Smiling	No rouge	86	94	88	56	63	60
	Rouge	99	74	88	75	82	60
Touching own nose	No rouge	0	0	0	6	7	7
	Rouge	0	0	19	25	70	73

Table 8.10 *The percentage of time the infant smiled and touched their nose while looking at their reflection in a mirror (Lewis and Brooks-Gunn 1979)*

demonstrated that children in the pre-operational stage of cognitive development (2–6 years) were unable to understand the perspectives of other people (see p.259). Harris's research indicates that children can 'decentre' at a much earlier age than Piaget originally suggested. Further support for Harris's findings comes from the work

of Simon Baron-Cohen whose research will be considered next when we consider the theory of mind.

Theory of mind

A **theory of mind** (often abbreviated to **ToM**) underpins our understanding of mental states (beliefs, desires, intentions, emotions, imagination) that cause action and reflects on the content of our own minds and other people's minds and the realization that these may differ (i.e. that what other people know, believe or feel about things may be different from one's own knowledge, beliefs and feelings). ToM allows us to make inferences about what others know, think and feel and to predict their motivations, what they are likely to do next and the reasons behind their actions (their intentions). Baron-Cohen (1993, 1995) also uses the term '**mind reading**' when discussing ToM because we mind read other people's mental states all the time without even noticing (although not, of course, in the literal sense).

The term ToM was first used by Premack and Woodruff (1978) when studying a chimpanzee's ability to predict a person's behaviour and has since been used by psychologists studying children's ability to perceive someone else's thoughts, wants, beliefs and/or feelings.

A ToM provides a common conceptual understanding that enables us to understand meaning and intentions. So if I say 'Have you got the time please?' I do not expect a 'yes/no' answer – you will understand that I want to know the time. A common understanding is important because it is essential for social interaction. It is also important for children's ability to play. Understanding mental and emotional states is not, however, quite as simple as it might sound. Read the following two statements and decide whether each one is true or false:

◾ 'Whales are fish'

◾ 'Jane believes that whales are fish'.

The first statement is straightforward because it is factually incorrect (whales are mammals). The second statement is, however, more difficult because it contains two components – a proposition (whales are fish) and a statement of belief regarding the proposition (Jane believes it to be the case). Statements of this latter type can therefore be true, even when the proposition is false.

Testing for ToM

An awareness that people may have different beliefs and feelings to our own enables us to empathize with others and also to manipulate and deceive them. Telling a lie is a structurally complex thing to do because it involves taking account of the mental state of the other person. To do this, Baron-Cohen (1993) claims a person needs to be able to represent a range of mental states such as pretending, imagining, guessing and deceiving. Baron-Cohen also found that children learn early on how to suspend the normal truth relations of propositional information, which may help to explain why children as young as four or five can understand stories involving deception as portrayed in much-loved children's stories (e.g. Little Red Riding Hood *thinks* it's her grandmother in the bed, but it's really the nasty wolf). By the age of four or five, a child begins to understand that he/she cannot always predict accurately what other people will do just from observing the situation itself – the other person's desires and beliefs may also affect the other person's behaviour and need to be taken into account.

Simon Baron-Cohen, professor of Developmental Psychopathology at Cambridge, is well known for his research on autism and theory of mind. He was awarded the Presidents' Award for Distinguished Contributions to Psychological Knowledge from the British Psychological Society in 2006

Two clinical psychologists – Alan Leslie and Simon Baron-Cohen – noted that children with autism appear to lack the ability to understand other people's minds (i.e. a ToM) and coined the phrase mindblindness to describe this ToM deficit (Baron-Cohen 1995). In an early study Baron-Cohen *et al.* (1985) investigated when children develop a ToM by studying normal children, children with autism (i.e. children with impaired social interaction, impaired communication skills and who exhibit repetitive patterns of behavior) and children with Down's syndrome (see Key research p.289). The three groups of participants were as follows:

◾ Normal children of average/above average intellectual ability for their chronological age and good social competence (control for the effects of maturation).

◾ The children with autism had average or above average intellectual ability but poor social competence.

◾ The children with Down's syndrome were socially competent but their intellectual ability was well below average (a control for intelligence).

A number of tests have been employed to investigate whether children have a ToM and the age at which it is acquired, including tests to infer what a person might want from the direction of their eye gaze (Baron-Cohen 2001), but in this section we will focus on **false-belief tasks**. A well-known false-belief task is the Sally-Anne task, developed by Baron-Cohen *et al.* (1985), which is outlined in the Key research opposite. It has become the most widely used, standard version of a false-belief task, adapted from a task that was originally devised by Wimmer and Perner (1983) and involved two dolls (Maxi and his mother) and the movement of chocolate belonging to Maxi from one location to another by the mother while Maxi is outside playing (this is sometimes referred to as the Maxi task). Baron-Cohen and colleagues simplified the 'Maxi' task so that it was suitable for use with autistic children. It is assumed that children who answer false-belief questions successfully have a developed ToM because they understand there are two different sets of beliefs (their own beliefs based on what they have seen and reasoned, and the beliefs of others based on what they have seen and reasoned).

Using a false-belief task to investigate theory of mind

Key research: Baron-Cohen, Leslie and Frith (1985)

Baron-Cohen and colleagues undertook a quasi-experiment (natural experiment) using the Sally-Anne false-belief task to test three groups of children (N = 61):

- 20 autistic children, aged between six and 16 (mean chronological age = 11.11 years) and a mean verbal mental age of 5.5 years.

- 14 children with Down's syndrome, aged between six and 17 (mean 10.11) and a mean verbal mental age of 2.11 years.

- 27 normal children, aged between three and five (mean 4.5) with a verbal mental age similar to their chronological age.

They hypothesized that the normal children and the children with Down's syndrome would have a ToM but that the autistic children would not. This prediction was based on the fact that children with autism have poor social competency and their ability to play is seriously compromised. The independent variable is the three groups of children and the dependent variable is success or failure on the task. Each child was seated at a table opposite the researchers and tested individually using two dolls – one named Sally and the other one, Anne.

The Sally-Anne task

Sally has a basket and Anne has a box. Sally has a marble and puts it into her basket and then goes out. Anne takes Sally's marble out of the basket and puts it into her box. Sally comes back and wants to play with her marble. The child is then asked the false-belief question: 'Where will Sally look for her marble?' The steps in the task are summarized in Figure 8.12. Three other questions were also asked: (i) a 'naming' question to confirm that the child knew the names of the two dolls (this question is asked at the outset); (ii) a 'reality' question ('Where is the marble really?') to check that the child had paid attention to the transfer of the marble from the basket to the box; and (iii) a 'memory' question (Where was the marble at the beginning?) to check that the child had not forgotten where Sally had left the marble. All of the control questions were correctly answered.

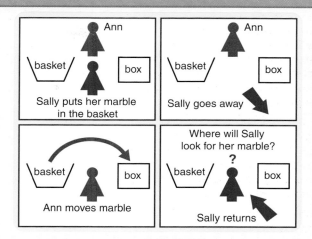

Figure 8.12 *The Sally-Anne task*

To be successful on this task, they needed to give the correct answer to the belief question (that Sally believes that the marble is in her basket). The results supported their hypothesis: 23 out of the 27 normal children (85 per cent) and 12 of the 14 children with Down's syndrome (86 per cent) answered the belief questions correctly, whereas 80 percent of the autistic children (i.e. 16 out of 20) failed to answer the questions correctly. The difference was statistically significant.

It is interesting to note that the autistic children performed significantly worse than the children with Down's syndrome, despite the fact that the verbal mental age of those with Down's syndrome was much lower (2.11 years compared with 5.5). This and other evidence has been used to suggest that children with autism lack a ToM (Baron-Cohen 1995).

Evaluation

A particular strength of the experimental method used by Baron-Cohen and colleagues is the precise control of variables. However, since it is known that autistic children do not play well, the use of dolls may be inappropriate. Children may also think that dolls cannot believe things, rendering the task artificial and lacking in validity. This study has also generated a significant amount of further research.

Further research using other false-belief tasks has reported similar findings. For example, Perner and colleagues (1989) used a 'Smarties task' where young children are shown a tube of smarties and asked, 'What do you think is inside?' They will invariably answer 'smarties'. They are then shown what is inside the tube and are surprised to discover that it contains pencils. The researcher then closes the tube and asks the child two belief questions:

1 'When I first showed you this tube what did you think was in here?' The child answers 'smarties'.

2 'And when the next child comes in who hasn't seen the tube, what will he or she think is inside here?'

The correct answer to the second question is smarties (a false-belief). Children from the age of three responded correctly whereas younger children struggled. To answer this and other similar questions correctly, a child must realize that what they know (e.g. the smarties tube has pencils in it) is not known by the other child; this is assumed to demonstrate a ToM. An incorrect answer, on the other hand, indicates that the child cannot distinguish what they know and what others would know.

Activity **Create your own false-belief task**

Work in a small group and create a false-belief test that is similar to the Sally-Anne task, including the required false-belief questions. Try to keep it simple by creating a first-order test (i.e. a test which only involves inferring one person's mental state). Try it out with one or two of your friends.

Then devise a more complex version (i.e. a second-order test which involves embedded mental states such as what X thinks that Y thinks) by introducing a third person who witnesses the event and would therefore have a different perspective. Ask questions about what false-belief this third person would have on behalf of the key player in your task. Try out this version with some of your friends and see how they respond.

Evaluation of theory of mind

- *Replication* – Since the early study by Baron-Cohen and colleagues in 1985, the findings have been replicated by other researchers (e.g. Happé 1994a and b). However there is also contradictory evidence (e.g. Mitchell 1997). A meta-analysis conducted on 187 studies by Wellman *et al.* (2001) concluded that ToM does develop during the pre-school years and is not an artifact of the tasks used.

- *Use of false-belief tasks* – Research using false-belief tasks suggests an understanding of ToM develops around the age of three, but other researchers have suggested that this ability is not fully developed until later. Chandler and Sokol (1999) claim that children's understanding of other people's minds develops long after they are successful at false-belief tasks. For example, Carpendale and Chandler (1996) showed children, aged between five and eight, an ambiguous drawing of a rabbit or duck face (see p.77). When asked what they saw, they would say a rabbit and a duck, indicating that they could identify both interpretations. However, when asked a question about what someone called Anne would see, they typically said either the rabbit, or the duck, or that they did not know. Furthermore, when asked why they did not know, they could not explain why it is difficult to predict someone else's interpretation. Children's ability to answer these questions correctly improved with age. There is therefore much to learn about ToM even after successful performance on false-belief tasks.

- *Is a false-belief task a valid test of ToM?* – Some claim that false-belief tasks are inherently difficult, partly because they require a child to reason about a belief that is false when beliefs are supposed to be true. Bloom and German (2000) suggest that false-belief tasks should be abandoned for two reasons: (i) successful performance on these tasks requires abilities other than ToM and (ii) ToM need not entail the ability to reason about false-beliefs.

- *Performance on false-belief tasks focusing on behaviour and emotion may differ* – It may be difficult for children to extrapolate successful performance on false-belief tasks to other contexts. An understanding of the relationship between false-beliefs and emotion, as demonstrated by the 'Ellie the elephant' task devised by Harris (1989), may develop more slowly than false-beliefs and behaviour (as indicated by the 'Sally-Anne' task).

- *Understanding deception* – Understanding deception is part of a ToM because it involves trying to make someone else believe that something is true when it is actually false. Peskin (1992) investigated the ability of three-, four- and five-year-olds to deceive two puppets into choosing a sticker they did not want. Children were shown four stickers and told they could select the one they liked best, but that they could not do this until two puppets had each selected a sticker. They were also told that one of the puppets was 'nice' and would not take the sticker that the child wanted and the other was 'nasty' and would. Before the puppets made their selections, each child was asked which sticker he/she wanted. Children of three and four years of age identified the sticker they wanted for themselves to the 'nice' and to the 'nasty' puppet. The nasty puppet then selected the sticker that the child wanted. Most of the five-year-olds, however, pointed to a sticker they did not want. All children were tested on a further four trials. The five-year-olds understood the task and the need to deceive the nasty puppet straight away, the four-year-olds rapidly learned that they had to deceive the nasty puppet, while the three-year-olds continued to be dismayed every time the nasty puppet chose the sticker that they wanted.

- *Stages in the development of ToM* – Wellman (1990) suggested that children's understanding of self and other people's minds develops in three stages:

1 Two-year-old children understand others through their own desires.

2 By the age of three this progresses to include not only a person's desires but also their beliefs about the world, which is why they can successfully perform false-belief tasks; at this stage they perceive beliefs as a representation of the real world and do not yet realize that they are interpretations of the real world.

3 At four years of age they realize that beliefs are not exact copies or photographs of the world, but rather they are interpretations that can sometimes be incorrect, as is the case with Sally's belief in the Sally-Anne task.

Wellman claims that ToM becomes progressively more sophisticated with age and experience, likening it to a scientist who has a theory that he tests to gather information which may or may not fit the existing theory. The scientist must either incorporate the information within the existing model or modify the theory to account for the incongruent information. This is what children do. They start with a simple desire-based interpretation and when this no longer accounts for the information, they modify it to a belief-desire one and then to the view that it is just one interpretation that can be wrong. Thus children's theory of mind progresses through several stages.

Development of children's understanding of others

Perspective-taking

Perspective-taking involves an understanding that another person has a different perspective (or view) from one's own and is important for the development of moral reasoning. Before reading on, please complete the activity below.

> **Activity Examples of perspective-taking**
>
> We have already considered some examples of perspective-taking in this chapter. Look back and make a note of the examples that you can identify. How reliable and valid do you think the tasks used to assess perspective-taking are in the examples you identified?

Piaget was one of the first psychologists to investigate perspective-taking when he used the three mountains task to study egocentrism in preoperational children and decentration in concrete operational children (see p.259). This is an example of a perceptual perspective-taking task because it was concerned with what the 'doll' could perceive (see). The Sally-Anne task, described on p.289, is another example of a test of perspective-taking (this is a ToM perspective-taking task).

According to Flavell *et al.* (1990), there are two levels of ability in perspective taking:

- Level 1: Children aged between two and three know that another person experiences something differently (perceptual perspective-taking).

- Level 2: Children aged between four and five begin to develop more complex rules for working out what someone else is able to see or experience (cognitive and emotional perspective-taking). False-belief tasks test cognitive perspective-taking.

Selman's stage theory of perspective-taking

One of the best-known ToM perspective-taking tests that focuses on the cognitive and emotional aspects was devised by Robert Selman (1980) and is described in the key research below.

Perspective-taking

Key research: Selman (1980)

To find out how children and adolescents think about a range of situations and how others might think about the same situations, Selman read participants various stories and then asked a series of questions about what the character in the story would do and how others would react to it. (Selman also used dilemmas like Kohlberg and Eisenberg.) One example is as follows:

'Holly is an 8-year-old girl who likes to climb trees. She is the best tree climber in the neighborhood. One day while climbing a tall tree she falls off the bottom branch but does not hurt herself. Her father sees her fall, and is upset. He asks her to promise not to climb trees any more, and Holly promises.

Later that day, Holly and her friends meet Sean. Sean's kitten is caught in a tree and cannot get down. Something has to be done right away or the kitten may fall. Holly is the only one who climbs trees well enough to reach the kitten and get it down, but she remembers her promise to her father' (Selman 1980).

Questions were then asked such as:

- Does Holly know how Sean feels about the kitten?
- How will Holly's father feel if he finds out that she climbed the tree?
- What does Holly think her father will do if he finds out she climbed the tree after promising that she wouldn't?
- What would you have done in this situation?

Selman clustered the answers and the reasoning for the answers given and was able to develop a five-stage model to describe the development of perspective-taking, based on age and maturity level (see Table 8.11). This reliable method depends on the strength of correlation between the answers within the age range. As with any stage approach using age as a defining criterion, there will be overlaps of ability in different stages. Selman has accounted for these individual differences in development by allowing for age overlap across his stages.

Undifferentiated (egocentric) perspective-taking	3–6 years	Recognizes the self and that others can have different thoughts and feelings, but these frequently become confused.
Social–informational perspective-taking	5–9 yrs	Understands that different perspectives can arise because individuals have access to different information and another person's perspective may or may not be similar to their own. The child tends to focus on his/her own perspective rather than attempting to co-ordinate a range of viewpoints.
Self-reflective perspective-taking	7–12 yrs	The first empathetic perspective whereby someone can see, think, feel and behave from another person's perspective (i.e. 'step into their shoes'). Also aware that others can do the same.
Third-party (or bystander) perspective-taking	10–15 yrs	A decentred view in the emotional/cognitive personal sense; the young person can see a situation from the perspective of a first, second and a neutral bystander.
Social and conventional system (societal) perspective-taking	14 to adulthood	Understands that the third-party perspective can be influenced by the societal and cultural context of the bystander.

Table 8.11 *Selman's developmental stage theory of perspective-taking*

Typical responses at the different stages

- Children at the undifferentiated perspective stage will say that Holly will save the kitten because she does not want it to get hurt. And her father will feel the same, i.e. he will be happy because he likes kittens. Children may possibly have ToM, but are unable to attribute another perspective which differs from their own to anyone else (this is similar to Stage 1 of Kohlberg's theory).

- Answers become more sophisticated in the social-informational perspective stage. Here children typically respond by saying that if her father was not privy to information about the kitten, then he would be angry. However, once Holly shows the kitten he might have a change of heart. This is comparable to Kohlberg's stage 2 which is highlighted by self-interest – here people realize that there are different perspectives but like their own best.

- Children in the self-reflective perspective stage claim that Holly does not think she would be punished, as her father will understand why she climbed the tree. This response assumes that Holly's point of view is influenced by her father being able to step into her shoes. This is comparable to Kohlberg's stage 3 which is highlighted by interpersonal relations and the ability to empathize with others.

- In the case of the third-party perspective stage, children answer that it was important to save the kitten but also realize the promise made not to climb trees. As long as Holly can get her father to understand why she climbed the tree she should not be punished. Hence both Holly's and her father's perspective are considered simultaneously. This is comparable to

Kohlberg's stage 4 which has a social order orientation.

- Finally in the societal-perspective stage, answers typically address the importance of humane treatment of animals to justify Holly's behaviour. And because this is a good value to hold, her father will not punish her. This is comparable to Kohlberg's stage 5 where social contracts and people's rights become paramount. Selman argued that as children mature they are able to consider more information and they realize that different individuals can and do react differently to the same situation. They develop the ability to consider simultaneously a multitude of perspectives based on the potential viewpoints of a bystander and furthermore, consider how these might be influenced by the bystander's social and cultural values.

Children's perspective-taking can enhance their understanding of themselves and can also improve the quality of their relationships with others. Selman's theory has been used in counselling situations (see the next HSW feature).

Evaluation of Selman's perspective-taking stage approach

- *Empirical support* – Keller and Edelstein (1991) used one of Selman's (1980) dilemmas based on friendship in a longitudinal study consisting of 121 participants (57 female and 64 male) aged 7, 9, 12 and 15. They found that the participants' responses reflected Selman's stages of perspective-taking and also Kohlberg's stages of moral development. Evidence to support Selman's approach also comes from biology (this evidence will be examined in the next and final section of this chapter). Sensory-motor systems, such

Pair therapy

With increasing violence occurring in the school environment, some parents are insisting that something should be done to ensure the safety of their children. Karcher (1996) and Selman et al. (1997) advocate the use of **pair therapy** as a means of helping children and adolescents who are experiencing emotional and behavioural difficulties. The underlying theoretical explanation as to why pair therapy is successful comes from Selman's perspective-taking stage approach which focuses on the cognitive-emotional facet of ToM (Selman 1980). Selman et al. (1997) showed that it is possible to improve children's and young people's skills of negotiation in interpersonal relationships by enhancing their perspective-taking so that the youngsters realize the need to talk through any differences in views in order to get along with their peers. Using this evidence, Selman was able to bridge the gap between perspective-taking (i.e. the thoughts) and interpersonal negotiation (i.e. the behaviour) in children with emotional and behavioural problems through pair therapy.

In pair therapy, pairs of children learn, with the guidance of a therapist, to manage a friendship or relationship using perspective-taking and negotiation skills appropriate to their age. More research is needed about the effectiveness of this therapy. It does make sense that if aggressive children are taught appropriate ways of achieving their goals and developing their moral values by understanding perspective-taking, they will no longer need to be aggressive towards others which can only be a positive thing.

Activity **Using Selman's perspective-taking approach in pair therapy**

Consider a child who is aggressive and bullies other children at school. Create a pair therapy schedule, using Selman's perspective-taking approach. What would you focus on and how would you develop the child's negotiation skills so that they can form and maintain friendships? Make a list of the kinds of issues you would address and the social skills you would help the child to develop.

as kinaesthetic stimulus–response, are involved when taking the perspective of another person. When participants imagine themselves in a video-clip, taking the first-person perspective, brain scans are different, compared with when they take a bystander perspective. The key difference was the level of activity in the sensory-motor area of the brain. The more we are able to draw conclusions from our own experiences, the better we might be at imagining how it would be for others. Children with sensory processing problems or problems of integrating sensory stimuli often find it difficult to make sense of cues required for perspective-taking.

- *Use of assessment interviews to validate the model* – Selman was rigorous in the assessment interviews used to validate his model. Selman tested the relationship between perspective-taking and how children negotiate relationships. A direct link was found between the stage of perspective-taking and the nature of the negotiations that children used in their friendships (Selman *et al.* 1997). Their findings showed that by improving children's perspective-taking skills, they became more competent and socially mature in their relationships with others.

- *Application of Selman's theory* HOW SCIENCE WORKS – Selman's stage theory of perspective-taking has been applied in pair therapy to help children and young people with emotional and behavioural difficulties to develop perspective-taking and negotiation skills appropriate to their age and help them manage their relationships with others. Further research is needed into the effectiveness of this therapeutic intervention.

Biological explanations of social cognition

An important question is whether we are biologically designed to be social beings who live co-operatively with each other? To understand each other, we need to be able to recognize both our own emotional states and those of others (including empathy), consider different perspectives and have a ToM. These skills help us to 'mind read' others and develop a sense of morality. Is there an underlying biological mechanism that ensures we develop the skills we need in order to be social animals? Have our brains evolved in such a way to enhance our sociability?

Important information about the working of the human brain has been obtained from patients with acquired damage to specific parts of the brain. For example, Adolphs *et al.* (1995) studied a 30-year-old patient, known as S.M., whose amygdala was destroyed by a metabolic disorder. The amygdala plays an important role in perceiving and experiencing negative emotions such as fear and anger. S.M. could not recognize fear shown in photos of faces that portrayed a range of emotional expressions and nor did S.M. experience fear. Another patient, known as N.M., also had damage to the amygdala. N.M. also found it difficult to recognize fear in facial expressions and could not identify bodily postures that expressed fear. These findings suggest a link between perception and behaviour. By studying brain deficits it is possible to establish the importance of being able to recognize other people's emotional states. For both S.M. and N.M. understanding other people and inferring other people's emotional state and their intentions from their behaviour would have been very difficult. Although some facets of their ToM would have been intact, the overall quality and depth of their understanding of others would have been compromised.

Measuring neural activity

A rapidly developing area of research employs modern neuro-imaging (such as positron emission tomography and **functional magnetic resonance imaging (fMRI)**) to measure brain activity. This can provide valuable information about areas of brain activity during the execution of qualitatively different types of task and the effects of cognitive development in the brain. More recently, this technology has been used to ascertain which part of the brain becomes most active when individuals are asked to simulate carrying out a task in the first or third person. Even though we are able to do this without much thought on a daily basis, it involves considerable co-ordination of different social cognitive skills. This type of **simulation**, which has been described by Decety and Ingvar (1990) as a 'conscious reactivation of previously executed actions' stored in memory, requires less effortful processing when carried out in the first person but is more difficult when undertaken from a third-person perspective. Hesslow (2002) claims that when actions are simulated we activate the motor areas of the brain in such a way that resembles the neural activation involved when doing the actual action itself. Furthermore the same phenomenon occurs when imagining something – the same area of the brain is activated as when something is actually being perceived in real time. In addition, Hesslow investigated the anticipation of something which also results in perceptual activity which would have occurred if the action was actually carried out in real time. This has also been demonstrated by Meister *et al.* (2004) in a study using fMRI scanning, where participants played the same piece of music on the piano under two conditions:

1   on a silent keyboard, and

2   imagining that they were playing the same piece.

They found that similar fronto-parietal neurons were activated regardless of whether the piano was played silently or on an imaginary basis.

Simulation studies where brain activity is measured using fMRI have enabled neuro-cognitive researchers to understand our capacity to interpret mental states such as intentions, feelings and beliefs in others. These studies typically involve a person mimicking the mental activity of someone else in order to understand someone else's behaviour while observing them, and often involve imagining ourselves carrying out the same behaviour. In order to do this we have to ignore our own current mental state and focus on that of the target. Electrophysiological studies have shown that when macaque monkeys observe actions carried out by other macaque monkeys, two areas of the brain are activated – the premotor cortex and the superior temporal sulcus. Some of the cells in the F5 area of the premotor cortex are sensorimotor neurons which become activated, regardless of whether the

monkey is performing the action or perceiving the action being carried out by another monkey (Rizzolatti *et al.* 1996). These sensorimotor neurons are also known as mirror neurons – so-called because they fire when an animal acts and also when the animal observes the same action performed by another animal of the same species. The discovery of mirror neurons has been one of the most important recent findings in neuroscience. Interestingly, these mirror neurons are also found in other areas of the brain, including the parietal cortex for actions carried out with objects. A study by Calvo-Merino *et al.* (2005) used fMRI scans to study the brain activity of three groups of participants: experts in classical ballet, experts in capoeira (Brazilian martial arts) and control participants. The next activity will enable you to find out more about this fascinating study.

HOW SCIENCE WORKS

Activity   **Investigating the role of mirror neurons**

Go to the NOVA Science NOW website at http://www.pbs.org/wgbh/nova/sciencenow/3204/01.html

(a)   First watch the short video (14 minutes) which provides an excellent introduction to mirror neurons and their importance for social interaction.

(b)   Read the Research Update and then listen to a short interview (nine minutes) with Daniel Glaser from University College London (Monkey Do, Monkey See) about the research he has carried out with an international group of researchers from the UK (University College London and the University of Oxford) and from Paris (France) and Madrid (Spain). Alternatively, you can read the transcript of this interview.

(c)   Write some notes on:
  ● the research study with ballet dancers carried out by Glaser and his colleagues
  ● the main findings of the study
  ● the possible practical implications of their findings.

(d)   **STRETCH AND CHALLENGE**   When you have completed this, discuss your notes with other students in your psychology class and create your own 'Key research feature' similar to the ones included in this and other chapters of this textbook which you can use for your revision.

What about social cognition?

What happens when we imagine the emotions or the pain experienced by someone else? Are similar mirror neurons activated when imagining the emotion or pain experienced by someone else as when a similar emotion or pain is experienced by oneself? This important question is central to the notion of ToM. Levenson and Ruef (1992) found that when two people experience the same emotion, they are more accurate at determining each other's intentions, and this finding has been supported by fMRI scans. For instance, when participants were asked to imitate or observe emotional expressions on faces, increased neural activity occurs in the areas of the brain related to understanding facial expression of emotions, as well as the premotor cortex which is normally active during the physical portrayal of emotional expression.

Recognition of the pain experienced by others is important for the emotion of empathy. Do we have mirror neurons that enable us to imagine and experience the pain of someone else? Morrison *et al.* (2004) compared the neural pattern of activation during the actual experience of pain and when observing pain in another person. Participants were given fMRI scans while experiencing a sharp probe, not unlike a needle, to the hand. In a second condition, participants were shown a video of someone's hand being pricked by a needle. The fMRI scans showed similar patterns of neural activity in both conditions: the anterior cingulated cortex (ACC) and anterior insula became activated. These findings have been replicated in numerous fMRI studies (e.g. Jackson *et al.* 2005, Botvinick *et al.* 2005). There are, however, qualitative differences in the areas of the ACC activated when experiencing pain in the first person (i.e. oneself) or the third person (in another person). This then might be the mechanism that allows us to differentiate between empathic responses to other's pain and our own distress. Furthermore, this may prevent us from actually experiencing the emotional distress or too much of an empathic response. When we empathize with other people it is important to be able to distinguish our own feelings from those of the other person (Decety and Jackson 2004). This may explain why the pattern of neural overlap is not quite the same in relation to the perception of pain perception. Another way that the system ensures we know our own experiences from someone else's is the role played by the right inferior parietal cortex. This part of the brain enables us to distinguish self-produced actions from actions performed by others (Blakemore and Frith 2003). Saxe and Wexler (2005) have taken this one step further by claiming that this region of the brain is

What perspective should a teacher take when modelling an action?

Key research: Jackson *et al.* (2005)

Participants were shown and asked to imitate a series of simple hand and foot movements from two different visual perspectives: (i) the first person perspective reflecting their own view and (ii) the mirror view (i.e. the third-person perspective).

Jackson and colleagues hypothesized that when the perspective matched their own, the time taken to imitate the movements would be less compared with the mirror perspective. This is because observation and imitation of movements will evoke stronger premotor cortex activity in the first than the third-person perspective. Sixteen individuals (eight males and eight females), aged between 29 and 65, participated in the study. They were shown five video clips of different hand and foot movements: 50 per cent in the first person and 50 per cent in the third person. They watched the video clips while in the fMRI scanner and were either instructed to watch (observation condition) the simple movements or to imitate them (imitation condition). In the case of the first-person perspective, the participants were watching or performing the movements from the same perspective. However, the third-person perspective was like imitating an action while watching another person who is facing you do it. A baseline level of brain activity was obtained when participants were looking at a static cross. The results showed that participants were faster at imitating a model seen from a first-person than a third-person perspective (see Figure 8.13).

The findings confirmed their hypothesis that the more similar the perspective of the model to the person's own perspective, the easier it is to imitate an action. The fMRI data also support the view that partly distinct neural mechanisms are used when different visual perspectives are taken (i.e. first-person versus third-person).

This suggests that the perspective a teacher should take when demonstrating an action should be determined by what the students already know. If a teacher wants to challenge students' ability to learn, demonstrating something using the third-person perspective might stimulate more effortful processing, resulting in transferable skills.

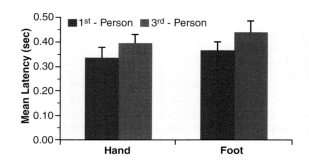

Figure 8.13 *Bar chart showing the mean latency when imitating actions as a function of perspective i.e. (first vs mirror view (third person)) and the limb used.*

specifically involved in ToM. The right inferior parietal cortex only becomes activated during simulated actions from someone else's perspective and not one's own. Furthermore, it is activated when imagining how another person would feel in an unpleasant situation but not when imagined for ourselves (Jackson *et al.* 2005).

Activity **Changing the perspective**

Make a video recording of someone carrying out four or five different 'moves' on a rubic's cube. Film the demonstration from two perspectives: the first person (own view) and the third person (a mirror view). Then try to imitate the moves under both conditions and use a stop-watch to time how long it takes to imitate each of the moves successfully. Which perspective did you find easier? Which perspective took longer to imitate?

Evaluation of biological explanations of social cognition

- *Use of mirror neurons* – Mirror neurons are needed to imitate behaviour; these become active in areas of the brain responsible for translating observation (perception) into action (behaviour). Numerous studies using fMRI scanning have shown this to be true, so this claim is based on replicated empirical evidence.

- *Understanding of social cognition* – To understand the intentions of others requires the ability not only to understand our own emotions but also those of others. fMRI scanning has enabled us to investigate how we do this. Mirror neurons in the premotor, parietal and the anterior cingulated cortex become differentially activated, depending on whether we are experiencing pain or an emotion in the first or third person. The pattern of mirror neuron activity is not exactly the same when an emotion or pain is personally experienced compared with when it occurs in the third person.

- *Differential mirror neuronal activity* – Differential mirror neuronal activity associated with personal experiences and the experience of others makes sense; although we may try to empathize with someone else's pain, we do not actually experience it in the same way.

- *Use of fMRI scanning* – fMRI scanning has demonstrated the importance of the right inferior parietal cortex in distinguishing our own actions from the actions of others. The right inferior parietal cortex is also involved in ToM. It is only activated during simulated actions from someone else's perspective and not one's own. This may be a means of protecting us from experiencing someone else's adversity.

- *Further research is needed* – This is a new and exciting field of research, with rapid advances in

technology enabling more accurate detection of neuronal activity in different areas of the brain. Although reports of mirror neurons have been confirmed by a number of scientists (e.g. Fogassi *et al.* 2005), there is also some evidence that questions the importance of motor neurons in the human brain (e.g. Dinstein *et al.* 2008). Further research is therefore required.

CHECK YOUR UNDERSTANDING

Check your understanding of the development of social cognition by answering the following questions. Try to do this from memory. You can check your answers by looking back through Topic 3.

1. In what ways do psychologists test for self awareness in very young infants?

2. What do we mean by ToM? What skills do we need to have in order to 'mind read' another person successfully?

3. When do children acquire ToM? What emotions do children need to develop to assist the acquisition of ToM?

4. How does Harris' (1989) research reflect ToM?

5. Describe a typical false-belief task. What do false-belief tasks actually test?

6. What is meant by the term 'perspective-taking'? What skills do children need in order for perspective-taking to be successful?

7. How has perspective-taking been applied in therapy? What does it aim to achieve?

8. What are mirror neurons and what do they enable us to do?

9. How has fMRI scanning helped us to understand the role of their mirror neurons and their involvement in both perception and social cognition?

10. What differences do fMRI scans show for mirror neural activity under conditions of imagining the self and others in adversity?

Piaget

- Theoretical description of conceptual mechanisms used (schema, assimilation, accommodation and equilibration)
- Description of four stages of cognitive development:
    1 Sensorimotor   3 Concrete operational
    2 Pre-operational   4 Formal operational

Evaluation of theory and methods

- Fixed sequence of stages
- Limited samples of children tested
- Descriptive account rather than explanatory
- Tasks more conceptually driven than child-centred
- Ignores demand characteristics
- Universality of stages challenged
- Language and social factors underestimated

Vygotsky

- Theoretical description of culture, ZPD and language
- Stages of language and thought development:
    1 Pre-intellectual, social speech
    2 Egocentric speech   3 Inner speech
- Stages of concept formation
    1 Vague syncretic   3 Potential concept stage
    2 Complex   4 Mature concept

Evaluation of theory and methods used

- Individual differences acknowledged
- More emphasis on social/cultural factors, less on biological
- Accounts for rare cases (e.g. feral children) and success at Piagetian tasks at an earlier age
- Lacks empirical support

Bruner

- Early work builds on Piaget, later work on Vygotsky
- Theory addresses social/cultural context and scaffolding
- Three modes of internal representation:
    1 Enactive   2 Iconic   3 Symbolic

Evaluation of theory and methods used

- Flexibility of mode application
- Publicized Vygotsky's work and extended his ideas
- Scaffolding enables application of ZPD
- Focuses mainly on the mother's role in scaffolding

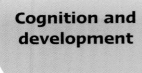

Cognition and development

Theories of cognitive development

Application of the theories of Piaget, Vygotsky and Bruner to education

Piaget's theory

- Discovery learning (e.g. Nuffield Maths project)
- Child-centred education
- Concept of developmental readiness
- Use of concrete examples to introduce abstract concepts

Vygotsky's theory

- Teaching assists child learning within the ZPD
- Reciprocal teaching develops children's reading skills
- Collaborative group work

Bruner's theory:

- Learning as an active process – the spiral curriculum
- Scaffolding provides a framework supporting attempts to understand new ideas and undertake new tasks
- Learning any subject is possible if presented effectively
- Should include intuition, analytical thinking and reasoning in the school curriculum
- Knowing is a process rather than a product (hence emphasis on learning process rarther than content)

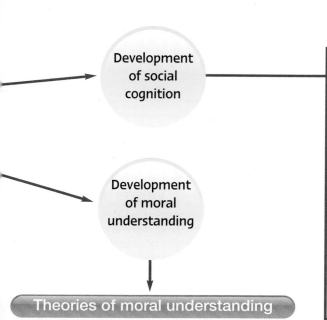

Development
of social
cognition

Development
of moral
understanding

- Self-recognition as awareness of self
- Understanding of emotions
- Theory of mind (ToM) enabling inferences of what others know, think and feel
- False-belief tasks as a means of testing ToM

Evaluation

- Replication of findings
- Is false belief a valid test of ToM?
- False-belief tasks can focus on behaviour or emotion (emotion may develop more slowly)
- Role of deception is paramount to ToM

Theories of moral understanding

Kohlberg's theory

- Theory based on three levels, subdivided into six stages:
  - Level 1 (Preconventional morality)
  - Level 2 (Conventional morality)
  - Level 3 (Postconventional morality)
- Method employed use of moral dilemmas

Evaluation of Kohlberg's theory

- Replication
- Cross-cultural support
- Gender bias
- Difficulty of scoring responses to dilemmas
- Emphasizes moral thought rather than behaviour
- Dilemmas are artificial tests emphasizing justice and fairness
- Cultural bias

Eisenberg's theory of prosocial reasoning

- Theory emphasizes emotional dimension of moral reasoning
- Method employed use of dilemmas involving conflict between own needs and those of others
- Five levels of prosocial reasoning identified

Evaluation

- Distinction between primitive empathetic and sympathetic distress
- Altruism motivated by experience of others' distress
- Provides practical guidance on how to socialize children

Development of children's understanding of others

- Role of perspective-taking
- Selman's (1980) five-stage theory of perspective-taking in children and young people

Evaluation

- Empirical support
- Neurological evidence
- Assessment interviews validate model
- Pair therapy as a practical application of model

Biological explanations of social cognition

- Studies of patients with acquired brain damage
- Use of functional magnetic resonance imaging (fMRI) to measure brain activity during task simulation supports existence of mirror neurons
- fMRI scans also show similar neural activity when experiencing a sharp probe and when watching another person's hand being pricked by a needle

Evaluation

- Empirical support for mirror neuron involvement in imitation
- Enables the understanding of others' emotions
- Differential mirror neuron activity between first-hand experience and third-person experience
- This supports why we can empathize with others without the real-time experience
- fMRI scanning shows the importance of the right inferior parietal cortex for separating our own actions from the actions of others and ToM

Claire Meldrum
Jane Willson

Psychopathology

INTRODUCTION TO PSYCHOPATHOLOGY

Psychopathology is the study of psychological disorders and their origins.

The AQA specification requires you to choose *one* mental disorder, chosen from schizophrenia, depression and anxiety disorders (either phobic disorders or obsessive-compulsive disorder), and consider that disorder from a variety of perspectives. However, there are some general points that apply to *all* mental disorders and you should read this introduction to psychopathology before you start looking at your chosen disorder in detail. You may also find it helpful to read more than one of the chapters on mental disorders, even if you are preparing to study only one disorder for exam purposes. By doing so, you will gain a wider understanding of the issues that arise in diagnosing, explaining and treating mental disorders.

Classification and diagnosis

Before we look at particular psychological disorders, we need to consider how and why the disorders have been identified in the first place. You will know from your AS course that abnormality is a difficult concept to define. One of the problems is trying to decide where normal behaviour stops and abnormal behaviour takes over. For example, we all feel a little 'down' sometimes when things are not going too well in our lives, but in most cases we are able to bounce back again fairly quickly. This is very different from the state of mind of someone who is suffering from clinical depression, where the low mood goes on for a long time and seriously disrupts daily functioning. For treatment purposes, it is important to be able to distinguish the normal ups-and-downs of everyday life from the serious, even life-threatening mood swings of depression.

Prior to the 20th century, there was a tendency to label people who behaved in a psychologically abnormal way as 'mad' or 'deviant'. This blanket description failed to take into account different types of abnormal behaviour. We now know that mental disorder can take many forms and that treatment varies tremendously depending on the particular type of disorder. For example, the behavioural therapies that can be so effective in reducing the distress caused by phobic disorders are not useful in helping people with schizophrenia. For this kind of reason, clinicians and researchers working in the field of psychopathology have developed **classification** systems to help them make an accurate **diagnosis**.

- **Classification**: the act of distributing things into classes or categories of the same type.

- **Diagnosis**: the recognition and identification of a disease or condition by its signs and symptoms.
  - *Signs* are the results of objective tests, such as those from blood or urine tests.
  - *Symptoms*, on the other hand, are reports from patients about how they feel, e.g. how much pain they are experiencing or how tired they feel.

Classifying and diagnosing mental disorders

Classification is central to scientific disciplines. It is used in psychopathology for a variety of reasons:

- To make *communication between professionals* working within the field of psychopathology easier.

- To understand the *implications of diagnosis* for predicting the outcome of the disorder and for choosing *appropriate treatment*.

- To understand more about the *possible causes* of mental disorders.

- To indicate possible *preventive measures*.

- To *stimulate research* and to make the research more reliable, i.e. to ensure that it is conducted with comparable groups.

Psychiatric classification raises particular controversies and challenges which are not the same for other scientific disciplines, including other branches of medicine. Mental disorders, for example, differ from physical disorders in several ways:

- *Underlying cause of disorder:* One major difference is that the underlying cause of the problem is usually apparent in physical illnesses but not in mental illnesses. For example, if someone goes to the doctor with a painful and swollen wrist, an X-ray could show that a broken bone was responsible. Similarly, a lab test could show that a sore, inflamed throat had been caused by a streptococcal infection. This is not the case with mental disorders and there are usually no handy blood or urine tests that will aid diagnosis. Clinicians are more dependent on the patients' accounts of their symptoms. However, with the arrival of modern brain scanning techniques (e.g. **PET** and **MRI**), more signs are now available to those working in the field of psychological disorder.

- *What is mental illness:* Another difference is that there is less agreement about what actually constitutes illness with regard to mental disorders as opposed to physical disorders. For example, no-one would disagree with the conclusion that someone having a heart attack is ill and needs treatment. However, there is less agreement about whether someone who is in a sad and depressed mood should be classified as 'mentally ill' and in need of treatment.

There are two major classification systems used in the field of psychopathology. These are called the International Classification System for Diseases (ICD) and the Diagnostic and Statistical Manual of Mental Disorders (DSM). We shall be looking at them in more detail below. Meanwhile see 'Definitions of mental disorders' in the box below.

Definitions of mental disorders by ICD and DSM

A mental disorder is defined in ICD-10 as follows:

'...a clinically recognizable set of symptoms or behaviour associated in most cases with distress and with interference with personal functions. Social deviance or conflict alone, without personal dysfunction, should not be included in mental disorder as defined here.'

A similar but slightly longer definition is given in DSM-IV-TR:

'...a clinically significant or behavioural or psychological syndrome or pattern that occurs in an individual and that is associated with present distress (e.g. a painful symptom) or disability (e.g. impairment in one or more important areas of functioning) or with a significantly increased risk of suffering death, pain, disability or an important loss of freedom.'

Unlike physical diagnostic categories, most psychiatric disorders are not based on theoretical concepts or assumptions about underlying causes, but upon recognizable, observable clusters of symptoms and behaviours. Clusters of symptoms and behaviours which regularly are found together in a particular combination are called '**syndromes**'.

Evaluation of classification and diagnosis of mental disorders

While most professionals working in the field of psychopathology acknowledge the usefulness of classification and diagnosis, some people think it is inappropriate in the context of psychological abnormality. See Table 2 (on the following page).

Current classification systems

In spite of some of their drawbacks, classification systems are widely accepted as important and useful. The most widely used systems in psychopathology, as already mentioned, are the International Classification System for Diseases (ICD) and the Diagnostic and Statistical Manual of Mental Disorders (DSM). They were first developed over 50 years ago, but have since been revised several times to reflect both changing views in psychiatric practice and new research evidence.

ICD

The current (tenth) edition, ICD-10, was published in 1991 by the World Health Organisation (WHO). It is a huge volume that includes 21 chapters of which only one, Chapter 5, is devoted to psychiatry. Mental disorders were not included in the ICD until its sixth revision in 1952. It is an international document and is available in most world languages. It is also available in slightly different versions for clinical work, research and primary health care. Chapter 5 is divided into ten main sections and is primarily a descriptive document used for classification and research rather than for diagnostic purposes. See Table 1 below.

The ten categories of mental disorder in ICD-10 are:

- Organic, including symptomatic, mental disorders (e.g. dementia in Alzheimer's disease)
- Mental and behavioural disorders due to psychoactive substance abuse (e.g. those arising from alcohol abuse)
- Schizophrenia, schizotypal and delusional disorders
- Mood (affective) disorders (e.g. recurrent depressive disorder)
- Neurotic, stress-related and somatoform disorders (e.g. anxiety disorders)
- Behavioural syndromes associated with physiological disturbances and physical factors (e.g. anorexia nervosa)
- Disorders of adult personality and behaviour (e.g. paranoia)
- Mental retardation
- Disorders of psychological development (e.g. childhood autism)
- Behavioural emotional disorders with onset usually occurring in childhood or adolescence (e.g. conduct disorders)

Table 1 *The ten categories of mental disorder in ICD-10*

Criticism	Response
The 'myth of mental illness' Some people have challenged the whole idea of treating mental disorder in the same way as physical disorder. Thomas Szasz (1962), for example, dismissed this approach as 'the myth of mental illness'. He believed that it encourages us to interpret problems of living as if they are illnesses. As a consequence, we remove all responsibility from individuals for solving their own problems and we run the risk of administering inappropriate, even damaging, treatments. If the concept of mental disorder is itself controversial, any classifications of mental disorders are likely to be controversial as well. If you wish to see and hear Szasz give a short talk about his anti-psychiatry views, go to: www.encefalus.com/clinical/thomas-szasz-short-talk/	Szasz's view is not accepted by many psychologists. There is considerable evidence for the existence of certain distinct syndromes, e.g. schizophrenia, and little support for the idea that such a devastating condition can be brought about simply by stressful living.  *Thomas Szasz*
Stigmatizing Some critics say that placing a patient in a diagnostic category distracts from understanding that person as a unique human being with an individual set of difficulties. This can lead to stigma whereby an individual with a 'mental illness' is wrongly judged, e.g. as dangerous, unpredictable, incurable, unemployable etc. Some sociologists have suggested that labelling socially deviant behaviour as illness simply increases the individual's difficulties, e.g. by attracting stigma.	It is not the diagnostic label that leads to stigma. People with mental disorders were stigmatiszed long before modern diagnostic categories were used. Stigma will only be reduced when there is better public understanding of the true nature of some mental illnesses. This process is helped by the recent trends for prominent people to talk publicly about their own mental illness, e.g. Stephen Fry. Clinicians working within psychopathology argue that mental illness should only be diagnosed in the presence of a range of symptoms, not solely in terms of socially deviant behaviour.
Failure to categorize some individuals Individuals do not all fit neatly into the diagnostic categories. Some meet the criteria for more than one and others do not fit into an existing category at all.	It is true that a few individuals do not fit into the existing categories, but this is not a good reason to abandon classification systems for the majority who do.
Abuse in psychiatric diagnosis There have also been cases of abuse in psychiatry where diagnoses have been made for political reasons. In the Soviet Union there were instances where psychiatrists colluded with the government to classify political dissidents as mentally ill. At: www.amnesty.ca/.../exposing_torture.php 	Fortunately, cases like this are rare, but it is very important that clinicians use psychiatric diagnoses carefully and appropriately. *Oryol Special Psychiatric Hospital in the USSR where political prisoners were subject to psychiatric torture*

Table 2 *Evaluating the usefulness of classification and diagnosis*

DSM

DSM was developed in America and is only available in the English language. Despite this, it is more widely used than ICD. It is currently in its fourth edition. DSM-IV was first published in 1994 and a text-revision – DSM-IV-TR was published in 2000. It is planned to publish DSM-V some time in 2011. Early versions of DSM were heavily influenced by the psychodynamic approach which was dominant in psychiatry at the time. Later editions were not biased in this way and contained much more detailed criteria in order to improve the reliability of diagnosis.

The DSM (but not the ICD) is multi-axial. This means that clinicians have to assess a patient in five separate axes (areas of information) before making a diagnosis. These axes provide information about the biological, psychological and social aspects of a person's condition and so lead to a more informed decision by the clinician. See Table 3.

Reliability and validity of classification systems

Any robust classification system should satisfy the following criteria:

- It should provide an *exhaustive system* that includes all types of abnormal behaviour.

- The classificatory *categories should be mutually exclusive*, i.e. the boundaries between different categories should not be 'fuzzy' and it should, therefore, be clear what disorder(s) a particular person is suffering from.

- It should be *valid*.

- It should be *reliable*.

Reliability in this context means that each time the classification system is used (to diagnose a particular cluster of symptoms and behaviours) it should produce the same outcome. The consistency with which the clinicians agree on a diagnosis for a particular set of symptoms is known as '**inter-rater reliability**'. For DSM and ICD to be reliable, those using it must be able to agree when a person should or should not be given a particular diagnosis.

Validity is concerned with the appropriateness of the classification categories – whether or not the system puts together the people whose symptoms come from the same causal factors and who respond to similar treatments. There are different kinds of validity. One of the most important types of validity for clinicians is **predictive validity** – in other words if someone is given, for example, a diagnosis of schizophrenia, it is expected that the person will respond to a particular kind of drug. If the person does not respond, it casts doubt on the validity of the original diagnosis.

Evaluation of reliability and validity of classification systems

- *Reliability:* The early editions of DSM contained rather vague descriptions and lacked reliability. In other words, clinicians using the manual to assess a particular patient could not agree on diagnosis. The current version, DSM-IV, was compiled very carefully and based on extensive research. The compilers

Axis I	Clinical syndromes	Axis I contains an extensive list of all the mental disorders thought to cause significant impairment, e.g. schizophrenia, anxiety disorder
Axis II	Personality disorders and mental retardation	Axis II contains a list of long-standing disorders which begin in childhood or adolescence
		People usually receive a diagnosis from either Axis I or Axis II but it is possible to be diagnosed in both categories
Axis III	Physical disorders	Physical conditions which could contribute to the mental disorder or make it worse, e.g. brain injuries, thyroid disorder
Axis IV	Severity of social stressors	Axis IV describes psychosocial and environmental problems, e.g. problems at school, work or in the family
Axis V	Highest level of adaptive functioning in the last year	A global scale of functioning is used to rate an individual's ability to function psychologically, socially and in terms of occupation on a scale from 1 to 100 – the lower the score, the more serious the dysfunction. See Chapter 7, p.220 of *Psychology AS for AQA A* for the Global Assessment of Functioning Scale.

Table 3 *The five axes of DSM-IV*

excluded some categories which had proven to be unreliable and included some new ones and also modified existing diagnostic criteria to reflect recent research findings. They then carried out field trials involving many clinicians and researchers to make sure that they were reliable. The current DSM appears to be considerably more reliable than earlier versions but there are still problems. For example, it is sometimes difficult to distinguish between certain types of mental disorder and clinicians do not always agree (for example, see Phobic disorders, Chapter 11a).

- *Validity:* Similarly, although levels of validity have improved, DSM-IV-TR is still criticized by people who believe some of the criteria and categories lack validity (for example, premenstrual dysphoric disorder, see Chapter 10 Depression, p.339), and that others reflect inherent gender bias (see, for example, Chapter 10 Depression, p.334), and cultural bias (see the Cultural issues box below).

Cultural issues in classification and diagnosis

One important goal of a satisfactory classification system is to identify and diagnose mental problems in the same way across different cultures. Certain disorders, such as schizophrenia and major depressive disorder, do seem to occur universally and follow a very similar pattern wherever they are found. However, there is evidence that people from different cultures sometimes present differently when they first ask for help. In many Asian cultures, for example, where it is not acceptable to show strong emotions, particularly negative ones, distressed individuals often seek help for physical rather than mental problems. For example, see Kua *et al.* (1993) on p.335 in Chapter 10.

Explanations in psychopathology

You will know from your AS course that there are many different approaches (models) within the field of psychology. There is no single dominant approach and all of them have strengths and limitations in explaining human behaviour. All the models also offer explanations for abnormal behaviours and these, in turn, give rise to different forms of therapy. See 'Explaining mental disorders' in the box opposite. At this point it would be a good idea to re-read pp.224–246 of *Psychology AS for AQA A* which discusses the different approaches used by psychologists (a) to explain psychopathology and (b) to underpin therapies.

Many modern clinicians take an eclectic view, which means that they combine aspects of different explanations (approaches) and therapies in order to best suit the needs of the individual patient. We will look at the various models and their strengths and limitations when we look at explanations for specific disorders.

If you have not already done so, you should read the Approaches section of the Introduction to the textbook (pp.2–18) where you will find a thorough discussion of the main approaches used in psychology. The main approaches used in explaining mental disorders are listed in the box below.

Therapies

As with explanations, we will consider therapies for mental disorders in more detail when we look at specific disorders. However, when you are thinking about therapies and preparing to evaluate them, there are some general issues about how science works that you need to take into account.

Explaining mental disorders

Psychologists use one or more of the following approaches to explain mental disorders:

Biological approach which includes the following explanations:

- Genetic
- Biochemical
- Neuroanatomical
- Evolutionary

Psychological approach which includes the following explanations:

- Psychodynamic
- Behavioural
- Cognitive

Researching the effectiveness and appropriateness of therapies

A therapy, from whichever theoretical approach, is intended to reduce suffering and to restore normality. Therapy can be expensive, time-consuming and, in certain cases, harrowing and uncomfortable for the recipient. The chosen therapy must have a likely chance of success, i.e. it should be appropriate for that particular individual and effectively bring about a change for the better in their condition.

Research is an important way of establishing which therapies are effective and for which disorders. However, there are many problems associated with research in this area which means that conclusions should be drawn with caution. Here are a few points for you to consider when you are evaluating research studies:

- *Operational definitions* – In order to carry out meaningful research, the investigator must define and measure precisely the concepts under investigation. A concrete measure of an abstract concept is called an 'operational definition'. If, for example, the research concerns depression, some agreed definition of what is meant by depression must be established. Researchers often use the current diagnostic manuals to provide operational definitions. However, these manuals are not totally reliable and decisions based on their criteria could lead to inclusion of participants in the research sample who have widely differing symptoms. For example, it is possible to diagnose two people with schizophrenia even though they might exhibit very different behaviours. Treatment outcomes for these different types of schizophrenia might vary. The research sample used to investigate treatment outcomes must, therefore, be recruited according to strict operational definitions otherwise the results will be misleading.

- *Allocation to treatment groups* – Ideally, participants should be allocated randomly to the different conditions of an experiment, so that there is no room for bias. This means that, in treatment outcome research, the group in the new treatment condition should not differ significantly from the group in the control condition. Truly random allocation can only occur with the consent of the patient and of their supervising clinician and, in practice, this rarely happens. Severely disturbed patients are often unwilling to take part in clinical trials and doctors are often reluctant to assign older patients or those with acute symptoms to experimental groups. This means that the result of research will not give an accurate picture of the effectiveness or appropriateness of the treatment.

- *The role of the therapist* – Research into a specific form of treatment is often instigated and carried out by people who are skilled in or committed to that particular therapy. It is known that the personal characteristics of the individual therapist can be important in the efficacy of a particular treatment. Factors such as skill, experience, age, gender, culture and even attractiveness have all been shown to affect treatment outcomes. It is, therefore, possible that promising results obtained in such research studies may not hold good when the treatment is used in everyday practice where the therapist may be more of a generalist and not as skilled in or committed to that particular therapy.

- *The effects of existing treatments* – Participants involved in treatment outcome research have often had some form of therapy for their disorder. It is important to ensure that the effects of the original treatment do not then confound the results of the research into the new treatment. For example, some drug therapies can affect levels of concentration and arousal. This means that they might be less responsive to a therapy such as **cognitive-behavioural therapy (CBT)** than they would be if they were drug free. It is important, therefore, to stop medication in all patients some time before they take part in research into an alternative therapy. However, for obvious ethical and practical reasons, this rarely happens.

- *The placebo effect* – There is an argument that therapy produces beneficial effects simply because attention is given to the patient and an expectation of success is created when treatment is offered (the **placebo effect**). In order to rule out this possibility, most well-controlled treatment outcome research includes a placebo group. For example, in a drug trial, the control group would receive an inert substance presented in exactly the same way as the real drug of interest and, in double-blind designs, neither the participants nor the doctors would know which group was receiving the genuine medication. If the drug group shows significantly greater improvement than the placebo group, it can be concluded fairly confidently that the effect is due to the pharmacological rather than the psychological properties of the drug. It is more difficult to control for the placebo effect when assessing psychological treatments such as CBT or psychodynamic therapy. It is also virtually impossible to carry out a double-blind design with these types of therapy. There is a further complication when comparing treatment and placebo groups. This is the phenomenon known as '*spontaneous remission*', where people simply recover over the course of time without any type of therapeutic intervention. The precise reasons for this are not known, but it has been estimated to occur in 30 to 60 per cent of cases (Bergin and Lambert 1978).

- *The concept of cure* – It is difficult to determine the criteria for deciding whether a particular treatment has been effective or not, because the concept of a 'cure' for mental disorders is hard to establish. For example, is a person with schizophrenia 'cured' if the major, psychotic symptoms are kept under control by drugs even though the symptoms may well return if the drugs are discontinued? Is someone with a rat phobia only 'cured' if they start keeping rats as pets or is it enough for them to show less anxiety about rats than they did before? A related problem is the issue of time. Some therapies take considerably longer than others to take effect. At what point should the measure of effectiveness take place?

EXPLAINING THE SPECIFICATION

Specification content	The specification explained
Psychopathology: schizophrenia as chosen disorder	If you have chosen schizophrenia as the disorder you wish to study, you need to be able to do the following.
Clinical characteristics and issues of classification and diagnosis (Topic 1)	In this part of the specification you should be familiar with the key features of clinical characteristics and issues of classification and diagnosis. To do this, you need to be able to:
Clinical characteristics of schizophrenia	■ Outline the main clinical characteristics (symptoms) of schizophrenia.
Issues surrounding the classification and diagnosis of schizophrenia including reliability and validity	■ Describe and evaluate at least two issues (potential problems) in classifying or diagnosing schizophrenia. If you concentrate on only two issues, these must be reliability and validity.
Explanations of schizophrenia (Topic 2)	In this part of the specification you should be familiar with the explanations of schizophrenia. To do this, you need to be able to:
Biological explanations of schizophrenia, for example genetics, biochemistry	■ Describe and evaluate at least two **biological explanations** of schizophrenia. To do this you will need to discuss relevant research findings. **Genetics** and **biochemistry** are suggested as examples of explanations that you might study but neither of these is specified as compulsory. The chapter discusses genetics, biochemistry, neuroanatomical explanations, pregnancy and birth factors.
Psychological explanations of schizophrenia. for example behavioural, cognitive, psychodynamic and socio-cultural	■ Describe and evaluate at least two psychological explanations of schizophrenia. To do this you will need to discuss relevant research findings. Four examples of explanations are suggested – behavioural, cognitive, psychodynamic and socio-cultural – but none of these is specified as compulsory. The chapter discusses the psychological explanations that have most commonly been used to explain schizophrenia: psychosocial factors, family relationships, expressed emotion, and cognitive impairments.
Therapies for schizophrenia (Topic 3)	In this part of the specification you should be familiar with the key features of therapies for schizophrenia. To do this, you need to be able to:
Biological therapies for schizophrenia including their evaluation in terms of appropriateness and effectiveness	■ Describe and evaluate at least two biological treatments for schizophrenia. Your evaluations should consider how (appropriate) suitable and how effective (successful) the treatments are. To do this you will need to discuss relevant research findings. The chapter briefly discusses early treatments such as ECT and psychosurgery and more fully considers drug treatment.
Psychological therapies for schizophrenia, for example behavioural, psychodynamic, and cognitive-behavioural, including their evaluation in terms of appropriateness and effectiveness	■ Describe and evaluate at least two psychological treatments for schizophrenia. You need to discuss how appropriate and effective the treatments are. To do this you will need to discuss relevant research findings. The chapter discusses family interventions, social skills' training and cognitive-behavioural therapy.

Before you begin reading about depression, it is essential that you have read the Introduction to psychopathology on pp.300–305.

Introduction

Schizophrenia is a serious mental disorder characterized by severe disruptions in psychological functioning and a loss of contact with reality. Schizophrenia is the condition most often associated with the term 'madness'. It is sometimes referred to as a psychosis, which is a broad term used to describe a range of severe psychiatric disorders. The term psychosis is no longer used by the major classification systems but it is a useful overarching descriptive label, still used by clinicians and researchers. The descriptive form of the word (i.e. psychotic) is also still widely used to describe behaviours characterized by the experience of hallucinations and delusions and general lack of ability to distinguish between subjective experience and external reality. The earliest clear descriptions of schizophrenia date from the end of the 18th century, but it was not until 1911 that the Swiss physician, Eugen Bleuler first coined the term 'schizophrenia'. Although the word literally means 'split mind', Bleuler was not referring to a split personality, but to a disorder associated with disconnected thought processes and a loss of contact with reality. These symptoms are among the clinical characteristics of schizophrenia that will be discussed in Topic 1 along with some of the issues of classification and diagnosis. In Topic 2, we shall look at biological and psychological explanations for schizophrenia and in Topic 3, we shall discuss the main therapies for the disorder.

Topic 1: Clinical characteristics and issues of classification and diagnosis

Psychology in context   Schizophrenia in the cinema

One of the problems of classification is that it can lead to people being stigmatized. Stigma and prejudice often arise because of public ignorance or misunderstanding about the nature of mental illness. There have been several Hollywood films that have featured people with mental disorders, and these have sometimes perpetuated myths and untruths. A particular problem has been the way such movies have used the schizophrenia label incorrectly to describe violent, aggressive and evil individuals with a split personality. Although people with schizophrenia can become hostile and aggressive, this is rare and, in any case, develops gradually rather than in the sudden outbursts favoured by film directors. Smith and Cooper (2006), in an article written for the *Student British Medical Journal*, focused on a particular example:

'One of the most outright misrepresentations of schizophrenia is found in *Me, Myself and Irene*. Jim Carrey plays a man with multiple personalities, diagnosed in the film as having "advanced delusionary schizophrenia with narcissistic rage". This fundamental inaccuracy caused widespread anger. In the United Kingdom alone, the Royal College of Psychiatrists and the mental health organizations Mind and the National Schizophrenia Fellowship made a joint protest against the film.'

The authors of the article also singled out the 1999 film *Fight Club*, in which the main character shoots a hole in his cheek to try to destroy his hallucinated alter ego

– and it is shown to work. They quote Ian Chovil, a patient diagnosed with schizophrenia, as follows: 'I know people who start to cut themselves to get rid of their delusions when their symptoms flare up. I hope none of them see this film.'

The 2001 film *A Beautiful Mind*, based on the true story of the mathematician John Nash, provides a more realistic, sensitive and optimistic portrayal of schizophrenia even though it still contains some inaccuracies.

Russell Crowe as John Nash in the film A Beautiful Mind *(2001)*

1 Why do you think Hollywood filmmakers see mental illness as a suitable topic for fictional movies?

2 Why is it important to show mental disorders like schizophrenia accurately?

Clinical characteristics

In most countries across the world, the lifetime risk of being diagnosed with schizophrenia is 1 per cent. The onset of the disorder usually occurs between the ages of 15 and 45. It is equally common in males and females, but it usually occurs in males four to five years earlier than in females.

There is a distinction between acute and chronic onset schizophrenia:

- *In chronic onset*, there is often an insidious change in an apparently normal young person who gradually loses drive and motivation and starts to drift away from friends. After months, or even years of this deterioration, more obvious signs of disturbance, such as delusional ideas or hallucinations, appear.

- *In acute onset*, obvious signs such as hallucinations can appear quite suddenly, usually after a stressful event, and the individual shows very disturbed behaviour within a few days.

People who have been diagnosed with schizophrenia will not all display the same behaviour, so the major classification systems include lists of symptoms only some of which need to be present before a diagnosis can

be made. You will remember from the Introduction to Psychopathology that the two main classification systems in current use are ICD-10 and DSM-IV-TR (see p.301). You can see the criteria for schizophrenia that are set out in ICD-10 by looking at Table 9.1 below. These are similar to the criteria in DSM-IV-TR, and the slight differences between the two systems will be considered on p.309. To gain a more detailed knowledge of the main classification systems, you should try the activity below.

STRETCH AND CHALLENGE

Activity ICD and DSM

You might like to look at the relevant pages in the ICD and DSM manuals yourself. These are large and complex documents, but you could look at the relevant sections on schizophrenia on the websites and compare them. The websites are:

www.who.int/classifications/icd/en/

www.apa.org/

Table 9.1 *ICD-10 Symptoms of schizophrenia*

In ICD-10, the following groups of symptoms are considered important. There is a minimum requirement for at least one of the symptoms listed under 1, or two of those listed under 2, to be present for a period of at least one month. Note that the examples given to illustrate the symptoms are included here for the purposes of clarification, but are not included in the ICD list of symptoms.

1 (a) *Thought control*
- *Thought withdrawal* – thoughts are being extracted from the person's mind.
- *Thought insertion* – unwelcome thoughts are being inserted into the person's mind.
- *Thought broadcast* – private thoughts have become accessible to other people.

   (b) *Delusions of control, influence and passivity* – A delusion is a distorted belief. The individual does not feel in control of their own thoughts, feelings and will (that is the ability to make things happen).

   (c) *Hallucinatory voices* – These are voices that do not exist, but feel real to the person hearing them. The content of the voices is very variable but often takes the form of a running commentary on the person's behaviour.

   (d) *Other persistent delusions* – These are distorted beliefs that are culturally inappropriate or involve impossible powers and capabilities (e.g. believing themselves to be great politicians or religious leaders).

2 (a) *Persistent hallucinations* – These are distorted perceptions arising from any of the senses and may be accompanied by delusions. Hallucinations are perceptions that occur in the absence of any external stimuli. They usually take the form of auditory hallucinations, i.e. hearing voices. However, they can involve any of the senses, i.e. touch, taste, smell, vision or sensations within the body, e.g. feeling a snake crawling around in the intestines.

   (b) *Incoherent or irrelevant speech* – This arises when the train of thought is disrupted and the person's speech is so jumbled that it becomes meaningless. Neologisms (made-up words) that make little sense to anyone else are often inserted into the conversation.

   (c) *Catatonic behaviour* – This refers to unusual body movements and includes the adoption of odd postures, uncontrolled limb movements and, sometimes, complete frozen immobility. See the case study on p.310.

   (d) *Negative symptoms* – These are the less florid symptoms associated with schizophrenia, and include apathy and a general lack of drive and motivation. Speech often conveys little meaning and is often repetitive. The individual shows flat affect, i.e. displays little emotional response to what is going on around them and speaks in a monotonous, expressionless tone. When emotion is displayed, it can be inappropriate, such as laughing at bad news or crying at a joke, and there can be sudden mood swings.

Issues of classification and diagnosis

Take a few minutes to look back to the section on classification and diagnosis in the Introduction to Psychopathology (see p.300), because some of the general points there (e.g. reliability and validity) are relevant to schizophrenia.

Reliability

There has been little consistency in how the diagnosis of schizophrenia has been applied over the years. Since it was first coined, the term schizophrenia has been used widely and indiscriminately so that, by the 1950s, it had been reduced to an overarching label for any kind of severe mental disorder. The diagnosis was more common in the USA than in European countries because earlier versions of DSM contained very broad diagnostic criteria.

As you saw in the Introduction to Psychopathology (pp.300–305), classification is only useful if it is based on a reliable system. The inconsistency between different early classification systems and the vagueness of the DSM led to very low reliability in diagnosis. This, in turn, hampered research into the underlying causes of schizophrenia and into effective treatments for the disorder. Clinicians came to realize that they needed to agree on a common, operational definition of schizophrenia if any progress was to be made.

First-rank symptoms

Kurt Schneider (1959), in an attempt to make the diagnosis more reliable, identified a group of symptoms characteristic of schizophrenia but rarely found in other mental disorders. He called these 'first-rank symptoms' because he saw them as having special value in helping clinicians to determine the diagnosis of schizophrenia. First-rank symptoms form the basis of the current ICD-10 classification. The major systems, ICD-10 and DSM-TR-IV have now become very similar, but not entirely identical. Some of the differences are outlined next.

Some differences between ICD-10 and DSM-TR-IV

- DSM requires symptoms to have been evident for a period of six months while ICD requires only one month.

- ICD places more emphasis on the first-rank symptoms whereas DSM emphasizes the course of the disorder and the accompanying functional impairment.

- DSM is multi-axial, which means that various factors are taken into consideration before a diagnosis is made (see p.303 Intro to Psychopathology p5.

- The two classification systems differ slightly in the way they categorize subtypes of schizophrenia: ICD lists seven subtypes; DSM identifies only five subtypes (see 'Different types of schizopheria' opposite).

Criteria for diagnosis

In addition, clinicians and researchers sometimes use alternative sets of criteria for diagnosis and research purposes, such as the St. Louis criteria (Feighner *et al.* 1972) and the Research Diagnostic Criteria (Spitzer *et al.* 1978). There is still no universally agreed definition of schizophrenia, although the criteria set by all these currently used systems share many similarities. This lack of consensus about how to define schizophrenia highlights the point that definitions of mental disorders are fairly arbitrary and liable to change according to prevailing influences. If a person is wrongly diagnosed as having schizophrenia, this can lead to long-term and even tragic outcomes. A remarkable person who only just avoided such an outcome is Janet Frame, the New Zealand poet, whose story was told in the film *An Angel at My Table* (1990).

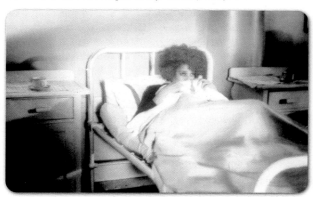

*Janet Frame was an introverted, awkward child who did not fit into her rural New Zealand background. As she grew up and became increasingly alienated, she retreated into a world of fantasy. Wrongly diagnosed as suffering from incurable schizophrenia, Janet spent eight years in an institution. She only just managed to leave before being subjected to **psychosurgery**. Eventually, she was able to travel and became a full-time writer, as she had always wished to do.*

Different types of schizophrenia

Many researchers believe that schizophrenia is not a single disorder and have suggested various subtypes. As already mentioned, ICD-10 distinguishes between seven different subtypes, whereas DSM identifies only five. The subtypes and their characteristics are as follows:

- *Paranoid schizophrenia* – Delusions (e.g. of persecution) and/or hallucinations are the predominant characteristics. Negative symptoms such as flattening of affect (emotion) and poverty of speech are less apparent than in other types. See the case study on p.310.

- *Hebephrenic schizophrenia* (called Disorganized schizophrenia in DSM-IV) – Behaviour is aimless and disorganized, and speech is rambling and incoherent. There is marked flattening and inappropriateness of affect.

- *Catatonic schizophrenia* – Motor abnormality (e.g. immobility) is the main characteristic of this subtype. Individuals sometimes adopt strange postures or flail their limbs around in an uncontrolled fashion. They often show negativism where they resist all instructions or attempts to move them. See the case study in the panel below.

- *Undifferentiated schizophrenia* – This is a sort of general category where individuals are placed who have insufficient symptoms for any of the subtypes, or so many symptoms that they do not fit neatly into any category.

- *Post-schizophrenic depression (not in DSM-IV)* – Criteria for schizophrenia have been met in the last 12 months but are not currently present. Depressive symptoms are prolonged and severe.

- *Residual schizophrenia* – Criteria for schizophrenia have been met in the past but are not met at the present time. However, there have been many signs of negative symptoms throughout the previous 12 months.

- *Simple schizophrenia (not in DSM-IV)* – There is slow but progressive development (over a period of at least a year) of social withdrawal, apathy, poverty of speech and marked decline in scholastic/occupational performance.

In all cases (apart from simple schizophrenia), the general criteria for a diagnosis of schizophrenia must be met as well as the specific criteria for each subtype. Two case studies of different subtypes of schizophrenia are described in the panel below.

Catatonic schizophrenia

Maria is a 19-year-old college student who has been psychiatrically hospitalized for more than a month. For days before her admission, and for the weeks she has been in the hospital, Maria has been mute. Rigidly posturing her body and staring at the ceiling, she spends most of the day in a trance-like state that seems impenetrable. Her family and college friends are mystified. In trying to sort out why and when she began showing such odd behaviour, the only incident that could be recalled was Maria's ranting and raving, just prior to going into the catatonic state, that one of her lecturers was a 'demon'.

Paranoid schizophrenia

Esther is a 31-year-old unmarried woman who lives with her elderly mother. A belief that the outside world is filled with radio waves that will insert evil thoughts into her head keeps Esther from leaving the house. The windows in her bedroom are 'protected' with aluminium foil that 'deflects the radio waves'. She often hears voices that comment on these radio signals.

Source: Halgin and Whitbourne (1993)

Type I and Type II syndromes

In practice, most British psychiatrists use the overarching category of schizophrenia and only make use of the subtypes outlined above for individuals who fit their criteria exactly. Crow (1985), however, made a further distinction:

- **Type I syndrome** – an acute disorder characterized by positive symptoms (additions or exaggerations of normal behaviour or thought processes), e.g. hallucinations, delusions and disorganized speech.

- **Type II syndrome** – a chronic disorder characterized by negative symptoms such as flattening of affect, apathy and poverty of speech.

Evaluating the use of subtypes in classification and diagnosis

- *Type I and Type II* – There are problems with this simple division because people do not always fit neatly into one or other category. However, it remains a useful distinction because, as you will see in the next section, the two types may have different underlying causes.

- *Blurred distinction between some subtypes* – There is a fine distinction between some of these different types of schizophrenia, and this distinction is blurred even more by the fact that some people diagnosed in one category later develop symptoms from another. This can weaken the reliability of diagnosis.

Validity

The large number of categories also raises issues of **validity**, i.e. do these different types of schizophrenia actually exist? Some issues relating to the validity of schizophrenia as diagnosed by DSM-TR-IV and ICD-10 are discussed next.

Schizophrenia-like disorders

There are some individuals who show symptoms similar to those seen in schizophrenia but who do not exactly meet the criteria. In addition to the subtypes of schizophrenia described above, a further set of disorders is described in ICD and DSM to accommodate this type of individual. These include schizophreniform psychosis, schizoaffective disorder, schizotypal disorder and schizoid personality disorder. You do not need to know the diagnostic criteria for these disorders. However, it is important to understand that so many variations exist. This is an indication of how difficult it can be to diagnose an individual presenting with schizophrenia-like symptoms. There is also some doubt about the validity of some of these classifications and the boundary between them is somewhat blurred. This has led some people to suggest that schizophrenia is not an 'all-or-nothing' condition as suggested by the categorical diagnostic systems (i.e. ICD and DSM).

Dimensional or categorical disorder?

Some psychologists believe that schizophrenia should be seen as a dimensional disorder. In other words, classification should relate to the degree to which problems are experienced, not simply the presence or absence of such problems. For example, it has been found that people who have not been diagnosed with schizophrenia can nevertheless experience one of its main symptoms (i.e. hearing voices), but they have strategies to cope with them and they do not feel disabled by them (Romme and Escher 1989). For these reasons, some people would prefer the classification systems to be dimensional rather than categorical.

Schizophrenia as a multiple disorder
People who have been diagnosed with schizophrenia can present with very different problems. According to both ICD and DSM, only two, potentially quite different, symptoms need to be present to warrant the diagnosis of schizophrenia. This suggests that there is no single, underlying causal factor – if there was, we would expect all people with schizophrenia to show exactly the same set of characteristics. Similarly, as we shall see in the section on therapies, people with schizophrenia do not all respond in the same way to treatments. This has led some researchers to question the validity of schizophrenia as a diagnosis and suggest that the term should be abandoned (e.g. Bentall, 1993) according to this view, each of the symptoms of schizophrenia should be seen as a disorder in its own right, each with its own particular cause and treatment.

Differential diagnosis
We have noted above that there are different subtypes of schizophrenia and also a number of related, schizophrenia-like, conditions. However, it can also be difficult for clinicians to distinguish between schizophrenia and other, seemingly quite separate, syndromes. For example, people with temporal lobe epilepsy often show symptoms similar to those of schizophrenia. Similarly, certain prescribed and recreational drugs can cause psychotic behaviour and it can be difficult to distinguish between drug-induced psychosis and schizophrenia. Such examples show how important it is for the clinician to carry out a thorough physical examination and a careful history-taking before making a diagnosis.

Dual diagnosis
It is fairly common for people diagnosed with one mental disorder simultaneously to show symptoms of another; this is called co-morbidity. Schizophrenia, for example, is accompanied often by symptoms of depression. In such cases, it is important for the clinician to make a dual diagnosis so that the individual is given appropriate treatment for both disorders. However, it has been suggested (e.g. Maj 2005) that the multi-axial classification system of DSM encourages multiple diagnoses to be made where it might not always be appropriate.

Cultural variations
Although schizophrenia occurs generally across cultures, it is a consistent finding in the USA and the UK that schizophrenia is diagnosed more frequently in African Americans and African-Caribbean populations than in other groups (Harrison *et al.* 1988). It is not clear whether this reflects greater genetic vulnerability, psychosocial factors associated with being part of a minority group or misdiagnosis. It could, for example, be the case that clinicians from the majority population misinterpret cultural differences in behaviour and expression as symptoms of schizophrenia. If this is the case, it demonstrates how important it is for clinicians to take particular care in their assessment of people from a different ethnic group.

Activity Characteristics of schizophrenia

Practise writing a concise outline of the characteristics of schizophrenia – something worth say five marks in an exam. Look through Topic 1 and select what you think are relevant points. Once you have made your selection, you should take no more than five or six minutes to write your outline.

Include a brief definition, types of onset with reference to Type I and Type II and two or three important symptoms. Avoid going into too much detail or becoming bogged down in issues to do with reliability and validity of diagnosis.

Some suggestions are given in the Answers to activities on p.603. ▶

CHECK YOUR UNDERSTANDING

Check your understanding of characteristics of schizophrenia and issues around classification and diagnosis in schizophrenia by answering the following questions. Try to do this from memory. You can check your answers by looking back through Topic 1.

1. What is the lifetime risk of developing schizophrenia in the normal population?

2. What is the difference between acute and chronic onset schizophrenia?

3. Outline some of the symptoms that characterize schizophrenia.

4. Why is it important to have a reliable system for diagnosing schizophrenia?

5. Briefly outline some differences between DSM-IV and ICD-10 in the classification of schizophrenia.

6. How does dimensional classification differ from categorical classification?

7. The consequences of misdiagnosis are very serious. What factors do you think clinicians need to take into account before reaching a diagnosis of schizophrenia? Consider issues to do with reliability and validity of classification and diagnosis.

Psychology in context — Schizophrenia and cannabis

As you will see in this section, there is no single explanation for schizophrenia and it is likely that different factors are responsible in different people. Most researchers now agree that biological factors play a key part in the origins of the disorder, but it has been difficult in the past to investigate brain structure and biochemical processes. New scanning techniques have opened up more precise ways of looking at human brains. In one interesting line of research, they have provided the means to investigate the link between schizophrenia and cannabis. Drug taking among young people is a controversial area and there has been much discussion in the media about the effects of taking cannabis and about its classification as either a B or C Class drug.

A newspaper article in the *Times* (Martyn Halle, 11 December 2005) reported on research into a causal link between cannabis and schizophrenia. This article provided details about a new scanning technique called 'diffusion tensor imaging', used by a team of researchers in New York headed by Dr Manzar Ashtari. They used the technique to look at the brains of 15 young, regular cannabis smokers who had all given up the drug a month before the study. The scans showed evidence of the same kind of white-matter damage that is commonly found in the brains of people with schizophrenia. No such damage was shown in the brains of a control group. Dr Ashtari is quoted in the article as saying:

'What we saw should cause alarm because the type of damage in cannabis smokers' brains was exactly the same as in those with schizophrenia and in exactly the same place in the brain. To me, this is proof of the damage cannabis can do and it is shown up graphically for the first time. All the research by psychiatrists so far has strongly suggested cannabis-smoking youngsters run a higher risk of developing psychotic behaviour. Now we have extremely strong evidence that shows what damage has been done.'

1 Robin Murray, a professor at the Institute of Psychiatry in London, is quoted in the article as saying: 'This does seem to be a landmark study, although we will need to see it repeated. For the first time, we are able to see the effects of cannabis smoking.' Why do you think that his response is rather cautious?

2 To what extent do you think that you can draw reliable conclusions from reading about scientific research in a newspaper? Think about issues to do with the validity of the data and the accuracy of the reporting.

Biological explanations of schizophrenia

We have seen that the diagnosis of schizophrenia is not straightforward and that people with schizophrenia vary considerably in terms of the problems they experience. The causes of schizophrenia are not fully understood, and it seems likely that the disorder arises from an interaction of various contributory factors (see the panel, 'Nature–nurture and schizophrenia' opposite). However, there is strong evidence that biological factors have an important part to play. See the Key research study Kety *et al.* 1994) opposite.

 IDA **Nature–nurture debate and schizophrenia**

The controversy about the origins of schizophrenia provides a good example of the nature–nurture debate. The dominant model (explanation) of schizophrenia is that it is due to biological factors and there is considerable evidence for a genetic contribution. However, this has been questioned by people who believe that environmental factors are more important. Most psychologists would now agree that schizophrenia arises from a combination of factors.

Biological explanations of schizophrenia

This prospective, longitudinal study was carried out in Denmark and began in 1962. Kety and colleagues identified 207 offspring of mothers diagnosed with schizophrenia (high-risk group) along with a matched control of 104 children with 'healthy' mothers (low-risk group). The children were aged between 10 and 18 years at the start of the study and were matched on age, gender, parental socio-economic status and urban/rural residence. Follow-up of the children was conducted in 1974 and in 1989. Results published by Parnas *et al.* (1993) strongly support a familial link with two psychotic disorders:

■ Schizophrenia was diagnosed in 16.2 per cent of the high-risk group compared with 1.9 per cent in the low-risk group.

■ Schizotypal personality disorder was diagnosed in 18.8 per cent of the high-risk group compared with 5.0 per cent in the low-risk group (see the panel below for a brief description of this disorder).

■ Combining the figures for the two disorders, the percentages are 35 per cent high-risk, compared with 6.9 per cent low-risk.

Another prospective study with offspring of patients with schizophrenia – the New York High-Risk Project – has reported similar findings at a 25-year follow-up by Erlenmeyer-Kimling *et al.* (1997).

Evaluation

Kety *et al.*'s study seems to provide good evidence of a genetic influence:

■ *Advantage of prospective study* – It has the advantage of any prospective study in that it looks at children before they show any symptoms of schizophrenia and does not rely on retrospective data. Retrospective data depend on people's memory and/or recorded data from schools, hospitals, etc., which is not always reliable. Kety and his team were able to select participants appropriately and follow them accurately because of the detailed life-long records that are kept on Danish citizens. The study was conducted over many years – this is important as schizophrenia can develop in individuals over the age of 40, even though it usually has a much earlier onset than this.

■ *Matching of relevant variables* – The children were carefully matched on relevant variables as detailed above. It is very important to take into account factors such as socio-economic status and whether the children live in urban or rural environments. This is because low socio-economic status and urban environments are known to be risk factors for schizophrenia.

■ *Genes versus environment* – In spite of the fact that this was a large, well-controlled study carried out over a number of years, there are some problems of interpretation. The main difficulty with family studies such as this is that they cannot differentiate between genetic and environmental influences because the children share the same environment as their mothers.

■ *Reliability of diagnosis* – We have also seen that the diagnosis of schizophrenia is not always reliable. The mothers of these children had all been diagnosed with schizophrenia before the modern diagnostic systems were available, so it is possible that they varied widely in their symptoms. It might even be the case that they would not have been given this diagnosis at all if later criteria had been used. People diagnosed with schizotypal personality disorder were also included in the overall figures, whereas this is different from schizophrenia and may have different causes. In fact, in DSM-IV-TR, it is regarded as a distinct personality disorder rather than a schizophrenic spectrum disorder.

These criticisms do not completely undermine the value of the study, but they do illustrate why we should treat such data with caution.

Schizotypal personality disorder

People with schizotypal personality disorder experience acute discomfort in close relationships, cognitive or perceptual distortions and display eccentric behaviour, such as wearing peculiar clothing and repeatedly organizing the contents of cupboards. They tend to lack humour and have flat or inappropriate emotions. One of the most distinctive symptoms of this disorder is digressive speech – conversing vaguely or over-elaborating statements. These symptoms may be similar to those of people with schizophrenia but they are seldom as extreme and do not represent a complete break with reality.

(Adapted from Comer 2004)

Genetic explanation for schizophrenia

It has been known for a long time that schizophrenia runs in families. This could be because family members share the same disadvantaged environment, but a large body of research evidence suggests that genetic factors are also important. This evidence comes from three major sources:

- family studies
- twin studies
- adoption studies.

Evidence from family studies

First-degree relatives (parents, siblings and offspring) share an average of 50 per cent of their genes, and second-degree relatives share approximately 25 per cent. To investigate genetic transmission of schizophrenia, studies compare rates of schizophrenia in relatives of diagnosed cases with relatives of controls. There is now a considerable body of evidence that suggests that the closer the biological relationship, the greater the risk of developing schizophrenia or a related psychotic disorder. For example, Kendler et al. (1985) have shown that first-degree relatives of those with schizophrenia are 18 times more at risk than the general population.

Evaluation of evidence

Family studies are often inconclusive because they are conducted retrospectively, that is, they are comparing a cross section of people who have already been diagnosed. A **prospective (longitudinal) study** can provide more reliable data because it follows the same group of people over a period of time and can make comparisons before and after any of the signs of illness occur. A number of large-scale projects have been undertaken in different parts of the world (see Key research on p.313).

Evidence from twin studies

Twin studies offer another way of establishing genetic links, by comparing the difference in concordance rates (i.e. the likelihood of both twins being affected with the disorder) for identical (MZ) and fraternal (DZ) twins. Both share the same environment, but only the MZ twins have identical genetic make-up. Many studies have been conducted and they all show a much higher **concordance rate** in MZ than in DZ twins. To separate out genetics conclusively from the environment, researchers have sought out MZ twins reared apart where at least one twin has been diagnosed with schizophrenia. Obviously, they are few in number and an added problem is that one of the reasons for separation may have been a problem in the family. Gottesman and Shields (1982) used the Maudsley twin register and found 58 per cent (seven out of 12 MZ twin pairs reared apart) were concordant for schizophrenia. If the genetic hypothesis is correct, then the offspring of a non-affected discordant MZ twin should still be high-risk. A study by Fischer (1971) found that 9.4 per cent of such offspring developed schizophrenia, which is a much higher incidence than in the general population (approximately 1 per cent). A study in London using the Maudsley Twin Register by Cardno et al. (1999) found a 40 per cent concordance rate in MZ twins, compared with 5.3 per cent in DZ twins.

Evaluation of evidence

Even in the rare cases where MZ twins are reared apart, they still share the same environment in the womb before birth, so the contribution of environmental factors cannot be entirely discounted.

Evidence from adoption studies

A more effective way of separating out the effects of environmental and genetic factors is to look at adopted children who later develop schizophrenia and compare them with their biological and adoptive parents. The Finnish Adoption Study, which Tienari began in 1969, identified adopted-away offspring of biological mothers who had been diagnosed with schizophrenia (112 index cases), plus a matched control group of 135 adopted-away offspring of mothers who had not been diagnosed with any mental disorder. Adoptees ranged from five to seven years at the start of the study and all had been separated from their mother before the age of four. The study reported that 7 per cent of the index adoptees developed schizophrenia, compared with 1.5 per cent of the controls (Tienari et al. 1987).

The Danish Adoption Study, reported by Kety et al. (1994), taking a national sample from across Denmark, found high rates of diagnosis for chronic schizophrenia in adoptees whose biological parents had the same diagnosis, even though they had been adopted by 'healthy' parents.

Evaluation of evidence

The data provided by these prospective studies have, so far, indicated a strong genetic link for schizophrenia. However, data from adoption studies have to be analysed carefully. Tienari et al. (2000) showed that the risk for developing schizophrenia was four times greater in adopted children with biological mothers suffering from schizophrenia than in adopted children with biological mothers without schizophrenia. Wahlberg et al. (2000) re-examined these same data and found that there was a strong interaction between genetic and environmental factors. It seemed that only children who were adopted into families with poor communication were at increased risk of developing schizophrenia. Another problem in these longitudinal studies is that diagnostic criteria for schizophrenia are continually being updated and changed.

Evaluation of genetic explanation of schizophrenia

Twin, adoption and family studies continue to provide reliable evidence that the degree of risk increases with the degree of genetic relatedness (see Fig. 9.1).

- *Research evidence* – There is now very strong evidence, particularly from adoption studies, that genetics are a clear risk factor for schizophrenia. Although studies have shown clearly that the risk of schizophrenia is increased if close relatives have been diagnosed with the disorder, the chances are never 100 per cent. Even if a MZ twin has the disorder, the risk for the other twin is less than 50 per cent. This suggests that genetics cannot offer a complete explanation. Furthermore, about 89 per cent of people with schizophrenia have no known relative who has been diagnosed with the disorder, so other factors are clearly responsible in these individuals.

- *Search for relevant genes* – Research into the location of specific genes has not yet produced definitive results, although several have been implicated. Without knowing which precise genes are involved, it is impossible to understand the underlying mechanisms that lead from the genetic risk to the symptoms of the disorder. The search for specific genes continues.

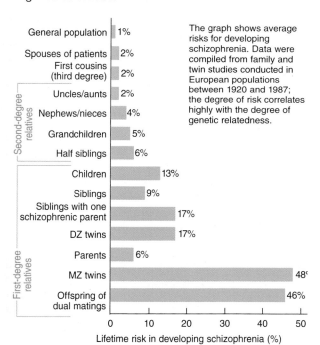

The graph shows average risks for developing schizophrenia. Data were compiled from family and twin studies conducted in European populations between 1920 and 1987; the degree of risk correlates highly with the degree of genetic relatedness.

Figure 9.1 *Genetic risk of developing schizophrenia (Source: Zimbardo et al. 1995)*

Biochemical explanations of schizophrenia

If genetic factors are important, they are likely to work by exerting an influence on the hardware of the brain. In other words, structural or biochemical abnormalities should be detectable in the brains of those diagnosed with schizophrenia. In particular, research interest has focused on the action of certain neurotransmitters (chemicals that act as messengers to transmit impulses from one nerve cell to another across the gap between adjacent nerve cells, called the synapse).

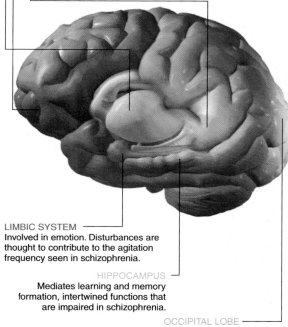

BASAL GANGLIA
Involved in movement and emotions and in integrating sensory information. Abnormal functioning in schizophrenia is thought to contribute to paranoia and hallucinations. [Excessive blockage of dopamine receptors in the basal ganglia by traditional antipsychotic medicines leads to motor side effects.]

AUDITORY SYSTEM
Enables humans to hear and understand speech. In schizophrenia, overactivity of the speech area [called Wernicke's area] can create auditory hallucinations-the illusion that internally generated thoughts are real voices coming from the outside.

FRONTAL LOBE
Critical to problem solving, insight and other high-level reasoning. Pertubations in schizophrenia lead to difficulty in planning actions and organizing thoughts.

LIMBIC SYSTEM
Involved in emotion. Disturbances are thought to contribute to the agitation frequency seen in schizophrenia.

HIPPOCAMPUS
Mediates learning and memory formation, intertwined functions that are impaired in schizophrenia.

OCCIPITAL LOBE
Processes information about the visual world. People with schizophrenia rarely have full-blown visual hallucinations, but disturbances in this area contribute to such difficulties as interpreting complex images, recognizing emotion, and reading emotions on others' faces.

Figure 9.2 *The brain in schizophrenia*

The dopamine hypothesis

Dopamine is a neurotransmitter that is found in the limbic system of the brain. It is thought that some of the symptoms of schizophrenia are a result either of an excess of dopamine in the brain or of a super-sensitivity of the dopamine receptors. In either case, schizophrenia is believed to occur as a result of over-activity in parts of the brain controlled by dopamine.

Interest in the neurotransmitter dopamine arose when it was found that phenothiazines (neuroleptic, antipsychotic drugs), which work by inhibiting dopamine activity, can reduce the symptoms of schizophrenia. Conversely, L-dopa (a synthetic dopamine-releasing drug) can induce symptoms resembling acute schizophrenia in non-psychotic people.

Studies of drugs like amphetamines and LSD, which are known to increase dopamine activity, have provided further support. These drugs can induce positive symptoms very similar to acute schizophrenia in healthy individuals and can exacerbate symptoms in people who are already vulnerable. In a study by Randrup and Munkvad (1966), behaviour similar to that found in those suffering from schizophrenia was induced in rats by administering amphetamines. The effects were then reversed by neuroleptic drugs.

Evaluation of the dopamine hypothesis

■ *Post-mortems and PET scans* – Further support for the dopamine hypothesis comes from post-mortems which are examinations of patients with schizophrenia after they have died. These have revealed a specific increase of dopamine in the left amygdala (Falkai *et al.* 1988) and increased dopamine receptor density in the caudate nucleus putamen (Owen *et al.* 1978). However, it is not clear whether these increases are a cause or a result of schizophrenia. Given the findings from post-mortems, and assuming that dopamine is the important factor in the action of antipsychotic drugs, then it would be expected that dopamine metabolism is abnormal in patients with schizophrenia. With the development of **PET (positron emission tomography) scans**, metabolic activity can now be monitored in living brains. PET scan research conducted by Wong *et al.* (1986) revealed that dopamine receptor density in the caudate nuclei is indeed greater in those with schizophrenia (particularly those with positive symptoms) than in controls. Unfortunately, neither post-mortems nor PET scans can reveal whether increased dopaminergic activity causes schizophrenia, or whether schizophrenia interferes with dopamine metabolism.

■ *Effectiveness of drug treatments* – Drugs alleviate positive symptoms, but are not so effective with negative symptoms. It is possible that the inconclusive findings in dopamine studies merely reflect two different forms of schizophrenia (Type I and Type II, see p.310). Amphetamines (known to affect dopamine activity) worsen positive symptoms associated with acute schizophrenia and lessen negative symptoms associated with chronic schizophrenia, whilst phenothiazines (antipsychotic drugs) alleviate positive symptoms, but are not so effective at lessening negative symptoms. However, there are some people with schizophrenia who do not respond at all to neuroleptic drugs, which suggests that a faulty dopamine system is not always a causal factor.

■ *Role of other neurotransmitters* – One of the most effective drugs in treating schizophrenia is clozapine (see p.323). This drug has its major effect on the serotonin system rather than the dopamine system, suggesting that other neurotransmitters could also be causal factors in schizophrenia.

■ *Role of dopamine in other disorders* – Dopamine is unlikely to be the only factor in schizophrenia because it has also been implicated in mania, and a number of other mental disorders which have quite different symptoms. Each of these disorders is alleviated by quite different drugs, yet the main evidence for the dopamine link in schizophrenia is the effectiveness of phenothiazines in alleviating symptoms.

■ *Reductionism* – Before reading further, look at the box below, which outlines the criticism that biochemical explanations of schizophrenia may be reductionist.

IDA **Reductionism in biochemical explanations**

A criticism of biochemical explanations of schizophrenia is that they are reductionist, i.e. they reduce a complex behaviour such as schizophrenia down to a relatively simple level of explanation, i.e. an imbalance in brain chemicals. The influence of brain chemicals such as dopamine is indisputable, but to argue that they cause schizophrenia is to neglect all other potential influences (such as stress or irrational thought processes) in the course of this disorder. To find out more about reductionism in psychology, turn to p.39.

Neuroanatomical explanations

Recent advances in technology have enabled the medical profession to examine the live brains of people with schizophrenia to see if there are observable brain abnormalities.

Magnetic resonance imaging

Magnetic resonance imaging (MRI) is a non-invasive technique used to record radio waves from the brain. These recordings are computerized and assembled into a three-dimensional picture of brain structures. MRI studies show quite definite structural abnormalities in the brains of many patients with schizophrenia. The development of this technique has been a tremendous breakthrough because it provides a picture of the living brain. Earlier research depended on post-mortem studies of the brains of people who had suffered from schizophrenia for many years. It was, therefore, difficult to be sure whether any structural damage was a causal factor or whether it was the result of drug therapy or the natural progression of the disorder.

Evidence for neuroanatomical explanations
Brown *et al.* (1986) found decreased brain weight and enlarged ventricles, which are the cavities in the brain that hold cerebrospinal fluid. Flaum *et al.* (1995) also found enlarged ventricles, along with smaller thalamic, hippocampal and superior temporal volumes. Buchsbaum (1990) found abnormalities in the frontal and pre-frontal cortex, the basal ganglia, the hippocampus and the amygdala. As more MRI studies are being undertaken, more abnormalities are being identified.

Structural abnormalities have been found more often in those with negative/chronic symptoms, rather than positive/acute symptoms, lending support to the belief that there are two types of schizophrenia: Type I (acute) and Type II (chronic). An argument against this is that many people with acute symptoms of schizophrenia go on later to develop chronic symptoms, which could indicate a further degeneration of the brain rather than two distinct types of schizophrenia.

The critical period for the onset of schizophrenia is not usually before adolescence. Therefore, if brain abnormalities precede the onset of clinical symptoms, this would confirm the view that schizophrenia is a developmental disorder. Weinberger (1987) claims that, despite much research, the evidence is still inconclusive as to whether there are progressive structural brain changes prior to the initial onset of schizophrenia or whether they follow the onset of clinical symptoms.

One of the main problems in trying to understand the causal direction is that, so far, brain imaging in relation to schizophrenia has been restricted mainly to people who have already been diagnosed. A study of monkeys by Castner et al. (1998) may shed some light on the direction of causality. The researchers subjected the monkeys to brain-damaging X-rays during foetal development and found that they showed no ill effects during childhood compared with the control group, but at puberty they developed symptoms of schizophrenia, such as hallucinations. These findings suggest that brain damage during the foetal stage of development caused the schizophrenic symptoms. Look now at the activity below.

HOW SCIENCE WORKS

Activity — **Evaluating studies using non-human animals**

When you are evaluating research that supports a particular hypothesis, you need to think carefully about methodological and ethical issues. Animal studies such as the one carried out by Castner et al. (1988) on monkeys and by Randrup and Munkvad (1966) (see p.316) have been used to investigate the origins of schizophrenia and have produced some useful and interesting evidence. However, there are considerable problems involved in using animals in research, particularly when the results are then generalized to humans. These problems can be practical and/or ethical and, because of this, animal experimentation is a very controversial area of research. There are several discussion points for you to consider.

- Why do you think non-human animals have been used at all in schizophrenia research, given the problems associated with their use?

- Try to think of as many ethical and practical problems as you can and then consider whether there are ways to overcome these difficulties. It might be helpful to bear in mind the advances in science which now allow more sophisticated methods of investigation into human brains. Remember that you need to discuss these problems in the context of research into schizophrenia, so do not be tempted to have a rant about the use of animal experimentation in general.

Evaluation of the neuroanatomical explanation

- *Conflicting findings about structural abnormalities* – Whilst MRI studies appear to provide conclusive evidence of structural abnormalities, it is worth noting that they do not always agree on the regions of the brain affected. For example, Flaum et al. (1995) found no abnormalities in the temporal lobe regions of those with schizophrenia, whereas Woodruff et al. (1997) found quite significant reductions in the temporal lobe, compared with controls.

- *Structural abnormalities as cause or effect* – Because most studies using MRI techniques have been carried out on people already diagnosed with schizophrenia, it is not clear whether structural abnormalities predispose to schizophrenia, or whether the onset of clinical symptoms cause structural changes. However, Wood et al. (2005) compared hippocampus size in 79 males deemed to be at high risk of developing schizophrenia and 49 healthy males with no predisposing factors and found that the high-risk group had significantly smaller hippocampuses than the control group. This suggests that brain abnormalities might exist before the onset of symptoms.

- *Types of study* – Prospective studies, which could shed light on the direction of causality, have been carried out mainly on non-human animals and it is difficult to generalize such findings to humans.

Pregnancy and birth factors as explanations for schizophrenia

Other avenues of research have been explored for alternatives to the genetic view of schizophrenia as a developmental disorder.

Winter births

Since the late 1920s, it has been noticed that an overwhelmingly high proportion of people diagnosed with schizophrenia were born in the winter and early spring (Hope-Simpson 1981). Bradbury and Miller (1985) conducted a review of the evidence and found that this was borne out in most countries in the northern hemisphere. A more recent study in England and Wales shows that this has remained consistent over the latter half of the century (Procopio and Marriott 1998). In southern hemisphere countries, a high proportion of those diagnosed with schizophrenia were born in July to September (i.e. their winter months). One possible reason for this is the greater likelihood of contracting a viral disease in the winter months.

Viral infections

Jones and Cannon (1998) found that young children who had viral infections were five times more likely to develop schizophrenia than those who did not. It has also been suggested that viral infections in the mother during pregnancy could be a causal factor. A number of viral infections, such as measles, scarlet fever, polio, diphtheria and pneumonia and, in particular, the virus Influenza A, have been suggested as an explanation (Torrey *et al.* 1988, Torrey *et al.* 1996). Influenza A is most prevalent in the winter and, if implicated in some way, could explain the high proportion of winter births in those diagnosed with schizophrenia. The suggestion is that if the mother is infected during pregnancy there is pre-birth exposure to the Influenza A virus. It is thought that the 25- to 30-week foetus is most vulnerable because of accelerated growth in the cerebral cortex at this time (Mednick *et al.* 1988). It is hypothesized that the viral infection enters the brain and gestates until it is activated by hormonal changes in puberty. Alternatively, there may be a gradual degeneration of the brain which eventually becomes so severe that symptoms of schizophrenia emerge.

Further support for the viral hypothesis comes from the observation that, throughout history, peaks in schizophrenia diagnosis have corresponded with major influenza epidemics (Torrey *et al.* 1988) although other researchers have not always been able to corroborate this (Battle *et al.* 1999)

Birth complications

There is now quite convincing evidence for both structural abnormalities and neurochemical abnormalities in the brains of people with schizophrenia, but there are conflicting views as to whether these abnormalities result from a genetic defect or from complications at birth leading to brain damage. A longitudinal study by Dalman *et al.* (1999) found significant links between birth complications and later development of schizophrenia, with pre-eclampsia being the most significant risk factor. This is a very serious complication of pregnancy which can lead to babies with growth problems.

Maternal stress

Some studies have provided evidence for the role of maternal stress in the development of schizophrenia. For example, Van Os and Selten (1998) found that children born to mothers who had experienced bombing raids during the Second World War were more likely to develop schizophrenia than comparison groups.

Evaluation of pregnancy and birth factor explanations

- *Methodological problems* – Although the evidence relating to viral infections is suggestive, there are some problems. For example, studies such as those of Torrey *et al.* (1988) were based on correlational data and so caution should be observed when attempting to infer causation. The data are also based on DSM-II diagnostic criteria for schizophrenia, which included a broader diagnostic range of patients than DSM-III onwards. Torrey *et al.* (1988) claimed that the link between viral infection and schizophrenia only occurs in those who are already genetically predisposed. If that were the case, however, 100 per cent concordance would be expected in MZ twins because they are in the uterus together and are both therefore exposed to the same viruses.

- *Birth complications and maternal stress* – It is unlikely that birth complications like pre-eclampsia could be the sole cause of schizophrenia, because this is a common problem and not all such infants go on to develop schizophrenia. It is very difficult to interpret data on maternal stress and links with schizophrenia because the precise contributory factor cannot be isolated. For example, stressed women might smoke more or drink more alcohol than other women.

Substance abuse and links to schizophrenia

If you have not already done so, read the Psychology in context 'Schizophrenia and cannabis' on p.312.

There is some evidence that taking cannabis can lead to schizophrenia. Cannabis raises levels of dopamine in the brain and could trigger psychotic episodes. Henquet *et al.* (2005) in a meta-analysis found that young, heavy users of cannabis were twice as likely as non-users to develop schizophrenia.

Evaluation of link between substance abuse and cannabis

Several studies have shown a link between smoking cannabis and schizophrenia. However, it seems likely that the increased risk only occurs in young people who have a particular genetic predisposition (Caspi *et al.* 2005). It has also been suggested (Peralta and Cuesta 1992) that people with early schizophrenic symptoms might take cannabis as a form of self-therapy to deal with their negative experiences, suggesting that the cannabis is not a causal factor.

Diathesis-stress model as an explanation for schizophrenia

Although it has been well established that biological factors are important in explaining the origins of schizophrenia, it is clear that environmental influences also have a part to play. One explanation that links biological vulnerability to environmental stressors is the 'diathesis-stress model'. The reasoning behind this theory is that certain individuals have a constitutional predisposition to the disorder, but will only go on to develop schizophrenia if they are exposed to stressful situations. The predisposition may be genetic and/or the result of illnesses or damage early in life. Stressful events in the environment, such as major life events, traumatic experiences, or dysfunctional families, may then act as a 'trigger' in a high-risk individual (see Fig. 9.3).

Evaluation of diathesis-stress model

- *Longitudinal studies* – Support for the 'diathesis-stress' model comes from prospective longitudinal studies. Even though such studies have provided compelling support for the importance of genetic factors, they have also shown that schizophrenia did not always develop in those thought to be genetically vulnerable. This led researchers back to the environment in the search for precipitating factors.

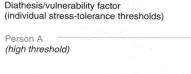

Diathesis/vulnerability factor
(individual stress-tolerance thresholds)

Person A
(high threshold)

Person B
(medium threshold)

Person C
(low threshold)

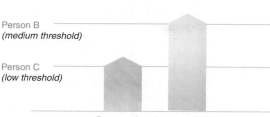

Degree of environmental stress

When environmental stressors (illustrated by the shaded arrows) penetrate the tolerance threshold for an individual, this results in physical or mental symptoms (illustrated by the darker shaded areas).

- A small number of stressors, such as minor ailments or failing a driving test, may penetrate the stress tolerance of person C (who has a low threshold).

- Additional stressors may penetrate the stress tolerance threshold of both person C and person B (who has a medium threshold).

- The cumulative effect of many stressors, or one significant or life-threatening event, may penetrate the stress-tolerance threshold of persons C and B and even of person A (who has a high threshold).

Figure 9.3 *Diathesis-stress model*

- *Studies on parenting* – The Finnish Adoption Study undertaken by Tienari *et al.* (1987) investigated environmental factors by assessing the quality of parenting through a battery of tests and interviews. All of the reported cases of schizophrenia occurred in families rated as 'disturbed'. Furthermore, where the rearing environments were rated as 'healthy' in the high-risk sample, the occurrence of schizophrenia was well below general population rates. However, this cannot be seen as evidence for a purely environmental aetiology because low-risk children from 'disturbed' families did not develop schizophrenia.

- The Israeli High Risk Study (Marcus 1987) investigated environmental factors by assessing the parents on hostility, inconsistency and over-involvement. All the reported cases of schizophrenia had poor parenting ratings. However, all of these cases also showed signs of neuropsychological abnormalities at the time of initial assessment (13 years previously), which raises the question of whether these abnormalities had influenced the parent-child interaction. These studies are ongoing but the evidence so far strongly supports the diathesis-stress model.

Psychological explanations of schizophrenia

If you think back to the AS topic of Psychopathology, you will recall that there are several main approaches or theoretical perspectives in this area. All of these approaches offer explanations for schizophrenia, but some of them have much less credibility than others. For example, the traditional behavioural approach and the psychodynamic approach have less convincing explanations of schizophrenia than some of the others.

- *The **behavioural approach*** – It explains schizophrenia in terms of conditioning and observational learning. It is difficult to see how the bizarre and complex pattern of schizophrenic behaviour can be acquired through these simple processes, although once diagnosed, it is possible that people with schizophrenia are unintentionally reinforced (e.g. paid special attention) for their odd behaviour by staff in hospitals or by

families in the home. The behavioural approach might, therefore, offer some understanding of how schizophrenic characteristics are maintained, but it contributes little to our understanding of the underlying causes of the disorder.

- ***Psychodynamic explanations*** – There have been several psychodynamic explanations, including the idea of the 'schizophrenogenic family' (see below). Another suggestion is that people with schizophrenia cannot resolve the conflict between the demands of the id and the overwhelming guilt imposed by the superego, and so they regress to an earlier, infantile stage of development. There is no evidence to support this view and, as with the behavioural approach, it fails to explain the complexity of the disorder.

Psychosocial factors

- *Socio-economic status* – One consistent finding is that schizophrenia occurs more in lower socio-economic groups. This could be explained in two ways: either low socio-economic status is itself a risk factor for schizophrenia or people with schizophrenia can no longer cope adequately with jobs and relationships and so 'drift' down the social-economic hierarchy. Fox (1990) examined data from his own and others' studies and found no evidence for the so-called 'social drift hypothesis'. It seems, then, that factors associated with living in poorer conditions, such as high levels of stress, may trigger the onset of schizophrenia.

- *Migrant populations* – A related finding is that schizophrenia occurs more frequently in migrant populations, i.e. people who move, usually from a different country, to settle in a new and unfamiliar environment. A particularly controversial finding is that there is an increased risk of being diagnosed with schizophrenia in the African-Caribbean population in the UK. It is not entirely clear why this should be the case, but it might reflect racial bias in diagnosis or factors associated with other migrant populations such as psychosocial adversity, stress of living with racial discrimination, cannabis use, etc.

- *Evaluation* – There is certainly evidence that acute life stresses can precipitate schizophrenia, but it is unlikely that social class or economic status can be anything other than a contributory factor.

Family relationships

- *Schizophrenogenic families* – In the past 50 years, there has been some interest in the idea that disturbed patterns of communication within families might be a factor in the development of schizophrenia. The term 'schizophrenogenic families' (coined by Fromm-Reichmann 1948) was used to describe families with high emotional tension, with many secrets, close alliances and conspiracies. Bateson *et al.* (1956) suggested the **'double-bind hypothesis'**, where children are given conflicting messages from parents who express care, yet at the same time appear critical. It was thought that this led to confusion, self-doubt and eventual withdrawal. Lidz *et al.* (1965) coined the term 'marital schism' to explain an abnormal family pattern where discord between parents was associated with schizophrenia in offspring.

- *Evaluation* – Such theories were based on methodologically flawed studies. For example, they did not include control groups and used poorly operationalized definitions of schizophrenia. One major problem was that families were studied retrospectively, long after the person's mental disorder may have affected the family system. Living with someone who is suffering from schizophrenia is difficult and distressing for the whole family. Routines are disrupted, often with one parent having to give up paid employment to care for the person. As families struggle to cope with schizophrenia, to suggest that they have caused the disorder is unhelpful, if not highly destructive.

Expressed emotion in the course of schizophrenia

By the mid-1970s, psychologists had become more interested in the part the family might play in the *course*, rather than the cause, of schizophrenia. Unfortunately, there is quite a high risk that someone who has had one episode of schizophrenia will experience another one. This means that it is possible to set up prospective studies to investigate the degree of relapse in people who have already been diagnosed. Most of the research into **expressed emotion (EE)** in families suggests that it acts to maintain schizophrenia rather than as causal factor for the first episode of schizophrenia.

Research relating to expressed emotion

Vaughn and Leff, working at the Medical Research Council in London, published a paper in 1976 suggesting that the extent of expressed emotion within a family was a strong predictor of relapse rates among discharged patients. Their research was stimulated by an earlier study by Brown (1972) showing that patients with schizophrenia who returned to homes where a high level of emotion was expressed (EE) – such as hostility, criticism, over-involvement and over-concern – showed a greater tendency to relapse than those returning to low-EE homes. Vaughn and Leff (1976) found similar results, with 51 per cent relapse in those in high-EE homes and only 13 per cent relapse in those in low-EE homes. Vaughn and

Leff included in their study the amount of time spent in face-to-face contact with relatives after discharge and found that relapse rates increased as face-to-face contact increased with high-EE relatives. Individuals who went to work or attended a day center and so spent less than 35 hours per week exposed to a negative home environment were significantly less likely to relapse.

Evaluation of the role of 'expressed emotion' in the course of schizophrenia

- *Accepted maintenance model* – EE has now become a well-established 'maintenance' model of schizophrenia and many prospective studies have been conducted which support the expressed-emotion hypothesis across many countries and cultures (e.g. Miklowitz 2004). So well accepted has this model become that treatment programmes for schizophrenia usually include education and training for family members in controlling levels of EE. Interestingly, it has been found that relapse rates are lower in countries like Nigeria and India, where there is less of a stigma attached to a diagnosis of schizophrenia and where extended families provide strong support and consequently exhibit lower levels of negative expressed emotion.

- *Relapse rates and estrangement from the family* – Despite the widely held acceptance of the EE model, it is not without its critics. Many patients with schizophrenia are either estranged from their families or have minimal contact and so, it is argued, they do not experience high EE and yet there is no evidence that such people are less prone to relapse (Goldstein 1988). There is no reason why this should negate the model, however, because presumably social involvement with anyone (not just family members) could be regarded as high or low EE. Research may focus more on families simply because they are usually the first and most frequent point of contact for those with schizophrenia.

- *High EE as a response to living with schizophrenia* – It should also be remembered that relationships within the family work both ways and there is some evidence that certain aspects of high-EE behaviour are associated with abnormalities in the patient (Miklowitz 2004). It has been found, for example, that high EE is less common in the families of first-episode patients than in those with frequent re-admissions. This suggests that high EE may well develop as a response to the burdens of living with a person suffering from schizophrenia.

Cognitive explanations of schizophrenia

Schizophrenia is characterized by profound thought disturbance. Cognitive psychologists suggest that disturbed thinking processes are the cause rather than the consequence of schizophrenia.

The role of attention

Much cognitive research has focused on the role of attention in schizophrenia. It is thought that the mechanisms that operate in normal brains to filter and process incoming stimuli are somehow defective in the brains of people with schizophrenia. Most people are able to focus attention selectively. It is suggested that people with schizophrenia cannot filter information in this way and they simply let in too much irrelevant information. This means that they are inundated by external stimuli, which they are unable to interpret appropriately, and so they experience the world very differently from the rest of us. Such ideas are supported by evidence that shows that some people with schizophrenia are poor at laboratory tasks that require them to pay attention to some stimuli, but to ignore others.

Physiological abnormality and cognitive malfunction

Cognitive psychologists believe that there are almost certainly physiological abnormalities associated with schizophrenia and that these lead to cognitive malfunctioning. Explanations that relate underlying biological impairments to psychotic symptoms are often referred to as 'neuropsychological theories'.

Failure to activate schemas

A neuropsychological theory proposed by Hemsley (1993) suggested that the central deficit in schizophrenia is a breakdown in the relationship between information that has already been stored in memory and new, incoming sensory information. Packages of information stored in our memories as **schemas** influence the way we interpret later events. For example, if we go out to eat in a restaurant, we know from past experiences what to expect and, therefore, know which aspects of the current situation need our attention and which we can take for granted. Such processing normally occurs very quickly and without conscious awareness. Hemsley suggests that this processing breaks down in schizophrenia and that schemas are not activated. As a result, people with schizophrenia are subjected to sensory overload and do not know which aspects of a situation to attend to and which to ignore. This means that superficial incidents might be seen as highly relevant and significant (e.g. a conversation at the next table is interpreted as being personally relevant) and could explain symptoms such as delusions. Hemsley further suggests that internal thoughts are sometimes not recognized as arising from memory and so are attributed to an external source and experienced as auditory hallucinations.

Faulty cognitive processes

Another neuropsychological theory was proposed by Frith (1992), who has attempted to explain the onset and maintenance of some of the positive symptoms of schizophrenia. His idea is that people with schizophrenia are unable to distinguish between actions that are brought about by external forces and those that are generated internally. He believes that most of the symptoms of schizophrenia can be explained in terms of deficits in three cognitive processes:

- inability to generate willed action (that is, any action that is under the voluntary control of the individual)

- inability to monitor willed action

- inability to monitor the beliefs and intentions of others.

Frith suggests that these three processes are all part of a general mechanism, which he calls 'meta-representation', that allows us to be aware of our goals and our intentions and to understand the beliefs and intentions of others. According to Frith, faulty operation of this mechanism is due to a functional disconnection between frontal areas of the brain concerned with action and more posterior areas of the brain that control perception. He has produced some evidence for his ideas by detecting changes in cerebral blood flow in the brains of people with schizophrenia when engaged in specific cognitive tasks.

Genetic links

Cognitive psychologists are attempting to find evidence for genetic links by examining whether malfunctioning cognitive processing is a family trait. Park et al. (1995) identified working memory deficits in people with schizophrenia and in their first-degree non-schizophrenic relatives, a study that has been supported by Faraone et al. (1999), who also found impairments in auditory attention. Faraone and colleagues claim that these memory and attention impairments are a manifestation of the genetic predisposition to schizophrenia and are even bold enough to claim that these are the cause of schizophrenia. They admit, however, that their data cannot explain why some relatives do not develop schizophrenia, even though they have the predisposing genes. They suggest that further work is needed to establish whether some people have a low 'dose' of the genes, or, alternatively, whether they have not been exposed to any environmental agents that may trigger the disorder. Cannon et al. (1994b), who also identified verbal memory and attention deficits in people with schizophrenia and their non-schizophrenic siblings, suggested that the mediating factors that determine the expression of these genes are birth complications (see p.318).

Evaluation of cognitive explanations

- *Limited scope of cognitive theories* – Cognitive theories in themselves do not really explain the causes of schizophrenia. They simply describe some of the symptoms of the disorder in cognitive terms. In order to explain the origins of schizophrenia, they need to be combined with the biological model (see the neuropsychological and genetic explanations outlined previously). Cognitive theories may not be able to offer a full explanation of schizophrenia, but they may help to explain the origins of particular symptoms (e.g. hallucinations and delusions).

- *Hemsley's model* – Hemsley has tried to link his cognitive model to an underlying neurological system, in particular to the hippocampus and related brain structures. There is currently very little clear-cut empirical evidence, but there has been some promising research with animals offering tentative support for his ideas.

- *Frith's theory* – Frith's theory has provided a comprehensive framework for explaining many of the symptoms of schizophrenia. However, research support is far from conclusive and the theory is still regarded as speculative. Some critics regard his

theory as too reductionist in that it fails to take into account the role of environmental factors.

- *A genetic origin* – Cognitive impairments thought to have a genetic origin have been implicated in a number of different mental disorders, e.g. Attention Deficit Hyperactivity Disorder. As an explanation for schizophrenia, this is a new area of research and, as yet, it is not possible to evaluate the validity of such a link.

CHECK YOUR UNDERSTANDING

Check your understanding of explanations of schizophrenia by answering the following questions. Try to do this from memory. You can check your answers by looking back through Topic 2.

1. What is meant by the 'nature–nurture' debate in the context of schizophrenia?

2. Explain why twin, family and adoption studies are useful in investigating the causes of schizophrenia.

3. Give a brief outline of the dopamine hypothesis.

4. Explain why the effectiveness of clozapine has cast some doubt on the dopamine hypothesis.

5. What are some of the problems of investigating biochemical and neuroanatomical factors?

6. Wood *et al.* (2005) compared people with a high risk of developing schizophrenia to a control group. How might he have selected his high-risk sample?

7. Outline the diathesis-stress model of schizophrenia.

8. Why do you think that migrant populations might be more at risk of developing schizophrenia than indigenous groups?

9. What is the possible role of the family in schizophrenia?

10. Give a brief outline and evaluation of a cognitive explanation of schizophrenia.

Topic 3: Therapies for schizophrenia

Psychology in context   Art therapy

One of the things that should be clear after reading the first sections of this chapter is that schizophrenia involves a wide range of symptoms and problems. It is unlikely that one type of therapy will address all of these, so clinicians tend to offer treatment programmes made up of different elements. A recent BBC news article (14 September 2008) reported on an interesting

suggestion for helping people with schizophrenia to combat feelings of isolation and social withdrawal. It reported on plans by the National Institute of Clinical and Health Excellence (NICE) to promote the use of programmes offering music, art and dance therapy, including activities such as playing musical instruments and creating collages. Schemes use trained therapists with degrees in art, music or dance, and encourage people with schizophrenia to be creative, as well as participating in group activities. On the basis of several research trials, this kind of therapy has proved effective, particularly with negative symptoms such as withdrawal and poor motivation. It is not entirely clear how or why it works, but it is useful because it is a non-threatening and accessible therapy that can help people express their feelings without the need to talk them over.

1. Why do you think this kind of art therapy might be helpful for people with schizophrenia?

2. How might you evaluate the effectiveness of art therapy for people with schizophrenia?

3. What difficulties might you encounter and how would you try to overcome them?

The treatment of schizophrenia is aimed at both reducing the symptoms of the acute illness and providing relief for any ongoing, chronic disability. The best treatment programmes combine aspects of biological and psychosocial treatments.

Biological therapies

Biological treatments arise from the medical model of abnormal behaviour, which considers mental disorder to be an illness or disease resulting from underlying biological factors. There are various biological treatments, such as drug therapy, **electro-convulsive therapy (ECT)** and **psychosurgery**. Most people with schizophrenia receive some form of medication (drug therapy). Drugs are administered in tablet form or, sometimes, by injection. We shall first look briefly at the earlier treatments of psychosurgery and ECT.

Early treatments for schizophrenia

In the past, many people with schizophrenia were hospitalized and spent years in institutions because no effective treatments were available. Wards became overcrowded and the priority for staff was to keep order rather than to offer humanitarian therapy. This was often achieved by restraint (see picture opposite) and punishment. One early form of treatment, first performed by Moniz in 1935, was the prefrontal lobotomy, a form of psychosurgery in which sizeable portions of brain tissue were destroyed (Moniz 1936). This operation was carried out extensively on a range of mentally ill patients, many of whom met the criteria for a diagnosis of schizophrenia. There was no evidence that this drastic treatment was effective but plenty of evidence to show that it caused serious, even life-threatening side effects and so was an inappropriate therapy. It was eventually abandoned as a therapy for schizophrenia in the 1950s, when antipsychotic drugs were discovered. With the introduction of more sophisticated equipment and techniques, psychosurgery is now a much more refined process. However, it is only used as a last resort and rarely, if ever, in cases of schizophrenia.

Should therapy ever be compulsory?

Read this excerpt from a BBC news report and consider whether people suffering from mental disorders such as schizophrenia should ever be compelled to undergo therapy?

Sword attacker's release condemned

A parishioner at a church where a schizophrenic man attacked the congregation with a samurai sword has condemned his early release from a secure mental hospital ... One of the seven people who over-powered and disarmed [the attacker] has grave concerns about his release ... [saying] his release made him as much a risk to himself as to the public. 'He could, tomorrow, just flatly refuse to take his medication and we are back to square one,' he said.

Source: BBC news report, 29 June 2002 (news.bbc.co.uk)

ECT is another controversial, early therapeutic technique, developed in the 1930s. ECT was developed as a treatment for schizophrenia, but it was found that it had little effect on the disorder and has now been largely abandoned. In a modified and less brutal form, it continues as a treatment for people with severe depression (see p.351).

In the past, restraints such as straitjackets were used to control mentally ill patients. Nowadays we use different methods, but is drug therapy just a chemical straitjacket?

Drug therapy

Drug therapy (**chemotherapy**), the most common treatment for schizophrenia, uses antipsychotic drugs. Some of these (called 'conventional/typical' antipsychotic drugs) are used to reduce the effects of dopamine, while others (called 'atypical' antipsychotic drugs) also work on reducing serotonin activity.

Blocking dopamine receptors

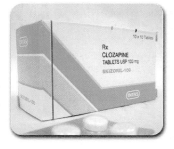

Clozapine blocks serotonin receptors.

As we have seen, biological researchers believe that dopamine plays an important part in the origins of schizophrenia. An important goal of antipsychotic drug therapy, then, is to reduce the amount of available dopamine or to reduce the number of dopamine receptor sites by blocking them. Phenothiazines (also known as neuroleptics) are a class of drugs which work by blocking dopamine receptors. One of the most frequently used is chlorpromazine. There is considerable evidence to suggest that these drugs can reduce the acute, positive symptoms (e.g. hallucinations) in many people with schizophrenia. They produce the maximum benefits within the first six months of use.

Blocking serotonin receptors

More recently, atypical antipsychotic drugs such as clozapine have been introduced. These seem to take their effect by blocking serotonin rather than dopamine receptors. Research suggests that these drugs are more effective than the conventional antipsychotic drugs (Julien 2005).

Evaluation of drug therapy

Effectiveness

■ *Antipsychotic drugs* – the management of schizophrenia has been revolutionized by antipsychotic drugs, which can rapidly reduce the most disturbing symptoms and can decrease the amount of time spent in hospital. Both conventional and atypical antipsychotic drugs have been shown in many studies to be an effective form of treatment. They produce a sedative effect and can significantly reduce psychotic symptoms of hallucinations and delusions. This enables patients to live a relatively normal life in the community and has transformed schizophrenia from a hospital 'long-stay' to a hospital 'short stay' condition. In fact many patients in Britain are now able to be treated on an outpatient basis.

The conventional drugs, though successful in reducing positive symptoms, have little effect, however, on negative symptoms (e.g. loss of motivation). Atypical drugs, on the other hand, also seem to improve negative symptoms (deLima *et al.* 2005).

■ *Relapse* – It has been found that symptoms often return if patients stop taking the drugs (Rzewuska 2002) and patients sometimes have to be kept on maintenance doses for long periods of time. This increases the risk of serious side effects.

Appropriateness

■ *Side effects* – The conventional antipsychotic drugs produce some very serious side effects which raise doubts about their appropriateness as a treatment for schizophrenia. One is the development of symptoms similar to those found in Parkinson's disease, such as stiffness, immobility and tremors. In its most serious form, it leads to a condition called 'tardive dyskinesia', which includes uncontrollable sucking and smacking of the lips and facial tics (see pictures above). It is thought that this is caused by phenothiazines destroying parts of the brain. This occurs in around 30 per cent of those taking the drugs and the risk increases with prolonged usage (Gualtieri 1991). Other side effects include: low blood pressure, blurred vision and constipation.

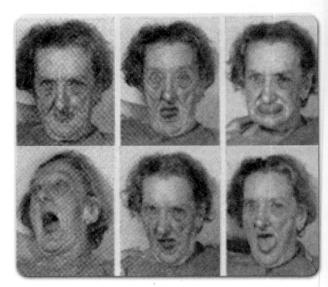

Uncontrollable lip smacking and sucking are symptoms of tardive dyskinesia, a side effect of the long-term use of conventional antipsychotic drugs.

The newer drugs are more effective and cause fewer side effects than the conventional drugs. However, clozapine has a potentially life-threatening side effect resulting in damage to the immune system. Other drugs then have to be administered to counteract this effect and regular blood tests are necessary. This makes the treatment very expensive and limits its availability. The other atypical drugs do not have this effect but they are also very expensive and can cause unwanted weight gain.

■ *Compliance* – Some patients refuse to comply with drug treatment regimes, possibly because of the side effects or sometimes because of poor memory. Research has indicated that if antipsychotic drugs are stopped abruptly, then symptoms recur (e.g. Davis *et al.* 1993). This has led to the 'revolving door syndrome' of continual discharge into the community followed by re-admission to hospital. One way of avoiding this problem is to provide depot antipsychotic medication. This is a special preparation of medication, which is given by injection into a large muscle (usually the buttock) so as to lessen any discomfort and swelling. It is usually administered by a nurse in the patient's home, in a doctor's surgery or in an outpatients' clinic. Depot injections release the medication slowly into the body over a number of weeks. The main advantage is that they only need to be given at intervals (once a week, or in some cases, once a month), which means that the patient does not have to remember to take several tablets a day.

Look at the panel 'Motivational interviewing' on the right to read about another strategy for improving compliance.

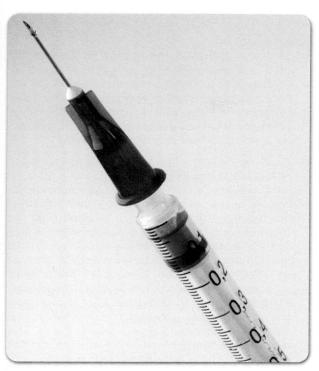

Depot injections, often given by nurses, consist of a quantity of antipsychotic drug given directly into the buttock, where it forms a depot or pocket of the drug, which is slowly released into the body. Depot injections are useful for people who may have difficulty in remembering to take their medication. (Source: www.niamh.co.uk)

Ethical issues – Some people have criticized whether the widespread use of drugs in the treatment of mental disorders is appropriate, referring to them as 'chemical straitjackets'. The argument is that the drugs are dehumanizing and take away any sense of personal responsibility or control. The ethical issue of informed consent is also a consideration. People in a psychotic state are not really in a position to give truly informed consent about their treatment

Psychological therapies

Before the introduction of antipsychotic drugs, psychotherapy was not really deemed appropriate for treating people with schizophrenia. Most patients were so detached from reality that they would not have been able to cope with the cognitive and verbal demands of such therapy. Now, psychological treatments are often used alongside drug therapy. The major approaches are family interventions and cognitive-behavioural therapies.

Family interventions/therapy

We have seen how the type of communication within a family can influence the maintenance of schizophrenia. One type of treatment is aimed at reducing the level of negative expressed emotion in the family. This type of treatment programme requires the involvement of several family members as well as the individual with schizophrenia. It also usually involves an educational element where family members are given information about the disorder and ways of managing it, e.g. improving communication styles, lowering expressed emotion, adjusting expectations and expanding social networks.

Evaluation of family interventions

A meta-analysis (Pharoah *et al.* 2003) found that family interventions of this type were effective in significantly reducing rates of relapse and of admission to hospital in people with schizophrenia. Family intervention may also be appropriate because it can improve compliance with taking medication, which, as we saw before, contributes to effective outcomes from drug therapy. However, the analysis revealed a wide range of outcomes so the results are not conclusive. The therapy is widely used in current practice, but is clearly most suited to patients who still live with or are in close contact with their families.

Social skills training

Individuals with schizophrenia have a number of problems with social skills, e.g. social interactions, self-care, coping with stressful situations, self-awareness, managing symptoms and appraising social situations. Social skills training programmes aim to teach complex interpersonal skills so that people with schizophrenia can manage their lives more effectively.

Evaluation of social skills training

The results of these interventions are generally positive, but it seems likely that the gains are not always maintained after the programme has ended. This kind of approach also seems to work better, and therefore be more appropriate, in conjunction with other therapies. For example, Hogarty (2002) found that patients on medication who also received social skills training adjusted to living in the community and avoided re-hospitalization more successfully than other groups on medication or social skills training alone.

Cognitive–behavioural therapy (CBT)

In the main, **cognitive-behavioural therapies (CBT)** used to be thought appropriate only for those who are capable of gaining reasonable insight into their problems. However, some therapists see a role for CBT with psychotic patients. CBT is based on the idea that people with mental disorders have irrational and unrealistic ways of thinking. The goal of CBT, therefore, is to adjust thinking patterns and alter inappropriate beliefs.

One particular type of cognitive intervention, called *belief modification*, teaches strategies to counter delusional beliefs and hallucinations and involves a process called cognitive challenge. Clients are taught to regard their negative responses to particular situations (in this case delusions and/or hallucinations) as hypotheses rather than reality. They then learn to challenge their initial negative interpretations.

Social skills training, combined with other therapies, can help people with schizophrenia manage their lives more effectively.

Evaluation of cognitive-behavioural therapy

Effectiveness

- *Evidence* – Several controlled trials have shown that CBT can be effective in treating schizophrenia. Turkington *et al.* (2000) for example, found CBT to have a significant effect on both positive and negative symptoms of schizophrenia and also that it could be effectively delivered via brief intervention programmes delivered by community psychiatric nurses.

- *Belief modification* – This is a relatively new approach to treating schizophrenia and there have not been many evaluative studies. However, Jones *et al.* (2000) carried out a **meta-analysis** on trials of belief modification and found that it reduced both the frequency and the intensity of hallucinations. It was less effective in changing delusional beliefs but it did seem to reduce the accompanying distress. Drury *et al.* (2000) reported on a study in which belief modification formed part of the treatment programme. Immediate and short-term gains were encouraging, but in a five-year follow-up the treatment group showed no advantage over a control group. This suggests that interim cognitive interventions might be required in order to achieve long-term benefits.

- *Further research on CBT effectiveness* – See the Key research panel opposite.

Appropriateness

- *Not a cure* – Although some studies have shown that CBT can improve certain symptoms of schizophrenia (see opposite) and new cognitive treatments continue to be developed, CBT does not offer a cure but rather a way of 'normalizing' symptoms.

- *Ethics* – CBT is a collaborative therapy and involves the active cooperation of the client. For this reason it often avoids the criticism made of drug therapy that the client becomes a passive recipient of treatment.

Methods for investigating the effectiveness of therapies

Key research: Pilling *et al.* (2002) and Broadshow (1998)

There are a number of ways in which psychologists can investigate the effectiveness of therapies. Two different examples of studies on the effectiveness of CBT are set out below:

1 Pilling *et al.* (2002) conducted a meta-analysis comparing family intervention with cognitive-behavioural therapy (CBT). A meta-analysis is a study that collects data from previously published studies on a related research hypothesis and uses statistical techniques to combine the data to provide a more complete set of findings. In this meta-analysis, they first completed a literature search to find randomized, controlled trials of four types of psychological intervention. They then subjected the data to meta-analysis on a variety of outcome measures. They found that:

- Family intervention had clear preventative effects on the outcomes of psychotic relapse and readmission, in addition to benefits in medication compliance.

- CBT produced higher rates of 'important improvement' in mental state and demonstrated positive effects on continuous measures of mental state at follow-up. CBT also seemed to be associated with low drop-out rates.

They concluded that family intervention should be offered to people with schizophrenia who are in contact with carers and that CBT could be useful for those with treatment-resistant symptoms. They suggested that both treatments should be further investigated in large trials across a variety of patients in various settings. In particular, the factors mediating treatment success in these interventions should be researched.

2 Bradshaw (1998) reported on a case study in which he assessed, over a period of four years, the impact of CBT on one young American woman who had been diagnosed with schizophrenia (undifferentiated). She was a high-school graduate from an upper-middle-class family with high academic expectations and strong Christian faith. She had been hospitalized 12 times in the seven years prior to the start of the CBT programme. At that time, she scored 30 on the Global Assessment of Functioning Scale (see Table 3 on p.303, the fine axes of DSM-IV) and was on daily medication. She received regular CBT sessions over a three-year period. Assessments of her progress showed significant improvement in her psychosocial functioning, her symptoms reduced dramatically and she had no hospital re-admissions. In a follow-up assessment a year later, she had maintained these benefits. This suggests that CBT might have an important role to play in preventing relapse in schizophrenia.

Activity — Comparing two methods for evaluating CBT

The two studies outlined in the key research panel are very different.

- Identify the major differences between the methods used by the two studies. If necessary, refer to Chapter X to refresh your memory on research methods.

- Try to think of some of the advantages and limitations of the two methods.

CHECK YOUR UNDERSTANDING

Check your understanding of therapies for schizophrenia by answering the following questions. Try to do this from memory. You can check your answers by looking back through Topic 3.

1 Why is it thought that phenothiazines can help people with schizophrenia?

2 Outline some of the strengths and limitations of using drug therapies for people with schizophrenia.

3 Why do people with schizophrenia often fail to comply with drug treatments and how do you think this can be improved?

4 What is meant by family intervention?

5 How can CBT help people with schizophrenia?

6 What is meant by motivational interviewing?

7 Why is it important to offer a range of therapies to people with schizophrenia?

Clinical characteristics (symptoms) of schizophrenia

- Thought disturbances (e.g. thoughts being inserted)
- Delusions of control and other persistent delusions
- Hallucinations (e.g. hearing voices)
- Disorders of speech (e.g. neologisms)
- Catatonic behaviour (e.g. immobility)
- Apathy and lack of drive (i.e. negative symptoms)

Clinical characteristics & issues of classification & diagnosis

Schizophrenia

Issues surrounding classification and diagnosis

Factors that affect the reliability and validity of classification and diagnosis:

- Different types of schizophrenia
- Schizophrenia-like disorders
- Schizophrenia as a multiple disorder
- Differential diagnosis
- Dual diagnosis
- Cultural issues

Therapies for schizophrenia

Psychological therapies

- Often used in conjunction with drug therapies.
- Particularly useful in addressing the negative symptoms of schizophrenia

Family interventions
(e.g. to improve communications)

Evaluation:

- Can significantly reduce relapse and also encourage compliance with medication

Social skills training
(e.g. to improve self-care and self-awareness)

Evaluation:

- Can be helpful in getting people with schizophrenia back in the community
- Gains are not maintained once the treatment programme is over

Cognitive-behavioural therapy
(e.g. to challenge irrational thinking)

Evaluation:

- Relatively new treatment for schizophrenia
- Promising results in dealing with hallucinations

Biological therapies

- Early therapies such as psychosurgery and ECT are no longer used
- Medication (drugs) is main therapy
- Variety of antipsychotic medication available
- Most work by influencing the dopamine availability in the brain and nervous system
- Newer, atypical drugs such as clozapine also affect other neurotransmitters (e.g. serotonin)

Evaluation

- Drugs are effective in reducing symptoms for many people with schizophrenia
- They do not work for everyone and tend to target positive rather than the negative symptoms.
- All anti-psychotic medication can produce side effects (e.g. tardive dyskinesia), particularly after long-term use

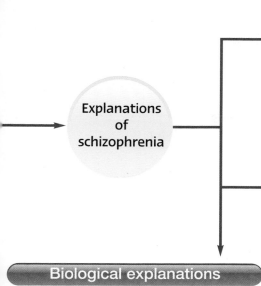

Diathesis-stress explanation

- Interaction between biological and environmental factors – individuals have genetic vulnerability for schizophrenia but only develop the disorder in the presence of triggering environmental factors

Explanations of schizophrenia

Psychological explanations

Psychodynamic

Evaluation:

- Little support for the various psychodynamic explanations

Behavioural

Evaluation:

- No convincing explanation for the origins of schizophrenia
- Could explain how some of the symptoms are maintained

Psychosocial factors
(e.g. socio-economic status)

Evaluation:

- Difficult to disentangle cause and effect
- No more than contributory factor

Family relationships
(e.g. schizo-phrenogenic families)

Evaluation:

- Studies are methodological flawed (e.g. no controls, retrospective)
- Seem to influence maintenance and relapse of schizophrenia rather than original cause

Expressed emotion

Evaluation:

- Accepted as maintenance and relapse model
- May be response to living with schizophrenia

Cognitive
(e.g. failure to filter information or activate relevant schemas)

Evaluation:

- More descriptive than explanatory
- Limited links to neurological underpinnings

Biological explanations

Genes

Evaluation:

- Support from family, twin and adoption studies
- 100% concordance not demonstrated
- Difficult to disentangle effects of environment

Biochemical factors (particularly dopamine)

Evaluation:

- Support from research, e.g. with PET scans
- Effective antipsychotic medication
- Difficult to distinguish cause and effect

Neuroanatomical factors

Evaluation:

- Research support, e.g. from MRI scans
- Difficult to distinguish cause and effect
- Structural abnormalities not found in all patients

Pregnancy and birth factors
(e.g. viral infections)

Evaluation:

- Limitations of correlational data from studies of viral infections and studies of maternal stress

Substance abuse (e.g. cannabis)

Evaluation:

- Known to raise dopamine levels and support from recent meta-analysis
- Genetic predisposition may interact with substance abuse
- Cannabis may be used as form of therapy to relieve symptoms and so not a causal factor

EXPLAINING THE SPECIFICATION

Specification content	The specification explained
Psychopathology: depression as chosen dosorder	If you have chosen depression as the psychopathology disorder you wish to study, you need to be able to:
Clinical characteristics and issues of classification and diagnosis of depression (Topic 1)	In this part of the specification you should be familiar with the key features of clinical characteristics and issues of classification and diagnosis. To do this, you need to be able to:
Clinical characteristics of depression	■ Outline the main clinical characteristics (symptoms) of depression.
Issues surrounding the classification and diagnosis of depression, including reliability and validity.	■ Describe and evaluate **at least two** issues (potential problems) in classifying or diagnosing depression. If you concentrate on only two issues, these must be reliability and validity.
Explanations of depression (Topic 2)	In this part of the specification you should be familiar with the explanations of depression. To do this you need to be able to:
Biological explanations of depression, for example, genetics, biochemistry.	■ Describe and evaluate **at least two** biological explanations of depression. To do this you will need to discuss relevant research findings. Genetics and biochemistry are suggested as examples of explanations that you might study but neither of these is specified as compulsory. The chapter discusses genetics, and biochemical and neuroanatomical explanations.
Psychological explanations of depression, for example, behavioural, cognitive, psychodynamic and socio-cultural.	■ Describe and evaluate **at least two** psychological explanations of depression. To do this you will need to discuss relevant research findings. Four examples of explanations are suggested – behavioural, cognitive, psychodynamic and socio-cultural – but none of these is specified as compulsory. The chapter discusses the psychological explanations that have most commonly been used to explain depression: psychodynamic, behavioural, cognitive and psychosocial.
Therapies for depression (Topic 3)	In this part of the specification you should be familiar with the key features of therapies for depression. To do this, you need to be able to:
Biological therapies for depression including their evaluation in terms of appropriateness and effectiveness	■ Describe and evaluate **at least two** biological treatments for depression. Your evaluations should consider how (appropriate) suitable and how effective (successful) the treatments are. To do this you will need to discuss relevant research findings. The chapter discusses drug therapy, ECT and psychosurgery.
Psychological therapies for depression, for example, behavioural, psychodynamic, and cognitive-behavioural, including their evaluation in terms of appropriateness and effectiveness.	■ Describe and evaluate **at least two** psychological treatments for depression. You need to discuss how appropriate and effective the treatments are. To do this you will need to discuss relevant research findings. The chapter discusses psychodynamic, behavioural, cognitive behavioural and psychosocial therapies.

Introduction

We all feel depressed from time to time and this is quite normal. Usually, it is short-lived and does not interfere too much with our everyday functioning; we carry on going to work, school or college, even though we might not feel much like socializing. This is not depression in the clinical sense. Clinical **depression** is when everyday functioning is seriously impaired. Depression often co-exists with other psychological problems and many people diagnosed with depression also meet the DSM and/or ICD (see Introduction to Psychopathology chapter, p.301) criteria for at least one other disorder.

The term **'unipolar disorder/depression'** is used to distinguish the mental disorder of depression from the quite different disorder once known as manic-depression. This is now called **'bipolar disorder'** because of the way an individual swings between the two extremes of mania (excessive, unreasonable elation and hyperactivity) and depression. For the purposes of the AQA specification, you are only required to study depression: a unipolar disorder.

The clinical characteristics (symptoms) of depression are discussed in Topic 1 along with some of the issues of classification and diagnosis. In Topic 2 we shall look at biological and psychological explanations for depression and in Topic 3 we shall discuss the main therapies for the disorder.

Many well-known people, including Kerry Katona, have struggled with depression.

Topic 1: Clinical characteristics and issues of classification and diagnosis

Psychology in context   Stigma of mental illness

The DSM and ICD classification systems are used by physicians, psychiatrists and researchers all over the world. However, some countries such as India, Pakistan and China continue to use their own classification systems. In particular, they object to the way in which Western classification systems place too much emphasis on the separation of mind and body. The Chinese Classification of Mental Disorders (CCMD-2-R), although largely based on ICD 10, has a category of *neurasthenia*, the core symptoms of which are identified as mental and/or physical fatigue, accompanied by at least two of seven symptoms (dizziness, dyspepsia (indigestion), muscular aches or pains, tension headaches, inability to relax, irritability, and sleep disturbance). In many Asian cultures, including Japan, it is considered a sign of weakness to admit to being depressed and a major reason that neurasthenia has survived as a common diagnosis in these cultures is that it is considered an acceptable medical diagnosis that conveys distress without the stigma of a psychiatric diagnosis.

Crown Princess Masako of Japan, who is married to the heir of the Emperor, has shocked the traditional Royal household and the Japanese public by retreating

Crown Princess Masako of Japan

from public life and confessing to suffering from depression. *The Times* (5 February 2008), see online address below, reported on this story as follows:

'In a country that cherishes above all the spirit of gaman — perseverance — the unspecified mental illness from which she is suffering is merely an obstacle she is too weak to overcome … The Crown Prince told The Times, "People see [depression], mistakenly, as something you simply have to fight hard to overcome, so any failure to do so is seen as a failure of the spirit."'

http://www.timesonline.co.uk/tol/news/world/asia/article3307711.ece

1 To what extent do you think that the criteria for neurasthenia and major depressive disorder differ?

2 Even though the diagnosis of depression is relatively common in Western culture, do you think that it stigmatises the people who are diagnosed? Give reasons for your answer.

Depression is an 'affective' (mood) disorder, characterized by feelings of sadness and a general withdrawal from those around us. The degree of impairment varies and can range from mild to severe, such that it causes an inability to feed or dress or maintain personal hygiene. Depression can be so serious that it leads to suicide.

Depression is one of the most common types of psychological abnormality and can occur at any age. About five per cent of the European population experience clinical depression at any one time (Paykel *et al.* 2005) and 17 per cent will experience significant depression at some time in their life (Angst 1999). Onset most commonly occurs between the ages of 20 and 50, but recent epidemiological studies suggest that the incidence of major depressive disorder is increasing in people younger than 20. A robust finding is that women are twice as likely to be diagnosed with depression as men (Keller *et al.* 1984). While some of this difference might be due to diagnostic practice, it also seems to reflect hormonal differences and the differing psychosocial stressors for men and women

DSM-IV lists two sub-types of depressive disorder:

- *'Major depressive disorder' (MDD)* – severe but can be short-lived. People with MDD sometimes develop symptoms such as delusions or hallucinations and are then given a diagnosis of 'severe depressive episode with psychotic symptoms'.

- *'Dysthymic disorder' (DD)* – may be less severe but is more chronic, i.e. it has a longer duration. If the depressive episode has lasted for two consecutive years and there have been fewer than two months without symptoms, then 'dysthymic disorder' is diagnosed.

See Table 1 below for the ICD-10 criteria for 'depressive episode'

In addition to the criteria, clinicians also take account of the severity of symptoms and the degree of functional impairment before deciding on the type of depression. ICD distinguishes between three types of depression: mild, moderate and severe.

Although lack of sex drive is common in people with depression, it is not specifically listed on ICD-10 but comes under the criterion 'loss of interest or pleasure in activities that are normally pleasurable'. Similarly, poor memory is one aspect of the general cognitive difficulties and concentration problems experienced by those with depression.

Look at the case study below and note the characteristics of depression experienced by Mr J.

A case study of depression

Mr J is a 51-year-old engineer who, since the death of his wife five years earlier, has been suffering from continual episodes of depression marked by extreme social withdrawal and occasional thoughts of suicide. His wife died in a car accident while on a shopping trip which he himself was to have made but had cancelled because of professional responsibilities. He blames himself for his wife's death and this feeling of guilt has deepened as the years passed. He began to drink, sometimes heavily and when intoxicated would plead to his deceased wife for forgiveness. He has lost all capacity for joy; friends cannot recall when they last saw him smile. Once a gourmet, he now has no interest in food or good wine and on the rare occasions when he is with friends he can barely manage to engage in small talk. His work has deteriorated markedly, with missed appointments and projects haphazardly started and then left unfinished.

(Adapted from Davison and Neale 2001)

General criteria which must be met for all categories of depressive disorder	From this category: at least two for diagnosis of mild and moderate depressive disorder; all three for diagnosis of severe depressive disorder	From this category: at least two for diagnosis of mild depressive disorder; at least three for diagnosis of moderate depressive disorder; at least four for diagnosis of severe depressive disorder
The depressive episode must last for at least two weeks	Depressed mood that is abnormal for the individual and that lasts most of the day almost every day	Loss of confidence or self-esteem
The episode cannot be attributed to psychoactive substance use (e.g. alcohol) or organic illness	Loss of interest or pleasure in activities that are normally pleasurable	Unreasonable feelings of self-reproach or guilt
		Recurrent thoughts of death or suicide
	Decreased energy or increased tiredness	Inability to concentrate and proneness to indecision
		Changes in psychomotor activity, e.g. agitation or lethargy
		Sleep disturbance of any type
		Change in appetite (decrease or increase) with corresponding weight change

Table 1 *Criteria for 'depressive episode' in ICD-10*

Activity **ICD and DSM**

You might like to look at the relevant pages in the ICD and DSM manuals yourself. These are large and complex documents but you could look at the relevant sections on depressive disorder on the websites and compare them.

www.who.int/classifications/icd/en/

www.apa.org/

Issues of classification and diagnosis

Take a few minutes to look back to the section on classification and diagnosis (in the Introduction to Psychopathology on p.301), because some of the general points there (e.g. about **reliability** and **validity**) are relevant to depression.

Reliability and validity of classification and diagnosis

There are a number of different factors that affect how reliably depression may be classified and diagnosed and how valid the diagnostic categories for depression are. Some of these are discussed next.

Types of depression

As described in the previous section, there are different types of depression that vary from one another in terms of severity and duration of symptoms. It can be difficult for clinicians to decide on the most appropriate category and this reduces reliability of diagnosis.

Different ways of classifying depressive disorder

■ *Underlying cause* – Historically, depressive disorders were sometimes classified into two kinds on the basis of the presumed underlying *cause* of the disorder. A distinction was made between *endogenous depression* (where the depression was caused by internal, biological mechanisms) and *reactive depression* (where the depression was assumed to be in response to external stressors). Endogenous depression was usually the more severe and longer-lasting form. Although these terms are still used by people working in the field of abnormal psychology, they are no longer considered helpful as an accurate or reliable means of distinguishing between types of depression and they are not used in either ICD or DSM.

■ *Types of symptoms* – Another way of distinguishing different types of depression is to consider the nature of the symptoms. Symptoms which appear to be of biological origin (e.g. appetite changes, weight loss, constipation, reduced sex drive, early morning waking) are called *melancholic symptoms* in DSM (called somatic in ICD). The difficulty here is that most patients with depression have some physical symptoms so it is not easy to decide where the defining line should be drawn between *melancholic depression* and non-melancholic depression. Despite this, there is agreement amongst clinicians (Parker *et al.* 1999) that melancholic depression is associated with more severe symptoms, poor response to placebo medication and good response to ECT (see section on therapies on p.348). This suggests that melancholic depression is a valid category, despite the difficulties with reliable diagnosis.

■ *Course of the disorder* – Yet another way of distinguishing between types of depression is by their course. One particular type of depression first identified by Rosenthal *et al.* (1984) has been called **'Seasonal Affective Disorder' (SAD)** (see p.339) because the symptoms appear mainly in the winter months. Another type of disorder is called 'brief recurrent depression' because the depressive episodes are fairly frequent but of very short duration. It is important to diagnose these types accurately as effective treatments are not the same as for other types of depression.

■ *Validity of diagnostic categories* – A related point concerns the validity of some of the sub-types found in the classification manuals. Some of these diagnostic categories are used mainly as criteria for research purposes and have not all been validated, e.g. premenstrual dysphoric disorder (pre-menstrual depression) which shares some of the characteristics of depression but also involves anxiety symptoms and some very specific somatic (physical) symptoms. It is only included in the appendix of DSM to help researchers and clinicians to investigate the validity of the syndrome. Whether this is a genuine syndrome in its own right remains a controversial issue. If necessary, see p.301 to remind yourself of what constitutes a syndrome.

Confirming the diagnosis

■ *Lack of reliable signs* – There is no clear objective measure to confirm the diagnosis of a mental disorder such as depression (see p.301 in the Introduction to psychopathology). Experienced clinicians take a careful history from their patients and, using the DSM axes (see p.303), try to consider the patient from many angles before deciding on a diagnosis. They also look out for signs in the way a patient presents him or herself. For example, depressed people commonly present with characteristic body language, e.g. furrowed brow, low blink rate, bent shoulders and downward gaze. However, many people who do not want to face up to the idea of having clinical depression will often try to smile and attempt to conceal their low mood from other people. If they consult a doctor, it is often on the pretext of a physical problem and they attempt to behave normally and

Sorrow *by Vincent Van Gogh. Sadness is the most prominent and widespread emotional symptom in depression. The painting is owned by Rijksmuseum, Amsterdam.*

hide any tell-tale signs. This can make it difficult for a busy GP to detect the depression and make an accurate diagnosis.

- *Who makes the diagnosis?* – Medical doctors specializing in psychopathology are called psychiatrists and they treat people with mental disorders in hospitals and outpatient clinics. In the UK, people who are depressed usually go to see their GP who can refer them to a psychiatrist if it is thought appropriate. GPs specialize in general medicine and it has been suggested that about 50 per cent of people who are showing depressive symptoms when they go to see their GP are not diagnosed with depression (Goldberg and Huxley, 1992). This clearly has implications for treatment.

Differential diagnosis

If a clinician is to make a valid diagnosis of depression it is important that they rule out other possibilities first.

- *Normal sadness* – As we have already noted, sadness is a universal emotion which we have all experienced from time to time, and it is a perfectly normal reaction to life events such as bereavement. The diagnosis of clinical depression should only be made when people clearly meet the diagnostic criteria.

- *Depression or anxiety*? – Mild depressive disorders can be difficult to distinguish from anxiety disorders. Clinicians have to make a judgement about the relative severity of depressive and anxiety symptoms before they make a diagnosis. It is important to get the judgement right as the two conditions respond to different treatments.

- *Depression or dementia*? – In middle and late adult life, it can be difficult to distinguish between patients with depressive symptoms and dementia. People with depression often perform quite badly on tests of cognitive functioning. A diagnosis of depression rather than dementia can sometimes only be confirmed when the individual's mood improves and normal cognitive function is restored.

- *Depression and physical illness* – Depression can sometimes occur in people as a result of a physical illness, e.g. hypothyroidism when the thyroid gland is not working properly. In these cases, the depression usually disappears when the physical condition is treated.

- *Depression in children* – Depression in children sometimes goes undiagnosed because they often present with other problems such as conduct disorders which can mask the symptoms of depression. They also sometimes show slightly different symptoms from adults. For example, childhood depression is often characterized by irritability.

Other issues affecting the validity of diagnosis

- *Treating depression as a disease* – How valid is it to treat depression as a disease? Some people argue that sad and depressed moods are normal human reactions to the problems of living and that it is wrong to classify depression as an illness and stick a disease label on an individual (see p.302 for discussion on 'The myth of mental illness'). The counter-argument is that depression can be extremely distressing for the individual and can lead to very severe consequences, e.g. suicide. Accurate diagnosis leads to appropriate treatment and relief for the person experiencing the symptoms.

- *Dual diagnosis* – Depression often occurs alongside other mental disorders within the same individual. This is referred to as co-morbidity. Commonly, co-morbid disorders are schizophrenia, anxiety disorder, eating disorders and substance abuse. In these cases, clinicians make a dual diagnosis but try to determine what they consider to be the primary condition and treat that first, but this is not always easy. However, it has been suggested (e.g. Maj 2005) that the multi-axial classification system of DSM (see p.303 in the Introduction to Psychopathology) encourages multiple diagnoses to be made where it might not always be appropriate.

- *Gender* – It has been found that rates of major depression are about twice as high in females as males and this finding holds good across cultures. Some people have suggested that this is a misleading statistic and reflects diagnostic practice rather than real gender differences. For example, it is 'more acceptable' for women to admit to the kinds of symptoms that characterize depression than men, and women may feel more willing to go and ask for help. However, it is unlikely that the increased rates in women are simply due to misdiagnosis. We will consider possible reasons for gender differences in Topic 2, p.347.

- *Effect of socio-cultural background* – Before making a diagnosis, clinicians should be aware of the cultural and social background of the individual. People from social minorities seem to have a higher level of mental health problems than others. It is not clear whether this reflects greater genetic vulnerability, psychosocial factors associated with being part of a minority group or misdiagnosis. It could, for example, be the case that clinicians from the majority population misinterpret cultural differences in behaviour and expression as symptoms of mental disorder. If this is the case, it demonstrates how important it is for clinicians to take particular care in their assessment of people from a different ethnic or social group.

- *Cultural differences* – One key difference across cultures is the emphasis a particular society places on physical symptoms as a means of expressing mental problems. People from eastern cultures, in particular, often express their distress through physical symptoms. Kua *et al.* (1993) reported that 72 per cent of people in China who first presented with chest or abdominal pains or headaches were later found to have a mental health problem. One reason that people do not mention emotional symptoms when they first present for treatment is the stigma associated with emotional or mental weakness (see Psychology in context on p.331).

Activity **Characteristics of depression**

Practise writing a concise outline of the main characteristics of depression – something worth about five marks in an exam. Look through Topic 1 and select what you think are relevant points. Once you have made your selection, you should take no more than five or six minutes to write your outline.

Some tips are given in the answer section on p.603. ▶

CHECK YOUR UNDERSTANDING

Check your understanding of characteristics of depression and issues around classification and diagnosis in depression by answering the following questions. Try to do this from memory. You can check your answers by looking back through Topic 1 on clinical characteristics and issues of classification and diagnosis of depression.

1 When are mood disturbances classified as depression?

2 What is meant by 'melancholic depression'?

3 Why might it be difficult to diagnose melancholic depression reliably?

4 What do you think are some of the problems of diagnosing depression in children?

5 Why might the axial system of DSM-IV lead clinicians to make dual diagnoses?

6 What are some of the factors clinicians have to consider when they are assessing people from different cultures?

7 Outline two factors that affect the reliability of diagnosing depression.

8 Outline two factors that clinicians must bear in mind if they are to make valid diagnoses of depression.

Topic 2: Explanations of depression

If you have not already done so, you should re-read the section in your AS textbook that discusses the different approaches used by psychologists to explain psychopathology (*Psychology for AS AQA A,* pp.224–36).

We have seen that the diagnosis of depression is not straightforward and that people with depression can vary from one another in the type and severity of their symptoms. There is no single explanation for depression that accounts for all cases and it is likely that different factors interact to produce depressive symptoms. We know that a depressive episode can often be triggered by stressful life events. Also, depressed people experience a greater number of such events during the month just before the start of the disorder than do other people (Kendler *et al.* 2004). However, many people experience stressful events and do not develop depressive disorder while some people diagnosed with depression do not have such a history. Stress, therefore, can only be one of many contributory factors. It is also the case that, whatever the underlying origin of the disorder, depressive symptoms express themselves through changes in the brain and the

---

IDA **Nature–nurture debate and depression**

The question as to whether depression arises from biological or environmental factors is a good example of the nature-nurture debate in psychology. People who support the nurture argument believe that all behaviours, including abnormal behaviours, are learned or acquired through interaction with the environment; people who support the nature argument believe that many of our characteristics are 'wired-in' or innate. In other words, we are genetically determined to behave in certain ways and to develop certain disorders. In the field of psychopathology, few people embrace either of these extreme views. It is now fairly widely accepted that disorders such as depression come about as a result of a variety of biological and environmental factors in combination.

To learn more about the nature–nurture debate in psychology, look at p.42 in Introduction to approaches, issues and debates in psychology

You will see in the following section that there are various explanations of depression. However, one finding about depression that is difficult to explain is the fact that the lifetime risk for developing the disorder has shown a steady increase in every decade since the 1930s. In addition, the age of onset has become gradually younger.

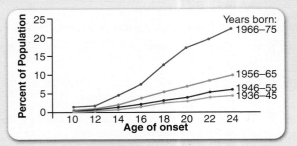

The lifetime prevalence of major depression in the United States in decades since 1936. Source Kessler et al. 2003.

No-one knows exactly why depression has increased so markedly across the world over the last few decades, but it is a robust finding that has been demonstrated in many studies. On the basis of such findings, Rosenhan and Seligman (1995) have suggested that we live in 'an age of melancholy'. As additional evidence for their claim, they point to the fact that the Amish community of Pennsylvania, who follow a simple pre-modern way of life, show much lower rates of unipolar depression than the population in the rest of the USA.

An article in the *Guardian* newspaper in 2008 described how a Government think tank called *Foresight* has put forward proposals for a nationwide campaign to combat rising rates of depression and other mental illnesses.

Members of the Amish community of Pennsylvania

Following a two-year enquiry, their report: '...warns that mental illness caused by stressful working conditions, a lack of exercise and a breakdown in family and social networks is likely to be exacerbated by the economic downturn and rising average age of the population. ... The proposed campaign, which would be akin to the "five portions of fruit and vegetables a day" guidelines promoted by the Food Standards Agency, identifies five actions that people can take to boost their mental health'.

1 What do you think Rosenhan and Seligman mean by the term 'age of melancholy'? Do you agree with them that we live in an age of melancholy?

2 What kind of things could a Government campaign suggest to help protect people from depression? You might like to look at the original article in the *Guardian* to give you some ideas. (http://www.guardian.co.uk/science/2008/oct/22/mental-health-illness-foresight) or compare your ideas with the five things suggested by the Foresight campaign (shown in the Answers section at the end of the book).

---

central nervous system. Most clinicians would now agree that unipolar depression is a result of an interaction of biological, psychological and socio-cultural factors.

Biological explanations of depression

There are several factors that suggest biological mechanisms may play a part in depression:

- *Physical changes* – The symptoms of depression include physical changes (e.g. sleep and appetite disturbance, weight change, fatigue, lack of energy).

- *Similar symptoms* – There is great similarity in the symptoms across cultures, races, gender and ages.

- *Families* – Depression runs in families (although this could be due to a shared environment).

- *Drug treatments* – Antidepressant medication can be successful in treating depression (although this does not in itself prove an underlying biological cause).

Genetic explanations

Depression seems to run in families and a number of studies have shown an increased risk for depression in first-degree relatives of people with unipolar depression. There seems to be a link between the biological closeness of the relationship and the likelihood of developing depression. Note also that people with a relative diagnosed with bipolar disorder (see p.331 for definition) have a three times greater risk of developing MDD than

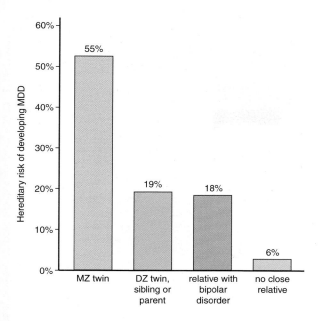

Figure 10.1 *The hereditary risk of developing MDD (adapted from Gershon et al. 1989)*

people who have no relatives suffering from either unipolar or bipolar disorder. This suggests that the two disorders might share some genetic component even though the main symptoms are different. See Fig. 10.1 above.

Research into the influence of genetics has been carried out in the form of family, twin and adoption studies.

Evidence from family studies

First-degree relatives (parents, siblings and offspring) share an average of 50 per cent of their genes, and second-degree relatives share approximately 25 per cent. To investigate genetic transmission of depression, studies compare rates of depression in relatives of diagnosed cases compared with relatives of controls.

Gershon (1990) reviewed ten family studies and found that the rates of unipolar depression in first-degree relatives ranged between seven per cent and 30 per cent, which is considerably higher than in the general population. Family studies have also shown that the younger people are when they are first diagnosed with depression, the more likely it is that their relatives also have depressive episodes. For example, relatives of people diagnosed before the age of 20 had an eight-times greater chance of being diagnosed with depression than relatives of non-depressed individuals (Weissman et al. 1984). However, it is not clear whether these findings are due to genetic influence or to a shared environment, and family studies often show inconclusive results.

Evidence from twin studies

Twin studies offer another way of establishing genetic links, by comparing the difference in concordance rates (i.e. the likelihood of both twins being affected with the disorder) for identical (MZ) and fraternal (DZ) twins. McGuffin et al. (1996) found 46 per cent concordance in MZ twins compared to 20 per cent in DZ twins in a total of 109 twin pairs, with no evidence of the effect of shared

environment. However, Bierut *et al.* (1999) carried out a study of 2,662 twin pairs in Australia and, although they reported concordance of between 36 and 44 per cent in MZ twins, they claimed that environmental factors played a larger role.

Evidence from adoption studies

Adoption studies provide the best way of disentangling genetic factors from environmental, since they look at depressed people who have been adopted at an early age and brought up away from the influence of their families. Most of these studies have shown an increased risk in the biological relatives of people with depression rather than in the adoptive relatives. Wender *et al.* (1986), for example, found that biological relatives were eight times more likely to have depression than adoptive relatives.

Before reading further, look at the How Science Works box below which outlines a different way of investigating the roles of genes in depression.

HOW SCIENCE WORKS

Genes and depression

One way of trying to resolve some of the problems with genetic research is to locate a particular gene that is present in all cases of depression. Studies exploring genetic patterns in families with bipolar disorder have been quite promising, but it has proved much more difficult with unipolar disorder. However, recent advances in the field of molecular biology have provided techniques that allow more accurate research. As a result, a number of studies have identified an abnormality in the 5-HTT gene in people who are depressed (Hecimovic and Gilliam 2006). This is the gene responsible for transmission of the neuro-chemical serotonin. As you will see in the section below, serotonin has been strongly linked to depression. This kind of research is relatively new and, although it is promising, it is too early to draw firm conclusions.

Evaluation of genetic explanations

- *Genes or environment?* – Although MDD has been consistently shown to run in families, it is not easy to disentangle the effects of genetics from the effects of the environment. Whilst there appears to be some degree of genetic evidence for depression, in most cases those diagnosed share the same environment, which means it may equally be a learned behaviour.

- *Risk factor only* – Although the concordance rate for MZ twins is greater than for those who are less closely related, the concordance is well short of 100 per cent. Genetics seem to be a risk factor for depression but not the whole explanation.

- *What aspects of depression are genetic?* – In one study of MZ and DZ twins, it was found that so-called 'negative' symptoms of depression (e.g. sleep disturbance, weight changes and appetite changes) seemed to be more influenced by heredity than by any stressful events in the twins' lives. However, the actual number of depressive episodes was linked more to life events (Kendler *et al.* 1992). There may be a genetic component operating as a predisposing factor, with additional precipitating causes (see the diathesis-stress model p.346).

- *Genetic uncertainty* – Even if genetic factors do play a part in the origins of unipolar depression, it is not yet clear what the precise mechanism is that is transmitted. Without knowing the specific genes involved, it is impossible to understand how they code for biological structures and functions that produce the symptoms of depression.

Biochemical explanations of depression

If genetic factors are important, they are likely to exert their influence on the hardware of the brain. In other words, structural or biochemical abnormalities should be found in the brains of people diagnosed with depression.

The role of neurotransmitters

Neurotransmitters are chemical messengers in the brain and nervous system that transmit nerve impulses from one nerve cell to another across the synapse (the gap between adjacent nerve cells).

The biochemical theory of depression emerged in the 1950s, when it was discovered that a certain class of drugs, known as tricyclic drugs, was effective in treating depression (see the section on therapy on p.350 for a discussion of antidepressant drugs). These are known to work by increasing the availability of a group of neurotransmitters in the brain called 'monoamines'. These neurotransmitters, especially serotonin, noradrenaline and dopamine, are important in the functioning of the limbic system in the brain, which plays a significant role in the regulation of drives such as appetite, and in the control of emotion.

Noradrenaline and serotonin

Post-mortems of depressed patients have not revealed any abnormality of noradrenaline concentration (Cooper 1988), but, there is some evidence from findings relating to the drug reserpine. Reserpine is known to act by reducing the availability of noradrenaline in the brain. When this drug is administered to patients to reduce high blood pressure, it can have the unwanted side effect of producing depressive symptoms and suicidal tendencies.

These findings originally led researchers to believe that depression was caused by low activity of either serotonin or noradrenalin. In the light of more recent research, this simple idea has now been challenged. It seems that people with depression might have an overall imbalance between several different neurotransmitters including serotonin, noradrenaline, dopamine and acetylcholine (Thase *et al.* 2002). The reason why serotonin appeared to be particularly important is because it might act as a neuromodulator (controller) of a variety of brain systems. When serotonin levels are low, activity in these other systems is disrupted and this results in depression.

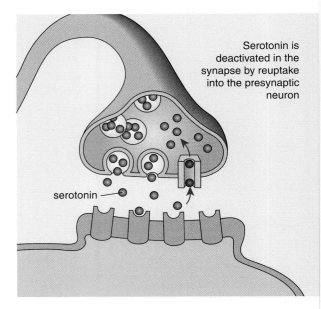

Figure 10.2 *The deactivation of serotonin*

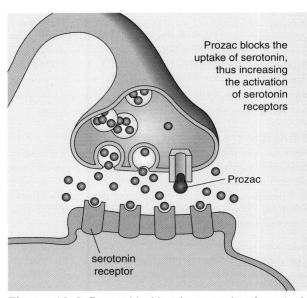

Figure 10.3 *Prozac blocking the reuptake of serotonin*

The drug Prozac, which has been found to be an effective antidepressant, works by increasing availability of serotonin in the brain, but does not seem to have any effect on noradrenaline. Advances in technology have enabled healthcare professionals to measure the action of neurotransmitters through **Positron Emission Tomography (PET)** scans (see p.300 in Introduction to Psychopathology). Mann *et al.* (1996) found impaired transmission of serotonin in people with depression.

Dopamine

Dopamine is thought to be especially involved in depression in old age, because the dopamine content of the brain diminishes considerably over the age of 45. However, the synthetic drug L-dopa (which replicates the action of dopamine) has no specific antidepressant effect.

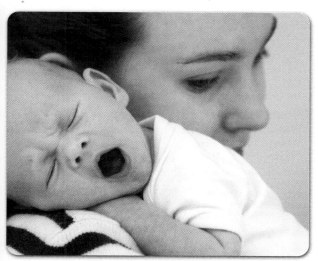

Post-natal depression is the name given to the depression suffered by some mothers in the months after the birth of their baby.

The role of hormones

Another biological explanation has emerged from endocrinology (the study of **hormones**). High levels of the hormone cortisol are found in those suffering from depression and techniques known to suppress cortisol secretion have been found to be successful in depressive patients (Carroll 1982). This suggests that there is over-activity in the hypothalamic-pituitary-adrenal cortex (see chapter on Stress in *Psychology AS for AQA A*, pp.148–79). However, this may be due to the stress of being ill, because increased cortisol secretion is a function of the stress response. A study by Nemeroff *et al.* (1992), however, has shown that there is marked adrenal gland enlargement in those suffering from major depressive disorder, which is not found in controls. Endocrine (hormonal) changes could account for depression relating to pre-menstrual, post-natal and menopausal phases. These types of depression can be very serious indeed, leading to suicide attempts.

- *Post-natal depression* – In the case of severe post-natal depression, psychotic elements can appear, such as fantasies and loss of contact with reality. In such cases, some mothers with severe post-natal depression may harm or even, in rare cases, kill their newborn child. Both oestrogen and progesterone increase greatly during pregnancy and then fall rapidly after childbirth, which may account for post-natal depression. Cooper (1988), however, found little difference between the number of women suffering from depression immediately after childbirth and a control group of non-pregnant women of a similar age.

- *Premenstrual dysphoric disorder* – Depression can occur in the week prior to menstruation and 25 per cent of women are affected, although most are not of diagnosable severity. An oestrogen-progesterone imbalance has been suggested (Dalton 1964), oestrogen levels being too high and progesterone levels too low.

- *Menopausal depression* – At menopause, oestrogen levels drop. Hormone replacement therapy appears to be reasonably effective for treating many (but not all) women who suffer from menopausal depression.

Research evidence for these hormone-imbalance theories is inconclusive (Clare 1985). Nevertheless, if hormonal changes are not implicated, then it is difficult to explain why these depressive states occur more frequently during periods of hormonal change. One of the problems in trying to ascertain hormonal links with depression is that there are invariably social changes occurring at the same time. A possible explanation is that hormonal changes interact with a genetic predisposition to depression, together with excessive tiredness and a stressful domestic situation.

Biological rhythms

It has been understood for a long time that the functioning of humans and other animals is influenced by **biological rhythms**, e.g. the 24-hour day cycle, monthly cycles etc. One type of biological rhythm that has attracted the interest of researchers is seasonal. In 1984, it was formally recognized that some people experience recurrent depressive episodes that start towards the end of Autumn and continue until Spring (Rosenthal *et al.* 1984).

Seasonal Affective Disorder

One explanation for Seasonal Affective Disorder (SAD) relates to changes in the number of daylight hours – either the person is not exposed to enough natural light, or they are adversely affected by too much artificial light. Special daylight light bulbs can now be purchased which can help those suffering from this type of depression.

Daylight SAD lamp

- *Melatonin* – The hormone melatonin, sometimes dubbed 'Dracula hormone' because it is only released in dark conditions, is implicated in SAD. Melatonin levels increase in the winter months and this has the effect of slowing us down and making us feel more fatigued. People with SAD seem to be particularly sensitive to these rises in melatonin levels.

- *Serotonin and noradrenaline* – There is some evidence to link SAD with brain chemicals, particularly serotonin and noradrenaline. Lam *et al.* (1996) found that treatments with antidepressant drugs which contain serotonin are effective, whereas those drugs containing noradrenaline had no effect. They concluded that SAD may be related to serotonergic mechanisms. However, the relationship cannot be causal because treatment does not cure the problem, which returns when drug treatment is ceased.

- *Genetic predisposition* – Although not a great deal of research has yet been conducted, some evidence is emerging for a genetic predisposition. For example, Madden *et al.* (1996) report a significant genetic

influence in winter-pattern SAD. Their data were collected from 4639 adult twins in Australia via a mailed questionnaire. However, it has been found that people do not always answer such questionnaires truthfully and so the results of such studies must be treated with caution.

Evaluation of biochemical explanations

- *Role of neurotransmitters* – There is a considerable body of evidence that supports the role of certain neurotransmitters in unipolar depression. However, theories based on excess or deficit of such chemicals in the brain are too simple. For example, antidepressant drugs have an immediate effect on increasing neurotransmitter availability, but typically take several weeks to have a significant effect on mood. Furthermore, much of the evidence implicating noradrenaline comes from observing the effects of reserpine and antidepressant drugs. However, these drugs do not simply affect levels of noradrenaline. It, may, therefore, be other properties of these drugs that relate to depression and not their reaction with

Methodological and ethical issues

Key Research: Seligman (1974)

When you are evaluating research that supports a particular hypothesis, you need to think carefully about methodological and ethical issues.

In the field of psychopathology, one major problem for investigators is that they often cannot use human patients directly in clinical research. They are able to conduct post-mortem examinations on people who have suffered from a mental disorder to see if any brain abnormalities can be detected. However, post-mortem studies of people who had suffered from depression in life are difficult to interpret. It is not clear whether brain changes reflect the origins of the disorder or whether they were caused by the depression and/or medication. It is worth remembering, however, that advances in science now allow more sophisticated methods of investigation into human brains. Techniques such as **Positron Emission Tomography (PET)** and **Magnetic Resonance Imaging (MRI)** scans can provide more detailed and accurate information. See p.5 in the Introduction for more information about MRI and other non-invasive techniques of studying the brain.

There are numerous ethical and practical limitations which prevent researchers from using patients who are still living. One way in which researchers can carry out their investigations without breaching ethical guidelines is to conduct what are called 'analogue experiments'. This means that they can simulate, for example, the symptoms of depression in

'substitutes' of some kind and then generalize their findings to people who are actually suffering from the disorder. Non-depressed human volunteers can be used as models or substitutes when it is ethical to do so. Seligman (1974), for example, has used this technique in investigating the **learned helplessness** theory of depression (see section on p.343). He has produced depression-like symptoms in non-depressed people by repeatedly subjecting them to unpleasant stimuli (e.g. loud noises, mild electric shocks, critical feedback) in situations where they have no control. Participants in these kinds of situations have a tendency to give up, become apathetic and lose their motivation. Seligman took this as supporting evidence for his ideas about learned helplessness leading to depression.

Evaluation

- We can never be sure from such analogue experiments that the behaviour shown in the laboratory is the same as that shown by people with genuine depression. If the similarities are only superficial, the researcher could draw the wrong conclusions. This is the major limitation of analogue experiments.

- You might be thinking that Seligman's studies were somewhat dubious in ethical terms. Even though he used volunteers, they were subjected to unpleasant experiences and this could have affected their self-esteem after they left the laboratory environment.

noradrenaline. Some biological researchers are beginning to think that depression is linked to damage within neurons (nerve cells). In particular, they believe that a chemical within the cell called brain-derived neurotrophic factor (BDNF) is deficient in people with depression (Julien 2005).

- *Isolating cause and effect* – It is difficult to disentangle cause and effect in many of the studies. It may be that depression causes biochemical changes rather than the other way round. See methodological and ethical issues box on the left.

- *Role of hormones* – Abnormal levels and regulation of cortisol suggested that depression may be related to impairment of the stress-response system. However, such irregularities are not found in all people with depression and are sometimes found in people with other kinds of mental disorder. Females are more likely to be diagnosed with depression than males, and female hormones have been suggested as a reason for this difference. However, evidence for their importance in depression is weak. For example, only a small minority of women suffer from severe post-natal depression, so this is not an inevitable response to hormonal changes.

Activity

Ethical issues in analogue studies

Read Key research: Methodological and ethical issues on the left.

Use your knowledge of ethical guidelines for psychological research to identify and discuss with some of your fellow students the ethical issues raised by the analogue studies carried out by Seligman.

- *Biological factors as predisposing factor* – There is no definitive evidence of biological features as the cause of depression, although there is a lot of support for the idea that they are a contributory factor. It is likely they predispose people to depression, but that environmental triggers are required before the disorder emerges.

Neuroanatomical explanations

Some brain abnormalities have been demonstrated in people with depression. Studies using **computerized tomography (CT)** and **magnetic resonance imaging (MRI)** have found enlarged ventricles, decreased volume in the hippocampus, basal ganglia and pre-frontal cortex grey matter in patients with severe or chronic depression. Similarly, PET and **functional Magnetic Resonance Imaging (fMRI)** scans have shown changes in cerebral blood flow in parts of the brain associated with emotional and attentional processing, e.g. the pre-frontal cortex, the amygdala and the thalamus. This suggests that severe depression might be associated with faulty interactions between a number of brain regions (Drevets *et al.* 2004). This is a promising area of research that has only been made possible by the development of sophisticated scanning techniques.

Evaluation of brain neuroanatomical explanations

- *Contradictory findings* – Numerous studies have been carried out but results have been contradictory for many methodological reasons, e.g. patient selection, current medication and differing imaging techniques.

- *Limited findings* – Brain abnormalities have not been found in all people with depression.

IDA   **Research using non-human animals**

Owing to the ethical issues raised by analogue studies using human participants, studies often use non-human animals. Animal studies have been used quite extensively in research into the biological underpinnings of mental disorders. Studies using animals have provided useful information which could not have been gathered from human participants. They can provide the basis for further hypothesis testing and for later, safer experimentation with humans. Animals can be easier to manipulate than humans and, although animals are protected by ethical guidelines and even legislation, they do not pose the same ethical problems as human participants. The use of animals in this kind of research is controversial and many people, including some scientists, object strongly to their use. They object mainly on ethical grounds but they also make the point that it is not possible to generalize findings from animals to humans, particularly in the field of mental illness.

Scientists who support their use believe that there are sufficient neurobiological similarities between animals (such as monkeys and rats) and humans to make the use of animal analogues acceptable.

As you can see, there are advantages and limitations in using animals to investigate disorders like depression. There are several discussion points for you to consider:

- Why do you think non-human animals have been used at all, given the problems associated with their use?
- Try to think of as many ethical and practical problems as you can and then consider whether there are ways to overcome these difficulties.

One important thing to remember is that you need to discuss these problems in the context of research into depression, so do not be tempted to have a rant about the use of animal experimentation in general.

Reductionism and biological explanations

IDA

A criticism of biological explanations of depression is that they are reductionist, i.e. they reduce the complex set of behaviours associated with depression down to a relatively simple level of explanation, i.e. an imbalance in brain chemicals or a faulty gene. The influence of brain chemicals such as serotonin seems to be widely accepted, but to argue that they cause depression is to neglect all other potential influences (such as stress or irrational thought processes) in the course of this disorder.

It is important to note that most researchers and clinicians in the field of psychopathology accept that depression is a result of an interaction of factors.

To learn more about reductionism, look at p.39 in the Introduction to the book.

Psychological explanations of depression

As we have seen, there is strong evidence for the importance of biological factors in depression. It should also be clear, however, that biological factors alone cannot account for all that we know about the disorder. There are several psychological and psychosocial explanations and we will consider them next.

Psychodynamic explanations

- *Psychoanalytic explanation* – Freud (1917) developed the first psychodynamic explanation of depression. He thought that depression occurs when the normal grieving process following the death of a loved one does not diminish with time. Depressed people cannot accept the loss and begin to merge their own personality with that of the loved one. During this period of so-called 'introjection', the depressed person directs all the feelings they had for the loved one inwards to themselves. These feelings can include both sadness and anger. Freud realized that many people become depressed without experiencing the death of someone close. He suggested that these people had experienced a 'symbolic loss', where an event such as losing a job, breaking up with a partner etc. is interpreted in the same way as the death of a loved one.

- *Relationship with parents* – A slightly different psychodynamic view relates depression in adulthood to the individual's early relationship with parents. Hostile feelings towards parent(s), it is claimed, are redirected towards the self in the form of self-accusation or self-hatred. These feelings may arise from a lack of love and care, support and safety, or from child abuse. In general terms, the psychodynamic view sees the repression of early trauma re-emerging in adulthood in the form of an anxiety disorder or depression. The case study of Robert (see box below) is an example of the longer-term effects of early trauma.

- *Effects of separation and loss* – In his theory of 'attachment and separation', John Bowlby (1973) suggested that separation from or loss of the mother in early childhood could result in severe depression in adulthood (see Chapter 4, Early social development, pp.116–47 in *Psychology AS for AQA A*). Support for this view comes from carefully conducted studies by Hinde (1977), who examined the effects of separating infant rhesus monkeys from their mother. These monkeys (both mother and child) very quickly

The psychoanalytic theory of depression likens it to grieving for a lost loved one.

Case study of Robert

Robert is in his early twenties and suffers from severe clinical depression. He was a small, thin child and from the start of junior school he was bullied by a group of boys. Pleas to his parents and to the school did not resolve the problem and he became more and more withdrawn. He felt abandoned and learned not to trust anyone.

His fear of being bullied also became an obsession and he began to ruminate in his head almost all of the time: for example, 'Will the bullies be waiting round the corner?', 'What would happen if I took another route?', 'Will I be able to escape?' These ruminations completely took over his thoughts and became an integral part of his personality, such that as an adult he now cannot cease to ruminate upon every single aspect of daily activity. These ruminations, together with his inability to trust others, are at the root of his depression.

displayed behaviours similar to the symptoms of depression in humans. However, Paykel (1981) subsequently reviewed 14 studies and found the evidence inconclusive, with seven studies supporting and seven not supporting the hypothesis. It should also be borne in mind that it may be unwise to use studies of primates to support theories about the causes of human disorders. Some support comes from studies with humans who have filled out questionnaires about their experiences in childhood and the quality of parental care. Depressed patients often report a parental style called 'affectionless control' (Martin *et al.* 2004).

Evaluation psychodynamic explanations

- *Difficult to test* – It is difficult to test Freud's ideas empirically because it is impossible to demonstrate unconscious motivations or abstract concepts such as 'symbolic loss'. There is some evidence that people with depression show more anger than non-depressed people, but findings have been inconsistent. In any case, the studies have been unable to show that this anger is directed inwards.

- *Effect of loss of parent* – There is some evidence that the loss of a parent in childhood is associated with later depression. However, such loss affects the environment in which the child lives as well as the child's psychological functioning. It might be that the social and financial hardships that such loss might entail create a vulnerability to depression. It has been found that family discord and lack of adequate care predispose people to depression even in families where there is no actual separation (Harris, 2001).

- *Significance of findings* – In many studies, only some children/monkeys reacted to loss with depressive symptoms. It has been estimated that fewer then 10 per cent of people who experience major losses in their early life go on to develop depression (Bonanno 2004)

Behavioural explanations of depression

Behavioural explanations typically focus on operant conditioning processes (learning theory).

Learning theory

Lewinsohn (1974) suggested that depression is caused by a reduction in positive reinforcement. For example, if someone experiences bereavement or loses a job, there may be less opportunity for them to enjoy pleasant experiences and receive positive reinforcement. Depression may then occur. There may also be a secondary gain in that the depressive behaviour may be positively reinforced by others in the form of sympathy or concern. However, this cannot explain why the depression continues long after sympathy from others has waned.

Learned helplessness

Seligman (1974) proposed a behavioural theory of 'learned helplessness' to explain reactive depression (i.e. depression caused by stressful events).

In the course of investigating the effects of fear conditioning in dogs, Seligman found that, after being placed in an inescapable and unavoidable stressful situation, the dog failed to initiate escape behaviour in another stressful situation where escape was possible. Seligman suggested that the effects of this 'learned helplessness' were similar to some of the symptoms of human depression. People are generally able to influence or control many aspects of their environment, but sometimes unpleasant things just happen, irrespective of their own behaviour. If this occurs too often, then people lose their motivation and just give up, because they have learned that they are unable to influence situations (that is, they have learned they are helpless).

Maier and Seligman (1976) tested this theory with humans. They subjected people to inescapable noise or shocks, and found that they later failed to escape from similar situations where escape was possible. See Key research box on p.340 for information about 'analogue studies' conducted by Seligman into learned helplessness.

Evaluation of behavioural explanations

- *Not a complete explanation* – Like many behavioural theories, learned helplessness is seen to be inadequate as a complete explanation because it does not take account of cognitive processes.

- *Limitations of 'analogue studies'* – See Key research: Methodological and ethical issues box on p.340.

- *Inconsistent findings* – Findings of learned helplessness in humans have not always been replicated. Some studies showed that helplessness actually facilitated subsequent performance (Wortman and Brehm 1975).

Cognitive-behavioural explanations of depression

In view of the inadequacy of the learned helplessness account, Seligman's theory was reformulated in cognitive, attributional terms, called the 'hopelessness theory of depression' (Abramson *et al.* 1978).

Hopelessness theory of depression

Hopelessness has been identified as one of the core characteristics of depression. Beck *et al.* (1974) developed a 'Hopelessness Scale' used to measure and quantify levels of hopelessness. The **hopelessness theory** suggested that when people experience failure, they usually try and attribute the failure to a cause. Causal explanations (attributions) operate on three dimensions of judgement:

- *internal-external* – personal or environmental

- *stable-unstable* – always so or just on this occasion

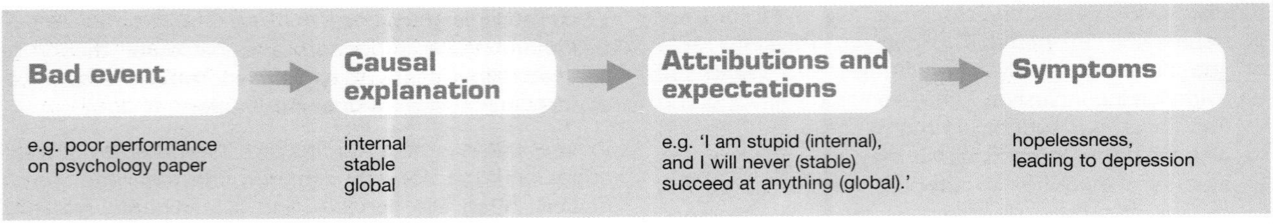

Figure 10.4 *An example of attributional judgements leading to depression.*

- *global-specific* – all-encompassing or specific to this situation.

A 'maladaptive attributional style' would involve attributing all negative events to internal, stable, global causes because these causal explanations tend to lead to negative expectations and feelings of hopelessness, which in turn can lead to symptoms of depression (see Fig.10.4 above).

Research supporting the hopelessness theory comes from studies using the 'Attributional Style Questionnaire', devised by Seligman (1974), which gives scores for internality, stability and globality of an individual's expectations. A study on grade aspirations in college students showed that most of those with poor results were depressed after the exams. Two days later, however, those who made unstable, specific attributions about their failure had recovered, whereas those who had made stable, global attributions remained depressed.

Activity **Activity on attributional style**

Look at Figure 10.4. Re-write the attributions and expectations about the bad event to avoid feelings of hopelessness and consequent depression.

Evaluation of hopelessness theory of depression

- *Research participants* – Most of Seligman's studies were conducted on college students, rather than on clinically depressed patients (see Key research box on analogue research p.340).

- *Perception of control* – One of the key elements of the hopelessness theory is that depressed people believe they have little control over their lives. Ford and Neale (1985), however, found that depressed students did not underestimate their degree of control.

- *Hopelessness as cause or effect?* – It is not clear whether hopelessness is a cause of depression, or whether it is a side effect of becoming depressed. If it is the cause, then it would have to precede the onset of depression. A five-year longitudinal study of children by Nolen-Hoeksema *et al.* (1992) found no connection between attributional style and depression in young children. However, they did find a connection as the children grew older, suggesting that attributional styles may develop over a number of years.

- *Hopelessness expectancy* – Abramson *et al.* (1989) further reformulated their theory of hopelessness, to include the role of expectancy. They outlined a sequence of events which they claimed led to hopelessness. This begins with a negative event which interacts with the person's already-held negative schemas, and a stable and global attribution is made about why the event occurred. These beliefs lead to 'hopelessness expectancy' for the future, which then results in depression. Abramson and colleagues have even suggested 'hopelessness depression' as a sub-type of depression. DeVellis and Blalock (1992), in a longitudinal study of 57 adults, found support for the link between expectancy and depression, but as a moderating, rather than mediating factor, i.e. it does not by itself cause the depression, merely the degree of the disorder.

Beck's cognitive theory of depression

Beck (1967), although trained as a psychoanalyst, was struck by the negative thinking shown by depressed clients. He suggested that depression is the result of negative thinking and catastrophizing (exaggerating the importance of negative events), which he called 'cognitive errors'.

The cognitive triad

Beck maintained that there are three main components to depression, which he called the '**cognitive triad**' (see Figure 10.5):

- negative views of the self as worthless and helpless

- negative views of the world as full of obstacles and a negative view of one's ongoing experience of the world

- negative views about the future as continuing in much the same way.

As these three components interact, they interfere with normal cognitive processing, leading to impairments in perception, memory and problem-solving abilities, with the person becoming completely obsessed with negative thoughts. These thoughts arise spontaneously and are not a result of conscious intention. Not surprisingly, constant exposure to these faulty cognitions can lead to depression. According to Beck, the cognitive triad is maintained by the interaction of negative self-schemas and cognitive distortions.

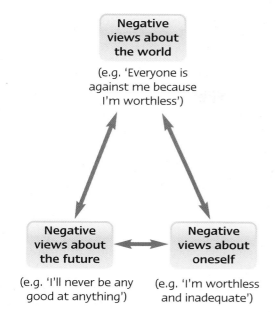

Figure 10.5 *The cognitive triad that leads to depression (Beck 1967)*

Negative self-schemas

In addition to the cognitive triad of negative cognitions, Beck believed that depression-prone individuals develop a '**negative self-schema**' – a set of beliefs and expectations about themselves that are essentially self-blaming and pessimistic. Beck claimed that negative schemas may be acquired in childhood as a result of traumatic events and/or negative treatment. Whenever the person encounters a situation that resembles the early negative or traumatic event the negative schema is triggered. Early experiences that might contribute to negative schemas include:

- death of a parent or sibling

- parental rejection, criticism, overprotection, neglect or abuse

- being bullied at school or excluded from peer group.

Gotlib and Macleod (1997) have supported the idea that negative schemas are deep-seated belief systems which develop early in life as the result of a series of negative events.

Cognitive distortions

People with negative self-schemas become prone to making logical errors in their thinking and they tend to focus selectively on certain aspects of a situation while ignoring equally relevant information. Beck referred to these logical errors as '**cognitive distortions**'. They include the following:

- *Arbitrary inference* – Drawing conclusions on the basis of insufficient or irrelevant evidence: for example, thinking you are worthless because an open-air concert you were going to see has been rained off.

-

- *Selective abstraction* – Focusing on a single aspect of a situation and ignoring others: for example, feeling responsible for your team losing a football match even though you are just one of the players on the field.

- *Overgeneralization* – Making a sweeping conclusion on the basis of a single event: for example, you get a D for an exam when you normally get straight As and you, therefore, think you are stupid.

- *Magnification and minimization* – Exaggerating or underplaying the significance of an event: for example, you scrape a bit of paintwork on your car and, therefore, see yourself as a totally awful driver; you get praised by your teachers for an excellent term's work, but you see this as trivial.

- *Personalization* – attributing the negative feelings of others to yourself. For example, your teacher looks really cross when she comes into the room, so she must be cross with you.

Personality types

Beck has adapted his theory over time and one important modification concerns personality differences. He thought that there were individual differences that determined the types of event that can trigger depressive episodes. For example, he identified the 'sociotropic personality' type, where a person based their self-esteem entirely on the approval and regard of others. For such a person, a perceived snub from a colleague, neighbour, boss, etc., might be enough to instigate depressive thoughts. The 'autonomous personality' type, on the other hand, would react badly to a situation where their sense of achievement or independence had been challenged, e.g. losing a game of tennis or having a decision overruled at work.

Evaluation of Beck's cognitive theory of depression

- *Research and therapies* – Cognitive explanations of depression have stimulated a huge amount of research into the disorder over the last few decades. This has contributed greatly to our understanding of the disorder and to the rise of cognitive-behavioural therapies, which have been very helpful in alleviating the symptoms of depression.

- *Studies into negative thinking* – There have been hundreds of studies which have investigated whether depressed people actually think more negatively than non-depressed people. On the whole, such studies have shown strong evidence for more negative thinking in depressed people. For example, it has been found that depressed people do have a tendency to maladaptive attitudes and beliefs and that the more of these they hold, the more severe is their depression (Evans *et al.* 2005). However, most studies are based mainly on correlational data and it is difficult to determine whether the negative thinking is a cause or an effect of depression.

- *Does negative thinking precede depression?* – There have been very few studies to investigate whether negative thinking precedes the onset of depression. The few longitudinal studies that have been reported do not show that cognitive vulnerability is a predictor of depression. If negative thinking is a vulnerability factor in depression, you would expect that depressed people would show more dysfunctional self-schemas than non-depressed people, even if they are not currently depressed and would, therefore, be more at risk of future episodes. However, numerous studies (reviewed by Segal and Ingram 1994) that have compared non-depressed and recovered depressed patients have found no difference on a variety of cognitive vulnerability measures. This suggests that negative thinking is a consequence of having depression rather than a causal factor.

Diathesis-stress model

It seems clear that no single explanation can account for depression; it is much more likely that various contributory factors interact to bring about the disorder. According to the **diathesis-stress model**, underlying predispositions, such as a genetic vulnerability, childhood loss or patterns of negative thinking, can give rise to depressive symptoms only if activated by stressors in the environment. There is considerable evidence that links stressful events such as bereavement, unemployment, divorce and serious illness to the onset of depression.

Psychosocial explanations: stressful life events

There is considerable evidence that the social environment plays an important role in the development of unipolar depression. Factors such as culture, gender, work environment, relationships can all contribute. One area that has attracted considerable research interest is the role of stressful life events.

In 1978, Brown and Harris published a very influential book, entitled *The Social Origins of Depression*, the result of a major study of depression among housewives in Camberwell, London. Brown and Harris identified two types of precipitating factors for depression: severe life events and long-term difficulties. These factors came into play when the person also experienced 'vulnerability factors', such as lack of paid employment outside the home, two or more children under the age of five, early loss of mother and, especially, the lack of a close confiding relationship. Further research into depression among working-class mothers is shown in the panel below, 'Depression among working-class mothers'.

Activity

Early life experiences and depression

With some of your fellow students, discuss why early-life experience might be a strong predictor of adult depression.

A more recent investigation into the role of stressful life events and personality as predictors of depression is discussed in the Key Research panel opposite.

HOW SCIENCE WORKS

Activity Predictors of depression

With reference to Mazure et al.'s (2000) study (see panel opposite) answer the following questions:

- The researchers were interested to find that 'need for control' was an important predictor of depressive episodes. Which psychological explanation of depression does this support?

- The researchers wrote in their report that 'a prospective study would provide a more definitive test of cognitive-personality characteristics as a risk factor for depression'. Find out what is meant by a prospective study. Explain how a prospective study could have provided more information.

- Cognitive-personality styles are learned patterns that are stable and long-lasting but potentially amenable to change. How might the findings of this study help therapists to develop prevention and treatment programmes for people at risk of depression?

Depression among working-class mothers

Brown and Harris (1978) originally identified people who were already depressed. However, they have continued to research their life-events theory to incorporate early-life experiences. They conducted a study in Islington with 404 working-class women who were single mothers living in an inner-city area. An eight-year follow-up (Brown et al. 1994) found:

- Early-life experience was a strong predictor of adult depression.
- The most significant childhood adversities were parental indifference and physical or sexual abuse.
- Early loss of mother was not significant unless it increased the chances of negative experiences.

A prospective study by Bifulco et al. (1998) confirmed these findings. They gathered data on 105 working-class mothers with vulnerability factors (e.g. negative close relationships and adverse early-life experiences), but who were not depressed. They found:

- Over a period of 14 months, 37 per cent of these women became depressed and, of these, two-thirds had experienced childhood neglect or abuse.
- Early loss of a parent was not significant, provided that subsequent care had been good, which does not support Bowlby's theory of the effects of early separation mentioned above (p.342).

Now try the activity on early life experiences and depression.

Gender differences

Women are twice as likely to be diagnosed with depression as men but the reasons for this are not entirely clear.

- *Biological factors* – Depression is often associated with hormonal changes in women, e.g. depression around the time of menstruation, after the birth of a baby and during the menopause. This suggests a biological reason but it cannot be the whole answer. Important social, emotional, even financial, factors that operate during these times could be the cause of the depression.

- *Poorer quality of life and cultural pressures* – It has been suggested that women have a poorer quality of life than men. They tend to have lower-paid and lower-status jobs and have more spill-over between job and home. In other words, once they have finished their paid employment, they come home and continue working at domestic chores (Bird and Rieker 1999). Women may also be more subject to cultural pressure than men, e.g. to be slim, attractive, good wife and mother etc. and this could add to their feelings of inadequacy if they do not meet expectations.

- *Attributional style* – Women are also more likely than men to attribute their failures to incompetence and their successes to luck than men (e.g. Beyer 1998). This is an attributional style associated with depression (see p.343–4).

- *Rumination* – Women also ruminate more than men when they feel down. In other words they think about what is making them feel sad and turn these thoughts over and over in their minds. Rumination is a predictor of depression (Nolen-Hoeksema and Corte, 2004).

- *Adverse early life experiences* – Veijola *et al.* (1998) conducted a study on gender differences in adult depression and found that adverse early-life experiences (such as sexual and physical abuse) predisposed females to depression in adulthood. They found no significant relationship between early-life experience and adult depression in males and suggested that, in males, early adverse experiences were more likely to be expressed in antisocial behaviour and alcoholism.

It seems that a number of factors interact to make women more vulnerable to depression than men.

Stressful life events, personality and depression

Key Research: Mazure *et al.* (2000)

A study carried out by Mazure *et al.* (2000) looked at stressful life events and personality style as factors in predicting depression (MDD).

They knew from previous research that stressful life events are known to precipitate episodes of MDD. However, they were interested to find out why only some people who experience adverse events go on to develop depression. Beck (see above) had suggested that cognitive personality style might modify the impact of any stressful experiences in some individuals. This background research gave them the idea for their own study. They aimed to examine the effects of stressful life events and cognitive-personality style in predicting:

1 the onset of a depressive episode in patients with unipolar depression versus controls

2 depressive symptom severity at the completion of a six-week standard antidepressant treatment programme.

Trained interviewers used standard scales to assess the number, severity and type of stressful events that had occurred in the previous six months in both 43 patients and 43 matched controls. Cognitive-personality characteristics were assessed by using Beck's measures of sociotropy (interpersonal dependency) and autonomy (need for independence and control).

They found that adverse life events, sociotropy and need for control were each significantly related to depressive episode onset. The type of stressful event also seemed to have an impact on the effectiveness of treatment

They concluded that:

- Adverse life events are a potent factor in predicting depression.

- However, certain cognitive-personality characteristics (e.g. need for control) also increase susceptibility to depression.

- Better treatment outcome is associated with occurrence of adverse interpersonal events (e.g. death of a loved one) rather than adverse achievement events (e.g. loss of job).

Evaluation

- This was a carefully controlled study that looked at several potentially important variables that might influence susceptibility to depression. However, it did not take into account factors such as social support networks, coping strategies and early trauma, and these would need to be considered in future research before firm conclusions could be drawn about the impact of personality style.

- The study also found some evidence of gender differences in response to treatment and this would also merit further investigation.

Evaluation of diathesis-stress explanation of depression

■ *Support for life-events theory* – The life-events theory has received a great deal of support and is now incorporated into the DSM diagnostic criteria under Axis IV, where social and environmental circumstances are assessed. The theory, however, does not explain why many patients fail to report critical life events at the onset of their depression, nor why many people have ongoing psychosocial stressors yet do not become clinically depressed.

STRETCH AND CHALLENGE

Activity **Culture and depression**

Cultural factors seem to be important in influencing vulnerability to depression. People from ethnic minorities often have higher levels of mental health problems than the rest of the population. Ethnicity in itself is not a cause for mental illness. The concept of ethnicity includes language, religion, culture, ancestry, forms of identity etc., and some or all of these factors probably contribute to greater vulnerability. One explanation is that people in ethnic minorities are exposed to higher levels of stress than the indigenous population because of racial prejudice, low socio-economic status and problems of adapting to a new and different culture. For example, Lai (2004) studied Chinese immigrants to Canada and found that the highest levels of depression were amongst the group who had resisted integrating into Canadian society and who maintained a higher level of identification with Chinese cultural values. Ethnicity is not the only factor that defines minority status.

● Can you think of any other social groups in the UK who form minorities? Try to find out more about links between minority status and depression. You might like to look at the website for the organisation 'Mind' to give you some more information. www.mind.org.uk/Information/Factsheets/Diversity/Factsheet

■ *Life events as triggering factors* – The diathesis-stress model provides a way of integrating the life events theory to some of the other explanations. Life events may be triggering factors that interact with vulnerability factors such as a genetic predisposition, personality factors, gender or adverse early-life experience. See also Fig. 9.3 on p.319.

CHECK YOUR UNDERSTANDING

Check your understanding of explanations of depression by answering the following questions. Try to do this from memory. You can check your answers by looking back through Topic 2, Explanations of depression.

1. What is meant by the nature-nurture debate with regard to depression?

2. Give three reasons why biological factors might be important in understanding the origins of depression.

3. Briefly outline the role of neurotransmitters in depression.

4. Evaluate research findings concerning biochemical explanations of depression.

5. Outline two strengths and two limitations of the biological explanations for depression.

6. Give a brief evaluation of Freud's theory of depression.

7. Explain what is meant by 'learned helplessness theory' and explain how this is different from 'hopelessness theory'.

8. Briefly outline and evaluate Beck's cognitive theory of depression.

9. What role might stressful life events have in the origins of depression?

10. Explain what is meant by the diathesis-stress model?

Topic 3: Therapies for depression

A **therapy** is a deliberate intervention designed to treat mental disorders either by producing a complete cure or by making the symptoms more manageable. Different therapies are used in the treatment of depression, each one based on a particular theoretical orientation regarding the underlying causes. You will already be familiar with these orientations or models of mental disorder from your AS-level studies into psychopathology. If you have not already done so you should re-read the section in your AS textbook that deals with treatments for psychopathology (*Psychology AS for AQA A*, pp.237–47).

There are considerable ethical and practical issues involved with therapeutic interventions and some of these points will be considered in the context of each type of therapy. There are, however, some important general issues surrounding the use of therapies. These are described in the Introduction to Psychopathology (pp.300–305), and you should start by reading about these first and then come back to them later on as you evaluate the various types of therapy.

Biological therapies

Biological therapies arise from the medical model of abnormal behaviour: mental disorder is seen as an illness which results mainly from a biochemical imbalance. Biological treatments are designed to redress this

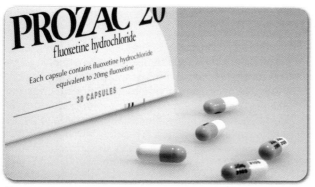
Prozac

imbalance through the administration of chemical drugs, electroconvulsive therapy (ECT) and, in rare cases, psychosurgery. In other words, they aim to alter abnormal behaviours by intervening directly in bodily processes.

Many people who are experiencing symptoms of depression go for help to their family doctor in the first instance. This means that the first line of treatment offered is usually medical. The most commonly prescribed treatment for depression is drug therapy, although this is often combined with psychological therapies to bring about the best outcomes.

Chemotherapy (drug therapy)

Since the 1950s, the use of drugs in the treatment of mental disorders has been widespread and they account annually for a large proportion of NHS prescriptions. So-called psychoactive drugs have a direct effect on the nervous system and, although they work in various ways, they essentially serve either to increase or decrease the availability of particular neurotransmitters.

Psychology in context — Treating depression with St John's wort

There has recently been a trend for people in the UK to reject processed foods and to buy organic or environmentally friendly foods. Similarly, there has been renewed interest in herbal remedies rather than manufactured chemical drugs.

The following extract is adapted from an article by Colin Brennan on the website:

http://www2.netdoctor.co.uk/special_reports/depression/stjwort.htm

You might like to look this up so that you can read the whole article.

One apparently wholesome, natural, inexpensive remedy that is available over the counter is St John's wort. Taken all over the world in huge quantities, it has become the pill to take without guilt or fear as a means of combating mild to moderate depression.

The Medicines Control Agency issued a warning on 1 March 2000 that patients who are on a long list of drugs should stop taking St John's wort until they have consulted their GP or pharmacist. Medications for asthma, epilepsy, depression, migraine and heart problems are all implicated. In the Irish Republic, St John's wort is only available on prescription.

A trial by Michael Philipp and his colleagues, involving 263 people, published in the *British Medical Journal* in December 1999, showed that St John's wort was better than placebo (dummy pills) and as good as the commonly prescribed antidepressant imipramine. The herbal remedy had fewer side effects and the researchers concluded it showed promise for the long-term treatment of moderate depression.

St John's wort, a 'wholesome' remedy for depression?

However, research has been contradictory and it has been claimed that some studies are too small to be reliable, that there is a lack of long-term data and that St John's wort has not been compared with the most effective prescription drugs like Prozac and Zoloft.

- Why do you think people take St John's wort tablets 'without guilt or fear'?

- Packets or bottles of St John's wort tablets often have pretty pictures of the flower on the front. What message do you think that the companies who produce them are trying to convey?

- What are the problems of self-medication for disorders such as depression?

- Why is it important to have properly controlled clinical trials of remedies such as St John's wort?

Antidepressant drugs

These drugs affect the availability of serotonin and noradrenaline which are the main neurotransmitters thought to be implicated in depression. Antidepressants include:

- monoamine-oxidase inhibitors (MAOIs)
- tricyclics (TCAs)
- selective serotonin re-uptake inhibitors (SSRIs).

Monoamine-oxidase inhibitors (MAOIs)

The first MAOI was Iproniazid. Its antidepressant effect was discovered by accident when it was tried as a new drug for tuberculosis and found to induce euphoria. MAOIs block the action of the enzyme that breaks down noradrenaline and serotonin, so increasing the availability of these neurotransmitters in the nervous system.

Tricyclics (TCAs)

Tricyclics were also discovered accidentally when the drug imipramine, initially trialled as an anti-schizophrenic drug, was found to be helpful in alleviating symptoms of depression. The most commonly used drug in the tricyclic group is Tofranil and it operates by blocking the re-uptake of noradrenaline and serotonin and so making more of these neurotransmitters available. Tricyclics are milder antidepressants than MAOIs and, although slower acting, they have fewer severe side effects. Although these drugs have an immediate effect on reuptake mechanisms they do not seem to provide relief from symptoms for at least 10 days. The reason for this seems to be that the drugs also slow down activity in the nerve cells that use serotonin and noradrenaline so that they release lower levels of the neurotransmitters. It seems to take the cells about 10 days to adapt to the tricyclic drugs and to begin releasing normal levels of the neurotransmitters.

It is important for people taking tricyclics to continue on the medication for some months after symptoms have improved. About 50 per cent of users relapse within a year if they stop the drugs too soon (Montgomery et al. 1993).

Selective serotonin re-uptake inhibitors (SSRIs)

A newer class of drugs called SSRIs, which include Prozac, inhibit the re-uptake of serotonin and thus make more of this neurotransmitter available. The original SSRIs did not affect other neurotransmitters such as noradrenaline. More recently, drugs have been developed that increase both serotonin and noradrenaline (SNRIs) and these seem to be more effective in treating the symptoms of depression but may have more severe side effects (Sir et al. 2005). As with tricyclics, users should not stop taking SSRIs abruptly or they run the risk of developing unpleasant symptoms such as dizziness, nausea, lethargy and headache.

More recently, the natural herb hypericum, commonly known as St John's wort, has been found in clinical trials to have antidepressant qualities (Holden 1997). It is thought that the herb alters serotonin function in some way (see Psychology in context on p.349).

Evaluation of antidepressant drugs

- *Effective in reducing symptoms* – Antidepressants have been tested in trials with placebos and found to be effective in reducing symptoms of severe depression in around 65 to 75 per cent of cases, compared with around 33 per cent for placebos (e.g. Prien 1988 and Gitlin 2002). See p.305 in the Introduction to Psychopathology for discussion of placebo effects.

- *Comparing effectiveness and side effects of MAOIs and TCAs* – Although MAOIs have been shown to be effective in reducing the symptoms of depression, they can have serious side effects. Patients have to stick to a strict diet regime and avoid foods or other medications which can interact with the drug to cause a potentially fatal reaction. A recently introduced MAOI in the form of a skin patch allows for slow continuous absorption of the drug into the nervous system and seems less likely to produce dangerous food interactions (Julien 2005). A study by Jarrett et al. (1999) found that MAOIs were much more effective than tricyclics for severe depression. Tricyclics are prescribed more often than MAOIs since they are milder antidepressants and, although slower acting, cause fewer adverse reactions and so are seen as more appropriate. However, they can cause side effects, the most serious being cardiac problems.

- *Prozac, the wonder drug?* – Prozac (an SSRI) was hailed as a 'wonder drug' when it was first introduced in the late 1980s and is currently the most frequently prescribed of all antidepressants. It is more expensive that tricyclics but was originally thought to have fewer side effects and to be less dangerous in overdose. Shortly after its introduction, doubts were raised about its safety and the drug became a media target because of many anecdotal reports of serious side effects, including a preoccupation with violence and suicide (Steiner 1991). A notorious case reported in America in 1991 concerned Joseph Wesbecker, who, while taking Prozac, shot 20 people at his former workplace before killing himself (Geoffrey 1991). More scientific studies have been conducted and the general conclusion seems to be that any very small risk of suicide or violent behaviour should be weighed against the benefits of taking SSRIs to reduce symptoms of depression. See Prozac box below.

- *Treating the symptoms, not the cause* – It has now become clear that drugs do not necessarily offer a long-term cure, because in many cases symptoms recur when the drugs are no longer taken. It is believed by many psychologists that biochemical imbalance is the result of, rather than the cause of, mental disorders. This leads to the claim that drugs merely treat the symptoms, but do not address the cause of the problem (*why* the person is depressed). Consequently, they can only provide short-term relief.

- *Combining drugs and psychological treatment* – For psychological therapies to be effective, clients or patients must have some insight, that is, they must recognize that they have a problem. Some people suffering from severe depression often have little or no insight and so psychological treatment is difficult. Short courses of antidepressant drugs can be worthwhile in cases of severe clinical depression, because without these drugs, patients often have no motivation to engage in psychological treatment. Antidepressants may even be essential as a first line of treatment for severe clinical depression, because of the high risk of suicide. In this way, biological treatment and psychological treatment can work together, rather than as alternative forms of treatment.

IDA — Ethical issues in drug therapy for depression

Some people have criticized the wide-spread use of drugs in the treatment of mental disorders referring to them as 'chemical straitjackets'. The argument is that the drugs are dehumanizing and take away any sense of personal responsibility or control. The ethical issue of informed consent is also a consideration. People in a seriously depressed state are not really in a position to give truly informed consent about their treatment.

Electroconvulsive therapy (ECT)

This controversial form of treatment was developed from the mistaken idea that schizophrenia was incompatible with epilepsy. It was thought that schizophrenia could be alleviated by artificially inducing epileptic seizures. Initially, seizures were induced by giving patients insulin. However, this proved to be extremely unreliable since it was difficult to judge the correct dosage and the side effects were very unpleasant. In 1938, Cerletti and Bini tested the technique of applying electric shocks to the brain in order to induce seizures. In the couple of decades following the introduction of this technique, ECT was widely used for a broad range of psychiatric disorders. The original procedure involved passing very high currents of electricity across both hemispheres of the brain and was known to lead to severe memory loss, speech disorders

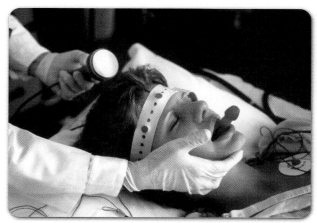

A patient receives electro-convulsive therapy (ECT).

and irreversible brain damage. Its use declined significantly with the arrival of the new psychoactive drugs in the 1950s. The decline was partly as a result of bad publicity because ECT was seen as a barbaric and punitive treatment that caused serious side effects. However, it soon became clear that the new drugs did not offer a complete solution and interest revived in ECT.

Procedure for administering ECT

- Modern techniques are much more humane and the patient is given muscle relaxants and a short-acting anaesthetic before ECT begins.

- The standard procedure is unilateral and involves administering a current of between 70 and 130 volts to the temple of one side of the head for between half a second to five seconds. This usually induces convulsions for a brief period after which the patient comes round from the anaesthetic with no recollection of the treatment.

- Usually a course of approximately six sessions will be given over a period of a few weeks.

Evaluation of ECT therapy for depression

- *Effectiveness* – Although ineffective as a treatment for schizophrenia, ECT has been found to be very effective in alleviating severe depression (includes melancholic depression, see p.333) in some patients where all other methods have failed. Studies indicate that 60 to 70 per cent of patients improve with ECT (e.g. Richards and Lyness 2006), although a large proportion of these become depressed again the following year (Sackeim *et al.* 2001). In spite of its effectiveness, the precise mechanism underlying its therapeutic action is not understood. An analogy has been drawn with banging the side of the television set to make it work (Heather 1976). It is likely that ECT increases the levels of available noradrenaline or serotonin in the brain, but it is such an invasive technique that it is difficult to isolate the element that brings about therapeutic change.

- *Appropriateness* – ECT should only be administered if antidepressant drugs have no effect and if there is a risk that the person will commit suicide (see Mental Health Act 2007). It works much more rapidly than antidepressant drugs or psychological therapies and hence is often the treatment of choice for patients who are severely depressed and at risk for suicide. Nowadays, ECT requires consent from the patient or a close relative. However, ECT has a history of abuse, being used as a means of punishing or controlling people in mental hospitals. Although techniques are improving, the decline in the use of ECT continues. As Comer (2007) argues, applying an electrical current to the brain is a frightening and forceful form of intervention. Even with the newer techniques there are still side effects, especially with repeated use. Effective antidepressant drugs now provide a more attractive alternative.

- *Side effects* – When ECT was first introduced, there were dangerous side effects, such as bone fractures, memory loss and confusion. There are no detectable changes in brain structure with the newer procedures and, as the technique is continually improved, side effects are being reduced. However, there is still concern that ECT can impair memory, particularly if it is administered to both sides of the brain (see Key research in panel below).

- *TMS – a new treatment method* – Researchers have looked for other, less invasive ways of helping people with severe depression as a replacement for ECT.

Transcranial magnetic stimulation (TMS) is a new technique (sometimes called 'magnetic therapy') which involves stimulating brain cells using magnetic fields but without any direct contact with the brain (see

In the film One Flew Over the Cuckoo's Nest, *the main character, McMurphy (played by Jack Nicholson), causes persistent problems for the staff – attempts are made to control him using drugs, ECT and finally psychosurgery.*

HOW SCIENCE WORKS

Unilateral versus bilateral ECT

Key Research: Sackheim *et al.* (2000)

There has been some controversy about the use of unilateral (UL, one side of the brain) versus bilateral (BL, both sides of the brain) ECT. BL is thought to produce more side effects but greater relief from depressive symptoms.

Sackheim *et al.* (2000) carried out a double-blind study in which 80 depressed patients were randomly allocated to four different treatment groups: UL-ECT, with electrical dosages 50 per cent, 150 per cent, or 500 per cent above the seizure threshold, or BL-ECT, with an electrical dosage 150 per cent above the threshold. Depression severity, cognitive functioning and memory for personal and general knowledge were assessed by trained interviewers before, during, immediately after, and two months after the period in which they were receiving a course of ECT.

Evaluation

- High-dosage UL- and BL-ECT were equally effective (65 per cent) and approximately twice as effective as low-dosage (that is, 50 per cent above seizure threshold) UL-ECT.

- During the week after the treatment, BL-ECT resulted in greater impairment in memory and general cognitive functioning than any dosage of UL-ECT. Two months after ECT, memory deficits were greatest among patients treated with BL-ECT.

- Thirty-three (53 per cent) of the 62 patients who responded to ECT relapsed, regardless of treatment group.

- UL-ECT at high dosage is as effective as high dosage BL-ECT, but produces less severe and persistent cognitive effects.

1 Why is it important to compare the efficacy of unilateral and bilateral ECT?

2 What is meant by a double-blind procedure and why is it used in this kind of study?

3 What ethical issues did the researchers need to consider in this study?

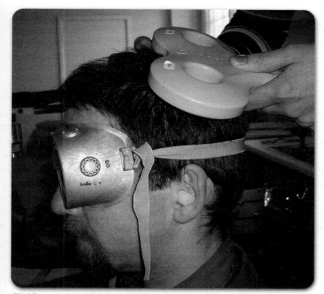
TMS – a new treatment for depression – involves stimulating brain cells using magnetic fields.

picture above). The treatment is painless and does not involve using anaesthetics, electrodes or surgery. TMS can influence various brain functions and there is some evidence that the procedure can have a lasting effect on mood. It is not clear exactly how TMS works but it is thought to increase the availability of serotonin and other neurotransmitters in the brain. In a comparison of TMS and ECT in the treatment of MDD, Schulze-Rauschenbach *et al.* (2005) found 46 per cent of patients in the ECT group showed significant improvement compared with 44 per cent in the TMS group. More importantly, while people in the ECT group showed some signs of memory impairment after ECT, this was not the case for the TMS patients. More research is needed but this suggests that TMS might prove to be a safer alternative to ECT.

Psychosurgery

Psychosurgery is an extreme form of biological treatment since it involves the destruction or removal of neural tissue in the brain. Modern psychosurgery techniques are a far cry from the crude surgical methods used between the 1930s and 60s. Surgeons now use sophisticated equipment to pinpoint exactly the relevant area of the brain, and tissue damage is now restricted to the absolute minimum. Psychosurgery is rarely used and is considered only in extreme cases where no other treatment has been successful. A technique known as subcaudate tractotomy is very occasionally used for people with severe, otherwise untreatable, depression.

Evaluation of psychosurgery

- *A last resort* – Psychosurgery continues to be regarded as the most controversial of all treatments for mental disorders and we might question whether it is appropriate to use such a drastic biological intervention to treat a psychological disorder.

- *Effectiveness* – The modern procedures are less invasive, but there are still dangers. According to Beck and Cowley (1990), however, the procedure can be beneficial in some cases of severe anxiety, depression and obsessive-compulsive disorders.

- *Issue of informed consent* – Psychosurgery is highly invasive and its effects on the brain are irreversible. For these reasons, psychosurgery is tightly regulated in the UK. In England and Wales, a panel appointed by the Mental Health Act Commission is required to assess the individual's ability to give full consent to psychosurgery and to weigh up the costs and benefits.

Psychological therapies

Psychological therapies address psychological rather than biological factors associated with mental disorders. Psychological treatments for depression include psychodynamic and cognitive-behavioural therapies.

Psychodynamic therapy

Psychoanalysis (a form of psychodynamic therapy) was first introduced by Freud at the beginning of the 20th century. The aim of psychodynamic therapy is not to 'cure' the patient's psychological problems in the same way that the medical profession might hope to find a cure for cancer. Psychoanalysts do not aim simply to remove the symptoms of mental disturbance, because this will not tackle the underlying problem – indeed, it might make the situation worse by creating a different set of symptoms (symptom substitution). Rather, the aim is to enable the person to cope better with inner emotional conflicts that are causing disturbance.

The purpose of therapy is to uncover unconscious conflicts and anxieties that have their origins in the past, in order to gain insight into the causes of psychological disturbance. After bringing these conflicts into consciousness, the client is encouraged to work through them by examining and dealing with them in the safety of the consulting room, and, in so doing, release the power they exert over behaviour – a process known as '**catharsis**'. An important aspect of this is that confusing or traumatic childhood experiences can be better understood with the benefit of adult knowledge.

In psychodynamic therapy, a variety of techniques is employed to facilitate the process of catharsis, including the following:

- *Free association* – The client is asked to allow the free flow of feelings, thoughts or images and then to express them in words, without censorship. The reasoning is that associations should arise from, and therefore reflect, internal dynamic conflict.

- *Word association* – The client has to respond to particular words with whatever comes instantly to mind.

- *Dream analysis* – The client is asked to recount their dreams and the analyst helps them to interpret the hidden meanings.

- *Transference* – This occurs when the client redirects feelings (e.g. of hostility) towards the therapist, that are unconsciously directed towards a significant person in their life (usually a parent), but which have been censored from the conscious mind.

- *Projective tests* – There are many types of projective test, the most well-known being the Rorschach Ink Blot and the Thematic Apperception Test. The client is asked to describe what they see in the ink blot or to tell a story around the picture.

All these techniques are used as tools to uncover recurrent themes that may reveal the unconscious needs and motives of the person.

The therapist expects that, in the course of treatment, the depressed person will become less dependent on others, cope with loss more effectively and make appropriate changes in their everyday lives.

Evaluation of psychodynamic therapies

- *Timescale of therapy* – Psychodynamic therapy is generally conducted over a number of years, which makes it expensive compared with other therapies for depression. However, more modern, brief psychodynamic therapies have emerged where the focus has been much more on current, rather than past, concerns and these can produce some quick improvements in functioning. These brief therapies have also made this type of therapy more affordable.

- *Suitability (appropriateness) for depression?* – It is often the case that depressed people are too passive, withdrawn and fatigued to participate in demanding therapy sessions. It is also in the nature of the disorder that people become easily disheartened and are likely to drop out of treatment long before it has had a chance to have any therapeutic effect. In the case of depressed patients with suicidal tendencies, psychodynamic therapy is inappropriate because they need a rapidly effective intervention to prevent suicide attempts.

- *Effectiveness - Does psychotherapy actually work?* – Probably the most-quoted indictment against psychodynamic therapy came from Eysenck (1952) who claimed that it simply does not work. However, other studies have been more supportive (see 'Critique of the effectiveness of psychotherapy' panel opposite and Key research box opposite.).

- *Danger of emotional harm* – Criticism has been levelled at psychodynamic therapies in relation to emotional harm. For example, a psychoanalyst may guide a client towards an insight that may prove emotionally distressing, yet is necessary for recovery from their current problem. The distress surrounding the new insight may prove to be greater than the distress of the current problem. Psychotherapists abiding by a professional code of ethics should warn their clients of this danger before engaging in therapy, and therapists should never work beyond their competence in dealing with what may arise in therapy.

- *Difficulties in evaluating the effectiveness of psychotherapy* – Problems that arise when trying to evaluate psychotherapy are discussed in Table 10.2 below. Although these are general points they are nevertheless valid when considering the effectiveness of psychotherapy for treating depression.

What is meant by 'cure'?	When to test for effectiveness?	Who decides when a therapy is effective?
Corsini and Wedding (1995) claim that, depending on the criteria involved, 'cures' from using psychotherapy range from 30 to 60 per cent. The concept of 'cure' is, however, inappropriate, and Bolger (1989) makes the point that much of the evaluative research is based on the medical model of problem behaviour that assumes that a psychological disorder follows a course similar to that of a physical disease.	It is now generally accepted that there are methodological difficulties in evaluating the effectiveness of psychodynamic therapy. Psychotherapy usually spans several years and the point at which it is assessed may be crucial to a measurement of efficacy. Corsini and Wedding (1995) also explain that there are too many variables involved to enable a controlled and statistically valid outcome study. Comparisons may be made between symptoms at the beginning and end of treatment, but during the course of therapy, other complications may arise as a direct result of insight during therapy. Because treatment is over such a long period, there may also be other factors occurring in the client's life during the course of therapy which impact upon the outcome.	Effectiveness is a subjective concept, measurable only by the extent to which clients feel that their condition has improved. Freud himself was quite modest about the therapeutic claims of psychoanalysis (Freud 1935).

Table 10.2 *Issues in evaluating effectiveness of psychotherapy*

Effectiveness of psychotherapy

Read 'Critique of the effectiveness of psychotherapy' in box below.

Why do you think investigators come to such different conclusions when they are investigating issues such as the effectiveness of therapy?

Behavioural therapies

Lewinsohn (1974) developed a **behavioural therapy** for depression based on helping clients to start taking up pleasurable activities again and to develop improved social skills. The therapist discusses various activities that the client has found pleasurable in the past and sets up an action plan for trying them again. The therapist then makes sure that any positive behaviours are rewarded while negative behaviours are ignored. Therapists often recruit other family members into the treatment

Critique of the effectiveness of psychotherapy

Eysenck (1952) reviewed two outcome studies, incorporating waiting-list controls, which showed that 66 per cent of the control group improved spontaneously, whereas only 44 per cent of psychoanalysis patients improved. He concluded that psychoanalysis did not work.

However, not everyone agreed with Eysenck's conclusions. In a review of the original data, Bergin (1971) reported that patients in one of the control groups were in fact hospitalized and those in the other group were being treated by their GP. He also found that by selecting different outcome criteria, improvement in the psychoanalysis group increased to 83 per cent and

the control groups dropped to 30 per cent.

Eysenck, however, was still defending his attack on psychotherapy in an interview in 1996 with Colin Feltham at Sheffield Hallam University (Feltham 1996). Eysenck referred to a meta-analysis published in 1991 (40 years after his initial indictment) conducted by Svartberg and Stiles. (Meta-analysis is a statistical technique for combining the data from a number of experiments.) In 19 studies comparing psychoanalysis with no treatment, no difference was found in outcome one year after the end of treatment. Eysenck said: 'Clearly there was no evidence that psychoanalysis or psychotherapy did any good'.

Research support for psychotherapy

Key Research: Thase et al. (1997), and Mufson et al. (1999)

A meta-analysis of six studies with a total of 595 patients diagnosed with major depressive disorder (MDD) was conducted by Thase *et al.* (1997). They compared the effectiveness of psychotherapy combined with antidepressants with psychotherapy alone. They reported that, over a 12-week period:

- With less severe patients, there was no significant difference in the outcome of psychotherapy either with or without additional medication, indicating that improvement was due to psychotherapy alone.

- However, with more severe patients, the combined psychotherapy and medication patients showed a much greater improvement than with psychotherapy alone (43 per cent compared with 25 per cent). This suggests that if the disorder is more severe, it is advisable to combine medication with therapy.

Mufson *et al.* (1999) conducted a 12-week clinical trial with 48 adolescents, aged between 12 and 18 years, diagnosed with major depression, and randomly

assigned to a psychotherapy group or a control group (with no therapy, but fortnightly assessment of functioning). After 12 weeks there was:

- A notably greater decrease in depressive symptoms and an increase in social functioning and problem-solving skills in 75 per cent of the psychotherapy group compared with 46 per cent of the control group.

Evaluation

- Ethical issues are raised by Mufson *et al.*'s study concerning which participants were allocated to the treatment group and which to the control group. Look back to p.305 for more discussion on allocation to treatment groups.

- Both the above studies were conducted over a 12-week period. However, it may not be possible to test the effectiveness of psychotherapy over such a short period. Some later research using adolescents (e.g. Horowitz *et al.* 2007) has shown that intervention effects from psychotherapy were not maintained at six-month follow-up.

programme so that reinforcement can be consistently applied. An important part of the treatment programme is the learning of social skills. These include basic verbal and non-verbal skills as well as learning to recognize cues in other people and to respond more appropriately. The practice gained from homework tasks seems to be important in the success of this treatment approach.

Evaluation of behavioural therapies

- *Whole package needed* – Lewinsohn's programme seems to be effective provided it is delivered as a whole package. Isolated elements of the treatment regime, e.g. just re-engaging with previously enjoyed activities, do not seem to be effective.

- *Combination of therapies* – Many behavioural therapists including Lewinsohn have started to combine traditional behavioural techniques with more cognitive approaches (see next section).

Cognitive-behavioural therapies

Cognitive-behavioural therapies (CBT) began in the 1960s and there are now several different types. Albert Ellis (1962) founded 'rational-emotive therapy' (RET) which he subsequently renamed **'rational-emotive behaviour therapy' (REBT)** and Aaron Beck (1976) developed a cognitive therapy specifically for depression.

Aims of CBT

The aim of all types of CBT is to help the client to identify their negative, irrational thoughts and to replace these with more positive, rational ways of thinking. A therapy session includes both cognitive and behavioural elements, with homework between sessions.

- *Cognitive element* – The therapist encourages the client to become aware of beliefs that contribute to anxiety or depression, or are associated with a general dysfunction in daily life. This involves direct questioning, such as: 'Tell me what you think about ...'. The client's beliefs are treated as hypotheses and examined for validity. Diagrams (such as the ABC model (devised by Ellis 1991) in Fig. 10.6) can be used to help the client understand better where their faulty cognitions are leading them.

- *Behavioural element* – The therapist and client decide together how the client's beliefs can be reality-tested through experimentation, either as role-play or as homework assignments. The aim is that by actively testing out possibilities, clients will themselves come to recognize the consequences of their faulty cognitions. The therapist and client then work together to set new goals for the client in order that more realistic and rational beliefs are incorporated into ways of thinking. These are usually in graded stages of difficulty so that clients can build upon their own success.

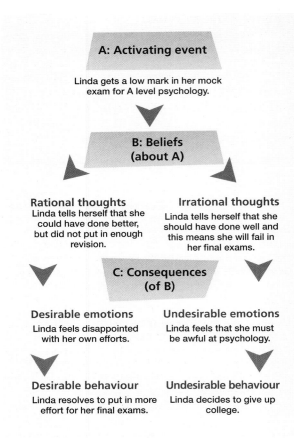

Figure 10.6 *An example of the ABC model in action*
Source: Adapted from Ellis (1991)

Rational-emotive behaviour therapy (Ellis 1962)

The rationale for CBT is that thoughts (cognitions) interact with, and have an enormous influence on, emotions and behaviour. When these thoughts are persistently negative and irrational, they can result in maladaptive behaviour. Ellis (1962) maintained that people can become so accustomed to their disturbed thoughts that this results in problems such as anxiety and depression. Ellis' ABC model illustrates how irrational, self-defeating thoughts can lead to maladaptive behaviour.

Rational-emotive behaviour therapy (REBT) can be effective in treating various mental disorders including depression. For example, Haaga and Davison (1989) found REBT to be effective for anger, aggression, depression and antisocial behaviour. Engels et al. (1993) examined quantitative data from 28 controlled studies which showed REBT to be superior to placebo and no treatment. A more recent appraisal by Haaga and Davison (1993) suggests that there are difficulties in evaluating the effectiveness of REBT because of the difficulty in defining and measuring 'irrational beliefs'. However, Beck's cognitive therapy was developed specifically to help people with depression and it is outlined next.

Cognitive (-behavioural) therapy (Beck 1976)

Beck's therapy is one of the most widely used therapies for depression. It aims to provide opportunities both inside and outside the therapy sessions that will change a client's negative talk to something more positive. During a therapy session a client's negative talk (i.e. their behaviour) is directly challenged with a view to changing the type of talk that is associated with destructive cognitions. For this reason, the therapy is often called a **cognitive-behavioural therapy** (CBT).

Beck's therapy involves four phases and is usually delivered over a period of 20 weeks:

- *Stage 1*: Clients are encouraged to draw up a schedule of activities and to become more active and confident.

- *Stage 2*: They are encouraged to recognize their automatic, negative thoughts (e.g. if I don't get A* grades I'll never go to university or get a good job) and to record them and bring them to the weekly CBT sessions. The therapist then helps them to test the reality of their thoughts (for example, by identifying people who have gone to university without getting A* grades)

- *Stage 3:* The therapist helps clients to recognize the underlying illogical thinking processes that produce negative thinking.

- *Stage 4:* The therapist helps clients to change their maladaptive attitudes, often by asking them to test them out in real-life situations. They are also encouraged to keep actively engaged in pleasurable activities.

Evaluation of cognitive-behavioural therapies

- *Clear goals* – Like the older behavioural therapies, cognitive-behavioural therapies are structured, with clear goals and measurable outcomes. They are increasingly becoming the most widely employed therapy by clinical psychologists in the National Health Service, not least because they are short term and economic.

- *Appeal of CBT* – CBT appeals to clients who find insight therapies (which delve into inner emotional conflicts) too threatening. Although CBT is criticized for ignoring the influence of unconscious dynamics and for minimizing the importance of past events, it does attempt to empower clients by educating them into self-help strategies. Despite this, some clients do become dependent upon their therapist.

- *Use and effectiveness of CBT* – CBT is thought to be particularly effective for depression and anxiety disorders, and sexual problems. A number of studies have compared this therapy with traditional antidepressant drugs in the treatment of major depression. Some have found CBT to be more effective (e.g. Seligman *et al.* 1979) whilst others have not. Most studies find both types of therapy equally effective although, of course, CBT has no physical side effects

and long-term follow-up studies have also shown that the relapse rate is lower in those who received CBT (Evans *et al.* 1992), (see 'Research on CBT and drug therapy' panel below). A study by Brent *et al.* (1997) with 107 adolescents diagnosed with major depression compared individual CBT, systematic behaviour family therapy and individual supportive therapy. They found CBT to be the most effective, with a more rapid and complete treatment response. Brent and colleagues felt that the rapidity of improvement was an important factor because a significant proportion of severely depressed adolescents commit suicide in their first episode of depression. They also view rapidity as an economic advantage for both patients and the health service.

- *Difficulty in evaluating therapies* – A difficulty in assessing the effectiveness of therapy for depression, according to Senra and Polaino (1998), is the measurement scale used to monitor the effects of treatment. They assessed 52 patients suffering from major depression with the Beck Depression Inventory, the Hamilton Rating Scale and the Zung Self-Rating Depression Scale (Beck *et al.* 1961, Hamilton 1960 and Zung 1965, respectively). They found different measures of improvement, depending on which scale they used, illustrating the difficulty of evaluating a therapy.

HOW SCIENCE WORKS

Research on CBT and drug therapy

A study by Jarrett *et al.* (1999) and Hollon *et al.* (1992)

A study by Jarrett *et al.* (1999) found CBT and MAOI antidepressant drugs to be equally effective with 108 patients with severe depression in a 10-week trial. Hollon *et al.* (1992) found no difference between CBT and treatment with tricyclics (antidepressant drugs) with 107 patients over a 12-week trial. They also found no difference between CBT alone and CBT combined with antidepressant drugs. Hollon and colleagues claimed that relapse often occurs when people cease medication; however, with CBT the effect is maintained beyond the termination of therapy. They point out, however, that only about 40 per cent of those who begin treatment – either drugs or psychological therapy – will complete it.

Evaluation

One of the difficulties with studies of this kind is that they are generally undertaken with small samples and over too short a period of time to assess the longer-term effectiveness. Another difficulty is that a control group (no treatment) is essential and these people often exert their right to withdraw in order to seek treatment themselves.

Psychosocial Therapy (Interpersonal psychotherapy – IPT)

One explanation of depression is that symptoms are triggered by social and cultural factors (see p.334). **Interpersonal psychotherapy (IPT)** was developed as a way of dealing with this kind of depression (Klerman *et al.* 1984). It integrates the psychodynamic perspective which emphasises childhood experiences and the cognitive-behavioural approach which focuses on current psychosocial stressors. The therapy usually involves weekly one-hour meetings, over a period of 20 weeks and maintains a focus on one to two key issues concerning interpersonal problems. Depression may not be caused by interpersonal events, but it often affects relationships and roles in those relationships. The precise focus of IPT is on interpersonal events (such as disputes and conflicts, interpersonal role transitions, complicated grief that goes beyond the normal bereavement period) that seem to be most important in the onset and/or maintenance of the depression. The first one to three sessions of IPT are usually devoted to assessment and identification of the specific interpersonal issue(s) that will be the focus of the remainder of the therapy.

Evaluation of IPT

- *Effectiveness* – IPT has been shown to be as effective as cognitive therapy i.e. the symptoms disappear in 50 to 60 per cent of patients who receive treatment (Weissman and Markowitz 2002). It has been shown to be effective in both adults and adolescents (Mufson 2004).

- *Appropriateness* – However, it is not suitable for all depressed people and works best where the depression is linked to social conflict or changes in career or social roles. It can be effective both in treating acute depression and in preventing relapse (Stuart and O'Hara 2002).

Activity — Advice from NICE on treating depression

The following is an extract taken from the website of Mind (The National Association for Mental Health).

'In December 2004, the National Institute for Health and Clinical Excellence (NICE) published guidelines on the treatment of depression. These suggest that antidepressants should not be used as a first treatment for mild to moderate depression, and that other treatments should be offered, including talking treatments and exercise regimes, which may be as effective as drug treatment. It also suggests "watchful waiting" – recognition of the fact that depression sometimes just goes away without any medical intervention and that active treatment may be unnecessary. The guidelines suggest that when an antidepressant is prescribed, it should be an SSRI because their side effects are better tolerated than those of the alternative antidepressants.'

- Using your knowledge of therapies for depression, consider to what extent you agree with this advice offered by NICE.

Which is the best therapy for depression?

No single treatment stands out as being the most effective therapy for all cases of depression. Symptoms of depression can vary tremendously depending on the individual and on the underlying causes of the disorder.

There is some evidence to suggest that different types of therapy can be equally effective. A large-scale, six-year investigation carried out by The National Institute of Mental Health (Elkin 1994), for example, compared groups of depressed patients allocated randomly to four different treatment groups:

- 16 weeks of Beck's cognitive therapy
- 16 weeks of interpersonal therapy
- 16 weeks of antidepressant drug imipramine
- 16 weeks of placebo.

The findings were that all three active treatments eliminated symptoms in 50 to 60 per cent of the participants opposed to only 29 per cent of the placebo group.

This study appears to show that there is not much to choose between the different types of therapy. However, it is thought that some depressed patients respond to certain treatments more than others. This means that the clinician needs to make a careful judgement of each individual patient before prescribing treatment. There is also some evidence that psychotherapy combined with drug therapy is slightly more effective that either therapy alone (Hollon *et al.* 2002). Many depressed patients receive a combination of therapies.

CHECK YOUR UNDERSTANDING

1. Identify the three main types of drug used to treat depression and outline some of the advantages and limitations of using antidepressants in the treatment of depression.

2. Give a brief evaluation of ECT as a treatment for depression. What new therapy might replace ECT?

3. Why is it particularly important to obtain informed consent from patients before they undertake any biological therapy?

4. What is the principal aim of psychoanalysis?

5. Describe three techniques used in psychoanalysis and summarize how effective psychoanalysis is for treating depression.

6. What are the goals of CBT?

7. Explain briefly how the ABC model (part of REBT) works.

8. Outline the procedures used in Beck's cognitive-behavioural therapy.

9. Outline two strengths and two weaknesses of CBT.

10. What is the principal focus of IPT and how effective is it?

Clinical characteristics (symptoms)

Clinical characteristics & issues of classification & diagnosis

A range of the following symptoms over a period of at least two weeks:

- Depressed mood
- Loss of interest in normally pleasurable activities
- Decreased energy/increased tiredness
- Loss of confidence/self-esteem
- Unreasonable feelings of guilt
- Recurrent thoughts of death and suicide
- Sleep disturbance
- Appetite disturbance
- Motor movement disturbance

Issues surrounding classification & diagnosis

Factors that affect the reliability and validity of classification and diagnosis:

- Different types of depression
- Validity of diagnostic categories
- Lack of objective criteria for confirming diagnosis
- Differential diagnosis
- Dual diagnosis
- Medicalization of a 'normal' state
- Cultural issues

Therapies for depression

Psychological therapies

Often used in conjunction with drug therapies

Psychodynamic therapy
(aims to uncover unconscious conflicts to gain insight into cause of depression)

Evaluation:

- Little convincing evidence to support this as effective therapy for depression

Behavioural approaches
(usually based on social skill training)

Evaluation:

- Can be useful in developing coping skills
- Seems to work best used alongside other therapies

Cognitive–behavioural therapy (CBT)
(aims to replace irrational thinking with more positive, rational ways of thinking)

Evaluation:

- Appeals to those who find insight therapies too threatening
- Evidence suggests that CBT is effective for depression
- Most effective when combined with drug treatment

Psychosocial therapy (e.g. interpersonal psychotherapy – IPT)
(used to treat depression caused by social and cultural factors)

Evaluation:

- Effective where depression is linked to social conflict

Biological therapies

- ECT sometimes used for severe depression particularly where there are suicidal intentions
- Medication (drugs) is main therapy
- Variety of antidepressant medication available:
  - MAOIs (e.g. Iproniazid)
  - TCAs (e.g. Tofranil)
  - SSRIs (e.g. Prozac)
- Most drugs work by influencing the availability of serotonin and noradrenaline in the brain and nervous system

Evaluation:

- Drugs are effective in reducing symptoms for many people with depression
- They do not work for everyone
- All antidepressant medication can produce side effects, particularly after long-term use
- ECT can be effective in severe cases, but can have side effects. TMS (magnetic therapy) may be a safer alternative

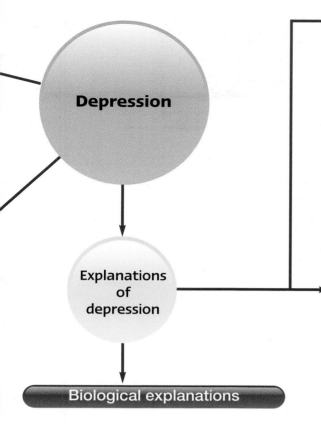

Diathesis-stress explanation

- Interaction between biological and environmental factors – individuals have genetic vulnerability but only develop depression in the presence of triggering environmental factors
- Predictors of adult depression include negative early life experiences, cognitive-personality characteristics (e.g. need for control)
- Women are twice as likely as men to be diagnosed with depression
- Cultural factors, e.g. people from ethnic minorities have higher levels of depression

Depression

Explanations of depression

Psychological explanations

Psychodynamic
(linked to loss of a loved one or symbolic loss)

Evaluation:

- Difficult to test the theory empirically
- Little evidence for the idea of 'anger turned inwards'
- Some evidence for loss of a parent in childhood pre-disposing to later depression, but many other variables could contribute

Behavioural (learned behaviour)

Evaluation:

- Some support for learned helplessness model but findings inconsistent
- Insufficient account taken of cognitive processes

Cognitive (e.g. faulty thinking patterns)

- Hopelessness theory – depression caused by maladaptive attributions (Abramson *et al.*)
- Cognitive triad, negative self-schemas and cognitive distortions (Beck)

Evaluation:

- Some evidence that depressed people have negative thinking patterns
- Gives rise to effective therapy
- Difficult to disentangle cause and effect

Biological explanations

Genes

Evaluation:

- Support from family, twin and adoption studies
- 100% concordance not demonstrated
- Difficult to disentangle effects of environment

Biochemical factors

- Neurotransmitters: serotonin and noradrenaline
- Hormones in post-natal, premenstrual and menopausal depression
- Hormone melatonin in SAD

Evaluation:

- Support from research, e.g. with PET scans
- Effective antidepressant medication
- Difficult to distinguish cause and effect

Neuroanatomical factors

Evaluation:

- Research support, e.g. from fMRI scans
- Difficult to distinguish cause and effect
- Structural abnormalities not found in all patients

CHAPTER **11A**

Claire Meldrum
Jane Willson

Phobic disorders

EXPLAINING THE SPECIFICATION

Specification content	The specification explained
Psychopathology: phobic disorders as chosen disorder	If you have chosen phobic disorders as the disorder you wish to study, you need to be able to:
Clinical characteristics and issues of classification and diagnosis of phobic disorders (Topic 1)	In this part of the specification you should be familiar with the key features of clinical characteristics and issues of classification and diagnosis. To do this, you need to be able to:
Clinical characteristics of phobic disorders	■ Outline the main clinical characteristics (symptoms) of phobic disorders. The chapter outlines specific phobia, social phobia and agoraphobia.
Issues surrounding the classification and diagnosis of phobic disorders, including reliability and validity	■ Describe and evaluate **at least two** issues (potential problems) in classifying or diagnosing phobic disorders. If you concentrate on only two issues, these must be reliability and validity.
Explanations of phobic disorders (Topic 2)	In this part of the specification you should be familiar with the explanations of phobic disorders. To do this, you need to be able to:
Biological explanations of phobic disorders, for example, genetics, biochemistry	■ Describe and evaluate **at least two** biological explanations of phobic disorders. To do this you will need to discuss relevant research findings. Genetics and biochemistry are suggested as examples of explanations that you might study but neither of these is specified as compulsory. The chapter discusses genetics, and biochemical and neuroanatomical explanations.
Psychological explanations of phobic disorders, for example, behavioural, cognitive, psychodynamic and socio-cultural	■ Describe and evaluate **at least two** psychological explanations of phobic disorders. To do this you will need to discuss relevant research findings. Four examples of explanations are suggested – behavioural, cognitive, psychodynamic and socio-cultural – but none of these is specified as compulsory. The chapter discusses the psychological explanations that have most commonly been used to explain phobic disorders: psychodynamic, behavioural and cognitive-behavioural explanations and the diathesis-stress model.
Therapies for phobic disorders (Topic 3)	In this part of the specification you should be familiar with the key features of therapies for phobic dosorders. To do this, you need to be able to:
Biological therapies for phobic disorders including their evaluation in terms of appropriateness and effectiveness	■ Describe and evaluate **at least two** biological treatments for phobic disorders. Your evaluations should consider how appropriate (suitable) and how effective (successful) the treatments are. To do this you will need to discuss relevant research findings. The chapter discusses two drug therapies (the most common biological treatments for phobic disorders) – anti-anxiety drugs and antidepressant drugs.

Specification content	The specification explained
Psychological therapies for phobic disorders, for example, behavioural, psychodynamic, and cognitive-behavioural, including their evaluation in terms of appropriateness and effectiveness	■ Describe and evaluate **at least two** psychological treatments for phobic disorders. You need to discuss how appropriate and effective the treatments are. To do this you will need to discuss relevant research findings. The chapter discusses behavioural, cognitive-behavioural and psychodynamic therapies.

Before you begin reading about phobic disorders, it is essential that you have read the Introduction to psychopathology on pp. 300–305.

Introduction

Phobic disorders (phobias) come under the general diagnostic category of anxiety disorders. **Anxiety disorders** are the most common type of mental disorder and, according to the American Psychological Association, the lifetime risk of developing an anxiety disorder is between 10 and 14 per cent. The major classification systems (e.g. DSM and ICD, see p.301 in Introduction to Psychopathology) list a number of anxiety disorders which differ from one another in significant ways, e.g. in the developmental timing of their first appearance, the types of stimuli that provoke anxiety, the pervasiveness of the anxiety, the way it manifests itself and the role of identifiable factors in the underlying cause. However, all anxiety disorders have certain characteristics in common:

■ high levels of anxiety

■ considerable emotional distress

■ avoidance behaviour.

In this chapter we shall look at three phobic anxiety disorders (specific phobia, social phobia and agoraphobia). Obsessive-compulsive disorder (OCD), another type of anxiety disorder, is discussed in Chapter 11b. Before reading further, try the Activity, 'Fear and anxiety'.

Activity — Fear and anxiety

Discuss the following with a few of your fellow psychology students:

1 some things that make you afraid (i.e. experience real fear)

2 some things that make you anxious

3 whether the things you identified as fearful are the same as, or different from, those that cause you anxiety

4 what you think the difference is between fear and anxiety.

Fear and anxiety: similarities and differences

The term 'anxiety' refers to a complex set of reactions in response to some real or imagined threat. Emotionally, physiologically and behaviourally, anxiety is the same as fear. There is, however, a difference in the way the two terms are used:

■ The term '*anxiety*' is used to describe the response to an unclear or diffuse source of danger.

■ The term '*fear*', on the other hand, is used mainly to describe the reaction to specific objects or situations.

The distinction between fear and anxiety, however, is not always clear cut, and the terms are often used interchangeably. We react to fearful situations on several levels:

■ *Emotionally* – We experience a sense of panic and alarm. If we experience fear over a long period of time, we also feel drained and overwhelmed.

■ *Cognitively* – We worry about what will happen and often anticipate dire consequences.

■ *Physiologically* – We show many involuntary physiological responses, such as a dry mouth, palpitations, tensed muscles, perspiration.

■ *Behaviourally* – We show a tendency either to freeze or to run away.

These are perfectly normal reactions in the face of a threatening stimulus. They are helpful to us because they allow us to anticipate impending danger and take action to deal with it. Such reactions only lead to anxiety disorders when they are out of all proportion to the threat posed or when they exist in the absence of any obvious danger.

Phobias (classified as anxiety disorders in DSM-IV TR and ICD-10) are defined as extreme fears out of all proportion to the actual danger posed by a particular object or situation. In Topic 1, we begin by considering the characteristics of phobic disorders and the issues that surround their classification and diagnosis. In Topics 2 and 3, we shall look at explanations and therapies for phobic disorders.

Psychology in context — School phobia

The following account is adapted from an article in *The Observer* in September (2008), which reported on the increasing problem of 'school phobia'. To read the complete article, go to:
www.guardian.co.uk/education/2008/sep/07/schools.youngpeople

"For tens of thousands of English and Welsh schoolchildren the start of the new school term … will be so traumatic that it will make them ill. Doctors and psychologists are seeing a significant increase in the numbers of children suffering from a condition dubbed 'school phobia'.

School phobia is already estimated to affect one in every 20 children and now experts believe the trend towards bigger schools in the UK, an increase in childhood obesity and bullying, is making the medically recognized condition far worse. The condition can, if left untreated, bring on physical symptoms such as vomiting, headaches, fatigue and panic attacks and sufferers run the risk of carrying anxiety phobias into adulthood.

Mark, 14, developed school phobia when he moved from his Wiltshire primary school into a large London suburban comprehensive. It took 18 months for him to be diagnosed, during which time his mother was threatened with being taken to court over his 'truancy'.

Dr Nigel Blagg, a psychologist and author of School Phobia and its Treatment, said: 'The saddest thing about children going undiagnosed was that the phobia can lead to lifelong problems. All the evidence shows that the best way to deal with this is to get the child back to school and routine as quickly as is possible.'

1 Do you think that school phobia is a valid diagnosis?

2 What do you think are the differences between school phobia and truancy?

3 Why do you think school phobia might be on the increase in the UK?

Clinical characteristics of phobic disorders

Phobias are the most common of all anxiety disorders. We all have aversions (strong dislikes, repugnance) to certain things or situations, which can make us feel a little squeamish or anxious – or even fearful – when we encounter them. This is quite normal. It is only when the aversion becomes an excessive and unreasonable fear that it is classified as a phobia. Even then, many people adapt their life in order to avoid or cope with their extreme fears. However, when they cannot do this, the fear or anxiety can become so severe that it interferes with everyday life. It is only then that the fear is classified as a mental disorder. People with phobias become extremely anxious just thinking about the feared object or situation. Most people with phobias recognize that their fear reaction is extreme and irrational, but this does not help them to overcome it.

Both DSM-IV-TR and ICD-10 list three main types of phobic anxiety disorders:

- specific phobia (e.g. fear of cats)

- social phobia (fear of social or performance situations)

- agoraphobia (fear of public places, with panic disorder and without panic disorder).

Onset appears to be earliest for animal phobias (a type of specific phobia), followed by other specific phobias and social phobia, with the latest onset being for agoraphobia (Kendler *et al.* 1992a).

Specific phobias

A **specific phobia** is a persistent, irrational fear of a specific object or situation (excluding social phobia and agoraphobia).

- *Prevalence* – About 12 per cent of individuals develop a specific phobia at some time in their lives. The number of people with a specific phobia at any one time is about eight per cent (Kessler *et al.* 2005). Specific phobia is the most common mental disorder in women and the second most common in men (second only to substance-related disorders).

- *More common in women* – Women are usually twice as likely to develop specific phobias as men, except in the case of blood-injection type phobias, where both men and women are equally vulnerable (Kaplan and Sadock 1997).

- *Fear response* – These fears relate to a specific object or situation. When the person encounters the feared object or situation, they show an immediate fear response (e.g. quickened breathing, heart beating faster, trembling and feeling nauseous). They will often anticipate situations where the phobic object might be encountered and will go to great lengths to avoid it.

- *Recognize fears are irrational* – People with specific phobias usually recognize that their fears are irrational and exaggerated, but this does not help them to deal with their anxiety.

Specific phobias are often given a Greek prefix to indicate the target of the phobia, e.g. arachnophobia (fear of spiders), acrophobia (fear of heights). Do not worry if you cannot remember these long names, many clinicians and researchers now adopt the simpler English terms.

Fear of spiders (arachnophobia), is a widespread phobia, more common in females than males.

Diagnostic criteria for specific phobias
The diagnostic criteria for specific phobia are similar in DSM-IV-TR and ICD-10:

- Marked and persistent fear that is excessive or unreasonable, cued by the presence of or anticipation of a specific object or situation.

- Exposure to phobic stimulus almost invariably provokes an immediate anxiety response (this may be in the form of a panic attack). Note: in children, anxiety might be expressed by crying, tantrums, freezing or clinging.

- The person recognizes the fear is excessive or unreasonable. Note: not always in children.

- The phobic situation(s) is avoided or else endured with intense anxiety or distress.

- The avoidance, anticipation or distress interferes significantly with the person's routine functioning.

- In individuals under the age of 18 years, the duration is of at least 6 months.

- The anxiety, panic attacks or phobic avoidance are not better accounted for by another mental disorder.

DSM also includes a list of distinctive types of specific phobia:

- animal type (e.g. horses, dogs, snakes)

- natural environment type (e.g. heights, thunderstorms, water)

- blood-injection types (i.e. fear of blood or syringes)

- situational type (e.g. plane, lifts, enclosed spaces)

- other type (e.g. phobic avoidance of situations that might lead to choking, vomiting or contracting an illness).

Theoretically, it is possible to develop a phobia to almost anything. However, some phobias are more common than

others and some occur in response to modern living. For example, with the increase in air travel, fear of flying is becoming one of the most widespread phobias, and many airlines now offer therapy programmes based on systematic desensitization (see p.380). Fear of dentists is also relatively common, and the specific focus of illness phobia often relates to current health scares, e.g. AIDS phobia.

Specific phobias that begin in childhood often disappear without treatment. However, if they persist into or begin in adulthood, they usually only disappear in response to some kind of therapeutic intervention.

Social phobia
A social phobia (sometimes also called social anxiety disorder) is an excessive and persistent fear of particular social situations:

- *Prevalence* – Social phobia often begins in late childhood and can continue into adulthood. It is estimated that about 12 per cent of the population in Western countries will develop social phobia at some time in their lifetime, and women are more susceptible than men by a ratio of 3:2 (Kessler *et al.* 2005).

- *Co-morbidity* – Social phobia is frequently co-morbid with (occurs alongside) other mental disorders, particularly depression and/or substance abuse.

- *More than shyness* – Many people are shy and slightly uneasy in social situations, but someone with a social phobia is afraid of particular activities performed in public, such as eating in public or going into a public lavatory. It has been suggested that social phobia is merely a case of excessive shyness, but this is not so. The difference between social phobia and shyness lies in the severe effects social phobia can have on everyday functioning. The lives of people with social phobia are dictated by the need either to avoid certain situations or to endure them with extreme anxiety. Social phobia disrupts normal life, interfering with career or social relationships. For example, a worker can turn down a job promotion because he can't give public presentations. The dread of a social event can begin weeks in advance, and symptoms can be quite debilitating.

Many actors who perform in public have admitted to being excessively shy. However, their shyness does not usually make them avoid situations such as eating in public.

Difference from specific phobias
Social phobia is different from specific phobias in that the phobic object is not the situation *per se*, i.e. being in a restaurant or a public lavatory; the fear is rather of the possibility of embarrassment or humiliation in front of other people (such as showing clear signs of anxiety, e.g. blushing, hand tremor, voice shaking).

Diagnostic criteria for social phobia

The DSM and ICD criteria for social phobia are similar to those for specific phobia (see p.301). The main difference from the specific phobia criteria is in the first point:

- A marked and persistent fear of one or more social or performance situations in which the person is exposed to unfamiliar people or to possible scrutiny by others. The individual fears that he or she will act in a way (or show anxiety symptoms) that will be humiliating or embarrassing. Note: in children, there must be evidence of capacity for age-appropriate social relationships with familiar people and the anxiety must occur in peer settings, not just in interactions with adults.

Case study of a phobia

Eddie had always been terrified of travelling in cars and had managed to avoid this for most of her life by using buses or trains. For some reason, she was not afraid to travel by these methods. Eddie finished her degree and got a good job with an advertising agency. They told her she would need to drive in order to visit clients and would have access to the pool car. Eddie knew she would have to overcome her fear and arranged driving lessons. To her surprise she did not find this as frightening as she had expected and passed on the second attempt. The first time she used the pool car, however, she tried to reverse out of a parking space and hit the adjacent car, doing considerable damage to both cars. The car park attendant told her the other car belonged to the Managing Director. Eddie lost her nerve and went straight home, resigning from her job immediately. After that Eddie stayed at home, refusing to go out socially or to find another job, even one which did not involve driving. Eddie was referred for treatment by her general practitioner (GP). She knew that her recent anxiety was related to the car accident, but she had no idea why she had been terrified of cars since she was a young child. She could not recall a car accident in her past.

STRETCH AND CHALLENGE

Activity ICD and DSM

You might like to look at the relevant pages for anxiety disorders in the ICD and DSM manuals yourself. These are large and complex documents but you could look at the relevant sections on anxiety disorders on the websites and compare them:

www.who.int/classifications/icd/en/

www.apa.org/

Agoraphobia

Agoraphobia is defined in similar ways in both DSM-IV and ICD-10. The DSM-IV-TR defines agoraphobia as 'Anxiety about being in places or situations from which escape might be difficult (or embarrassing) or in which help may not be available in the event of having an unexpected or situationally predisposed panic attack or panic-like symptoms'(APA, 2000). These places are often public places, and DSM uses examples of being outside the home alone, being in a crowd, standing in a line, being on a bridge, and travelling in a bus, train, or automobile. The ICD-10 definition is similar, but states that the anxiety must be restricted to two out of four specific situations – crowds, public places, travelling alone, or travelling away from home. Both classification systems state avoidance of the feared situation as a *diagnostic criterion*.

Agoraphobia is especially debilitating because it can result in people being afraid to go out of their home, meaning they are unable to go to work or even shop for provisions. For these reasons it is thought to be the most serious of all phobias.

- *Agoraphobia with panic disorder* – Many people with agoraphobia are also prone to panic attacks when they venture into public places. Agoraphobia is closely associated with 'panic disorder', as people with panic disorder fear public places because they are likely to induce a panic attack. Indeed, DSM-IV-TR classifies two types of panic disorder: with and without agoraphobia. However, agoraphobia can continue even if the person has not had a panic attack in years.

- *Prevalence* – About 2.7 per cent of the population suffer from panic disorder with agoraphobia in any one year and the lifetime risk of developing agoraphobia is about five per cent (Kessler *et al.* 2005).

- *Onset* – Onset of agoraphobia is generally in early adulthood and is twice as likely in females as in males. People diagnosed with agoraphobia can be clingy and dependent and have often experienced separation anxiety in childhood (Gittelman and Klein 1984). See Early Social Development (pp.129–32) in *Psychology AS for AQA A*.

Agoraphobia is a debilitating condition that makes people avoid public places.

Difference from specific and social phobias

Agoraphobia differs from specific phobias in that it is not the shop or the workplace itself that induces the fear reaction; the fear is focused on the inability to escape from the situation. It differs from social phobias in that it is not fear of the scrutiny of other people that provokes anxiety; the fear is of having a panic attack, losing control and being unable to escape (see panel on p.367).

Activity A fear of cars

Read the case study of a phobia and discuss with a small group of fellow psychology students:

- what type(s) of phobia Eddie is suffering from
- possible reasons for her fear of cars since her childhood
- ideas as to how Eddie could be helped to overcome her phobia.

Keep a note of your ideas so that you can compare them with the explanations and therapies for phobias discussed later in the chapter.

Issues of classification and diagnosis of phobic disorders

Look back to the section on classification and diagnosis in the Introduction to Psychopathology on p.301. You will find that some of the general points there (e.g. about reliability and validity) are relevant to phobias.

A question of validity

Medicalization of normal human behaviour

Fear is a normal adaptive response. Phobias should only be diagnosed, therefore, in people who meet the stringent requirements of the DSM or ICD criteria if the diagnosis is to be valid. Critics of the medical model of mental disorder object to the idea that normal human emotions (such as fear) and behaviours (such as avoidance) are 'medicalized' (i.e. seen as 'medical' problems that require fixing).

Differences in the classification systems

The two main classification systems, DSM-IV-TR and ICD-10, list very similar criteria for phobias. The main difference between them is the way in which they classify agoraphobia. In DSM, cases with more than four panic attacks (see panel, 'Panic attacks') in four weeks are classified, not as agoraphobia but as panic disorder with secondary agoraphobic symptoms. In ICD, there is a requirement for at least two definitive anxiety symptoms to be present before panic disorder with secondary agoraphobic symptoms is diagnosed.

Reliability of diagnosis

The overlap between agoraphobia and panic disorder highlights a problem for diagnosing phobic disorders:

- *Specific phobias* – As far as specific phobias are concerned, there is usually little difficulty in making a diagnosis. Occasionally, a person with obsessive disorder (see Chapter 11b) first shows symptoms of fear and avoidance of objects such as knives. Clinicians need to take a careful history and to carry out a detailed examination of the person's mental state to see if there are any obsessional thoughts that underlie the fear, e.g. thoughts about killing someone.

Panic attacks

During a panic attack a person may experience palpitations, chest pains and dizziness.

A panic attack is a recurrent, short bout of panic that occurs without warning, reaches a peak in about 10 minutes and then gradually subsides. Panic attacks can occur several times in a week or, in extreme cases, even in a day.

A number of symptoms are experienced during a panic attack, such as heart palpitations, chest pains, trembling, tingling in the hands and feet, shortness of breath, sweating, dizziness, faintness and choking sensations.

Many people report that they feel they 'are going mad', 'are going to die' or 'are going to lose control'. People with agoraphobia often fear going out in case they have a panic attack and have no means of escape.

- *Social phobias and shyness* – As discussed earlier, social phobias need to be distinguished from normal shyness. Like many mental illnesses that have things in common with natural reactions (e.g. anxiety), there is a continuum, from being slightly shy and retiring through to a totally non-functioning social phobia. At some point along that continuum – and that point varies with the individual – simple shyness turns into a diagnosable disorder. So a person can be severely shy, but as long as it is not impairing their life, they would probably not be diagnosed with social phobia. Another person, however, may be less shy but diagnosable because their life has become greatly affected by their shyness. It is important to note that some people with social phobia do not give the outward impression of being shy. They can be completely at ease with people most of the time, but particular situations, such as using a public toilet or giving a presentation, can cause them intense anxiety.

- *Generalized and non-generalized social phobia* – A related issue is the possibility that there are two types of social phobia: generalized where the individual fears a wide variety of social situations; non-generalized where the individual has one particular fear, e.g. speaking in public, but otherwise is socially competent. There is some support from genetic studies for this distinction (see p.369).

- *Shared characteristics* – Social phobia shares some common characteristics with other mental disorders as well. For example, people with schizophrenia sometimes avoid social situations and show extreme anxiety. The main difference is that people with social phobia understand that their behaviour is irrational but people with schizophrenia do not. There is also considerable overlap with other anxiety disorders. Social phobia is present in 30 to 50 per cent of individuals with panic disorder (Magee *et al.*1996).

Dual diagnosis

Phobias often occur alongside other mental disorders. This is called co-morbidity. For example, social phobia frequently co-exists with depression, presenting clinicians with the diagnostic challenge of distinguishing social withdrawal due to depression from fearful social avoidance. It has been suggested that social phobia can actually be a predictor of depression and that it not only increases the risk of developing depression, but also increases the severity of the symptoms. This has implications for treatment. If social phobia can be accurately diagnosed and treated at an early stage, it might prevent the onset of depression in some individuals (Kessler *et al.* 1999). Similarly, alcohol-related disorders occur twice as often in those affected by social phobia as in those without (Schneier *et al.* 1991). Social anxiety disorder usually precedes alcohol abuse, and about 20 per cent of those treated for alcohol-related disorders have social phobia (Randall *et al.* 2001). If undetected, the risk of rapid relapse is high, since psychosocial treatments, which are often a central aspect of treating alcohol abuse, may be difficult or impossible to attend. Importantly, when the phobia is treated in alcohol abusers, both social anxiety and alcohol use appear to improve.

Who is diagnosed?

However, there are probably many people in the community who meet the diagnostic criteria for a phobia but who do not come forward for treatment because they recognize the irrationality of their behaviour. Some people may recognize that they have a problem, wish for help but do not want to be stigmatized with a mental illness label. Other people manage their lives so that they can avoid the feared object without experiencing major disruption in their lives. For example, if someone with an obvious phobia of snakes lives, for instance, in London, the chances of coming into contact with a snake are pretty limited. A person with a phobia of pigeons, on the other hand, would run the constant risk of seeing them and so experience much more disruption to their daily life.

Cultural differences

Phobias sometimes present (are exhibited) in ways that reflect the cultural background of the individual. For example, there is a condition found in the Inuit population called kayak angst. This is a feeling of panic associated with being out alone in a kayak in Arctic conditions. It seems to be a variation on agoraphobia. In Japan, there is a variation on social phobia called taijin kyofusho (TKS). This differs from a Western diagnosis of social phobia in that the anxiety is focused on the shame associated with offending or harming other people in social situations. This reflects the Japanese cultural norm of pronounced politeness towards others (Kirmayer 1991). According to Huffman (2002) the difference between Western social phobias and TKS exemplifies how 'individualistic cultures (like ours) emphasize the individual, whereas collectivist cultures (like Japan) focus on others'.

Activity | **Characteristics of phobic disorders**

Practise writing a concise outline of the main characteristics of phobic disorders – something worth about 5 marks in an exam. Look through Topic 1 and select what you think are the relevant points. Once you have made your selection, you should take no more than 5 or 6 minutes to write your outline.

Useful tips are given in the answer section at the end of the book. ▶

CHECK YOUR UNDERSTANDING

Check your understanding of characteristics of phobic disorders and issues surrounding the classification and diagnosis of phobic disorders. Try to do this from memory. You can check your answers by looking back through Topic 1.

1 What is the difference between anxiety and fear?

2 What characteristics are shared by all anxiety disorders?

3 What is meant by a specific phobia?

4 For which type of specific phobia are males and females equally vulnerable?

5 Which type of phobia is considered to be the most serious and why?

6 How does social phobia differ from agoraphobia?

7 How can social phobia be distinguished from normal shyness?

8 What is meant by co-morbidity?

9 What diagnostic challenges do clinicians face when a patient shows symptoms of both social phobia and depression?

10 Why is it important to make an early diagnosis of social phobia?

Psychology in context

Needle phobia

Some objects are much more likely to elicit a phobic response than others. Fear of needles/injections has recently been acknowledged as a genuine phobia and is included in the blood/injection/injury category in DSM-IV (see p.303). Needle phobia is not a transient fear and it is not confined to children. It is difficult to obtain precise statistics, but it has been estimated to affect between about 5 and 20 per cent of the population. People with needle phobia are reluctant to go to see doctors or to visit hospitals for fear of routine needle procedures. Needle phobia can have important consequences: fear of blood testing or immunization can deter people from travelling or, in some cases, from applying for immigration or employment; some women choose not to have children because they fear that they will have to have blood tests during pregnancy. There have even been cases where people involved in accidents have been charged by police for failing to provide blood samples.

The physiological reaction to the feared object (the needle) is different from that of other types of phobic reaction. In most phobias, exposure to the feared object increases heart rate and blood pressure. In needle phobia, after this initial reaction, blood pressure drops and heart rate declines rapidly. This can lead to pallor, fainting and, in some reported cases, death. It is thought that there is a strong genetic component in needle phobia, although environmental factors are also believed to play a part (Hamilton 1995).

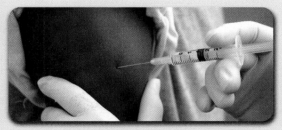

Fear of needles can deter people from being immunized.

1 Why do you think that needle phobia has only been recognized within the last 20 years?

2 How do you think needle phobia differs from other types of phobia?

3 Why is it important to find out what causes people to become needle phobic?

All the models of psychopathology which you looked at on your AS course offer explanations for phobias. There are slightly different explanations depending on the type of phobia. In exam questions about explanations of phobic disorders, you can take a broad, overarching approach looking at phobias in general, or you can discuss the different types of phobia.

> **IDA** **Nature–nurture debate and phobic disorders**
>
> The question as to whether phobic disorders arise from biological or environmental factors is a good example of the nature–nurture debate in psychology. People who support the nurture argument believe that all behaviours, including abnormal behaviours, are learned or acquired through interaction with the environment. People who support the 'nature' argument believe that many of our characteristics are 'wired-in' or innate. In other words, we are genetically determined to behave in certain ways and to develop certain disorders.
>
> In the field of psychopathology, few people embrace either of these extreme views. It is now fairly widely accepted that disorders such as phobias come about as a result of a combination of a variety of biological and environmental factors.

Biological explanations of phobic disorders

Biological explanations of phobias (and other anxiety disorders) include the following propositions:

- We have an evolutionary predisposition to fear what posed a danger to our ancestors.

- Some of us inherit a (genetic) predisposition to become anxious.

- Anxiety is caused by disrupted biochemistry or other abnormal brain activity.

In the following section, we shall consider genetic, biochemical and neuroanatomical explanations. We shall return to the evolutionary explanation for phobias when we consider preparedness theory (a modification, based on evolutionary theory, of the behavioural explanation) on p.374. Note, however, that preparedness theory also qualifies as a biological explanation.

Genetic explanation

Fear and anxiety have evolutionary advantages for survival because they trigger our 'fight-or-flight' mechanisms, i.e. the release of certain brain chemicals which give us a spurt of energy in threatening or dangerous situations either to attack or to escape faster. We know, therefore, that fear and anxiety are part of the genetic make-up of many species, including humans. However, not all humans develop such extreme fears that they become phobias, and most phobias are related to things which are not potentially harmful. Genetic research, therefore, is attempting to establish whether there is a familial genetic link, i.e. whether the tendency to develop phobias is hereditary. Research into phobias has focused mainly on:

- *family studies* – with first-degree relatives (parents, children, siblings) and, in a few cases, with second-degree relatives (aunts, uncles, nieces, nephews)

- *twin studies* – a small number, but almost no adoption studies.

Family history studies

First-degree relatives share an average of 50 per cent of their genes and second-degree relatives share approximately 25 per cent. To investigate genetic transmission of phobic disorders, studies compare rates of phobic disorder in relatives of diagnosed cases compared with relatives of controls (patients who do not have the disorder):

- A study by Solyom *et al.* (1974) of 47 phobic patients found a family history of psychiatric disorder in 45 per cent of the cases (30 per cent of their mothers had phobias), in contrast to only 19 per cent in families of a non-phobic control group of patients.

- Noyes *et al.* (1986) found a higher-than-normal rate of agoraphobia (11.6 per cent) and panic disorder (17.3 per cent) in first-degree relatives, using the family interview method. In this method, family members were interviewed to see if any of them reported symptoms of agoraphobia and panic disorder.

- Another family interview study by Fyer *et al.* (1990) of 49 first-degree relatives of people with a specific phobia found that 31 per cent of relatives were also diagnosed with phobias, but only two people had the same type.

- In another family study looking specifically at social phobia, Fyer *et al.* (1993) found that 16 per cent of first-degree relatives also had social phobia, compared with five per cent in a control group. Interestingly, they found that the disorder was more common in siblings than in parents.

- Mannuza *et al.* (1995) carried out an extension of Fyer *et al.*'s (1993) study but made a distinction between generalized and non-generalized social phobia. Some people, with a diagnosis of social phobia, have one particular focus of anxiety, e.g. eating in a restaurant or speaking to a group of people. Others have a more diffuse sense of anxiety generalized to a range of situations. Mannuza and colleagues found that 16 per cent of first-degree relatives also had social phobia in the generalized group, compared with only six per cent in the non-generalized group. This study is interesting because it suggests that the two types of social phobia are distinct and have different origins, i.e. generalized social phobia is more likely to have a genetic component, whereas non-generalized social phobia might have developed in response to some particular learning experience.

Twin studies

Twin studies offer another way of establishing genetic links, by comparing the difference in concordance rates (i.e. the likelihood of both twins being affected with the disorder) for identical (**MZ**) and fraternal (**DZ**) twins. Only MZ twins have identical genetic make-up.

There is some evidence that there is a genetic component in phobic disorders:

- A study conducted by Torgersen (1983) found 31 per cent concordance in 13 MZ twin pairs for panic disorder and agoraphobia versus zero concordance in 16 DZ twin pairs, although none of the concordant twins shared the same phobia.

- Kendler *et al.* (1992a) interviewed 722 female twins with a lifetime history of phobia. They found that MZ twins had significantly lower concordance rates for agoraphobia than DZ twins, which runs counter to the genetic hypothesis. The researchers suggested that this finding might reflect a protective effect of the close emotional bond between MZ twins. For specific phobias, they found that a shared environment, rather than shared genes, provided a more likely explanation.

- However, Kendler *et al.* (1992), in a study of over 2000 female twin pairs where one had been diagnosed with social phobia, found 24 per cent concordance for MZ twins compared with 15 per cent concordance in DZ pairs.

Evaluation of genetic explanation

- *Family studies* – Most of the family studies show that the relatives of those with phobias are more likely to suffer phobias themselves compared with relatives of non-phobic controls. However, there are methodological difficulties with family studies, the main problem being that in most instances family members share the same environment and could equally, therefore, have learned the behaviour. Furthermore, many family studies of phobic disorders use the family interview technique where family members provide self-reports. Data collected using the family interview method are vulnerable to memory lapses and distortions, as well as to demand characteristics such as trying to impress/please the interviewer.

- *Twin studies* – Twin studies offer more reliable data to test the genetic hypothesis, but unfortunately very few have been conducted. Adoption studies would provide more convincing evidence, but such studies have been sparse.

- *Role of genetic factors* – There is some evidence for genetic factors in the development of phobias. However, this is more likely to be a tendency to inherit a physiological predisposition towards anxiety in general, rather than to be a predisposition specific to phobias. Even if genetics do play a role, it is not clear exactly what is passed on genetically. One suggestion is that people at high risk for developing phobias inherit a genetic oversensitivity of the sympathetic nervous system. See pp.149–151 of *Psychology AS for AQA A* for more information on the role of the sympathetic nervous system in the body's response to stress.

Biochemical explanation

If genetic factors are important, they are likely to work by exerting an influence on the hardware of the brain. In other words, structural or biochemical abnormalities should be detectable in the brains of those diagnosed with phobic disorders.

The role of GABA

Research indicates that people who develop phobias are those who generally maintain a high level of physiological arousal which makes them particularly sensitive to their external environment. It has been suggested that phobias arise because of a dysfunction in the neurones that inhibit anxiety. The dysfunction is caused by low activity levels of the neurotransmitter GABA. **Neurotransmitters** are chemicals that act as messengers to transmit impulses from one nerve cell (neurone) to another across the synapse (the gap between adjacent nerve cells). GABA is a neurotransmitter that is automatically released in response to high levels of arousal. It binds to receptors on excited neurones, which underlie the experience of anxiety, and inhibits their activity. This produces a reduction of arousal levels and, therefore, a decrease in anxiety.

Evaluation of biochemical explanation

■ *Effect of benzodiazepines* – Evidence to support the GABA hypothesis comes from studies of people treated with benzodiazepines such as Valium and Librium. These drugs work like GABA by binding to neuroreceptors and decreasing arousal and anxiety. While there is some evidence for the anxiety-reducing effects of benzodiazepines in adults, the effects seem to be short term (Roy-Byrne and Cowley 1995). In children, benzodiazepines produce only marginally better relief than placebos (chemically inert substances) (Taylor 1994).

Neuroanatomical explanations

The amygdala is a part of the brain that is activated in response to threat. There is some evidence from **PET** scans that people with phobias have increased blood flow in the amygdala when they experience anticipatory anxiety, compared with controls (Tilfors *et al.* 2001). When people with a specific phobia were exposed to the phobic stimulus, they had a startled response and increased activity was observed in the amygdala and hippocampal areas (Frederickson and Furmark 2003).

Evaluation of neuroanatomical explanations

■ *Treatment with drugs* – Successful treatment with the drug citalopram or with cognitive behaviour therapy has been shown to decrease blood flow in the amygdala region (Furmark *et al.* 2002).

■ *Inconclusive evidence* – However, not all people with phobias show blood flow abnormalities and, in any case, it is not clear whether they are a causal factor or a result of phobic disorder.

Psychological explanations of phobic disorders

We now turn our attention to the psychological explanations that have been proposed for phobic disorders. You might find it helpful at this point to refresh your memory of psychological approaches to psychopathology in *Psychology AS for AQA A* (pp.227–36). In the following section, we shall look at psychodynamic, behavioural (including preparedness and social learning theory) and cognitive-behavioural explanations. We end with a consideration of the diathesis-stress model of phobias.

Psychodynamic explanations of phobic disorders

The **psychodynamic** explanation of phobic disorders is that the anxiety experienced about an object or situation is a displacement of internal underlying anxiety. In other words, the phobia is not related to the obvious external stimulus but to an internal source of anxiety. The psychoanalytic view is that phobias are associated with unconscious sexual fears (or 'id' impulses) and that they operate through the defence mechanisms of repression and displacement. The original source of the fear is repressed into the unconscious and the fear is then displaced onto some other person, object or situation. Thus the fear appears to be irrational because there is no conscious explanation for it.

Freud's theory of phobias

Freud's theory of phobias rests on his 1909 case study of a boy named Little Hans who developed a fear of horses (Freud 1909). Freud believed that the boy's phobia was directly related to his unconscious fear of his father, associated with the Oedipal phase. See Key research panel, 'The case study of Little Hans' on p.372.

Bowlby's theory of phobias

Bowlby (1973) suggested that phobias can be explained by his theory of 'attachment and separation' (see *Psychology AS for AQA A*, pp.120–2, 129–31). For instance, agoraphobia is said to relate to a fear of losing someone to whom the person has become attached (most often the mother). He maintained that the origins of phobic disorder lie with 'separation anxiety' in early childhood, particularly where parents are overprotective.

The case study of 'Little Hans'

Key research: Freud (1909)

Freud conducted a case study into a five-year-old child, referred to by the pseudonym 'Little Hans'. Freud had already written a paper on childhood sexuality in 1905 and used the case of Little Hans to support his theory. The parents of Little Hans were Freud's friends and were admirers of Freud's work. Freud only met Hans once for a therapeutic session during the two years of the case study and conducted his analysis through Hans's father, Max Graf. Graf carried out various analytical techniques under the supervision of Freud. Techniques included analysis of fantasies, observation and interpretation of Hans's general behaviour and fears, and analysis of his dreams. The details of the case study are complex and cannot be described at length here. If you want to find out more, there is a good, readable account in Gross (2003) *Key Studies in Psychology* (4th edn), Chapter 19.

The relevance of this case study for phobias is that Little Hans had developed a phobia of horses – he believed that a white horse would bite him and this made him fearful of going out on the streets in Vienna where he lived and where horses would have been seen everywhere. Freud interpreted Hans's phobia in terms of a displaced fear. He believed that Hans liked having his mother to himself and, therefore, at an unconscious level, felt hostility towards his father and wished that he would go away, or even die. He was also fearful of his father because of the father's power to punish – in particular, Little Hans feared that he would be castrated. Such fear and hostility was unacceptable to the child at a conscious level so he displaced his fear to horses (Freud suggested that the black skin around the horse's mouth and its blinkers represented his father's moustache and glasses.)

Graf explained this process to Little Hans and this appeared to help him recover from his phobia and to enjoy a fearless relationship with his father.

Evaluation

- *Limitations of this case study* – Case studies, such as this of 'Little Hans', provide rich and detailed information. However, they are open to various interpretations and cannot be generalized to other people. With respect to this particular case, Freud had already developed his ideas about child sexuality and so was looking for opportunities to support his theory. This could have led to researcher bias in his report of Little Hans's case. Furthermore, Freud gathered most of his information from second-hand accounts provided by Hans's father, who was already a follower of Freud's ideas and so unlikely to be entirely objective in his approach.

- *An alternative explanation* – A good scientific theory should be parsimonious; this means that it should explain all the known facts as simply and succinctly as possible. Freud's explanation of phobias lacks parsimony. Hans reported that he had seen a horse fall down in the street and start kicking its legs about. Hans was terrified, and it was after this incident that he became frightened of horses. The behavioural explanation therefore provides a much simpler account of his subsequent phobia (see p.373).

- *Spontaneous recovery* – Little Hans did recover from his phobia of horses. However, it is often the case that animal phobias, which are very common in childhood, disappear spontaneously without any therapeutic intervention.

Evaluation of psychodynamic explanations

- *Lack of empirical evidence* – Freud's theory about the origins of phobias is based almost entirely on case studies and there is no direct evidence to support his ideas. Despite the lack of empirical evidence to support Freud's theory directly, cross-cultural studies (e.g. Whiting 1966) do indicate that anxieties and phobias are more common in cultures characterized by strict upbringing and punishment.

- *No evidence of symptom substitution* – Psychodynamic theory predicts that a phobia can only be treated by uncovering the real, underlying fear – simply removing the displaced 'surface' fear will result in 'symptom substitution', i.e. the development of another displaced fear. However, when phobias are

removed, e.g. by behavioural treatments, there is no evidence of symptom substitution.

- *Inconsistent evidence for Bowlby's theory* – The evidence for Bowlby's theory with regard to phobias is inconsistent. For example, Parker (1979) found that being overprotected during early childhood correlated with the development of social phobias later on. On the other hand, the development of agoraphobia was found to correlate with having parents who had tended to display a lack of affection. Many studies indicate no relationship at all between parental rearing styles and types of anxiety disorders.

- *Links with early abuse* – There is some evidence of an association between childhood sexual and/or physical abuse and social phobia in adults, particularly women (Stein et al, 1996). However, the data are correlational and do not demonstrate cause and effect.

Behavioural explanations for phobic disorders

Behavioural explanations typically focus on classical and operant conditioning processes (learning theory) and learning through observation (social learning theory). A modified behavioural approach called preparedness theory is also considered below.

Learning theory

Learning theory proposes that, first, a panic attack occurs spontaneously in response, for instance, to being trapped in a lift. This results in an association being established between anxiety and that particular lift (*classical conditioning*). Subsequently, this anxiety becomes generalized to all lifts (*stimulus generalization*). Consequently, the person will actively avoid using lifts in the future. Avoidance of lifts is further reinforced by the reduction in anxiety experienced when the person adopts alternative strategies, such as using the stairs (*operant conditioning*).

Evaluation of the learning theory explanation

- *Support for conditioning explanation* – The conditioning explanation for phobias has been extensively researched and is supported by early studies on humans and animals (many of which would now be considered unethical). In a now classic study, Watson and Rayner (1920) apparently conditioned a 10-month-old boy, named Little Albert, into developing a phobia towards a white rat, using classical conditioning techniques. However, this study was very flawed and has been misreported in numerous text books (see Activity, 'Little Albert').

- *Support for behavioural explanations not replicated* – Although there has been considerable support for the behavioural explanation of phobias, more recent studies have failed to replicate their findings. Munjack (1984) studied a group of people with driving phobia and found that only 50 per cent of them had actually had a frightening experience in a car. In addition, 50 per cent of the control group in Munjack's study who did not have a phobia had had a frightening experience in a car, many of these involving an accident. The behavioural explanation cannot account for such individual differences.

Munjack (1984) found that only 50 per cent of people with a driving phobia had had a frightening experience in a car.

- *Selectivity of phobias* – If phobias are simply learned through classical conditioning, it should be possible to develop a phobia for virtually anything. In fact, phobias are quite selective. Try the Activity, 'Objects of phobia', then read the panel, 'Research into preparedness' on p.374.

Activity Little Albert

For this activity you will need to have refreshed your memory of the Little Albert study by rereading the account given in your AS textbook (*Psychology AS for AQA A*, p. 232). The study of Little Albert raises a number of important issues:

- Using primary sources – One issue concerns the problem of reporting studies. Watson and Rayner wrote up the results of their study at the time, but their procedures were quite complex and subsequent writers have condensed the study so much that they have distorted the actual findings. Interestingly, even Watson contradicted himself in later articles. This shows the importance of looking at primary sources instead of relying on the interpretation of a later textbook writer!

- Ethical issues – The study also raises important ethical issues because Little Albert was only 11 months old and he was subjected to some frightening experiences. It is also unclear whether Watson and Rayner obtained consent from his mother. She took Albert away soon after the study, so Albert was never 'desensitized' to his fears. Think about modern ethical guidelines. Would this kind of study be allowed today?

You can find out more about this study by looking at an article by Ben Harris, 'Whatever happened to Little Albert?':

www.sussex.ac.uk/psychology/documents/harris_-1979.pdf

You can also see film footage of Little Albert on Youtube at:
www.youtube.com/watch?v=KxKfpKQzow8

Activity Objects of phobias

Look at the various things shown above. Which of these do you think are most likely to be the objects of phobia. Why might this be so?

Research into preparedness: Öhman et al. (1976)

Öhman et al. (1975) used a classical conditioning paradigm (procedure) to induce fear in a group of volunteer, non-fearful participants using various stimuli. In the fear-relevant condition, participants were shown pictures of snakes or spiders (i.e. stimuli that are potentially dangerous), whereas in the fear irrelevant condition, they were shown pictures of houses, flowers and mushrooms. Presentations of the pictures were paired with brief electric shocks. The intensity of the shock level was individualized for each participant to make sure that the shock was uncomfortable, but not painful. Participants were then shown the pictures again without shocks, and their response was tested by skin conductance levels and finger-pulse-volume response (FPVR). The findings were as follows:

- Fear conditioning occurred rapidly in the fear-relevant (prepared) condition after only one pairing.
- It took approximately five pairings to condition a fear response in the fear-irrelevant (unprepared) condition.

The conclusion was that humans were more likely to learn a fear response to potentially dangerous things than to neutral objects. In later variations on this study, Öhman and colleagues found that the fear conditioned by the neutral stimuli soon extinguished, whereas the fear to the fear-relevant stimuli remained strong.

Activity | Research into preparedness

After you have read the panel 'Research into preparedness', answer the following questions:

1 What is the advantage of carrying out a laboratory study when investigating this kind of topic?

2 Why did the researchers individualize the intensity of the shock?

3 What ethical considerations should the researchers have taken into account?

Preparedness theory

The recognition that some phobic reactions are more common than others has prompted the suggestion that there is a species-specific, biological predisposition to fear certain stimuli, dating back to our ancestors. This **preparedness theory** was researched by Seligman (1971) who proposed the concept of biological 'preparedness': all species are innately 'prepared' to avoid certain stimuli because they are potentially dangerous. A classic study by Garcia and Koelling (1966) showed that rats could easily be conditioned to avoid life-threatening

stimuli, such as shocks or toxic liquids, but not to avoid stimuli which carried no adverse consequences, such as flashing lights. Human phobias, such as fear of the dark or fear of heights, are consistent with preparedness theory (see the panel, 'Research into preparedness' for an example of a study of preparedness).

Preparedness theory can explain why people are more likely to develop phobias for snakes than for lambs.

Evaluation of the preparedness theory explanation

- *Explains some phobias, but not others* – Preparedness theory can account for the fact that certain objects, animals (e.g. spiders and snakes) and situations are more likely to induce phobic reactions than others. However, it is possible to develop phobias of things like buttons and feathers, although these are much rarer, and it is more difficult for the theory to explain them.

- *Explains irrationality of phobias* – Preparedness theory also accounts for the irrationality of phobias, i.e. the fact that phobias persist in the face of logical argument. In Öhman's study, for example, the participants were assured at the end of the experiment that no more shocks would be delivered. The conditioned fear to the neutral items extinguished immediately, but the conditioned fear to the fear-relevant stimuli was much more resistant to extinction.

- *Explains ease of developing phobias* – The theory suggests why people can develop a phobia without any memory of a traumatic event. There is evidence that 'prepared' fear conditioning can be acquired with the minimum contact with the feared stimulus. Mineka et al. (1984), for example, found that rhesus monkeys developed a persistent phobia for snakes after brief exposures to the sight of their parents behaving fearfully in the presence of a toy snake. However, the theory does not explain why there are such wide individual differences in the tendency to acquire phobias. See the panel, 'The evolutionary approach to explaining phobias'.

- *What is the real fear?* – Further criticism of the theory of 'biological preparedness' comes from a study by McNally and Steketee (1985). They found that in 91 per cent of cases of snake and spider phobias, the cause for concern was not a fear of being harmed, but rather a fear of having a panic attack. The exception was dog phobias, where most people were afraid of being bitten.

The evolutionary approach to explaining phobias

Preparedness theory is an evolutionary explanation of phobic disorders. Such explanations emphasize that disorders such as phobias would not have persisted in the gene pool unless they conferred net benefits by doing so. An evolutionary explanation is valuable because it offers us an insight into the possible adaptive nature of phobias that would have led to their evolution in the first place. However, a response that has evolved through natural selection because it was adaptive may nowadays be activated in circumstances that make it psychologically maladaptive.

Explaining phobic fears in terms of biological preparedness also assumes that all members of a species would share such predispositions. There are, however, distinct cultural differences. In many areas of Africa, the spider is revered as a wise creature and its dwelling places are cleaned and protected by the local people (Renner 1990). In some areas of the world, spiders are frequently eaten as a delicacy, including those that are most lethal to humans (Bristowe 1945). Many cultures consider spiders to be symbols of good fortune rather than fear. For example, it is common practice in Egypt to place a spider in the bed of a newly married couple (Bristowe 1958).

You will find more information about evolutionary explanations of behaviour in the Introduction to this book, p.6. ▶

Social learning theory

The ease with which certain phobias can develop could equally be accounted for in terms of **social learning** (also known as vicarious learning) – modelling our behaviour on the observed behaviour of others. If certain stimuli are potentially dangerous, then from an early age we are likely to observe others (often our parents) avoiding them. In the same way, we also learn that certain non-dangerous stimuli are commonly avoided within a given culture. This could explain phobias for stimuli that are not necessarily life-threatening, for example snakes and large spiders, most of which are not dangerous. Bandura and Rosenthal (1966) asked participants to watch someone (actually a confederate of the experimenters) who appeared to be receiving a painful electric shock every time a buzzer sounded. After witnessing this, the participants showed a fear response when they, themselves, heard the buzzer even though they had never directly experienced the shocks.

Evaluation of the social learning theory explanation

- *Inconsistency in the development of phobias* – Many people who seek treatment for phobias report never having observed others showing the same fear. Similarly, many people who have been exposed to phobic models do not go on to develop phobias themselves.

- *Social learning as part explanation* – It appears that vicarious learning may lead to phobic reactions in some, but it cannot provide a complete explanation of how phobias are acquired.

Cognitive-behavioural explanation

If you have not already done so, you should read the section on the cognitive-behavioural approach in the Introduction to the book on p.15.

The **cognitive-behavioural explanation** for phobias extends the behavioural view of the conditioning of physiological reflexes to the cognitive domain of 'thinking'. Leading theorists in this field, such as Albert Ellis (1962) and Aaron Beck (1963), suggest that catastrophic thoughts and irrational beliefs contribute to the development of phobias.

For example, an experience of feeling 'hemmed in' while in a crowded lift might be maintained later on by thoughts such as 'I might suffocate if I were trapped in a lift again'. This then turns into a fear of lifts, which is then generalized to other similar situations, resulting in the onset of claustrophobia. Therefore, it is not only exposure to a fearful situation that initiates the phobia; rather it is also the person's *irrational* thoughts about the future possibility of the fearful situation arising again.

According to Beck, people with phobias know, at a rational level, that danger is minimal, yet they also truly believe that their feared object or situation will cause them physical or psychological harm. Beck *et al.* (1985) found that 'danger beliefs' were activated when the person was in close proximity to the phobic stimuli. When at a distance, however, the person stated that the probability of harm was almost zero. The fear of being in danger gradually increased as the person came closer to the feared situation/object. Beck and colleagues also found that people with phobias were more preoccupied with their 'fear of fear' than the actual object or situation itself.

Williams *et al.* (1997) examined this concept by subjecting people with agoraphobia to a hierarchy of increasingly scary tasks, while monitoring their thoughts throughout. The results supported Beck and colleagues: participants' tape-recorded statements were mainly preoccupied with their current anxiety rather than their safety.

Negative self-appraisal appears to be a key feature in social phobia, together with the need for perfectionism. A study by Bieling and Alden (1997) found that people with social phobia scored significantly higher than controls on the need for perfectionism and had lowered perceptions of their social ability.

Evaluation of the cognitive-behavioural explanation

■ *Research support* – The cognitive-behavioural explanation has found considerable support from numerous studies (e.g. Williams *et al.* 1997). It can also explain why certain people are more prone to develop phobias than others. However, it is difficult to ascertain whether irrational thoughts are the cause of phobias, or merely a symptom of the disorder.

■ *Success of therapy* – Cognitive-behavioural therapy is very effective in reducing phobic anxiety (p.381), although this in itself does not verify the underlying theory.

Diathesis-stress model explanation of phobias

The diathesis-stress model proposes an interaction between various factors and may explain individual differences in susceptibility to stress and anxiety. It is suggested that we all have our own individual tolerance thresholds that form a predisposition to stress; this is known as our 'diathesis' or 'vulnerability' factor. The origin of this predisposition to vulnerability is not certain. It may be genetically inherited or it may be acquired through early experience. The interaction between this vulnerability factor and the degree of life stress a person encounters (major life events and/or minor hassles) is thought to determine the likelihood that anxiety will reach a degree where it becomes dysfunctional, and from this phobias may develop. See Fig. 11a.1.

Diathesis/vulnerability factor
(individual stress-tolerance thresholds)

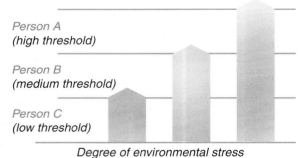

Person A
(high threshold)

Person B
(medium threshold)

Person C
(low threshold)

Degree of environmental stress

Figure 11a.1 Diathesis-stress model

As with the other psychological disorders considered in this book, the diathesis-stress model suggests an interaction between vulnerability factors and triggering events. Major life events have long been regarded as important contributing factors in all anxiety disorders, including phobias. Holmes and Rahe (1967) explained the cumulative effects of major life events, and the work of Kobasa (1979) highlighted the effects of everyday minor hassles (see *Psychology AS for AQA A*, pp. 157–62).

Evaluation of the diathesis-stress model explanation

■ *Research evidence* – Kleiner and Marshall (1987) found that in a group of agoraphobics, 84 per cent had experienced family problems prior to the onset of their first panic attack, and this finding has been confirmed by a number of other studies. However, the difficulty with the life-events theory is that many people who experience the most adverse life events do not develop an anxiety disorder.

■ *Role of vulnerability factors* – There is some evidence to support the behavioural view of conditioning and, indeed, many people with specific phobias do report fearful experiences as the onset of their phobias. Nevertheless, many people who have similar experiences do not develop phobias. This suggests that other vulnerability factors play a part and lends support for the diathesis-stress model. The vulnerability factor is the key to the aetiology (cause) of phobias. This could be a physiological vulnerability, or a deeper underlying problem expressing itself in a phobia or in negative ways of thinking. However, we all have fears and anxieties; they only become mental disorders when they are so extreme that the person's life has become dysfunctional.

CHECK YOUR UNDERSTANDING

Check your understanding of explanations of phobic disorders. Try to do this from memory. You can check your answers by looking back through Topic 2.

1 Briefly outline and evaluate what family and twin studies have told us about the origins of phobias.

2 How might GABA be involved in the origin of phobias?

3 Give a brief outline and evaluation of the psychodynamic explanation of phobias.

4 Explain how a phobia might be acquired through classical conditioning and maintained through operant conditioning.

5 Outline the ethical issues raised by the study of 'Little Albert' (Watson and Rayner 1920).

6 Outline and evaluate the preparedness theory of phobias.

7 How does the cognitive-behavioural approach explain phobias?

8 What is the diathesis-stress model and how does it explain phobias?

A **therapy** is a deliberate intervention designed to treat mental disorders either by effecting a complete cure or by making the symptoms more manageable. A number of different therapies are used in treating phobic disorders, each one based on a particular theoretical approach regarding the cause of the disorder. You will already be familiar with these approaches or models of mental disorder from your AS-level studies into Psychopathology; you may wish to refresh your memory on these before starting this topic, as this background knowledge is essential to an understanding of therapies (see *Psychology AS for AQA A*, pp. 237–46).

There are considerable ethical and practical issues involved with therapy and intervention, and these have important implications for all of those involved in mental health, whether recipients or practitioners. Some of these points will be considered in the context of each type of therapy. There are, however, some important general issues surrounding the use of therapies. These are described on pp. 304–5 in the Introduction to psychopathology, and we recommend that you start by reading about these first and also come back to them later on as you evaluate the various types of therapy.

Biological therapies

Biological therapies arise from the medical model of abnormal behaviour, that is, mental disorder is viewed as an illness which results mainly from a biochemical imbalance. Biological treatments are designed to redress this imbalance through the administration of chemical drugs, electroconvulsive therapy (ECT) and, in rare cases, psychosurgery. They aim to alter abnormal behaviours by intervening directly in bodily processes. Many people who are experiencing psychological problems or who show disturbed behaviour patterns go for help to their family doctor. This means that the first line of treatment offered is usually medical. In the case of phobias, drug treatment is the most usual form of biological therapy.

Drug therapy (chemotherapy)

Since the 1950s, the use of drugs in the treatment of mental disorders has been widespread, and they account annually for a large proportion of NHS prescriptions. There are different types of drugs for different mental disorders.

Drugs used to treat mental disorders are called psychoactive drugs and they work by affecting the nervous system. Neurons (nerve cells) communicate with one another via a number of different chemical messengers called neurotransmitters. There are many different types of neurotransmitter, but the main ones are:

- dopamine
- acetylcholine
- serotonin
- GABA
- noradrenaline (called norepinephrine in the United States).

Psychoactive drugs work in various ways, but essentially they serve either to increase or decrease the amount of available neurotransmitter.

Psychology in context Therapy on line

It is thought that many people with phobias, particularly with social phobia, do not come forward for treatment, possibly because they are embarrassed to seek help or because they cannot face the social demands of one-to-one therapy. There are often long waiting lists to see fully trained

therapists. One way of trying to address this problem is to provide self-help therapies on the internet. A study by Carlberg *et al.* (2007) investigated the effectiveness of such a programme. They investigated 60 people with social phobia who met their strict inclusion criteria and allocated 30 to the treatment group and 30 to the waiting-list group. The treatment was based on cognitive-behavioural therapy (CBT) methods as described in a self-help book (Furmark *et al.* 2006) and adapted for the internet into nine

modules. Participants sent homework assignments in by e-mail and received feedback within 24 hours. They also received a weekly phone call from a therapist to provide positive feedback and to answer any questions. They found that people in the treatment groups showed significant improvement on all measures (e.g. lowered social anxiety, avoidance behaviours, depression and general anxiety) whereas people in the waiting-list group did not.

This study suggests that there is real promise in offering on-line therapies to people with social phobias.

1 Why do you think some people with social phobias might prefer on-line therapy?

2 Why is it important to carry out well-controlled research studies to check the efficacy of on-line therapy?

3 What do you think are some of the advantages and limitations of using on-line therapy for people with mental disorders?

Anti-anxiety drugs

Diazepam is used to reduce anxiety levels.

Anti-anxiety drugs consist of a class of drugs called 'benzodiazepines' – minor tranquillizers designed to reduce levels of anxiety. Benzodiazepines (which work like GABA to decrease arousal) are sedatives that inhibit the nervous system and produce muscle relaxation and an overall calming effect.

Benzodiazepines, such as Librium and Valium, were introduced in the 1950s and 1960s and soon became the most prescribed drugs in the world. They were taken up eagerly by GPs because they offered an apparently safe way to alleviate anxieties in patients. They did not lead to fatality when taken in overdose, unlike opioids, such as morphine and laudanum. These had been the only drugs previously available and doctors were loath to prescribe them because of the dangers of addiction, severe side effects, overdose and potential fatality.

- *Behaviour therapy* (see p.379) is usually the treatment of choice for *specific phobias*, but anti-anxiety drugs are also sometimes prescribed to help reduce symptoms of panic.

- *Anti-anxiety drugs* are sometimes used for people with *agoraphobia* and *social phobia*, but usually only in the short term to help them cope with a particularly important engagement while they are waiting for another treatment to take effect.

- *Alprazolam* is a high-potency compound benzodiazepine that does not have the sedative effect of some other drugs in this class. It is used in the US to treat people with agoraphobia and panic attacks but its use is not now recommended in the UK (National Institute for Clinical Excellence 2004). Marks *et al.* (1993) found that it was only half as effective as behavioural therapy in treating agoraphobia and that relapse after treatment was more frequent.

Antidepressant drugs

Prozac is effective in reducing panic.

This class of drug is primarily intended to enhance the mood of people with depression, but antidepressants have also been used to treat some kinds of phobia, particularly by helping to reduce panic.

Antidepressants affect the availability of serotonin and noradrenaline, which are the neurotransmitters thought to be implicated in depression. The main antidepressants are monoamine-oxidase inhibitors (MAOIs), tricyclics (TCAs) and selective serotonin re-uptake inhibitors (SSRIs), and they have all been used in the treatment of phobias, particularly agoraphobia and social phobia.

- *Monoamine-oxidase inhibitors (MAOIs)* – The first MAOI was Iproniazid. Its antidepressant effect was discovered by accident when it was tried as a new drug for tuberculosis and found to induce euphoria. MAOIs block the action of the enzyme that breaks down noradrenaline and serotonin, so increasing the availability of these neurotransmitters in the nervous system. These drugs can reduce panic symptoms in people with phobias but they are used infrequently because they interact adversely with other drugs and foodstuffs.

- *Tricyclics (TCAs)* – Tricyclics, such as Tofranil, operate in a similar way to MAOIs, but are milder antidepressants and, although they are slower acting, have fewer severe side effects. The drug imipramine has been used successfully with people with agoraphobia but a high rate of relapse occurs when the medication stops (Zitrin *et al.* 1978).

- *Selective serotonin re-uptake inhibitors (SSRIs)* – The SSRIs, such as Prozac, inhibit the re-uptake of serotonin and thus make more of this neurotransmitter available. These drugs have been effective in reducing panic in people with agoraphobia and social phobia, and seem to be more effective than imipramine and alprazolam (Boyer 1995)

For more information about antidepressant drugs see Chapter 10, Depression, pp. 338–41.

Evaluation of drug therapy

- *Effectiveness* – Benzodiazepines have been found to be effective in reducing symptoms of anxiety and panic. Gelernter *et al.* (1991) found them to be more effective than a placebo for social phobia, and Lecrubier *et al.* (1997) found that around 60 per cent of patients with panic disorder remained free of panic while on medication.

- *Dangers of dependence* – Anti-anxiety drugs offered an easy solution for GPs, who could write a prescription rather than engage in counselling (for which few GPs are trained). Unfortunately, benzodiazepines did not prove to be a magic solution, because they created dependence on the drug, sometimes for years. The frequency and willingness with which GPs prescribed benzodiazepines in the 1960s/70s has led to the recent development of self-help groups for people trying to overcome long-term dependence. Most GPs now restrict such drugs to short courses. Dependence leads to physical withdrawal symptoms, such as tremors and insomnia when the person stops taking the drug. However, Linden *et al.* (1998) found that neither the dosage nor length of treatment were major factors in dependence. When patients were asked to take a three-week drug-holiday programme, withdrawal occurred before the programme began, indicating that the dependency was psychological, not physical.

How appropriate? Treating the symptoms not the cause – It is argued that one of the main problems with anti-anxiety drugs is that they do not treat the cause of the anxiety. This is illustrated by the fact that there is around a 90 per cent relapse rate when benzodiazepine medication is ceased (Fyer *et al.* 1987). Some psychologists believe that biochemical imbalance is the result, rather than the cause, of mental disorders. This leads to the claim that drugs merely treat the symptoms (e.g. the anxiety or depression), but do not address the cause of the problem (e.g. why the person is anxious or depressed). Consequently, drugs can only provide short-term relief and may not be an appropriate or effective long-term solution for anxiety.

Costs versus benefits – Given that there are also numerous side effects from drugs, it is arguable whether the benefits outweigh the costs, particularly if the initial problems still remain. Furthermore, there are dangers of complying with medication when drugs have not been accurately prescribed or when anti-anxiety drugs are taken along with other medication. The actor Heath Ledger, who died of an accidental overdose of prescription drugs in January 2008, was reported to have taken two anti-anxiety drugs including Valium, along with other prescribed medication.

Heath Ledger, the actor who died of an accidental drug overdose which included two anti-anxiety drugs.

Many people, however, prefer drugs. This may be because taking medicine is a familiar activity, whereas psychological treatment is unfamiliar territory.

Combining drugs and psychological treatment – For psychological therapies to be effective, clients or patients must have some insight, that is, they must recognize that they have a problem. Some people suffering from severe agoraphobia or social phobia are so distressed that they cannot attend psychotherapy sessions. For this reason, drugs are sometimes prescribed to help them deal with their overwhelming anxiety symptoms so that they become more open to other treatments.

Ethical issues in drug therapy

Some people have criticized the widespread use of drugs in the treatment of mental disorders, referring to them as 'chemical straitjackets'. The argument is that the drugs are dehumanizing and remove any sense of personal responsibility or control.

The ethical issue of informed consent also arises, as people who are seriously anxious may not be in the best position to give fully informed consent about their treatment.

Activity   Placebos

Gelernter *et al.* (1991) found that benzodiazepines were more effective for treating social phobia than a placebo (see Evaluation of drug therapy).

1 What is a placebo?

2 How would you design a study to compare the effects of Benzodiazepines with the effects of a placebo?

3 What ethical issues might arise in a study of this type? How would you try to overcome them?

Psychological therapies

Psychological therapies address psychological rather than biological factors associated with mental disorders. Psychological treatments for phobic disorders include behavioural therapies, cognitive-behavioural therapy (CBT) and psychodynamic therapy. You might find it helpful to re-read the section on psychological therapies for psychopathology in Psychology AS for AQA, pp. 240–6.

Behavioural therapies

Behavioural therapies emerged in the 1950s. The main assumption of the behavioural view is that abnormal behaviour is acquired in the same way as normal behaviour, through the principles of classical and operant conditioning, and through social learning. Behavioural therapists, therefore, suggest that maladaptive behaviours can be 'unlearned' and replaced with new, more desirable behaviours. The therapy is usually targeted at specific, well-delineated anxiety disorders, such as phobias and compulsions. Behavioural techniques have been shown to be highly effective in the treatment of phobia and it is the most widely used form of treatment for this disorder.

Over the past 30 or 40 years, a number of therapeutic techniques have been developed with the overall aim of encouraging adaptive strategies to enable the person to function more effectively in the environment. The first stage in behavioural therapy is a '*functional analysis*'. The aim of this is to:

- assess the person's level of functioning

- identify the antecedents to maladaptive responses (i.e. what came before)

- decide upon the most appropriate treatment techniques.

Techniques used in the treatment of phobias are:

- *desensitization and flooding* – based on classical conditioning

- *modelling* – based on social learning theory.

These techniques are collectively called exposure treatments.

Systematic desensitization

'**Systematic desensitization**', devised by Wolpe (1958), is a technique developed specifically to counter-condition phobias and anxieties. Counter-conditioning is a process whereby a fearful reaction is replaced by another emotional response that is incompatible with fear. This is usually achieved by teaching the individual deep muscle relaxation techniques. The therapist then works with the client to compile a hierarchical list of feared situations, starting with those that arouse minimal anxiety, progressing to those that are the most frightening. After this preliminary training, the desensitization procedure can begin. Muscular relaxation is induced and the client is then asked to visualize the situation associated with the least anxiety-provoking item in the hierarchy. After several repetitions without anxiety, the treatment continues by repeating the process for every rung in the hierarchy. The client can indicate a feeling of anxiety at any stage in the process, usually by raising their hand. The therapist will then immediately stop the visualization, recreate the relaxation state and then return to the item again. Treatment is complete when the client is able to work through the entire hierarchy without anxiety. This technique can be conducted either '*in vitro*' (through imagined imagery) or '*in vivo*' (in real life). Therapists often advise clients to place themselves in progressively more anxiety-provoking real-life situations between therapy sessions in order to help them move from merely imagined to actual situations. *In vivo* techniques are usually more effective than *in vitro* techniques for specific phobias (Menzies and Clarke 1993).

Activity Tackling fears

In pairs or small groups, try the following:

1 Think about a specific fear that one of you has, *although you must make sure that you do not cause anyone distress.*

2 Write down a hierarchy of graded exposure in line with systematic desensitization, starting with the least fearful situation relating to the specific fear, through a number of systematic steps of increasing fearfulness, and ending with the most frightening situation.

Flooding

Research into the effectiveness of systematic desensitization has shown that visualization can occasionally bring about therapeutic change even without relaxation. This finding has led to the development of an extinction treatment called 'flooding'. **Flooding** involves exposing clients to a phobic object in a non-graded manner with no attempt to reduce prior anxiety. This technique can be used *in vivo* but, for ethical and practical reasons, it is often conducted *in vitro* (in this case, it is known as **implosion therapy**) after the therapist has first ensured that the person is in good physical health.

Typically, the client is placed alone in the phobic situation, for example, in an enclosed space in the case of claustrophobia, and is required to remain there until there is a marked decrease in anxiety. In implosion therapy, the client would be asked to imagine themselves in such a situation. Physiologically, it is not possible to maintain a state of high anxiety for a very long period, and so eventually anxiety will subside. This can take about an hour and it is important not to remove the person from the feared situation too early. If this happens, the person will be released when anxiety is still high and this will merely serve to reinforce the original fear. In the initial stages of the treatment, anxiety is very high, but it will reduce fairly quickly as emotional exhaustion and/or habituation set in and the client realizes that they are still safe and that nothing dreadful has happened to them. Thus the fear should be extinguished.

More recently therapists have started to use virtual reality (VR) therapy. This is a technique that uses 3D computer graphics to simulate real-world objects and situations. Now try the activity 'Virtual reality techniques'.

STRETCH AND CHALLENGE   HOW SCIENCE WORKS

Activity Virtual reality (VR) techniques

You might like to find out a bit more about virtual reality techniques.

A report in *The Times* in May 2008 reported on the effectiveness of this therapy for a range of disorders, including phobias. Dr P. Anderson from Georgia State University has used the technique successfully for people with fears of public speaking and flying.

> "Dr Anderson's study indicated that the patients who use VR therapy did as well as those treated with real-life flying. So why use VR? 'Facing fears in a virtual world is much more appealing than facing them in real-life,' says Dr Anderson. 'This may make treatment more accessible.' For patients with a fear of public speaking, she can make the audience look bored, talk among themselves, raise hands, or fall asleep. She can even make virtual mobile phones ring mid-talk."

If you would like to look up the original article, go to:

www.timesonline.co.uk/tol/life_and_style/health/articl e3945251.ece

1 Why do you think virtual reality therapy might be preferable to *in vivo* flooding therapy?

2 How do you think the two techniques differ?

3 How realistic do you think the virtual reality is?

A headset used in VR therapy.

Evaluation of techniques based on classical conditioning

- *Appropriate treatment for anxiety disorders* – Behavioural therapies based on classical conditioning are particularly appropriate for treating phobias. They are relatively quick (a few weeks or months) in contrast to psychodynamic therapies that can last for years. There are minimal side effects and none of the dependency problems associated with drug therapy.

- *Effectiveness* – The efficacy of behavioural techniques has been shown to be quite high: McGrath *et al.* (1990) found systematic desensitization effective for around 75 per cent of people with specific phobias. In their review, Barlow and Lehman (1996) reported that for specific phobias, graded exposure (systematic desensitization) was very effective and the preferred choice of patients. They also reported that for blood/injection/injury types of phobias, 90 per cent of patients were cured in around five sessions of graded exposure. Ost *et al.* (1991) conducted a study where the whole hierarchy of feared stimuli were presented in a single session over several hours to 20 patients with spider phobias. They found that, no matter how severe the phobia, 90 per cent were much improved or completely recovered at a four-year follow-up. Ost *et al.*, however, noted that the recovery might not have been a direct consequence of the single behavioural therapy session received four years earlier.

- *Effectiveness for treating agoraphobia* – Agoraphobia is one of the most difficult phobias to treat, yet systematic desensitization has helped improve between 60 and 80 per cent of cases (Craske and Barlow 1993). However, improvements are shown to be only partial, and in 50 per cent of cases relapses occur.

- *Combining treatments* – Behaviour therapies are sometimes used in conjunction with other therapies. A number of studies comparing different types of therapy have found systematic desensitization to be equally effective for phobias when administered alone, or in combination with other treatments, such as medication or cognitive-behavioural therapy (e.g. Burke *et al.* 1997). However, a study by Beurs et al. (1995) of 96 patients found that systematic desensitization combined with medication was the most effective treatment for panic disorder with agoraphobia.

- *Symptom substitution* – Critics of behavioural methods point out that, quite often, people with phobias have no recollection of any traumatic experience involving the object of their fear. Psychoanalytic therapists claim that this is because the phobia is merely a symptom, a signal from the unconscious that something is wrong. They claim that removing the phobia through behavioural techniques will simply result in a new phobia emerging because the treatment does not resolve the underlying conflict. However, there is no evidence that such symptom substitution occurs after behavioural therapy.

- *Unpredictable effects of therapy* – When agreeing to a particular therapy, patients and, to some degree, even therapists, cannot always anticipate what may occur during the course of therapy. This has been a major criticism of behavioural therapies, in particular the technique of 'flooding'. Even when conducted in vitro rather than *in vivo*, there may be dangerous consequences, such as hyperventilation, raised blood pressure or heart attacks. It would be unethical and inappropriate, therefore, for flooding to be undertaken without adequate training and proper medical supervision.

Modelling therapy

Modelling therapy is based on Bandura's (1969) 'social learning theory'. This is an extension of learning theory, to include learning through observing the behaviour of others. According to social learning theory, phobias can develop when we observe the fears of significant others and model our behaviour upon those observations. In therapy, the individual is given the opportunity to observe the therapist handling the phobic object (e.g. a spider or a snake) confidently and without any dire consequences. Modelling emphasizes the acquisition of appropriate behavioural skills and a feeling of competence. In participant modelling, individuals are encouraged to engage with the therapist and handle the object themselves.

Modelling therapy is successful in treating specific phobias.

Evaluation of modelling therapy

- *Effectiveness* – Bandura and Menlove (1968) and Bandura *et al.* (1969) have provided evidence to support the effectiveness of using modelling in the treatment of phobias. In clinical studies of nursery children with dog phobias and adults with snake phobias, they claimed a 90 per cent success rate.

Cognitive-behavioural therapy

The aim of **cognitive-behavioural therapy (CBT)** is to help the client identify their negative, irrational thoughts and replace these with more positive, rational ways of thinking. A therapy session usually includes both cognitive and behavioural elements, with homework between sessions. Cognitive-behavioural therapists use a number of different techniques to bring about change in the client, for example:

- *Cognitive restructuring* – which helps people to review their irrational beliefs and expectations and to develop more rational strategies for coping with anxiety.

- *Thought stopping* – based on the idea that a sudden distracting stimulus, such as a loud noise (e.g. the therapist shouting 'Stop!'), will interrupt unhelpful or obsessional thoughts. Clients learn to say this mentally to themselves as a way of self-regulating intrusive thoughts.

- *Cognitive rehearsal* – which allows clients to rehearse adaptive approaches to difficult situations. This is particularly useful for people with, for example, social phobias, where their fear cannot easily be simulated in a clinical setting.

Aaron Beck has developed one of the most important forms of cognitive-behavioural therapy (Beck *et al.* 1985). His therapy has been used mostly in the treatment of depression but it has also been found to be effective in treating anxiety. He believes that people with anxiety disorders have a fundamental tendency to devalue themselves and their ability to solve problems, and to overestimate the degree of threat posed by a difficult situation.

Beck's cognitive therapy, which usually consists of between five and 20 sessions, includes the following:

- At the start of therapy, the therapist takes a history to obtain some background information and to try to find the original causes of the anxiety.

- Most of the therapy is then focused on providing tasks for the client that will help him or her to cope with difficult situations more effectively. The therapist encourages the client to talk openly about their anxieties and is empathetic.

- The therapist helps the client to examine their own thoughts for evidence of cognitive distortions and to substitute more rational thoughts.

- Together, the client and therapist decide how the client's beliefs can be tested against reality, e.g. using role-play or homework assignments.

For more information about cognitive-behavioural therapies, see Chapter 10, pp. 356–7, where they are discussed in the context of depression.

Evaluation of cognitive-behavioural therapy
- *Advantages* – Like the older behavioural therapies, cognitive-behavioural therapies are structured, with clear goals and measurable outcomes. They are increasingly becoming the most widely employed therapy by clinical psychologists in the National Health Service, not least because they are short term and economic.

- *Appropriateness and appeal of CBT* – CBT appeals to, and is appropriate for, clients who find insight therapies (which delve into inner emotional conflicts) too threatening. Although subject to the criticism that it does not address underlying causes, CBT attempts to empower clients by educating them into self-help strategies. Despite this, many clients do become dependent upon their therapist.

- *Evidence of effectiveness* – In a review of behavioural versus CBT for anxiety disorders, Barlow and Lehman (1996) found CBT to be the more effective for generalized anxiety disorder and social phobia, but behavioural therapy was found to be more effective for specific phobias and obsessive-compulsive disorder. However, a study by Thorpe and Salkovskis (1997) reported significant improvements in patients with spider phobia after just one session of CBT, compared with no therapy. More recently, it has been shown to be helpful for people with agoraphobia and social phobia (Heimberg and Becker 2002).

- *Combination with other therapies* – There is some evidence that cognitive techniques work more effectively when combined with exposure training and social-skills training (Butler 1989). A number of studies have compared graded exposure treatment (systematic desensitization) with CBT and graded exposure combined. Burke *et al.* (1997) hypothesized that graded exposure would be more effective if the rationale was presented in cognitive terms (i.e. as an opportunity to challenge negative thoughts), rather than in strictly behavioural terms. See Key research, 'Comparing CBT and systematic desensitization' opposite for an account of Burke and colleagues' findings.

- *Effect of the therapist* – There is a suggestion that the nature and expertise of the therapist can have an important effect on the efficacy of cognitive therapy. For example, Huppert *et al.* (2001) found that more experienced therapists achieved better outcome measures with clients with anxiety disorders than less experienced colleagues, even though they were all fully trained.

Psychodynamic therapy

Psychodynamic therapy has been used to treat people with phobias. The aim of the therapy is to uncover the repressed conflicts that are believed to have caused the phobic behaviour. The therapist does not focus on the phobia directly because it is assumed that the phobia has arisen as a way of protecting the individual from repressed conflicts that are too painful to confront. If the phobia is removed, therefore, without tackling the underlying cause, psychodynamic therapists believe that it will simply reappear in another form (symptom substitution).

The therapist uses a variety of psychoanalytic techniques, such as free association and dream analysis, to uncover and, eventually, resolve the repressed conflict. For more detail about psychodynamic therapy, see Chapter 10, Depression, pp. 342–3, where psychoanalytic techniques are described.

Comparing CBT and systematic desensitization (graded exposure)

Key research: Burke *et al.* (1997)

Burke *et al.* (1997) tested two groups of females with agoraphobia, balanced for age, severity and duration of the phobia, and the presence of panic.

The study began with 39 participants. One group experienced behavioural therapy, that is, they were exposed to systematic desensitization (graded exposure) alone. The other group were first taught to identify and challenge negative thoughts using CBT and then experienced graded exposure along with the cognitive rationale (explanation) for the treatment. Each group was given ten sessions, and was assessed at the end of the sessions and six months later. Both groups were found to have improved equally, with no significant difference six months after treatment.

It was concluded that CBT does not add to the effectiveness of graded exposure (systematic desensitization) in the treatment of agoraphobia.

Evaluation

- *The sample size was very small* – the study started with only 39 people and 13 dropped out. With only 26 participants completing the course, it is difficult to draw any firm conclusions about the relative merits of the two treatment programmes that could be generalized confidently. Although the two groups were carefully balanced at the start of the study, losing one-third of the participants most likely unbalanced the grouping of those who remained.

- *Length of study* – Burke and colleagues themselves also point out that a six-month follow-up may not have been long enough to test whether CBT is more effective in preventing relapse.

- *Other evidence* – Beurs *et al.* (1995) conducted a similar study with people diagnosed with agoraphobia. They also found that CBT combined with graded exposure was not superior to graded exposure alone. Although CBT has been found to be effective in a number of comparative studies, it has not been found to add to the effectiveness of behavioural treatments for phobic disorders. It should be borne in mind, however, that these studies did not test CBT alone versus graded exposure alone.

Evaluation of psychodynamic therapy

- *Difficulties in evaluating the effectiveness of psychotherapy* – The main problems in trying to evaluate psychotherapies are discussed in Table 10.2 on p.338. The points discussed are general but they remain valid when considering the effectiveness of psychodynamic treatments for anxiety disorders.

- *Lack of evidence* – There is no evidence that psychoanalytic therapy is effective for people with phobic disorders. It is also time-consuming and expensive and can actually make people feel worse by stirring up unwelcome memories and feelings. Even psychoanalytic therapists themselves acknowledge that clients need to be exposed to the feared object if they are to show any improvement (Wolitzky and Eagle 1990).

CHECK YOUR UNDERSTANDING

Check your understanding of therapies for phobic disorders. Try to do this from memory. You can check your answers by looking back through Topic 3.

1. What type of drug is benzodiazepine?

2. Why are antidepressant drugs sometimes used for people with phobias?

3. Outline some of the advantages and disadvantages of using drugs to treat phobias.

4. Outline two behavioural therapies for phobias based on the principles of classical conditioning.

5. What is participant modelling? Give an example of when this might be used.

6. What is virtual reality therapy? When might it be useful?

7. What is the aim of CBT? Outline three techniques used by cognitive-behavioural therapists to effect positive change in clients suffering from anxiety disorder.

8. Outline advantages and limitations of using cognitive-behavioural therapies to treat phobias.

9. What is the aim of psychoanalysis? Describe two psychoanalytic techniques used by analysts.

10. How effective is psychoanalysis for treating phobias?

Clinical characteristics (symptoms)

Criteria differ depending on the type of phobia (i.e. specific phobia, social phobia or agoraphobia), but characteristics broadly similar. In all cases, individuals experience emotional, cognitive, physiological and behavioural anxiety symptoms:

- Marked and persistent fear that is excessive or unreasonable, cued by the presence of or anticipation of a specific object or situation.
- Exposure to phobic stimulus almost always provokes an immediate anxiety response (e.g. panic attack)
- The person recognizes the fear is excessive or unreasonable.
- The phobic situation(s) is avoided or else endured with intense anxiety or distress
- Avoidance, anticipation or distress interferes significantly with person's routine functioning

Issues surrounding classification & diagnosis

Factors that affect the reliability and validity of classification and diagnosis:

- Different types of phobic disorder
- Medicalization of a 'normal' state – the validity of the diagnosis?
- Differences in classification systems
- Fear of stigma
- Differential diagnosis – problems with reliability
- Dual diagnosis
- Cultural issues

Clinical characteristics & issues of classification & diagnosis

Therapies for phobic disorders

Psychological therapies

Often used in conjunction with drug therapies

Behavioural therapies
(e.g. systematic desensitization, flooding and modelling, based on classical conditioning and social learning)

Evaluation:

- Quick and effective treatment for specific phobias
- Support from research studies
- No side-effects although techniques such as flooding can be overwhelming
- Not always effective for social phobia and agoraphobia

Combination treatment
Evaluation:

- Some evidence that treatments are more effective if combined, e.g. medication with CBT.

Cognitive–behavioural therapy (CBT)
(to challenge irrational thinking)

Evaluation:

- Research evidence suggests CBT effective for phobic disorders
- Empowers the client
- No side-effects
- Effectiveness depends on the skill/experience of the therapist

Psychodynamic therapy
(uncover repressed conflicts believed to cause phobic disorder)

Evaluation:

- No convincing evidence to support this as effective for phobic disorders

Biological therapies

- Medication (drugs) can be used but usually only in short-term
- Variety of anti-anxiety drugs available
- Antidepressant medication can be helpful for people with social phobia or agoraphobia

Evaluation:

- Drugs can be effective in reducing symptoms for people with phobic disorders
- They do not work for everyone
- All anti-anxiety and antidepressant medication can produce side-effects particularly after long-term use
- People can become dependent on drugs, particularly anti-anxiety drugs
- Drugs can relieve symptoms but do not provide a cure
- Use of drug therapy raises ethical issues

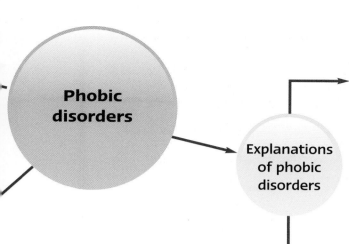

Phobic disorders

Explanations of phobic disorders

Psychodynamic (phobias are displaced fears (Freud) or related to early separation from carer (Bowlby))

Evaluation:

- Difficult to test the theory empirically
- Explanation lacks parsimony
- Llittle evidence for the idea of 'symptom substitution'
- Loss of a parent in childhood may predispose to later phobic disorders, but evidence is mixed

Behavioural (learned behaviour)

Evaluation:

- Some support for the idea that phobias are acquired through classical conditioning and maintained through operant conditioning (e.g. Watson and Rayner's 'Little Albert' study)
- Not everyone with a phobia has had a conditioning or social learning experience. Some people who have experienced a really frightening event do not go on to develop phobias
- Insufficient account taken of cognitive processes

Preparedness theory
(extension of basic learning theory)

- We are innately 'prepared' to fear certain stimuli that are potentially dangerous

Evaluation:

- Some good supporting evidence (e.g. Mineka *et al.* 1984)
- Explains the apparent irrationality of phobias
- Can explain some phobias (e.g. of snakes) better than other phobias (e.g. of buttons)

Cognitive-behavioural
(e.g. faulty thinking patterns as contributory factor)

Evaluation:

- Some research evidence to support explanation (e.g. Beck *et al.* 1985)
- Explains individual differences in acquiring phobias
- Gives rise to effective therapy
- Difficult to disentangle cause and effect

Biological explanations

Genes
(inherited predisposition to develop phobias)

Evaluation:

- Support from family, twin and adoption studies
- 100% concordance not demonstrated
- Difficult to disentangle effects of environment

Biochemical factors (GABA hypothesis)

Evaluation:

- Effective anti-anxiety medication that works by regulating GABA levels.
- Difficult to distinguish cause and effect

Neuroanatomical factors
(e.g. increased blood flow in amygdala)

Evaluation:

- Research support, e.g. from PET scans showing decreased blood flow following drug treatment
- Blood flow abnormalities not found in all patients
- difficult to disentangle cause and effect

Diathesis-stress explanation

- Interaction between biological and environmental factors
- Individuals have a genetic vulnerability for phobic disorder, but only develop the disorder in the presence of triggering environmental factors such as major life events and accumulating daily hassles

EXPLAINING THE SPECIFICATION

Specification content	The specification explained
Psychopathology: obsessive-compulsive disorder as chosen disorder	If you have chosen obsessive-compulsive disorder (OCD) as the psychopathology disorder you wish to study, you need to be able to:
Clinical characteristics and issues of classification and diagnosis surrounding obsessive-compulsive disorder (OCD) (Topic 1)	In this part of the specification you should be familiar with the key features of clinical characteristics and issues of classification and diagnosis. To do this, you need to be able to:
Clinical characteristics of obsessive-compulsive disorder	■ Outline the main clinical characteristics (symptoms) of obsessive-compulsive disorder.
Issues surrounding the classification and diagnosis of obsessive-compulsive disorder, including reliability and validity.	■ Describe and evaluate **at least two** issues (potential problems) in classifying or diagnosing OCD. If you concentrate on only two issues, these must be reliability and validity.
Explanations of OCD (Topic 2)	In this part of the specification you should be familiar with the explanations of obsessive-compulsive disorder. To do this, you need to be able to:
Biological explanations of obsessive-compulsive disorder, for example, genetics, biochemistry.	■ Describe and evaluate **at least two** biological explanations of OCD. To do this you will need to discuss relevant research findings. Genetics and biochemistry are suggested as examples of explanations that you might study but neither of these is specified as compulsory. The chapter discusses genetics, and biochemical and neuroanatomical explanations.
Psychological explanations of obsessive-compulsive disorder, for example, behavioural, cognitive, psychodynamic and socio-cultural.	■ Describe and evaluate **at least two** psychological explanations of OCD. To do this you will need to discuss relevant research findings. Four examples of explanations are suggested – behavioural, cognitive, psychodynamic and socio-cultural – but none of these is specified as compulsory. The chapter discusses psychodynamic, behavioural and cognitive-behavioural explanations.
Therapies for OCD (Topic 3)	In this part of the specification you should be familiar with the key features of therapies for obsessive-compulsive disorder. To do this, you need to be able to:
Biological therapies for obsessive-compulsive disorder, including their evaluation in terms of appropriateness and effectiveness.	■ Describe and evaluate **at least two** biological treatments for OCD. Your evaluations should consider how appropriate (suitable) and how effective (successful) the treatments are. To do this you will need to discuss relevant research findings. The chapter discusses drug therapy and psychosurgery.

Specification content	The specification explained
Psychological therapies for obsessive-compulsive disorder, for example, behavioural, psychodynamic, and cognitive-behavioural, including their evaluation in terms of appropriateness and effectiveness.	■ Describe and evaluate **at least two** psychological treatments for OCD. You need to discuss how appropriate and effective the treatments are. To do this you will need to discuss relevant research findings. The chapter focuses on behavioural and cognitive therapies.

Before you begin reading about phobic disorders, it is essential that you have read the Introduction to psychopathology on pp.300–305.

Introduction

Obsessive-compulsive disorder (OCD) comes under the general diagnostic category of anxiety disorders. **Anxiety disorders** are the most common type of mental disorder and the lifetime risk of developing one is between 10 and 14 per cent. (Phobic disorders, another class of anxiety disorders, are discussed in Chapter 11a.) The major classification systems list a number of anxiety disorders that differ from one another in significant ways, for example in the developmental timing of their first appearance, the types of stimuli that provoke anxiety, the pervasiveness of the anxiety, the way it manifests itself and the role of identifiable factors in the underlying cause. However, all anxiety disorders have certain characteristics in common:

■ high levels of anxiety

■ considerable emotional distress

■ avoidance behaviour.

The term 'anxiety' refers to a complex set of reactions to a real or imagined threat or danger (i.e. a fearful situation). We react to fearful situations on several levels:

■ *Emotionally* – We experience a sense of panic and alarm. If we experience fear over a long period of time, we also feel drained and overwhelmed.

■ *Cognitively* – We worry about what will happen and often anticipate dire consequences.

■ *Physiologically* – We show many involuntary physiological responses, such as a dry mouth, palpitations, tensed muscles, perspiration.

■ *Behaviourally* – We show a tendency either to freeze or to run away.

These are perfectly normal reactions in the face of a threatening stimulus. They are helpful to us because they allow us to anticipate impending danger and take action to deal with it. Such reactions only lead to anxiety disorders when they are out of all proportion to the threat posed or when they exist in the absence of any obvious danger.

In Topic 1, we consider the characteristics of OCD and the issues surrounding its classification and diagnosis. In Topics 2 and 3, we shall look at explanations and therapies for OCD.

Topic 1: Clinical characteristics and issues of classification and diagnosis

Clinical characteristics of OCD

Obsessive-compulsive disorder (OCD) is a mental disorder characterized by intrusive, unwelcome thoughts (obsessions) and a need to perform repetitive and ritualistic behaviour (compulsions) along with intense anxiety when these behaviours are suppressed.

Most of us have obsessional thoughts at times, often related to underlying fears and, on occasions, have a compulsion or impulse to act in ways that are strange and out of character. Many of us have certain ritualistic or routine ways of doing things, such as always putting on our clothes in a particular order or eating food in a

particular way, and many of us have certain superstitious beliefs. For someone with 'obsessive-compulsive disorder' (OCD), these thoughts and rituals are so invasive and taken to such an extreme, and are accompanied by such severe anxiety, that the person cannot function effectively in their daily life. OCD is probably the most severe of all anxiety disorders and is one of the most difficult to treat.

People with OCD are generally aware that their obsessional thoughts and behaviours are illogical, but they are powerless to overcome them. Often they attempt to hide them from others. Most, but not all, people diagnosed with OCD experience both obsessions and compulsions.

Psychology in context Diagnosing mental disorders

In November 2008, the BBC broadcast two programmes in the *Horizon* documentary series with the title: *How Mad Are You?* The following is an extract from the BBC Headroom site:

'Take ten volunteers, half have psychiatric disorders, the other half don't – but who is who?

Follow this two-part social experiment to see if you can tell which of the people have a mental health diagnosis.

Over five days the group are put through a series of challenges – from performing stand-up comedy to mucking out cows. The events are designed to explore the character traits of mental illness and ask whether the symptoms might be within all of us.

Three leading experts in mental health attempt to spot which volunteers have been diagnosed with a mental health condition. But will the individuals who have suffered from mental illness reveal themselves?'

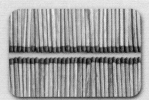

An obsession with orderliness is a symptom of OCD.

This programme was designed to remove some of the stigma attached to mental illness labels. The three clinicians, whose task it was to identify who had been diagnosed with a mental illness, were not given the opportunity to take case histories from any of the participants and had to base their judgements purely on observations. Not surprisingly, the experts were not very successful and only managed to identify two people correctly. Interestingly, their most confident decision concerned a young man called Dan who had OCD. This was mainly because Dan was unable to hide his uneasiness in some of the tasks he was asked to do.

You might like to look at the website yourself to find out a bit more about the programme and to see an interview with Dan.

1 Why is it so important for clinicians to take a detailed case history before making a diagnosis of mental illness?

2 From what you know about OCD, why do you think it might have been reasonably straightforward for the experts to recognize this disorder in one of the participants?

3 The extract refers to a 'social experiment'. How does such a television entertainment programme differ from a properly conducted psychology experiment?

Obsessions

Obsessions are persistent and recurrent thoughts, images, beliefs and impulses that enter the mind apparently uninvited and that cannot be removed. The content of these obsessions is various and wide-ranging but can usually be grouped into one or other of the following six categories:

1 dirt and contamination

2 aggression

3 orderliness

4 illness

5 sex

6 religion.

Obsessional symptoms can take various forms:

- *Obsessional thoughts* – Repeated, intrusive words or phrases which are distressing or even offensive to the individual. Attempts are usually made to resist them.

- *Ruminations* – Internal debates which are endlessly reviewed, presenting arguments for and against even the simplest of actions. Ruminations can also include repeated worrying themes about complex issues beyond the control of the individual, e.g. the end of the world.

- *Doubts* – Repeated worrying themes, often concerning actions that have or have not been carried out, e.g. locking the door after leaving the house, or turning off the cooker.

- *Impulses* – Repeated urges to carry out actions, usually actions that could be aggressive, dangerous or socially embarrassing, e.g. running into the road in front of a bus or shouting obscenities in a library. It is important to note that, although such impulses are strong, people with OCD rarely behave in violent or immoral ways.

- *Obsessional phobias* – Symptoms associated with avoidance as well as anxiety, such as obsessional impulses to stab someone with a knife, might lead to the avoidance of knives or even places where knives might be available, e.g. kitchens.

Compulsions

The compulsive element of OCD is the irresistible urge to carry out repetitive acts ritualistically in order to ward off some imagined dire consequence.

Again, **compulsions** can take many forms, but there are four particularly common types:

- *checking rituals* (e.g. checking and re-checking that the door has been locked or the cooker has been turned off)

- *cleaning rituals* (e.g. repeated hand-washing or continual scrubbing and bleaching of surroundings, especially sinks, toilets and doorknobs)

- *counting rituals* (e.g. usually silent counting in particular groupings, such as in threes, or counting objects around them)

- *dressing rituals* (e.g. putting clothes on in a particular order).

Natalie Appleton, the former 'All Saints' singer, is obsessed with cleanliness and broke down in tears when she had to touch a tree on the reality show I'm a Celebrity Get Me Out of Here.

Compulsions cause considerable difficulties for the individual carrying them out:

- They may be directly harmful, e.g. excessive hand-washing can cause serious skin problems.

- They interfere with everyday living because they are so time-consuming.

- They offer only very temporary relief from the anxiety associated with the underlying obsession and, in the long run, only seem to serve to maintain the obsessions.

See the case study of OCD, which describes a woman's obsession with fiery colours.

Onset and prevalence

The age of onset for OCD is usually in late teens and early twenties, and it affects around two per cent of the population across the world (Kessler *et al.* 2005). The disorder seems to occur equally in men and women, and equally in people of different ethnic and race groups.

Criteria for diagnosis

The criteria for a diagnosis of OCD are very similar in both ICD-10 and DSM-IV TR.

Diagnostic criteria for OCD (adapted from ICD-10):

- Either obsessions or compulsions (or both) are present on most days for a period of at least two weeks

---

Case study of OCD (A research study based on Rachman and Hodgson 1980)

A middle-aged woman complained of an obsession concerning colours and heat, 'The main problem is colours. I cannot look at any of the colours that are in the fire, red, orange or pink.'

She believed the colours blue, green, brown, white and grey were neutral and she used these colours to 'neutralize' the fiery colours. If she saw a fiery colour she would immediately look at some other colour to cancel it out. She used to walk around with a small piece of green carpet in order to neutralize the effects of any orange colours she might happen upon and see or imagine. She described the feelings that images of hot colours provoked, 'It starts in my mind and when I look at the colour, I start to tremble and I go hot all over... I can't stand up. I've got to sit down or else I'll fall... I feel sick... I know it can't hurt me physically although it does harm me mentally'.

(Neutralizing intrusive thoughts is discussed further in the cognitive-behavioural explanations of OCD on p.396.)

- Obsessions and compulsions share the following features *all* of which *must* be present:
  - acknowledged by the patient as originating in their own mind and not imposed by outside persons or influences
  - repetitive and unpleasant – at least one obsession or compulsion acknowledged as excessive or unreasonable must be present
  - patient tries to resist them – at least one obsession or compulsion that has been unsuccessfully resisted must be present
  - experiencing the obsessive thought or carrying out the compulsive act is not in itself pleasurable (to be distinguished from the temporary relief of tension or anxiety).

- The obsessions or compulsions cause distress or interfere with the patient's social or individual functioning, usually by wasting time.

- The obsessions or compulsions are not the result of other mental disorders, e.g. a mood disorder.

Activity ICD and DSM

You might like to look at the relevant pages in the ICD and DSM manuals yourself. These are large and complex documents, but you could look at the relevant sections on OCD on the websites and compare them:

www.who.int/classifications/icd/en/
www.apa.org/

Issues surrounding the classification and diagnosis of OCD

Look back to the Introduction to psychopathology section on **classification** and **diagnosis** on p.300. You will find that some of the general points there (e.g. about reliability and validity) are relevant to OCD.

When is a diagnosis valid?

Medicalization of normal behaviour

Many of us have transient, intrusive thoughts and sometimes carry out ritualistic behaviours like avoiding cracks in the pavement. This suggests that obsessive-compulsive behaviours in a mild form are not uncommon. However, as with other anxiety disorders, obsessive-compulsive behaviour probably exists on a continuum. The disorder is only diagnosed in people where the thoughts/behaviours are so overwhelming and disruptive that they interfere with everyday living. A valid diagnosis of OCD requires evidence of dysfunction and persistence.

Different subtypes

Given the range of content in both obsessions and compulsions, it has been suggested that OCD is not a single disorder but a group of rather different disorders. Jakes (1996) for example, believes that there are subgroups of patients who differ in the nature of their compulsions, e.g. some have mainly checking compulsions, while others engage mainly in cleaning rituals. He has suggested that these subtypes might have different origins and might respond to different treatments. However, many OCD sufferers have a mixture of types of obsession/compulsion and these can also change over time. Studies looking at people with apparently different types of symptoms have, in fact, found very few fundamental differences. Rasmussen and Eisen (1991) found certain factors that seem to be present in virtually all diagnosed cases:

- All experience anxiety as their overwhelming emotion.
- All fear that something terrible will happen, either to them or to other people, for which they will be responsible.
- They all believe that compulsive behaviours serve to provide temporary relief from obsessions.

How reliable is the diagnosis?

Differential diagnosis

Certain symptoms of OCD can be found in other mental disorders:

- OCD symptoms can resemble the delusional beliefs of schizophrenia when the nature of the obsessional thoughts is particularly bizarre. However, provided that the clinician makes a careful assessment of the patient and their other symptoms, the two disorders are usually readily distinguishable. Obsessions are recognized by individuals as their own and they are

In the film The Aviator, *Leonardo DiCaprio played the part of American millionaire, Howard Hughes, who suffered from OCD.*

not attributed to an external force. It is important that the clinician takes a careful history from the patient before making a diagnosis.

- Obsessions and compulsions occur in a number of other disorders. DSM-IV-TR specifically warns clinicians not to diagnose OCD when the obsessions and compulsions are restricted to another disorder (e.g. obsessive behaviour with regard to food in an eating disorder, concern with physical appearance in a body dysmorphic disorder, preoccupation with having a serious illness in hypochondriasis, etc.).

- There can be some overlap between OCD and obsessive personality disorder (called anankastic personality disorder in ICD-10). This diagnosis is given to people who are inflexible, obstinate, rigid and apt to focus on unimportant detail. They are frequently indecisive, humourless and judgemental. Their need for perfectionism, rigidity and indecisiveness can make it impossible for them to hold down a job. They often seem quite controlled but can become violent towards people who disrupt their careful, ordered routine. Although there are some similarities between this personality type and people with OCD, many people with OCD have other types of personality – most commonly, avoidant and dependent (Baer *et al.* 1990). Moreover, people with obsessive personality disorder are more likely to develop depression than OCD.

Dual diagnosis

OCD often occurs alongside other mental disorders – this is called co-morbidity. For example, OCD frequently occurs with depression and it can be difficult to disentangle the two disorders. Estimates suggest that about 67 per cent of people with OCD also have depression (Gibbs 1996). OCD is also often co-morbid with social phobia, panic disorder and specific phobia, and people with OCD are commonly also diagnosed with either avoidant or dependent personality disorder. Another closely related disorder which frequently co-exists with OCD is BDD (body dysmorphic disorder) in which people are obsessed with imagined flaws in their appearance.

Who is diagnosed?

There are probably many people in the community who meet the diagnostic criteria for OCD, but who do not come forward for treatment. It is a characteristic of OCD that individuals recognize the irrationality of their behaviour.

Some people recognize they have a problem but do not want to be stigmatized with a mental illness label. Some people with OCD try to hide their symptoms from other people because they realize that they look ridiculous to other people. It has been estimated that only about 40 per cent of people with obsessive-compulsive symptoms come forward for treatment (Kessler & Zhao 1999).

Cultural factors

OCD appears to affect people from all cultures and has been reported in countries such as India, Taiwan and Israel (Yaryura-Tobias and Neziroglu 1997).

Activity **Characteristics of OCD**

Practise writing a concise outline of the main characteristics of OCD – something worth about five marks in an exam. Look through Topic 1 and select what you think are relevant points. Once you have made your selection, you should take no more than five or six minutes to write your outline.

Useful tips are given on p.610. ▶

CHECK YOUR UNDERSTANDING

Check your understanding of characteristics of OCD and issues surrounding the classification and diagnosis of OCD. Try to do this from memory. You can check your answers by looking back through topic 1.

1 What characteristics are shared by all anxiety disorders?

2 List four symptoms of obsession.

3 What is the difference between obsessions and compulsions?

4 Give three reasons why compulsions cause difficulties for people with OCD.

5 What is meant by co-morbidity?

6 How do the obsessions of OCD differ from the delusions of schizophrenia?

7 Explain how OCD and obsessive personality disorder differ from one another.

8 Why do the majority of people who experience symptoms of OCD not come forward for treatment?

Topic 2: Explanations of OCD

Psychology in context   Attitudes towards OCD

The footballer David Beckham admitted in 2006 that he suffers from OCD. The following is adapted from an article in *The Independent* newspaper (3 April 2006).

The footballer has spoken for the first time of his addiction to rearranging hotel rooms and lining up cans of soft drinks to make 'everything perfect'.

'I've got this obsessive compulsive disorder where I have to have everything in a straight line or everything has to be in pairs. I'll put my Pepsi cans in the fridge and if there's one too many then I'll put it in another cupboard somewhere'... Asked if he wanted to stop his obsessive behaviour, he said: 'I would like to. I've tried and can't stop.'

The England captain said that his wife, Victoria, calls him a 'weirdo' because of his condition. Beckham said that ... players at his former club, Manchester United, would deliberately rearrange his clothes in hotel rooms or move magazines around to make them 'wonky' to infuriate him.

A spokesman for the charity OCD UK said: 'There is still a lot of stigma about the condition and even

GPs are not very good at picking up on it. Young men in particular are often reluctant to come forward and ask for treatment, so to have someone like David Beckham talk about it is very good.'

David Beckham

1 The World Health Organization lists OCD as among the ten biggest causes of disability, yet many sufferers keep their illness hidden and the condition is often the subject of scepticism and derision. Why do you think this is the case? What do you think about the reactions of Beckham's wife and team mates?

2 Do you think that it is helpful for people in the media to 'admit' to suffering from mental disorders?

3 Why do you think that people, particularly young men, are reluctant to come forward for treatment?

All of the models of psychopathology which you looked at on your AS course offer explanations for OCD.

Biological explanations of OCD

Biological explanations of OCD (and other anxiety disorders) include the following propositions:

- Some of us inherit a predisposition to develop anxiety that may take the form of OCD.

- Anxiety is caused by disrupted biochemistry or other abnormal brain activity.

In the following section we shall consider genetic, neuroanatomical and biochemical explanations.

Genetic explanation

Genetic research attempts to establish whether there is a familial genetic link, i.e. whether the tendency to develop OCD is hereditary. Research is mainly based on family studies with first-degree relatives (parents, children, siblings) and on twin studies.

Family studies

First-degree relatives share an average of 50 per cent of their genes. To investigate the genetic transmission of OCD, studies compare rates of OCD in relatives of diagnosed cases compared to relatives of controls:

- Pauls et al. (1995) reported a prevalence of up to 10 per cent in first-degree relatives of those with OCD compared with approximately two per cent prevalence in the general population.

- Nestadt et al. (2000), who compared 80 patients with OCD and 73 patients without mental illness (controls), found that first-degree relatives of those with OCD had an 11.7 per cent risk of developing the condition at some time in their lives. First-degree relatives of the control patients had only a 2.7 per cent risk.

Twin studies

Twin studies offer another way of establishing genetic links, by comparing the difference in concordance rates (i.e. the likelihood of both twins being affected with the disorder) for identical (**MZ**) and fraternal (**DZ**) twins. Both share the same environment, but only the MZ twins have identical genetic make-up. A number of studies have been conducted and most seem to show a significantly higher concordance rate in MZ than in DZ twins:

- Carey and Gottesman (1981), in a study using the Maudsley Twin Register, found 87 per cent concordance for MZ twins and 47 per cent for DZ twins.

- Lambert and Kinsley (2005), in a review of studies, found 53 per cent concordance in MZ twins and 23 per cent in DZ twins.

Gene research

More recently, researchers have started to conduct more direct genetic studies to try to identify the precise gene or gene combination that predisposes people to OCD. This work is still at an early stage and no firm conclusions can yet be drawn.

Evaluation of the genetic explanation

- *Not 100 per cent concordance* – No study has yet shown 100 per cent concordance in MZ twins, suggesting that other factors also have a contributory role. For example, in all the twin studies, people shared the same environment, suggesting that environmental factors might also have a strong influence.

- **HOW SCIENCE WORKS** *Differences in concordance rates* – Twin and family studies have not all found the same concordance rates, e.g. Andrews et al. (1990) found no evidence for a higher concordance rate in MZ twins versus DZ twins. Some of the differences in concordance rates found in family and twin studies of OCD may reflect the different diagnostic criteria used to identify people with OCD in the various studies. Pauls et al. (1995), for example, found much higher rates of concordance if people who had some obsessive-compulsive symptoms but did not qualify for a full diagnosis were included in the study. You need to be aware of this when you evaluate research.

- *Non-specific predisposition* – Most researchers do now accept that there is some genetic contribution to OCD but that it might be a somewhat non-specific predisposition to anxiety (MacKinnon and Foley 1996). However, it is not clear exactly what is passed on genetically.

- *Fixed action patterns* – It has been suggested (e.g. Rapoport 1989) that obsessions and compulsions result from fixed action patterns in the brain that have *evolutionary* significance for survival. In stressful and dangerous situations, certain action patterns are triggered, but most people cease to perform actions when their purpose has been completed. For people with OCD, the inherited, fixed action patterns are inappropriately triggered by their own perceptions of danger. You can find more information about evolutionary explanations of behaviour on pp. 6–7 in the Introduction to the book. See also the panel, 'The evolutionary explanation of OCD' below.

> ### IDA The evolutionary explanation of OCD
>
> According to the evolutionary approach, the ritual behaviours associated with OCD are exaggerations of adaptive strategies that once enhanced the chances of our ancestors reproducing successfully. For example, involuntary feelings of disgust or fear regarding particular objects or events would lead some individuals to avoid common dangers without the need to experience them in real life. Individuals who possessed this trait would have an advantage over those who did not. This would result in the trait becoming widespread within the population. This view is supported by the fact that unwanted intrusive thoughts and compulsive rituals are universal phenomena across cultures. However, responses that have evolved through natural selection because they were once adaptive may nowadays be activated in circumstances that make them psychologically maladaptive.

Neuroanatomical explanations

It is possible that genetic factors might work by influencing the brain's structure. One suggestion is that a structural dysfunction in the central nervous system (CNS) underlies OCD (see Fig. 11b.1).

The main areas of the brain that have been implicated are the orbito-frontal cortex (OFC) (an area in the frontal lobe just above the eye) and the caudate nuclei (structures located in a part of the brain called the basal ganglia). These are regions of the brain which form a circuit whose function seems to be to convert sensory information into thoughts and actions. Impulses arising in the OFC are passed to the caudate nuclei, which act as filters screening out irrelevant or unimportant impulses. The most powerful impulses are then passed on to the thalamus. It is only when impulses reach the thalamus that the individual is driven to think any more about them and to take action. Many researchers now believe that parts of this brain circuit are damaged in people with OCD, so inappropriate impulses are not suppressed and the individual is overwhelmed by troublesome thoughts and actions (Lambert and Kinsley 2005).

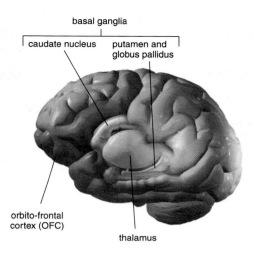

Figure 11b.1 *A three-dimensional view of the human brain (with parts shown as they would if the overlying cerebral cortex were transparent), showing areas that appear to be too active in people with OCD (Adapted from Rapoport 1989, p.85).*

Evaluation of neuroanatomical explanations

- *Evidence* – There is growing evidence that links OCD to impaired functioning of the basal ganglia, e.g. OCD is often co-morbid with disorders where the basal ganglia are known to be implicated (Wise and Rapoport 1989). These disorders include Parkinson's disease (a degenerative neurological disorder, characterized by tremors, slowness of movement and rigidity); Tourette's syndrome (a neurological disorder characterized by sudden involuntary movements and vocal outbursts, called tics), and Huntington's disease/chorea (an inherited neurological disorder that results in a progressive loss of the control of movement and mental ability, and changes in personality). It has also been demonstrated that OFC or basal ganglia damage, resulting from head injury and illnesses such as encephalitis and brain tumours, can give rise to OCD (Coetzer 2004). The development of brain scanning techniques has allowed researchers to examine the living brains of people with OCD. However, although results from neuro-imaging studies have been encouraging, they are rather inconclusive and basal ganglia impairment has not always been found in OCD patients when compared with controls (Piggot et al. 1996)

- *Therapies* – There is also some support from certain therapeutic interventions. For example, psychosurgery which disconnects the basal ganglia from the OFC can reduce symptoms in severe OCD (Rapoport *et al.* 1994). It has also been found that the symptoms of OCD can be relieved using SSRI medication (see section on therapies, pp. 398–400, for more detail). SSRIs are thought to inhibit activity in the OFC.

Research investigating brain structures

When you are evaluating research that supports a particular hypothesis, you need to think carefully about methodological and ethical issues.

A major problem for those investigating brain structures or systems in the field of psychopathology, is that they often cannot use human patients directly in clinical research. There are numerous ethical and practical limitations which prevent researchers from using patients who are still living.

Researchers are able to conduct post-mortem examinations on people who have suffered from a mental disorder to see if any brain abnormalities can be detected. However, post-mortem studies of people who had suffered from a mental disorder in life are difficult to interpret. It is not clear whether brain changes reflect causal factors or whether they developed because of the disorder or as a result of treatments.

Newer, more sophisticated techniques such as PET and MRI scans can provide more detailed and accurate information. **Magnetic resonance imaging (MRI)** is a technique in which radio waves in the brain are recorded, computerized and assembled into a three-dimensional picture of brain structures. Menzies *et al.* (2007) used MRI scans to compare the brains of people diagnosed with OCD, their unaffected first-degree relatives and a group of healthy, unrelated controls. Menzies and her team were interested in investigating the endophenotypes (heritable traits) that might predict genetic susceptibility to OCD.

Brain structure of all the participants was measured using magnetic resonance imaging (MRI), and behavioural performance was measured using a stop-response task (the participants were given a repetitive task which they were instructed to stop at the sound of a pre-learned signal). OCD patients and their relatives (even though they did not have OCD) were less able to stop the task than the controls. It was also found that the OCD patients and their relatives had lower amounts of grey matter in the OFC than the controls, and greater amounts of grey matter in the cingulated regions. They concluded that these variations in brain systems related to motor control might be endophenotypes for OCD.

Evaluation

- *Well-designed study* – This was a carefully controlled study using sophisticated technical equipment. MRI scans allow detailed and accurate images of brain structures to be recorded. However, MRI scanners are expensive and only available for researchers working in large, well-funded research centres.

- *Control group* – We know that OCD runs in families and is more likely to occur in close relatives; the investigators were trying to identify some underlying factor that occurs in vulnerable families. It was important to choose the control group carefully to make sure that none of them had any signs of OCD.

- *Future research* – Although the study was relatively small scale (31 participants in each group) it found significant difference in the brains of OCD patients and relatives from those of normal controls. This provided testable hypotheses for further studies.

Biochemical explanations

Neurotransmitters are chemical messengers in the brain and nervous system that transmit nerve impulses from one nerve cell to another across the synapse (the gap between adjacent nerve cells). Some researchers believe that OCD results from a deficiency of the neurotransmitter serotonin or a malfunction in serotonin metabolism. This idea is based on the rather surprising finding that OCD can be relieved by antidepressant drugs, especially those which increase levels of serotonin in the brain. It is now clear that OCD differs from other anxiety disorders in that it responds preferentially to drugs that affect serotonin rather than other neurotransmitters. Originally, it was assumed that OCD was caused by deficiencies in serotonin. However, it now seems clear that the link between OCD and serotonin is more complex. One suggestion is that serotonin acts as a neuromodulator (a neurotransmitter which regulates the levels of other neurotransmitters) in OCD. If this is the case, it is assumed that disruption of serotonin levels has a knock-on effect on regulating the levels of other important neurotransmitters. The other neurotransmitters that seem to be important are glutamate, GABA and dopamine. (Lambert and Kinsley 2005)

The role of neurotransmitters is linked to the neuroanatomical explanations (see p.393). Serotonin and the other implicated neurotransmitters (glutamate, GABA and dopamine) are important in the functioning of the OFC and the caudate nuclei. It is possible that abnormal neurotransmitter levels underlie the impaired functioning in these brain areas.

Evaluation of biochemical explanations

- *Medication* – Support for the biochemical explanation comes from the effectiveness of medication. In particular, drugs which inhibit the re-uptake of the neurotransmitter serotonin have been found beneficial for up to 60 per cent of patients with OCD (Zohar *et al.* 1996). However, they seem to provide only partial alleviation of the symptoms, which recur when medication is ceased (Lydiard *et al.* 1996), indicating that medication is not a cure.

- *Cause or effect of OCD* – It may be that neurotransmitter levels fluctuate as a result, rather than a cause, of OCD.

Psychological explanations of OCD

We now turn our attention to the psychological explanations that have been proposed for OCD. You might find it helpful at this point to refresh your memory of psychological approaches to psychopathology in *Psychology AS for AQA A* (pp. 227–36).

Given the lack of consistent findings from studies investigating the biological causes of OCD, it seems likely that psychological factors may also be important. In the following section we shall look at psychodynamic, behavioural and cognitive-behavioural explanations.

Psychodynamic explanations

Freud offered a psychoanalytic explanation for the symptoms of OCD. Alfred Adler, a onetime colleague of Freud's, offered a somewhat different **psychodynamic explanation**.

Freud's psychoanalytic explanation

Freud explained OCD in terms of his **psychoanalytic theory** (the first psychodynamic theory) – OCD is most likely to occur in people who are anally fixated and who, therefore, show anal personality characteristics. Such people are excessively neat, orderly and punctual. Freud believed that OCD stems from a fixation at the anal stage of development at around the age of two years. He thought that children at this stage derive pleasure from their bowel movements, both as a physical release and as a creative act. During toilet training, the child has to accept the will of the parents and be neat and clean when its natural preference is to be messy and aggressive. The child feels rage at this restraint but parental pressure also makes the child feel guilty, ashamed and dirty. This gives rise to an intense conflict between the id (wanting to let go) and the ego (wanting to control). When this conflict is particularly strong and parental restrictions are too strict, development is arrested and so the issues related to this stage become issues in adulthood as well and may produce the symptoms of OCD. However, because this takes place at an unconscious level, the adult really believes that they are concerned with keeping themselves clean. For example, an individual fixated at the anal stage may use the defence mechanism, reaction formation, to resist the urge to soil and become compulsively neat and tidy.

Adler's 'inferiority complex' explanation

According to Adler (1931) some parents dominate their children and prevent them from developing a sense of their own competence. When this happens, an 'inferiority complex' may result so that later, as adults, these people may adopt compulsive rituals (such as ordering items in a drawer) in order to carve out an area in which they exert control of *something* and can feel competent.

Evaluation of psychodynamic explanations

- *Difficult to test* – It is hard to test the idea of unconscious motivation experimentally. There is no convincing evidence to support the psychoanalytic view of OCD, and psychoanalysis has proved of little use in helping people to overcome OCD.

- *Adler's theory* – Adler's theory of the 'inferiority complex' resembles some of the ideas contained within humanistic psychology, i.e. that the best route to mental health and wellbeing is to become autonomous and take responsibility for oneself. Child-rearing practices that impede such development, therefore, may result in mental disorders. Support for the importance of feeling capable and being able to exercise control comes from stress research. You may recall from your AS studies that the 'hardy personality', which helps people resist the negative effects of stress, contains a 'control' element – the belief that you can influence what happens in your life. Adlerian therapy focuses on helping clients gain self-confidence.

Behavioural explanations

Behavioural explanations typically focus on the two processes of classical and operant conditioning. The behavioural explanation of OCD is based on the two-process model of Mowrer (1947):

1. Fear of specific stimuli is acquired through a process of classical conditioning (e.g. touching a doorknob in a dirty environment might become associated with the frightening idea of contamination).

2. Fear is maintained by operant conditioning (once the fear of dirty doorknobs had been acquired, the individual learns that hand-washing relieves the feeling of fear).

Unlike in phobic disorders (see Chapter 11a), the anxiety of OCD is hard to escape. Therefore, individuals try to relieve their anxiety by covert or overt ritual behaviours. These 'substitute' escape rituals (e.g. compulsively checking and re-checking that the doors are locked) produce short-term anxiety relief but they maintain longer-term anxiety because the individual never learns that nothing bad happens in the absence of the rituals.

Evaluation of behavioural explanations

- *Research evidence* – There is evidence that people who engage in compulsive behaviour are rewarded by a reduction in anxiety (Rachman and Hodgson 1980).

- *Effective behavioural therapy* – There is some evidence for the effectiveness of treatments based on behavioural theory (see ERP therapy on p.400). Studies (e.g. Baxter *et al.* (1992) and Schwartz *et al.* (1996)), have found that behavioural therapies not only reduce symptoms of OCD, but also bring about changes in biochemical activity. Marks (1981) found behavioural therapy to be very effective in treating compulsive cleaning and checking behaviour, but not so effective for obsessional thoughts. However, just because a behavioural therapy successfully treats a particular disorder, this does not mean that the cause of the disorder can best be explained in behavioural terms. To assume so would be to commit what is known as the treatment aetiology fallacy. After all, as Hewstone *et al.* (2005) point out, 'few people would argue that because aspirin relieves headache, headache is actually due to the lack of aspirin in the body'.

Cognitive-behavioural explanations

If you have not already done so, you should read the section on the cognitive approach in the Introduction to the book on p.15.

According to the cognitive view, OCD is a consequence of faulty and irrational ways of thinking taken to an absolute extreme. Most people experience involuntary, intrusive thoughts from time to time but are usually able to ignore them. People with OCD, on the other hand, do not seem able to dismiss these thoughts and, in addition, blame themselves for having them and for the terrible things that will happen as a consequence of the thoughts (Shafran 2005). In order to try to ward off the awful consequences, people with OCD attempt to neutralize their thoughts. Two methods are used to do this: actions and thought suppression.

Actions to neutralize intrusive thoughts
Neutralizing intrusive thoughts usually involves carrying out actions (e.g. repeated hand-washing to neutralize thoughts about contamination) that are intended to reduce any potential threat (Salkovskis *et al.* 2003). These neutralizing acts bring about a temporary relief in anxiety and so, in behavioural terms, act as reinforcement. Reinforced behaviours are then repeated, and a pattern of repetitive, ritualistic behaviour begins (look again at the case study of OCD on p.398).

Repeated hand-washing is a cleaning ritual associated with OCD.

Research has shown that, compared with controls, people with OCD do, indeed, experience more intrusive thoughts, develop more elaborate methods to neutralize these thoughts and are more likely to experience temporary relief from anxiety after carrying out the neutralizing acts (Salkovskis *et al.* 2003).

Suppression to neutralize intrusive thoughts
Another way in which people with OCD try to neutralize their thoughts is to suppress them. Paradoxically, it has been found that thought suppression actually leads to greater preoccupation with the thought. Wegner *et al.* (1987), for example, asked two groups of normal college students either to think about a white bear or not to think about a white bear. One group was asked to think about the bear and, after an interval, were told to stop thinking about it. The other group were told not to think about the bear (i.e. suppress thoughts) and then, after an interval, were asked to start thinking about it. The participants had to ring a bell every time they thought about the bear. Interestingly, students in the second group thought more about the bear after the suppression than students in the first group. In other words, deliberate attempts to suppress a particular thought can lead to an increase in those thoughts later. Similar findings have been demonstrated in people with OCD. Salkovskis and Kirk (1997) asked some of their OCD clients to keep a diary in which they recorded all their intrusive thoughts. They were instructed on some days to try to suppress these thoughts and, on other days, simply to record them in the diary with no attempt at suppression. It was found that the OCD clients recorded almost twice as many intrusive thoughts on the days that they tried to suppress them as on other days.

Activity Suppressing intrusive thoughts

Try a 'white bear' study (Wegner *et al.* 1991) for yourself. You could substitute 'pink elephant' (or something similar) for white bear if you wished. When planning your study, think about the following:

- What timescale will you use?
- How will your participants record when they have intrusive thoughts?
- Are there any ethical issues to be considered when you are deciding on what you will ask participants to think (or not think) about?

After you have carried out your study, consider the following:

- What are the shortcomings of collecting data in this way?
- Do your findings support those of Wegner *et al.*?

Evaluation of cognitive-behavioural explanations

■ *More description than explanation* – Cognitive-behaviourists describe fairly accurately what happens in the thought processes of people with OCD, but they do not really explain *why* people develop OCD in the first place. We all have intrusive thoughts occasionally, but we do not all go on to develop OCD. OCD seems to be associated with particular characteristics:
- People with OCD are also likely to be more depressed than other people (Hong *et al.* 2004).
- They set themselves unrealistically high moral and personal standards (Rachman 1993).
- They believe that they should be in perfect control of all their thoughts and actions (Coles *et al.* 2005).

This suggests that certain vulnerability factors predispose people to OCD. It does not, however, explain why they think in such an irrational fashion.

■ *Success of therapies* – Cognitive-behavioural therapies (see pp. 400–402) have been shown to be reasonably effective in treating OCD (e.g. Emmelkamp *et al.* 1988). However, this does not, in itself, support the underlying cognitive explanation (see treatment aetiology fallacy on p.396).

Summing up

It is clear that no single explanation can account for a complex disorder such as OCD. It used to be thought that OCD, like other anxiety disorders, was caused by psychosocial factors. However, there is increasing evidence from biological research that physiological factors also have a part to play. It seems likely that OCD develops as a consequence of an interaction between biological, psychological and social factors. This approach (called the **diathesis-stress model**) proposes that certain individuals have an underlying biological vulnerability to OCD. However, they only develop the full-blown disorder in response to environmental triggers. To see an illustrative diagram of the diathesis-stress model turn to Chapter 11a Phobic disorders, Figure 11a.1 on p.376.

CHECK YOUR UNDERSTANDING

Check your understanding of explanations of OCD. Try to do this from memory. You can check your answers by looking back through Topic 2.

1. How can family and twin studies help us to understand genetic factors involved in OCD? Briefly outline the findings from these studies.

2. Briefly outline a neuroanatomical explanation of OCD.

3. Outline the main findings from the MRI study conducted by Menzies *et al.* (2007).

4. What is a neurotransmitter?

5. Why has serotonin been implicated in OCD?

6. Briefly outline and evaluate the psychodynamic explanations for OCD.

7. What is meant by the two-process explanation of OCD?

8. Why is the behavioural two-process explanation of OCD inadequate?

9. Outline two ways in which people with OCD try to deal with intrusive thoughts (according to the cognitive-behavioural explanation of OCD). How successful is each of these two ways?

10. Explain what is meant by the treatment aetiology fallacy.

Topic 3: Therapies for OCD

A **therapy** is a deliberate intervention designed to treat mental disorders either by effecting a complete cure or by making the symptoms more manageable. A number of different therapies and treatments for mental disorders will be outlined, each one based on a particular theoretical approach regarding the basis of human nature and the causes of psychological problems. You will already be familiar with these approaches or models of mental disorder from your AS-level studies of psychopathology; you may wish to refresh your memory on these before starting this topic, as this background knowledge is essential to an understanding of therapies.

There are considerable ethical and practical issues involved with therapy and intervention and these have important implications for all of those involved in mental health, whether recipients or practitioners. Some of these points will be considered in the context of each type of therapy. There are, however, some important general

Activity   The concept of cure

The concept of cure is difficult to establish for mental disorders such as OCD. In small groups, discuss the following:

1 How much improvement in their OCD symptoms might clients be expected to show or experience before they are considered cured?

2 How might improvement be measured?

3 Who should decide that a cure has been achieved?

issues surrounding the use of therapies. These are described in the section on therapies in the Introduction to Psychopathology on p.304, and we recommend that

Psychology in context Self-help for OCD

Robert Eddison, an actor and playwright, now in middle-age, wrote an article for *The Times* newspaper in April 2003 about his early experience of OCD. The following is an adapted extract from the article:

'At 14 I was taken out of school on the cusp of a nervous breakdown, powered by a pathological dread of losing possessions, thoughts or even my own identity. So extreme was my fear of disorder and loss that it confined me, on bad days, to my room – and even to my bed. This meant that I had almost no secondary education. My parents' response was too extreme to be helpful. In colluding with my rituals, Mum exacerbated them, while my father was too intransigent.

Without the benefit of modern OCD treatments and medication, I had to bare-knuckle my way to recovery. I continued cramming and scrabbled together the requisite four A levels for my place at Cambridge, where I duly arrived, feeling tense and ill-prepared. Three years later I emerged OCD-free. How had I done it? I had noticed that my OCD got worse when I was tired or had not eaten properly, so I started to live more healthily. Then came positive thinking. I filled each day with things I enjoyed doing. My rapid (and permanent) improvement enabled me to do well at Cambridge and to follow a normal career path as a journalist and playwright.

Scientific validation for my recovery strategy has come recently with *The Mind and the Brain*, a revolutionary new book on OCD, co-authored by Jeffrey Schwartz (2002), an authority on OCD. He demonstrates that we have the power to use our minds to rewire our physical brain – and that we can do this ourselves without outside help.'

- Why do you think it would have been difficult to get effective treatment for OCD in the 1950s and 1960s?
- Do you think that it is possible to overcome mental disorders like OCD through 'strength of mind'?
- Do you think that the idea of 'self-help' puts an unnecessary responsibility on people who are suffering from a serious, distressing mental disorder?

Is positive thinking enough to overcome OCD?

you start by reading about these and also come back to them later on as you evaluate the various types of therapy. Now try the activity, 'The concept of cure' on p.397.

Biological therapies

Biological therapies arise from the medical model of abnormal behaviour. According to this model, mental disorder is an illness which results mainly from a biochemical imbalance. Biological treatments are designed to redress this imbalance through the administration of chemical drugs, electroconvulsive therapy (ECT) and, in rare cases, psychosurgery. They aim to alter abnormal behaviours by intervening directly in bodily processes. Many people who are experiencing psychological problems or who show disturbed behaviour patterns go for help to their family doctor. This means that the first line of treatment offered is usually medical. In the case of OCD, drug therapy is the most usual form of biological therapy, although psychosurgery has been used in extreme cases.

Drug therapy (chemotherapy)

There are several broad classes of drugs that are used in the treatment of mental disorders. Although there are a number of different types of anti-anxiety drugs, antidepressant drugs are actually the first choice for people with OCD. Two particular types of antidepressant drug have been used with OCD: tricyclics (e.g. Tofranil) and SSRIs (e.g. Prozac):

- Research findings on the effectiveness of tricyclics (which work by increasing the availability of noradrenaline and serotonin) on OCD have been mixed. There is some suggestion that they are only effective for people who are also depressed and, in any case, that any benefits of therapy are short-lived (Pato *et al.* 1988).

- SSRIs, which increase the availability of serotonin levels, seem to be a more effective form of treatment and produce more relief from symptoms than either tricyclics or placebo. About 50 to 70 per cent of OCD clients have reported some reduction in symptoms, compared with five per cent on placebo (an inert substance) (Dolberg *et al.* 1996). See the Introduction to Psychopathology, p.305, for more information about the use of placebo.

For more information about antidepressant drugs, turn to Chapter 10 Depression, p.330.

Evaluation of drug therapy

- *Limited effectiveness* – While antidepressants, especially SSRIs, have helped people with OCD, it seems that approximately 30 to 50 per cent of clients derive no benefit from them. Relapse rates are very high (as much as 90 per cent) when the drugs are discontinued. Therefore, drugs do not provide a permanent 'cure' for the disorder. In order to have long-lasting benefits, clients need to stay on the drug for long periods of time. This is not desirable as the drugs have some unpleasant side effects.

- *Combined therapy* – There is some evidence, however, that relapse is reduced when the drugs are combined with exposure treatments (Simpson *et al.* 2004). Exposure treatments are discussed later, on p.400.

- *Appropriateness of drug therapy* – see Ethical issues box below.

IDA | Ethical issues in use of drugs

Some people have criticized the widespread use of drugs in the treatment of mental disorders, referring to them as 'chemical straitjackets' and, therefore, as inappropriate treatment for psychological conditions. The argument is that the drugs are dehumanizing and take away any sense of personal responsibility or control. Furthermore, drugs may have serious side effects. The ethical issue of informed consent is also a consideration. People whose lives are seriously disrupted by OCD may not be in a position to give fully informed consent about their treatment.

Psychosurgery

Psychosurgery is sometimes used in the case of treatment-resistant OCD. However, it is important to understand that such therapy is considered only as a last resort if all other treatment options have failed to work. The most commonly used psychosurgical treatments for OCD involve the use of radio-frequency waves to destroy a small amount of brain tissue that disrupts a specific circuit in the brain that has been implicated in OCD. (See neuroanatomical explanations, p.393.) This area is the corticostriatal circuit, and it is comprised of the orbito-frontal cortex, the caudate nucleus, the thalamus, and the anterior cingulate cortex.

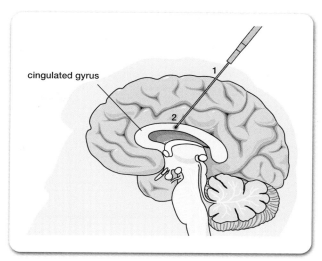

Figure 11b.2

1 *Probes are inserted through the skull into the cingulated gyrus, a bundle of connections that regulate the circuit that is hyperactive in OCD.*

2 *The probes' tips are heated and tissue is burned. The operation can also be done with external radiation.*

Various techniques are used, including anterior cingulotomy, capsulotomy and limbic leucotomy. These are generally considered safe procedures that do not usually affect a patient's memory or intellect, but the safest method appears to be the **cingulotomy**. This is a procedure to destroy a small area of tissue in the cingulated gyrus, which links the prefrontal cortex to the limbic system of the brain. The limbic system is involved in emotion and behaviour. See Figure 11b.2.

There are some slightly less permanent, brain-based techniques, such as vagus nerve stimulation, deep brain stimulation and transcranial magnetic stimulation (TMS). Though only fairly recently introduced, TMS has shown promising results (see TMS box below).

TMS – a new treatment method

Transcranial magnetic stimulation (TMS) is a new technique (sometimes called 'magnetic therapy') which involves stimulating brain cells using magnetic fields but without any direct contact with the brain.

The treatment is painless and does not involve using anaesthetics, electrodes or surgery. It is not clear exactly how TMS works but it is thought to increase the availability of serotonin and other neurotransmitters in the brain.

Activity Psychosurgery

Psychosurgery is a very controversial treatment for a variety of reasons. Because of this, its use is strictly controlled in the UK. You might like to find out a bit more about the Mental Health Act (1983) and the regulations that apply to psychosurgery. You can look at the Mental Health Act and also a number of interesting articles about psychosurgery on the website of the UK charity Mind.

www.mind.org.uk/

Evaluation of psychosurgery

- *Effectiveness* – Baer *et al.* (1995) reported that cingulotomy was successful in decreasing anxiety and OCD behaviour. More recently, however, Cosgrove (2000) found that the procedure produced marked benefits in only 30 per cent of patients. The evidence about the efficacy of psychosurgery, therefore, is inconsistent, although it has been estimated that long-term effectiveness in alleviating symptoms is somewhere between 25 to 70 per cent depending on the criteria used for assessing success. However, all these techniques are drastic and irreversible and can cause seizures.

- *Appropriateness* – Psychosurgery also raises ethical issues in terms of informed consent: patients who are disturbed enough to warrant consideration for psychosurgery might well not have the insight to understand the implications of such therapies.

Psychological therapies

Psychological therapies address psychological rather than biological factors associated with mental disorders. Psychological treatments for OCD include behaviour therapy and cognitive therapy. First, however, since Freud offered a psychoanalytic explanation for OCD, we shall have a brief look at psychoanalytic therapy.

Psychoanalytic therapy

Psychoanalytic therapy aims to uncover the unconscious conflicts that the individual has repressed from childhood. Traditional psychoanalysis uses a variety of techniques, including free association and dream analysis (see Chapter 10 Depression, p.330 for more about these techniques). However, there has been no controlled study of its effectiveness with OCD, and it is not generally thought to be appropriate for people with OCD.

Behavioural therapy

We shall consider two **behavioural therapies**: modelling, and exposure and response prevention, the latter being the most commonly used psychological therapy for OCD.

Modelling

One very straightforward behavioural technique that has been tried with OCD is **modelling** – based on Bandura's (1969) 'social learning theory'. This is an extension of learning theory, to include learning through observing the behaviour of others. Modelling involves the therapist demonstrating 'fearless' behaviour, e.g. the therapist might handle an object which the patient regards as contaminated. In later sessions, the client is asked to handle the object. Although this therapy can be helpful for people with phobias, because the focus of their fear is fairly specific, it is of less use for OCD, where the anxiety is more diffuse.

Exposure and response prevention (ERP)

Although compulsions serve to reduce anxiety in the short term, in the longer term, they might actually increase anxiety levels. **Exposure and response prevention (ERP)** is a method aimed to stop people carrying out compulsive behaviours. It was first developed by Meyer (1966) and is now one of the most widely used forms of treatment for OCD.

In ERP, clients are repeatedly exposed to objects or situations that normally arouse anxiety in them. They are then encouraged to avoid their normal 'safety' rituals. This is extremely difficult for them at the beginning of the therapy programme, and relaxation techniques are taught to help clients cope with the high levels of physiological arousal associated with their fear. Other techniques include verbal persuasion, continuous monitoring and the encouragement of alternative behaviour. Sometimes, the therapist uses modelling techniques to provide the client with an example of how to behave. Deliberate forceful intervention is counterproductive and can lead to non-compliance. There is some evidence that close family members can sometimes unwittingly collude with the OCD clients in maintaining their rituals. For this reason, other family members are sometimes invited to take part in the therapy sessions to help stop the ritualistic behaviour. Clients are also sometimes given homework assignments so that they can try to apply the learned strategies outside the therapy session. For example, Emmelkamp (1982) reported on homework assignments given to a woman with a cleaning compulsion:

- Do not mop the floor of your bathroom for a week. After this, clean it within three minutes, using an ordinary mop. Use this mop for other chores as well, without cleaning it.

- You, your husband and children all have to keep their shoes on. Do not clean the house for a week.

- Drop a cookie on the contaminated floor, pick the cookie up and eat it.

Now try the 'Ritual behaviours' activity.

Activity   Ritual behaviours

Work in a small group to discuss:

- the kind of ritual behaviours the woman in Emmelkamp's report might have carried out before treatment
- why the homework assignments would be very difficult for her
- ways family members might unwittingly collude with someone suffering from OCD to maintain their rituals.

Evaluation of behavioural therapies

- *Effectiveness* – ERP has been shown in a number of studies to be an effective treatment for OCD. It seems that betweeen 55 to 85 per cent of OCD clients improve significantly with ERP, and the therapeutic effects appear to be long-lasting (e.g. Hollon *et al.* 2006). See also the Activity, 'Evidence in support of ERP' on p.402. When ritual behaviour reduces in response to ERP, obsessional thoughts also seem to diminish. However, behavioural treatment is much less successful for people who experience obsessional thoughts without the accompanying rituals (e.g. sexual obsessions). Further evidence in support of behavioural therapy comes from Greist *et al.* (2002) – see Key research, 'Computer-guided therapy' below.

- *Effects of ERP on brain* – Recent research (Saxena *et al.* 2008) has demonstrated that when ten patients were given four weeks of intensive ERP therapy, they showed significant improvements in their OCD symptoms. In addition, PET scans showed improved brain functioning (e.g. decrease in thalamus activity) in the patients. Saxena and his colleagues claim their research demonstrates that psychological treatments such as ERP can have beneficial biological effects.

Computer-guided therapy

Key research: Greist *et al.* (2002)

It seems clear that behavioural therapy can be very effective in helping people with OCD. Unfortunately, the demand for effective therapy exceeds its supply by trained therapists, both in the US and the UK. One way of trying to cut waiting lists is to offer computer-guided therapy, which does not depend on one-to-one contact with a therapist. If this is going to be a viable option, it is important to make sure that such therapy does produce some therapeutic change.

Greist *et al.* (2002) set out to test such a therapy programme.

Potential participants were screened by a clinician and verified as meeting the DSM-IV-TR criteria for OCD. 218 patients were selected from eight clinics in North America. They were randomly assigned to one of three groups for ten weeks of therapy:

- computer-guided therapy accessed by telephone and supported with a user workbook (N = 74)
- behaviour therapy provided by a trained therapist (N = 69)
- systematic relaxation guided by an audiotape and a manual (N = 75).

Effectiveness was measured by scores on a well-validated Obsessive-Compulsive Scale. It was found that:

- the mean improvement in scores was greater for people in the therapist-led group (8.0 points) than in the computer-guided group (5.6 points)

- both computer-guided and therapy groups showed significantly greater improvement than people in the relaxation group (1.7 points).

The researchers concluded that computer-guided therapy was effective in treating OCD, although clinician-guided therapy was even better. Systematic relaxation was found to be an ineffective treatment for OCD.

Evaluation

- *Validity of OCD diagnosis was high* – All participants were carefully screened by a qualified clinician, using recognized DSM criteria for OCD.

- *A large number of participants were used* – 218 patients were drawn from eight different clinics, increasing the potential for results to be generalized to other people diagnosed with OCD.

- *Application of findings* – The existing shortage of trained clinicians to treat OCD is a serious problem. The findings from this study suggest that computer-guided therapy could be a helpful first step in treating clients with OCD when treatment from a trained clinician is unavailable.

- *Speed of therapy* – Behaviour therapy programmes may be seen as appropriate because they are relatively short (approximately three to eight weeks) and, unlike drugs, do not produce side effects. However, as many as 25 per cent of clients offered ERP experienced no improvement in their symptoms (Foa *et al.* 2005). Also, because of the difficulty of resisting compulsions, it is quite common for clients to drop out of therapy or refuse to comply with assignments.

HOW SCIENCE WORKS

Activity **Evidence in support of ERP as a treatment for OCD**

Rachman et al. (1970) reported the progress of a client who underwent ERP for his compulsive cleaning behaviour. The results, showing a steady decline in the daily washing, are illustrated in Fig. 11b.3.

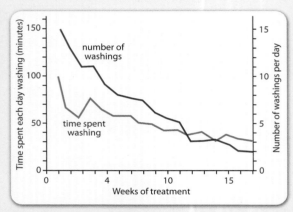

Figure 11b.3 *When treated for his compulsive cleaning, the client showed a steady decline in both the total time he spent washing and in the number of times he washed daily.*

Source: Adapted from Rachman *et al.* (1970)

- Why do you think it is important that the graph shows the decline in both the number of daily washings and the minutes per day spent washing?
- The results of this study are based on data from one individual client. What do you call this type of study and what are its limitations?

Cognitive therapy

Cognitive therapies focus on changing the irrational thinking that is believed to underlie obsessions and compulsions. Cognitive therapists use various strategies:

- *Information* – They provide information to educate clients about their misinterpretations of intrusive thoughts and about the futility of neutralising acts.
- *Challenge* – They challenge inappropriate thoughts (testing the reality of clients' negative expectations).
- *Thought stopping* – They teach thought stopping (distracting the client from inappropriate thoughts by literally shouting out 'Stop!' and then encouraging them to divert their thinking to a pre-prepared image or thought). Clients gradually develop the skill of stopping their own thoughts when these threaten to overwhelm them.

HOW SCIENCE WORKS

Activity **Computer-guided therapy for OCD**

These questions relate to Greist *et al.*'s (2002) research into computer-guided therapy (see Key research on p.401).

- Why was it important to have one group of participants in a systematic relaxation group?
- What are some of the ethical issues that arise in this kind of study?
- Why is it important to use a well-validated scale to measure outcome effectiveness?
- What do you think are some of the advantages and disadvantages of offering computer-guided therapy to people with OCD?

Evaluation of cognitive therapies

■ *Effectiveness* – It seems that pure cognitive interventions are not as effective as ERP, but, in combination, they are more effective than either on its own (VanOppen *et al.* 1995).

■ *ERP as a cognitive-behavioural therapy* – Note that ERP is sometimes classed as a cognitive-behavioural therapy, as the exposure element may involve exposure to fearful thoughts as well as to compulsive behaviours. Therefore, evaluations of ERP as a cognitive-behavioural therapy are relevant here also.

Turn to p.381 in Chapter 11a to read more about cognitive-behavioural therapy (CBT) as a treatment for anxiety disorders.

CHECK YOUR UNDERSTANDING

Check your understanding of therapies for OCD. Try to do this from memory. You can check your answers by looking back through Topic 3.

1 Which antidepressant drugs are effective in reducing OCD symptoms and how do they work?

2 Briefly outline and evaluate the use of psychosurgery in the treatment of OCD.

3 Outline techniques used in ERP.

4 Why do you think people often drop out of ERP therapy?

5 Write a paragraph evaluating the effectiveness of ERP therapy.

6 Rank the following in order of their effectiveness in treating OCD: systematic relaxation; behaviour therapy provided by a trained clinician; computer-guided therapy.

7 Outline some of the strategies used by cognitive therapists to treat OCD.

8 Why is ERP sometimes considered to be a cognitive-behavioural (as opposed to just cognitive) therapy?

Clinical characteristics (symptoms) of OCD

- Overwhelming feeling of anxiety
- Either obsessions or compulsions (or both) are present over a period of time
- Obsessive thoughts – recurrent, unwanted, intrusive and distressing
- Compulsive behaviour – repetitive, ritualistic actions that bring temporary relief from anxiety
- Acknowledgement that behaviour is irrational
- Individual attempts to resist the obsessive thoughts and compulsive behaviours

Clinical characteristics & issues of classification & diagnosis

Issues surrounding classification and diagnosis

Factors that affect the reliability and validity of classification and diagnosis:

- Medicalization of a 'normal' state – validity of diagnosis?
- Some people reluctant to come forward for diagnosis
- Different subtypes of OCD
- Differential diagnosis – problems with reliability
- Dual diagnosis
- Cultural issues

Therapies for OCD

Psychological therapies

- Often used in conjunction with drug therapies

Psychodynamic therapy
(e.g. to reveal hidden conflicts)

Evaluation:

- No convincing evidence to support this as effectiv therapy for OCD

Behavioural therapies (e.g. mainly modellin and exposure and response prevention (ERP))

Evaluation:

- Modelling alone not very effective
- ERP is effective and long-lasting
- ERP does not work for everyone
- No side effects from ERP
- Non-compliance with ERP quite high because therapy so difficult
- ERP not so effective for those with obsessions or

Biological therapies

- Medication (drugs) is main biological therapy
- Antidepressant medication, particularly SSRIs, which work by influencing the availability of serotonin in the brain and nervous system
- Psychosurgery (e.g. cingulotomy) used in extreme cases

Evaluation

- Drugs effective in reducing symptoms for many people with OCD but high relapse rates
- Drugs do not work for everyone
- All medication can produce side effects, particularly after long-term use
- Relapse reduced when drugs combined with exposure treatment
- Psychosurgery highly invasive and effects irreversible – only undertaken when all other treatments have failed and then only under regulated conditions
- Use of drugs and psychosurgery raise ethical issues

Cognitive-behavioural therapy
(e.g. to challenge irrational thinking)

Evaluation:

- Not as effective as ERP but very effective when used in combination with ERP

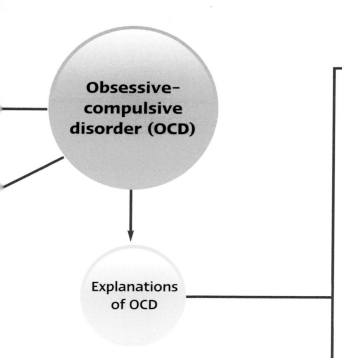

Obsessive-compulsive disorder (OCD)

Explanations of OCD

Psychodynamic

- Freud – OCD arises from intense conflict between id and ego in the anal stage
- Adler – OCD result of inferiority complex

Evaluation:

- Difficult to test unconscious motivation empirically
- No convincing evidence to support explanations

Behavioural (learned behaviour)

Evaluation:

- Some support for the idea that compulsions are acquired through classical conditioning and maintained through operant conditioning
- Effective therapy arises from this theory
- Does not explain where obsessions come from
- Insufficient account taken of cognitive processes

Cognitive (e.g. faulty thinking patterns and attempts to neutralize intrusive thoughts)

Evaluation:

- Descriptive rather than explanatory
- Some research evidence to support idea that people with OCD have different ways of thinking
- Effective therapy arises from this theory but beware the treatment aetiology fallacy

Biological explanations

Genes (inherited predisposition to develop OCD)

Evaluation:

- Support from family and twin studies
- 100% concordance not demonstrated
- Difficult to disentangle effects of environment
- Non-specific predisposition to anxiety (rather than to OCD)
- Evolutionary perspective

Biochemical factors (particularly serotonin)

Evaluation:

- SSRIs can be effective in treating symptoms of OCD
- Difficult to distinguish cause and effect

Neuroanatomical factors
(involvement of the OFC and caudate nuclei)

Evaluation:

- Research support, e.g. from MRI scans
- Support from psychosurgical interventions
- Difficult to distinguish cause and effect
- Structural abnormalities not found in all patients

Diathesis-stress explanation

- Interaction between biological and environmental factors – individuals have genetic vulnerability for OCD but only develop the disorder in the presence of triggering environmental factors

EXPLAINING THE SPECIFICATION

Specification content	The specification explained
Media influences on social behaviour (Topic 1)	The specification focuses on media psychology. In this part of the specification you are required to look at and understand the concept of 'media effects', i.e. different effects the media may have (positive or negative) on those who are exposed to them. To do this you will need to be able to:
Explanations of media influences on pro- and antisocial behaviour	■ Describe and evaluate at least two explanations of media influences on antisocial (e.g. aggressive) behaviour. ■ Describe and evaluate at least two explanations of media influences on prosocial (e.g. helping) behaviour.
The effects of video games and computers on young people	■ Describe and evaluate explanations and research relating to their possible effects on young people (e.g. increasing aggressive behaviour). Note that the terms 'video games' and 'computers' are used synonymously so would not need to be treated separately.
Persuasion, attitude and change (Topic 2)	In this part of the specification you are required to consider psychological insights into how attitudes and behaviour might be influenced through the media. To do this you will need to be able to:
Persuasion and attitude change, including Hovland-Yale and Elaboration Likelihood models	■ Describe and evaluate the relationship between persuasion and attitude change. Note the Hovland-Yale and elaboration likelihood models are specific requirements and can be named in an exam question.
The influence of attitudes on decision making, including roles of cognitive consistency/dissonance and self-perception	■ Describe and evaluate explanations of how attitudes influence the process of decision making. ■ Describe cognitive consistency (which includes cognitive dissonance). Note self-perception explanations are specific requirements and can be named in an exam question.
Explanations for the effectiveness of television in persuasion	■ Describe and evaluate at least two explanations for the effectiveness of television. Although not stated, the most obvious example of the effectiveness of television is through TV advertisements.
The psychology of 'celebrity' (Topic 3)	In this part of the specification you are required to consider the public's attraction to and behaviour towards celebrity figures. To do this you will need to be able to:
The attraction of 'celebrity', including social psychological and evolutionary explanations	■ Describe and evaluate social psychological and evolutionary explanations (e.g. parasocial relationships) of the attraction of celebrity. Note there is, of course, no such thing as an 'evolutionary' explanation of celebrity, but we can speculate *why* celebrities hold a fascination for people.
Research into intense fandom, for example, celebrity worship, stalking	■ Describe and evaluate research into the extreme behaviour of 'fans'. Note: celebrity worship and stalking are used only as examples, therefore cannot be specified in an exam question.

Introduction

The study of 'media' as distinct from other forms of 'communication' is a relatively new area of psychology. Although the use of the term 'media' (or sometimes 'mass media') includes many different forms (including written media, the Internet and various forms of broadcast media), for many the term is synonymous with television. Yet, as media scholar Marshall McLuhan reminds us, each new medium shapes society in its own ways so we can never have a universal definition of 'the media'. Giles (2003) suggests that psychology's lack of interest in the media in the past has been based partly on cultural snobbery and partly on a concern for the subject's scientific integrity, surely compromised by the study of such a vague area as 'the media'. Yet it is precisely the concern for scientific integrity that has prompted many psychologists to take up the challenge to provide answers to important questions concerning, for example, the effects on young people of viewing (or playing) violent media. It seems obvious that the media must have some effect on our behaviour, otherwise why would advertisers spend such a lot of money on trying to convince consumers to change their behaviour? Policy makers and the general public alike are frequently guilty of seeking simple answers to what are very complex questions concerning the influence of the media in our daily lives. Does the media have an effect on our behaviour, and if so what sort of effect? In this chapter we examine the psychology behind these questions.

Psychology in context — Island airs good news on TV for children

A child in St Helena.

'Behaviour among children exposed to television for the first time improves, according to a unique study published in 1997, which contradicts the stereotypical belief that television increases violence and antisocial behaviour.

The "remarkable" results have been taken from a study among children in St Helena, a remote British dependency in the South Atlantic, which had no access to live television until 1995.

Professor Tony Charlton, who has been leading the research, said that the study suggested that it was wrong to blame television for society's failings.

There have been fears in the past that television violence could be responsible for rises in levels of crime and violence in real life, particularly following statistics which suggested that the average American child would see (on television) 32 000 murders, 40 000 attempted murders and, altogether, 250 000 acts of violence before the age of 18.

The St Helena study, now in its sixth year, collected data on the children's leisure-time pursuits and behaviour prior to and following the introduction of television. Content analysis of the programmes received suggested a similar level of violence as in those broadcast in the United Kingdom.

While St Helena children have always been among the best-behaved in the world – only 3.4 per cent of 9- to 12-year-olds on the island have behavioural problems, whereas in London the figure is 14 per cent – the researchers said that the most recent findings show that "in classrooms and playgrounds, young children in St Helena are at least as well-behaved now as they were two years ago, before the availability of television. Moreover, they are significantly less likely to display temper tantrums, tease other children and engage in fighting".'

Source: *The Independent*, 21 July 1997

1 This ongoing study suggests that the link between media violence and violent behaviour is not as clear cut as some commentators would like to make out. Use the Internet to find out what has happened since these results were first published in 1997. Have the standards of good behaviour been maintained?

2 Most of the teenagers admitted they watched 'some' violence on television. One said: 'When we come home in the afternoon, we watch a bit of violence ... Some of the films on Hallmark are packed with horror and violence. Blood and brains ... ugh'. What does this tell you about the way media violence is received by children on St Helena?

3 Students said it was difficult to misbehave on St Helena because 'everyone watches you ... everyone knows you'; 'you've just got to behave, if you don't ... someone will see you'. What does this tell you about the relationship between media violence and violent behaviour generally?

Media influences on antisocial behaviour

'There can no longer be any doubt that heavy exposure to televised violence is one of the causes of aggressive behavior, crime and violence in society.' (Eron 1992)

'We need to be aware that media violence can affect any child from any family. The psychological laws of observational learning, habituation/desensitisation, priming, and excitation transfer are immutable and universal.' (Huesmann *et al.* 2003).

As these statements illustrate, some psychologists believe strongly and even passionately that **media violence** is harmful. More than this, they claim a convergence of many theories and a convergence of many different research methods, all pointing to harm (Grimes *et al.* 2008). Public opinion, by and large, well supports their concerns about harm. Most surveys indicate that, when asked directly, three out of four people will agree that media violence is a cause of crime and violence in society (Cumberbatch 2009). In this opinion, intriguingly, most people also believe they are, themselves, not influenced by the media, but that 'other people' probably are. This has been called the '**third person effect**'. Even among children, the concern about 'others' is remarkable: ten-year-olds will declare themselves immune to media effects but will express concern about their younger brothers and sisters (Andsager and White 2007).

Although there are many theoretical reasons for hypothesizing a link between media violence and aggression, it is probably fair to say that most studies have focused effort on establishing a link rather than developing theories of media influence. Huesmann *et al.* (1984) admitted that, over the 22 years of their **longitudinal study**, they progressed through four different theoretical interpretations of the results, and have moved on since. This may indicate that theories in this area tend to be retrospective (i.e. the link is established first and then explained).

Explanations of media influences on antisocial behaviour

This section looks at observational learning before going on to access other explanations for behaviour, such as cognitive priming and desensitization.

The bobo doll experiments

Key research: Bandura (1986)

Albert Bandura's series of experiments have become something of a classic. His participants were three- to five-year-olds, mostly from the university crèche. Bandura showed them specially prepared film clips of a model (in some experiments this was an adult, in others a child) behaving aggressively towards a Bobo doll (see p.43). When struck, these large knock-down dolls would bounce back up again due to their weighted base. As Bandura describes it, 'The model pummels it on the head with a mallet, hurls it down, sits on it and punches it on the nose repeatedly ...'. Each of these acts was repeated three times in the clip. Following exposure to these curious antics, the children were led to the laboratory containing various toys, including the Bobo doll seen in the clip. On the way, they passed some attractive toys which the researcher invited them to admire but told them they were not allowed to play with. The children, described by Bandura as 'frustrated', were then ostensibly left alone to play with the toys, but hidden observers monitored their free

play. Acts were defined as imitative aggression when the children who had seen the film clips imitated the aggressive behaviour, and where these actions were not demonstrated by any children in a control group who had not seen the film clip. The results were dramatic – up to 88 per cent of pre-school children imitated the aggressive acts shown in the film clip.

Evaluation

Demand characteristics – There is a concern that even young children might respond to the demand characteristics of the experiment. For example, Noble quotes one shrewd four-year-old who, on her first visit to the laboratory, was heard to whisper to her mother: 'Look, mummy! There's the doll we have to hit!' (Noble 1975). The novelty of the toy was also a factor – children unfamiliar with the doll were five times more likely to imitate than those with previous experience.

An artificial setting – An additional issue is that the experiment was structured to show behaviours not normally demonstrated in children, and learning was maximized by repeating the act three times. It is questionable whether the behaviours observed should be defined as aggression – they might be better classed as rough-and-tumble play (Smith *et al.* 2004).

Observational learning

The concern that people may copy what they see on stage or screen is one of the most enduring. Bandura (1986) argued that television can shape the forms that aggressive behaviour takes (see Key research). Television can teach skills that may be useful for committing acts of violence, and it can direct the viewer's attention to behaviours that they may not have considered. For example, young people may mimic martial arts moves or may learn effective tactics for committing violent crime. There is frequent anecdotal evidence that bizarre violent events have followed soon after their depiction on television, suggesting a form of copycat behaviour.

Evaluation of observational learning

- *Lack of research support* – Perhaps largely due to ethical concerns, laboratory experiments along the lines of Bandura began to die out in the 1980s and so very little attention has been paid to developing theories of imitation. More naturalistic studies rarely find imitation – Noble (1975) commented, 'in my own studies, where children watch media violence in small groups, I have rarely found more than 5 per cent imitation after viewing'.

- *Inconsistent effects?* – The kinds of media violence that are typically condemned by the 'effects model' are limited to fictional programmes. The acts of violence that appear daily on our television screens on news programmes are somehow exempt from this condemnation. There is an inconsistency to this argument. If antisocial acts shown in television drama have such a profound effect on viewers, it is puzzling that the antisocial activities that are so frequently in the news and other documentaries do not have similar effects. This is even more puzzling when we consider the fact that in fictional drama, most antisocial acts have negative consequences for the perpetrator, but in documentary depictions of violent acts, there are few apparent negative consequences for those who perform them. The basic question of why the media should induce people to imitate its content has never been answered (Gauntlett 1998).

Cognitive priming

Aggressive ideas in violent films can activate other aggressive thoughts in viewers through their association in memory pathways (Berkowitz 1984). Immediately after a violent film, the viewer is primed to respond aggressively because a network of memories involving aggression is retrieved. Huesmann (1982) suggests that children learn problem-solving scripts in part from their observations of others' behaviour. These scripts are cognitive expectations about a sequence of behaviours that may be performed in particular situations. Frequent exposure to scenes of violence may lead children to store scripts for aggressive behaviour in their memories, and these may be recalled in a later situation if any aspect of the original situation – even a superficial one – is present.

Desensitization

This argument assumes that under normal conditions, anxiety about violence inhibits its use. Those who are not used to media violence would, presumably, be shocked at witnessing an act of violence in the real world, yet frequent viewing of television violence causes such events to appear more commonplace and so may cause viewers to be less anxious and less sensitive about actual violence. Therefore, someone who becomes desensitized to violence may perceive it as more 'normal', become less likely to intervene when they witness violence and be more likely to engage in violence themselves. Related to this view is the finding that boys who are heavy watchers of television violence show lower than average physiological arousal to new scenes of violence, i.e. they are less shocked by violence and less inhibited about using it themselves.

> ### Ethical issues in media research
>
> In testing explanations of the effects of exposure to media violence, ethical considerations have greatly limited the amount of 'violence' to which participants might be exposed, particularly if any resultant aggression is believed to persist beyond the time spent within the laboratory. Clearly it would be unacceptable to put people in situations where actual physical violence may be elicited as a result of their participation in the study.

Research on media violence

Belson (1978) is still the most rigorous and comprehensive study of media violence and one of the largest.

In the last decade, longitudinal studies, examining how early media exposure predicts later aggression, have become surprisingly popular (given they are so expensive). The idea of a **sleeper effect** whereby media violence at a critical age leads to later aggression is an attractive one (e.g. Hopf *et al.* 2008). However, apart from Belson (1978) who controlled for 236 variables which could cause both media consumption and aggression, no other study has been systematic in this even with social class (Chowhan and Stewart 2007). Slater *et al.* (2003) showed that personality traits such as sensation seeking and aggressivity lead to both selective exposure to media violence and aggressive behaviour. They conclude that this might call into question many of the relationships claimed even in longitudinal studies. Although claims that the evidence on media violence extend to real-life crime and violence, the most recent meta-analyses do not support concerns that media violence is associated with criminal aggression (Savage and Yancey 2008).

Children and media violence

The vast literature on media effects has only rarely allowed the voices of children to be heard. Most of the research

Belson studied 1565 youths who were a representative sample of 13- to 17-year-old males living in London. The boys were interviewed on several occasions about their exposure to a variety of violent television programmes. The level and type of violence in these programmes were rated by members of a BBC viewing panel. As a result, it was possible to obtain a measure of how much violent television they watched and also the type of violent television they had been exposed to (e.g. realistic, fictional). To assess violent behaviour, Belson assessed how often he had been involved in any of 53 categories of violence over the previous six months. These ranged from only slightly violent aggravation (such as taunting), to very violent behavior such as 'I bashed a boy's head against a wall'. When Belson compared the behaviour of boys who had higher exposure to televised violence with those who had lower exposure (and had been matched on a wide variety of other possible contributing factors such as social class), he found that boys who had enjoyed high levels of exposure to television violence when they were younger committed 49 per cent more acts of serious violence than those who had enjoyed little television violence. However, this does not tell the whole story. Belson's results actually showed a curvilinear relationship between exposure to televised violence and violent behaviour, with exposure to very high levels of televised violence being associated with 50 per cent less violent behaviour than moderate or high levels.

One potential weakness in the study is that the boys were asked about their viewing habits and preferences when they were younger. Belson argues that because the boys gave the same answers when asked on two occasions, this shows that the answers were valid. However, it merely shows that the same answer is given reliably. The answers might be inaccurate. Nevertheless, more recently, Belson's methodology has been vindicated (Potts *et al.* 2008).

assumes that children are extremely vulnerable to negative media influences. As Huesmann *et al.* (2003) seem to put it, the mass media can steal any child from any family: 'the psychological laws are immutable and irreversible'. Psychological research into media effects has tended to represent young media users as 'the inept victims of products, which can trick children into all kinds of ill-advised behaviour' (Gauntlett 1998). Those who have chosen to listen with respect to the perspectives of children have emerged with quite the opposite, optimistic conclusions. Research which seeks to establish exactly what children can and do understand about the media has shown that

children are able to talk intelligently (and cynically) about the media (Buckingham 1996) and that children as young as seven are able to make thoughtful, critical and 'media literate' utterances themselves. The pioneering work of Australian researchers such as Hodge and Tripp (1986) has only recently blossomed into a *Zeitgeist* where empowering young people is seen as the priority. Buckingham's challenge to the media effects' tradition was based on listening to how young people understand, negotiate and respond to media content which parents might consider to be upsetting or nasty. This 'active viewer' perspective has accelerated the growth of research on the subject of media literacy (Buckingham 2008).

Evaluation of media influences on antisocial behaviour

- *The inconclusive case for media violence effects* – More than almost any other area of social psychology, the issue of media violence provokes fierce debate between those who believe that violence on the screen does promote violence in those who are exposed to it (e.g. Huesmann and Moise 1996), and those who believe evidence does not support this conclusion (e.g. Freedman 2002).

- *The nature of the audience* – A further complication for those who subscribe to the media effects model is the finding by Hagell and Newburn (1994) that young offenders watched less television and video than their non-offending counterparts, had less access to the technology in the first place and had no particular interest in specifically violent programmes.

- *Methodological problems with media violence research* – Because experiments are narrowly focused on specific causal hypotheses, they tend not to examine the real-world influences that might actually lessen or

Cross-sectional surveys

These are often described as 'correlational' studies because they examine the link or correlation between two 'variables' such as a measure of how many hours of television people watch and measure of how often they think of punching someone in the face. The aim of such research would be to examine whether these two measures co-vary in their amounts. If a lot of one is associated with a lot of the other then they are positively correlated and have something in common.

Correlations are measures only of *association* between two things and do not prove that one thing (e.g. watching violent videos) *causes* the other (aggression). In fact, the reverse may be true: that being aggressive may 'cause' people to be attracted to aggressive programming. Thus, such studies have a serious limit to their contribution to knowledge, but it is often argued that if no association exists, then it is unlikely that there will be any casual link.

even eliminate the aggressive reactions observed in experiments. Participants may also react differently in the laboratory when they realize that their expressions of aggression will not be punished (Gunter 1983). In addition, claims Freedman (1992), many participants may choose to provide the responses they believe the researcher wants (demand characteristics). It is particularly problematic that the more naturalistic or 'ecologically valid' a research design, the less likely it is that any effects will be observed, suggesting that beliefs or behaviours learned under experimental conditions cannot be generalized to viewers' everyday lives (Livingstone 2001).

- *Desensitization* – The desensitization hypothesis claims that excessive media violence diminishes the distaste with which we normally view violence and makes us more blasé about its consequences. Research fails to support this fundamental claim. Indeed, some research shows the exact opposite. Goldstein (1976), for example, found that immediately after seeing a violent movie, men were more concerned about murder, and more punitive towards those who commit murder. This finding was confirmed

across four different countries, and showed no support for the desensitization hypothesis. Furthermore, in a comparison of towns with and without television, those *with* television scored higher in terms of their anxiety about aggression compared with those *without* television (Schramm *et al.* 1961).

Media influences on prosocial behaviour

The history of the mass media is also a history of popular concerns about the harm which they might cause to society – especially to young people. By the 1930s there had been a series of substantial social science studies exploring the influence of motion pictures on youth. By far the largest research effort to date has been on television. Electronic transmissions began in the UK and the USA before World War II, but sales of sets did not take off until the early 1950s when they did so so rapidly as to make TV by far the predominant mass medium within a decade. There is an enormous range of different ways in which television might affect people (Mazarella 2007). However, anxieties have centred on crime and violence which children might imitate. The extent to which TV is also saturated with prosocial fare has been relatively neglected. Nevertheless, various studies have claimed to demonstrate both positive content and positive effects of television.

prosocial research has become marginalized since the 1980s. For example, in the **meta-analysis** by Mares and Woodard (2005) the most recent study had been published some 16 years earlier! They note with regret that 'The question of prosocial effects should not languish as the topic of the 1970s'. From the 1970s millions of dollars of American funding prioritized projects on antisocial behaviour, thus eclipsing interests in other areas. Occasionally, some measure of prosocial behaviour is also included in research on aggression, but it is usually quite cursory (e.g. Ostrov *et al.* 2006). It is true that work on *Sesame Street* and similar educational prosocial programmes has continued, but this is among a very small number of committed researchers (see, for example, Cole *et al.* 2008).

Explanations of media influences on prosocial behaviour

As with aggressive behaviour, there are many explanations regarding media influences on prosocial behaviour. This section covers the pervasiveness of television and exposure to prosocial messages. We will then go on to consider social learning theory, and developmental trends in prosocial influences.

The pervasiveness of television

On average, in most of the Western world, television consumption runs at around 25 hours per week. It increases rapidly from around seven hours per week in two-year-olds to around 20 hours by the age of six, then declining during the teen years, rising through adulthood

---

Activity **External validity**

Many experimental studies of media effects can be criticized on the grounds that they use a restricted sample (students) in an artificial environment (the laboratory). As a result, it may be argued, the data acquired may bear very little resemblance to real-life media experience. These criticisms may be countered by the argument that such studies are not *meant* to be realistic, rather they are intended to show that under controlled conditions short-term effects *can* be created. Similarly, responses to the stimuli presented should be subject to universal laws of cause and effect, therefore the actual population studied is irrelevant. However, Giles (2003), claims that some researchers have not always been so modest in the interpretation of their findings, often claiming that they demonstrate a direct causal link between everyday media (such as television) and everyday behaviour (e.g. aggression). Nowadays researchers are more sensitive to these concerns and take steps to design experimental studies that use more 'realistic' stimuli and more varied populations than just students.

1 Use the Internet to track down some experimental studies of media effects.

   (a) What population did they use (e.g. students, schoolchildren)?

   (b) How 'realistic' was the type of media used (i.e. how true to real life)?

   (c) Were the conclusions from these studies justified given your answers to (a) and (b) above?

to peak among the elderly. All viewers are exposed to an enormous amount of prosocial, as well as aggressive, behaviour on television.

Exposure to prosocial messages

Although there are periodic **moral panics** concerning the exposure of children to violence on television, children are also exposed to a fair proportion of prosocial acts. An early content analysis of US broadcasting found that, on average, there were 11 **altruistic** acts and six sympathetic behaviours per hour of programming (Sprafkin *et al.* 1975). However, as in real life, these prosocial acts frequently appeared in the context of *antisocial* behaviour, with one study finding that among the favourite television programmes of 8- to 12-year-olds, there were an average of 42.2 acts of antisocial behaviour and 44.2 acts of prosocial behaviour in an average hour (Greenberg *et al.* 1980). Since then such approaches have become very sporadic and idiosyncratic, making time trends impossible to discern (e.g. Smith *et al.* 2006). Although there have been relatively few recent content analyses of prosocial content on television, studies have continued to demonstrate that prosocial content on television is clearly as evident as antisocial content.

Teletubbies

As may be readily observed, even very young viewers can demonstrate enthusiastic pleasure and understanding of televisual material. Howard and Roberts (2002) studied toddlers from the age of 14 months watching the UK pre-school programme *Teletubbies*. Responses included **parasocial behaviour** such as joining in with the action (e.g. by singing and dancing or clapping at the end of a scene). In addition, they would interact with any viewing companions present by turning to them, smiling at them, pointing to the screen and so on and even go up to the TV set and talk to the characters, answering their questions. These kinds of activities have been observed before in older children of four or five years old (Palmer 1986). The parasocial responses may be seen as examples of what Penner *et al.* (2005) described as 'micro-level prosocial tendencies'. Wilson (2008) argued that young children learn about the nature and causes of different emotions from media characters and often experience empathy with them. Others go further, arguing that in watching, children 'are learning important and complex structures

of meaning and developing capacities for thinking and judgement that are a necessary part of the process of socialization' (Hodge and Tripp 1986).

Social learning theory

How might children learn prosocial messages having been exposed to them? Bandura's social learning theory (Bandura 1965) suggests that children learn by first observing a behaviour, then later imitating it if the expectation of reward is greater than the expectation of punishment for that behaviour. The process of social learning works in the same way for learning prosocial acts seen on television as it does for learning antisocial acts. Unlike the depiction of *antisocial* acts, however, the depiction of prosocial acts (such as generosity or helping) is likely to be in accordance with established social norms (e.g. the need to be generous and helpful to others). Assuming that these social norms have been internalized by the viewer, the imitation of these acts, therefore, is likely to be associated with the expectation of social reinforcement, and so the child is motivated to repeat these actions in their own life.

Developmental trends in prosocial influence

We might expect there to be developmental trends in the influence of prosocial messages because many of the skills associated with prosocial reasoning develop with age. prosocial behaviours have been shown to be contingent on the development of prosocial skills, such as perspective-taking, empathy and level of moral reasoning, which continue to develop throughout childhood and into adolescence (Eisenberg *et al.* 1987). For example, research has shown that young children are less able to recognize the emotional state of others (Hoffman 1976) and are less sure of how to help (Mares 1996). It is also evident from research that young children have more difficulty understanding abstract prosocial messages, and may be less affected by prosocial messages if these portrayals are more complex than the simple modelling of a specific behaviour (Mares 1996).

Evaluation of media influences on prosocial behaviour

- *Exposure to prosocial messages* – A number of studies have found that the prosocial messages in programmes are getting through to children and are influencing their values and behaviour. Evidence from the meta-analyses carried out by Hearold (1986) and Mares (1996) add testimony to this claim. Many of these studies, however, have demonstrated that children fail to generalize from the specific act seen on screen to new and different situations. Some specially constructed prosocial programmes, used primarily in educational settings, have been criticized for not being of the same production quality as broadcast material, and for failing to provide sufficient opportunity for children to rehearse the key behaviours being portrayed (Zielinska 1985). prosocial behaviours depicted in educational programming seem only to enhance the extent to which young children exhibit similar behaviours if sufficient opportunities are provided for rehearsing these behaviours (Gunter and McAleer 1997).

- *Social learning theory* – Exposure to filmed models has less effect than exposure to real-life models. prosocial programming *does* appear to have an effect, but the effect tends to be relatively short-lived and may not generalize to new settings. Nonetheless, although filmed models may have less influence on prosocial behaviour than live models, it is likely that prolonged viewing of prosocial programming could result in substantial and enduring increases in children's prosocial behavior (Eisenberg 1983). Social learning theory also requires that children *notice* a particular act or message, and must then remember it so that they can recreate it some time in the future. A characteristic of many antisocial acts is that they have high impact value, whereas prosocial acts tend to be more subtle and abstract, and therefore less memorable. An additional problem for young children arises when two segments of a story line are separated by adverts, and therefore lose some of their impact.

- *Developmental trends in prosocial influence* – Research has tended to show that prosocial messages have a greater effect on young children than on adolescents. This is contrary to what we might expect given the development of prosociality proposed by Eisenberg *et al.* (1987). However, when younger and older children do imitate prosocial behaviours they have seen modelled on television, their motives might be quite different. Midlarsky and Hannah (1985) suggest that younger children have more egocentric motives in that they may imitate prosocial behaviours if they believe these will bring them rewards or help them avoid punishment. In contrast, adolescents are better able to understand the underlying principle of abstract prosocial messages and are more likely to act for altruistic reasons (Roker *et al.* 1998).

Research on media influences on prosocial behaviour

A meta-analysis in this area was carried out by Mares (1996). Mares included four different categories of prosocial behaviour in her analysis, spread over 39 different studies. These are the main findings and the effect size for each category of prosocial behaviour:

- *Positive interaction* – This included friendly/non-aggressive interactions, expressions of affection and peaceable conflict resolution. Children who viewed positive interactions tended to act more positively in their own interactions with others, compared with those who viewed neutral or antisocial content. The effect size was found to be moderate.

- *Altruism* – This included sharing, donating, offering help and comforting. Children who viewed explicitly modelled altruistic behaviours tended to behave more altruistically than those who viewed neutral or antisocial content. The effect size was found to be moderate to large. Where altruism was not explicitly modelled, but required generalization from one context to another, the effect size was much smaller.

- *Self-control* – This included resistance to temptation, obedience to rules, ability to work independently and persistence at a task. Children who viewed models exercising self-control tended to show more self-control in their own behaviour, particularly when compared with those who saw a model behaving *antisocially* (e.g. disobeying rules). The effect size was moderate when comparisons were made with neutral content, but large when comparisons were made with antisocial content.

- *Anti-stereotyping* – This included the effects of counter-stereotypical portrayals of gender and ethnicity on attitudes and beliefs. Children who viewed counter-stereotypical themes showed less evidence of stereotyping and prejudice in their own attitudes and beliefs. The effect size was moderate, but was much larger when exposure to counter-stereotypical themes in the context of a school classroom was accompanied by extra classroom activities designed to expand on the issues viewed.

- *Justifying aggression* – Lovelace and Huston (1983) also observed that negative effects might occur if the prosocial behaviours were not shown in clear contrast to the antisocial behaviours. A study by Liss and Reinhardt (1979) supported this conclusion. They found an increase in aggressive behaviour in children who had watched a cartoon series *Superfriends*. Although both prosocial and antisocial behaviours were modelled in this series, characters usually demonstrated some justification for their aggressive behaviour, and so legitimized it for those watching.

In most of the studies analysed by Mares (1996), results were not broken down by sex. However, in those that were, and consistent with earlier research findings, more positive effects were discovered for girls. Also, prosocial messages have a greater effect with primary age children than with adolescents. Many studies have found that prosocial effects were limited to those situations which were similar to the prosocial act seen in the television programme. This perhaps highlights the need to be specific when attempting behaviour change through this medium, and contrasts with the typical finding that viewers are able to generalize *antisocial* behaviours from one context to another more readily than they can *prosocial* behaviours. A good example of real-life prosocial programming is the study by Cole *et al.* (2003), which evaluated the impact of a *Sesame Street* series of programmes aimed at teaching mutual respect and understanding among Israeli and Palestinian children. The series, *Rechov Sumsum/Shara'a Simsim* was bilingual but contained relatively more Hebrew for Israeli TV broadcasts and more Arabic for the Palestinian version. In all, 275 four- and five-year-olds were interviewed before and after the series. Encouragingly, in the before measures few held strong negative stereotypes of each other, but the after results showed an increase in positive attributes to describe the other group and an increase in prosocial justifications to resolve conflicts. In a more recent study, Mares and Woodard (2005) concluded that, overall, males and females were equally positively affected by prosocial content and that there were no ethnic or racial differences. However, effects were stronger among higher socio-economic groups.

Sesame Street has been associated with increases in prosocial behaviour.

The effects of video games and computers

Byron (2008) states, 'The most persistent and controversial question concerning video games and children is the question of violent content and it's (sic) potential influence on aggressive behaviour. This has been the subject of public debate over recent years and has been reviewed on various occasions both by Government and industry…The research remains highly controversial and inconclusive'.

Research into the effects of video games

Anderson *et al.* (2007) report even more powerful effects of violent **video games** in a series of studies including a longitudinal survey at two points in a school year. Although the sample size is generous enough (n=430), the measurement of media violence was as cursory as usual. Thus, the youngsters were asked to name their three favourite TV shows, their three favourite video or computer games, and their three favourite movies or videos. For each named media product, participants were asked to rate how frequently they watched or played (on a five-point scale) and how violent they considered them to be (on a four-point scale). Despite the short time lag between measures of media use at time '1' and aggression at time '2', the effect size for violent video games was remarkably high, accounting for 8.8 per cent of the variance in aggression. This is well above that reported for substance abuse (0.4 per cent) or abusive parents (0.8 per cent) or poverty (0.8 per cent).

Another interesting piece of research is that by Gentile *et al.* (2004) – see below.

Violent video games

Key research: Gentile *et al.* (2004)

Gentile *et al.* (2004) carried out a survey in Midwestern US schools of 607 students (mean age 14), who were asked to name their three favourite video games. For each game, participants were asked to say how often they played (from '1 = rarely' to '7 = often') and to rate how violent the game was (from '1 = a little' to '7 = extremely violent'). These two measures were multiplied to give a score for violent video game exposure. In addition, participants were asked about the amount of time they spent playing video games, how often their parents limited this, whether they had got into a fight in the last year and how often they got into arguments with their teachers. A key measure was that of **trait hostility** since they hypothesized that those who were most at risk of aggression would be the most influenced by violent video games.

Although the authors claim support for this hypothesis, their final results indicate that the amount of play did not correlate significantly with arguments with teachers or physical fights. Violent video game exposure, while significant, correlated only very weakly with having arguments with teachers (+0.10) and with having physical fights (+0.07). In other words, only half of one per cent of the variability in physical fights could be statistically 'explained' by violent video game exposure. However, even if the results had been more impressive, they may merely illustrate that those who score low on hostility measures rarely get into fights or have much appetite for violent media.

Media violence and physiology

There is evidence to suggest that exposure to violent media may alter the activity of brain structures that regulate aggressive behaviour. The anterior cingulate cortex (ACC) is thought to play an inhibitory role in the regulation of aggression in humans.

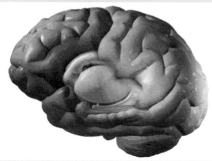

Figure 12.1 *The brain*

A recent study by Boes *et al.* (2008) found that aggressive behaviour was associated with decreased ACC volume, particularly in boys. Weber et al. (2006) used **functional magnetic resonance imaging (fMRI)** to test possible links between exposure to violent video games, ACC activity and aggression. They found that engaging in virtual violence led to decreased activity in the rostral (i.e. towards the front) ACC. Other research (Matthews *et al.* 2005) has also shown that both individuals with disruptive behaviour disorder (with aggressive features) and individuals who self-reported high exposure to violent media showed reduced ACC function compared with clinically normal individuals who self-reported low exposure to violent media.

given by the control group, lasted one half of one second and weren't even loud!' (Cumberbatch 2004). In this study the participants were not even allowed to deliver actual blasts to a real person, their responses were delivered to a computer. It seems inconceivable that even first-year psychology students would think a person would receive a noxious stimulus in an experiment, particularly as most would already be familiar with the obedience experiments of Stanley Milgram.

- *Should violent video games be banned?* – Media violence, including violent video games, tends to provoke a moral panic among many members of the public. It is worth noting, however, that in the UK all reviews of the research evidence on media violence commissioned by regulatory bodies have decided that conclusions are not possible on such weak data. These include Cumberbatch and Howitt (1989) Broadcasting Standards Commission, Harris (2001) Home Office, and Byron (2008) Department for Children, School and Families.

- *Can video games be cathartic?* – Despite most reviews rejecting any idea that media violence can be cathartic (i.e. allowing people to discharge their aggressive feelings through video games) some have argued that this remains a distinct possibility. In the meta-analysis, Sherry (2007) concludes that the theory is reasonably well supported – especially so since the catharsis theory has not been adequately tested (such as using participants who are anger aroused) and the evidence on harmful effects is so weak.

Evaluation of research into the effects of videogames

- *Unsubstantiated claims* – The overall pattern in research is one of inconsistent findings, which would not normally lead us to expect researchers to make any strong claims about the effects of video games. However, this is far from the case. As with other research on media violence, some of the strongest claims are made on the most flimsy of evidence. A recent example is a study by Anderson and Dill (2000), which attracted considerable media attention in its claim that violent video games are 'potentially more harmful than exposure to violent television and movies which are known to have substantial effects on aggression and violence'. However, it is evident that 'substantial' is one adjective which does not seem very appropriate for the rag bag of findings in this area. So what evidence did Anderson and Dill offer? That after playing a 'violent video game', the student volunteers gave 'significantly longer noise blasts' to an opponent in another room. These 'significantly longer blasts turn out to be just two per cent longer than those

The validity of scientific knowledge

One of the problems with scientific knowledge is that the medium of publication is that of the refereed journal. For material to be judged worthy of publication, normally significant results are required. This means that non-significant findings tend to be lost from sight. Indeed, it is not unusual for some researchers such as Anderson simply to gloss over the results of some measures. One critic of Anderson and Dill's (2000) study pointed out that the authors had both fabricated results and suppressed findings that failed to support their argument (Cumberbatch 2004). Fergusson (2007) suggested a way of taking into account the 'publication bias' of journals in a meta-analysis of research on video games. He concluded that when a correction is made for this bias, the size of the effect becomes non-significant and near zero.

Check your understanding of media influences on behaviour by answering these questions. Try to do this from memory. You can check your answers by looking back through Topic 1, Media influences on social behaviour.

1 Summarize the key features of the 'observational learning' explanation as it applies to media violence.

2 Summarize the key features of the 'cognitive priming' and 'desensitization' explanations as they apply to media violence.

3 Outline the claim that media violence research suffers from a lack of external validity.

4 Outline two critical points relating to each of these three explanations.

5 What specific ethical issues are important in a study of media violence?

6 Summarize the key features of each of 'exposure to prosocial messages', 'social learning theory', and 'developmental trends' explanations as they apply to prosocial media.

7 Outline one critical point relating to each of these explanations.

8 Outline research relating to the effects of video games on young people.

9 What is the link between violent game play and physiology?

10 Should violent video games be banned? Give reasons for your answer.

Topic 2: Persuasion, attitude and change

Psychology in context   Advertising

Levi 501s commercial

Although the 'science' of persuasion can be traced back to the development of propaganda by the Nazis during World War II, to most of us 'persuasion' is synonymous with advertising, particularly advertising on the television. The success of television advertising campaigns is vividly illustrated in the mid-1980s commercials for Levis 501 jeans. In this advert, model Nick Kamen strips to his boxers in a launderette so he can wash his precious 501s while Marvin Gaye's 1960s hit *I heard it through the grapevine* plays in the background. Giles (2003) comments how this advert had multiple effects on consumer behaviour. In the year following the introduction of the advertisement, sales of Levis 501s increased by 800 per cent. *I heard it through the grapevine* was re-released and went straight to Number 1, sparking a succession of re-released 'oldies' that were catapulted to the top of the charts following their exposure as TV advertising soundtracks. Even boxer shorts became increasingly popular as essential underwear for young men!

1 Discuss advertisements that stick in your mind. What was there about these examples that you found so compelling and why?

2 What 'tricks' do you think advertisers use to make consumers want to buy their product?

Persuasion

This section will introduce two different models which try to explain the psychology of persuasion: the Hovland-Yale model and the elaboration likelihood model.

The Hovland-Yale model

Towards the end of World War II, Carl Hovland was recruited by the US War Department to investigate how propaganda could be used to help support the American war effort in the closing stages of the war. After the war Hovland and his research team continued their work at Yale University, producing insights into the psychology of persuasive communication that became known as the

'Hovland-Yale' model (Hovland *et al.* 1953). Hovland and his colleagues at Yale suggested that the key to discovering when a communication was likely to be persuasive was understanding the characteristics of the person presenting the message (the 'source'), the contents of the message itself, and the characteristics of the receiver of the message (the 'audience').

The source

Hovland *et al.* found that source characteristics played an important role in determining the persuasive nature of any communication. For example, they found that experts are usually more persuasive than non-experts and that 'attractive' sources (e.g. through celebrity endorsement in product advertisements) are also instrumental in enhancing consumer demand for a particular product. Bochner and Insko (1966) found that 'credible' (i.e. expert) sources were effective at influencing an audience even when there was a significant discrepancy between what the audience already believed and the arguments contained in the message. Bochner and Insko found that if a non-expert source presented arguments that were too discrepant with an audience's existing views, the audience would resist and even look for ways of discrediting the communicator. However, with an expert source this was less likely to happen, and in this study a highly credible witness (supposedly a Nobel prize-winning sleep researcher) was able to convince an audience that one hour of sleep per night was the optimum.

The message

Several message variables have been researched as part of this explanation of persuasive communication. These include:

- *One- versus two-sided arguments* – In a persuasive communication we may decide to present both sides of an argument or just one. For example, a Norwich Union car insurance TV advert in 2008 stated that customers who applied for Norwich Union insurance would also be informed of the prices and products of its rivals – even if they were cheaper. If an audience is fairly intelligent, or likely to be hostile toward the arguments being presented, then it is more effective to present both sides of the argument. However, if the audience is less intelligent or already favourably disposed toward the product, a one-sided argument is more effective (McGinnies 1966).

- *Repetition* – In the advertising world, it is commonly accepted that messages must be repeated several times if they are to have an impact on consumers. Repeated exposure to a person or object increases familiarity and liking, and research by Arkes *et al.* (1991) suggested that mere repetition of a statement can make it appear more true!

- *Fear* – We have all been exposed to messages at some time that have used fear as a way of changing our behaviour. This may have been a message warning of the perils of unprotected sex, drink driving or smoking, but how effective is fear at changing attitudes? Early work by Janis and Feshbach (1953),

which used the perils of tooth decay as the message, found that high-fear messages were far less effective at changing attitudes than low- or moderate-fear messages. How can we explain this? At low levels of fear an audience may not be sufficiently motivated to attend to the message. As the level of fear content increases, so the audience pays attention to the message, but at very high levels of fear, the panic or anxiety caused by the message may obscure its factual content, thus making it less effective. Other research (e.g. Witte *et al.* 1998) has shown that fear-inducing messages are more likely to work if they also include an effective way of coping with the danger.

Campaigns like this one from the NHS were effective because as well as highlighting the dangers of unprotected sex (i.e. the greater likelihood of sexually transmitted diseases), they also included information about how to avoid them, in this case by wearing a condom.

The audience

Hovland *et al.* identified several characteristics of audiences that determine how easily they are influenced by a persuasive communication. These include self-esteem, i.e. how good an audience feels about themselves, and age. Hovland *et al.* originally believed that the relationship between self-esteem and persuasibility was fairly straightforward, with low self-esteem individuals being more easily persuaded than high self-esteem individuals. However, McGuire (1968) suggested that this relationship was actually curvilinear. People with low or high esteem would be less easily persuaded than those with moderate levels of self-esteem. McGuire reasoned that people with low self-esteem would be less attentive or more anxious when processing a message, and therefore less influenced by its factual content. Those with high self-esteem would also be difficult to persuade, presumably because they are more self-assured about their current beliefs. Age, as an audience variable, is less easily linked to persuasion. Tyler and Schuller's 'lifelong openness' hypothesis (Tyler and Schuller 1991) claims that age is generally irrelevant, people are to some extent susceptible to attitude change as a result of persuasive communications throughout their life. In contrast to this view, Visser and Krosnick (1998) argue for a 'life changes' hypothesis, claiming that there is a curvilinear relationship between age and persuasion, with high susceptibility during early adulthood and later life, but a lower susceptibility throughout middle adulthood.

Evaluation of the Hovland-Yale model

■ *Individual differences in audience effects* – Rhodes and Wood (1992) conducted a meta-analysis of studies on social influence and found evidence to support the claim that people lower in intelligence were more prone to persuasion. When a message is simple, clear and straightforward and thus readily received by all parties, the only difference in persuasion should be in the tendency to yield to such a message. Individual differences in intelligence appear to be particularly relevant to this yielding stage. Rhodes and Wood argue that people high in intelligence should be less likely to yield to persuasive messages because they are

confident of their own opinions, and are more likely to critically evaluate the message.

■ *Age as an audience effect* – Evidence supporting the 'life changes' (or life stages) hypothesis comes from Rutland's (1999) research on the development of prejudiced attitudes in children. He questioned 329 children in a photograph evaluation task. National prejudice and group favouritism were not apparent in young children, but emerged at age 12, reaching a peak at age 16.

The elaboration likelihood model

Petty and Cacioppo (1986) believed that the key to successful persuasion was whether or not an individual was motivated to elaborate on a particular message. When people receive a persuasive communication (such as an advertisement) they think about the arguments it makes. However, they do not always think very deeply about these arguments because to do so involves making considerable mental effort. In some situations, therefore, people are sufficiently motivated to analyse the content of message, but in other situations the persuasive nature of the message is less to do with the arguments used and more to do with the 'context' of the message. With this in mind, Petty and Cacioppo identified two routes to persuasion: the 'central' route, which involves elaboration and analysis of the message, and the 'peripheral' route, which does not.

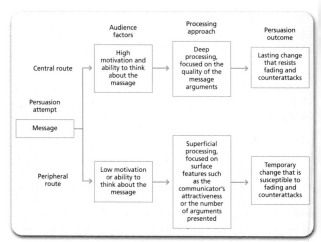

Figure 12.2 *The elaboration likelihood model*

The central route to persuasion

In the 'central route', it is the message itself which is most important. The arguments are followed closely and we may even indulge in mental counter-arguments if we disagree with some of them. For a communication to be effective via the central route, the arguments have to be convincing. However, no matter how convincing the arguments, the communicator cannot dictate how they are received by the individual receiving them. If an individual finds a message interesting or personally involving, and if they have the ability to understand the arguments being used, then it is likely that they will process a message (such as an advertisement) through the central route. Petty and Cacioppo believed that attitudes formed as a result of central route processing would be stronger and more resistant to change than those formed through the peripheral route. Central route processing is more likely when the message is seen as personally relevant (e.g. about global warming for someone who is concerned about the environment) or important (e.g. a charity appeal following a disaster).

The peripheral route to persuasion

In contrast, individuals who are not particularly motivated to think deeply about a communication are assumed to undergo attitude change through what is referred to as the 'peripheral route' to persuasion. In the peripheral route, individuals are more likely to be influenced by contextual cues (e.g. mood, emotional cues, image etc.). It is assumed that attitudes acquired via the peripheral route are comparatively more susceptible to change than those acquired via the central route. Communications that are considered less important by the individual or less personally relevant are more likely to be processed via the peripheral route.

This advert for the Audi Q7 unashamedly takes the peripheral route to persuasion.

Need for cognition

Cacioppo and Petty (1982) claim that individuals differ in their **need for cognition** (NC), i.e. the degree to which they enjoy thinking about information they receive and analysing problems. NC is a stable individual difference and individuals high in NC are assumed to have an inherent tendency to search for, scrutinize and reflect upon information in an effort to better understand the world around them. In contrast, those individuals who are low in NC are assumed to rely primarily on the opinions of credible others, the context of the persuasive communication etc. when making decisions.

Evaluation of the elaboration likelihood model

Need for cognition – Research by Haugtvedt et al. (1992) provided support for the claim that high need for cognition individuals would be more influenced by central route communications than would individuals low in need for cognition. In their research, the attitudes of high need for cognition individuals were based more on an evaluation of product attributes in advertisements than were the

attitudes of low need for cognition persons. In addition, the attitudes of low need for cognition individuals were based more on simple peripheral cues inherent in the advertisements than were the attitudes of high need for cognition individuals.

Application of need for cognition to a real-life problem – The claim that NC is a key factor in determining whether the central or peripheral route will be more successful in producing attitude change is supported in a study of smoking relevant to risk perception. Vidrine et al. (2007) measured NC among 227 college students, who were required to evaluate a fact-based (central route) or emotion-based (peripheral route) smoking risk pamphlet. Among participants with higher NC, the fact-based message produced the greatest increase in risk perception, whereas among participants with lower NC, the emotion-based message produced the greatest change.

Can attitude change be temporary? – Attitude change via the peripheral route is described by Petty and Cacioppo as 'transitory', but if attitudes are 'enduring positive or negative feelings toward an object' (Petty and Cacioppo 1986), is it possible for change to be 'transitory'? Petty and Cacioppo therefore appear to be arguing that peripheral route processing leads to attitude 'formation' rather than attitude 'change'. However, some studies have shown that peripheral route processes can be successful even when a prior attitude is held about an object. For example, a study by Mackie and Worth (1989) found that participants were more persuaded by expert rather than non-expert sources regarding the issue of gun control even when they already held an attitude on the issue prior to the experiment.

The influence of attitudes on decision making

In the next section we will focus on research into how attitudes can influence decision making. A number of theories will be covered, including cognitive dissonance, post-decisional dissonance, self-perception theory and the overjustification effect.

The role of cognitive consistency

In the late 1950s social psychologists hit upon a very simple idea, that people like their cognitions, i.e. their attitudes, beliefs and behaviours to be 'consistent' with each other. If they are, we are in a state of balance, if they are not, we are forced to think about the inconsistencies in order to reorganize our thinking and restore consistency. For example, if we have a negative attitude towards a particular type of car (perhaps believing that only a certain sort of person would drive one), then we buy one (because it was such a good deal), there is inconsistency between the attitude we hold and our decision to act in a certain way. We find this inconsistency unpleasant and are motivated to reduce it. Although there were a number of consistency theories that could explain this process, the most enduring of these was Leon Festinger's **cognitive dissonance** theory.

Cognitive dissonance

Festinger (1957) described the desired state of consistency between the different cognitions as 'consonance'. When one or other of our cognitions is inconsistent with the others (such as in the example above), we are in a state of 'dissonance'. For Festinger, anything that was represented in a person's mind (such as a specific belief or an awareness of a past behaviour) counted as a cognition. Three types of relationship could exist between these cognitions. They might be:

- 'irrelevant' to each other, e.g. 'I like psychology' and 'yesterday I washed my car'

- 'consonant', e.g. 'I like psychology' and 'psychology is a valuable subject to study'

- 'dissonant', e.g. 'I like psychology' and 'I never go to my psychology classes'. Festinger claimed that if people detect that they are harbouring a cognitive inconsistency, they experience dissonance and will attempt to reduce it.

Dissonance can be removed in a number of ways. The simplest way is to change one of the cognitions (e.g. start going to psychology classes or stop liking it). An alternative way is to introduce another cognition which explains the dissonant relationship. For example, 'I like psychology but don't go to the classes because the teacher is rubbish'.

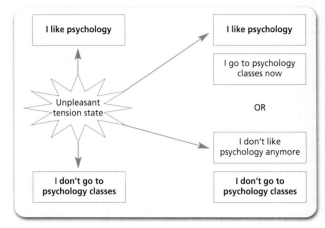

Figure 12.3 *Ways of removing cognitive dissonance*

Counter-attitudinal behaviour

Key research: Festinger and Carlsmith (1959)

Festinger and Carlsmith (1959) carried out a classic study to demonstrate how dissonance could be produced when an individual engages in **counter-attitudinal behaviour**, i.e. behaviour contrary to what the individual really believes. Participants were required to complete a very boring task. At the end of the study, each participant was asked if they would act as a research assistant and greet the next participant. They were to tell the new participant that the task was really interesting. In return for doing this, they were told they would be paid. Some were told they would be paid $20 and some just $1. After they had greeted the new participant (and told their 'lie'), they were then asked to rate how interesting 'they' had found the task when they had been the participant.

You may expect that the $20 participants would have enjoyed it more, but this was not the case. In fact the $1 participants rated the task as more interesting. Knowingly telling the new participant a lie would have created dissonance, but for one group (those paid $20), the money was sufficient justification for their behaviour and so the dissonance was overcome. For those paid just a measly $1, however, the money was insufficient justification, therefore the only way left to reduce the dissonance was to convince themselves that they really had enjoyed the task (i.e. attitude consistent with behaviour). The $1 participants were also more willing to take part in similar experiments in the future.

Figure 12.4 *The effect of different incentives on the evaluation of a boring task (Festinger and Carlsmith 1959)*

Figure 12.5

Post-decisional dissonance

We have all probably experienced a situation where we are forced to choose between two alternatives, be they cars, holiday destinations or even who to go out with. Making a decision in such situations invites a state of dissonance. Suppose you are weighing up a choice between a Honda and a Renault. You choose the Renault but then experience post-decisional dissonance, the uneasy feeling that you may have made the wrong decision and should have bought the Honda. This type of dissonance can be overcome by selectively exposing yourself to information about the two types of car. For example, you might avoid reading anything about the rejected choice while happily reading reports on the car you have chosen. In this way any potential dissonance (e.g. 'I bought the Renault but the Honda is a better car') can be avoided.

Evaluation of cognitive dissonance

- *Cognitive dissonance in real life* – Cognitive dissonance might be dismissed as an artefact of the artificial conditions of the laboratory, but its predictions were also upheld in an ingenious real-life study. Festinger and his colleagues (Festinger *et al.* 1956) infiltrated a doomsday cult who believed that their leader (referred to as 'Mrs Keech') was in touch with the 'Elders of the Planet of Clarion'. The Elders had informed Mrs Keech of an impending natural disaster but said that they would send a spaceship to rescue her and her followers. Of course, the natural disaster did not strike and the followers of Mrs Keech were now in possession of beliefs that were disconfirmed by subsequent events (i.e. a state of dissonance). The followers were able to make sense of this disconfirmation and reduce their dissonance by strengthening their beliefs in the power of the cult (which had somehow managed to avert the disaster).

- *Does inconsistency always lead to dissonance?* – Cooper and Fazio (1984) argued that a detected inconsistency between cognitions does not automatically arouse dissonance, and that most people are content to be only partially consistent beings. Cooper and Fazio suggested that an individual would only experience dissonance under conditions of cognitive inconsistency *if* they perceive that inconsistency as having possible aversive consequences for them *and* if they accept personal responsibility for the inconsistency (e.g. they chose to act in a certain way). Even when dissonance is aroused, they will only be motivated to act to reduce it if it is experienced as unpleasant.

- *Post-decisional dissonance* – Although some research has supported the idea of selective exposure to information following decisions, other studies have failed to support the idea. Festinger (1964) believed that this selective exposure would only occur in certain situations. For example, if someone is very confident in their decision they may expose themselves to apparently contradictory information because they believe they could explain it away, thus supporting the decision that they had already made. Selective exposure to information need not follow decision-making, but is likely to do so in situations where it could help to reduce any dissonance caused by the decision.

Self-perception theory

Self-perception theory is an explanation of attitude change developed by Bem (1965). Bem claimed that we have the same knowledge of our own behaviour that another person would have, and so we therefore develop our attitudes by observing our own behaviour and inferring from that what attitudes must have caused them.

Self-perception theory differs from cognitive dissonance theory in that it does not claim that people have to experience the negative state of dissonance prior to attitude change. Instead, people simply infer their attitudes from their own behaviour in the same way that an outside observer might.

Self-perception or cognitive dissonance?

Bem ran his own version of Festinger and Carlsmith's cognitive dissonance experiment. Participants listened to a tape of a man enthusiastically describing a tedious peg-turning task. Some participants were told that he had been paid $20 for his enthusiastic commentary and others were told that he was paid $1. Those in the latter condition thought that the man must have enjoyed the task more than those in the $20 condition. Bem argued that the participants did not judge the man's attitude to the task in terms of cognitive dissonance (which was how Festinger and Carlsmith had judged the behaviour of their own participants), but rather that any attitude change the man might have experienced was the result of his own self-perception.

The overjustification effect

In the self-perception, attributions are made concerning the likely causes of behaviour. For example, an individual may conclude that the reason they watch a lot of sport on television must be because they like sport. These self-attributions have important implications for motivation. If someone is offered significant financial inducements for performing a behaviour, then the reason for engaging in that task is attributed externally and motivation to perform decreases. However, in the absence of external factors to which performance can be attributed, the person attributes the motivation internally (e.g. enjoyment or commitment). This has been called the **overjustification effect**, where motivation to perform a task is reduced if there is significant external 'justification' for that behaviour. Hogg and Vaughan (2008) suggest that an implication of this position is that perhaps antisocial behaviour might be less appealing if people were rewarded for engaging in it rather than punished.

Evaluation of self-perception

- *The facial feedback hypothesis* – Evidence for the link between self-perception and attitude change comes from evidence that facial movements can influence emotional experience, e.g. an individual who is forced to smile during a social event will actually find the event more enjoyable. Strack *et al.* (1988) asked participants to hold a pencil in their mouth in such a way that it helped them to smile or inhibited smiling while they were rating cartoons. Those participants who smiled reported a more positive emotional experience than those who did not when presented with the same cartoons.

■ *Research evidence for the overjustification effect* – Support for the existence of an overjustification effect in self-perception comes from a study by Lepper *et al.* (1973) who asked nursery school children to draw pictures. Half of the children were given the promise of a reward for drawing, while the rest drew of their own free will. A few days later the children were observed playing. Those who had been rewarded for drawing now spent half as much time drawing compared with those who had drawn of their own free will.

£0 per week and £180 000 per week. Which of them play because they enjoy it?

The effectiveness of television

Television has long been considered an extremely effective method of advertising. The next section considers the different methods of television advertising, and the psychology behind them. We will then go on to consider celebrity product endorsement, and the impact of television given our changing viewing habits.

Psychology and advertising

The connection between psychology and persuasion is frequently seen as synonymous with advertising. Psychological ideas, such as those exemplified in Petty and Cacioppo's 'elaboration likelihood model' quickly found a home in the many attempts to persuade viewers, either to change unhealthy behaviours (e.g. to stop smoking or to drive slower) or more usually to change 'consumer' behaviour. This has led to a focus on the 'effectiveness' of adverts in changing behaviour, a different approach from the study of media effects in the first part of this chapter.

Hard and soft sell advertising

Consumer research has shown a shift away from '**hard sell**' advertising, where the viewer is presented with factual information about the product, and '**soft sell**' advertising, where advert is oriented more towards the consumers themselves than it is towards the product. Products may suggest a lifestyle towards which the viewer might aspire; for example, buying frozen foods from a particular store will turn mealtimes from mundane experiences into veritable social feasts. Likewise, buying a particular car will make you feel young, funky, sexy and so on. Jhally (1990) suggests that advertising is less about how people are acting, and more about how they are dreaming.

Research suggests that hard and soft sell approaches have different effects on different people. Snyder and de Bono (1985) found that participants who scored high on 'self-monitoring' (i.e. were concerned with the image of a product than its factual properties) had more favourable attitudes to soft sell adverts, and were more likely to change their behaviour as a result of exposure to them. Those who were low in self-monitoring, on the other hand, take a more pragmatic approach to life, and preferred advertisements that presented the factual information about a product than the moods or associations present in the soft sell approach.

Based on research such as this, companies have begun to focus their advertising strategies on specific consumer profiles, commissioning particular types of adverts to fit a specific target audience. This type of profiling, where advertising is designed to appeal to the profile of a particular target audience (e.g. women rather than men, younger rather than older viewers and so on) is known as 'psychographics'.

> **Activity** **You and advertising**
>
> Tear yourself away from your studies for just an hour or so. Watch some television adverts. Would you classify the adverts you see as 'hard sell' or 'soft sell'? Which do you think had the greater effect on you (allowing for personal relevance of course, e.g. men are unlikely to be affected by adverts for tampons)? What, if anything, does this tell you about you?

When researching the effectiveness of adverts, researchers have to rely on 'attitudinal studies' rather than studies on actual changes in behaviour. For example, they may ask participants how much they like a particular advert, how much they like the product being advertised, or even how likely they might actually be to buy the product. These are indirect measures of the effectiveness of adverts, because what such studies cannot tell us is whether these people do buy the product advertised. Giles (2003) suggested that it might be possible to study consumer behaviour directly by observing consumer behaviour over a period of time. Alternatively, people might be asked to keep a diary of programmes (and adverts) watched and subsequent purchases over a specific period of time. Although such methods are likely to be cumbersome and subject to inaccuracies, they would at least provide us with a real-life assessment of changes in consumer behaviour as a direct result of advertising, and therefore a direct measure of its effectiveness.

1 Watch a selection of programmes on commercial television (e.g. ITV and Channel 4) that you think appeal to a specific type of audience (e.g. *Desperate Housewives, Big Brother* etc.). Are the advertisements associated with these programmes designed with a specific target audience in mind?

2 Discuss with other members of your class occasions when you feel you have brought a product as a direct result of a television advert. What was there about the advert that convinced you the product was worth buying?

3 Design a study that could assess the relationship between exposure to a particular advert and subsequent consumer behaviour (i.e. product purchase). How would you measure 'effectiveness' in this study?

Tough, resilient and not afraid of a bit of rough terrain. Davidoff were quick to cash in on Ewan McGregor's real-life motorcycling exploits in this advert for aftershave.

A clever advert? We are told the dog's name but not the product.

Product endorsement

Many of the products that we buy are bought on the advice of a friend, and while advertisers cannot personalize their adverts in such a personally relevant way, they can still make use of the 'ready made' friendships that exist between viewers and well-known celebrities (Giles 2002). These 'friendships', known as **parasocial relationships** (see p.426) provide the trustworthy and reliable endorsement of a product that makes us more willing to 'give it a go'. One way in which celebrity endorsement might work is by transforming the image of the product through its association with a particular celebrity. Walker *et al.* (1992) investigated the qualities that viewers associated with particular products using different celebrity endorsements. They found that the same participants rated the same products differently when endorsed by different celebrities. For example, a video recorder was rated differently when promoted by

the singer Madonna than when promoted by model Christie Brinkley.

Giles (2003) describes an advertising campaign run by the insurance company 'More Th>n' in 2001. This campaign featured a poster with a crude black and white photograph of an Airedale/collie cross under the slogan 'Where's Lucky?'. There was no mention of the sponsor's name, let alone any product information. We might expect such advertising to be particularly pointless, but Giles argues that the lack of explicit information in these posters is precisely why they were so memorable. He cites the elaboration likelihood model (Petty and Cacioppo 1986) as an explanation. In order to link the posters with a subsequent television campaign, viewers needed to make extra cognitive effort that eventually paid off in terms of recall and recognition and (so the sponsors would hope) greater attitude change in terms of their particular product. In terms of Cacioppo and Petty's concept of 'need for cognition', the differential effects of advertising are associated with individual preferences for 'thinking'. The 'Where's Lucky?' campaign succeeded because it required central route processing and subsequently a more effective and long-lasting attitude change.

Evaluation of the effectiveness of television

- *Does celebrity endorsement work?* – Although there are lots of anecdotal accounts of the success of celebrity product endorsement (e.g. actor Ewan McGregor's endorsement of Davidoff aftershave), research evidence for its effectiveness is somewhat less conclusive. In a study of the 'persuasiveness' of over 5000 TV commercials, Hume (1992), concluded that celebrity endorsement did not enhance the persuasive communication of the advert.

- *The impact of advertising* – As Giles (2003) points out, television and cinema advertising have been hugely successful because their adverts generally have a captive audience. However, claims Giles, television audiences have more options open to them when it comes to the viewing of adverts. According to a study by Comstock and Scharrer (1999), 80 per cent of viewers were likely to leave the room when the adverts came on, and viewers who watch recorded television on video or DVD have the option to fast forward through the adverts, therefore minimizing their impact. Research also suggests that adverts appearing in the commercial breaks of some types of programme have less impact than those in other types of programme. For example, Bushman (1998) found that both violent and humorous programmes were associated with low levels of recall for advertised material, presumably because the emotional response to the television shows blunts the degree of attention that viewers can pay to the adverts themselves.

Advertising and children

Every year, round about early November, the annual run up to Christmas begins on the television. This period is characterized by increasing numbers of advertisements for toys and games, and activates the beginning of what some commentators refer to as 'pester power' as children put pressure on their parents to add the advertised toys to their already bulging Christmas list. In Sweden this is taken so seriously that the Swedish government has placed a ban on all television adverts aimed at the under 12s.

Do children understand the difference between programmes and adverts?

Young (1990) coined the term 'advertising literacy' to refer to an individual's understanding that advertising has both a source that is distinct from other television programming and also that has a persuasive intent, i.e. to persuade us to change our behaviour in some way. In a meta-analysis of studies, Martin (1997) found evidence of a strong positive correlation between age and comprehension of persuasive intent. Now read about an earlier study by Robertson and Rossiter (1974) in the Key research below.

Advertizing literacy

Key research: Robinson and Rossiter (1974)

Robertson and Rossiter (1974) investigated whether children could discern the difference between commercials as distinct from regular programmes. They used 289 Catholic primary schoolchildren from Philadelphia, who were interviewed using **open-ended questions** relating to their understanding of television commercials. They collected data on whether children of different ages could discriminate between regular programmes and commercials, whether they attributed persuasive intent to advertisements, whether they trusted and liked advertisements, and whether they wanted all the products advertised. The results are shown in Table 12.1 below.

The results of this study show that as children get older, they are better able to discriminate between commercial advertisements and regular programming (73.5 per cent of five-year-olds could do this and 100 per cent of nine-year-olds). Similarly, about half of the five-year-olds attributed persuasive intent to commercials, but nearly all did so at age nine. The findings also suggest that when a child attributes persuasive intent to commercials they trust them less, like them less and are less likely to want the products advertised.

Age	Percentage		
	5 years	7 years	9 years
Can discriminate between programming and commercials	73.5	90.1	100
Attributes persuasive intent to commercials	52.7	87.1	99.0
Trusts all commercials	64.8	30.4	7.4
Likes all commercials	68.5	55.9	25.3
Wants all products advertised	53.3	26.7	6.4

Table 12.1 *The development of advertising literacy in young children*

Pester power and the effectiveness of children's advertising

It is a widely held belief that repeated presentations on television of advertisements for toys and games lead children to make demands on parents for products that the parents may not easily be able to afford. The effectiveness of this form of advertising was investigated by Pine and Nash (2001), in a study of the relationship between television exposure and gift requests to Father Christmas. They found a direct positive correlation between the amount of commercial television watched by children and the number of goods on their list to Father Christmas. This correlation was particularly strong for children who tended to watch television on their own, suggesting that parents may have a mediating influence on the connection between product exposure and any subsequent request. The researchers did not, however, find any relationship between exposure to specific products advertised and subsequent gift requests. Rather they found evidence of a general, more materialistic culture among those children exposed to a large number of television adverts. The researchers also compared their findings with data collected in Sweden (where advertising aimed at under 12s is banned) and found that among Swedish children's letters to Santa there were significantly fewer gift requests.

Figure 12.6 *The power of television. Research suggests that children who watch a lot of commercial television ask Santa for a lot more toys at Christmas! (© www.cartoonstock.com)*

Evaluation of advertising to children

- *Difficulties in establishing the role of television in behaviour* – Trying to establish the effectiveness of television in changing the behaviour of children (e.g. in making them buy more or want more products) is extremely difficult. Pine and Nash's study showed that parental mediation during television watching plays an important role in subsequent behaviour, but we must also consider the important role played by peers in a child's consumer behaviour. We cannot be certain of the conversations children have with their peers, nor of the influence of those conversations in shaping subsequent behaviour. It is entirely possible that many of these conversations may be related to television advertisements ('Did you see the advert for…?'), so it becomes impossible to disentangle the two influences.

- *Implications for legislation on advertising to children* – If children, particularly young children, are so influenced by television adverts, then should the UK, as is the case in Sweden, ban advertising aimed at such a vulnerable age group? Giles (2003) argues that a ban on advertising direct to young children would not rule out their influence over parental purchases of family goods, such as holiday destinations and the family car. Giles points out that modern-day children occupy a different position in the family regarding decision making, having considerable power over parental choice.

CHECK YOUR UNDERSTANDING

Check your understanding of persuasion, attitude and change by answering these questions. Try to do this from memory. You can check your answers by looking back through Topic 2.

1. What, according to the Hovland-Yale study, are the key features of a persuasive communication?

2. Outline two critical points relating to this model.

3. Distinguish between the 'central' and 'peripheral' routes to persuasion. When is each likely to work?

4. Outline two critical points relating to this (elaboration likelihood) model.

5. Explain the process of cognitive dissonance.

6. What is the difference between cognitive dissonance and self-perception explanations of decision making?

7. Outline one critical point relating to each of these explanations.

8. Summarize two explanations for the effectiveness of television.

9. Outline two critical points relating to these explanations.

10. How, specifically, are children influenced by television advertising?

Psychology in context

Membership of the 'human club'

Celebrities and gossip seem to go hand in hand, with part of the attraction of celebrities being the opportunity they offer the rest of us to analyse their lives in fine detail with our friends. Do you have a tendency to gossip? Try the following items from the 'Tendency to Gossip Questionnaire' (Nevo *et al.* 1993).

- I like analysing with a friend the compatibility of celebrity couples.
- I like talking with friends about the personal appearance of celebrities.
- I enjoy analysing with my friends the motives and reasons for the behaviour of celebrities.
- I tend to talk with friends about the love affairs of celebrities.
- I like reading biographies of famous people.

Did you mostly agree with the above statements? No need to worry, Medini and Rosenberg (1976) coined the term 'same-boat phenomenon' to explain how gossiping about famous people serves to confirm our membership of the 'human club'. Hearing about famous people's lives, particularly when they engage in behaviour that is frowned upon (such as getting drunk in public) or that would cause conflict (such as having an affair), tells us that we are not the only person on this planet who engages in such behaviour or who experiences that conflict. Gossip breaks down inhibitions, lifts the 'public mask' and illuminates the 'private face', to find that the private face is not that bad after all (Medini and Rosenberg 1976).

Explanations of the attraction to celebrity

The attraction to celebrity has many possible explanations, and the social psychological explanations are outlined below.

Social psychological explanations

Over half a century ago, Horton and Wohl (1956) summarized the phenomenon of celebrity attraction:

'One of the striking characteristics of the new mass media – radio, television, and the movies – is that they give the illusion of face-to-face relationship with the performer. The conditions of response to the performer are analogous to those in a primary group. The most remote and illustrious men are met *as if* they were in the circle of one's peers… We propose to call this seeming face-to-face relationship between spectator and performer a *para-social relationship*.'

Horton and Wohl observed that, for much of the time, the characters we see on television (whether factual or fictional) face the viewer, use modes of direct address and talk as if conversing personally and privately. Of course the crucial difference between this experience and face-to-face ones, 'obviously lies in the lack of effective reciprocity, and this the audience cannot normally conceal from itself'.

Over the years television has evolved to become a potentially powerful force for such parasocial relationships. Ashe and McCutcheon (2001) observed that 'By design, television news has increasingly come to resemble celebrity gossip'. Intimate details of celebrities become the subject of mass mediated knowledge, thus encouraging feelings of knowing the media figures as if they were in our own circle. As Cashmore (2006) observed, media coverage of celebrities has, for many, replaced that of 'legitimate' news.

Parasocial relationships

In the history of television there is little doubt that *Big Brother* has been a landmark. It allowed 'ordinary people' to become celebrities and earn fortunes. The parasocial process was encouraged by a revolutionary concept in television: to broadcast (on mainstream terrestrial TV) highlights of the programme, but, in addition, to narrowcast (i.e. on a digital channel) raw footage of the show. Here, the participants could be observed in real time more intimately than anyone's flatmates and with the added spice of very provocative interactions rarely allowed in communal living. The American dream, represented by Barack Obama, was that anyone with talent, however unlikely their birth background, could become president of the United States. *Big Brother* has a wider apparent reality that virtually anyone, regardless of talent, can become a celebrity and earn millions.

Research on parasocial relationships

Parasocial interaction was not really investigated until McQuail *et al.* (1972) revealed that it occurred in soap opera audiences, with audience members empathizing with the plights of characters. They concluded that the parasocial relationships developed from this form of 'interaction' were generally utilized by audiences for companionship and personal identity purposes.

Schiappa *et al.* (2007) examined all studies (not just psychological) where the word 'parasocial' appeared and selected empirical studies where the data could allow a meta-analysis.

Overall, parasocial relationships were best predicted by:

1 Perception of television characters as attractive (36 per cent of variance, seven studies)

2 Perception of homophily (similarity) with television characters (23 per cent of variance, five studies)

3 Perception of TV characters as real (23 per cent of variance, seven studies)

4 Parasociability (12 per cent of variance, four studies)

5 Affinity for watching television (7 per cent of variance, 12 studies)

6 Internal locus of control (7 per cent of variance, four studies)

7 Being female (3 per cent of variance, eight studies)

8 Being shy/lonely (2 per cent of variance, 10 studies).

Age (comprising five studies) did not appear as a predictor, despite speculation (e.g. Giles and Maltby 2004) that this is an adolescent phenomenon.

So, Schiappa et al. concluded that characters who were seen as attractive (1 above) and similar in some way to the viewer (2 above) were the most likely to be the object of a parasocial relationship. However, an important additional factor was that they were perceived to be real (3 above), meaning that however unlikely the fictional settings, such as *Buffy the Vampire Slayer*, the character was seen to react in a believable way.

It seems likely that this realism may well be related to similarity, in that in reacting in a believable way, viewers can compare how they would behave in similar situations. Moreover, as the characters reveal credible information about themselves, this disclosure may be assumed to encourage a feeling of intimacy. Although Schiappa et al. do not distinguish between fictional and real-world characters, it is probable that this would be equally true of celebrities.

Evaluation of parasocial relationships

- *Are parasocial relationships dysfunctional?* – Rubin et al. (1985) cast doubt on the popular belief that parasocial relationships are based on dysfunctional loneliness. They found that loneliness was not a significant factor in parasocial interaction. Instead, people merely need to perceive a media figure as similar to themselves (and real) in order to rely upon that figure for companionship. Although much of the early research in this area focused on the development of parasocial relationships as indicative of social isolation and limited activity, more recent research suggests this is not the case, with results consistently revealing that people who are socially active and socially motivated are more likely to engage in such relationships (Sood and Rogers 2000).

- *Are parasocial relationships real?* – Giles (2002) points out that much of the theorizing implicitly pathologizes individuals who form strong parasocial attachments. However, although the relationships established with media celebrities are imagined by the viewer, they are none the less real in the sense that they can lead to attitudinal and behavioural changes.

The 'Absorption-Addiction model' and body image

In recent years there has been considerable research on the association between the mass media and eating disorders, with one of the most feared effects being that by glamorizing thin celebrities, the media may promote body shapes that are unrealistic and unattainable for many young people (Maltby et al. 2005). Increasingly, researchers have moved away from the simplistic idea that mere 'exposure' to thin celebrities is enough by itself to trigger eating disorders. McCutcheon et al. (2002) proposed an 'Absorption-Addiction' model which explained how a compromised identity structure in some individuals leads to a psychological absorption with a celebrity in an attempt to establish an identity.

Maltby et al. (2005) carried out a study to investigate the relationship between this model and body image within the perspective of parasocial relationships with celebrities. They found that when celebrity worship was related to poorer body image it tended to be among female adolescents between the ages of 14 and 16 years. The relationship was not evident among males, and Maltby et al. claim that this relationship tends to disappear at the onset of adulthood (between 17 and 20 years).

Evaluation of the 'Absorption-Addiction model' and body image

This study also suggests that parasocial relationships with celebrities perceived as having a good body shape may lead to a poor body image in female adolescents. However, this appears only to be the case with those adolescents who have an 'intense-personal' relationship with 'their' celebrity (i.e. they do not discuss the celebrity with their friends, and prefer to retain an exclusive interaction with the celebrity – see p.428). This finding suggests that it is the 'type' of interaction an individual has with celebrities in the media that determines whether there will be any effect on body image.

Evolutionary explanations of the attraction to celebrity

In contrast to the social psychological explanations regarding the attraction to celebrity, there are other, more evolutionary based explanations. These are discussed in the next section.

Preferences for creative individuals

A particular characteristic of human beings is our love of novelty (known as 'neophilia'). Before the arrival of television and computers, our ancestors would have had to amuse each other and neophilia would have led to ever-more creative displays from potential mates. This would explain many of the characteristics that are universally and uniquely developed in humans, such as music, art and humour, all of which are highly valued during mate choice (Miller 1998). We might, therefore, explain our attraction to celebrities as an extension of our love of these characteristics. We are drawn to individuals who display these creative skills, and the magnification of such characteristics that are broadcast regularly into our living rooms makes our attraction to such figures even greater.

The mating mind (Miller 2000) claims that sexual selection through mate choice was important in human mental evolution; especially the more 'self-expressive' aspects of human behaviour, such as art, humour and creativity. Miller argued that whereas natural selection might tend to favour minds with survival-enhancing skills, sexual selection might favour minds prone to inventing attractive, imaginative fantasies, the kinds of fantasy that nowadays we witness in the work of artists, film stars and musicians. Sexual selection can, therefore, explain why most people prefer fiction to non-fiction and myth to scientific evidence. Celebrities represent this world of fantasy, therefore we are attracted to them because of their association with it.

Evaluation of attraction to creative individuals
Comparative evidence – Darwin (1871) argued that neophilia was an important factor in the diversification and rapid evolution of bird song, with females being attracted to males who display the most complex songs. Among human beings neophilia is especially strong, with boredom often cited as a reason for terminating romantic relationships (Duck 1982). Partners who offer more cognitive variety and creativity in their relationships may have had longer, more reproductively successful relationships.

Celebrity gossip
Even if we can explain the intense interest that we have in other people who are socially important to us, how can we possibly explain the seemingly useless interest that we have in the lives of reality show contestants, movie stars, and celebrities of all kinds? One possible explanation may be found in the fact that celebrities are a recent occurrence, evolutionarily speaking. In our ancestral environment, any person about whom we knew intimate details of his or her private life was, by definition, a socially important member of the in-group. Barkow (1992) points out that evolution did not prepare us to distinguish between members of our community who have genuine effects on our lives and the images and voices that we are bombarded with by the entertainment industry. Thus, the intense familiarity with celebrities provided by the modern media trips the same gossip mechanisms that have evolved to keep up with the affairs of in-group members. After all, anyone whom we see that often and know that much about must be socially important to us. This will be especially true for television actors in soap operas or news anchors who are seen on a daily basis; these famous people become familiar friends. In our modern world, celebrity gossip may also serve another important social function. According to De Backer (2005), gossip serves a similar function to social grooming; it initiates and maintains alliances, but does it more efficiently. It takes up less time and is not necessarily a one-to-one exchange, thereby allowing larger social networks (e.g. fan clubs) to form.

Figure 12.7 © www.CartoonStock.com

Evaluation of evolutionary explanations of celebrity gossip
- *Research support* – De Backer *et al.* (2007) carried out a survey of 838 participants and in-depth interviews with 103 individuals to test which of two competing evolutionary explanations best explained our fascination with celebrity gossip. The learning hypothesis explains interest in celebrity gossip as a by-product of an evolved mechanism that is useful for acquiring relevant survival information. The parasocial hypothesis sees celebrity gossip as a diversion of this mechanism, leading individuals to misperceive celebrities as people who are part of their social network. In support of the learning hypothesis, age was a strong predictor of interest in celebrities. In partial support of the parasocial hypothesis, media exposure was a strong predictor of interest in celebrities.

Research into intense fandom

While many people have an interest in celebrities, some take this interest to an extreme. Celebrity worship, stalking, and the newer form of cyberstalking, are discussed below.

Celebrity worship
Giles and Maltby (2006) review some of the progress made in understanding the psychology of celebrity worship. They report that a recent factor analysis of data from 1723 UK respondents revealed three types of celebrity worship:
- *Entertainment-social* – Fans are attracted to a favourite celebrity because of their perceived ability to entertain and to become a source of social interaction and gossip. Items include, 'My friends and I like to discuss what my favourite celebrity has done' and, 'Learning the life story of my favourite celebrity is a lot of fun'.

- *Intense-personal* – The intense-personal aspect of celebrity worship reflects intensive and compulsive feelings about the celebrity, akin to the obsessional tendencies of fans often referred to in the literature.

Items include, 'My favourite celebrity is practically perfect in every way' and, 'I consider my favourite celebrity to be (sic) my soul mate'.

- *Borderline pathological* – This dimension is typified by uncontrollable behaviours and fantasies about their celebrities. Items include, 'I would gladly die in order to save the life of my favourite celebrity' and, 'If I walked through the door of my favourite celebrity's house, she or he would be happy to see me'.

Although the relative frequency of these is not revealed, an earlier paper by Maltby *et al.* (2004) suggested that in a sample of 372 people aged 18–47, less than 2 per cent could be considered 'borderline pathological'; just over 5 per cent 'intense-personal' and some 15 per cent 'entertainment-social'. The authors show that these categories relate to the personality dimensions proposed by Eysenck (1991): psychoticism, neuroticism and extroversion respectively.

The extrovert/social aspects of fandom are the predominant ones. Here 'worship' may be too strong a word and 'celebrity' too restrictive. People who are avid followers of television series, such as *Star Trek* and *Doctor Who,* might display enthusiasm bordering on the obsessional. But in these cases the fandom is rarely for an individual. This is equally true of football supporters who are fans of their clubs above individual players. Indeed almost all of the characteristics of celebrity fandom as summarized by Giles and Maltby can probably be found in an enormous range of clubs where members meet to celebrate their common purpose. Parasocial bereavement was the term used by Giles (2003) to describe the grief felt at the death of a celebrity. The two examples he takes are Diana Princess of Wales and Jill Dando the BBC presenter, who both died in tragic circumstances. Most striking of all was the phenomenon of people only realizing after the celebrity's death how much they would miss them. Latent celebrity worshippers were revealed by such comments as: 'I was taken by surprise by my depth of feeling for her on hearing of her death.'

Evaluation of celebrity worship

- *Celebrity worship as pathological behaviour* – Research suggests two contrasting views of celebrity worship. One of these represents celebrity worship as pathological in nature and representing fans' apparent confusion between celebrities' fictional roles and their real lives (Giles 2000). McCutcheon *et al.* (2002) provided evidence to support this view. They analysed a large set of questions about celebrity worshipping behaviours. They found evidence of a hierarchy of celebrity worship that spanned many different types of celebrity including actors, musicians and sports figures. At the top of this hierarchy, behaviour is characterized by over-identification with the celebrity as well as obsession with details of the celebrity's life. Further support comes from Maltby *et al.* (2001) who found a negative correlation between celebrity worship and psychological wellbeing (see Key research below).

Celebrity worship

Key research: Maltby *et al.* (2001)

Maltby *et al.* (2001) tested the assumption that celebrity worship is accompanied by poorer psychological wellbeing. They administered the Celebrity Attitude Scale (CAS) and the General Health Questionnaire (GHQ) to an opportunity sample of 126 men (mean age 26.97 years) and 181 women (mean age 27.67) from workplaces and community groups in South Yorkshire. The CAS measures attitude to celebrities on three subscales (see p.428)

The GHQ is a screening device designed to reveal symptoms of poor psychological health, including somatic (physiological) symptoms, anxiety, social dysfunction and severe depression.

Scores on the entertainment-social subscale of the CAS correlated positively (and significantly) with social dysfunction, anxiety and depression scores on the GHQ. Scores on the intense-personal and borderline pathological subscales correlated positively (and significantly) with anxiety and depression scores.

Maltby *et al.* conclude that the significant relationship between celebrity worship and poorer psychological wellbeing is the result of (failed) attempts to escape, cope or enhance the individual's daily life. This conclusion, they claim, holds even for the initial stages of celebrity worship that do not appear pathological.

Evaluation

Ethical issues are important in studies such as this because of the sensitive nature of the information being collected. Participants were told that their responses were confidential and that the purpose of the study was to examine a number of psychological factors that may be related to individuals' interest in famous people.

A methodological issue in this study concerns the use of the GHQ to measure psychological wellbeing. This measure is designed for a non-clinical population therefore would not cover the mental health issues and that might be expected in the borderline pathological subscale of the CAS.

■ *The benefits of celebrity worship* – Contrary to the pathological view of celebrity worship is the view that this form of behaviour is potentially beneficial to the individual (Maltby *et al.* 2001), provided the individual is participating in a social network of fans. Maltby *et al.* suggest that in this context, sharing information and experiences with friends (or over the Internet), such behaviours might promote productive social relationships and serve as a buffer against everyday stressors.

HOW SCIENCE WORKS

Activity **Research into celebrity worship**

Read the Key research 'Celebrity worship' on p.429 and then answer the following three questions:

1 What other ethical issues might arise in this study, and how would you address them?

2 How might researchers have assessed the reliability of the CAS?

3 There is the possibility of an order effect when two different scales are used. How might researchers have dealt with a possible order effect in this study?

Answers are given on p.610. ▶

Stalking

Oscar Wilde once famously remarked that the only thing worse than being talked about is not being talked about. Celebrities may share this ambivalence about public attention. Fandom in more obsessional forms can result in stalking. Stalking is defined in the British Crime Survey as 'A course of conduct involving two or more events of harassment causing fear, alarm or distress' (Walby and Allen 2004). Giles (2000) gives an example of one fan sitting on the steps of a recording studio for 110 days in the hope of meeting her idol. However, stalking victims may be surprisingly prevalent in the general population. McIvor *et al.* (2008) carried out a survey of 324 psychiatrists attached to a 'large mental health institution' in London to find that more than one in five (21 per cent) had been stalked and, in a third of these cases, received physical threats.

A recent text book on stalking (Pinals 2007) concluded, somewhat unhelpfully, that the various studies indicate a lifetime risk rate of being stalked for women of between eight per cent and 33 per cent while for men estimates ranged from three per cent to 46 per cent. A more typical figure in community surveys suggests around 12 per cent of people may fall victim to such behaviour (Dressing *et al.* 2005).

Although widely regarded as a simple nuisance, threats and acts of violence are not uncommon. In Mullen *et al.*'s (1999) study of 145 stalkers referred for treatment, 63 per cent had made threats and 36 per cent were assaultive. Rosenfeld (2004), in a meta-analysis of 13 studies of stalking, estimated the overall risk of violence was 39 per cent. Here the best correlates were given by a prior intimate relationship (the ex) and a previous history of violence. However, these figures would exaggerate the risk of violence in most stalking which may go unreported – especially if it involves an ex-partner about whom the victim has ambivalent feelings, including perhaps residual affection and guilt. Purcell *et al.* (2001) point out that studies which are community based provide quite different figures from mental health services. Around one-third of stalkers referred for psychiatric treatment are women compared with around 12 per cent in community studies. Interestingly, in the Purcell study of 190 stalkers, same-gender victims were chosen by half the women (48 per cent) compared with only nine per cent of men. Not surprisingly, many studies indicate that women are two to three times more likely to be victims than men (Sheridan *et al.* 2003).

Perhaps the most outrageous examples of stalking behaviour, where violence is attempted, can only be understood in terms of the pathology of the attacker. James *et al.* (2008) concluded that attempts to attack British royalty have been by quite disturbed individuals – over two-thirds were mentally ill (48 per cent showed psychotic behaviour and 20 per cent demonstrated mental disorder). This has long been recognized. William Gladstone, when Prime Minister to Queen Victoria, offered reassurance to her that foreigners usually had political motives for trying to assassinate their monarchs. However, those who attempted to kill the British Royalty were just madmen (Glancy 2008).

Cyberstalking

The evolution of modern technologies such as mobile phones sand the Internet has offered stalkers a new medium for their behaviours. Examples of **cyberstalking** would include compiling information about the victim in order to harass them later online (e.g. through text or e-mail communication) and offline (i.e. through more traditional face-to-face behaviours), repeated unsolicited e-mailing, instant messaging, spamming and sending electronic viruses to the target individual. In one large study of cyberstalking involving over 4000 female undergraduates, 13 per cent reported having been stalked, with one-quarter of these reporting having received e-mails from their stalker (Fisher and Cullen 2000). Similarly Finn (2004) reported that in a study of 339 students, 15 per cent had received e-mails or instant messages that were insulting, harassing or threatening. Campbell (2005) cited a National Children's Home study (2002) where one in four children reported being bullied by other children on the Internet or by mobile phone.

The Internet offers an attractive alternative to 'offline' stalking for would-be harassers. Advantages, such as anonymity and the opportunities for disinhibited behaviour, can promote greater risk-taking and antisocial behaviour (Finn 2004). Similarly it has been proposed that messages sent between mobile phones (i.e. SMS 'texts') are also attractive to stalkers because there is no direct contact and therefore stalker apprehension is reduced (Eytan and Borras 2005).

Evaluation of cyberstalking

- *Tolerance to cyberstalking* – Sheridan and Grant (2007) argue that 'offline' stalking may be more reinforcing than cyberstalking because stalkers are better able to observe the impact of their activities on the victim. Research suggests that cyberstalkers may develop a tolerance to Internet-based harassment such that they need more and more extreme activities to experience the same 'rush'.

- *Perceptions of cyberstalking* – Research suggests that cyberstalking may not be taken as seriously as 'offline' stalking. For example, Alexy et al. (2005) presented students with a vignette based on a real-life case of cyberstalking. Despite the fact that this very serious case resulted in prosecution, only 30 per cent of the students judged the behaviours concerned to be 'stalking'.

IDA   Stalking and attachment

Research on attachment has suggested that attachment patterns learned in childhood have long-term behavioural effects. Hazan and Shaver (1987) found, for example, that adult romantic relationships were generally consistent with childhood attachments. Individuals who recalled having secure attachments with parents tended to form secure attachments with their adult partners. On the other hand, those who recall inconsistent or rejecting parents were less likely to be securely attached to their adult partners.

McCutcheon et al. (2006) suggested that attachment patterns in childhood may contribute to other adult problems such as stalking. If insecurely attached children are more likely to have relationship difficulties as adults, then they might be tempted to have more parasocial relationships. Such a relationship, they argue, might be appealing to the insecurely attached individual because it makes few demands and, because they do not have a 'real' relationship with the celebrity, they do not run the risk of criticism or rejection.

Kienlen (1998) has hypothesized that insecure attachment patterns may lead to stalking behaviour, although the motivations of such insecurely attached individuals may differ according to the type of insecure attachment. Kienlen suggests that the people classified as the **anxious/ambivalent attachment** type experience anxiety over social rejection and therefore would be more likely to seek the approval of the object of their obsession. The **avoidant attachment** type individual, on the other hand, tends to maintain emotional distance from others. They are less likely to seek approval and more likely to pursue the target individual in order to retaliate against some perceived wrongdoing. There is some support for the link between insecure attachment and stalking behaviour. A study by McCutcheon et al. (2006), using 300 college students, found that those who reported insecure attachments as children were more likely to condone behaviours indicative of celebrity stalking.

HOW SCIENCE WORKS

Study of stalkers

Key research: Mullen *et al.* (1999)

Mullen *et al.* (1999) set out to investigate the behaviours, motivations and psychopathology of stalkers. They used a sample of 145 stalkers who had been referred to a forensic psychiatry centre in the US for treatment. Most of these stalkers were men (79 per cent), and many were unemployed (39 per cent) and over half had never had an intimate relationship. The most common victims were ex-partners (30 per cent), although work contacts and strangers were also victims of stalking. From this sample, five types of stalkers were identified: rejected, intimacy seeking, incompetent, resentful and predatory. Delusional disorders were common particularly among intimacy-seeking stalkers, and those with personality disorders were more common among rejected stalkers. The duration of stalking was from 4 weeks to 20 years (mean = 12 months), and was longer for rejected and intimacy-seeking stalkers than for the other types. Sixty three per cent of the stalkers had made threats towards their victim, and 36 per cent had committed an assault on them. Resentful stalkers were more likely to make threats and commit property damage, but rejected and predatory stalkers committed more physical assaults on their victims. The researchers concluded that stalkers have a range of motivations, from reasserting power over a partner who rejected them to the quest for a loving relationship. Most stalkers are lonely and socially incompetent, but all have the capacity to frighten and distress their victims.

Check your understanding of the psychology of celebrity by answering these questions. Try to do this from memory. You can check your answers by looking back through Topic 3, The psychology of celebrity.

1 What is meant by a 'parasocial relationship' and how are these experienced with celebrities?

2 What has research discovered about the role of parasocial relationships in shaping body image?

3 Summarize two evolutionary explanations for our attraction to celebrities.

4 Outline one critical point for each of the above explanations.

5 What have psychologists discovered from research into celebrity worship?

6 What are the three levels of the 'Absoption-Addiction' model of celebrity?

7 Give one behaviour that might be considered indicative of each of these three levels.

8 What have psychologists discovered about 'stalking' as a form of extreme fandom?

9 What is 'cyberstalking' and what do psychologists know about this phenomenon?

10 Outline the link between stalking and attachment.

Antisocial influences

Explanations

- Observational learning – imitation (Bobo doll studies), but little research support for this
- Demand characteristics and artificial setting
- Cognitive priming
- Desensitization

Research

- Some studies suggest a sleeper effect for media influence
- Research suggests that children are 'media literate'

  Evaluation of media research
  - inconclusive case for media effects
  - the nature of the audience (Hagell and Newburn)
  - methodological problems (lab and naturalistic studies)
  - studies lack external validity

prosocial influences

Explanations

- The pervasiveness of television
- Exposure to prosocial messages clearly evident
- Social learning theory
- Developmental trends in prosocial influence

  Evaluation
  - children fail to generalize from specific to general
  - prosocial messages more subtle than antisocial themes
  - greater effect on young children, contrary to developmental trends

Research

- Mares (1996): evidence for influence on positive interaction, altruism, self-control and anti-stereotyping
- More consistent effects found for girls than boys
- Effects stronger among higher socio-economic groups

Video games

- Anderson et al (2007) report powerful effects on aggression for violent video games
- Gentile *et al.* (2004) – amount of video game play did not correlate with arguments or physical fights
- Violent video game play associated with decreased activity in anterior cingulate cortex (ACC)

  Evaluation
  - unsubstantiated claims – evidence far from conclusive
  - Should violent games be banned? Conclusions not possible on such weak data
  - Can they be cathartic? Remains a possibility
  - validity of knowledge – evidence of a publication bias in research in this area

Persuasion

The Hovland-Yale model

- Source characteristics (attractive, credible)
- The message
- The audience

  Evaluation
  - gender bias in research
  - Rhodes and Wood (1992): low IQ more susceptible
  - Rutland (1999): support for 'life stages' hypothesis

The elaboration likelihood model

- Central route – high motivation; deep processing; lasting change
- Peripheral route – low motivation; superficial processing; temporary change
- Need for cognition (NC) – stable individual difference

  Evaluation
  - research supports NC as key factor in influence
  - NC relevant to real-life problem (smoking risks)
  - peripheral route processing long-lasting change

Decision making

Cognitive dissonance

- Experienced when two cognitions are in conflict
- Counter-attitudinal behaviour (Festinger and Carlsmith 195
- Post-decisional dissonance

  Evaluation
  - real-life relevance?
  - inconsistency does not always lead to dissonance
  - inconsistent research support for post-decisional dissonance

Self-perception theory

- Attitudes inferred by observing our own behaviour
- Bem (1965): different results from replication of Festinger and Carlsmith's experiment
- Overjustification effect – intrinsic motivation less important extrinsic rewards provided

  Evaluation
  - research support – facial feedback
  - overjustification supported by childrens' drawings study

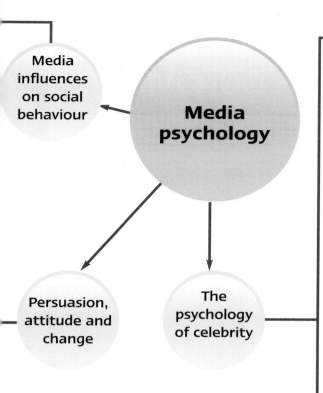

Attraction of celebrity

Social psychological explanations

- Parasocial relationships – formed with celebrities but one-sided
- Best predicted by perception of characters as attractive, similar and real
- Absorption-Addiction model
- Levels can be linked to body image

  Evaluation
  - parasocial relationships not always dysfunctional
  - real for the people who have them
  - links to body image only for female adolescents

Evolutionary explanations

- Preferences for creative individuals – neophilia
- Linked to sexual selection
- Celebrity gossip – celebrities as 'real people'
- Equivalent to social grooming

  Evaluation
  - neophilia supported in comparative studies and relationship dissolution
  - De Backer *et al.* (2007) support for adaptive value of celebrity gossip

Effectiveness of television

Psychology and advertising

- Hard sell – factual information on product
- Soft sell – focused more on consumers (particularly high self-monitors)
- Problem in determining actual changes in behaviour
- Celebrity endorsement may make use of parasocial relationships

  Evaluation
  - research suggests celebrity endorsement makes little difference
  - impact of advertising minimized by audience choice of whether to watch adverts

Advertising and children

- Age and comprehension of persuasive intent
- 'Pester power' linked to exposure to commercial TV

  Evaluation
  - importance of parental mediation
  - implications for legislation

Intense fandom

Celebrity worship

- Giles and Maltby – factor analysis shows three levels:
  1. entertainment-social
  2. intense-personal
  3. borderline-pathological
- Linked to Eysenck's personality dimensions

  Evaluation
  - Maltby *et al.* (2001) celebrity worship negatively correlated with psychological wellbeing
  - may have benefits (e.g. as buffer against stressors)

Stalking

- Both men and women are stalked but women more
- Prior intimate relationship best predictor of violence
- Cyberstalking – use of e-mail and SMS, etc.
- May be attractive because more opportunity for disinhibited behaviour
- Mullen *et al.* (1999) – identified five types of stalker

  Evaluation
  - statistics may underestimate stalking rates
  - may be linked to insecure attachment patterns
  - tolerance to cyberstalking may be greater
  - cyberstalking perceived as 'less serious'

Specification content	The specification explained
Models of addictive behaviour (Topic 1)	This opening section asks you to consider three major psychological approaches in terms of how they might be applied to help us understand the nature of addictive behaviours. For each model, you must be clear about how initiation, maintenance and relapse of addictive behaviour is accounted for and be able to:
Biological, cognitive and learning models of addiction, including explanations for initiation, maintenance and relapse	■ Describe and evaluate the biological model of initiation, maintenance and relapse of addictive behaviour. ■ Describe and evaluate the cognitive model of initiation, maintenance and relapse of addictive behaviour. ■ Describe and evaluate the learning model of initiation, maintenance and relapse of addictive behaviour.
Explanations for specific addictions, including smoking and gambling	■ Describe explanations of specific addictions – you must include smoking and gambling but may consider other addictions as well. ■ Evaluate explanations of specific addictions – you must include smoking and gambling but may consider other addictions as well.
Factors affecting addictive behaviour (Topic 2)	In this section you are asked to consider individual and social processes underlying addictive behaviour, in particular, how these might affect resistance or vulnerability. In this section 'research' can refer to theory or studies or a mixture of both. You should be able to:
Vulnerability to addiction including self-esteem, attributions for addiction and social context of addiction	■ Describe research into the role of at least three factors which may affect vulnerability to behavioural addiction (you must include self-esteem, attributions and social influences). ■ Evaluate research into the role of at least three factors which may affect vulnerability to behavioural addiction (you must include self-esteem, attributions and social influences).
The role of media in addictive behaviour	■ Describe research into ways in which media might influence addictive behaviour. ■ Evaluate research into ways in which media might influence addictive behaviour. (Note: 'media' is a plural term so you should know about more than one 'medium'.)

Specification content	The specification explained
Reducing addictive behaviour (Topic 3)	**Here you are asked to study ways in which addictive behaviours might be managed, with particular emphasis on those that need to be prevented from occurring, or reduced, or eradicated once established. You are also asked to assess the effectiveness of particular types of intervention. You should be able to:**
Models of prevention, including theory of reasoned action and theory of planned behaviour	■ Describe models of prevention of addictive behaviour. You must include both theories of reasoned action and planned behaviour. ■ Evaluate models of prevention of addictive behaviour. You must include both theories of reasoned action and planned behaviour but may include others as a means of comparison.
Types of intervention, including biological, psychological, public-health interventions and legislation, and their effectiveness	■ Describe the four named types of intervention into addictive behaviour. You must include biological, psychological, public-health interventions and legislation. ■ Evaluate the four types of intervention: biological, psychological, public-health interventions and legislation, including their effectiveness.

Introduction

In this chapter, a number of observations will be made based on the empirical literature surrounding the psychology of addiction. More importantly, this chapter will highlight that:

■ There is a growing movement that views a number of behaviours as potentially addictive, including those that do not involve the ingestion of a drug (e.g. gambling).

■ Addiction can be examined in many different ways but there appear to be key features and components, such as salience, tolerance, withdrawal, mood modification, conflict and relapse.

■ There are numerous models of addictive behaviour (e.g. disease/medical model, moral model, experiential model, genetic model).

■ There are many different kinds of theories of addiction, including biological perspectives, behavioural perspectives and cognitive perspectives. However, addiction is by nature **biopsychosocial** and it is this eclectic perspective that provides the most all-encompassing view of addictive behaviour.

■ There are many factors involved in the development of addictive behaviours, including attributions, individual differences (self-esteem), media and advertising influences. Addiction is thus a highly complex behaviour.

■ There are many different types of treatment that have been used to help reduce addictive behaviour, including behavioural therapies, cognitive therapies, medical/biological interventions, psychotherapies, self-help therapies, online therapies, harm minimization and a wide range of idiosyncratic therapies. Research has concluded that it is better to be treated than not treated and that a variety of simultaneous treatments (i.e. a multi-modal approach appears to be the most beneficial).

In Topic 1, we discuss the problems of defining addictive behaviour and its components, and look at different models (approaches) that attempt to explain addictive behaviour. Two specific addictions, smoking and gambling, are then examined in more detail, and we outline the argument for an eclectic, biopsychosocial approach.

In Topic 2, we look at factors affecting vulnerability to addictive behaviour, and the role of the media in influencing addictive behaviour, while Topic 3 is devoted to ways of reducing addictive behaviour, including stages and models of prevention and types of intervention.

Psychology in context   Addiction stories

Open any paper or check any news website on almost any day and there will be a story on addiction. Here are some typical headlines and stories:

First free NHS clinic for gambling addicts opens

'The first NHS clinic offering free treatment for gamblers will open in September in what campaigners are hailing as a landmark development in the fight against the growing addiction to traditional and online betting. An estimated 600 000 people have an unhealthy relationship with gambling, but the few clinics able to treat them are either run by charities or are private and charge large sums of money – something addicts have very little of.'

The Independent, 18 June 2008

Cocaine addiction 'gene' discovered

'A study of 670 cocaine addicts found they were 25 per cent more likely to carry the gene variant than people who did not use the drug.'

Daily Telegraph, 11 November 2008

Drug-addicted teens increases by third

'The number of 16 and 17-year-olds being treated for drug addiction has soared by 30 per cent in two years. And cocaine is fast catching up with cannabis as the drug of choice for teenagers. There were 7857 youngsters aged 16 and 17 on drug treatment programmes in England in 2007/08 – up from 6058.'

Daily Mail, 2 October 2008

Duchovny's sex addiction tops 2008 scandal list

'David Duchovny's sex addiction scandal has been named the year's most surprising by readers of American weekly magazine Parade. More than 30 per cent of voters selected the star's confession and subsequent rehab stint as 2008's Most Shocking Scandal.'

Yahoo News, 31 December 2008

Elderly drug and alcohol abuse often undetected

'Memory loss, disorientation, shaky hands, mood swings, depression and chronic boredom are often normal to the aging process. These behaviors can, though, signal something less benign. Grandma or Grandpa may have a substance abuse problem.'

Google News, 27 November 2008

The first things you may notice about these headlines are that:

- addiction covers a wide range of behaviours in today's society
- addiction affects people right across the lifespan
- addiction stories range from the frivolous to the scientific
- the public appears to have an almost insatiable appetite for stories about addiction.

This topic will explore addiction from many different psychological approaches. First, just take a few minutes to think about the following questions:

1 When you hear the word 'addiction', what pops into your head?

2 Does the study of addiction interest you? Why? Why not?

3 What types of activities do you associate with addiction?

4 Who is most likely to become addicted? Are addicts born or made?

Defining addiction

How to define addiction has been a matter of great debate for decades. For many, the concept of addiction involves the taking of drugs. Therefore, it is perhaps unsurprising that most official definitions concentrate on drug ingestion. Here are some typical definitions:

'Addiction is the compulsive uncontrolled use of habit forming drugs' (*Webster's New International Dictionary*).

'Addiction is a state of periodic or chronic intoxication produced by repeated consumption of a drug, natural or synthetic' (*World Health Organization*).

Despite such definitions, there is now a growing movement which views a number of behaviours as potentially addictive, including those that do not involve the ingestion of a drug. These include behaviours as diverse as gambling (Griffiths 2006), overeating (Orford 2001), sex (Carnes 1991), exercise (Allegre *et al.* 2006), videogame playing (Griffiths 2007), love (Peele and Brodsky 1975), Internet use (Widyanto and Griffiths 2006) and work (Griffiths 2005a). In fact, you can become addicted to almost anything. Such diversity has led to new all encompassing definitions of what constitutes an addictive behaviour. One such definition is that of Marlatt *et al.* (1988), who define addictive behaviour as:

'A repetitive habit pattern that increases the risk of disease and/or associated personal and social problems. Addictive behaviours are often experienced subjectively as 'loss of control' – the behaviour contrives to occur despite volitional attempts to abstain or moderate use. These habit patterns are typically characterized by immediate gratification (short term reward), often coupled with delayed deleterious effects (long term costs). Attempts to change an addictive behaviour (via treatment or self initiation) are typically marked with high relapse rates'.

The key idea here that is common to previous ideas about chemical addictions is the idea of 'loss of control'. The person with the addiction is not able to regulate their

---

Activity Defining addiction

1 Spend five to ten minutes on your own trying to devise your own definition of 'addiction'.

2 Share your definition with others in the class and discuss the problems in trying to define it.

3 Post-task discussion: Was the task difficult? Easy? What were the parameters you were working within? Do your definitions cover all types of addiction? If not, why not?

Some suggestions are given in the Answers to activities on p.603. ▶

---

behaviour as they would like and their behaviour becomes extreme.

Components model of addiction

All kinds of addictive behaviour have elements in common which are summed up in the clinical criteria for diagnosing substance dependence (addiction) to alcohol, nicotine or other drugs (see Table 13.1). However, it is clear that some individuals engage in behaviours that have addictive elements without it necessarily being a full-blown addiction. For instance, if someone has no negative **withdrawal** effects after stopping their excessive cocaine use or gambling, are they really addicted? If the cocaine use or gambling does not conflict with anything else in that person's life, can it be said to be an addiction? In very simple terms, the difference between an excessive enthusiasm and an addiction is that enthusiasms add to life whereas addictions take away from it.

Salience

The importance of the behaviour to the individual – addictive behaviours become the most important activity for a person so that even when they are not doing it, they are thinking about it. Some addictive behaviours, such as smoking (nicotine) and drinking (alcohol), can be engaged in concurrently with other activities and so do not tend to dominate an addict's thoughts or lead to total preoccupation, e.g. a smoker can carry cigarettes and still engage in other activities. However, when a smoker is unable to smoke for a long period (such as a 24-hour plane flight), smoking totally dominates their thoughts and behaviour. This could be termed 'reverse salience', with the addictive activity becoming the most important thing in that person's life when they are prevented from engaging in it.

Mood modification

The experience people report while carrying out their addictive behaviour – people with addictive behaviour patterns commonly report a 'rush', a 'buzz' or a 'high', e.g. when taking their drugs or when gambling. Interestingly, a person's drug or activity of choice can have the capacity to achieve different **mood-modifying** effects at different times, e.g. a nicotine addict may use cigarettes first thing in the morning for the arousing 'nicotine rush' they need to get going for the day. By the end of the day, they may be using nicotine as a way of de-stressing and relaxing, rather than for its stimulant qualities. It appears that addicts can use their addiction to bring about mood changes, and this is as true for gamblers as it is for drug addicts.

Tolerance

The increasing amount of activity that is required to achieve the same effect – the classic example of **tolerance** is a heroin addict's need to increase the size of their 'fix' to get the type of feeling (e.g. an intense 'rush') they once got from much smaller doses. In gambling, tolerance may involve the gambler gradually having to increase the size of the bet to experience a mood-modifying effect that was initially obtained by a much smaller bet. It may also involve spending longer and longer periods gambling.

Withdrawal symptoms

The unpleasant feelings and physical effects that occur when the addictive behaviour is suddenly discontinued or reduced – this can include 'the shakes', moodiness and irritability. These symptoms are commonly believed to be a response to the removal of a chemical that the person has developed a tolerance to. However, these effects can also be experienced by gamblers (see Orford 2001), so the effects might be due to withdrawal from the behaviour as well as the substance.

Conflict

People with addictive behaviours develop conflicts with the people around them, often causing great social misery, and also develop conflicts within themselves. Continual choosing of short-term pleasure and relief leads to disregard of adverse consequences and long-term damage, which in turn increases the apparent need for the addictive activity as a coping strategy.

Relapse

The tendency for repeated reversions to earlier patterns of the particular activity to recur and for even the most extreme patterns, typical of the height of the addiction, to be quickly restored after many years of abstinence or control. The classic example of **relapse** behaviour is in smokers, who often give up for a period of time only to return to full-time smoking after a few cigarettes. However, such relapses are common in all addictions, including behavioural addictions such as gambling (Griffiths 2002).

Table 13.1 *Components of addictive behaviour (from Griffiths 2005a)*

STRETCH AND CHALLENGE

Activity — **Applying the components of addictive behaviour**

In the introduction to this chapter it was suggested that it is possible to become addicted to overeating, sex, exercise, videogame playing, love, Internet use and work.

1 Choose any one of these.

2 How well does it apply to each of the components of addictive behaviour listed in Table 13.1? Give examples.

3 What difficulties with this can you identify?

Some suggestions are given in the Answers to activities on p.603. ▶

Models of addictive behaviour

The model we use to explain addiction affects how we view the person with the addictive behaviour and also how we decide to 'treat' their behaviour in order to change it. The word 'treat' is in inverted commas because what we are really talking about here is not making someone better from the measles but changing their behaviour to make them more socially acceptable. We can only really call this 'treatment' if addiction is a disease. There are numerous models of addictive behaviour and some examples of the many different approaches are shown in Table 13.2. We then develop these ideas further, looking at biological, behavioural and cognitive explanations. Although there are clear differences between the theories, they do overlap, and all contribute to our understanding of the complex behaviours we call addictions.

The disease model

Suggests that addiction comes from a disorder of the body such as a neurochemical imbalance – in this model, the individual has limited control over their behaviour in the same way that you have limited control over whether you get measles or not.

The genetic model

Suggests there is a genetic disposition towards addictive behaviour – it is known that the biggest risk factor for becoming a smoker is having parents who smoke, but does this show evidence of a genetic disposition or family influence? There is evidence that shows a higher incidence of certain genes in people with addictive behaviours (see below).

The experiential model

Commonly associated with Stanton Peele (1990) – in brief, this model suggested that addictive behaviours are much more temporary and dependent on the situation we are in than either of the previous two models would suggest. In fact, people often move on (or grow out of) their addictive behaviours as their life circumstances change.

The moral model

Suggests that the key issue with addiction is a lack of character – in this view, addiction is a result of weakness, or moral failure in the individual. The treatment is clearly to get people to repent and then to develop their moral strength.

Table 13.2 *Some models of addictive behaviour*

Biological models of addictive behaviour

The biological explanation is much easier to understand in relation to chemical addictions, such as nicotine, than to behaviour, such as gambling. Biological explanations of addiction focus on neurotransmitter substances in the brain, and on genetic differences between people with addictions and people without addictions. In biological models of addictive behaviour, a person would be most susceptible to addiction during the *initiation phase*, because they have a predisposed biological vulnerability. Biological predispositions are much less likely to have an effect during the maintenance of the addiction. However, if a person managed to give up their addiction, a biological predisposition would make them more susceptible to relapse (i.e. repeating the behaviour).

Neurotransmitters

Simply, a neurotransmitter is a chemical that moves in the gaps between nerve cells to transmit messages. If the chemical is blocked or replaced, for example, then the message changes and there is an effect on the physiological systems, and also on cognition, mood and behaviour. The neurotransmitter that is most commonly implicated in all this is dopamine, but other chemicals have also been found to have an effect (Potenza 2001). Not only do neurotransmitters play a role in chemical addictions but they have also been implicated in behaviours such as gambling (Comings *et al.* 1996) and videogame playing (Koepp *et al.* 1998).

Genetics

Until relatively recently, the main way of investigating genetic factors in human behaviour was to study family relationships. More recently, it has been possible to carry out genetic analysis and look for differences in the genetic structure of people with and without addictive behaviours. The two methods tend to point to different answers. The family studies tend to emphasize the role of environmental factors in the development of addictive behaviours. A study of over 300 monozygotic (MZ) twins (identical) and just under 200 same-sex dizygotic (DZ) twins (fraternal) estimated the contribution of genetic factors and environmental factors to substance use in adolescence. It concluded that the major influences on the decision to use substances were environmental rather than genetic (Han *et al.* 1999). Some family studies, however, suggest there is a link between addictive behaviour and personality traits. For example, a study of over 300 MZ twins and over 300 DZ twins looked at the relationship between alcohol use and personality. The study suggests that there is a connection between genetics and antisocial personality characteristics (including attention seeking, not following social norms, and violence), and between these personality characteristics and alcoholism (Jang *et al.* 2000). Similar findings have also been claimed for behavioural addictions such as gambling addiction (Comings *et al.* 1996).

Reinforcement

The biological explanation overlaps with the behavioural explanation (see pp.442) when we look at **reinforcement**. Reinforcement is defined as being anything that increases the probability that the behaviour will recur in similar circumstances. The term commonly refers to learned associations, acquired through **operant conditioning** or

classical conditioning (see pp.445 and 447), but it may also be applied to other forms of learning.

A possible answer to the question of what makes something reinforcing comes from the discovery of 'pleasure centres' in the brain. Olds and Milner (1954) found that rats would press a lever for the reward of mild electrical stimulation in particular areas of the brain. The rats would continue to press the lever in preference to other possible rewards, such as food, drink or sexual activity. The researchers did not record whether the animals had silly smiles on their faces, but the areas of the brain are now commonly referred to as 'pleasure centres'.

The experience of pleasure is very important for our healthy development. If, for example, we found food or sex boring, then our species would probably starve to death or fail to breed. The feelings of pleasure associated with these activities act as a reinforcement. If we associate these pleasure feelings with other activities, then they too will be reinforced. So, the pleasure that encourages essential behaviours is also the pleasure that can encourage damaging behaviour. Could it be that the threat of addiction is the price we pay for pleasure?

Evaluation of biological explanations of addictive behaviour

- *Biological explanations help explain susceptibility* – There are countless instances of people who live in exactly the same environment (e.g. two siblings) but addiction is only present in some cases. Biological explanations help to account for inherent vulnerabilities and susceptibilities (i.e. at the initiation stage, some people are predisposed towards addictive behaviour) and also provide a reason as to why some people may be more resistant to addiction treatment and more prone to **relapse**.

- *Neurotransmitters' complex effects are not fully understood* – The difficulty with looking at which neurotransmitter produces which reward is that the brain is remarkably complex, and the effects of even one drug

Twin studies have long been a favourite way of attempting to unravel the **nature–nurture** debate with respect to many aspects of human behaviour, including addictive behaviours. Differences between genetically identical twins should be largely due to environmental influences, and comparing identical twins reared together or apart should enable us to tease out how much the environment contributes. If there is a genetic component to addictive behaviours, we would expect to find twins who were reared apart to be equally susceptible to addiction, irrespective of the environmental conditions in which they were raised.

can be very diverse. Ashton and Golding (1989) suggest that nicotine can simultaneously affect a number of systems, including learning and memory, the control of pain, and the relief of anxiety. In fact, it is generally believed that smoking nicotine can increase arousal and reduce stress – two responses that ought to be incompatible. This means that it is difficult to pin down a single response that follows smoking a cigarette.

- *Interaction with social context is neglected* – A deeper problem with the neurochemical explanations is the neglect of the social contexts of the behaviours. The pleasures and escapes associated with taking a drug are highly varied and depend on the person, the dose, the social situation they are in and the wider social context of the society they live in (Orford 2001). For example, drug taking in Vietnam was highly prevalent, but most soldiers' addictive drug use stopped spontaneously in their US home environment (Robins *et al.* 1975); the effects of Ecstasy are likely to differ depending on the presence or absence of 'rave' music (Larkin and Griffiths 2004). Biological explanations that neglect social context are thus too **reductionist** to be complete.

- *Genotypes are not the whole story* – Studies that analyse the genetic structure of individuals (their **genotype**) tend to emphasize the role of genetics rather than the environment in addictive behaviours. Some genes have attracted particular attention and have been shown to appear more frequently in people with addictive behaviours than in people without. The problem is that these genes do not occur in all people with the addictive behaviour and they do appear in some people without it. For example, a gene referred to as DRD2 (nothing to do with *Star Wars*) has been found in 42 per cent of people with alcoholism. It has also been found in 50 per cent of pathological gamblers, 45 per cent of people with Tourette's syndrome, and 55 per cent of people with autism. It has also been found in 25 per cent of the general population. This means that DRD2 appears more frequently in people with these behavioural syndromes, but it cannot be the sole explanation for the behaviour (Comings 1998).

IDA   Addiction and reductionism

As with other psychological disorders, criticism of biological explanations of addiction is that they are reductionist: they reduce a complex behaviour such as addiction down to a relatively simple level of explanation, i.e. an imbalance in brain chemicals or a particular genetic variation. The influence of brain chemicals, such as dopamine, in addiction is indisputable, but to argue that they cause addiction is to neglect all other potential influences (such as personality variables, cognitive biases) in the development of this disorder.

Cognitive explanations of addictive behaviour

The cognitive explanation is much easier to understand in relation to behavioural addictions, such as gambling, than to chemical addictions, such as alcoholism and cigarette smoking. Cognitive explanations of addiction focus on faulty thinking processes and biases, and it is assumed that a person would be most susceptible to addiction during the *maintenance* phase. Faulty cognitions are less likely to have an effect during the initiation phase of the addiction, as the cognitive model also assumes that all individuals are equally susceptible to developing an addictive behaviour. However, if someone managed to give up their addiction, those with faulty cognitions would be more susceptible to relapse unless they undergo some kind of cognitive correction treatment.

Faulty thinking

Cognitive explanations focus on the way that we process information. If we are making faulty judgements then we might develop addictive behaviours. This explanation is not nearly as clear cut as it sounds, because faulty thinking is what keeps us going. Look at it this way, you will exist for just a few moments in the great expanse of time and your impact on the whole scheme of things amounts to very little (at best). And yet it does all seem to matter, so please don't give up your psychology course now. The faulty thinking around gambling is that we will win or at least be able to control the odds, using our 'lucky numbers' on the lottery – so lucky that you've never won anything with them.

Irrational biases

Despite the fact that the odds of almost all activities are weighted strongly in favour of the gambling operator, gamblers continue to believe they can win money from gambling. This observation leads to the conclusion that gambling may be maintained by irrational or erroneous beliefs (Griffiths 1994). For example, people overestimate the extent to which they can predict or influence gambling outcomes, and tend to misjudge how much money they have won or lost. This hypothesis has been confirmed in numerous studies (Langer 1975; Langer and Roth 1983) showing that people overestimate the degree of skill or control that can be exerted in chance activities. For a more detailed examination of cognitive bias in gamblers read the Key research by Griffiths (1994) opposite.

Gamblers' irrational cognitive biases

An experiment demonstrated that gamblers have irrational cognitive biases concerning their gambling behaviour and that they use a variety of heuristics (flexible attributions, hindsight bias, illusory correlations, etc.) when gambling (see panel, 'Applied heuristics' on p.445). Griffiths' aim was to investigate cognition and gambling and, in particular, to find out whether regular gamblers (RG) think and behave differently from non-regular gamblers (NRG).

Participants were volunteers who responded to a poster placed in the local university (30 RG and 30 NRG). The RGs included 29 males and one female, whereas the NRG group had 15 males and 15 females. RGs were defined as those who gambled on slot machines at least once a week and NRGs were those who gambled on slot machines once a month or less.

The experiment took place in a real amusement arcade. The independent variable was whether the gamblers were regular or non-regular. The methods included:

1 measuring the winnings and time spent gambling
2 content analysis of 'thinking aloud' recordings
3 semi-structured interviews.

All participants gambled on the same slot machine ('Fruitskill'), and were randomly allocated to the thinking aloud (TA) group or the non-thinking aloud (NTA) group. Each participant was given £3 (equivalent of 30 plays), and they were asked to stay on the machine for 60 plays. This meant, in effect, that they had to break even. Any winnings after 60 plays they could keep, or they could carry on playing. There were seven dependent variables (see Table 13.3).

Only two results were significant (i.e. were different at p<.05):

1 RGs had a higher play rate
2 RGs who thought aloud had a lower win rate in plays.

Griffiths also found that winning was not necessarily the main aim – staying on the machine for as long as possible was more important, for playing was enjoyable in itself.

The participants in each condition (NG and NRG) were randomly assigned to two groups: thinking aloud (TA) and non-thinking aloud (NTA). In the TA condition the participants were encouraged to say whatever came into their heads while playing. These were qualitative and quantitative data. The results were recorded at the time and written up within 24 hours (see Table 13.4).

Griffiths showed there were cognitive differences between the two groups:

■ *Irrational verbalizations* – The RG were more likely to have irrational verbalizations (e.g. personifying the machine, talking and swearing at it). Examples of personification are: 'the machine hates me', 'this fruity is in a good mood'. Typical explanations for explaining away losses involved hindsight bias, with players predicting events after they happened: 'I had a feeling it wasn't

DV: Behavioural Findings	Non-Regular NTA	Regular NTA	Non-Regular TA	Regular TA
Total plays = number of plays per session	47.8	56.3	55.7	65.6
Total time = minutes in play per session	8.4	8.5	11.5	9.9
Play rate = number of plays per minute per session	6.5	7.5	5.3	8.4
End stake = winnings	4.0	0	7.3	13.9
Win = total number of wins	6.1	8.0	8.3	6.0
Win rate (time) = minutes between each win	2.0	1.0	1.7	1.8
Win rate (plays) = number of plays between each win	12.5	7.5	8.0	14.6

Table 13.3 *Summary of behavioural differences between regular gamblers (n=30) and non-regular gamblers (n=30)*

going to pay very much after it had just given me a feature'. 'I had a feeling it was going to chew up those tokens fairly rapidly.' 'I had a feeling it had paid out earlier because it's not giving me a chance.' Some players had completely erroneous perceptions: 'I'm only gonna put one quid in to start with because psychologically I think it's very important...it bluffs the machine - it's my own psychology'.

- *Rational verbalizations* – The NRG were more likely to record confusion and lack of understanding of the game, whereas the RG were more likely to refer to winning situations.

In conclusion, there are only minor behavioural differences between RGs and NRGs, but there are important cognitive differences in both their rational and irrational verbalizations. The results support explanations of gambling that are based on cognitive bias and heuristics.

Evaluation

Why the players should demonstrate these biases and where they come from is not so clear. It may be that there is a general tendency to personify machines with which people spend a lot of time. Furthermore, it is difficult to predict when a heuristic will be used. It is also unclear whether use of heuristics depends on intrinsic factors (psychological mood state) and/or extrinsic factors (gambling history). Based upon these findings, it has been suggested that irrational thinking may be related to problematic gambling behaviour (Wagenaar 1988; Parke et al. 2007), with persistent behaviour thought to be the result of people's overconfidence in their ability to win money (Wagenaar 1988; Walker 1992).

DV: Content analysis. Examples of findings	NRGs (% verbalization)	RGs (% verbalization)
Machine personification	1.14	7.54
Explaining losses	0.41	3.12
Talk to machine	0.90	2.64
Swear at machine	0.08	0.06
Reference to skill	1.47	5.34
Verbalizing confusion	4.81	1.72

Table 13.4 *Summary of verbal differences between regular gamblers (n=15) and non-regular gamblers (n=15)*

Evaluation of cognitive explanations of addictive behaviour

- *Cognitive explanations help explain individual differences* – There are countless instances of people engaged in exactly the same activity (e.g. playing the same slot machine) but addiction is only present in some cases. Cognitive explanations help to account for individual differences while engaged in the activity (e.g. during the development and maintenance stage, those who develop faulty cognitive biases may be more likely to develop problems).

- *Irrationality is an erratic predictor of addictive behaviour* – A problem with the cognitive approach to studying addictions like gambling is that irrationality does not appear to co-vary with other observable facets of gambling, such as the level of risk taking or reinforcement frequency. This is a problem because cause and effect of cognitive bias cannot be established.

- *Cognitive explanations may be limited to particular addictions* – Cognitive explanations may have less of an effect in chemical addictions like heroin addiction but a more pronounced effect in gambling or videogame addictions.

- *Experiential factors may play a role* – Griffiths (1994) found that regular gamblers had greater difficulty than occasional players in verbalizing their thoughts while they were gambling. Regular players seemed capable of gambling without attending to what they were doing ('on automatic pilot'), suggesting that cognitive processes did not play a major role in the maintenance of their behaviour.

- *Skill perception varies across individuals* – Many cognitive processes thought to underlie gambling behaviour are more likely to be observed when activities are perceived as having some skill component (Griffiths 1995). However, beliefs about skill in gambling are neither completely irrational nor consistent across players. This means that cause and effect of such relationships cannot be established with any certainty.

- *Need to control variations in perceived skill* – Even in activities where outcomes are chance-determined, there are likely to be variations in the extent to which gamblers perceive that the outcomes are solely chance-determined (e.g. playing slot machines is seen by some players as very skilful).

Applied heuristics

Heuristics are basically 'rules of thumb', and are often used by gamblers as a way of simplifying decisions or justifying their behaviour (Griffiths 1994). For instance, some gamblers will say after a gambling session that they knew what was going to happen (*hindsight bias*), attribute any wins to their own skill and any losses to other influences (*flexible attribution*) and solely concentrate on how much they won, ignoring how much they lost to get it (*absolute frequency bias*). The gaming industry also uses heuristics to attract gamblers. For instance, winners are often highly publicized as a way of making it seem as though there are more winners than losers (*availability bias*).

Behavioural (learning) explanations of addictive behaviour

Behavioural (i.e. learning) explanations take as their starting point the theories of both classical and operant conditioning (see below and p.447). For instance, in classical conditioning, a drug addict might experience a craving for heroin at the sight of a hypodermic needle, or a gambling addict might get a strong craving to gamble walking past a casino or bookmakers. (See Explanations of addictions to gambling, p.447, for more detail on classical and operant conditioning in relation to gambling.)

Operant conditioning

In operant conditioning, addicts change their behaviour in response to changes in the environment, such as rewards and punishments (e.g. an alcoholic drinking a bottle of whisky may experience positive feelings of pleasure, or the drinking of the whisky might relieve withdrawal symptoms). These rewards (reinforcers) and punishments can bring about changes in mood (e.g. pleasure, see biological models above), or material changes (e.g. money, in the case of gambling). One of the striking findings that Skinner (1953) discovered in his work with animals was that he was able to achieve greater behavioural change if he gave less reinforcement rather than more. This effect was further amplified if he made the arrival of these reinforcements less predictable. The schedule for producing the strongest behavioural change he found was the **variable ratio**, which describes a situation where rewards are given not every time you do the behaviour but, on average, every fifth time you do it (does this remind you of anything?).

Susceptibility

In behavioural (learning) models of addictive behaviour, it is assumed that a person would be most susceptible to addiction during both the *initiation* phase (because initial rewards can shape future behaviour) and the *maintenance phase* (because continued rewards can maintain behaviour). The behavioural model also assumes that all individuals are equally susceptible to developing an addictive behaviour. However, if a person managed to give up their addiction, relapse might be less likely if they have 'unlearned' the addictive behaviour.

Activity — Rewarding behaviour

Can you think of examples in your own life when:

1 an aspect of your behaviour is rewarded so much that you cease to feel motivated to do it

2 an aspect of your behaviour is reinforced regularly so you keep it up

3 an aspect of your behaviour is reinforced irregularly and unpredictably so you keep it up?

Some suggestions are given in the Answers to activities on p.603. ▶

Evaluation of learning explanations of addictive behaviour

▪ *Learning explanations help explain individual differences* – In the countless instances of people engaged in exactly the same activity (e.g. drinking two or three pints of beer), addiction is only present in some cases. Learning explanations help to account for individual differences while engaged in the activity, during the development and maintenance stage, (e.g. those who get constant rewards from their alcohol drinking may be more likely to develop problems).

▪ *Neither conditioning explanation is sufficient on its own* – Despite evidence supporting both theories, neither is entirely satisfactory on its own. Classical conditioning theory seems useful to explain people's motivation in initiation of a gambling session, but appears less useful to explain maintenance of gambling behaviour. Conversely, while operant conditioning might explain maintenance of behaviour, it appears less useful in explaining why people initiate gambling or recommence gambling after a prolonged period of abstinence (Griffiths 1995).

▪ *Findings contrary to operant theory* – Researchers have also raised questions about the extent to which behaviours like excessive gambling adhere to operant theory at all, since gamblers lose more than they win and because reinforcement magnitudes are not independent of player responses, e.g. stake sizes (Delfabbro and Winefield 1999).

▪ *Operant explanations are not equally successful* – Difficulties plague attempts to develop general operant theories of very specific activities such as gambling. Some activities appear more suited to this form of explanation, e.g. slot machines and scratchcards, where there is a short time-interval between stake and outcome, and where outcomes are entirely determined by chance. It seems more difficult to apply these principles to skilled gambling games such as blackjack, poker and sports betting, where player decisions can significantly influence outcomes.

■ *Learning theories cannot stand in isolation* – As with other psychological theories, learning (conditioning) theories cannot explain why people exposed to similar stimuli respond differently; why some smoke, drink or gamble whereas others do not, or why some people smoke, drink or gamble more than others. In addition, the effectiveness, or strength, of the conditioning effect may be a function of motivational factors and type of activity. Some, but not all, people engage in these behaviours for excitement or relaxation and, as discussed, people satisfy these needs by different activities. Thus, it is unlikely that classical conditioning will affect all types of addictive behaviour in the same way.

Explanations for specific addictions

Explanations of addiction to smoking

Smoking addiction occurs when a person has formed an uncontrollable dependence on cigarettes to the point where stopping smoking would cause severe emotional, mental, or physical reactions (Leshner 1999). Most smokers want to stop but only one in three succeeds in stopping permanently before the age of 60. Nicotine is the drug in tobacco that causes physiological addiction. Nicotine is a psychoactive drug with stimulant effects on brain activity. It can also have calming effects, especially at times of stress. Smoking nicotine causes activation of 'pleasure centres' in the brain (e.g. the mesolimbic dopamine system), which may explain the pleasure and addictiveness of smoking (Berke and Hyman 2000). Smokers develop tolerance to nicotine. Many of the unpleasant effects of cigarette withdrawal are due to lack of nicotine. Other biological explanations include genetic susceptibility (see Key research, Thorgeirsson et al. 2008, below).

Studies show that tobacco use usually begins in early adolescence, and those who begin smoking at an early age are more likely to develop severe nicotine addiction than those who start later (Griffiths 1996b). Despite the essentially physiological nature of nicotine addiction, social and psychological factors also play an important role in the addiction process. In smoking addiction, psychosocial factors determine the initial exposures. Addiction may subsequently develop if the drug has pharmacological effects that people like or find rewarding.

Learned conditioning in smoking

Another explanation for nicotine addiction is that it is essentially a learning process, in that smokers learn when, where and how to take the drug to get the most rewarding effects. The taste, smell, visual stimuli, handling, and other movements closely associated with the rewarding pharmacological effects gradually become rewarding themselves. This is another example of conditioning: environmental cues are paired in time with an individual's initial drug-use experiences and, through classical conditioning, take on conditioned stimulus properties. When those cues are present at a later time, they elicit

Genetic susceptibility to smoking

Key research: Thorgeirsson et al. (2008)

Recent research has indicated that genetics may also underpin addiction to smoking. A study in Iceland by Thorgeirsson and colleagues suggests that particular genetic variants make people more addicted to nicotine once they start smoking.

The team began the study with a smoking-history questionnaire distributed to over 50 000 Icelanders, in which respondents were asked to say whether they had ever smoked, were still smokers, and, if so, how many cigarettes they smoked per day. The research group then studied the DNA of over 10 000

current and former smokers who had responded to the original questionnaire.

They found that a particular pattern of gene variation at two points of chromosome 15 was more common among people who developed lung cancer (and were dependent on nicotine), than among those who remained healthy. In their sample, the genetic variant had an effect on the number of cigarettes smoked per day and there was a highly significant association with nicotine dependence.

Evaluation

Interestingly, the variant was less common among smokers who smoked less than ten cigarettes per day than it was among non-smokers, supporting the notion that the variant does not influence smoking initiation, but rather confers risk of nicotine dependence among those who start. Although this was one of the largest ever studies on the genetics of smoking, the findings showed a correlation and not causation.

anticipation of a drug experience and thus generate tremendous drug craving (Leshner, 1999). These become linked with its rewards and with the relief of withdrawal. They come to serve as signals or triggers for the urge or craving for nicotine's effects (for example, straight after eating dinner, drinking substances such as coffee or alcohol, social situations such as meeting new people, breaking up the working day, speaking on the telephone, when experiencing particular psychological states (anxiety, anger, joy)). There are numerous triggers that stimulate the urge to smoke as smoking takes place in so many situations (Leshner 1999).

Evaluation of explanations of addiction to smoking

- *Biological approaches are too simplistic* – Modern science has demonstrated that it is too simplistic to pit biology in opposition to social and psychological behaviour. Addiction to smoking involves inseparable biological, behavioural and psychological components.

- *Physiological versus psychological addiction is outdated* – Confusion comes about (in part) because of the somewhat out-of-date distinction between whether specific drugs like nicotine are 'physically' or 'psychologically' addictive.

- *Biological underpinnings are similar across addictions* – As has been shown, a body of scientific evidence is developing that points to an array of cellular and molecular changes in specific brain circuits and genetic bases for addictive behaviour. However, many of these brain changes and genetic variants are common to all chemical addictions, and some also are typical of other behavioural addictions, such as pathological gambling and pathological overeating (Leshner 1999).

- *Relapse can be caused by environmental factors* – Those who became addicted in their home setting are constantly exposed to the cues conditioned to their initial nicotine use, such as the locality where they live, other smokers, or where they bought cigarettes. Simple exposure to those cues automatically triggers craving and can lead to relapses. This is one reason why someone who apparently overcame nicotine cravings at another dwelling (e.g. prison, residential treatment centre) could quickly revert to use upon returning home.

Explanations of addiction to gambling

As we saw with smoking, addictions always result from an interaction and interplay between many factors, including the person's biological and/or genetic predisposition, their psychological constitution (personality factors, unconscious motivations, attitudes, expectations and beliefs, etc.), their social environment (i.e. situational characteristics) and the nature of the activity itself (i.e. structural characteristics) (Griffiths 1999a). Gambling addiction is no different. This 'global'

view of addiction highlights the interconnected processes and integration between individual differences (i.e. personal vulnerability factors), situational characteristics, structural characteristics, and the resulting addictive behaviour. Each of these general sets of influences (i.e. individual, structural and situational) can be subdivided much further depending on the type of addiction.

As we saw earlier, one possible explanation for problem gambling and gambling addictions may be the role of cognitive bias (i.e. faulty thinking), (see Key research, Griffiths (1994), p.443). However, there are many individual (personal vulnerability) factors that may be involved in the acquisition, development and maintenance of gambling addiction, such as personality traits (see Key research Parke *et al.* (2004), p.448), biological processes, unconscious motivations, learning and conditioning effects, thoughts, beliefs and attitudes. There are also some more idiosyncratic factors in the case of gambling addiction, such as financial motivation and economic pressures.

Classical and operant conditioning in gambling

Both classical and operant conditioning principles have been applied to the study of gambling. In operant explanations for problem gambling (e.g. Delfabbro and Winefield 1999), persistent gambling is seen as a conditioned behaviour maintained by intermittent schedules of reinforcement, most likely a variable-ratio schedule. This involves the provision of infrequent rewards after varying numbers of responses. On the other hand, proponents of classical conditioning models (e.g. Anderson and Brown 1984) argue that people continue to gamble as a result of becoming conditioned to the excitement or arousal associated with gambling, so that they feel bored, unstimulated and restless when they are not gambling. Both the classical and operant perspectives have been central to the development of measures of 'impaired control' over gambling, in which the self-restraint which most people exercise over recreational gambling breaks down (Baron *et al.* 1995; Dickerson and O'Connor 2006).

| Activity | **Evaluating Parke *et al.*'s (2004) study** |

Read the research panel 'Personality traits in gamblers' and then try and answer the following evaluation questions in relation to Parke *et al.*'s study:

1 What was this the first-ever study to do?

2 What traits do the authors claim might be risk factors for pathological gambling?

3 What finding suggests that the population studied was unrepresentative of gamblers as a whole?

4 Even though the sample was unrepresentative, what was the advantage in this particular case?

Some suggestions are given in the Answers to activities on p.603. ▶

Personality traits in gamblers

Key research: Parke *et al.* (2004)

To date, research into personality traits among gamblers has been largely inconsistent. A study by Parke and colleagues assessed the predictive values of three personality traits on pathological gambling (**sensation seeking**, deferment of gratification and competitiveness) – two of which (deferment of gratification and competitiveness) had never been investigated before.

They administered a questionnaire to an opportunity sample of 114 gamblers (91 males and 23 females) of whom 38 per cent were classified as pathological gamblers according to DSM-IV criteria for pathological gambling (American Psychiatric Association 1994). For purposes of this particular study, a participant was defined as a gambler if they participated in any or any combination of the following activities: betting on the outcome of sporting events, playing the National Lottery, playing AWPs (slot machines), playing any casino games or playing bingo. The questionnaire included the Sensation Seeking Scale (Zuckerman 1984), the Deferment of Gratification Scale (Ray and Najman 1986) and the Gambling Competitiveness Scale constructed by the authors specifically for this study.

It was hypothesized that:

1 pathological gamblers would have higher levels of sensation seeking than non-pathological gamblers

2 pathological gamblers would have lower levels of deferment of gratification (i.e. less able to tolerate waiting for desired things) than non-pathological gamblers

3 pathological gamblers would have higher levels of competitiveness than non-pathological gamblers.

The results showed that two of the three hypotheses were supported. Competitiveness had a strong, positive predictive value for pathological gambling, and, deferment of gratification had a relatively strong, negative predictive value (see Chapter 17, p.558, Data analysis and reporting). Sensation seeking was shown not to be a significant predictor of pathological gambling.

Situational characteristics

Situational characteristics are also central to understanding gambling addiction. These are the factors that often facilitate and encourage people to gamble in the first place (Griffiths and Parke 2003). Situational characteristics are primarily features of the environment (e.g. accessibility factors, such as location of the gambling venue, number of venues in a specified area and possible membership requirements) but can also include internal features of the venue itself (décor, heating, lighting, colour, background music, floor layout, refreshment facilities) or facilitating factors that may influence gambling in the first place (e.g. advertising, free travel to and/or accommodation at the gambling venue, free bets or gambles on particular games) or influence continued gambling (e.g. the placing of a cash dispenser on the casino floor, free food and/or alcoholic drinks while gambling) (Griffiths and Parke 2003; Abbott 2007). (See p.453 for context in the development of chemical addictions.)

Structural characteristics

In gambling, structural characteristics can also be important in the development and maintenance of addictive behaviour. For example, slot machines are known to be one of the most addictive types of gambling (Griffiths 1999a, 2002; Parke and Griffiths 2006). Structural factors that are unique to slot machines (e.g. fast game speed, large jackpots, lots of 'near misses', short payout interval) are specifically incorporated into the machine by the designers and operators in the gaming industry to keep people gambling once they have started. Many other characteristics are also used to influence gambling behaviour, including light and colour, music and sound effects, and pseudo-skill features (see Parke and Griffiths 2007, for an extensive overview).

Evaluation of explanations of addiction to gambling

- *Addiction is addiction whatever the focus* – Behavioural addictions such as gambling addiction can be just like chemical addictions. Furthermore, the biopsychosocial explanatory model is just as relevant to behavioural addictions as to chemical addictions, see p.442.

- *Behavioural explanations are limited* – Despite evidence supporting both operant and classical conditioning theories of gambling, neither is entirely satisfactory on its own. Classical conditioning theory seems useful to explain people's motivation to commence a gambling session, but appears less useful to explain persistent gambling behaviour. Conversely, while operant conditioning might explain ongoing behaviour, it appears less useful in explaining why people commence gambling or recommence gambling after a prolonged period of abstinence.

- *Biopsychosocial factors are not the only factors involved in gambling addiction* – In the case of gambling, these factors are not the only major sets of influences in the development of addictive behaviour. Different structural characteristics (e.g. event frequency, near misses) may have implications for the gambler's motivations and, subsequently, have a wider social impact.

- *Structural characteristics apply to chemical addictions too* – It is for this reason, above all others, that a structural approach could be potentially useful. For drug addictions, structural characteristics would include things such as the dose amount, the drug's toxicity, and the route of administration.

The case for an eclectic approach

As we have seen, all singular approaches have major shortcomings in providing a comprehensive explanation for addictive behaviour. Addiction is a multifaceted behaviour strongly influenced by contextual factors that cannot be encompassed by any single theoretical perspective. These factors include variations in behavioural involvement and motivation across different demographic groups, structural characteristics of activities/substances, and the developmental or temporal nature of addictive behaviour.

While increased involvement with a particular behaviour seems likely to contribute to loss of control over behaviour, development of irrational beliefs and greater psychological dependence, it is important to determine what makes some people more susceptible to these factors than others. Central to research into biological and personality factors is discovering whether addicts possess qualities that would predispose them to excessive gambling. Biological and dispositional (i.e. personality/character) accounts assume that such factors should override other environmental or contextual factors and allow for the development of a general theory of gambling addiction. However, this is clearly not so. Apart from the conceptual difficulties associated with determining a causal relationship between characteristics and behaviour, dispositional theories are unable to account for the full diversity of addictive patterns and behaviour, nor can they explain why some activities are more 'addictive' than others and why the structural characteristics of specific activities (e.g. slot machines) can influence behaviour.

Therefore, it appears that addictive gambling is likely to result from both dispositional and psychological factors and the complex interaction between them. Psychological explanations must play a role because of the obvious importance of external factors (e.g. environmental and situational variables) in the development of gambling habits. However, it is also clear that internal factors influence how certain individuals respond to these situations.

A unified theory of addiction will, therefore, be complex, and research and clinical interventions are best served by a biopsychosocial approach that incorporates the best strands of contemporary psychology, biology and sociology (Griffiths 2005b; 2008b).

| **Activity** | **Understanding addiction** |

There are number of things to consider when looking at addictive behaviours. After reading the text on addictive behaviours, try to come to your own decisions about some of them by answering these questions:

1 How much control do people have over their behaviour? Your answer to this will affect how strongly you support the various models of addictive behaviour.

2 What are similarities and differences between chemical addictions and behavioural addictions?

3 Is addiction something that can happen to anyone (like catching measles), or are some people more likely to develop these behaviours than others? If so, why? Is it due to chemical imbalances or genes or family background or something else inside them?

4 How can we obtain evidence for our theories? Are the methods of asking people to describe their experience the best way of capturing what is going on? Are there other ways of collecting reliable evidence?

Some suggestions are given in the Answers to activities on p.603. ▶

CHECK YOUR UNDERSTANDING

Check your understanding of models of addictive behaviour by answering the questions below. Try to do this from memory. You can check your answers by looking back through Topic 1, Models of addictive behaviour.

1 What types of activity can people become addicted to?

2 According to Griffiths (2005), what are the six components of addictive behaviour?

3 Name four models of addictive behaviour.

4 What neurotransmitter is most commonly associated with addictive behaviour?

5 Why are twin studies a good method for examining the role of genetics in addictive behaviour?

6 What are 'heuristics' and why do they help us in understanding addictive behaviour?

7 Outline three criticisms of the biological approach to addictive behaviour.

8 Outline three criticisms of the cognitive approach to addictive behaviour.

9 Outline three criticisms of the behavioural (learning) approach to addictive behaviour.

10 Why might a biopsychosocial approach be useful in studying addictive behaviour?

Psychology in context — Super-casinos and gambling addiction

One of the most hotly contested issues towards the end of Tony Blair's premiership in 2007 was whether Britain should have 'Las Vegas-type' casinos. Eight bids from around the country applied for a licence for one of these new 'super-casinos'. Originally, eight national super-casinos were thought to be likely but Parliament decided in the end that only one city should be awarded a licence, and that only those towns and cities that were the most deprived should be allowed to bid for a super-casino. Most observers assumed that the likely winner of the licence would be Blackpool (although some thought it would be London). To most people's surprise, Manchester won the bid.

Opponents of super-casinos (supported by a high-profile campaign run by the *Daily Mail*) said that such casinos were a 'scourge on society' and would lead to a large rise in gambling addiction nationally. Supporters said that super-casinos would economically regenerate the area that got the licence. When Gordon Brown became Prime Minister, one of his first decisions was to order an enquiry into the economic and psychosocial impact of casinos. Many people fed into various reviews, including psychologists. Since 2008, the introduction of a new super-casino has been put 'on hold' and it is unclear whether Britain will now get such a casino. However, this has not stopped the debates about whether we should introduce these new types of casino into the country.

In the previous section, the evidence on the factors that contribute to the development of gambling addictions was briefly overviewed. Imagine you were in control of government policy; based on what you read earlier, how would you answer these questions?

1 Was the Prime Minister right to put the decision 'on hold'?

2 Would you allow Britain to have a new super-casino? If so, why? If not, why not?

3 What psychological evidence is there that the introduction of (one or) a few super-casinos would lead to a rise in gambling addiction?

4 Given the fact that anyone with access to a computer has almost instant access to hundreds of on-line casinos, would it make a difference if one more large off-line casino was introduced?

5 Who is responsible for gambling addiction? The individual gambler? The gaming industry? The government?

When we are looking for factors that change behaviour, we can look:

- inside the individual for personal characteristics that make people vulnerable to addiction, e.g. their explanations of their behaviour (attributions) and their sense of self-worth

- outside the individual for features of the environment that encourage addictive behaviours, e.g. availability and media cues.

Personal vulnerability explanations of addictions

There is a long tradition of psychological research into individual differences of addictive behaviour. Much of this research appears to show that addicts share many characteristics and traits. For instance, longitudinal research following children from childhood through to adulthood generally shows that adolescents who are

Problems with defining addiction

Griffiths and Larkin (2004) note that it is important to acknowledge that the meanings of 'addiction', as the word is understood in both daily and in academic usage, are contextual and socially constructed. They ask whether the term 'addiction' actually identifies a distinct phenomenon – something beyond problematic behaviour – whether socially constructed or physiologically based. If we argue that it is hypothetically possible to be addicted to anything, it is still necessary to account for the fact that many people become addicted to alcohol but very few to gardening. Implicit within our understanding of the term 'addiction' is some measure of the negative consequences that must be experienced in order to justify the use of this word in its academic or clinical context.

'rebellious' and have 'less conventional attitudes' (i.e. have antisocial traits) are more likely to abuse alcohol, nicotine and illicit drugs (McMurran 1994). There has also been extensive research examining the link between personality dimensions (neuroticism, psychoticism, extraversion) and drug addictions (Eysenck 1997). Correlational research has generally shown that those addicted to drugs (alcohol, heroin, benzodiazepines, nicotine) have higher than normal scores on neuroticism and psychoticism (Teeson *et al.* 2002). In this section, we focus more closely on aspects such as self-esteem, attributional style and social context.

Self-esteem, addictive personality and individual differences

In a comprehensive overview of addiction, Orford (2001) noted that self-esteem is not well represented in research on taking up alcohol, tobacco or other drug use. There appears to be more work in areas such as eating disorders/addictions which shows that those with lower self-esteem are at significantly greater risk of developing problems with their behaviour (e.g. Button *et al.* 1997). Jessor (1987) reports low self-esteem as predictive of involvement in problematic behaviours such as addiction, although some studies suggest that no such association exists. For instance, Van Hasselt *et al.* (1993) compared adolescent substance abusers and a comparative adolescent group who did not abuse drugs. Although the adolescent drug abusers were more likely to be depressed, there were no differences between them in terms of self-esteem. An earlier study by Newcomb *et al.* (1986) examining risk factors for substance abuse found that in order of importance, self-esteem ranked behind peer drug use, general deviance, perceived drug use by adults, early alcohol use, sensation seeking, poor relationship with parents, low religiosity, poor academic achievement and psychological distress. Much of this type of research on individual differences suggests that certain personality traits might be associated with addictive behaviour. In fact, many people believe in the concept of '**addictive personality**'.

Those who believe in the concept of addictive personality claim that some people are more prone to addiction than others (Nathan 1988). Addictive personality is a concept that was used to explain addiction as the result of pre-existing character defects in individuals. An addictive personality also suggests that some people will inevitably become dependent on drug taking or some other activity because of a personality fault. However, personality is complex and the role of personality in addiction is uncertain. It is difficult to disentangle the effects of personality on addiction from the effects of addiction on personality (Teeson *et al.* 2002).

Evaluation of individual differences explanations of addiction

- *Common traits found in addiction may not be specific to addictive behaviour* – Although there is lots of research showing that certain traits are common among addicts, this does not prove that these are

specific to addictive behaviour. For instance, although there is some evidence that addicts have low self-esteem, this is not a trait that is predictive of addiction, as there are individuals who have low self-esteem but are not addicted to anything.

- *If addictive personality exists there need to be accepted 'standards of proof'* – According to Nathan (1988) there must be standards of proof to show that valid links between personality and addictive behaviour exist. He reported that for addictive personality to exist, the personality trait or factor must:

  1 either precede the initial signs of the disorder or be a direct and lasting feature of the disorder

  2 be specific to the disorder rather than antecedant, coincident or consequent to other disorders/behaviours that often accompany addictive behaviour

  3 be discriminative

  4 be related to the addictive behaviour on the basis of independently confirmed empirical, rather than clinical, evidence.

- *There is little evidence of an addictive personality* – Research has shown that no personality trait guarantees addiction and that, in relation to an addictive personality trait, Nathan's 'standards of proof' have not been met. In short, there is little evidence for an addictive personality as such.

Attributions

Attribution theory relates to how people explain the behaviour of others in an attempt to make sense of the world. Attribution theory has been used to illustrate how the use of addiction as a label can promote irresponsibility, learned helplessness and passivity (Preyde and Adams 2008). Similarly, there is concern that the label of 'addict' may lead to a self-fulfilling prophecy fostering hopelessness, dependency and low self-efficacy (Preyde and Adams 2008). Therefore, what people think about addiction is important.

Davies (1996) argues that the explanations people make for their behaviour are functional. He asserts that people make different attributions for the same event in different contexts. For example, Davies and Baker (1987) showed that heroin users reported different attributions for their own drug use to another heroin user from those they

The attributional stages of addiction

Key research: Davies (1996)

Davies suggests in a 1996 study that as addiction develops, there are five attributional stages that a person might progress through. Each of these stages is marked by a different attribution style and can vary in terms of:

- *purposiveness* – i.e. how intentional the behaviour is portrayed
- *hedonism* – i.e. how positively the behaviour is described
- *contradictoriness* – i.e. whether attributions contradict across the course of a given time period
- *addiction self-ascription* – i.e. whether attributions make use of the concept of addiction as an explanation for behaviour.

To formulate and confirm the attributional stages, Davies interviewed 20 drug addicts and alcoholics, both in and out of treatment. Interviews were transcribed and coders rated the attributions given in each interview in terms of the dimensions outlined in Table 13.5. The investigators assigned each respondent to one of the five stages based upon those ratings. Consensus between four judges rating the same participants was good. The average agreement between the judges was 71 per cent (ranging from 0.49 to 0.75). In all instances, the judges never disagreed by more than one stage.

The five stages:

1 *Stage 1* – Before the drug-using behaviour becomes a problem, people's attributions for their drug use are high on purposiveness and hedonism (i.e. people enjoy using the drug and consider it under their control).

2 *Stage 2* – As problems begin to arise, people's discourse becomes contradictory, and varies from context to context (between positive and negative aspects of drug use) and the controlled and uncontrolled aspects of their drug use. These attributions reflect the ambivalence that emerges during the development of addiction.

3 *Stage 3* – People refer to themselves as addicted, explain their drug use as out of their control, and view it as negative.

4 *Stage 4* – People begin to reject the usefulness of the 'addiction' concept in the explanation of their behaviour, and their discourse again becomes mixed and contradictory.

5 *Stage 5* – People can be either positive or negative. Whatever the version, their attributions are relatively stable at this stage and do not contradict in different contexts. Furthermore, they do not refer to their drug-using behaviour in terms of addiction. In the positive version, people might have given up drugs or alcohol, but return to a view of their past behaviour as controllable and a description of their drug use that highlights both the positive and negative aspects of that behaviour. In the negative version, although the concept of addiction has been dropped, people continue to use drugs and see themselves as 'down and out'. Here, their behaviour is uncontrollable and their drug use is negative.

Although these stages tend to relate to the progression of an addiction, people can move back and forth between stages. The one exception to this, according to Davies, is an irreversible transition from the second to third stage, which often occurs when people enter treatment and may persist long after.

Attributional style	Purposiveness	Hedonism	Contradictoriness	Addicted self-ascription
Stage 1 (pre-problem)	High	High	Absent	Absent
Stage 2 (as problems develop)	Mixed	Mixed	Present	Absent
Stage 3 (problem recognition)	Low	Low	Absent	Present
Stage 4 (reconsideration)	Mixed	Mixed	Present	Present
Stage 5+ (substance use in the past	High	Mixed	Absent	Absent
Stage 5– ('down and out')	Low	Low	Absent	Absent

Table 13.5 *Summary of attributional styles (n=20)*

reported to someone whose drug use was unknown to them. This is because attributions we make about ourselves serve to protect self-esteem and preserve self-concept (Schlenker *et al.* 1990). Davies argues that attributions help serve the self-protective function in relation to an addiction. Davies (1996) subsequently tested his attribution model through interviews with 20 drug and alcohol users (see Key research: Davies, 1996, opposite).

Evaluation of the attributions theory of addiction

- *There is good evidence about the reliability of addiction attributions* – Davies demonstrated good reliability of his model (i.e. ability of coders to identify the attribution patterns associated with each stage) and stated that these stages related to the stages of an addiction.

- *There are doubts about the validity of addiction attributions* – Davies did not provide information about how the attributional stages correspond to the actual temporal progression of addiction in his interviewees (e.g. whether the majority of participants classified as Stage 3 were in treatment at the time of the interview). Given his claim that movement between at least two of the stages is irreversible, which contradicts established research on addiction stages (see Prochaska, Norcross and DiClemente, 1994), further research is needed to verify the model.

- *The addiction attributions are based on only a small sample size* – Although Davies developed his model based on years of observations and interviews of drug users, he only tested it on 20 people.

- *The addiction attribution model needs further testing* – Given the theoretical basis of the model (i.e. that attributions vary according to context), it is important to test this model and its stages in different samples of substance users and different settings.

- *Further validity testing is needed on predicting change versus reflecting change* – Nelson (2004) argues that Davies' model of attribution change needs to be validated, but argues that the model is important for the questions it raises. For instance, if these attribution patterns reliably correspond to different stages of an addiction, it is important to determine whether these attributions predict change (e.g. provide explanations that refer to being addicted as precursors of treatment-seeking behaviour) or reflect change (e.g. provide explanations that refer to being addicted as an attempt to understand and explain past behaviour within the treatment context). Both possibilities (i.e. predictive and reflective) stress the importance of a person's subjective understanding and interpretation of behaviour in guiding future behaviour. As Nelson concludes, this attribution-behaviour cycle is a crucial, often neglected, piece of the study of addictions.

Social context: Addiction and availability

There are a number of environmental factors that affect the incidence of addictive behaviours in a society. One factor that affects the level of alcoholism is the availability of alcohol and the average consumption of alcohol by the general population. Comparison studies have found near perfect correlations between the number of deaths through liver cirrhosis (generally attributed to alcohol abuse) and the average consumption of alcohol in different countries (for a discussion see Orford 2001). The availability factor also affects the consumption of cigarettes and gambling.

If we examine the pattern of cigarette consumption compared with the retail price of cigarettes in the UK, we can observe a remarkable relationship. Figure 13.1 shows how the curve for consumption is the mirror image of the curve for retail price (Townsend 1993). Since 1970, any increase in price has brought about a decrease in smoking. At the time of the study, there was a slight decrease in the price of cigarettes (figures adjusted to take account of inflation) and a corresponding rise in smoking. This rise in smoking was particularly noticeable in young people and, according to Townsend (1993), regular smoking by 15-year-old boys increased from 20 per cent to 25 per cent and by 16- to 19-year-old girls from 28 per cent to 32 per cent. This connection between price and consumption suggests an obvious policy for governments who want to reduce smoking.

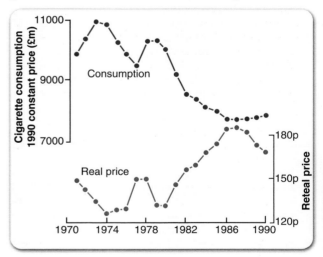

Figure 13.1 *The relationship between the price of cigarettes and consumption 1971–1990 (Townsend 1993)*

In relation to gambling, Volberg (1994) found in a study of five US states that prevalence of pathological gambling increased after significant increase in gambling accessibility. Furthermore, Volberg (1997) indicated that problem-gambling prevalence was proportional to the length of time elapsed since the new gambling opportunities had been available to the public. The US National Research Council (1999) performed a meta-analysis of prevalence studies across different periods of time regarding gambling accessibility. They found results similar to Volberg's, and concluded that increased opportunity to gamble was correlated with increased problem-gambling prevalence. In a UK Family Expenditure Survey, Grun and McKeigue (2000) found that the percentage of families spending more than £20 per week on gambling increased from 0.8 to 2.5 following the introduction of the National Lottery. Moreover, it was revealed that the percentage of families spending more than 10 per cent of their income on gambling activities increased from 0.4 to 1.7 following the introduction of the National Lottery.

Evaluation of social context explanations of addiction

- *The relationship between addiction and accessibility is correlational* – Much of the evidence examining the relationship between accessibility and addiction is correlational in nature (e.g. smoking and price), so we cannot establish causality. Furthermore, the massive reduction in smoking over recent decades is unlikely to be because of price and accessibility restriction.

- *Social context can change over time* – Although Volberg (1994) showed a correlation between increased availability of gambling opportunities and problem gambling, she then reported that in a number of replication studies problem-gambling rates had stabilized or decreased. Looking at these jurisdictions in more detail, she reported that all of them had introduced comprehensive services for problem gamblers, including public awareness campaigns, helplines, and professional counselling programmes. She concluded that the relationship between increased opportunities to gamble and problem gambling may be moderated by the availability of problem-gambling services. In areas of the US (like Montana and North Dakota) that saw an increase in problem gambling following the introduction of casinos, no public awareness campaigns or services for problem gamblers were introduced.

- *Social context can be affected by third-party initiatives* – Collins (2007) also reviewed this evidence and concluded that if a jurisdiction introduces new forms of gambling *and does nothing else*, it will most likely see an increase in problem gambling. However, if the jurisdiction combines the introduction of new forms of gambling with appropriate prevention and treatment services, it is likely to decrease numbers of problem gamblers. Collins and Barr (2006) note, in the national South African gambling-prevalence study, that the country witnessed a decline in problem gambling over a two-year period following the introduction of the National Responsible Gambling Program. This may be because of the 'adaptation hypothesis' (see panel, 'Gambling and the adaptation hypothesis').

Gambling and the adaptation hypothesis

Abbott (2007) proposes that with increased access to gambling opportunities, gambling problems may increase initially, but then level out and actually decrease over time. This is known as the adaptation hypothesis. This hypothesis has been supported by various national prevalence studies. For example, prevalence of problem gambling in New Zealand in 1995 and 1999 was shown to be lower than prevalence rates in 1991. Also, in the 1999 Australian national survey, prevalence rates were shown to be 2.1 per cent, substantially lower than the initial 1991 prevalence rate determined at 6.6 per cent.

Media and advertising influences on addiction

Media effects

The media (television, radio, newspapers, etc.) are an important channel for information and communication. Knowledge about how the mass media work may influence both the promotion of potentially addictive behaviour (as in advertising), and the promotion of health education (such as promoting abstinence or moderation) (McMurran 1994). Much of the research on advertising is done by the companies themselves and thus remains confidential (Wilde 1993). The media, especially television and film, often portray addictions (e.g. heroin addiction in the film *Trainspotting*, marijuana use in the TV show *Weeds*, gambling addiction in the TV show *Sunshine*). Such portrayals by television and film dramas often create controversy because of claims that they glorify addictive behaviour. The popularity of media drama depicting various addictions requires an examination of their themes and the potential impact on the public.

A fairly recent study examining sex and drug depiction in the top 200 grossing films showed that whilst drug taking in film may not be as prevalent as other risky behaviours (e.g. unprotected sex), portrayals were overwhelmingly positive (see Key research, Gunakesera *et al.* (2005) opposite). It could be argued that seeing drug use in this context is a form of observational learning similar to advertising through product placement. A similar study by Roberts *et al.* (2002) examined drug use within popular music videos. Whilst depictions of illicit drugs or drug use were relatively rare in pop videos, when they did appear they were depicted on a purely neutral level, as common elements of everyday activity.

The makers of such drama argue that presenting this material reflects the fact that addictions are everywhere and cut across political, ethnic and religious lines. Addiction is certainly an issue that affects all communities. However, it is important to consider possible impacts that these depictions might have on society. Empirical research suggests that the mass media can potentially influence behaviours, e.g. that the more adolescents are exposed to movies with smoking, the more likely they are to start smoking (Dalton *et al.* 2003). Furthermore, research has shown that the likeability of film actors and actresses who smoke (both on-screen and off-screen) relates to their adolescent fans' decisions to smoke (Distefan *et al.* 1999). Perhaps unsurprisingly, films tend to stigmatize drinking and smoking less than other forms of drug taking (Cape 2003). However, the media transmit numerous positive messages about drug use and other potential addictions (Will *et al.* 2005), and it is plausible that such favourable portrayals lead to more use by those who watch them. Anecdotally, some things may be changing. For instance, there appears to be more emphasis on the media's portrayal of alcohol as socially desirable and positive, as opposed to smoking that is increasingly being regarded as antisocial and dangerous.

HOW SCIENCE WORKS

Film portrayals of sex and drug use

Key research: Gunakesera *et al.* (2005)

A study by Gunakesera and colleagues (2005) analysed the portrayal of sex and drug use in the most popular movies of the last 20 years using the Internet Movie Database list of the top 200 movies of all time. The researchers excluded a number of films, including those released or set prior to the HIV era (pre-1983), animated films, films not about humans, and family films aimed at children. The top 200 films following the exclusions were reviewed by one of two teams of two observers using a data extraction sheet tested for **inter-rater reliability**. They recorded sexual activity, sexually transmitted disease (STD) prevention, birth-control measures, drug use and any consequences discussed or depicted.

There were 53 sex episodes in 28 (32 per cent) of the 87 movies reviewed. There was only one suggestion of condom use, which was the only reference to any form of birth control. There were no depictions of important consequences of unprotected sex, such as unwanted pregnancies, HIV or other STDs. Movies with cannabis (8 per cent) and other non-injected illicit drugs (7 per cent) were less common than those with alcohol intoxication (32 per cent) and tobacco use (68 per cent) but tended to portray their use positively and without negative consequences. There were no episodes of injected drug use. The researchers concluded that sex depictions in popular movies of the last two decades lacked safe-sex messages. Drug use, though infrequent, tended to be depicted positively. They also concluded that the social norm being presented in films was of great concern given the HIV and illicit drug pandemics.

Advertising effects

In their response to the Health of the Nation strategy (Department of Health, 1992), the British Psychological Society (1993) called for a ban on the advertising of all tobacco products. This call was backed up by the government's own research (Department of Health 1999), which suggested a relationship between advertising and sales. In four countries that have banned advertising (New Zealand, Canada, Finland and Norway), there has been a significant drop in tobacco consumption.

However, public policy is not always driven by research findings, and the powerful commercial lobby for tobacco has considerable influence. In her reply to the British Psychological Society, the Secretary of State for Health (at the time) rejected a ban, saying that the evidence was unclear on this issue and efforts should be concentrated elsewhere. This debate highlights how issues of addictive behaviours cannot be discussed just within the context of health; there are also political, economic, social and moral contexts to consider. Later, the British government and European Community made commitments to ban tobacco advertising, though they found it difficult to bring the ban in as quickly as they hoped. It is now rare to see smoking advertised anywhere in the UK, but there is a new trend in television drama and films to set the action in a time or location where smoking was part of the way of life (e.g. the US television series *Mad Men*).

While the British government have now banned cigarette advertising and smoking in public places, they have also deregulated gambling, through the introduction of the 2005 Gambling Act. This Act came into effect on 1 September 2007 and allowed all forms of gambling to be advertised in the mass media for the first time. This has led to a large number of nightly television adverts for betting shops, online poker and online bingo. Whether this large increase in gambling advertising will affect gambling participation and gambling addiction remains to be seen. There have been very few studies that have examined gambling advertising, and those that have been carried out are usually small scale and lack representativeness (see Key research, Youn *et al.* (2000), p.456). A worldwide review on gambling advertising and its impact on problem gambling concluded that the empirical base was too small to make any firm conclusions (Griffiths, 2005c).

Evaluation of the role of media in addictive behaviour

- *Glamorization versus reality is complicated* – Although drama producers hope to depict various addictions accurately, they still need to keep ratings up. Clearly, positive portrayals are more likely to increase ratings,

The third-person effect

Key research: Youn et al. (2000)

A US study by Youn et al., (2000) examined the 'Third-person effect' (TPE) in relation to gambling advertising. The TPE postulates that people believe media messages have a greater impact on others than they do on themselves (Davison 1983). Youn and colleagues hypothesized that some people believe that lottery and casino advertising campaigns adversely affect other people but do not affect themselves. Therefore, those who claim they are unaffected might support censorship of gambling advertising.

Youn and colleagues carried out a survey of 194 adults in a US mid-western city where lottery and casino gambling are legal. These people were asked about their gambling behaviour, their attitudes to gambling advertising on themselves and other people, and questions concerning gambling censorship. Most people were defined as 'ordinary' gamblers who gambled two or three times a month. The results showed a significant relationship between the third-person perception and gambling advertising (in both casino and lotteries). People did indeed think that casino and lottery advertising had more impact on others than on themselves. They also found that the perceived effects of gambling advertising predicted their desire to censor the advertisements. While this is an interesting study, it suffers from the usual limitations (e.g. representativeness of the sample), and it fails to differentiate between different advertising forms. For instance, the effect might be more powerful with broadcast media than print media. It would also be interesting to carry out this research among problem gamblers.

and so programmes might favour acceptance of drug use over depictions of potential harms.

- *Research on the role of media effects is inconclusive* – More research on how the media influence drug use is needed in order to evaluate the impact of such drama. With media and addiction, it is important to walk with caution, as the line between reality and glamorization is easy to cross. More research is needed that investigates direct, indirect and interactive effects of media portrayals on addictive behaviour.

- *Relationship between advertising and addictive behaviour is mostly correlational* – The literature examining the relationship between advertising on the uptake of addictive behaviour is not clear cut and mostly correlational in nature, hence it is not possible to make causal connections.

- *There could be different media effects for different addictions* – Although there appears to be some relationship between tobacco advertising and tobacco uptake, this does not necessarily hold for all addictive behaviours. For instance, Nelson (2001) claims that virtually all econometric studies of alcohol advertising expenditures come to the conclusion that advertising has little or no effect on market-wide alcohol demand.

- *Research done to date may not be suitable* – Survey research studies have failed to measure the magnitude of the effect of advertising on youth intentions or behaviour in a manner that is suitable for policy analysis. As a consequence, policy makers may introduce (and/or change) policy that is ineffective or not needed on the basis of research that was unsuitable in answering a particular question.

Activity — The media, advertising addictions, and you

Can you think of examples when you have seen:
1 Addictive behaviours being advertised?
   - Where do these occur: on television; in the print media; at an event?
   - What effect (if any) do they have on you?
2 Films that reinforce the idea that potentially addictive substances or activities are good for you?
   - What films were they?
   - What effect (if any) did they have on you?
3 Films that reinforce the idea that potentially addictive substances or activities are bad for you?
   - What films were they?
   - What effect (if any) did they have on you?

Activity — Applying components of addiction to film

A study by Griffiths (2004) empirically analysed the film *The Gambler*. To ascertain whether the film accurately portrayed the 'typical' gambling addict, the DSM criteria for pathological gambling were used to assess the gambling pathology of the film's main character.

1 Watch a film that features an addict as its central character (e.g. *Trainspotting*, *Leaving Las Vegas*).
2 Using either the six components of addiction (see Table 13.1) or some other measure of addiction (e.g. DSM criteria), decide to what extent the core addiction components are portrayed in the film you selected.

Some suggestions are given in the Answers to activities on p.603. ▶

Check your understanding of factors affecting addictive behaviour by answering the questions below. Try to do this from memory. You can check your answers by looking back through Topic 2, Factors affecting addictive behaviour.

1 What types of factor can affect whether someone develops an addiction?

2 What types of personality factor have been associated with addiction?

3 What is an 'addictive personality'? Does it exist?

4 What is attribution theory and how can it be applied to addiction research?

5 According to Davies (1996), what are the four ways in which attributional style may vary in addicts?

6 What problems might occur for a person if they are labelled an 'addict'?

7 Give an example of how a psychologist might study the relationship between accessibility and addiction.

8 What is the adaptation hypothesis?

9 What types of media can affect addictive behaviour?

10 Give an example of how a psychologist might study the relationship between media effects and addiction.

Topic 3: Reducing addictive behaviour

Psychology in context — Stopping and starting addictions

Almost every day, newspapers and magazines feature stories and photographs of high-profile celebrities – e.g. the singer Amy Winehouse, the actor Robert Downey Jr., ex-football players Paul Gascoigne and Tony Adams – who appear to be out of control because they are addicted to alcohol, drugs, gambling or some other addiction (Hollywood actors Michael Douglas and David Duchovny have said they were unfaithful to their wives because of sex addiction). As a result of their addictions, their careers suffer and their personal relationships are put at risk. They may get into financial trouble because they are spending too much on a drug like heroin or cocaine, or on an activity like gambling. So what can be done to help reduce addictive behaviour and get the behaviour back under control? For celebrities, there is something quite fashionable about going into 'rehab' (i.e. a rehabilitation centre) like *The Priory*. For the rest of us, however, it is very difficult and unglamorous to change our behaviour dramatically and escape from our addiction to smoking, drinking alcohol or gambling.

Of course, the best solution to addiction is not to start it in the first place. A lot of effort is put into stopping people starting the behaviours. Unfortunately, there are even more pressures encouraging you to start than there are to stop. And the reason for that is that the people selling you the activity, product or service stand to make a lot of money if you become addicted to it. This is why major tobacco companies give away cigarettes to children in developing countries; they are not being generous, they are just investing in the future (McGreal 2008).

1 What is it about celebrities and their lifestyle that seems to make them succumb to addictive behaviour?

2 Do you think celebrities are more addiction-prone than the general public?

3 If you thought you were addicted to a drug or an activity, how would you go about trying to regain control of your behaviour?

Stages of prevention

Prevention efforts targeting mental health and addictive disorders are widely used, but there is limited data available on their effectiveness. In the area of substance-abuse prevention, there have been large-scale, structured investigations into the effectiveness of individual programmes (e.g. Drug Abuse Resistance Education, or project DARE; Clayton *et al.*, 1996), although findings are often inconclusive. Prevention has historically been divided into three stages (Force 1996), see Table 13.6. These divisions of prevention focus on different targets, with primary efforts tending to target the general population, secondary efforts targeting at-risk or vulnerable groups, and tertiary efforts targeting individuals with an identified disorder.

Primary prevention

Describes measures employed to prevent the onset of a targeted condition.

Secondary prevention

Describes measures that identify and treat asymptomatic persons who have already developed risk factors or pre-clinical disease but in whom the condition is not clinically apparent.

Tertiary prevention

Describes efforts targeting individuals with identified disease in which the goals involve restoration of function, including minimizing or preventing disease-related adverse consequences.

Table 13.6 *The three stages of prevention*

Primary prevention

If we look at how to prevent addictions, then clearly the best route is to stop people developing the addictive behaviours in the first place. These campaigns have been spectacular in their failure. Millions of pounds have been spent on campaigns to prevent smoking, excessive drinking and drug taking. Latest evidence suggests a small decline in smoking and rises in the other two. 'Just say "No!"' is not enough. The content and impact of primary prevention is strongly influenced by knowledge of the impact of the behaviour or disorder. For example, prevention efforts targeting tobacco smoking have changed significantly as more information concerning the health impact of tobacco smoke has become available (Slovic, 2001).

Secondary and tertiary prevention

General evidence shows that accurate knowledge about healthy and unhealthy behaviours (including, to some degree, attitudes towards these behaviours) does not necessarily affect the behaviour itself (Durlak 2003; Botvin 2001). Thus, it is premature to draw definite conclusions about:

- what type of preventive intervention works in terms of behavioural change related to addiction

- what type of prevention programme works with regard to enduring behavioural changes

- whether the positive effects reported have any long-lasting effect.

Nevertheless, findings from universal cognitive-based approaches demonstrate that inappropriate perceptions related to addictive activities can be corrected (Hayer *et al.* 2005). To increase effectiveness, prevention models must:

1 increase awareness of addiction and its consequences

2 enhance knowledge about addiction and its consequences

3 change attitudes towards addiction and adopt a more balanced view

4 teach effective coping and adaptive skills

5 correct inappropriate cognitions related to addiction.

In the future, one of the main goals must be to connect research findings, theory and prevention science with practice. It would seem reasonable that such prevention programmes should be aimed at adolescents, given that many addicts report that their first experiences with their drug or behaviour of choice in their youth (Griffiths 1995).

Models of behaviour change and prevention

Since social psychology first started, psychologists have been trying to understand why people do the things they do and, sometimes, how to stop them doing it or encourage them to do something else. During this time, they have developed a wide range of theories and models to explain these behaviours. However, no one theory has been able to explain more than a narrow set of behaviours. Perhaps this is not surprising given that even the most thoughtful and reflective people often struggle to explain their own behaviour.

STRETCH AND CHALLENGE

Activity Giving up

In a small group, think of two addictive behaviours (one chemical addiction and one behavioural addiction) and ask yourselves the following:

1 What factors are important in trying to give up the behaviour?

2 What are the problems and barriers that might be faced by the addict?

3 Are there any differences between trying to overcome chemical addictions and behavioural addictions?

Some suggestions are given in the Answers to activities on p.603. ▶

The Theory of Reasoned Action

Research examining the link between attitudes and behaviour has led to the development of predictive models aimed at demonstrating how a person's attitude can provide a reliable indication of their actual behaviour. The Theory of Reasoned Action demonstrated how a person's actions are controlled by their behavioural intentions. These behavioural intentions are, in turn, derived from a number of cognitive components including the following:

- *Personal beliefs about the behaviour* – derived from the person's expectation of the outcome of performing the behaviour, and their evaluation of that outcome.

- *The subjective norm* – the person's perception of how others would view the behaviour, and the individual's motivations to comply with social convention.

Research consistently showed that the theory had strong predictive utility (Sharma 2007). However, the theory was deficient in explaining behaviour, especially of people who have, or feel they have, little power over their behaviours (such as addictions). As a result, a new construct was added that resulted in the Theory of Planned Behaviour.

Theory of Planned Behaviour

Azjen (1991) (see also Fishbein and Ajzen 1975) designed the Theory of Planned Behaviour (TPB) to address how various disparate factors combine to form an intention to act a certain way (see Fig. 13.2). The theory has been adapted for use as a model for addiction prevention.

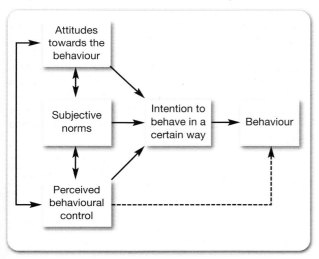

Figure 13.2 *The Theory of Planned Behaviour*

The Theory of Planned Behaviour included not only personal beliefs and subjective norms, but an additional component:

- *perceived behavioural control* – the extent to which the person believes that a behaviour is actually attainable or possible.

Subsequent research has shown the Theory of Planned Behaviour to be an accurate predictor of a person's behaviour in a number of areas, including cigarette smoking (Norman and Tedeschi 1989; Godin *et al.* 1992 – see Key research below), alcohol use (McMillan and Conner 2003), marijuana use (Ajzen *et al.* 1982), LSD, illicit drug use (i.e. ecstacy and amphetamines; McMillan and Connor 2003) and gambling behaviour (Wood and Griffiths 2004).

Predicting cigarette smoking

Key research: Godin *et al.* (1992)

A study by Godin *et al.* (1992) aimed to verify the basic assumptions underlying the Theory of Planned Behaviour for the prediction of cigarette smoking intentions and behaviour among adults of the general population. In this study, baseline data about their smoking behaviour was collected from participants by trained interviewers and with the use of a questionnaire. Self-report on behaviour was obtained six months after the baseline data collection. The results showed that the most important predictors for smoking intention were perceived behavioural control, attitudes and subjective norm. The most important predictors of actual smoking behaviour were perceived behavioural control and habit. The study suggested that promotional programmes should help smokers to know and develop their willpower regarding non-smoking of cigarettes and should be informed of the effort required in order to modify smoking behaviour.

Stages of change model

One model that has been used with some success in changing the behaviour of people with addictions is the 'Stages of change' model (Prochaska *et al.* 1992). If you have ever attended a smoking cessation clinic, then it is likely that this model was behind the structure of the event. This model identifies an individual's 'readiness for change' and tries to get them to a position where they are highly motivated to change their behaviour. The individual stages of this model are explained in Table 13.7.

The spiral model of change

The model shown in Fig. 13.3 presents change as a spiral. This takes account of the observation that most people who take action to change a habit are not successful at the first attempt. Prochaska *et al.* (1992) suggest that smokers commonly make three or four action attempts before they reach the maintenance stage.

Precontemplation stage

The person has no intention to change their behaviour and probably does not even perceive that they have a problem. The problem might be obvious to the person's family and friends, but the person might well respond to these concerns by saying 'I know I have some faults but there is nothing I really need to change'.

Contemplation stage

The person is aware that they have a problem and think they should do something about it. However, they have not yet made a commitment to take action. People can stay in this stage indefinitely, and the authors quote their own research that observed some smokers who were stuck in the contemplation stage for the full two years of the study.

Preparation stage

The person is intending to take action in the near future and may well have already started to do something. Most commonly, they will have reduced the number of cigarettes they smoke, or delayed the time of the first cigarette each day. If this were a race, then people in this stage are at the 'get set' point, just before they start to run.

Action stage

People change their behaviour, or their experience, or their environment so that they can overcome their problem. A person is said to be in the action stage if they have successfully altered their behaviour for a period of between one day and six months. In the case of smoking, the change must involve not smoking at all. People often incorrectly see the action stage as the main part of change and overlook the importance of the preliminary stages that prepare the person for change, and the efforts that are required to maintain the change.

Maintenance stage

The person works to prevent a relapse and to consolidate the changes they have made. Someone is said to be in the maintenance stage if they are able to remain free from the problem behaviour for more than six months.

Table 13.7 *Stages of change model*

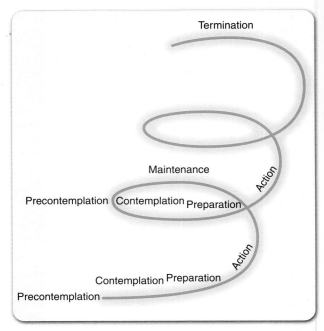

Figure 13.3 *The spiral model of change proposed by Prochaska et al. (1992)*

People can stay in one stage for a long time; unassisted changes, such as 'maturing out' or 'spontaneous remission' (McMurran, 1994), are also possible. Various techniques can be used to help people prepare for readiness, including motivational techniques, behavioural self-training, skills training, stress-management training, anger-management training, relaxation training, aerobic exercise, relapse prevention and lifestyle modification. The goal of treatment can be either abstinence or simply to cut down.

Evaluation of Theories of Reasoned Action and Planned Behaviour, and of models of change

- *Theory of Reasoned Action is deficient in explaining addictive behaviour* – The theory was deficient in explaining behaviour, especially that of people who have little or feel they have little power over their behaviours (such as addictions).

- *Theory of Planned Behaviour explains addictive behaviour better than the Theory of Reasoned Action* – Research has also shown that the Theory of Planned Behaviour can in some circumstances be used successfully to help prevent potentially addictive behaviours (e.g. teenage smoking; Winge 2003).

- *The Theories of Reasoned Action and Planned Behaviour are limited in scope* – There has been criticism that both these theories are limited to conscious and deliberate behaviours, and do not predict well behaviours that are not consciously intended (Bohner 2001), which could include addictive behaviours.

- *Other models may provide better alternatives for behaviour change* – Given the limitations of the Theories of Reasoned Action and Planned Behaviour, other models such as the 'Stages of change' model may be more productive in explaining non-conscious behaviours such as addiction.

Types of intervention

Helping addicts to stay in treatment

Successful treatment outcomes often depend upon treating the person long enough for them to gain the full benefits. As a consequence, strategies for keeping addicts in help programmes are critical. Whether an addict stays in treatment depends on factors associated with both the individual and the treatment programme. Individual factors related to engagement and retention include:

- motivation to change addictive behaviour
- degree of support from family and friends
- pressure to stay in treatment from the criminal justice system, child protection services, employers, and/or the family.

Within the programme, successful counsellors are able to establish a positive, therapeutic relationship with the addict. The counsellor has to ensure that a treatment plan is established and followed so that the addict knows what to expect during treatment (National Institute on Drug Abuse, 1999).

The intervention and treatment options for the treatment of addiction include, but are not limited to, biological/medical/pharmacological interventions, counselling/psychotherapies, behavioural therapies, cognitive-behavioural therapies, self-help therapies, and combinations of these (i.e. multi-modal treatment packages). The following sections include a selection of interventions that give a flavour of what is on offer.

Biological (medical) interventions

Pharmacological interventions (pharmacotherapy) basically consist of addicts being given a drug to help overcome their addiction. These are mainly given to those people with chemical addictions (e.g. nicotine, alcohol, heroin) but are increasingly being used for those with behavioural addictions (e.g. gambling, sex). For instance, some drugs produce an unpleasant reaction when used in combination with the drug of dependence, replacing the positive effects of the drug of dependence with a negative reaction.

Aversive agent treatment
The only available treatment of this kind is disulfiram (Antabuse) which, when combined with alcohol, produces nausea and possibly vomiting.

Agonist maintenance (methadone) treatment
This treatment is usually given to opiate addicts in outpatient settings. Here, long-acting synthetic opiates (methadone) are administered orally to prevent withdrawal symptoms, block the effects of illicit opiate use, and decrease craving. Addicts using methadone can engage more readily in counselling and other behavioural interventions essential to recovery and rehabilitation.

Narcotic antagonist (naltrexone) treatment
This treatment is usually given to opiate addicts in outpatient settings, although initiation often begins after detoxification in a residential setting. Detoxification provides interventions to ensure that the physical withdrawal process to eliminate the drug of dependence is completed with safety and comfort. Experience in many different countries has shown that relapse following detoxification is extremely common unless followed by an appropriate rehabilitation programme. Naltrexone is a long-acting synthetic opiate antagonist with few side effects, which blocks the effects of self-administered opiates (e.g. euphoria). The theory behind this treatment is that the repeated lack of the desired opiate effects breaks the drug habit. Due to addict non-compliance, effective counselling or psychotherapy is often used as an adjunct. More recently, antagonists have also been used in other addictions, such as alcoholism and gambling addiction. Partial agonists (such as buprenorphine) can also be used.

Evaluation of biological interventions
- *Biological interventions may ignore the underlying reason(s) for addiction* – The main criticism of all these treatments is that although the symptoms may be being treated, the underlying reasons for the addictions may be being ignored.

- *Addicts may return to their addictive behaviour when pharmacotherapy is stopped* – On a more pragmatic level, what happens when the drug intervention is taken away? It is very likely the addict will return to their addiction if this is the only method of treatment used.

- *Substitute drugs help stabilize behaviour* – Methadone maintenance has been shown to be safe and very effective on a variety of measures, including preventing illicit drug use. Buprenorphine is probably equally effective, although it is more expensive in some countries (Luty 2003). The value of these 'substitution therapies' lies in the opportunity they provide for addicts to stabilize their health and social functioning and reduce their exposure to risk behaviours before addressing the physical adaptation dimension of addiction.

Psychological interventions

Classical conditioning therapies

Behavioural therapies are based on the view that addiction is a learned maladaptive behaviour and can therefore be 'unlearned'. A wide range of behavioural techniques has been applied on this basis in the treatment of addictions. These have mainly been based on the classical conditioning paradigm and include aversion therapy, *in vivo* desensitization, imaginal desensitization, systematic desensitization, relaxation therapy, covert sensitization, and satiation therapy (see Table 13.8). All of these therapies focus on cue exposure, and relapse triggers (e.g. the sight and smell of alcohol/drugs, walking through a neighbourhood where casinos are abundant, pay day, arguments, pressure). By repeated exposure to relapse triggers in the absence of the addiction, the addict learns to stay addiction-free in high-risk situations. There is some evidence that such therapies are effective in stopping the addictive behaviour, but there is also evidence that just treating the symptom means that the underlying problem is still present and that other addictive behaviours can replace the one that has ceased (Griffiths 1995).

Aversion therapy

The pairing of an aversive stimulus (electric shock or an emetic) with a specific addiction response, or it may be randomly interspersed while engaging in the addictive behaviour.

In vivo desensitization (IVD)

Pairing cues for addiction with no addiction behaviour and feelings of boredom. Typically the addict is taken to the environment where the addiction usually takes place and stands by, without enaging in the addictive behaviour, for extended periods of time. The therapist suggests that the whole situation is uninteresting.

Imaginal desensitization

Differs from IVD by having the addict imagine the cues for addiction and then pairing these imagined cues with a competing response, such as feelings of boredom.

Systematic desensitization

A gradient of increasingly powerful cues for the addiction. At each step, any arousal that the addict is experiencing is extinguished by imagined scenes of tranquillity or direct muscular relaxation.

Relaxation therapy

Training in relaxation techniques that can be used when the urge to engage in the behaviour arises.

Satiation therapy

Involves presenting the addict with no other stimuli and no other activities but those associated with the addiction.

Table 13.8 *Types of behavioural therapy for addictive behaviour (adapted from Walker 1992)*

Operant conditioning therapies

One way to reduce substance abuse is to give people rewards for not taking the substance. There are two psychological ways of looking at this; to see it as:

1 reinforcement for the behaviour

2 a distracter from the pleasurable reinforcement of the substance.

One of the biggest challenges in treating addiction is getting addicts to stay in treatment long enough to take the first difficult steps toward recovery. However, the voucher-based approach developed by Higgins and colleagues (see Key research: Higgins *et al.* 1994, opposite) may help drug addicts take those vital first steps. It also suggests that under some circumstances operant therapies can be an effective treatment approach for some types of addicts.

Activity | **Would you recommend the voucher system?**

Read a summary of the study 'The voucher-therapy approach' (see Key research: Higgins et al., 1994, opposite), then discuss the following issues in a group:

1 Given the apparent success of the programme, would you recommend the approach to government think tanks? If yes, why? If no, why not?

2 Given the fact that drug users are basically being paid to keep drug-free, do you think this is good use of taxpayers' money? Are there any circumstances when it might be morally right (e.g. a pregnant addict who would be helping protect an unborn baby)?

3 What other operant-type incentives could be used instead of money? Do you think they would be as effective as the voucher system?

Some suggestions are given in the Answers to activities on p.603. ▶

Cognitive-behavioural therapy

A more recent development in the treatment of addictive behaviours is the use of cognitive-behavioural therapies (CBT) (Marlatt and Gordon, 2005; Harris, 1989). There are many different CBT approaches that have been used in the treatment of addictive behaviours, including rational emotive therapy, motivational interviewing and relapse prevention. The techniques assume that addiction is a means of coping with difficult situations, dysphoric mood and peer pressure.

Motivational interviewing

The therapeutic approach of motivational interviewing (MI) has gained many adherents since its inception in the early 1980s. MI borrows strategies from cognitive therapy,

Operant conditioning treatment: The voucher-therapy approach

Key research: Higgins *et al.* (1994)

A programme in the USA, reported by Higgins and colleagues, tried to change the behaviour of people with a serious cocaine problem.

The 28 cocaine addicts (all white males from Vermont) on the programme had their urine tested several times a week for traces of cocaine, and every time it was clear of any cocaine they were given vouchers. The vouchers started with a value of $2.50, but every time they were clear of cocaine the value went up by $1.50, so that if they had ten consecutive clear tests they would receive $17.50 for the next clear test. If they had one test that showed traces of cocaine then the payments went back to $2.50 again. The best way to cash in on this programme, then, was to stay clear of cocaine for as long as possible. The vouchers were backed up with counselling on how best to spend the money, so they were encouraged to spend it on, for example, sports equipment to take up a hobby, or a family meal in a restaurant to help build up relationships which might have been damaged by the substance use.

The voucher-therapy approach was reported to have good results. The norm for drug-treatment programmes is a drop out rate of 70 per cent within six weeks. However, on this programme, around 85 per cent stayed in the programme for 12 weeks, and around two-thirds stayed in for six months. The voucher-based treatment was also compared with a more traditional outpatient counselling programme over a 12-week period. In a follow-up, 11 of the 13 patients assigned to the behaviour-change programme completed 12 weeks of treatment, compared with five of the 15 patients in the traditional programme. The researchers found that patients in behavioural treatment had significantly longer periods with cocaine-free urine. The findings

were much the same for a subsequent study of 38 cocaine addicts over 24 weeks.

According to the study authors, the voucher-based system creates an alternative, builds coping skills and strengthens social relationships. Furthermore, the approach involves more than regular urine tests and vouchers for points; it also includes intensive counselling directed at employment, recreation, relationships, skills training and structuring the day, and family and friends are brought into the counselling process.

Evaluation

■ Although this study reported good results, and showed that behaviour could be modified using operant conditioning techniques, many would argue that in real life, drug addicts are unlikely to be rewarded with financial incentives like the ones in this study. The fact that it also includes intensive counselling directed at employment, recreation, relationships, skills training, and structuring the day suggests there may be other confounding variables that could account for some of the programme's success.

■ The research was carried out on white males in Vermont, a rural state. Therefore, further studies are needed to determine the effectiveness of the vouchers over longer periods of time and among women, urban populations and other cultural groups.

■ The scheme's biggest problem is its political palatability. Even if the voucher scheme was shown to be the best treatment in the world, the fact that drug users will be paid for simply obeying the law and keeping off drugs would not sit too well with the tax-paying public.

client-centred counselling, systems theory and the social psychology of persuasion, and contains elements of both directive and non-directive therapeutic approaches. It is based on theories of **cognitive dissonance** and attempts to promote a favourable attitude change. Briefly, instructing addicts on the problems of dependency and the advantages of abstinence tends to provoke contradictory arguments from the client. Motivational interviewing encourages clients to give their own reasons for attempting to change their drug use.

Miller and Rollnick (2002) are the main proponents of this approach and argue that MI is primarily about the motivational aspects of changing people's behaviour in the therapeutic setting, particularly for those people who engage in addictive behaviours (alcohol and other drug use, gambling, eating disorders, etc.). The underlying theme of such a therapeutic approach is the issue of

ambivalence, and how the therapist can use MI to resolve it and allow the client to build commitment and reach a decision to change. Miller and Rollnick argue that integral to MI's theoretical basis is the assertion that motivation is not a personality problem and that there is little evidence for an 'addictive personality'.

Motivational interviewing highlights Prochaska *et al.*'s (1982) 'Stages of change' model (see Table 13.7), which seeks to explain how people change either with or without a therapist. The method employed in MI consists of using a mnemonically structured (A–H) list of eight effective motivational strategies:

1 giving Advice

2 removing Barriers

3 providing Choice

4   decreasing Desirability

5   practising Empathy

6   providing Feedback

7   clarifying Goals

8   active Helping.

This is intertwined with the five general principles of MI:

1   expressing empathy

2   developing discrepancy

3   avoiding argumentation

4   rolling with resistance

5   supporting self-efficacy.

The therapist attempts to elicit self-motivational statements (through non-confrontational approaches) to bring the individual to a point of making a decision to change (e.g. problem recognition, expression of concern, intention to change, optimism about change). MI involves avoiding labelling, asking evocative questions, listing advantages and disadvantages, acknowledging positives, reversing roles and summarizing as methods of getting people to come to a decision themselves about changing their behaviour. There is growing evidence that this is an effective treatment for addictive behaviour (Arkowitz *et al.* 2007).

Relapse prevention

Another common strategy, often used as part of cognitive-behavioural therapy in helping people overcome their addictions, is relapse prevention (Marlatt and Gordon 2005). Here, the therapist helps to identify situations that present a risk for relapse, both intrapersonal and interpersonal:

■   On an intrapersonal level, this may include acknowledging unpleasant emotions, physical discomfort and pleasant emotions; testing personal control and urges/temptations.

■   On an interpersonal level, this is likely to include conflicts and social pressures.

Relapse prevention provides the addict with techniques to learn how to cope with temptation (positive self-statements, decision review and distraction activities), coupled with the use of covert modelling (i.e. practising coping skills in one's imagination). There is now a lot of evidence that this can be an effective part of the CBT treatment process for addictive behaviour (Marlatt and Gordon 2005).

Psychotherapies

Psychotherapy can include everything from Freudian psychoanalysis and transactional analysis, to more recent innovations like drama therapy, family therapy and minimalist intervention strategies (Griffiths and MacDonald 1999). The therapy can take place on an individual, couple, family or group level and is basically viewed as a 'talking cure', consisting of regular sessions

HOW SCIENCE WORKS

Changing cognitions and changing behaviour

Key research: Dijkstra and De Vries (2001)

Dijkstra and De Vries investigated the extent to which self-help interventions change specific cognitions, and the extent to which changes in these cognitions are related to behaviour.

They carried out a field experiment with follow-ups after 2 weeks and 12 weeks. Over 1500 smokers were randomly assigned to one of four conditions offering self-help materials to aid giving up smoking. The research used two types of information:

1   information about the outcomes of smoking, such as shorter life expectancy and various unpleasant diseases

2   self-efficacy information telling people how to be successful at giving up.

The four groups were given the information as follows:

Group 1: Just given information about the outcome of continuing to smoke

Group 2: Just given self-efficacy enhancing information

Group 3: Given outcome and self-efficacy information

Group 4: Given no information

The response rate of the smokers was 81 per cent after 2 weeks and 71 per cent after 12 weeks, which is good for this sort of study. Table 13.9 shows the proportion of people after 12 weeks who had not smoked for the previous 7 days (7 days quit) and the number of people who had attempted to quit during the previous 12 weeks (quit attempt).

	7 days quit	Quit attempt
Group 1	4.8	25.5
Group 2	8.5	27.3
Group 3	8.1	24.6
Group 4	3.2	15.6

Table 13.9 *Proportion of people reporting smoking behaviour after 12 weeks (data in percentages)*

Evaluation

Table 13.9 highlights that about a quarter of the smokers had attempted to quit but most had started smoking again. This might be a bad thing because it gives them an experience of failure and hence lowers self-efficacy, though it might well be a learning experience that helps them to be successful in the future. The main conclusion from the study is that self-efficacy information seems to be effective, and the outcome information had no significant effect.

with a psychotherapist over a period of time. Most psychotherapies view maladaptive behaviour as the symptom of other underlying problems. Psychotherapy is often very eclectic by trying to meet the needs of the individual and helping the addict develop coping strategies. If the problem is resolved, the addiction should disappear. In some ways, this is the therapeutic opposite of pharmacotherapy (which treats the symptoms rather than the underlying cause). Although there is generally little evaluation of psychotherapy as a treatment for addictive behaviour, there is general agreement that it is a useful adjunct to other therapies and that clients do like some form of psychotherapeutic intervention as part of the harm-reduction process (Tatarsky 2003).

Evaluation of psychological interventions

- *Behavioural therapy may eliminate the behaviour but not the problem* – It would seem that behavioural therapies can curtail addictive behaviour, but to achieve a long-term improvement the addict must learn how to satisfy their needs in more adaptive ways. It could be argued that if the addiction is caused by some underlying psychological problem (rather than a learned maladaptive behaviour), then behavioural therapy would at best only eliminate the behaviour but not the problem, so the person may engage in a different addictive behaviour instead. For instance, there are case studies in the literature of gambling addicts being treated with aversive therapy, only for the gambling to stop but for alcohol addiction to take its place (Griffiths 1995).

- *Behavioural therapy and psychotherapy are often used as an adjunct to other addiction treatments* – It is hard to evaluate treatment effectiveness in some studies because behavioural therapy and psychotherapy are often used with other treatment techniques (e.g. self-help groups, counselling, pharmacotherapy).

- *Treatment success for addicts might be overshadowed by public reaction* – The problem with an operant conditioning treatment approach for addiction does not concern its success rate but the reaction of other people to the idea of giving drug users money not to take drugs. The hostile reaction of politicians and the general public to this sort of programme is likely to be similar to that met by harm-minimization programmes seeking to reduce the dangers to health in people carrying out risky behaviours, e.g. giving out clean needles to drug addicts.

- *Cognitive therapies appear to be reasonably successful, but not necessarily better than other addiction treatments* – Reasonable evidence exists for the effectiveness of techniques such as motivational interviewing and relapse prevention (Luty 2003). Furthermore, CBT approaches are better researched than many of the other psychological methods in addiction but are probably no more effective, although

CBT appears to be the current technique of choice by therapists in the addiction field (Luty 2003).

- *Some types of therapy or combined therapy may be more effective than others* – There is some evidence that some forms of psychodynamic psychotherapy do not appear to be particularly effective (Luty, 2003). It is also hard to establish whether 'success' is due to the psychotherapy, some other treatment intervention (pharmacotherapy or attendance at a self-help group), or an interaction between therapies.

- *Gaining control of behaviour may be just as good a treatment objective as abstinence* – There can sometimes be the added problem of defining what a 'successful' outcome is. Although abstinence from the behaviour might appear to be a clear objective, many would argue that improvement in the lifestyle of the addict – regardless of whether they have stopped the behaviour – is just as valid as an obtainable objective.

Self-help therapies

The most popular self-help therapy worldwide is the **Minnesota Model** 12-step programme (e.g. Alcoholics Anonymous, Gamblers Anonymous, Narcotics Anonymous, Overeaters Anonymous, Sexaholics Anonymous). This treatment programme uses a group therapy technique and only ex-addicts as helpers (Griffiths 1995). Addicts attending 12-step groups become involved in accepting personal responsibility and come to view the behaviour as an addiction that cannot be cured but merely arrested. For the therapy to work, the 12-step programme asserts that the addict must come to them voluntarily and must really want to stop engaging in their addictive behaviour. Further to this, they are only allowed to join once they have reached 'rock bottom'.

Typically, 12-step groups meet once a week and each member of the group talks about their personal experiences. (These testimonies are in fact called therapies.) Meetings focus on the 12 steps to recovery (e.g. '*We admitted we were powerless over [the addiction] and that our lives had become unmanageable*', '*We came to believe that a Power greater than ourselves could restore us to a normal way of thinking and living*'). The therapeutic aims are to:

- instil hope, openness and self-disclosure
- develop social networks
- focus on abstinence and loss of control
- rely on others for help
- develop spiritually.

However, it should be noted that the spiritual development and references to a 'Higher Power' may put off some people from continuing with the group. The 12-step programmes claim to help fill the void left by not engaging in the addiction, by focusing attention on the demands of the next meeting, and through social rewards (i.e. praise from other members) for non-participation in the addiction.

Evaluation of self-help therapies

To date, there has been little systematic study of 12-step groups. There are a number of problems preventing this, particularly anonymity, sample bias and criterion for success (Walker, 1992). These points relate specifically to gambling addiction.

- *Anonymity* – No case records are kept; no attempt is made at objective evaluation, and the only evidence is the subjectively based self-report of the member. As there is little in the way of data that an external body can audit or evaluate, there is no evidence that this is an effective treatment for gambling addiction.

- *Sample bias* – 12-step groups only accept those who come voluntarily and have reached 'rock bottom'. Membership is continually changing and some members attend multiple meetings. As Gamblers Anonymous (GA) only accepts a certain type of client (one who is at 'rock bottom') from a group that is self-selected, there is no way of knowing whether they are offering an effective treatment and/or whether it is only effective to those in an extremely vulnerable state. These factors also rule out the possibility of comparison with a control group, making evaluation of the treatment almost impossible.

- *Criterion for success* – In 12-step groups, the criterion for success is complete abstention. Among those who drop out and those who 'fall', there is no measure of the success that the 12-step programme has achieved. It could be the case that some of those who attended for a small number of meetings gained the strength to resist the urge to gamble compulsively without needing to attend further meetings. Alternatively, those who dropped out may have simply found the therapy ineffective. Neither success nor non-success is measured, and the measure itself is very strict. It could be that some gamblers regain control of their gambling, which GA would count as a failure, as abstention is their therapeutic goal.

Public-health interventions and legislation

Interventions can also come in the shape of public-health interventions and legislation. In this section, and by way of example, we will consider what could be done about teenage gambling addiction, based on what has been done legislatively and from a public-health perspective for other potentially addictive behaviours. For example, given the increasing amount of research showing that adolescent gambling is widespread and causing harm for a significant minority of teenagers (Griffiths 1995; 2002), the government could legislate (i.e. introduce a restriction initiative) to make it illegal for those under 18 years to play on slot machines (the activity most associated with teenage gambling). They could also legislate to stop gaming companies advertising gambling on television before the 21h 'watershed'. Such simple measures could greatly curtail adolescent gambling.

> ### Norwegian slot-machine gambling
>
> In the early 2000s, Norway witnessed a huge increase in numbers of slot machines from numerous slot-machine operators. In 2007, the Norwegian government took the extreme step of banning slot machines as a way of stopping the large increase in slot machine proliferation and reducing gambling addiction in the country. However, this led to an increase in illegal slot machines and did not stop people having problems with them. In June 2008, the Norwegian government reintroduced slot machines operated by just one company as a way of controlling the supply. It is too early to tell whether the government's intervention has successfully reduced problems with slot-machine gambling.

From a public-health perspective, problem gambling needs to be embedded into public-health policy and practice (Shaffer and Korn 2002). These include the following:

- *Adopt strategic goals* for gambling, to provide a focus for public-health action and accountability, including:

  - preventing gambling-related problems among individuals and groups at risk of gambling addiction

  - promoting balanced and informed attitudes, behaviours, and policies towards gambling and gamblers by both individuals and communities

  - protecting vulnerable groups from gambling-related harm.

- *Endorse public-health principles* consisting of three primary principles that can guide and inform decision-making to reduce gambling-related problems. These would ensure that prevention is a community priority:

  - with the appropriate allocation of resources to primary, secondary and tertiary prevention initiatives

  - incorporating a mental-health promotion approach that builds community capacity, incorporates a holistic view of mental health, and addresses the needs and aspirations of gamblers, individuals at risk of gambling problems, or those affected by them

  - fostering personal and social responsibility for gambling policies and practices.

- *Adoption of harm-reduction strategies* directed at minimizing the adverse health, social and economic consequences of gambling behaviour for individuals, families and communities. These initiatives should include:

  - healthy-gambling guidelines for the general public (similar to low-risk drinking guidelines)

- vehicles for the early identification of gambling problems

- non-judgemental moderation and abstinence goals for problem gamblers

- surveillance and reporting systems to monitor trends in gambling-related participation and the incidence and burden of gambling-related illnesses.

Activity **Addiction and culture**

It could perhaps be argued that addiction is merely an invention of Western culture. Addiction treatment mainly exists in Western cultures even though third-world societies engage in potentially addictive behaviours.

In class, discuss the extent to which addiction is universal:

1 Do you think that addiction is an invention of Western culture?

2 Is it connected to the role and the rise of the mass media?

3 Are addictions more or less prevalent in third world countries?

Some suggestions are given in the Answers to activities on p.603. ▶

Addiction treatment: Conclusions

When examining all the literature on the treatment of addiction, and taking the cautions into account, a number of key conclusions can be drawn, as outlined in Table 13.10. For all the money and effort put into behaviour change, perhaps people will just give up anyway. Some people argue that giving up is a natural consequence of developing a strong or excessive appetite (Orford 2001). This argument points out that expert treatments only have a limited success, and that the success occurs regardless of the treatment that is used. Treatments that are very different in intensity or in theory have a similar beneficial effect. Orford concludes that there is a lot of evidence that people give up excessive appetites (or addictions) without the help of experts.

Treatment must be readily available.
No single treatment is appropriate for all individuals.
It is better for an addict to be treated than not to be treated.
It does not seem to matter which treatment an addict engages in, as no single treatment has been shown to be demonstrably better than any other. However, psychosocial interventions have been demonstrated to be effective in rehabilitation and relapse prevention, both in out-patient and residential settings, in particular cognitive-behavioural therapy, motivational interviewing and contingency management, employment and vocational training, counselling and legal advice.
Undergoing a variety of treatments simultaneously appears to be beneficial to the addict.
Individual needs of the addict have to be met (i.e. the treatment should be fitted to the addict, including being gender-specific and culture-specific). Effective treatment attends to the multiple needs of the individual, not just their addiction. An individual's treatment plan must be assessed continually and modified as necessary to ensure that the plan meets the person's changing needs.
Clients with co-existing addiction disorders should receive services that are integrated.
Remaining in treatment for an adequate period of time is critical for treatment effectiveness.
Medications are an important element of treatment for many patients, especially when combined with counselling and other behavioural therapies.
Recovery from addiction can be a long-term process and frequently requires multiple episodes of treatment.
There is a direct association between the length of time spent in treatment and positive outcomes. One of the challenges is retaining clients in addiction treatment.
The duration of treatment interventions is determined by individual needs, and there are no pre-set limits to the duration of treatment.

Table 13.10: *Key conclusions about treatment (National Institute on Drug Abuse 1999; Zerger 2002; United Nations/WHO 2008)*

Evaluation of addiction treatments

- *Defining 'success' in treatment can be difficult* – In addiction treatment, there are many problems defining whether an intervention has been successful, e.g. is success defined as complete abstinence or does reducing the amount of addictive behaviour and/or getting the addictive behaviour under control count as a successful outcome? For example, if someone reduces their own smoking by 50 per cent, does that indicate effective treatment?

- *Effectiveness may depend on the addiction* – The effectiveness of different interventions would appear to depend on the nature of the addiction. Although this has not been investigated with any empirical rigour, biological (pharmacotherapeutic) interventions might be more likely to work with chemical addictions than with behavioural addictions, whereas psychological interventions might be the opposite.

- *Interaction effects are likely in addiction treatment* – It should also be emphasized that there are likely to be interaction effects between interventions and treatment effectiveness (i.e. the effectiveness of any intervention is likely to depend in part on the factors that produced the addiction in the first place).

CHECK YOUR UNDERSTANDING

Check your understanding of reducing addictive behaviour by answering the questions below. Try to do this from memory. You can check your answers by looking back through Topic 3, reducing addictive behaviour.

1. In what way does the Theory of Planned Behaviour differ from the Theory of Reasoned Action?

2. According to Prochaska *et al.* (1992), what are the 'stages of change' involved in changing human behaviour such as addictions?

3. Name four different types of pharmacotherapy in the treatment of addictive behaviour.

4. Outline two main criticisms of pharmacotherapy in the treatment of addictive behaviour.

5. Outline three main criticisms of behavioural therapy in the treatment of addictive behaviour.

6. Outline three main criticisms of self-help therapy in the treatment of addictive behaviour.

7. According to Walker (1992), what are the six types of behavioural therapy in treating addictive behaviour?

8. In motivational interviewing, what (mnemonically A–H) are the eight effective motivational strategies for effecting behaviour change?

9. What is the most effective type of treatment for addictive behaviour?

Further resources

Davies, J.B. (1997) *The Myth of Addiction* (2nd edn), London: Routledge.

This provocative, challenging and easy-to-read book applies attribution theory to addiction and suggests that addiction is a myth.

Mayer, G., Hayer, T. and Griffiths, M.D. (2009) *Problem Gaming in Europe: Challenges, Prevention, and Interventions*, New York: Springer.

This book provides a comprehensive overview of gambling addiction on a country-by-country basis in Europe.

McMurran, M. (1994) *The Psychology of Addiction*, London: Taylor and Francis.

This overview of the psychology of addictive behaviour is focused on alcohol and drug addictions but covers all the key concepts in an easy-to-read book.

Orford, J. (2001) *Excessive Appetites: A Psychological View of Addictions* (2nd edn), Chichester: Wiley.

This was the first book to compare chemical and non-chemical addictions (such as gambling, eating and sex) psychologically across the spectrum.

Websites

http://www.peele.net/

Stanton Peele is a psychologist who has been influential in the addiction field. He has pioneered the idea that addiction occurs with a range of experiences, and the 'harm reduction' approach to addiction. This site contains much of his widely published writing, as well as his opinions, and communications with people with addictive problems.

http://www.responsiblegambling.org/en/research/library.cfm

This site provides access to over 12,000 articles on gambling and gambling addiction and is an excellent resource for students and researchers.

http://www.netaddiction.com/

This site run by Kimberly Young concentrates on addictions that occur on the internet and has a lot of resource material about excessive behaviour on the internet (sex addiction, gaming addiction, internet addiction, etc.)

Models of addictive behaviour

Biological models of addictive behaviour

- Biological predisposition
- Neurotransmitters (dopamine)
- Genetics
- Reinforcement

Evaluation:

- Help explain differential susceptibility in same environment
- Neurotransmitters' complex effects not fully understood
- Reductionist: interaction with social context is neglected
- Genotypes not the whole story

Cognitive explanations of addictive behaviour

- Faulty thinking
- Irrational biases

Evaluation:

- Help explain individual differences
- Irrationality an erratic predictor of addictive behaviour
- Explanations may be limited to particular addictions
- Experiential factors may play a role
- Skill perception varies across individuals

The case for an eclectic approach

- Singular approaches inadequate
- Individual susceptibility largely unexplained
- A unified theory will be complex and biopsychosocial

Factors affecting addictive behaviours

Explanations for specific addictions

Addiction to smoking

- Effects of nicotine
- Withdrawal effects
- Genetic underpinning?
- Social and psychological factors

Evaluation:

- Biological approaches too simplistic
- Physiological vs psychological addiction is outdated
- Biological underpinnings similar across addictions
- Relapse can be caused by environmental factors

Addiction to gambling

- Multiple determinants: individual, structural and situational
- Personal vulnerability
- Financial motivation
- Inconsistent evidence re. personality
- Slot machines most addictive

Evaluation:

- Behavioural explanations limited
- Biopsychosocial factors not the only factors involved
- Structural characteristics apply to chemical addictions too

Behavioural (learning) explanations

- Based on classical and operant conditioning
- Reinforcers and punishments can change mood
- Rewards initiate and maintain behaviour
- Relapse after giving up less likely if addictive behaviour has been 'unlearned'

Evaluation:

- Help explain individual differences
- Neither conditioning explanation sufficient on its own
- Findings contrary to operant theory
- Operant explanations not equally successful
- Difficulty explaining why people exposed to similar stimuli respond differently

Personal vulnerability explanations of addictions

Self-esteem, addictive personality and individual differences

Evaluation:

- Common traits found in addiction may not be specific to addictive behaviour
- Need for accepted 'standards of proof'
- Little evidence of an addictive personality

Attributions

- How we explain own and others' behaviour

Social context

- Addiction and availability

Evaluation:

- Correlational relationship
- Social context can change over time
- Social context affected by third-party initiatives

Addictive behaviour

→ **Reducing addictive behaviour**

Definitions of addiction

- Compulsive, uncontrolled drug use
- Chronic intoxication through repeated drug consumption
- Addictive behaviours, e.g. smoking, gambling, Internet use
- Excessive enthusiasm vs addiction
- Central concept = 'loss of control'

Components of addiction

- Salience
- Mood modification
- Tolerance
- Withdrawal symptoms
- Conflict
- Relapse

Media and advertising influences on addiction

- Media effects
- Advertising effects

Evaluation:

- Glamorization vs reality is complicated
- Research on the role of media effects inconclusive
- Relationship between advertising and addictive behaviour mostly correlational
- Could be different media effects for different addictions
- Research done to date may not be suitable

Biological (medical) interventions

- Aversive agent treatment (Disulfiram – Antabuse)
- Agonist maintenance (Methadone)
- Narcotic antagonist (Naltrexone)

Evaluation:

- May ignore the underlying reason(s) for addiction
- Addicts may relapse when pharmacotherapy stopped
- Substitute drugs help stabilize behaviour

Public health interventions & legislation

- Teenage gambling addiction controllable through legislation?
- Bans may encourage illegal gambling
- Embed problem gambling into public health policy and practice

Addiction treatment: Conclusions

- People may just give up
- Cessation may naturally follow excess
- Success not specific to type of individual or treatment
- Treatment better than no treatment
- May be lengthy and repeated
- Longer treatment correlates with success

Evaluation:

- Hard to define 'success' in treatment
- Effectiveness may depend on the addiction
- Interaction effects are likely in addiction treatment

Models of behaviour change and prevention

1. The theory of reasoned action
2. Theory of planned behaviour
3. Stages of change model

Evaluation:

- Deficiencies in **1**
- **2** an improvement
- **1** and **2** limited in scope
- **3** may be better

Psychological interventions

- **Classical conditioning** therapies – aversion therapy, desensitization, satiation therapy
- **Operant conditioning** therapies
- **Cognitive–behavioural** therapy
- **Psychotherapies** – variety of 'talking cures'

Evaluation:

- Behavioural therapies may eliminate behaviour not problem
- Used as adjuncts to other treatments
- Treatment success might be overshadowed by public reaction
- Cognitive therapies not necessarily better than others
- Gaining control may be just as good an objective as abstinence

Self-help therapies

- The Minnesota Model 12-Step Programme (e.g. Alcoholics Anonymous)
- Group therapy; ex-addicts as helpers

Evaluation:

- Little systematic study of 12-Step groups
- Methodological problems: anonymity, sample bias, criterion for success
- Some gamblers regain control

Anomalistic psychology

EXPLAINING THE SPECIFICATION

Specification content	The specification explained
Theoretical and methodological issues in the study of anomalous experience (Topic 1)	The specification focuses on the paranormal, familiar astrological beliefs and UFOology. Anomalistic psychologists aim to investigate behaviour and experiences that are extraordinary and which fall outside the bounds of what we might think of as everyday and explainable. The key issue is that, because so many people have a belief in anomalous phenomena, it deserves explanation. In this first section you should be able to:
Issues of pseudoscience and scientific fraud	■ explain what is meant by pseudoscience in the context of paranormal and related claims ■ explain what is meant by scientific fraud in the context of parapsychology ■ evaluate the scientific status of parapsychology and the role of scientific fraud in the context of parapsychology
Controversies relating to Ganzfeld studies of ESP and studies of psychokinesis	■ outline the Ganzfeld procedure ■ describe studies of ESP that used the Ganzfeld procedure ■ describe studies of psychokinesis ■ evaluate studies of ESP that used the Ganzfeld procedure and studies of psychokinesis
Factors underlying anomalous Experience (Topic 2)	In this section you are asked to study individual, social and cultural aspects of anomalous experience in order to understand the similarities and differences that exist between individuals. In this section 'research' can refer to theory or studies or a mixture of both. You should be able to:
Cognitive, personality and biological factors underlying anomalous experience	■ describe research into cognitive, personality and biological factors underlying anomalous experience ■ evaluate research into each of these three underlying factors
Functions of paranormal and related beliefs, including their cultural significance	■ identify the functional significance of paranormal and related beliefs for individuals ■ identify ways in which paranormal beliefs might have functional significance for cultural groups ■ evaluate research into the functions of paranormal and related beliefs
The psychology of deception and self-deception, superstition, and coincidence	■ describe psychological explanations of deception and self deception with respect to anomalous experience ■ describe psychological explanations of superstition ■ describe psychological explanations of coincidence ■ evaluate research into each of these three areas

Belief in exceptional experience (Topic 3)	In this section you are asked to study the psychological processes underlying three aspects of anomalous experience. You should be able to:
Research into psychic healing	■ describe psychological research into psychic healing ■ evaluate psychological research into psychic healing
Research into out-of-body and near-death experience	■ describe psychological explanations of both out-of-body and near-death experiences ■ evaluate psychological research into both out-of-bodyand near-death experiences
Research into psychic mediumship	■ describe psychological research into psychic mediumship ■ evaluate psychological research into psychic mediumship

Introduction

Opinion polls from around the world consistently show high levels of belief in the **paranormal**, and a significant minority of the population claim to have had direct personal experience of the paranormal. Moore (2005) reported the results of a telephone survey of 1002 American adults. The levels of belief in different types of paranormal phenomena were as follows: extrasensory perception (ESP) 41 per cent; haunted houses 37 per cent; ghosts 32 per cent; telepathy and astrology 25 per cent; communication with the dead 21 per cent; and reincarnation 20 per cent. Furthermore, when we consider such beliefs from a cross-cultural perspective, we find that there is no society in the world, either geographically or historically, where paranormal belief and claims of paranormal experience are not common. Does this indicate that paranormal forces really do exist? **Parapsychologists** have, for well over a century, attempted to prove this, but it is not generally accepted by the wider scientific community. If paranormal forces do not exist, how can we explain why so many people believe in the paranormal and even claim to have personally experienced paranormal phenomena? **Anomalistic psychology** attempts to provide answers to this question.

In a study of 1002 American adults, Moore (2005) found 32 per cent believed in ghosts.

The field of anomalistic psychology 'attempts to explain paranormal and related beliefs and apparently paranormal experiences in terms of known (or knowable) psychological and physical factors. It is directed at understanding bizarre experiences that many people have, without assuming *a priori* that there is anything paranormal involved' (French 2001a). It is important to note that although anomalistic psychologists generally adopt the working hypothesis that paranormal forces do not exist, they also accept that it is at least conceivable that parapsychologists might, at some point in the future, produce high quality evidence that paranormal forces really do exist. If that happens, anomalistic psychologists will still have provided a useful service for parapsychologists by helping them to distinguish genuine paranormal phenomena from those which only appear to be paranormal but are in fact explicable in other ways.

Given the complementary relationship between anomalistic psychology and **parapsychology**, it is important to define the latter. Parapsychologists would typically endorse the following definition provided in the glossary of volume 71, p.203 (Spring/Fall 2007 issue) of the *Journal of Parapsychology*, an affiliated publication of the Parapsychological Association and the most respected parapsychology journal in the world: 'The scientific study of certain paranormal or allegedly paranormal phenomena, in particular, ESP and PK.' Many parapsychologists would also want to include evidence relating to the possibility of life after death within the remit of parapsychology. This definition still needs a little bit of unpacking. What is meant by 'paranormal', for example? The same glossary provides the following definition on p.203: 'Term for any phenomenon that in one or more respects exceeds the limits of what is deemed physically possible according to current scientific assumptions.' The term **psi** is often used as a generic term to refer to any aspect of the paranormal.

'**ESP**' stands for **extrasensory perception** and parapsychologists distinguish between three different types. The first is **telepathy**, the alleged ability of direct mind-to-mind contact, popularly known as 'mind-reading'. The second is **clairvoyance**, the alleged ability to pick up information from remote locations and events without using the known sensory channels. Examples of this would include the claims of so-called 'psychic detectives' that they can help police to solve crimes by telling them where missing bodies can be found or the identity of murderers. The final type of ESP is **precognition**, the alleged ability to foretell future events other than by the use of inference. Examples of this would include the claim that Nostradamus accurately foretold many major historical events and the idea that dreams sometimes provide a glimpse into the future.

Whereas ESP refers to the sensory side of the paranormal, PK or **psychokinesis** refers to the motor side. Psychokinesis is the alleged ability to influence the external world by thought alone. Parapsychologists typically distinguish between **macro-PK** and **micro-PK**. Examples of macro-PK would include mediums levitating tables, chairs and even themselves during séances, or people claiming that they can bend metal simply by gently stroking it. Such effects would be plainly visible if they really occurred. Micro-PK, on the other hand, refers to much weaker effects that would only be evident as a result of statistical analysis. For example, participants might be asked to influence the roll of a dice or the output

from a random event generator (see p.200). It would not be clear on a trial-by-trial basis whether PK had been operating, but if the results differed from what one would expect on the basis of chance alone, this might be taken as being indicative of the operation of PK.

It should be noted that parapsychologists typically restrict their attention to just the areas of ESP, PK and life after death, whereas the public and the media would also consider many other phenomena as being paranormal, such as alien abduction claims, astrology, the Loch Ness monster, and so on. Anomalistic psychologists tend also to adopt this looser definition of the paranormal on the grounds that similar psychological mechanisms may underlie belief in and experience of a range of bizarre phenomena. For example, it seems plausible to argue that similar processes underlie belief in and experience of readings by both mediums and astrologers, but it is only the former that fit within the stricter definition of the paranormal.

It should also be noted that many definitions of parapsychology, including the one provided, refer to the scientific study of 'ostensibly paranormal phenomena' as being within the remit of the discipline. Thus, anomalistic psychology might be considered by some to be a sub-discipline of parapsychology. In practice, most parapsychologists focus primarily upon attempting to produce evidence that supports the existence of genuine paranormal phenomena and have only a secondary interest in what looks like it is psychic but is not. For anomalistic psychologists, the situation is reversed and they would tend to see their field of investigation as being a sub-discipline of psychology rather than parapsychology.

In the first topic, we will consider the theoretical and methodological issues associated with the study of anomalous experiences. We will do this first by considering the claim that parapsychology is a **pseudoscience** which simply has the superficial appearance of being a true science. We will also consider the role of scientific fraud in the context of parapsychology, as well as evaluating the controversial findings from studies of ESP using the **ganzfeld technique** and studies of psychokinesis. The second topic considers some of the cognitive, personality and biological factors that may underlie anomalous experiences, and also the psychological functions that paranormal beliefs may serve. The psychology of deception and self-deception is also described, with particular attention to the psychology of superstitions and coincidences. The final topic considers research into **psychic healing**, **out-of-body** and **near-death experiences** and **mediumship**.

Astrology is studied by anomalistic psychologists, yet it does not fit into the strict definition of the paranormal.

Psychology in context

Science and the paranormal

'Theories of telepathy and afterlife cause uproar at top science forum' according to a headline on the *TimesOnline* website (Henderson 2006). The article proceeded to describe the 'furious row' that had broken out because the organizers of the British Association for the Advancement of Science (the BA) meeting had allowed a session to take place featuring the research of Rupert Sheldrake, Peter Fenwick and Deborah Delanoy, all known to be proponents of the paranormal, with no participation by anyone representing the opposing viewpoint. Peter Atkins, a Professor of Chemistry at the University of Oxford, stated that in his view, 'Work in this field is a complete waste of time. [...] there is absolutely no reason to suppose that telepathy is anything more than a charlatan's fantasy'. The article also claimed that 'Some [critics] said telepathy had already been found wanting in experiments, and had no place at a scientific meeting'. But only Professor Atkins, who admitted in a subsequent live radio debate with Sheldrake on *BBC Radio Five Live* that he had not actually read any of the relevant research, seemed to be prepared to be named as endorsing such extreme views.

Now answer the following:

1 Do you feel that the BA deserved to be criticized in this way?

2 How might they avoid such criticism in future?

3 Does Professor Atkins' attitude show science in a good light?

Some suggestions are given in the Answers to activities on p.603. ▶

As described in the Introduction, parapsychologists and anomalistic psychologists tend to approach the study of anomalous experience from different perspectives. Parapsychologists often assume that paranormal forces do exist and direct their efforts towards providing evidence to support this assumption. Indeed, some parapsychologists (e.g. Radin 1997, 2006) argue strongly that the available evidence already proves beyond reasonable doubt that this assumption is true and that parapsychologists should now place less emphasis upon proof-oriented research and instead adopt a process-oriented approach. By this, they mean that parapsychology should be more focused upon *how* paranormal forces operate not *if* they operate. Critics of parapsychology, including most anomalistic psychologists, remain unconvinced that the available

evidence actually does offer strong support for the existence of psi. Their focus therefore is to look for and, where possible, test alternative explanations for evidence put forward in support of the psi hypothesis.

Parapsychology is often criticized (e.g. Alcock 1981, 2003) for having made little progress in terms of theory development despite over a century of research, mainly due to the lack of reliable empirical data upon which to base such development. In terms of both theory and methodology, anomalistic psychology is based firmly upon well-established approaches developed and empirically supported by psychologists working in all of the various sub-disciplines of psychology.

Issues of pseudoscience and scientific fraud

Some critics go so far as to claim that parapsychology is in fact a pseudoscience, based upon little more than wishful thinking, poor reasoning, shoddy methodology and fraud. Such claims are discussed next, where we will attempt to assess the scientific status of parapsychology and also to consider the important role that fraud has played in its history.

What is pseudoscience?

Critics (e.g. Alcock 1981; Radner and Radner 1982) often claim that parapsychology is a pseudoscience. They maintain that, in common with other pseudosciences such as astrology and creationism, the discipline may have some of the superficial trappings of true science but that closer examination reveals that this is an illusion. Lilienfeld (2005) provided a useful list of features to help students distinguish between real science and pseudoscience, which is summarized in Table 14.1 and elaborated upon here. Pseudosciences are said to be characterized by:

- *A tendency to invoke ad hoc hypotheses, which can be thought of as 'escape hatches' or loopholes, as a means of immunizing claims against falsification* – One classic example of this is the claim made by some creationists that God made the Earth with signs of prior aging, such as fossils in rocks, already in place. This essentially renders the claim that the Earth is only a few thousand years old unfalsifiable.

- *An absence of self-correction and an accompanying intellectual stagnation* – Western astrology has changed remarkably little over the last 2500 years (Hines 2003) not because it is valid but because astrologers simply ignore all the empirical evidence that shows that it is invalid (e.g. Dean *et al.* 1996).

- *An emphasis on confirmation rather than refutation* – Astrologers, for example, accepted results of a study by Mayo *et al.* (1978) that initially appeared to support the predictions of sun-sign astrology regarding personality, but did not accept subsequent findings which showed the results to be spurious (Eysenck and Nias 1982).

- *A tendency to place the burden of proof on sceptics, not proponents, of claims* – Pseudoscientists appear to assume that if sceptics cannot supply completely watertight explanations for every single case that is put before them, then they should admit that the pseudoscientific claim is valid. This is a particularly popular approach amongst UFOlogists and those investigating hauntings and poltergeist cases (Hines 2003). But this is unreasonable. It will often be the case that, even if the claimed phenomena did in fact have quite ordinary causes, the evidence to establish this is simply no longer available. The burden of proof in science always rests with those making a claim.

- *Excessive reliance on anecdotal and testimonial evidence to substantiate claims* – Such reliance is typical, for example, of those arguing in favour of claims of psychic healing (French 1996a) and alternative medicines generally (Singh and Ernst 2008), when in fact the best way to test such claims is by subjecting them to double-blind, randomized, clinical trials (see p.497).

- *Evasion of the scrutiny afforded by peer review (see Chapter 15)* – Peer review is one important mechanism of quality control within science. Pseudoscientists will therefore often prefer to avoid peer review altogether by publishing in books, magazines, or even directly on to the Internet.

- *Absence of 'connectivity' [...], that is, a failure to build on existing scientific knowledge* – Alcock (1981) also took parapsychology to task for its lack of overlap with normal science. In fact, he argued, many of the claims within parapsychology run counter to normal science. The latter is supported by a huge amount of empirical research. If the foundations of normal science are to be overturned, it must be on the basis of better evidence than parapsychology has so far been able to produce.

- *Use of impressive-sounding jargon whose primary purpose is to lend claims a façade of scientific respectability* – Many proponents of the paranormal, especially those promoting New Age therapies such as psychic healing, often use scientific-sounding terminology such as 'vibrations', 'energy', 'fields', 'harmonization' and so on, in ways that bear little resemblance to the precisely defined meanings that such terms have when used by scientists. However, such imprecise usage is, by and large, not a feature of articles published in peer-reviewed journals within parapsychology.

- *An absence of boundary conditions [...], that is, a failure to specify the settings under which claims do not hold* – There are two aspects to this. On the one hand, pseudoscientists often claim initially that the wondrous phenomenon they are claiming to have

proven has universal or near-universal application. Thus alternative therapies such as psychic healing are said to be beneficial to all ailments, unlike conventional medicine where specific therapies are applied to specific ailments. On the other hand, pseudoscientists often resort to providing spurious explanations of why their claims were not supported in

- A tendency to invoke *ad hoc* hypotheses.
- An absence of self-correction resulting in intellectual stagnation.
- An emphasis on confirmation rather than refutation.
- A tendency to place the burden of proof on sceptics of claims.
- Excessive reliance on anecdotal evidence to substantiate claims.
- Evasion of the scrutiny afforded by peer review.
- Absence of 'connectivity' with other areas of science.
- Use of impressive-sounding jargon.
- An absence of boundary conditions.

Table 14.1 *List of features typically found in a pseudoscience, based upon those proposed by Lilienfeld (2005).*

Psychology as science: Is pseudoscience a useful concept?

In the same way that philosophers of science have failed to produce a set of definitive criteria to demarcate between science and non-science, it has not proven possible to characterize pseudoscience definitively. Some commentators (e.g. Truzzi 1996; McNally 2003) have even argued that the concept is not useful. Truzzi (1996), for example, argued that 'there are good reasons to purge the term *pseudoscience* from our disputes. It may simply prove more useful and less incendiary to speak of *bad*, *poor*, or even *stupid* theories without entanglement in the demarcation problem.' Lilienfeld *et al.* (2003) on the other hand, argued that: '[...] the fuzziness of such categories does not mean that distinctions between science and pseudoscience are fictional or entirely arbitrary. As psychophysicist S.S. Stevens observed, the fact that the precise boundary between day and night is indistinct does not imply that day and night cannot be meaningfully differentiated [...]. From this perspective, pseudosciences can be conceptualized as possessing a fallible, but nevertheless useful, list of indicators or "warning signs". The more such warning signs a discipline exhibits, the more it begins to cross the murky dividing line separating science from pseudoscience.'

well-controlled studies, even though they may have agreed in writing before the test was carried out that it was, in fact, a fair test.

Although other commentators have proposed alternative sets of criteria, Lilienfeld's is fairly typical. Not all commentators, however, are convinced that the pseudoscience concept is useful (see panel below: Psychology as science: Is pseudoscience a useful concept?).

The scientific status of parapsychology

Having described the typical characteristics of pseudoscience, we can now consider the scientific status of parapsychology as a discipline. Anyone can call themselves a parapsychologist and there is no doubt that many of those who do would fit the bill as pseudoscientists perfectly. For this reason, we need to be very clear what we mean by parapsychology in this context as it would obviously not be fair to judge any discipline as a whole on the basis of its worst practitioners. The type of parapsychology that we will consider is that exemplified by contributions to the *Journal of Parapsychology* and the research carried out by members of the Parapsychological Association which became an affiliated organization of the American Association for the Advancement of Science (AAAS), amid much controversy, in 1969.

In a true scientific spirit, we will draw upon the empirical approach taken by Mousseau (2003) in addressing this issue. She compared the contents of a sample of mainstream scientific journals (e.g. *British Journal of Psychology, Molecular and Optical Physics*) with a sample of 'fringe' journals (e.g. *Journal of Parapsychology,*

Journal of Scientific Exploration) with respect to several common criteria of pseudoscience. In general, her analysis showed that parapsychology appears to meet the implicit criteria of science, to a greater or lesser extent, rather better than it meets the criteria of pseudoscience. In some cases, parapsychology actually fared better than mainstream science. For example, with respect to an alleged emphasis on confirmation, Mousseau (2003) found that, in her sample, 'almost half of the fringe articles report a negative outcome (disconfirmation). By contrast, no report of a negative result has been found in my sample of mainstream journals.' With respect to an alleged absence of self-correction, '... 29 per cent of the fringe-journal articles [...] discuss progress of research, problems encountered, epistemological issues. This kind of article is completely absent from the mainstream sample.' (Mousseau 2003). Overall, the only reasonable conclusion is that parapsychology, at its best, is a true science.

Fraud in parapsychology

Fraud occurs in all areas of science (Broad and Wade 1982), but it is often claimed by critics of parapsychology that it is particularly prevalent within this domain. The motivations to cheat on the part of scientists in general are many and varied. A scientist may become so convinced that their theory is correct that they feel justified in presenting data that strongly support it – even if the results of the studies actually have to be altered somewhat to bring this about! Of course, if the underlying theory is actually correct, such fraud may never be detected, but if other scientists simply cannot replicate the claimed results, suspicions of data manipulation may be raised.

Scientists may be tempted to cheat simply to get their papers published in the best scientific journals. This will enhance their reputation amongst their peers, increasing the likelihood that their work will be cited, and of them receiving awards, large grants and career promotion. Failure to publish in prestigious journals may lead to unemployment or employment at low status institutions. Scientific fraud is, however, an extremely risky venture, as discovery will result in disgrace and instant dismissal. Honesty and integrity are seen as being essential to the scientific enterprise.

The most notorious case of deliberate fraud on the part of a parapsychologist is probably that of S.G. Soal and relates to research published in the 1930s and 1940s (e.g. Soal and Goldney 1943). This is described in the panel on the next page: Confirmed fraud within parapsychology. Soal is by no means the only parapsychologist to have engaged in fraud. Other examples include Walter Levy, who was caught red-handed faking data in a study of precognition in rats in the 1970s and dismissed from his post as director of research at the Institute of Parapsychology in North Carolina (Rogo 1985). This came just months after the publication of a paper describing 12 other cases of definite or probable fraud in parapsychological laboratories during the 1940s and 1950s (Rhine 1974).

Activity **HOW** SCIENCE WORKS

Pseudoscience within psychology

Use the Internet and the library to find out about some of the more controversial therapeutic claims within clinical psychology, possibly including some of those on the fringes of the discipline, such as 'New Age' therapies, used to treat psychological problems. Examples might include psychoanalysis, neurolinguistic programming (NLP), and even homoeopathy.

1 Assess your choices by applying Lilienfeld's (2005) characteristics of pseudoscience to them. For each characteristic, decide whether it definitely applies, probably applies, probably does not apply, definitely does not apply, or else is simply not applicable. Do not expect all characteristics to apply to all controversial claims.

2 To what extent do your choices qualify as science or pseudoscience?

See p.612 for some suggestions. ▶

Confirmed fraud within parapsychology

Soal claimed to have found strong evidence for ESP in a series of experiments in which a sender would attempt telepathically to communicate to a distant receiver which picture they were looking at on each trial. The results were highly statistically significant and appeared to have been obtained under exceptionally well-controlled conditions. Although rumours were circulating for a long time that Soal had manipulated his data, it took over forty years for this to be definitively established (for full details of the fascinating detective work that led to this discovery, see Hyman (1985a) and Markwick (1985)). Throughout this period, Soal's research was often presented as the strongest evidence ever obtained in support of ESP.

Dishonesty on the part of experimenters is not the only concern within parapsychology. Participants may also be tempted to cheat, especially those who are claiming to possess special psychic powers. Once again, the motivations may vary from a deliberate attempt to fool investigators in order to enhance the fake psychic's reputation for financial gain, or simply the desire to prove that scientists can be fooled. There are numerous such cases described in the parapsychological literature. During the Victorian era, it was very common for mediums to be caught red-handed using trickery to produce the allegedly paranormal phenomena of the séance room, but many scientists pronounced such effects as genuine (Hyman 1985a). Indeed, the whole Spiritualist movement was launched in 1848 in Hydesville, New York, by a schoolgirl prank that got out of hand (see p.500, later in this chapter).

Nicol (1985) described many other cases of fraudulent children in psychical research, including the dozens of 'mini-Gellers' that suddenly appeared in the 1970s claiming that they could bend metal psychokinetically, just like Uri

Project Alpha

Key research: Randi (1983a, 1983b)

In 1980, James Randi set out to test the ability of parapsychologists to detect frauds, in an investigation which he called Project Alpha (Randi 1983a, 1983b). He had two collaborators, young conjurors by the names of Steve Shaw and Michael Edwards, present themselves at the newly established McDonnell Laboratory for Psychical Research at Washington University claiming to possess psychic powers. Over a period of more than two years, the two were investigated by laboratory staff whilst they performed all the standard tricks: metal bending, mind reading, reading the contents of sealed envelopes, and so on. The deceptions were carried out in relatively simple ways but at no time were they caught cheating. The McDonnell researchers described them as 'gifted psychic subjects'. This exercise strongly reinforces the idea that it is often sensible to employ the services of a skilled conjuror if one wishes to expose fake psychics. Scientific expertise alone is unlikely to be sufficient.

Evaluation
Strengths

- *Real world testing vs speculation* – Prior to Project Alpha, many critics of parapsychology, especially those with some knowledge of conjuring techniques, were convinced that most parapsychologists simply did not possess the expertise to avoid being fooled by fake psychics. Parapsychologists in general, whilst acknowledging that their predecessors may sometimes have been fooled, felt that they were now capable of ruling out fraud on the part of the psychic claimants they

tested. But both sides in the debate were speculating about the current state of parapsychology on the basis of its past history. In the past, psychic claimants had occasionally been caught red-handed in the act of cheating, but their intention would have been to get away with their deception if they could. Project Alpha was the first systematic test of the ability of parapsychologists to detect deception carried out with the intention of the fraudsters openly admitting their deception even if they were not caught red-handed, which they weren't!

- *Positive consequences* – This public demonstration of the failure of a parapsychological laboratory to detect fraud on the part of two alleged 'psychics' was extremely embarrassing for the parapsychological community as a whole. However, many parapsychologists did accept that such research did require greater involvement of magicians than had occurred in the past if such embarrassment was to be avoided in the future. As reported by Thalbourne (1995) in 1983 the Council of the Parapsychological Association adopted a resolution which included the following: '[...] the PA Council has voted unanimously to request from organizations such as the International Brotherhood of Magicians, Society of American Magicians and the Psychic Entertainers Association a list of their members who, regardless of their opinions on the existence of psi, would be willing to consult with PA members regarding adequate controls against fraud. We look forward to a fruitful professional relationship with these individuals.'

Weaknesses

- *Failure to distinguish between exploratory versus formal research* – Thalbourne (1995) has presented a detailed critique of Project Alpha in which he claimed that Randi misrepresented important aspects of the case. One of his strongest criticisms is that Randi did not acknowledge the distinction between exploratory research and formal experimentation. Exploratory research with psychic claimants may often take place under relatively relaxed, poorly controlled conditions in order for the experimenter to decide whether or not there is a phenomenon worth investigating further and in order for a rapport to develop between the claimant and the experimenter. It is often expensive and time-consuming to set up properly controlled tests and many parapsychologists believe that such conditions tend to inhibit psi. They thus prefer to begin with relaxed informal testing and to gradually increase the degree of experimental control. None of the tests carried out at the McDonnell laboratory were considered by the researchers concerned to be formal experiments.

- *Ethical issues* – Project Alpha clearly involved deception, and publication of the results was extremely embarrassing for the McDonnell researchers concerned. As such, the project would have been very unlikely to have been passed by any ethics committee adhering to any of the ethical guidelines produced by professional societies such as the British Psychological Society. Randi and his colleagues are not, of course, psychologists and, as such, were not professionally bound by such guidelines. It is to some degree a matter of personal judgement whether one feels that lessons learned from the exercise justify the project from an ethical perspective. It is difficult to see how the point could have been made in any more ethically acceptable way.

Geller. Many of them were caught red-handed using distinctly non-paranormal methods to produce the effects reported. Indeed, when it comes to the whole range of effects produced by Geller, it has been demonstrated that basic conjuring skills are all that is required (Marks 2000; Randi 1982). If Geller is producing these effects using paranormal powers, he is doing it the hard way!

IDA — Whistle-blowing within parapsychology

In terms of ethical issues, fraud in science is clearly one of the most serious. However, exposing such fraud can also raise ethical issues. Blackmore (1987a, 1996a) raised concerns regarding the results of ganzfeld studies of telepathy (described on p.480) following a visit to Sargent's parapsychology laboratory in Cambridge. She was not sure whether apparent errors in the protocol were evidence of deliberate fraud or not, but knew that any suggestion of fraud would be likely to tarnish Sargent's reputation and make her few friends amongst the parapsychological community. It took great moral courage on Blackmore's part to publicly raise her concerns regarding a colleague who, at the time, was held in great esteem. Sargent consistently refused to make his data available to others to allow proper investigation and left the field of parapsychology.

Susan Blackmore, who faced ethical issues when exposing possible fraud.

Although there is no reason to believe that fraud is any more common in parapsychology than in any other area of science, it is important, given the history of the discipline in this regard, that the possibility of fraud is reduced to an absolute minimum. The wider scientific community would only be prepared to accept the existence of paranormal forces if the evidence in favour of them is very strong, as to do so would require that many aspects of the current scientific world-view would have to be revised. In the words of Carl Sagan, 'Extraordinary claims require extraordinary evidence.' If any particular paranormal claim could be replicated reliably by independent researchers, this would greatly reduce the possibility of explaining it away as based upon fraud.

Evaluation of issues of pseudoscience and scientific fraud

- *Pseudoscience: a grey area* – The value of the very concept of pseudoscience has been questioned by some critics. Nevertheless, scientists in general feel that it is helpful to evaluate disciplines in terms of the criteria typically put forward in order to distinguish between science and pseudoscience. Although there is inevitably a grey area between the two, there are many examples of pseudoscience, such as astrology and creationism, which would be widely accepted as such by virtually all scientists. Regrettably, there are also many pseudoscientific claims within psychology, particularly within clinical psychology.

- *The scientific status of parapsychology* – Although parapsychology is often lambasted as a pseudoscience by its critics, an empirical approach to evaluating such accusations tends not to support them. Parapsychology does not meet very many of the criteria typically put forward as characteristic of pseudosciences and, on some, even appears to be better than some mainstream sciences.

- *Impact of fraud in parapsychology and in science generally* – There are many documented instances of fraud within parapsychology, either on the part of investigators or on the part of participants. However, there is no strong evidence that fraud is any more common within parapsychology than it is within science generally. The implications of accepting the existence of psi are profound for the wider scientific community. If psi exists, much of our current scientific understanding of the universe is mistaken. Because our current scientific world-view is based upon strong empirical foundations, the evidence required to overturn it would have to be robust, reliable and completely above suspicion. It is for that reason that fraud is such an important issue within parapsychology. The single most powerful weapon against fraud as a possible explanation of an alleged paranormal effect is a high level of replication by independent investigators around the world.

Controversies relating to ganzfeld studies of ESP and studies of psychokinesis

Two of the areas of research that parapsychologists most often highlight as providing strong evidence for the existence of psi are ESP studies using random event generators (REGs), and studies of psychokinesis (the alleged ability to influence the external world by will). The controversial findings from these studies are considered in this section. The ganzfeld technique is 'a technique used to test for telepathy in which a sender attempts to transmit mentally the identity of a randomly selected target … to a receiver who is perceptually deprived.'

Perhaps surprisingly, most commentators find the evidence put forward for subtle micro-PK effects (only detectable through statistical analysis) somewhat more compelling than that for macro-PK (plainly visible) effects. This is mainly because the latter have never been convincingly demonstrated under conditions that would rule out the possibility of fraud.

Ganzfeld studies of ESP

The term *ganzfeld* is German for 'entire field'. The ganzfeld technique is based upon the assumption that, if ESP exists, the ESP signal is probably very weak and usually drowned out by the input from our normal sensory channels. This technique therefore aims to reduce this background noise by having a receiver in a state of mild perceptual deprivation. This is usually achieved by having the receiver's eyes covered with half ping-pong balls, directing a red light at them and playing them white noise through headphones. The receiver reclines on a comfortable chair or mattress. Typically, this induces a pleasant, mildly altered state of consciousness during which the receiver experiences a series of mental images. At pre-specified times, a sender in a remote location (which could either be a room down the corridor or a room several thousand miles away) attempts to telepathically transmit information about a randomly selected target, usually a picture or a video clip, to the receiver. The receiver verbally describes their imagery at this time. Subsequently, the receiver judges which of four possible targets (that is, the actual target plus three decoys) is most similar to the images they experienced. By chance, one would expect a hit-rate of 25 per cent but an early review of this literature by Honorton (1978) claimed that 23 of 42 experiments using this technique had produced significantly higher hit rates.

This replication rate of 55 per cent across studies is well in excess of what would be expected purely on the basis of chance, but it has not gone unchallenged. See Hyman's (1985a, 1985b) challenge to Honorton (1978).

HOW SCIENCE WORKS

Hyman's (1985a, 1985b) challenge to Honorton (1978)

Hyman (1985a, 1985b) reviewed the same studies much more critically. For example, he pointed out that the replication rate depended upon what one was willing to count as a replication. One study which had been counted as a successful replication included twelve experiments, only one of which produced significant results. Hyman's estimate of the replication rate was 30 per cent. He also criticized the use of different criteria for scoring hits across studies, increasing the probability of obtaining spuriously significant effects, as well as noting procedural flaws, such as inappropriate randomization, statistical errors, including the actual target picture in the set to be judged rather than a duplicate (signs of wear could influence judges), and insufficient details of procedure.

Honorton (1985) responded to Hyman's critique, but the overall outcome was very constructive. The following year, Hyman and Honorton (1986) issued a joint communiqué in which they outlined the points upon which they agreed and disagreed:

'We agree that there is an overall significant effect in this data base that cannot reasonably be explained by selective reporting or multiple analysis. We continue to differ over the degree to which the effect constitutes evidence for psi, but we agree that the final verdict awaits the outcome of future experiments conducted by a broader range of investigators and according to more stringent standards.'

The stringent standards which they spelled out in the report were summarized (see Table 14.2) and elaborated by Bem and Honorton (1994) as follows:

- *Strict security precautions against sensory leakage* – In order to conclude that information has been transmitted telepathically, it is essential that the possibility of information transfer via the known senses is strictly excluded. Sensory leakage refers to experimental situations where information might 'leak' via normal sensory channels. Some commentators have suggested that this might happen sometimes in Ganzfeld studies (e.g. Wiseman *et al.* 1996).

- *Testing and documentation of randomization methods for selecting targets and sequencing the judging pool* – Proper randomization of the selection of targets for use in ESP studies and for presenting items for judging is essential because any departure from true

randomness may bias results. For example, if such a non-random bias were to result in targets always being presented as either the second or third choice out of four (people have a natural tendency to avoid picking the end choices, French 1992), this would artefactually inflate the hit rate. Therefore the random sequences used must be generated properly and then shown to be truly random.

- *Statistical correction for multiple analyses* – If no such correction is made for the fact that data have been analysed in several different ways prior to obtaining a significant effect, this will lead to the reporting of spuriously significant results.

- *Advance specification of the status of the experiment* – Pilot testing is a standard part of experimental psychology and parapsychology when setting up a formal study. It allows the investigator to check out all procedures and equipment prior to the commencement of formal testing. However, unless it is clear in advance whether a particular experiment was intended to be a pilot study or a formal confirmatory experiment, the investigator may be tempted to ignore (rightly) results of pilot experiments which fail to obtain significant results but to report (wrongly) the results of pilot testing which produces significant results, without making it clear that the results are from a pilot study.

- *Full documentation in the published report of the experimental procedures* – This is essential if independent researchers are going to have the information they need to attempt replications.

HOW SCIENCE WORKS

Meta-analyses of ganzfeld studies

Key research: Milton and Wiseman (1999)

Meta-analysis is often used in science to evaluate controversial claims. In a meta-analysis, the basic unit of analysis is a whole experiment. Relevant experiments can be coded in various ways such as in terms of size, quality, and so on, to allow conclusions to be drawn regarding not only whether the data base as a whole yields significant effects overall, but also whether positive outcomes are related to other factors. Milton and Wiseman (1999) published a meta-analysis of 30 ganzfeld studies carried out in seven independent laboratories according to the same stringent guidelines as those used by Bem and Honorton (1994). The studies started in 1987 and were all published by February 1997. The combined data set consisted of 1198 individual trials. Participants were found not to score above chance expectation. In other words, in this meta-analysis, participants did not achieve overall more hits than would be expected on the basis of guesswork. As is often the case within parapsychology, however, there is a sting in the tail. The cut-off date of February

1997, which was set in advance by Milton and Wiseman, meant that at least one large-scale study with positive results was not included in the meta-analysis. If it had been, the overall effect would have actually reached statistical significance.

Some commentators (e.g. Bem *et al.* 2001) have argued that Milton and Wiseman's (1999) meta-analysis did not find a significant overall effect because it failed to distinguish between proof-oriented studies employing the more 'standard' ganzfeld set-up and more exploratory process-oriented studies attempting to assess the effects of varying experimental factors. It is claimed that the former 'standard' studies did produce significant results but that the latter often failed to do so. However, a review by Palmer (2003) acknowledges that it is still unclear why there is such variability in results across studies. The conditions required to establish a reliably positive outcome in ganzfeld studies have yet to be specified.

■ *The status of statistical tests* – Sometimes, when a researcher fails to obtain an anticipated significant result from the statistical analysis that was initially planned, they may be tempted to try analysing the data in alternative ways (e.g. using alternative statistical tests, removing 'outliers', etc.). While such practices are common and generally acceptable, it is good practice to make clear to readers exactly what was done. If the main planned analysis fails to reveal significant results, this weakens the strength of the evidence presented, even if some significant effects are found with later tests. Although the latter may be suggestive of interesting effects, one would want to confirm that such effects were real by carrying out follow-up studies.

- Strict security precautions against sensory leakage.
- Testing and documentation of randomization methods for selecting targets and sequencing the judging pool.
- Statistical correction for multiple analyses.
- Advance specification of the status of the experiment.
- Full documentation in the published report of the experimental procedures.
- The status of statistical tests.

Table 14.2 *Summary of the stringent standards recommended by Hyman and Honorton (1986) as summarized by Bem and Honorton (1994).*

IDA   Approaches

The ganzfeld experiments illustrate the fact that many techniques within modern parapsychology adopt a **cognitive** approach. ESP, if it exists, is seen as being simply another type of information processing and many parapsychological experiments are similar in rationale and methodology to standard cognitive experiments, the only difference being that all normal modes of information transfer are excluded.

STRETCH AND CHALLENGE

Other ways of testing for telepathy

There are other ways of testing for telepathy than the ganzfeld procedure. Rupert Sheldrake's website (http://www.sheldrake.org/homepage.html) includes many different online tests of telepathy that you could try with friends. What problems might arise with respect to collecting valid data via such online experiments?

In 1983, Honorton and colleagues began work using an improved version of the ganzfeld technique which they called the **autoganzfeld**. Essentially, they attempted to avoid all of the methodological problems identified by Hyman and others and introduced the innovations of computer control of the experimental procedure to minimize human bias, and the use of video clips as targets. Bem and Honorton (1994) reviewed the results of 11 new autoganzfeld studies carried out by Honorton, which they claimed provided strong and replicable evidence for 'an anomalous process of information transfer' – in other words, ESP. They acknowledged, however, that the final verdict would await the results of replication attempts by a broad range of independent investigators. See *Meta-analyses of ganzfeld studies* (p.481) for the results of subsequent investigations using the ganzfeld technique.

Studies of psychokinesis

If macro-PK existed, it ought to be very easy to demonstrate it under controlled conditions, but to date there is no compelling evidence that this has occurred. Instead, many mediums and psychics have been caught red-handed engaged in trickery, or else they have simply refused to be tested under properly controlled conditions (French 1996b; Hyman 1985a). Attention has thus focused instead on the more subtle micro-PK effects. Such experiments often involve asking participants to influence the output of a random-event generator (REG). An REG is a device which produces an output, based, for example, upon radioactive decay or electronic noise, that is intended to be truly random. This output can be displayed in various ways to provide feedback to the participant, such as by using a binary random output to determine if a point on a computer screen goes up or down as it traverses from left to right. The effects reported in such studies are tiny but, because this technique allows large data sets to be accumulated very quickly, they are often highly statistically significant.

The use of REGs in PK research was originally championed by Schmidt (1973) and subsequently by Jahn and colleagues (2000). Alcock (1990) criticized Schmidt's research programme on a number of grounds, including the fact that Schmidt's research programme was unusually disjointed (varying across experiments in terms of type of REG employed, type of feedback and task instructions given, and type of participant employed, including both humans and non-humans), as well as his failure to apply consistently proper randomization checks to his target series. Meta-analyses of the results of PK studies have produced conflicting results. Meta-analyses by Radin and Nelson (1989), Radin (1997), and Radin and Nelson (2003) appeared to support the existence of a real PK effect, both in studies using dice-throwing and REG studies. The most recent meta-analysis of this literature by Bösch *et al.* (2006) came to a very different conclusion.

Meta-analyses of PK studies

Bösch *et al.* (2006) criticized previous meta-analyses (e.g. Radin and Nelson 1989; Radin 1997; Radin and Nelson 2003) which had concluded that REG studies demonstrated a PK effect. From their own meta-analysis of 380 REG-PK studies, Bosch *et al.* concluded that there appeared to be a very small but significant overall effect which, 'even if incredibly small, is of great fundamental importance'. However, they also noted that 'study effect sizes were strongly and inversely related to sample size and were extremely heterogeneous'. They argued that the most parsimonious explanation for their results was in fact in terms of publication bias, with early small-scale studies producing large significant effects that were not replicated by subsequent large-scale studies. In other words, the apparent PK effect was not real but was, instead, an artefact of publication practices.

Evaluation of issues relating to ganzfeld studies of ESP and psychokinesis

- *Disagreement over Ganzfeld studies of ESP* – Data from the ganzfeld and autoganzfeld studies of ESP are often highlighted as being amongst the strongest sources of evidence for the existence of telepathy. Bem and Honorton's (1994) meta-analysis of results from studies using the improved autoganzfeld technique concluded that 'an anomalous process of information transfer' had been demonstrated. However, a meta-analysis by Milton and Wiseman (1999) of subsequent studies using this technique failed to find evidence of ESP. The ongoing controversy relating to this evidence highlights the strengths and limitations of meta-analysis. Decisions relating to the coding of the information entered into a meta-analysis can have a major effect upon the results obtained.

- *Disagreement over studies of psychokinesis (PK)* – Claims relating to macro-PK have failed to convince the wider scientific community mainly because such effects can be reproduced by conjurors using non-paranormal techniques and have never been demonstrated convincingly under controlled conditions that would effectively rule out such non-paranormal explanations. Evidence from micro-PK studies (e.g. using REGs) has generally been judged to be stronger. These studies have been criticized on methodological grounds (e.g. Alcock 1990) but others have argued, on the basis of meta-analyses, that PK effects have indeed been demonstrated (e.g. Radin 1997). However, these meta-analyses were strongly criticized by Bösch *et al.* (2006). Their own analysis suggested that a small but significant effect was to be found in the database but that it was more likely to be the result of publication bias rather than a genuine PK effect, once again highlighting the fact that meta-analyses of the same research literature can sometimes lead to dramatically different conclusions.

- *Experimenter effects in parapsychology* – Within science generally, **experimenter effects** are seen as undesirable. Such a situation is common within parapsychology and has a number of possible explanations (Smith 2003). Those with a positive attitude towards the possibility that paranormal forces exist tend to be more likely to get significant results than those who are more sceptical. If paranormal forces really do exist, experimenter effects within parapsychology may be a result of pro-paranormal researchers communicating this positive attitude to their participants, thus affecting their performance, or it may even be that the experimenters' own paranormal influence plays a part. If, on the other hand, paranormal forces do not exist, experimenter effects may reflect procedural sloppiness or even deliberate fraud on the part of pro-paranormal experimenters.

CHECK YOUR UNDERSTANDING

Check your understanding of theoretical and methodological issues in the study of anomalous experience by answering these questions from memory. Check your answers by looking back through Topic 1, Theoretical and methodological issues in the study of anomalous experience.

1. What is the main aim of anomalistic psychology?

2. Define parapsychology.

3. Name and define the three different types of ESP.

4. What is the difference between macro-PK and micro-PK?

5. What are the main characteristics of pseudoscience?

6. Assess the scientific status of parapsychology.

7. Describe two examples of fraud within parapsychology.

8. Why is it a good idea to make use of the expertise of conjurors when testing psychic claimants?

9. Outline the ganzfeld procedure, including the rationale behind the technique.

10. By consulting published research on the Internet, outline the procedure and findings of two studies using the ganzfeld procedure and two studies of psychokineses.

11. What are experimenter effects within parapsychology and how might they be explained?

12. Evaluate the evidence for the existence of PK obtained from studies using REGs.

Psychology in context — Superstitions and sense of control

Research shows that groups with the highest levels of superstitious belief tend to be those for whom the success or failure of their activities can often be affected by events outside of their direct control, such as politicians, actors, soldiers, fisherman, gamblers, students doing exams, and sports stars. Superstitions provide at least an illusory sense of control and may, in sports for example, actually aid performance by providing a calming mental focus prior to a game. Tennis champion, Goran Ivanisevic, attributed his success at Wimbledon in 2001 partly to the complex superstitious rituals he followed during the tournament, including starting the day with an episode of *Teletubbies*, eating a specific menu (soup, lamb cutlets and chips), refusing to shave or cut his hair, and banning female family members from watching him play. Of course, if performers are prevented from engaging in their favourite ritual for some reason, this may have the opposite effect, resulting in a self-fulfilling prophecy. Thus, Serena Williams knew exactly why she failed to win the 2007 French Open: 'I didn't tie my laces right and I didn't bounce the ball five times and I didn't bring my shower sandals to the court with me' (MacGregor 2008).

Are you aware of any idiosyncratic superstitious habits that you or people close to you have adopted? Have you noticed an increased tendency to engage in superstitious behaviour when control of a situation is difficult?

Goran Ivanisevic, who partly attributes his success at Wimbledon 2001 to his superstitious rituals.

STRETCH AND CHALLENGE

Activity — Hearing voices

Consider what factors determine how a person interprets the experience of hearing voices and the way in which such reports are treated by others. Why is it that sometimes such reports are taken as indicating psychic ability (as in mediums allegedly talking to the dead), sometimes as indicating a religious experience (as in talking to God), and sometimes as an indication of psychopathology (as in schizophrenia)? How relevant are context and culture to such issues?

If paranormal forces really do exist, then many anomalous experiences that people report would obviously be best explained in paranormal terms. However, as discussed above, the scientific evidence put forward in support of psi is far from overwhelming. For this reason, many psychologists have considered the possibility that anomalous experiences might be explicable without having to invoke paranormal forces. This section considers some of the wide range of psychological factors that may be of relevance in helping us to understand anomalous experiences. It goes on to discuss some of the functions that paranormal and related beliefs may serve, at both the individual and group level. The section concludes with some discussion of the psychology of deception and self-deception, superstition and coincidence.

Cognitive, personality and biological factors underlying anomalous experience and paranormal belief

A wide range of different factors have been considered as possibly playing a role in causing anomalous experiences. This section will focus on some of the cognitive, personality and biological factors that have been investigated.

While each factor will be discussed separately, it is important to recognize that all three are related in complex ways.

Research into cognitive factors

A considerable amount of research has explored the possibility that cognitive biases may sometimes lead people to misinterpret experiences as necessarily involving the operation of paranormal forces, when in fact they are better explained in non-paranormal terms (for reviews, see French 1992; French and Wilson 2007). For example, poor or faulty reasoning may lead people to draw invalid conclusions from available evidence. One example of a potentially relevant cognitive bias is our tendency to make errors on certain types of deductive reasoning tasks known as **syllogistic reasoning**, a type of reasoning in which conclusions are drawn which logically follow from other given statements (known as premises) if those statements are true. An example of an invalid syllogism which some people would accept as valid is as follows:

> If this psychic is genuine then they will be able to describe my personality accurately.
>
> This psychic can describe my personality accurately.
>
> Therefore, this psychic is genuine.

As we will see later, there are other ways besides genuine psychic ability for a psychic reading to be accurate. Wierzbicki (1985) was the first to present evidence suggesting that believers in the paranormal may be worse on such reasoning tasks than non-believers. Since then, numerous investigators have replicated this finding (e.g. Roberts and Seager 1999). As French and Wilson (2007) conclude their review of the relevant literature, believers in the paranormal also 'have a more distorted concept of randomness leading them to see meaning where there is none, are more susceptible to experiencing anomalous sensations and are, in certain circumstances, more suggestible.'

Although there is now considerable evidence supporting the idea that some supposedly paranormal experiences can be adequately explained in terms of the effects of cognitive biases upon perception, memory and judgement, there is considerable variability in findings in this area. It should also be borne in mind that the generally negative picture to emerge of paranormal believers from this research may well be related to the fact that most of the investigations have been carried out by anomalistic psychologists who themselves tend to be sceptical regarding the paranormal. It is possible that sceptics may also demonstrate cognitive biases under certain conditions, but this is a topic which has to date received little research attention.

Research into personality factors

A number of personality variables have been shown to correlate with paranormal belief and the tendency to report paranormal experiences (e.g. Irwin 1993; Irwin and Watt 2007). For example, numerous studies have shown a correlation between **schizotypy** and paranormal belief/experience (e.g. Goulding 2004, 2005; Irwin and Green 1998–1999; Thalbourne 1994, 1998; Thalbourne et al. 1995; Thalbourne and French 1995; Williams and Irwin 1991). Schizotypy refers to the tendency to experience milder sub-clinical forms of symptoms associated with schizophrenia such as magical thinking and unusual experiences, such as hallucinations or bizarre interpretations of events. Several other factors generally associated with poor psychological health have also been shown to correlate with paranormal belief and anomalous experience, including tendency towards bipolar (manic)

Non-conscious processing and ostensibly paranormal experiences

Sometimes when we have to make a decision, we feel a strong urge to go with one particular course of action for reasons that we cannot put into words. We just feel we are acting on a hunch. Men may prefer to call it 'gut instinct' where women may opt for 'female intuition'. If our choice turns out to be the right one, we may even take that as evidence of some kind of psychic ability. One alternative explanation is that our decision may have been influenced by information that we had actually been exposed to but had not processed consciously.

This possibility was investigated in an experiment carried out by Crawley et al. (2002). Participants in this study were under the impression that they were taking part in a computerized test of ESP requiring them to guess which symbol the computer would randomly select on each trial. Participants were not aware that on half of the trials the correct answer was subliminally presented to them by flashing it up on the screen so briefly that it could not consciously be perceived. As with all studies involving subliminal processing, great care was taken to ensure that the subliminal stimuli really were unavailable to consciousness by carrying out awareness checks as a second phase in the experiment.

All participants also completed a scale designed to measure **transliminality**, a concept proposed by parapsychologist Michael Thalbourne and most recently described by him as heightened sensitivity to psychological material originating in the unconscious or the external environment (Thalbourne and Maltby 2008). On primed trials, transliminality scores correlated with the number of hits obtained on the 'ESP guessing' task, but no such correlation was found for the unprimed trials. It would therefore be quite reasonable for high transliminals to consider the possibility that their higher than expected scores might be due to genuine ESP ability as they would be unaware of the real reason for their performance. Transliminality is highly correlated with paranormal belief/experience.

depression (see Chapter 10, p.331) (Thalbourne and French 1995) and tendency to dissociate (e.g. French et al. 2008; Irwin 1994). Dissociation refers to the tendency for different aspects of consciousness which are usually integrated (e.g. thoughts, feeling, memories, sense of identity) to become disrupted. The correlations reported are, however, not high and it would be a gross over-simplification to equate reports of seemingly paranormal experiences with mental illness. Furthermore, there are also positive psychological correlates of paranormal belief and experience, such as creativity and reduced fear of death (e.g. Irwin 1993; Irwin and Watt 2007).

Approaches

An **evolutionary approach** allows us to answer the question of why our cognitive systems are affected by biases, some of which may underlie paranormal beliefs and experiences. At first sight, it may appear that evolution should have favoured cognitive systems that are not susceptible to such biases. But in terms of evolutionary survival, a cognitive system that operates upon the basis of heuristics (i.e. rules of thumb) and quickly comes to decisions that are *usually* right is likely to be favoured over a much slower system that is right a little more often.

One personality feature which has been the focus of a great deal of interest is that of fantasy proneness (e.g. Lynn and Rhue 1988; Rhue and Lynn 1987; Wilson and Barber 1983). Fantasy prone personalities show high levels of hypnotic susceptibility and, as the name suggests, have rich fantasy lives. They have very vivid imaginations and

Activity **Are UFO abductees and contactees fantasy prone?**

The biographical approach adopted by Bartholomew *et al.* (1991) to answer the above question illustrates the wide range of techniques that can be used to investigate hypotheses within anomalistic psychology. Essentially, these investigators carried out content analysis of 'biographies' of 152 abductees and contactees to determine how many of them showed evidence of the typical characteristics of the fantasy prone personality as originally described by Wilson and Barber (1983). These include such characteristics as hypnotic susceptibility, self-reported psychic ability, healing, out-of-body experiences, religious visions and apparitional experiences. The biographies analysed ranged from a single paragraph to several volumes. The analysis revealed that 132 of the 152 cases showed evidence of one or more of the major characteristics of fantasy proneness.

In your judgement, how much potential is there for subjective bias in this approach?

UFO

sometimes confuse reality and imagination. Fantasy proneness has been shown to correlate reliably with paranormal belief and reports of anomalous experiences (Irwin 1990, 1991). French (1993) and French and Wilson (2006) have highlighted the fact that many of the variables that correlate with paranormal belief and experience, such as fantasy proneness and dissociativity, also correlate with susceptibility to false memories, raising the possibility that at least some reports of allegedly paranormal experiences may be based upon false memories. Recent experiments provide support for this hypothesis (e.g. Clancy *et al.* 2002; Wilson and French 2006).

Fantasy proneness has received considerable attention as a possible factor underlying claims of alien contact and abduction (e.g. Clancy 2005; French 2001b; French *et al.* 2008; Holden and French 2002). Interestingly, studies which have adopted a biographical analysis approach (Bartholomew *et al.* 1991) have tended to conclude that contactees and abductees do indeed show typical characteristics of fantasy proneness. However, with few exceptions (French *et al.* 2008), studies which have employed standard scales to assess fantasy proneness have usually failed to find significant differences between such claimants and control groups (Spanos *et al.* 1993). This may reflect nothing more than the transparency of typical fantasy proneness scales and the fact that alien abductees and contactees are unlikely to complete questionnaires in a way that implies that they have over-active imaginations.

Research into biological factors

Unusual activity in the temporal lobes of the brain is associated with a variety of anomalous experiences. As discussed below, there is clear evidence that unusual activity in the temporal lobes of the brain plays an important role in out-of-body and near-death experiences (e.g. Blackmore 1993, 1996b; French 2005). Persinger and colleagues claim to have induced a variety of anomalous experiences, including a 'sense of presence' (Cook and Persinger 1997, 2001) and even a full-blown apparitional experience (Persinger *et al.* 2000), by exposing the temporal lobes of the brain to transcerebral complex magnetic fields using a purpose-built helmet device. Individuals scoring highly on Makarec and Persinger's (1990) Temporal Lobe Signs (TLS) scale are said to be particularly susceptible to such electromagnetically induced anomalous experiences. Granqvist *et al.* (2005) reported the only direct attempt to replicate such effects to date. However, these investigators failed to find any relationship between transcerebral stimulation and anomalous experiences, arguing instead that such reports were explicable in terms of suggestibility.

Another example of how biological factors can explain a range of anomalous experiences is the phenomenon of sleep paralysis (French and Santomauro 2007; Santomauro and French, in press). In its most basic form, sleep paralysis is very common and refers to a situation where someone is half-asleep and realizes that they cannot move. However, about five per cent of the population also experience (at least once in their lives) sleep paralysis with accompanying symptoms, such as visual hallucinations (e.g. monstrous figures or lights moving around), auditory hallucinations (e.g. voices, footsteps, or mechanical sounds), a strong sense of presence, difficulty breathing and intense fear. Sleep paralysis episodes are known to play an important role in alleged nocturnal spiritual encounters and alien abduction claims (e.g. Clancy 2005; French 2001b; Holden and French 2002). During REM-stage sleep, the muscles of the body are relaxed, presumably to prevent one from physically acting out one's dreams. Physiologically, sleep paralysis appears to be an abnormal state involving aspects of both REM-sleep and normal waking consciousness. Subjectively, the temporarily paralysed sufferer experiences dream imagery combined with normal sensory input. Although often terrifying, sleep paralysis episodes are usually brief and harmless.

One explanation for alien abduction claims is sleep paralysis.

Evaluation of research into cognitive, personality and biological factors underlying anomalous experience

- *The psychological profile of typical paranormal believers* – Research into cognitive, personality and biological factors allows us to describe the psychological profile of the 'typical believer' in the paranormal. Such a person would tend to be somewhat poorer than average with regard to some types of reasoning and possibly influenced by information that they had processed non-consciously. They would tend to score higher than average on such factors as schizotypy, tendency to dissociate, and fantasy proneness. They may also suffer from sleep paralysis and be susceptible to unusual activity in the temporal lobes of the brain. However, it must be emphasized that such differences are not pronounced and only show up in group comparisons between those high and low in terms of paranormal belief. It is probable that the profile would be more likely to be found in those who report personal experience of the supposedly paranormal as opposed to believing in the paranormal for other reasons (e.g. belief based upon stories in the media).

- *Implications for the psi hypothesis* – Although such findings are consistent with a sceptical perspective that assumes seemingly paranormal experiences are purely psychological in origin, other interpretations are possible. For example, it may be that genuinely paranormal phenomena really do occur but that one has to have the type of psychological profile described in order to be 'open' to them.

- *Cause or effect* – Alternatively, the psychological profile noted may be a consequence (not a cause) of apparently paranormal experiences, which would again leave open the question of whether or not the explanation for such experiences was purely psychological or whether genuine paranormal forces were involved (if indeed such forces exist). Such questions could, in principle, be answered by longitudinal research strategies that followed the psychological development of individuals to see if the psychological profile typically exists prior to experiences of an allegedly paranormal nature or is produced by such experiences.

Functions of paranormal and related beliefs

Paranormal belief is not unidimensional. Different types of paranormal belief are likely to serve different psychological functions and, indeed, the same paranormal belief may serve different functions for different individuals. Zusne and Jones (1989), amongst others, argued that paranormal belief is one aspect of a broader world-view which has been adopted in order to make sense of the world, in the same way that religious beliefs do for some people. One common theme that runs through the literature on the functions of paranormal and related beliefs is the need for a sense of control over the essential unpredictability of life (Irwin 1993). The way in which superstitious beliefs may serve this function for people generally is described later in this chapter, but the following section considers the possibility that for some people the tendency towards paranormal beliefs may develop from and be maintained by the need for a sense of control that originates during the experiencing of childhood trauma.

Functional significance of paranormal beliefs

Lindeman (1998) argued that paranormal and pseudoscientific beliefs are the result of the interplay between basic social motives and our everyday mode of thinking. The basic social motives she refers to are widely accepted as being important in the maintenance of psychological health: our need to understand ourselves and the world around us, to have a sense of control over

events, to feel part of a community, to feel that the world is benevolent, and to maintain self-esteem. A paranormal world-view serves many of these basic functions somewhat more readily than a scientific world-view. Following Epstein (1994) and others, Lindeman (1998) made a distinction between two basic modes of thought. One mode of thinking, that of rational thought, is slow, deliberate, unemotional and generally accurate. It is a relatively recent development in evolutionary terms. However, for most of our everyday lives, during which we have to make quick decisions based upon incomplete information, we rely upon experiential thinking. This is an evolutionarily more primitive mode of thought, which is rapid, automatic, and influenced by emotions. Furthermore, beliefs based upon experiential thinking are much more resistant to change than those based upon rational thinking. According to Lindeman, paranormal and related beliefs are usually based upon experiential thinking. We will focus in this section (and in the subsequent section on superstition) on the way in which paranormal and related beliefs might serve to give us a sense of control, albeit illusory, and help us to cope with life's uncertainties.

As one fascinating example of this, Irwin (1992) demonstrated a link between paranormal belief and reports of childhood trauma, an association which has been replicated in several subsequent studies (Lawrence *et al.* 1995). Fantasy proneness is also known to be associated with reports of a traumatic childhood and it has been argued that fantasy proneness may develop as a psychological defence mechanism (Lynn and Rhue 1988; Rhue and Lynn 1987), with the child attempting to escape from harsh reality into a fantasy world where he or she has at least the illusion of control. Similarly, dissociativity is also known to correlate with reports of childhood trauma (Mulder *et al.* 1998) and it has again been argued that dissociation may provide a psychological escape from the harsh reality of a traumatic childhood.

Perkins and Allen (2006) predicted that individuals reporting a history of physical abuse during childhood would show higher levels of belief in paranormal phenomena for which previous research had suggested that the beliefs in question were associated with a sense of personal efficacy and control (e.g. psi, precognition and spiritualism) but not for others (e.g. extraordinary life forms). They assessed paranormal belief using Tobacyk's (2004) Revised Paranormal Belief Scale, a widely used measure of paranormal belief which, in addition to providing a global measure of paranormal belief, also provides a number of sub-scale scores measuring belief in different paranormal phenomena. History of childhood physical abuse was assessed using the Assessing Environments III Questionnaire (Berger and Knutson 1984), a retrospective self-report measure assessing childhood trauma events. In general, the results were in line with the hypothesis, with those reporting a history of childhood physical abuse scoring higher on control-related beliefs but not others.

The idea that paranormal belief is associated with an illusory sense of control is supported by a number of empirical studies using a range of different approaches (Blackmore and Troscianko 1985; Brugger *et al.* 1991; Rudski 2004). Blackmore and Troscianko, for example, had participants engage in a computerized coin-tossing task. Even on blocks of trials where it was impossible to exert any influence over the result of the coin toss, believers in the paranormal tended to feel that they were exerting some control.

The relationship between paranormal beliefs and the need for control is also supported by a number of studies that show a general trend for such beliefs to correlate with an external locus of control (Dag 1999; Irwin, 1986a; Tobacyk and Tobacyk 1992). Individuals with an external locus of control tend to feel that events in their lives are largely the result of external forces beyond their control, whereas those with an internal locus of control believe such events to be largely dependent upon their own decisions and actions. It is impossible to determine from the results of such correlational studies whether paranormal beliefs are a consequence of innate differences in locus of control or vice versa.

Cultural significance of paranormal beliefs

The relationship between culture and paranormal beliefs is reciprocal. It is a truism to state that the particular types of paranormal belief that an individual adopts will be influenced by exposure to their own particular wider culture (e.g. Alcock 1981; Irwin and Watt 2007). This exposure will come from various sources such as family members, peers, religious leaders and, in industrialized societies, the media. Many such beliefs will be based upon the teachings of influential members of that particular society and those teachings will often be based upon the personal anomalous experiences of the opinion leaders involved. Often, the views expressed will serve to reinforce wider belief systems such as religions (especially with respect to life after death) or New Age philosophies. Personal anomalous experiences themselves appear to be shaped to some extent by the culture in which they occur. One example of this is that when individuals report encounters with spiritual beings during a near-death experience, they almost always report beings that are consistent with their own culture's religion. For example, Christians do not encounter Hindu gods and vice versa (Blackmore 1993).

Illusory control and paranormal belief

Key research: Blackmore and Troscianko (1985)

Blackmore and Troscianko (1985) asked participants to take part in a computerized coin-tossing task in which they were to try to make a simulated 'coin' fall as either heads or tails with control exerted via a push-button. Unbeknownst to the participants, they could in fact only influence the outcome on half of the trials, the outcome being randomly determined on the other half. As predicted, believers in the paranormal believed themselves to be exerting more control than the disbelievers, even on trials where no control was possible. Paradoxically, however, the believers' retrospective estimates of their scores on the task were

lower than those of the disbelievers. This apparent paradox was resolved by asking participants for estimates of the score they would expect just by chance. Whereas the disbelievers were relatively accurate at estimating their chance scores, the believers significantly underestimated what their scores should be, leading them to conclude erroneously that their chance level performance was actually evidence that they had exerted some control. This was a novel way to examine these issues and provided evidence in support of the notion that both illusory control and poor understanding of probability underlie paranormal belief.

The influence of belief upon reincarnation claims

A strong argument can be made that apparent memories of past lives, whether spontaneously recalled or 'recovered' by the use of hypnotic regression, are almost certainly false memories based upon cultural beliefs and expectations (e.g. Edwards 1996; French 2003; Spanos 1996). Spontaneous past-life memories always correspond to the cultural expectations of the society in which they occur. For example, if the religion of a particular culture maintains that individuals never change gender between different incarnations, this is what is found. In other cultures without this belief, cross-gender reincarnations may well be reported. Spanos *et al.* (1991) demonstrated similar effects in a study of hypnotic past-life regression. Whether or not reincarnation is real, it is likely to have psychological benefits for those that believe in it including reduced fear of death, helping to cope with bereavement, and increased social cohesion.

Ethics: Challenging cherished beliefs

Given that paranormal and related beliefs often seem to serve beneficial psychological functions for those that adopt them, is it ethically justified for psychologists to challenge such beliefs? Most scientists would probably answer this question affirmatively, arguing that science is more concerned with the quest for truth rather than happiness based upon unfounded beliefs.

Cultural bias: Is Western science biased against parapsychology?

Many parapsychologists would probably answer this question positively, agreeing with Milton's (1994) assertion 'that there are legitimate areas of scientific research that are being neglected for non-scientific reasons; that a subtle form of scientific censorship is being applied to such research; and that, as a result, important scientific discoveries may be ignored, or even lost to us entirely.' The prevalent belief amongst scientists that parapsychology is a pseudoscience may be an example of such bias. Of course, even if such a bias does exist, it does not follow automatically that paranormal forces really do exist, but the appropriate attitude to adopt to paranormal claims is the same as that to any other scientific claim: one of open-minded scepticism.

Evaluation of research into the functions and cultural significance of paranormal beliefs

- *Paranormal belief and lack of control* – Providing a sense of control in an unpredictable universe appears to be one of the psychological functions of belief in the paranormal. Data supporting this hypothesis come from a wide variety of different approaches, ranging from experimental tasks to personality measures.

- *Paranormal belief and childhood trauma* – A number of studies have also reported an association between reports of traumatic childhood, fantasy proneness, dissociativity and paranormal belief experience. This pattern of findings is consistent with theories of paranormal belief that maintain that fantasy proneness and dissociativity develop as psychological defence mechanisms to deal with the stress of childhood trauma, resulting in a psychological profile that is susceptible to hallucinations and false memories. However, alternative interpretations of this pattern of findings are possible.

- *Reciprocal relationship between paranormal beliefs and culture* – The surrounding culture directly influences the particular beliefs that an individual is likely to adopt simply through direct instruction, and the adoption of those beliefs is likely to reinforce the believer's sense of belonging to a particular culture. In turn, the belief system adopted is likely to have an influence upon aspects of certain common anomalous experiences (such as sleep paralysis episodes, near-death experiences, or past-life memories). The relationship between paranormal beliefs and experiences and the particular culture in which they are found is clearly reciprocal.

- *Positive aspects of paranormal and related beliefs* – Although evidence suggests that, in general, there are modest but significant correlations between various measures of psychopathological tendencies and paranormal beliefs/experiences, this should not be taken as necessarily implying that paranormal beliefs do not serve positive psychological functions. As indicated above, paranormal and related beliefs may help people in numerous ways, such as to find meaning in their lives, cope with stressful situations by providing an illusory sense of control, and reduce fear of death. However, none of these benefits are of any relevance to assessing whether the beliefs themselves are actually true.

Deception, self-deception, superstition and coincidence

We have already seen how fraud on the part of psychic claimants of various kinds has plagued the history of parapsychology, and we have discussed the need for professional conjurors to take part in testing such claimants. The techniques of the professional conjuror are also relevant to those with an interest in the actual psychology of deception, as conjurors base their art of 'honest deception' upon a keen appreciation of lay psychology. The same applies, of course, to professional con artists. Many of the same psychological processes that allow us to be fooled by others are also responsible for our susceptibility to self-deception, superstitious thinking and our fascination with coincidences.

Deception and self-deception

Anomalistic psychologists believe that many seemingly paranormal experiences can be explained in terms of deception and self-deception (e.g. Alcock 1981; French 1992; Gilovich 1991; Sutherland 1992; Wiseman 1997). In both cases, we may draw the wrong conclusions from available evidence because of our reliance upon cognitive heuristics that are prone to systematic error. One of the most pervasive cognitive biases that has been identified is that of **confirmation bias**, defined by Nickerson (1998) as 'the seeking or interpreting of evidence in ways that are partial to existing beliefs, expectations, or a hypothesis in hand'. Similarly, Marks (2000) referred to **subjective validation** which he describes thus: 'This occurs when two unrelated events are perceived to be related because a belief, expectancy, or hypothesis demands or requires a relationship'.

Such biases are likely to come into play when a believer in the paranormal is evaluating a reading that supposedly applies to them uniquely. Often the statements in such readings are of a kind that will give rise to a phenomenon known as the **Barnum effect**. This refers to the tendency for people to accept vague, ambiguous and general statements as descriptive of their unique personalities, even though in fact they apply to virtually everybody (for reviews, see Dickson and Kelly 1985; Furnham and Schofield 1987; Snyder, Shenkel and Lowery 1977). Typical Barnum statements include, 'You have a great deal of unused capacity which you have not used to your advantage', 'While you have some personality weaknesses, you are generally able to compensate for them' and, 'You have found it unwise to be too frank in revealing yourself to others'. The Barnum effect is one element of a technique known as **cold reading**, which enables deliberate con artists to give the impression that they know all about complete strangers whom they have never met before (Hyman 1977; Rowland 2002). This does not mean that all self-professed psychics and astrologers are deliberate con artists. It is likely that many of them are making use of the same strategies as deliberate cold readers without realizing it, thus fooling themselves as well as their clients.

HOW SCIENCE WORKS

Magicians in the laboratory

Conjurors are experts at exploiting the foibles of human cognition in order to amaze spectators with feats that apparently defy the laws of physics and bear a striking resemblance to similar exploits performed by psychics allegedly using psychic powers. Psychologists have recently begun to study the techniques used by conjurors to achieve their effects (Lamont and Wiseman 1999; Macknik *et al*. 2008). One example of this is a study by Wiseman and Greening (2005) investigating eyewitness testimony for apparent psychokinetic metal-bending. They presented participants with a video of an alleged psychic apparently bending a key in the way made famous by Uri Geller. Once the key had been bent by sleight of hand and was put down in full view on a table, half of the participants heard the 'psychic' suggest that the key was still bending while the other half were not presented with this suggestion. Around 40 per cent of the participants who heard the suggestion reported that they thought the key did indeed continue to bend whereas virtually none of the participants in the other condition did so. This reinforces findings relating to the unreliability of eyewitness testimony that Wiseman and colleagues have found in previous studies using faked séances (Wiseman *et al*. 2003).

IDA Approaches: Cognitive psychology and paranormal experiences

Most cognitive psychologists agree that we rely upon a mental model of the world around us and of our place in it in order to interact with our surroundings. This model is constantly updated on the basis of input from our senses (bottom-up information) interacting with our stored knowledge, beliefs and expectations about the world (top-down influences). Top-down influences will have the strongest effect upon our interpretation of our surroundings when sensory input is ambiguous or degraded in some way. Many examples of allegedly paranormal experiences involve such degraded or ambiguous information, meaning that our prior beliefs about the paranormal are likely to influence what we perceive and remember.

Activity Satanic messages in rock music?

One of the most impressive demonstrations of the power of top-down processing relates to the claim made by some American fundamentalist Christians that rock music contains subliminal satanic messages that can only be heard when the music is played backwards. They allege that the messages can still influence behaviour without conscious awareness even if the music is played normally. Such claims are completely without foundation (McIver 1988). The best example is a clip from Led Zeppelin's *Stairway to Heaven*. Visit the site http://jeffmilner.com/backmasking.htm for this and other examples. First, play the reversed clip without knowing what you are supposed to hear. Then try it again once you know what you are supposed to hear. You will be amazed by the difference. Once you have the expectation that a particular message is there to be heard, top-down processing will kick in and you will hear it.

Superstitious beliefs and behaviour

Superstitions have long been of interest to psychologists (e.g. Jahoda 1969; Vyse 1997; Wargo 2008). Some superstitions are culturally transmitted, shared by many members of a particular society, and are generally acquired from family and peers during childhood (Opie and Opie 1959). Others are more idiosyncratic and personal, such as valuing lucky charms or believing that the chances of success in some activity are increased by engaging in particular rituals. Cognitive psychologists would explain the latter in terms of the formation of illusory correlations (e.g. Chapman and Chapman 1967; Smedslund 1963), a form of confirmation bias in which we come to believe that two events are related when in fact they are not. Behaviourists (see Behaviourism and superstition opposite) would highlight the role that operant conditioning may play.

Superstitious thinking and behaviour increase in situations where there is a heightened sense of uncertainty, stress and unpredictability (Keinan 2002). Dudley (1999) reported two experiments that suggest that such thinking may actually be beneficial in such circumstances. In one experiment, students were shown to increase in their level of superstitious thinking following attempts to solve puzzles that were, unbeknownst to them, unsolvable. No such increase was found in students exposed to solvable puzzles. In the other experiment, all participants attempted to solve unsolvable puzzles and were then exposed to an anagram task consisting of solvable anagrams. Students with high levels of superstitious thinking were found to perform better on the anagrams task than their less superstitious counterparts. It appears that those who were superstitious were able to attribute their failure on the first task to external forces beyond their control and thus their subsequent performance was less affected by their initial failure.

Lack of control and illusory pattern perception

Whitson and Galinsky's (2008) series of studies investigating the effects of lack of control on illusory pattern perception is particularly noteworthy because of the wide range of tasks used across the six experiments. In addition to changes in superstitious thinking, other tasks measured the tendency to see images in noise, to form illusory correlations in stock market information, and to perceive conspiracies. Additionally, perceived control was also manipulated using a range of different techniques. The fact that the hypothesis was supported across the series as a whole suggests that the basic effect is robust and that similar psychological processes underlie a wide range of superficially disparate examples of illusory pattern recognition.

A recent paper by Whitson and Galinsky (2008) reported the results of six experiments investigating the hypothesis that lack of control increases the tendency to see meaningful patterns in random noise. In one experiment (experiment 3), they manipulated the degree of perceived control by having participants remember situations in which they either had complete control or lacked any control. Participants were then presented with three scenarios involving superstitious beliefs (e.g. knocking on wood before an important meeting and getting one's idea approved). Those who had been asked to remember a situation where they lacked control perceived a stronger connection between the superstitious behaviour and the outcome than those who recalled a situation where they had been in control. This shows that even merely recalling situations involving a lack of control will increase superstitious thinking.

IDA — Behaviourism and superstition

A **behavioural approach** also provides insight into superstitious behaviour. Skinner (1948) described an experiment in which pigeons were individually placed inside a box and simply presented with a food pellet once every 15 seconds, regardless of their behaviour. Surprisingly, however, after a few minutes the birds had developed various little idiosyncratic rituals, such as walking round in circles, bobbing their heads up and down and so on. Although behaviourists would reject such mentalistic notions, it looked for all the world as if the pigeons thought their strange little routines were causing the release of the food even though in reality their was no relationship between their behaviour and the release of food whatsoever. Skinner's explanation for this phenomenon was that the accidental pairing of the release of food early on in the process with whatever the bird happened to be doing was enough to reinforce that particular type of activity. Many personal superstitions, such as the wearing of lucky hats or the adoption of rituals, probably have their origins in such coincidental reinforcement.

The psychology of coincidences

People are generally poor at estimating probabilities in everyday life (Kahneman et al. 1982). This is illustrated by the classic 'Birthday problem': 'How many people would you need to have at a party to have a 50:50 chance that two of them share the same birthday (ignoring year)?' The correct answer of 23 seems far too low to most people. Many supposedly paranormal claims, such as dreams apparently 'coming true', are often rejected by sceptics on the basis that the match may have been simply a coincidence. The psychology of coincidences is, therefore, of great interest to anomalistic psychologists (Watt 1990–1991).

Mathematicians Diaconis and Mosteller (1989) identified four factors that can account for the majority of coincidences. First, there may be a 'hidden cause' that actually explains what appears to be a coincidence. For example, imagine you are walking down the street with a close friend that you have known since schooldays, both lost in your own thoughts, when your friend suddenly says, 'I wonder whatever happened to Rob that used to go to our school?' Amazingly, you were just thinking about Rob yourself, for the first time in years. An amazing coincidence? Or maybe even evidence of a psychic link? Perhaps. But it may be that as you were walking down the street you both saw something that reminded you of Rob, such as someone who resembled him or an object in a shop window that related to one of his hobbies. By the time your friend mentioned Rob's name, you had both forgotten what made you think of him in the first place, so it was not really a coincidence at all.

Second, there is the consideration of 'multiple end points'. If a coincidence is an exact match, then it is much less likely than if it is just 'close' because there are so many ways in which it could be 'close', most of which we are not consciously aware of until they happen. For example, we may be most impressed if someone we have just met has exactly the same birthday as us. But we might also be somewhat impressed if it was the day after or the day before or the same date but a different year. By allowing these 'multiple end points' to count as a match, we make it much more likely that we will find coincidences.

Third, there is the 'Law of Truly Large Numbers'. Given enough opportunities for even very unlikely coincidences to occur, they will occur. Thus, Paulos (1988) showed that we should expect numerous reports of apparently precognitive dreams every year purely on the basis of coincidence given the fact that billions of people dream every single night. What would be truly spooky would be if no one ever had a dream that seemed to 'come true'.

Finally, Diaconis and Mosteller (1989) discussed a number of psychological factors that played a role in the way that we notice and interpret coincidences (see also Watt 1990–91). Although a full discussion of all these factors is beyond the scope of this chapter, we will mention a classic study of the psychology of coincidences that was carried out by Falk (1989). She showed that we find coincidences that we are personally involved in much more surprising and impressive than those which happen to other people. This egocentric bias suggests that we can be more objective in considering other people's coincidences. As Watt (1990–1991) puts it, 'Although we can appreciate that coincidences happening to others represent only one of a large range of possible events, when coincidences occur to us personally we do not see ourselves as "part of the statistics".'

It seems plausible then that biases in probability estimation might underlie various paranormal experiences and beliefs. Blackmore and Troscianko (1985) reported that believers in the paranormal generally performed more poorly than disbelievers on a range of probability estimation tasks, sometimes significantly so. Subsequent studies have, however, generally failed to find such differences between believers and disbelievers (Matthews and Blackmore 1995; Roberts and Seager 1999). Musch and Ehrenberg (2002) did find a significant correlation between paranormal belief and errors on probabilistic reasoning tasks, but claimed that this was best accounted for by the lower cognitive ability of the believers. However, several previous studies have failed to find relationships between general basic measures of cognitive ability and paranormal belief (Irwin and Watt 2007), and so this finding requires replication.

Blackmore (1997) reported an interesting test of the probability misjudgement hypothesis based upon the idea that believers in the paranormal may be more impressed by psychic readings because they fail to appreciate that statements that are true for them are also likely to be true for others simply on the basis of chance. Through a newspaper survey, she obtained data from 6238 respondents. Each respondent was asked to look at ten statements corresponding to the type of information that psychics typically produce during readings (e.g. 'I have a scar on my left knee', 'There is someone called Jack in my family'). Each respondent was asked firstly whether each statement was true for them and secondly how many of the statements they would expect to be true for a randomly selected person. She hypothesized that although people generally would underestimate the number of statements that were true for others, this bias would be stronger for believers. In fact, these predictions were not supported, although the believers did claim that more of the statements were true for them compared with the non-believers.

Activity

Probability misjudgement and belief in the paranormal

Consider Blackmore's (1997) newspaper survey study and answer the following questions:

1 How ecologically valid was the test as an analogue of a real psychic reading? Do you think this might be important in terms of motivational factors that might influence how participants responded to the survey?

2 Do you think that Blackmore might have found different results if she had used a between-participants design in which half the participants indicated how many statements were true for them personally and the other half estimated how many statements would be true for a randomly selected person?

Answers are given on p.613. ▶

Evaluation of research into the psychology of deception and self-deception, superstition and coincidence

- *Conjurors and con artists vs genuine paranormal feats* – Psychologists are beginning to study systematically the techniques used by conjurors and con artists in order to understand the psychology of both deception and self-deception, as the same psychological processes are often involved in both. With a few notable exceptions, the history of psychology reveals little interest in such techniques until relatively recently, which is surprising given the way that skilled deceivers can reliably cause us to misperceive and misremember events. By studying such effects under controlled laboratory conditions, we can obtain great insights into the foibles of human cognition more generally. The fact that conjurors and con artists can duplicate seemingly paranormal feats does not prove that such feats are never performed using genuine paranormal powers. But unless this can be done under controlled conditions that would rule out any possibility of the use of deceptive techniques, it is not unreasonable for sceptics to remain unconvinced.

- *Superstition as beneficial* – Although there is a long tradition of psychological research interest in this topic, the level of interest appears to have risen in recent years. As with paranormal beliefs generally, a convincing body of evidence now exists to demonstrate that superstitious thinking increases in situations where we feel we lack control, and may even be beneficial in such situations.

- *Poor intuitive statisticians* – There is little doubt that we now have a good understanding of many of the factors involved in the psychology of coincidence, not least the fact that we are all very poor intuitive statisticians. The promising hypothesis that believers in the paranormal may be somewhat poorer intuitive statisticians compared with non-believers has, however, received limited support at best.

CHECK YOUR UNDERSTANDING

Check your understanding of factors underlying anomalous experience by answering these questions from memory. You can check your answers by looking back through Topic 2, Factors underlying anomalous experience.

1. How might cognitive biases lead someone to think that they had had a paranormal experience when in fact they had not?

2. Describe some of the personality factors that are associated with paranormal belief.

3. What evidence suggests that some reports of ostensibly paranormal experiences may be based upon false memories?

4. What evidence is there that biological factors may play a role in anomalous experiences?

5. How might one account for the apparent relationship between paranormal belief and reports of traumatic childhood?

6. What is the Barnum effect?

7. Why is the concept of top-down processing important in understanding anomalous experiences?

8. What insights can professional conjurors and con artists provide into the psychology of deception and self-deception?

9. In what ways might being superstitious actually enhance performance?

10. Why is the psychology of coincidences relevant to anomalistic psychology?

Topic 3: Belief in exceptional experience

Psychology in context   Most Haunted

Most Haunted is Living TV's most popular programme. In each programme, a team of parapsychologists and ghost-hunters investigate an allegedly haunted location with the help of mediums who claim to be able to communicate directly with the spirits involved. For many years, the star of the show was Derek Acorah. He would often appear to become possessed by the spirits on location and has always insisted that any information relayed was coming to him through paranormal means. According to Ciaran O'Keeffe, one of the parapsychologists employed on the show, Acorah is actually deceiving the public with 'showmanship and dramatics' (Roper 2005). On one occasion, to test Acorah's honesty, he was deliberately fed false background information concerning a fictional South African jailer called Kreed Kafer. The 'spirit' of Kreed Kafer subsequently 'possessed' Acorah on camera. Kreed Kafer is an anagram of 'Faker Derek'. Acorah still enjoys a very lucrative career as a successful medium. Why do you think that such paranormal programmes are so popular? Do all viewers watch for the same reasons? What is the main motivation of the programme makers and how might that affect the integrity of the programmes?

One of the major reasons given for believing in many paranormal phenomena is direct personal experience. This is certainly the case with respect to the phenomena discussed in this section: psychic healing, out-of-body and near-death experiences, and mediumship. The challenge for those who are not convinced that these phenomena actually involve anything paranormal is therefore twofold: first, to evaluate critically the evidence offered in support of paranormal explanations of these phenomena and, secondly, to develop and test alternative non-paranormal explanations.

Research into psychic healing

Psychic healing is known by a variety of names including mental healing, spiritual healing, faith healing, psi healing, divine healing, miracle healing paranormal healing, laying-on of hands, non-medical healing and shamanistic healing. It refers to the alleged ability to treat and cure diseases by exerting some kind of paranormal influence and without the use of recognized physical curative agents. Psychic healers often attempt to cure people by passing their hands over their patients' bodies, sometimes lightly touching them, sometimes not. Many psychic healers claim to be able to exert a curative influence even from a distance (French 1996a). If psychic healing really works, it would be an example of a psychokinetic effect.

Understanding the nature of illness

It is very natural to assume that if we feel better after taking some form of treatment when we are ill, the treatment must have caused the improvement. But that is not necessarily the case. First, patients almost always experience fluctuations with respect to how well they feel even in the complete absence of treatment. Therefore, any improvement one experiences after taking treatment might have occurred even without that treatment. Second, our bodies have amazing natural recuperative powers. We will recover fully from most minor ailments even without treatment. Third, we must also consider the possibility that any improvement following treatment was simply a **placebo effect** (French 2001c). This is the term used to describe any subjective improvement reported by patients who believe themselves to have been given some form of effective treatment but who have in fact received some inactive substitute. For these reasons, anecdotal evidence offered in support of psychic healing claims can never be particularly compelling.

Randomized controlled trials

It follows from the nature of illness that the best evidence in support of any form of treatment is that obtained from double-blind **randomized controlled trials** (RCTs). Ideally, in such trials neither the patient nor the person administering the treatment knows whether the patient is receiving the active treatment or the placebo. If the active treatment group show significantly greater levels of improvement than the placebo control group, then the treatment would appear to be effective. Surveys of the literature that have tested psychic healing claims using such methodology have generally concluded that the available evidence does not support the claim that the effects of psychic healing are anything more than placebo effects, whilst acknowledging that placebo effects, can have a noticeable effect on the subjective aspects of disease such as pain and discomfort. The words of Schouten (1992–1993) are fairly typical:

> 'An overview of the research on the effectiveness of "psychic" healing on human subjects indicates that psychic healing can be effective, especially on subjectively experienced state of health. Objectively measured effects are much less pronounced. However, the strength of the effect of psychic healing seems strongly dependent upon the patient's knowledge that treatment is attempted and appears to be mainly related to psychological variables associated with the patient and with the healer-patient interaction.'

HOW SCIENCE WORKS

Testing the therapeutic effectiveness of intercessory prayer

Millions of people around the world believe that praying for those who are ill can bring about real improvements in health. Although any such effects, if real, would be seen by most people to be the results of God responding to the requests for healing, it is of interest to consider the results of double-blind RCTs of the power of intercessory prayer (i.e. prayers on behalf of another). Some early studies (e.g. Byrd 1988) appeared to produce evidence in favour of the power of prayer, but they have been criticized on methodological grounds (Chibnall et al. 2001). The most recent and largest study to date was reported by Benson et al. (2006). Patients recovering from coronary artery bypass graft surgery were randomly allocated to one of three groups: the first group (n = 604) received prayer after being informed that they may or may not do so; the second group (n = 597) did not receive prayer after being told the same; and the final group (n = 601) received prayer after being told that they would definitely do so. Prayer was provided for two weeks, beginning the night before surgery. The incidence of post-operative complications did not differ between the two groups who were uncertain about receiving prayer but, surprisingly, was actually somewhat higher in the group that knew they were being prayed for. The results clearly do not support claims of beneficial effects of intercessory prayer.

Single case studies

Although replicable evidence from double-blind RCTs would provide the most persuasive evidence for any form of treatment, most proponents of psychic healing are convinced upon the basis of evidence from case studies. Provided that stringent conditions are met, such case studies might indeed provide valid evidence in support of such claims. Randi (1987) proposed the criteria summarized in Table 14.3.

(1) The disease must not normally be self-terminating.

(2) The recovery must be complete.

(3) The recovery must take place in the absence of any medical treatment that might normally be expected to affect the disease.

(4) There must be adequate medical opinion that the disease was present before the application of whatever means were used to bring about the miracle.

(5) There must be adequate medical opinion that the disease is not present after the application of whatever means were used to bring about the miracle.

Table 14.3 *Conditions for accepting psychic healing*

In fact, as pointed out by French (1996a), Randi's criteria would not rule out cases involving initial misdiagnosis by qualified doctors (which inevitably occasionally occurs) or cases of spontaneous regression or remission. For example, Buckman and Sabbagh (1993) noted that spontaneous regressions of cancer occur approximately once in every 100 000 cases; that is to say, occasionally it happens that properly diagnosed cancer sometimes simply goes away for no obvious reason. French provided details of a number of anecdotal cases that have been presented as evidence of psychic healing but which, upon closer inspection, would have failed to satisfy Randi's criteria. Other reviews have drawn similarly negative conclusions (e.g. Hines 2003; Randi 1987).

HOW SCIENCE WORKS

Activity · Investigating single case studies

Morris Cerullo, an American evangelical faith healer, was challenged to produce details of his 'best cases' in 1992 by Peter May, MD (May 1993–1994). None of the cases put forward provided convincing evidence for faith healing. Consider the McHale case summarized here in terms of Randi's criteria. Georgine McHale claimed to have been cured of a fibroid. Her medical records revealed that a fibroid had never actually been diagnosed, although a test had been arranged to investigate that possibility. The test, carried out three weeks after the alleged miracle cure, revealed two ovarian cysts, but no fibroid. In other cases, patients really did have the medical conditions that they thought they had (e.g. spinal degeneration, poor vision, hip displacement), but they still had them after the alleged miracle cures. May (1993–1994) described another case as follows: 'Alfred Coombes was an elderly man who claimed to have been healed of a malignancy in his gullet. He readily admitted that he had just had a course of fifteen sessions of radiotherapy, and thanked God for the skill of his doctors'.

Fraudulent techniques

Although many, perhaps the majority of, psychic healers are probably sincere (albeit mistaken) in their claims, there are also many known cases of deliberate fraud. Amongst many other cases, Randi (1987) described how 'psychic surgeons' in the Philippines use sleight of hand to create the impression that they were operating upon seriously ill patients without the use of surgical instruments. He also described the case of the Reverend Peter Popoff, an American fundamentalist preacher, who claimed that God was speaking to him directly in order to give him details of the medical conditions of members of his congregation with whom he had never spoken. In fact, the information was provided to Popoff by his wife via a radio receiver disguised as a hearing aid.

Therapeutic touch

Psychic healers typically believe that they are able to diagnose and heal people using subtle forms of energy that are not detectable by any currently available scientific instruments. One example of this approach is known as 'therapeutic touch' (TT), developed in the 1970s and particularly popular with nurses in the USA. Rosa *et al.* (1998) tested the claim that 21 TT practitioners could detect a human energy field, as claimed, using a very simple and direct approach. On each trial, they simply asked the practitioners to say which of their hands, left or right, was closer to the investigator's hand which was held a few centimetres above one of the practitioner's hands but shielded from view. By chance alone, the practitioners would be expected to obtain a hit rate of 50 per cent. They scored 44 per cent, below the average rate that would be obtained simply by guessing, this offering no support whatsoever for their claims.

IDA · Ethics: The placebo effect and healing

The placebo effect is a component of the response to all forms of treatment, including those which can be shown on the basis of clinical trials to have an effect over and above the placebo effect itself. Psychic healers and practitioners of other forms of complementary and alternative medicine (CAM) are usually sincerely convinced regarding their ability to heal a wide range of diseases and often provide lengthy consultations during which they treat all of the patient's symptoms with concern and sympathy. Conventional GPs, on the other hand, usually have very little time for each consultation and are obliged to give accurate information regarding the treatments on offer, including alerting patients to any unpleasant side effects. Given that psychic healers are likely to induce a stronger placebo effect because of such differences, is it ethical for scientists to undermine the likely placebo effect by pointing out that psychic healing and other forms of CAM appear to be nothing more than placebo treatments?

Testing therapeutic touch

There are several notable features about the study by Rosa *et al*. (1998) including the simplicity of the design. Direct tests of the fundamental tenets of paranormal healing claims are clearly to be preferred over expensive studies with complicated designs and statistical analyses whenever possible. This particular test was conceived of and carried out by Emily Rosa when she was nine years old.

Evaluation of research into psychic healing

- *The nature of illness* – It is important to understand the nature of illness if one is to appreciate why no amount of anecdotal evidence put forward in support of claims of psychic healing will ever amount to proof of efficacy. People can recover from an illness following the administration of therapeutically worthless treatments for a variety of reasons, including the natural fluctuations in the course of the illness, the natural recuperative powers of the body and the placebo effect.

- *Double-blind randomized controlled trials (RCTs)* – Given the nature of illness, it is clear that the therapeutic effectiveness of any form of treatment, including psychic healing, is best assessed using double-blind RCTs. In this form of clinical trial, patients are assigned at random to the treatment condition(s) and the control conditions, typically including a placebo condition and possibly a no treatment condition. When such trials have been carried out to assess the therapeutic effectiveness of psychic healing, the results typically indicate some improvement of subjective aspects of illness due to the placebo effect but little or no improvement in objective aspects of the disease.

- *Criteria for single case studies* – Randi (1987) has proposed a set of criteria that must be met by any single case study put forward as evidence of psychic healing. In fact, his criteria would not rule out cases of inadvertent misdiagnosis by doctors and rare cases of spontaneous regression or remission. Even so, Randi was unable to find any cases that met his criteria.

- *Fraudulent techniques* – Although most self-proclaimed psychic healers are probably sincere, if mistaken, in their claims, there are numerous cases of the use of fraudulent techniques.

Research into out-of-body and near-death experiences

Reports of out-of-body experiences (OBEs), during which consciousness appears to become separated from the physical body, and more elaborate near-death experiences (NDEs), which may involve apparent trips to spiritual realms, have been recorded for centuries. There is little doubt that such experiences have often been accepted as providing strong support for the idea of life after death, supplying, as they appear to do, proof that the mind (or soul) is not entirely dependent upon the underlying neural substrate as modern neuroscience assumes. But how convincing are such arguments when examined closely?

Out-of-body experiences

Blackmore (1982) defines an out-of-body experience (OBE) as 'an experience in which a person seems to perceive the world from a location outside the physical body'. Here is an example (from Blackmore, 1996c):

> 'Some time into the earlier part of the lecture, imagine my surprise when I found *myself* looking at *me* giving the lecture, and remarking to myself "This is going absolutely perfectly – I wonder where *he* is getting all those words from..." and then I was back again lecturing as normal. During the experience I was standing watching myself lecture from the left front of the audience at a distance of about 10–12 feet.'

Such experiences are surprisingly common. Surveys show that some 15–20 per cent of the population will experience an OBE at least once in their lives. Spontaneous OBEs often occur just before sleep, but the OBE is also a common component in the more dramatic near-death experience to be described later. The experience of OBEs is not related to age, gender, education level, religion, or psychological problems. However, OBEs are more frequent in the hypnotically susceptible, the fantasy prone, and people who report psychic experiences, good memory for dreams and lucid dreaming. Indeed, all of these variables intercorrelate positively. Drugs, hypnosis and mental training can all be used to induce OBEs (Blackmore 1982, 1996c).

Explanations of out-of-body experiences

Blackmore (1996c) considered three possible explanations for OBEs. Most people who have had a striking OBE experience are convinced that something, the soul perhaps, left the body temporarily. They often report a stronger belief in life after death as a consequence. A second possibility is that OBEs involve a combination of imagery or hallucination with ESP. Thus, although it may appear to OBErs that their minds are actually present at some location distant from their physical bodies, it is argued that in fact this is not so. The information they acquire is, it is suggested, obtained via ESP. The information is presented to the conscious mind in such a way that it appears to the OBEr that they were at the distant location, but this is an illusion. However, as Blackmore pointed out, this is simply trying to explain one mysterious phenomenon in terms of another. The third type of theory attempts to explain OBEs in purely psychological terms and does not assume the existence of a soul.

Blackmore's (1982, 1996a) own theory is based on the idea, widely accepted within cognitive psychology, that we are all constantly creating and revising mental models of the world and our position in it on the basis of incoming sensory information and our expectations and knowledge. This leads to a situation where we usually perceive our 'selves' to be 'behind our eyes' because we base our current model of the world on mainly visual input. Another important aspect of our current overall model of the way things are is our own self-schema. To a large extent this is based upon our body image, i.e. our model of our body's position, again based upon sensory input and expectations. In certain situations, especially those involving reduced sensory input and deep absorption, the normal body and self-image may break down. The cognitive system would then attempt to construct the best model that it can and this would be taken as 'reality' by the individual. In the absence of strong sensory input to correct the model, a model based more or less entirely upon memory and imagination will become dominant. According to Blackmore, when this happens we are likely to experience an OBE. This model accounts for both the conditions under which OBEs usually occur and the nature of the experience itself. The OBE world is often like the world of imagination. Walls may be transparent, the individual may feel that they can see great distances, or move to distant stars and planets. Even less spectacular views are likely to be the product of imagination, given the mix of correct and incorrect details that typifies the OBE.

HOW SCIENCE WORKS

OBEs and the 'bird's eye view'

Memory images often involve a 'bird's eye' view in which a scene is pictured from above. This is referred to as the 'observer' perspective, in contrast to memories that reflect a so-called 'field' perspective, i.e. the memory reflects the original viewpoint of the subject. Blackmore (1987b), on the basis of her model, predicted that people who experience OBEs should be more likely to use observer perspectives in recall, imagery and dreams, and should be better able to switch imagined perspectives. In a series of three studies, participants were asked to report, for example, how clearly they could visualize the room they were in from different perspectives or the perspective of remembered dreams. OBErs were more likely to use the observer perspective for dream recall (see also Irwin 1986b) but not recall of real-life events. Furthermore, they were found to be better able mentally to switch perspectives, thus offering considerable support for the model. OBErs have also been shown to have better spatial imagery (Cook and Irwin 1983) and to have superior dream control skills (Blackmore 1986).

OBEs and veridical information

Blackmore (1982, 1996a) considered the claim that some OBErs report veridical information (i.e. accurate information corresponding to facts in the real world) that they obtained during their OBE. There have, for example, been many reports of individuals obtaining veridical knowledge during OBEs which occurred as part of near-death experiences (NDEs). Many of the major NDE researchers seem to be convinced that individuals can indeed paranormally obtain veridical information from distant locations during such episodes. Unfortunately, the evidence is largely anecdotal and corroboration is often lacking. The accounts may be offered by just the NDEr and possibly one or two others, almost always after they have discussed the event. As Blackmore (1996a) writes:

> 'There is no doubt that people describe, reasonably accurately, events that have occurred around them during their NDE. However, this need not entail paranormal powers. Alternatives include information available at the time, prior knowledge, fantasy or dreams, lucky guesses and information from the remaining senses. Then there is selective memory for correct details, incorporation of details learned between the NDE and giving an account of it, and the tendency to tell a good story. Can these explain why people are able to "see" during NDEs?'

Blackmore felt that such factors may well account for the most impressive reports in the literature. While the available evidence offers reasonable support for the idea that spontaneous OBEs are typically the result of difficulties in integrating bottom-up and top-down sources of information to produce a stable mental model of reality, recent research has shown that OBEs can be induced by deliberately disrupting the integration of different sources of sensory (bottom-up) information. A number of investigators (e.g. Ehrsson 2007; Lenggenhager *et al.* 2007) have used virtual reality technology to present participants with the view of their own backs that would be seen from a perspective, say, two metres behind their actual position. If the experimenter touches the participant's chest (which is out of view) with a rod at the same time as apparently touching their 'illusory body' by moving a rod towards a location just beneath the camera, the strong illusion is created within participants that their centre of consciousness is located behind the position of their real bodies.

Research into near-death experiences

The OBE is a common component of near-death experiences (NDEs), during which people often report viewing their own physical bodies from above, sometimes during frantic attempts at resuscitation. NDEs are vivid and dramatic experiences reported by a sizeable minority of people who come close to (or believe themselves to have come close to) death. Other components which are commonly reported include a feeling of bliss, moving down a dark tunnel towards a bright light, entering the light, meeting with spirits (either of dead friends and relations or

OBEs induced by direct stimulation of the cortex

Key research: Blanke *et al.* (2002, 2004)

Blanke and colleagues have published a number of papers relating to OBEs induced by direct electrical stimulation of the cortex and OBEs associated with neurological conditions (e.g. Blanke *et al.* 2004; Blanke *et al.* 2002). Blanke *et al.* (2004) argued that OBEs 'are related to a failure to integrate proprioceptive, tactile and visual information with respect to one's own body (disintegration in personal space) and by a vestibular dysfunction leading to an additional disintegration between personal (vestibular) space and extrapersonal (visual) space.' Both types of integration failure are said to be caused by abnormal activity in the temporo-parietal junction during a period of impaired consciousness. Blanke *et al.* (2002) describe how OBEs were repeatedly induced in a 43-year-old woman by direct cortical stimulation of the right angular gyrus of the brain as she was being evaluated for epilepsy treatment. Some commentators (e.g. Neppe 2002; Holden *et al.* 2006) have argued that OBEs produced by electrical stimulation of the brain differ from spontaneous OBEs in that they do not feel as realistic, stable and continuous as the latter. However, as French (in press) notes, this may well reflect differences in context, given that patients undergoing direct brain stimulation would be well aware of the cause of their anomalous sensations. Furthermore, the electrical stimulation would be administered in short bursts, unlike the unusual neural activity assumed to underlie spontaneous OBEs.

religious figures), moving through idyllic landscapes or beautiful cities, a life review, reaching a point of no return, and returning to the physical body. NDEs are often life-changing for those that experience them, resulting in greatly decreased fear of death, a more spiritual, less materialistic outlook on life, and a greater concern for the wellbeing of others and for environmental issues.

Explanations of NDEs

There are essentially two possible interpretations of the NDE. On the one hand, the NDE is often viewed as providing a glimpse of an afterlife. This is sometimes referred to as the 'transcendental hypothesis' and is the view taken by most people who actually have an NDE as well as the majority of NDE researchers. If true, this hypothesis has profound implications with respect to the nature of the relationship between mind and brain. It would mean that mind is not entirely dependent upon the underlying neural substrate, that consciousness can

become separated from the physical brain, and that consciousness survives the death of the physical body. Modern neuroscientists, on the other hand, tend to favour the notion that the NDE is an entirely subjective experience brought about by unusual activity within the brain. This is often referred to as the 'dying-brain hypothesis' although it should be noted that both sides in this debate agree that one does not have to be objectively near death in order to experience an NDE.

The evidence in favour of the transcendental hypothesis is largely anecdotal in nature, with a particular emphasis upon those few cases that appear to involve veridical perception of information from remote locations during an NDE. As stated above, Blackmore (1993, 1996a) listed a number of factors that may contribute to explaining such cases in non-paranormal terms. Augustine (2007a) presented a detailed critical review of such cases, concluding that they can all be explained without the need to invoke paranormal forces. Furthermore, Augustine (2007b) presented compelling evidence that NDEs are indeed hallucinatory in nature.

Arguments in favour of the dying-brain hypothesis largely rest upon the fact that experiences similar to each of the components of the NDE are known to occur independently of the NDE and we have a reasonable understanding of the physiological causes of these experiences. As already described above, the OBE commonly occurs outside of the NDE context and can be induced by such means as direct electrical stimulation of the cortex and by disrupting the integration of proprioceptive, tactile and visual information with respect to one's own body. With respect to OBEs and other components of the NDE, it has been pointed out that reduction of oxygen to the brain (hypoxia) produces many of the same symptoms as reported during NDEs (Whinnery 1997), as does the build up of carbon dioxide (hypercarbia) in the blood (Meduna 1950). Carr (1982) has argued that many aspects of the NDE could be explained in terms of endorphin release, such as the generally positive affective tone of the experience. Morse *et al.* (1989) have proposed that serotonin may be involved in the generation of NDEs and Jansen (1989, 1997, 2001) developed a neurotransmitter-based model of NDEs based upon the similarities between NDEs and ketamine-induced experiences.

The temporal lobes and OBEs/NDEs

Augustine (2007c) recently reviewed several lines of evidence indicating that unusual activity in the temporal lobes is strongly implicated in the generation of OBEs and other aspects of NDEs. For example, Britton and Bootzin (2004) presented evidence of a direct link between NDEs and altered functioning in the temporal lobes in that more epileptiform EEG activity was recorded from the temporal lobes of NDErs (usually on the left) than from a control group.

Approaches: An integrated model of NDEs

Physiological models of the various components of the NDE sometimes appear to offer plausible accounts for some aspects of NDEs at the expense of virtually ignoring others. Blackmore (1993, 1996b) proposed an integrated physiological model of the NDE, essentially a synthesis of suggestions from previous commentators plus some novel explanations of particular components. For example, she argued that the tunnel experience could be explained in terms of neural disinhibition of the visual cortex. The main advantage of the dying-brain approach is that it generates testable hypotheses, whereas it is difficult to see what possible observations could not be made to fit with the transcendental hypothesis. As the latter is not falsifiable, it is arguable whether it is actually a scientific hypothesis at all.

Debates: A challenge to neuroscience?

A number of NDE researchers have claimed that findings from recent prospective studies of NDEs in cardiac arrest survivors (Greyson 2003; Parnia *et al.* 2001; van Lommel *et al.* 2001) constitute a major challenge to the reductionist approach of modern neuroscience. In the words of van Lommel *et al.* (2001), 'How could a clear consciousness outside one's body be experienced at the moment that the brain no longer functions during a period of clinical death with flat EEG?' French (2001d, 2005, in press) pointed out that this question is misleading as it is not at all clear when the NDEs actually take place in these cases. It has further been pointed out that a flat surface EEG does not equate to clinical death (Crislip 2008) and that there can still be sufficient activity at sub-cortical levels to produce hallucinatory experiences even when surface EEG records are flat (Braithwaite 2008).

Evaluation of research into out-of-body and near-death experiences

- *Paranormal theories of OBEs and the mind–body problem* – There are two paranormal theories of OBEs: first, that consciousness can in some way leave the body and move to distant locations and, second, that information which is obtained via ESP is presented to the conscious mind in such a way as to produce the illusion that the mind has left the body. The former suffers from all of the same philosophical difficulties as any other dualist theory of mind–body interaction. How can an immaterial mind ever interact with a material brain? The latter theory, while avoiding these complications, simply tries to explain one mysterious phenomenon in terms of another. The evidence supporting the claim that veridical information can be obtained during an OBE is not compelling when closely examined.

- *Support for psychological theories of OBEs* – Blackmore, amongst others, has proposed a psychological explanation of the OBE. Essentially, she argues that under certain circumstances the model of reality adopted by the mind is one that is based upon imagination and memory rather than incoming sensory input. This model is supported by a considerable amount of empirical data.

- *Problems with transcendental theories of NDEs* – Such theories tend to assume that NDEs are exactly what they appear to be to the person having the experience: the soul departing from the physical body and being given a glimpse of the afterlife. The main arguments put forward in support of this focus upon allegedly veridical information obtained during the OBE component and the claim that other aspects of the NDE (e.g. 'clear consciousness in the clinically dead') cannot be explained in terms of modern neuroscience. The latter claims appear to be based upon a misrepresentation of neuroscientific models of the NDE. Furthermore, transcendental theories of NDEs appear to be non-falsifiable in many ways and therefore non-scientific.

- *More plausible neuroscientific theories of NDEs* – The alternative viewpoint, favoured by most neuroscientists, is that NDEs reflect abnormal activity in the brain. This is often referred to as the 'dying brain hypothesis' even though it is accepted that NDEs can occur in people who are not objectively close to death. Such explanations draw upon the fact that all of the commonly reported NDE components are known to occur outside of the NDE context and it is assumed, therefore, that similar neuropsychological processes are involved in both situations. Although neuroscience is still some distance from providing a definitive account of the NDE, real progress has been made. Furthermore, neuroscientific models have the advantage of generating testable hypotheses for future research.

Research into mediumship

Although people have believed in paranormal phenomena since ancient times, we can date the origins of modern interest in such phenomena very precisely. In March 1848, in a house in Hydesville, New York, two young sisters by the name of Kate and Margaret Fox reported hearing strange rapping noises and eventually discovered that they could communicate with 'the other side' using a simple code. They claimed that the noises were made by the spirit of a peddlar who had been murdered and buried in the cellar. This marked the birth of the Spiritualist movement. Soon others claimed also to be able to communicate with the dead and séances spread like wildfire across America and Europe.

Many strange phenomena were said to occur during séances.

Séances eventually came to involve other phenomena too, including movement of tables and objects, the playing of musical instruments by unseen hands and lips, strange lights in the dark, levitation of objects, the table or even the medium, the disappearance or materialization of objects, the materialization of hands, faces, or even complete spirit forms (seemingly composed of 'ectoplasm'), disembodied voices, spirit paintings and photographs, and written communications from the spirit world.

Séances and spiritualism

In fact, many scientists investigated séances and several, including some of the finest of the day, pronounced them genuine. Hyman (1985a) discussed in detail the cases of Robert Hare, an eminent American chemist, Alfred Russel Wallace, cofounder of the theory of evolution, and Sir William Crookes, the discoverer of thallium. All three were attacked by the scientific establishment for expressing views in favour of the reality of spiritualist phenomena. The attacks were often unfair and do not show the scientific establishment in a good light. In particular, many of those who attacked Hare, Wallace and Crookes refused to accept invitations to observe the phenomena for themselves. However, this does not mean that Hare, Wallace and Crookes were correct in their conclusions.

For example, Crookes was most impressed by a medium named Florence Cook. A typical séance with Florence would involve her entering a cabinet and apparently going into a trance. After a while a white-robed female form wearing a turban would emerge and claim to be 'Katie King', a materialized spirit. There was an uncanny resemblance between Florence and Katie which was noted by many sceptics. Crookes claimed that there were also crucial differences. However, even before the sessions with Crookes, 'Katie King' had been grabbed by a certain Mr Volckman and shown to be none other than Florence Cook. She was also caught red-handed in the act of cheating in sessions following those with Crookes. Yet Crookes was convinced that she was genuine.

Although one could cite many other scientists who were convinced by what they witnessed with their own eyes under the dim lights of the séance room, many others considered the whole thing to be a hoax. In fact, it was a rare medium that was not caught cheating. Strangely, as with Crookes, this rarely deterred their supporters, who would argue that sometimes the mediums felt obliged to cheat if the spirits were not coming through so as not to disappoint the public.

The spirit of Katie King bore a striking resemblance to the medium Florence Cook.

In an attempt to resolve the controversy, the Society for Psychical Research was founded in the United Kingdom in 1882 (a similar group was formed in America three years later). Many of the founder members, all of them eminent scholars, were motivated primarily by the urge to prove that the soul survived bodily death. Darwin's theory had caused a great stir amongst thinking people, with its obvious implication that humans were not God's special creation. If Darwin was right, how could one justify belief in an immortal soul? This issue troubled many scientists with strong Christian beliefs. A second event which had kept interest in psychical phenomena high was the arrival in this country of D.D. Home, considered by many to be the greatest medium ever. In fact, his performances were very similar to a stage magician with an emphasis upon physical effects. Many witnesses claimed that he could levitate tables, objects and himself, and produce a variety of other spectacular effects.

Initially there was cooperation with the Spiritualist movement, but as the scientists of the SPR insisted on tougher controls at séances, cooperation declined. At the time, many of the scientists who declared these phenomena as genuine felt that their qualifications as scientists, and therefore professional impartial observers, were enough to ensure that they could not be fooled. In fact, most scientists are no better than anyone else at detecting charlatans. The people with the real know-how are conjurors, as already discussed.

As stated, the rise of the Spiritualist movement was one of the major factors underlying the formation of the SPR in 1882. Six years later, in 1888, Margaret Fox admitted that the original rapping, noises produced 40 years earlier when she was a schoolgirl, were not in any way psychic. They were produced in a variety of ways, but mainly by cracking her toe and ankle joints, a skill which she demonstrated in public. What had begun as a prank had got out of hand and the sisters had then felt unable to own up. Typically, Spiritualists simply refused to believe the confession and the movement continues to this day.

The first three decades of the last century were a time of transition for psychical research. Investigators were becoming increasingly disillusioned with investigations of mediums as they were notoriously difficult to carry out under properly controlled conditions. Furthermore, so many mediums were shown to be frauds that many investigators concluded that they all were. Amongst the phenomena which were most studied during this time were the so-called mental phenomena of psychics and mediums (i.e. mediums would go into trances and pass back messages from departed loved ones, either vocally or through automatic writing, e.g. Leonora Piper, Gladys Osborne Leonard, Eileen Garrett). Another line of research focused on physical phenomena of the type produced by Home (Eusapia Palladino is one famous example – although frequently caught cheating, her supporters insist that she could produce genuine effects).

Modern mediums still claim to be able to communicate directly with the dead but, as already described, it is possible to give such an impression by the deliberate use of the deceptive art of cold reading. It seems likely, however, that the majority of mediums and psychics genuinely believe that they have some kind of special gift but are, in fact, unintentionally picking up on the same sources of information as the cold reader. Schouten (1994) traced the techniques used by parapsychologists over recent decades in attempting to investigate the claims of psychics. In his words (Schouten 1994):

'The main question asked in most of these studies was whether a significant number of correct statements deviated significantly from chance expectation. Another question, less often addressed, was whether psi ability was necessary to explain the correct statements. The present study indicates that the number of studies with significant positive results is rather small. Moreover, in most of

How not to test a psychic?

Key research: Schwartz *et al*. (2001)

Schwartz *et al*. (2001) claimed to have proved that mediums really could contact the dead. As part of the study, which involved two sitters and five mediums, the sitter sat behind an opaque screen while the medium did their reading. The medium was allowed only to ask questions requiring 'yes/no' answers which the sitters were required to answer out loud. The sitters subsequently judged the mediums' statements for accuracy, claiming that 80 per cent of them were 'definitely true'. It was claimed that a control group only managed to obtain 36 per cent accuracy.

Wiseman and O'Keefe (2001) presented a detailed critique of this study in terms of:

(a) the potential for judging bias

(b) the use of an inappropriate control group and

(c) inadequate safeguards against sensory leakage (see also Hyman 2002, 2003; Schwartz 2003).

The potential for judging bias is present in the study because Schwartz *et al*. did not use a blind-judging procedure. Such a procedure would involve presenting both statements which were generated by the medium specifically for a particular sitter and statements generated for another sitter, with the sitter not knowing which were which. Instead, the sitters judged statements which they knew were directed specifically at them, and judged around 80 per cent of the statements to be 'definitely true'. But many statements produced by psychics are highly ambiguous and a sitter who is motivated to find evidence for after-death communication may well be able to come up with some aspect of their life to judge the statement a hit.

The original study also used an inappropriate control group and method in trying to rule out the possibility that the high hit rate might be due to intelligent guesswork. Schwartz *et al*. (2001) selected 70 statements from the original transcripts and turned them into questions, e.g. 'Your son is very good with his hands' might be turned into 'Who is very good with his hands?' A group of undergraduates were then presented with the questions and asked to guess the answers. They were right only 36 per cent of the time. But, as Wiseman and O'Keefe (2001) pointed out, this is like testing one group of archers by getting them to shoot arrows wherever they like and then drawing targets around them, and then testing a second group by asking them to fire at the targets.

Finally, the steps taken to isolate the sitters from the mediums were rudimentary to say the least. Essentially, for many of the sittings, they were separated by a large opaque screen. For much of the proceedings, however, the sitters responded to the mediums statements with 'yes/no' responses. Much emotional significance can be read from this by a skilled cold reader, not to mention other possible auditory cues to emotional state. This would give the medium a definite advantage in knowing when he was on the right track. Overall, the Schwartz *et al*. (2001) study was very poorly controlled and did not deserve the massive amount of media attention it received. When O'Keeffe and Wiseman (2005) tested the alleged abilities of several professional mediums using properly controlled methodology, no evidence for any kind of psychic ability was found.

these, one or more potential sources of error were present that might have influenced the outcome. It seems, therefore, that there is little reason to expect psychics to make correct statements about matters unknown at the time more often than would be expected by chance.'

Evaluation of research into mediumship

- *Early research into mediumship fraud* – Although there have always been people who claimed to be able to communicate with the dead, it was the birth of Spiritualism in 1848 that marked the beginning of modern interest in mediumship. Séances became very fashionable in the Victorian era, initially in America and then throughout Europe. Some scientists were convinced that genuine paranormal forces were at work, but many others considered that all of the effects were produced by trickery. It was a rare medium who was not caught red-handed in the act of cheating, but this rarely deterred their supporters.

- *Conjurors can duplicate mediumship* – Mental mediums typically go into an apparent trance in order to communicate with the dead, whereas physical mediums focus upon physical effects, such as materializations and levitation of objects. Modern mediums tend to focus on mental phenomena. In both cases conjurors can duplicate such effects, although this does not necessarily rule out genuine mediumship.

- *Modern tests of mediumship* – Despite the much publicized claims that Schwartz *et al.* (2001) had proven that communication with the dead was possible, closer examination reveals that this was a very poor study indeed from a methodological point of view. Better controlled studies typically fail to find any evidence to support the claims of mediums.

CHECK YOUR UNDERSTANDING

Check your understanding of belief in exceptional experience by answering these questions. Try to do this from memory. You can check your answers by looking back through Topic 3, Belief in exceptional experience.

1. What is psychic healing?

2. What is the placebo effect and why is it relevant to claims of psychic healing?

3. Why are double-blind randomized clinical trials required to assess claims relating to psychic healing?

4. List the criteria that must be met if single case studies are to be accepted as providing evidence suggestive of psychic healing.

5. Describe three approaches to explaining OBEs.

6. Outline Blackmore's psychological theory of OBEs.

7. Briefly describe the typical components of NDEs commonly reported in Western cultures.

8. What is the 'dying-brain hypothesis'?

9. How might physiological factors contribute to NDEs?

10. List some of the methodological problems with Schwartz's (2001) study of mediums.

Further resources

The following books provide useful background reading relating to the topics covered in this chapter:

Carroll, R.T. (2003) *The skeptic's dictionary: A collection of strange beliefs, amusing deceptions and dangerous delusions*. A series of informative entries providing a sceptical perspective on everything from acupuncture to zombies. The same information can be found on-line at www.skepdic.com.

Della Sala, S. (ed.). (2007) *Tall tales about the mind and brain: Separating fact from fiction.* New York: Oxford University Press. This book explores a wide range of commonly held but mistaken beliefs about the mind and brain. Of particular relevance to this course are chapters on the psychology of paranormal beliefs and experiences, conjuring, deception, intuition, cold reading, the neuropsychology of anomalous experiences, sleep paralysis, and out-of-body experiences.

Hines, T. (2003) *Pseudoscience and the paranormal: A critical examination of the evidence.* 2nd ed. Amherst, NY: Prometheus. This book provides an excellent introduction to several of the topics dealt with in this chapter.

Irwin, H.J., and Watt, C. (2007). *An introduction to parapsychology.* 5th ed. Jefferson, NC: McFarland & Co. Even-handed evaluation of the evidence for and against the paranormal.

You may also find it useful to visit the following websites:

www.goldsmiths.ac.uk/apru

The website of the Anomalistic Psychology Research Unit provides details of the research activities of the APRU, including many downloadable publications.

http://www.parapsych.org/

Website of the Parapsychology Association.

Parapsychology and anomalistic psychology

- Many parapsychologists assume that paranormal forces exist
- Many believe they should now focus on how not if paranormal forces operate
- Critics of parapsychology, such as anomalistic psychologists, remain unconvinced
- They investigate alternative explanations for evidence for psi

Theoretical & methodological issues in the study of anomalous experience

Issues of pseudoscience and scientific fraud

What is pseudoscience?

- Tendency to invoke *ad hoc* hypotheses
- Absence of self-correction – intellectual stagnation
- Emphasis on confirmation rather than refutation
- Tendency to place the burden of proof on sceptics
- Excessive reliance on anecdotal evidence
- Evasion of the scrutiny afforded by peer review
- Absence of 'connectivity' with other areas of science
- Use of impressive-sounding jargon
- Absence of boundary conditions

The scientific status of parapsychology

- Parapsychology meets the criteria of science better than those of pseudoscience (Mousseau 2003)
- Parapsychology, at its best, is a true science

Fraud in parapsychology

- Fraud in all areas of science (Broad & Wade 1982)
- May remain undetected if underlying theory correct
- Pressure to publish may motivate fraud
- Famous cases in parapsychology: Soal; Levy
- Trickery by Victorian mediums and 'mini Gellers'
- Scientists would benefit from advice of skilled conjurors to expose fake psychics Project Alpha (Randi 1983a, 1983b).
- Bravery of whistle-blowers (Blackmore 1987a, 1996a)

Evaluation of issues of pseudoscience and scientific fraud

- Pseudoscience – a grey area
- The scientific status of parapsychology
- Impact of fraud in parapsychology and in science generally

Controversies relating to ganzfeld studies of ESP and studies of psychokinesis

Ganzfeld technique tests for telepathy

- Above chance 'hit rates' claimed (Honorton, 1978)
- Hyman's (1985) challenge
- Meta-analyses of ganzfeld studies are controversial

Psychokinesis: macro-PK and micro-PK

- No compelling evidence for macro-PK
- REGs used to test micro-PK (Schmidt 1973)
- Conflicting results from meta-analyses of PK studies
- Publication bias and different sample sizes responsible?

Evaluation of issues relating to ganzfeld studies of ESP and psychokinesis

- Disagreement over ganzfeld studies of ESP
- Disagreement over studies of psychokinesis (PK)
- Experimenter effects in parapsychology

Cognitive, personality & biological factors

Research into cognitive factors

- Cognitive biases and faulty (e.g. syllogistic) reasoning
- Much research by sceptical anomalistic psychologists

Research into personality factors

- Schizotypy, manic depression, dissociation and fantasy proneness
- Correlation with susceptibility to false memories

Research into biological factors

- Role of temporal lobe activity in OBEs and NDEs
- Association with sleep paralysis

Evaluation of issues relating to ganzfeld studies of ESP and psychokinesis

- Psychological profile of typical paranormal believers
- Implications for the psi hypothesis
- Cause or effect?

Anomalistic psychology

Factors underlying anomalous experience

Belief in exceptional experience

Research into psychic healing
- Understanding the nature of illness
- Randomized controlled trials
- Single case studies – could provide evidence for psychic healing
- Fraudulent techniques (Randi 1987)
- Therapeutic touch

Evaluation
- The nature of illness
- Double-blind randomized controlled trials (RCTs)
- Criteria for single case studies: Randi (1987)
- Fraudulent techniques

Research into out-of-body and near-death experiences

Out-of-body experiences
- OBEs are common and linked with NDEs
- Positive correlation between OBEs and psychological characteristics
- OBEs can be induced
- Explanations of out-of-body experiences
- OBEs and veridical information

Near-death experiences
- Can be life-changing
- Explanations of NDEs

Evaluation
- Paranormal theories of OBEs and the mind–body problem
- Support for psychological theories of OBEs
- Problems with transcendental theories of NDEs
- More plausible neuroscientific theories of NDEs

Functions of paranormal and related beliefs
- Functional significance of paranormal beliefs
- Cultural significance of paranormal beliefs

Evaluation of research
- Paranormal belief and lack of control
- Paranormal belief and childhood trauma
- Reciprocal relationship between of paranormal beliefs and culture
- Positive aspects of paranormal and related beliefs

Deception, self-deception, superstition and coincidence
- Deception and self-deception
- Superstitious beliefs and behaviour
- The psychology of coincidences

Evaluation of research
- Conjurors and con-artists vs genuine paranormal feats (if any)
- Superstition as beneficial
- Poor intuitive statisticians

Research into mediumship

Séances and spiritualism
- Early scientific studies uncovered frauds
- Scientists vs conjurors
- Cold reading
- Results no better than chance in controlled tests

Evaluation of research
- Early research into mediumship fraud
- Conjurors can duplicate mediumship effects
- Modern tests of mediumship

EXPLAINING THE SPECIFICATION

Specification content	The specification explained
The application of scientific method in psychology	In this part of the specification you are required to know about how psychologists apply scientific method when planning and carrying out research. To do this, you need to be able to:
The major features of science – for example, replicability, objectivity (Topic 1)	■ Describe the main characteristics of science, how science works and what distinguishes science from other types of activity. ■ Discuss why it is so important to replicate research studies. ■ Explain why objectivity is an important concept in any scientific research, including psychological research.
The scientific process, including theory construction, hypothesis testing, use of empirical methods, generation of laws/principles (e.g. Popper, Kuhn) (Topic 2)	■ Outline the steps involved in the scientific process: – the construction and testing of theory; – the testing of hypotheses; – the use of empirical research methods to collect data; and – the ways in which laws and principles are generated and tested, including Karl Popper's views about the role of falsification (as opposed to verification) as a means of testing scientific laws and Thomas Kuhn's ideas about the revolutionary character of scientific progress, based on abandoning one set of assumptions and replacing them with another set, i.e. revolution rather than incremental changes.
Validating new knowledge and the role of peer review (Topic 3)	■ Discuss the ways in which new research knowledge is validated and the important contribution of peer review by members of the scientific community in this process.

Introduction

This chapter is divided into three topics. The first of these will examine the key features of science that set scientific activity and scientific knowledge apart from other forms of knowledge.

Topic 2 focuses on the **scientific process** (which is sometimes called the scientific method). We will consider how scientists work by constructing theories, testing hypotheses and using empirical methods to test the theory/hypothesis. We will also examine different views about the way in which scientific laws and principles are generated.

Topic 3 will consider the ways in which new psychological knowledge is validated and the important role of expert reviews by members of the wider research community to establish the credibility of research.

Psychology in context

Magazines, newspapers and TV/radio programmes often report the latest scientific discovery resulting from the work of eminent scientists. In September 2008 the media were full of news of the launch of a gigantic scientific instrument – the Large Hadron Collider – the world's largest and highest-energy particle accelerator, located deep underground on the Swiss/French border near Geneva. There has been a lot of discussion about the exciting discoveries about the universe that scientists, including Professor Stephen Hawking, hope will result from the experiments they plan to carry out over the coming months and years.

1 What are the key characteristics of scientific knowledge and of common-sense knowledge? What do you think is the main difference between these two forms of knowledge?

2 Which type of knowledge do you think is more trustworthy and why?

3 Would you recommend that policy or practice should be based on the findings of a single, large-scale, well-designed research study? Give reasons for your answer.

The Large Hadron Collider

Discuss your ideas with other members of your psychology class and/or your teacher.

Topic 1: The major features of science

You may be aware that 'How science works' is one of the important elements of the AS and A2 psychology specification and is designed to help you understand how scientists investigate specific phenomena as they attempt to explain particular aspects of the world around us. Science aims to find things out by describing and explaining specific aspects of the physical and social world in which we live. This chapter will contribute to your understanding of 'How science works'.

The goals of science

Researchers claim that science offers a method of distinguishing what is true and real from what is not. In fact, some would go even further and argue that science is the *only* way of doing this, and not just a more reliable process of generating knowledge.

So how do scientists support this claim? All scientific investigation involves a detailed examination of the subject matter that is being studied and this is done in a systematic and objective way. It begins with detailed description, then, as Allport famously stated, it aims to achieve '…understanding, prediction and control above the levels achieved by unaided common sense' (Allport 1947). Psychological science thus has four key objectives:

- description (finding out *what* happens)

- understanding (finding out *how* and *why* something happens).

Once something can be explained, it may be possible to:

- predict what will happen in a specific context

- control a phenomenon (where appropriate).

We will look at each of these goals briefly in turn.

Description

In psychology the first step towards understanding and explaining behaviour is to describe it accurately. For example, parents know through experience (observation) that children begin to talk around the age of 14 months, but may not be able to explain why this occurs at this point in their cognitive development. Detailed and unbiased observation is a key link between the real world and more abstract scientific ideas; it enables psychologists to be clear about the nature of their subject matter and to describe specific phenomena, which can later lead to possible explanations.

Understanding

Once something has been described the next step is to develop our understanding to explain *how* and *why* it occurs, i.e. how can we account for and explain why something happens? To do this, psychologists, like other scientists, develop explanatory theories and test these theories systematically to find out what they can and cannot explain.

Psychologists usually start by deriving a hypothesis (a testable statement) from a theory and then gather evidence to see whether the hypothesis, and thus the underpinning theory, is supported. For example, a hypothesis based on learning theory might be that, compared with girls, boys are reinforced (rewarded) more often for physically aggressive acts. It would be possible to design a research study to test this and see if boys do, indeed, receive more reinforcement than girls for their aggressive acts. If this were found to be the case, the explanation would be that 'Boys are more physically aggressive than girls because they are rewarded more often than girls for physically aggressive behaviour'.

As a first step in testing explanations of phenomena, researchers look for patterns and trends in the data they collect. If the analysis of the data suggests a degree of certainty, then they can be more confident about their explanation (see pp.515). If this is not the case, then alternative explanations may need to be provided.

Different types of relationship

It is essential to remember the difference between cause-and-effect and correlational relationships.

A correlational relationship enables the researcher to claim that there is an association between specific variables. If, for example, a relationship is found between the number of reported instances of colds/'flu and the time of year (winter), it would be possible to claim that these two variables are related in some way, but *not* that colds/flu are caused by winter weather. (See pp.20–22 of *Psychology AS for AQA A*.) Some other variable may be responsible and in this case it is because the explanation lies in the fact that viruses transmit colds and 'flu and viruses spread more easily between people when they spend more time together indoors during the winter months. A correlational relationship, therefore, enables us to *predict* that X is likely to occur alongside Y.

A cause-and-effect relationship, on the other hand, enables the researcher to claim that X causes Y. Cause-and-effect relationships can only be identified through well-designed, tightly controlled experimental research (see pp.13–17 of *Psychology AS for AQA A*) and, once established, enable us to *understand/explain* the phenomenon of interest.

Prediction

After describing and attempting to explain a particular aspect of behaviour, psychologists will usually try to predict when that behaviour is likely to occur (i.e. what variables are associated with its occurrence). For example, we know that lacking a sense of control over aspects of our life is associated with stress symptoms such as migraine and gastric ulcers. We might therefore predict that people whose work is monotonous, repetitive and regulated by others would be more likely to have high rates of stress and absenteeism than people whose job allows them more freedom to organize their work. Specific predictions, such as this, can be tested.

Control

Finally, scientists aim to control or modify a specific phenomenon by manipulating the factors that cause it. In certain circumstances it may be desirable to modify behaviour. Take, for example, the use of token economy to encourage self-care and social skills in people with learning disabilities. Tokens, used to reward any examples of desired behaviour, can be collected and then exchanged for privileges (see Chapter 7 of *Psychology AS for AQA A* for more information on this and other therapies that are based on operant conditioning).

Prediction and control are particularly important for applied psychologists who use psychological knowledge and theories to bring about improvements in many aspects of people's lives.

A traditional view of science

Ideas about the nature of science have changed during the 20th century. The traditional view of science focused on its objectivity achieved through such methods as careful observation and tightly controlled experiments. Personal values and biases are assumed to have no place in scientific thinking: all research is assumed to be value free.

Objectivity is embedded in the scientific tradition through the separation of the research participant from the investigator. As we shall see when we discuss the use of **empirical methods** (on p.516), our modern view of science as being empirically based and objective emerged in the 17th century as a reaction to previously accepted ways of thinking. Up until this point in history, the Bible and the writings of ancient Greek philosophers, such as Aristotle, were the main sources of 'scientific' knowledge about the world. These philosophers had developed a powerful and consistent explanation of the cosmic system based on a combination of observation and logical reasoning. The term 'empirical' is used to describe evidence which can be experienced through the human senses and thus measured, shared and made publicly observable.

Scientists are expected to provide objective evidence to support any scientific claims they make. Science does not allow people to make specific claims about either the physical or the social world based on their personal views and beliefs without any evidence to support the claim being made. Just think about some of the outrageous claims that might be made by prejudiced individuals about, say, immigrants, without the need for any objective evidence to support their claims.

In an attempt to ensure objectivity, the early behaviourists, such as Watson (1913), argued that the subject matter of psychology should be restricted to observable behaviour. This meant that important psychological concepts, such as the mind or self, could not be studied and were not considered to have a place in the scientific study of behaviour. However, over the years this traditional view of science, held by behaviourists and some other scientists, has been challenged. As we shall see, some have argued robustly against the view that all behaviour can be observed objectively.

Modern views of science

Following vigorous debate about the key features of scientific enterprise, some consensus is emerging about the main characteristics that distinguish science from other types of activity:

1 **Objectivity**: although it is now recognized that total objectivity may not be achievable, it is still regarded as an important feature of science. Scientific data should be gathered in a way that strives to be as objective as possible.

2 **Replicability**: research findings need to be replicable (consistent or repeatable) to avoid basing policy, practice and actions on findings that are either unreliable or based on a 'fluke' occurrence.

3 The importance of scientific **paradigms**: a paradigm is a world-view or general theoretical orientation that is accepted by the majority of scientists working in a given discipline, such as psychology; it determines how researchers approach their work and also what is deemed to be acceptable evidence by the research community.

We will look at each of these key features in turn and how they apply to psychology.

Objectivity

As we have seen, the traditional view of science is that all scientific observation is wholly objective. However, more recently it has been acknowledged that total objectivity may not be achievable, even though it is still regarded as being important.

Popper (1972) challenged the assumption of total objectivity in any science when he argued that all people, including scientists, have beliefs, preferences, expectations and interests and that these influence the observations they make and could introduce bias into their scientific investigations. According to Popper, it is simply not possible to observe something without having some idea of what you are looking for. He demonstrated this during a lecture when he told his audience to 'Observe!' Predictably, the response of the audience was 'Observe what?' What we observe may partly depend on what we expect to see and in a research context is driven by relevant hypotheses or theories (i.e. the researcher's theoretical orientation). Attempt the activity 'Ways in which psychologists strive to be objective' before reading on.

Activity | **Ways in which psychologists strive to be objective**

In your AS course you considered a number of techniques that psychologists use to maximize objectivity and minimize bias.

Look back at either your AS textbook or your notes and make a list of the main ways in which objectivity is achieved when carrying out an experiment which is often regarded as being the 'gold' standard in terms of maximizing objectivity in research.

The control of variables is regarded as a key means of enhancing objectivity in experimental research. However, it could be argued that what is controlled and what is not controlled is based on the researcher's judgement, i.e. what he or she thinks is important to control and also what it is possible and/or desirable to control.

Activity | **Objectivity**

Below are a series of statements. Think carefully about each one and decide which ones you think are objective and which are not:

- People who want to understand themselves better should study psychology.
- Based on 2005–7 data, the mean life expectancy at birth for men living in the United Kingdom is 77.2 years and 81.5 years for women, compared with 73.4 years for men and 78.8 years for women in 1991–3.
- There are usually more road accidents during the winter months because there are more hours of darkness each day.
- Girls are more motivated to succeed at school than boys and therefore girls' examination performance is better.
- A colour name can be read faster when it is written in the same coloured ink than when it is written in a conflicting coloured ink (the Stroop effect).
- Specific eating disorders are far more prevalent in girls/women than they are in boys/men.

When you have completed this activity by yourself, compare your answers with other students in your psychology class.

Moreover, it may not be possible for an experimenter to be confident that a given stimulus is identical for all participants and has a standard effect. We have seen in Chapter 2 that there is an important distinction between what the eye sees (the sensation) and what the individual actually sees (perception). Perception involves the interpretation of sensory data and is affected by a vast range of factors, including an individual's past experience, expectations and motivation. This determines the meaning that is attributed to it, which in turn will influence a participant's response. To illustrate this, consider what happens when you think you have seen someone you know and are preparing to greet them. Suddenly you realize this person is a complete stranger. The image on our retinas has not changed, just our knowledge and expectations. Clearly, there is no one-to-one correspondence between the image on the retina and the experience of seeing; as Hanson (1958) describes it: 'There is more to seeing than meets the eyeball'. It could be argued, therefore, that experimental stimuli do not exist in a purely objective way and may differ from individual to individual.

There is also increased interest in the social context of scientific activity and its implications for claims of objectivity (Woolgar 1988). A psychological experiment may be regarded as a social situation, involving expectations of the participants. Orne (1962) studied the social psychology of psychological experiments and described the demand characteristics that occur when participants try to make sense of the situation they find themselves in and act in accordance with what they perceive its demands to be (see p.16 and p.60 of *Psychology AS for AQA A*). Examples from your AS studies include Asch's studies of conformity (1956) and Milgram's study of obedience (1963).

Mitroff (1974) studied a group of lunar rock scientists who suggested that the idea of science being entirely objective was both naive and misguided. The scientists claimed that good scientists had their own beliefs and points of view, which they defend robustly, and these influenced their thinking and therefore the way they carried out their research.

Some psychologists, including those who support a social constructivist viewpoint, also argue that data can never be wholly objective, but rather that our knowledge and understanding of the social world is based on social constructions. That is to say, our interpretation of psychological data is determined by prevailing cultural, social and historical influences.

Taken together, it can be argued that there are no facts 'out there' waiting to be observed because the very act of observation is not neutral and never can be. This undermines the idea that scientists can achieve total objectivity through careful observation from a perspective outside of what is being studied. It implies that objectivity is a matter of degree and it is unrealistic to expect total objectivity in any science, even physics. If this is the case, it is clearly even more difficult, and some would argue impossible, to achieve total objectivity in psychology, as it focuses on the study of human behaviour, mental processes and experience, involving people studying other people.

It is important to remember that researchers using qualitative research methods (such as unstructured

Moscovici (1981) suggested that shared beliefs within a specific social/cultural group could be used to explain social events. Scientific theories are initially communicated and discussed within the research community. However, the media can intervene in this process. You may have noticed that when the British Psychology Society's annual conference takes place in the spring, you often read about specific studies in the newspaper or on the Internet, or hear about them on the radio or television. Not surprisingly, these studies are usually selected for their newsworthiness and their ability to astound/engage the general public.

Scientific ideas communicated to the wider public in this way are sometimes applied more widely than intended by the researcher(s) and used to explain things not originally intended. Moscovici and Hewstone (1983) highlighted this in the context of split-brain research. Some specific, and quite limited, findings relating to significant differences between the left and right brain, which were carefully presented and interpreted by the researchers, became incorporated into more general claims about innate differences between men and women. The evidence for such beliefs is, however, extremely limited and very weak. Great care is therefore needed when reading any account of research that is not published in a reputable scientific journal. We will return to this issue in Topic 3.

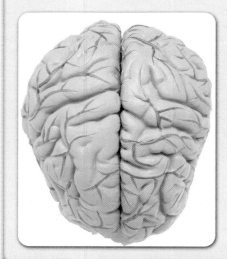

The left and right brain

interviews) do not necessarily view objectivity as an indication of the worth of their research in the same way as quantitative researchers do. Qualitative researchers are far more concerned with understanding meanings and people's inner worlds; they often use participant's subjective feelings and reflections as a key source of data. Rather than focusing on objectivity, qualitative researchers aim to demonstrate the confirmability of their findings by drawing on other sources of data and/or additional perspectives in an attempt to verify any claims they make.

Replicability

Another fundamental aspect of any scientific research is that researchers working in a particular field can validate (check) each other's findings. Confidence in research findings is increased when investigations are replicated (repeated) and the results are similar. Replication is essential in any scientific discipline, including psychology. It serves two important purposes. Firstly, it guards against scientific fraud (see p.475). Secondly, and of equal importance, it enables scientists to check whether particular results were a one-off, fluke occurrence because of the particular way the study was carried out, or the people studied (e.g. a small atypical sample was tested), or the place where the study was carried out. Replication is particularly important in a discipline such as psychology, which studies complex human behaviour using fairly small samples in order to generalize the findings to the wider population from which the sample was drawn. If findings cannot be replicated then we can have no confidence in them and they should not be applied or used to inform policy.

Tightly controlled laboratory experiments usually allow good replicability, as long as the details of the study have been carefully reported. An experiment that has been carried out over and over again and the same findings have been reported indicates high **internal validity** and high replicability. Replicability is therefore usually higher when the research situation is tightly controlled in a laboratory, but tends to be lower for experiments undertaken outside a laboratory setting (e.g. social psychology experiments carried out in natural settings).

However, it could be argued that any experiment is a unique event in just the same way that any cake you bake is unique (even though you follow the same recipe). So perhaps it is more accurate to state that what is replicated are the essential characteristics of a specific quantitative research study.

Qualitative researchers, on the other hand, are not concerned with replicating studies. Instead, they provide what is sometimes referred to as an 'audit trail' (or 'decision trail') which enables others to trace any specific claims made by the researcher back to the original data to check whether they seem to be appropriate. The audit trail provides a detailed account of the thoughts and decisions of the researcher to help the reader understand the logic and development of the study, including making explicit any biases of the researcher(s).

Replicability and reporting

To enable others to replicate a particular study, psychologists are expected to publish full and precise details of their research. This should include:

- exactly what they did
- how the study was carried out
- the number of participants, their key characteristics and how they were selected
- where the study was carried out
- what raw data were collected and how they were analysed.

When writing the 'Method' section of a report of quantitative research, it is essential to keep the need for replicability in mind. A reader should be able to replicate the study exactly after reading this section of the report, which is usually subdivided into four sections: Design, Participants, Apparatus/materials and Procedure (see p.577 for further detail).

If a study is replicated and the findings differ from the original, the research community needs to decide the reasons for this. It could be that the effect being investigated is small or that it is not there at all and the original researchers just happened to collect data which led them to make a Type 1 error (see 'Replicability and hypothesis testing' below). On the other hand, it could be that procedural details in the original research were poorly reported so the replication attempt differed in some important way which led to the difference in the findings. Attention to detail is thus essential when preparing any research report for publication and dissemination to the wider psychology community.

Replicability and hypothesis testing

The discussion of Type 1 and Type 2 errors (on p.563) highlights that the use of **probability** means it is possible to observe an effect, even when the null hypothesis is true (a **Type 1 error**). Alternatively, it is possible to miss an effect that is actually there (a **Type 2 error**). A single research study could fall into either of these traps and lead the researcher to make an error of optimism (a Type 1 error) or an error of pessimism (a Type 2 error) which would result in the null hypothesis being wrongly accepted or wrongly rejected respectively. The replication of research studies guards against this happening. If another researcher also finds statistically significant differences that confirm the results of previous research, then the likelihood is far lower that the original findings were a fluke. Since it would be very unwise to base any policy or practice on research evidence that turned out to be a fluke, replication is essential.

The role of paradigms

A scientific **paradigm** (a term that comes from the Greek word for pattern) determines how researchers approach their work and also what is deemed to be acceptable evidence by the research community. It provides a general theoretical orientation (a world-view or perspective) that is accepted by the majority of scientists working in a given discipline and is used to assess the appropriateness or otherwise of specific studies. As we shall see, when we consider Kuhn's views about the development of scientific knowledge over time, there is ongoing debate about the importance and contribution of paradigms.

In Topic 2 we will examine how the key features of objectivity, replicability and paradigms contribute to the scientific process, which describes the range of activities that psychologists and other scientists engage in when undertaking research.

CHECK YOUR UNDERSTANDING

Check your understanding of the major features of science by answering the following questions. Try to do this from memory. You can check your answers by looking back through Topic 1, The major features of science.

1 List the four main goals of science and provide a brief description and example of each.

2 Clear evidence has been observed for a relationship between smoking behaviour and the incidence of lung cancer. Is this a cause-and-effect or a correlational relationship?

3 What is the traditional view of scientific objectivity and how is it achieved?

4 Explain why it may not be possible for scientists to achieve total objectivity.

5 Explain why replicability is an important feature of science. What is needed to enable researchers to replicate the work of others?

6 Describe what is meant by the term 'paradigm'.

Topic 2: The scientific process

What distinguishes scientific evidence from a common-sense understanding of the world is the systematic ways in which research is carried out that can be consciously articulated (see Table 15.1). As you already know from your AS studies, there are specific rules and procedures that determine how research is conducted and this allows us to evaluate scientific evidence generated through research. To ensure that a proposed study is worthwhile and appropriate, researchers must try to find out what research has already been undertaken by reading the literature relating to the topic of interest.

The scientific process involves building theories, designing studies to test specific aspects of a theory by testing hypotheses (specific predictions about the relationship between key variables), collecting and analysing data to provide evidence that can be used to support, adjust, or reject the theory. Look back at your AS textbook or your notes to remind yourself about research aims, research questions and the formulation of hypotheses (see pp.37–9 of *Psychology AS for AQA A*).

Theory construction

A **theory** is a general model of how events are related to one another in the real world and which attempts to explain observed phenomena; it relates to the scientific objective of understanding (see p.507).

Theorizing in everyday life

You may be surprised to discover that we formulate theories all the time in the course of our day-to-day life. For example, you may have noticed that a cup of tea is particularly good when you warm the teapot and use tealeaves rather than a teabag. Previous experience has led you to associate a particular set of circumstances (in this case, warming the teapot and using tealeaves) with a particular outcome (a good cup of tea). It can therefore be said that you have developed a theory, based on your previous observations, about how to make a good cup of tea. This theory provides a possible explanation that increasing the temperature of the teapot prior to pouring boiling water on the tealeaves is responsible. Your theory offers a potential explanation (understanding) of the factors that can influence the quality of a cup of tea, but you cannot be certain on the basis of your observations that this explanation is correct.

Scientific knowledge	Common-sense knowledge
Strives to be objective	Is typically subjective
Is reliable	Can be unreliable
Is intolerant of contradictory evidence	Can be contradictory (e.g. many hands make light work vs too many cooks spoil the broth)
Is replicable	Can be difficult to replicate because people's common-sense insights can be highly individual
Is based on empirical evidence	Can be based on unchecked evidence such as rumour, hearsay and prejudices

Table 15.1 *Scientific versus common-sense knowledge*

Activity Theorizing

Think about this theory of how to make a good cup of tea (discussed earlier):

1 What further observations could you carry out to test whether the explanation is correct?

2 What outcomes would suggest that the explanation is incorrect?

See p.613 for some commentary on this activity. ▶

Everyday theories, such as the one outlined above, are sometimes referred to as 'implicit theories' to distinguish them from scientific theory, but they are still theories. The important point here is that we are already familiar with the concept of theory construction in the course of our everyday lives. This includes the process of formulating and testing theories, using evidence from observations to make sense of, and explain, aspects of the world in which we live.

Scientific theorizing

Like implicit theories, scientific theories are formulated in an attempt to explain behaviour that has been repeatedly observed. Once a scientific theory has been constructed it must be subjected to rigorous testing to see whether the gathered evidence supports (confirms) or challenges (questions) the theoretical explanation about why something happens. Theories need to be tested in order to add to our body of scientific knowledge. Theory construction equates to the understanding/explanation goal of science that was discussed on p.507.

A hypothetical example will be used to illustrate the process of theory construction, focusing on a topic that continues to generate a lot of interest, namely the growing incidence of aggression in young people. A psychologist would start by examining a range of factors that might explain aggression in young people. Using a nature–nurture framework, the possible factors responsible for aggression might include:

- genetic factors – aggressive tendencies are inherited from their parents

- learning – children learn patterns of aggressive behaviour through observing and imitating those around them

- the influence of the media – young people may hear about a lot of violent behaviour in the news and see a lot of violence in films.

To formulate a testable theory, a psychologist would draw on and try to extend existing work by consulting the research literature to find out what research has been carried out by other experts in the field and which of the possible causes would be most fruitful to investigate further. You may have noticed that researchers demonstrate how their work is connected to previous studies and justify the direction their research will take in the 'Introduction' section of the research report. In this way, a connected body of knowledge is built up in a specific field over time, avoiding the patchiness and inconsistency that could result if individual researchers ignored what others had done before them.

Returning to our example, let's assume that the psychologist decides to focus on exposure to violence on television and formulates a theory that children and young people who are exposed to high levels of violence on TV exhibit more aggressive behaviour. Using systematic observation, a psychologist could test out the predicted relationship between exposure to aggression on TV and observed levels of violence.

Role of theory in knowledge generation and testing

Scientific progress is made when clear and explicitly formulated theories are developed and systematically tested by research and are either validated, modified or rejected on the basis of research evidence. As we have seen above, a key feature of scientific theory is its potential to make predictions about how key elements of the theory relate one to another, and what should happen if the theory was correct or incorrect. These predictions enable the researcher to deduce specific relationships that are testable (see the section on hypothesis testing below).

It is important to appreciate the tentative nature of scientific knowledge. Scientific explanations (i.e. scientific theories and models) represent our best, current understanding of a phenomenon, based on evidence that has been accepted by the scientific community through peer review, critical scrutiny and academic debate (see p.521).

Some previous scientific theories have been found to be inadequate or wrong, as illustrated by Eysenck's theory of personality (discussed on p.519), so it is important to appreciate that some of our current theories may also be flawed, and this will be revealed through rigorous and systematic testing over time.

If research evidence that has been replicated does not support an existing theory that it was designed to test, then that theory must either be modified to accommodate all the available evidence or rejected and, possibly, replaced with a new theory. Scientific knowledge advances when new evidence becomes available that provides a better explanation of scientific observations. Such evidence must have been demonstrated to be reliable, valid and reproducible. The scientific community constantly scrutinizes the **reliability** and validity of any new evidence and the robustness of any conclusions drawn on the basis of new evidence.

In summary, a scientific theory represents the best and most parsimonious explanation of available evidence, but can never be regarded as the absolute truth. Rather, a scientific theory is provisional and can be supported, modified or abandoned in the light of new research evidence that is judged to be reliable and valid. In the course of your A2 studies you are required to study a number of psychological theories, including Piaget's theory of cognitive development, Eisenberg's theory of prosocial reasoning and Baron-Cohen's theory of mind in Chapter 8, and Gardner's theory of multiple intelligences (in Chapter 7). When reading about any psychological theory, it is important to evaluate the strengths and weaknesses of the theory by using your knowledge and understanding of alternative theories or concepts.

Research that is undertaken in the absence of a theoretical framework is sometimes criticized because the researcher may be attempting to gather evidence to confirm their own personal views (biases) relating to a specific issue.

Scientific assumptions about the world

Theory building is a fruitless exercise unless we accept certain key assumptions that scientists make about the world:

- *Order* – events are connected in such a way that lawful relationships can be uncovered.
- *Determinism* – events have causes and do not happen randomly or haphazardly.
- *Empiricism* – directly sensed, publicly observable data should be the basis of scientific knowledge.
- *Parsimony* – the best theories are those which account adequately for a phenomenon in the most economical way.

Hypothesis testing

Hypotheses are derived from theory, using a process of deduction, and are systematically tested through research. A **hypothesis** is a precise, testable statement of the expected outcome of a research study.

Psychological theories and models are tested by generating specific, testable hypotheses from the theory and investigating whether the evidence supports them (i.e. validates the underpinning theory) or requires aspects of the theory to be modified to accommodate the findings. Sometimes the accumulating evidence raises such difficulties for a theory that it has to be rejected (see p.519 for a brief discussion of Eysenck's (1967) biological theory of personality).

Testing a single hypothesis cannot usually test an entire theory. Instead, specific hypotheses are generated and tested in order to test elements of the theory. A theory, or more likely an aspect of a theory, is challenged if research evidence does not support the predictions articulated within the hypothesis when they are tested. Note the use of the word 'support' here. Scientific evidence may support a theory, but cannot prove that a theory is true. We persist with the theory that provides the best explanation of all the available data that accumulate over time.

Let's return once more to the theory that exposure to violence in the media may explain levels of aggression in children and young people. A naturalistic experiment could test the following directional hypothesis: 14-year-olds who regularly watch films known to include violent episodes and/or play violent computer games for more than 15 hours each week exhibit more aggressive behaviour on a school trip than those who do not. A study designed to investigate levels of violent behaviour in 14-year-olds is outlined on p.515.

When experimental data confirm specific predictions (hypotheses) derived from a theory or model, researchers become more confident that the theory or model is valid. As we have seen, confidence in research findings is enhanced by replication. Confidence is also determined to some extent by the probability level of the results. For example, if the probability is found to be less than .01 ($p < .01$), the likelihood of a Type I error is reduced, compared with $p < .05$. As we shall see in Chapter 17, statistical analysis is a powerful tool that enables a researcher to decide whether a particular result is due to chance variation, or whether there are genuine differences in performance between different groups due to the manipulation of variables (see p.509).

The scientific process, summarized in Table 15.2, indicates how scientists investigate aspects of the physical and social world to generate new knowledge.

An observation study to investigate levels of violent behaviour in 14-year-olds

All 14-year-olds who attend a large, inner-city school are asked to record:

a) How many hours of TV they watched over a four-week period.

b) What they watched on TV during this four-week period.

c) How long they spent playing computer games.

d) What computer games they played.

These data are used to categorize the young people into two groups: those who spent 15 or more hours per week watching films or playing computer games that score high on violent content (the HIGH group) and those who spent less than three hours a week (the LOW group) on these activities.

An observation schedule is developed and piloted that can be used to categorize behaviour on a three-day school trip attended by 40 of the 14-year-olds (see pp.44–5 of *Psychology AS for AQA A*), including eight in the HIGH group and eight in the LOW group.

During the school trip a film was made of key activities and events. After the trip, three adults, who were not aware of (i.e. blind to) the allocation of the young people to groups, watched 10 hours of recorded film in order to categorize the recorded behaviour during the trip, using the pre-prepared observation schedule. The reliability of the categorizations was checked.

The incidence of behaviour categorized as 'aggressive' was compared for those in the HIGH group and those in the LOW group to see if there was a statistically significant difference.

Activity **Designing a study to test theory**

Choose one of the psychological theories you have studied and design a research study to investigate a specific aspect of your chosen theory. Think about and make notes on the following:

- What hypothesis/hypotheses would be tested? Is the hypothesis directional or non-directional?
- What research design would be used?
- Who would the participants be? How many participants would there be? How would they be selected?
- What kind(s) of data would be collected?

When you have completed this activity, ask another member of your psychology class to look at your proposal and you look at theirs. Give each other some constructive feedback on how well you think the proposed study will test the theory, suggesting possible improvements where appropriate.

Stage 1 Induction
Step 1: Carry out detailed observations of the topic of interest.
Step 2: Identify any patterns or trends from the observation data.
Step 3: Suggest a possible explanation for any patterns that have been noted by generating explanatory theory that will account for the observations and is amenable to testing.
Stage 2 Deduction
Step 4: One or more hypotheses (specific predictions derived from theory or systematic observations) are deduced to test aspects of the theory.
Step 5: Carry out research to test the hypothesis; check whether the evidence that is systematically gathered and analysed supports the predictions derived from the theory.
Step 6: Assuming that the research evidence is valid, reliable and has been replicated, the theory is either supported by the evidence, adjusted to accommodate the evidence, or rejected because it fails to account for the research findings.
Step 7: Undertake further research to attempt to test further aspects of the theory. If findings are replicated this provides additional support for the theory. If not, the accumulating evidence may suggest that the theory needs to be adjusted or even abandoned.

Table 15.2 *The scientific process*

The scientific process involves the two complementary processes of **induction** and **deduction**. The inductive method is a form of reasoning that rests on the following assumption. If a researcher makes a sufficient number of observations of events at various times and places, and if the findings are fairly uniform, then it is legitimate to generalize from the observations to a general law or scientific principle. The inductive method progresses from specific observations (Step 1) to generalized statements/predictions (Step 2) and the generation of theory (Step 3). For example, if a number of independent observations have recorded that mercury expands when heat is applied, the inductive method would generate the universal law that mercury expands when it is heated.

The inductive process is particularly important in an entirely new research field where there is no existing theory. Qualitative research methods, such as grounded theory, contribute to theory construction rather than theory testing.

Theories generated through induction progress from particular instances (specific observations) to more generalized principles/statements (or laws) based on systematic investigation using deduction (Steps 4–7). These latter four steps are sometimes referred to as the **hypothetico-deductive method**. This term captures the process of systematically generating and testing hypotheses, using the process of deduction, which results in research findings that either support or challenge the underpinning theory.

As presented, the steps in Table 15.2 appear neat and linear. As you might guess, this is a gross oversimplification of what actually happens. Scientists often start the scientific process by generating hypotheses (i.e. at Step 4) because they already know a lot about the phenomenon they intend to study or theories have already been constructed that need testing. They therefore start by examining ideas about why certain things occur. This involves working out what might be responsible for specific aspects of behaviour they are interested in, using their intuition/experience to generate specific predictions that can be tested (hypotheses). Alternatively, they use existing theory to generate testable predictions.

The 'Introduction' section of a research report indicates how a specific study is connected to previous studies, providing a rationale for the study that has been undertaken and is being reported. In this way, a useful and interconnected body of knowledge is built up in a specific field over time; this avoids the patchiness and inconsistency that could occur if researchers ignored what others had done before them. However, some psychologists may choose to work in unusual niche areas where there is little or no previous research.

What should be apparent by now is that psychological research is carried out in a systematic and rigorous fashion and can generate insights that go beyond our common-sense knowledge of the world.

Use of empirical methods

A fundamental characteristic of science is its reliance on the **empirical methods** of observation and measurement, i.e. methods that rely on direct sensory experience. It was Francis Bacon (1561–1626) who first insisted that in order to understand the world better, it was necessary to consult it, rather than rely on the writings of ancient philosophers, such as Aristotle, and the Bible. He claimed that only through the careful observation and measurement of nature would this enable scientists to understand their world better. He argued that the test of whether observations and the conclusions drawn from them were correct should be whether or not they were able to exert control over nature to achieve practical results. Bacon laid the foundations of modern science, and empiricism subsequently became accepted as a key feature of science.

Francis Bacon
(1561–1626)

Empiricism is the name given to the belief that the only source of true knowledge is through our senses, and that careful observation and measurement are needed to generate this form of knowledge. Bacon and other empiricists (such as John Locke) argued that reality consists of what is available to the senses and, therefore, only phenomena that are publicly observable and can be agreed upon by others can be validated as knowledge (i.e. provide the basis of our understanding).

This led to the assertion that all scientific evidence should be empirical, which is a statement about the type of evidence that is accepted by the scientific community. All scientific knowledge must be based on evidence received via our senses through direct observation, direct experience or measurement (known as **empirical evidence**), rather than on intuition, personal opinions or beliefs. Thoughts, feelings and subjective experiences can only be studied, therefore, if they can be made observable. However, observation is only one aspect of empiricist thinking; the other part involves the use of the inductive method described (on p.516).

The early empiricists claimed that scientists needed to empty their minds of preconceived ideas and control carefully the specific aspect of the world they were observing to ensure their observations were free from error. This is how the idea of experimental research was first introduced. The early empiricists would say that no interpretation should be involved because the 'facts' are simply 'out there' waiting to be systematically studied.

Empiricists argued that *all* scientific ideas (theories) must be subjected to empirical investigation through careful observation or investigation of perceivable events or phenomena, and that this test should be the final test of their truth. Science has emerged as a trusted approach to knowledge generation because of its reliance on direct, sensory experience. The empirical methods used by psychologists include well-designed experiments and non-experimental research such as observation (see Topic 2 in Chapter 1 of *Psychology AS for AQA A*). Scientific claims, based on accumulated empirical evidence, can be judged as true, using criteria that are public and available for all to see and judge, because of the emphasis on the objectivity of empirical evidence.

In 1690, the empiricist philosopher, John Locke, published an essay in which he claimed that the human mind was a *tabula rasa* (i.e. a blank slate) at birth on which experience made its mark. He was proposing an empiricist view of learning. Behaviourism, which greatly influenced psychology in the 20th century, emerged out of Locke's early ideas. Supporters of the 'nurture' view within the nature–nurture debate are referred to as empiricists because they hold the view that all knowledge is gained through experience (see p.514 for a discussion of the nature–nurture debate in the context of perceptual development).

Activity   **Refining our understanding through research**

Imagine you have overheard a conversation between two people on a bus, discussing a newspaper article based on some new research, which claims that eating fat is good for you. In the course of their conversation they dismiss 'all this scientific nonsense' and suggest that scientists can't be believed because they 'keep changing their minds and contradicting themselves'.

How would you explain the scientific process to these two people to help them understand the process by which our scientific understanding of something (such as the food we eat) is refined over time?

When you have completed this activity, look back to p.515 to check you have included all the key points.

General laws and principles

Scientists aim to generate knowledge that can be generalized, i.e. the results can be applied to other individuals who were not tested, to locations other than the one(s) tested and to different times. An example of this is the replication of Milgram's research by Burger (2009). Ideally, psychologists would study a target population (i.e. the entire group of people who share a given set of characteristics about which a researcher wishes to draw conclusions). However, the target population is usually far too large for each individual to be included, so a subset of the population – a sample – is investigated instead (see pp.58–60 of *Psychology AS for AQA A*). If, and only if, a sample is truly representative of the target population, can it be used as a basis for generalizing the results of the study and any conclusions drawn to the remainder of the target population.

IDA   **Cross-cultural issues**

Cross-cultural studies are important in psychology because they test whether specific findings can be generalized from one culture to another. It is also important to remember the challenges of generalizing findings within cultures. For example, it cannot be assumed that psychology students (who are often participants in psychology research, particularly in the US) are representative of all adult human beings, or that North American men and women are representative of all men and women in the Western world. In these examples, **population validity** cannot be assumed and care may be needed when interpreting research findings based on unrepresentative cultural groups.

Based on the principles of replicability and **generalizability**, it should be possible for quantitative researchers to generate general laws/principles as the empirical evidence accumulates based on observed commonalities. However, unlike physicists, psychologists rarely talk about general **laws** or scientific principles. One exception to this is, perhaps, the *law of reinforcement* on which much operant conditioning is based. This law states that the probability of a given response occurring increases if that response is followed by a reward (such as positive reinforcement). While working in the field of learning theory, Thorndike put forward the *law of effect*, which states that actions followed by a positive state of affairs are more likely to be repeated and actions that are not reinforced are likely to die out. For the most part, however, psychologists are only able to generate tentative theoretical explanations of events for the reasons outlined below, rather than claim they have identified general laws or scientific principles that hold true at all times and under all circumstances.

As we have seen, the inductive method is the process whereby scientists decide, on the basis of a series of observations or experiments, that a particular theory or scientific principle is supported. Inductive inferences are based on a finite number of past observations (specific cases) which are used to draw a generalized conclusion about how something will always be. The difficulty lies in knowing just how many observations are needed to ensure that what is being claimed is correct. In fact, no amount of corroborated empirical evidence about what has happened in the past can guarantee that it will continue to be so for all time and prove a theory to be true. All that can be claimed is that the theory, which produced the confirmed prediction, remains a useful explanation and can predict outcomes, but it can never lead to certainty. It is, therefore, a confirmation of the theory's continuing usefulness and not of its truth. A good example comes from zoology: the discovery that the platypus (a mammal) lays eggs overturned the previous theory, based on huge numbers of observations of mammals, that mammals do not lay eggs and they all suckle their young. So, if the evidence for a particular scientific theory or principle is simply that this has always been found to be so in the past, how can we be sure that it will not be disproved sometime in the future?

Platypus

Popper's principle of falsifiability

In response to the problem associated with induction outlined above, Popper (1969), a philosopher of science, argued that one of the hallmarks of science, which distinguishes it from non-science, is the principle of **falsifiability** (sometimes referred to as refutability). Since there is no logical way in which theories can be proved to be true using induction, scientists should aim to demonstrate they are wrong by ruling out alternative explanations of a specific phenomenon. They should generate theories and hypotheses that can potentially be refuted (disproved) by research. This is a very different approach from the principle of verification, based on repeated confirmatory evidence from replicated studies (i.e. the inductive process), which only allows the scientist to argue that the theory has not yet been disconfirmed.

Karl Popper (1902–1994)

The following everyday example should help you understand the power behind the principle of falsifiability. No amount of observation of swans can ever prove that they are always white, even though our everyday experience might suggest that this is the case. Just a single observation of a black swan, however, would lead to certainty that the theory ('all swans are white') is false. Thus the theory would have been disproved in spite of there being masses of confirming evidence. (See also the example of the discovery that the platypus lays eggs, which overturned the previous theory that mammals do not lay eggs and they all suckle their young.)

HOW SCIENCE WORKS

Continuing uncertainty about the structure of the universe

One of the possible discoveries that may arise from the Large Hadron Collider (LHC) is the detection of the 'Higgs particle' (the last unobserved particle from those predicted by an important theory), and some physicists consider this finding to be highly likely. They cannot, however, be certain about it until many tests have been carried out. In a BBC interview, Professor Stephen Hawking (the well-known physicist who works at the University of Cambridge) acknowledges this uncertainty when he said, 'I think it will be much more exciting if we don't find the Higgs. That will show something is wrong, and we will need to think again. I have a bet of 100 dollars that we won't find the Higgs.' He goes on to state 'Whatever the LHC finds, or fails to find, the results will tell us a lot about the structure of the universe'.

Popper declared that it was relatively easy for scientists to gather evidence to support a theory. In fact, his main criticism of Freud's psychoanalytic theory was that it is formulated in such a way that it can be used to explain anything! Freud's account of personality permitted him to place interpretations on behaviour, which could not be shown to be wrong. For example, he might predict on the basis of his theory of 'penis envy' that women would prefer to have boy babies rather than girl babies. When he subsequently found that most women desired girls, he interpreted this finding as an unconscious reaction, which disguised women's true but unacceptable desires that had been repressed. Since observational and experimental data are usually *interpreted* in the light of the underpinning theory that is being tested, it can be quite easy to verify the theory. In the above example, both wanting boy babies and not wanting them could be cited as support for Freud's theory. Kline (1981) claimed that there is very little evidence to support the idea of penis envy.

Therefore, according to Popper, advances in scientific understanding are based on scientific theories that are formulated in such a way that precise predictions can be tested and can, potentially, be disproved by evidence. A challenge to a theory, therefore, can be a more stringent and effective way to advance our scientific understanding. If a precise prediction is not supported by evidence generated by a well-designed study, this demonstrates that the theory is wrong and needs to be adjusted or even abandoned. The well-known psychologist, Hans Eysenck, formulated a biological theory of personality that was clearly articulated in such a way that it was falsifiable (Eysenck 1967). The theory predicted that individuals who scored highly on neuroticism should be physiologically more responsive than those who had a low score. Most of the studies that have tested this theory did not find evidence to support this prediction: Eysenck's biological theory of personality has, therefore, been falsified.

Over the course of the centuries, many universal laws (such as the laws of motion and of gravity) have been generated which most scientists accept. This is not the case in the social sciences, including psychology, and probably never will be so. One possible reason for this is that the social world is far more complex than the physical world, which makes it very difficult to propose scientific laws and principles that sit above theories as absolute truths. Some people argue that the idea of universal laws is simply not applicable to human behaviour because there are many reasons for how we behave, and not merely causes of it.

The social, cultural and scientific context of the scientific process

It is also important to recognize that scientific theorizing is carried out in a social, cultural and scientific context and that scientists will inevitably be influenced by their own beliefs which can affect the way they approach their work. Kuhn (1970), for instance, argued that there are social aspects to all scientific activity, introducing the possibility of subjectivity. Scientists use their social and cultural knowledge and understanding when defining a scientific problem and also when evaluating their own interpretation and explanations of their own findings and those of other scientists. According to Cook and Campbell (1979), when a theory, such as Newton's (they are referring to Newton's theory of gravitation), accurately predicts an enormous range of observed phenomena, then there may be a tendency to overlook a few wrong predictions. These wrong predictions are the very issues that Popper argues

are so important in terms of his principle of falsifiablity, highlighting a tension between falsifiability and the wider social context of scientific activity.

Thomas Samuel Kuhn (1922–1996)

Feyerabend (1988) went as far as to argue that when competing theories co-exist, which are supported by research evidence, scientific progress may sometimes be based on publicity and visibility rather than any scientific criterion. He suggested that scientists who shouted the loudest and generated the most interest in their work tended to have the greatest influence, and that this could even be more important than the quality of their research.

Views about what research is permissible may also change over time – this is particularly evident in relation to ethical issues. It is highly unlikely, for instance, that a research ethics committee in the UK today would give permission for Milgram's (1963) study of obedience to be replicated in its original form. Furthermore, once there is clear-cut evidence of a particular psychological outcome or that a specific psychological intervention is effective, it would be regarded unethical to continue to recruit participants to similar studies. In fact, studies may even be cut short if the effectiveness of an intervention is shown to be overwhelming in the course of an experimental trial *before* all the intended sample of participants have been recruited and tested.

Kuhn and the influence of scientific paradigms

The contextual framework of research includes a set of assumptions about what should be studied, the ways in which the subject matter should be studied (i.e. the research methods that can be used) and what should be considered to be legitimate data and acceptable evidence. This scientific context is sometimes referred to as a 'paradigm', which is the name given to the implicit views scientists hold that are shared by communities of scientists and that influence the way research is done.

In the early 1960s, Kuhn (a physicist who became a philosopher of science) challenged the idea of our scientific understanding being a cumulative process (Kuhn 1962/1970). He claimed that rather than building systematically on what went before, science develops in a revolutionary way by abandoning one paradigm (world-view) and replacing it with another (for example, when the Aristotelian approach was replaced by the empirical method, or when Newtonian physics was replaced by Einstein's theory of relativity). He defined a paradigm (Kuhn 1970) as 'the shared set of assumptions about the subject matter of a discipline and the methods appropriate to its study', and suggested that there are three stages to the development of any scientific discipline:

- The first stage is *pre-science* and refers to the period when there is a range of views about the most appropriate theoretical approach to adopt, so there is no generally accepted paradigm.

- *Normal science* is said to occur when there is a generally accepted paradigm, which determines the research that is carried out within the discipline.

- The third stage is *revolutionary science*, which occurs when there is a paradigm shift and a new paradigm replaces the previous one. One example of this is the Copernican revolution in the 16th century, when the astronomer, Copernicus, overthrew the then dominant belief that the earth was at the centre of the universe.

According to Kuhn (1970), major scientific discoveries tend to occur through revolution caused by a paradigm shift, rather than through steady logical development towards an ultimate goal. A 'crisis' occurs when more and more things cannot be explained and there is tension between those scientists who wish to maintain the *status quo* by retaining the current paradigm and those proposing a new one. In fact, it could be argued that Kuhn's view is itself a paradigm shift in terms of how we view the process of science.

As you may already be aware, the science of psychology has a fairly short history of around 130 years. Prior to 1879, when the German physiologist and psychologist Wilhem Wundt founded the first laboratory for experimental psychology in Leipzig, it was considered to be a branch of philosophy. The activity on the right encourages you to think about the contribution of paradigms in psychology.

Scientific evidence is of potential benefit to society by influencing policy, practice and decision-making in many areas of our everyday lives, including education, health and social care and so on. As we have seen, it is important to remember that current scientific knowledge based on the best available evidence may be found to be incomplete by future research. Just as we have seen that the work of scientists may be influenced by the social, cultural and scientific context so, too, may policy, practice and decision-making be influenced by the external context. This is likely to include public opinion, the media, the views of special interest groups, as well as the

Activity Paradigms in psychology

Think about your psychology studies so far. Make a note of the various approaches in psychology, such as behaviourism and cognitive psychology, and the various branches of psychology, such as neuropsychology and psychobiology.

Which of the three stages identified by Kuhn (1970) best identifies the current position in psychology? Give reasons for your answer and then discuss your views with the rest of your psychology class and your teacher. Are you finally all able to agree that psychology is currently located at a particular stage?

See p.613 for some commentary on this activity. ▶

personal beliefs and vested interests of those involved (see the *How science works* feature on p.521).

CHECK YOUR UNDERSTANDING

Check your understanding of the scientific process by answering the following questions. Try to do this from memory. You can check your answers by looking back through Topic 2, The scientific process.

1. Outline the main stages of the scientific process.

2. Define what is meant by the term 'theory'. What is the role of theory in knowledge generation and testing?

3. What is the main difference between an implicit theory and a scientific theory?

4. What are the main limitations of the inductive method?

5. What is the hypothetico-deductive method and what does it contribute to knowledge generation and testing?

6. Is the statement 'a theory can be never be proved' true or false? Give reasons for your answer.

7. Explain what is meant by the term 'empirical evidence'. Why is empirical evidence deemed to be important in science?

8. Explain the principle of falsifiability as articulated by Popper. Why is it considered to be an important hallmark of science?

9. What is a paradigm and why might paradigms be considered to be useful?

10. What, according to Kuhn, are the three stages in the development of any scientific discipline?

Scientists are self-regulating and adopt a common set of values and responsibilities based on the common aim of progressing scientific knowledge and understanding. One of the key responsibilities of members of this self-regulating scientific community is to validate new knowledge. This process of validation starts with the critical scrutiny of research proposals and ends with the peer review of all new contributions to the body of psychological knowledge, prior to publication and wider dissemination.

External scrutiny of research proposals

Even before a research study is carried out, it will be carefully scrutinized. If a study is externally funded, the funding body will usually send the research proposal to a number of experts for their views on all aspects of the planned study in order to maximize the likelihood of the study achieving its aims. The research councils and other funding agencies only support research that is robust, well designed and likely to contribute to the body of knowledge.

A research ethics committee will also scrutinize any research proposal that involves human participants to ensure high ethical standards are met at all stages of the research process (see Chapter 16). Members of a research ethics committee include people drawn from different walks of life so that they are able to represent the interests and concerns of the general public, as well as those with research expertise. The views and judgement of the research ethics committee will determine what investigations are permitted to go ahead and the research methods that are used.

Publicly available evidence

Once a study has been completed and the data have been analysed and interpreted, the researcher is expected to share their ideas and findings with their colleagues in the wider research community. This spirit of openness helps to encourage academic debate and to inspire others working in the same field. However, before any formal report of a research study is permitted to enter the public domain, members of the scientific community are expected to assess the quality of the research to ensure that it is worthy of wider dissemination.

There are a number of different routes for dissemination (communication) such as conferences, scientific meetings and publishing in reputable academic journals. In psychology there is a wide range of journals, including generalist journals, e.g. the *British Journal of Psychology*, and highly specialist journals such as the *Journal of Social and Personal Relationships*. Some psychologists also publish their work in professional journals in order to disseminate the evidence and insights to readers who may be able to apply the research findings to their professional practice (for example, in education and health and social care).

Researchers are expected to uphold the important principle that their reputation and possible individual advancement is less important than the greater good of the scientific discipline. Accurate reporting of findings is therefore considered to be essential and more important than recognition of success for the individual or team concerned (see the discussion of scientific fraud on p.475 in Chapter 14). Although researchers may be disappointed if there are no statistically significant differences in outcome to report, such findings can be informative in their own right and may be worthy of publication, assuming of course that the study was well designed and well executed.

It is also important to remember that solutions to scientific problems are often generated when different teams of researchers publish conflicting evidence. When this happens, it becomes necessary to explain any inconsistencies in the data and any unexpected or anomalous findings. Inconsistent data can therefore provide a stimulus for further scientific investigation. This might involve refinements of the research technique(s) used (in the light of any reported weaknesses of previous studies) or the construction and testing of new theories or new hypotheses in an attempt to eliminate possible alternative explanations.

The external review process

Scientists are expected to use their knowledge and expertise to question and evaluate scientific explanations offered by other researchers and to contribute to academic and public debates about specific claims that are made in the name of science.

The standard format of most research papers (see p.576) is determined by the need for researchers to communicate effectively and concisely with each other. It also enables important links to be made to existing knowledge in the review of existing research in the 'Introduction' section, and in the 'Discussion' section where the new findings are considered in the light of existing evidence.

Research reports are required to include sufficient detail to enable other researchers to repeat the study (to meet the requirement for replicability), and also so that others can assess the contribution of a particular study to the developing body of scientific knowledge.

To safeguard the quality of published research, all reputable academic journals employ a robust review process of all research papers (even papers that have been specifically commissioned by the journal) *before* they are accepted for publication.

Journal editor, editorial board and external reviewers

The editor of the journal will be an internationally recognized expert in the field and will usually be supported by one or more associate editors and an editorial board of UK and international experts. The

Scientists are expected to question the reliability and validity of all new evidence and the robustness of any conclusions that stem from research evidence.

Various kinds of validity are important and each type of validity influences how trustworthy a study is regarded to be. A study has **internal validity** if it is well designed and so can be trusted to indicate whether or not an effect is present. A study has **external validity** if the findings have relevance to different times (historical validity), places (ecological validity) and samples of people (population validity). That is to say, the findings can be generalized to a wider group than those actually studied.

Careful reporting allows members of the research community to scrutinize both the reliability and validity of each other's studies. This is achieved through the formal system of peer review of work submitted for publication outlined below. (Validity is discussed on pp.52–3 of *Psychology AS for AQA A*.)

names of all these individuals usually appear at the front of every issue of the journal because its credibility and reputation will largely depend on the expertise, standing and networks of these key individuals.

The editorial board of a journal is supported by a 'bank' of external reviewers with expertise in a range of areas that reflect the aims and scope of the journal. If a submitted paper is deemed to meet the journal's aims and scope, it is typically sent to two external reviewers selected for their expertise in the specific area of the study. These reviewers are expected to read the draft carefully and provide detailed commentary on all key aspects of the study. This is usually provided in the form of structured feedback to the editor. This will include commentary on:

- the appropriateness of the overall research design, including the methods used to collect and analyse the data
- any ethical issues
- the sampling technique used
- any potential sources of bias
- the operationalization and control of key variables
- the reliability, validity and interpretation of the findings
- the appropriateness of any conclusions drawn.

An external reviewer is expected to assess all these issues carefully and arrive at an independent judgement about whether or not the research is worthy of publication in their particular journal.

The research findings may be judged to be flawed or unclear, either because of weak research design or because of poor reporting. The latter can sometimes be addressed by requesting clarification or further details of the study, prior to publication. Poor research design, on the other hand, usually means that the study and its findings will not be published. Journal reviewers, therefore, have a crucial role as controllers of the quality of published research that enters the public domain.

Double-blind peer review process

Reviewers are not told who has undertaken the research they are reviewing (or where the research was carried out) – hence the term 'blind' review. Double-blind review indicates that at least two people were involved in the 'blind' independent review process, which is designed to minimize bias or the publication of research evidence that is flawed. The critical evaluation of research should be based on its intrinsic scientific merit rather than on the views and prejudices of any individual reviewer. In this context, peers are fellow research psychologists with expertise in the particular area of the study or specific methodological expertise.

Once the editor has received the reviews of a particular paper, he/she will respond to the author(s) of the report. This response will indicate whether the paper will be published without any changes (a highly unusual outcome), with minor modifications requested by the reviewers, with major modifications (in which case the report may need to be reviewed again) or rejected. Just as the reviewers are not told whose work they are reviewing, so the author(s) of the report will not know who reviewed their paper. Again, this is designed to maximize the objectivity of the review process.

A similar external review process is employed when selecting conference papers that will be presented at major psychology conferences such as those run by the British Psychological Society (BPS).

As we saw in Topic 1 of this chapter, replicability is an important characteristic of science, providing the research community with the opportunity to repeat a study and further test specific explanations and either confirming them or refuting them and providing an alternative explanation (see p.511). When research findings have been replicated in a number of studies carried out by different researchers/research teams, and have been published in reputable academic journals, the scientific community can have greater confidence in the results because they are deemed to be valid and reliable (dependable and consistent).

Reading research

When looking at any psychology journal it should be clear whether double-blind peer review is employed. When it is, readers can be more confident about the quality of the papers they read because they have already been subjected to detailed scrutiny by experts. For some journals the rejection rate, following peer review, may be as high as 80 per cent, suggesting high levels of quality control.

You will notice when reading a published research report that researchers use scientific terminology (which is often unhelpfully dismissed by many students unused to psychology as 'jargon') and language very precisely in order to avoid confusion. For example, in his theory of

Activity — Using primary and secondary sources

As we have seen, the media and pressure groups may be highly selective in the evidence they present to support a particular viewpoint and influence public opinion (see Moscovici and Hewstone (1983) in the HSW feature on p.610). It is clearly important that policy makers and decision makers do not make key decisions on the basis of flawed or incomplete evidence.

Think about the following sources of evidence that are available to policy makers and decision makers:

a) A journal article that was written by the researcher(s) who carried out the study (a primary source) and has been subject to double-blind peer review prior to publication in a reputable scientific journal.

b) A systematic review of research evidence undertaken by a range of different researchers that has been subject to double-blind peer review prior to publication in a reputable scientific journal.

c) An article summarizing the findings of a research study that was carried out by others (a secondary source), published in a professional journal and that has not been peer reviewed.

1 Which of these three sources do you think is likely to be *most* reliable and therefore useful to a policy maker? Give your reasons.

2 Which of these three sources do you think is likely to be the *least* reliable? Give your reasons.

3 Explain how inaccuracies might creep in to a secondary source.

4 When might a secondary source be useful to a psychology student?

See p.614 for some commentary on this activity.

the source of any external funding and any potential conflict of interest. Particular care is needed when reading a report of externally funded research; it is important to satisfy yourself of the reliability and validity of the findings, their interpretation and any conclusions drawn.

Primary and secondary sources

When reading articles describing research it is important to distinguish between primary and secondary source material. A research report written by the researcher(s) who actually carried out the study is a **primary source** of information. If someone who was not involved in the original research reads the primary source and then writes their own account of it, the information becomes a **secondary source**. Errors and misunderstandings can easily creep into a secondary source, making it a less reliable source of research evidence. Research reports published in reputable psychology journals will usually be primary sources.

Literature reviews, including **systematic reviews**, are also published in academic journals. Technically speaking these are secondary sources, but since they are prepared using an agreed methodology that involves rigorous literature search and careful review, analysis and synthesis of relevant research, a systematic review provides a valuable overview of the research evidence on a particular topic. **Meta-analysis** is often employed in systematic reviews in order to re-analyse quantitative data from different studies on the same topic, to draw conclusions about the validity of a specific outcome based on the combined data. This gives more weight to any conclusions that are drawn than is possible on the basis of the findings of a single study. Systematic reviews should be useful to policy makers and decision makers who need to base recommendations on the best available research evidence.

CHECK YOUR UNDERSTANDING

Check your understanding of the ways in which new knowledge is validated by answering the following questions. Try to do this from memory. You can check your answers by looking back through Topic 3, Validating new knowledge and the value of peer review.

1 What kinds of behaviour are expected of members of a self-regulating scientific community?

2 At what points is a funded research study involving human participants likely to be critically scrutinized before it is published in a reputable scientific journal?

3 What elements of a draft research paper will an external reviewer be expected to comment on?

4 What are the main differences between external review and double-blind peer review?

5 Why are the principles of openness and transparency important for a scientific community?

6 How do primary sources and secondary sources differ? Which is likely to provide the most reliable source of research evidence?

cognitive development Piaget uses a number of key psychological concepts, such as assimilation and accommodation, to communicate his findings clearly (see Chapter 8). This enables the research community to understand scientific concepts and explanations fully and to test these further should it be appropriate to do so.

In spite of a robust review process prior to publication, it is still essential to evaluate carefully any published research evidence that you read. In addition to assessing methodological issues, it is important to consider the possible effect of the source of any funding that supported the study. Scientific research is funded via a number of routes, including public funding, government research agencies, charities and commercial companies (such as drug companies). Organizations which fund research sometimes have vested interests in the findings, raising the possibility that these interests may influence the focus and direction of the research, and also the validity of any claims made. It is important, therefore, for researchers to declare

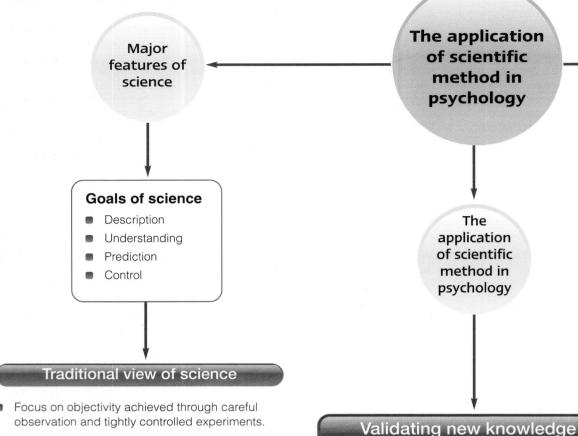

Goals of science

- Description
- Understanding
- Prediction
- Control

Traditional view of science

- Focus on objectivity achieved through careful observation and tightly controlled experiments.

Modern view of science

- Strive to be as objective as possible, recognizing that total objectivity may not be achievable.
- Research evidence needs to be replicable, enabling others to validate the findings.
- Scientific paradigms determine how scientists working in a particular discipline approach their work and also what is deemed to be acceptable evidence.

Validating new knowledge and the role of peer review

External scrutiny of research proposals

- including by a research ethics committee

External review process

- including double-blind peer review process, prior to wider dissemination in reputable academic journals or at major scientific conferences

Publicly available evidence

- Primary sources of research evidence
- Secondary sources of research evidence, including systematic reviews

The scientific process

Induction

- *Step 1:* Carry out **detailed observation** of the phenomenon of interest.
- *Step 2:* Identify any **patterns/trends** from the observation data.
- *Step 3:* **Theory construction** – Suggest a possible explanation for any patterns noted by generating explanatory theory that will account for the observations and is amenable to testing. (This process is not very different from theorizing in everyday life.)

Use of empirical methods

- Empirical methods rely on direct sensory experience.
- All scientific knowledge must be based on evidence received via our senses through direct observation, direct experience or measurement (empirical evidence).

Deduction

Scientific theories are subject to rigorous testing, using deduction.

- *Step 4:* One or more hypotheses are deduced to test specific elements of the theory (**generation of hypotheses**).
- *Step 5:* **Hypothesis testing** – research is undertaken to test the hypothesis to find out whether the evidence supports the hypothesis (and thus the underpinning psychological theory).
- *Step 6:* If the research evidence is deemed to be **valid**, **reliable** and has been **replicated**, the theory is either supported, adjusted to accommodate the new evidence or rejected because it does not account for the research findings.
- *Step 7:* Undertake **further research** to attempt to test further aspects of the theory.

Scientific theories represent our best, current understanding of a phenomenon, but cannot be regarded as the absolute truth, highlighting the tentative nature of scientific knowledge.

General laws/principles

- Scientists aim to generate knowledge that can be generalized.
- Based on the principles of replicability and generalizability, research can generate general laws/principles.
- Inductive inferences are based on a finite number of specific observations to draw a generalized conclusion about how something will always be, but no amount of corroborated empirical evidence can prove a theory to be true.
- Popper argued instead for the principle of falsifiability (refutability): researchers should generate theories that can potentially be refuted (disproved) by research.

Kuhn and scientific paradigms

- Paradigms reflect the implicit views shared be communities of researchers that influence the way research is carried out and what is considered to be acceptable evidence.
- Kuhn proposed three stages in the development of any scientific disciplines:
  1. pre-science
  2. normal science
  3. revolutionary science.

Designing psychological investigations

Specification content	The specification explained
Designing psychological investigations	**In this part of the specification you are required to build on your knowledge and skills developed at AS level and demonstrate your understanding of how psychological investigations are designed. You are encouraged to practise your skills by designing and conducting small-scale investigations. You need to be able to:**
Selection and application of appropriate research methods (Topic 1)	■ Discuss how psychologists select and apply appropriate research methods when designing and conducting research.
Implications of sampling strategies, for example, bias and generalizing (Topic 2)	■ Describe random and non-random sampling strategies (opportunity sampling and volunteer sampling). ■ Discuss how the sampling technique can introduce possible bias into a study and affect the generalizability of the findings.
Issues of reliability, including types of reliability, assessment of reliability, improving reliability. Assessing and improving validity (internal and external) (Topic 3)	■ Describe different types of reliability, including experimenter reliability, internal reliability, external reliability and inter-rater reliability. ■ Discuss ways in which reliability can be assessed, including the split-half and the test–retest methods. ■ Discuss ways in which the reliability of psychological research can be improved. ■ Discuss ways of assessing and improving internal and external validity, including face validity, content validity, concurrent validity and predictive validity.
Ethical considerations in the design and conduct of psychological research (Topic 4)	■ Explain how the application of clear ethical principles and standards by psychologists can help protect the public from harm when participating in psychological research, including the role of ethics committees, use of informed consent, confidentiality and anonymity, the right to withdraw, use of deception and debriefing. ■ Discuss how the British Psychological Society Code of Ethics and Conduct can affect the design and conduct of psychological research. ■ Demonstrate your understanding of ethical issues by identifying specific areas of concern in research that might harm the participants.

Psychology in context

'Near death experience' and 'Out of body experience'

About 30 years ago, an American – Raymond Moody – coined the term 'Near-Death Experience' (NDE). Having survived life-threatening situations (e.g. medical emergencies requiring resuscitation), some people recalled, for example, experiencing an overwhelming sense of warmth and wellbeing, meeting with deceased relatives, and feeling as though they were moving through a tunnel to a source of light. For some, there is also an 'Out-of-Body Experience' (OBE) which might involve a sense of floating above the scene.

Reports such as these have led scientists to wonder what it is like to experience the physical processes in one's dying brain and whether it is possible to think of the mind and body as separate. This relationship between mind and body has, in fact, preoccupied philosophers and scientists for centuries.

NDEs are not uncommon (some estimate the figure to be one per 10 cardiac arrests), but NDEs with OBEs are comparatively rare. Finding ways of monitoring physical changes, when people have these NDEs, is challenging for researchers. Demonstrating that an associated OBE has happened and quantifying its physical and psychological dimensions is particularly difficult.

Some aspects of OBEs are surprisingly simple to test. As people having an OBE often report a feeling of floating above the scene of their own emergency, symbols and images could be placed on a high shelf, where they can only be seen from ceiling level. If, after recovering, people report seeing these images, it would provide fascinating insights into the nature of consciousness and whether it is possible for it to be separate from the physical body.

In September 2008, 25 hospitals in the UK, Europe and North America began a major three-year research project to study the experiences of 1500 survivors of NDEs in which cardiac arrest has occurred. The AWARE (AWAreness during REsuscitation) study should enable us to find out whether it is possible to continue to see and hear during cardiac arrest.

- What assumptions about the relationship between mind and body are being made in NDE and OBE research?
- What kind of images could be used to check the reliability of people's recall following an OBE?
- Why do researchers only study the natural occurrence of OBEs?
- Are there any other ways in which OBEs could be studied?

When planning research, psychologists have to choose from a range of research methods (see Topic 2, pp.12–32, in Chapter 1 of *Psychology AS for AQA A*). Decisions about which method to use depend on the nature of the research question, as well as a range of practical and ethical considerations. There is a series of stages to work through when planning and designing any research project.

Topic 1 begins by considering how to generate appropriate research aims, questions and hypotheses, and how these lead us to select particular research methods. We then discuss experiments, naturalistic observation, questionnaires and interviews. For each method, a number of practical considerations that arise when applied to research questions will be discussed.

Topic 2 focuses on the procedures for selecting research participants and their implications for the extent to which findings can be more widely generalized. Topic 3 examines ways in which the reliability (consistency) and validity (relevance) of research can be assessed and improved. Finally, in Topic 4, we consider the importance of ethical issues in research and how these can be identified and addressed.

The research methods used by psychologists range from highly controlled, laboratory-based studies that generate **quantitative data** at one extreme, to field-based exploratory studies that generate **qualitative data** at the other. It is important to choose the most appropriate method for the research question and to design the study carefully so that the research community can have confidence in the findings.

Aims, research questions and hypotheses

The purpose of a research study can be expressed as an aim, research question and/or a hypothesis, which shapes the design of the investigation. We will consider what is meant by each of these terms, starting with the research aim.

Generating a research aim

The starting point for any psychological research study is for the researcher to think carefully about what the investigation is trying to discover, and then generate an appropriate aim that makes the focus of the study explicit. In order to generate the research aim(s), the researcher needs to be clear about the purpose of the investigation. In some observational or survey research, the research aim may be fairly broad – for instance, describing what is happening rather than measuring something to test a statement, e.g. 'To describe the incidence of cigarette smoking in 12- to 16-year-olds in the United Kingdom'. In an experimental investigation, on the other hand, the aim may be to test a hypothesis to see whether smoking habits differ between boys and girls aged between 12 and 16 years.

The aim of a research study may be further refined into a research question (or questions) and, in the case of most quantitative research, into a hypothesis (or hypotheses).

Generating research questions

Research questions differ in their breadth. Some are very precisely worded and indicate how the research study will focus on a specific issue, e.g. 'How do children aged between five and seven react to the news that a sibling has recently been diagnosed as having a life-threatening illness?' Others are deliberately worded in such a way that they allow the researcher to explore issues more widely, such as, 'What meanings do young children attach to the diagnosis of a life-threatening disease?'

Formulating hypotheses

A **hypothesis** can be defined quite simply as a statement that is testable. This statement is made at the outset of an investigation and sums up what the researcher expects to find. This statement is based on the researcher's knowledge of theory and previous research in a particular

field. It is essential to phrase a hypothesis carefully so that it is precise, unambiguous and testable through the statistical analysis of quantitative data collected during the research study. This process of generating and refining a hypothesis is known as hypothesis formulation.

Consider, for example, the research hypothesis that 'The use of leading questions affects eyewitness testimony'. Stated in this rather general way, it raises too many questions and could not, therefore, be tested precisely. For instance, what kind of leading question are we talking about, and in what ways is the testimony of witnesses affected? If this statement is to be testable on the basis of the data collected in an investigation, its wording must be clear and unambiguous. A more tightly worded hypothesis would be: 'Witnesses exposed to a leading question, suggesting the existence of a knife as a murder weapon, are subsequently more likely to report seeing a knife in a crime scene than witnesses who are not exposed to the leading question'.

The process of formulating hypotheses highlights a fundamental issue relating to research. If the wording of the research hypothesis is too general, it will be difficult to test. On the other hand, when a hypothesis is clearly defined and testable, it may lack more general application, so a careful balance needs to be achieved.

Two different forms of hypothesis are important when analysing and interpreting the results of research – the alternative hypothesis and the null hypothesis.

Alternative hypothesis
The **alternative hypothesis** (in an experiment this is often referred to as the experimental hypothesis) states that the expected effect of the manipulated independent variable on the outcome is statistically significant.

Consider an experiment investigating the effect of a mnemonic on memory recall (a mnemonic is a device for aiding memory, such as using the phrase '**R**ichard **O**f **Y**ork **G**ave **B**attle **I**n **V**ain' to remember the order of the colours in a rainbow). In this experiment, the alternative hypothesis might state that there is a difference in rates of recall between those in the experimental condition who use a mnemonic and those in the control group who do not. If the investigation is well designed, the researcher will be left with just one plausible explanation for the results (i.e. that the **independent variable** – in this case the use of a mnemonic – is responsible for any observed difference in the outcome). In practice, this can be quite challenging to achieve, as we shall see when we consider issues that need to be addressed when designing an experiment.

The alternative hypothesis can be either directional or non-directional:

- A **directional hypothesis**, as its name suggests, states the direction in which results are expected to occur. For example, 'More words are recalled from a list when using rehearsal as a mnemonic technique than when no mnemonic technique is used'. In this case, we are stating not only that there is a difference in the number of words recalled, but that more will be recalled by participants in the condition where a mnemonic technique is used, than in the control group where it is not used.

- A **non-directional hypothesis** does not state the expected direction of outcome. For example, 'There is a difference in the number of words recalled from word lists presented with or without the presence of background music'. In this statement a difference is indicated, but not the direction of the difference, i.e. which of the two conditions will result in better recall.

Directional and non-directional hypotheses are sometimes referred to (not entirely accurately) as one-tailed and two-tailed hypotheses respectively. In this textbook, we use the terminology directional and non-directional hypothesis.

Null hypothesis

The **null hypothesis** states that there is no effect in a study. For example, in an experiment investigating the effect of a mnemonic on rate of recall, the null hypothesis would state that the difference between the memory scores for the two conditions is zero or close enough to zero to be statistically non-significant. If small differences occur, these are assumed to be due to random variation, rather than the manipulation of the independent variable (in this case, the use of a mnemonic). Statistical techniques enable the researcher to decide whether to retain or reject the null hypothesis (see Chapter 17, p.563). If the null hypothesis is rejected, then the alternative hypothesis is the most plausible explanation of the findings.

Some key considerations when designing psychological investigations

Some key design decisions

When planning a research study, a number of important design issues need to be considered. These include the following:

- *Choosing an appropriate research method* – It is important to decide which is the most appropriate research method (or methods) to address the research aim. If the research design is purely qualitative, textual data might be gathered (e.g. transcripts of what people say), or a study could generate quantitative data suitable for statistical analysis, or it could involve a mixture of both. If the purpose is to describe and understand the nature and/or meaning of something, qualitative research methods (e.g. naturalistic observation, content analysis, case studies or unstructured interviews) could be used. However, each of these methods can also generate quantitative data that can be analysed statistically, using descriptive or inferential statistics (see Chapter 17,

p.568). A researcher who wants to measure the outcome (an effect) is more likely to select a research method that generates quantitative data (e.g. an experiment to compare samples of data gathered under different conditions).

- *Deciding how many participants to study* – Researchers conducting any kind of research have to decide how many participants to recruit for the study. This decision is based on practical and financial considerations, and, most importantly, on the number of participants needed to provide findings that can be trusted. We will return to this when we consider sampling issues in Topic 2.

- *Using an appropriate sampling method* – The researcher will have in mind a particular **target population** of individuals who would be suitable research participants. A **sample** of participants is usually selected and it is important to do this in such a way that the sample adequately represents the wider population from which it is drawn. Findings from a **representative sample** can be generalized to the target population. (See Topic 2, p.541.)

- *Deciding how to brief participants* – It is important to decide whether participants should be made aware, or remain unaware, of the specific nature of the investigation or even that they are taking part in research. This raises the important ethical issue of informed consent (discussed in Topic 4, p.547). Researchers sometimes disclose their intention to participants – this is usual in survey research using questionnaires or interviews and in many experiments. The researcher may even spend some time getting to know the participants before the research is carried out in order to put them at their ease prior to participating in the study. It is hoped that this encourages more natural behaviour. With naturalistic observation, the researcher may choose whether or not to inform participants that they are being studied. If participants are not asked to give their informed consent, the researcher needs to consider very carefully the ethical issues that arise from such a decision.

- *Deciding how to record the data and the techniques to be used* – A written record may be made (often by the participant in the case of questionnaires and some experiments), or behaviour may be recorded for subsequent analysis (e.g. on video/audio tape or using computer software). A combination of these methods may be used. The researcher also needs to decide which behaviour to record and which to ignore. If a written record is made, the researcher may need to devise an appropriate coding system for recording behaviour. The technique used may be highly structured (as in many experiments, research using questionnaires or structured interviews, and some observation studies), or it may be unstructured (as in unstructured interviews). The main aim is to collect data that can be appropriately analysed.

Conducting pilot studies

An important step in designing a good research study is to undertake a **pilot study**. This is a small-scale trial run of a specific research investigation in order to test out the planned procedures and identify any flaws and areas for improvement, before time and money are invested in carrying out the main study. It is carried out on a small number of participants to find out whether there are any problems with:

- the design
- the clarity of any standardized instructions for participants and the procedures
- the measuring instrument(s) employed, including the use of behavioural categories in observational research.

A questionnaire or interview schedule should always be piloted on people from the appropriate target population.

A pilot study also enables the researcher to practise carrying out the research task and provides information on how long it takes, which can be useful when recruiting and briefing participants and when creating a schedule for the actual study. The researcher will inform participants that they are taking part in a pilot study and ask them to highlight any problematic areas or ambiguities they come across during the trial run. In the light of direct experience and feedback from the pilot study, the researcher will make changes to address any issues raised by the pilot study before the main study is conducted.

The relationship between researchers and participants

When psychologists study fellow human beings, the research situation has its own social dimensions, so it is possible for a relationship to develop between the researcher and the participants. A research investigation is, therefore, liable to be influenced by those who are taking part. Research participants may be affected by **demand characteristics**, while investigators themselves may have unintended effects (known as **investigator effects**) on the outcome of research.

Demand characteristics

In any social situation, people will usually try to work out how they are expected to behave. This is also true in a research context. Demand characteristics are those elements in a research situation that lead participants to behave in accordance with what they perceive the research situation demands of them, which may be different from how they would typically behave outside the research situation. Well-designed research aims to minimize the effects of demand characteristics as much as possible.

Demand characteristics might lead to any of the following forms of **participant reactivity**:

- *Faithfulness and faithlessness* – Participants try to guess the purpose of the research and act in a way they feel is helpful to the researcher or, alternatively, in a way that is deliberately unhelpful. Either way, such distortions can make the data unreliable and invalid.

- *Evaluation apprehension* – Participants may change their behaviour because the research situation makes them feel they are being evaluated in some way. This could make them feel anxious about being found wanting in comparison to others (for example, less intelligent or less capable). This, in turn, could interfere with their performance or, alternatively, it could trigger participants to try even harder; both would have a distorting effect on the data.

- *Social desirability bias* – Participants might be concerned about how others see them and so, rather than being completely honest, change their behaviour in order to create a favourable impression and, by so doing, distort the research findings. This is particularly likely to happen when a sensitive issue, such as an aspect of social responsibility, is being investigated and individuals are questioned about their moral beliefs or personal standards.

Investigator effects

An undesired effect of a researcher's expectations or behaviour on participants or on the interpretation of data is known as an investigator effect. Participants' behaviour could be affected by something as basic as their reactions to researchers who look a particular way or who have (or don't have!) good social skills. Investigator effects are a risk in any research situation, particularly if it involves some form of face-to-face interaction. Many different features of the investigator could potentially influence the participants, including their age, gender, ethnic group, appearance, facial expressions and communication style.

Investigator expectation effects can also occur if a researcher is committed to, or even unconsciously biased towards, interpreting the findings in a certain way. This can be a particular risk if events can be interpreted in more than one way – for example, it could be difficult to decide whether children are fighting or simply indulging in rough-and-tumble play. Deliberate fraud through 'massaging' the data to produce the desired results is a further possibility, although highly unlikely (see Chapter 14, p.472).

Experimental design

Experiments involve the manipulation of variables in order to investigate cause-and-effect relationships. Selecting an appropriate experimental design is essential for the success of any experimental research. It involves balancing the advantages and weaknesses of different designs. The aim of successful experimental design is to:

- provide an overall plan for all stages of the experiment
- ensure high levels of control over the **independent variable** (IV) and **dependent variable(s)** (DV)
- eliminate all potential sources of ambiguity or bias
- ensure appropriate and precise measurement of the key variables
- enable the data collected to be analysed appropriately.

You studied the experimental method in psychology as part of your AS studies. Look back at your notes and/or AS textbook to remind yourself of the details of laboratory experiments, quasi-experiments, field experiments and natural experiments (see *Psychology AS for AQA A*, pp.13–19). The activity below is designed to help you consolidate your understanding of these four types of experiments.

HOW SCIENCE WORKS

Activity **Do children learn aggressive habits from TV?**

There are at least four ways that an experiment could be designed to address the research question: 'Do children learn aggressive habits from being exposed to aggressive role models on television?'. These are shown in Table 16.1. Briefly describe the design you would use for each of these experiments. Discuss your ideas with other students in your psychology class.

TYPES OF EXPERIMENT	IV VARIES	
THE RESEARCH ENVIRONMENT IS	by deliberate manipulation	naturally
controlled by the experimenter	Laboratory experiment	Quasi-experiment
naturally occurring/home territory for the participants	Field experiment	Natural experiment

Table 16.1 *Four types of experiment research*

Some suggestions are given in the Answers to activities on p.603. ▶

Defining and operationalizing variables

A **variable** is something that may vary or change in some way and which can either be categorized or measured. IQ, memory span, personality and stress levels are some examples of variables that psychologists study. The control, manipulation and measurement of variables are central to psychological research. Psychologists need to be able to define variables clearly if their research is to be scientifically credible and worthwhile. This is not an easy task. Think for a moment about how you might define aggressive behaviour. Your definition might include different kinds of physical or verbal aggression, but did you also think about things such as spitting, ignoring, swearing, glaring or invading personal space? Even a smile can sometimes have aggressive intent. It is even more challenging to define variables when they are less tangible, such as 'stress' or 'concentration levels'. For example, psychologists may be able to measure the visible signs of the effects of stress on a person, and also attempt to measure its effects on a specific aspect of behaviour, but can they be confident that they are actually measuring stress?

Operational definitions
Operational definitions are descriptions of variables phrased in terms that are sufficiently precise to enable them to be identified and measured.

In experimental research, the key variables are the independent variable (IV) and the dependent variable (DV). The IV is the variable that is systematically manipulated by the researcher in order to bring about changes in the DV. The DV is an outcome variable that is measurable. Operationalizing variables usually results in narrowing the research focus. For example, the general statement that 'mnemonics (the IV) improve memory (the DV)' might be refined into an independent variable that specifies the presence or absence of imagery, and a dependent variable that specifies the number of words correctly recalled. This process can have important implications for the extent to which research findings can be generalized. The more precise the operational definition, the narrower the research focus and the more limited the extent to which results can be generalized. There is a balance to be achieved between precision and what is meaningful in the real world.

Choosing an experimental design

When deciding on an appropriate design, the researcher must consider carefully:

- the precise nature of the experimental task
- how to control the relevant variables
- the availability of participants.

This section focuses on three types of experimental design:

1 an **independent groups design** – different participants are used in each condition of the experiment

2 a **repeated measures design** – the same participants are used in each condition of the experiment

3 A matched pairs design – each participant in one group/condition is carefully matched on all the variables considered to be relevant to the investigation with a participant in another group/condition.

Experiments using these designs typically involve a *control condition* and an *experimental condition*; the group of participants who receive the experimental treatment (IV) is referred to as the **experimental group** and the group that does not receive the experimental treatment is the **control group**. Results from the control group provide the baseline data against which to compare the effect of the IV on the experimental group. The **Stroop effect**, outlined in the activity on p.534, is an example of a classic study with an experimental and a control condition (Stroop 1935).

Alternatively, an investigation might compare *two experimental conditions*. It is sometimes impossible or meaningless to eradicate the IV from one condition. For example, when investigating the effect of gender (IV), the researcher would compare males and females, or when investigating the effectiveness of two reading schemes (the IVs), Scheme A and Scheme B would be compared. It would be impossible to remove gender from one condition or meaningless to compare the reading skills of participants who have been taught to read with those who have not. For these reasons, two levels of the IV are compared using two experimental conditions.

Counterbalancing in a two-condition experiment:

Participant number	First condition undertaken	Second condition undertaken
1	A	B
2	B	A
3	A	B
4	B	A

... and so on.

Counterbalancing in a three-condition experiment:

Participant number	First condition undertaken	Second condition undertaken	Third condition undertaken
1	A	B	C
2	B	C	A
3	C	A	B
4	A	C	B
5	B	A	C
6	C	B	A

... and so on.

Figure 16.1 *Allocation of participants in three different experimental designs*

The simplest form of experiment involves just two conditions, but it is possible to compare a control condition with a number of experimental conditions in more complex studies, or to compare two or more experimental conditions in situations where a control group cannot be used. Figure 16.1 summarizes how participants could be allocated to conditions in the three experimental designs outlined below.

Independent groups design

An independent groups design involves using different participants in each condition of the experiment. (This may also be referred to as an independent measures/participants/subjects/samples design, or a between groups/participants/subjects/samples design.)

Ideally, participants should be allocated randomly to the conditions (i.e. allocated in such a way that every participant has an equal chance of being selected for a particular group or condition). **Random allocation** aims to ensure that characteristics of the participants (sometimes referred to as participant variables) do not differ systematically between the conditions at the start of the study. If they did, any individual differences relevant to the investigation might become a **confounding variable** (see under Constant error, p.535). For example, a study of learning ability would be poorly designed if all the fast learners were allocated to the same condition.

Random allocation cannot guarantee equivalent groups of participants. The researcher may still fail to eliminate individual differences if, for instance, the fastest learners happened to be allocated by chance to one of the groups. Fortunately, the likelihood of this occurring is minimal. Imagine, for example, the likelihood of the numbers one to six inclusive coming up in that order on the National Lottery, or the probability of dealing all four suits of a pack of cards in both suit and number order. The chances of events such as these happening are extremely remote but, of course, any single combination is as statistically likely to occur as any other single combination. By randomly allocating participants to groups, a researcher also aims to avoid any conscious or subconscious bias in the allocation of participants to groups. When an independent groups design is used and there is a sufficient number of participants in each group, it is highly unlikely that individual differences between the groups will be a confounding factor.

The random allocation of participants to conditions can be achieved in several ways. The simplest method is to draw names randomly from the proverbial hat. In reality, more sophisticated methods are usually employed, involving the generation of random numbers from tables or computer programs that can then be used to allocate participants to conditions. Sometimes, the nature of a particular IV will determine the allocation of participants to conditions. For example, if gender or different reading schemes are the IV, the allocation of participants to the conditions of the study has already been established and the experimenter cannot control it. See Table 16.2 for the advantages and weaknesses of an independent groups design.

1 Independent groups design

Advantages	■ There is no problem with order effects which occur when participants' performance is positively or negatively affected by taking part in two or more experimental conditions. For example, performance in a second or subsequent condition may be improved through practice of a task carried out in a previous condition, whereas negative effects may result from fatigue or boredom. An independent groups design has a wide range of potential uses and can be used where problems with order effects would make a repeated measures design impractical (e.g. an investigation of the effect of background noise or no noise on the performance of a problem-solving task).
Disadvantages	■ There is the potential for error resulting from individual differences between the groups of participants taking part in the different conditions. Also, if participants are in short supply, then an independent groups design may represent an uneconomic use of those available to participate, since twice as many participants are needed to collect the same amount of data as would be required in a repeated measures design with two conditions.

2 Repeated measures design

Advantages	■ Individual differences between participants are removed as a potential confounding variable. Also, fewer participants are required, since data for all conditions are collected from the same group of participants.
Disadvantages	■ The range of potential uses is smaller than for the independent groups design. For example, it is inappropriate to use two different reading schemes to teach young children to read within the same group of children – only an independent groups design could be employed in this case.
	■ Order effects may result when participants take part in more than one experimental condition. Order effects can confound the results in two ways – either negatively through the effects of fatigue or boredom, or positively through the effects of learning or practice.

3 Matched pairs design

Advantages	■ A matched pairs design combines the advantages of both an independent groups and a repeated measures design.
Disadvantages	■ Achieving matched pairs of participants can be difficult and time consuming. It depends on the use of reliable and valid procedures for pre-testing participants to identify the matched pairs. Complete matching of participants on all variables that might affect performance can rarely be achieved. Matched pairs designs are, therefore, relatively uncommon, with their use restricted to specific situations where a matching process is highly desirable in order that experimental success can be achieved. For example, in a study of the effect of psychological stress on recovery time following physical illness or on wound healing, the researcher would need to match the particpants carefully in terms of variables such as age, family support, family income and history of illness.

Table 16.2 *Advantages and disadvantages of different experimental designs*

Repeated measures design

This design involves exposing every participant to each of the experimental conditions, which means that participants are used as their own controls. (This design may also be referred to as a related measures, related samples, within participants or within subjects design.) Figure 16.1, above, provides an example of how participants might be arranged in an experiment using this design. One of the conditions in a repeated measures design may be a control condition, which serves the same purpose as the control condition in an independent groups design, i.e. it provides a baseline against which the responses from an experimental condition can be compared. (See the description of the Stroop effect at the beginning of the activity on p.535 for an example of this.) Alternatively, a researcher may compare two levels of the IV.

Table 16.2 summarizes the advantages and weaknesses of a repeated measures design. The weakness associated with order effects can be minimized in two ways: either by counterbalancing or randomization.

Matched pairs design

A matched pairs design aims to achieve the key advantages of an independent groups design (i.e. no problems with order effects because different people are used in each condition), and of a repeated measures design (i.e. a reduced risk of problems resulting from individual differences because participants are matched). This design is sometimes referred to as a matched participants design or a matched subjects design.

A matched pairs design involves matching each participant in one of the experimental conditions as closely as possible

Counterbalancing

Counterbalancing involves equal numbers of participants undertaking the required tasks in different orders. Figure 16.2 shows two examples of how this might take place, with participants performing the conditions alternately until all participants have been tested. Note that there needs to be an even number of participants if counterbalancing is to be implemented fully. In the first example in Figure 16.2, a multiple of two participants would be required, and in the second a multiple of six, reflecting the number of possible task orders in each case.

Occasionally, however, it is not appropriate to apply counterbalancing as a strategy to minimize order effects. Problems can occur, for example, when performing one condition helps the performance on another more than the other way round.

Consider the following memory experiment:

- *Condition A:* Learning a set of words presented randomly.
- *Condition B:* Learning a matched set of words using a mnemonic technique to assist memory.

There may be no problem when participants undertake Condition A first, followed by Condition B. However, when Condition A is presented after Condition B, it is likely that participants will still have the mnemonic technique fresh in their minds. As a result, Condition B might help performance on Condition A more than A helps performance on B, which is likely to confound the results. In such circumstances, using repeated measures with counterbalancing would not solve the problem; the researcher would need to employ an independent or matched groups design instead.

Counterbalancing in a two-condition experiment:

Participant number	First condition undertaken	Second condition undertaken
1	A	B
2	B	A
3	A	B
4	B	A
		... and so on.

Counterbalancing in a three-condition experiment:

Participant number	First condition undertaken	Second condition undertaken	Third condition undertaken
1	A	B	C
2	B	C	A
3	C	A	B
4	A	C	B
5	B	A	C
6	C	B	A
			... and so on.

Figure 16.2 *Examples of counterbalancing in experiments with two and three conditions*

Randomization

Randomization involves adopting a strategy for randomly determining the order of presentation of experimental conditions by, for example, drawing lots or tossing a coin. This procedure, however, fails to provide a guarantee that the presentation order of conditions will not influence results, since it is still possible that by chance differences will remain in the number of participants who experience the conditions in a particular sequence.

Randomization can also be used as a technique for deciding the order of presentation of, for example, individual stimuli within a condition. It works best when there are a large number of items in each condition. For example, suppose an investigation involves presenting 20 photographs of faces to participants, which they must later try to identify when mixed in with a set of 80 new faces. If all participants viewed the 20 original faces in the same order, then biases might occur. For example, the photos seen first and last might be more memorable than those in the middle of the presentation, because of primacy and recency effects. Randomizing the order of presentation would help to protect against an order effect.

Activity   The Stroop effect

In one of many experiments, Stroop (1935) selected five colour names – red, blue, green, brown and purple. In the experimental group, each word was printed several times in a grid, but always in a colour that did not match its name (for example, the word 'red' written in blue ink). Each colour name appeared an equal number of times in each of the other four colours. The control group experienced the same arrangement of the five ink colours, but this time, each one appeared as a coloured block.

The times taken by participants to name all the ink colours in each condition were compared. On average, it took participants 47 seconds longer to name the ink colours in the experimental condition compared with the control condition.

1 What is the independent variable (IV) in this experiment?

2 What is the dependent variable (DV)?

3 How many conditions are there in this experiment?

4 Are the data qualitative or quantitative?

5 What cause-and-effect relationship is this study designed to investigate?

6 In small groups, prepare two stimulus sheets as described above. Formulate an experimental and a null hypothesis, and choose an appropriate experimental design to investigate the Stroop effect, using a small sample of, say, 10 to 12 participants. Calculate the mean response times for the two conditions. How do your results compare with the original findings?

7 When you have studied Chapter 17 you may wish to return to this small-scale investigation and select an appropriate non-parametric test to analyse your data in order to see whether the null hypothesis is supported by your data or whether it can be rejected.

Answers to questions 1 to 5 are given in the Answers to activities on p.603. ▶

Activity   Vitamins and IQ

Imagine you want to design a study on GCSE students to see whether a vitamin supplement improves their grades in mathematics.

● Make a note of the merits and limitations of using (i) an independent groups design, (ii) a repeated measures design and (iii) a matched pairs design.

● Which design do you think would be most appropriate?

Answers are given in the Answers to activities on p.603. ▶

Control of extraneous variables

In experimental research there will always be a certain aamount of interference from unwanted variables that cannot be fully controlled or about which the researcher may be unaware. These variables are a source of unwanted 'noise' and are known as **extraneous variables** (EVs). EVs need to be controlled because they can obscure the effect that is being investigated so, wherever possible, the researcher will aim to minimize their influence through good experimental design. Extraneous variables may result from random error or constant error.

Random error

The effects of random error cannot be predicted. Possible sources of random error include:

▪ a participant's state of mind

▪ a participant's level of motivation

▪ incidental noise

▪ room temperature

▪ previous experiences on the day of the study (e.g. an argument with a friend).

The aim is to ensure that random error resulting from variables such as these will not systematically affect one condition of an experiment more than any another condition. By allocating participants randomly to experimental conditions, psychologists usually assume that random errors balance out across the experimental conditions. Such errors might, however, result in some loss of sensitivity of the results.

Constant error

Constant errors affect the dependent variable in a consistent way and, therefore, create a more serious problem for the researcher than random error, as they may not affect all conditions of an experiment equally. Constant errors might include:

▪ a failure to counterbalance or randomize the presentation order of experimental conditions

with another participant in the second condition on all the variables considered to be relevant to performance in the study. For example, pairs of participants might be matched for age, gender and scores on intelligence and personality tests. Once pairs of participants have been identified, members of each pair are randomly allocated to the conditions (see Fig. 16.1). The assumption is made that members of each pairing are sufficiently similar on the relevant variables that they can, for research purposes at least, be treated as if they are the same person. At the same time, however, participants perform in one condition of the experiment only, thereby eliminating the problem of order effects. See Table 16.2 for the advantages and weaknesses of a matched pairs design.

We know that distinctive faces are more easily recognized, but why should this be? Valentine (2001) has proposed the face-space model to explain this. It is proposed that we have many stored images of faces and most faces we encounter are 'average', so when presented with an average face, we have many others to compare it to and are less efficient in deciding whether we have seen it before. Distinctive faces are less common and take up less space in our memory, so when presented with a distinctive face, we have fewer comparisons to make and are therefore more efficient in deciding whether it is familiar.

The Psychological Image Collection at Stirling University (PICS) is a database of faces freely available to the research community, as long as the source is properly acknowledged. It provides many possibilities for research. You can access it online at: http://pics.psych.stir.ac.uk/

1 Formulate an experimental hypothesis and a null hypothesis to test the claim of the face-space model that distinctiveness plays a part in face recognition.

2 What is the independent variable and the dependent variable?

3 Operationalize the variables in the hypothesis. You will need to think carefully about how to determine distinctiveness and how to measure ease of recognition.

4 How will you decide which faces to include? You will also need to consider any extraneous variables (EVs), specifically related to the faces, that you will need to control (e.g. orientation, hairstyle).

5 Identify your target population of potential participants.

6 How will you select a sample from this target population? How many participants will you recruit? How will you allocate the participants to conditions?

7 What ethical issues are important in this study?

8 How will you brief and debrief participants?

9 How will you present faces to participants?

10 What EVs associated with the experimental procedure will you need to control (e.g. presentation order)?

11 How will you test and score efficiency of face recognition?

12 Now carry out the study you have designed and collect some data. When you have completed Chapter 17 you might like to return to these data and decide how you would analyse them in order to determine whether or not you can reject the null hypothesis.

Answers are given in the Answers to activities on p.603. ▶

● participant differences affecting one condition more than another

● errors of measurement that affect one condition more than another.

An uncontrolled constant error in an experiment, which brings about a *systematic* change in a dependent variable, is known as a *confounding variable*. For example, failure to counterbalance may introduce an uncontrolled order effect, which leads to higher scores in one condition, obscuring the effect that is being investigated.

IDA **Reductionism in psychological research**

Some psychologists argue that experimental research reduces complex human behaviour to statistical statements about narrowly defined variables and probabilities. It could be argued that this loses sight of the essence of what it means to be human. Instead, they advocate the use of qualitative research methods, as these generate the kind of data that preserve the wholeness, meaningfulness and complexity of human behaviour and experience.

Naturalistic observation design

A key design issue with naturalistic observation studies is deciding how to sample the behaviour to be studied. The possibilities include:

● *time interval sampling* – observing and recording what happens in a series of fixed time intervals (e.g. every 10 minutes or other suitable time interval)

● *time point sampling* – observing and recording the behaviour that occurs at a series of given points in time (e.g. meal times)

● *event sampling* – observing and recording a complete event, such as a teacher encouraging a pupil.

A further issue that needs careful consideration relates to behavioural categories, i.e. the way in which data are organized and recorded. Possible methods include:

● preparing written notes

● producing a checklist or tally chart

● using a rating scale.

Figure 16.3 shows a simple tally chart that was developed for an observational study on the state of a baby. Figure 16.4 is a simplified example of a tally chart devised by

Bales (1970) as part of the Interaction Process Analysis (IPA) technique he developed, which can be used to observe and record interactions within small groups.

State of baby during 30-second time period	No. of observations
Deep sleep:	ℕ ℕ ℕ
Active sleep:	ℕ ℕ ℕ ℕ ℕ
Quiet awake:	ℕ ℕ ℕ ℕ ℕ ℕ
Active awake:	ℕ ℕ
Crying, fussing:	ℕ ℕ ℕ

Figure 16.3 *Specimen checklist of behaviours and tally chart (the behavioural categories are taken from Bee and Boyd 2007)*

Questionnaire and interview design

We will examine some important issues that need to be considered when designing questionnaires and interviews.

Questionnaires

Questionnaires can be administered face to face, by post or online via the internet.

Some of the key decisions that need to be made when designing a questionnaire are outlined in Table 16.3.

Once a questionnaire has been developed it should always be piloted. Piloting allows the researcher to check that all the questions can be answered and that they contribute to the purpose of the research. Any ambiguity or other issue that comes to light during piloting can be rectified before the questionnaire is used to gather data in an actual research study.

Each observer records the interactions of one participant for the period of the discussion, which lasts for 10 minutes. This 10-minute period can be divided into two 5-minute halves to allow comparison between behaviours over time. From this sheet, the total number, type and direction of a participant's interactions can be calculated and compared with those of other participants.

Name of observed person _____

Person being addressed

Categories	Person A		Person B		Person C		Person D		Person E		The group	
	1st half	2nd half	1st half	2nd half	1st half	2nd half	1st half	2nd half	1st half	2nd half	1st half	2nd half
Seems friendly												
Jokes												
Agrees												
Gives suggestion												
Gives opinion												
Gives guidance												
Asks for guidance												
Asks for opinion												
Asks for suggestion												
Disagrees												
Shows tension												
Seems unfriendly												

Figure 16.4 *Simplified version of a tally sheet used by Bales (1970)*

Closed or open questions?	■ Closed questions are frequently used in questionnaires because they are easy to score and analyse. Closed questions invite the respondent to choose an answer from various possible answers (e.g. by answering 'yes' or 'no', ticking a category – it is important that the categories are non-overlapping – or placing a list of options in order from the most important to the least important).
	■ Open questions, on the other hand, do not constrain respondents, allowing them to answer in whatever way they like. They may, therefore, generate more informative answers, but the disadvantage is that these can be more difficult to analyse. Any question – whether open or closed – that is long or complex is liable to be misunderstood by respondents and should be avoided.
Number of questions and question order	■ Only questions that are absolutely necessary for the purpose of the research should be included. However tempting it might be, it is not appropriate to add extra questions just in case they might generate some interesting information! Questions relating to demographic characteristics (e.g. age, gender, marital status, sexual orientation) are usually included at the end of a questionnaire. An important principle is that any highly sensitive questions should not be placed at the beginning of a questionnaire if it can be avoided.
Use clear language	■ Plain English should always be used, so that the wording of every question is clear and unambiguous. Questions that are ambiguous are likely to be interpreted in different ways by respondents, making meaningful comparisons impossible at the data analysis stage.
	■ Jargon or technical language should be avoided wherever possible. For example, 'Do you support affirmative action in employment?' To answer this question respondents would need to be familiar with the concept of 'affirmative action'. If this understanding cannot be assumed, an explanation of any technical terms used should be provided before the particular question is asked.
Avoid leading, biased or value-laden questions	■ Question wording should never lead the respondent towards a particular answer. It is better to ask 'What colour was the young boy's shirt?' than 'Was the boy's shirt green or blue?'
	■ Questions should not include any value judgements. Here is an example of a biased, value-laden question: 'Do you think the British government should allow immigrants to settle in our overcrowded country now that the European Union has been enlarged to include 27 member states?'
Ask one question at a time	■ It is sometimes tempting to ask two separate questions rolled into one, but this does not allow the respondent to give a different answer to each part of the question and therefore the response to each part of the question is likely to be unclear. It is important therefore to avoid questions such as 'Do you think that life is more stressful today than it was 30 years ago, or do you find that modern technology has reduced the stresses of modern living?' Instead, two separate questions should be asked.
Avoid using emotive language when asking questions	■ Use of emotive language can bias the response. The question 'Do you think that the use of defenceless animals in psychological laboratory studies should stop?' (which is both leading and emotive) could be rephrased as: 'What do you think about the use of animals in psychological laboratory studies?'
Ask questions that are clear and unambiguous	■ It is important to avoid asking questions that are vague or ambiguous. For example, 'Do you take time off work? (please tick one): ▢ Never ▢ Rarely ▢ Sometimes ▢ Often' Using categories such as these is problematic because each category may mean something different to different people responding to this question. All participants need to treat a particular question in the same way if the data collected are to be meaningful and produce useful results. Instead, the possible responses could be presented as: ▢ Never ▢ 1–5 days a year ▢ 6–10 days a year ▢ 11–20 days a year ▢ More than 20 days a year
Avoid making inappropriate or insensitive assumptions	■ Avoid asking questions that incorporate an assumption and could therefore cause embarrassment to some respondents. For example, the question 'What is your occupation?' assumes that every respondent is employed. Instead, the question could be asked: 'Are you currently in paid employment? Yes/No' If your answer is 'yes', is your employment: ▢ Full-time (30 or more hours per week) ▢ Part-time (16–29 hours per week) ▢ Part-time (15 hours or less per week)

Table 16.3 *Designing effective questionnaires*

Interviews

Interviews may be conducted face to face or by telephone. Table 16.4 provides a useful checklist when planning interviews.

1	The preliminaries to the interview	Have you: ☐ clearly described the research problem? ☐ stated the aim of the interview? ☐ linked the problem to an appropriate theory? ☐ identified the general categories of data that you will need to collect?
2	The questions	Have you: ☐ generated an appropriate set of questions? ☐ planned the order in which the questions will be presented? ☐ planned the interview to obtain the required balance between structured and unstructured interviewing?
3	The interview procedure	Have you: ☐ considered the issues of self-presentation? ☐ identified and approached potential respondents? ☐ planned the pre-interview meeting? ☐ planned the post-interview debriefing? ☐ decided how the information is to be recorded in the interview? ☐ considered the ethical issues raised by the proposed research and sought advice if necessary?

Table 16.4 *A checklist for planning interviews (based on Dyer 1995)*

Table 16.5 is an example of an interview schedule that would generate qualitative data, which was prepared for a study of gender identity.

Now try the activities on page 540 to generate and pilot your own interview schedule.

Title of project: A study of the development of gender identity

Topic: Contribution of early school experiences

Date of interview:

1 Can you begin by giving me a general description of the school you attended at the age of 5, so I can begin to understand what kind of a place it was?
2 Looking back, how did your school deal with the issue of gender in general? For example, were boys and girls treated in different ways? Could you give me some examples of that?
3 How did this compare with what you experienced at home?
4 How was children's behaviour dealt with? For example, was a clear distinction made between what was considered appropriate behaviour for boys compared with girls?
5 Did the school generally reinforce or challenge stereotyped gender definitions? Can you give me some examples of that?
6 How do you now think this affected you during your early school life? Can you give me some examples?
7 Can you give me some examples of the kind of thing that would have happened if a boy behaved in a way the teachers thought was more appropriate to a girl?
8 Can you give me any examples of the ways in which the rules about appropriate behaviour were enforced? How do you feel about them now?
9 What would have happened if you had been found breaking a rule like that?

Table 16.5 *An example of an interview schedule (based on Dyer 1995)*

Activity Devising a closed questionnaire

This activity is based on cognitive interviewing, which is a technique for improving eyewitness memory (see pp.106–8 of *Psychology AS for AQA A*).

1 Using fellow students as actors, make a short film (a minute is sufficient) of a staged non-violent crime (e.g. theft of belongings while the owner is distracted).

2 Show the film to a group of participants acting as witnesses.

3 After showing the film, give the 'witnesses' a sheet with about 20 questions, asking them to recall specific details about the physical objects, the people present and what was said and done.

4 After a suitable time interval has passed, ask the witnesses to cover their answer sheets.

5 Now give half of the group of witnesses a new sheet of four questions that are entirely unrelated to the video, but which require some careful thought. This acts as the control condition.

6 Give the other half of the group (the experimental condition) a sheet of questions asking them to:

- mentally recreate the context of the video (e.g. the colours, the lighting and how they felt while watching it)
- recall any other details they can
- mentally replay the film in reverse order in their mind
- mentally replay the film from the perspective of one of the actors.

7 Finally, ask everyone to turn over their sheet of about 20 questions and allow a short period of time for them to add to, or amend, their answers.

8 Mark each answer as correct or incorrect and collate the scores.

9 Decide how to present these data in graphical form.

After studying Chapter 17, you will be able to practise using the Mann-Whitney U test to analyse your data and decide whether there is a statistically significant difference between the two conditions.

Comments on this activity are given in the Answers to activities on p.603. ▶

Activity Devising and piloting a semi-structured interview schedule

It can be surprisingly difficult to devise clear and unambiguous questions, so this activity is best carried out in a small group so that you can discuss question wording.

Bearing in mind ethical considerations, decide on a suitable topic area. This must be something potential participants could be expected to know about and be interested in, and not something that might make them angry or upset. For example, interviewing A2 students about their experiences of the transition between GCSE and AS level would, hopefully, fit these criteria and provide useful information for students and their teachers.

1 Prepare a short introductory statement which you will use at the beginning of the interview (e.g. introduce yourself, welcome the interviewee and briefly summarize the purpose of the interview). You should not let the interviewee feel that you are the expert, so try to convey that your understanding is incomplete and that you value what they have to say.

2 Decide on your first question. Think of this as a warm-up question that focuses attention on the chosen topic and puts the interviewee at ease (e.g. 'How did you decide which subjects to study at AS level?').

3 Prepare six to eight open-ended questions (i.e. questions which do not trigger a yes/no answer) to tap into the topic of interest. Ask about beliefs, feelings and behaviour. Try not to put ideas into your interviewee's head by asking leading questions. Create some

standardized prompts to be used if an interviewee needs some further help in thinking about a question that has been asked. For example:

- 'What do you think are the main differences between studying at GCSE and AS level?'
  Prompts: personal choice; level of difficulty; study hours.
- 'In what ways did your feelings about your studies change?'
  Prompts: more positive/negative, more/less enjoyable.
- 'How have your study habits changed?'
  Prompts: level of responsibility; study patterns.

4 Include at least one open-ended question that allows the interviewee to raise any issues you may not have thought of.

5 Finally, prepare a statement to thank the interviewee for their participation.

Pilot your interview schedule with a willing volunteer and revise it in the light of feedback received. When you are happy with the interview schedule, carry out and record at least one interview. You could use the qualitative data you collect to carry out a thematic analysis, as described in Chapter 17, p.574.

Comments on this activity are given in the Answers to activities on p.603. ▶

Activity **What makes a research method scientific?**

1 What makes a research method scientific?

2 Can qualitative research be regarded as scientific? If not, what is the contribution of qualitative research to psychological knowledge and why should psychologists continue to undertake it?

Answers are given in the Answers to activities on p.603. ▶

CHECK YOUR UNDERSTANDING

Check your understanding of the selection and application of appropriate research methods by answering the following questions. Try to do this from memory. You can check your answers by looking back through Topic 1.

1 Distinguish between a research aim, a research question and a research hypothesis.

2 What is a null hypothesis?

3 What is the purpose of a control condition?

4 How might you counterbalance a two-condition experimental design?

5 What is meant by randomization?

6 When and why would you use counterbalancing or randomization?

7 Prepare an operational definition of happiness.

8 Give two examples of a constant error.

9 What is meant by the term 'demand characteristics'?

10 Explain one way in which participant reactivity could manifest itself in psychological research.

11 Identify and define three ways of sampling behaviour in a naturalistic observation study.

12 In interview- or questionnaire-based research, what is a leading question, a closed question and an open-ended question?

Topic 2: Sampling strategies and their implications

Populations and samples

A target population is the total collection of people who share a given set of characteristics (e.g. all students registered for AS psychology examinations in a given year in the UK). However, many target populations are too large for a researcher to study everyone in a way that is practical or financially feasible. For these reasons, a subset of the population – a sample – is typically investigated instead.

A representative sample is a selection of individuals from the target population, which shares all the main characteristics of the population despite its smaller size. If, and only if, a sample is truly representative, can it be used as a basis for generalizing the results of the study, and any conclusions drawn, to the rest of the target population. A sample that is not truly representative, on the other hand, may result in wasted time and effort because the results would only apply to the specific sample studied and cannot be generalized to the target population.

In practice, there will nearly always be some degree of **sampling error** that results in the sample differing in some way from the target population. If the sampling error is large, then generalizations to the target population are unlikely to be accurate. Researchers can minimize sampling error by choosing their sampling technique carefully in order to be able to generalize with confidence. Samples can be selected in several different ways. We consider three methods: random sampling, opportunity sampling and volunteer sampling.

Activity **Defining target populations**

For each of the following, list the characteristics that define the target population they represent:

1 Robbie Williams

2 This textbook

3 A chimpanzee trained to use sign language

4 You

Answers are given in the Answers to activities on p.603. ▶

Random sampling

In a random sample, every person or item in a given target population has an equal chance of being selected for inclusion. This means that it is necessary to have a list that identifies every person or item in the target population (this is known as a sampling frame). Random number tables or random number generators can then be used to select a random sample in an unbiased way. However, selecting a random sample does not guarantee a sample that is totally representative of the population concerned. Nor does it mean that any two random samples drawn from the same target population will share identical characteristics. By its very nature, a random sample can only guarantee that it has been selected in an entirely unbiased manner. As long as the target population and sample size have been chosen carefully, the laws of probability predict that the chance of selecting a biased sample through **random sampling** techniques is minimal.

Opportunity sampling

Opportunity sampling involves the researcher selecting anyone who is available to take part in a study from a defined population such as the staff or students in a particular college. Opportunity sampling is a non-random method of sampling, widely used because it is convenient (in fact, this type of sample is sometimes referred to as a convenience sample). Its main weakness is that it is unlikely to generate a sample that is representative of the target population. This means that the findings gathered from an opportunity sample are unlikely to be representative of the target population and may be biased, so should not be generalized to the wider population.

Volunteer sampling

Volunteer sampling (also referred to as self-selected sampling) is another non-random sampling technique that involves participants selecting themselves to take part in a research study, often by replying to an advertisement. This type of sampling has been widely used in psychological research. A well-known example was in Milgram's research on obedience in the 1960s (Milgram 1963, 1974). Potential weaknesses of using a volunteer or self-selected sample are that the majority of a given target population are unlikely to respond to the request to participate. Those who do respond (i.e. volunteers) may have particular characteristics, such as a greater than average need for attention or a desire to please, that makes them atypical of the target population. Compared with random sampling, data gathered from a potentially biased, volunteer sample are less likely to be representative of the target population and so the findings of the study should not be generalized to all its members.

Sample bias

The aim of sampling is to keep sampling error to a minimum in order to represent the target population accurately. Ideally, this means that every member of the target population has an equal chance of being selected. However, **sample bias** can occur if some members of a target population are more likely to be selected than others. Three ways in which bias might be introduced are through choice of sampling technique, choice of target population and sample size.

Choice of sampling technique

In the three sampling techniques outlined above, recruitment depends on individuals agreeing to participate, so there is inevitably an element of bias towards self-selection. Potential participants have the right not to participate in research, which means that the characteristics of people who choose not to participate are lost, and the sample becomes biased towards those who are willing to take part. Even in random sampling, which is the only technique in which all members

of a target population have an equal chance of being selected, there is still an element of self-selection, which increases sampling error. Researchers have to accept this because it is unacceptable on ethical grounds to coerce anyone to participate in research against their will. Furthermore, in opportunity sampling, researchers, being human, may introduce bias by unwittingly recruiting people they, personally, find approachable.

Even when a sampling technique is carefully applied, a sample may still be biased if certain members of a population, who might be prepared to take part, are not represented. This can happen if there are minority subgroups (e.g. female students far outnumber male students in some undergraduate psychology programmes). Any one of the three sampling techniques described could, therefore, fail to recruit males and be entirely biased in favour of females. The solution is to specify the characteristics of the subgroups in advance and then select from each group in the same proportions that appear in the target population. This is known as stratification. If the selection is then carried out using random sampling, the technique is known as **stratified random sampling**. If it is carried out using opportunity sampling, the technique is known as **quota sampling**. It is also possible to do this with volunteer sampling, but it depends on sufficient numbers of volunteers presenting themselves.

HOW SCIENCE WORKS

Activity Sampling issues

Imagine that you want to select a random sample of A-level psychology students. You have been told that psychology attracts about 90 per cent female students and 10 per cent male students:

- What danger might there be in using simple random sampling?
- How might this limitation be overcome?

Answers are given in the Answers to activities on p.603. ▶

Choice of target population

No matter how careful a researcher is to select a representative sample in order to be able to generalize findings to the target population, sample bias can occur if certain populations are persistently targeted at the expense of others. This could lead to a body of psychological knowledge that is based on a limited subset of individuals who are alike in various ways but different from other people. For example, there may be gender bias in research which under-represents women (see the debate between Kohlberg and Gilligan on moral development in Chapter 8, p.281) or culture bias in research that is based in the developed Western world and under-represents different cultures (see cross-cultural explanations of gender in Chapter 6, pp.211–12). It is not necessarily wrong to target specific populations, as long as researchers recognize the limits that this places on their ability to generalize the findings.

However, it is also important to recognize the diversity that exists among potential participants and try to ensure that all voices are heard, rather than just those of the dominant group.

Small samples

Small samples may be biased if they happen to contain individuals with particular characteristics that are unlike the majority in the target population. A general principle is that the larger the sample, the more likely it is to provide a good approximation of the population from which it was drawn (for example, the means derived from larger samples tend to be closer to the population mean than those derived from small samples). Determining sample size, therefore, depends on balancing the need to represent the target population accurately on the one hand, and practical considerations, such as saving money and participants' and researchers' time, on the other. Statistical techniques can be used to decide on the sample size needed to achieve acceptable levels of sampling error in target populations of different sizes. It should be noted, however, that small samples should not automatically be discounted; they are sometimes used to good effect (e.g. in research concerning clinical groups with relatively rare conditions).

IDA · Sampling bias

A frequent criticism is that many of the classic psychological research studies have been based on samples of easily available, predominantly white, males, many of whom were undergraduate students. Graham (1992) examined 20 years of publications in six of the American Psychological Association's journals and claimed that fewer than 4 per cent of the 15 000 published articles studied African–Americans. Since then, awareness has been increasing about how this type of bias has affected what psychologists study, how they do it and how widely the findings are applicable. Whenever you read about a research study, pause to consider:

- when it was done
- where it was done
- the nature of the sample
- how the participants were recruited
- how applicable the findings might be to other times, places and people.

Is it possible that the findings could be quite different if another sample of participants had been used?

STRETCH AND CHALLENGE

Activity · Is bigger always better in terms of sample size?

When evaluating a research study, students often write that it would have been better to use a bigger sample.

1 Do you think that this is always true? Give your reasons.

2 Identify some research where N = 1. What have we learned from such studies that is more widely applicable?

3 How might you find and recruit individuals with rare characteristics?

Answers are given in the Answers to activities on p.603. ▶

CHECK YOUR UNDERSTANDING

Check your understanding of sampling strategies and their implications by answering the following questions. Try to do this from memory. You can check your answers by looking back through Topic 2.

1 What is a 'target population' in psychological research?

2 Give two reasons why a researcher may study a sample rather than the target population.

3 Why is it important that a sample is representative of the target population?

4 What is sampling error?

5 Describe a procedure for selecting a random sample.

6 Identify three potential sources of sample bias and suggest ways of minimizing each one.

Psychologists need to gather data that are both reliable and valid. There are several different types of **reliability** and **validity** and this section outlines some of the ways in which reliability and then validity can be assessed and how they can be improved.

Reliability

Types of reliability

When carrying out psychological research it is essential that the chosen approach is used consistently. Any variation in how a researcher conducts a study and/or in the tools used to collect data can introduce unwanted variation that can reduce the quality of the research evidence and, possibly, obscure the effects being investigated.

- **Researcher reliability** refers to the extent to which a researcher acts entirely consistently when gathering data. In experimental research this is referred to as **experimenter reliability** and in non-experimental research, such as observational research or clinical assessment, where more than one researcher may be involved in data collection, it is known as **inter-observer** or **inter-rater reliability**.

- **Internal reliability** refers to the consistency of the measures used in an investigation. For example, in psychometric tests, such as those measuring personality, it is important that all items used to assess a particular personality type perform similarly to each other (i.e. they are internally consistent) and that there are no 'rogue' items, which produce unpredictable responses from participants.

- **External reliability** refers to the consistency of a measure from one occasion to another (for example, the extent to which a psychological test or clinical diagnostic procedure can be depended on to generate a similar result if used twice with the same individual).

Assessing researcher reliability

Assessing intra-researcher reliability

The consistency of researchers' behaviour is important in all research situations, irrespective of the research method being used. **Intra-** (within) **researcher reliability** is achieved if a researcher performs consistently. Reliability is assessed by measuring the extent to which a researcher produces similar results when observing or scoring the same/similar situations on more than one occasion. In other kinds of research, such as observational and other non-experimental studies, reliability is typically assessed by correlating the sets of data obtained on two separate occasions to establish the degree of similarity between the scores. **Intra-observer** (or **intra-rater**) **reliability** is achieved if there is a

statistically significant positive **correlation** between the scores obtained on the different occasions. (Look back at pp.20–22 of *Psychology AS for AQA A* to remind yourself about correlation.)

Assessing inter-researcher reliability

Inter-researcher reliability is important when there is more than one researcher working on a particular project. The researchers need to act in entirely similar ways. In experimental research, this would involve different researchers carrying out exactly the same procedures. In observation research, *inter-observer* (or *inter-rater*) reliability is a measure of the extent to which different observers agree on what they have observed. Each observer records their data independently and the scores are then correlated to establish the degree of similarity. Inter-observer reliability is achieved if there is a statistically significant positive correlation between the scores of the different observers.

Improving researcher reliability

Since variability in the way researchers operate can introduce unwelcome extraneous variation into a research study and lead to reduced confidence in the research findings, it is important to ensure high intra- and inter-researcher reliability. There are two main ways in which these can be improved:

1 *Careful design of a study*, taking into account issues discussed in Topic 1 of this chapter, is critical to improving both intra- and inter-researcher reliability. For example, piloting research procedures and the materials used can improve their precision and also make them less likely to be open to interpretation due to personal biases of the researcher. This might include standardized briefing, instructions and debriefing materials, and carefully planned procedures, such as the use of a structured interview schedule, designed to minimize human variation and error.

2 *Careful training of researchers* in the procedures and use of materials can, and should, take place prior to data collection, so that variability in their behaviour is reduced and reliability is improved both within and between researchers. Researchers should know exactly how to carry out the research procedure(s) and how to record the data. From the outset, operational definitions of the key terms should be clear and fully understood by all those involved. Thorough preparation is crucially important. For example, in an observation study, the researcher(s) should be clear what qualifies as, say, an example of physical aggression in children's play and how to record a particular behaviour. In an experimental study, the researcher should know how to record participants' responses in a consistent manner.

Assessing and improving internal and external reliability

Another important issue concerns the internal and external reliability (or consistency) of the measures employed by psychologists in their research. Although this is important for any form of psychological measurement, it is particularly clearly illustrated in psychometric testing of intelligence and personality. Psychologists use several methods to improve test reliability, including the split-half method and the test–retest method.

The split-half method of assessing internal reliability

This can be used as a way of assessing the extent to which individual items in a particular psychological test or questionnaire are consistent with other items within the same test. The method involves splitting the psychological test or questionnaire into two parts after the data have been collected from the participants. This splitting might be done, for example, by:

- comparing the results obtained from odd- and even-numbered questions
- comparing the results from the first half of the test with those from the second half
- randomly splitting the test/questionnaire into two parts.

Whichever method is used, the two sets of responses are then correlated. A statistically significant positive correlation for the two sets of responses indicates that the test or questionnaire is reliable. If the correlation is not statistically significant, the researcher would need to check individual test items by removing each one in turn and retesting to see if the overall reliability of the measuring instrument improves. Certain statistical software packages will do this and highlight the items that are the most inconsistent. The overall aim is to improve the internal reliability of a particular test or questionnaire so that the split-half correlation is at least +.8.

The test–retest method for external reliability

Test–retest reliability is used to assess the consistency or stability of a psychological test or questionnaire over time. This method involves presenting the same participants with the same test or questionnaire on two different occasions, with no feedback given after the first presentation. The time interval between presentations needs to be selected carefully. If it is too short, participants may remember their previous answers, and if it is too long the participants may have changed in some way relevant to the test or questionnaire. (Sometimes, alternate equivalent forms of a test are available, in which case, testing with counterbalancing can be done with little or no time interval in between.)

Correlational techniques are again used to calculate the test stability. If there is a statistically significant positive correlation between the scores obtained in the test–retest phases, the test is deemed to be stable. If not, individual test items can be checked for consistency and/or the testing procedures can be revised (e.g. by rephrasing the instructions) and the reliability retested to see if a statistically significant correlation is obtained.

Validity

Like other scientists, psychologists aim to conduct research that is valid – that is to say, the research is sound, it does what it claims to do, and any research effect can be trusted to be real and not contaminated by unwanted variables. Any psychological test or measuring instrument must have **internal validity**, i.e. it must measure what it is intended to measure. Research findings should also have **external validity**, by which we mean they should be generalizable beyond the specific context in which the study was carried out.

Assessing and improving internal validity

Internal validity refers to the overall quality of a research design and is relevant to any kind of research. For example, in a well-designed experiment we can be confident that any differences in the results are due to the manipulation of the independent variable and not to the action of some other unwanted (extraneous) variable, such as individual differences or order effects. Poor internal validity can result in failure to find an effect in a research study when one actually exists. It is important, therefore, to pay close attention to all aspects of the research process, from formulating the research question, through planning, designing, conducting the study and analysing the data, so that the research community can have confidence in the findings.

Techniques to assess and improve internal validity

Psychologists use various techniques to assess and improve the validity of specific tests and measures. Four of these are outlined below:

- *Face validity* – This is the simplest type of validity and refers to whether a test or measuring instrument appears, on the surface, to be doing what it should and is self-evident. One or more judges with some relevant expertise assess whether the test or measuring instrument appears to be appropriate, and they may make suggestions for how it might be improved.

- *Content validity* – This is similar to face validity, focusing on whether the content of a test or measuring instrument covers the whole of the topic area. The assessment and improvement of content validity also involves asking independent experts to assess the validity of the measure. However, the procedures are more rigorous, involving a detailed and systematic examination of all the component parts of the test or measuring instrument, typically by comparing them against specific standards, until it is agreed that the content is appropriate.

- *Concurrent validity* – This involves obtaining two sets of scores at the same time – one from the new procedure with unknown validity, and the other from an alternative procedure or test for which validity has already been established. The scores obtained from both the new and the existing test will then be correlated to assess the validity of the new procedure. A statistically significant positive correlation coefficient would suggest that the new procedure is valid. For example, a new procedure for the diagnosis of a psychopathological condition might be compared with an established method of diagnosis for which the success rate is already known. If the correlation obtained is not sufficiently high, the new test or measuring instrument would need to be further refined to improve its internal validity, as indicated by its concurrent validity.

- *Predictive validity* – This involves a similar strategy to that used to assess concurrent validity, but the two sets of scores are obtained at different points in time. For example, students' GCSE grades might be converted into points and compared with the total number of points achieved at A level. A statistically significant positive correlation would indicate that the use of GCSE points is a valid predictor of achievement at A level. Teachers may then decide to use this information when selecting students for A-level courses and when setting A-level target grades. Using more precise measures, such as the actual marks

awarded instead of the grades, may increase the predictive validity. Predictive validity may also be improved by adding further relevant predictors, such as motivation to study and parental support.

External validity

The term 'external validity' is concerned with the extent to which results can be generalized across people, places and times, i.e. to other situations beyond those in which the study was actually carried out. The three different types of external validity are sometimes referred to as:

- **Context validity** – This refers to the extent to which research findings can be generalized to settings other than that of the original research. Psychologists often call this '**ecological validity**'. Ecological validity is sometimes assumed to mean applicable to everyday life or 'real' life, implying that this means 'naturalistic'. However, ecological validity more accurately means applicable across different contexts whatever these may be.

- **Temporal validity** – This is concerned with the 'shelf life' of research findings and whether they are able to endure over time.

- **Population validity** – This refers to the extent to which research findings can be generalized to people other than those actually involved in the original research.

Milgram's classic studies of obedience in the 1960s and 1970s can be used to illustrate how each type of external validity can be assessed (Milgram 1963). The original research took place in a laboratory at the prestigious Yale University and it was shown that the findings could be reproduced, but at a lower level, when the study was replicated in a less prestigious office building (context validity). The temporal validity of the original findings has also been tested: some studies have reported that rates of obedience have reduced over time, suggesting that later generations may be less deferential, although a recent study by Burger (2009) found the effect is still remarkably robust. In addition, rates of obedience have also been studied across a range of cultures, so the population validity of the original findings has also been tested.

Varying places, times and populations have generated results that differ from Milgram's original findings. This is not to say that the original research was flawed. The results were trustworthy in their particular setting, historical context and with the specific participants studied. However, the variation does highlight the importance of researchers testing their findings in a variety of settings, at different historical times and with different populations in order to claim external validity. Refinements to studies and a great deal of replication may be necessary to improve external validity but, once this has been done, the findings can be generalized with confidence. (The importance of replicability is discussed in Chapter 15, p.511.)

HOW SCIENCE WORKS

Activity **Improving internal validity**

Apply what you know about good experimental design to improve the internal validity of the study described below.

A researcher is interested in the relationship between parenting style and students' academic achievement at GCSE level. Students in Year 12 in a large comprehensive school each filled in a questionnaire about their parents' behaviour. Scores from the questionnaires were used to select a sample of students whose parents were predominantly democratic and another sample whose parents were predominantly authoritarian. Students' GCSE grades were then converted into points (A* = 6, A = 5, B = 4, etc.) and added together to give an overall achievement score for each student. These scores were compared using a Mann-Whitney U test and it was concluded that students with democratic parents were higher achievers than those with authoritarian parents.

Comments are given in the Answers to activities on p.603. ▶

CHECK YOUR UNDERSTANDING

Check your understanding of reliability and validity by answering the following questions. Try to do this from memory. You can check your answers by looking back through Topic 3.

1 What is meant by the term 'reliability'?

2 What is the difference between internal and external reliability?

3 What is the difference between intra- and inter-rater reliability? How can they be assessed?

4 Explain two ways in which researcher reliability can be improved.

5 What is the split-half method and how can it be used to assess and improve internal reliability?

6 What is the test–retest method? How can it be used to improve external reliability?

7 What is meant by the term 'validity'?

8 What is the difference between internal and external validity?

9 Briefly describe four techniques that can be used to assess and improve the internal validity of psychological tests and measuring instruments.

10 What are the three types of external validity? How might each of these be assessed and improved?

Topic 4: Ethical considerations in the design and conduct of psychological research

Psychologists recognize that some research undertaken previously would now be regarded as questionable, based on today's standards with regard to how research participants should be treated when participating in psychological research. Two studies that are frequently discussed in this context were both undertaken in the United States of America in the 1960s and 1970s: Milgram's study of obedience to authority (Milgram 1963, 1974) and the prison simulation study (Zimbardo 1973, Zimbardo *et al*. 1973). Arguments continue to this day about whether these studies should ever have been permitted and whether the results justified the means. However, it is sometimes forgotten that both studies would have had to be approved before they were carried out. This approval would have been based on the then current **ethical guidelines** that have since been regularly reviewed and updated.

British Psychological Society *Code of Ethics and Conduct*

When undertaking research, psychologists are expected to follow guidelines about **ethics** (moral responsibilities and standards of conduct) set out by whichever professional body they belong to. Since there are no absolutes about what is deemed to be 'right' or 'wrong', different groups determine what is considered to be acceptable or unacceptable for their members. In the United Kingdom, the British Psychological Society (BPS) is responsible for promoting ethical behaviour among psychologists and has developed ethical principles to protect all research participants from harm. The BPS acknowledges that psychologists owe a debt of gratitude to everyone who agrees to take part in research studies, and requires its members to treat participants with high standards of consideration and respect. The guidelines also protect psychologists as they go about their work.

The latest BPS *Code of Ethics and Conduct* (BPS 2006a) outlines the guiding principles that all psychologists should apply, including those who carry out research, and those in practice. Unfortunately, the mere existence of a code does not guarantee ethical practice; for this to happen, the code has to be implemented conscientiously. Good psychological research is only possible if there is mutual respect and confidence between the investigator and participants. For sound ethical reasons, some areas of human experience and behaviour may no longer be investigated.

1 Respect

Psychologists should respect people's dignity and their rights to privacy and to have a say in what happens to them (this is known as self-determination); they must also be sensitive to issues regarding perceived authority and influence over those with whom they work. This means that psychologists should respect individual and cultural differences, including those relating to age, disability, education, ethnicity, family status, gender, race, religion, sexual orientation and socio-economic status.

Informed consent

Psychologists should ensure that all participants are helped to understand fully all aspects of the research that are likely to influence their willingness to participate, including the nature and objectives of the investigation, so they can give their fully informed consent to take part. Special care is needed when planning to carry out research with children or other vulnerable individuals. Wherever possible, the real consent of children and of adults with impairments in understanding should be obtained. If an individual is unable to give his or her own consent, a parent/guardian (if the child is under the age of 16) or legal representative can provide additional consent, making this decision on what is in the individual's best interests.

Where the researcher is in a position of authority or influence over the participants (e.g. students or employees), care needs to be taken to ensure that this relationship does not cause individuals to feel obliged to agree to take part in, or remain in, an investigation.

If a study is carried out over an extended period of time or if there is any significant change in the focus of the study, it may be necessary to seek additional informed consent.

Proposed alternatives for when it is not possible to gain fully informed consent are shown in the panel on the right.

Confidentiality and anonymity

Except where disclosure is required by law or has been agreed at the outset, participants have the right to expect that all data collected during a research study remain confidential and will be stored securely in accordance with the UK Data Protection Act, 1998. If the findings are published, the data should remain anonymous and should be presented in such a way that specific information cannot be linked to particular individuals. Participants should be warned at the start of a study if confidentiality and anonymity cannot be guaranteed, prior to giving their consent to take part.

Right to withdraw at any time

At the outset it should be made clear to participants their right to withdraw from a research investigation at any time, without having to give a reason and to request that any data relating to them that have been collected are removed from the study and destroyed. This right applies in all situations, including when financial payments have been made. Participants should also be informed of their right to decline to answer specific questions or to participate in a particular aspect of a study.

Deception

Withholding information or misleading participants about the purpose of a study is unacceptable if the participants subsequently become uneasy when they have been debriefed about its true purpose at the end of the study. If there is any doubt about the possible impact of deception, careful consultation should take place prior to the investigation.

Intentionally deceiving participants about the purpose and nature of the investigation should be avoided wherever possible and is only ever deemed to be acceptable in very exceptional circumstances. Information should only be withheld from participants if it is crucial to do so in order to maintain the integrity of the research. If any form of deception is used, the nature of the deception should be disclosed to participants at the earliest possible opportunity and participants have the right to request that their data are excluded from the study and destroyed. Proposed alternatives to using deception are outlined in the panel on the left.

Observation research

Studies based on observation should always respect the privacy and psychological wellbeing of the individuals studied. Unless those being observed give their informed consent, observational research is only acceptable in public places where those being observed would expect to be observed by strangers. Careful account should be taken of local cultural values – researchers should avoid the possibility of invading the privacy of individuals for whom it is important that they are not being observed, even though they are in a public space (e.g. when taking part in a religious ceremony).

2 Competence

Psychologists should be committed to the *Code of Ethics and Conduct* and to maintaining their levels of competence, while at the same time acknowledging any limits of their knowledge, skills, education and experience. This means that they should recognize and resolve the ethical dilemmas that arise out of a proposed research study and be able to defend all their decisions and actions on ethical grounds.

Table 16.6 *British Psychological Society Code of Ethics and Conduct (BPS 2006a)*

3 Responsibility

Psychologists undertaking research should understand their responsibilities to the general public, including their research participants, which includes their protection from harm or undue risk at all times.

Protection of research participants

- *Risk of harm* – Investigators have a key responsibility to protect all participants from physical and mental harm during research – the risk of harm should normally be no greater than in their everyday life. Therefore, psychologists should always think very carefully about both the ethical implications and psychological consequences of the research for the participants. This involves considering the study from the participants' perspective to eliminate any foreseeable threats to physical health, psychological wellbeing, personal dignity or values.

- *Understanding the implications of an investigation* – The researcher may not, however, have sufficient knowledge about the implications of an investigation for all participants, particularly if they are drawn from different groups in terms of key factors such as age, cultural background, disability, gender, education, ethnicity, language, marital status, race, religion, sexual orientation and social background. In which case it may be necessary to consult others who are more knowledgeable – the best judges of whether an investigation is likely to cause offence are members of the same population from which the research participants are to be drawn.

- *Protection from stress* – Where research involves behaviour or experiences that are considered to be personal and private, the participants should be protected from undue stress, and given assurance that they need not answer personal questions.

- *Inducements* – Financial incentives or other inducements should not be used to encourage individuals to take part in research and risk harm beyond that which they would normally risk without payment in their normal, everyday life.

- *Professional advice* – A researcher has a responsibility to inform a participant of any psychological or physical problem that emerges during the course of research, and about which the participant seems to be unaware, if the problem identified is likely to affect his/her future wellbeing adversely. If any professional advice is requested in the course of research, a referral should be suggested to someone who is suitably qualified to deal with the matter raised.

- *Non-human animals* – When carrying out research with non-human animals the highest standards of animal welfare should be observed; the animals should not be subjected to any more pain, discomfort, suffering, fear, distress, frustration, boredom than is absolutely necessary. All decisions and actions must be strictly justified and should adhere to the BPS *Guidelines for Psychologists Working with Animals*.

Debriefing

At the end of an investigation where the participants were aware they had taken part in a study, the researcher should take time to discuss the study with the participants. This is known as debriefing and should involve informing the participants about the nature and outcomes of the research. During the debriefing session the researcher should also discuss the participant's experience of the study in order to identify any unforeseen discomfort, distress or other negative effect of the research, and offer professional support should this be deemed necessary. Care is required to avoid making any evaluative statements during a debriefing session since these can take on unintended significance when provided by a psychologist, especially when discussing results involving children with their parents, teachers or those in *loco parentis*.

As a result of debriefing or in the light of experience of the investigation, a participant has the right to withdraw any consent given retrospectively, and to require that all their personal data be removed from the study and destroyed.

A researcher should never use the provision of debriefing sessions as justification for any unethical aspects of an investigation.

4 Integrity

Psychologists should be honest, accurate, clear and fair in all their dealings with people, including research participants. They should also seek to promote integrity in all scientific activity. In the context of research, this should include being accurate and honest when recording and analysing data, and when reporting research findings and acknowledging any limitations of the results and the conclusions drawn.

It is also important to emphasize that participating in research is entirely voluntary and there should never be overt or covert coercion to do so. It needs to be clear that participation in research will not affect in any way the provision of resources or services to which the individual is otherwise entitled. This is particularly important when the researcher is in a position of authority or power over the participants (e.g. a teacher and his/her students). Someone who is unwilling to participate or who withdraws during the course of a study would receive exactly the same services and resources as those who participated.

The scientific community shares the responsibility for the ethical conduct of research and ethical treatment of research participants. A psychologist who believes that another person may be carrying out research in the UK that is not in accordance with the BPS *Code of Ethics and Conduct* is expected to encourage that investigator to re-evaluate the study and make changes where appropriate.

(Adapted from *the BPS Code of Ethics and Conduct 2006*)

Table 16.6 *continued British Psychological Society Code of Ethics and Conduct (BPS 2006a)*

Table 16.6 summarizes the main points of the BPS *Code of Ethics and Conduct* (BPS 2006a), using as main headings, the four ethical principles on which the guidance is based:

- respect
- competence
- responsibility
- integrity.

It outlines how these principles are put into practice in the context of research.

The BPS has also produced additional guidance for researchers:

- *Ethical principles for conducting research with human participants* (BPS 2004a and currently under review)
- *Guidelines for minimum standards of ethical approval in psychological research* (BPS 2004b and currently under review)
- *Guidelines for ethical practice in psychological research online* (BPS 2007a)
- *Guidelines for psychologists working with animals* (BPS 2007b).

STRETCH AND CHALLENGE

Activity

Ethics in Internet-mediated research (IMR)

The growth in different forms of electronic communication in recent years has extended opportunities to recruit research participants online and to access a wide range of information that could form useful data for psychological research. Use Table 16.6 to help you think about and note down any special ethical issues that might be raised by IMR.

When you have completed this activity and discussed your ideas with other students in your psychology class, you might like to look at the guidelines on IMR on the BPS website: http://www.bps.org.uk

Comments are given in the Answers to activities on p.603.

Views of what constitutes ethical conduct and ethical research are not fixed, so codes of ethics are regularly reviewed and updated. For example, some recent additions include the ethical implications for psychologists working with the media on television (BPS 2007c). The latest versions of all the guidance documents, including the Code of Ethics and Conduct (BPS 2006a) are available on the BPS website, so you might like to download your own copies for reference purposes.

Psychologists sometimes need to find creative ways of applying the guidelines in order to carry out particular kinds of research, while still ensuring that the rights of the participants are fully protected. Two special cases of informed consent and deception are described in the

HOW SCIENCE WORKS

Activity

Ethical issues in the study of parenting style and academic achievement

Look again at the study outlined in the 'Improving internal validity' activity on p.546. What ethical issues does it raise and how could these be addressed?

Comments are given in the Answers to activities on p.603.

Alternatives to fully informed consent

Alternatives to informed consent may be used in situations when revealing the true purpose of the investigation to the participants would invalidate the research findings. Two alternatives are outlined below:

Presumptive consent – A psychologist may select a large, random sample of individuals from the target population and introduce the participants to the purpose of the study and its design, including the use of deception. If the participants agree that they would still have given voluntary informed consent had they known the true aims of the investigation, then the researcher can presume that they represent the views of that population. Another sample from the same population could then be selected for use in the study without being told its true purpose.

Prior general consent – In this case, potential participants are told that participants are sometimes misinformed about the true purpose of a study. Only those who agree that such a practice is acceptable would subsequently be selected to participate in the study. They are therefore deemed to have given general informed consent, but they do not know whether or not the actual study they participate in involves any misleading information.

panels 'Alternatives to fully informed consent' above and 'Alternatives to the use of deception' opposite.

The role of research ethics committees

Psychologists are required to apply the BPS guidelines when designing research and this provides the first line of defence in protecting the public from harm. However, researchers are not permitted to proceed to data collection until they have gained formal approval from an ethics committee. In universities and other institutions where research is carried out, this is the responsibility of a research ethics committee whose job is to scrutinize and rigorously evaluate ethical standards in research proposals and protect participants from harm. This provides a second line of defence for ensuring that participants are fully protected.

Types of committee

The BPS sets out minimum standards of ethical approval in psychological research (BPS 2004b). Any university department running courses accredited by the BPS is required to apply these minimum standards, which indicate that psychological research carried out by staff and students must be approved by one or more of the following committees:

- a departmental ethics committee
- an institutional ethics committee
- an external ethics committee.

Departmental ethics committee (DEC)

Every psychology department in which research is carried out is required to have a DEC, which is responsible for scrutinizing all undergraduate and postgraduate research proposals. The DEC must consist of at least three people with appropriate expertise and no vested interest in the proposed research. The research proposal is first screened by the project supervisor(s) and then formally submitted to the DEC. After careful consideration, the DEC may approve the research or refuse to approve it, although in the latter case the committee will more usually

request that the proposal is modified and resubmitted. If the project is approved, the Chair of the DEC will authorize the research to proceed. The ultimate responsibility for the ethical conduct of 'routine' research (i.e. research that does not involve any risk and does not study minors or vulnerable groups) lies with the head of the department.

A member of a DEC may sometimes indicate that he or she is not impartial or sufficiently expert to assess a particular research proposal or may feel that the research does not qualify as routine, possibly because of the procedures used or the level of potential risk to participants. Alternatively, the proposed research may involve researchers from more than one discipline. In such cases, the DEC can refer the proposal to an IEC, which is a higher-level group operating at institutional level.

Institutional ethics committee (IEC)

An IEC consists of academics from psychology and other disciplines and may also include one or two lay members. This committee will not only have wider expertise, but also knowledge of practical issues such as insurance and the law. The Chair of the IEC will also either not approve a project, or ask for modifications and re-submission, or will give formal permission for the research to proceed.

External ethics committee (EEC)

Some research proposals cannot be approved by either a DEC or an IEC and will need to be referred to an EEC. This tends to depend on the type of research participant the researcher wishes to use. For example, if National Health Service (NHS) patients or staff are involved in a proposed research study, the National Research Ethics Service (NRES) is responsible for the approval process. EECs also consist of experts and lay people with no vested interest in the research studies that are being scrutinized. Meanwhile, all research in the UK involving non-human animals needs to be approved by the Home Office.

Enforcing ethical guidelines

The monitoring of ethical standards is the third and final means of protecting research participants. Should psychologists be found to be contravening the published guidelines, or a formal complaint is made about them, the BPS Investigatory Committee has the power to apply disciplinary procedures of varying severity. This committee can recommend whether a complaint should be dismissed or followed up by a disciplinary body. The psychologist may subsequently be officially reprimanded, have their Chartered Psychologist status suspended or removed (so they are no longer an approved practitioner) or, in extreme cases, be expelled from the society. Fortunately, complaints to the BPS Investigatory Committee are relatively rare: the BPS reports that there are about 120 complaints a year (out of a total membership of 42 000). Some of these complaints were about psychologists in practice and others were about researchers. Of these, only between 10 and 15 are referred to a full hearing (BPS 2006b). These figures do not, however, represent all psychologists, as membership of the BPS is voluntary. This means that not all research psychologists are directly governed by the Society's rules and would, instead, be bound by the rules of the institution that employs them.

The impact of the *BPS Code of Ethics and Conduct* on psychological research

Origins and shaping of the guidelines

The origins of the formal codes of ethics and conduct available today (developed by such organizations as the American Psychological Association (APA) and the BPS) can be traced back to World War II, when psychologists' work became increasingly visible. This made it desirable to devise guidelines to ensure that professional standards were adhered to. Towards the end of the 1940s, members of the APA were asked to report any work-related incidents they had encountered which had involved an ethical issue or decision. Over 1 000 incidents were reported and these were used to develop the first version of the APA's guidelines, which was published in 1953. In 1978 the BPS published an early version of its ethical guidelines entitled *Ethical principles for research on human subjects*. The *Code of Ethics and Conduct* was first published in 1985 as part of the conditions of its Royal Charter. These guidelines are regularly reviewed and revised to ensure they reflect the latest thinking on ethical issues.

The early APA ethical guidelines not only shaped the research that was undertaken but were also shaped by the research. Milgram (1963) and Zimbardo (1973) would have been required to adhere to the APA guidelines when they carried out their early studies into obedience and would have gained approval from an ethical standards committee. Nevertheless, the nature of their research raised new questions about what research psychologists should be allowed to do and about how participants should be treated. As a result, the guidelines were revised and it is now inconceivable that their original studies would be approved today. For example, the level and nature of deception would be regarded as particularly problematic.

Means before ends

Changes in ethical guidelines over time illustrate how they can and do impact on what is done, how it is done, and by whom and on whom it is done. Over 50 years have elapsed since the first official APA guidelines were published and, during that time, changes in the *Zeitgeist* (that is, the intellectual mood of the time) and tremendous technological advances have occurred. With regard to the *Zeitgeist*, research ethics committees are currently primarily concerned with protecting participants. There has, therefore, been an important shift – the means (i.e. how the research is conducted) is now regarded as being more critical than the end (i.e. what it will find out).

Participants not subjects

It is now difficult to conceive of a research question that would be deemed to be so important it would take precedence over the rights and dignity of the research participants. There is now a far greater awareness of human rights and legal sanctions. For example, current BPS guidelines state that psychology undergraduates are no longer permitted to carry out any form of research with anyone under the age of 18 or with vulnerable groups. Moreover, any psychologist who works with such people must have clearance from the Criminal Records Bureau. In addition, research participants are now viewed more as collaborators in research and are no longer referred to as 'subjects' (a term that could be said to indicate psychological 'distance' between the person being studied and the person doing the research). This drive towards equality has also led to the inclusion of guidance on how to avoid sexist or racist language in any aspect of their work in the BPS *Code of Ethics and Conduct* (BPS 2006a).

Media and communications

Developments in information and communications technology has meant that greater openness and accountability to a wider audience is now possible and this has led to concerns about how research findings are communicated. As we saw earlier, there are now guidelines about how psychologists should conduct themselves with the media and what is expected of them (BPS 2007b), and about how to conduct Internet-based research (BPS 2007a). All the ethical guidelines produced by the BPS are primarily concerned with protecting participants, as well as protecting psychologists.

Bias and benefits

In addition to protecting psychologists and research participants, research ethics committees can act as gatekeepers, not only limiting the way in which research is carried out, but also what research is undertaken and the kinds of research question that are asked. In Topic 2, we saw how the choice of certain target populations at the expense of others could lead to bias and how this has resulted in the marginalization of the concerns of females and others who are not part of the dominant group. So, although members of ethics committee strive to maintain their neutrality, the dominant ideas and values of the time may still influence their decision-making. This awareness has led to the approval of more research for the benefit of women, people who are elderly, and other previously marginalized groups. In addition to safeguarding participants, ethics committees also have a responsibility to try to address any biases, so that the benefits of research are distributed equitably.

Identifying ethical issues in research proposals

Ethics committees focus, above all else, on the protection of research participants, and this demands detailed and rigorous evaluation of all aspects of a proposed study. A committee will therefore require extensive documentation, including the research proposal, a copy of the consent form, and any other material, such as the invitation to participate, questionnaires or interview schedules, behaviour checklists, record-keeping documents and evidence of legal and insurance cover.

The activity, 'Writing a research proposal' opposite, will help you consolidate and apply your understanding of ethics in the context of the design and conduct of psychological research. This activity gives an indication of what a researcher needs to do in order to persuade an ethics committee to allow a study to proceed. It will encourage you to identify ethical issues in two very different types of research and to think about how they could be addressed. The two research papers are not only different in method, but were also published about 40 years apart. So, when you are preparing the proposals, think about the context of the original research, how that shaped the form they took, and how a proposal for the research by Bandura *et al.* (1963) might be received now.

Constructing a consent form for a research ethics committee focuses the researcher's attention on how to communicate the details of the research with potential participants. According to the BPS guidelines (BPS 2004b), a consent form should include:

- the name of the institution responsible for overseeing the research

- the title of the project

- a clear statement of the purpose of the study and an invitation to participate

- who the researcher is and where they work or where they are studying and their contact details

- what participants will be asked to do, what data will be recorded, likely risks or discomfort, and any payment

- how anonymity and confidentiality will be ensured and who will have access to the data

- assurance that participants can withdraw at any point during the study

- a statement that the participant has read and understood what they are agreeing to and have had any questions about the research answered; space for both the participant and researcher to sign the consent form (the participant can initial or make another mark to protect their identity)

- contact details of the Chair of the relevant ethics committee, should the participant want to discuss any issues later.

Once a researcher has prepared all the documentation that an ethics committee needs, it is circulated to the committee members so they can familiarize themselves with it. The committee then meets to consider the proposal and decide whether to reject it outright, approve it, or ask for further clarification and/or modifications before the study is permitted to proceed. The decision of the ethics committee will be based on consideration of the general principles outlined in the panel, 'Checklist of ethical

Activity   Writing a research proposal

Download a copy of the two research papers listed below (you will be using them again in the activities in Chapter 17):

'Imitation of film-mediated aggressive models' This paper by Bandura *et al.* (1963) can be found at: http://des.emory.edu/mfp/BanduraPubsByYear.html

'A qualitative study of GPs' views of treating obesity' This research paper by Epstein and Ogden (2005) can be found at: http://scholar.google.co.uk/

Choose one of the papers and prepare a proposal, using the following headings to guide you. You might like to carry out this activity in a small group.

1   Title of the research project

2   Aim and rationale of the project

3   The research method to be used and the kind of data to be collected

4   Participants: who will be recruited and how? Who will be excluded and included?

5   Documentation: information for participants (e.g. an invitation to take part, consent form, debriefing)

6   Ethical issues raised by the proposed research and how they will be addressed

7   Expected duration of the research project

When you have done this, discuss your proposal with another group who prepared a research proposal for the other paper. How did your two research proposals differ?

Comments are given in the
Answers to activities on p.603. ▶

principles', which are drawn from BPS recommendations (BPS 2004a). Approval is granted for a specified period of time; once this period has lapsed, it would need to be reconsidered. This ensures that changes in ethical guidelines, the law and the *Zeitgeist* are taken into account and the proposed research remains acceptable.

Once research has been approved and carried out, the findings will need to be analysed and reported, which is the focus of Chapter 17. Formal approval by an ethics committee is just one of the elements of quality control that research must pass before it can be disseminated to the wider research community. Other important quality assurance mechanisms, such as peer review of journal articles and conference papers, were outlined in Chapter 15.

Checklist of ethical principles

Are potential participants told:

- about the purpose of the study and the credentials of the researcher?
- what is expected of them as participants?
- of any potential risks and benefits associated with taking part?
- that their participation is voluntary and they can withdraw from the study at any time without any form of penalty?
- of the procedures for obtaining fully informed consent (e.g. signed consent)?
- that they can choose not to answer questions if they wish?
- of procedures to ensure confidentiality and anonymity?
- that they can expect a full debrief?

Is there:

- intention to mislead or deceive the participants?
- any physical or psychological risk to potential participants?

Are participants to be recruited from:

- vulnerable groups, such as under-18s, patients, people with learning or communication difficulties, in legal custody or involved in criminal activity?

Check your understanding of ethical considerations in the design and conduct of psychological investigations by answering the following questions. Try to do this from memory. You can check your answers by looking back through Topic 4.

1 What are the four main aspects of ethical responsibility in the BPS *Code of Ethics and Conduct* (BPS 2006a)? Briefly explain the meaning of each one.

2 What alternatives are there to fully informed consent and the use of deception?

3 What are the two major responsibilities of an ethics committee?

4 Give two reasons why a departmental ethics committee might refer a research proposal to an institutional ethics committee.

5 What are the three possible recommendations that an ethics committee might make after it has formally considered a research proposal?

6 What sanctions can be brought to bear if a psychologist in the UK is found to have breached the BPS ethical guidelines?

7 Give an example of how changes in both the *Zeitgeist* and technological changes have influenced ethical guidelines.

8 Identify two ways in which changes in ethical guidelines have restricted access to potential participants.

Further resources

Flanagan, C. (1998) *Practicals for Psychology: A student workbook*, London: Routledge.

This book is written in the style of a manual with suggestions for practical projects that you could try (with ethical approval of course), using a range of research methods and ways of analysing the data.

Harris, P. (2008) *Designing and Reporting Experiments in Psychology* (3rd edn), Buckingham: Open University Press.

This book is written in an accessible, interactive style. It concentrates mainly on experimental research and covers many of the issues discussed in this chapter and Chapter 17 in more depth.

Websites

www.socialresearchmethods.net
  Bill Trochim's Centre for Social Research Methods provides a rich source of information on both quantitative and qualitative research methods. Click on 'Knowledge Base' and then 'Content' (listed on the left in very small type). Use the A2 specification to help you select from this extensive list.

subscribe-rd@bps.lists.org.uk
  Send a blank email to this address to subscribe to the British Psychological Society's Research Digest and receive fortnightly summaries of up-to-date research.

http://www.bps.org.uk/
  The BPS *Code of Ethics and Conduct* and other information relevant to research ethics can be found on this website.

http://www.opsi.gov.uk
  The Office of Public Sector Information gives access to the latest version of the Data Protection Act.

Aims, research questions and hypotheses

Generating research aims

- Research aims clarify the focus of the study
- Aims vary according to type of research
- Typically refined into research questions (qualitative research) or hypotheses (quantitative research)

Generating research questions

- Questions can be very specific and focused

OR

- Can be worded to allow for exploration of an issue or topic

Formulating hypotheses

- A research hypothesis is a precise, unambiguous, testable statement formulated on the basis of theory and/or previous research
- The alternative hypothesis can be directional or non-directional
- The null hypothesis states that there is no effect in a study
- Statistical analysis is used to decide between the null and alternative hypothesis on the basis of the data

Selection & application of appropriate research methods

Investigation design

Some key design decisions

- Choose from a range of quantitative and qualitative research methods
- Determine the number of participants
- Choose the sampling method
- Decide how to brief participants
- Decide how to record the data

Conducting pilot studies

- Small-scale dummy run
- Test and refine design, procedures and materials

The relationship between researchers and participants

- Research situations have demand characteristics
- Participant reactivity may result in evaluation apprehension
- Investigator effects may influence participants and data analysis

Experimental design

Defining and operationalizing variables

- Create clear and unambiguous definitions of the IV and DV

Choosing an experimental design

- Independent groups design
- Repeated measures design
- Matched pairs design

Control of extraneous variables

- Extraneous variables
- Confounding variables
- Random error
- Constant errors

Design of naturalistic observation

Behaviour categories

Behaviour sampling

- Time interval sampling
- Time point sampling
- Event sampling

Design of questionnaires and interviews

Questionnaires

- Administered face to face, by post or online via the Internet
- Open or closed questions
- Question order
- Question wording

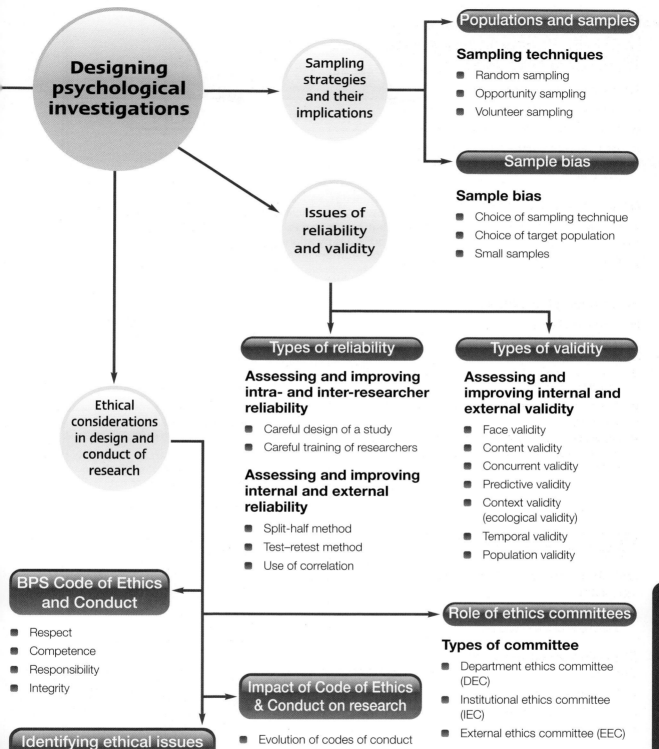

Designing psychological investigations

Sampling strategies and their implications

Sampling techniques
- Random sampling
- Opportunity sampling
- Volunteer sampling

Sample bias

Sample bias
- Choice of sampling technique
- Choice of target population
- Small samples

Issues of reliability and validity

Types of reliability

Assessing and improving intra- and inter-researcher reliability
- Careful design of a study
- Careful training of researchers

Assessing and improving internal and external reliability
- Split-half method
- Test–retest method
- Use of correlation

Types of validity

Assessing and improving internal and external validity
- Face validity
- Content validity
- Concurrent validity
- Predictive validity
- Context validity (ecological validity)
- Temporal validity
- Population validity

Ethical considerations in design and conduct of research

BPS Code of Ethics and Conduct
- Respect
- Competence
- Responsibility
- Integrity

Role of ethics committees

Types of committee
- Department ethics committee (DEC)
- Institutional ethics committee (IEC)
- External ethics committee (EEC)

Enforcing ethical guidelines
- Investigate
- Dismiss complaint
- Suspend or remove chartered status
- Expel from the BPS

Impact of Code of Ethics & Conduct on research
- Evolution of codes of conduct
- Ethical codes shape research and are shaped by it
- Impact of changes in *Zeitgeist* and technology
- Ethics committees as gatekeepers

Identifying ethical issues in research proposals
- Writing a research proposal
- Constructing a consent form
- How an ethics committee works

EXPLAINING THE SPECIFICATION

Specification content	The specification explained
Data analysis and reporting on investigations	In this part of the specification you are required to build on your knowledge and skills developed at AS level and know about how psychological data are analysed and reported in such a way that others can replicate the study. You will need to practise your skills by analysing quantitative (numerical) and qualitative (non-numerical) data and writing up small-scale investigations you have conducted. To do this you need to be able to:
Appropriate selection of graphical representations	■ Describe a range of ways of representing data graphically, including tables, graphs, bar charts, histograms, frequency polygons and scattergraphs. ■ Demonstrate your understanding of when a particular method of graphical representation can be used by selecting and evaluating appropriate methods.
Probability and significance, including the interpretation of significance and Type 1/Type 2 errors (Topic 1)	■ Demonstrate your understanding of the concept of probability and how it applies when statistical tests are used to calculate the statistical significance of quantitative (numerical) data. ■ Explain how Type 1 and Type 2 errors can arise and how these can affect the interpretation of the results of statistical analyses.
Factors affecting choice of statistical test, including levels of measurement	■ Describe the four levels of measurement: nominal, ordinal, interval and ratio. ■ Outline the factors that affect the choice of statistical test. ■ Demonstrate your understanding of the factors affecting the choice of statistical test by selecting the appropriate test to analyse specific data sets.
The use of inferential analysis, including Spearman's *Rho*, Mann-Whitney, Wilcoxon and Chi-squared tests (Topic 2)	■ Outline the use of inferential tests to analyse quantitative (numerical) data and assess whether the data are statistically significant. ■ Describe when the following inferential tests are used: Spearman's *rho*, Mann-Whitney, Wilcoxon and chi-squared. ■ Demonstrate your understanding of the use of inferential analysis to test for statistical significance by analysing and interpreting some small sets of quantitative data.
Analysis and interpretation of qualitative data	■ Discuss ways in which qualitative (non-numerical) data can be analysed and interpreted. ■ Demonstrate your understanding of the analysis and interpretation of qualitative data by analysing and interpreting some qualitative data.
Conventions of reporting on psychological investigations (Topic 3)	■ Describe the conventions for reporting psychological investigations, including the structure of the report.

Thinking statistically about alien abductions

In 2002, Holden and French considered neuroscientific explanations of people's reported experiences of alien abduction. Sometimes the memory of the abduction is conscious and sometimes it is recalled only under hypnosis. People usually report being taken from their bed at night, but some describe being taken from their car or while out walking. Often these experiences have features in common, for example, seeing bright lights, a feeling of lost time, waking up feeling paralyzed, a sensation of flying and unexplained scars on the body. Holden and French concluded that there is still no clear explanation even though there are some neurological clues about what is happening. In the meantime, there is still the indisputable fact that many people believe in aliens and some also believe that they have been abducted by them.

Blackmore (1998) examined some data provided by The Roper Organization, which carries out surveys of public opinion in America. In 1992, a large sample of 5947 adults were asked to indicate which, if any, of five common features of alien abduction they had experienced, e.g. 'waking up paralyzed with a sense of a strange person or presence or something else in the room'. If people answered yes to four or more of these questions it was thought possible that they had experienced alien abduction. Blackmore continues:

'From there, the stunning conclusion of the Roper Poll was reached. Out of the 5947 people interviewed, 119 (or two per cent) had four or five of the indicators. Since the population represented by the sample was 185 million, the total number was 3.7 million – hence the conclusion that nearly four million Americans have been abducted by aliens' (Blackmore 1998).

http://www.csicop.org/si/9805/abduction.html

- Work through the figures in Blackmore's quotation to see if you arrive at the same result. Can you account for any differences?
- Could self-selection by respondents have had an effect on the result?
- Was it appropriate to conclude that experiencing four out of five indicators meant that abduction had occurred?

Most people react with incredulity to the idea of 3.7 million abductees, so you know intuitively that data from even the most reliable of sources will always be flawed to some degree. These statistics alone leave you not really knowing what the truth is. It is possible that they are an accurate measure of something, but not alien abduction. It could also be that the statistics are misleading; perhaps the survey respondents were mischievously not telling the truth, perhaps those who had experienced the indicators were over-eager to report them, or it could be both of these. Psychologists need to be able to trust data and need to know how and from whom the data were obtained and for what purpose. Most importantly, they need to think carefully how to interpret and communicate them, since even the most responsible reporting can quickly be misrepresented, especially if it concerns something as sensational as alien abduction.

Introduction

At A2 level you are required to extend your understanding of data analysis and become familiar with how psychologists communicate their research findings between themselves and with the wider scientific community. With regard to data analysis, it will be necessary to revisit certain ideas from your AS-level studies and take them further. You considered a range of **descriptive statistics**, including three measures of central tendency (the **mean**, **median** and **mode**), three measures of dispersion (the **range**, the **interquartile range** and the **standard deviation**). Look back at your AS-level textbook now if you need to refresh your memory about any of these descriptive statistics.

Here you will be revisiting graphs, histograms, bar charts, frequency polygons and scattergraphs, but now you will be constructing them yourself. At A2 level, you will also learn about how psychologists choose and apply a range of **inferential statistical tests**. Choosing a test depends partly on the design of your investigation and partly on the nature of the data to be analysed, particularly the level of measurement used. Here you will have experience of a range of tests that detect differences or correlation and will learn about how psychologists determine whether a test result is meaningful or, to use the correct terminology, statistically significant.

Qualitative methods have always been part of the psychologist's toolkit and they are enjoying increasing popularity. The question is 'What do I do with information that is not in numerical form?' For example, you may have a written account of something (a transcript) such as a diary, a case history or an interview transcript. Sometimes it makes sense to reduce this kind of data to numbers and apply statistical procedures. However, at other times it is important to preserve the qualitative data in a way that is close to the original textual form, so that the richness of the data is not lost. Both of these approaches will be discussed.

Finally, we will look at ways in which psychologists share their research findings with each other. They do this by writing reports of their studies that usually conform to conventions, which have developed over time. The reports are published in scientific journals; each issue of a journal consists of a collection of research papers. Issues of journals are published at regular intervals throughout the year and, typically, a year's collection of issues is referred to as a 'volume'. *The British Journal of Psychology* is one example of a journal published in the United Kingdom. Other journals specialize in a particular area of research (e.g. *The British Journal of Social Psychology* or *Neuropsychologia*) or in a way of doing research (e.g. *Qualitative Inquiry*). The editors of a journal scrutinize work submitted by researchers and subject each paper to a system of peer review, as a means of quality control prior to publication. Each journal will have its own particular 'house-style', but there are broad similarities. We will examine how a typical research report is constructed.

Appropriate selection of graphical representations

Look back at your AS textbook or your notes for examples of how to tabulate data so they communicate their message clearly. There are, however, other recommended formats. For example, the American Psychological Association (APA) publishes a manual that includes recommendations for presenting all aspects of a report, including data. Hints are available online: www.apastyle.org

Graphing and charting

It is important to remind yourself of the ways in which data can be presented visually, using graphs, bar charts, histograms, frequency polygons and scattergraphs, by looking back at your Psychology AS textbook [pp. 62–66 of *Psychology AS for AQA A*]. Below is a brief, further reminder of the main types.

Graphs
Graphs tend to be used to show change over time or trials. For example, Peterson and Peterson's (1959) duration of STM study. Time or number of trials is usually plotted on the horizontal axis (the x-axis) and the measure you are interested in is presented on the vertical axis (the y-axis).

Frequency diagrams
As the name suggests, frequency diagrams give a visual impression of how often certain measures occur. There are rules to do with how the data are measured that determine which ones to use when; you will read more about this later in this chapter. Frequency is always

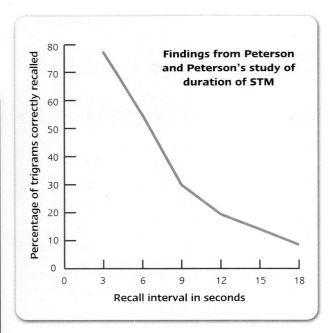

Figure 17.1 *Findings from Peterson and Peterson's study of duration of STM*

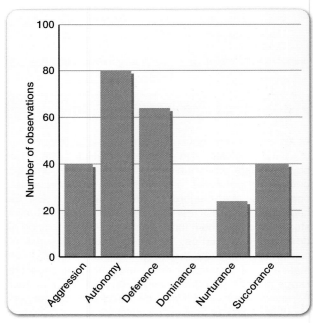

Figure 17.2 *Bar chart showing the number of observations of different behaviours in a group of children*

recorded on the vertical axis and the frequency of the variable of interest is plotted on the horizontal axis. Here are some key points.

Bar charts

Bar charts are best for showing frequencies of **nominal data** or **ordinal data**, or for showing averages of different data sets on the same set of axes. Bar charts are also used to plot data in the form of percentages and means.

Presentation tips:

- Use the 75 per cent or (because opinions vary) the 80 per cent rule that the vertical axis should be 75 per cent or 80 per cent of the length of the horizontal axis to avoid giving a distorted impression.

- Use plain paper with no gridlines, as the area of each of the bars is immaterial.

- Make the bars a sensible width and leave small gaps between them. You can plot more than one sample of data for comparison purposes on a clustered bar chart, leaving gaps between each cluster of bars.

- Use alphabetical order on the horizontal axis if the data are nominal and the natural order if the data are ordinal.

Histograms and frequency polygons

Histograms and frequency polygons are most suitable for use with interval and ratio data and choosing between them may be determined by the nature of the scores to be presented. Discrete data are in the form of whole units, e.g. number of goals in a football league table. Such units are more meaningful if they are not sub-divided. Continuous data are measured in units that can

theoretically be sub-divided *ad infinitum* (e.g. physical measurements such as reaction times). You may, therefore, prefer to use a histogram for discrete data and a frequency polygon for continuous data, although you will sometimes see them used interchangeably.

Presentation tips:

- In histograms it is important that the bars touch.

- In frequency polygons a continuous line joins the midpoints of each bar or of each class interval.

- In both cases, you may need to group categories on the horizontal axis into about six to eight class intervals and recalculate the frequencies in each for the sake of clarity.

- In both cases, the area contained in the bars or under the line (in the case of frequency polygons) is informative, so it is appropriate to use graph paper.

Scattergrams

Drawing a scattergram is an essential first step when carrying out any correlation analysis. It gives an initial indication of whether there is a relationship between two variables and, if so, whether it is positive or negative. A scattergram also shows whether correlation analysis is suitable. For example, if there are anomalies, such as unusual scores in the data set that stand apart from other points on the scattergram (these are known as **outliers**), the correlation might be unduly affected (either increased or decreased). As a general rule, if you think that one variable predicts another – for example, children's age might predict their attention span – the predictor variable (age) is presented on the horizontal axis (x-axis).

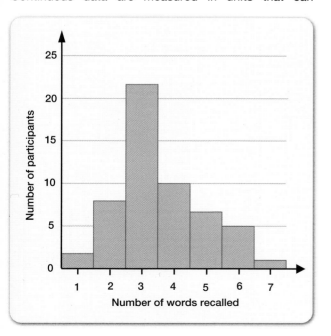

Figure 17.3 *Histogram showing the number of words recalled in a memory experiment*

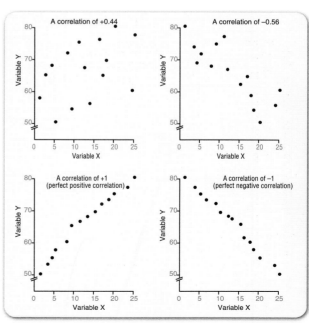

Figure 17.4 *Scattergraphs illustrating different correlation coefficients*

Check your understanding of graphical representations by completing the exercises below.

Construct a clustered bar chart

Two schools entered students in the same year for each of five core GCSE subjects. Table 17.1 shows the percentage of students in each school who gained A or A* grades.

Subject	School A	School B
English Language	51	30
English Literature	39	26
Science	41	17
Mathematics	39	17
French	30	45

Table 17.1 *Percentage of A and A* grades by subject*

1 Apply the guidelines on drawing bar charts to plot the data by subject for Schools A and B on the same chart.
2 Consider each school individually: what observations can you make about the performance of students in the various subjects?
3 Now compare the two schools: what similarities and differences are there?

Construct a histogram and a frequency polygon

Table 17.2 indicates the numbers of hours that students spent preparing for an exam. Use the guidelines about drawing histograms and frequency polygons to present these data.

1 Group the hours of exam preparation into six class intervals (1–3 hours, 4–6 hours, 7–9 hours, etc.) and recalculate the frequencies in each class interval.
2 Use these frequencies to construct a histogram. What does the histogram show?
3 Now treat the hours of preparation as continuous data. You can do this by marking the mid-point of the class interval at the top of each bar on your histogram, and joining them with straight lines. Continue the lines to meet the horizontal axis at 0 and 20, at each end. These values represent the mid-points of the notional class intervals above and below the ones you have used.
4 If you were the teachers of these students, what could you learn from these two diagrams?
5 What do you notice about the area in the bars of the histogram compared to the area under the frequency polygon?

Construct a scattergram

1 Table 17.3 shows the marks awarded to 20 students for two practical reports. Use these data to construct a scattergram.
2 What do you notice about the pattern of scatter?
3 Estimate what you think the correlation coefficient would be.
4 What problem is evident in the scattergram and how would you resolve it?
5 If you could resolve this problem and recalculate the correlation coefficient, what do you think it would now be?

The answers can be found on p.619. ▶

Hours of exam preparation	Number of students (frequency)
18	1
17	0
16	3
15	5
14	5
13	4
12	10
11	6
10	10
9	8
8	7
7	5
6	5
5	1
4	4
3	5
2	2
1	0
TOTAL	**N = 81**

Table 17.2 *Frequency table showing the number of hours spent preparing for an exam*

Student	Report 1	Report 2
1	64	52
2	50	54
3	68	65
4	48	39
5	47	44
6	61	53
7	35	32
8	41	54
9	66	58
10	47	40
11	26	64
12	59	64
13	52	35
14	70	60
15	53	48
16	46	40
17	73	76
18	60	71
19	48	39
20	63	75

Table 17.3 *Marks of 20 students for two practical reports*

Topic 1: Probability and significance

The ways of describing data you learned about in your AS studies – descriptive statistics (see pp. 66–71 of *Psychology AS for AQA A*) – are not the only statistical techniques available to psychologists. There are also inferential statistics that enable them to go further and use the samples of data they have collected, as the name suggests, to make inferences about the populations from which the samples were drawn. So how is this done? If you find that girls and boys perform differently in an academic test, how do you decide whether this difference is meaningful or, in statistical terms, significant? The difference is judged to be significant (or not) by carrying out an inferential test on the data that have been gathered. In this case, you would use a test that compared sample means and apply rules of **probability** and **statistical significance** to assess the result formally. If it is decided that a test result is statistically significant (in this case that the difference between the mean scores for boys and girls is meaningfully large), practical consequences, such as policy changes in the way boys and girls are educated, might well follow.

The concept of statistical significance is central to inferential statistics and to any decision about whether to retain or reject the null hypothesis. You will have studied hypotheses on your AS course (see pp. 38–9 of *Psychology AS for AQA A*). You can also use the Glossary at the end of this book to remind yourself about the **null hypothesis** and **alternative hypothesis**. Hypotheses can be directional, i.e. they specify the direction of a difference ('Sample A has larger scores than Sample B') or the type of correlation ('Samples C and D are positively correlated'). They can also be non-directional and simply state that there is a difference or a correlation, but not indicate a direction. When testing statistical significance, a **one-tailed test** is applied to a **directional hypothesis** and a **two-tailed test** is applied to a **non-directional hypothesis**.

You might hear it said that a statistical result is significant if it is unlikely to be due to chance. However, it is actually more accurate to say that assuming the null hypothesis is true (i.e. no effect is observed), the probability of observing the test result obtained is very small and that other influences, such as the experimental manipulation, are likely to be at work.

Level of significance

How do you know when to reject a null hypothesis and when to retain it? The answer to this question lies in the concept of **level of significance** (or significance level). The significance level for the result of any statistical test is expressed as a probability value, which can be anything from 0 to 1. This value indicates the probability that the null hypothesis is true and so it follows that a researcher would want a very small probability value in order to be able to claim that the test result is statistically significant. Probability values may be written as percentages or decimals, for example:

- The *5 per cent level of significance* can also be written as $p = .05$ (where p = the probability of the result occurring if the null hypothesis were true).

- The *1 per cent level of significance* can also be written as $p = .01$.

The choice of significance level is largely conventional: five per cent is usually regarded as being the minimum acceptable value for deciding whether a test result is statistically significant. When the 5 per cent significance level is achieved in quantitative research, such as an experiment, providing that the study has been carefully designed and executed, a more likely explanation is that the result is due to the effects of the manipulated independent variable. The null hypothesis is, therefore, rejected.

The 5 per cent level of significance is by no means the only one that is used by psychologists. Sometimes more stringent significance levels are needed. Such a situation might occur if people would be at risk if a finding that was not highly reliable were applied in real-life situations (e.g. in certain kinds of medical research). Examples of more stringent levels include the 1 per cent level of significance *(or $p = .01$)*, the 0.5% level ($p = .005$) and the 0.1% level ($p = .001$).

Statistical software will provide the exact p for a test statistic, but when you carry out statistical tests by hand, you may not know the exact figure. When this happens, the usual way of expressing significance is to use the symbol < which means less than, but you may also see ≤ which means 'less than or equal to'. If the 5 per cent level of significance, or less, is achieved (expressed as $p \leq .05$), this means that the probability of observing that particular result, if the null hypothesis is true, is 1 in 20 (or 5 per cent) or less. Non-significant results are expressed using > (greater than), so would be followed with $p > .05$.

Be careful not to mix up the different ways of expressing levels of significance. A common error is to add a percentage symbol onto the end of a decimal version (e.g. $p = .05$ per cent is a very different value to $p = .05$).

Type 1 and Type 2 errors

The 5 per cent level of significance, which is typically adopted by psychologists, is easier to understand in the context of Type 1 and Type 2 errors. As mentioned earlier, you should not talk about proving hypotheses because you are dealing with statistical probabilities rather than certainty. Test statistics give indications of what is true in the real world, but there is still a possibility that errors will be made when deciding what to do with the null hypothesis.

- A *Type 1 error* occurs when a null hypothesis is rejected when it should not have been. The likelihood of making such an error is equal to the level of significance employed. For example, at $p = .05$ the risk of making a Type 1 error is 1 in 20 (5 per cent). This type of error can occur when an insufficiently stringent significance level is adopted (for example, $p = .1$).

■ A **Type 2 error** occurs when a null hypothesis is retained when it should not have been. There is a failure to detect an 'effect' (e.g. a difference or a correlation); this may occur when significance levels are too stringent.

HOW SCIENCE WORKS

Activity Probability values

What is the percentage probability of making a Type 1 error at the following significance levels?

$p \leq .01$
$p < .005$
$p \leq .001$ The answers can be found on p.620. ▶

Now you can see exactly what psychologists achieve by adjusting significance levels. It is often considered preferable to run a higher risk of making a Type 2 error rather than a Type 1 error, and this is why psychologists might choose a more stringent level of significance. It is better scientific practice to err on the side of caution, especially when the potential consequences of applying a weak finding would be serious. For the most part, however, choosing $p = .05$ as a default value strikes an acceptable balance between the likelihood of Type 1 and Type 2 errors.

A tip to help you remember the difference between Type 1 and Type 2 errors

A Type 1 error is often called an error of **O**ptimism: you claim to have found an effect, but are wrong because it is not actually there. A Type 2 error is an error of **P**essimism and occurs when you say you do not have an effect, but are wrong because, actually, there is an effect. O comes before P and 1 comes before 2. O and 1 go together and come first, P and 2 go together and come second.

CHECK YOUR UNDERSTANDING

Check your understanding of probability and significance by answering the questions below. Try to do this from memory. You can check your answers by looking back through Topic 1, 'Probability and significance'.

1 Describe the concepts of: (a) probability, (b) statistical significance and (c) level of significance

2 'A statistically significant result is one which is highly unlikely to have occurred by chance.' Is this statement accurate? Explain your answer.

3 Is a significance level of $p = .001$ more or less stringent than a significance level of $p = .05$?

4 When might a researcher choose to use more stringent levels of statistical significance?

5 Explain what is meant by a Type 1 and a Type 2 error.

6 What type of error would you be more likely to make if you were using the following levels of significance instead of the 5% level ($p = .05$):
(i) a 10 per cent level of significance ($p = .10$)
(ii) a 1 per cent level of significance ($p = .01$)?

7 Outline how inferential statistical techniques can be used to decide whether to retain or reject a null hypothesis.

Factors affecting choice of statistical tests, including levels of measurement

During your AS psychology course you will have learned about descriptive statistics for measuring such things as central tendency and spread and for presenting data visually. You will also have been taught that there are rules for choosing, say, a mean rather than a median or a bar chart rather than a histogram. The same is true of inferential tests. There is a wide variety of tests to choose from, but it is important to apply the most appropriate one. If you do not, the test result, and the conclusions drawn from it, will not be trustworthy.

What are the tests making inferences about? The short answer is 'populations'. Strictly speaking, in a statistical context, the term 'population' refers to a complete data set rather than to a sample (a subgroup) of the population. However, in the real world of research, psychologists almost always work with samples of data drawn from populations of data for practical reasons. As long as the sample is carefully selected and the research study is well designed, it should be possible to generalize the findings from the sample to the wider population from which the sample was drawn. In other words, statistical tests are applied to the data collected from the sample in order to infer the characteristics of the wider population.

HOW SCIENCE WORKS

Activity Defining a population

What qualifies someone to contribute to a population of data? Imagine you want to collect a sample of IQ scores from British eight-year-old children. What attributes should these eight-year-olds have in order to be eligible to provide the population of IQ data? Think about the criteria you would use that would include certain children while excluding others.

Some suggestions are given on p.620. ▶

Factors affecting choice of statistical test

Think back to your AS studies to remind yourself about research techniques that generate quantitative data (numbers); these include experimental research, correlational research and some survey research. Two main factors affect test choice:

- *The type of research design*, which is determined by the research question that you want to answer – If you have conducted an experiment, you will need a test to detect differences between the samples of data from the two or more conditions. The test you use will depend on whether the design of your experiment was independent or related (matched pairs or repeated measures). If you are looking for a correlation you will need a test that detects linear relationships in samples of paired data and if you are looking for a difference in frequency counts, you will need a test that will show if one exists.

- *The type of data* – The data will be measured on either a nominal, ordinal, interval or ratio scale. These scales differ in the qualities that they have and determine which type of graphical representation is appropriate. Along with the research design, they also determine which statistical test should be applied. Relatively complex statistical procedures can be applied to interval or ratio data and, for the most part, it is not

necessary to focus on the distinction between these two levels of measurement because the same procedures can be applied to both. However, it is important to be able to distinguish interval/ratio data from ordinal and nominal data to which only relatively simple statistical procedures can be applied. The four levels are explained in ascending order of complexity in Table 17.4.

Arguing about levels of measurement

There is often debate between psychologists about what level of measurement their data represent. For example, some people treat numbers of words recalled in a memory task as interval data, whereas others treat such data as ordinal on the grounds that all words are not equally easy to recall. This highlights an important point: data do not arrive with a label attached to them, signifying the level of measurement; the researcher needs to decide the appropriate level at which data are to be treated.

Nominal data	Nominal scale of measurement simply involves setting up mutually exclusive levels, or categories, of a variable. (The term 'nominal' comes from the Latin word *nomen*, which means 'name'.) Data are allocated to categories such as male/female, smoker/non-smoker or left-handed/right-handed. Nominal data are sometimes referred to as 'categorical data' or 'frequency data' because once the categories have been set up, data are in the form of frequencies. The category labels are merely names so there is no inherent order in them (see Table 17.6 on p.572 for an example). This is the simplest of the four levels of measurement.
Ordinal data	A scale which consists of rankings or ratings is ordinal. This allows you to make statements about the relative **magnitude** (size) of scores, i.e. that one value is higher than, lower than or equal to another. However, the extent of the comparison is limited; for example, if you ranked Olympic medalists into first second and third place, you would know that the person who came first is the best, followed by the second and third, but you do not know by how much. This is because the intervals between the units on the scale are not necessarily equal.
	Ordinal measurement is sometimes seen in attitude scales in which participants indicate their level of agreement with statements by choosing from: strongly agree, agree, neither agree nor disagree, disagree and strongly disagree.
	Strongly agree would score 5 down to strongly disagree, which would score 1. Responses to a number of statements would then be added up to give the overall scale score which could be used to compare participants.
Interval and ratio data	An interval scale involves measurements that, like ordinal data, can be compared in terms of magnitude; however there are **equal intervals** between the units on the scale because they are based on some standard unit of measurement. Most temperature scales and, some would argue, IQ scales are good examples of **interval data**. However, the zero point on these scales is arbitrary and does not indicate absolutely nothing.
	Ratio data are also measured on a scale that has magnitude and equal intervals but, in addition, has a genuine zero point (an **absolute zero**), for example, height in centimetres or weight in kilograms. The fixed zero point allows ratio statements to be made, i.e. to claim that someone whose height is 1.9 metres is twice as tall as someone who is 95 cm. The ratio scale is the most complex of the four levels of measurement.

Table 17.4 *Levels of measurement*

Using measurement scales in practice

Measuring intelligence

What type of measurement scale do you think IQ scores represent? Try to make a case for them being ordinal data and then interval/ratio data. When you have done this, decide which case is the more convincing.

Measuring motivation

A psychologist measures the motivation of a group of A-level students on a scale of 0 to 100, using an ordinal level of measurement. Person A achieves a score of 50 and Person B a score of 25. Can the psychologist claim that Person A is twice as motivated as Person B? Give reasons for your answer.

Some suggestions are given on p.620. ▶

Deciding which test to use

Identifying which research design has been used is the easier part of test choice. Once you have done this, your options are immediately narrowed. There are many tests to choose from. In particular, there is a range of tests, known as **parametric test**s, which you should only use if the samples of data meet particular standards. For example, they should only be applied to interval or ratio data. The tests you need to know about for the A2 exam are all **non-parametric test**s and do *not* require such high levels of measurement. Three of the four statistical tests you will learn about in the next section – the Mann-Whitney *U* test, the Wilcoxon matched pairs signed ranks test and Spearman's *rho* test – each requires data that are at least on an ordinal scale of measurement. The chi-squared test is used to analyse nominal data.

So what happens if the data collected are on an interval or ratio scale? Assume, for example, that you have samples of data such as the time in seconds taken for rats to run a particular maze. Seconds are fixed units of measurement that you could treat, correctly, as being on a ratio scale. However, you could allocate rank orders to these scores, thereby converting them to an ordinal scale. Alternatively, you could group the scores into categories

such as 'number of rats running the maze in less than 40 seconds' and 'number of rats taking 40 seconds or more to run the maze'. In this case, you are now treating the data as nominal. It is usually possible to make a more complex measurement scale into a simpler one but not the other way round. As you will see in the test calculations that follow, converting the data to an ordinal scale by ranking them in some way is a key part of the procedure. The one exception is the chi-squared test, which is the only one of the four tests that can be used with nominal data.

Table 17.5 provides you with a decision tree for choosing between the four tests that you need to know about for your A2 course.

Choosing the right test

Use the section 'Factors affecting test choice' and Table 17.5 to help you decide which test would be appropriate for each of the following examples:

1. You have sorted a group of 18-year-old students into four groups according to whether they are male or female and whether they have or do not have a full driving license. You want to know if there is a difference between the frequencies you have collected.

2. Now, considering just the students who have a full driving license, what test would you apply to compare the number of hours of driving tuition men and women had before passing their test?

3. What test would you apply to see if there is a relationship between the 18-year-olds' self-confidence in their driving and the number of hours of pre-test tuition they had?

4. Imagine you were able to test the 18-year-olds' driving self-confidence immediately after passing their driving test and again after one year's experience of driving. What test would you apply to see if the 18-year-olds' self-confidence in their driving had changed.

Some suggestions are given on p.621. ▶

Decision 1: What are you looking for?			
Differences			**Correlation**
Decision 2: What level of measurement do the data represent?			Spearman's r_s (Spearman's *rho*)
Nominal	**Ordinal (or interval/ratio)**		
Chi squared test	Decision 3: What experimental design was used?		
	Independent groups	**Related**	
	Mann Whitney *U* test	Wilcoxon matched pairs signed ranks test	

Table 17.5 *Selecting a statistical test*

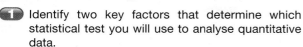

Check your understanding of statistical test choice by answering the questions below. Try to do this from memory. You can check your answers by looking back through the previous section: 'Factors affecting choice of statistical tests, including levels of measurement'.

1 Identify two key factors that determine which statistical test you will use to analyse quantitative data.

2 Give an example of a measurement scale for each of the following: (a) nominal data, (b) ordinal data, (c) interval data and (d) ratio data.

3 What is meant by: (a) magnitude, (b) equal intervals and (c) absolute zero in relation to levels of measurement?

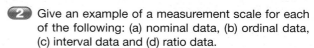 Topic 2: The use of inferential tests

In each of the following tests, a formula is applied to the data to calculate a test statistic. The next step is to assess this statistic to find out whether it indicates a significant effect. Statistical software will normally do this for you, but here you will be doing it manually. For each test there is a table of critical values and, for certain tests, the calculated statistic must equal or exceed a particular critical value but, in others, it must be equal to or less than the critical value in order to be deemed significant. The critical value you need to use is determined by whether you are carrying out a one- or two-tailed test, and by the level of significance you have decided on. A one-tailed test is used when the hypothesis is directional and a two-tailed test when the hypothesis is non-directional (see also p. 39 of *Psychology AS for AQA A*). You will also need to take into account the sample size(s) and there are various ways of doing this, depending on the test you are using.

Four non-parametric inferential statistical tests will now be considered, starting with the Mann-Whitney *U* test.

The Mann-Whitney *U* test

The Mann-Whitney *U* test is a test of difference that is suitable for comparing data gathered from two groups in an experiment using an **independent groups design**. It can be used with ordinal data. It can also be used with interval or ratio data since they are converted to an ordinal level measurement by rank ordering the data as part of the test procedure. (See pp. 41–2 in *Psychology AS for AQA A* for information about an independent groups design and Table 17.4 on p.565 for a reminder of levels of measurement.)

Specimen calculation of *U*

In the following example, data were obtained from a memory experiment (see below). There are different people in each condition (independent groups) and no more than 20 observations in each condition. The experimental (alternative) hypothesis is that more words are recalled in the experimental condition than in the control condition; the hypothesis is therefore directional.

Condition 1			Condition 2		
Participant no.	No. of words recalled (control condition)	Rank order	Participant no.	No. of words recalled (experimental condition)	Rank order
1	7	2	10	20	19
2	6	1	11	14	11
3	8	3.5	12	14	11
4	12	8	13	18	17
5	9	5	14	15	13
6	14	11	15	17	16
7	8	3.5	16	13	9
8	11	7	17	16	14.5
9	10	6	18	19	18
			19	16	14.5

Σ (sum of) ranks for Condition 1 (the smaller sample) = 47

1. Place the data to be analysed into the appropriate columns of a table prepared in a similar way to the one shown on the previous page.

2. Rank the data, from the lowest value (allocated rank 1) to the highest value (rank N). *Notice that both data sets are ranked in a single sequence and that the ranks are shared for any scores that are the same.* See Appendix 1 for guidance on how to place data in rank order.

3. Calculate the sum of the ranks for the smaller of the two samples and call this value T. If both samples contain the same number of observations, calculate the sum of the ranks for either sample. In the example $T = 47$.

4. Substitute in the following formula:

$$U = N_1 N_2 + \frac{N_1(N_1 + 1)}{2} - T$$

Here,

$U =$ the observed (i.e. the calculated) value of the Mann-Whitney statistic.

$N_1 =$ the number of values in the smaller sample (or in the sample for which the sum of the ranks has been calculated if both are the same size).

$N_2 =$ the number of values in the larger sample (or in the sample for which the sum of the ranks has not been calculated if both are the same size).

Here,

$$U = (9 \times 10) + \frac{9 \times (9 + 1)}{2} - 47$$

$$U = (9 \times 10) + \frac{90}{2} - 47$$

$$U = 90 + 45 - 47 = 88$$

$U = 88$. This is the observed value of U.

5. Substitute in the following formula:

$$U' = N_1 N_2 - U$$

Here, $U' = (9 \times 10) - 88$

$$U' = 90 - 88$$

$$U' = 2.$$

This is the observed value of U'.

6. Select the smaller value of U and U'. In this example, U' has the smaller value of 2. Whichever is the smallest value becomes the value of U.

7. Consult the table in Appendix 2 to obtain the critical values of U; a critical value of U is the maximum value of U that is significant at a given level of significance. (Statistical significance was discussed earlier in this chapter on p.563.) In order to obtain this, you need to know:

(a) the values of N_1 and N_2 (in this case 9 and 10 respectively)

(b) whether a one-tailed or two-tailed test is required; the experimental hypothesis was directional, so a one-tailed test is appropriate. (The concept of directional and non-directional hypotheses is discussed on p. 39 of *Psychology AS for AQA A*.)

Take the smaller of the observed values of U and U'. In this case the smaller is U', which = 2. If this value is equal to or less than the critical value for a given level of significance, the null hypothesis can be rejected. (Levels of significance are discussed earlier in this chapter on p.563.)

A minimum significance level of $p = .05$ will be assumed in this case. From Appendix 2, Table 4, the critical value of U for $N_1 = 9$ and $N_2 = 10$ for a one-tailed test at p = .05 is 24. As the observed value of U (2) is less than the critical value (24), the probability of these results occurring if the null hypothesis is true is less than 5% *(p < .05)*.

In this case, the null hypothesis can be rejected and the experimental hypothesis, that more words are recalled in the experimental condition than in the control condition, is a more likely explanation of the results.

Note: If the observed value had been greater than the critical value, then the probability of these results occurring if the null hypothesis is true would have been greater than 5 per cent. The null hypothesis would not, therefore, have been rejected.

For samples of more than 20 in each condition, a different formula should be applied as explained in Coolican (2009).

The Wilcoxon matched pairs signed ranks test

The Wilcoxon matched pairs signed ranks test is a test of difference, suitable for use with data gathered from an experiment using a related (**matched pairs** or **repeated measures**) design. It can be used on ordinal data. Interval or ratio data can also be used because they are converted to an ordinal level as part of the test calculations. (See pp. 42–4 in *Psychology AS for AQA A* for a discussion of a related design, and Table 17.4 on p.565 for a discussion of levels of measurement.). The method described here is appropriate when there is a maximum of 25 pairs of observations (see specimen calculation below). In this example, the experimental (alternative) hypothesis is that more words are recalled in the experimental condition than in the control condition; the hypothesis is therefore directional.

Specimen calculation of T

Below is a specimen calculation of the Wilcoxon matched pairs signed ranks test, which is suitable for situations where there is a maximum of 25 pairs of observations. The data below are taken from a memory experiment.

Participant no.	No. of words recalled (control condition)	No. of words recalled (experimental condition)	Difference	Rank order
1	17	20	-3	4
2	12	14	-2	2.5
3	16	14	+2	2.5
4	12	19	-7	9
5	16	15	+1	1
6	14	19	-5	6
7	13	13	0	(omitted)
8	11	16	-5	6
9	13	19	-6	8
10	11	16	-5	6

1 Place the data to be analysed into the appropriate columns of a table prepared in a similar way to that in the table opposite.

2 Calculate the difference between each pair of scores (see the 'Difference' column in the table below). It is essential that the direction of any difference is recorded.

3 Rank the data in the difference column, from the lowest value (allocated rank 1) to the highest value (rank N). Notice that when you do this:

(a) any zero differences are disregarded

(b) positive and negative signs are disregarded

(c) the ranks are shared for any scores which are tied. (See Appendix 1 for how to rank data.)

4 Calculate the sum of the ranks, which correspond to:

(a) the differences with the + sign; and

(b) the differences with the – sign.

Call the smaller of these values T. In the example below:

Sum of the ranks which correspond to the differences with the + sign = 2.5 + 1 = 3.5

Sum of the ranks which correspond to the differences with the – sign

= 4 + 2.5 + 9 + 6 + 6 + 8 + 6 = 41.5

The smallest sum of ranks is T. Therefore, the observed value of $T = 3.5$.

5 Consult the table in Appendix 3 to obtain the critical values of T (a critical value is the maximum value of T that is significant at a given level of probability).

In order to obtain the critical value of T, you need to know:

(a) the value of N (the number of pairs of scores). Note that pairs of scores with a difference of zero are not included. In this example, the number of pairs of scores is therefore 9.

(b) whether a one-tailed or two-tailed test is required; the experimental hypothesis was directional, so a one-tailed test is appropriate. (The concept of directional and non-directional hypotheses is discussed on p.39 of *Psychology AS for AQA A*.)

If the observed value of T is equal to, or less than, the critical value for a given level of significance, the null hypothesis can be rejected.

A minimum significance level of $p = .05$ will be assumed in this case. (Levels of significance are discussed earlier in this chapter on p.563.) From Appendix 3, the critical value of T for $N = 9$ for a one-tailed test *at p = .05* is 8. As the observed value of T (3.5) is less than the critical value (8), the likelihood of the results occurring if the null hypothesis is true is less than 5% *(p < .05)*. The experimental hypothesis that more words are recalled in the experimental condition than in the control condition is supported. In this case, the null hypothesis can be rejected and the experimental (alternative) hypothesis is supported as a more likely explanation of the results.

Note: If the observed value had been greater than the critical value, then the likelihood of results such as these occurring if the null hypothesis is true would have been greater than 5 per cent. The null hypothesis would not, therefore, have been rejected.

For samples with more than 25 pairs of observations a different formula should be applied as explained in Coolican (2009).

Spearman's rank order correlation coefficient (r_s)

Spearman's rank order correlation coefficient (r_s) is a test of correlation suitable for use with pairs of scores. It can be used with ordinal data. It can also be used with interval or ratio data because they are converted to an ordinal level for the purposes of the test. The test gives a correlation coefficient with a value between +1.00 and –1.00. The sign

Participant no.	Psychology test score	Rank order	Biology test score	Rank order	d	d²
1	95	10	92	9	1	1
2	27	2	36	2	0	0
3	47	4	40	3	1	1
4	68	7	57	5	2	4
5	50	5	61	6	−1	1
6	94	9	91	8	1	1
7	33	3	41	4	−1	1
8	26	1	35	1	0	0
9	93	8	93	10	−2	4
10	59	6	70	7	−1	1
						$\Sigma d^2 = 14$

indicates the direction of the relationship (positive or negative) and the number indicates the strength of the relationship, where one is a perfect correlation and a value between 0 and + or − 1 is an imperfect correlation.

Specimen calculation of r_s

The example below uses data obtained from a study investigating the possible correlation between psychology test scores and biology test scores of a group of participants studying both subjects. The direction of the relationship, if any, is uncertain and so the alternative hypothesis (that there is a correlation between psychology and biology test scores) is non-directional.

1 Draw a scattergraph (sometimes referred to as a scattergram) of the data sets that you wish to correlate. This is important as this technique measures only straight-line relationships, and drawing a scattergraph can help you to decide if this is the case (see pp. 64–65 of *Psychology AS for AQA A*).

2 Place the data to be analysed into the appropriate columns of a table prepared in a similar way to the table above.

3 Rank each set of scores separately, giving the lowest score rank 1 and the highest score rank *N*. (See Appendix 1 for how to rank data.)

   Note: Accuracy is diminished if this test is used when ranks are shared for any scores that are tied. In such cases, the appropriate procedure is to carry out correlation analysis using Kendall's *tau*, especially for small samples. However, unless there are large numbers of ties, the effects on the outcome are likely to be very small.

4 Find the difference *(d)* between each pair of rank order scores (see *d* column in the table above).

5 Square each of the *d* values (see d^2 column in the table above).

6 Calculate the sum of (Σ) the d^2 values. This is the value described as d^2 in the table above.

7 Substitute in the following formula:

$$r_s = 1 - \left(\frac{6 \Sigma d^2}{N(N^2 - 1)} \right)$$

Here,

r_s = the observed (i.e. calculated) value of Spearman's correlation coefficient

Σd^2 = the sum of the squared differences

N = the number of pairs of scores being correlated.

Here,

$$r_s = 1 - \left(\frac{84}{10(100 - 1)} \right)$$

$$= 1 - \left(\frac{84}{10 \times 99} \right)$$

$$= 1 - \frac{84}{990}$$

$$= 1 - 0.0848$$

$$= 0.9152$$

This is the observed value of r_s, which is more neatly expressed as .92

8 Consult the table in Appendix 4 to obtain the critical values of r_s (a critical value is the minimum value of r_s that is significant at a given level of probability). In order to obtain this you need to know:

   (a) the value of *N* (the number of pairs of scores)

   (b) whether a one-tailed or two-tailed test is required. In this case, the hypothesis was non-directional, so a two-tailed test is appropriate. (The concept of directional and non-directional hypotheses is discussed on p. 39 of *Psychology AS for AQA A*.)

If the observed value of r_s is equal to or greater than the critical value for a given level of significance, the null hypothesis can be rejected.

A minimum significance level of $p = .05$ will be assumed in this case. (Levels of significance are discussed earlier in this chapter on p.563.) From Appendix 4, when $N = 10$, the critical value of r_s for a two-tailed test at $p = .05$ is .648. As the observed value of r_s (.9152) is greater than the critical value (.648), the likelihood of results such as these occurring if the null hypothesis is true is less than 5 per cent. In this case, the null hypothesis can be rejected and the alternative hypothesis that there is a relationship between psychology and biology test scores is a more likely explanation of the results.

Note: If the observed value had been less than the critical value, the likelihood of such results occurring if the null hypothesis were true would be greater than 5 per cent. In which case, the null hypothesis could not have been rejected, but rather would have accounted for the results (i.e. there is no relationship between the psychology and biology test scores).

The chi-squared test for independent samples (χ^2)

The chi-squared test for independent samples (χ^2) is a test of association for use with data gathered from independent samples that are measured at a nominal level in the form of frequencies. It tests for differences by examining the association that exists between data categorized into rows and columns. It compares observed frequencies (those actually obtained) with expected frequencies (the frequencies which would be observed if the null hypothesis were true).

You need to be aware of the following limitations on the use of the chi-squared test:

- The chi-squared test should only be used in situations where each observation belongs in just one category. If an observation can go in more than one category, the data are not independent and the test cannot be used.

- The observations used in the test must be actual frequencies of occurrence. Data, such as averages, percentages or proportions, should not be used.

- The probability of making a Type 1 error is increased when there are expected frequencies of less than 5, especially when the total sample size is small (i.e. less than 20). A chi-squared test could still be used in such situations, although the potential for error increases with small samples or with an increase in the number of expected frequencies less than 5. Using a larger sample size can minimize this potential problem. (Type 1 errors are discussed earlier in this chapter on p.563.)

Specimen calculation of χ^2

What follows is a specimen calculation of the chi-squared test for independent samples, using data from an

	No. of children able to solve problem	No. of children unable to solve problem	Row total
4-year-old children	Cell 1 8	Cell 2 12	RT1 20
5-year-old children	Cell 3 17	Cell 4 3	RT2 20
Column total	CT1 25	CT2 15	GT 40

investigation into children's thinking. The non-directional hypothesis to be tested is that there is a difference in the problem solving ability of four- and five-year-old children.

where RT1 and RT2 are row totals, CT1 and CT2 are column totals and GT is the grand total.

1 Place the observed values to be analysed into the appropriate boxes of a table prepared in a similar way to the table shown above. This kind of table is called a 'contingency table'; in this case it is a 2 x 2 contingency table because there are two rows and two columns of data. Other numbers of rows and columns are possible using this same test (e.g. 2 × 3).

2 Calculate the expected frequency for each cell, using the formula:

Expected frequency $(E) = \left(\dfrac{RT \times CT}{GT}\right)$

3 Subtract the expected frequency (E) from the observed frequency (O) for each cell:

Cell 1: $O - E = 8 - 12.5 = -4.5$
Cell 2: $O - E = 12 - 7.5 = 4.5$
Cell 3: $O - E = 17 - 12.5 = 4.5$
Cell 4: $O - E = 3 - 7.5 = -4.5$

4 Calculate $(O - E)^2$ for each cell:

Cell 1: $-4.5^2 = 20.25$
Cell 2: $4.52 = 20.25$
Cell 3: $4.52 = 20.25$
Cell 4: $-4.52 = 20.25$

5 Calculate $\dfrac{(O - E)^2}{}$ for each cell:

Cell 1: $20.25 \div 12.5 = 1.62$
Cell 2: $20.25 \div 7.5 = 2.7$
Cell 3: $20.25 \div 12.5 = 1.62$
Cell 4: $20.25 \div 7.5 = 2.7$

6 Add the answers to step 5 to obtain the observed value of χ^2:

$1.62 + 2.7 + 1.62 + 2.7 = 8.64$.
This is the observed value of χ^2.

Note: Steps 2 to 6 can be represented by the following formula:

$\chi^2 = \Sigma \left[\dfrac{(O - E)^2}{E} \right]$

7 Calculate the number of degrees of freedom using the formula:

Degrees of freedom *(df)* = (No. of rows − 1) × (No. of columns − 1)

(Degrees of freedom are the number of cell values that are free to vary, given that row totals and column totals are known.)

In the example above:
df = (2 − 1) × (2 − 1)
df = 1.

8 Consult the table in Appendix 5 to obtain the critical values of χ^2; a critical value of χ^2 is the minimum value of χ^2 that is significant at a given level of significance. (Statistical significance is discussed earlier in this chapter on p.563.) In order to obtain this you need to know:

(a) the number of degrees of freedom (in this case *df* = 1)

(b) whether a one-tailed or a two-tailed test is required. In this case, a non-directional hypothesis was used, so a two-tailed test is appropriate.

If the observed value of χ^2 is equal to or greater than the critical value for a given level of significance, the null hypothesis can be rejected. (Levels of significance are discussed earlier in this chapter on p.563.)

HOW SCIENCE WORKS

Activity **Carrying out statistical tests**

1 An experiment was carried out to see whether drinking regular or decaffeinated coffee before doing an IQ test had any effect on people's scores. Use the Mann-Whitney *U* test for small samples on the independent groups of data in Table 17.6 to see whether scores in the two conditions vary. Decide on an appropriate significance level and whether to use a one- or a two-tailed test. Assess the significance of the result and state whether you can reject the null hypothesis. Try to explain the result.

2 The data in Table 17.1 summarize the number of A and A* grades achieved by students in two schools. The data are in pairs matched by subject and you want to find out if they differ. Carry out a Wilcoxon matched pairs signed ranks test. Decide on an appropriate significance level and whether to use a one-tailed or a two-tailed test. Assess the significance of the result and decide whether you can reject the null hypothesis. Try to explain the result.

3 Using the data in Table 17.3 showing student's marks for two practical reports, carry out a Spearman's *rho* correlation test. Decide on an appropriate significance level and whether to use a one-tailed or a two-tailed test. Assess the significance of the result and decide whether you can reject the null hypothesis. Try to explain the result.

4 A school requires all its students to study one humanities subject only at GCSE and the staff are curious to know whether there is an association between the gender of students and their choice of subject. Use the data in Table 17.7 to carry out a chi-squared test. Decide on an appropriate significance level and whether to use a one-tailed or a two-tailed test. Assess the significance of the result and state whether you can reject the null hypothesis. Try to explain the result.

Participant	Regular coffee	Participant	Decaffeinated coffee
1	106	11	97
2	108	12	97
3	110	13	100
4	113	14	103
5	117	15	105
6	119	16	108
7	120	17	109
8	122	18	110
9	128	19	113
10	130	20	116

Table 17.6 *IQ scores after drinking regular or decaffeinated of coffee*

Gender	Subject		
	Geography	History	Religious studies
Male	20	28	15
Female	22	17	27

Table 17.7 *Subject choices by gender*

The answers can be found on p.621. ▶

A minimum significance level of $p = .05$ will be assumed in this case. From Appendix 5, the critical value of χ^2 for $df = 1$ and a two-tailed test at $p = .05$ is 3.84. As the observed value of χ^2 (8.64) is greater than the critical value (3.84), the likelihood of these results occurring if the null hypothesis is true is less than 5 per cent $(p < .05)$. In this case, the null hypothesis would be rejected and the alternative hypothesis that four- and five-year-old children differ in their problem-solving ability is a more likely explanation of the results.

Note: If the observed value had been less than the critical value, then the probability of results such as these occurring if the null hypothesis is true would have been greater than 5 per cent. In which case, the null hypothesis would not have been rejected because the alternative hypothesis is not supported by the results.

CHECK YOUR UNDERSTANDING

Check your understanding of inferential statistics by answering the following questions. Try to do this from memory. You can check your answers by looking back through Topic 2, 'The use of inferential tests'.

1 What does the use of inferential statistical techniques enable a researcher to do that descriptive statistics do not?

2 Name two tests for differences between two samples of data. What is the essential difference between them?

3 What information is given by (a) the sign (+ or −) of a correlation coefficient and (b) its numerical value?

4 How do tests that require at least ordinal data deal with interval or ratio data?

5 Explain the independence assumption in the chi-squared test.

6 When is it appropriate to use a one-tailed test and when should a two-tailed test be used?

Analysis and interpretation of qualitative data

In Chapter 2 of *Psychology AS for AQA A*, a number of research techniques that may generate qualitative data were discussed, including naturalistic observation, questionnaires that include open-ended questions and unstructured and semi-structured interviews. Each of these may generate qualitative data in the form of text, although these data can be simplified by converting them into quantitative data.

There are many different methods for analysing qualitative data so just two examples will be included here. Content analysis is the first to be expanded upon: it involves reducing qualitative data to make it quantitative data. The second method involves analysing text to identify themes and does not involve any numbers.

Content analysis

In *Psychology AS for AQA A*, content analysis was described as a systematic research technique for analysing transcripts of interviews, documents or text (visual or written), including advertisements, children's books, TV programmes, cartoons, films, song lyrics, newspapers and magazines, and websites (see pp. 73–75). The researcher creates a coding system of predetermined categories (e.g. age groups of 16–25 and 26–35) at the outset of the study, which is then applied to the materials in a consistent manner. A pilot study is often used to generate and test the coding system to be employed. Care is needed to ensure that the categories are discrete and do not overlap.

Manstead and McCulloch (1981) carried out one of the earliest British studies of sex-role stereotyping in TV advertisements. They focused on adverts that featured an adult playing a leading part, analysing the role played by the adult, the product used, the type of argument they voiced, and the basis of their credibility (i.e. whether they were an expert on the product, a user of it, or neither).

HOW SCIENCE WORKS

Activity Content analysis of TV advertisements

1 Gather some data by looking at a series of advertisements and, for each one, decide which cell it belongs in. Record your data in a table similar to the one below. It is important to ensure that adverts are not classified in the table more than once. Dependent characters are defined as being shown in relation to someone else (e.g. husband, girlfriend, employee, relative). Autonomous characters appear to be alone

	Male	**Female**
Dependent		
Autonomous		
Other		

and independent (e.g. a celebrity). Use the 'other' category only if you really cannot decide.

2 When you have sufficient data, count up the total in each category and analyse the data, using a chi-squared test. Are gender and role independent of each other or are they associated? Is there is a difference and, if so, does it suggest sex-role stereotyping?

3 Now devise a table for recording another aspect of advertisements based on the type of product being used (e.g. domestic, cosmetic). Pilot it to ensure that the categories are workable and mutually exclusive. Again, is there an association that suggests sex-role stereotyping?

Suggestions are given on p.623.

Stereotypically, men portrayed an autonomous role (e.g. as a professional), gave factual information about a product and were experts on it. Women tended to be shown in dependent roles (e.g. as a wife), gave opinions about products and were product users.

Ten years later, Cumberbatch (1990) also used content analysis to study the portrayal of men and women on TV and found an additional age bias in favour of portraying younger women along with persistent gender stereotyping. Such research continues to be relevant, not only because of the need to understand the impact of ever-increasing communications technology, but also because it enables the monitoring of whether equal opportunities legislation is being observed. The 'Content analysis of TV advertisements' activity gives you some experience of this method.

Evaluation of content analysis

Reductionism – It could be argued that converting qualitative data to numbers is reductionist, meaning that the richness and complexity of the qualitative data are lost. In an advert, for example, the whole is greater than the sum of its parts and so breaking it down results in a loss of subtleties and nuances about how its message is constructed. On the other hand, it could be argued that such analysis preserves the essence of the content of complex material by making it more manageable and much easier to understand.

Illusion of objectivity – Transforming qualitative data into numbers appears to be scientifically rigorous because of the trust people tend to place on 'hard' data and statistics. However, this apparent objectivity could be illusory since the system of categorization may be biased by what the researcher personally believes to be important. The findings may therefore not be as trustworthy or valid as they might appear initially.

Reliability checking – Creating a coding system and training different researchers to use it allows them to compare their data to check whether they are the same. This is a form of reliability checking. If the findings are consistent, it indicates that the coding system is well designed and that the researchers are well trained. Most importantly, it tells you that the findings can be replicated by at least two different people, so you can have greater confidence in them.

Statistical procedures become possible – Once qualitative content has been converted into quantitative data, a range of statistical procedures can be used to identify patterns in the data that are not otherwise apparent. It becomes easier to compare findings from similar studies which, again, acts as a kind of reliability check for particular effects, giving you greater confidence in findings that seem to be consistent.

Thematic analysis

There are some complex techniques available for analysing textual information, which take time and training to master. **Thematic analysis** is one of the simplest and easiest to grasp. Braun and Clarke (2006 p.79) state that:

> 'Thematic analysis is a method for identifying, analysing and reporting patterns (themes) within data. It minimally organises and describes your data set in (rich) detail. However, frequently it goes further than this, and interprets various aspects of the research topic.'

Thematic analysis involves taking a body of text (qualitative data) and organizing it into specific themes so that the content can be summarized. Braun and Clarke distinguish between inductive and theoretical analysis. **Inductive analysis** involves approaching the data with no preconceptions about which themes might emerge. **Theoretical analysis**, on the other hand, usually means that the researcher already has some ideas about what themes may emerge, based on previous research, so they examine data to see whether these themes are present. Furthermore, Braun and Clarke distinguish between semantic analysis and latent thematic analysis. Latent thematic analysis involves first analysing themes at a semantic level and then 'drilling down' to try to understand why a text has been structured in a particular way. This is much more complex and difficult than semantic thematic analysis on its own and so only the latter will be illustrated here. Semantic thematic analysis looks at the meaning and form of text without going beyond this.

1.	Transcribe the data if you need to, number each line and read the text through several times until you know it well. As you read the text, make notes of any ideas that occur to you about it.
2.	Divide the text into meaning units using a forward slash (/) between every apparent change in meaning or subject.
3.	Search the entire text for meanings that seem to have a similar theme and group these together. You could highlight these using different colours on the computer screen or on paper if you prefer.
4.	Keep adjusting the themes as you continue to sort through the data.
5.	Once you are satisfied that there are no more themes to find you will need to define and name each theme.
6.	Write up the report. In the results section you will need to present a case for each theme and provide some supporting verbatim quotations from the text, using the original line number so that it can be located if necessary.

Table 17.8 *Stages in thematic analysis*

Starting thematic analysis

Here is a brief example of how a portion of an interview transcript might be analysed and interpreted. For this analysis, lines have been typed and numbered and then split into meaning units. Some interpretation using emergent themes is also given. Text in square brackets has been added to the transcription for clarification purposes and is not analysed.

1 I'm having to decide / whether to have my baby vaccinated [with the triple MMR

2 vaccine] and I'm in a total state of confusion about it. / Of course it's important / but

3 you hear so many scare stories / about autism and that / but then you're told

4 there's no evidence for it / or the risks are so low. / They scare you another way

5 too / by going on about how dangerous the real illness is / and how children can

6 go deaf or blind or even die / ...so you're weighing it up. / The other thing they do /

7 is give you a guilt trip / about herd immunity / and how a few unvaccinated babies /

8 can upset the whole thing. / 'You never see polio any more' / they say / 'but once it

9 was really common / that's what modern medicine can do for you'. / I've thought

10 about asking for the three separate vaccines / to let things settle in between. /

11 Three at once seems like lot for a little baby to cope with / but then it's only once./

12 How they scream when it happens though. / You're cuddling them, / feeling really

13 tense, smiling away at the nurse / but thinking 'This is awful what have I done?' /

14 and then anxiously watching them like a hawk for the whole of the next week. /...so

15 what's to do? / Three needles or one? / I just don't know.../

Two semantic themes that can be extracted from this transcript are outlined below. When writing a report you would need to introduce each theme and add some commentary to justify and explain each theme.

Theme 1: Uncertainty
Lines 1–2   I'm having to decide and I'm in a total state of confusion about it
Line 6   ...so you're weighing it up...
Lines 14–15   ...so what's to do? / I just don't know...

Theme 2: Intense negative feelings
Lines 4–5   They scare you another way too...
Lines 12–13   ...feeling really tense...
Line 13   ...thinking 'This is awful what have I done?'
Line 14   ...anxiously watching them like a hawk for the whole of the next week.

Having decided to ask a particular research question you would need to gather some textual data. This might mean conducting face-to-face interviews or the data may already be in written form. Sometimes texts are unique (e.g. Princess Diana's interview with Martin Bashir in 1995 (which is available online at http://www.bbc.co.uk/politics97/diana/panorama.html) and sometimes it is possible to gather a number of accounts (e.g. eyewitness accounts of the events of 9/11 in New York). The method of analysis can be the same, but multiple accounts also allow for comparisons to be made. Once you have the text, a typical way to proceed is outlined in Table 17.8 on the left.

Evaluation of thematic analysis

Accessibility – Although it is important not to underestimate the effort involved in learning to carry out thematic analysis and do it well, it is one of the more accessible ways of analysing text and, according to Braun and Clarke (2006), should be the starting point for an aspiring qualitative researcher. A positive side-effect of its

Activity Continuing thematic analysis

Another possible theme could be 'Consequences of actions'. Extract material from the transcript in the box to support this theme.

Suggestions are given on p.623. ▶

accessibility is that the reports also tend to be understandable and meaningful to people the general public; this allows psychologists to share their findings more easily with others who might benefit from them.

Subjectivity – In spite of having a set of procedures for content analysis, there is a risk that individual researchers could interpret the same text in very different ways and so qualitative reports could appear to be nothing more than journalism. This increased risk of subjectivity, or openness to personal bias, makes it difficult for some critics to believe they could have enough confidence in the findings to apply them. However, just as with quantitative research, there are procedures to reduce bias. Qualitative researchers could, for example, carefully and deliberately reflect and report on how they tried to take account of any possible biases. They can also double-check their interpretation with the participants involved. Nevertheless, it is debatable whether any researcher could be fully aware of all his/her own biases, or that any participant would truly be in a position to judge the quality of the written report.

Quality – Some critics argue that it is difficult to ensure the quality of research that is purely qualitative because the aspects of quantitative research that are typically valued, such as control, objectivity and replicability, are missing. This is essentially a philosophical argument about how psychologists should do research – either using the traditional ways of science or more flexible and newer approaches. A possible solution is to use different criteria for assessing quality. For example, it is impossible to replicate a unique interview, but it is possible to use a technique called **data triangulation** and examine other sources of information about a particular interviewee. If these additional sources of data support the researcher's analysis then it has greater credibility.

Topic 3: Reporting psychological investigations

Psychologists communicate their research findings by means of articles published in scientific journals and these articles have to be written in the 'house style' of the journal concerned. For quantitative studies, such as experiments, reporting style is similar across all journals and most conform to the guidelines which will be outlined here. The main sections in a quantitative report are summarized in Table 17.9.

Title
Abstract (or Summary)
Introduction
Method • Participants • Design • Apparatus (or Materials) • Procedure
Results • Descriptive analysis of data (as appropriate) • Inferential analysis of data (as appropriate)
Discussion
References
Appendices

Table 17.9 *Section headings in a typical quantitative research report*

Qualitative reporting is less formulaic, mainly because of the wide variety of research methods available. Those that adopt a qualitative method, such as an unstructured or semi-structured interview, but then reduce the text to numbers using some kind of content analysis, usually look very much like a traditional report. Those that are entirely qualitative and adopt a type of non-numerical textual analysis, resemble traditional reports in many respects, but look entirely different in the results section, sometimes combining textual analysis and discussion. To get an idea of how different kinds of research might be reported, have a look at some examples in the *Research Digest* of the British Psychological Society and in *Google Scholar* listed in Further Resources at the end of this chapter. There are some full-text articles available in the archive.

In this section we will consider the conventions of reporting research in academic journals, with opportunities to discover the sections of a published research paper and to compare the way in which quantitative and qualitative research is reported. You might like to prepare a short report, using ideas for data collection in this chapter (see Content analysis activity) and in other parts of this book. There is no substitute for hands-on experience in helping you to understand the entire research process, from initial planning and ethics approval, through to writing a report suitable for publication.

Reporting psychological investigations

The final stage of carrying out research is to write the report. This section provides detailed guidance on how to organize and present a report in a way that would be suitable for publication. Each journal has its own style but, essentially, published articles follow a similar structure to that summarized in Table 17.9.

Tips about writing style
Here are some general points:

- Reports are usually written using the third person in the passive voice (e.g. 'An investigation was carried out' rather than 'I carried out an investigation').

- Reports are written in the past tense. Researchers report what has taken place, rather than what they plan to do.

- When writing a report, it should be borne in mind that it is being written for someone who is unfamiliar with the investigation. However, the reader should be able to replicate it from the description provided. A good way to check this would be to give it to someone else to read and ask them whether they could replicate the study exactly.

A report typically has the following sections.

Title
The title should provide a clear indication of the focus of the study. However, selecting an informative title is not always as easy as it might seem. A very general title gives the reader little information about the nature of the investigation (e.g. 'A study of short-term memory'). At the same time, a title that is too long and complicated should also be avoided (e.g. 'A study to investigate gender differences in self-reported health behaviours and stress levels of a group of 14- to 16-year-old young people who attend a large, inner-city comprehensive school').

A useful way of thinking about a title is to consider the key variables involved in the investigation; for example, 'The relationship between health and stress levels' or 'The effect of visual imagery on encoding in short-term memory'.

Abstract
Although it is the first thing to appear in a report, the abstract (or summary) is often the last section the researcher writes. The abstract provides a clear and concise account of the entire investigation in about 150–200 words so that readers can gain an overview of the study and decide whether or not the rest of the report is likely to be of interest. When researchers are reviewing existing research, abstracts provide useful snapshots of what is often a considerable amount of literature, not all of which will be relevant so, in this sense, abstracts constitute a kind of academic speed-dating!

Within this short section, information is provided on:

- the background idea of the investigation, including the previous research that it was based on

- the aim of the investigation and the experimental (alternative) hypotheses tested

- a brief description of the research method used and, if appropriate, the design (e.g. repeated measures design)

- the sample of participants and the setting

- a brief description of the findings, including the statistical tests used, the statistical significance of the results and how the findings were interpreted

- the conclusions drawn and any key limitations or important implications of the study.

It can be challenging to capture all of this in around 150–200 words; the skill of writing a good abstract takes time to master.

Introduction, aim(s) and hypotheses
The introduction to a report should review existing research literature in the area of interest and provide a clear rationale for the work to be undertaken. Coolican (2004) provides a helpful way of thinking about this process, suggesting that writing an introduction should be regarded as a logical 'funnelling' process. As it progresses, it should move closer and closer to the specific focus of the investigation. When you read the introduction of a report, you should be able to see a logical flow of ideas from the general research topic through to the research aim and find yourself persuaded about the reasons for carrying out the study. It is essential to be clear about the aim of the research and you may or may not find a formally stated hypothesis at the end of the introduction. Null hypotheses should only be mentioned in relation to statistical tests and nowhere else in the report. Hypotheses are inappropriate in any research that is entirely qualitative.

Method
Precise details are given about how the investigation was carried out in the method section. A key aim of this section is replicability, so there should be sufficient detail to enable another researcher to replicate the study exactly. For the sake of clarity, the method section is often divided into subsections:

- *Design* – This gives an overview of the structure of the study and justifies the decisions to conduct it in a particular way (e.g. by way of a particular experimental design or non-experimental method). The reader should be able to see what variables were involved and what controls, if relevant, were in place. Many reports deal with ethical issues in this section, as these are a key aspect of good research design.

- *Participants* – Demographic information about participants is described here, together with details of number, sampling and recruitment procedures. In qualitative research it is increasingly common for the researcher to reflect here on how their personal interests might influence the research.

- *Apparatus/materials* – Here the researcher explains what is needed to carry out the research (e.g. particular hardware and software, consent forms, recording devices, interview schedules or questionnaires).

- *Procedure* – This section describes how the investigation was carried out. Once again, the key issue is replicability, so it is important that the reader knows exactly the design that was used, what was done, who the participants were and what materials were used. Sufficient detail is needed to enable others to replicate the study.

Results
In a report of quantitative research, this section will consist of appropriate descriptive and inferential statistics presented in summary tables and figures with brief explanations. Raw data and analyses tend not to appear in published work, but would be seen by the journal editors and reviewers prior to accepting the work for publication. Reports of qualitative research or of studies that combine quantitative and qualitative methods will naturally differ. In some qualitative reports, the analysis of the results and the final discussion are interwoven.

Discussion
This section is used to review the findings, compare them to existing research, assess the overall quality of the study and make suggestions about what research could be done next. It usually includes:

- *An explanation of findings* – the writer will summarize the main findings, assess the findings and offer an interpretation of them.

- *Relationship to previous research* – the findings are discussed in relation to those of other studies, usually the ones mentioned in the introduction. The similarities are highlighted and an explanation is offered for any differences.

- *Assessment of methodology (internal validity)* – although the researcher will have tried to design an exemplary study, it is important to have the humility to scrutinize its internal validity, in other words, to question whether it was well designed and how far the results can be trusted. If, with the benefit of hindsight, the design could be improved, the researcher should describe how. In reality, research that is poorly designed and flawed is unlikely to be published.

- *Assessment of implications (external validity)* – assessing external validity involves considering the wider practical and/or theoretical implications of the findings; for example, are there any implications for society, education, specific psychological theories or equal opportunities policies?

- *Suggestions for further research* – possible follow-up studies may be suggested.

Conclusion
There will usually be a brief conclusion that sums up the main findings.

References
All the sources that the researcher used to inform the report, and are cited in it, must be included here.

Appendices
Published research occasionally has numbered appendices which might include raw data, statistical calculations, a copy of a questionnaire or interval schedule or other materials that would overload the main report.

Examples of published research
The 'Imitation of film-mediated aggressive models activity opposite provides an example of how quantitative research is reported. This classic study by Bandura and colleagues (1963) investigated the conditions under which children learn aggressive behaviour from others. The activity entitled 'A qualitative study of GPs' views of treating obesity' provides an example of a qualitative research report.

Good practice in reporting research
As well as observing the rules of the 'house style' of a particular journal, there are at least two more aspects of good practice that research psychologists need to bear in mind when preparing reports.

Avoiding plagiarism
As you saw in Chapter 15, it is important in any scientific community to share research ideas and findings so that knowledge is built up in an open and systematic way. However, this sharing should never lead to researchers passing off other people's work or ideas as their own. To do this is **plagiarism** (or intellectual theft) which is regarded as a serious academic offence. There are rules about how to use other people's work or ideas and how to acknowledge them both within a research report and in the references. The existence of these rules and other guidelines for reporting research helps to guard against accusations of copying.

Using primary source material
One way to guard against plagiarism and to improve the quality of your work is to use and acknowledge primary sources of information when writing a report. In the activities on p.579, involving research articles, you have been reading **primary sources** or first-hand reports of psychologists' research. In addition, they provided references to other related work and this allows other researchers to track down the original papers to read for themselves if they so wish. It is nearly always better to read the original than to depend on a **secondary source** (i.e. someone else's account of it). This is because inaccuracies can creep in as information is passed from one person to another and this can compromise the integrity of psychological knowledge. A story originating from World War II illustrates the dangers. A message that apparently originated as 'Send reinforcements, we're going to advance' was passed along until it eventually became 'Send three and fourpence, we're going to a dance'. A visit to the website for 'Classics in the History of Psychology' given in the *Further Resources* will enable you to read first-hand accounts of classic studies that are

Activity: Imitation of film-mediated aggressive models

Download a copy of a classic study undertaken by Bandura *et al.* (1963), entitled 'Imitation of film-mediated aggressive models', from: http://des.emory.edu/mfp/BanduraPubsByYear.html Dates are listed at the top of the screen. Click on 1963 to find the paper amongst the publications listed for that year. When you have read the paper, try to answer the following questions:

1 Identify the journal that the article appeared in.

2 The opening paragraph is the Abstract. Compare this to the six points about abstract content on p.577. How does the house style of the journal differ from these?

3 Who financed the research? Does it affect its credibility?

4 The introduction makes a case for the study that was carried out. Identify three different sources of information that the authors draw on. Are these primary or secondary sources?

5 What are the two research predictions?

6 Ethical considerations are not explicitly reported in the method. Suggest two ethical issues that would have been addressed.

7 What conditions were compared?

8 What experimental design was used?

9 How were the data collected?

10 From the total aggression scores presented in Table 1, identify the least and the most aggressive group.

11 In Table 2, the Wilcoxon test was used to compare treatment conditions. Which differences in total aggression scores were significant?

12 What general conclusion was drawn about the effect on aggressive behaviour of the relationship between the sex of the model and sex of the child?

13 From the discussion, identify:
- a link to related research
- a strength and a limitation of the study
- an implication of the study
- a proposed extension of the study.

The answers can be found on p.623. ▶

Activity: A qualitative study of GPs' views of treating obesity

This qualitative research paper by Epstein and Ogden (2005) can be found at: http://scholar.google.co.uk/ The second author is Professor Jane Ogden who is the author of the chapter on 'Eating behaviour' in this textbook (Chapter 5).

Type 'Epstein and Ogden and obesity 2005' into the search term box. The paper should appear at the top of the list. Click on the link and on 'PDF (215K)' which appears on the next screen.

When you have read the paper, try to answer the following questions:

1 Which journal is this article published in?

2 What information is there about the paper to convince the reader of its quality?

3 Compare the abstract to the one in the paper by Bandura *et al.* (1963) on film-mediated aggressive models. What differences do you notice?

4 What kind of sources does the introduction draw on? How do these compare to those used in the paper written by Bandura and colleagues?

5 Is there a hypothesis or research aim as in the paper by Bandura *et al.*?

6 How do you know that ethical issues have been addressed?

7 How is the method section constructed compared with the one in the paper by Bandura *et al.*?

8 How were the data collected and what form were they in?

9 How does the presentation of the results differ between the paper by Bandura *et al.* and this one?

10 Try to identify the following features in the Discussion section:
- a link to related research
- a strength and a limitation of the study
- an implication of the study
- an extension of the study.

The answers can be found on p.624. ▶

often misrepresented in secondary sources and avoid some of the pitfalls of using secondary source material.

CHECK YOUR UNDERSTANDING

Check your understanding of reporting psychological investigations. Try to do this from memory. You can check your answers by looking back through Topic 3, 'Reporting psychological investigations'.

1 What is the purpose of a research journal?

2 What is the purpose of an abstract?

3 Why is it preferable to use primary source material rather than secondary source material?

4 What is meant by plagiarism and how can it be avoided?

5 Identify two key differences between a quantitative and a qualitative research report.

Further resources

American Psychological Association (2005) *Concise Rules of APA Style*, Washington DC: American Psychological Association.
  This abridged version of the APA's publication manual includes the essentials on reporting style.

AQA assessment criteria
The assessment criteria for the A2 examination are included in the Psychology A-level specification, available on the AQA website at: www.aqa.org.uk

Ethical guidelines
British Psychological Society (2006) *Code of Ethics and Conduct*, Leicester: British Psychological Society.

British Psychological Society (2007) *Report of the working party on conducting research on the Internet. Guidelines for ethical practice in psychological research online.*

These ethical guidelines are essential reading for any psychology student undertaking practical work. They are available at www.bps.org.uk

Reference texts
Coolican, H. (1996) *Introduction to Research Methods and Statistics in Psychology* (2nd edn), London: Hodder and Stoughton.

Coolican, H. (2009) *Research Methods and Statistics in Psychology* (5th edn), London: Hodder and Stoughton.

These two reference texts offer detailed information on the research methods you need to learn about during your A2 studies.

A large collection of psychology papers can be accessed at:
http://scholar.google.co.uk/

http://psychclassics.yorku.ca/index.htm
  This site (for 'Classics in the History of Psychology') is an archive of key publications from many famous psychologists and includes many classic research papers.

Holloway, I. (2001) 'Ethical dilemmas in qualitative research', *Psychology Review*, 8(2), pp.28–31.
  This paper discusses ethical issues in qualitative research.

Searle, A. (1999) *Introducing Research and Data in Psychology*, London: Routledge.
  This book provides a user-friendly introduction for those who find research methods and statistics daunting.

Research Digest from the British Psychological Society (BPS)
You can subscribe to the British Psychological Society's Research Digest and receive fortnightly summaries of up-to-date research by sending an e-mail to subscribe-rd@bps.lists.org.uk
Alternatively, you can search the archives online.

Appendix 1: Method for ranking data in statistical tests

1 Organize the data into ascending order of values (see specimen data below).

2 Allocate rank 1 to the lowest value.

3 Allocate ranks to the remaining values, averaging the ranks for any tied scores (see below).

4 A useful check that you have done this correctly is that the last rank value you use should be the same as N, unless, of course, it was tied.

Scores	Rank	Notes
10	1	Both scores of 12 are given the average rank of positions 2 and 3. Note that the next score is ranked 4, not 3.
12	2.5	
12	2.5	
15	4	
17	5	
18	7	The three scores of 18 are each given the average rank of positions 6, 7 and 8, i.e. 7. Note that the next score is rank 9, not 8.
18	7	
18	7	
20	9	
25	10	

Appendix 2: The critical values of U

Table 1: Critical values of U for a one-tailed test at $p = .005$; two-tailed test at $p = .01$ (Mann-Whitney)

																				N_1
N_2		1	2	3	4	5	6	7	8	9	10	11	12	13	14	15	16	17	18	19	20
	1	-	-	-	-	-	-	-	-	-	-	-	-	-	-	-	-	-	-	-	-
	2	-	-	-	-	-	-	-	-	-	-	-	-	-	-	-	-	-	-	0	0
	3	-	-	-	-	-	-	-	-	0	0	0	1	1	1	2	2	2	2	3	3
	4	-	-	-	-	-	0	0	1	1	2	2	3	3	4	5	5	6	6	7	8
	5	-	-	-	-	0	1	1	2	3	4	5	6	7	7	8	9	10	11	12	13
	6	-	-	-	0	1	2	3	4	5	6	7	9	10	11	12	13	15	16	17	19
	7	-	-	-	0	1	3	4	6	7	9	10	12	13	15	16	18	19	21	22	24
	8	-	-	-	1	2	4	6	7	9	11	13	15	17	18	20	22	24	26	28	30
	9	-	-	0	1	3	5	7	9	11	13	16	18	20	22	24	27	29	31	33	36
	10	-	-	0	2	4	6	9	11	13	16	18	21	24	26	29	31	34	37	39	42
	11	-	-	0	2	5	7	10	13	16	18	21	24	27	30	33	36	39	42	45	48
	12	-	-	1	3	6	9	12	15	18	21	24	27	31	34	37	41	44	47	51	54
	13	-	-	1	3	7	10	13	17	20	24	27	31	34	38	42	45	49	53	56	60
	14	-	-	1	4	7	11	15	18	22	26	30	34	38	42	46	50	54	58	63	67
	15	-	-	2	5	8	12	16	20	24	29	33	37	42	46	51	55	60	64	69	73
	16	-	-	2	5	9	13	18	22	27	31	36	41	45	50	55	60	65	70	74	79
	17	-	-	2	6	10	15	19	24	29	34	39	44	49	54	60	65	70	75	81	86
	18	-	-	2	6	11	16	21	26	31	37	42	47	53	58	64	70	75	81	87	92
	19	-	0	3	7	12	17	22	28	33	39	45	51	56	63	69	74	81	87	93	99
	20	-	0	3	8	13	18	24	30	36	42	48	54	60	67	73	79	86	92	99	105

*Dashes in the body of the table indicate that no decision is possible at the stated level of significance. For any N_1 and N_2, the observed value of U is significant at a given level of significance if it is equal to or less than the critical values shown.

Table 2: Critical values of U for a one-tailed test at $p = .01$; two-tailed test at $p = .02$* (Mann-Whitney)

N_2 \ N_1	1	2	3	4	5	6	7	8	9	10	11	12	13	14	15	16	17	18	19	20
1	-	-	-	-	-	-	-	-	-	-	-	-	-	-	-	-	-	-	-	-
2	-	-	-	-	-	-	-	-	-	-	-	-	0	0	0	0	0	0	1	1
3	-	-	-	-	-	-	0	0	1	1	1	2	2	2	3	3	4	4	4	5
4	-	-	-	-	0	1	1	2	3	3	4	5	5	6	7	7	8	9	9	10
5	-	-	-	0	1	2	3	4	5	6	7	8	9	10	11	12	13	14	15	16
6	-	-	-	1	2	3	4	6	7	8	9	11	12	13	15	16	18	19	20	22
7	-	-	0	1	3	4	6	7	9	121	12	14	16	17	19	21	23	24	26	28
8	-	-	0	2	4	6	7	9	11	13	15	17	20	22	24	26	28	30	32	34
9	-	-	1	3	5	7	9	11	14	16	18	21	23	26	28	31	33	36	38	40
10	-	-	1	3	6	8	11	13	16	19	22	24	27	30	33	36	38	41	44	47
11	-	-	1	4	7	9	12	15	18	22	215	28	31	34	37	41	44	47	50	53
12	-	-	2	5	8	11	14	17	21	24	28	31	35	38	42	46	49	53	56	60
13	-	0	2	5	9	12	16	20	23	27	31	35	39	43	47	51	55	59	63	67
14	-	0	2	6	10	13	17	22	26	30	34	38	43	47	51	56	60	65	69	73
15	-	0	3	7	11	15	19	24	28	33	37	42	47	51	56	61	66	70	75	80
16	-	0	3	7	12	16	21	26	31	36	41	46	51	56	61	66	71	76	82	87
17	-	0	4	8	13	18	23	28	33	38	44	49	55	60	66	71	77	82	88	93
18	-	0	4	9	14	19	24	30	36	41	47	53	59	65	70	76	82	88	94	100
19	-	1	4	9	15	20	26	32	38	44	50	56	63	69	75	82	88	94	101	107
20	-	1	5	10	16	22	28	34	40	47	53	60	67	73	80	87	93	100	107	114

Table 3: Critical values of U for a one-tailed test at $p = .025$; two-tailed test at $p = .05$* (Mann-Whitney)

N_2 \ N_1	1	2	3	4	5	6	7	8	9	10	11	12	13	14	15	16	17	18	19	20
1	-	-	-	-	-	-	-	-	-	-	-	-	-	-	-	-	-	-	-	-
2	-	-	-	-	-	-	-	0	0	0	0	1	1	1	1	1	2	2	2	2
3	-	-	-	-	0	1	1	2	2	3	3	4	4	5	5	6	6	7	7	8
4	-	-	-	0	1	2	3	4	4	5	6	7	8	9	10	11	11	12	13	13
5	-	-	0	1	2	3	5	6	7	8	9	131	12	13	14	15	17	18	19	20
6	-	-	1	2	3	5	6	8	10	131	13	14	16	17	19	21	22	24	25	27
7	-	-	1	3	5	6	8	10	12	14	16	18	20	22	24	26	28	30	32	34
8	-	0	2	4	6	8	10	13	15	17	19	22	24	26	29	31	34	36	38	41
9	-	0	2	4	7	10	12	15	17	20	23	26	28	31	34	37	39	42	45	48
10	-	0	3	5	8	11	14	17	20	23	26	29	33	36	39	42	45	48	52	55
11	-	0	3	6	9	13	16	19	23	26	30	33	37	40	44	47	51	55	58	62
12	-	1	4	7	11	14	18	22	26	29	33	37	41	45	49	55	57	61	65	69
13	-	1	4	8	12	16	20	24	28	33	37	41	45	50	54	59	63	67	74	76
14	-	1	5	9	13	17	22	26	31	36	40	45	50	55	59	64	67	74	78	83
15	-	1	5	10	14	19	24	29	34	39	44	49	54	59	64	70	76	80	85	90
16	-	1	6	11	15	21	26	31	37	42	47	53	59	64	70	75	81	86	92	98
17	-	2	6	11	17	22	28	34	39	45	51	57	63	67	75	81	87	93	99	105
18	-	2	7	12	18	24	30	36	42	48	55	61	67	74	80	86	93	99	106	112
19	-	2	7	13	19	25	32	38	45	52	58	65	72	78	85	92	99	106	113	119
20	-	2	8	13	20	27	34	41	48	55	62	69	76	83	90	98	105	112	119	127

Table 4: Critical values of *U* for a one-tailed test at *p* = .05; two-tailed test at *p* = .10* (Mann-Whitney)

N_2 \ N_1	1	2	3	4	5	6	7	8	9	10	11	12	13	14	15	16	17	18	19	20
1	-	-	-	-	-	-	-	-	-	-	-	-	-	-	-	-	-	-	0	0
2	-	-	-	-	0	0	0	1	1	1	1	2	2	2	3	3	3	4	4	4
3	-	-	0	0	1	2	2	3	3	4	5	5	6	7	7	8	9	9	10	11
4	-	-	0	1	2	3	4	5	6	7	8	9	10	121	12	14	15	16	17	18
5	-	0	1	2	4	5	6	8	9	121	12	13	15	16	18	19	20	22	23	25
6	-	0	2	3	5	7	8	10	12	14	16	17	19	21	23	25	26	28	30	32
7	-	0	2	4	6	8	11	13	15	17	19	21	24	26	28	30	33	35	37	39
8	-	1	3	5	8	10	13	15	18	20	23	26	28	31	33	36	39	41	44	47
9	-	1	3	6	9	12	15	18	21	24	27	30	33	36	39	42	45	48	51	54
10	-	1	4	7	11	14	17	20	24	27	31	34	37	41	44	48	51	55	58	62
11	-	1	5	8	12	16	19	23	27	31	34	38	42	46	50	54	57	61	65	69
12	-	2	5	9	13	17	21	26	30	34	38	42	47	51	55	60	64	68	72	77
13	-	2	6	10	15	19	24	28	33	37	42	47	51	56	61	65	70	75	80	84
14	-	2	7	11	16	21	26	31	36	41	46	51	56	61	66	71	77	82	87	92
15	-	3	7	12	18	23	28	33	39	44	50	55	61	66	72	77	83	88	94	100
16	-	3	8	14	19	25	30	36	42	48	54	60	65	71	77	83	89	95	101	107
17	-	3	9	15	20	26	33	39	45	51	57	64	70	77	83	89	96	102	109	115
18	-	4	9	16	22	28	35	41	48	55	61	68	75	82	88	95	102	109	116	123
19	-	4	10	17	23	30	37	44	51	58	65	72	80	87	94	101	109	116	123	130
20	-	4	11	18	25	32	39	47	54	62	69	77	84	92	100	107	115	123	130	138

*Dashes in the body of the table indicate that no decision is possible at the stated level of significance. For any N_1 and N_2, the observed value of *U* is significant at a given level of significance if it is equal to or less than the critical values shown.
Source: Runyon and Haber (1976)

Appendix 3: The critical values of T for the Wilcoxon Matched Pairs Signed Ranks test

Level of significance for a one-tailed test			
.05	.025	.01	.005

Level of significance for a two-tailed test			
N	.10	.05	.02	.002

N	.10	.05	.02	.002
5	0			
6	2	0		
7	3	2	0	
8	5	3	1	0
9	8	5	3	1
10	10	8	5	3
11	13	10	7	5
12	17	13	9	7
13	21	17	12	9
14	25	21	15	12
15	30	25	19	15
16	35	29	23	19
17	41	34	27	23
18	47	40	32	27
19	53	46	37	32
20	60	52	43	37
21	67	58	49	42
22	75	65	55	48
23	83	73	62	54
24	91	81	69	61
25	100	89	76	68

Value of T that is equal to or less than the tabled value is significant at or beyond the level indicated.
Source: Taken from Table 1 of McCormack (1965) *With permission of the publisher.*

Appendix 4: Critical values of Spearman's Rank Order Correlation Coefficient (r_s)

Level of significance for two-tailed test			
.10	.05	.20	.01

Level of significance for one-tailed test

N	.05	.025	.01	.005
4	1.000			
5	.900	1.000	1.000	
6	.829	.886	.943	1.000
7.	714.	786	.893	.929
8.	643.	738	.833	.881
9	.600	.700	.783	.833
10	.564	.648	.745	.794
11	.536	.618	.709	.755
12	.503	.587	.671	.727
13	.484	.560	.648	.703
14	.464	.538	.622	.675
15	.443	.521	.604	.654
16	.429	.503	.582	.635
17	.414	.485	.566	.615
18	.401	.472	.550	.600
19	.391	.460	.535	.584
20	.380	.447	.520	.570
21	.370	.435	.508	.556
22	.361	.425	.496	.544
23	.353	.415	.486	.532
24	.344	.406	.476	.521
25	.337	.398	.466	.511
26	.331	.390	.457	.501
27	.324	.382	.448	.491
28	.317	.375	.440	.483
29	.312	.368	.433	.475
30	.306	.362	.425	.467

Values of r_s that equal or exceed the tabled value are significant at or below the level indicated.
Source: Zar (1972)
With permission of the author and publisher

Appendix 5: Critical values of χ^2

Level of significance for a one-tailed test						
df	.10	.05	.025	.01	.005	.0005
1	1.64	2.71	3.84	5.41	6.64	10.83

Level of significance for a two-tailed test						
df	.20	.010	.05	.02	.01	.001
1	1.64	2.71	3.84	5.41	6.64	10.83
2	3.22	4.60	5.99	7.82	9.21	13.82
3	4.64	6.25	7.82	9.84	11.34	16.27
4	5.99	7.78	9.49	11.67	13.28	18.46
5	7.29	9.24	11.07	13.39	15.09	20.52
6	8.56	10.64	12.59	15.03	16.81	22.46
7	9.80	12.02	14.07	16.62	18.48	24.32
8	11.03	13.36	15.51	18.17	20.09	26.12
9	12.24	14.68	16.92	19.68	21.67	27.88
10	13.44	15.99	18.31	21.16	23.21	29.59
11	14.63	17.28	19.68	22.62	24.72	31.26
12	15.81	18.55	21.03	24.05	26.22	32.91
13	16.98	19.81	22.36	25.47	27.69	34.53
14	18.15	21.06	23.68	26.87	29.14	36.12
15	19.31	22.31	25.00	28.26	30.58	37.70
16	20.46	23.54	26.30	29.63	32.00	39.29
17	21.62	24.77	27.59	31.00	33.41	40.75
18	22.76	25.99	28.87	32.35	34.80	42.31
19	23.90	27.20	30.14	33.69	36.19	43.82
20	25.04	28.41	31.41	35.02	37.57	45.32
21	26.17	29.62	32.67	36.34	38.93	46.80
22	27.30	30.81	33.92	37.66	40.29	48.27
23	28.43	32.01	35.17	38.97	41.64	49.73
24	29.55	33.20	36.42	40.27	42.98	51.18
25	30.68	34.38	37.65	41.57	44.31	52.62
26	31.80	35.56	38.88	42.86	45.64	54.05
27	32.91	36.74	40.11	44.14	46.96	55.48
28	34.03	37.92	41.34	45.42	48.28	56.89
29	35.14	39.09	42.69	46.69	49.59	58.30
30	36.25	40.26	43.77	47.96	50.89	59.70
32	38.47	42.59	46.19	50.49	53.49	62.49
34	40.68	44.90	48.60	53.00	56.06	65.25
36	42.88	47.21	51.00	55.49	58.62	67.99
38	45.08	49.51	53.38	57.97	61.16	70.70
40	47.27	51.81	55.76	60.44	63.69	73.40
44	51.64	56.37	60.48	65.48	68.71	78.75
48	55.99	60.91	65.17	70.20	73.68	84.04
52	60.33	65.42	69.83	75.02	78.62	89.27
56	64.66	69.92	74.47	79.82	83.51	94.46
60	68.97	74.40	79.08	84.58	88.38	99.61

Calculated value of χ^2 must equal or exceed the table (critical) values for significance at the level shown.
Source: abridged from Fisher and Yates (1974).

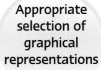

Appropriate selection of graphical representations

Probability and significance

Graphing and charting

Graphs

- Show change over time or trials
- Time or trials on x-axis
- Variable being measured on y-axis

Frequency diagrams

(Frequency on y-axis, variable measured on x-axis)

Bar charts

- Nominal or ordinal data
- Percentages or means
- 80% rule
- Plain paper
- Gaps between bars
- Alphabetical (nominal) or natural order (ordinal)

Histograms or frequency polygons

- Interval or ratio data
- Bars in a histogram touch
- Class-interval mid-points are joined in a frequency polygon
- Use 6 to 8 class intervals
- Area contained in bars or under the line is important

Scattergrams

- Used for plotting paired variables
- Predictor (if appropriate) on x-axis
- Indicate direction of a linear relationship
- Can help identify unusual scores or non-linear patterns
- Give a clue about the correlation coefficient value

Level of significance

- Probability (p) is expressed as a value between 0 and 1
- It expresses the p that the null hypothesis is true
- The conventional level is $p \leq .05$
- If $p \leq .05$, the alternate H could be a more likely explanation of the results – the result is said to be statistically significant
- More stringent levels (e.g. $p \leq .01$) may be favoured if applying an unreliable finding would be risky
- One-tailed tests are applied to directional hypotheses
- Two-tailed tests are applied to non-directional hypotheses

Type I and Type II errors

- A Type 1 error is an error of optimism: the null H is wrongly rejected
- A Type 2 error is an error of pessimism: The null hypothesis is wrongly retained
- p expresses the probability of making a Type 1 error

Factors affecting the choice of statistical tests

Factors affecting choice

Type of research design

- Experiment – independent or related design
- Correlation
- Differences in frequency counts

Type of data

- Nominal (frequency counts; categorical data)
- Ordinal (has magnitude)
- Interval (has magnitude and equal intervals)
- Ratio (has magnitude, equal intervals and absolute zero)

Deciding which test to use

- Chi-squared test – for differences samples of nominal (frequency) d
- Mann-Whitney U test – for differences in independent, ordina (or better) data from experiments
- Wilcoxon test – for differences in related, ordinal (or better) data fro experiments
- Spearman's rho – for linear relationships in samples of paired data

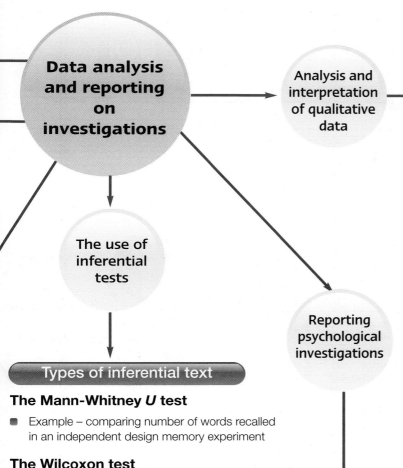

Data analysis and reporting on investigations

Analysis and interpretation of qualitative data

The use of inferential tests

Reporting psychological investigations

Content analysis

- Mixes qualitative and quantitative techniques
- Systematic technique for analysing visual or textual data
- Coding system of discrete, mutually exclusive categories is created
- Data are sorted into the categories
- Data can be treated statistically, e.g. using the chi-squared test

Evaluation of content analysis

- **Reductionism** – richness and complexity of data can be lost
- **Illusion of objectivity** – categorization may be affected by researchers' personal biases
- **Reliability checking** – researchers can cross-check their analyses for consistency
- **Statistical procedures become possible** – may uncover patterns not otherwise apparent

Thematic analysis

- A transcribed body of text is analysed into themes
- Inductive analysis identifies emergent themes
- Theoretical analysis checks for the presence of themes already believed to be important

Evaluation of thematic analysis

- **Accessibility** – a relatively simple method with results understandable to the non-specialist
- **Subjectivity** – risk of personal biases affecting interpretation (may be reduced by reflective practices)
- **Quality** – has to be assessed differently from quantitative research, e.g. through data triangulation

Types of inferential text

The Mann-Whitney *U* test

- Example – comparing number of words recalled in an independent design memory experiment

The Wilcoxon test

- Example – comparing number of words recalled in an related design memory experiment

Spearman's *rho*

- Example – relationship between psychology and biology test scores

Chi-squared test

- Example – difference between the number of four and five year olds who can and cannot solve a problem

Reporting psychological investigations

Tips about writing style

- Third person, passive voice
- Past tense
- Replication possible
- Sections – Title, Abstract, Introduction, Method, Results, Discussion, References, Appendices

Examples of published research

- Quantitative – Bandura *et al.* (1963) 'Imitation of film-mediated aggressive models'
- Qualitative – Epstein and Ogden (2005) 'A qualitative study of GP's views of treating obesity'

Introduction

Examinations are generally amongst the most dreaded times in our lives. The stress of the lead-up period, the pressure to do well, the impenetrable questions and then those awful two months when we fear that the examiners are doing all they can to undo our best efforts. However, it does not have to be like that. Just as an athlete trains for the Olympics, a student preparing for an A-level exam simply needs to know how to harness all their talent and energy in the most cost-effective way.

This final chapter aims to provide an understanding of the A2 examination, including how questions are set and marked, so that you can prepare for the exam with this in mind. If you use this chapter in conjunction with the other chapters that provide the psychological knowledge, you should be well prepared to achieve your best possible grade.

In Topic 1 we start by looking at how to prepare for the A2 exam by considering its structure and requirements and

some revision strategies that you might use. We turn our attention to how you can maximize your performance in the exam itself in Topic 2. Finally, in Topic 3, we consider how your answers will be marked by the examiners.

Topic 1: Preparing for the A2 exam

The A2 exam for AQA Psychology A specification assesses three skills which are known as 'assessment objectives'. These are the same skills as those assessed at AS level and are:

AO1: The ability to demonstrate knowledge and understanding of psychology.

AO2: The ability to use, apply and evaluate your knowledge of psychology.

AO3: The ability to demonstrate your understanding of how science works in psychology.

For a more detailed account of the assessment objectives turn to *Psychology AS for AQA A*, pp.250–2.

Structure of the A2 specification and assessment

The A2 part of the AQA A specification consists of two units (Unit 3 and Unit 4). Unlike the AS part of the specification (i.e. Unit 1 and Unit 2), both A2 units allow an element of choice in the topics you study.

Unit 3: Topics in psychology

Specification

Unit 3 of the specification consists of eight topics and you must study a minimum of three of these. The eight topics are:

- Biological rhythms and sleep
- Perception
- Relationships
- Aggression
- Eating behaviour
- Gender
- Intelligence and learning
- Cognition and development

Unit 3 assessment (PSYA3)

The Unit 3 exam lasts for **one hour and 30 minutes**. There are eight questions – one question on each topic – and you are required to answer **three** questions.

Each question is worth 25 marks. The weighting of the assessment objectives for questions in the Unit 3 exam is shown in Table 18.1 opposite.

Unit 4: Psychopathology, Psychology in Action and Research Methods

Specification

Unit 4 of the specification is divided into three sections:

- **Section A: Psychopathology** – you are expected to study **one** of the following disorders: schizophrenia, depression, anxiety disorders (either phobic disorders or obsessive compulsive disorder) and apply your knowledge of models, classification and diagnosis to your chosen disorder.

- **Section B: Psychology in Action** – you are expected to study in detail **one** of the following contemporary applications of psychology: media psychology, psychology of addictive behaviour, anomalistic psychology. In the context of your chosen application, you are expected to apply your knowledge and understanding of research methods, approaches, issues and debates and to appreciate the relationship between research, policy and practices in applying psychology in everyday life.

- **Section C: Psychological Research and Scientific Method** – you are expected to extend the knowledge, understanding and skills of research design, data analysis and data interpretation and reporting that you gained at AS level and to understand the nature of science and scientific method.

Unit 4 assessment (PSYA4)

The Unit 4 exam lasts for **two hours**. It is divided into three sections which reflect the sections of the specification outlined above. The weighting of the assessment objectives for the questions in each section of the Unit 4 exam is shown in Table 18.1 below.

- **Section A: Psychopathology** – there are three questions in this section, one for each disorder. Each question is worth 25 marks. You are required to answer **one** question from this section.

- **Section B: Psychology in Action** – There are three questions in this section, one for each of the Psychology in Action topics. Each question is worth 25 marks. You are required to answer **one** question from this section.

- **Section C: Psychological Research and Scientific Method** – There is one compulsory question (worth 35 marks) in this section. This question is always divided into several parts and you are required to answer **all parts** of the question.

The wording of exam questions

When writing an examination paper, the A2 Principal Examiners follow a number of basic rules and guidelines. The main guidelines are as follows:

- All questions must be drawn from the specification, using similar wording wherever possible. The questions set will fit into the structure of the examination outlined above.

- Specification content which is preceded by the words 'should include' or 'including' can be specified in an exam question.

- Content which is preceded by the words 'for example' cannot be specified in a question, but may appear as an example to help jog your memory about suitable material.

- There are no rules regarding repetition of questions: the fact that a topic area is examined one year does not mean it will not be examined the next. Similarly, the fact that a particular topic has not been examined for a year or two does not mean that it will automatically be examined soon.

- When exam questions are set, the AQA employ a 'Reviser' who checks that the questions are appropriate in terms of standard and complexity, and that they could be answered within the time. The Reviser must also check that the 'rules' outlined above are adhered to. For example, the following question would be rejected by the Reviser:

Discuss two biological explanations for anorexia nervosa.   (25 marks)

Although anorexia appears under the third sub-section of 'Eating behaviour' in Unit 3 of the specification, it is included as an example of an eating disorder that might be considered, so this would not be an appropriate question. In other words, you do not have to study anorexia and so a question cannot be asked specifically about it. The topic of 'Eating behaviour' is discussed in Chapter 5 on pp.161–72 and focuses on obesity.

Terms commonly used in A2 examinations

As indicated above, the AQA examination tests your ability in three main skill areas – AO1, AO2 and AO3. Each exam question tests all these skills. You will already be aware of these terms from your AS course and so should be familiar with them in practice, but what do they mean in the context of an A2 exam?

Assessment objectives	Unit 3 (PSYA3) Mark allocation	Unit 4 (PSYA4) Mark allocation		
		Section A	Section B	Section C
AO1	9	9	9	3
AO2	12	12	12	4
AO3	4	4	4	28

Table 18.1 *Weighting of assessment objectives for Unit 3 and Unit 4 exam questions*

The best way of thinking about them is to see AO1 as a narrative (i.e. giving information and showing understanding) and AO2 as a commentary (i.e. offering some comments about the narrative, such as evaluating the points made or showing how they fit into a wider body of knowledge). AO3 can be seen as describing, explaining, interpreting, analysing and evaluating methodology and research findings.

The following terms are commonly used to assess the requisite skills in essay-type questions in the exams for Units 3 and 4.

AO1 terms
- **Describe, Outline, Define** – these terms require you to demonstrate AO1 skill by providing information. In addition:
  - **Outline** requires a summary description only (more breadth than detail/depth).
  - **Define** requires a statement of what is meant by a particular term.

AO2 terms
- **Evaluate, Assess, Analyse** – these terms require you to provide commentary as evidence of AO2 skill.

AO1 and AO2 terms
- **Discuss, Critically consider** – these terms require evidence of AO1 *and* AO2.

AO3 skills
AO3 skill involves *knowledge* about how science works and the ability to use that knowledge to *evaluate*, *interpret* and *analyse* how science works.

Your AO3 *knowledge* may be assessed, for example, by asking you to:

- Identify an appropriate inferential test of statistical significance to analyse a set of data and explain why it is a suitable test.

- Identify ethical issues associated with a study that has been outlined for you. You may also be asked to explain ways in which these issues could be addressed.

Your ability to *evaluate/interpret/analyse* how science works may be assessed, for example, by asking you to:

- Analyse and evaluate the methodology used in an investigation.

- Discuss evidence for and against biological explanations of one psychopathological disorder.

- Discuss the benefits and risks for the individual and for society of using biological therapies to treat one psychopathological disorder.

Unlike AO1 and AO2, there are rarely explicit AO3 injunctions (instructions) in essay questions. You need to remember that every 25-mark essay question includes four marks for AO3 material. For example, consider the following possible question from a Unit 3 exam paper:

Discuss one theory of moral understanding. (25 marks)

The instruction in this question is 'discuss', which we can translate as requiring a description (the AO1 requirement) and an evaluation (the AO2 requirement) of one theory of moral understanding. To ensure that you gain the four AO3 marks available (as well as the nine AO1 and twelve AO2 marks), you could evaluate the methods used and the results obtained in the studies of moral understanding that are relevant to the theory you are discussing. For example, you could evaluate:

(i) the appropriateness of the methods used in terms of the ethical issues they raise, and

(ii) the value of the results in terms of their practical applications. Moral understanding is part of the 'Cognition and development' topic which is discussed in Chapter 8 of this book.

Qualifiers
- *One or more, two or more* – It is acceptable to focus on one or two theories in depth or more theories in less detail. Bear in mind, however, that a superficial review of several theories might mean that you do not do adequate justice to any of them. (See 'Specific demands within questions' on p.598).

Other terms
- *Evidence* – Material from studies or theories that may be used to support or contradict an argument or theory.

- *Findings* – The outcome or product of research.

- *Research* – The process of gaining knowledge through the examination of data derived empirically (i.e. through studies) or theoretically (i.e. through theories, explanations or models).

- *Study* – An investigation providing evidence which may be empirical or non-empirical (such as meta-analysis).

- *Theory* – A complex set of inter-related ideas/assumptions/principles intended to explain or account for certain observed phenomena.

- *Model* – An explanation which may be less complex/elaborate than a theory although the terms 'model' and 'theory' are often used interchangeably.

- *Applications* – Actual or possible ways of using psychological knowledge in an applied/practical setting.

Innovative and effective AO2 and AO3

Twelve marks are awarded for AO2 skills in each essay-type A2 exam question. It is worth spending some time practising your AO2 skills before you sit the exam. Unfortunately for many students, AO2 involves merely dismissing whatever psychological theory or research findings they have previously described.

There are, however, many valid opportunities for 'commentary' (a generic term for analysis and evaluation) when addressing the AO2 and AO3 components of A2 questions. There are two important points to remember when constructing your commentary material:

- make your commentary obvious
- make your commentary effective.

Making AO2 commentary obvious

AO2 skills can take various forms which broaden the possibilities for you to maximize your marks for these assessment objectives. To make AO2 obvious, it is often useful to employ a short, lead-in phrase as illustrated below:

- **'So we can see...'**
  For example: *So we can see that the research findings provide support for the adaptive nature of coping behaviours when faced with relationship breakdown.*

- **'This would imply...'**
  For example: *This would imply that there are two forms of schizophrenia, as positive symptoms are alleviated by drug therapy but negative symptoms are not.*

- **'One consequence of this would be...'**
  For example: *One consequence of this would be that people begin to discriminate against members of the out-group because they are evaluated more negatively compared to members of the in-group.*

- **'This is supported by...'**
  For example: *The social learning theory of aggressive behaviour is supported by Bandura's (1965) studies where it was found that children, who had watched an adult play aggressively with a Bobo doll (an inflatable clown), were most likely to copy the adult's aggressive behaviour if they had seen the adult being rewarded.*

- **'This is challenged by...'**
  For example: *This is challenged by Mandel (1998) who found little evidence of the types of 'blind obedience' proposed by Milgram in his studies of real-life events during the Holocaust.*

- **'Not everyone reacts in the same way, for example ...'**
  For example: *Not everyone reacts in the same way – for example, Wood and Duck (1995) point out that we know very little about relationships between lesbian, gay, disabled or other marginalized groups in society.*

- **'There may be cultural variations...'**
  For example: *There may be cultural variations in this behaviour, and so many of these explanations may not be applicable or relevant to non-Western cultures. They represent a narrower view of human behaviour, which is, in turn, the product of researchers whose own views are inevitably shaped by the same cultural experience.*

- **This has been applied to ... situation'**
  For example: *The argument that powerful social psychological processes caused the behaviour found in the Stanford Prison experiment has also been applied to help explain the abuse of Iraqi prisoners at Abu Ghraib prison.*

Each of the examples above demonstrates a different form of commentary on the material. Some of these ('So we can see ...', 'This would imply ...') are nothing more than pointing out what may seem entirely obvious to you, but they indicate to the examiner that you understand the conclusions that could be drawn, as well as the implications of a particular study or point of view. Others (such as 'This is supported by ...', 'This is challenged by ...') demonstrate that you appreciate the degree to which a theory has been backed up by actual research evidence. It is important to remember when choosing your commentary that you still have to represent it in an evaluative form rather than simply adding more descriptive material. If you look back at the example concerning cultural variations, you will see this does more than simply identify cultural variations, but indicates why these variations are problematic for the explanation in question. This is our next challenge. How do we ensure that whatever points of analysis or evaluation we make, we do so *effectively*? We will now look at some AO3 commentary to illustrate how to do this.

Effective AO3 commentary

Effective AO3 commentary is more than just identifying a methodological point of evaluation. To give your commentary real impact, you should first identify and then develop a point. Having identified a point of commentary, you need to ensure that:

- It is *appropriate* to the material being evaluated – Is it relevant?

- It is *justified* – How do I know that?

- It is *elaborated* – So why exactly is this a problem?

For example:

- *This study lacked ecological validity* ...: 'This study lacks ecological validity *(identification)* because ...... attempts to replicate the findings in other situations have been largely unsuccessful *(justification)* ... This means that the results of the study cannot be generalized beyond this situation *(elaboration)*.'

- *'The study was unethical...'*: 'The study was unethical *(identification)* because by allowing the 'guards' to engage in antisocial behaviour against the 'prisoners', Zimbardo effectively gave the pursuit of scientific knowledge priority over the welfare of his participants *(justification)*. A consequence of this decision has been a tightening of ethics guidelines to give other psychologists shared responsibility for the research behaviour of their colleagues *(elaboration)*.'

The expansion necessary to give your commentary real weight means that you have to be a bit more selective about the number of AO2 and AO3 points you make. To earn high marks your answer must be well focused and provide sound analysis and understanding, as well as coherent elaboration; a few well-chosen points coherently analysed and elaborated will be awarded more marks than a long list of evaluative points with little analysis or elaboration (see Table 18.5 for AO2/AO3 marking allocations on p.600).

Synoptic assessment and stretch and challenge

Synoptic assessment

The term **synoptic assessment** in psychology refers to the assessment of your knowledge and understanding of the *breadth* of theoretical and methodological approaches, issues and debates in the subject.

The PSYA3 and PSYA4 exams are *synoptic*. In other words, both papers assess your knowledge and understanding of psychology as a whole. This is done by assessing your knowledge and understanding of issues, debates and approaches *within the context of the topics you have studied*. In order to gain marks in the higher mark bands (see p.600), you will need to use issues, debates and approaches as tools of analysis and evaluation (i.e. to demonstrate synopticity) in your answers. For more information about issues, debates and approaches look at the Introductory chapter to this textbook.

How to demonstrate synopticity

You can demonstrate your knowledge and understanding of the theoretical and methodological approaches, issues and debates in psychology in a variety of ways, including the following:

- *Different explanations or perspectives relating to the topic area* – for example, schizophrenia (see Chapter 9) can be explained from many different perspectives; different perspectives also have different positions in the nature–nurture and free will versus determinism debates.

- *Different methods used to study the topic area* – for example, the origins of psychopathological conditions might be studied using twin studies, cross-cultural studies and so on (see Chapters 9, 10 11a and 11b).

- *Overarching issues relating to the topic area* – for example, the use of biological explanations for psychopathology might be discussed in terms of the issue of reductionism (see Chapter 10 Depression), or nature/nurture (see Chapter 11b Obsessive-compulsive disorder) and treatments might be discussed in terms of the ethical issues they raise (see Chapter 10 Depression).

- *Links with other areas of the specification* – for example, phobias might be seen as having an adaptive role within human evolution (see Chapter 11a Phobic Disorders).

- *Psychology-wide concerns and issues* such as reliability and validity, cultural variations and aspects of research design (e.g. demand characteristics and participant reactivity).

Stretch and challenge

The AQA psychology specification is designed in such a way that there are opportunities for you to be stretched and challenged while you are studying *and* also when you are being assessed. An example from the topic of Aggression illustrates this:

In an essay, one student might state that genetic explanations of aggression are deterministic. However, another student who understands the social and legal implications of such a statement could go on to consider how the treatment of aggressive offenders might be affected if their aggressive behaviour was viewed as genetically determined rather than as a product of their free will. (The issue of free will and aggressive behaviour is discussed in Chapter 4 on p.131.)

Throughout this book you will find *Stretch and Challenge* features and activities. These encourage you to undertake independent research, contextualize topics in psychology, think about sensitive issues and extend your skills of critical thinking. Look back through the topics you have studied and check that you have taken full advantage of the opportunities to engage with the Stretch and Challenge activities.

Revision strategies

Now that you are aware of the structure and skill requirements of the exam and the type of wording used in exam questions, you may still be wondering 'How do I best revise for the exam?' This is one of the most frequently asked questions before any exam. We will focus on some important points that have specific relevance to the A2 Psychology exam.

Know what you should be revising

To know what you should be revising, you need to know what the examination will require of you. This has been summarized in the first part of this chapter. It is important, however, that you are familiar with the complete AQA Psychology specification. If you do not have a copy of this, go to: www.aqa.org.uk/qual/gce/psychology_a_new.php

On the AQA website you will find details of the specification, including information about the AS and A2 exams. You will also find specimen question papers (and, in due course, there will be some past question papers) with mark schemes. These will help inform you about what to expect in your own exams and about how to achieve high marks. To recap, in preparing for the exams, you need to revise *at least* three topics for PSYA3 and *at least* three topics for PSYA4 because you are required to answer three questions in each exam.

Note that each topic is divided into three sub-topics. Whichever topics you select to study, it is vital that you revise *everything* (i.e. all the sub-topics) within your chosen topics and not just the bits that you like. For example, if you choose the topic of 'Cognition and development', you must revise Development of thinking *and* Development of moral understanding *and* Development of social cognition. AQA guarantees that one question will be set on this topic but only one!

The eight topics in Unit 3 and the first six topics of Unit 4 correspond to the first 14 chapters of this book. Chapters 15, 16 and 17 cover Psychological Research and Scientific Method.

You will have noticed that at the start of each chapter, the relevant area of the specification is given and explained. As you revise a topic, take a moment to check that your notes encompass *all* the requirements highlighted in the right-hand column of the 'Explaining the specification' feature. Take steps to fill in any gaps you discover. A comprehensive set of notes is an essential starting point if your revision is to cover all the material that might be assessed in the exam.

Revise actively

Merely reading material in textbooks is not necessarily the most productive way of using your time. In the A2 exam, you will be given a specific set of instructions which tells you what you should write about. All questions require you to demonstrate not only knowledge and understanding (AO1 skills), but also the skills of analysis and evaluation (AO2 skills) and an appreciation of methodological issues (AO3 skills). Students often do less well than they deserve to do in exams because, for example, they describe theories in great detail, but do not provide any evaluative commentary. In your revision notes, therefore, it can be helpful to highlight those points that are part of the narrative and those that are part of your commentary.

Practise the skills on which you will finally be assessed and try to do this under conditions as close as possible to those you will encounter in the exam.

Learn to summarize

Many of the questions in the A2 exam will require you to focus on more than one theory, therapy or explanation. This means allocating your time carefully and not in a random way. Take a look at Piaget's theory of cognitive development in Chapter 8 (pp.256–63). How long would it take you to provide an effective outline of this theory? No more than nine marks are allocated to AO1 descriptions/outlines in exam questions and so it is important to acquire the skill of précis (summary) before you go into the exam room. Try the next activity.

Activity   Writing a précis

In the exam, part of a question might ask you to 'Outline **two** theories' or 'Outline **one or more** theories' – for example, 'Outline **one or more** theories of intelligence' (9 marks) or 'Outline **two** explanations of institutional aggression.' (9 marks)

Look back over the chapters you have read in this book and select a topic where this type of exam question might be asked and do the following:

- In approximately nine minutes, construct a description of *one* appropriate theory/explanation.
- Now, in the same time (nine minutes), construct a description of *two* theories/explanations.
- Repeat this with as many theories/therapies/ explanations as you like until you feel confident you can repeat this skill in an exam.

Organize your revision

It is never too early to plan your revision. As the exams get closer, your precious time will seem to become scarcer than ever. Decide (realistically) just how much of the specification you are going to revise and make a plan of what you are going to revise and when. Above all, remember you are studying psychology! Try to use your knowledge of psychology to help you make this a profitable time. For example:

- *Avoid interference effect* – Don't cram too much into one session.
- Remember the value of *spaced practice* – Don't expect to remember everything perfectly immediately after the first revision session.
- Use *positive reinforcement* – Reward yourself when you have had a productive session.
- Enjoy *positive feedback* and *avoid negative thinking* – Do not spend time worrying about what you should be doing – just do it and then congratulate yourself on a job well done.

Reading and interpreting questions

Before you start writing in an exam it is important to spend a few minutes reading the instructions and the questions carefully and then highlighting the questions you are going to answer. Highlight *all parts of any parted questions* so that you do not miss anything.

A vital skill in tackling examinations is interpreting what is actually required by a particular question. There is no substitute for practice, so get hold of as many specimen and past papers as possible and 'deconstruct' the questions into their constituent skills and parts. Try the activity below.

Activity | **What do exam questions actually require?**

Deconstruct the following two questions. What skills are required for 1(a) and 1(b)? How should you use the quotation in Question 2?

1(a) Outline one theory of cognitive development.
(9 marks)

(b) Evaluate applications of this theory to education.
(16 marks)

2 'Violent video games are potentially harmful to children and should be banned.' Discuss the effects of video games on young people.
(25 marks)

Tackling innovative questions in PSYA4

Questions on psychopathology

In Section A (Psychopathology) of PSYA4, it is possible that the examiner may set the same question for all disorders. For example: 'Discuss issues surrounding the classification and diagnosis of schizophrenia OR depression OR one anxiety disorder. (25 marks)

On the other hand, the examiner may set a different question for each disorder. For example:

1. Outline and evaluate **two** explanations for schizophrenia. Refer to research evidence in your answer. (25 marks)

2. **(a)** Outline clinical characteristics of depression. (5 marks)

(b) Explain issues associated with classification and diagnosis of depression. (10 marks)

(c) Outline and evaluate **one** explanation of depression. Refer to research evidence in your evaluation. (10 marks)

3. Discuss **one or more** psychological treatments for either phobic disorder or obsessive-compulsive disorder. (25 marks)

Read the questions carefully before you begin to write and remember that your answer should relate to one disorder. If, however, you are asked to answer a question about issues of classification and diagnosis or about therapies for a specific disorder, remember there are general points that apply to all disorders (e.g. the validity of the classification categories and the problems associated with evaluating the effectiveness of therapies). These general points (outlined on pp.300–303 can be used effectively, provided that you contextualize them in relation to your chosen disorder. All the material on specific mental disorders is provided in Chapters 9, 10, 11a and 11b.

Stimulus material in questions

It is not only in Section C (Research methods) of PSYA4 that you may encounter stimulus material as an integral part of a question. In Sections A and B of PSYA4, examiners may also include some stimulus material in a question. This could take the form of data in a diagram, graph or table, which you are required to translate into another form. You might, on the other hand, be asked to refer to, or evaluate, the conclusions of a study as part of a question. Consider the following two example questions. Question 1 illustrates a possible type of question from Section B on 'The psychology of addictive behaviour'. Question 2 illustrates a possible type of question from Section A on Schizophrenia.

> Example 1. With reference to the findings in Table 18.2 below, outline public health interventions and/or legislation that have attempted to reduce addictive behaviour. Evaluate these attempts in terms of their effectiveness. (25 marks)

A meta-analysis by Fichtenberg and Glantz (2002) of 26 studies carried out in four countries on the effects of smoke-free workplaces found that:

- Smoke-free workplaces reduce the prevalence of smoking as well as consumption (number of cigarettes smoked).

- The combined effects of people stopping smoking and reducing consumption reduces total cigarette consumption by 29 per cent.

They concluded that to achieve similar results through taxation would require cigarette taxes to increase from £3.44 to £6.59 per pack in the United Kingdom.

Table 18.2 *Smoke-free workplaces and smoking prevalence among employees*

If you are studying the topic of 'Reducing addictive behaviour' you could use this question for practice. The material required to answer the question is provided in Chapter 13 on pp.458–68.

Example 2. Summarize what the graph in Figure 18.1 illustrates with respect to the genetic explanation for schizophrenia.   (5 marks)

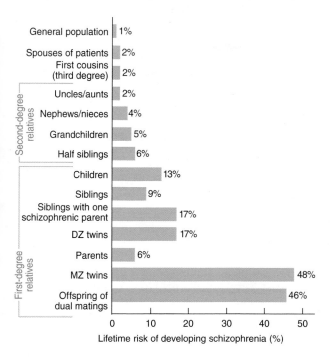

Figure 18.1: *The graph shows average risks for developing schizophrenia. Data were compiled from family and twin studies conducted in European populations between 1920 and 1987*

The genetic explanation for Schizophrenia is discussed in Chapter 9 on pp.314–15 where this graph is also interpreted.

Research methods

The assessment of research methods (in PSYA4, Section C) takes the form of a compulsory question presented in a series of parts. A description of a study (called the question stem/scenario) is given, followed by a number of questions prompted by the scenario.

The questions may take a variety of forms, including the following:

- Identify (a) the target population for the study and (b) the sampling technique the researcher(s) used to select their participants.

- Explain one limitation of the sampling technique used by the researcher(s).

- Use the data in the table to construct a bar chart/histogram/scattergram.

- Why was a related/independent groups design used in this study?

- Give one reason why the researcher used a one-tailed/two-tailed test of significance to analyse the data in the study.

- Explain what is meant by '$p \leq 0.01$'?

- What is meant by a Type 1/Type 2 error?

- Explain why the researchers used the Mann-Whitney *U*/Wilcoxon/Chi-squared/Spearman's Rho test to analyse the data in the study.

- With reference to the data in the table, what conclusions can you draw from the findings of the study?

- Give two reasons why the researchers in this investigation carried out a pilot study.

Chapter 15	Chapter 16	Chapter 17
Designing a study to test a theory (p.514)	Choosing a research method (p.529)	Presenting data graphically (p.562)
Refining our understanding through research (p.517)	Types of experiments – Do children learn aggressive habits from TV? (p.531)	Probability values (p.564)
Using primary and secondary sources (p.523)	Questions on the Stroop effect experiment (p.535)	Defining a population (p.564)
	Designing a study – the effect of vitamins on IQ (p.535)	Using measurement scales (p.566)
	Designing an experiment on face recognition (p.536)	Choosing the right test (p.566)
	Devising a closed questionnaire (p.540)	Carrying out statistical tests (p.572)
	Devising a semi-structured interview (p.540)	Content analysis of TV advertisements (p.573)
	Defining target populations (p.541)	Continuing thematic analysis (p.575)
	Sampling issues (p.542)	Imitation of film-mediated aggressive models – questions on a research paper (p.579)
	Thinking about reliability and validity (p.547)	
	Improving internal validity (p.546)	
	Ethics in Internet-mediated research (p.550)	
	Ethical issues in the study of parenting style and academic achievement (p.550)	A qualitative study of GPs' views of treating obesity – questions on a research paper (p.579)
	Writing a research proposal (p.553)	

Table 18.3 *Activities on research methods in Chapter 15, 16 and 17*

- Design a study to investigate…

- How would you assess the reliability of the personality/aptitude/intelligence test used in this study?

- Identify two ethical issues raised by the study and explain how these might be addressed.

- Describe one technique for analysing and interpreting qualitative data and explain one of its key limitations.

- What is meant by the term 'peer review' and how does it contribute to the process of validating new scientific knowledge?

To answer these questions you need a thorough grasp of the material on psychological research and scientific method provided in Chapters 15, 16 and 17. Within each of these chapters, there are many activities (with answers where appropriate) that enable you to practise the skills you need to do well on this part of your exam. Some of the activities are listed in Table 18.3 p.595. Specimen questions with marking guidelines are also available on the AQA website.

Take care that you attempt *all parts* of the research methods' question. Check and double-check that you have not missed any part of the question. There is likely to be an implicit logic to the order in which the questions are asked, but you can decide the order in which you answer the parts of the question. You must, however, label all parts of your answer clearly.

Moving on

When you feel confident in working out exactly what is required in each exam question, you are ready to move on to the next stage – planning an effective response. Although this may seem a fairly straightforward process, things can go wrong! This section looks at some of the typical errors that can creep in at this stage.

Answering questions

What can go wrong?

When answering exam questions, many students tend to wander off the point, use the wrong sort of information or the right information but in the wrong place. The problem is largely due to not thinking carefully enough about a question before answering it and/or losing focus while answering it. Try the activity on p.597. The answer to the question reads quite well, but there are a number of reasons why it is not effective.

What went wrong?

This essay includes a lot of good psychological knowledge which is accurate, but how well does it fit the question?

Part (a)

- The first paragraph is totally wasted. Do not waste precious time saying what you are going to do, just get straight on and do it.

- The second paragraph is interesting but unnecessary. There is no requirement to define terms in this way because the question has already made very specific demands. Students often feel obliged to include this sort of information, as if they will be penalized for leaving it out. This is not the case.

- The third paragraph is not outlining the theory but outlining a study related to social learning theory. An examiner would be able to pick a couple of implicit points out of this, but far better that the assumptions of the theory had been made explicit in the first place.

- The deindividuation paragraph gives an excellent description but is too long for an outline that is worth only 4.5 marks!

- The last paragraph of part (a) is also wasted, as this is a third theory when the question only asked for two. An examiner might even choose this as being better than social learning theory, except that it has not been addressed in part (b) and so could not earn any AO2 or AO3 marks.

Part (b)

- The first paragraph is simply a description of a study that might be relevant, but it is not used in an evaluative way (e.g. do the results support or challenge the assumptions of the theory?). Having already described this study in part (a), the student is struggling to find any more to say.

- The second paragraph will not gain any marks because it is general evaluation, rather than evaluation in terms of 'relevant research studies'.

- The final paragraph does refer to a relevant study, and mentions ethical issues but fails to elaborate on these in relation to deindividuation. The paragraph only describes the study and also fails to include any reference to deindividuation at all.

What does this tell us?

This answer to the exam question is hugely imbalanced, with over 450 words for part (a) and under 250 words for part (b). This student has not allocated the time appropriately; hence part (b) is rushed and therefore short (even though it is worth 16 marks). There is a lot of irrelevant information throughout the essay, demonstrating that they have not thought about what might be relevant to the question and, perhaps more importantly, what might earn marks. Examiners must follow the instructions of the mark scheme, which means they can only give marks for material that answers the question set. It does not matter how interesting or insightful something is, it can only be awarded marks if it maps onto the mark scheme. In this case, part (a) would

Here is a question that could be set about the topic of aggression. An example answer is given below. Using the marking allocations for AQA Unit 3 in Tables 18.4 and 18.5 on p.600, give this answer a mark for each part of the question.

(a) Outline **two** social psychological theories of aggression. (9 marks)

(b) Evaluate each of the theories you outlined in part (a) in terms of relevant research studies. (16 marks)

(a) In this essay I intend to say first what is meant by aggression, and look at different types of aggression. Then I will move on to describe different social-psychological theories of aggression. These will be social learning theory and deindividuation theory. In the second part of the question I will evaluate my theories of aggression by looking at research evidence. I will look at the strengths and weaknesses of each theory as part of my evaluation.

Aggression is usually thought to be antisocial, including any behaviour that is intended to inflict harm on another person. However, some aggression can be prosocial such as when police shoot a terrorist who has murdered hostages and is threatening others. Other types of aggression are sanctioned by society, such as in cases of self-defence, e.g. when a woman injures a rapist whilst defending herself.

The social learning theory of aggression is demonstrated in Bandura's study with the Bobo doll (Bandura *et al.* 1961). This involved children observing aggressive and non-aggressive adult models and then being tested to see if they imitated any of the behaviours modelled by the adult. Children who watched an adult behaving aggressively showed a good deal of physical and verbal aggression when given the opportunity to interact with the Bobo doll. Children who had seen a model behaving non-aggressively towards the Bobo doll, later showed virtually no aggressive behaviour in their own interactions with the doll.

My second theory is deindividuation theory (Zimbardo 1969). Deindividuation is a process whereby the normal constraints on behaviour are weakened as people lose their sense of individuality. People are likely to become deindividuated when they join a crowd or a large group. Factors that contribute to deindividuation include anonymity (for example, if people wear a uniform) and altered states of consciousness due to drugs or alcohol. Deindividuated people tend to behave aggressively because the loss of individuality

leads to reduced self-restraint. This leads to impulsive behaviour and reduced attention to how our behaviour might be evaluated by others. When we are in a crowd, being anonymous has the consequence of reducing inner restraints and increasing those behaviours (such as aggression) that are usually inhibited. In large groups or in crowds, people have greater anonymity and therefore a reduced fear of negative evaluation of their actions and of feelings of guilt for any deviant behaviour.

Another theory of aggression is relative deprivation theory, where people may feel frustrated because they do not feel that they have what they deserve (e.g. decent jobs and living conditions, freedom from harassment by police). This can produce feelings of anger and may be responsible for many of the riots (e.g. Toxteth and St Pauls) that have happened over the last 20 years.

(b) In the Bobo doll studies, children aged between three and five years were used. Half of these were exposed to aggressive models and half were exposed to non-aggressive models. These models displayed some distinctive physically aggressive acts (such as hitting the doll with a mallet) accompanied by verbal aggression. Children were then frustrated by being shown attractive toys and not being allowed to play with them. As I stated earlier, children in the aggressive condition (who had seen a model acting aggressively towards the Bobo doll) reproduced a lot of the aggressive behaviour (both physical and verbal) they had seen from the model.

A strength of social learning theory is that this can explain differences between individuals (who may or may not have been exposed to aggressive models) and within individuals. People may behave differently in different situations because they have observed different consequences for aggressive behaviour in those situations.

Zimbardo carried out a study on deindividuation in his prison study. He took normal students and divided then into prisoners and guards in a mock prison. He found that the guards bullied the prisoners and that the prisoners became very upset. He had to stop the study before the end. This study has been criticized because of the ethics of exposing people to such stress. Critics have said that Zimbardo lost sight of what the study was really about, and let his participants suffer far too much before ending the study.

get 5 marks (nearly all for deindividuation), and part (b) would get only 3 marks because it is weak, muddled and incomplete with ineffective use of material.

Next time you sit down to answer an exam question, take a little time to think about how best to fit what you know to the specific demands of the question.

Specific demands within questions

One, two or more

A2 questions frequently invite you to write about either 'one or more' of something. Although you may think that you would get more marks for including more theories, studies or whatever, this is not necessarily the case. What it tells you is that if you do not have enough material to write about just one theory, for example, then you can write about more than one. There is no hidden agenda here – it is up to you which route you take. When making your decision, be careful to consider the *breadth and depth* of your answer. The very best AO1 marks are awarded for evidence of depth and/or breadth which can be achieved by either route. See the mark scheme for AO1 in Table 18.4 on p.600.

Use of quotations

If quotations are used in a question, there may (or may not) be an instruction to refer to the quotation. Where a question includes a phrase such as 'With reference to the above quotation…' you will lose marks unless you do so. To earn good marks you need to engage with the quotation throughout your answer. However, *read the question carefully* as this is what you are required to answer, not the quotation.

The following is an example of a possible question where it is essential to engage with the quotation:

'Pseudoscientists rely excessively on anecdotal and testimonial evidence to substantiate their claims and commonly avoid peer review by publishing in books, magazines, or even directly on to the Internet.'

With reference to the issues raised in the quotation, discuss the issues of pseudoscience and scientific fraud.
(25 marks)

The material you need to answer this question is provided in Chapter 14 on pp.475–83.

When is evaluation not evaluation?

The answer to this riddle is – when it is just more description. This is most common when introducing alternative theories/explanations or studies that may (or may not) support the conclusions of the material in question. For example, in the question 'Discuss one explanation of insomnia', you may choose to introduce other explanations that offer a different perspective to the one you have chosen for your AO1 description. Likewise, you may introduce studies that support (or challenge) your explanation. The trick is to use this material to construct an evaluative argument that is focused on your chosen theory/explanation. This may involve pointing out how the weak points of your chosen explanation are overcome in the alternative explanation, or how your chosen explanation is superior to the alternative on some appropriate criterion. The same applies to research studies. These may either support or challenge the conclusions of your AO1 material, but it is up to you to make this clear, rather than leaving it to the examiner to

make links on your behalf. The section on 'Innovative and effective AO2 and AO3' on p.590 provides some ideas on how to do this.

Parted questions

Some essay questions are divided into two or three parts. Split questions require careful planning to ensure you do not slip up in your response. The two parts of the question may or may not be tied together (e.g. 'in this theory …' is definitely tied, whereas 'in such theories…' is not) or the second part of the question may make quite specific demands in terms of the AO2/AO3 component of your answer. For example:

(a) Outline **one** explanation for psychological androgyny and gender dysphoria.   (9 marks)

(b) Evaluate the explanation that you outlined in part (a) in terms of relevant research studies.   (16 marks)

In the above example, you are asked to evaluate 'in terms of relevant research studies'. In such a question, more general evaluation that is not in the form of research studies would not receive any credit.

Time management

Having decoded the requirements of the questions, the next hurdle is to manage your time effectively in the exam. This involves time management both between and within questions.

Between questions

This really should present no problems to the well-prepared student. In PSYA3, each question requires a 30-minute response. If you extend the time you give to one question, you are effectively stealing it from another. You should also remember that these 30 minutes include thinking and planning time. This means that you actually only have around 25 or so minutes of writing time for each question. Imagine the following two scenarios. Two students spend different amounts of time on their three essays in PSYA3 and receive the marks shown:

Student A		Student B	
Time (mins) per essay	Mark	Time (mins) per essay	Mark
40	18	30	16
40	18	30	16
10	6	30	16
Total:	**42**	**Total:**	**48**

It is much easier to push a mark up from 10 to 16 than from 16 to 20 as student 'A' found to his/her cost. It is rarely cost effective to extend any one individual essay beyond the 30 minutes allocated to it within the confines of a one-and-a-half-hour exam.

The PSYA4 exam last for two hours. You are required to answer three questions, two of which are worth 25 marks each and then the compulsory research methods question which is worth 35 marks. A rough calculation shows that approximately 50 minutes should be allocated to the compulsory question and 35 minutes to each of the other two. You may find that the short answers needed for parts of the research methods questions are quick to produce because they require only a few words (e.g. 'Identify the experimental design used'). However, other parts of the question will require answers worth up to 12 marks (e.g. 'Design a study to investigate ....'). These answers need careful planning. Try not to underestimate the time required to do justice to the various demands of the research methods question.

Within questions

The second challenge is to manage your time within a question, so that all the different aspects and requirements of the question are covered. We will take a typical essay question as an example:

Describe and evaluate research (explanations and/or studies) into the influence of the media on antisocial behaviour.   (25 marks)

With only 30 minutes to answer this question, you may be tempted to start writing straight away and run the risk of getting only half or two-thirds of the way through the whole question when the 30 minutes are up. To perform effectively and maximize your marks for any particular question, you need a strategy. There are many such strategies, but a particularly effective one is as follows:

- Decide exactly what is required in each question or part of a question. Remember that in the A2 exams, essay questions earn only 9 marks for AO1 content, but 12 marks for AO2 and 4 marks for AO3.

- Calculate how much time should be allocated to each aspect of the question.

- Divide the answer into about six paragraphs of about 100 words (or five minutes per paragraph).

- Plan carefully what will go into each paragraph, bearing in mind the required balance of AO1, AO2 and AO3 material.

- Finally, stick to your plan and try not to exceed the allocated time.

This strategic method has a number of advantages. Firstly, it makes sure that you are answering all parts of the question (provided your planning is appropriate). Secondly, it ensures that you do not get caught short of time before you have made significant progress into the question. Finally, it makes the whole process of writing an essay less daunting. Writing a series of pre-planned, 100-word chunks is much easier than writing one 600-word essay. If the thought of writing 100 words worries you, then you may be interested to know that there are 100 words in this paragraph.

Activity **Planning an essay**

Take the example essay question above (or any other essay question in this chapter) and plan your answer, using the six-paragraph system outlined above.

Topic 3: Examination marking

Marking schemes

This part of the exam process may not appear to be something you can actively take part in, but knowing how papers are marked can certainly help you in your quest for the highest marks. The AQA uses a separate marking grid for AO1 and for AO2/AO3. An adapted version of these marking grids is presented in Tables 18.4 and 18.5 on p.600. Try the next activity to help you get to grips with the criteria used by examiners when they mark your exam answers.

Activity **Marking your own essays**

The next time you write an essay, mark it yourself using the marking guidelines given in Tables 18.4 and 18.5. Try to place your answer in an appropriate mark band descriptor for each of the assessment objectives (AO1 and AO2/AO3).

Next, you should justify the mark you have awarded – if it is not in the top band, why not? What would be needed to gain a mark in the top band? If you get used to doing this, and following the guidance from your teachers, you will effectively become an examiner for your own work.

Marks	Content
9–8 marks	**Sound**
	• Knowledge and understanding are accurate and well detailed. • A good range of relevant material has been selected. There is substantial evidence of breadth/depth. • Organization and structure of the answer are coherent.
7–5 marks	**Reasonable**
	• Knowledge and understanding are generally accurate and reasonably detailed. • A range of relevant material has been selected. There is evidence of breadth and/or depth. • Organization and structure of the answer are reasonably coherent.
4–3 marks	**Basic**
	• Knowledge and understanding are basic/relatively superficial. • A restricted range of material has been presented. • Organization and structure of the answer are basic.
2–1 marks	**Rudimentary**
	• Knowledge and understanding are rudimentary and may be muddled and/or inaccurate. • The material presented may be very brief or largely irrelevant. • Lacks organization and structure.
0 marks	• No credit worthy material.

Table 18.4 *AO1 marking allocations for AQA Unit 3 and Unit 4 essay questions*

Marks	Content
16–13 marks	**Effective** • Evaluation demonstrates sound analysis and understanding. • The answer is well focused and shows coherent elaboration and/or a clear line of argument. • Issues/debates/approaches are used effectively. • There is substantial evidence of synopticity. • Ideas are well structured and expressed clearly and fluently. Consistently effective use of psychological terminology. Appropriate use of grammar, punctuation and spelling.
12–9 marks	**Reasonable** • Evaluation demonstrates reasonable analysis and understanding. • The answer is generally focused and shows reasonable elaboration and/or a line of argument is evident. • Issues/debates/approaches are used in a reasonably effective manner. • There is evidence of synopticity. • Most ideas appropriately structured and expressed clearly. Appropriate use of psychological terminology. Minor errors of grammar, punctuation and spelling only occasionally compromise meaning.
8–5 marks	**Basic** • Analysis and evaluation demonstrate basic, superficial understanding. • The answer is sometimes focused and shows some evidence of elaboration. • Superficial reference may be made to issues/debates/approaches. • There is some evidence of synopticity. • Expression of ideas lacks clarity. Limited use of psychological terminology. Errors of grammar, punctuation and spelling are intrusive.
4–1 marks	**Rudimentary** • Analysis and evaluation is rudimentary, demonstrating very limited understanding. • The answer is weak, muddled and incomplete. Material is not used effectively and may be mainly irrelevant. • If reference is made to issues/debates/approaches, it is muddled or inaccurate. • There is little or no evidence of synopticity. • Deficiency in expression of ideas results in confusion and ambiguity. The answer lacks structure, often merely a series of unconnected assertions. Errors of grammar, punctuation and spelling are frequent and intrusive.
0 marks	• No creditworthy material is presented.

Table 18.5 *AO2/AO3 marking allocations for AQA Unit 3 and Unit 4 essay questions*

How examiners approach marking

Contrary to popular opinion, examiners do not try to find ways to award the lowest possible marks, but neither can they award 'sympathy' marks for essays that are good psychology yet not relevant to the question set. There is a lot involved when examining at this level and some of the basic rules are outlined below:

- *Examiners are realistic* – All answers are marked at the level of a notional 18-year-old who is writing under exam conditions. What this means in practice is that examiners do not look for a 'perfect' answer and are realistic in what they expect a student to write in the time available.

- *Positive marking* – Examiners engage in a process known as 'positive marking' which means that they do not look for opportunities to take marks off (because of errors), but rather for opportunities to add marks on (for correct and appropriate material). If you write something that is wrong, the examiner effectively ignores it, and looks for content that can be credited under the terms of the question.

- *No prescribed single right answer* – One of the features of psychology is that there are many ways to approach exam questions and many different perspectives to take when answering them. Students often worry that they might be answering a question in the 'wrong' way. Provided that their answer is relevant to the question, it will be credited by the examiner. Examiners often learn things from students, so it is gratifying to know that your work is being marked by an appreciative audience.

- *Marking guidelines* – Examiners do not mark with ideas of pass and fail in their mind, nor of the grades that they think an answer might be worth. Examiners will award marks according to the marking guidelines illustrated in Tables 18.4 and 18.5 opposite, together with any special requirements of the question (for example, have the candidates included two theories if asked to do so?).

- *Names and dates* – These are not as important as you might imagine. Students often spend a great deal of their time revising as many names and dates as they can, perhaps under the impression that it is the weight of such detail that gets the high marks. This impression is bolstered when you read learned academic journals, which often appear to be brimming over with research names and dates. While they do serve an important function in a journal, they are less important in A-level exams. Including a researcher's name or the date of the research certainly helps to place the research in context, but as long as a piece of research is recognizable and is described in a way that is both accurate and relevant to the question, it will gain as many marks as if it were anchored to a name and date.

- *Quality of written communication (QWC)* – QWC is assessed in both PSYA3 and PSYA4. The criteria for QWC are incorporated into the mark bands (see opposite) and include accurate, well structured and clearly expressed ideas, the use of psychological terminology, and good grammar, punctuation and spelling.

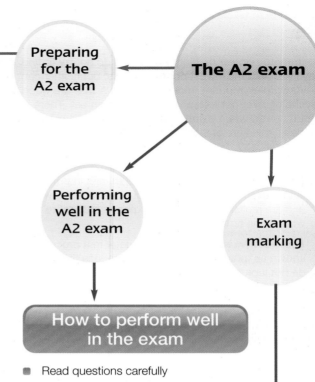

Prepare for the A2 exam by knowing about ...

Assessment objectives
- AO1, AO2 and AO3

Structure of specification
- Unit 3:
  - eight topics
  - you should study at least three
- Unit 4:
  - seven topics (three in Section A: Psychopathology; three in Section B: Psychology in action; one in Section C: Psychological research and scientific method)
  - you should study at least one from each section

Structure of assessment
- PSYA3:
  - one hour and 30 minutes
  - answer three questions
- PSYA4:
  - two hours
  - answer three questions

Exam terms
- Terms commonly used in exam questions, e.g. describe, discuss, evaluate

AO2 and AO3 commentary
How to produce good AO2 and AO3 commentary:
- Make it obvious (e.g. with lead-in phrases)
- Make it effective (e.g. identify, justify, elaborate)

Synoptic assessment
- Assesses your understanding of:
  - breadth of different theoretical and methodological approaches
  - issues and debates in psychology

Stretch and challenge
- Develop high-level analytical skills and the ability to think like a psychologist

Revision
How to revise effectively, e.g. by:
- being active and organized
- practising answering exam-type questions

How to perform well in the exam

- Read questions carefully
- Note specific demands of questions (e.g. the use of quotations, parted questions)
- Be prepared for innovative questions (e.g. the use of graphs or diagrams in questions)
- Think before writing – plan what you will include in your answer
- Manage your time between and within questions

What you need to know about A2 exam marking

- The AO1 and AO2/AO3 marking allocations (mark bands) for Unit 3 and Unit 4
- Examiners mark positively and use the marking schemes
- Marks are available for quality of written communication
- Be your own examiner by marking your own essays

Answers to activities

Chapter 1: Biological rhythms and sleep

Melatonin and jet lag, p. 54

There is evidence that certain specific neurones in the brain control biological rhythms. These neurones have receptor sites (areas on the surface) that melatonin can bind (attach) to. When they bind to these neurones they alter their activity and this alteration resets the biological rhythm back to where it 'should be' (i.e. it is 'resynchronized').

A study by Takahashi *et al.* (2002) demonstrated that melatonin reduced the symptoms of jet lag by speeding up the resynchronization of biological rhythms following an 11-hour flight.

Chapter 2: Perception

The slimming effect of stripes, p. 71

Thompson (2008) suggests that the reason for the illusion might be that horizontal stripes make an image appear more three-dimensional and so the apparent width is reduced with the impression of depth.

However, the *Times* (12 September 2008) offered a different, unscientific, explanation: 'Women's bodies are by their very nature curvy things. Stripes are straight. If you put a straight vertical stripe on a curvy bottom, the line of the stripe will be distorted by the body beneath – which will only serve to accentuate the bulge.' This highlights the importance of carefully evaluating what you read to distinguish between plausible scientific explanations and unscientific explanations.

Perceptual set, p. 76

1 The lack of obvious contours surrounding the dog makes it difficult to distinguish it from its background.

2 Once a *perceptual set* has been established by the clue 'there's a dog', the observer's expectations help them to separate the figure of the Dalmatian from its background. The verbal clue 'sets' the observer to interpret the figure in a particular way.

Research into face recognition, p. 83

1 Think about the age of the infants and their tendency to fall asleep. Think, too, about the risk of experimenter bias influencing the collection of data.

2 Infants might have a preference for complex images (rather than human faces). See the comments on p. 83 by Flavell (1985) and Bremner (2003) who investigated this interpretation.

The 'Thatcher illusion', p. 94

Photo B has been created by cutting out the eyes and mouth and inverting these within the face. Because it is difficult to perceive the relationship between the features in the inverted faces, we lose holistic processing and tend to miss the strangeness of the grotesque face.

Chapter 5: Eating behaviour

Thinking about food preferences, p. 163

Food preferences are influenced by basic learning processes such as exposure, modelling, observations, reinforcement and association. Evidence indicates that although our preferences are learned throughout our lives, many are established during childhood.

An analysis of healthy-eating adverts, p. 168

- Is the advert giving information? If so, what information?

- Is it trying to change beliefs? If so, what beliefs?

- You may have noticed that much of the healthy-eating advertising focuses only on knowledge and on education and overlooks the many reasons why we behave in the way we do.

Developing and testing health education advice, p. 169

Research indicates that when we try not to think about something or behave in a particular way, we can become preoccupied with the very thing we are trying not to think about. Health-education campaigns often fall into this trap by telling us not to do something which may make us want to do it all the more! An alternative approach would be to explore more creative, positive messages, such as 'Be active' and 'Eat more fruit and vegetables', rather than emphasize the negative messages associated with the consequences of not doing something.

Having designed some health education advice, an experiment could be designed to test its effectiveness. A group of school children (aged 14 and above) could be randomly divided into two groups (an independent groups design). The health education advice could be presented to the first group (the experimental group) during a 45-minute session run by a school nurse. After the presentation, the participants would have an opportunity to ask questions about how to eat healthily and to discuss the healthy eating advice in small groups. The other group (the control group) would be invited to a session of the same length by the school nurse, during which they would watch a short, general film about food, followed by small group discussion about the film.

Both groups would then be asked to record in a food diary everything they eat, including snacks, during the next seven days. The school nurse would then be asked to examine each food diary, without knowing which group the individual had attended, and categorize the food intake for the week as 'very healthy', 'healthy' or 'unhealthy'. If a significantly higher number of school children in the experimental group had eaten a diet that was categorized as either 'very healthy' or 'healthy' than in the control group, then the health education advice was successful. The data could be analysed using a chi-squared test.

Changing eating behaviour, p. 171

Some people manage successfully to avoid certain foods without developing a craving for that food for the following reasons:

- They have changed their behaviour for ideological and moral reasons.
- They are motivated by religion or politics.
- They do not actually like the food they are avoiding any more.
- They do not place themselves into a position of denial.

Design a study to investigate the influence of social and biological drives on eating behaviour, p. 177

It is very hard to demonstrate empirically either the nature (evolutionary) or the nurture (learning) side of any debate. However, methods could include:

- the use of twins and adoptees (see p. 185.)
- investigating how people change as they migrate from one culture to another
- changes over time.

To explore the role of learning, it would be necessary to demonstrate that very young babies can learn to prefer different foods because of their environment.

Looking at your environment, p. 177

Things you might have noticed that are part of the obesogenic environment include:

- lots of people driving cars and motorbikes
- few people walking or cycling
- fast-food outlets
- many more cafes and restaurants
- fewer local shops selling fresh fruit and vegetables.

Aspects of the obesogenic environment such as these affect the imbalance between energy intake and energy expenditure by reducing the likely energy expenditure while increasing the energy input.

Activity levels past and present, p. 182

From talking to your parents and/or grandparents, you may well have found the following:

- They walked and cycled more than you do and they travelled by car and/or public transport less often than you do. Very few of the people they knew had their own cars.
- They played more sports and were required to carry out regular physical activity every week at school.
- They watched less TV and there were no computer games, videos or DVDs.
- They became more independent and were allowed out after dark at an earlier age than you because their parents were less focused on the dangers of cars, traffic and physical/sexual assault.

Patterns of eating then and now, p. 184

From talking to your parents and/or grandparents, you may well have discovered some of the following:

- You eat less at breakfast than they did.
- You eat more in the evenings than they did.
- You snack more between meals.
- You eat more meat and you eat meat more frequently than they did.
- You eat more foods that contain a lot of fat than they did, including crisps and chips.
- You eat more processed food than they did and more food from fast-food outlets.
- You eat fewer vegetables on a daily basis than they did.

Developing a treatment intervention for obesity, p. 184

If you wanted to manage and treat obesity, you might well try out some of the approaches listed below:

- Explore the roles that food plays in the person's life.
- Discuss with the person why and when they eat and what they gain from eating.
-

Try to find alternative ways for them to gain some of the same benefits (e.g. emotional satisfaction, a treat, a celebration, a family occasion).

▣ Discuss ways to change their diet that are small and manageable to start with.

▣ Avoid setting up a process of denial.

▣ Alongside changes in eating behaviour, encourage the person to be more physically active, including walking up the stairs instead of taking a lift or escalator, and engage in some form of regular exercise, such as a sport they enjoy.

Chapter 6: Gender

The appearance of gender schemas (Bauer 1993), p. 195

1 By adopting this innovative method, researchers can get a more informed idea of when gender schema develops and what causes this. What can be said from Bauer's findings is that 2-year-old boys are already aware of what are typically male and female activities and so they must have developed an understanding of gender schema before they can ascribe what is male and female activity.

2 Another explanation for why boys differentiate gender consistent and gender inconsistent information more than girls might relate to the fact that a man's role is more defined whereas a woman's role is more diverse, especially since women's right to work and still have a family is supported in our society. Girls therefore see their mother involved with a more diverse set of activities and roles. Boys who model on their father have a more straight forward role model.

Lenses of gender (Bem 1993), p. 195

1 The connection between Bem's Lenses of Gender and Gender Schema Theory is a matter of socialisation which reinforces gender from generation to generation.

2 It is through the process of socialisation that parents instil the norms of society and more importantly how a boy and girl should behave: masculinity versus femininity.

3 In the case of Bem's Lenses of Gender, androcentrism describes a society based on the male ideal. Gender polarisation and biological essentialism support androcentric views about what is appropriate and this includes boys' and girls' toys.

4 Children are socialized to adopt appropriate gender roles and according to Gender Schema Theory they self socialize by observing gender-appropriate behaviour in other same sex role models.

Designer personalities, p. 197

1 According to Bem it is healthy to adopt personality traits that suit one's temperament, rather than being forced to behave in a society-prescribed masculine and feminine manner. Given the diverse roles that females can have, adopting cross-gender activity can become easier to do. It is more acceptable for instance for girls to play football, in fact we have female footballers playing competitively at amateur level.

2 It is possible but unlikely. The fact remains that we are rather accepting of our gender roles and would only want to change in a very minor way. It is likely that your male friends will continue to adopt typical masculine traits whereas your female friends might be more flexible in their choices – some traits overlapping with male traits. It is likely that your same-sex friends will be similar to yourself – birds of a feather flock together.

Androgyny in cross-sex behaviour, p. 198

1 This is a difficult one to answer, because being female offers more protection against illness and a variety of genetic conditions: so if anyone gets colds or ill it is more likely to be boys than girls and if feminized boys are more like girls then perhaps they too should be more protected against ailments! It really does depend on what we mean by feminized – if we are talking about boys who just act in a feminine way then they are still not genetically endowed with the same protection against illnesses as females are. They may be less likely to have contact with their parents if they are away in hospital due to illness but it is more likely that this connection is derived from a spurious correlation inherent in the study.

2 If a male foetus does not secrete testosterone during prenatal development then the natural pathway of development is that of a female. It is very likely that he will show ambiguous genitalia (appearing more like female genitalia) at birth and the brain might not have masculinized in the usual way. However, at pubescence there is another developmental surge of testosterone which might help develop secondary male sexual characteristics. If high levels of female hormones were given to an adult man however, there would be subtle changes to appearance and behaviour. The skin will become smoother and there would be changes to hair growth pattern. There will be more feminine behaviour arising such as less aggression and risk taking behaviour.

3 If a female foetus is exposed to testosterone during prenatal development, it is possible that her genitalia might be on the ambiguous side at birth, However, it is more likely that she will show cross-gender behaviour but still appear feminine. If high levels of male hormones were given to an adult woman however, there would be subtle changes to appearance and behaviour. Male pattern hair growth and possible male pattern baldness might occur due to testosterone intake, but female genitalia would not suddenly become ambiguous and change to that of a man. This would require special surgery as would the removal of breast tissue. Differences in behaviour might occur such as becoming more aggressive (if not physically then possibly verbally) and sexual activity might also show an increase.

Gender dysphoria as a psychological condition, p. 200

1   The common thread that seems to connect the approaches of psychoanalysis, behaviourism and cognitive psychology is the process of identifying with the same-sex model. In all cases there appears to be an emphasis on faulty identification whatever the reason behind that may be. For instance, psychoanalysis sees the mother figure as fragmented making it very difficult for the daughter to model and identify with her – so instead she identifies with her father resulting in her gender dysphoria. The same problem occurs for behaviourism – the imprinting process makes associative learning of who the female is, and what behaviour should therefore be mimicked by a young girl, very difficult. The cognitive approach is similar for there is emphasis on developing gender concept which improves as the brain matures. But children must develop gender identity and this again relies on knowing what sex one is and this comes through identifying with the same-sex model.

2   Testing these approaches must rely upon observation of behaviour because for ethical reasons researchers could not tamper with the natural course of events. One could introduce male and female toys, with male or female role models playing with them, then observe to see which model is copied by very young children.

Sex hormones in animals and humans, p. 205

1   Hormones have set actions which cannot be modified – they are designed to do what they do. During gestation the uterus is bathed in hormones so it goes without saying that the inter-uterine environment is bound to have an influence over developing foetuses. Of course the foetus produces its own hormones appropriate to its sex. However, if there are many foetuses developing in a confined space, then it is possible that hormones of the opposite sex could seep through the umbilical cord and influence the development to some degree of the opposite sexed foetus. This is what these experiments are showing. There are not enough opposite sex hormones to create a problem for the developing foetus (as it is producing its own hormones) but it may just slightly influence behaviour.

2   Both contrived and naturally occurring experiments appear to support one another in that findings suggest the same conclusions. Given what we know about hormones these findings are not really that surprising. Furthermore, given that contrived experiments are in support of findings from naturally occurring experiments, one could conclude that these studies are very well thought out.

An experiment in child-rearing, p. 206

1   Think about the differences in cognitive strengths between men and women. If men are better visuo-spatially than women could this influence their strategies for attaining food? Men are stronger – again what impact could that have for hunting and building shelters? It is likely that there would be a difference in the way males and females solve problems on the island – their strategies might be different.

2   In order to try and tease out nature and nurture contributions, a baseline level of their behaviour would have to be recorded without them knowing whilst on the island – in this way we know what and how they approached survival without any human intervention. Then, back in 'civilisation', their behaviour could be observed and any modifications shown in their behaviour could be down to human intervention.

3   It would be problematic to look at the brain whilst they were on the island which is why it is very important to do cognitive-based tests and brain scanning as soon as they were brought back to civilisation before their 'natural' behaviour became confounded by human intervention.

The runaway selection hypothesis, p. 207

1   It is possible that this sexual selection will continue until the 'fittest' peacocks become extinct due to being eaten by tigers. Only peacocks that have lighter, smaller tails that enable them to out-run the tigers will survive.

2   Their fitness would decrease, as the number of offspring produced by large-tailed peacocks would be less due to the high number being killed prior to mating. As these peacocks can no longer escape from their predators, peahens mate with the less 'fit' peacocks who have a lighter tail and can therefore out-run their predator and live to mate and pass on their genes. Thus peacocks with a smaller tail-display increase within the population. They would then become the more 'fit' peacocks as a higher proportion of their genes will be passed onto future generations.

3   Yes as the peahen unwittingly will continue to mate with the peacock she considers to be most fit, which will still be the ones with the largest tail display.

4   We can only speculate on whether it can be stopped. The sexual selection process can't naturally be stopped but peacocks and peahens could be kept incarcerated so that peacocks are protected from tigers and peahens are forced to select the fittest amongst a motley crew!

Pre-natal hormones and looking preferences, Lutchmaya et al (2002), p. 209

1   It would appear that sexual selection did have a hand in the development of gender-role differences. This can be seen from an early age in the studies devised by Lutchmaya and Connellan. There are already differences in preference for certain objects at day one. Baby boys prefer to look at mechanical objects and baby girls at social objects such as the human face. These differences reflect a temperamental demarcation: girls are more socially inclined.

2 The levels of testosterone have already had an effect in the morphological differences between males and females and this has an impact on the way the brain functions. Even at 24 hours, newborns are showing preferential looking time at objects relating to their gender role. For male newborns this is mechanical objects and for female newborns this is the face – they are already prepared for being in touch with their socio-emotional side, a skill that is very useful for forming relationships and nurturing offspring. The connection between hormone level and observing faces is the trait for sociability in females and, in the case of males, the fact that testosterone means less interest in faces. The fact newborns have had very little experience with the world lends greater weight to the argument that these differences are due to inherent characteristics of males and females, rather than nurture effects.

Patriarchy and power, p. 211

1 The statement implies that women are disadvantaged by the mere virtue of giving birth to offspring and nurturing them. At some point in a given society this has hindered women from doing things other than looking after children and enabled men to be the providers and play a more active role in pursuing other activities. Hence this has meant that men have ruled the roost and therefore defined what constitutes status. This theory could be tested by comparing different cultures in which women experience different levels of childcare burden, to see whether patriarchy continues to exist when childcare responsibilities are reduced.

2 The way of addressing this statement would be to compare different types of society: patriarchal and matriarchal. Differences of attitude regarding trait status across these two types of culture would demonstrate who is making the rules regarding which traits (male or female) are regarded in a positive light. You could note the differences between these two types of culture in terms of traits regarded as positive and do a content analysis to see if differences between the two types of culture truly exist.

3 Behaviours of men and women which are linked to their child-caring contributions: so nurturing the children at home in the case of women and working to support the family in the case of men.

Gender and food-getting (Ember 1978), p. 211

1 There are noticeable differences of women's contribution towards subsistence which can be explained using an evolutionary approach. In our evolutionary past it was the responsibility of men to hunt for food whereas women gathered fruit and vegetables – a foraging strategy that didn't require as much strength and energy expenditure. Both studies suggest that men are more involved with hunting and fishing and women with other forms of food harvesting.

2 The second study shows more validity than the first because the number of societies examined was much higher (862 compared to 181), and more strategies of subsistence were considered which means that women were more likely to be represented which is what was found.

Formal socializing agents across cultures, p. 213

There are bound to be some differences in gender-role across cultures and different eras. For instance the law changes with the times and what was illegal behaviour at some point in history is now legal and socially acceptable. Different countries have different laws such that some behaviours are permissible and others not – this pertains to gender-role too. In some cultures women are not allowed to have more than one child whereas in other cultures they must have children as abortion is not permitted legally so there are inevitably differences in gender role. But what we can say is that the fundamental differences between men and women are preserved cross-culturally and remain constant regardless of country and Zeitgeist. These fundamental differences of gender-role relate to differences in reproduction and the ability to carry and give birth (in the case of females) and to nurture children.

The young child's gender schema, p. 215

1 They wanted to consider all possible angles that could explain and account for the way in which the parents socialized their children.

2 In Fagot and Leinbach's study, parents were given a series of questionnaires to complete. This was good practice as they wanted to know how the parents' attitudes impacted on the interactions that they had with their children.

3 If the parents were very traditional in their views towards how men and women should behave, then they would be very controlling in ensuring that their boys behaved like boys and girls like girls. The interactions that they had with their children would be reflective of these views.

4 Yes it did. By including all the different measures that they used they were able to rule out any possible confounding variables which might have interfered with their findings or at the very least make it more difficult to come to a conclusion.

5 This was a compact and well considered study. They tried to take account of the many different variables that could have accounted for their findings. This method enabled them to deduce a likely explanation for their findings.

The evolution of school books, p. 217

1 Although an archival search is used, the actual method of data extraction involves the qualitative method of

content analysis. Here the research devises a list of traits/labels/categories of information that is considered relevant to understanding gender role and gender depictions. By looking at books used in education, a tick is put beside the relevant category every time it appears in the books considered.

2 It is difficult to exclude bias from this kind of research. A major problem is that the traits/labels/categories used are subjective and could be biased. Furthermore, the content in the books considered might not always fall easily into a particular category

A thought experiment on gender, p. 218

Considering studies that look at gaze preference from day one, toy choice and type of play, it appears that children already have a predisposition for certain objects, toys and games and parents merely reinforce these interests. Also, given our knowledge about the influence of pre-natal hormones on brain development, it is not surprising that certain games and toys would appeal more to boys and others to girls.

1 If you had to design an experiment as a way of answering this question what would you do?

2 Parents read gender-stereotyped books to their unborn foetus (studies have shown that the foetus has a well-developed auditory system and can actually recognize the mother's voice once born and they also recognize stories that have been read to them) such that they read 'girly' books to male or female foetuses or 'boy' books to male or female foetuses. These books are highly gender stereotyped and reinforce gender socialisation. It would be interesting to see which of the babies under both conditions would want to hear the books they heard as a foetus. Previous studies have used the sucking reflex that babies have as a means of switching on a recording of the book they are familiar with. Would male babies still want to hear 'girly' books or female babies 'boy' books? Would nature override this?

3 It is important to consider variables that are harmless and don't interfere with what parents would have done anyway. Obviously with the study devised above, parents would have to be on board and not mind or perceive reading gender-biased material to their unborn child a problem.

The six cultures study, p. 220

1 Gender plays an important role in demarcating the work load. As most Kenyans work on the land, the work is demanding and effortful. Females do typically female work related to what their level of strength and stamina will enable them to do, whereas males do the more labour intensive work because their build enables them to do so.

2 The working patterns between males and females are more segregated and defined in Kenyan culture than American. As lifestyle in America is less dependent on the land and more on money exchange for goods, children can bide their time and obtain an education that will give them good career prospects and therefore money. These opportunities will be open to both males and females and therefore the divide in career prospects is less likely to be vastly different for males and females: therefore gender role might be more diffused.

3 As nomadic people are literally on the move and have temporary fixed abodes, their major concern must be first to secure a food supply and shelter for the family. This is on-going and repetitive. The likelihood is that gender roles will be more defined, rigid and hierarchically organized so that every member of the family/group know what their role is and what is expected of them. This is necessary as nomadic people often travel through and stop at very hostile environments with conditions that make survival difficult. Being organized, and knowing and accepting one's capabilities (and that includes limitations and strengths of each gender role) is paramount for the cohesiveness and successful functioning of the group.

Emics and etics in cross-cultural research, p. 221

1 Cultural bias can be reduced by considering the observable rather than interviewing. If the behaviour of the tribal people (one specific tribal group considered at a time) is considered long-term, in time their relationships, sexual, warfare and everyday behaviour would become apparent. If they behave in a specific manner then this would be eventually observed.

2 And to convert this to emic fact, this behaviour would have to be deemed as peculiar to the tribal people considered *per se* and not a select few.

3 This element of behaviour could be compared with other cultures to see if there is something special about the tribal people considered, so supporting an etic fact.

Comparing theories (Part 1), p. 267

	Piaget	Vygotsky
Role of innate factors and biological processes	Cognitive development is biologically driven, occurring as a result of the maturation of innate structures in the brain.	Although the contribution of biological processes was not ruled out it was not highlighted.
Role of experience	The role of experience intertwined with nature is acknowledged; children construct their knowledge in response to their experience.	Emphasized nurture over nature. Experience is crucial – children are not born with knowledge, it is acquired through social interactions with peers and adults. Knowledge is not, therefore, independent of the social context.
Social/cultural influence	The role of social and cultural factors is overlooked.	The central importance of social and cultural factors is emphasized.
What drives (motivates) cognitive development?	The brain has matured to a point of 'readiness' and new information/experiences cannot be assimilated into the child's existing understanding challenges their thinking.	The cultural context determines the child's immediate social environment and drives the development of higher mental functions which shape language and make thought possible.

Comparing theories (Part 2), p. 270

	Bruner
Role of innate factors and biological processes	Bruner's early work was influenced by Piaget's ideas about cognitive development and the role of biological processes.
Role of experience	Bruner's early work was behaviourist in its approach, emphasizing the role of experience.
Social/cultural influence	Over the years Bruner increasingly focused on the influence of the social and cultural context (influenced by Vygotsky's work).
What drives (motivates) cognitive development?	Particularly interested in how knowledge is represented and organized through different modes of representation, based on muscle memories, images and symbols.

Comparing theories (Part 3), p. 274

	Piaget	Vygotsky	Bruner
Role of teaching in cognitive development	Piaget believed that children are curious and intrinsically motivated to learn. Role of teacher is not, therefore, to teach but to create opportunities for children to explore and learn about the world for themselves (discovery learning).	Children learn best through interaction with others (collaborative learning). The role of the teacher (a more knowledgeable other) is to assist a child's performance through the ZPD, emphasizing stretch and challenge. Vygotsky predicted that the greatest learning occurred at the edge of the ZPD.	Bruner wrote several books on education. Like Piaget, Bruner sees learning as an active process (not passive recipients of adult instruction) with teachers having an active instructional role. Scaffolding is one of the teacher's key roles, enabling the learner to become an increasingly active participant in the learning process (a shift from regulation by others to self-regulation). His spiral curriculum approach reflects the importance of teachers being sufficiently flexible to accommodate learners' differing needs, making use of different modes of representation.

Chapter 9: Schizophrenia

Characteristics of schizophrenia, p.3 11

Include a brief definition, types of onset with reference to Type I and Type II and two or three important symptoms. Avoid going into too much detail or becoming bogged down in issues to do with reliability and validity of diagnosis.

Chapter 10: Depression

Characteristics of depression, p. 335

Include a brief definition of depression that distinguishes between clinical depression and normal feelings of sadness. Outline three or four of the main clinical symptoms for severe depressive disorder (called major depressive disorder in DSM). Avoid going into too much detail about symptoms or becoming bogged down in issues to do with reliability and validity of diagnosis.

Five steps to happiness recommended by Foresight think tank, p.336

Connect
Developing relationships with family, friends, colleagues and neighbours will enrich your life and bring you support.

Be active
Sports, hobbies such as gardening or dancing, or just a daily stroll will make you feel good and maintain mobility and fitness.

Be curious
Noting the beauty of everyday moments as well as the unusual, and reflecting on them, helps you to appreciate what matters to you.

Learn
Fixing a bike, learning an instrument, cooking – the challenge and satisfaction brings fun and confidence.

Give
Helping friends and strangers links your happiness to a wider community and is very rewarding.

Chapter 11a: Phobic Disorders

Characteristics of phobic disorders, p. 368

You could take a broad, overarching approach, outlining the main characteristics of phobias in general, or you could select one type of phobia (e.g. specific) and outline its characteristics. Whichever approach you adopt, outline two or three symptoms (e.g. excessive, persistent fear that interferes with everyday life; avoidance behaviour; awareness of irrationality), using brief examples where appropriate. Avoid going into too much detail or becoming bogged down in issues to do with reliability and validity of diagnosis.

Chapter 11b: Obsessive Compulsive Disorders

Characteristics of OCD p. 391

Include a brief definition and two or three important symptoms to illustrate obsessions and compulsions. You can use an illustrative example, but keep it brief. Avoid giving too much detail and do not become bogged down in issues to do with reliability and validity of diagnosis.

Chapter 12: Media psychology

Research into celebrity worship, p. 430

1   Participants should also be informed of their right to withdraw from the study at any time, even if it means withdrawing data after the study is completed. Participants should be able to withdraw retrospectively having given their consent and demand that any data relating to them is destroyed. If data is to be published, participants have the right to expect that it will not be identifiable as theirs. In this study, if anonymity cannot be guaranteed, the participant must be warned of this in advance of agreeing to participate.

2   There are several methods for assessing the reliability of a measure, but the one most relevant in this situation is test-retest reliability, where a group of participants complete the measure then the same group of participants complete it again some time in the future. The two sets of scores are then correlated, with a higher positive correlation between the two sets of scores indicating greater reliability.

3   The order effect might have been minimized by counterbalancing, i.e. half of the participants would have completed the CAS followed by the GHQ, and the other half the GHQ followed by the CAS.

Chapter 13: Psychology of Addictive Behaviour

Defining addiction, p. 439

This exercise has no right or wrong answers. By trying to devise your own 'addiction' definition, you may realize that the whole is more than the sum of its parts, i.e. giving examples of addictive behaviour is easier than trying to define it. Sharing your definitions will show how others are likely to have different parameters and boundaries. All definitions of 'addiction' must be operationally defined.

Applying the components of addictive behaviour, p. 440

Here is what we might expect each component to look like if someone were addicted to videogame playing:

Salience – Videogame playing becomes the most important activity in the person's life, dominating their thinking, feelings and behaviour, e.g. even when not actually playing, the person would be thinking about the next time they would be.

Mood modification – The videogame player finds playing arousing, giving them a 'buzz' or a 'high', or alternatively, a way of 'escape' or relieving stress.

Tolerance – The videogame player gradually increases the amounts of playing, needing to play for longer to get the mood-modifying effects.

Withdrawal symptoms – The videogame player experiences unpleasant feeling states and/or physical effects when play is discontinued or suddenly reduced, e.g. the shakes, moodiness, irritability.

Conflict – The videogame player experiences conflicts with other people and with other activities, or internal conflicts (e.g. feelings of loss of control) arising from spending too much time engaged in playing video games.

Relapse – The videogame player reverts to earlier excessive patterns of play after a period of abstinence.

The difficulties of applying the components model to behavioural addictions include the fact that components like 'tolerance' and 'withdrawal' are derived from (and typically consequences of) chemical addictions and may not always have direct equivalents in behavioural addictions such as excessive videogame playing. In addition, the person may not ever have tried to give up and, therefore, not have experienced relapse.

Rewarding behaviour, p. 445

Again in this activity there is no right or wrong answer. Examples you think of might include:

1 eating your favourite food every day; winning easily on your favourite video game

2 smoking; drinking alcohol; getting good marks for your psychology essays

3 playing a slot machine at the seaside; eating your favourite chocolate bar; seeing your favourite football team win.

Evaluating Parke et al.'s (2004) study, p. 447

1 This is the first-ever study to show empirically that competitiveness and deferment of gratification appear to be important risk factors in pathological gambling.

2 Competitiveness and deferment of gratification.

3 For 38 per cent of the sample to be classified as pathological gamblers, is exceedingly high and unrepresentative of the population of 'people who gamble'.

4 The high level of problem gambling was fortuitous as the increased numbers of pathological gamblers in the study added weight to the statistical findings.

Understanding addiction, p. 449

The answers you come to will depend on which theories or models you find most convincing and useful.

1 This will depend on whether you believe that some people are predisposed towards addiction or that people are fully responsible for their own actions.

2 The components model looks for similarities across all addictive behaviour but all addictions are idiosyncratic to some extent. All chemical addictions involve the ingestion of a psychoactive substance whereas behavioural addictions don't. This means that biological factors may be more prominent in chemical addictions and cognitive factors may be more important in behavioural addictions. Learning factors might be equally important irrespective of addiction type. Some addictions feature aspects unique to that addiction (such as the role of a 'competitive trait' in gambling addiction).

3 Again, the answer to these questions depends on how you evaluate the literature. It could be argued that all addicts have some kind of predisposing factors, but for some this may be based on biological heredity (e.g. genetics), others on social heredity (e.g. social learning).

4 There are many ways of collecting data about addictive behaviours. These include self-report methods (questionnaires, interviews), observation methods (participant observation, non-participant observation), experiments (laboratory-based, ecologically valid experiments, natural experiments), chemical testing (e.g. urine tests, hair analysis), and corroborative evidence (archive data, parental and peer reports).

Applying components of addiction to film, p. 456

Some components may be easy to spot (e.g. relapse, withdrawal symptoms, mood modification, conflict), whereas others may need to be inferred (salience, tolerance). You may notice other symptoms and consequences (e.g. loss of control, cravings) that are particular to the addiction being studied. This activity should give you an insight into whether the addiction has been faithfully depicted on the screen or whether the writer and/or director has taken 'artistic liberties'.

Giving up, p. 458

1 There are many factors involved in trying to give up an addiction, such as whether the addict actually wants to give up the behaviour, whether a third party wants the addict to give up the behaviour (spouse, legal system),

whether the addict has a good social-support system, and whether there are local services to access. Some addicts may engage in their addiction with all their friends (e.g. drinking buddies in the pub). Giving up their addiction may also mean giving up their social-support network.

2   There are many barriers that an addict might face, depending on the addiction in question. An alcoholic might have a choice of local AA groups but a gambling addict might have to travel 20 miles to the nearest meeting; an internet addict may have no self-help group to go to at all. Addicts may not be able to avoid the environments where their addiction takes place. An alcoholic may live next to a pub. A gambling addict may work next to a betting shop or an amusement arcade. Addictions may be co-occurring, adding a complicating factor.

3   Many chemical addictions may involve the total abstention of the activity but most behavioural addictions may be difficult or impossible to give up (No sex? No food? No computer use? No exercise?). The treatment goal in behavioural addictions may be more about control of the activity rather than abstention from it. There may be more resources for help with chemical addictions than for other less common behavioural addictions.

Would you recommend the voucher system? p. 462

How you respond to this question depends on whether you think the means justifies the ends. There is certainly evidence that this type of intervention can work but there may be a political backlash if such a scheme were introduced in the UK. There is also a moral dimension about whether addicts should be positively rewarded for engaging in a behaviour that the general public may perceive in a very negative way.

Addiction and culture, p. 467

The answers to these questions depend on how addictions are operationally defined and how each individual culture views a particular behaviour.

The taking of drugs in a third-world culture might be very socially acceptable and the behaviour will not be pathologized in the same way as in our own culture.

The mass media could be said to reflect societal addictions rather than be a cause of them, although as we saw earlier in the chapter, advertising and the media can certainly play a part in the initiation of addictive behaviours.

Chapter 14: Anomalistic psychology

Psychology in context: Science and the paranormal, p. 475

The BA possibly deserved some criticism for not ensuring that all viewpoints were represented in a session dealing with such a controversial area. The BA should certainly allow proper debate and coverage of such areas, and should ensure this occurs in future. Professor Atkins' views can only be seen as reflecting his own personal prejudices, given his admission that he had not read the relevant research. Proper scientific criticism can only be based upon careful consideration of the available evidence and arguments.

Pseudoscience within psychology, p. 477

Unfortunately, there is a lot of pseudoscience within psychology, especially clinical psychology (Lilienfeld *et al.* 2003). The following brief notes give some indication of the kind of things you might consider when assessing controversial clinical claims within psychology.

Psychoanalysis: Founded by Sigmund Freud (1856-1939), psychoanalytic theory encompassed human development, personality, psychopathology and therapy. Its scientific status has long been disputed along the following lines:

▪   Tendency to invoke *ad hoc* hypotheses (e.g. so-called *reaction formation*, whereby if psychoanalytic reasoning suggests that an individual should demonstrate certain psychological tendencies, it is also seen as supportive of psychoanalytic theory if that person actually demonstrates the exact opposite);

▪   Absence of self-correction (e.g. Freudian psychoanalysis is largely unchanged since Freud's day);

▪   Also, emphasis on confirmation, excessive reliance on anecdotal evidence, absence of connectivity with other areas of science, and the use of impressive-sounding jargon.

Neurolinguistic Programming (NLP): NLP was founded by Richard Bandler and John Grinder in the 1970s (e.g. Bandler and Grinder 1979). It is claimed by its proponents to be a powerful theory and therapy to allow people to lead more fulfilled lives. It is allegedly derived from a model of interpersonal communication which takes into account characteristic patterns of thought and emotion based upon underlying neuropsychology. It has been criticized in terms of:

▪   Tendency to invoke *ad hoc* hypotheses (e.g. rejecting empirical studies which failed to support the claims of NLP on the grounds that the practitioners involved were inadequately trained);

▪   Absence of connectivity with other areas of science (the allegedly scientific basis for NLP is in fact based upon what has been referred to as 'neuromythology', i.e. oversimplification and unjustified extrapolation from genuine neuroscience);

- Use of impressive-sounding jargon (e.g. even the phrase 'neurolinguistic programming' itself implies links with neuroscience, linguistics, and computing that in fact do not exist);

- All other characteristics of pseudoscience listed in Table 14.1 appear to apply to NLP.

Homoeopathy: Homoeopathy is an alternative medicine in which solutions of active ingredients are diluted to such an extent that it is mathematically almost certain that not one molecule of the active compound remains in the solution which the patient finally receives. In terms of conventional science, therefore, homoeopathic treatments are simply pure water and cannot therefore have any effect other than a placebo effect. Homoeopaths argues that, when properly prepared, water retains a 'memory' of the active ingredient which can then have real therapeutic effects but this is not supported by good empirical evidence. Many of the criteria of pseudoscience previously outlined would apply to homoeopathy, but the following are particularly noteworthy:

- an absence of self-correction

- excessive reliance on anecdotal evidence

- absence of 'connectivity'

- use of impressive-sounding jargon

- absence of boundary conditions.

Childhood trauma and paranormal belief, p. 489

1 The use of retrospective questionnaires to assess history of childhood trauma is somewhat problematic insofar as the investigators have no independent proof of whether or not childhood abuse actually did or did not occur. Some fantasy prone respondents may provide inaccurate reports of their childhood. A preferable (but much more difficult) methodology to employ would be to carry out a longitudinal study following development throughout childhood.

2 It may be that individuals who score highly on fantasy proneness and/or dissociativity possess the appropriate psychological profile to experience genuine paranormal phenomena (if such phenomena actually exist).

Probability misjudgement and belief in the paranormal, p. 493

1 The newspaper survey was quite different to a real psychic reading insofar as, in contrast to a typical psychic reading, it would be obvious to respondents that they were not reading statements that were intended to apply specifically to them. Believers are likely to be highly motivated to find evidence that supports their belief in the paranormal (i.e. confirmation bias) and would therefore be likely to endorse more statements in the context of a psychic reading compared to the newspaper survey.

2 The fact that all respondents were asked to indicate both how many statements were true for them and to estimate how many would be true for a randomly selected stranger may well lead many to realize that these numbers are likely to be similar (in the absence of any other information). A between-participants design might have produced results more in line with Blackmore's initial hypothesis.

Chapter 15: Scientific method

Theorizing, p. 513

1 There are two possible factors in our implicit theory – use of tealeaves and warming the pot. To test whether this theory is correct and identify which of the factors determines the outcome, you could carry out a series of further observations, including:

a warming the teapot and using tealeaves;
b not warming the teapot but using tealeaves;
c making the tea using teabags and warming the pot beforehand; and
d making the tea with a teabag without warming the teapot.

You would ask others, who are unaware of the theory that is being tested, to assess the overall quality of the resulting cups of tea.

If our implicit theory is correct that both the use of tealeaves and warming the pot are important, then only (a) would produce a good cup of tea.

If it is the use of tealeaves rather than a teabag that is crucial, then (a) and (b) should both produce a good cup of tea.

If it is the warming of the teapot that is crucial, then (a) and (c) should both produce a good cup of tea.

2 The theory would be deemed to be entirely incorrect if only method (d) was found to make a good cup of tea. In which case we would be forced to conclude that warming the teapot and using tealeaves does not determine the quality of a cup of tea and would need to revise our theory.

Paradigms in psychology, p. 520

As you may have realized in the course of your discussion, there is no simple answer to this question. Some psychologists would argue that psychology is at the *pre-science* stage because of its diversity in terms of its subject matter and the range of perspectives that it encompasses. As a result there is no common agreement on a general theoretical orientation or single paradigm. In 1970, Kuhn claimed that psychology had not yet developed a dominant paradigm because of its fragmentation and diversity. Others, such as Valentine (1992), have argued that behaviourism is a paradigm because of the dominant position it has occupied within psychology in determining what is studied and also how it is studied. This would locate psychology at the *normal science* stage.

Yet others claim that each of the main approaches in psychology (physiological, evolutionary, behavioural, psychodynamic and cognitive) represents a paradigm and there is no dominant paradigm in psychology (Kline 1988). Whatever your views about paradigms, it could be argued that they provide a useful way of conceptualizing how different claims about how to generate knowledge in a rigorous way can coexist.

Using primary and secondary sources, p. 523

Pressure groups are often highly selective in the evidence they present in order to support a particular viewpoint and influence public opinion. It is important that policy makers and decision-makers do not base their actions on incomplete or flawed evidence, rather they should always consult primary sources (i.e. an account of a study written by the actual researcher) rather than secondary sources. In the course of reporting other people's work and ideas, inaccuracies can creep in to secondary sources and they can become highly unreliable, particularly if secondary sources are based on other secondary sources, so that the details of the original account become more and more vague. You only have to think about the game of Chinese whispers to illustrate this point about the potential unreliability of secondary sources!

Systematic reviews, particularly those using meta-analysis, provide the most reliable source of evidence for policy makers because the conclusions are based on the combined data from a series of similar studies.

Secondary sources can sometimes be useful to psychology students as a starting point to orient themselves to a particular topic and identify the primary sources that need to be read.

Chapter 16: Designing psychological investigations

Choosing a research method, p. 529

Some suggestions are given below. You may have come up with different ones. Be sure that you can provide a good rationale for your choice.

1 This research question could be addressed using an experiment to compare the two learning conditions. Independent judges (unaware of which condition an individual has been allocated to) could assess participants' level of skill after training to see whether it differs according to the learning schedule.

2 The focus here is on understanding an experience that is personal, subjective and difficult to quantify. An unstructured interview might be the best method to use (i.e. qualitative research), although a questionnaire, which allows some flexibility in the responses, could also provide a more general view.

3 To address this question it is important for the researcher to canvas opinion as widely as possible, so a questionnaire survey might be the most suitable research method.

4 This question begs a quantitative answer and so a way of measuring individual's internet usage and face-to-face social skills would need to be devised. Data could then be correlated to test for the hypothesized negative relationship (a study using correlational analysis). Alternatively, the skills of individuals categorized as 'high' and 'low' internet users could be compared (a natural experiment).

5 Accounts of dreams from samples of boys and girls would need to be recorded. Content analysis of these accounts, using either qualitative, textual methods or a coding system to count themes, could be applied. In the latter case, the numerical data could be statistically analysed to quantify the differences between boys' and girls' dreams.

6 Examples of extreme neglect such as this are rare and unique. The method of choice is an in-depth case study, which would document all aspects of the child's current linguistic abilities, alongside the child's cognitive development, physical and mental health, and domestic circumstances.

Do children learn aggressive habits from TV? p. 531

TYPES OF EXPERIMENT	IV VARIES ⁻	
THE RESEARCH ENVIRONMENT IS ⁻	by deliberate manipulation	naturally
controlled by the experimenter	LABORATORY EXPERIMENT Children are brought into a psychological laboratory and their behaviour is observed and recorded to establish a baseline. They are then systematically exposed to different types of TV content. They are subsequently tested in the laboratory to assess any related changes in their behaviour. (This approach is highly contrived and not very practical.)	QUASI-EXPERIMENT Children with parents who control or do not control their exposure to aggression on TV are studied in a laboratory setting to assess their levels of aggression.
naturally occurring/home territory for the participants	FIELD EXPERIMENT The behaviour of children in residential care is observed and recorded to establish a baseline. They are then systematically exposed to different types of TV content in their natural environment and then observed again to assess any related changes in their behaviour.	NATURAL EXPERIMENT Children in a remote location with no prior access to TV are exposed to TV when the technology is available to transmit it to them. Their behaviour is observed in their natural environment before and after TV is introduced to assess any related changes in their behaviour.

The Stroop effect, p. 535

1 The independent variable is the way in which colours were presented: either as colour names written in conflicting coloured ink (e.g. the word 'red' written in blue ink) or as blocks of colour.

2 The dependent variable is the time taken by participants to name all the colours in each of the conditions.

3 There are two conditions in this experiment: the control condition based on colour blocks and the experimental condition with colour names written in a conflicting coloured ink.

4 The data are quantitative (numerical). The total time in seconds taken to complete the control and experimental condition were measured.

5 The cause-and-effect relationship investigated was whether changing the presentation form affected the speed with which participants could name the colours.

Vitamins and IQ, p. 535

Independent groups design

▦ In this design, it is relatively straightforward to allocate participants to conditions randomly.

▦ In comparison with a repeated measures design, however, greater numbers of participants would be needed, which is costly in time and money.

▦ Random allocation might, by chance, still result in groups that are not the same. Individual differences are greater than in the other two designs.

Repeated measures design

▦ Fewer participants are needed in a repeated measures design than in either an independent groups design or a matched pairs design, as individuals are tested in each condition, thereby reducing the overall number of participants that need to be recruited.

▦ Participants act as their own controls thereby reducing the effect of individual differences.

▦ Participants would need to take part in a control condition, which would take a long time. They could drop out of the study between testing sessions and their data would therefore be lost.

▦ Order effects are a risk, so counterbalancing or randomization would need to be used. If these measures are judged to be inadequate, another design would be necessary.

Matched pairs design

▦ In comparison with the repeated measures design, greater resources, including numbers of participants, are needed which is costly in time and money.

▦ Good matching of participants may be difficult to achieve.

▦ If one member of a pair drops out, the partner participant is also lost from the study.

▦ There are no order effects, so the study should have a lower dropout rate than a repeated measures design.

▦ Control of individual differences is better than in an independent groups design.

In a study of this nature, in which participants may be needed for some time and in which counterbalancing might be time-consuming, a repeated measures design is the most risky experimental design. Of the two remaining designs, the matched pairs design is better than an independent groups design because individual differences are better controlled (unless large numbers of participants are recruited to an independent groups design, which would increase the cost of the study).

Designing an experiment on face recognition, p. 537

1 Hypothesis: Distinctive faces are recognized more efficiently than average faces. This is a directional hypothesis, which is justified on the basis of the theory.

   Null hypothesis: There is no difference in recognition efficiency of distinctive and average faces.

2 The independent variable is the level of distinctiveness of faces, previously categorized as average or distinctive by a panel of independent judges. The dependent variable is the number of faces correctly identified as having been seen before (a recognition task).

3 To operationalize the key variables in the hypothesis, you could either use overall distinctiveness or choose a particular facial feature such as eyebrows. You could also count instances of correct face recognition or measure decision time.

   In the following example, general distinctiveness and accuracy counts are used: the faces categorized as distinctive are accurately recognized more frequently than faces categorized as being average.

4 To decide which faces to include, you could assemble a variety of images of faces and ask a panel of independent judges to rate them for distinctiveness. These ratings could then be used to select a suitable, equal number of 'distinctive' and 'average' faces. Extraneous variables specifically related to the faces that could be controlled to ensure that facial distinctiveness alone is being studied include gender, orientation, ethnic origin, colour, age, facial hair, hairstyle, hair colour and facial expression.

5 When identifying the target population of potential participants, it is important to consider gender, age and ethnic group in relation to the stimulus pictures you have chosen, as these variables have been shown to affect face perception. Consider also participants' ability to take part in the study (e.g. their vision or ability to concentrate or understand what they are required to do).

6 You will need to decide between random, volunteer or opportunity sampling and gather sufficient data to carry out the analysis chosen for question 12. You could use an independent groups design, a matched pairs design or a repeated measures design. Random allocation of participants to conditions is an important consideration when using an independent groups or a matched pairs design.

7 Ethical issues include permission to use the images and formal acknowledgement of their origin in any written report. You should also consider the major ethical concerns of respect, competence, responsibility and integrity.

8 This study would be invalidated if participants were informed of the hypothesis in advance, so an element of deception is involved. The briefing should therefore give clear instructions without mentioning the precise purpose of the study and should emphasize a participant's right to withdraw at any point in the study. Ethical responsibilities require the researcher to explain the true purpose of the study when debriefing participants at the end, and giving them the right to withdraw their data should they wish.

9 It would be best to present the faces on screen using a computer programme, which automatically randomizes and times the presentation. A repeated measures design would work well, as participants act as their own controls.

10 Extraneous variables associated with the experimental procedure that would need to be controlled include exposure time, orientation to participant, illumination of stimuli, order effects (controlled by randomization), standardized instructions, recall time allowed (which should be the same for every participant).

11 To test and score the efficiency of recognition, the original faces would need to be mixed with a large number of new faces and presented in random order to participants who are required to indicate which ones they have seen before. The total number of correct identifications of 'distinctive' and 'average' faces would be recorded for each participant.

12 To analyse the data you could calculate the mean score and standard deviation for the 'distinctive' and 'average' faces to compare average recognition scores and variability. If the experimental design used was repeated measures or matched pairs, the Wilcoxon matched pairs signed ranks test could be used to find out whether the difference in recognition between the distinctive and average faces is statistically significant. The Mann-Whitney U test should be applied if an independent groups design was used. Using a one-tailed test with $p \leq .05$, the null hypothesis can be rejected if the probability of the test statistic is less than $p = 0.05$ and if the distinctive condition has the higher scores (as indicated by the mean).

Devising a questionnaire, p. 540

Table 16.3 provides some useful tips on question wording. When carrying out this activity you will need to think carefully about:

▪ what to include in the short film

- how to recruit participants
- who you will approach
- how you will brief and debrief them.

Participants should not be aware that there are two different types of question sheet during the second stage, so there is an element of deception that will need to be handled sensitively. Control-group questions will need to be neutral but sufficiently interesting to engage participants' attention. In studies such as these, participants usually enjoy watching the film again to check their recall. Allow time for this when planning the study.

Devising and piloting a semi-structured interview schedule, p. 540

Devising a good interview schedule is far more difficult than it might initially appear. It is important to think carefully about question wording and create a series of questions that encourage the interviewee to give detailed responses. This activity also encourages you to think about the actual conduct of an interview in terms of your approach to the interviewee and the practicalities of beginning and ending the interview.

What makes a research method 'scientific'? p. 541

1 Science aims to describe, predict, understand and control its subject matter. It makes assumptions that there is order in the subject matter, events are determined and that empirical evidence and extremely cautious explanations are best. It seeks to build theories using the hypothetico-deductive method, and values studies that are replicable.

2 Quantitative research methods fit these criteria fairly easily, while purely qualitative methods do not. Qualitative researchers defend their position by arguing that the criteria on which the quality of their work is assessed should be different – for example, the richness and meaningfulness of qualitative data are valued over measurement precision and replicability.

Defining target populations, p. 541

The characteristics that define the target population they represent are:

1 Robbie Williams – an ex-band member, solo artist, pop singer, white, British, Caucasian male of a particular age, millionaire.

2 This textbook – all the textbooks of the same edition that have been written and edited by the same team. Alternatively, the population could be all A2 psychology textbooks written for the AQA A specification in a particular year.

3 A chimpanzee trained to use sign language – this could include all captive and free-living chimpanzees of a particular breed that have been taught to use the same system of sign language. They could be living

and/or dead, depending on whether archival material can be accessed about chimpanzees who have since died.

4 You – only you can answer this!

Sampling issues, p. 542

1 When selecting a random sample of A-level psychology students, care would be needed to ensure that female students were not over-represented. It is possible that a small sample of students selected randomly would have no males in it (because 90 per cent of students are female). It is also statistically possible, although unlikely, that males could be overrepresented in the sample.

2 A representative sample should reflect the population in miniature and share its characteristics. One way of ensuring an appropriate proportion of males and females would be to split the population into two groups, called 'strata', and select a random sample from both. To represent the population of A-level students, the sample should comprise 10 per cent males and 90 per cent females. This is called 'stratified random sampling' and is only worth doing if gender is deemed to be an important variable in a study.

Is bigger always better in terms of sample size? p. 543

1 A sample should be sufficiently large to represent the target population adequately, while still remaining practical. Sample size can be determined using statistical techniques. Some classic psychological studies have been based on quite small samples, such as Zimbardo's (1973) prison simulation study, which recruited just 22 volunteers.

2 Many case studies focus on just one person – for example, Freud's Anna O and Little Hans, Watson and Rayner's Little Albert, Milner's HM and Phineas Gage. In each case, a great deal was learned that could be more widely applied to a particular subject area and used to validate findings involving different research methods.

3 Individuals with rare characteristics are often aware of others in a similar position, especially in these days of internet communication. One way to recruit such people is to use a technique known as 'snowball sampling'. An individual with particular rare characteristics is asked to approach or nominate others with similar characteristics so that they can be asked to participate in research. Those individuals will then be asked to nominate others and so on.

Improving internal validity, p. 546

Some suggestions about how the internal validity of a study investigating parenting style and GCSE achievement could be improved are outlined below. You may have thought of other equally valid ideas which you may like to discuss with your teacher.

Operationalization of the independent variable (parenting style) – Assessment of parental behaviour/parenting style, using a self-report questionnaire completed by students, is not necessarily invalid. However, it could be highly subjective because students may have had little or no direct experience of other parental behaviour; this would also be the case if parents were asked to complete self-assessments. An independent assessment of parenting style would be better.

Operationalization of the dependent variable (academic achievement) – As students study different combinations and numbers of subjects at GCSE, point scores will not be readily comparable (although a mean point score could be calculated). It may be better to take scores from the core subjects that are common to all students. It would be even better to be able to use the actual marks from GCSEs rather than the grade conversions.

Selection of sample – This could be considered to be a population study, as all eligible students were included. It may not, however, have been necessary to test everyone. A random sample could have been studied instead. See the 'extraneous variables' below.

Extraneous variables – There is no attempt to establish whether a student lives with one parent, both parents, neither parent, or with both parents but at different times. It has not been established whether parents are consistent in their parenting style. Others in the household have not been taken into account (e.g. older siblings, grandparents and step-relatives). These things would need to be as uniform as possible for the participants. Other factors that may impact on academic achievement, such as a student's motivation, personality, mental and physical health and any other personal circumstances, would ideally also need to be taken into account.

Study design – An independent groups design was used. However, given the range of extraneous variables it might have been better to attempt to match students on the basis of at least some of the extraneous variables identified above. A repeated measures design is not possible for this study.

Thinking about reliability and validity, p. 547

1 Content validity – the entrance test is comprised of questions that junior school children can be expected to know about.

2 Inter-observer reliability (or corroborative evidence).

3 Concurrent validity (although head size is unlikely to correlate with IQ!).

4 This question refers to test–retest reliability, using the alternate forms procedure. Two equivalent forms of the same test can be used in quick succession, thereby avoiding the risk of order effects, in order to check external reliability.

5 Predictive validity – universities use A-level grades as an indication of whether applicants can be expected to succeed on a degree course.

6 External validity and more specifically population validity – the researchers want to find out if the findings for male participants are also relevant to females.

Ethics in Internet-mediated research (IMR), p. 550

The BPS guidelines on IMR are organized under 10 headings. Check these against the issues you identified:

1 Difficulties in verifying the identity of participants.

2 Blurred distinction between public and private space.

3 Difficulties in obtaining fully informed consent.

4 Compromised levels of control over participants and the research environment.

5 Special measures needed to enable participants to withdraw.

6 Special measures needed to debrief participants at any stage of participation.

7 There must be a very strong justification for any form of deception.

8 Monitoring of research designs is essential to avoid any undesirable consequences of participation, which may not fully be dealt with by debriefing.

9 Protection of participants through safeguarding participant anonymity, and of researchers by being aware of the legal position with regard to 'spamming' and maintaining a professional distance.

10 Awareness of data protection legislation (Data Protection Act 1998).

Ethical issues in the study of parenting style and academic achievement study, p. 550

Respect – Care should be taken to ensure the wellbeing of participants and their parents, especially as the students are under 18. Permission would be needed from parents or those in *loco parentis*. Confidentiality and anonymity must be assured. Students and their parents need to know that they can withdraw from the study at any time. A degree of deception would be necessary, as this is a single-blind study. This would apply to the students, but their parents/guardians would need to be fully informed beforehand.

Competence – The researchers need to be well trained and prepared to deal with any ethical issues arising at any time before, during or after the study.

Responsibility – The researchers must recognize that students might find it uncomfortable to consider parental behaviour and parenting style, particularly those who have difficult relationships with their parents. It should be clear to students that they are under no pressure from peers, staff, parents or researchers to complete the questionnaire or to divulge their answers to anyone.

Integrity – It is important to be open about the findings and present them in a way that is accessible and which does not make claims unwarranted by the data. If poorly handled, awkward conversations between parents and students could ensue. Parents might feel guilty or responsible for not parenting in a particular way. Students might pressurize authoritarian parents to change their style. Such issues would need to be anticipated and dealt with carefully at the debriefing stage and when findings are presented.

Writing a research proposal, p. 553

Writing a proposal for scrutiny by others is a good discipline and helps a researcher to identify the key ethical issues and how these might be addressed. A research ethics committee would require copies of all relevant documentation associated with the proposed study (e.g. letters of invitation to participants and any other recruitment procedures, briefing and de-briefing documents, and consent forms). Although you are not expected to prepare all of this, the activity provides the opportunity to create a model consent form.

Chapter 17: Data analysis and reporting on investigations

Practising how to present data graphically, p. 562

Construct a bar chart

1 See chart below.

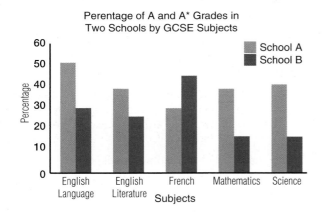

Perentage of A and A* Grades in Two Schools by GCSE Subjects

2 The percentage A/A* rate in each subject can be read from the data table or bar chart. In School A, just over half of English Language grades are A/A* (51%) and this is the highest of all five subjects. English Literature, Mathematics, and Science all score similarly at 39–41% and French is the lowest at 30%. The biggest difference (21%) is between English Language and French (51% and 30% respectively). Over all 500 grades, 40% were A or A*.

French is the highest scoring subject in School B with 45% at A/A*, followed by English Language at 30% and English Literature at 26%. Mathematics and Science score the lowest at 17% each. The biggest difference (28%) is between French and Mathematics/Science (45%/17% respectively). Over all 500 grades, 27% were at A/A*.

3 School A outperforms School B in all subjects except for French. The highest percentage A/A* grades are for English Language in School A (51%) and the lowest for Mathematics and Science equally in School B (17%). The difference is most marked in Mathematics and Science, where over twice as many grades (39% and 41%) are at A/A* in School A compare to School B (17%). The schools differ by just 7% in English Literature (School A 39% and School B 26%). In French, School B has 50% more A/A*% grades than School A (45% and 30% respectively). Although School A's grades are higher, in both schools, students perform similarly in Mathematics and Science. Apart from that the differences outweigh the similarities.

Construct a histogram and a frequency polygon

1

Class interval of study time in hours	1–3	4–6	7–9	10–12	13–15	16–18
Frequency	7	10	20	26	14	4

2

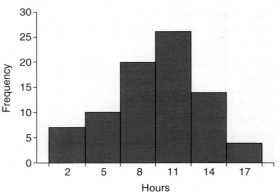

Histogram Showing Hours Spent Preparing for an Exam

The majority of students spend 10–12 hours preparing for an exam. Over half (46/81) spend between 7 and 12 hours preparing for an exam. A minority of 4 spend 16–18 hours preparing, fewer than those 7 who spend just 1–3 hours revising. The histogram is very slightly negatively skewed with a little over half the scores occurring towards the higher end of the scale, but this is not marked. It could be argued that the distribution of scores appears to be normal with a majority of scores occurring in the middle section of the scale and fewer at each of the tails.

3

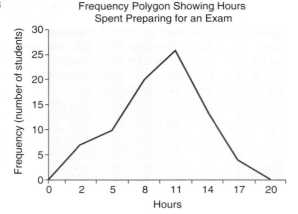

Frequency Polygon Showing Hours Spent Preparing for an Exam

(y-axis: Frequency (number of students); x-axis: Hours)

4 The interpretation of these graphs would be similar to answer 3 above. It is encouraging to see that all students spend some time working but, for a teacher, this is only useful in a practical context. The teacher would have an idea about what constituted reasonable effort for the exam in question and would be interested in whether effort was related to achievement. This would be helpful when advising students about how much effort they need to invest in the future.

5 They should be the same. This illustrates the point made in the chapter (on p.561) that the area of histogram bars and under a frequency polygon are meaningful.

Construct a scattergram

1 Notice that the axes have been started from 20 to eliminate white space.

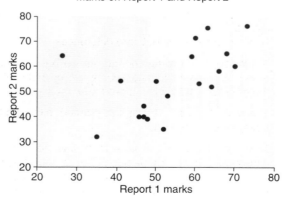

Scattergram to Show the Relationship Between Marks on Report 1 and Report 2

(y-axis: Report 2 marks; x-axis: Report 1 marks)

2 The pattern of scatter seems to show an imperfect positive correlation, but there is one outlier in the top left.

3 It is likely to be about +.60

4 Outliers need special consideration. It may be that you can explain the anomaly and have grounds to discard the data. If not, it could be included and its effect noted. Alternatively, more data could be gathered to see if the pattern becomes clearer.

5 The correlation coefficient would be increased, but not by a great deal. In a larger data set it would have little or no effect.

Probability values, p. 564

Less than or equal to 1%

Less than 0.5%

Less than or equal to 0.1%

Defining a population, p. 564

Clearly you would want to select a sample from British eight-year-olds but think carefully about what being eight years old and British means. A seven-year-old is in the eighth year of life and, on their eighth birthday, begins their ninth year. By eight-years-old we usually mean the latter. The concept of 'Britishness' is rather more complex. It can be by birth, by descent, by adoption, by registration or by naturalization, therefore, place of birth and first language would be considerations.

Important selection criteria will also be determined by the IQ test you intend to use. You would need to find out about the characteristics of the eight-year-old children who initially provided the data on which it was standardized. This information will be provided in the test manual and will determine which children have the physical and intellectual ability to take the test.

Using measurement scales in practice, p. 566

To qualify as ratio data, scores should have magnitude, equal intervals and absolute zero. To qualify as interval data they need to have magnitude and equal intervals but not an absolute zero. To be ordinal they just need to have magnitude. In practice, the distinction between interval and ratio measurement when choosing statistical procedures is immaterial since both types of scale are suitable.

Measuring intelligence

It is easy to argue that IQ scores are at least ordinal as test-takers can score more than, less than or the same points as each other and so can be placed in rank order. It could be argued that the intervals between points are equal and there is absolute zero with certain kinds of IQ scale, especially if scores depend on physical measurement, such as mental speed, but measurement is rarely that precise. So really, you cannot answer this question unless you know how IQ has been measured!

Measuring motivation

No, a psychologist cannot claim Person A is twice as motivated as Person B as an ordinal scale shows only that B is less motivated than A by 25 scale points. As an ordinal scale does not have equal intervals or an absolute zero, it is not possible to make meaningful statements in the form of ratio statements.

Choosing the right test, p. 566

1 Chi-squared test

2 Mann-Whitney U test

3 Spearman's *rho*

4 Wilcoxon test

Carrying out statistical tests, p. 572

1 Steps 1 to 3

Table 17.6 IQ scores after drinking regular or decaffeinated of coffee

P	Regular coffee	Rank order	P	Decaff coffee	Rank order
1	106	6	11	97	1.5
2	108	7.5	12	97	1.5
3	110	10.5	13	100	3
4	113	12.5	14	103	4
5	117	15	15	105	5
6	119	16	16	108	7.5
7	120	17	17	109	9
8	122	18	18	110	10.5
9	128	19	19	113	12.5
10	130	20	20	116	14
					T = 68.5

Step 4

$$U = N_1 N_2 + \frac{N_1(N_1 + 1)}{2} - T$$

$$U = 10 \cdot 10 + \frac{10(10 + 1)}{2} - 68.5$$

$$U = 100 + 55 - 68.5$$

$$U = 86.5$$

Step 5

$$U' = N_1 N_2 - U$$

$$U' = 100 - 86.5$$

$$U' = 13.5$$

Step 6

Select the smaller of U' *or* U. In this case it is 13.5.

Step 7

Select a one-tailed p level of .05 on the grounds that caffeine could improve alertness and mental speed. This means using Table 4 in the Appendices. Where N1 and N2 both equal 10, the critical value is 27. As U is less than this, we can conclude that the null hypothesis can be rejected. The data table indicates that regular coffee scores occupy higher ranks than the decaffeinated coffee scores and this is in line with a directional prediction. Calculation of the medians (Regular = 118, Decaff = 106.5) confirms this. If we can be confident that the presence or absence of caffeine was the only difference between the two groups of participants, it would appear that this is responsible for the difference in outcome. To be really sure, we should have taken baseline IQ measures without coffee of any kind and compared these to the experimental data. It could be that a warm drink is relaxing and actually depresses scores compared to baseline and caffeine simply protects from this. Comparison to baseline data would enable us to check this possibility out.

2 Steps 1 to 3

Table 17.1 Total A and A* grades by subject

Subject	School A	School B	Difference	Rank order
English Language	51	30	21	3
English Literature	39	26	13	1
Science	41	17	24	5
Mathematics	39	17	22	4
French	30	45	−15	2

Step 4

Sum of ranks for differences with a + sign:

3 + 1 + 5 + 4 = 13

Sum of ranks for differences with a – sign: 2

T = 2

Step 5

Number of pairs without zero differences = 5

A two-tailed test is appropriate as we have no prior reason for assuming one school will be better than the other. $p = .05$ is also appropriate.

The critical value = 0. This is assumed, although the table does not show it.

T is not equal to or less than this so the null hypothesis cannot be rejected: T = 2, p > .05 (two tailed). This non-significant result is surprising as the raw data give the opposite impression but this is a risk in small samples. French results buck the trend and have a disproportionate effect.

3 Step 1

The scattergram constructed earlier showed an outlier. We do not have a good reason to discard it, so should proceed with the full data set.

Steps 2 to 6

Table 17.3 Marks of 20 students for two practical reports

Student	Report 1	Rank 1	Report 2	Rank 2	d	d²
1	64	16	52	9	7.00	49.00
2	50	9	54	11.5	-2.50	6.25
3	68	18	65	17	1.00	1.00
4	48	7.5	39	3.5	4.00	16.00
5	47	5.5	44	7	-1.50	2.25
6	61	14	53	10	4.00	16.00
7	35	2	32	1	1.00	1.00
8	41	3	54	11.5	-8.50	72.25
9	66	17	58	13	4.00	16.00
10	47	5.5	40	5.5	.00	.00
11	26	1	64	15.5	-14.50	210.25
12	59	12	64	15.5	-3.50	12.25
13	52	10	35	2	8.00	64.00
14	70	19	60	14	5.00	25.00
15	53	11	48	8	3.00	9.00
16	46	4	40	5.5	-1.50	2.25
17	73	20	76	20	.00	.00 18
60	13	71	18	-5.0	0	25.00
19	48	7.5	39	3.5	4.00	16.00
20	63	15	75	19	-4.00	16.00

$$\Sigma d^2\ 559.5$$

Step 7

$$r_s = 1 - \frac{6\Sigma d^2}{N(N_2 - 1)}$$

$$r_s = 1 - \frac{3357}{7980}$$

$$r_s = 1 - 0.42$$

$$r_s = .58$$

Step 8

Consult the table in Appendix 5 to obtain the critical values of r_s. We need to know:

(a) the value of N (the number of pairs of scores). Here, N = 20

(b) whether a one-tailed or two-tailed test is required. In this case, let us assume a one-tailed test, that is, that students perform consistently across the two assignments and that p = .05 is acceptable.

The critical value = .38. As the calculated r_s exceeds this value the null hypothesis can be rejected:

$$r_s = .58, p < .05 \text{ (one-tailed)}$$

In fact r_s exceeds the critical value at p = .005 as well, so we could say that p < .005 instead of < .05. This shows that, if the null hypothesis were true we would see our result five times in a 1000. The result suggests that students' performance is consistent across the two occasions, but we don't know the precise reason for this. It could indicate consistent ability or effort or a combination of both.

When the analysis is run without the outlier, the correlation coefficient increases to .72. If the tutor could identify the student concerned and, perhaps, find that there were exceptional circumstances at the time report 1 was produced, there could be grounds for discarding that pair of scores.

4 **Step 1 Observed frequencies**

	Subject			Row totals
Gender	Geography	History	Religious studies	
Male	20	28	15	63
Female	22	17	27	66
Column totals	42	45	42	Grand total 129

Step 2 Expected frequencies

	Subject		
Gender	Geography	History	Religious studies
Male	20.51	21.98	20.51
Female	21.49	23.02	21.49

Step 3 Observed frequency – Expected frequency for each cell

20 – 20.51 = -0.51
28 – 21.98 = 6.02
15 – 20.51 = -5.51
22 – 21.49 = 0.51
17 – 23.02 = -6.02
27 – 21.49 = 5.51

Step 4 (O – E)² for each cell

0.26
36.24
30.36
0.26
36.24
30.36

Step 5 (O – E)²/E for each cell

0.26/20.51 = 0.01
36.24/21.98 = 1.65
30.36/20.51 = 1.48

$0.26/21.49 = 0.01$
$36.24/23.02 = 1.57$
$30.36/21.49 = 1.41$

Step 6 Add together the answers from Step 5
$^2 = 6.13$

Step 7 Calculate the df
df = (Rows − 1) × (Columns − 1)
df = (2 − 1) × (3 − 1)
df = 1 × 2 = 2

Step 8
With 2 df and at the .05 level for a two-tailed test, the critical value is 5.99. As the calculated value of 6.13 exceeds this, it is possible to reject the null hypothesis. The result shows that there is a significant association between gender and subject choice.

$^2 = 6.13$, $p < .05$ (two-tailed test)

A bar graph showing the percentage of males and females in each subject would help us to understand the effect but, as the totals for each subject are similar, we can hazard a guess that Geography would show a fairly even split while History would attract more males than females and Religious Studies would attract more females than males. Interestingly, research has linked this to gender in that Geography tends to attract androgynous types, History attracts more masculine types and Religious Studies attracts more feminine types.

Content analysis of TV advertisements, p. 573

When you have collected your data, follow the procedure for calculating and assessing the chi squared statistic. You could also draw a clustered bar chart with role on the horizontal axis. Calculate the percentage of dependent characters that were male or female and plot these as a pair of bars. Repeat this with the other two categories until you have three pairs of bars on the chart. Use this to help you interpret the test result.

Continuing thematic analysis, p. 575

Here are some 'Consequences of actions'. These might subsequently be further subdivided into consequences of vaccinating or not vaccinating.

Line 3   …autism and that…

Line 5–6   …how children can go deaf or blind or even die…

Line 7–8   …herd immunity / and how a few unvaccinated babies / can upset the whole thing./ '

Line 12   How they scream when it happens though.

Line 14   …and then anxiously watching them like a hawk for the whole of the next week/…

Imitation of film-mediated aggressive models, p. 579

1 *The Journal of Abnormal and Social Psychology*

2 No background studies are mentioned explicitly.
A general hypothesis is stated.
Experimental conditions are mentioned but not the design.
The sample is not explicitly described. The setting is described in general terms.
Findings are described in general, but not in statistical terms.
A conclusion is drawn but no implication is offered.

3 The footnote on page 3 names the National Institute of Health and Stanford University. These funding bodies would only finance high-quality research.

4 The press – San Francisco Chronicle – this is probably a secondary account of a crime written by a journalist.

The research literature (e.g. Bandura and Huston 1961) is a primary source of which Bandura himself was an author.

Books (e.g. Mowrer 1960) which would contain both primary and secondary source material.

5 '… subjects who manifest high aggression anxiety would perform significantly less imitative and non-imitative aggression than subjects who display little anxiety over aggression' (p.4)

'…subjects who observed aggressive models would display significantly more aggression when subsequently frustrated than subjects who were equally frustrated but who had no exposure to models exhibiting aggression' (p.4)

6 Fully informed parental consent would have been needed, especially as frustration and deception was involved.
Protection of the children from harm e.g. adverse consequences of having participated in the study.

7 The control condition was compared to conditions with a real-life model, a filmed model and a cartoon style filmed model (p.4).

8 Matched pairs (p.4).

9 Children were observed through a one-way mirror in the test room for 5-second intervals over 20 minutes, yielding 240 observations per child during which behaviour was categorized according to a predetermined checklist (pp.5–6).

10 Most aggressive: boys who observed a real life male model (mean aggression score = 131.8.)

11 Least aggressive: control group girls (mean aggression score = 36.4).

12 Live vs. control, film vs.control and cartoon vs. control.

13 The authors conclude: '…the influence of models in promoting social learning is determined, in part, by the sex appropriateness of the model's behaviour' (p. 8).

- Lovaas (1961) is supportive and Schramm *et al.* (1961) is not supportive (p.9).
- In the opening paragraph of the discussion, the authors highlight the strength of the effect aggressive human and cartoon aggression on film were nearly twice as aggressive as controls.
- There was a failure to link children's predisposition to aggression and their aggression in the experimental context. This may have been due to weaknesses in the predictor measures (p.10).
- '… a good deal of human imitative learning can occur without any reinforcers delivered either to the model or the observer' (p.11).
- A test of the effect of vicarious reinforcement on imitation was planned in which children will observe adult models being reinforced or unrewarded for their behaviour.

A qualitative study of GPs' views of treating obesity, p. 579

1 *The British Journal of General Practice.* This professional journal is clearly aimed at GPs, but is also of interest to health psychologists.

2 The acknowledgements state that the work was carried out as part of a Masters degree, which was supervized by Professor Jane Ogden. Incidentally, the journal is a respected, peer-reviewed publication (p.754).

3 The journal's house style requires the authors to present the abstract under sub-headings, which correspond closely to the advice given earlier in the chapter.

4 The introduction draws on a variety of primary and secondary sources such as Ogden's own research papers, others' research papers, and reports from Government organizations and committees. Bandura's introduction is built on a similarly credible body of evidence.

5 The authors explicitly state that quantitative research has not addressed the issue they are interested in, so a hypothesis is inappropriate. They say they want to use '…qualitative methods to explore in-depth how GPs feel about obesity within the context of their own attempts at management and their own interactions with obese patients' (p.751).

6 The ethics committee that approved the research is named on p.754. Bandura *et al.* would also have had ethical approval for their work, but would not have needed to declare it openly as is now required.

7 The method sections in the two papers are very similar in structure, although they differ in content and detail.

8 Semi-structured interviews were used to collect the data, which were then transcribed into text form.

9 This is where the greatest difference between the two kinds of report lies. Quantitative data can be tabulated and treated statistically. Epstein and Ogden have used a technique for analysing textual data called Interpretative Phenomenological Analysis. They use chunks of text as evidence for the findings they lay claim to in this section and use it to achieve their aim to explore the research issue.

10 The layout of the paper makes it very obvious that these points have been covered.

Glossary

Ablation: surgical removal of brain tissue.

Absolute zero: a quality of a measurement scale such that zero signifies absolutely nothing and below which it is impossible to go. This is in contrast to other scales, such as degrees centigrade on which zero signifies a temperature below which there are minus values.

Accommodation: the process of modifying an existing schema by expanding it or creating a new one when new information, a new object or a new situation cannot be assimilated into the original schema.

Aggression: the delivery of an aversive stimulus from one person to another, with intent to harm and with an expectation of causing such harm, when the other person is motivated to escape or avoid the stimulus (Geen, 1990).

Agoraphobia: a fear and avoidance of public places.

Adaptive response (or characteristic): an evolved behaviour (or trait) that increases the likelihood of the individual's survival and successful reproduction.

Addictive personality: a concept that some (usually lay people) use to explain why some people are more prone to addiction than others. It also suggests nthat some people will inevitably become dependent on drug taking or some other activity because of a personality fault.

Alien abduction: alleged phenomenon of individuals being taken against their will by extraterrestrial beings, often involving them being taken on board spaceships and subjected to medical examination.

Alpha bias: the tendency of some theories and research to assume real and enduring differences between men and women – for example, by overvaluing or devaluing women.

Alpha-biased: refers to theories and research which assume real and enduring differences between men and women. Sometimes alpha biased theories heighten the value of women, and sometimes they are used to devalue women.

Alternative hypothesis (may also be referred to as the **research hypothesis** or, in an experiment, the **experimental hypothesis**): states that something other than chance variation has determined the results obtained. In a well-designed experiment, this should be due to the effect of the independent variable.

Altruistic: helping another person with no personal gain and some cost to the person doing the helping.

Androcentric: refers to the tendency of some theories to offer an interpretation of women, based on an understanding of the lives of men (i.e. a male perspective).

Androcentrism: a view of human behaviour that is based on and concerning males only.

Androgyny: the tendency in a female body to approximate to that of a male and vice versa.

Anomalistic psychology: sub-discipline of psychology primarily concerned with developing and testing non-paranormal explanations for ostensibly paranormal experiences and related beliefs.

Anorexia nervosa: a form of eating disorder that involves under-eating and weight loss (see also **restricting anorexia** and **binge eating/purging anorexia**).

Antagonists: a drug which 'acts against' or blocks the action of a naturally occurring substance in the body. For example, antipsychotic drugs work by blocking receptors for the neurotransmitter dopamine, thus preventing it from stimulating post-synaptic nerve cells.

Anti-anxiety drugs: minor tranquillizers designed to reduce levels of anxiety.

Anxiety disorders: the most common of adult mental disorders, characterized by such severe anxiety and fear that the sufferer cannot lead a normal life. Phobic disorder is the most common type of anxiety disorder.

Anxious/ambivalent attachment – someone who both seeks and rejects intimacy and social interaction.

Approaches: in psychology the term 'approach' refers to what was once called a 'school of thought' – a group of psychologists who share a common way of thinking about things and share common assumptions and characteristic methods for studying phenomena.

Appropriateness of a therapy: refers to both the effectiveness of the treatment in producing a cure for or improvement in the condition and the suitability of the therapy e.g. in terms of its side effects and the ethical issues it raises.

Arboreal: tree-living.

Arousal threshold: a measure of how hard it is to wake someone up.

Arranged marriage: although there are many variations, the traditional arranged marriage is one in which the parents choose a bride or bridegroom for their son or daughter.

Assimilation: the process of fitting new information and experiences into existing schemas (i.e. into what a child already knows and understands).

Astrology: the notion that the position of celestial bodies at the time of one's birth can influence one's personality and events in one's life.

Attachment disorder: a child is unable to form healthy social relationships, particularly with a primary caregiver and eventually with other adults.

Attachment theory: a strong emotional and reciprocal bond between two people, especially between an infant and its caregiver(s). Attachments serve to maintain proximity between infant and caregiver because each experiences distress when separated.

Attitudes: beliefs that people hold about specific aspects of their world but which also involve an evaluative component (i.e. favourable/positive or unfavourable/negative feelings).

Attribution (of causality): the way in which we infer the causes of our own or another person's behaviour according to a set of cognitive rules and biases. As a result of these strategies we decide whether a person's behaviour is caused by their own stable characteristics, or whether it is a result of situational influences.

Atypical antipsychotic drugs: sometimes called second-generation antipsychotic drugs, they work on both serotonin and dopamine receptors in the treatment of schizophrenia.

Autoganzfeld: improved version of the ganzfeld technique which attempts to minimize the possibility of human bias by automating procedures under computer control wherever possible.

Autonomic nervous system (ANS): part of the nervous system that maintains the normal functioning of the body's inner environment. The ANS has two sub-divisions: (a) the sympathetic division whose activity mobilizes energy resources and prepares the body for action, and (b) the parasympathetic division whose activity tends to conserve the body's energy resources and restore inner calm.

Avoidant attachment style: an attachment style characterized by a suppression of attachment needs, based on the fact that previous attempts to be intimate have been rebuffed. Individuals with this attachment style find it difficult to develop intimate relationships.

Barnum effect: the tendency for people to accept vague, ambiguous and general statements as descriptive of their unique personalities.

Behavioural approach: concerned only with behaviour that can be observed, the view that all behaviour can be explained in terms of learning and the environment (i.e. nurture rather than nature).

Behavioural explanations (of mental disorders): the view that mental disorders are caused by maladaptive, learned responses through the processes of classical and operant conditioning and social learning.

Behavioural therapies: therapeutic techniques of changing behaviour that are based on the principles of classical conditioning. The term 'behaviour modification' is more usually used for techniques derived from operant conditioning.

Beta bias: the tendency of some theories and research to ignore or minimize differences between men and women.

Beta-biased: the tendency of some theories to ignore or minimize differences between men and women. They have done this either by ignoring questions about the lives of women or by assuming that findings from studies of men apply equally well to women.

Bias: a leaning in a particular direction, a systematic distortion in one's attitudes and beliefs based on prejudices or pre-existing ideas.

Binge eating/purging anorexia: a form of anorexia that involves episodes of restricted eating, followed by episodes of bingeing and/or purging through self-induced vomiting, the misuse of laxatives, diuretics or enemas.

Biochemistry: the study of chemical events within the body. In the context of psychopathology, the biochemical approach is particularly concerned with the role of neurotransmitters in the brain (chemical messengers that transmit impulses between adjacent nerve cells).

Biological approach: the view that behaviour can be explained in terms of physiological, genetic or evolutionary factors.

Biological explanations (of mental disorders): the view that mental disorders are caused by physical factors such as genes or biochemistry.

Biological rhythms: cycles of activity that occur with some regularity in an organism. Infradian rhythms occur less than once a day (e.g. human menstrual cycle), circadian rhythms repeat themselves every 24 hours (e.g. sleep/waking cycle), and ultradian rhythms more than once a day (e.g. stages of sleep during one night).

Biological (somatic) therapies: an approach to the treatment of mental disorders that relies on the use of physical or chemical methods.

Biopsychosocial approach: an eclectic approach to studying human behaviour that incorporates the best strands of contemporary psychology, biology and sociology; it assumes that human behaviour is multifaceted and strongly influenced by contextual factors that cannot be encompassed by any single theoretical perspective.

Biosocial model: an alternative evolutionary theory to that proposed by Darwin whereby psychological sex differences are a product of physical sex differences. There is a denouncement of adaptive pressures such as natural and sexual selection to account for sex role differences.

Bipolar depression/disorder (manic-depressive disorder): a mood disorder characterized by extremes of mania and depression.

Body mass index (BMI): a measure of the ratio between a person's weight (in kilograms) and their height (in metres) squared (i.e. weight in kg/height in metres) which is used to assess which category a person belongs to in terms of their body weight (normal weight, overweight, clinical obesity or severe obesity).

Bottom-up/direct theory of perception: proposes that there is sufficient information in the sensory (visual) stimulus to allow us to make sense of our environment without the involvement of stored knowledge or problem-solving skills.

Bulimia (sometimes referred to as bulimia nervosa): an eating disorder characterized by a recurrent cycle of bingeing (eating a lot of food in a short period of time) and purging in order to try to get rid of the food (e.g. by vomiting, taking laxatives or exercising excessively).

Cataplexy: a condition where the skeletal muscles suddenly give way as a person collapses and falls asleep. Cataplexy most frequently follows strong emotions such as laughter, excitement or rage.

Catharsis: the process in psychoanalysis whereby a client is helped to recall previously repressed conflicts and is encouraged to work through them by examining and dealing with them in the safety of the consulting room, and, in so doing, release the power they exert over behaviour.

CAT (computed axial tomography) scans: *see* **CT scans**.

Chemoreceptors: specialized neurons (brain cells) that detect specific chemicals in the blood.

Chemotherapy: treatment by using drugs.

Cingulotomy: a procedure to destroy a small area of tissue in the cingulated gyrus, which links the prefrontal cortex to the limbic system of the brain. The limbic system is involved in emotion and behaviour.

Circadian rhythm: (from the Latin words *circa* 'about' and *dies*, 'day') a biological rhythm that takes place over approximately 24 hours, such as sleep/wake cycle.

Clairvoyance: the ability to pick up information from remote locations without using the known sensory channels.

Classical conditioning: a form of learning where a neutral stimulus is paired with a stimulus that already produces a response, such that, over time, the neutral stimulus also produces that response.

Classification: the act of distributing things into classes or categories of the same type.

Cognition: a person's knowledge, understanding, thoughts or ideas.

Cognitive approach: cognitive psychologists are interested in how mental processes affect behaviour, likening the mind to a computer or an information-processing machine.

Cognitive-behavioural explanation (of mental disorder): an extension of the behavioural explanation to include the role of irrational thinking as a cause of mental disorders.

Cognitive-behavioural therapies: techniques that involve helping clients to identify their negative, irrational thoughts and to replace these with more positive, rational ways of thinking.

Cognitive developmental theory: there are two sub-theories Kohlberg's Gender Consistency Theory and Gender Schema Theory. Both approaches explain the way in which people are active agents and masters of their own gender-role socialisation.

Cognitive dissonance: a condition of conflict or anxiety resulting from inconsistency between one's beliefs and one's actions, such as opposing the slaughter of animals and eating meat.

Cognitive dissonance theory: states that when a person behaves in a way that does not fit with an existing attitude or belief, they will experience an unpleasant state of dissonance because the action conflicts (is dissonant) with the belief. To reduce the dissonance, they may later re-evaluate the experience.

Cognitive distortions: according to Beck, these are logical errors commonly found in the thinking of those with depression. They include drawing conclusions on basis of insufficient evidence, making sweeping conclusions on basis of a single event and focusing on a single aspect of a situation and ignoring others.

Cognitive explanations (of mental disorders): the view that mental disorders are caused by disturbed thought processes.

Cognitive therapies: therapies that focus on changing the irrational thinking that is believed to underlie psychological abnormality.

Cognitive triad: according to Beck, the cognitive triad comprises the three components of depression – negative views of self; negative views of the world; negative views about the future.

Cold reading: a technique used by deliberate con artists in order to convince complete strangers that they know all about them.

Collectivist culture (collectivism): a culture that values group loyalty, prefers collective to individual decisions and where the needs of the group outweigh the needs of the individual.

Comparison level: the comparison between the rewards and costs of a reference (i.e. current) relationship and what we have been used to in the past or believe is appropriate given the nature of the relationship.

Comparison level for alternatives: the comparison of the rewards and costs associated with a current relationship and the rewards and costs of possible alternative relationships.

Compulsion: the irresistible urge to carry out repetitive acts ritualistically in order to ward off some imagined dire consequence.

Concordance rate: in a sample of twin pairs, if one twin of each pair has a particular disorder, the concordance rate refers to the number of times that the other twin also shows that disorder. In a sample of 200 pairs of twins, if 90 have the disorder, then the concordance rate is 45 per cent.

Confirmation bias: the seeking or interpreting of evidence in ways that are partial to existing beliefs and expectations.

Confounding variable: a variable, other than the independent variable (IV), that has a systematic effect on the dependent variable and which could distort, mask or replace the effect of the IV.

Conspecifics: individuals who belong to the same species.

Context validity: refers to the extent to which research findings can be generalized to settings other than that used in the original research even though there may be some variation. Psychologists often refer to this as **ecological validity**.

Continuous positive airway pressure (CPAP): a system that provides air under pressure to a person who has difficulty with snoring or sleep apnoea.

Contra-gender: this is the opposite gender.

Control group: this is the group in an experimental design used as a baseline against which to compare the performance of the experimental group.

Correlation: a statistical technique for determining the strength and direction (positive or negative) of a linear relationship between paired samples of data. The correlation coefficient expresses this in a value from $+1.00$ to -1.00.

Cortex: the outer layer of the brain: grey in appearance (hence sometimes called the 'grey matter').

Counter-attitudinal behaviour: any behaviour that is inconsistent with its underlying attitude e.g. believing that racist behaviour is wrong yet behaving in a racist manner.

Counterbalancing: a measure that is routinely applied to repeated measures designs in order to control for possible order effects. In a two-condition experiment the ABBA design is routinely used.

Cross-gender behaviour: this describes behaviour normally exhibited in the opposite gender.

Cross-sectional design (or cross-sectional study or cross-sectional research): research carried out at one point in time and the data gathered on one occasion only. Comparisons between different age groups are achieved by recruiting groups of children at the appropriate ages and testing them at a single time (rather than studying the same participants over time at different ages in a longitudinal study).

CT (computed tomography) scans: a non-invasive, multiple X-ray procedure for creating images of the brain.

Cuckoldry: when a woman deceives her partner into investing in (e.g.

providing for, protecting) offspring conceived with another man.

Cultural schema: cognitive structures that contain knowledge relating to everyday interactions in an individual's cultural environment. Cultural schema guide our behaviour in familiar situations.

Culture: the beliefs, customs and practices that a group of people shares.

Cyberstalking: a form of behaviour in which one person harasses (stalks) their victim using electronic communication, such as e-mail or instant messaging.

Data triangulation: A method of checking on the reliability of research findings that involves collecting a different type of evidence about the same phenomenon to see if there is correspondence between them.

Debate: a discussion where two (or more) contrasting points of view are presented; a formalized system of logical argument.

Deduction (or the deductive process): a logical process involving rules to derive a conclusion from specific premises.

Deindividuation: A psychological state in which individuals have lowered levels of self-evaluation (e.g. when in a crowd or under the influence of alcohol) and decreased concerns about evaluation by others.

Demand characteristics: features of a research situation that participants perceive they must respond to, sometimes leading to changes in behaviour that become a source of extraneous variation in the study.

Dependent variable: in an experiment, the DV is the factor that is affected by the manipulation of the IV. It is the outcome measure in an experiment.

Depression (unipolar disorder): a type of mood disorder where the person experiences feelings of great sadness, worthlessness and guilt, and finds the challenges of life overwhelming.

Descriptive statistics: numerical techniques used to describe or characterize samples of data.

Determinism: the philosophical doctrine that an individual's behaviour is shaped or controlled by internal or external forces rather than an individual's will to do something.

Diabetes (diabetes mellitus): an illness that occurs when the level of glucose (sugar) in a person's blood is higher than normal. There are two forms of diabetes: **Type 1 diabetes** usually occurs in people over 40. Diet, weight control and physical activity are the first-line approaches to treatment. If this is not successful, then tablets are needed or, in some cases, insulin

injections. **Type 2 diabetes** usually develops in children or young people when the body no longer manufactures insulin and therefore the onset of the illness is faster (it is sometimes called early-onset diabetes or insulin-dependent diabetes) and is treated with insulin injections and also dietary restrictions.

Diagnosis: the recognition and identification of a disease or condition by its signs and symptoms

Diagnostic and Statistical Manual (DSM) of Mental Disorders: a classification, definition and description of over 200 mental health disorders which groups disorders in terms of their common features. The latest version is DSM-IV-TR published in 2000.

Diathesis-stress model (of mental disorders): general model of disorders postulating that people develop mental disorders when they possess both a constitutional vulnerability (diathesis) and are exposed to stressful events.

Dilemmas: scenarios used to study moral development. Normally a story/scenario is presented to the participant where he or she is confronted with two possible behavioural choices such that by selecting one violates one set of moral percepts and selecting the other violates another set.

Directional hypothesis: a hypothesis that states the direction of a research outcome, e.g. the mean of sample A is higher than the mean of sample B, or the correlation between A and B is positive.

Disinhibition: overeating which is triggered by a number of factors, such as a preload, anxiety, smoking cessation or alcohol. It reflects the abandonment of control.

Diurnal: active during the day.

Dizygotic (DZ) (fraternal) twins: twins that develop from different zygotes (eggs) and are no more likely to be similar than any pair of siblings.

Dopamine: a neurotransmitter (a chemical messenger used to transmit impulses from one nerve cell to another). The over-activity of dopamine has been linked to schizophrenia.

Double-bind hypothesis: the claim that children may experience confusion, self-doubt and eventual withdrawal if they are given conflicting messages from parents who express care, yet at the same time appear critical.

Double blind peer review: a process whereby two (or more) reviewers evaluate a research paper prior to publication in a reputable academic journal without knowing who wrote the paper.

DSM: see **Diagnostic and Statistical Manual.**

Ecological validity: the extent to which research findings can be generalized to other settings.

Effectiveness of a therapy: refers to how successful a treatment is in improving or removing the symptoms of the disorder being treated.

Egocentrism: a feature of thinking in the young child, characterized by an inability to understand the perspective of another person.

Electroconvulsive therapy (ECT): a treatment involving passing an electrical current through the brain by the application of between 70 and 130 volts which induces a convulsion or epileptic seizure.

Electroencephalography (EEG): In electroencephalography electrodes attached to the scalp record the gross electrical activity of the brain and allow researchers to classify different levels of arousal.

Empathy: the ability to understand another person's emotions.

Empirical evidence: a type of evidence that can be observed, experienced or measured through the human senses.

Empirical methods: methods that rely on sensory data gathered through observation, experience or measurement using the human senses.

Empiricism: the name given to the belief that the only source of true knowledge is through our senses, and that careful observation and measurement are needed to generate this type of knowledge.

Endogenous pacemakers: the scientific term for 'biological clock'. Brain mechanisms that control an animal's cycles.

Environmental determinism: an approach that views the source of determinism as being outside the individual.

Environment of evolutionary adaptiveness (EEA): the environment to which a species is adapted and the set of selection pressures that operated at that time. The EEA is generally regarded to be the African Savannah, sometime between 10 000 and five million years ago.

Epidemiological data: data about why, when and where diseases occur within human communities.

Equal intervals: A property of a measurement scale such that the distance between whole units on a scale is the same amount irrespective of where the unit is on the scale e.g. the distance between 1 and 2 cm is the same as the distance between 21 and 22 cm.

Equilibration: a state of equilibrium or balance is attained through the processes of assimilation and accommodation as described by Piaget. This enables a natural balance between the individual and the world.

Equity theory: a theory of relationships which stresses that people strive to achieve fairness in their relationships and feel distressed if they perceive unfairness.

Estrocentrism: a view of human behaviour that is based on and concerning females.

Ethical guidelines: prescriptive guidance on the conduct of psychologists in research and practice. These represent the key issues that face psychologists in their work with humans and animals, and are regularly updated by the organizations that issue them.

Ethics: morals are that which is deemed right or wrong in terms of human behaviour; ethics are the moral standards and rules of conduct used by a group of professionals such as doctors, lawyers or psychologists.

Ethnocentrism: the term used to describe the belief in the superiority of one's own ethnic and cultural group.

Ethnographic approach: this is a qualitative method employed primarily by social anthropologists. It involves the observation techniques and meticulous recording of observations of different peoples using a diary format.

Evolutionary approach: the view that behaviours can be explained in terms of the principles of natural selection, i.e. any behaviour that is adaptive is more likely to be perpetuated in future generations. Selection is made at the level of the genes.

Exposure and response prevention (ERP): a technique to stop people carrying out compulsive behaviours. Clients are repeatedly exposed to situations that make them anxious, but they are encouraged to avoid carrying out the 'safety' rituals (compulsive behaviours) that they previously used to reduce anxiety.

Experimental group: a group of participants who are exposed to the treatment/intervention that is being investigated through the manipulation of an independent variable in experimental research.

Experimenter effect: a term used to describe a situation where one experimenter consistently obtains significant positive results but another, apparently following the same procedures, consistently fails to replicate these results.

Experimenter reliability: this refers to the extent to which an experimenter is consistent in the way in which experimental procedures are carried out.

Expressed emotion (EE): in the context of schizophrenia, this refers to the amount of hostility and criticism that other people (often family members) direct towards the person with schizophrenia.

External reliability: refers to the consistency of a measure from one occasion to the other.

External validity: the extent to which findings can be generalized across people (others who were not involved in the original research), places (other contexts beyond the research setting) and times.

Extraneous variable: an uncontrolled source of variation (or 'noise') in a research study that needs to be kept within reasonable limits in order not to obscure the effect that is being investigated.

Extrasensory perception (ESP): the alleged ability to receive information without the use of the known sensory channels, often sub-divided into telepathy, clairvoyance, and precognition.

Face recognition: an area of psychological research concerned with pattern recognition, which investigates how we process and recognize faces.

False-belief tasks: a type of task used to test for theory of mind; to perform these tasks successfully, children need to understand that there can be different sets of beliefs (their own beliefs based on what they have seen or reasoned) and the beliefs of others (based on what they have seen and reasoned). The Sally-Anne task is a well-known example of a false-belief task.

Falsifiability: the principle that good scientific theories can potentially be disproved by empirical evidence.

Fatal familial insomnia: a genetic sleep disorder, which strikes during middle age and results in death. It affects an area of the brain responsible for sleep, the thalamus. Sleep, blood pressure and body core temperature are all affected by the interruption of the body's circadian rhythms which is a direct result of the degeneration of the thalamus.

Femininity: a social concept to describe a cluster of traits typifying traditional female qualities and behaviour.

Fitness: a measure of the number of offspring left behind by an individual compared to the number of offspring left behind by other members of the same species.

Flooding: a treatment for phobic disorder based on classical conditioning. The client is exposed to a phobic object or situation in a non-graded manner (in contrast to systematic desensitization) with no

attempt to reduce prior anxiety and remains there till anxiety decreases.

fMRI (functional magnetic resonance imaging): a form of magnetic resonance imaging (neuroimaging) used to study activity in the brain. It shows which areas of the brain are most active during specific mental operations. (*See also* **Imaging techniques** and **MRI**.)

Formal socializing agents: these are institutions such as education and law within a given society that reinforce expectations, customs, mores and the behaviour of citizens.

Freewill: the philosophical doctrine that individuals are capable of making their own choices, i.e. that they are self-determining and free from coercion.

Functional magnetic resonance imaging (fMRI): *see* fMRI.

Ganzfeld technique: A technique used to test for telepathy in which a sender attempts to mentally transmit the identity of a randomly selected target (usually a picture or a video clip) to a receiver who is perceptually deprived.

Gender: the social/psychological element of a person's sex (masculinity and femininity) as distinct from the biological category of male and female.

Gender bias: the treatment of men and women in psychological research and /or theory in a way which offers a view of behaviour and experience that might not fully represent the characteristics of both genders.

Gender bias: the treatment of men and women in psychological research and/or theory in a way which offers a view of behaviour and experience that may not adequately represent the characteristics of both genders.

Gender consistency theory: this is one approach of the cognitive-developmental theory. Kohlberg coined the term and claims that there are stages which children must go through in order to fully understand their gender. These sages are in the order of gender identity, gender stability and gender consistency. Children will imitate same-sex models as a means to understanding.

Gender consistency: a concept used to describe when children have achieved the knowledge that their sex will not change even if they dress up as the opposite sex.

Gender differences: this is used to point out that there are differences of behaviour, personality and cognition between boys and girls and men and women as a consequence of their gender roles.

Gender dysphoria: this is a gender identity disorder, where the individual feels that he or she was born to the

wrong sex. This can be so disturbing that they seek sex reassignment to change the external genitalia and secondary sexual characteristics to the desired sex.

Gender identity: a concept used to describe when children understand which sex they are.

Gender labelling: this occurs when people, usually parents, define what and how their baby boys and girls should appear and behave. Parents may label their children by deciding to dress their girls in pink and boys in blue.

Gender role: a set of expectations that describe how males and females should think, act and feel.

Gender schema theory: this is a cognitive-developmental theory. Martin and Halverson coined the term and claim that children develop (concept clusters such as stereotypes) as soon as they recognize that there is a difference between men and women.

Gender stability: a concept used to describe when children understand that their sex will remain the same throughout their life.

Gender stereotypes: these are social categories enveloping a host of characteristics. In the case of gender stereotypes being female will conjure up a series of 'typical' traits of what it is to be female – likewise for males.

Gender-typed play behaviour: this is play behaviour specific to males or to females only. So rough and tumble games are normally associated with play in boys and not girls.

Generalizability: the ability of researchers to offer a justifiable extension of their findings beyond the actual sample of participants used to a wider population of people.

Genetic: refers to influences that are biologically inherited in the form of genes, rather than learned as a result of experience.

Genetics: the part of biological science concerned with the study of heredity and the role of genes throughout one's life.

Genotype: the genetic makeup, as distinguished from the physical appearance, of an organism or a group of organisms.

Group display: a type of behaviour which is adopted by the group as a whole or by individuals within the group to signal group membership, e.g. aggressive responses to outsiders and ritualized behaviours performed uniquely by group members.

Hard sell: a persuasive and highly pressured approach used to sell a product or service. Hard sell advertising usually focuses on the merits of a particular product, therefore is likely to involve central route processing.

Hawthorne effect: the effect on human performance resulting from the participants' knowledge that they are being observed or studied.

Health belief model: an example of a social cognition model that consists of different cognitions and is used to understand and predict health-related behaviours such as diet and smoking.

Heuristics: 'rules of thumb' that are used cognitively by people to simplify decision-making.

Holistic approach: an approach to explaining behaviour or experience that emphasizes the whole person (or situation) rather than individual elements. This approach was adopted by Gestalt psychologists to explain the recognition of objects based on the overall shape and structure of the object rather than on the constituent parts.

Holistic processing: in the area of face recognition, this refers to processing based on the overall shape and structure, rather than on individual elements of the face.

Homeostasis: the notion that the body is constantly striving to achieve an optimal physiological state (e.g. body temperature). Homeostasis is maintained via a negative feedback loop, which assumes that any given bodily variable has a set point (or range) and the actual value of this variable is compared by the body to where it should be and adjusted accordingly.

Hopelessness theory of depression: a cognitive theory, stating that depression rises from a 'maladaptive attributional style' where negative events are attributed to internal, stable and global causes. See attribution (of causality).

Hormones: chemicals released by the endocrine system into general circulation.

Hypnagogic hallucinations: dreamlike experiences that occur when still awake and are often difficult to distinguish from reality. Hypnagogic hallucinations most frequently occur around the onset of sleep.

Hypocretin: a protein in the brain that is involved in the regulation of sleep. People that have low levels of hypocretin often develop narcolepsy.

Hypothalamus: an area of the brain involved in motivation and lying a little behind the eyes.

Hypothesis: a precisely worded, testable statement formulated by a researcher to indicate the expected outcome of a study.

Hypothetico-deductive method: a method of recording observations, developing explanatory theory and testing hypotheses derived from the theory in order to test the theory.

ICD: *see* **International Classification of Disorders**.

Imaging techniques: *see* **CT, fMRI, MEG, MRI** and **PET** scans.

Implosion therapy: a treatment for phobic disorder. The technique is the same as that for flooding except that the therapy is conducted *in vitro* (using imagination) rather than *in vivo* (a real-life situation).

Inclusive fitness: a measure of how successful individuals are in passing on a high proportion of their genes to succeeding generations. This may be achieved *directly* (through their own offspring) or *indirectly* (by helping close genetic relatives with whom they share a proportion of their genes). The total number of their genes passed on in these ways determines the individual's *inclusive* fitness.

Independent groups design: this type of experimental design involves using different participants in each condition of the experiment.

Independent variable: the variable in an experiment that is deliberately and systematically manipulated by the experimenter in order to observe and measure its effects on a dependent variable.

Individualist culture (individualism): a culture where self-interest and individual rights are promoted, rather than the needs and interests of others.

Inductive analysis: a type of thematic analysis of qualitative textual data which involves approaching the data with no preconceptions about which themes you might find and allows them to emerge as analysis progresses.

Induction (or the inductive process): a process of drawing conclusions and constructing theory from observed data.

Inferential statistics: statistical tests used to analyse samples of data to enable us to infer or draw conclusions about the population from which the sample is drawn.

Infidelity: unfaithfulness, e.g. sexual infidelity – when a man or a woman has sexual relations with someone other than their partner.

Informal socializing agents: these are parents and peers and anyone close to the family who socialize their children according to the expectations, customs, mores and model behaviour expected by the society they live in.

Infradian: rhythmical cycles that occur less often than once a day (*infra* is Latin for 'below'). An example would be the human menstrual cycle.

Initiation rituals: special rituals and requirements for new members of a group. Some initiation rituals are painful and stressful.

Insomnia: problems with sleep patterns and in particular difficulties falling asleep or maintaining sleep. Can be sub-divided into primary insomnia where the main problem is a disrupted sleep pattern and secondary insomnia where the lack of sleep may is the secondary consequence of for example Parkinson's disease.

Institutional aggression: violent behaviour that exists within, and may be a defining feature of, certain institutions and groups. It can also refer to other forms of collective violence *between* social groups (such as the violent behaviour observed in riots and intergroup conflict).

Interactionist approach: an approach adopted, for example, by many developmental psychologists who concentrate on how both nature (inherited characteristics) and nurture (the environment in which the child is raised) interact to shape a child's development.

Internal reliability: the consistency with which measures within a test or measure perform (e.g. the items from a personality test).

Internal validity: the extent to which a test (or measure) tests what it is meant to test (or measure).

Internal working model: an inner representation of the parent–child bond that subsequently becomes an important part of an individual's personality. It serves as a set of expectations about the availability of attachment figures and the likelihood of receiving support from them. This model becomes the basis for all future close relationships during childhood, adolescence and adult life.

International Classification of Disorders (ICD): a classification of physical and psychological disorders published and regularly updated by the World Health Organization. The current edition is ICD-10, published in 1992.

Inter-observer (or inter-rater) reliability: this refers to the extent to which two or more observers (or raters) are consistent when observing the same event.

Interpersonal psychotherapy (IPT): used to treat depression, IPT focuses on interpersonal events (e.g. personal conflicts, long-lasting grief) that seem important in the onset or maintenance of the disorder. IPT combines aspects of psychodynamic and cognitive-behaviour therapy.

Interquartile range: the range of the middle 50 per cent of scores in a set of rank ordered data.

Inter-rater reliability: refers to the consistency with which observers agree on the classification or scoring of the behaviour being observed. Inter-rater reliability between clinicians is achieved when there is significant agreement on a diagnosis for a particular set of symptoms.

Inter-researcher reliability: this refers to the consistency of performance between different researchers.

Interval data: Units of measurement that can be placed in a logical order and the intervals between adjacent units on the scale are equal because they are based on some standard unit of measurement (e.g. the Celsius temperature scale).

Intra-observer (or intra-rater) reliability: the extent to which an observer (or rater) is consistent when observing or scoring the same events on different occasions.

Intra-researcher reliability: this refers to a researcher's own consistency of performance.

Invasive methods: techniques for investigating the brain that involve penetrating through the skull into brain tissue. Examples include electrical stimulation and lesions.

Investigator effects: an undesired effect on the responses of research participants, arising from the researcher's behaviour or expectations (these effects may operate at an unconscious level).

Jealousy: A state of fear or suspicion caused by a real or imagined threat to one's current status. In evolutionary psychology, males are believed to be more vulnerable to *sexual* jealousy (potential loss or infidelity of a sexual partner) and females to *emotional* jealousy (potential loss of access to the male's resources).

Law: a universal scientific principle that holds true at all times and under all circumstances.

Learned helplessness: a psychological state produced as a result of being exposed to uncontrollable events. Observed in people who give up trying to cope because previous attempts have been frustrated and led to failure.

Lesioned: producing a structural change in an organ or tissue as a result of injury, disease or surgical manipulation.

Lesioning: injuring brain tissue, e.g. by heating the top of an implanted electrode so that a small area of tissue is destroyed.

Level of significance: the value between 0 and 1 (typically .05) used by researchers to determine the probability of observing a particular result if the null hypothesis were true.

Longitudinal study: an investigation where participants are studied over an extended period of time.

Longitudinal study - the study of an individual or group of individuals at regular intervals over a relatively long period of time.

Long-term memory (LTM): an unlimited capacity system for storing information for long periods.

Lynch mob: a group of people without legal authority who execute someone for a presumed offence.

Macro-PK: psychokinesis operating on such a scale that the effects are immediately observable.

Magnitude: a property of a measurement scale that allows us to judge values in terms of relative size i.e. larger than, smaller than, the same size.

Masculinity: a social concept to describe a cluster of traits typifying traditional male qualities and behaviour.

Matched pairs design: an experimental design in which participants are paired up on the basis of variables which it is believed need to be controlled. The members of each pair are then randomly allocated to one or other of the experiment's conditions.

Median: a measure of central tendency which is the middle value in a set of data which have been ranked in order of size.

Mean: a measure of central tendency which is the arithmetic average of a sample of scores. It is the sum of scores divided by the number of scores.

Media: various means of communication such as television, radio, and the Internet. The term 'mass media' is also used as an alternative.

Media violence: acts of aggressive behaviour portrayed on television, DVD, computer games and other media. The media effects argument suggests that exposure to such acts of aggression influences viewers to engage in similar acts of aggression in their own lives.

Medium: a person who claims to be able to communicate with the dead.

Mediumship: believed by its adherents to be a form of communication with spirits.

Medulla: the caudal (rear) part of the brain stem.

MEG (magneto-encephalography): non-invasive technique for visualizing (imaging) the brain by recording tiny magnetic fields produced by active neurons.

Meta-analysis: a method of combining a number of studies on the same theme in order to detect trends in the behaviour being studied; this technique is often used in systematic reviews.

Methodology: a way of conducting research in order to test theories and explanations.

Micro-PK: psychokinesis operating in such a way that it can only be demonstrated by statistical analysis of data showing that some distribution of possible outputs had deviated from what would be expected upon the basis of chance alone.

Mindblindness: a term coined by Simon Baron-Cohen (2005) to describe the autistic children's lack of ability to understand other people's minds (i.e. a ToM deficit).

Mind–body problem: the problem of determining the relationship between the physical realm (the body) and the mental realm (the mind).

Mindreaders: a term coined by Simon Baron-Cohen to account for our ability to understand what others may be thinking, their feelings and desires.

Minnesota Model: a treatment programme using a group therapy technique and only ex-addicts as helpers. Groups (e.g. Alcoholics Anonymous, Gamblers Anonymous, Narcotics Anonymous, Overeaters Anonymous, Sexaholics Anonymous) follow a 12-step programme that involves them accepting personal responsibility for their actions. This model views the behaviour as an addiction that cannot be cured but merely arrested.

Mirror neurons: these sensorimotor neurons are located in different areas of the brain but primarily in the premotor cortex and superior temporal sulcus; they are responsible for enabling us to observe actions being carried out and trying to imitate them.

Mode: a measure of central tendency which is the most frequently occurring value in a sample of scores.

Modelling therapy: a treatment for phobic disorder based on social learning theory, in which clients observe the therapist handle the feared object (e.g. spider) with confidence, and thereby lose their fear of the object.

Modes of representation: a term introduced by Jerome Bruner to represent how we mentally represent the world; he identified three different levels: enactive, iconic and symbolic.

Monogamy: the practice of being married to only one partner at a time.

Monozygotic (MZ) (identical) twins: twins that develop from the same zygote (egg) and are therefore genetically identical.

Mood modification: the result of engaging in any behaviour that facilitates a change of mood, e.g. getting aroused (a 'high' or 'buzz') from taking drugs, or engaging in a behaviour to help tranquillize (i.e. escape).

Moral development: the process by which children internalize standards of right and wrong, and ultimately make their own decisions concerning moral issues.

Moral panic: an intense feeling expressed by a large number or people when they feel that something

(such as media violence) is threatening to undermine the social order).

Motion parallax: movement of an object's image across the retina, owing to movements of the observer's head.

MRI (magnetic resonance imaging): a non-invasive technique for picturing (imaging) the brain (or other soft tissue of the body) by subjecting it to a sequence of pulsed radio waves while the head (or other body part) is held in a powerful magnetic field.

Narcolepsy: is a general term used to describe the frequent occurrence of periods of sleepiness throughout the day.

Natural selection: the part of Darwin's theory which states that those animals that are well adapted to their environment will leave behind more offspring than those animals that are less well adapted.

Nature: those aspects of behaviour that are inherited. Nature does not simply refer to abilities present at birth, but to any ability determined by genes, including those that appear through maturation.

Nature–nurture debate: the controversy about the relative contributions of genetic factors (nature) versus environmental factors (nurture) in determining a person's characteristics and abilities.

Near-death experience (NDE): an experience reported by some people who have come close to death or believe themselves to have come close to death, sometimes involving such components as feeling bliss, an out-of-body experience, travelling down a tunnel towards a light, meeting spirits, a life review, and returning to the physical body.

Need for cognition: a personality variable which reflects an individual's preference for, and tendency to engage in effortful cognitive activities.

Negative self-schemas: in Beck's theory of depression, these are a set of beliefs and expectations that are self-blaming and pessimistic.

Neophobia: a fear of new things; used in eating research to describe a fear of novel foods.

Neurotransmitters: chemical messengers (e.g. serotonin and dopamine) that transmit nerve impulses from one nerve cell to another across the synapse (the gap between neurons).

Nocturnal: active during the night.

Nominal data: data on this most basic scale of measurement simply involve distinguishing between different and mutually exclusive categories of a variable (e.g. smokers/non-smokers; male/female; right-handed/left-handed). The category labels are

merely names, so there is no inherent order between the categories.

Non-directional hypothesis: a hypothesis that gives no indication of the direction of the predicted difference or correlation between two variables.

Non-parametric test: a test of statistical significance that does not make any assumptions about the parameters underlying the distribution of the quantitative data (e.g. the data do not have to be normally distributed) and so can be more widely used than parametric tests.

Null hypothesis: a statement that no effect exists; used to state results that do not support the research hypothesis. Under the null hypothesis, the results obtained are more likely to be due to chance variation.

Nurture: aspects of behaviour that are acquired through experience, i.e. are learned from interactions with the physical and social environment.

Obesogenic environment: factors in the environment which promote an unhealthy lifestyle and can ultimately lead to obesity (e.g. cars and fast-food outlets).

Objectivity: a factual stance that is unaffected by beliefs, opinions, feelings or expectations.

Object permanence: the knowledge that things continue to exist when they can no longer be seen.

Observational learning: this is based on Bandura's modelling theory whereby we can learn through watching others – sometimes referred to as vicarious learning.

Obsessions: persistent and recurrent thoughts, images, beliefs and impulses that enter the mind apparently uninvited and that cannot be removed.

Obsessive-compulsive disorder (OCD): a mental disorder characterized by intrusive, unwelcome thoughts (obsessions) and a need to perform repetitive and ritualistic behaviour (compulsions) along with intense anxiety when these behaviours are suppressed.

Oestrus: a regularly occurring period of fertility and sexual receptivity during the reproductive cycle of female mammals. It is generally assumed that women do not display oestrus, but research now suggests that when fertile in their reproductive cycles, women are particularly sexually attracted to a variety of features in men that are indicators of genetic quality.

One-tailed test: A statistical procedure applied to test a directional hypothesis.

Open-ended question – a question for which there is no set answer, thus requiring the respondent to answer in their own words.

Operant conditioning: an explanation of learning that sees the consequences of behaviour as of vital importance to the future appearance of that behaviour. If a behaviour is followed by a desirable consequence, it becomes more frequent; if it is followed by an undesirable consequence, it becomes less frequent.

Opportunity sampling: a way of selecting a group of participants simply because they are available and fit the criteria needed for them to take part in a research study.

Optic tract: the nerve fibres that travel from the eyes to the back of the brain where visual processing begins.

Ordinal data: data on an ordinal scale of measurement can be organized into categories (as for nominal data) but these categories can also be place in a logical order, based on their meaning (e.g. categories used to measure social class). The differences between the various categories on an ordinal scale are not, however, standard.

Outliers: data points that stand out because they are either a lot smaller or a lot larger than the rest of the data set.

Out-of-body experience (OBE): an experience during which a person feels as if their consciousness has left their physical body, often involving looking down on their body and surroundings from above.

Overjustification effect: this occurs when an external incentive (e.g. money) decreases any intrinsic motivation to perform a particular behaviour.

Pair therapy: a psychological intervention involving pairs of children learn, with the guidance of a therapist, to manage a relationship using perspective-taking and negotiation skills appropriate to their age.

Paradigm: a world-view or general theoretical orientation that is accepted by the majority of scientists working in a given discipline; it determines how researchers approach their work and also what is deemed to be acceptable evidence by the research community.

Paradoxical sleep: a recurring sleep state during which dreaming and rapidly shifting eye movements occur.

Parametric test: a more powerful test of statistical significance that makes assumptions about the parameters underlying the distribution of the quantitative data (e.g. the data have to be normally distributed). These assumptions must be satisfied before a parametric test can be used to analyse data.

Parasocial behaviour: when individuals 'interact' with a media representation of a person as if the person were actually present.

Parasocial relationships: a one-sided 'relationship' whereby one person knows a great deal about the other person and feels intense affection for them, yet the recipient of this affection may not be aware of that person's existence. For example, a person feeling they have a friendship or intimate relationship with a television personality, based on the frequent appearance (on the television) of that character in the person's life.

Paranormal: a term that refers to any phenomenon which is beyond explanation in terms of conventional science.

Parapsychology: scientific study of paranormal or ostensibly paranormal phenomena, typically restricted to extrasensory perception, psychokinesis, and evidence relating to life after death.

Parapsychologists: psychologists who apply scientific method to the study paranormal phenomena including ESP and PK and, in some cases the possibility of life after death.

Parental investment: any parental expenditure (time, energy etc.) that benefits one offspring at a cost to parents' ability to invest in other offspring.

Parentification: a child taking on the role of parent to his or her own parents, a situation where the child provides a level or type of care that is developmentally inappropriate.

Participant reactivity: extraneous variation introduced into the research situation by the way in which participants construe the situation and respond to it; participants maybe helpful, hostile or anxious about being evaluated.

Perceptual development: the systematic change of perceptual abilities and processes that develop as a result of maturation and experience.

Perceptual organization: the structure of experiences based on sensory activity and the underlying processes that produce that perceived structure.

Personality variables: internal causes of differences in behaviour between people such as extraversion or openness to new experiences.

Perspective-taking: a term that describes our ability to understand the perspectives of other people.

PET (positron emission tomography) scans: a non-invasive technique for visualizing (imaging) the activity in the brain by measuring the accumulation of a radioactive substance in various regions of the brain. A battery of detectors scans the brain after the radioactive substance has been injected into the bloodstream.

Phobic disorders (phobias): a type of anxiety disorder where a person experiences extreme fear out of all proportion to the actual danger posed by a particular object or situation.

Physiological approach: explains behaviour in terms of bodily systems, such as nerves and hormones.

Pilot study: a small-scale trial of a research study designed to identify problems with testing procedures and materials so that they can be dealt with prior to the main study.

Pineal gland: a small pea-shaped secretory gland in the middle of the brain. Produces melatonin.

Placebo effect: any subjective improvement reported by patients who believe themselves to have been given some form of effective treatment but who have in fact received some inactive substitute.

Plagiarism: 'academic theft'; the crime of stealing someone else's ideas or work and passing it off as one's own.

Polygyny: the practice of being married to more than one woman at a time.

Population validity: the extent to which research findings can be generalized to other groups of people.

Post-traumatic stress disorder (PTSD): a type of anxiety disorder that arises as a result of some traumatic event. The symptoms began shortly after the event and may last for years.

Precognition: the ability to receive information about future events without the use of inference or the known sensory channels.

Predictive validity: the extent to which test scores (or classifications) can predict later behaviour (or attitudes). For example, if someone is given a valid diagnosis of depression we would expect (predict) that they would respond positively when given medication/treatment known to alleviate depressive symptoms.

Preload/taste-test method: a procedure used in the laboratory to investigate the impact of eating a controlled amount of food (the preload) on the amount eaten during a subsequent taste test session during which food is freely available.

Preparedness theory: all species are innately 'prepared' to avoid certain stimuli because they are potentially dangerous.

Primary source: a first-hand account of something (e.g. a report of a research study written by the individual(s) who carried out the study).

Probability: a numerical measure of the chance that something will happen on a scale from 0 (indicating never) to 1 (indicating certainty).

Prosopagnosia: a failure to recognize familiar faces despite intact intellectual functioning.

Prosocial behaviour: an act that benefits others but which may appear to have no direct benefit for the person performing it.

Prosocial reasoning: an area of thinking concerned with helping or comforting others, sometimes at a personal cost.

Prospective data: data that are gathered over the forward passage of time in either a longitudinal study or a prospective study; a prospective study begins with an examination of presumed causes (e.g. overeating) and then continues forward in time to observe presumed effects (e.g. obesity).

Prospective (longitudinal) study: an investigation where the participants are studied over an extended period of time.

Protection motivation theory: a social cognition model that is based on a number of cognitions; similar to the health belief model, except that it includes fear as one of the key cognitions.

Proximate cause: the explanation of a particular trait or behaviour in terms of immediate (e.g. physiological, environmental) causes, to be contrasted with an **ultimate** cause.

Pseudohermaphroditism: this is a problem of limited male hormone testosterone production during prenatal development resulting in ambiguous genitalia at birth. Once puberty hits testosterone production changes the genitalia to that of the typical male.

Pseudoscience: a field of intellectual activity which has the superficial appearance of being scientific but actually differs from true science in important ways.

Psi: a generic term, used as both a noun and an adjective, to refer to any aspect of the paranormal, covering both ESP and PK.

Psychic healing: the alleged ability to treat or cure disease by the use of mental energy alone.

Psychoanalysis: therapeutic method in which a person is given insights into the unconscious psychological conflicts that are seen as the cause of their symptoms.

Psychoanalytic theory (of mental disorders): the theory, first developed by Freud, that abnormal psychological functioning is caused by unconscious conflicts.

Psychoanalytic therapy: see **psychoanalysis**.

Psychodynamic approach: any approach that emphasizes the dynamics of behaviour, i.e. the forces that motivate it. This approach is associated with psychoanalytic theories.

Psychodynamic explanations (of mental disorders): the view that mental disorders are caused by underlying psychological forces of which the individual is probably unaware.

Psychodynamic therapies: treatments that help clients to uncover past traumatic events and the conflicts that have resulted from them. These conflicts can then be resolved so that the client is able to restore an adaptive level of functioning.

Psychokinesis (PK): the alleged ability to influence the external world by will-power alone, often sub-divided into micro-PK and macro-PK.

Psychological androgyny: a term introduced by Bem used to perceive men and women as the same. Notions of masculinity and femininity become redundant as people become increasingly similar in behaviour and personality.

Psychological disorder: a term used synonymously with 'mental disorder', it refers to a level of functioning that is harmful and distressing to the individual or to those around them. Psychological disorders are usually defined and described according to some current classification system such as DSM-IV-TR.

Psychological explanations (of mental disorders): these are explanations, other than biological, for mental disorders. They include psychodynamic, behavioural and cognitive explanations.

Psychological therapies: more commonly called 'psychotherapies', they cover any treatment that addresses psychological rather than biological factors associated with mental disorder. Each psychological approach has its own therapies. For example, psychoanalysis is based on the psychodynamic approach, and systematic desensitization (for phobias) is based on the behavioural approach.

Psychopathology: the study of the origins and course of psychological disorders.

Psychosurgery: cutting brain tissue in order to alleviate the symptoms of severe psychological disorder.

Qualitative data: a type of data based on words (text and what people say) rather than numbers (numerical data).

Qualitative methods: a type of research method used to generate qualitative data (i.e. non-numerical data); for example, some case study research and interviews involving open-ended questions.

Quantitative data: numerical data resulting from some form of measurement.

Quantitative methods: a type of research method used to generate quantitative (numerical) data; for example, experimental research and some survey research).

Quota sampling: a target population is divided into subgroups (strata) and opportunity samples are taken from each of them in the same proportions that exist in the target population.

Random allocation: a way of allocating participants to conditions in such a way that every participant has an equal chance of being selected for each condition (e.g. by tossing a coin to decide which condition someone is allocated to).

Randomization: this term is sometimes used interchangeably with random allocation. Randomization also refers to allowing chance to decide the order in which multiple stimuli should be presented.

Randomized controlled trial (RCT): a clinical trial in which patients are assigned at random to the various treatment and control conditions, the control conditions often being a placebo condition and/or a no treatment condition.

Random sampling: a way of selecting a group of participants by ensuring that each one has an equal chance of being selected. Usually, they would all be allocated a number, then the selection would be made using random number tables or generators.

Range: a measure of spread which is the difference between the highest and lowest score in a sample of scores.

Rapid-eye-movement sleep (**REM**): also called **paradoxical sleep**.

Ratio data: measurements on a scale that has equal intervals and also a genuine zero point (e.g. height in centimetres or weight in kilograms). With a fixed zero point it is possible to make ration statements such as someone who height is two metres is twice as tall as someone who is one metre tall.

Rational-emotive behaviour therapy (REBT): a form of psychotherapy, based on the work of Ellis, where the therapist actively confronts clients about their irrational thinking.

Reaction range: this concept indicates how people's genes provide the potential range for specific characteristics (such as height, weight, creativity, personality) to develop. Their environment determines the extent to which they achieve the maximum of their range for specific characteristics.

Receptor: molecules on the surface a neuron where chemicals called neurotransmitters become attached in order to initiate the firing of a neuron (brain cell), or in some cases to cause inhibition of firing of a neuron.

Reductionism: the act of breaking complex phenomena down into more simple components. A belief in reductionism implies that complex phenomena are best understood in terms of a simpler level of explanation.

Reductionist: an approach to behaviour that explains a complex set of facts, entities, phenomena, or structures by another, simpler set (e.g. explaining addiction as due solely to synaptic changes or a genetic predisposition).

Regression: a reversion to childhood behaviours and desires.

Reinforcement: the process by which a response is strengthened and thereby reinforced.

Relapse: falling back into a former state, especially after apparent improvement, e.g. someone who has given up smoking for a period of time starts smoking again after a particular trigger event.

Reliability: in the context of classification systems, this refers to the consistency with which clinicians agree on a diagnosis for a particular set of symptoms. For a classification system to be reliable, those using it must be able to agree when a person should or should not be given a particular diagnosis. It is also the degree to which a description or score is consistent over time or across different observers (sometimes called consistency or dependability). If the findings of research are consistently replicable then they can be called reliable.

REM behaviour disorder (RBD): a special form of sleep walking where a person acts out their dream.

Repeated measures design: a type of experimental design in which every participant is exposed to each of the conditions, so, in effect, participants are used as their own controls.

Replicability: a characteristic of research that involves repeating the study to find out whether the findings are the same.

Representative sample: a selection of individuals from the target population, which shares all the main characteristics of the population despite its smaller size. Findings from a truly representative sample can be generalized to the target population from which it was drawn.

Reproductive fitness: a measure of the success of an individual in passing on their genes to the next generation and beyond.

Restricting anorexia: a form of anorexia nervosa that involves restricted eating without episodes of bingeing and purging.

Research aim: the aim identifies the purpose and focus of a research study.

Research question: the question a researcher is trying to answer by carrying out an investigation.

Researcher reliability: this refers to the consistency of a researcher's behaviour; different terminology is used according to the type of research being carried out (e.g. experimenter reliability, intra- and inter-researcher reliability, inter-observer reliability or inter-rater reliability).

Reward/need satisfaction model: the view that relationships are based ion the rewards they provide or the needs they satisfy.

Salience: in addiction research, when the behaviour is the most important thing in that person's life, so they neglect and/or compromise other areas of their life and functioning (e.g. job, relationship).

Sample: a sub-group of a target population, which is chosen in a particular way so that it represents the target population.

Sample bias: this can occur if a certain kind of participant is persistently recruited for research at the expense of others, so that other subgroups are not adequately represented in the body of psychological knowledge.

Sampling error: an indication of the extent to which a sample differs from the target population.

Scaffolding: this metaphor was first used by Wood *et al.* (1976) to describe the ideal role of the 'more knowledgeable other' who is providing graduated assistance to a learner, withdrawing adult/peer control and support as the learner's mastery of a given task increases.

Schema: Piaget used the term schema (sometimes referred to as 'scheme') to describe a psychological structure representing everything known about an object or event; an internalized representation of the world. It is a cluster of interrelated concepts that tell us about how things function in the world, e.g. a schema about television would include our knowledge about how TVs work and what sort of programmes they are likely to display.

Schizophrenia: a serious mental disorder that is characterized by severe disruptions in psychological functioning and a loss of contact with reality.

Schizotypy: tendency towards milder (sub-clinical) forms of symptoms associated with schizophrenia.

Science: a body of knowledge, or a method of study devoted to developing this body of knowledge, gained through systematic observation and experimentation.

Scientific process: a systematic method of investigation involving induction and deduction.

Seasonal affective disorder (SAD): a mood disorder related to changes in season. A period of depression in winter is the most common.

Secondary source: a 'second-hand' account of a primary source of research, e.g. a summary of a piece of research carried out by someone else.

Self-conscious emotions: emotions, such as guilt, shame, embarrassment and pride, which rely on some understanding of how others perceive you.

Self-disclosure: sharing significant personal information with others that they would not normally know or discover.

Self-socialization: socialization is the process by which individuals acquire the attitudes, beliefs, values and social skills that enable them to become a part of a particular social group through formal and informal agents. In the case of self-socialization as referred to in children, the child itself is responsible for acquiring these.

Sensation seeking: the need for varied, novel and complex sensations and experiences, and the willingness to take physical and social risks for the sake of such experience.

Sensory adaptation: the ability of the sensory systems to adapt to a change in the environment.

Serotonin: a neurotransmitter (a chemical messenger used to transmit impulses from one nerve cell to another). Abnormal activity of serotonin has been linked to depression and OCD.

Sexual differentiation: this occurs at about six weeks of prenatal development where the sexes develop along the male or female pathway. This involves a host of developmental differences such as the secretion of sex-specific androgens which promote the growth of sex appropriate genitalia.

Sex differences: this is used to point out that there are differences of behaviour, personality and cognition between boys and girls and men and women as a consequence of their sex.

Sexual dimorphism: this describes the differences of physical appearance and size between men and women. Men are generally larger and muscular.

Sexual selection: the observation that individuals possess features that make them attractive to members of the opposite sex (intersexual selection), or help them to compete with members of the same sex for access to mates (intrasexual selection).

Simulation: a conscious reactivation of previously executed actions which have been stored in memory.

Sleep apnoea: the inability to breathe whilst asleep for various periods of time ranging from a matter of seconds to a matter of minutes.

Sleeper effect: a 'hidden' effect whereby there is no immediate effect on the person (possible because a persuasive communication comes from an unreputable source), but after a period of time the effect is experienced.

Sleep paralysis: an inability to move just prior to falling asleep or waking.

Slow-wave sleep (SWS): the four stages of sleep (1-4) outside of REM. So called due to the appearance of slow wave EEG activity.

Social cognition: the area of social psychology concerned with how people think about other individuals or other groups of people.

Social cognition models: models made up of a number of different cognitions that are used to frame research and also to develop treatment interventions.

Social-cognitive theory: an explanation of the way in which people monitor their own behaviour with reference to what is appropriate.

Social desirability: when used in the context of interpersonal attraction, refers to any trait or characteristic that makes an individual attractive or desirable as a partner.

Social learning theory: an explanation of the way in which people learn by observing and imitating the behaviour of others, mentally rehearsing the behaviours and then later imitating them in similar situations.

Socially desirability bias: a tendency for respondents (e.g. in a questionnaire) to respond in such a way that would represent them in a favourable light.

Socially sensitive research: any research that may have direct social consequences for those participating in the study or the class of people they represent.

Social exchange: a perspective that sees all social behaviour as being subject to the goal of maximizing benefits and minimizing costs.

Socialization: the process by which an individual acquires the attitudes, beliefs, values, social skills and so on that enable them to become a part of a particular social group.

Social learning theory: an explanation of the way in which people learn by observing and imitating the behaviour of others.

Socio-cultural explanations (of mental disorders): the view that social and cultural factors (e.g. social class, child rearing, gender) cause or contribute towards mental disorders.

Social phobia: an excessive and persistent fear and avoidance of particular social situations.

Soft sell: compared with the '**hard sell**' approach, a more subtle form of advertising that is likely to involve peripheral route processing such as the use of mood or music to make an impact.

Somnambulism: sleep walking.

Specific phobia: irrational, persistent fear and avoidance of a specific object or situation (excluding social phobia and agoraphobia). When the person encounters the feared object or situation, they show an immediate fear response.

Standard deviation: a statistical measure of variation about the mean in a set of scores.

Statistical significance: a conclusion drawn from the data collected in a research study that the null hypothesis is unlikely to be true and, therefore, the effect that was expressed in the alternative hypothesis is probably meaningful.

Stratified random sampling: a target population is divided into subgroups (strata) and random samples are taken from each of them in the same proportions that exist in the target population.

Stroop effect: refers to how colour name words have an interfering effect on the time taken to name the ink colours of non-matching colours.

Subjective validation: a belief, expectancy or hypothesis that a person holds which leads them to perceive two unrelated events as being related.

Suprachiasmatic nucleus (SCN): a small region of the hypothalamus that is found just above the point where the optic fibres from each eye cross over and travel to the opposite hemisphere.

Syllogistic reasoning: a type of deductive reasoning involving drawing conclusions from given premises typically of the form 'If A then B', e.g. *If you revise hard you will do well in your exams. You do revise hard. Therefore, you will do well in your exams.*

Synaptic connections: the area where neurons make contact with each other.

Syndrome: a cluster of symptoms and behaviours regularly found together in a particular combination.

Systematic desensitization: a behavioural therapy used to treat phobias and anxieties. After being trained in relaxation techniques, the phobic person is gradually exposed to situations that are more and more anxiety provoking until the fear response is replaced by one of relaxation.

Systematic review: a rigorous literature search and review using strict criteria for the inclusion of studies and evaluation. It may also involve meta-analysis (i.e. amalgamating statistical data from different studies).

Target population: the total number of individuals or data points that fit a set of defined criteria.

Telepathy: direct mind-to-mind contact.

Temporal validity: this refers to the 'shelf life' of findings, i.e. how durable they are over time.

Thalamus: an evolutionary ancient area of the forebrain sitting on top of the brain stem that largely determines how much sensory information reaches higher centres.

Thematic analysis: a method for examining qualitative, textual data, where the text is sorted into specific themes so the content can be organized and summarized. See also **inductive analysis** and **theoretical analysis**.

Theoretical analysis: a type of thematic analysis of qualitative, textual data; the researcher already has some ideas about what themes may emerge, based on previous research, so they examine data to see whether the themes are present

Theory: a set of interrelated ideas or principles that can be used to explain observed phenomena.

Theory of mind (often abbreviated to ToM): ToM underpins our understanding of mental states (beliefs, desires, intentions, emotions, imagination) that cause action and reflects on the content of our own minds and other people's minds and the realization that these may differ (i.e. that what other people know, believe or feel about things may be different from one's own knowledge, beliefs and feelings). It allows us to make inferences about what others know, think and feel and predict their motivations, what they are likely to do next and the reasons behind their actions (their intentions).

Theory of planned behaviour: an extension of the theory of reasoned action that includes perceived behavioural control.

Theory of reasoned action: a social cognition model made up of attitudes and social norms that are assumed to predict behavioural intentions and subsequent behaviour.

Therapy: a systematic intervention to help people overcome their psychological difficulties.

Third person effect: a tendency, among many people for them to believe that *they* are not influenced by the media, but that others probably are.

Tolerance: for those developing an addiction, the need to increase the amounts of drug or increase the amounts of behaviour to get mood-modifying effects, when previously they would have needed lesser amounts.

Top-down/indirect (constructivist) theory of perception: emphasizes the need for several sources of information in order to construct our perception of the world; in addition, we need to use higher cognitive processes to interpret the information appropriately.

Trait hostility: an underlying characteristic of the individual that determines the likelihood of an aggressive response in certain situations.

Transliminality: (literally, 'going beyond the threshold') A heightened sensitivity to psychological material originating in the unconscious or the external environment which is highly correlated with paranormal belief/experience.

Transsexualism: this is when individuals who feel uncomfortable about themselves – their sex in particular and they want to be the other sex.

Transsexuals: individuals characterized by the belief that one is of the wrong sex. Individuals feel discomfort and distress over their sexual anatomy and wish to change their sexual anatomy through surgery.

Transvestites: these are individuals who enjoy cross-dressing and in some cases find this sexually arousing.

Two-tailed test: a statistical procedure applied to test a non-directional hypothesis.

Type 1 and Type 2 diabetes: see diabetes.

Type 1 error: this type of error occurs when, following statistical analysis of the data, the null hypothesis is wrongly rejected because it is actually true; it is more likely to occur when the significance level is set at more than .05. A Type 1 error usually becomes apparent when the research is replicated.

Type I syndrome: in the context of schizophrenia, an acute disorder characterized by symptoms such as hallucinations, delusions and disorganized speech.

Type 2 error: this type of error occurs when, following statistical analysis of the data, the null hypothesis is accepted as being true when it is actually false; it is more likely to occur when the significance level is set at .01 or less. Like a Type 1 error, a Type 2 error usually becomes apparent when the research is replicated.

Type II syndrome: in the context of schizophrenia, a chronic condition, characterized by symptoms such as flattened affect, apathy and poverty of speech.

Ultradian: rhythmical cycles that last more than a day (*ultra* is Latin for beyond). An example might be sleep stages such as bouts of REM.

Ultimate cause: the explanation of a particular trait or behaviour in terms of ancestral (i.e. adaptive, functional) causes, to be contrasted with a **proximate** cause.

Unipolar disorder/depression: see **Depression**.

Validity: the degree to which a test, measurement or experimental manipulation is doing the job it has been designed to do. In the context of classification systems, predictive validity is particularly important where someone given a particular diagnosis should respond to the therapy recognized as effective for the diagnosed condition. If the person does not respond, it casts doubt on the original diagnosis. It is also the extent to which data, and their interpretation, reflect the phenomenon that is being investigated without bias. Evidence is unlikely to be valid unless it is also reliable. *Internal validity* is a term used tin experimental research to indicate the extent to which research findings are regarded as being genuinely caused by the manipulation of the independent variable. *External validity* indicates the extent to which quantitative research findings can be generalized to other people (*population validity*), other places (*ecological* validity).

Variable: any measurable characteristic or event that varies (or changes) in some way.

Variable ratio: in operant conditioning, a schedule of reinforcement where a response is reinforced after an unpredictable number of responses, creating a high, steady rate of responding. Gambling and lottery games are good examples of a reward based on a variable-ratio schedule.

Video games: an electronic game played on a computer. In the context of the media effects debate, this mainly concerns games with an aggressive content.

Visual agnosias: agnosia means not knowing; visual object agnosia is not recognizing familiar objects presented visually.

Visual constancies: the tendency for objects to provide the same perceptual experience despite changes in the viewing conditions.

Visual information processing: the transformation of a visual input into a meaningful perceptual experience.

Visual perception: the processes by which we transform sensory information from the eyes to produce an experience of depth, distance, colour, etc.

Volunteer sampling: a group of participants which is invited and agrees to take part in a research study. Such a sample is self-selected.

Withdrawal: physiological and/or psychological symptoms experienced by addicts if they are unable to engage in their behaviour or drug of choice (e.g. going 'cold turkey' in heroin addicts).

Zeitgebers: 'time giver' stimuli that alter the biological clock on a daily basis. Examples include light and heat.

Zone of proximal development (ZPD): the term used by Vygotsky to describe the distance between a child's current abilities when working unassisted and their potential ability based on what they can do with assistance from a 'more knowledgeable other'.

Abbott, M.W. (2007) 'Situational factors that affect gambling behavior', in G. Smith, D. Hodgins and R. Williams (eds.), *Research and Measurement Issues in Gambling Studies,* New York: Elsevier, pp.251–278.

Abraham, U., Gwinner, E. and Van't Hof, T.J. (2000) 'Exogenous melatonin reduces the resynchronization time after phase shifts of a nonphotic zeitgeber in the house sparrow (*Passer domesticus*)', *Journal of Biological Rhythms*, 15, pp. 48–56.

Abramson, L.Y., Seligman, M.E.P. and Teasdale, J.D. (1978) 'Learned helplessness in humans: critique and reformulation', *Journal of Abnormal Psychology*, 87, pp.49–74.

Abramson, L.Y., Metalsky, G.I. and Alloy, L.B. (1989) 'Hopelessness depression: a theory-based subtype of depression', *Psychological Review*, 96, pp.358-72.

Adams, K. (1981) 'Former mental patients in a prison and parole system: A study of socially disruptive behavior', *Criminal Justice and Behavior*, 10, pp.358–84.

Adler, A. (1931) *What Life Should Mean to You,* New York: Capricorn.

Adolphs, R., Tranel, D., Damasio, H. and Damasio, A. (1995) 'Fear and the human amygdale', *Journal of Neuroscience*, 15, pp.5879–91.

Ainsworth, M.D.S. and Bell, S.M. (1970) 'Attachment, exploration, and separation: illustrated by the behavior of one-year-olds in a Strange Situation', *Child Development*, 41, pp.49–65.

Ajzen, I. (1985) 'From intention to actions: A theory of planned behavior', in J. Kuhl and J. Beckman (eds) *Action Control: From cognition to behaviour*, Heidelberg: Springer-Verlag, pp.11–39.

Ajzen, I. (1991) 'Theory of planned behavior', *Organizational Behaviour and Human Decision Processes*, 50, pp.179–211.

Ajzen, I., Timko, C. and White, J.B. (1982) 'Self-monitoring and the attitude-behaviour relation', *Journal of Personality and Social Psychology*, 42, pp.426–435.

Akert, R. (1998) *Terminating Romantic Relationships: The role of personal responsibility and gender*, unpublished manuscript, Massachusetts: Wellesley College.

Alcock, J. E. (1981) *Parapsychology: Science or magic? A psychological perspective.* Oxford: Pergamon.

Alcock, J. E. (1990) *Science and supernature: A critical appraisal of parapsychology.* Buffalo, NY: Prometheus.

Alcock, J. E. (2003) 'Give the null hypothesis a chance: Reasons to remain doubtful about the existence of psi.' *Journal of Consciousness Studies*, 10, 29–50.

Aldrich, M. S. (1993) 'Narcolepsy', *Neurology*, 42, pp.34–43.

Alexander, R.D. (1974) 'The evolution of social behavior', *Annual Review of Ecology and Systematics*, 5 (1), pp.325–83.

Alexy, E.M., Burgess, A.W., Baker, T. and Smoyak, S.A. (2005) 'Perceptions of cyberstalking among college students', *Brief Treatment and Crisis Intervention*, 5(3), pp.279–89.

Allgeier, B.R. and Wiederman, N.W. (1991) 'Love and mate selection in the 1990s', *Free Inquiry*, 11, pp.25–7.

Allegre, B., Souville, M., Therme, P. and Griffiths, M.D. (2006) 'Definitions and measures of exercise dependence', *Addiction Research and Theory,* 14, pp.631–646.

Allport, F.H. (1955) *Theories of Perception and the Concepts of Structure*, New York: John Wiley & Sons.

Allport, G. (1947) *The Use of Personal Documents in Psychological Science*, New York: Science Research Council.

American Psychiatric Association (2000) *Diagnostic and Statistical Manual of Mental Disorders* (4th Edition, Text Revision), Washington: American Psychiatric Association.

American Psychiatric Association (1994) *Diagnostic and Statistical Manual of Mental Disorders* (4th edn) DSM-IV, Washington, DC: APA.

American Psychiatric Association (1994) *Diagnostic and Statistical Manual for Mental Disorders* (4th edn), Washington DC: APA.

American Psychiatric Association (2007) *Annual Report*, Conference at San Diego, California.

Ancoli-Israel, S. and Roth, T. (1999) 'Characteristics of insomnia in the United States: results of the 1991 National Sleep Foundation Survey, *Sleep*, 22 (Suppl 2), pp.347–53.

Anderson, C. and Dill, K. (2000) 'Video Games and Aggressive Thoughts, Feelings, and Behavior in the Laboratory and in Life', *Journal of Personality and Social Psychology*, 8(4), pp.772–90.

Anderson, C.A., Gentile, D.A. and Buckley, K.E. (2007) *Violent Video Game Effects on Children and Adolescents: Theory, Research, and Public Policy*, New York, NY: Oxford University Press.

Anderson, C.M. (1986) 'Predation and primate evolution', *Primates*, 27, pp.15–39.

Anderson, G. and Brown, R.I.F. (1984) 'Real and laboratory gambling, sensation seeking and arousal: Toward a Pavlovian component in general theories of gambling and gambling addictions', *British Journal of Psychology, 75*, 401–11.

Anderson, J.W., Johnstone, B.M., Remley, D.T. (1999) Breast-feeding and cognitive development: a meta-analysis, *American Journal of Clinical Nutrition*, 70, pp.525–35.

Anderson, K.G., Hillard, KKaplan, H.. and Lancaster, J.B. (1999), 'Paternal Care by Genetic Fathers and Stepfathers I: Reports from Albuquerque Men', *Evolution and Human Behavior*, 20, pp.405–31.

Andersson, M. (1982) 'Female choice for extreme tail length in widow bird', *Nature*, 299, pp.818–19.

Andrews, G., Stewart, G. and Allen, R. (1990) 'The genetics of six neurotic disorders: a twin study', *Journal of Affective Disorders*, 19, pp.23–9.

Andrews, P.W. (2006) 'Parent–offspring conflict and cost–benefit tradeoffs in adolescent suicidal behavior: The effects of birth order and maternal conflict on attempt incidence and severity', *Human Nature*, 17 (2), pp.190–211.

Andsager, J.L. and White, H.A. (2007) *Self versus Others; media, messages, and the third-person effect*, Hove: Lawrence Erlbaum.

Angermeier, W.F. (1984) *The Evolution of Operant Learning and Memory*, Basel: Karger.

Angst, J. (1999) 'The epidemiology of depressive disorders', *European Neuropsychopharmacology* (Suppl), pp.95–M.

Archer, J. (1989) 'Childhood gender roles: Structure and development', *The Psychologist, 12*, pp.367–70.

Archer, J. (1991) 'The influence of testosterone on human aggression', *British Journal of Psychology*, 82, pp.1–28.

Archer, J. (1992) Childhood gender roles: Social context and organisation. In: H. McGurk (Ed.), Childhood social development: Contemporary perspectives. Hillsdale (NJ): Lawrence Erlbaum.

Archer, J. and Lloyd, B. (1992) *Sex and Gender,* Cambridge: Cambridge University Press.

Archer, J. and Coyne, S.M. (2005) 'An integrated review of indirect, relational, and social aggression', *Personality and Social Psychology Review*, 9 (3), pp.212–30.

Argyle, M. (1992) *The Social Psychology of Everyday Life*, London: Routledge.

Argyle, M. (1994) *The Psychology of Interpersonal Behaviour* (5th edn), London: Penguin.

Arkes, H.R., Boehm, L. and Xu, G. (1991) 'Determinants of judged validity', *Journal of Experimental Social Psychology,* 27, pp.576-605.

Arkowitz, H., Westra, H.A., Miller, W.R. and Rollnick, S. (2007) *Motivational Interviewing in the Treatment of Psychological Problems*, New York: Guilford Press.

Aronoff, J. and Crano, W.D. (1975) 'A re-examination of the cross-cultural principles of task segregation and sex role differentiation in the family', cited in W. Wood and A.H. Eagly (2002) 'A cross-cultural analysis of the behaviour of women and men: Implications for the origins of sex differences' p. 706, *Psychological Bulletin*, 128, pp.699–727.

Aronson, E. (1999) *The Social Animal* (7th edn), New York: W.H. Freeman.

Arora, R.C. and Meltzer, H.Y. (1989) 'Serotonergic measures in the brains of suicide victims: 5-HT2 binding sites in the frontal cortex of suicide victims and control subjects', *American Journal of Psychiatry*, 146, pp.730–6.

Arslan, A.S. (2000) *Ders Kitaplarinda Cinsiyetçilik (Gender Bias in School Textbooks)*, Ankara, Turkey: KSSGM Textbooks.

Asch, S.E. (1956) 'Studies of independence and conformity: a minority of one against a unanimous majority', *Psychological Monographs*, 70(9), No.416, p.70.

Aserinsky, E. and Kleitman, N. (1953) 'Two types of ocular motility occurring in sleep', *Journal of Applied Physiology*, 8, pp.1–10.

Ashe, D.D. and McCutcheon, L.E. (2001) 'Shyness, loneliness, and attitude toward celebrities', *Current Research in Social Psychology*, 6(9), pp.124–33.

Ashton, H. and Golding, J. (1989) *Smoking and Human Behaviour,* Chichester: John Wiley & Sons Inc.

Ashton, W., Nanchahal, K. and Wood, D. (2001) 'Body mass index and metabolic risk factors for coronary heart disease in women', *European Heart Journal*, 22, pp.46–55.

Augustine, K. (2007a) 'Does paranormal perception occur in near-death experiences?' *Journal of Near-Death Studies*, 25, 203–236.

Augustine, K. (2007b) 'Near-death experiences with hallucinatory features', *Journal of Near-Death Studies*, 26, 3–31.

Augustine, K. (2007c) 'Psychophysiological and cultural correlates undermining a survivalist interpretation of near-death experiences', *Journal of Near-Death Studies*, 26, 89–125

Axelson, M.L., Brinberg, D. and Durand, J.H. (1983) 'Eating at a fast food restaurant: A social psychological analysis', *Journal of Nutrition Education*, 15, pp.94–8.

Azar, B. (1997) 'Nature, nurture: not mutually exclusive', *APA Monitor* at http://www.apa.org/monitor/may97/twinstud.html

Badawy, A. (2006) 'Alcohol and violence and the possible role of serotonin', Criminal Behaviour and Mental Health, 13(1), pp.31–44.

Badcock, C. (2000) *Evolutionary Psychology: A critical introduction*, Cambridge: Polity Press.

Baer, L., Rauch, S.L. and Ballanline, H.T. Jr (1995) 'Cingulotomy for intractable obsessive-compulsive disorder: A prospective, long-term follow up of 18 patients', *Archives of General Psychiatry*, 52, pp.384–92.

Bahrick, H.P., Bahrick, P.O. and Wittlinger R.P. (1975) 'Fifty years of memory for names and faces: a cross sectional approach', *Journal of Experimental Psychology: General*, 104, pp.54–75.

Bain J., Langevin, R., Dickey, R. and Ben-Aron, M. (1987) 'Sex hormones in murderers and assaulters', *Behavioral Science and the Law*, 5, pp.95–101.

Baker, R. and Bellis, M. (1995) *Human Sperm Competition*, New York: Chapman Hall.

Bales, R.F. (1970) *Personality and Social Behaviour*, New York: Holt Rinehart and Winston.

Bandler, R. and Grinder, J. (1979) *Frogs into princes: The introduction to neuro-linguistic programming*. London: Eden Grove Editions.

Bandura, A. (1965) 'Influence of a model's reinforcement contingencies on the acquisition of imitative responses', *Journal of Personality and Social Psychology*, 1, pp.589–95.

Bandura, A. (1969) *Principles of Behaviour Modification*, New York: Holt, Rinehart & Winston.

Bandura, A. (1977) 'Self-efficacy: toward a unifying theory of behaviour change', *Psychological Review*, 84, pp.191–215.

Bandura, A. (1986) 'The social learning perspective: Mechanisms of aggression', in H. Toch (ed.) *Psychology of Crime and Criminal Justice*, Prospect Heights, IL: Waveland Press.

Bandura, A. (1986) *Social Foundations of Thought and Action*, Englewood Cliffs, NJ: Prentice-Hall.

Bandura, A., Ross, D. and Ross, S. (1963) 'Imitation of film-mediated aggressive models', *Journal of Abnormal and Social Psychology*, 66, pp.3–11.

Bandura, A. and Walters, R.H. (1963) *Social Learning and Personality Development*, New York: Holt, Rinehart and Winston.

Bandura, A. and Rosenthal, T. (1966) 'Vicarious classical conditioning as a function of arousal level', *Journal of Personality and Social Psychology*, 3, pp.54–62.

Bandura, A. and Menlove, F.L. (1968) 'Factors determining vicarious extinction of avoidance behaviour through symbolic modelling', *Journal of Personality and Social Psychology*, 8, pp.99–108.

Bandura, A., Blanchard, E.B. and Ritter, B. (1969) 'Relative efficacy of desensitization and modelling approaches for inducing behavioural, affective and attitudinal changes', *Journal of Personality and Social Psychology*, 13, pp.173–99.

Bandura, A., Underwood, B. and Fromson, M.E. (1975) 'Disinhibition of aggression through diffusion of responsibility and dehumanization of victims', *Journal of Personality and Social Psychology*, 9, pp.253–69.

Banyard, P. and Hunt, N. (2000) 'Reporting research: something missing?', *The Psychologist*, 13, pp.68–71.

Barkow, J.H. (1992) 'Beneath new culture is old psychology: Gossip and social stratification', in: Barkow, J.H., Cosmides, L. and Tooby, J. *The Adapted Mind: Evolutionary psychology and the generation of culture*, NY: Oxford University Press, pp.627–37.

Barlow, D.H. and Lehman, C.L. (1996) 'Advances in the psychosocial treatment of anxiety disorders', *Archives of General Psychiatry*, 53, pp.727–35.

Baron, E., Dickerson, M. and Blaszczynski, A. (1995) 'The scale of gambling choices: Preliminary development of an instrument to measure impaired control of gambling behaviour', in J. O'Connor (ed.), *High Stakes in the Nineties*, Sixth National Conference of the National Association for Gambling Studies, Fremantle, Western Australia, pp.153–167.

Baron, R.A. and Byrne, D. (1997) *Social Psychology* (8th edn), London: Allyn & Bacon.

Baron-Cohen, S. (1993) 'From attention-goal psychology to belief-desire psychology: The development of a theory of mind and its dysfunction', in S. Baron-Cohen, H. Tager-Flusberg and D.J. Cohen (eds) *Understanding Other Minds: Perspectives from autism*, Oxford: Oxford University Press, pp.59–82.

Baron-Cohen, S. (1995) *Mindblindness: An Essay on Autism and Theory of Mind*, Boston: MIT Press.

Baron-Cohen, S. (2001) 'Theory of mind in normal development and autism', *Prisme*, 34, pp.174–83.

Baron-Cohen, S. (2008) *Autism and Asperger Syndrome: The Facts*, Oxford: Oxford University Press.

Baron-Cohen, S., Leslie, A.M. and Frith, U. (1985) 'Does the autistic child have a "theory of mind"?' *Cognition*, 21, pp.37–46.

Barrett-Connor, E., Von Muhlen, D.G. and Kritz-Silverstein, D. (1999) 'Bioavailable testosterone and depressed mood in older men: The Rancho Bernardo study', *Journal of Clinical Endocrinology and Metabolism*, 84, pp.573–577.

Barry, H. and Schlegel, A. (1986) 'Cultural customs that influence sexual freedom in adolescence', *Ethnology*, 25, pp.151–62.

Bartholomew, R. E., Basterfield, K. and Howard, G. S. (1991) 'UFO abductees and contactees: Psychopathology or fantasy proneness?' *Professional Psychology: Research and Practice*, 22, 215–222.

Bartlett, F.C. (1932) *Remembering*, Cambridge: Cambridge University Press.

Barton, J.J.S., Press, D.Z., Keenan, J.P. and O'Connor, M. (2002) 'Lesions of the fusiform face area impair perception of facial configuration in prosopagnosia', *Neurology*, 58, pp.71-8.

Bateson, G., Jackson, D.D., Haley, J. and Weakland, J. (1956) 'Toward a theory of schizophrenia', *Behavioural Science*, 1, pp.251–64.

Bateson, P. (1986) 'When to experiment on animals', *New Scientist*, 109, pp.30–2.

Batson, C. (1991) *The Altruism Question: Towards a social psychological answer*, Hillsdale, NJ: Lawrence Erlbaum Associates.

Battle, Y.L., Martin, B.C. and Dorfman, J.H. (1999) 'Seasonality and infectious disease in schizophrenia: the birth hypothesis revisited', *Journal of Psychiatric Research*, 33, pp.501–9.

Bauer, P.J. (1993) 'Memory for gender-consistent and gender-inconsistent event sequences by 25 month old children', *Child Development*, 64(1), pp.285–97.

Baumeister, R.F. (2001), *Social Psychology and Human Sexuality*, Philadelphia, RA: Psychology Press (Taylor and Francis).

Baumrind, D. (1964) 'Some thoughts on ethics of research after reading Milgram's "Behavioural study of obedience"', *American Psychologist*, 19, pp.421–3.

Baumrind, D. (1985) 'Research using intentional deception: ethical issues revisited', *American Psychologist*, 40, 165–74.

Baxter, L.R., Schwartz, J.M., Bergman, K.S., Szuba, M.P., Guze, B.H. and Mazziotta, J.C. (1992) 'Caudate glucose metabolic rate changes with both drug and behaviour therapy for obsessive-compulsive disorder', *Archives of General Psychiatry*, 49, pp.681–689.

Beal, E.W. and Hochman, D. (1991) *Adult Children of Divorce*, New York: Delacorte Press.

Beauchamp, G.K. and Moran, M. (1982) 'Dietary experience and sweet taste preference in human infants', *Appetite*, 3(2), pp.139–52.

Beck, A.T. (1963) 'Thinking and depression', *Archives of General Psychiatry*, 9, pp.324–33.

Beck, A.T. (1967) *Depression: Clinical, Experimental and Theoretical Aspects*, New York: Harper and Row.

Beck, A. T. (1976) *Cognitive Therapy and the Emotional Disorders*, New York: International Universities Press.

Beck, A.T., Ward, C.H., Mendelson, M., Mock, J. and Erlbaugh, J. (1961) 'An inventory for measuring depression', *Archives of General Psychiatry*, 4, pp.561–71.

Beck, A.T., Weissman, A., Lester, D. and Trexler, L. (1974) 'The measurement of pessimism: the hopelessness scale', *Journal of Consulting and Clinical Psychology*, 42 (6), pp.861–5.

Beck, A.T., Emery, G. and Greenberg, R.L. (1985) *Anxiety Disorders and Phobias: A Cognitive Perspective*, New York: Basic Books.

Beck, A.T. and Cowley, G. (1990) 'Beyond lobotomies', *Newsweek*, 26 March 1990, p.44.

Becker, M.H. and Rosenstock, I.M. (1984) 'Compliance with medical advice', in A. Steptoe and A. Mathews (eds) *Health Care and Human Behaviour*, London: Academic Press.

Bee, H. and Boyd, D. (2007) *The Developing Child* (11th edition), Boston: Pearson Education.

Beecher, H.K. (1959) *Measurement of Subjective Responses: Quantitative effects of drugs*, New York: Oxford University Press, pp.352–63.

Bell-Gredler, M.E. (1986) *Learning and Instruction: Theory into practice*, London: Collier Macmillan.

Belson, W. (1978) *Television violence and the adolescent boy*, Farnborough, England: Saxon House, Teakfield Limited.

Bem, D.J (1965) 'An experimental analysis of self-persuasion', *Journal of Experimental Social Psychology*, 1, pp.199–218.

Bem, D. J. and Honorton, C. (1994) Does psi exist? Replicable evidence for an anomalous process of information transfer. *Psychological Bulletin*, 115, 4–18

Bem, D. J., Palmer, J. and Broughton, R. S. (2001) Updating the ganzfeld database: A victim of its own success? *Journal of Parapsychology*, 65, 207–218.

Bem, S.L. (1974) 'The measurement of psychological androgyny', *Journal of Consulting and Clinical Psychology*, 42, pp.155–62.

Bem, S.L. (1975) 'Sex role adaptability: One consequence of psychological androgyny', *Journal of Personality and Social Psychology*, 31, pp.634–43.

Bem, S.L. (1976) 'Probing the promise of androgyny', in A.G. Kaplan and J.P. Bean (eds) *Beyond sex-role stereotypes: Readings toward a psychology of androgyny* (pp.48–62), Boston: Little, Brown.

Bem, S.L. (1989) 'Genital knowledge and gender constancy in pre-school children', *Child Development*, 60, pp.649–62.

Bem, S.L. (1993) *The Lenses of Gender: Transforming the Debate on Sexual Inequality*, New Haven, CT: Yale University Press.

Benedek, E. (1985) 'Premenstrual syndrome: a new defence?', in J. Gold (ed.) *The Psychiatric Implications of Menstruation*, Washington: American Psychiatric Press, Inc.

Benington, J.H. and Frank, M.G. (2003) 'Cellular and molecular connections between sleep and synaptic plasticity', *Progress in Neurobiology,* 69, pp.77–101.

Benson, D.F. and Greenberg, J.P. (1969) 'Visual form agnosia', *Archives of Neurology,* 20, pp.82–89.

Benson, H., Dusek, J. A., Sherwood, J. B., Lam, P., Bethea, C. F., Carpenter, W., Levitsky, S., Hill, P. C., Clem, D. W., Jain, M. K., Drumel, D., Kopecky, S. L., Mueller, P. S., Marek, D., Rollins, S. and Hibberd, P. L. (2006) 'Study of the Therapeutic Effects of Intercessory Prayer (STEP) in cardiac bypass patients: A multicenter randomized trial of uncertainty and certainty of receiving intercessory prayer', *American Heart Journal,* 151, 934–942.
http://www.ahjonline.com/article/PIIS0
002870305006496/abstract - article-
footnote-1

Bentall, R.P (1993) 'Deconstructing the concept of schizophrenia', *Journal of Mental Health,* 2, pp.223–38.

Berger, A. M. and Knutson, J. F., (1984) *Assessing Environments III,* Iowa City: The University of Iowa.

Berger, R.J. and Phillips, N.H. (1995) 'Energy conservation and sleep', *Behavioural Brain Research,* 69, pp.65–73.

Bergin, A.E. (1971) 'The evaluation of therapeutic outcomes', in A.E. Bergin and S.L. Garfield (eds) *Handbook of Psychotherapy and Behaviour Change: An Empirical Analysis,* New York: Wiley.

Berk, L.E. (1994) 'Why children talk to themselves', *Scientific American,* November, 271 (5), pp.78–83.

Berk, L.E. and Garvin, R.A. (1984) 'Development of private speech among low-income Appalachian children', *Developmental Psychology,* 20 (2), pp.271–86.

Berke, J.D. and Hyman, S.E. (2000) 'Addiction, dopamine, and the molecular mechanisms of memory', *Neuron,* 25, pp.515–32.

Berkowitz, L. (1984) 'Some effects of thoughts on anti- and prosocial influences of media events: A cognitive-neoassociation analysis', *Psychological Bulletin,* 95, pp.410–27.

Berkowitz, M.W. and Gibbs, J.C. (1983) 'Measuring the developmental features of moral discussion', *Merrill-Palmer Quarterly,* 29, pp.299–410.

Berry, J. (1971) 'Müller-Lyer susceptibility: culture, ecology, or race?', *International Journal of Psychology,* 6, pp.193–7.

Betzig, L. (1989) 'Causes of conjugal dissolution: a cross-cultural study', *Current Anthropology,* 30, pp.654–76.

Beurs, E., van Balkom, A.J.L.M., Lange, A., Koele, P. and van Dyck, R. (1995) 'Treatment of panic disorder with agoraphobia', *American Journal of Psychiatry,* 152, pp.683–91.

Beyer, S. (1998) 'Gender differences in causal attributions by college students of performance on course examinations', *Current Psychology,* 17(4), pp.346–58.

Bianchi, B. and Bakeman, R. (1978) 'Sex-typed affiliation preferences observed in preschoolers: Traditional and open school differences', *Child Development,* 49(3), pp.910–12.

Bierut, L.J., Heath, A.C., Bucholz, K.K., Dinwiddie, S.H., Madden, P.A.F., Statham, D.J., Dunne, M.P. and Martin, N.G. (1999) 'Major depressive disorder in a community-based twin sample', *Archives of General Psychiatry,* 56, pp.557–63.

Bieling, P.J. and Alden, L.E. (1997) 'The consequences of perfectionism for patients with social phobia', *British Journal of Clinical Psychology,* 36, pp.589–97.

Binkley, S. (1979) 'A timekeeping enzyme in the pineal gland', *Scientific American,* 240, pp.66–71.

of exposure on two-year-old children's food preferences', *Appetite,* 3(4), pp.353–60.

Birch, L.L., Zimmerman, S. and Hind, H. (1980) 'The influence of social affective context on pre-school children's food preferences', *Child Development,* 55, pp.431–9.

Bird, C.E. and Rieker, P.P. (1999) 'Gender matters: an integrated model for understanding men's and women's health', *Social Science and Medicine,* 48, pp.745–55.

Bischof-Kohler, D. (1988) 'Uber der Zusammenhang von Empathie und der Fahigkeit, sic him Spiegel zu erkennen', cited in Smith, P., Cowie, H. and Blades, M. (2003) *Understanding Children's Development,* Oxford: Blackwell Publishing, p.181.

Blackmore, S. (1998) 'Abduction by aliens or sleep paralysis?' *Skeptical Inquirer,* 22, pp.23–8.

Blackmore, S. J. (1982) *Beyond the body: An investigation of out-of-the-body experiences.* London: Paladin, p.1.

Blackmore, S. J. (1986) Spontaneous and deliberate OBEs: a questionnaire survey. *Journal of the Society for Psychical Research,* 53, 218–224.

Blackmore, S. J. (1987a) A report of a visit to Carl Sargent's laboratory. *Journal of the Society for Psychical Research,* 54, 186–198.

Blackmore, S. J. (1987b) 'Where am I? Perspectives in imagery, and the out-of-body experience.' *Journal of Mental Imagery,* 11, 53–66.

Blackmore, S. J. (1993) 'Dying to live: Science and the near-death experience.* London: Grafton.

Blackmore, S. J. (1996a) *In search of the light: The adventures of a parapsychologist.* Amherst, NY: Prometheus, p.480.

Blackmore, S. J. (1996b) Near-death experiences. In G. Stein (ed.), *The Encyclopedia of the paranormal.* Amherst, NY: Prometheus Books. Pp. 425–441, 471.

Blackmore, S. J. (1996c) 'Out-of-body experiences' In G. Stein (ed.) *Encyclopedia of the paranormal.* Amherst, NY: Prometheus. Pp. 471–483.

Blackmore, S. J. (1997) 'Probability misjudgement and belief in the paranormal: A newspaper survey', *British Journal of Psychology,* 88, 683–689.

Blackmore, S. J. and Troscianko, T. (1985) ,Belief in the paranormal: Probability judgements, illusory control, and the "chance baseline shift"', *British Journal of Psychology,* 76, 459–468.

Blades, M. (1998) Intelligence, in P. Scott and C. Spencer, (eds) *Psychology: A Contemporary Introduction,* pp.583–616, Blackwell: Oxford.

Blakemore, C. and Cooper, G.F. (1970) 'Development of the brain depends on the visual environment', *Nature,* 228, pp.477–8.

Blakemore, S.J. and Frith, C.D. (2003) 'Self-awareness and action', *Current Opinion in Neurobiology,* 13 (2), pp.219–24.

Blalock, H.M. (1967) *Toward a Theory of Minority-Group Relations,* New York: Wiley.

Blanke, O., Landis, T., Spinelli, L. and Seeck, M. (2004) ,Out-of-body experience and autoscopy of neurological origin', *Brain,* 127, 243–258.

Blanke, O., Ortigue, S., Landis, T. and Seeck, M. (2002) Stimulating illusory own-body perceptions. *Nature,* 419, 269–270.

Blau, P.N. (1964) *Exchange and Power in Social Life,* New York: Wiley.

Blaye, A., Light, P., Joiner, R. and Sheldon, S. (1991) 'Collaboration as a facilitator of planning and problem solving on a computer-based task', *British Journal of Educational Psychology,* 61, pp.471–83.

Bloom, P. and German, T.P. (2000) 'Two reasons to abandon the false-belief task as a test of theory of mind', *Cognition,* 77 (1), pp.B25–B31.

Blos, P. (1967) 'The second individuation process of adolescence', *The Psychoanalytic Study of the Child,* 22, pp.162–86.

Blundell, J.E. and Hill, A.J. (1988) 'On the mechanism of action of dexfenfluramine: Effect on alliesthesia and appetite motivation in lean and obese subjects', *Clinical Neuropharmacology,* 11, S121–34.

Blundell, J.E., Hill, A.J. and Lawton, C.L. (1989) 'Neurochemical factors involved in normal and abnormal eating in humans', in R. Shepherd (ed.) *Handbook of the Psychophysiology of Human Eating,* New York: John Wiley, pp.85–112.

Blundell, J.E., Lawton, C.L., Cotton, J.R. and Macdiarmid, J.I. (1996) 'Control of human appetite: Implications for the intake of dietary fat', *Annual Review of Nutrition,* 16, pp.285–319.

Blundell, J.E. and Macdiarmid, J.I. (1997) 'Fat as a risk factor for over consumption: Satiation, satiety and patterns of eating', *Journal of the American Dietetic Association,* 97, pp.563–9.

Bochner, S. and Insko, C.A. (1966) 'Communicator discrepancy, source credibility, and opinion change', *Journal of Personality and Social Psychology,* 4, pp. 614–21.

Boes, A.D., Tranel, D., Anderson, S.W. and Nopolulos, P. (2008) 'Right anterior cingulate cortex volume is a neuroanatomical correlate of aggression and defiance in boys', *Behavioural Neuroscience,* 122(3), pp.677–84.

Bohner, G. (2001) 'Attitudes', in M. Hewstone and W. Stoebe (eds), *Introduction to Social Psychology,* Oxford: Blackwell, pp.239–282.

Bolger, T. (1989) 'Research and evaluation in counselling', in W. Dryden, D. Charles-Edwards and R. Woolfe (eds) *Handbook of Counselling in Britain,* London: Routledge.

Bolton-Smith, C. and Woodward, M. (1994) 'Dietary composition and fat to sugar ratios in relation to obesity', *International Journal of Obesity,* 18, pp.820–8.

Bonanno, G.A. (2004) 'Loss, trauma and human resilience', *American Psychologist,* 59 (1), pp.20–8.

Book, A.S., Starzyk, K.B. and Quinsey, V.L. (2001) 'The relationship between testosterone and aggression: a meta-analysis', *Aggression and Violent Behaviour,* 6, pp.579–99.

Booth, A., Granger, D.A., Mazur, A. and Kivlighan, K.T. (2006) 'Testosterone and social behavior', *Social Forces,* 85, pp.167–91.

Bornstein, M.H., Tamis-LeMonda, C.S., Tal, J., Ludermann, P., Toda, S., Rahn, C.W., Pecheux, M., Azuma, H. and Vardi, D. (1992) 'Maternal responsiveness to infants in three societies: the United States, France and Japan', *Child Development,* 63, pp.808–21.

Bosch, H., Steinkamp, F. and Boller, E. (2006), 'In the eye of the beholder: Reply to Wilson and Shadish (2006) and Radin, Nelson, Dobyns, and Houtkooper', *Psychological Bulletin,* 132, pp. 497, 517, 533–7.

Botvin, G.J. (2001) 'Prevention of substance abuse in adolescents', in N.J. Smelser and P.B. Baltes (eds), *International Encyclopedia of the Social and Behavioral Sciences,* Oxford: Pergamon Press, pp.15255–15259.

Botvinick, M., Jha, A.P., Bylsma, L.M., Fabian, S.A., Solomon, P.E. and Prkachin, K.M. (2005) 'Viewing facial expression of pain engages cortical areas involved in the direct experience of pain', *NeuroImage,* 25 (1), pp.312–9.

Bouchard, C., Trembley, A., Despres, J.P., Nadeu, A., Dupien, P.J. and Formet, G. (1990) 'The response to long-term overfeeding in identical twins', *New England Journal of Medicine,* 322, pp.1477–82.

Bouchard, T.J. Jr., Lykken, D.T., McGue, M., Segal, N.L. and Tellegen, A. (1990) 'Sources of human psychological differences: the Minnesota Study of Twin Reared Apart', *Science,* 250, pp.223–8.

Bower, T.G.R. (1965) 'Stimulus variables determining space perception in infants', *Science,* 149, pp.88–9.

Bower, T.G.R. (1966) 'The visual world of infants', *Scientific American,* 215, pp.80–92.

Bower, T.G.R. (1977) *The Perceptual World of the Child*, London: Fontana/Open Books.

Bower, T.G.R. (1982) *Development in Infancy* (2nd edn), San Francisco: W.H. Freeman.

Bower, T.G.R. and Wishart, J.G. (1972) 'The effects of motor skill on object permanence', *Cognition*, 1, pp.165–72.

Bowlby, J. (1973) Attachment and Loss, Vol. 2, *Separation, Anxiety and Anger*, New York, Basic Books.

Bowlby, J. (1982) *Attachment and Loss, Volume I: Attachment*, New York: Basic Books (first published 1969).

Boyer, W. (1995) 'Serotonin uptake inhibitors are superior to imipramine and alprazolam in alleviating panic attacks: A meta-analysis', *International Clinical Psychopharmacology*, 10, pp.45–9.

Bradbury, T.N. and Miller, G.A. (1985) 'Season of birth in schizophrenia: a review of evidence, methodology and etiology', *Psychological Bulletin*, 98, pp.569–94.

Bradshaw, J.L. and Wallace, G. (1971) 'Models for the processing and identification of faces', *Perception and Psychophysics*, 9, pp.443–8.

Bradshaw, W. (1998) 'Cognitive-Behavioral Treatment of Schizophrenia: A Case Study', *Journal of Cognitive Psychotherapy*, 12, (1), pp.13–25.

Braithwaite, J. J. (2008) Towards a cognitive neuroscience of the dying brain. [UK] *Skeptic*, 21(2), 8–16.

Braun, V. and Clarke, V. (2006) 'Using thematic analysis in psychology', *Qualitative Research in Psychology*, 3, pp.77–101.

Breedlove, S.M., Rosenzweig, M.R. and Watson, N.V. (2007) Biological Psychology: An Introduction to Behavioral, Cognitive and Clinical Neuroscience, Massachusetts: Sinauer.

Breland, K. and Breland, M. (1951) 'A new field of applied animal psychology', *American Psychologist*, 6, pp.202–4.

Bremner, G. (2003) 'Perception, knowledge and action', in A. Slate and G. Bremner (eds) *An Introduction to Developmental Psychology*, Oxford: Blackwell Publishing.

Brent, D.A., Holder, D., Kolko, D., Birmaher, B., Baugher, M., Roth, C., Iyengar, S. and Johnson, B.A. (1997) 'Clinical psychotherapy trial for adolescent depression comparing cognitive, family and supportive therapy', *Archives of General Psychiatry*, 54, pp.877–85.

British Association for the Advancement of Science (1990) *Animals and the Advancement of Science*, London.

British Nutrition Foundation (2007) *The eatwell plate*, London: British Nutrition Foundation.

British Psychological Society (1978) *Ethical Principles for Research on Human Subjects*, Leicester: BPS.

British Psychological Society (1993), *The Quit For Life Programme: An Easier Way To Quit Smoking and Not Start Again*, Leicester: British Psychological Society.

British Psychological Society (2004a and currently under review) *Ethical Principles for Conducting Research with Human Participants*, Leicester: BPS.

Minimum Standards of Ethical Approval in Psychological Research, Leicester: BPS.

British Psychological Society (2006) *Code of Ethics and Conduct*, Leicester: BPS.

British Psychological Society (2006a) *Code of Ethics and Conduct*, Leicester: BPS.

British Psychological Society (2006b) 'How the investigatory committee works', (Ethics column no. 5), *The Psychologist*, 19(3), p.169.

British Psychological Society (2007) *Guidelines for Psychologists Working with Animals*, Leicester: BPS.

British Psychological Society (2007a) *Conducting Research on the Internet: Guidelines for ethical practice in psychological research online*, Leicester: BPS.

British Psychological Society (2007b) *Guidelines for Psychologists Working with Animals*, Leicester: BPS.

British Psychological Society (2007c) *Ethical Implications for Psychologists Working on TV: A guide for production companies*, Leicester: BPS.

Britton, W. B. and Bootzin, R. R. (2004) 'Near-death experiences and the temporal lobe', *Psychological Science*, 15, 254–258.

Bristowe, W.S. (1945) 'Spider superstitions and folklore', *Transactions of the Connecticut Academy for Arts and Science*, 36, pp.53–90.

Broad, C. D. and Wade, N. (1982) *Betrayers of the truth*. New York: Simon & Shuster.

Brodbar-Nemzer, J.Y. (1986) 'Marital relationships and self-esteem: How Jewish families are different', *Journal of Marriage and the Family*, 48, pp.89–98.

Broughton, R., Billiings, R., Cartwright, R., Doucette, D., Edmeads, J., Edwardh, M., Ervin, F., Orchard, B., Hill, R. and Turrell, G. (1994) 'Homicidal somnambulism: A case report', *Sleep*, 17, pp.253–64.

Brown, G.L., Ebert, M.H., Goyer, P.F., Jimerson, D.C., Klein, W.J., Bunney, W.E. and Goodwin, F.K. (1982) 'Aggression, suicide, and serotonin: relationships to CSF amine metabolites', *American Journal of Psychiatry*, 139, pp.741–6.

Brown, G.W. (1972) 'Influence of family life on the course of schizophrenic disorders: a replication', *British Journal of Psychiatry*, 121, pp.241–8.

Brown, G.W. and Harris, T.O. (1978) *The Social Origins of Depression*, London: Tavistock.

Brown, G. W., Harris, T. O., and Hepworth, C. (1994) 'Life events and endogenous depression. A puzzle re-examined', *Archives of General Psychiatry* 51, pp.525–34.

Brown, R., Colter, N. and Corsellis, J.A.N. (1986) 'Post-mortem evidence of structural brain changes in schizophrenia: differences in brain weight, temporal brain area, and parahippocampal gyrus compared with affective disorder', *Archives of General Psychiatry*, 43, pp.36–42.

Brown, R. and Ogden, J. (2004) 'Children's eating attitudes and behaviour: A study of the modelling and control theories of parental influence', *Health Education Research: Theory and practice*, 19, pp.261–71.

Bruce, V. and Young, A.W. (1986) 'Understanding face recognition', *British Journal of Psychology*, 77, pp.305–27.

Bruce, V. and Green, P.R. (1990) *Visual Perception: Physiology, Psychology and Ecology* (2nd edn), Hove: Lawrence Erlbaum.

Bruch, H. (1965) 'Anorexia nervosa and its differential diagnosis', *Journal of Nervous and Mental Disease*, 141, pp.556–66.

Brugger, P., Regard, M. and Landis, T. (1991) 'Belief in extrasensory perception and illusory control: A replication.' *Journal of Psychology*, 125, 501–502.

Bruner, J.S. and Minturn, A.L. (1955) 'Perceptual identification and perceptual organisation', *Journal of General Psychology*, 53, pp.21–8.

Bruner, J.S. (1957) 'On perceptual readiness', *Psychological Review*, 64, pp.123–52.

Bruner, J.S. (1960) *The Process of Education*, Cambridge, MA: Harvard University Press [A second edition was published in 1977].

Bruner, J.S. (1966) *Toward a Theory of Instruction*, Cambridge, MA: Harvard University Press.

Bruner, J.S. (1983) *Children's Talk: Learning to use language*, Oxford: Oxford University Press.

Bruner, J.S. (1996) *The Culture of Education*, Cambridge, MA: Harvard University Press.

Bruner, J.S. and Kenney, H.J. (1966) *The Development of the Concepts of Order and Proportion in Children*, New York: Wiley.

Bruner, J.S., Goodnow, J.J. and Austin, G.A. (1956) *A Study of Thinking*, New York: Wiley.

Bruner, J.S., Olver, R.R. and Greenfield, P.M. (1966) *Studies in Cognitive Growth: A collaboration at the Centre for Cognitive Studies*, New York: John Wiley.

Brunner, H., Nelen, M., Breakefield, X., Ropers, H. and van Oost B. (1993) 'Abnormal behavior associated with a point mutation in the structural gene for monoamine oxidase A', *Science*, 262, pp.578–80.

Bryant, P.E. and Trabasso, T. (1971) 'Transite inferences and memory in young children', *Nature*, 232, pp.456–8.

Buchsbaum, M.S. (1990) 'The frontal lobes, basal ganglia, and temporal lobes as sites for schizophrenia', *Schizophrenia Bulletin*, 16, pp.379–89.

Buckingham, D. (1996) *Moving Images: Understanding Children's Emotional Responses to Television*, Manchester: Manchester University Press.

Buckingham, D. (2008) *The Media Literacy of Children and Young People: A review of the literature*, London: Ofcom.

Buckman, R. and Sabbagh, K. (1993) *Magic or medicine? An investigation into healing*. London: Macmillan.

Buitelaar, J.K. (2003) 'Review: atypical antipsychotics and psychosocial interventions, alone or in combination, may reduce youth aggression', *Evidence Based Mental Health*, 26(3), p.79.

Bullen, B.A., Reed, R.B. and Mayer, J. (1964) 'Physical activity of obese and non-obese adolescent girls appraised by motion picture sampling', *American Journal of Clinical Nutrition*, 4, pp.211–33.

Burger, J.M. (2009) 'Replicating Milgram: Would people still obey today?' *American Psychologist*, 64 (1), pp.1–11.

Burke, M., Drummond, L.M. and Johnston, D.W. (1997) 'Treatment choice for agoraphobic women: exposure or cognitive-behavioural therapy?', *British Journal of Clinical Psychology*, 36, pp.409–19.

Burton, A.M. and Bruce, V. (1993) 'Naming faces and naming names', *Memory*, 1, pp.457–80.

Burton, A.M., Bruce, V. and Johnston, R.A. (1990) 'Understanding face recognition with an interactive activation model', *British Journal of Psychology*, 81, pp.361–80.

Bushman, B.J. (1998) 'Effects of television violence on memory of commercial messages', *Journal of Experimental Psychology: Applied*, 4, pp.291–307.

Buss, D. (1999) *Evolutionary Psychology*, Boston: Allyn & Bacon.

Buss, D., Larsen, R., Western, D. and Semmelroth, J. (1992) 'Sex differences in jealousy: Evolution, physiology and psychology', *Psychological Science*, 3, pp.251–5.

Buss, D.M. (1989) 'Sex differences in human mate preferences: Evolutionary hypotheses tested in 37 cultures', *Behavioral and Brain Sciences*, 12, pp.1–49.

Buss, D.M. (1995) 'Psychological sex differences: Origins through sexual selection', *American Psychologist*, 50, pp.164–8.

Buss, D.M. (1999) 'Adaptive individual differences revisited', *Journal of Personality*, 67 (2), pp.259–64.

Buss, D.M. and Schmitt, D.P. (1993) 'Sexual strategies theory: An evolutionary perspective on human mating', *Psychological Review*, 100, pp.204–32.

Buss, D.M. and Shackelford, T.K. (1997) 'From vigilance to violence: Mate retention tactics in married couples', *Journal of Personality and Social Psychology*, 72(2), pp.346–361.

Buss, D.M. and Duntley, J.D. (2006), 'The evolution of aggression', in M. Schaller, D.T. Kenrick and J.A. Simpson (eds), *Evolution and social psychology* (pp. 263–86), New York: Psychology Press.

Bussey, K. and Bandura, A. (1992) 'Self regulatory mechanisms governing gender development'. *Child Development*, 63, pp.1236–50.

Bussey, K. and Bandura, A. (1999) 'Social cognitive theory of gender development and differentiation', *Psychological Review*, 106, pp.676–713.

Butler, G. (1989) 'Issues in the application of cognitive and behavioural strategies to treatment of social phobia', *Clinical Psychology Review*, 9, pp.91–106.

Button, E.J., Loan, P., Davies, J. and Sonuga-Barke, E.J.S. (1997) 'Self-esteem, eating problems, and psychological well-being in a cohort of schoolgirls aged 15-16: A questionnaire and interview study', *International Journal of Eating Disorders*, 21, pp.39–47.

Button, T., Scourfield, J., Martin, N. and McGuffin, P. (2004) 'Do aggressive and non-aggressive antisocial behaviors in adolescents result from the same genetic and environmental effects?' *American Journal of Medical Genetics Part B: Neuropsychiatric Genetics*, 129B (1), pp.59–63.

Buysse, D.J., Reynolds, C.F. III, Monk, T.H., Berman, S.R. and Kupfer, D.J., (2000) 'The Pittsburgh Sleep Quality Index: A New Instrument for Psychiatric Practice and Research', pp.193–213. Modified from: J. Rush Pincus, H.A. First, M.B. Blacker, D. Endicott, J. Keith, S.J. I. (2000) *Handbook of Psychiatric Measures*, Washington DC: APA.

Byerly, M.J., Fisher, R., Carmody, T. and Rush, A.J. (2005) 'A trial of compliance therapy in outpatients with schizophrenia or schizoaffective disorder', *Journal of Clinical Psychiatry*, 66, pp.997–1001.

Byrd, R. J. (1988) 'Positive therapeutic effects of intercessory prayer in a coronary care unit population', *Southern Medical Journal*, 81, 826–829.

Byrne, D. and Clore, G.L. (1970) 'A reinforcement model of evaluative responses', *Personality: An International Journal*, 1, pp.103–28.

Byrne, R. W. (1994) *Behaviour and Evolution*, Cambridge: Cambridge University Press.

Byrnes, J.P., Miller, D.C. and Schafer, W.D. (1999) 'Gender differences in risk taking', *Psychological Bulletin*, 125(33), pp.367–83.

Byron, T. (2008) *Safer Children in a Digital World*, p.147, www.dcfs.gov.uk/byronreview

Cacioppo, J.T. and Petty, R.E. (1982) 'The need for cognition', *Journal of Personality and Social Psychology*, 42, pp.116–31.

Calvo-Merino, B., Glaser, D.E., Grèzes, J., Passingham, R.E. and Haggard, P. (2005) 'Action observation and acquired motor skills: An fMRI study with expert dancers', *Cerebral Cortex*, 15 (8), pp.1243–9.

Camilleri, J.A. (2004) 'Investigating sexual coercion in romantic relationships: A test of the cuckoldry risk hypothesis', Unpublished master's thesis, Saskatoon, Canada: University of Saskatchewan.

Campbell, M.A. (2005) 'Cyber bullying: An old problem in a new guise?', *Australian Journal of Guidance and Counselling*, 15, pp.68–76.

Campbell, S.S. and Murphy, P.J. (1998) 'Extraocular circadian phototransduction in humans', *Science*, 279, pp.366–9.

Campos, J.J., Langer, A. and Krowitz, A. (1970) 'Cardiac response on the cliff in pre-locomotor human infants', *Science*, 170, pp.196–7.

Cannon, T.D., Zorrilla, L.E., Shtasel, D., Gur, R.E., Gur, R.C., Marco, E.J., Moberg, P. and Price, R.A. (1994b) 'Neuropsychological functioning in siblings discordant for schizophrenia and healthy volunteers', *Archives of General Psychiatry*, 51, pp.651–61.

Cape, G.S. (2003) 'Addiction, stigma, and movies', *Acta Psychiatrica Scandinavica*, 107, pp.163–169.

Caplan, M.Z. and Hay, D.F. (1989) 'Preschoolers' responses to peer distress and beliefs about bystander intervention', *Journal of Child psychology and Psychiatry*, 30, pp.231–42.

Cardno, A.G., Marshall, E.J., Coid, B., Macdonald, A.M., Ribchester, T.R., Davies, N.J., Venturi, P., Jones, L.A., Lewis, S.W., Sham, P.C., Gottesman I.I., Farmer, A.E., McGuffin, P., Reveley, A.M. and Murray R.M. (1999) 'Heritability estimates for psychotic disorders', *Archives of General Psychiatry*, 56 (4), pp.162–8.

Carey, G. and Gottesman, I. (1981) 'Twin and family studies of anxiety, phobic, and obsessive disorders', in D. Klein and J. Rabkin (eds) *Anxiety: New Research and Changing Concepts*, New York: Raven Press.

Carlberg, P., Gunnarsdttir, M., Hedesjo, L., Andersson, G., Ekselius, L. and Furmark, T. (2007) 'Treatment of social phobia: randomised trial of internet-delivered cognitive-behavioural therapy with telephone support', *The British Journal of Psychiatry*, 190, pp.123–128.

Carlson, N.R. (2002) *Foundations of Physiological Psychology*, Boston: Allyn and Bacon.

Carnes, P. (1991) *Don't Call It Love: Recovery from Sexual Addiction*, New York: Bantam Books.

Carpendale, J.I.M. and Chandler, M.J. (1996) 'On the distinction between false belief understanding and subscribing to an interpretive theory of mind', *Child Development*, 67 (4), pp.1686–1706.

Carr, D. B. (1982) 'Pathophysiology of stress-induced limbic lobe dysfunction: A hypothesis relevant to near-death experiences', *Anabiosis: The Journal of Near-Death Studies*, 2, 75–89.

Carrier, D.R. (2007) 'The short legs of great apes: evidence for aggressive behaviour in australopiths', *Evolution: International Journal of Organic Evolution*, 61 (3), pp. 596–605.

Carroll, B.J. (1982) 'The dexamethasone suppression test for melancholia', *British Journal of Psychiatry*, 140, pp.292–304.

Cases, O. (1995) 'Aggressive behavior and altered amounts of brain serotonin and norepinephrine in mice lacking MAOA', *Science*, 268, pp.1763–6.

Cashmore, E. (2006) *Celebrity/Culture*, Oxford: Routledge.

Caspi, A., McClay, J., Moffitt, T.E., Mill, J., Martin, J., Craig, I.W., Taylor, A. and Poulton, R. (2002) 'Role of genotype in the cycle of violence in maltreated children', *Science*, 297, pp.851–4.

Caspi, A., Moffitt, T.E., Cannon, M., McClay, J., Murray, R., Harrington, H., Taylor, A., Arseneault, L., Williams, B., Braithwaite, A., Poulton, R. and Craig, I.W. (2005) 'Moderation of the effect of adolescent-onset cannabis use on adult psychosis by a functional polymorphism in the catechol-O-methyltransferase gene: longitudinal evidence of a gene X environment interaction', *Biological Psychiatry*, 57, pp.1117–27.

Castner, S.A., Algan, O., Findlay, H.A., Rakic, P. and Goldman-Rakie, P.S. (1998) 'Fetal Xirradiation in monkeys impairs working memory after but not prior to puberty', *Society of Neuroscience*, 24, Part 1, p.225.

Cavior, N. and Boblett, P. J. (1972) 'Physical attractiveness of dating versus married couples', *Annual Convention of the American Psychological Association*, 7, pp.175–6.

Ceci, S. J. (1990) *On intelligence...more or less: A bio-ecological treatise on intellectual development*, Englewood Cliffs, NJ: Prentice-Hall.

Cerlettii, U. and Bini, L. (1938) 'L'lettroshock', *Archives of General Neurology, Psychiatry and Psychoanalysis*, 19, pp.266–8.

Chagnon, N.A. (1988) 'Life histories, blood revenge, and warfare in a tribal population', *Science*, 239, pp.985–92.

Chandler, M.J. and Sokol, B.W. (1999) 'Representation once removed: Children's developing conceptions of representational life', in I.E. Sigel (ed.) *Development of Mental Representation: Theories and applications*, Mahwah, NJ: Lawrence Erlbaum Associates, pp.201–30.

Chapman, L. J. and Chapman, J. P. (1967) 'Genesis of popular but erroneous psychodiagnostic observations', *Journal of Abnormal Psychology*, 72, 193–204

Chibnall, J. T., Jeral, J. M. and Cerullo, M. A. (2001) 'Experiments on distant intercessory prayer: God, science, and the lesson of Massah', *Archives of Internal Medicine*, 161, 2529–2536.

Chinn, S. and Rona, R.J. (2001) 'Prevalence and trends in overweight and obesity in three cross sectional studies of British children, 1974–1994', *British Medical Journal*, 322, pp.24–6.

Chodorow, N. (1978) *The Reproduction of Mothering*, Berkeley: University of California Press.

Chowhan, J. and Stewart, J. (2007) 'Television and the Behaviour of Adolescents: Does Socio-economic Status Moderate the Link?', *Social Science and Medicine*, 65(7), pp.1324–36.

Chung, W.C.J., De Vries, G.J. and Swaab, D. (2002) 'Sex differentiation of the bed nucleus of the stria terminalis in Humans may extend into adulthood', *Journal of Neuroscience*, 22 (3), pp.1027–33.

Cialdini, R.B., Kenrick, D.T. and Bauman, D.J. (1982) 'Effects of mood on prosocial behaviour in children and adults', in N. Eisenberg-Berg (ed.) *The Development of Prosocial Behavior*, New York: Academic Press, pp.339–56.

Clare, A.W. (1985) 'Hormones, behaviour and the menstrual cycle', *Journal of Psychosomatic Research*, 29, pp.225–33.

Clancy, S. A. (2005) *Abducted: How people come to believe they were kidnapped by aliens*. Cambridge, MA: Harvard University Press.

Clancy, S. A., McNally, R. J., Schacter, D. L., Lenzenweger, M. F. and Pitman, R. K. (2002) 'Memory distortion in people reporting abduction by aliens', *Journal of Abnormal Psychology*, 111, 455–461.

Clark, M.S. and Mills, J. (1979) 'Interpersonal attraction in exchange and communal relationships', *Journal of Personality and Social Psychology*, 37, pp.12–24.

Clark, R.D. and Hatfield, E. (1989) 'Gender differences in receptivity to sexual offers', *Journal of Psychology and Human Sexuality*, 2, pp.39–55.

Clark, T.W. (2006) 'Ordem e progresso? A structural analysis of Brazilian lynch mob violence', Unpublished PhD dissertation, University of Minnesota.

Clayton, R., Cattarello A.M. and Johnstone, B.M. (1996) 'The effectiveness of Drug Abuse Resistance Education (project DARE): 5-year follow-up results', *Prevention Medicine*, 25, pp.307–318.

Clutton-Brock, T.H. and Vincent, A.C. (1991) 'Sexual selection and the potential reproductive rates of males and females', *Nature*, 351, pp.58–60.

Coates, T.J., Jeffrey, R.W. and Wing, R.R. (1978) 'The relationship between a person's relative body weights and the quality and quantity of food stored in their homes', *Addictive Behaviours*, 3, pp.179–84.

Coccaro, E.F., Bergeman, C.S., Kavoussi, R.J. andSseroczynski, A.D. (1997), 'Heritability of aggression and irritability: A twin study of the Buss-Durkee aggression scales in adult male subjects', *Biological Psychiatry*, 41 (3), pp.273–84.

Cochrane, R. and Sashidharan, S.P. (1995) 'Mental health and ethnic minorities: a review of the literature and implications for services', Paper presented to the Birmingham and Northern Birmingham Health Trust.

Coetzer, B.R. (2004) 'Obsessive-compulsive disorder following brain injury: A review', *International Journal of Psychiatric Medicine*, 34, pp.363–377.

Cohen, C. (1981) 'Person categories and social perception: testing some boundaries of the processing effects of prior knowledge', *Journal of Personality and Social Psychology*, 40, pp.441–52.

Cohen, D.B. (1979) Sleep and Dreaming: Origins, Nature and Functions, Pergamon Press: Oxford.

Coie, J.D. and Dodge, K.A. (1997) 'Aggression and antisocial behaviour' in W. Damon and N. Eisenberg (eds) *Handbook of Child Psychology (Vol.3): Social, Emotional and Personality Development*, New York: Wiley pp.779–862.

Colby, A. and Kohlberg, L. (1987) *The Measurement of Moral Judgment*, New York: Cambridge University Press.

Cole, C.F., Arafat, C., Tidhar, C., Tafesh, W.Z., Fox, N.A., Killen, M., Ardila-Rey, A., Leavitt, L.A., Lesser, G., Richman, B.A. and Yung, F. (2003) 'The educational impact of Rechov Sumsum/Shara'a Simsim: A *Sesame Street* television series to promote respect and understanding among children living in Israel, the West Bank, and Gaza', *International Journal of Behavioural Development, 27*, pp.409–22.

Cole, C.F., Labin, D.B. and del Rocio Galarza, M. (2008) 'Begin with the children: What research on Sesame Street's international coproductions reveals about using media to promote a new more peaceful world', *International Journal of Behavioral Development, 32*(4), pp.359–65.

Coles, M.E., Heimberg, R.G., Frost, R.O. and Steketess, G. (2005) 'Not just right experiences and obsessive-compulsive features: experimental and self-monitoring perspectives', *Behaviour Research and Therapy, 43*, pp.153–67.

Collins, P. (2007) 'Gambling and governance', in G. Smith, D. Hodgins and R. Williams (eds), *Research and Measurement Issues in Gambling Studies*, New York: Elsevier, pp.617–639.

Comer, R.J. (2004) *Abnormal Psychology* (5th edn), New York: Worth Publishers.

Comer, R.J. (2007) *Abnormal Psychology* (6th edn), New York: Worth Publishers.

Comings, D.E. (1998) 'Why different rules are required for polygenic inheritance: lessons from studies of the DRD2 gene', *Alcohol*, 16, pp.61–70.

Comings, D.E., Rosenthal, R.J., Lesieur, H.R., Rugle, L.J., Muhleman, D., Chie, C., Dietz, G. and Gade, R. (1996) 'A study of dopamine D2 receptor gene in pathological gambling', *Pharmacogenetics, 6*, pp.223–234.

Comstock, G. and Scharrer, E. (1999) *Television: What's On, Who's Watching, and What it Means*, San Diego, CA: Academic Press.

Conel, J.L. (1951) *The Postnatal Development of the Cerebral Cortex* (Vol. 3), Cambridge: Harvard University Press.

Connellan, J., Baron-Cohen, S., Wheelwright, S., Batki, A. and Ahluwalia, J. (2000) 'Sex differences in human neonatal social perception', *Infant Behaviour and Development, 23*, pp.113–8.

Conner, M. and Norman, P. (eds) (2005) *Predicting Health Behaviour* (2nd edn), Maidenhead: Open University Press/McGraw Hill Education.

Conner, M., Fitter, M. and Fletcher, W. (1999) 'Stress and snacking: A diary study of daily hassles and between meal snacking', *Psychology and Health*, 14, pp.51–63.

Cook, A. M. and Irwin, H. J. (1983) 'Visuospatial skills and the out-of-body experience', *Journal of Parapsychology, 47*, 23–35.

Cook, C. M. and Persinger, M. A. (1997) 'Experimental induction of the "sensed presence" in normal subjects and an exceptional subject', *Perceptual and Motor Skills*, 85, 683–693.

Cook, C. M. and Persinger, M. A. (2001) 'Geophysical variables and behaviour: XCII. Experimental elicitation of the experience of a sentient being by right hemispheric, weak magnetic fields: Interaction with temporal lobe sensitivity', *Perceptual and Motor Skills*, 85, 683–693.

Cook, T.D. and Campbell, D.T. (1979) *Quasi-experimentation: Design and analysis issues for field settings*, Chicago, Illinois: Rand McNally.

Coolican, H. (2009) *Research Methods and Statistics in Psychology* (5th edn), London: Hodder and Stoughton.

Cools, J., Schotte, D.E. and McNally, R.J. (1992) 'Emotional arousal and overeating in restrained eaters', *Journal of Abnormal Psychology*, 101, pp.348–51.

Cooper, C. (2002) *Individual Differences* (2nd ed.), London: Arnold.

Cooper, J., and Fazio, R. H. (1984) 'A new look at dissonance theory', *Advances in Experimental Social Psychology*, 17, pp.229–65.

Coren, S. (1996) *Sleep Thieves*, New York: Free Press.

Coren, S., Ward, L.M. and Enns, J.T. (2004) *Sensation and Perception*, Hoboken, NJ: Wiley.

Cosgrove, G.R. (2000) 'Surgery for psychiatric disorders', *CNS Spectrums 2000*, 5, pp.43–52.

Cosmides, L. and Tooby, J. (1987) 'From evolution to behavior: evolutionary psychology as the missing link', in J. Dupre (ed.) *The Latest on the Best: Essays on evolution and optimality*, Cambridge, MA: The MIT Press.

Costa, P.T., Terracciano, A. and McCrae, R.R. (2001) 'Gender differences in personality traits across cultures: Robust and surprising findings', *Journal of Personality and Social Psychology, 81*(2) pp.322–31.

Courage, M.L. and Adams, J. (1996) 'Infant peripheral vision: the development of monocular visual acuity in the first three months of postnatal life', *Vision Research*, 36, pp.1207–15.

Craske, M.G. and Barlow, D.H. (1993) 'Panic disorder and agoraphobia', in D.H. Barlow (ed.) *Clinical Handbook of Psychological Disorders: A Step-by-Step Treatment Manual* (2nd edn), New York: Guilford.

Crawley, S. E., French, C. C., & Yesson, S. A. (2002) 'Evidence for transliminality from a subliminal card guessing task', *Perception*, 31, 887–892.

Crick, N.R. and Rose, A.J. (2000) 'Toward a gender-balanced approach to the study of social-emotional development: A look at relational aggression', in M. Cole, S. R. Cole and C. Lightfoot (eds) *The Development of Children*, New York: Worth Publishers, p.554.

Crislip, M. (2008) 'Near death experiences and the medical literature', [US] *Skeptic*, 14(2), 14–15.

Crow, T.J. (1985) 'The two-syndrome concept: origins and current status', *Schizophrenia Bulletin*, 11, pp. 471–86.

Culp, R.E., Cook, A.S. and Housley, P.C. (1983) 'A comparison of observed and reported adult-infant interactions: Effects of perceived sex', *Sex Roles*, pp.475–9.

Cumberbatch, G. (1990) 'Television advertising and sex role stereotyping: a content analysis', Working paper IV for the Broadcast Standards Council Communications Research Group, Birmingham: Aston University.

Cumberbatch, G. (2000) 'Only a game?', *New Scientist, 2242*, pp.44–5.

Cumberbatch, G. (2004) Video Violence: villain or victim, videostandards.org.uk/downloads/video_violence

Cumberbatch, G. (2009) 'Effects', in D. Albertazzi and P. Cobley (eds) *The Media: An Introduction* (3rd edn), Harlow, Essex: Pearson Education

Cumberbatch, G. and Howitt, D. (eds) (1989) *A Measure of Uncertainty: Effects of Mass Media*, Broadcast Standards Council Research Monograph Series, London: John Libbey.

Cunningham, M.R. (1988) 'Does happiness mean friendliness? Induced mood and heterosexual self-disclosure', *Personality and Social Psychology Bulletin*, 14, pp.283–97.

Curtiss, S. (1977) *Genie: A Psycholinguistic Study of a Modern-day 'Wild Child'*, London: Academic Press.

Cuthill, I. (1991) 'Field experiments in animal behaviour', *Animal Behaviour*, 42, pp.1007–14.

Czeisler, C.A., Moore-ede, .C. and Coleman, R. . (1982) 'Rotating shift work schedules that disrupts sleep are improved by applying circadian principles', *Science*, 217, pp.460–3.

Dag, I. (1999) 'The relationships among paranormal beliefs, locus of control and psychopathology in a Turkish college sample', *Personality and Individual Differences*, 26, 723–737.

Dalman, C., Allebeck, P., Cullberg, J., Grunewald, C. and Koster, M. (1999) 'Obstetric complications and the risk of schizophrenia: a longitudinal study of a national birth cohort', *Archives of General Psychiatry*, 56 (3), pp.234-40.

Dalton, K. (1964) *The Premenstrual Syndrome*, London: Heinemann.

Dalton, M.A., Sargent, J.D., Beach, M.L., Titus-Ernstoff, L., Gibson, J.J., Aherns, M.B. and Heatherton, T.F. (2003) 'Effect of viewing smoking in movies on adolescent smoking initiation: A cohort study', *Lancet*, 362, pp.281–285.

Daly, M. and Wilson, M. (1978) *Sex, Evolution and Behavior*, Belmont, CA: Duxbury Press.

Daly, M. and Wilson, M. (1988) *Homicide*, Hawthorne, NY: Aldine de Gruyter.

Daly, M. and Wilson, M. (1994) 'Evolutionary psychology of male violence', in J. Archer (ed), *Male Violence*, London: Routledge pp.253–88.

Daly, M., Wilson, M. and Weghorst, S.J. (1982) 'Male sexual jealousy', *Ethology and Sociobiology, 3*, pp.11–27.

Damon, W. (1977) *The Social World of the Child*, San Francisco: Jossey-Bass.

Davies, J.B. (1996) 'Reasons and causes: Understanding substance users' explanation for their behaviour', *Human Psychopharmacology*, 11(Supp. 1), S39–S48.

Davies, J.B. and Baker, R. (1987) 'The impact of self-presentation and interviewer bias effects on self-reported heroin use', *British Journal of Addiction*, 82, pp.907–912.

Davis, J.D., Kane, J.M., Marder, S.R., Brauzer, B., Gierl, B., Schooler, N., Casey, D.E. and Hassan, M. (1993) 'Dose response of prophylactic antipsychotics', *Journal of Clinical Psychiatry*, 54 (3), pp.24–30.

Davison, W.P. (1983) 'The third-person effect in communication', *Public Opinion Quarterly*, 47, pp.1–15.

Darley, J.M. (1992) 'Social organization for the production of evil', *Psychological Inquiry*, 3 (2), pp.199–218.

Darwin, C. (1859) *On the Origin of Species by Means of Natural Selection*, London: John Murray.

Darwin, C. (1871) *The Descent of Man and Selection in Relation to Sex*, London: John Murray. For a general source book of Darwin's original writings, see Porter, D.M. and Graham, P.W. (eds) (1993) *The Portable Darwin*, Harmondsworth: Penguin Books.

Darwin, C. (1871) 'The descent of man and selection in relation to sex', in J. Archer and B. Lloyd (eds) *Sex and Gender*, Cambridge: Cambridge University Press, pp.55–61.

Dasen, P.R. (ed.) (1977) *Piagetian Psychology: Cross-cultural contributions*, New York: Gardner Press.

Dasen, P.R. (1994) 'Culture and cognitive development from a Piagetian perspective', in W.J. Lonner and R.S. Malpass (eds) *Psychology and Culture*, Boston: Allyn and Bacon, pp.145–9.

Davis, C. (1928) 'Self-selection of diets by newly weened infants', *American Journal of Disease of Children*, 36, pp.651–79.

Davis, C. (1939) 'Results of the self selection of diets by young children', *The Canadian Medical Association Journal*, 41, pp.257–61.

Davis, L. (1997) *Hazing in the Workplace*, Ann Arbor, MI: UMI.

Davison, G.C. and Neale, J.M. (2001) Abnormal psychology (8ᵗʰ edn), New York: John Wiley & Sons.

Dawkins, R. (1976) *The Selfish Gene*, Oxford: Oxford University Press.

Day, R.H. (1990) 'The Bourdon illusion in haptic space', *Perception and Psychophysics*, 47, pp.400–4.

Dean, G., Mather, A. and Kelly, I. W. (1996) 'Astrology' In G. Stein (ed.) *Encyclopedia of the paranormal*. Amherst, NY: Prometheus. Pp. 47–99.

Deary, I.J., Whalley, L.J., Lemmon, H., Crawford, J.R. and Starr, J.M. (2000) 'The Stability of Individual Differences in Mental Ability from Childhood to Old Age: Follow-up of the 1932 Scottish Mental Survey', *Intelligence*, 28, pp.49–55.

Deary, I.J. (2001) *Intelligence: A very short introduction*, Oxford: Oxford University Press.

Deaux, K., Dane, F.C. and Wrightsman, L.S. (1993) *Social Psychology in the '90s*, Pacific Grove, CA: Brooks-Cole.

De Backer, C. (2005) *Media Gossip in Evolutionary Perspective*, Human Nature and Society Conference, Los Angeles: University of California Los Angeles.

De Backer, C. (2007) 'Like Belgian Chocolate for the Universal Mind', *Interpersonal and Media Gossip from an Evolutionary Perspective*, News release, University of Leicester.

Decety, J. and Ingvar, D.H. (1990) 'Brain structures participating in mental simulation of motor behaviour: a neuropsychological interpretation', *Acta Psychologica*, 73, pp.13–24.

Decety, J. and Jackson, P.L. (2004) 'The functional architecture of human empathy', *Behavioural Cognitive Neuroscience Review*, 3, pp.71–100.

Delamont, S. (1990) *Sex Roles and the School*, London: Routledge, p.3.

Delfabbro, P.H. and Winefield, A.H. (1999) 'Poker machine gambling: An analysis of within session characteristics', *British Journal of Psychology*, 90, pp.425–439.

DeLima, M.S., de Jesus Mari, J., Breier, A., Costa, A.M., de Sena, E.P. and Hotopf, M. (2005) 'Quality of life in schizophrenia: A multi-center, randomised , naturalistic, controlled trial comaparing olanzapine to first generation antipsychotics', *Journal of Clinical Psychiatry*, 66 (7), pp.831–8.

DeLisi, M., Berg, M.T. and Hochstetler, A. (2004), 'Gang members, career criminals and prison violence: Further specification of the importation model of inmate behavior', *Criminal Justice Studies*, 17 (4), pp.369–83.

Dement, W.C. (1974) *Some Must Watch While Some Must Sleep*, San Francisco: W.H. Freeman.

Denmark, F., Russo, N.F., Frieze, I.H and Sechzer, J.A (1988) 'Guidelines for avoiding sexism in psychological research', *American Psychologist,* 43 (7), pp.582–5.

Dennis. W. (1960) 'Causes of retardation among institutional children: Iran', *Journal of Genetic Psychology*, 96, pp.47–59.

Denton, D. (1982) *The Hunger for Salt*, Berlin: Springer-Verlag.

Department of Health (1992) *The Health of the Nation: A strategy for health in England*, London: HMSO.

Department of Health (1999) *Saving Lives: Our Healthier Nation*, London: HMSO.

Deregowski, J. (1972) 'Pictorial perception and culture', *Scientific American*, 227, pp.82–8.

Deregowski, J. (1980) 'Illusions, patterns and pictures: a cross-cultural perspective', London: Academic Press.

Derrick, J.L., Gabriel, S. and Tippin, B. (2008) 'Parasocial relationships and self-discrepancies: Faux relationships have benefits for low self-esteem individuals', *Personal Relationships*, 15, pp.261–80.

Desor, J.A., Maller, O. and Turner, R.E. (1973) 'Taste and acceptance of sugars by human infants', *Journal of Comparative and Physiological Psychology*, 84, pp.496–501.

DeVellis, B.M. and Blalock, S.J. (1992) 'Illness attributions and hopeless depression: the role of hopelessness expectancy', *Journal of Abnormal Psychology*, 101, pp.257–64.

Devlin, B., Daniels, M. and Roeder, K. (1997) 'The heritability of IQ', *Nature*, 388, pp.468–71.

Diaconis, P. and Mosteller, F. (1989) Methods for studying coincidences. *Journal of the American Statistical Association*, 84, 853–862.

Diamond, M. and Sigmundson, H.K. (1997) 'Management of intersexuality: guidelines for dealing with persons with ambiguous genitalia', Archives of *Pediatrics and Adolescent Medicine*, 151, pp.1046–50.

Dickerson, M.G. and O'Connor, J. (2006) *Gambling as an Addictive Behaviour: Impaired Control and its Relationship to Other Variables*, Cambridge: Cambridge University Press.

Dickson, D. H. and Kelly, I. W. (1985) 'The "Barnum effect" in personality assessment: A review of the literature.' *Psychological Reports*, 57, 367–382.

Diener, E., Lusk, R., DeFour, D. and Flax, R. (1980) 'Deindividuation: Effects of group size, density, number of observers, and group member similarity on self-consciousness and disinhibited behavior', *Journal of Personality and Social Psychology*, 39, pp.449-59.

Dijkstra, A. and de Vries, H. (2001) 'Do self-help interventions in health education lead to cognitive changes, and do cognitive changes lead to behavioural change?' *British Journal of Health Psychology*, 6, pp.121–34.

Distefan, J.M., Gilpin, E.A., Sargent, J.D. and Pierce, J.P. (1999) 'Do movie stars encourage adolescents to start smoking? Evidence from California', *Preventive Medicine*, 28, pp.1–11.

Dinstein, I., Hasson, U., Rubin, N. and Heeger, D.J. (2008) 'Brain areas selective for both observed and executed movements', *Journal of Neurophysiology*, 98 93), pp.1415–27.

Dobash, R.E. and Dobash, R.P. (1984) 'The nature and antecedents of violent events', *British Journal of Criminology*, 24, pp.269–88.

Dolberg, O.T., Iancu, I., Sasson, Y. and Zohar, J. (1996) 'The pathogenesis and treatment of obsessive-compulsive disorder', *Clinical Neuropharmacology*, 19(2), pp.129–147.

Donaldson, M. (1978) *Children's Minds*, London: Fontana.

Dressing, H., Küehner, C. and Gass, P. (2005) 'Lifetime prevalence and impact of stalking in a European population, Epidemiological data from a middle-sized German city', *British Journal of Psychiatry*, 187, pp.168–72.

Drevets, W.L., Gadde, K.M. and Krishnan, K.R. (2004) 'Neuroimaging studies of mood disorder', In D. Chorey and E.J.Netsker (eds) *Neurobiology of mental illness*, pp.461–490, Oxford: Oxford University Press.

Driesen, N.R. and Raz, N. (1995) 'The influence of sex, age, and handedness on corpus callosum morphology: A meta-analysis', *Psychobiology 23*, (3) pp.240–7.

Drury, V., Bichwood, M. and Cochrane, R. (2000) 'Cognitive therapy and recovery from acute psychosis: a controlled trial. 3: Five-year follow-up', *British Journal of Psychiatry*, 177, pp.8–14.

Duck, S. W. (1982) 'A Topography of Relationship Disengagement and Dissolution', in S.W. Duck (ed), *Personal Relationships 4: Dissolving Personal Relationships*, London: Academic Press.

Dunbar, R.I.M. (1992) 'Neocortex size as a constraint on group size in primates', *Journal of Human Evolution*, 20, pp.469–93.

Dunbar, R.I.M. (1995) 'Are you lonesome tonight?', *New Scientist*, 11 February, pp.26–31.

Dunbar, R.I.M., Duncan, N. and Nettle, D. (1995) 'Size and structure of freely forming conversational groups', *Human Nature*, 6, pp.67–78.

Duncan, H.F., Gourlay, N. and Hudson, W. (1973) 'A study of pictorial representation among the Bantu and white primary school children in South Africa', Johannesburg: Witwatersrand University Press.

Dudley, R.T. (1999) 'The effect of superstitious belief on performance following an unsolvable problem', *Personality and Individual Differences*, 26, 1057–1064.

Durkin, K. (1995) *Developmental Social Psychology*, Oxford: Blackwell.

Durlak, J.A. (2003) 'Effective prevention and health promotion programming', in T.P. Gullotta and M. Bloom (eds), *Encyclopedia of primary prevention and health promotion*, New York: Kluwer, pp.61–69.

Dusek, J.B. (1987) 'Sex roles and adjustment' in D.B. Carter (ed) *Current Conceptions of Sex Roles and Sex Typing: Theory and Research,* New York: Praeger, pp.211–22.

Eagly, A. H. (1978) 'Sex Differences in Influenceability', *Psychological Bulletin*, 85(1), pp.86–116.

Eagly, A.H. and Carli, L.L. (1981) 'Sex of researchers and sex-typed communications as determinants of sex differences in influenceability: A meta-analysis of social influence studies', *Psychological Bulletin*, 90, pp.1–20.

Eckensberger, L.H. (1983) 'Research on moral development', *The German Journal of Psychology*, 7 (3), pp.195–244.

Eckensberger, L.H. (1994) 'Moral development and its measurement across cultures', in W.J. Lonner and R.S. Malpass (eds) *Psychology and Culture*, Boston: Allyn and Bacon, pp.71–8.

Eckensberger, L.H. (1999) 'Socio-moral development', in D. Messer and S. Millar (eds) *Exploring Developmental Psychology: From Infancy to Adolescence*, London: Edward Arnold, pp.302–22.

Edwards, P. (1996) *Reincarnation: A critical examination*. Amherst, NY: Prometheus.

Ehrhardt, A. and Money, J. (1967) 'Progestin-induced hermaphroditism: IQ and psychosexual identity in a study of ten girls' in G. C. Davidson and J. M. Neale (eds) *Abnormal Psychology*, New York: John Wiley & Sons p.383.

Ehrsson, H. H. (2007) 'The experimental induction of out-of-body experiences', *Science*, 317, 1048.

Eisenberg, N. (1983) 'Children's differentiations among potential recipients of aid', *Child Development*, 54, pp.594–602.

Eisenberg, N. (1986) *Altruistic Emotion, Cognition, and Behavior*, Hillsdale, NJ: Lawrence Erlbaum Associates.

Eisenberg, N. (1996) 'In search of the good heart', in M.R. Merrens and G.G. Brannigan (eds) *The Developmental Psychologists: Research adventures across the lifespan*, New York: McGraw-Hill, pp.89–104.

Eisenberg, N. and Hand, M. (1979) 'The relationship of preschoolers' reasoning about prosocial moral conflicts to prosocial behavior', *Child Development*, 50 (2), pp.356–63.

Eisenberg, N., Lennon, R. and Roth, K. (1983) 'Prosocial development: A longitudinal study', *Developmental Psychology*, 19, pp.846–55.

Eisenberg, N., Shell, R., Pasternak, J., Lennon, R., Beller, R. and Mathy, R.M. (1987) 'Pro-social development in middle childhood: A longitudinal study', *Developmental Psychology*, 23 (5), pp.712–8.

Eisenberg, N., Miller, P.A., Shell, R., McNalley, S. and Shea, C. (1991) 'Prosocial development in adolescence: A longitudinal study', *Developmental Psychology*, 27 (5), pp.849–57.

Eisenberg, N., Carlo, G., Murphy, B. and Van Court, P. (1995) 'Prosocial development in late adolescence', *Child Development*, 66, pp.1179–97.

Eisenberg, N., Guthrie, I.K., Murphy, B.C., Shepard, S.A., Cumberland, A. and Carlo, G. (1999) 'Consistency and development of prosocial dispositions: A longitudinal study', *Child Development*, 70 (6), pp.1360–72.

Eisenberg, N., Cumberland, A., Guthrie, I.K., Murphy, B.C. and Shepard, S.A. (2005) 'Age changes in prosocial responding and moral reasoning in adolescence and early adulthood', *Journal of Research on Adolescence*, 15 (3), pp.235–60.

Eklund, P.L.E., Gooren, L.J.G. and Bezemer, P.D. (1988) 'Prevalence of transsexualism in the Netherlands', *British Journal of Psychiatry*, 152, pp.638–40.

Elkin, I. (1994) 'The NIMH Treatment of Depression Collaborative Research Program: Where we began and where we are', In A.E. Bergin and S.L. Garfield (Eds) *Handbook of psychotherapy and behaviour change* (4th edn), New York: Wiley.

Ellis, A. (1962) *Reason and Emotion in Psychotherapy*, New York: Citadel.

Ellis, A. (1991) 'The revised ABCs of rational-emotive therapy', *Journal of Rational-Emotive and Cognitive-Behaviour Therapy*, 9, pp.139–92.

Ellis, H.D. (1986) 'Processes underlying face recognition', in R. Bruyer (ed.) *The Neuropsychology of Face Perception and Facial Expression*, Hove: Laurence Elbaum Associates.

Elms, A.C. (1972) *Social Psychology and Social Relevance*, Boston: Little, Brown.

Ember, C.R. (1978) 'Myths about hunter-gatherers' cited in Wood, W. and Eagly, A.H. (2002) 'A cross-cultural analysis of the behaviour of women and men: Implications for the origins of sex differences' p.703, *Psychological Bulletin*, 128, pp.699–727.

Emmelkamp, P.M. (1982) 'Exposure in vivo treatments', in A. Goldstein and D. Chambless (eds) *Agoraphobia: Multiple perspectives on theory and treatment*, New York: Wiley.

Emmelkamp, P.M., Visser, S. and Hoekstra, R.J. (1988) 'Cognitive therapy vs exposure in the treatment of obsessive compulsives', *Cognitive Therapy Research*, 12(1), pp.103–14.

Emmerlich, W., Goldmann, K., Kirsh, K. and Sharabany, R. (1977) 'Evidence for a transitional phase in the development of gender constancy', *Child Development*, 48, pp.930–6.

Engels, G.I., Garnefski, N. and Diekstra, R.F.W. (1993) 'Efficacy of rational-emotive therapy: a quantitative analysis', *Journal of Consulting and Clinical Psychology*, 61(6), pp.1083–90.

Epstein, L.C. and Lasagna, L. (1969) 'Obtaining informed consent', *Archives of Internal Medicine*, 123, pp.682–8.

Epstein, L. and Ogden, J. (2005) 'A qualitative study of GPs' views of treating obesity', *The British Journal of General Practice*, 55 (519), pp.750–4.

Epstein, S. (1994) 'Integration of the cognitive and the psychodynamic unconscious', *American Psychologist*, 49, 709–724.

Erikson, E.H. (1968) *Identity: Youth and crisis*, New York: Norton.

Erikson, E.H. (1978) *Adulthood*, New York: Norton.

Erlenmeyer-Kimling, L., Hilldoff-Adamo, U., Rock, D., Roberts, S.A., Basset, A.S., Squires-Wheeler, E., Cornblatt, B.A., Endicott, J., Pape, S., Gottesman, I.I. (1997) 'The New York High-Risk Project: prevalence and co-morbidity of axis I disorders in offspring of schizophrenic parents at 25-year follow-up', *Archives of General Psychiatry*, 54, pp. 1096–1102.

Eron, L.D. (1992) *The impact of televised violence*. Testimony on behalf of the American Psychological Association before the Senate Committee on Governmental Affairs, Congressional Record, 18 June 1992, p.14.

Espelage, D.L. (2002) 'Bullying in early adolescence: The role of the peer group', *ERIC Digest* (Accession No. ED471912). Champaign, IL: ERIC Clearinghouse on Elementary and Early Childhood Education.

Evans, J., Heron, J., Lewis, G., Araya, R. and Wolke, D. (2005) 'Negative self-schemas and the onset of depression in women: Longitudinal study', *British Journal of Psychiatry*, 186 (4), pp.302–07.

Evans, M.D., Hollon, S.D., DeRubeis, R.J. and Associates (1992) 'Differential relapse following cognitive therapy and pharmacotherapy for depression', *Archives of General Psychiatry*, 49, pp.802–8.

Everson, C.A., Bergmann, B.M. and Rechtschaffen, A. (1989) 'Sleep deprivation in the rat: III. Total sleep deprivation', *Sleep*, 12, pp.13–21.

Eysenck, H.J. (1952) 'The effects of psychotherapy: an evaluation', *Journal of Consulting Psychology*, 16, pp.319–24.

Eysenck, H.J. (1967) *The Biological Basis of Personality*, Springfield, Illinois: Charles Thomas.

Eysenck, H. (1991) 'Dimensions of personality: 16: 5 or 3? Criteria for a taxonomic paradigm', *Personality and Individual Differences*, 12, pp.773–90.

Eysenck, H.J. (1997) 'Addiction, personality and motivation' *Human Psychopharmacology: Clinical and Experimental*, 12, S79–S87.

Eysenck, H. J. and Nias, D. K. B. (1982) *Astrology: Science or superstition?* Harmondsworth, UK: Penguin.

Eysenck, M.W. and Keane, M.T. (2005) *Cognitive Psychology: A Student's Handbook* (5th edn), Hove: Psychology Press, p.113.

Eytan, A. and Borras, L. (2005) 'Stalking through SMS: a new tool for an old behaviour', *The Australian and New Zealand Journal of Psychiatry*, 39(3), p.204.

Fabes, R.A., Fultz, J., Eisenberg, N., May-Plumlee, T. and Christopher, F.S. (1989) 'Effects of rewards on children's prosocial motivation: A socialization study', *Developmental Psychology*, 25 (4), pp.509–15.

Fagot, B.I. (1974) 'Sex differences in toddlers' behaviour and parental reaction', *Developmental Psychology*, 4, pp.554–8.

Fagot, B.I. (1983) 'Fagot Interactive Behaviour Code', in B. Fagot and M.D. Leinbach (eds) 'The young child's gender schema: Environmental input, internal organisation, *Child Development*, 60, pp.603–72.

Fagot, B.I. (1985) 'Beyond the reinforcement principle: Another step toward understanding sex role development', *Developmental Psychology*, 21, pp.1097–104.

Fagot, B. and Leinbach, M.D. (1989) 'The young child's gender schema: Environmental input, internal organisation', *Child Development*, 60, pp.603–72.

Falk, R (1989) 'Judgment of Coincidences: Mine versus Yours', *The American Journal of Psychology*, 102, (4) pp.477–93.

Falkai, P., Bogerts, B., and Rozumek, M. (1988) 'Limbic pathology in schizophrenia', *Proceedings of the National Academy of Science, USA*, 2, pp.560–3.

Fantz, R.L. (1961) 'The origin of form perception', *Scientific American*, 204 (5), pp.66–72.

Farah, M.J. (2004) *Visual Agnosia* (2nd edn), Cambridge, Massachusetts: MIT Press, pp.106.

Farah, M.J., Levinson, K.L. and Klein, K.L. (1995) 'Face perception and with-category discrimination in prosopagnosia.' *Neuropsychologia*, 33, pp.661–74.

Farah, M.J. and Aguirre, G.K. (1999) 'Imaging visual recognition: PET and fMRI studies of functional anatomy of human visual recognition', *Trends in Cognitive Science*, 3, pp.179–86.

Faraone, S.V., Doyle, A.E., Mick, E. and Biederman, J. (2001) 'Meta-analysis of the association between the 7-repeat allele of the dopamine D(4) receptor gene and attention deficit hyperactivity disorder', *American Journal of Psychiatry*, 158(7), pp. 1052–7.

Faraone, S.V., Seidman, L.J., Kremen, W.S., Toomey, R. and Pepple, J.R. (1999) 'Neuropsychological functioning among the nonpsychotic relatives of schizophrenic patients: a four-year follow-up study', *Journal of Abnormal Psychology*, 108, pp.176–81.

Farooqi, I.S., Jebb, S.A., Cook, G. *et al.* (1999) 'Effects of recombinant leptin therapy in a child with leptin deficiency', *New England Journal of Medicine*, 16, 879–84.

Feeney, J.A., Noller, P. and Callan, V.J. (1994) 'Attachment style, communication and satisfaction in the early years of marriage', *Advances in Personal Relationships*, 5, pp.269–308.

Feighner, J.P., Robins, E. and Guze, S.B. (1972) 'Diagnostic criteria for use in psychiatric research', *Archives of General Psychiatry*, 26, pp.57–63.

Feltham, C. (1996) 'Psychotherapy's staunchest critic: an interview with Hans Eysenck', *British Journal of Guidance and Counselling*, 24, pp.423–35.

Ferguson, C.J. (2007) 'Evidence of a publication bias in video game violence effects literature: A meta-analytic review', *Aggression and Violent Behaviour*, 12, pp.470–82.

Fergusson, D.M., Lynskey, M.T. and Horwood, L.J. (1995) 'The adolescent outcomes of adoption: a 16-year longitudinal study', *Journal of Child Psychology and Psychiatry*, 36(4), pp.597–615.

Ferrari, P.F., van Erp, A.M.M., Tornatzky, W. and Miczek, K.A. (2003) 'Accumbal dopamine and serotonin in anticipation of the next aggressive episode in rats', *European Journal of Neuroscience*, 17, pp.371–378.

Festinger, L. (1957) *A Theory of Cognitive Dissonance*, Palo Alto, CA: Stanford University Press.

Festinger, L. (ed.) (1964) *Conflict, Decision and Dissonance*, Stanford, CA: Stanford University Press.

Festinger, L. and Carlsmith, J. M. (1959) 'Cognitive consequences of forced compliance', *Journal of Abnormal and Social Psychology*, 58, pp.203–10.

Festinger, L., Riecken, H. W. and Schachter, S. (1956) *When prophecy fails: A social and psychological study of a modern group that predicted the destruction of the world*, Minneapolis: University of Minnesota Press.

Feyerabend, P.K. (1988) *Against Method: Outline of an anarchist theory of knowledge* (revised edn), New York: Verso of New Left Books.

Fine, M. and Gordon, S.M. (1989) 'Feminist transformations of/despite psychology', in M. Crawford and M. Gentry (eds) *Gender and Thought: Psychological Perspectives*, New York: Springer-Verlag.

Finn, J. (2004) 'A survey of online harassment at a university campus', *Journal of Interpersonal Violence*, 19(4), pp.468–83.

Fischer, M. (1971) 'Psychosis in the offspring of schizophrenic monozygotic twins and their normal co-twins', *British Journal of Psychiatry*, 118, pp.43–52.

Fishbein, M. and Ajzen, I. (1975) *Belief, attitude, intention, and behavior: An introduction to theory and research*, Reading, MA: Addison-Wesley.

Fisher, B. and Cullen, F. (2000) *Extent and Nature of the Sexual Victimization of College Women: A National-level Analysis*, Rockville, MD: National Criminal Justice Reference Service.

Fisher, H. (1992) *Anatomy of Love: The natural history of monogamy, adultery, and divorce*, New York: Simon and Schuster.

Fisher, R.A. and Yates, F. (1974) *Statistical Tables for Biological, Agricultural and Medical Research* (6th edn), Harlow: Longman Group Ltd.

Fiske, S.T. (2004) *Social Beings: A core motives approach to social psychology*, New York, Wiley.

Flaum, M., Swayze II, V.W., O'Leary, D.S., Yuh, W.T.C., Ehrhardt, J.C., Arndt, S.V. and Andreasen, N.C. (1995) 'Effects of diagnosis, laterality and gender on brain morphology in schizophrenia', *American Journal of Psychiatry*, 152 (2), pp.704–14.

Flavell, J.H. (1985) *Cognitive Development* (2nd edn), Englewood Cliffs, NJ: Prentice-Hall.

Flavell, J.H., Green, F.L., and Falvell, E.R. (1990) 'Developmental changes in young children's knowledge about the mind', *Cognitive Development*, 5, 1–27.

Fleeson, F. (2001) 'Toward a Structure- and Process-Integrated View of Personality Traits as Density Distributions of States', *Journal of Personality and Social Psychology*, 80(6), pp.1011–27.

Flinn, M.V. (1989) 'Household composition and female reproductive strategies', in A. Rasa, C. Vogel and E. Voland (eds.) *Sexual and Reproductive Strategies*, London: Chapman and Hall, pp.206–33.

Flynn, J.R. (1994) 'IQ gains over time', in R.J. Sternberg (ed.) *Encyclopedia of Human Intelligence*, New York: Macmillan, pp.617–23.

Flynn, J.R. (1999) 'Searching for justice: The discovery of IQ gains over time', *American Psychologist*, 54, pp.5–20.

Flynn, J.R. (2007) *What is Intelligence?: Beyond the Flynn Effect*, Cambridge: Cambridge University Press.

Foa, E.B., Liebowitz, M.R., Kozak, M.J., Davies, S., Campeas, R. and Franklin, M.R.E. (2005) 'Randomised placebo-controlled trial of exposure and ritual prevention, Clomipramine, and their combination in the treatment of obsessive compulsive disorder', *American Journal of Psychiatry*, 162 (1), pp.151–161.

Fodor, G. (1983) *The Modularity of Mind*, Cambridge, MA: MIT Press.

Fogassi, L., Ferrari, P.F., Gesierich, B., Rozzi, S., Chersi, F. and Rozzolati, G. (2005) 'Parietal lobe: From action organization to intention understanding', *Science*, 308, No.5722, pp.662-7.

Force, U.S.P.T. (1996) *Guide to clinical preventative services* (2nd edn), Baltimore, MD: Williams & Wilkens.

Ford, C. and Neale, J.M. (1985) 'Effects of a helplessness induction on judgements of control', *Journal of Personality and Social Psychology*, 49, pp. 1330–6.

Fossey, D. (1984) 'Infanticide in mountain gorillas (*Gorilla gorilla beringei*) with comparative notes on chimpanzees', in G. Hausfater and S. Blaffer-Hrdy (eds) *Infanticide, Comparative and Evolutionary Perspectives*, New York: Aldine, pp. 217–35.

Foster, C. (2000) 'The limits to low fertility: A biosocial approach', *Population and Development Review*, 26(2), pp.209–34.

Fouts, H.N., Hewlett, B.S. and Lamb, M.E. (2005) 'Parent–offspring weaning conflicts among the Bofi farmers and foragers of Central Africa', *Current Anthropology*, 46 (1), pp.29–50.

Fox, J.W. (1990) 'Social class, mental illness, and social mobility: the social selection-drift hypothesis for serious mental illness', *Journal of Health and Social Behaviour*, 31, pp.344–53.

Fraley, R.C. (1998) *Attachment Continuity from Infancy to Adulthood: Meta-analysis and dynamic modeling of developmental mechanisms*, Colloquium speaker, University of California, Berkeley.

Frayling, T.M., Timpson, N.J., Weedon, M.N. and 29 other colleagues (2007) 'A common variant in the FTO gene is associated with body mass index and predisposes to childhood and adult obesity', *Science*, 316 (5826), pp.889–94.

Frederickson, M. and Furmark, T. (2003) 'Amygdaloid regional cerebral blood flow and subjective fear during symptom provocation in anxiety disorders', *Annals of New York Academy of Science*, 985, pp.341–7.

Freedman, J.L. (1992) 'Television violence and aggression: What psychologists should tell the public', in P. Suedfeld and P. Tetlock (Eds), *Psychology and social policy*, New York: Hemisphere Publishing, pp.179–89.

Freedman, J.L. (2002) *Media violence and its effect on aggression: Assessing the scientific evidence*, Toronto: University of Toronto Press.

Freeman, J. (1996) *Highly Able Girls and Boys*, Northampton: NACE.

French, C. C. (1992) 'Factors underlying belief in the paranormal: do sheep and goats think differently?' *The Psychologist*, 5, 295–299.

French, C. C. (1996a) 'Psychic healing' In G. Stein (ed.) *Encyclopedia of the paranormal*. Amherst, NY: Prometheus. Pp. 597–604.

French, C. C. (1996b) 'Psychokinesis' In G. Stein (ed.) *Encyclopedia of the paranormal*. Amherst, NY: Prometheus. Pp. 605–612.

French, C. C. (2001a) 'Why I study anomalistic psychology', *The Psychologist*, 14, 356–357.

French, C. C. (2001b) 'Alien abductions' In Roberts, R. and Groome, D. (eds.) *Parapsychology: The science of unusual experience*. London: Arnold. Pp. 102–116.

French, C. C. (2001c) 'The placebo effect' In Roberts, R. and Groome, D. (eds.) *Parapsychology: The science of unusual experience*. London: Arnold. Pp. 35–47.

French, C.C. (2001d) 'Dying to know the truth: visions of a dying brain, or false memories?' *Lancet*, 358, (9298) 2010–2011.

French, C. C. (2003) 'Fantastic memories: The relevance of research into eyewitness testimony and false memories for reports of anomalous experiences', *Journal of Consciousness Studies*, 10, 153–174.

French, C. C. (2005) 'Near-death experiences in cardiac arrest survivors', *Progress in Brain Research*, 150, 351–367.

French, C. C. (in press) 'Near-death experiences and the brain', In C. Murray (ed.) *Psychological scientific perspectives on out-of-body and near-death experiences*. New York: Nova Science Publishers.

French, C.C., Haque, U., Bunton-Stasyshyn, R., and Davis, R. (2009) 'The "Haunt" Project: An attempt to build a "haunted" room by manipulating complex electromagnetic fields and infrasound', *Cortex* 45(5), pp.619–29.

French, C. C. and Santomauro, J. (2007) 'Something wicked this way comes: Causes and interpretations of sleep paralysis', In S. Della Sala (ed.) *Tall Tales About the Mind and Brain: Separating Fact from Fiction*. Oxford: Oxford University Press. Pp. 380–398.

French, C.C., Santomauro, J., Hamilton, V., Fox, R. and Thalbourne, M. (2008) 'Psychological aspects of the alien contact experience', *Cortex*, 44, 1387–1395.

French, C. C. and Wilson, K. (2006) 'Incredible memories: How accurate are reports of anomalous events?' *European Journal of Parapsychology*, 21, 166–181.

French, C. C. and Wilson, K. (2007) 'Cognitive factors underlying paranormal beliefs and experiences' In S. Della Sala (ed.) *Tall tales about the mind and brain: separating fact from fiction*. Oxford: Oxford University Press. Pp. 3–22.

Freud, S. (1917) 'Introductory lectures on psychoanalysis' in J. Strachey (Ed) *The Complete Psychological Works of Sigmund Freud*, Vol 16, New York: Norton.

Freud, S. (1920) *A General Introduction to Psychoanalysis*, New York: Basic Books.

Freud, S. (1935) *A General Introduction to Psychoanalysis*, New York: Washington Square Press.

Freud, S. (1990, original work published in 1909) 'Case study of Little Hans' in *Sigmund Freud 8, Case Histories I*, London: Penguin Books.

Freund, L.S. (1990) 'Maternal regulation of children's problem-solving behavior and its impact on children's performance', *Child Development*, 61 (1), pp.113–26.

Frey, C.U. and Rothlisberger, C. (1996) 'Social support in healthy adolescents', *Journal of Youth and Adolescence*, 25 (1), pp.17–31.

Friedman, S.L. and Stevenson, M. (1980) 'Perception of movements in pictures', in M. Hagen (ed.) *Perception of Pictures*, Vol. 1, *Albert's Model: The Projective Model of Pictorial Information*, New York: Academic Press.

Frith, C.D. (1992) *The Cognitive Neuropsychology of Schizophrenia*. LEA: London

Fromm-Reichmann, F. (1948) 'Notes on the development of treatment of schizophrenics by psychoanalytic psychotherapy', *Psychiatry*, 11, pp.263–73.

Furmark, T., Holmstrom, A. and Sparthan, E. (2006) *Social Phobia – Effective Treatment with Cognitve-Behavioural Therapy*, Sweden: Liber.

Fyer, A., Leibowitz, M., Gorman, J., Compeas, R., Levin, A., Davies, S., Goetz, D. and Klein, D (1987) 'Discontinuation of alprazolam treatment in panic patients', *American Journal of Psychiatry*, 144, pp.303–8.

Fyer, A.J., Mannuzza, S., Gallops, M.S., Martin, L.Y., Aaronson, C., Gorman, J.M., Liebowitz, M.R. and Klein, D.F. (1990) 'Familial transmission of simple fears and phobias', *Archives of General Psychiatry*, 40, pp.1061–4.

Fyer, A.J., Mannuzza, S., Chapman, T.F., Liebowitz, M.R. and Klein, D.F. (1993) 'A direct interview family study of social phobia', *Archives of General Psychiatry*, 50(4), pp.286–93.

Gallagher, R. and Appenzeller, T. (1999) 'Beyond reductionism', *Science*, 284 (5411), p.79.

Gallo, P.S., Smith, S. and Mumford, S. (1973) 'Effects of deceiving subjects on experimental results', *Journal of Social Psychology*, 89, pp.99–107.

Gallup, G.G. Jr. (1975) 'Towards an operational definition of self-awareness' in R.H.Tuttle (ed.) *Socioecology and psychology of primates* (pp.309–41), The Hague, Netherlands: Mouton.

Garcia, J., Hankins, W.G. and Rusiniak, K.W. (1974) 'Behavioral regulation of the milieu interne in man and rats', *Science*, 185, pp.824–31.

Garcia, J. and Koelling, R.A. (1966) 'Relation of cue to consequence in avoidance learning', *Psychonomic Science*, 4, pp.123–4.

Garcia, J., Runsiniak, K.W., and Brett, L.P. (1977) 'Conditioning food-illness aversions in wild animals: caveant canonici' in H. Davis and H.M.B. Hurwitz (eds.) *Operant-Pavlovian interactions*, Hillsdale, N.J.: Lawrence Erlbaum Associates.

Gardner, B.T. and Gardner, R.A. (1969) 'Teaching sign language to a chimpanzee', *Science*, 165, pp.664–72.

Gardner, H. (1983) *Frames of mind: The theory of multiple intelligences*, New York: Basic Books.

Gardner, H. (2006) *Multiple Intelligences: New Horizons*, New York: Basic Books.

Garn, S.M., Bailey, S.M., Solomon, M.A. and Hopkins, P.J. (1981) 'Effects of remaining family members on fatness prediction', *American Journal of Clinical Nutrition*, 34, pp.148–53.

Gauntlett, D. (1998) 'Ten Things Wrong With the Media 'Effects' Model', in R. Dickinson, R. Harindranath and O. Linn (Eds) *Approaches to Audiences: A Reader*, London: Arnold.

Gauthier, I. and Tarr, M.J. (2002) 'Unravelling mechanisms for expert object recognition: Bridging brain activity and behaviour', *Journal of Experimental Psychology: Human Perception and Performance*, 28, pp.431–46.

Gauthier, I., Behrmann, M. and Tarr, J.J. (1999) 'Can face recognition really be dissociated from object recognition?', *Journal of Cognitive Neuroscience*, 11, pp.349–70.

Geen, R.G. (1990) *Human Aggression*, Milton Keynes: Open University Press.

Geher, G., Fairweather, K., Mollette, N., Ugonabo, U., Murphy, J.W. and Wood, N. (2007) 'Sex differences in response to cues of parental investment: An evolutionary social psychological perspective', *Journal of Social, Evolutionary and Cultural Psychology*, 1, pp.18–34.

Geis, F.L. (1993) 'Self fulfilling prophecies: A social psychological view of gender', in A.E. Beall and R.J. Sternberg (eds) *The Psychology of Gender*, New York: Guilford pp. 9–54.

Geldard, F.A. (1972) *The Human Senses*, New York: Wiley

Gelernter, C.S., Uhde, T.W. and Cimbolic, P. (1991) 'Cognitive-behavioural and pharmacological treatments of social phobia - a controlled study', *Archives of General Psychiatry*, 49, p.938.

Gender Recognition Act (2004) Available online: http://www.opsi.gov.uk/acts/acts2004/ukpga_20040007_en_1 <http://www.opsi.gov.uk/acts/acts2004/ukpga_20040007_en_1>

Gentile, D.A., Lynch, P.J., Linder, J.R. and Walsh, D.A. (2004) 'The effects of violent video game habits on adolescent aggressive attitudes and behaviors', *Journal of Adolescence*, 27, pp.5–22.

Geoffrey, C. (1991) 'A Prozac backlash'. *Newsweek*, 1 April, p.64.

Gergen, K.J., Morse, S.J. and Gergen, M.M. (1980) 'Behavior exchange in cross-cultural perspective', in H.C. Triandis and R.W. Brislin (eds.) *Handbook of Cross-Cultural Psychology, (Vol. 5)* Boston: Allyn and Bacon.

Gershon, E.S., Berrettini, W.H. and Golin, L.R. (1989) 'Mood disorders: Genetic aspects', In H.I. Kaplan and B.J. Sadock (eds) *Comprehensive textbook of psychiatry* (5th ed) Baltimore: Lippincott Williams and Wilkins.

Gershon, E.S. (1990) 'Genetics in manic depressive illness,' in F.K. Goodwin and K.R. Jamison (Eds) *Manic-depressive illness*, New York: Oxford University Press, pp.373–401.

Gerra, G., Zaimovic, A., Avanzini, P., Chittolini, B., Giucastro, G., Caccavari, R., Palladino, M., Maestri, D., Monica, C., Delsignore, R. and Brambilla, F. (1997) 'Neurotransmitter-neuroendocrine responses to experimentally induced aggression in humans: influence of personality variable', *Psychiatry Research*, 66, pp.33–43.

Geschwind, N. and Galaburda, A.M. (1987) 'Cerebral lateralisation: Biological mechanisms, associations and pathology', in M. Corballis (ed) *The Lopsided Ape: Evolution of the Generative Mind*, Oxford: Oxford University Press, p.296.

Gewertz, D. (1981) 'A Historical Reconsideration of Female Dominance among the Chambri of Papua, New Guinea', *American Ethnologist*, 8, pp.94–106.

Ghiglieri, M.P. (1999) *The Dark Side of Man: Tracing the Origins of Violence*, Reading, MA: Perseus Books.

Gibbs, N.A. (1996) 'Nonclinical populations in research on obsessive-compulsive disorder: A critical review', *Clinical Psychological Review*, 16(8), pp.729–73.

Gibson, D.R. (1990) 'Relation of socio-economic status to logical and socio-moral judgment of middle-aged men', *Psychology and Aging*, 5, pp.510–3.

Gibson, E.J. and Walk P.D. (1960) 'The visual cliff', *Scientific American*, 202, pp.64–71.

Gibson, J.J. (1950) *The Perception of the Visual World*, Boston: Houghton Mifflin.

Gibson, J.J. (1979) *The Ecological Approach to Visual Perception*, Boston: Houghton Mifflin.

Giles, D.C. (2000): *Illusions of immortality: A psychology of fame and celebrity*. London: Macmillan.

Giles, D.C. (2002) 'Parasocial interaction: A review of the literature and a model for future research', *Media Psychology*, 4, pp.279–305.

Giles, D.C. (2003) *Media Psychology*, Mawah, NJ: Lawrence Erlbaum.

Giles, D.C. and Maltby, J. (2004) 'The role of the media in adolescent development: relations between autonomy, attachment and interest in celebrities', *Personality and Individual Differences*, 36, pp.813–22.

Giles, D.C. and Maltby, J. (2006) 'Praying at the alter of the stars', *The Psychologist*, 19, pp.82–5.

Gilligan, C. (1982) *In a Different Voice: Psychological Theory and Women's Development*, Cambridge, MA: Harvard University Press.

Gilovich, T. (1991) *How we know what isn't so: The fallibility of human reason in everyday life*. New York: Free Press.

Gitlin, M.J. (2002) 'Pharmacological treatment of depression'. In I. H. Gotlib and C. L. Hammen (eds), *Handbook of depression*, pp.360–82, New York: Guilford Press.

Gittelman, R. and Klein, D.F. (1984) 'Relationships between separation anxiety and panic and agoraphobic disorders', *Psychopathology*, 17, pp.56–65.

Glancy, G.D. (2008) 'Commentary: attacks on royalty – the more we know, the more we can classify', *Journal of the American Academy of Psychiatry and the Law*, 36, pp.68 –73.

Glenny, A.M., O'Meara, S., Melville, A., Sheldon, T.A. and Wilson, C. (1997) 'The treatment and prevention of obesity: A systematic review of the literature', *International Journal of Obesity*, 21 (9), pp.715–37.

Glucklich, A. (2001) *Sacred Pain: Hurting the Body for the Sake of the Soul*, New York: Oxford University Press.

Godin, G., Valois, P., LePage, L. and Desharnais, R. (1992) 'Predictors of smoking behaviour: An application of Ajzen's theory of planned behaviour', *British Journal of Addiction*, 87, pp.1335–1343.

Goetz, A.T. and Shackelford, T.K. (2006) 'Sexual coercion and forced in-pair copulation as sperm competition tactics in humans', *Human Nature*, 17, pp.265–82.

Goldberg, D. and Huxley, P. (1992) *Common mental disorders: a biosocial model*, London: Routledge.

Goldsmith, T.H. and Zimmerman, W.F. (2001) *Biology, Evolution and Human Nature*, Wiley: New York.

Goldstein, J.H. (1976) *Aggression and Crimes of Violence*. New York: Oxford University Press.

Goldstein, M.J. (1988) 'The family and psychotherapy', *Annual Review of Psychiatry*, 39, pp.283–99.

Goodchild, S. (2006) 'The 200-year-old Asbos (they make Blair's Britain seem a soft touch', *The Independent* 19 March 2006 www.independent.co.uk

Goodwin, R., Adatia, K., Sinhal, H., Cramer, D. and Ellis, D. (1997) 'Social support and marital well-being in an Asian community', *Social Policy Research*, Joseph Rowntree Foundation, York: York Publishing Ltd.

Gooren, L. (2006) 'The biology of human psychosexual differentiation', *Hormones and Behavior*, 50, pp.589–601.

Gotlib, I.H. and Macleod, C. (1997) 'Information processing in anxiety and depression: a cognitive-developmental perspective', in J. Burack and J. Enns (eds), *Attention, Development and Psychopathology*, New York: Guilford Press.

Gottesman, I.I. (1963) 'Heritability of personality: a demonstration', *Psychological Monographs*, 77 (Whole no. 572).

Gottesman, I.I. and Shields, J. (1982) *Schizophrenia: The Epigenetic Puzzle*, Cambridge: Cambridge University Press

Gould, S.J. (1981) *The Mismeasure of Man*. New York: Norton and co.

Goulding, A. (2004) 'Schizotypy models in relation to subjective health and paranormal beliefs and experiences', *Personality and Individual Differences*, 37, 157–167.

Goulding, A. (2005) 'Healthy schizotypy in a population of paranormal believers and experients', *Personality and Individual Differences, 38*, 1069–1083.

Gove, M. (1988) http://wwwguardian.co.uk/2008/aug/04/6

Graham, S. (1992) 'Most of the subjects were white and middle class: trends in published research on African-Americans in selected APA journals 1970–1989', *American Psychologist*, 47 (5) 196–8.

Grammer, K. und Thornhill, R. (1994) 'Human facial attractiveness and sexual selection: the roles of averageness and symmetry', *Journal of Comparative Psychology*, 108 (3), pp.233–42.

Granqvist, P., Fredrikson, M., Unge, P., Hagenfeldt, A., Valind, S., Larhammar, D. & Larsson, M. (2005) 'Sensed presence and mystical experiences are predicted by suggestibility, not by the application of transcranial weak complex magnetic fields', *Neuroscience Letters*, 375, 69–74.

Grant, V.J. and France, J.T. (2001) 'Dominance and testosterone in women', *Biological Psychology*, 58, pp.41–47.

Green, S. (1994) *Principles of Biopsychology*, Hove: Erlbaum.

Greenberg, B. S., Edison, N., Korzenny, F., Fernandez-Cllado, C., and Atkin, C. K. (1980) 'Antisocial and prosocial behaviors on television', in B.S.Greenberg (ed.) *Life on television: Content analyses of U. S.*

TV drama, Norwood, NJ: Ablex Publishing, pp.99–128.

Greeno, C.G. and Wing, R.R. (1994) 'Stress-induced eating', *Psychological Bulletin*, 155(3), pp.444–64.

Greiling, H. and Buss, D.M. (2000) 'Women's sexual strategies: The hidden dimension of extra-pair mating', *Personality and Individual Differences*, 28, pp.929–63.

Greist, J.H., Marks, I.M., Baer, L., Kobak, K.A., Wenzel, K.W., Hirsch, M.J., Mantle, J.M. and Clary, C.M. (2002) 'Behaviour therapy for obsessive-compulsive disorder guided by a computer or by a clinician compared with relaxation as a control', *Journal of Clinical Psychiatry*, 63, pp.138–145.

Gregory, R.L. (1997) *Eye and Brain: The Psychology of Seeing*, Princeton, NJ: Princeton University Press.

Gregory, R.L. and Wallace, J. (1963) *Recovery from Early Blindness*, Cambridge: Heffer.

Greyson, B. (2003) 'Incidence and correlates of near-death experiences in a cardiac care unit', *General Hospital Psychiatry*, 25, 269-276.

Griffin, G. (2007) 'What mode marriage? Women's partner choice in British Asian cultural representation', *Women*, 18 (1), pp.1–18.

Griffiths, M.D. (1994) 'The role of cognitive bias and skill in fruit machine gambling', *British Journal of Psychology*, 85, pp.351–369.

Griffiths, M.D. (1995) *Adolescent Gambling*, London: Routledge.

Griffiths, M.D. (1996b) 'Behavioural addictions: An issue for everybody?', *Journal of Workplace Learning*, 8(3), pp.19–25.

Griffiths, M.D. (1999a) 'Gambling technologies: Prospects for problem gambling', *Journal of Gambling Studies*, 15, pp.265–283.

Griffiths, M.D. (2002) *Gambling and Gaming Addictions in Adolescence*, Leicester: British Psychological Society/Blackwells.

Griffiths, M. (2004) 'An empirical analysis of the film "The Gambler"', *International Journal of Mental Health and Addiction*, 1(2), pp.39–43.

Griffiths, M.D. (2005a) 'Workaholism is still a useful construct', *Addiction Research and Theory*, 13, pp.97–100.

Griffiths, M.D. (2005b) 'A "components" model of addiction within a biopsychosocial framework', *Journal of Substance Use*, 10, pp.191–197.

Griffiths, M.D. (2005c) 'Does advertising of gambling increase gambling addiction?', *International Journal of Mental Health and Addiction*, 3(2), pp.15–25.

Griffiths, M.D. (2006) 'An overview of pathological gambling', in T. Plante (ed.) *Mental Disorders of the New Millennium*, vol. I: Behavioural issues, New York: Greenwood, pp. 73–98.

Griffiths, M.D. (2007) 'Videogame addiction: fact or fiction? in T. Willoughby and E. Wood (eds.) *Children's learning in a digital world*, Oxford: Blackwell, pp. 85–103.

Griffiths, M.D. (2008b) 'The biopsychosocial and "complex" systems approach as a unified framework for addiction', *Behavioral and Brain Sciences*, 31, pp.446–447.

Griffiths, M.D. and Larkin, M. (2004) 'Conceptualizing addiction: The case for a "complex systems" account', *Addiction Research and Theory*, 12, pp.99–102.

Griffiths, M.D. and MacDonald, H.F. (1999) 'Counselling in the treatment of pathological gambling: An overview', *British Journal of Guidance and Counselling*, 27, pp.179–190.

Griffiths, M.D. and Parke, J. (2003) 'The environmental psychology of gambling', in G. Reith (ed.), *Gambling: Who wins? Who Loses?*, New York: Prometheus Books, pp.277–292.

Grimes, T., Anderson, J. and Bergen, L. (2008) *Media Violence and Aggression: Science and ideology*, Thousand Oaks, CA: Sage.

Gross, R. (2003) *Key Studies in Psychology* (4th edn), London: Hodder & Stoughton.

Gross, R.D. (2003) *Themes, Issues and Debates in Psychology*, 2nd edn, London: Hodder & Stoughton.

Grun, L. and McKeigue, P. (2000) 'Prevalence of excessive gambling before and after induction of a national lottery in the United Kingdom: Another example of a single distribution theory', *Addiction*, 95(6), pp.959–966.

Gualtieri, C. (1991) *Neuropsychiatry and Behavioural Pharmacology*, New York: Springer-Verlag.

Gulevich, G., Dement, W. and Johnson, L. (1966) 'Psychiatric and EEG observations on a case of prolonged (264 hours) wakefulness', *Archives of General Psychiatry*, 15, pp.29–35.

Gunakesera, H., Chapman, S. and Campbell, S. (2005) 'Sex and drugs in popular movies: An analysis of the top 200 films', *Journal of the Royal Society of Medicine*, 98, pp.464–470.

Gunter, B. (1983) 'Do aggressive people prefer violent television?', *Bulletin of the British Psychological Society*, 38, pp.166–8.

Gunter, B. and McAleer, J. (1997) *Children and Television*, London: Routledge.

Haaga, D.A. and Davison, G.C. (1989) 'Outcome studies of rational-emotive therapy', in M.E. Bernard and R.D. DiGiuseppe (eds) *Inside Rational-Emotive Therapy*, San Diego, CA: Academic Press.

Haaga, D.A. and Davison, G.C. (1993) 'An appraisal of Rational-Emotive Therapy', *Journal of Consulting and Clinical Psychology*, 61 (2), pp.215–20.

Hadjikhani, N. and de Gelder, B. (2003) 'Seeing fearful body expressions activates fusiform cortex and amygdala', *Current Biology*, 13, pp.2200–4.

Hagell, A. and Newburn, T. (1994) *Young Offenders and the Media*, London, Batisford.

Hagen, M. and Jones, R. (1978) 'Cultural effects on pictorial perception: how many words is one picture really worth?', in R. Walk and H. Pick (eds) *Perception and Experience*, New York: Plenum Press.

Haier, R.J., Siegel, B.V. Jr., Nuechterlein, A. and Soderling, E. (1992) 'Regional glucose metabolic changes after learning a complex visuospatial/motor task: a positron emission tomographic study', *Brain Research*, 570, pp.134–43.

Haith, M.M. (1990) *Rules that Babies Look By*, Hillsdale, NJ: Erlbaum.

Halpern, D.F. (1997) 'Sex difference in intelligence: Implications for education', *American Psychologist*, 52, pp.1091–102.

Halpern, D.F. (2000) *Sex Differences in Cognitive Abilities*, Mahwah, NJ: Erlbaum.

Hamer, D.H. (2002) 'Rethinking behavior genetics', *Science*, 298, pp.71–72.

Hamilton, M. (1960) 'A rating scale for depression', *Journal of Neurology, Neurosurgery and Psychiatry*, 23, pp.56–62.

Hamilton, J.G. (1995) 'Needle phobia: A Neglected Diagnosis', *Journal of Family Practice*, 41, p.169–179.

Hamilton, W.D. (1963) 'The evolution of altruistic behaviour', *The American Naturalist*, 97, pp.354–6.

Hamilton, W.D. (1964) 'The genetic evolution of social behavior', *Journal of Theoretical Biology*, 7, pp.17–8.

Hampson, P.J. and Morris, P.E. (1996) *Understanding Cognition*, Oxford: Blackwell.

Han, C., Mcgue, M.K. and Iacono, W. G (1999) 'Lifetime tobacco, alcohol and other substance use in adolescent Minnesota twins: univariate and multivariate behavioral genetic analyses', *Addiction*, 94, (7), pp.981–93.

Hanson, N.R. (1958) *Patterns of Discovery: An inquiry into the conceptual foundations of science*, Cambridge: Cambridge University Press.

Happé, F. (1994a) 'An advanced test of theory of mind: Understanding of story characters' thoughts and feelings by able autistic, mentally handicapped and normal children and adults', *Journal of Autism and Developmental Disorders*, 24, pp.129–54.

Happé, F. (1994b) *Autism: An introduction to psychological theory*, London: University College London Press.

Hare-Mustin, R.T. and Marecek, J. (1988) 'The meaning of difference: gender theory, post-modernism, and psychology', *American Psychologist*, 43, pp.455–64.

Harer, M. and Steffensmeier, D. (1996) 'Race and Prison Violence', *Criminology*, 34, pp.323–55.

Harlow, H.F. and Harlow, M.K. (1962) 'Social deprivation in monkeys', *Scientific American*, 207(5), pp.136–146.

Harris, C.R. (2003) 'A review of sex differences in sexual jealousy, including self-report data, psychophysiological responses, interpersonal violence, and morbid jealousy', *Personality and Social Psychology Review*, 7, pp.102–28.

Harris, J. (2001) 'The effects of computer games on young children – a review of the research', *RDS occasional paper*, 72, Home Office, U.K.

Harris, J.L. (1989) 'A model for treating compulsive gamblers through cognitive-behavioural approaches', *Psychotherapy Patient*, 11, pp.211–226.

Harris, J. R. (1998) *The Nurture Assumption: Why children turn out the way they do*, New York: The Free Press.

Harris, J.R. (2006) *No Two Alike: Human Nature and Human Individuality*, New York: W.W. Norton.

Harris, P.L. (1989) *Children and Emotion: The development of psychological understanding*, Oxford: Blackwell Publishing.

Harris, T. (2001) 'Recent developments in understanding the psychological aspects of depression', *British Medical Bulletin*, 57, pp.17–32.

Harrison, G., Owens, D. and Holton, A. (1988) 'A prospective study of severe mental disorder in Afro-Caribbean patients', *Psychological Medicine*, 18, pp.643–57.

Hart, D., Burock, D., London, B. and Atkins, R. (2003) 'Prosocial tendencies, antisocial behaviour, and moral development', in A. Slater and G. Bremner (eds) *An Introduction to Developmental Psychology*, Oxford: Blackwell, pp.334–56.

Hartshorne, H. and May, M.A. (1928) *Studies in the Nature of Character, Vol. 2: Studies in service and self-control*, New York: Macmillan.

Harvey, P.H. and Harcourt, A. (1984) 'Sperm competition, testes size, and breeding systems in primates', in R.L. Smith (ed.) *Sperm Competition and the Evolution of Animal Mating Systems*, Orlando: Academic Press.

Harvey, P.H. and May, R.M. (1989) 'Copulation dynamics: out for the sperm count?', *Nature*, 337, pp.508–9.

Haselton, M.G., Mortezaie, M., Pillsworth, E.G., Bleske-Recheck, A.E. and Frederick, D.A. (2007) 'Ovulation and human female ornamentation: Near ovulation, women dress to impress', *Hormones and Behavior*, 51, pp.41–5.

Hatfield, E. and Sprecher, S. (in press/2009) 'Matching hypothesis', in H. Reis and S. Sprecher (eds.) *Encyclopedia of Human Relationships*, New York: Sage.

Haugaard, J.J. and Hazan, C. (2003) 'Adoption as a natural experiment', *Development and Psychopathology*, 15, pp.909–26.

Haugtvedt, C.P., Petty, R.E., and Cacioppo, J.T. (1992) 'Need for Cognition and Advertising Understanding the Role of Personality Variables in Consumer Behavior', *Journal of Consumer Psychology*, 1, pp.239–60.

Hay, D.C. and Young, A.W. (1982) 'The human face', in A.W. Ellis (ed.) *Normality and Pathology in Cognitive Functions*, London: Academic Press.

Hayer, T., Griffiths, M.D. and Meyer, G. (2005) 'The prevention and treatment of problem gambling in adolescence', in T.P. Gullotta and G. Adams (eds), *Handbook of adolescent behavioral problems: Evidence-based approaches to prevention and treatment*, New York: Springer, pp.467–486.

Hayes, N. (1994) *Principles of Comparative Psychology*, Hove: Psychology Press.

Haynie, D. (2003) 'Contexts of risk? Explaining the link between girls' pubertal development and their delinquency involvement', *Social Forces*, 82 (1), pp.355–97.

Hays, R.B. (1985) 'A longitudinal study of friendship development', *Journal of Personality and Social Psychology*, 48, pp.909–24.

Hazan, C. and Shaver, P. (1987) 'Romantic love conceptualized as an attachment process', *Journal of Personality and Social Psychology*, 52, pp.511–24.

Hearold, S. (1986) 'A synthesis of 1043 effects of television on social behavior', in G. Comstock (ed.) *Public communication and behavior*, 1, New York: Academic Press, pp.65–133.

Heather, N. (1976) *Radical perspectives in psychology*, London: Methuen.

Heatherton, T.F., Herman, C.P., Polivy, J.A., King, G.A. and McGree, S.T. (1988) 'The (mis)measurement of restraint: An analysis of conceptual and psychometric issues', *Journal of Abnormal Psychology*, 97, pp.19–28.

Heatherton, T.F., Polivy, J. and Herman, C.P. (1991) 'Restraint, weight loss and variability of body weight', *Journal of Abnormal Psychology*, 100, pp.78–83.

Hebb, D.O. (1958) *A Textbook of Psychology*, Philadelphia: W.B. Saunders.

Hecimovic, H. and Gilliam, F.G. (2006) 'Neurobiology of depression and new opportunities for treatment', In F.G. Gilliam, A.M. Kanner and Y.I. Sheline (eds) *Depression and brain dysfunction*, pp.51–84, New York: Taylor & Francis.

Heimberg, R.G. and Becker, R.E. (2002) *Cognitive-behavioural Group Therapy for Social Phobia*. New York: Guilford Press.

Heine, S.J., Lehman, D.R., Peng, K. and Greenholtz, J. (2002) 'What's wrong with cross-cultural comparisons of subjective Likert scales? The reference-group effect', *Journal of Personality and Social Psychology*, 82, pp.903–18.

Heisenberg, W. (1927) 'Uber den anschlauchichen Inhalt der quantentheoretischen Kinetik und Mechanik'. *Zeitschrift für Physik*, 43, pp.172–98.

Helvacıo lu, F. (1996) 'Ders kitaplarında cinsiyetçilik 1928–1995', in A. A. Özdo ru, G. Aksoy, N, Erdo an and F. Gök (eds) *Content Analysis for Gender Bias in Turkish Elementary School Textbooks*, taken from an unpublished thesis, 2002.

Hemsley, D. (1993) 'Perceptual and cognitive abnormalities as the basis for schizophrenic symptoms', in A.S. David and J. Cutting (eds) *The Neuropsychology of Schizophrenia*, Hove, UK: Lawrence Erlbaum Associates Ltd.

Henderson, M. (2006) *Theories of telepathy and afterlife cause uproar at top science forum* [Electronic version]. Retrieved 28 November, 2008, from http://www.timesonline.co.uk/tol/news/uk/article629413.ece

Henquet, C., Murray, R. and Linszen, D. (2005) 'The environment and schizophrenia: The role of cannabis use', *Schizophrenia Bulletin*, 31, pp.608–12.

Herman, C.P. and Mack, D. (1975) 'Restrained and Unrestrained Eating', *Journal of Personality*, 43, 646–60

Herman, C.P. and Polivy, J. (1975) 'Anxiety, restraint and eating behavior', *Journal of Abnormal Psychology*, 84(6), pp.666–72.

Herman, C.P. and Polivy, J. (1980) 'Restrained eating', in A.J. Stunkard (ed.) *Obesity*, Philadelphia, PA: W.B. Saunders.

Herman, C.P. and Polivy, J.A. (1984) 'A boundary model for the regulation of eating', in A.J. Stunkard and E. Stellar (eds) *Eating and its Disorders*, New York: Raven Press, pp.141–56.

Herman C.P. and Polivy, J.A. (1988) 'Restraint and excess in dieters and bulimics', in K.M. Pirke and D. Ploog (eds) *The Psychobiology of Bulimia*, Berlin: Springer-Verlag.

Herzog, D.B., Greenwood, D.N., Dorer, D.J., Flores, A.T., Ekeblad, E.R., Richards, A., Blais, M.A. and Keller, M.B. (2000) 'Mortality of eating disorders: A descriptive study', *International Journal of Eating Disorders*, 28, pp.20–6.

Hesslow, G. (2002) 'Conscious thought as simulation of behaviour and perception', *Trends in Cognitive Science*, 6, pp.242–7.

Hetherington, E.M. and Parke, R.D. (1993) *Child Development: A contemporary viewpoint,* New York: McGraw Hill.

Hewstone, M., Fincham, F.D. and Foster, J. (2005) *Psychology*, Oxford: BPS Blackwell, pp.153–4.

Hewstone, M., Stroebe, W., Codol, J.P. and Stephenson, G.M. (1988) *Introduction to Social Psychology: A European perspective*, Oxford: Blackwell.

Higgins, S.T., Budney, A.J., Bickel, W.K., Foerg, F., Donham, R. and Badger, G.J. (1994) 'Incentives improve outcome in outpatient behavioral treatment of cocaine dependence', *Archives of General Psychiatry*, 51, pp.568–576.

Hill, K. and Kaplan, H. (1988) Trade offs in male and female reproductive strategies among the Ache: part 1. In L. Betzig, M.M. Bogerhoff and P. Turke. (eds.), (1988), Human Reproductive Behaviour: a Darwinian perspective, Cambridge: Cambridge University Press, pp 277-289

Hill, K.R. and Hurtado, A.M. (1996) *Aché Life History*, New York: Aldine de Gruyter, pp.118.

Hill, R.B. (1972) *The Strengths of Black Families*, New York: Astoria Press.

Hill, S.E. and Flom, R. (2006) '18- and 24-month-olds' discrimination of gender-consistent and inconsistent activities', *Infant Behavior and Development*, 30, pp.168–73.

Hinde, R.A. (1970) *Animal Behaviour: A synthesis of ethology and comparative psychology*, New York: McGraw-Hill.

Hinde, R.A. (1977) 'Mother-infant separation and the nature of inter-individual relationships: experiments with rhesus monkeys', *Proceedings of the Royal Society of London* (B), 196, pp.29–50.

Hines, T. (2003) *Pseudoscience and the paranormal: A critical examination of the evidence.* 2nd ed. Amherst, NY: Prometheus.

Hochberg, J. and Brooks, V. (1962) 'Pictorial recognition as an unlearned ability. A study of one child's performance', *American Journal of Psychology*, 75, pp.624–8.

Hodge, R. and Tripp, D. (1986) *Children and Television: A Semiotic Approach,* Cambridge: Polity, p.10.

Hoffman, M.L. (1976) 'Empathy, role-taking, guilt, and development of altruistic motives', in T. Lickona (ed.), *Moral Development and Behavior: Theory, Research, and Social Issues*, New York: Holt, Rinehart & Winston.

Hofling, C.K., Brotzman, E., Dalrymple, S., Graves, N. and Pierce, C.M. (1966) 'An experimental study in nurse–physician relationships', *Journal of Nervous and Mental Disease*, 143, pp.171–80.

Hofstede, G. (1980) *Culture's Consequences: International Differences in Work-related Values,* Beverley Hills, CA: Sage.

Hogarty,G.E. (2002) *Personal therapy for schizophrenia and related disorders: A guide to individualized treatment.* New York: Guilford Press.

Hogg, M.A. and Vaughan, G.M. (1998) *Social Psychology* (2nd edn) Hemel Hempstead: Prentice Hall/Harvester Wheatsheaf.

Hogg, M.A. and Vaughan, G.M. (2008) *Social Psychology* (5th edn) London: Prentice Hall.

Holden, C. (1997) 'National Institute of Health to explore St John's Wort', *Science*, 278, p. 391.

Holden, J. M., Long, J. and MacLurg, J. (2006) Out-of-body experiences: All in the brain? *Journal of Near-Death Studies*, 25, 99–107.

Holden, K. J. and French, C. C. (2002) 'Alien abduction experiences: Clues from neuropsychology and neuropsychiatry', *Cognitive Neuropsychiatry*, 7 (3), 163–178.

Hollis, K.L. (1984) 'The biological function of Pavlovian conditioning: the best offence is a good defence', *Journal of Experimental Psychology: Animal Behaviour Processes*, 10, pp.413–25.

Hollis, K.L. (1990) 'The role of Pavlovian conditioning in territorial aggression and reproduction', in D. A. Dewsbury (ed.) *Contemporary Issues in Comparative Psychology*, Sunderland, MA: Sinaur Associates.

Hollis, K.L., Pharr, V.I. Dumas, M.J., Britton, G.B. and Field, J. (1997) 'Classical conditioning provides advantages for male blue gouramis (*Trichogaster trichopteros*)', *Journal of Comparative Psychology*, 111, pp.219–25.

Hollister, L.E. (1971) 'Hunger and appetite after single doses of marihuana, alcohol, and dextroamphetamine', *Clinical Pharmacology and Therapeutics*, 12, pp.44–9.

Hollon, S.D., DeRubeis, R.J., Evans, M.D., Wiemer, M.J., Garvey, M.J., Grove, W.M. and Tuason, V.B. (1992) 'Cognitive therapy and pharmacotherapy for depression: singly and in combination', *Archives of General Psychiatry*, 49, pp.774–809.

Hollon, S.D., Haman, K.L. and Brown, L.L. (2002) 'Cognitive behavioural treatment of depression', In I. H. Gotlib and C. L. Hammen (eds) *Handbook of depression*, pp.383–403, New York: Guilford Press.

Hollon, S. D., Stewart, M. O. and Strunk, D. (2006) 'Cognitive behaviour therapy has enduring effects in the treatment of depression and anxiety', *Annual Review of Psychology*, 57, pp.85–315.

Holmes, T.H. and Rahe, R.H. (1967) 'The social readjustment rating scale', *Journal of Psychosomatic Research*, 11, pp.213–18.

Homan, R. (1991) *Ethics of Social Research*, Harlow: Longman.

Hong, J.P., Samuels, J., Bienvenue, O.J., Cannisraro, P., Grados, M. and Riddle, M.A. (2004) 'Clinical correlates of recurrent major depression and obsessive-compulsive disorder', *Depression and Anxiety*, 20(2), pp.86–91.

Honorton, C. (1978) Psi and internal attention states: Information retrieval in the ganzfeld. In B. Shapin & L. Coly (Eds.) *Psi and states of awareness.* New York: Parapsychology Foundation. Pp. 79–90.

Honorton, C. (1985) Meta-analysis of psi ganzfeld research: A response to Hyman. *Journal of Parapsychology*, 49, 51–91.

Hopf, W.H., Huber, G.L. and Weiss, R. (2008) 'Media violence and youth violence: a 2-year longitudinal study', *Journal of Media Psychology*, 20(3) pp.79–96.

Hopkins, B., Jacobs, D.M. and Westrum, R. (1992) *Unusual Personal Experiences: An analysis of data from three national surveys conducted by the Roper Organization*, Las Vegas: Bigelow.

Horne, J. (1988) *Why we sleep*, Oxford: Oxford University Press.

Horne, J.A. and Östberg, O. (1976) 'A self-assessment questionnaire to determine morningness-eveningness in human circadian rhythms', *International Journal of Chronobiology*, 4, pp.97–110.

Hope-Simpson, R.E. (1981) 'The role of season in the epidemiology of schizophrenia', *Journal of Hygiene*, 86, pp.35–47.

Horowitz, F.D. (1993) 'The need for a comprehensive new environmentalism', in R. Plomin and G.E. McClearn (1993) (eds) *Nature, Nurture and Psychology*, Washington, DC: American Psychological Association.

Horowitz, J.L., Garber, J., Ciesla, J.A., Young, J.F. and Mufson, L. (2007) 'Prevention of depressive symptoms in adolescents: A randomized trial of cognitive-behavioural and interpersonal prevention programs', *Journal of Consulting Clinical Psychology*, 75 (5), pp.693–706.

Horr, D.A. (1977) 'Orangutan maturation: Growing up in a female world', in S. Chevalier-Skolnikoff and F.E. Poirer (eds) *Primate Biosocial Development: Biological, social and ecological determinants*, Garland Publishing, pp.289–322.

Horrobin, D.F. (1998) 'Schizophrenia: the illness that made us human', *Medical Hypothesis*, 50, pp.269–88.

Horton, D. and Wohl, R.R. (1956) 'Mass communication and para-social interaction', *Psychiatry*, 19, pp.215–29.

Hovland, C.I., Janis, I.L. and Kelley, H.H. (1953) *Communication and Persuasion: psychological studies of opinion change,* New Haven: Yale University Press.

Howard, S. and Roberts, S. (2002) 'Winning hearts and minds: television and the very young audience', *Contemporary Issues in Early Childhood*, 3(3), pp.315–37.

Howitt, D. and Owusu-Bempah, J. (1994) *The Racism of Psychology: Time for change*, Hemel Hempstead: Harvester.

Hrdy, S. (1999) *Mother Nature: A History of Mothers, Infants, and Natural Selection,* New York: Pantheon Books.

Huang, W. J. (2005) 'An Asian perspective on relationship and marriage education', *Family Process,* 44 (2), pp.161-173.

Hudson, W. (1960) 'Pictorial depth perception in sub-cultural groups in Africa', *Journal of Social Paychology*, 52, pp.183–208.

Hudson, W. (1962) 'Pictorial perception and educational adaptation in Africa', *Psychologica Africana*, 9, pp.226–39.

Huesmann, L.R. (1982) 'Television violence and aggressive behavior', in D. Perl, L. Bouthilet, and J. Lazar (eds), *Television and Behavior: Ten years of programs and implications for the 80s,* Washington, DC: U.S. Government Printing Office, pp.126–37.

Huesmann, L.R. (1988) 'An information processing model for the development of aggression', *Aggressive Behavior*, 14, pp.13–24.

Huesmann, L.R. and Moise, J. (1996) 'Media violence: A demonstrated public threat to children', *Harvard Mental Health Letter, 72(12), pp.5–7.

Huesmann, L.R., Eron, L.D., Lefkowitz, M.M. and Walder, L.O. (1984) 'Stability of aggression over time and generations', *Developmental Psychology*, 20, pp.1120–34.

Huesmann, L.R., Moise-Titus, J., Podolski, C. and Eron, L.D. (2003) 'Longitudinal relations between children's exposure to TV violence and their aggressive and violent behavior in young adulthood: 1977–1992', *Developmental Psychology*, 39, pp.201–21.

Huffman, K. (2002) *Psychology in Action* (6th edn), New York: John Wiley, p. 496.

Hughes, M. (1975) *Egocentrism in Pre-school Children*, Unpublished PhD thesis, University of Edinburgh [Some of Hughes' research is described in detail by Donaldson, M. (1978) *Children's Minds*, London: Fontana.]

Hulshoff Pol, H.E., Cohen-Kettenis, P.T., Van Haren, N.E., Peper, J.S., Brans, R.G., and Cahn, W. (2006) 'Changing your sex changes your brain: Influences of testosterone and estrogen on adult human brain structure', *European Journal of Endocrinology*, 155 (Suppl. 1), S107–S114.

Hume, S. (1992) 'Best ads don't rely on celebrities', *Advertising Age*, p.20.

Humphrey, N.K. (1982) 'Consciousness: A just-so story' *New Scientist, 95*, pp.474–8.

Huppert, J.D., Bufka, L.F., Barlow, D.H., Gorman, J.M., Shear, M.K. and Woods, S.W. (2001) 'Therapists, therapist variables and cognitive-behavioural therapy outcome in a multicentre trial for panic disorder', *Journal of Consulting and Clinical Psychology*, 69, pp.745–55.

Hutchings, B. and Mednick, S.A. (1973) 'Biological and adoptive fathers of male criminal adoptees', in *Major Issues in Juvenile Delinquency*, Copenhagen: World Health Organization, pp.47–60.

Hyatt, M. (1999) 'Race, ritual, and responsibility', in A. Jones and A. Stephenson, *Performing the Body, Performing the Text*, London: Routledge.

Hyman, R. (1985a) A critical historical overview of parapsychology. In P. Kurtz (ed.) *A skeptic's handbook of parapsychology*. Buffalo, NY: Prometheus. Pp. 3–96.

Hyman, R. (1985b) ''The ganzfeld psi experiment: A critical appraisal', *Journal of Parapsychology*, 49, 3–49.

Hyman, R. (2002) How not to test mediums: Critiquing the afterlife experiments. *Skeptical Inquirer*, 27(1), 20–30.

Hyman, R. (2003) ,Hyman's reply to Schwartz's 'how not to review mediumship research', *Skeptical Inquirer*, 27(3), 61–64.

Hyman, R. and Honorton, C. (1986) 'A joint communiqué: The psi ganzfeld controversy.' *Journal of Parapsychology*, 50, 351–364.

Imperato-McGinley, J., Guerrero, L., Gautier, T. and Peterson, R.E. (1974) 'Steroid 5a-reductase deficiency in man: An inherited form of pseudohermaphroditism', in G.C. Davidson and J.M. Neale (eds) *Abnormal Psychology*, New York: John Wiley & Sons, pp.382–383.

Irons, W. (2001) 'Religion as a hard-to-fake sign of commitment', in R. Nesse (ed.), *Evolution and the capacity for commitment*, New York: Russell Sage Foundation, pp.292–309.

Irwin, H. J. (1986a) 'The relationship between locus of control and belief in the paranormal', *Parapsychological Journal of South Africa*, 7, 1–23.

Irwin, H. J. (1986b) 'Perceptual perspective of visual imagery in OBEs, dreams and reminiscence', *Journal of the Society for Psychical Research*, 53, 210–217.

Irwin, H. J. (1990) 'Fantasy proneness and paranormal beliefs', *Psychological Reports*, 66, 655–658.

Irwin, H. J. (1991) 'A study of paranormal belief, psychological adjustment and fantasy proneness. *Journal of the American Society for Psychical Research*, 85, 317–331.

Irwin, H. J. (1992) 'Origins and functions of paranormal belief: The role of childhood trauma and interpersonal control.' *Journal of the American Society for Psychical Research*, 86, 199–208.

Irwin, H. J. (1993) 'Belief in the paranormal: A review of the empirical literature', *Journal of the American Society for Psychical Research, 87*, 1–39.

Irwin, H. J. (1994) 'Paranormal belief and proneness to dissociation', *Psychological Reports, 75*, 1344–1346.

Irwin, H. J. and Green, M. J. (1998–1999) 'Schizotypal processes and belief in the paranormal: a multidimensional study', *European Journal of Parapsychology*, 14, 1–15.

Irwin, H. J. and Watt, C. A. (2007) *An introduction to parapsychology.* 5th ed. Jefferson, NC: McFarland & Co.

Irwin, J. and Cressey, R. (1962) 'Thieves, convicts, and the inmate culture', *Social Problems*, 10, pp.142–55.

Iwasa, N. (1992) 'Postconventional reasoning and moral education in Japan', *Journal of Moral Education*, 21 (1), pp.3–16.

Jacklin, C.N. and Maccoby, E.E. (1978) 'Social behaviour at 33 months in same-sex and mixed-sex dyads', *British Journal of Social Psychology*, 25, pp. 33–41.

Jackson, P.L., Meltzoff, A.N. and Decety, J. (2005) 'How do we perceive the pain of others? A window into the neural processes involved in empathy', *Neuroimage*, 24 (3), pp.771–9.

Jahoda, G. (1971) 'Retinal pigmentation, illusion perceptibility and space perception', *International Journal of Psychology,* 6, pp.199–208.

Jakes, I. (1996) *Theoretical Approaches to Obsessive-compulsive Disorder*, Cambridge: Cambridge University Press.

James, D.V., Mullen, P.E., Pathe, M.T., Meloy, J.R., Farnham, F.R., Preston, L. and Darnley, B. (2008) 'Attacks on the British Royal Family: The role of psychotic illness', *Journal of the American Academy of Psychiatric Law,* 36(1), pp.59–67.

Jang, K.L., Vernon, P.A. and Livesley, W.J. (2000) 'Personality disorder traits, family environment and alcohol misuse: a multivariate behavioural genetic analysis', *Addiction*, 95(6), pp.873–888.

Jahn, R.G., Dunne, B. J., Dobyns, Y. H., Nelson, R. D. and Bradish, G. J. (2000) 'ArtREG: A random event experiment utilising picture-preference feedback', *Journal of Scientific Exploration*, 14, 383–409.

Jahoda, G. (1969) *The psychology of superstition*. London: Penguin.

Janis, I.L. and Feshbach, S. (1953) 'Effects of fear-arousing communications', *The Journal of Abnormal and Social Psychology*, 48, pp.78–92.

Jankowiak, W. and Fischer, E. (1992) 'Romantic love: A cross-cultural perspective', *Ethnology*, 31 (2), pp.149–55.

Jansen, K. L. R. (1989) 'Near-death experience and the NMDA receptor', *British Medical Journal*, 298, 1708–1709.

Jansen, K. L. R. (1997) T,he ketamine model of the near-death experience: A central role for the N-methyl-D-aspartate receptor', *Journal of Near-Death Studies*, 16, 79–95.

Jansen, K. L. R. (2001) *Ketamine: Dreams and realities*. Sarasota, FL: Multidisciplinary Association for Psychedelic Studies (MAPS)

Jarrett, R.B., Schaffer, M., McIntire, D., Witt-Browder, A., Kraft, D. and Risser, R.C. (1999) 'Treatment of atypical depression with cognitive therapy or phenalzine: a double-blind placebo-controlled trial', *Archives of General Psychiatry*, 56, pp.431–7.

Jarvis, M. (2000) *Theoretical approaches in Psychology*, London: Routledge.

Jessor, R. (1987) 'Problem behavior theory, psychosocial development, and adolescent problem drinking', *British Journal of Addiction*, 82, pp.331–342.

Jhally, S. (1990) *The Codes of Advertising*, London: Routledge.

Johnston, A., DeLuca, D., Murtaugh, K. and Diener, E. (1977) 'Validation of a laboratory play measure of aggression', *Child Development, 48*, pp.324–7.

Johnston, J. and Ettema, J.S. (1982) *Positive Images: Breaking Stereotypes with Children's Television*, London: Sage.

Jones, C., Cormac, I. and Mota, J. (2000) 'Cognitive behaviour therapy for schizophrenia (Cochrane Review)', *The Cochrane Library*, Issue 3. Oxford: Update Software.

Jones, D. and Elcock, J. (2001) *History and Theories of Psychology: A critical perspective*, London: Hodder.

Jones, P. and Cannon, M (1998) 'The new epidemiology of schizophrenia', *Psychiatric Clinics of North America*, 21, pp.1–25.

Julien, R.M. (2005) (10th edn) *A primer of drug action*, New York: Worth Publishers.

Jouvet, M. (1975) 'The function of dreaming: a neuropsychologist's point of view', In M. S. Gazzaniga and C. Blakemore (eds), *Handbook of Psychology*, New York: Academic Press, pp.499–527.

Jurkovic, G.J., Thirkield, A. and Morrell, R. (2001) 'Parentification of adult children of divorce: A multidimensional analysis', *Journal of Youth and Adolescence*, 30, pp.245–57.

Kahn, A., O'Leary, V.E., Krulewitz, J.E. and Lamm. H. (1980) 'Equity and equality: Male and female means to a just end', *Basic and Applied Social Psychology*, 1, pp.173–97.

Kahneman, D., Slovic, P. and Tversky, A. (1982) *Judgement under uncertainty: Heuristics and biases*. Cambridge: Cambridge University Press.

Kalat, J.W. (2004) *Biological Psychology*, London: Thomson.

Kales, A. and Kales, J. D. (1984) *Evaluation and treatment of insomnia*, Oxford: Oxford University Press.

Kalick, S.M., and Hamilton. T.E. (1986) 'The matching hypothesis re-examined', *Journal of Personality and Social Psychology*, 51, pp.673–82.

Kaminski, J.A., Sloutsky, V.M. and Heckler, A.F. (2008) 'Learning theory: the advantage of abstract examples in learning maths', *Science*, 320 (5875), pp.454–5.

Kandel, E.R. (1979) *Behavioural Biology of Aplysia*, San Francisco: W.H. Freeman & Co.

Kaplan, H.I. and Sadock, B.J. (1997) (8th edition) *Synopsis of Psychiatry*, Philadelphia: Lippincott Williams & Wilkins.

Karcher, M.J. (1996) 'Pairing for the prevention of prejudice: Pair counselling to promote intergroup understanding', *Journal of Child and Youth Care Work*, 36, pp.119–43.

Kawai, M. (1965) 'Newly-acquired pre-cultural behavior of the natural troop of Japanese Monkeys on Koshima Islet', *Primates*, 6(1), pp.1–30.

Kaye, K.L. and Bower, T.G.R. (1994) 'Learning and intermodal transfer of information in new-borns', *Psychological Science*, 5, pp.286–8.

Keenan, J.P., Gallup, G. and Falk, D. (2003) *The Face in the Mirror*, New York: Harper Collins.

Keinan, G. (2002) ,The effects of stress and desire for control on superstitious behavior', *Personality and Social Psychology Bulletin*, 28, 102–108.

Keller, M. and Edelstein, W. (1991) 'The development of socio-moral meaning making: Domains, categories, and perspective-taking', in W.M. Kurtines and J.L. Gerwitz (eds) *Handbook of Moral Behavior and Development, Vol. 2: Research*, Hillsdale, NJ: Lawrence Erlbaum, pp.89–114.

Keller, M.B., Klerman, G.L. and Lavori, P.W. (1984) 'Long-term outcome of episodes of major depression: clinical and public health significance', *Journal of the American Medical Association*, 252, pp.788–92.

Keller, M. and Wang, H-M. (2005) 'Inmate assaults in Texas county jails', *The Prison Journal*, 85(4), pp.515–34.

Kemp R., Kirov, G. and Everitt, B. (1998) 'Randomised controlled trial of compliance therapy: 18 month follow-up', *British Journal of Psychiatry* 172, pp.413–19.

Kemp, R., Towell, N. and Pike, G. (1997) 'When seeing should not be believing: Photographs, credit cards and fraud.' *Applied Cognitive Psychology*, 11 (3), pp.211–222.

Kessler, R.C., Berglund, P., Demler, O., Jin, R., Koretz, D., Merikangas, K.R., Rush, A.J., Walters, E.E., and Wang, P.S. (2003) 'The epidemiology of major depressive disorder: results from the National Comorbidity Survey Replication (NCS-R)', *Journal of the American Medical Association*, 289, pp.3095–3105.

Kendler, K.S., Kuhn, J.W. and Prescott, C.A. (2004) 'Childhood sexual abuse, stressful life events and risk for major depression in women', *Psychological Medicine* 34 (8), pp.1475–82.

Kendler, K.S. Masterson, C.C. and Davis, K.L. (1985) 'Psychiatric illness in first degree relatives of patients with paranoid psychosis, schizophrenia and medical controls', *British Journal of Psychiatry*, 147, pp.524–31.

Kendler, K.S., Neale, M.C., Kessler, R.C., Heath, A.C., and Eaves, L.J. (1992) 'Familial influences on the clinical characteristics of major depression: A twin study', *Acta Psychiatrica Scandinavica*, 86, pp.371–8.

Kendler, K.S., Neale, M.C., Kessler, R.C., Heath, A.C. and Eaves, L.J. (1992) 'Major depression and generalized anxiety disorder', *Archives of General Psychiatry*, 49, pp.716–22.

Kessler.R.C. and Zhao, S. (1999) 'The prevalence of mental illness', in A.V. Horwitz and T.L. Scheid (eds) *A handbook for the study of mental health: Social contexts, theories and systems*, Cambridge: Cambridge University Press.

Kessler, R.C., DuPont, R.L., Berglund, P. and Wittchen, H.U. (1999) 'Impairment in pure and co-morbid generalized anxiety disorder and major depression at 12 months in two national surveys', *American Journal of Psychiatry*, 156 (12), pp.1915–23.

Kessler, R.C., Berglund, P., Demler, O., Jin R., Walters, E.E. (2005) 'Lifetime prevalence and age of onset distributions of DSM-IV disorders in the national Co-morbidity Survey Replication', *Archives of General Psychiatry*, 62, pp.593–602.

Kety, S.S., Wender, P.H., Jacobsen, B., Ingraham, L.J., Jansson, L., Faber, B. and Kinney, D.K. (1994) 'Mental illness in the biological and adoptive relatives of schizophrenia adoptees', *Archives of General Psychiatry*, 51, pp.442–55.

Kienlen, K.K. (1998) 'Developmental and social antecedents of stalking' in J.R. Meloy (ed.), *The Psychology of Stalking*, San Deigo: Academic Press.

Kiernan, M., King, A.C., Kraemer, H.C., Stefanick, M.L. and Killen, J.D. (1998) 'Characteristics of successful and unsuccessful dieters: An application of signal detection methodology', *Annals of Behavioral Medicine*, 20, pp.1–6.

Kilham, W. and Mann, L. (1974) 'Level of destructive obedience as a function of transmitter and executant roles in the Milgram obedience paradigm', *Journal of Personality and Social Psychology*, 29, pp.696–702.

Kim, U. and Berry, J.W. (eds) (1993) *Indigenous Psychologies*, Newbury Park, CA: Sage.

Kimmel, A.J. (1996) *Ethical Issues in Behavioural Research: A Survey*, Cambridge, MA: Blackwell.

Kirchler, E., Palmonari, A. and Pombeni, M.L. (1993) 'Developmental tasks and adolescents' relationship with their peers and their family', in S. Jackson and H. Rodriguez-Tome (eds.) *Adolescence and its Social Worlds*, Hove: Erlbaum, pp.145–67.

Kirkley, B.G., Burge, J.C. and Ammerman, M.P.H. (1988) 'Dietary restraint, binge eating and dietary behaviour patterns', *International Journal of Eating Disorder*s, 7, pp.771–8.

Kirmayer, L.J. (1991) 'The place of culture in psychiatric nosology: Taijin Kyofusho and DSM-III-R', *Journal of Nervous and Mental Disease*, 179(1), pp.19–28.

Kissileff, H.R., Pi-Sunyer, F.X., Thornton, J. and Smith, G.P. (1981) 'C-terminal octapeptide of cholecystokinin decreases food intake in man', *American Journal of Clinical Nutrition*, 34, pp.154–60.

Kleiner, L. and Marshall, W.L. (1987) 'Interpersonal problems and agoraphobia', *Journal of Anxiety Disorders*, 1, pp.313–23.

Kleitman, N. (1963) *Sleep and Wakefulness*, Chicago: University of Chicago Press.

Klerman, G.L, Weissman, M.M., and Rounsaville, B.J. (1984) *Interpersonal psychotherapy of depression*, New York: Basic Books.

Kline, P. (1981) *Fact and Fantasy in Freudian Theory* (2nd edn), London: Methuen.

Kline, P. (1988) *Psychology Exposed*, London: Routledge.

Knapp, R. (1997) 'Stuttering', http://www.rogerknapp.com/medical/stutter.htm. Accessed December 2003.

Knowler, W.C., Pettitt, D.J., Saad, M.F., Charles, M.A., Nelson, R.G., Howard, B.V., Bogardus, C. and Bennett, P.H. (1991) 'Obesity in the Pima Indians: Its magnitude and relationship with diabetes', *American Journal of Clinical Nutrition*, 53, pp.1543S–51S.

Kobasa, S.C. (1979) 'Stressful life events, personality, and health: an enquiry into hardiness', *Journal of Personality and Social Psychology*, 37, pp.1–11.

Koepp, M.J., Gunn, R.N., Lawrence, A.D., Cunningham, V.J., Dagher, A., Jones, T., Brooks, D.J., Bench, C.J. and Grasby, P.M. (1998) 'Evidence for striatal dopamine release during a video game', *Nature*, 393, pp.266–268.

Koerner, S.S., Wallace, S., Lehman, S.J. and Raymond, M. (2002) 'Mother-to-daughter disclosure after divorce: Are there costs and benefits?' *Journal of Child and Family Studies*, 11 (4), pp.469–83.

Kohlberg, L. (1963) 'The development of children's orientations toward a moral order. 1: Sequence in the development of moral thought', *Vita Humana*, 6, pp.11–33.

Kohlberg, L. (1966) 'A cognitive-developmental analysis of children's sex-role concepts and attitudes', in E.E. Maccoby (ed) *The Development of Sex Differences* Stanford, CA: Standford University Press pp.82–173.

Kohlberg, L. (1969) *Stages in the Development of Moral Thought and Action*, New York: Holt, Rinehart and Winston.

Kohlberg, L. (1976) 'Moral stages and moralization: The cognitive-developmental approach', in T. Lickona (ed.) *Moral Development and Behavior: Theory, research, and social issues*, New York: Holt, Rinehart and Winston, pp.31–53.

Kohlberg, L. and Elfenbein, D. (1975) 'The development of moral judgments concerning capital punishment', *American Journal of Orthopsychiatry*, 54, pp.614–60.

Kohlberg, L., Levine, C. and Hewer, A. (1983) *Moral Stages: A current formulation and response to critics*, Basel: Karger.

Kopelman, P. (1999) 'Aetiology of obesity II: Genetics', Chapter 6 in *Obesity: The Report of the British Nutrition Foundation Task Force*, Oxford: Blackwell Science.

Kouri, E.M., Lukas, S.E., Pope, H.G.J. and Oliva, P.S. (1995) 'Increased aggressive responding in male volunteers following the administration of gradually increasing doses of testosterone cypionate', *Drug and Alcohol Dependence*, 40, pp.73–9.

Kreuz, L.E. and Rose, R.M. (1972) 'Assessment of aggressive behavior and plasma testosterone in a young criminal population', *Psychosomatic Medicine*, 34, pp.321–32.

Kruijver, F.P., Zhou, J.N., Pool, C.W., Hofman, M.A., Gooren, L.J., and Swaab, D.F. (2000) 'Male-to-female transsexuals have female neuron numbers in a limbic nucleus', *Journal of Clinical Endocrinology and Metabolism*, 85, pp.2034–41.

Kua, E.H., Chew, P.H. and Ko, S.M. (1993) 'Spirit possession and healing among Chinese psychiatric patients', *Acta Psychiatrica Scandinavica*, 88, pp. 447–50.

Kudo H, Dunbar R.I.M. (2001) 'Neocortex size and social network size in primates', *Animal Behaviour*, 62, pp.711–22.

Kurian, G. (1991) 'Socialization of South Asia immigrant youth', in S.P. Sharma, A.M. Ervin and D. Meintel (eds.) *Immigrants and Refugees in Canada*, Saskatoon: Department of Anthropology and Archeology, University of Saskatchewan, pp.47–57.

Kuhn, D., Nash, S.C. and Brucken, L. (1978) 'Sex role concepts of two- and three-year-old children', *Child Development*, 49, pp.445–51.

Kuhn, T.S. (1962) *The Structure of Scientific Revolutions*, Chicago: University of Chicago Press.

Kuhn, T.S. (1970) *The Structure of Scientific Revolutions* (2nd edn), Chicago, Illinois: University of Chicago Press.

Kuhn, T.S. (1977) *The Essential Tension: Selected studies in scientific tradition and change*, Chicago, Illinois: University of Chicago Press.

Lai, D.W. (2004) 'Impact of culture on depressive symptoms of elderly Chinese immigrants', *Canadian Journal of Psychiatry*, 49, pp. 820–7.

Lakatos, I. (1970) 'Falsification and the methodology of scientific research programmes', in I. Lakatos and A. Musgrave (eds) *Criticism and the growth of knowledge*, Cambridge: Cambridge University Press.

Lalumière, M.L., Harris, G.T., Quinsey, V.L. and Rice, M.E. (2005) *The causes of rape: Understanding individual differences in male propensity for sexual aggression*, Washington, DC: APA Press.

Lam, R.W., Zis, A.P., Grewal, A., Delgado, P.L., Charney, D.S. and Krystal, J.H. (1996) 'Effects of rapid tryptophan depletion in patients with seasonal affective disorder in remission after light therapy', *Archives of General Psychiatry*, 53, pp.41–4.

Lambert, M.J. and Kinsley, C.H. (2005) *Clinical neuroscience: The neurobiological foundations of mental health*, New York: Worth Publishers.

Lamont, P. and Wiseman, R. (1999) *Magic in theory: An introduction to the theoretical and psychological elements of conjuring*. Hatfield, UK: University of Hertfordshire Press.

Langer, E.J. (1975) 'The illusion of control', *Journal of Personality and Social Psychology*, 32, pp.311–328.

Langer, E.J. and Roth, J. (1983) 'Heads you win, tails it's chance: The illusion of control as a function of the sequence of outcomes in a purely chance task', *Journal of Personality and Social Psychology*, 32, pp.951–955.

Langlois, J.H. and Downs, A.C. (1980) 'Mothers, Fathers, and Peers as Socialization Agents of Sex-typed Play Behaviors in Young Children', *Child Development*, 51, (4) pp.1237–47.

Langlois, J.H., Roggman, L.A., Casey, R.J., Ritter, J.M., Rieser-Danner, L.A. and Jenkins, V.Y. (1987) 'Infant preferences for attractive faces: Rudiments of a stereotype?', *Developmental Psychology*, 23, pp.363–69.

Larkin, M. and Griffiths, M.D. (2004) 'Dangerous sports and recreational drug-use: Rationalising and contextualising risk', *Journal of Community and Applied Social Psychology*, 14, pp.215–232.

Lauer, R.H. and Lauer, J.C. (1994) *Marriage and Family: The Quest for Intimacy*, Madison, WI: Brown and Benchmark.

Laughlin, R. (2005) *A Different Universe: Reinventing Physics from the Bottom Down*, Cambridge: Basic Books.

Lavine, R. (1997) 'Psychopharmacological treatment of aggression and violence in the substance using population', *Psychoactive Drugs*, 29, pp.321–29.

Lawrence, T., Edwards, C., Barraclough, N., Church, S. and Hetherington, P. (1995) ,'Modelling childhood causes of paranormal belief and experience: Childhood trauma and childhood fantasy', *Personality and Individual Differences*, 19, 209–215.

Le, B. and Agnew, C.R. (2003) 'Commitment and its theorized determinants: A meta-analysis of the investment model', *Personal Relationships*, 10, pp.37–57.

Leakey, R. and Lewin, R. (1992) *Origins Reconsidered: In Search of What Makes us Human*' London: Little, Brown.

Lean, M.E.J., Han, T.S. and Seidall, J.C. (1998) 'Impairment of health and quality of life in people with large waist circumference', *Lancet*, 351, pp.853–6.

Lecrubier, Y., Baker, A. and Dunbar, G. (1997) 'Long term evaluation of paroxetine, clomiphramine and placebo in panic disorder', *Acta Psychiatrica Scandinavica*, 95, pp.153–60.

Leeper, R.W. (1935) 'A study of a neglected portion of the field of learning: The development of sensory organization.' *Journal of Genetic Psychology*, 46, pp.41–75.

Leibowitz, S.F. (1986) 'Brain monoamines and peptides: Role in the control of eating behaviour', *Federation Proceedings*, 45, pp.1396–1403.

Lenard, H.G. and Schulte, F.J. (1972) 'Polygraphic sleep study in craniopagus twins (Where is the sleep transmitter?)', *Journal of Neurology, Neurosurgery, and Psychiatry*, 35, pp.756–62.

Lenggenhager, B., Tadi, T., Metzinger, T. and Blanke, O. (2007) 'Video ergo sum: Manipulating bodily self-consciousness', *Science*, 317, 1096–1099.

Lepper, M.R., Greene, D. and Nisbett, R.E. (1973) 'Undermining children's intrinsic interest with extrinsic reward: A test of the "overjustification" hypothesis', *Journal of Personality and Social Psychology*, 28, pp.129–37.

Lepper, M., Sagotsky, G., Dafoe, J.L. and Greene, D. (1982) 'Consequences of superfluous social constraints: Effects on young children's social inferences and subsequent intrinsic interest', *Journal of Personality and Social Psychology*, 42, pp.51–65.

Lerner, R.M. and Steinberg, L. (eds) (2004) *Handbook of Adolescent Psychology* (2nd edn), New York: Wiley.

Leshner, A.I. (1999) 'Science-based views of drug addiction and its treatment', *Journal of the American Medical Association*, 282, pp.1314–1316.

Levenson, R.W. and Ruef, A.M. (1992) 'Empathy: a physiological substrate', *Journal of Personality and Social Psychology*, 63, pp.234–46.

Levine, R., Sato., S., Hashimoto, T. and Verma, J. (1995) 'Love and marriage in eleven cultures', *Journal of Cross-cultural Psychology*, 26, pp.554–71.

Lewinsohn, P.M. (1974) 'A behavioural approach to depression', in R.J. Friedman and M.M. Katz (eds) *The Psychology of Depression: Contemporary Theory and Research*, Washington, DC: Winston Wiley.

Lewis K. A. (2001) 'Comparative study of primate play behaviour: implications for the study of cognition', *Folia Primatologica*, 71, pp.417–21

Lewis, M. (2000) 'The emergence of human emotions', in M. Lewis and J.M. Haviland-Jones (eds) *Handbook of Emotions* (2nd edn), New York: Guilford Press, pp.265–80.

Lewis, M. and Brooks-Gunn, J. (1979) *Social Cognition and the Acquisition of Self*, New York: Plenum Press.

Li, H.Z., Bhatt, G., Zhang, Z., Pahal, J. and Cui, Y.P. (2006) 'Defining relationships: Comparing Canadians, Chinese and Indians', *Asian Journal of Social Psychology*, 9 (3), pp.236–44.

Liben, L.S. and Signorella, M.L. (1993) 'Gender-schematic processing in children: The role of initial interpretation of stimuli', *Developmental Psychology*, 29, pp.141–9.

Lidz, T., Fleck, S. and Cornelison, A. (1965) *Schizophrenia and the family*. New York: International Universities Press.

Lilienfeld, S. O. (2005) 'The 10 commandments of helping students distinguish science from pseudoscience in psychology', *APS Observer*, 18(9), 39–40 and 49–51.

Lilienfeld, S. O., Lynn, S. J. and Lohr, J. M. (eds) (2003) *Science and pseudoscience in clinical psychology.* New York and London: Guilford Press, p. 5.

Lin, L., Faraco, J., Li, R., Kadotani, H., Rogers W., Lin, X., Qiu, X., de Jong, P., Nishino, S. and Mignot, E. (1999) 'The sleep disorder canine narcolepsy is caused by a mutation in the hypocretin (orexin) receptor 2 gene', *Cell*, 98, pp.365–76.

Linden, M., Bar, T. and Geiselmann, B. (1998) 'Patient treatment insistence and medication craving in long-term, low-dosage benzodiazepine prescriptions', *Psychological Medicine*, 28, pp.721–9.

Liss, M.B. and Reinhardt, L.C. (1979) *Behavioral and attitudinal responses to prosocial programs*, Paper presented at the meeting of the Society for Research in Child Development, San Francisco, CA.

Littlefield, T.R., Kelly, K.M., Pomatto, J.K. and Beals, S.P. (1999) 'Multiple-birth Infants at Higher Risk for Development of Deformational Plagiocephaly', *Pediatrics*, 103, pp.565–69.

Livingstone, S. (2001) 'Media effects research', *Psychology Review*, 7(3), pp.28–31.

Locke, J. (1690) *An Essay Concerning Human Understanding*, Harmondsworth: Penguin (originally London: Tegg.).

Lothstein, L.M. (1979) 'Psychodynamics and sociodynamics of gender dysphoric states', *American Journal of Psychotherapy*, 33, pp.214–8.

Lott, B.E. (1994) *Women's Lives: Themes and variations in gender learning* (2nd edn), Pacific Grove, CA: Brooks/Cole Publishing.

Lovelace, V. and Huston, H.C. (1983) 'Can television teach prosocial behavior?', *Prevention in Human Services*, 2, pp.93–106.

Lowe, C.F., Dowey, A. and Horne, P. (1998) 'Changing what children eat', in A. Murcott (ed.) *The Nation's Diet: The social science of food choice*, London: Longman.

Lujansky, H. and Mikula, G. (1983) 'Can equity theory explain the quality and stability of romantic relationships?' *British Journal of Social Psychology*, 22, pp.101–12.

Lutchmaya, S., Baron-Cohen, S. and Raggatt, P. (2002) 'Foetal testosterone and eye contact in 12-month-old human infants', *Infant Behaviour and Development*, 25, pp.327–35.

Luty, J. (2003) 'What works in drug addiction?', *Advances in Psychiatric Treatment*, 9, pp.280–288.

Luxen, M.F. (2007) 'Sex differences, evolutionary psychology and biosocial theory: Biosocial theory is no alternative', *Theory Psychology*, 17(3), pp.383–94.

Lydiard, R.B., Brawman-Mintzer, O. and Ballenger, J.C. (1996) 'Recent developments in the psychopharmacology of anxiety disorders', *Journal of Consulting and Clinical Psychology*, 64, pp.660–8.

Lynn, S. J. and Rhue, J. W. (1988) 'Fantasy proneness: Hypnosis, developmental antecedents, and psychopathology', *American Psychologist*, 43, 35–44.

Ma, R. (1996) 'Computer-mediated conversations as a new dimension of intercultural communication between East Asian and North American college students', in S.C. Herring (ed.) *Computer-mediated Communication: Linguistic, social, and cross-cultural perspectives*, New York: John Benjamins, pp.173–85.

Maccoby (ed) *The Development of Sex Differences*, Stanford, CA: Stanford University Press, pp.56–81.

Maccoby, E.E. and Jacklin, C.N. (1974) *The Psychology of Sex Differences*, Stanford, CA: Stanford University Press.

MacGregor, F. (2008) *Mind games: Sporting superstitions*. [Electronic version]. Retrieved 23 December 2008 from: http://thescotsman.scotsman.com/features/-Mind-games-sporting-superstitions.4651184.jp

Mackie, D.M. and Worth, L.T. (1989) 'Processing deficits and the mediation of positive affect in persuasion', *Journal of Personality and Social Psychology*, 57, pp.27–40.

MacKinnon, A. and Foley, D. (1996) 'The genetics of anxiety disorders', in H.G. Westenberg, J.A. Den Boer and D.J. Murphy (eds), *Advances in the neurobiology of anxiety disorders*, Chichester, England: Wiley, pp.39–59.

Mackintosh, N.J. (1981) 'Learning', in D.J. McFarland (ed.) *Oxford Companion to animal behaviour*, Oxford: Oxford University Press, pp.336–46.

Mackintosh, N.J. (1998) *IQ and Human Intelligence*, Oxford: Oxford University Press.

Macknik, S. L., King, M., Randi, J., Robbins, A., Teller, Thompson, J., Martinez-Conde, S. (2008) 'Attention and awareness in stage magic: turning tricks into research', *Nature Reviews: Neuroscience*, 9, 871–879.

McBurnett, K., Lahey, B.B., Rathouz, P.J. and Loeber, R. (2000) 'Low salivary cortisol and persistent aggression in boys referred for disruptive behavior', *Archives of General Psychiatry*, 57, pp.38–43.

McClure, E. (2000) 'A meta-analytic review of sex differences in facial expression processing and their development in infants, children, and adolescents', *Psychological Bulletin*, 126, pp.242–453.

McCorkle, R.C. (1993) 'Fear of victimization and symptoms of psychopathology among prison inmates', *Journal of Offender Rehabilitation*, 19(1/2), pp.27–41.

McCorkle, R.C., Miethe, T.D. and Drass, K.A. (1995) 'The roots of prison violence: A test of the deprivation, management, and "not-so-total" institution models', *Crime and Delinquency*, 41, pp.317–31.

McCormack, R.L. (1965) 'Extended tables of the Wilcoxon matched pairs signed ranks statistic', *Journal of the American Statistical Association*, 60, pp.864–71

McCrae, C.S., Rowe, M.A., Tierney, C.G., Dautovich, N.D., DeFinis, A.L. and McNamara, J.P.H. (2005) 'Sleep complaints, subjective and objective sleep patterns, health, psychological adjustment, and daytime functioning in community-dwelling older adults', *Journal of Gerontology Series B: Psychological Sciences and Social Sciences*, 60 B, pp.182–9.

McCutcheon, L.E., Scott, J.R., Aruguete, M. and Parker, J. (2006) 'Exploring the link between attachment and the inclination to obsess about or stalk celebrities', *North American Journal of Psychology*, 8, pp.289–300.

McCutcheon, L.E., Lange, R. and Houran, J. (2002) 'Conceptualization and measurement of celebrity worship', *British Journal of Psychology*, 93, pp.67–87.

McGarrigle, J. and Donaldson, M. (1974) 'Conservation accidents', *Cognition*, 3, pp.341–50.

McGinnies, E. (1949) 'Emotionality and perceptual defence', *Psychological Review*, 56, pp.244–51.

McGinnies, E. (1966) 'Studies in persuasion III: Reactions of Japanese students to one-sided and two-sided communication', *Journal of Social Psychology*, 70, pp.87–93.

McGrath, T., Tsui, E., Humphries, S. and Yule, W. (1990) 'Successful treatment of a noise phobia in a nine-year-old girl with systematic desensitization *in vivo*', *Educational Psychology*, 10(1), pp.79–83.

McGreal, C. (2008) 'Nigeria takes on big tobacco over campaigns that target the young', *The Guardian*, Tuesday January 15.

McGrenere, J. and Ho, W. (2000) 'Affordances: clarifying and evolving a concept', in *Proceedings of Graphic Interface 2000*, 15–17 May 2000, Montreal, pp.179–86.

McGuffin, P. and Gottesman, I.I. (1985) 'Genetic influences on normal and abnormal development', in M. Rutter and L. Hersoy (eds) *Child and Adolescent Psychiatry: Modern Approaches* (2nd edn) Oxford: Blackwell Scientific, pp.17–33.

McGuffin, P., Katz, R., Watkins, S. and Rutherford, J. (1996) 'A hospital-based twin register of the heritability of DSM-IV unipolar depression', *Archives of General Psychiatry*, 53, pp.129–36.

McGuire, W. J. (1968) 'Personality and susceptibility to social influence', in E. Borgatta and W. Lambert (eds), *Handbook of Personality Theory and Research*, Chicago, Rand McNally, pp.1130–87.

McIver, T. (1988) 'Backward masking, and other backward thoughts about music', *Skeptical Inquirer*, 13(1), 50–63.

McIvor, R.J., Potter, L. and Davies, L. (2008) 'Stalking Behaviour By Patients Towards Psychiatrists in a Large Mental Health Organization', *International Journal of Social Psychiatry*, 54(4), pp.350–7.

McMillan, B. and Conner, M. (2003) 'Using the theory of planned behaviour to understand alcohol and tobacco use in students', *Psychology, Health & Medicine*, 8, pp.317–328.

McMillan, B. and Conner, M. (2003) 'Applying an extended version of the Theory of Planned Behavior to illicit drug use among students', *Journal of Applied Social Psychology*, 33, pp.1662–1683.

McMurran, M. (1994) *The Psychology of Addiction*, London: Taylor and Francis.

McNally, R. J. (2003) 'Is the pseudoscience concept useful for clinical psychology? The demise of pseudoscience.' *The Scientific Review of Mental Health Practice*, 2(2), 97–101.

McNally, R.J. and Steketee, G.S. (1985) 'The etiology and maintenance of severe animal phobias', *Behaviour Research and Therapy*, 23(4), pp.431–5.

McNaughton, S. and Leyland, J. (1990) 'The shifting focus of maternal tutoring across different difficulty levels on a problem-solving task', *British Journal of Developmental Psychology*, 8 (2), pp.147–55.

McNeil, J.E. and Warrington, E.K. (1993) 'Prosopagnosia: A face specific disorder', *Quarterly Journal of Experimental Psychology: Human Experimental Psychology*, 46A, pp.1–10.

McNicholas, T.A., Dean, J.D., Mulder, H., Carnegie, C. and Jones, N.A. (2003) 'A novel testosterone gel formulation normalizes androgen levels in hypogonadal men, with improvements in body composition and sexual function', *British Journal of Urology International*, 91, pp.69–74.

McQuail, D., Blumler, J. and Brown, R. (1972) 'The television audience: a revised perspective', in D. McQuail (ed.), *Sociology of Mass Communication*, London: Longman.

Madden, P.A.F., Heath, A., Rosenthal, N.E. and Martin, N.E. (1996) 'Seasonal changes in mood and behaviour', *Archives of General Psychiatry*, 53, pp.47–55.

Madsen, S.D. (2001) 'The salience of adolescent romantic experiences for romantic relationships in young adulthood', Unpublished dissertation, University of Minnesota.

Maes, H.H., Neale, M.C. and Eaves, L.J. (1997) 'Genetic and environmental factors in relative body weight and human adiposity', *Behavior Genetics*, 27(4), pp.325–51.

Magee, W.J., Eaton, W., Wittchen, H.U., McGonagle, K.A. and Kessler, R.C. (1996) 'Agoraphobia, simple phobia and social phobia in the national comorbidity survey', *Archives of General Psychiatry*, 53 (2), pp.159–68.

Maguire, E.A., Gadian, D.G., Johnsrude, I.S., Good, C.D., Ashburner, J., Frackowiak, R.S. and Frith, C.D. (2000) 'Navigation-related structural change in the hippocampi of taxi drivers', *Proceedings of the National Academy of Science*, 97(8), pp.4398–403.

Mahowald, M.W. and Schenck, C.H. (1992) 'Dissociated states of wakefulness and sleep', *Neurology*, 42 (6), pp.44–52.

Maier, S.J. and Seligman, M.E.P. (1976) 'Learned helplessness: theory and evidence', *Journal of Experimental Psychology: General*, 105, pp.2–46.

Maj, M. (2005) 'Psychiatric co-morbidity: an artefact of current diagnostic systems?', *British Journal of Psychiatry*, 186, p.182–4.

Makarec, K. and Persinger, M. A. (1990) 'Electroencephalographic validation of a temporal lobe signs inventory', *Journal of Research in Personality*, 24, 323–337.

Malamuth, N. and Check, J. (1981) 'The effects of mass media exposure on acceptance of violence against women: A field experiment', *Journal of Research in Personality*, 15, pp.436–46.

Malinowski, B. (1922) *Argonauts of the Western Pacific*, New York: Dutton.

Maltby, J., Day, L., McCutcheon, L.E., Gillett, R., Houran, J. and Ashe, D. (2004) 'Celebrity worship using an adaptational-continuum model of personality and coping', *British Journal of Psychology*, 95, pp.411–28.

Maltby, J., Giles, D.C., Barber, L. and McCutcheon, L.E. (2005) 'Intense personal celebrity worship and body image: Evidence of a link among female adolescents', *British Journal of Health Psychology*, 10, pp.17–32.

Maltby, J., McCutcheon, L.E., Ashe, D.D. and Houran, J. (2001) 'The self reported psychological well-being of celebrity worshippers', *North American Journal of Psychology*, 3, pp.441–52.

Mann, J.J., Malone, K.M., Diehl, D.J., Perel, J., Cooper, T.B. and Mintun, M.A. (1996) 'Demonstration in vivo of reduced serotonin responsivity in the brain of untreated depressed patients', *American Journal of Psychiatry*, 153, pp.174–82.

Mann, J., Underwood, M. and Arango, V. (1996) 'Postmortem studies of suicide victims', in S.J. Watson (ed.) *Biology of Schizophrenia and Affective Disorders*, Washington: American Psychiatric Press, pp.197–221.

Mann, L. (1981) 'The baiting crowd in episodes of threatened suicide', *Journal of Personality and Social Psychology*, 41, pp.703–709.

Mann, J., Arango, V. and Underwood, M. (1990) 'Serotonin and suicidal behavior', *Annals of the New York Academy of Science*, 600, pp.476–84.

Mannuzza, S., Schneier, F.R., Chapman, T.F., Liebowitz, M.R., Klein, D.F. and Fyer, A.J. (1995) 'Generalized social phobia: Reliability and validity', *Archives of General Psychiatry*, 52(3), pp.230–7.

Manstead, A. and McCulloch, C. (1981) 'Sex role stereotyping in British studies of television advertisements', *British Journal of Social Psychology*, 20, pp.171–80.

Manstead, A.S.R. and Hewstone, M. (eds) (1995) *The Blackwell Encyclopedia of Social Psychology*, Oxford: Blackwell.

Maquet, P., Laureys, S., Peigneux, P., Fuchs, S., Petiau, C., Phillips, C., Aerts, J., Del Fiore, G., Degueldre, C., Meulemans, T., Luxen, A., Franck, G., Van der Linden, M., Smith, C. and Cleeremans, A. (2000) 'Experience-dependent changes in cerebral activation during human REM sleep', *Nature Neuroscience*, 3, pp.831–6.

Marcus, D.E. and Overton, W.F. (1978) 'The development of cognitive gender constancy and sex role preferences', *Child Development*, 49(2), pp.434–44.

Marcus, J., Hans, S.L., Nagier, S., Auerbach, J.G., Mirsky, A.F. and Aubrey, A. (1987) 'Review of the NIMH Israeli Kibbutz-City and the Jerusalem infant development study', *Schizophrenia Bulletin*, 13, pp.425–38.

Mares, M. (1996) 'The role of source confusions in television's cultivation of social reality judgments', *Human Communication Research*, 23(2), pp.278–97.

Mares, M.L. and Woodard, E. (2005) 'Positive effects of television on children's social interactions: A meta-analysis', *Media Psychology*, 7, pp.298, 301–22.

Marks, D. (2000) *The psychology of the psychic*. 2nd ed. Amherst, NY: Prometheus, p.41.

Marks, I.M. (1981) 'Review of behavioural psychotherapy: obsessive-compulsive disorders', *American Journal of Psychiatry*, 138, pp.584–92.

Marks, I.M., Swinson, R.P. and Basoglu, M. (1993) 'Alprazolam and exposure alone and combined in panic disorder and agoraphobia: a controlled study in London and Toronto', *British Journal of Psychiatry*, 162, pp.776–87.

Markwick, B. (1985) 'The establishment of data manipulation in the Soal-Shackleton experiments', In P. Kurtz (ed.) *A skeptic's handbook of parapsychology*. Buffalo, NY: Prometheus. Pp. 287–311.

Marlatt, G.A., Baer, J.S., Donovan, D.M. and Kivlahan, D.R. (1988), 'Addictive behaviors: Etiology and treatment', *Annual Review of Psychology*, 39, pp.223–252.

Marsh, P., Rosser, E. and Harre, R. (1978) *The Rules of Disorder*, London: Routledge.

Martin, C.L., Eisenbud, L. and Rose, H. (1995) 'Children's gender-based reasoning about toys', *Child Development*, 66, pp.1453–71.

Martin, C.I. and Halverson, C.F. (1983) 'Gender constancy: A methodological and theoretical analysis', *Sex Roles*, 9, pp.775–90.

Martin, C.I. and Little, J.K. (1990) 'The relation of gender understanding to children's sex-typed preferences and gender stereotypes', *Child Development*, 61, pp.1427–39.

Martin, G., Bergen, H.A., Roeger, L., and Allison, S. (2004) 'Depression in young adolescents: Investigations using 2 and 3 factor versions of the Parental Bonding Instrument', *Journal of Nerv Mental Disorders*, 192 (10), pp.650–7.

Martin, M.C. (1997) 'Children's understanding of the intent of advertising: A meta-analysis', *Journal of Public Policy and Marketing*, 16, pp.205–16.

Mason, D.A. and Frick, P.J. (1994) 'The heritability of antisocial behavior: A meta-analysis of twin and adoption studies', *Journal of Psychopathology and Behavioral Assessment*, 16, pp.301–23.

Massó-González, E.L., Johansson, S., Wallander, M-A. and García-Rodriguez, L.A. (2009) 'Trends in the prevalence and incidence of diabetes in the UK – 1996 to 2005', *Journal of Epidemiology and Community Health*, doi: 10.1136/jech.2008.080382.

Masters, J.C., Ford, M.E., Arend, R., Grotevant, H.D. and Clark, L.V. (1979) 'Modelling and labelling as integrated determinants of children's sex-typed imitative behaviour', *Child Development*, 50, pp.364–71.

Mathews V.P., Kronenberger, W.G., Wang, Y., Lurito, J.T., Lowe, M.J. and Dunn, D.W. (2005) 'Media violence exposure and frontal lobe activation measured by functional magnetic resonance imaging in aggressive and nonaggressive adolescents', *Journal of Computer Assisted Tomography*, 29, pp.287–92.

Matlin, M.W. (2005) *Cognition* (6th edn), Hoboken, NJ: Wiley.

Matthews, R. and Blackmore, S. (1995) Why are coincidences so impressive? *Perceptual and Motor Skills*, 80, 1121–1122.

May, J.L. and Hamilton, P.A. (1980) 'Effects of musically evoked affect on interpersonal attraction', *Motivation and Emotion*, 4, pp.217–28.

May, P. (1993–1994) The faith healing claims of Morris Cerullo. *Free Inquiry*, Winter 1993/94, 5–11.

Mayo, J., White, O. and Eysenck, H. (1978), 'An empirical study of the relation between astrological factors and personality', *Journal of Social Psychology*, 105, 229–36.

Mazarella, S.R. (ed) (2007) *Kid Stuff: 20 Questions about Youth and the Media*, New York: Peter Lang.

Mazure, C.M., Bruce, M.L., Maciejewski, P.K. and Jacobs, S.C. (2000) 'Adverse life events and Cognitive-personality Characteristics in the Prediction of Major Depression and Antidepressant Response', *American Journal of Psychiatry*, 157, pp.896–903.

Mead, M. (1935) *Sex and Temperament in Three Primitive Societies*, William Morrow and Company, pp.280.

Mead, M. (1949) *Male and Female: A Study of the Sexes in a Changing World*, New York: Morrow.

Meddis, R. (1975) 'The Function of Sleep', *Animal Behaviour*, 23, pp.676–91.

Meddis, R. (1977) The Sleep Instinct, London: Routledge.

Medicine, B. (1997) 'Changing Native American roles in an urban context and changing Native American sex roles in an urban context', in S. Jacobs, W. Thomas and S. Lang (eds) *Two Spirited People*, Champaign, Illinois: University of Illinois Press.

Medini, G., Rosenberg, E.H. (1976) 'Gossip and psychotherapy', *American Journal of Psychotherapy*, 30(3), pp.452, 459.

Mednick, S.A., Machon, R.A., Huttunen, M.O. and Bonett, D. (1988) 'Adult schizophrenia following prenatal exposure to an influenza epidemic', *Archives of General Psychiatry*, 45 (2), pp.189–92.

Meduna, L. J. (1950) *Carbon dioxide therapy*. Springfield, Illinois: Charles C. Thomas.

Meeus, W.H.J. and Raaijmakers, Q.A.W. (1986) 'Administrative obedience: carrying out orders to use psychological-administrative violence', *European Journal of Social Psychology*, 16, pp.311–24.

Meister, I.G., Krings, T., Foltys, H., Müller, M., Töpper, R. and Thron, A. (2004) 'Playing piano in the mind: An fMRI study on music imagery and performance in pianists', *Cognitive Brain Research*, 19, pp.219–28.

Mela, D.J. and Rogers, P.J. (1998) *Food, Eating and Obesity: The psychobiological basis of appetite and weight control*, London: Chapman and Hall.

Mellbin, T. and Vuille, C. (1989) 'Further evidence of an association between psychosocial problems and increase in relative weight between 7 and 10 years of age', *Acta Paediatrica Scandinavica*, 78, pp.576–80.

Mendola, J. (2003) 'Contextual shape processing in human visual cortex: Beginning to fill in the blanks', in L. Pessoa and P. De Weerd (eds), *Filling In: From Perceptual Completion to Cortical Reorganisation*, New York: Oxford University Press, pp.38–58.

Menzies, L., Achgard, S., Chamberlain, S.R., Fineberg, N., Chen, C.H., del Campo, N., Sahakian, B., Robbins, T.W. and Bullmore, E. (2007) 'Neurocognitive endophenotypes of obsessive-compulsive disorder', *Brain*, 130(12), pp.3223–36.

Menzies, R.G. and Clarke, J.C. (1993) 'A comparison of *in vivo* and vicarious exposure in the treatment of childhood water phobia', *Behavioural Research Therapy*, 31(1), pp.9–15.

Meyer, V. (1966) 'Modification of expectations in cases with obsessional rituals', *Behaviour Research and Therapy*, 4, pp.273–280.

Mezzanotte, W.S., Tangel, D.J. and White, D.P. (1992) 'Waking genioglossal electromyogram in sleep apnea patients versus normal controls (a neuromuscular compensatory mechanism)', Journal of Clinical Investigation, 89, pp.1571–9.

Midlarsky, E. and Hannah, M.E. (1985) 'Competence, reticence, and helping among children and adolescents', *Developmental Psychology*, 21, pp.534–91.

Miklowitz, D.J. (2004) 'The role of family systems in severe and recurrent psychiatric disorders: A developmental psychopathology view', *Development and Psychopathology (Special issue: Family Systems and Developmental Psychopathology)*,16 (3), pp.667–688.

Miles, D.R. and Carey, G. (1997) 'Genetic and environmental architecture of human aggression', *Journal of Personality and Social Psychology*, 72, pp.207–17.

Milgram, S. (1963) 'Behavioral study of obedience', *Journal of Abnormal and Social Psychology*, 67, pp.371–8.

Milgram, S. (1964) 'Issues in the study of obedience: A Reply to Baumrind', *American Psychologist*. 19, pp.848–52.

Milgram, S. (1965) 'Some conditions of obedience and disobedience to authority', *Human Relations*, 18, pp.57–76.

Milgram, S. (1974) *Obedience to Authority*, New York: Harper & Row.

Miller, G.F. (1998) 'How mate choice shaped human nature: A review of sexual selection and human evolution', in C. Crawford and D. Krebs (eds) *Handbook of Evolutionary Psychology: Ideas, issues and applications*, Mahwah, NJ: Lawrence Erlbaum, pp.87–129.

Miller, G.F. (2000) 'Sexual selection for indicators of intelligence', in G. Bock, J. Goode, and K. Webb (eds), *The nature of intelligence*, Novartis Foundation Symposium 233, John Wiley, pp.260–75.

Miller, G., Tybur, J.M. and Jordan, B.D. (2007) 'Ovulatory cycle effects on tip earnings by lap dancers: economic evidence for human estus?' *Evolution and Human Behavior*, 28, pp.375–81.

Miller, J.G., Bersoff, D.M. and Harwood, R.L. (1990) 'Perception of social responsibilities in India and the United States: Moral imperatives or personal decisions', *Journal of Personality and Social Psychology*, 58, pp.33–47.

Miller, W.R. and Rollnick, S. (2002) *Motivational Interviewing: preparing people to change addictive behaviour*. New York: The Guilford Press.

Milner, B. (1966) 'Amnesia following operation on the temporal lobes', in C.W.M. Whitty and O.L. Zangwill (eds) *Amnesia*, London: Butterworth.

Milton, J. and Wiseman, R. (1999) 'Does psi exist? Lack of replication of an anomalous process of information transfer' *Psychological Bulletin*, 125, 387–391.

Mischel, W. (1966) 'A social learning view of sex differences in behaviour', in E.E.

Mischel, W. (1968) *Personality and Assessment*, New York: Wiley.

Mischel, W. (1970) 'Sex typing and socialization', in: P.H. Mussen (ed) *Carmichael's Manual of Child Psychology*, Vol. 2, (3rd edn), New York: Wiley.

Mitchell, P. (1997) *Introduction to Theory of Mind: Children, autism and apes*, London: Edward Arnold.

Mitroff, I.I. (1974) 'Studying the lunar rock scientists', *Saturday Review World*, 2 November, pp.64–5.

Mixon, D. (1972) 'Instead of deception', *Journal of the Theory of Social Behaviour*, 2, pp.139–77.

Moeller, K. and Stattin, H. (2001) 'Are close relationships in adolescence linked with partner relationships in midlife? A longitudinal, prospective study', *International Journal of Behavioral Development*, 25, pp.69–77.

Moghaddam, F.M., Taylor, D.M. and Wright, S.C. (1993) *Social Psychology in Cross-Cultural Perspective*, New York: W.H. Freeman.

Mokdad, A.H., Serdula, M.K., Dietz, W.H., Bowman, B.A., Marks, J.S. and Koplan, J.P. (1999) 'The spread of the obesity epidemic in the United States, 1991–1998', *Journal of the American Medical Association*, 282, pp.1519–22.

Money, J., Hampson, J.G. and Hampson, J.L. (1955) 'Hermaphroditism: Recommendations concerning assignment of sex, change of sex and psychological management'

Money, J., Hampson, J.G. and Hampson, J.L. (1956) 'Sexual Incongruities and Psychopathology: The Evidence of Human Hermaphrodites', *Bulletin of the Johns Hopkins Hospital*, 98, pp.43–57.

Money, J., Hampson, J.G. and Hampson, J.L. (1957) 'Imprinting and the Establishment of Gender Role', *American Medical Association Archives of Neurology and Psychiatry*, 77, pp.333–6.

Money, J. and Norman, B.F. (1987) 'Gender identity and gender transposition: longitudinal outcome study of 24 male hermaphrodites assigned as boys', *Journal of Sex Marital Therapy*, 13, pp.75–92.

Money, J. and Ehrhardt, A.A. (1972) *Man and Woman, Boy and Girl*, Baltimore: Johns Hopkins University Press.

Money, J. (1995) *Gendermaps: Social Constructionism, Feminism, and Sexosophical History*, New York: Continuum.

Moniz, E. (1936) Tentatives Opératoires dans le Traitement de Certaines Psychoses, Paris: Masson

Montague, C.T., Farooqi, I.S., Whitehead, J.P. (1997) 'Congenital leptin deficiency is associated with severe early onset obesity in humans', *Nature*, 387, pp.903–8.

Montgomery, S.A., Bebbington, P., Cowen, P., Deakin, W., Freeling, P., Hallstrom, C., Katona, C., King, D., Leonard, B., Levine, S., Phanjoo, A., Peet, M. and Thompson, C. (1993) 'Guidelines for treating depressive illness with antidepressants: A statement from the British Association for Psychopharmacology', *Journal of Psychopharmacology*, 7, pp.19–23.

Moore, C. and Frye, D. (1986) 'The effect of the experimenter's intention on the child's understanding of conservation', *Cognition*, 22, pp.283–98

Moore, D.W. (2005) *Three in four Americans believe in paranormal: Little change from similar results in 2001.* Retrieved 3 October 2008 from: http://www.gallup.com/poll/16915/Three-Four-Americans-Believe-Paranormal.aspx

Moorcroft, W.H. (1993) *Sleep, dreaming, and sleep disorders: An introduction*, Landham, MD: University Press of America.

Morley, K. and Hall, W. (2003) 'Is there a genetic susceptibility to engage in criminal acts?' *Australian Institute of Criminology: Trends and Issues in Crime and Criminal Justice*, 263, pp.1–6.

Morris, C. (1866) 'The making of Man', *American Naturalist*, 20, pp.493–504.

Morris, N. (2006) 'Courts issue 3,500 Asbos but over half are ignored', *The Independent*, 7 December 2006.

Morrison, I., Lloyd, D., di Pellegrino, G. and Robets, N. (2004) 'Vicarious responses to pain in anterior cingulate cortex: is empathy a multisensory issue?', *Cognition, Affect and Behavioural Neuroscience*, 4, pp.270–8.

Morrison, T.L., Urquiza, A.J. and Goodlin-Jones, B.L. (1997) 'Attachment and the representation of intimate relationships in adulthood', *The Journal of Psychology*, 131 (1), pp.57–71.

Morse, M.L., Venecia, D. and Milstein, J. (1989) ‚Near-death experiences: A neurophysiological explanatory model' *Journal of Near-Death Studies*, 8, 45–53.

Moscovici, S. (1981) 'On social representations', in Forgas, J.P. (ed.) *Social Cognition: Perspectives on everyday understanding*, London: Academic Press.

Moscovici, S. and Hewstone, M. (1983) 'Social representations and social explanations: from the "naive" to the "amateur" scientist', in Hewstone, M. (ed.) *Attribution Theory: Social and functional extensions*, Oxford: Basil Blackwell.

Moss, E. (1992) 'The socio-affective context of joint cognitive activity', in L.T. Winegar and J. Valsiner (eds) *Children's Development Within Social Context, Vol. 2: Research and methodology*, Hillsdale, NJ: Erlbaum.

Mousseau, M-C. (2003) 'Parapsychology: Science or pseudo-science?' *Journal of Scientific Exploration*, 17, 271–282.

Mowrer, O.H. (1947) 'On the dual nature of learning: A reinterpretation of "conditioning" and "problem-solving"', *Harvard Educational Review*, 17, pp.102–148.

Mufson, L. (2004) 'A randomised effectiveness trial of interpersonal psychotherapy for depressed adolescents', *Archives of General Psychiatry*, 61, pp.577–84.

Mufson, L., Weissman, M.M., Moreau, D. and Garfinkel, R. (1999) 'Efficacy of interpersonal psychotherapy for depressed adolescents', *Archives of General Psychiatry*, 56, pp.573–9.

Mulder, R. T., Beautrais, A. L., Joyce, P. R. and Fergusson, D. M. (1998) 'Relationship between dissociation, childhood sexual abuse, childhood physical abuse, and mental illness in a general population sample' *American Journal of Psychiatry*, 155, 806–811.

Mullen, B. (1986) 'Atrocity as a function of lynch mob composition: a self-attention perspective', *Personality and Social Psychology Bulletin*, 12, pp.187–97.

Mullen, P.E., Pathé, M., Purcell, R. and Stuart, G.W. (1999) 'Study of stalkers', *American Journal of Psychiatry*, 156(8), pp.1244–9.

Munjack, D.J. (1984) 'The onset of driving phobias', *Journal of Behaviour Therapy and Experimental Psychiatry*, 15, pp.305–8.

Munroe, R.H., Shimmin, H.S. and Munroe, R.L. (1984) 'Gender understanding and sex role preference in four cultures', *Developmental Psychology*, 20, pp.673–82.

Murdock, G.P. (1967) 'Ethnographical atlas', cited in W. Wood and A.H. Eagly (2002) 'A cross-cultural analysis of the behaviour of women and men: Implications for the origins of sex differences' p. 703, *Psychological Bulletin*, 128, pp.699–727.

Murdock, G.P. and White, D.R. (1969) 'Standard cross-cultural sample', cited in W. Wood and A.H. Eagly (2002) 'A cross-cultural analysis of the behaviour of women and men: Implications for the origins of sex differences', p. 703, *Psychological Bulletin, 128*, pp.699–727.

Murdock, G.P. (1981) *Atlas of World Cultures*, Pittsburgh: The University of Pittsburgh Press.

Murdoch, S. (2007) *IQ: The Brilliant Idea that Failed*, London: Duckworth.

Murstein, B.I. (1972) 'Physical attractiveness and marital choice', *Journal of Personality and Social Psychology*, 22, pp.8-12.

Musch, J. and Ehrenberg, K. (2002) 'Probability misjudgement, cognitive ability, and belief in the paranormal' *British Journal of Psychology*, 93, 169–177.

Must, A., Spadano, J., Coakley, E.H., Field, A.E., Colditz, G. and Dietz, W.H. (1999) 'The disease burden associated with overweight and obesity', *Journal of the American Medical Association*, 282, pp.1523–9.

Myers, D.G. (2001) *Psychology*, New York: Worth.

Myers, J.E., Madathil, J. and Tingle, L.R. (2005) 'Marriage satisfaction and wellness in India and the United States: A preliminary comparison of arranged marriages and marriages of choice', *Journal of Counselling and Development*, 83, pp.183–90.

Myers, L.B. and Brewin, C.R. (1994) 'Recall of early experiences and the repressive coping style', *Journal of Abnormal Psychology*, 103, pp.288–92.

Nakajima, S., Arimitsu, K. and Lattal, K.M. (2002) 'Estimation of animal intelligence by university students in Japan and the United States', *Anthrozoös*, 15, pp.194–205.

Nangle, D.W., Erdley, C.A., Newman, J.E., Mason, C.A. and Carpenter, E.M. (2003) 'Popularity, friendship quantity and friendship quality: Interactive influences on children's psychological adjustment', *Journal of Clinical Child and Adolescent Psychology*, 32, pp.546–55.

Nathan, P.E. (1988) 'The addictive behavior is the personality of the addict', *Journal of Consulting and Clinical Psychology*, 56, pp.183–188.

National Audit Office (2001) *Tackling Obesity in England*, Report by the Comptroller and Auditor General, HC 220, Session 2000–2001: 15 February 2001, London: The Stationery Office.

National Children's Home (2002) *1 in 4 children are the victims of "on-line bullying"*.

National Institute for Clinical Excellence (2004) *Anxiety: management of anxiety (panic disorder with and without agoraphobia, and generalised anxiety disorder) in adults in primary, secondary and community care*, 22, London: National Institute for Clinical Excellence.

National Institute on Drug Abuse (1999) *Principles of drug addiction treatment: A research-based guide*, New York: National Institute of Health.

National Research Council (1999) *Pathological gambling: A critical review*, Washington, DC: National Academy Press.

National Statistics, Statistics of Education: School Workforce in England (2004 edition, including teachers' pay for England and Wales). Available from: http://www.statistics.gov.uk

Neave, N. (2007) *Hormones and Behaviour: A psychological approach*. Cambridge: Cambridge University Press, p121.

Neel, J. (1962) 'Diabetes mellitus: a thrifty genotype rendered detrimental by "progress"', *American Journal of Human Genetics*, 14, pp.353–62.

Neemann, J., Hubbard, J. and Masten, A. S. (1995) 'The changing importance of romantic relationship involvement to competence from late childhood to late adolescence', *Development and Psychopathology*, 7, pp.727–50.

Nelson, J.P. (2001) 'Alcohol advertising and advertising bans: A survey of research methods, results, and policy implications', in M.R. Baye and J.P. Nelson (eds), *Advances in Applied Microeconomics, Volume 10: Advertising and Differentiated Products*, Amsterdam: Elsevier Science, Ch. 11.

Nemeroff, C.B., Krishnan, R.R., Reed, D., Leder, R., Beam, C. and Dunnick, N.R. (1992) 'Adrenal gland enlargement in major depression', *Archives of General Psychiatry*, 49, pp.384–7.

Neppe, V. M. (2002) '"Out-of-body experiences" (OBEs) and brain localisation: A perspective' *Australian Journal of Parapsychology*, 2, 85–96.

Nestadt, G., Samuels, J., Riddle, M., Bienvenu, O.J., Liang, K.Y., LaBuda, M., Walkup, J., Grados, M. and Hoehn-Saric, R. (2000) 'A family study of obsessive-compulsive disorder', *Arch Gen Psychiatry*, 57(4), pp.358–63.

Nevo, O., Nevo, B. (1993) 'Gossip and counseling: The tendency to gossip and its relation to vocational interests', *Counseling Psychology Quarterly*, 6(3), p.229.

Newcombe, M.D., Maddahian, E. and Bentler, P.M. (1986) 'Risk factors for drug abuse among adolescents: Concurrent and longitudinal analyses', *American Journal of Public Health*, 76, pp.525–531.

Nichols, C. (1985) 'Sociobiology: Some probative problems', *Canadian Review of Sociology and Anthropology*, 22 (2), pp.227–32.

Nickerson, R. S. (1998) 'Confirmation bias: A ubiquitous phenomenon in many guises' *Review of General Psychology*, 2, 175–220.

Nicol, J. F. (1985) 'Fraudulent children in psychical research' In P. Kurtz (ed.) *A skeptic's handbook of parapsychology*. Buffalo, NY: Prometheus. Pp. 275–286.

Nicolson, P. (1999) 'Evolutionary psychology is not the answer to everything', *Proceedings of the British Psychological Society Annual Conference*.

Nisan, M. and Kohlberg, L. (1982) 'Universality and variation in moral judgment: A longitudinal and cross-sectional study in Turkey', *Child Development*, 53 (4), pp.865–76.

Noble, G. (1975) *Children in Front of the Small Screen*, London: Constable, p.134.

Nolen-Hoeksema, S. and Corte, C. (2004) 'Gender and self-regulation', In K.D. Vohs and R.F Baumeister (eds) *Handbook of self-regulation: Research, theory and applications*, pp.411–21, New York: Guilford Press.

Nolen-Hoeksema, S., Girgus, S. and Seligman, M.E.P. (1992) 'Predictors and consequences of childhood depressive symptoms: a five-year longitudinal study', *Journal of Abnormal Psychology*, 101, pp.405–22.

Norman, N.M. and Tedeschi, J.T. (1989) 'Self-presentation, reasoned action, and adolescents' decisions to smoke cigarettes', *Journal of Applied Social Psychology*, 19, pp.543–558.

Noyes, R., Crowe, R.R., Harris, E.L., Hamra, B.J., McChesney, C.M. and Chaudhry, D.R. (1986) 'Relationship between panic disorder and agoraphobia: a family study', *Archives of General Psychiatry*, 43, pp.227–32.

Nuffield Mathematics Project (1967) *Mathematics Begins*, London: Newgate Press.

O'Connor, D. J. (1971) *Free Will*, New York: Doubleday.

Ofcom (2003) Media Literacy Audit: Report on media literacy among children. http://www.ofcom.org.uk/

Ogden, J. (1993) 'The measurement of restraint: Confounding success and failure?' *International Journal of Eating Disorders*, 13, pp.69–76.

Ogden, J. (1994) 'The effects of smoking cessation, restrained eating and motivational states on food intake in the laboratory', *Health Psychology*, 13, pp.114–21.

Ogden, J. (2000) 'The correlates of long-term weight loss: A group comparison study of obesity', *International Journal of Obesity*, 24, pp.1018–25.

Ogden (2003) *The Psychology of Eating: From healthy to disordered behaviour*, Oxford: Blackwell.

Ogden, J. (2007) *Health Psychology: A textbook* (4th edn), Maidenhead: Open University Press/McGraw-Hill Education.

Ogden, J. and Fox, P. (1994) 'An examination of the use of smoking for weight control in restrained and unrestrained eaters', *International Journal of Eating Disorders*, 16, pp.177–86.

Ogden, J. and Hills, L. (2008) 'Understanding sustained changes in behaviour: The role of life events and the process of reinvention', *Health: An International Journal*, 12, pp.419–37.

Ogden, J., Reynolds, R. and Smith, A. (2006) 'Expanding the concept of parental control: A role for overt and covert control in children's snacking behaviour', *Appetite*, 47, pp.100–6.

Ogden, C.L., Troiano, R.P., Briefel, R.R., Kuczmarski, R.J., Flegal, K.M. and Johnson, C.L. (1997) 'Prevalence of overweight among preschool children in the United States: 1971 through 1994', *Pediatrics*, 99, pp.E11–7.

Ohman, A., Erixon, G., and Lofberg, I. (1975) 'Phobias and preparedness: phobic versus neutral pictures as continued stimuli for human autonomic responses', *Journal of Abnormal Psychology*, 84, pp.41–5.

Olds, J. and Milner, P. (1954) 'Positive reinforcement produced by electrical stimulation of the septal area and other regions of the rat brain', *Journal of Comparative and Physiological Psychology*, 47, pp.419–27.

Oliver, G. and Wardle, J. (1999) 'Perceived effects of stress on food choice', *Physiology and Behavior*, 66(3), pp.511–5.

Oliver, G., Wardle, J. and Gibson, E.L. (2000) 'Stress and food choice: A laboratory study', *Psychosomatic Medicine*, 62(6), pp.853–65.

Olivera, S.A., Ellison, R.C., Moore, L.L., Gillman M.W., Garrahie, E.J. and Singer, M.R. (1992) 'Parent–child relationships in nutrient intake: The Framingham children's study', *American Journal Clinical Nutrition*, 56, pp.593–8.

Olweus, D., Mattsson, A., Schalling, D. and Loew, H. (1980) 'Testosterone, aggression, physical and personality dimensions in normal adolescent males', *Psychosomatic Medicine*, 42, pp.253–69.

Opie, I. and Opie, P. (1959) *The lore and language of school children*. London: Oxford University Press.

Orford, J. (2001) *Excessive Appetites: A Psychological View of the Addictions*, (2nd edn), Chichester: Wiley.

Orne, M.T. (1962) 'On the social psychology of the psychology experiment with particular reference to demand characteristics and their implications', *American Psychologist*, 16, pp.776–83.

Orne, M.T. and Holland, C.C. (1968) 'On the ecological validity of laboratory deceptions', *International Journal of Psychiatry*, 6 (4), pp.282–93.

Ost, L.G., Salkovskis, P.M. and Hellstrom, K. (1991) 'One-session therapist-directed exposure vs self-exposure in the treatment of spider phobia', *Behavior Therapy*, 22, pp.407–22.

Ostrov, J., Gentile, D.A. and Crick, N.R. (2006) 'Media exposure, aggression and prosocial behaviour during early childhood: a longitudinal study', *Social Development*, 15(4) pp.612–27.

Oswald, I. (1980) Sleep, Harmondsworth: Penguin Books.

Owen, F., Cross, A.J., Crow, T.J. and Poulter, M. (1978) 'Increased dopamine receptor sensitivity in schizophrenia', *Lancet*, 2, pp.223–6

Özdoˇru, A.A., Aksoy, G., Erdoˇan, N. and Gök, F. (eds) (2002) *Content Analysis for Gender Bias in Turkish Elementary School Textbooks*, Unpublished manuscript, University of Boˇaziçi, Istanbul, Turkey.

Özdogru, A. A., Aksoy, G., Erdogan, N. and Gök, F. (2004) 'Content analysis for gender bias in Turkish elementary school textbooks', Proceedings of the sixteenth annual Ethnographic and Qualitative Research in Education conference, Albany: New York.

Pagel, M. and Bodmer, W. (2003) 'A naked ape would have fewer parasites', *Biology Letters, Proceedings of the Royal Society of London, B (Supplement)*, 270, S117–19.

Palmer, J. (2003) 'ESP in the ganzfeld: Analysis of a debate' *Journal of Consciousness Studies*, 10, 51–68.

Palmer, P. (1986) *The Lively Audience: A Study of Children Around the Television Set*, North Sydney: Allen & Unwin.

Palmer, S.E. (1999) *Vision Science: Photons to Phenomenology*, Cambridge, MA: MIT Press.

Palmer, S.E. (1975a) 'Visual perception and world knowledge: Notes on a model of sensory-cognitive interaction', in D.A. Norman and D.E. Rumelhart (eds) *Explorations in Cognition*, San Francisco: W.H. Freeman, pp.279–307.

Palmer, S.E. (1975b) 'The effects of contextual scenes on the identification of objects', *Memory and Cognition*, 3 (5), pp.519–26.

Palmer, S.E. (2003) 'Visual perception of objects', In A.F. Healy, R.W. Proctor and I.B. Weiner (eds) *Handbook of Psychology*, 4, Hoboken, NJ: Wiley and Sons, pp.179–211.

Pankhurst, B. (1994) *Working with Boys*, London Borough of Merton.

Park, S., Holtzman, P.S. and Goldman-Rakic, P.S. (1995) 'Spatial working memory deficits in the relatives of schizophrenic patients', *Archives of General Psychiatry*, 52, pp.821–8.

Parke, J. and Griffiths, M.D. (2006) 'The psychology of the fruit machine: The role of structural characteristics (revisited)', *International Journal of Mental Health and Addiction*, 4, pp.151–179.

Parke, J. and Griffiths, M.D. (2007) 'The role of structural characteristics in gambling', in G. Smith, D. Hodgins and R. Williams (eds), *Research and Measurement Issues in Gambling Studies*, New York: Elsevier, pp.211–243.

Parke, A., Griffiths, M.D. and Irwing, P. (2004) 'Personality traits in pathological gambling: Sensation seeking, deferment of gratification and competitiveness as risk factors', *Addiction Research and Theory*, 12, pp.201–212.

Parke, J., Griffiths, M.D. and Parke, A. (2007) 'Positive thinking among slot machine gamblers: A case of maladaptive coping?' *International Journal of Mental Health and Addiction*, 5, pp.39–52.

Parker, G. (1979) 'Reported parental characteristics of agoraphobics and social phobics', *British Journal of Psychiatry*, 135, pp.555–60.

Parker, G., Roy, K., Wilhelm, K., Mitchell, P., Austin, M-P., Hadzi-Pavlovic, D., Little, C. (1999) 'Sub-grouping non-melancholic depression from manifest clinical features', *Journal of Affective Disorders*, 53, pp.1–13.

Parker, S.T. and Gibson, K.R. (1979) 'How the child got his stages', *Behavioural and Brain Sciences*, 2 (3), pp.399.

Parkes, J.D. (1985) Sleep and its Disorders, Philadelphia: Saunders.

Parnas, J., Cannon, T.D., Jacobsen, B., Schulsinger, H., Schulsinger, F. and Mednick, S.A. (1993) 'Lifetime *DSM-III-R* diagnostic outcomes in the offspring of schizophrenic mothers', *Archives of General Psychiatry*, 50, pp.707–714.

Parnia, S., Waller, D. G., Yeates, R. and Fenwick, P. (2001) 'A qualitative and quantitative study of the incidence, features and aetiology of near death experiences in cardiac arrest survivors' *Resuscitation*, 48, 149–156.

Passer, M., Smith, R., Holt, N., Bremner, A.J., Sutherland, E., and Vliek, M. (2008) *Psychology: The science of mind and behaviour*, London, UK: McGraw-Hill, pp.28.

Pato, M.T., Zohar-Kadouch, R., Zohar, J. and Murphy, D.L. (1988) 'Return of symptoms after discontinuation of clomipramine and patients with obsessive-compulsive disorder', *American Journal of Psychiatry*, 145, pp.1521–1525.

Paulos, J. A. (1988), *Innumeracy: Mathematical illiteracy and its consequences*, London: Penguin.

Pauls, D.L., Alsobrooke, J.P., Goodman, W., Rasmusses, S. and Leckman, J.F. (1995) 'A family study of obsessive-compulsive disorder', *American Journal of Psychiatry*, 152, pp.76–84.

Pavlov, I.P. (1927) *Conditioned Reflexes*, Oxford: Oxford University Press.

Paykel, E.S. (1981) 'Have multivariate statistics contributed to classification?', *British Journal of Psychiatry*, 139, pp.357–62.

Paykel, E.S., Brugha, T. and Fryers, T. (2005) 'Size and burden of depressive disorders in Europe', *European Neuropsychopharmacology*, 15, pp.411–23.

Pearce, J.M. (2008) *Animal Learning and Cognition: An Introduction*, Hove: Psychology Press.

Peele, S. (1990) 'Addiction as a cultural concept', *Annals of the New York Academy of Sciences*, 602, pp.205–220.

Peele, S. and Brodsky, A. (1975) *Love and Addiction*, New York: Taplinger.

Penfield, W. (1958) 'Functional localization in temporal and deep Sylvian areas', *Research Publications of the Association for Research into Nervous and Mental Disease*, 36, pp.210–26.

Penner, L.A., Dovidio, J.F., Piliavin, J.A. and Schroeder, D.A. (2005) 'Prosocial behavior: Multilevel perspectives', *Annual Review of Psychology,* 56, pp.365–92.

Penton-Voak, I.S., Perrett, D.I., Castles, D.L., Kobayashi, T., Burt, D.M., Murray, L.K. (1999) 'Menstrual cycle alters face preference', *Nature*, 399, pp.741–2.

Peralta, V. and Cuesta, M.J. (1992) 'Influence of cannabis abuse on schizophrenic psychopathology', *Acta Psychiatrica Scandinavica*, 85, pp.127–30.

Perilloux, C. and Buss, D.M. (2008) 'Breaking up romantic relationships: Costs experienced and coping strategies deployed', *Evolutionary Psychology*, 6, pp.164–81.

Perkins, S. L. and Allen, R. (2006) ,Childhood physical abuse and differential development of paranormal belief systems' *Journal of Nervous and Mental Disease*, 194, 349–355.

Perner, J., Frith, U., Leslie, A.M. and Leekum, S.R. (1989) 'Exploration of the autistic child's theory of mind: Knowledge, belief, and communication', *Child Development*, 60, pp.689–700.

Perrett, D.I., May, K.A. and Yoshikawa, S. (1994) 'Facial shape and judgments of female attractiveness', *Nature*, 368, pp.239–42.

Persinger, M. A., Tiller, S. G. and Koren, S. A. (2000) 'Experimental simulation of a haunt experience and elicitation of paroxysmal electroencephalographic activity by transcerebral complex magnetic fields: Induction of a synthetic "ghost"?' *Perceptual and Motor Skills*, 90, 659–674.

Peskin, J. (1992) 'Ruse and representations: On children's ability to conceal information', *Developmental Psychology*, 28 (1), pp.84–9.

Peterson, L.R. and Peterson, M. (1959) 'Short-term retention of individual verbal items', *Journal of Experimental Psychology*, 58, pp.193–8.

Petty, R.E. and Cacioppo, J.T. (1986) *Communication and Persuasion: Central and peripheral routes to attitude change*, New York: Springer-Verlag.

Pharoah, F.M., Rathbone, J. and Mari, J.J. (2003) *Family intervention for schizophrenia*, 4: CD000088, Cochrane Database of Systematic reviews.

Philipp, M., Kohnen, R. and Hiller, K-O. (1999) 'Hypericum extract versus imipramine or placebo in patients with moderate depression: randomised multicentre study of treatment for eight weeks', *British Medical Journal*, 11, 319(7224), pp. 1534–9. .

Piaget, J. (1926) *The Language and Thought of the Child*, New York: Harcourt Brace Jovanovich.

Piaget, J. (1932/1965) *The Moral Judgment of the Child*, New York: Free Press.

Piaget, J. (1952) *The Origins of Intelligence in Children*, Oxford: International Universities Press.

Piaget, J. (1970) 'Piaget's theory', in P.H. Mussen (ed.) *Carmichael's Manual of Child Psychology*, Vol. 1 (3rd edn), New York: Wiley, pp.703–732.

Piaget, J. (1977) *The Development of Thought: Equilibration of cognitive structures*, New York: Viking Press.

Piaget, J. and Inhelder, B. (1956) *The Child's Conception of Space*, London: Routledge and Kegan Paul.

Piaget, J. and Inhelder, B. (1969) *The Psychology of the Child*, New York: Basic Books.

Picariello, M.L., Greenberg, D.N. and Pillemer, D.B. (1990) 'Children's sex-related stereotyping of colours', *Child Development,* 61, pp.1453–60.

Pick, H.L. (1987) 'Information and the effects of early perceptual experience', in N. Eisenberg (ed.) *Contemporary Topics in Developmental Psychology*, New York: Wiley.

Pigott, T.M., Myers, K.R. and Williams, D.A. (1996) 'Obsessive compulsive disorder: a neuropsychiatric perspective', in R. Rapee (ed.) *Current controversies in anxiety disorders*, New York: Guilford Press.

Pilling, S. I., Bebbington, P., Kuipers, E., Garety, P., Geddes, J., Orbach, G. and Morgan, C. (2002) 'Psychological treatments in schizophrenia: Meta-analysis of family intervention and cognitive behaviour therapy', *Psychological Medicine*, 32 (5), pp.763–782.

Pinals, D.A. (2007) *Stalking: Psychiatric perspectives and practical approaches,* New York: Oxford University Press.

Pine, K.J. and Nash, A. S. (2002) 'Dear Santa: The effects of TV advertising on children', *International Journal of Behavioural Development*, 26(6), pp.529–39.

Pinel, J.P J. (2003) *Biopsychology*, Boston: Allyn and Bacon.

Pinker, S. (1994) *The Language Instinct*, Harmondsworth: Allen Lane.

Pinker, S. (2008) 'Crazy love', *Time Magazine*, 28 January 2008.

Pirchio, M., Spinelli, D., Fiorentini, A. and Maffei, L. (1978) 'Infant contrast sensitivity evaluated by evoked potentials', *Brain Research*, 141, pp.179–84.

Platek, S.M. and Shackelford, T.K. (eds) (2006) *Female Infidelity and Paternal Uncertainty: Evolutionary Perspectives on Male Anti-Cuckoldry Tactics*, Cambridge University Press: New York.

Plomin, R., DeFries, J.C., McClearn, G.E. and Rutter, M. (1997) *Behavioural genetics*, New York: Freeman.

Plomin, R. (1988) 'The nature and nurture of cognitive abilities' in R. Sternberg (ed.) *Advances in the psychology of human intelligence*, Vol. 4, pp.1–33). Hillsdale, NJ: Lawrence Erlbaum.

Plomin, R. and Daniels, D. (1987) 'Why are children in the same family so different from each other?', *Behavioral and Brain Sciences*, 10, pp.1–16.

Plomin, R., Chipuer, H.M., and Neiderhiser, J.M. (1994) 'Behavioral genetic evidence for the importance of nonshared environment', in E. M. Hetherington, D. Reiss, and R. Plomin (eds.), *Separate social worlds of siblings: The impact of nonshared environment on development* pp.1–31, Hillsdale, NJ: Lawrence Erlbaum Associates.

Plomin, R., DeFries, J.C., McClearn, G.E. and McGuffin, P. (2001) *Behavioral Genetics (4th ed.)*, New York: Worth Publishers.

Plotnik, J.M., de Waal, F.B.M. and Reiss, D. (2006) 'Self-recognition in an Asian elephant', *Proceedings of the National Academy of Science, USA*, 103, pp.17053–7.

Plowden Report (1967) *Children and their Primary Schools*, London: Her Majesty's Stationery Office.

Polivy, J. and Herman, C.P. (1985) 'Dieting and bingeing: A causal analysis', *American Psychologist*, 40, pp.193–201.

Polivy, J. and Herman, C.P. (1999) 'Distress and eating: Why do dieters overeat?' *International Journal of Eating Disorders*, 26(2), pp.153–64.

Pollack, R.H. (1963) 'Contour detectability thresholds as a function of chronological age', *Perceptual and Motor Skills*, 17, pp.411–7.

Pollack, R.H. and Silvar, S.D. (1967) 'Magnitude of the Müller-Lyer illusion in children as a function of pigmentation of the Fundus oculi', *Psychonomic Science*, 8, pp.83–4.

Poole, E.D. and Regoli, R.M. (1983) 'Violence in juvenile institutions', *American Society of Criminology*, 21 (2), pp.213–32.

Pope Jr, H.G., Kouri, E.M. and Hudson, J.L. (2000) 'Effects of supraphysiologic doses of testosterone on mood and aggression in normal men', *Archives of General Psychiatry*, 57, pp.133–40.

Popma, A., Vermeiren, R., Geluk, C.A.M.L., Rinne, T., van den Brink, W., Knol, D.L., Jansen, L.M.C., van Engeland, H. and Doreleijer, T.A.H. (2007) 'Cortisol moderates the relationship between Testosterone and Aggression in Delinquent Male Adolescents', *Biological Psychiatry*, 61(3), pp.405–11.

Popper, K. (1959) *The Logic of Scientific Discovery*, New York: Basic Books.

Popper, K.R. (1969) *The Logic of Scientific Discovery* (2nd edn), New York: Basic Books.

Popper, K.R. (1972) *Objective Knowledge: An evolutionary approach*, Oxford: Oxford University Press.

Popper, R., Smits, G., Meiselman, H.L. and Hirsch, E. (1989) 'Eating in combat: A survey of U.S. marines', *Military Medicine*, 154, pp.619–23.

Potenza, M.N. (2001) 'The neurobiology of pathological gambling', *Clinical Neuropsychology*, 6, pp.217–26.

Potts, R., Belden, A. and Reese, C. (2008) 'Young adults' retrospective reports of childhood television viewing', *Communication Research*, 35(1), pp.39–60.

Povey, R., Conner, M., Sparks, P., James, R. and Shepherd, R. (2000) 'The theory of planned behaviour and healthy eating: Examining additive and moderating effects of social influence variables', *Psychology and Health*, 14, pp.991–1006.

Povinelli, D.J. (2000) *Folk physics for apes*, Oxford: Oxford University Press.

Povinelli, D.J., Landau, K.R. and Perilloux, H.K. (1996) 'Self-recognition in young children using delayed versus live feedback: Evidence of a developmental asynchrony', *Child Development*, 67 (4), pp.1540–54.

Power, F.C., Higgins, A. and Kohlberg, L. (1989) *Lawrence Kohlberg's Approach to Moral Education*, New York: Columbia University Press.

Premack, D. and Woodruff, G. (1978) 'Does the chimpanzee have a theory of mind?', *Behavioral and Brain Sciences*, 1 (4), pp.515–26.

Prentice, A.M. (1995) 'Are all calories equal?' in R. Cottrell (ed.) *Weight Control: The current perspective*, London: Chapman and Hall.

Prentice, A.M. and Jebb, S.A. (1995) 'Obesity in Britain: Gluttony or sloth?' *British Medical Journal*, 311, pp.437–9.

Prentice-Dunn, S. and Rogers, R.W. (1989) 'Deindividuation and the self-regulation of behavior', in P.B. Paulus (ed.), *The Psychology of Group Influence* (2nd ed.) Hillsdale, NJ: Erlbaum, pp.86–109.

Preyde, M. and Adams, G. (2008) 'Foundations of addictive problems: Developmental, social and neurbiological factors', in C. Essau (ed.), *Adolescent Addiction: Epidemiology, Assessment and Treatment*, San Diego: Elselvier, pp.3–16.

Prien, R.F. (1988) 'Somatic treatment of unipolar depressive disorder', in A.J. Frances and R.E. Hales (eds) *Review of Psychiatry*, Washington, DC: American Psychiatric Press.

Prins, K.S., Buunk, B.P. and Van Yperen, N.W. (1993) 'Equity, normative disapproval and extramarital relationships', *Journal of Social and Personal Relationships*, 10, pp.39–53.

Prochaska, J.O., DiClemente, C.C. and Norcross, J.C. (1992) 'In search of how people change: Applications to addictive behaviours', *American Psychologist*, 47, pp.1102–1114.

Prochaska, J.O., Norcross, J.C. and DiClemente, C.C. (1994) *Changing for good: a revolutionary six-stage program for overcoming bad habits and moving your life positively forward*, New York: Avon.

Procopio, M. and Marriott, P.K. (1998) 'Is the decline in diagnosis of schizophrenia caused by the disappearance of a seasonal aetiological agent? An epidemiological study in England and Wales', *Psychological Medicine*, 28, pp.367–73.

Purcell, R., Pathé, M. and Mullen, P.E. (2001) 'A study of women who stalk', *American Journal of Psychiatry*, 158, pp.2056–60.

Qualter, P. and Munn, P. (2005) 'The friendships and play partners of lonely children', *Journal of Social and Personal Relationships*, 22, pp.379–97.

Quinn, W.G., Sziber, P.P. and Booker, R. (1979) 'The *Drosophila* memory mutant amnesiac', *Nature*, 77, pp.212–4.

Qureshi, S. (1991) 'The Muslim family: A scriptural framework', in E.H. Waugh, S.M. Abu-Laban and R. Qureshi (eds.) *Muslim Families in North America*, Edmonton: University of Alberta Press, pp.32–67.

Raats, M.M., Shepherd, R. and Sparks, P. (1995) 'Including moral dimensions of choice within the structure of the theory of planned behavior', *Journal of Applied Social Psychology*, 25, pp.484–94.

Rachels, J. 1990 'Created from Animals: The Moral Implications of Darwinism', New York, NY: Oxford University Press.

Rachels, J. (1991) *Created from Animals: The Moral Implications of Darwinism*. Oxford: Oxford University Press.

Rachman, S. and Hodgson, R. (1980) *Obsessions and Compulsions*. Englewood Cliffs, NJ: Prentice–Hall.

Rachman, S. (1993) 'Obsessions, responsibility and guilt', *Behavioural Research Therapy*, 31(2), pp.149–154.

Rachman, S., Hodgson, R. and Marzillier, J. (1970) 'Treatment of an obsessional-compulsive disorder by modelling', *Behavioural Research Therapy*, 8, pp.385–392.

Radin, D. I. (1997) *The conscious universe*. San Francisco: Harper Edge

Radin, D. (2006) *Entangled minds: Extrasensory experiences in a quantum reality.* New York: Paraview Pocket Books.

Radin, D. I. and Nelson, R. D. (1989) 'Evidence for consciousness-related anomalies in random physical systems'. *Foundations of Physics*, 19, 1499–1514.

Radin, D. I. and Nelson, R. D. (2003) 'Research on mind-matter interactions (MMI): Individual intention' In W. B. Jonas and C. C. Crawford (eds.) *Healing, intention and energy medicine: Research and clinical implications*. Edinburgh: Churchill Livingstone. Pp. 39–48.

Radner, D. and Radner, M. (1982) *Science and unreason.* Belmont, CA: Wadsworth.

Ragsdale, J.D. and Brandau-Brown, F.E. (2007) 'Could relational maintenance in marriage really be like grocery shopping? A reply to Stafford and Canary', *Journal of Family Communication*, 7 (1), pp.47–60.

Rand, C.S.W. and McGregor, A.M.C. (1991) 'Successful weight loss following obesity surgery and the perceived liability of morbid obesity', *International Journal of Obesity*, 15, pp.577–9.

Randall, C.L., Thomas, S. and Thevos, A.K. (2001) 'Concurrent alcoholism and social anxiety disorder: A first step toward developing effective treatments', *Alcoholism: Clinical and Experimental Research*, 25(2), pp.210–20.

Randi, J. (1982) *The truth about Uri Geller.* Buffalo, NY: Prometheus.

Randi, J. (1983a) 'The Project Alpha experiment: Part 1. The first two years' *Skeptical Inquirer*, 7(4), 24–33.

Randi, J. (1983b) 'The Project Alpha experiment: Part 2. Beyond the laboratory' *Skeptical Inquirer*, 8(1), 36–45.

Randi, J. (1987) *The faith healers*. Buffalo, NY: Prometheus, p.25.

Randrup, A. and Munkvad, I. (1966) 'On the role of dopamine in the amphetamine excitatory response', *Nature*, 211, p.540.

Raphael, R. (1988) *The Men From The Boys: Rites of Passages in Male America*, Lincoln, NE & London, England: University of Nebraska Press.

Rapoport, J., Swedo, S. and Leonard, H. (1994) 'Obsessive compulsive disorder', in M. Rutter, E. Taylor and L. Hersov (eds) *Child and Adolescent Psychiatry: Modern Approaches*, (3rd edn), London: Blackwell, pp.441–454.

Rapoport, J.L. (1989) 'The biology of obsessions and compulsions', *Scientific American*, March, pp.82–89.

Rapoport, L. (2003) *How We Eat*, London: Independent Publishing Group.

Rasmussen, S. and Eisen, J.L. (1991) 'Phenomenology of OCD: Clinical subtypes, heterogeneity and coexistence', in J. Zohar, T. Insel and S. Rasmussen (eds) *The Psychobiology of Obsessive-Compulsive Disorder*, New York: Springer.

Ravussin, E. and Bogardus, C. (1989) 'Relationship of genetics, age, and physical activity to daily energy expenditure and fuel utilization', *American Journal of Clinical Nutrition*, 49, pp.968–75.

Ray, J.J. and Najman, J. (1986) 'The generalisability of deferment of gratification', *Journal of Social Psychology*, 126, pp.117–119.

Regan, T. (2004) *The Case for Animal Rights* (updated edn), Berkeley, CA: University of California Press.

Reicher, S.D. and Haslam, S.A. (2006) 'Rethinking the psychology of tyranny: The BBC Prison Experiment', *British Journal of Social Psychology*, 45, pp.1–40.

Renner, F. (1990) *Spinnen: Ungeheuer Sympathisch*, Kaiserslautern: Verlag.

Rest, J.R. (1983) 'Morality', in J.H. Flavell and E.M. Markman (eds) and P.H. Mussen (Series ed.) *Handbook of Child Psychology, Vol. 3: Cognitive development*, New York: Wiley, pp.556–629.

Rest, J.R., Narvaez, D., Bebeau, M.J. and Thoma, S.J. (1999) 'DIT-2: Devising and testing a revised instrument of moral judgment', *Journal of Educational Psychology*, 91 (4), pp.644–59.

Retz, W., Rosler, M., Supprian, T., Retz-Junginger, P. and Thome, J. (2003) 'Dopamine D3 receptor gene polymorphism and violent behavior: relation to impulsiveness and ADHD-related psychopathology', *Journal of Neural Transmission*, 110 (5), pp.561–72.

Rhee, S.H. and Waldman, I. (2002) 'Genetic and environmental influences on antisocial behavior: A meta-analysis of twin and adoption studies', *Psychological Bulletin*, 128, pp.490–529.

Rhine, J. B. (1974) 'Security versus deception in parapsychology' *Journal of Parapsychology*, 38, 99–121.

Rhodes, N. and Wood, W. (1992) 'Self-esteem and intelligence affect influenceability: The mediating role of message reception', *Psychological Bulletin*, 111, pp.156–71.

Rhue, J. W. and Lynn, S. J. (1987) 'Fantasy proneness: Developmental antecedents' *Journal of Personality*, 55, 121–137.

Richard I.R. and Lyness, J.M. (2006) *Psychiatry for Neurologists*, Totowa, NJ: Humana Press.

Richardson, K. (1986) 'Theory? Or tools for social selection?', *Behavioral and Brain Sciences*, 9, pp.579–81.

Ridley, M. (1997) *The Origins of Virtue*, London: Penguin.

Ridley, M. (2003) *Nature via Nurture: Genes, Experience and What Makes Us Human*, London: Fourth Estate.

Riesen, A.H. (1965) 'Effects of early deprivation of photic stimulation.' In S. Oster and R. Cook (Eds), *The biosocial basis of mental retardation*, Baltimore: John Hopkins University Press.

Rissanen, A.M., Heliovaara, M., Knekt, P., Reunanen, A. and Aromaa, A. (1991) 'Determinants of weight gain and overweight in adult Finns', *European Journal of Clinical Nutrition*, 45, pp.419–30.

Rizzolatti, G., Fadiga, L., Fogassi, L. and Gallese, V. (1996) 'Premotor cortex and the recognition of motor actions, *Cognitive Brain Research*, 3, pp.131–4.

Roberts, C.W., Green, R., Williams, K. and Goodman, M. (1987) 'Boyhood gender identity development: A statistical contrast of two family groups', *Developmental Psychology*, 23, pp.544–57.

Roberts, D.F., Christenson, P.G., Henriksen, L. and Bandy, E. (2002) *Substance Use in Popular Music Videos*, Office of National Drug Control Policy, located at: http://www.scenesmoking.org/research/SubstanceUseinMusic.pdf

Roberts, M. J. and Seager, P. B. (1999) 'Predicting belief in paranormal phenomena: a comparison of conditional and probabilistic reasoning' *Applied Cognitive Psychology*, 13, 443–450.

Roberts, S.C., Havlicek, J., Flegr, J., Hruskova, M., Little, A.C., Jones, B.C., Perrett, D.I. and Petrie, M. (2004) 'Female facial attractiveness increases during the fertile phase of the menstrual cycle', *Proceedings of the Royal Society London, B (Supplement)*, 271, pp.270–72.

Robertson, T.S., and Rossiter, J. R. (1974) 'Children and commercial persuasion: An attribution theory analysis', *Journal of Consumer Research*, 1, pp.508–12.

Robins, L.N., Helzer, J.E. and Davis, D.H, (1975) 'Narcotic use in Southeast Asia and afterward', *Archives of General Psychiatry*, 32, pp.955–961.

Robinson, R.G., McHigh, P.R. and Folstein, M.F. (1975) 'Measurement of appetite disturbances in psychiatric disorder', *Journal of Psychiatric Research*, 12, pp.59–68.

Rock, I. (1995) *Perception*, New York: Scientific American Library.

Rodin, J., Bray, G.A., Atkinson, R.L., Dahms, W.T., Greenway, F.L., Hamilton, K. and Molitch, M. (1977) 'Predictors of successful weight loss in an outpatient obesity clinic', *International Journal of Obesity*, 1, pp.79–87.

Roes, F. and Raymond M. (2003) 'Belief in moralizing Gods', *Evolution of Human Behaviour*, 24, pp.126–35.

Rogers, R.W. (1985) 'Attitude change and information integration in fear appeals', *Psychological Reports*, 56, pp.179–82.

Rogo, D. S. (1985) 'J. B. Rhine and the Levy scandal' In P. Kurtz (ed.) *A skeptic's handbook of parapsychology*. Buffalo, NY: Prometheus. Pp. 313–326.

Roker, D., Player, K. and Coleman, J. (1998) 'Exploring adolescent altruism: British young people's involvement in voluntary work and campaigning', in M. Yates and J.Youniss (eds), *Community Service and Civic Engagement in Youth: International Perspectives*, Cambridge: Cambridge University Press.

Rollie, S.S. and Duck, S.W. (2006) 'Stage theories of marital breakdown', in J.H. Harvey and M.A. Fine (eds.) *Handbook of Divorce and Dissolution of Romantic Relationships*, Mahwah, NJ: Lawrence Erlbaum, 176–93.

Romero-Corral, A.R., Montori, V.M., Somers, V.K., Korinek, J., Thomas, R.J., Allison, T.G., Mookadam, F. and Jimenez, F.L. (2006) 'Association of body weight with total mortality and with cardiovascular events in coronary heart disease: A systematic review of cohort studies', *Lancet*, 368, pp.666–78.

Romme, M.A. and Escher, A.D. (1989) 'Hearing voices', *Schizophrenia Bulletin*, 15, pp.209–216.

Roper, M. (2005) *Spooky truth: TV's Most Haunted con exposed TV* (sic) [Electronic version]. Retrieved 27 December 2008 from: http://www.mirror.co.uk/news/tm_objectid=16303507&method=full&siteid=94762&headline=spooky-truth—tv-s-most-haunted-con-exposed-tv—name_page.html

Rosa, L., Rosa, E., Sarner, L. and Barrett, S. (1998) 'A close look at therapeutic touch' *Journal of the American Medical Association*, 279, 1005-1010.

Rose, S. (1997) *Lifelines: Biology, Freedom, Determinism*, London: Penguin.

Rose, S.A. and Blank, M. (1974) 'The potency of context in children's cognition: An illustration through conservation', *Child Development*, 45, pp.499–502.

Rosenfeld, B. (2004) 'Violence risk factors in stalking and obsessional harassment: A review and preliminary meta-analysis', *Criminal Justice and Behavior*, 31(1), pp.9–36.

Rosenhan, D.L. and Seligman, M.E.P. (1995) *Abnormal Psychology* (3rd edn), New York: Norton.

Rosenthal, N.E., Sack, D.A., Gillin, J.C. (1984) 'Seasonal Affective Disorder: a description of the syndrome and preliminary findings with light therapy', *Archives of General Psychiatry*, 41, pp.72–80.

Rosenthal, R. (1966) *Experimenter effects in behavioural research*, New York: Appleton-Century-Crofts.

Rosenwasser, A. M., Boulos, Z. and Ternan, M. (1981) 'Circadian organisation of food intake and meal patterns in the rat', *Physiology and Behaviour*, 27, pp.33–9.

Ross, C.E. (1994) 'Overweight and depression', *Journal of Health and Social Behaviour*, 35, pp.63–78.

Roth, I. and Bruce, V. (1995) *Perception and Representation*. Milton Keynes: Open University Press, pp.144.

Rothenberg, D. (1998) '*Los Linchamientos* – The meaning of mob action in the wake of state terror in Guatemala', *Native Americas*, XV(1).

Rowland, I. (2002) *The full facts book of cold reading*. 3rd ed. London: Ian Rowland Limited.

Rowland, N.E., Li, B.H. and Morien, A. (1996) 'Brain mechanisms and the physiology of feeding', in W.D. Capaldi (ed.) *Why we Eat What we Eat: The psychology of eating*, Washington DC: American Psychological Association, pp.173–206.

Roy-Byrne, P.P and Cowley, D.S. (1995) 'Course and outcome of panic disorder: a review of recent studies', *Anxiety*, 1, pp.151–60.

Rozin, P. (1982) 'Human food selection: The interaction of biology, culture and individual experience', in L.M. Barker (ed.) *The Psychobiology of Human Food Selection*, Westport, Connecticut: AVI, pp.225–54.

Rubens, A.B. and Benson, D.F. (1971) 'Associative visual agnosia', *Archives of Neurology*, 24, pp.305–16.

Rubin, A.M., Perse, E. M. and Powell, R. A. (1985) 'Loneliness, para-social interaction, and local television news viewing', *Human Communication Research*, 12, pp.155–80.

Rubin, Z., Hill, C.T., Peplau, L.A. and Dunkel-Schetter, C. (1980) 'Self-disclosure in dating couples: Sex roles and the ethic of openness', *Journal of Marriage and the Family*, 42 (2), pp.305–17.

Ruderman, A.J. and Wilson, G.T. (1979) 'Weight, restraint, cognitions and counter-regulation', *Behaviour Research and Therapy*, 17, pp.581–90.

Rudski, J. (2004) 'The illusion of control, superstitious belief, and optimism' *Current Psychology: Developmental, Learning, Personality, Social*, 22, 306–315.

Ruffle, B. and Sosis, R. (2005) 'Does it pay to pray? Evaluating the economic return to religious ritual', Unpublished manuscript, Ben-Gurion University, Beer Sheva, Israel.

Rumbaugh, D.M. (1977) *Language learning by a chimpanzee: the Lana project,* London: Academic Press.

Runyon, R. and Haber, A. (1976) *Fundamentals of Behavioral Statistics* (3rd edn), Reading, MA: McGraw Hill.

Rusak, B. and Zucker, I. (1975) 'Biological rhythms and animal behaviour', *Annual Review of Psychology*, 26, pp.137–71.

Rusbult, C.E. (1983) 'A longitudinal test of the investment model: The development (and deterioration) of satisfaction and commitment in heterosexual involvements', *Journal of Personality and Social Psychology*, 45, pp.101–17.

Rusbult, C.E. and Martz, J.M. (1995) 'Remaining in an abusive relationship: An investment model analysis of non-voluntary commitment', *Personality and Social Psychology Bulletin*, 21, pp.558–71.

Russell, M.J., Switz, G.M. and Thompson, K. (1980) 'Olfactory influences on the human menstrual cycle', *Pharmacology, Biochemistry and Behaviour*, 13, pp.737–8.

Rutland, A. (1999) 'The development of national prejudice, in-group favouritism and self-stereotypes in British children', *British Journal of Social Psychology*, 38, pp.55–70.

Ryle, G. (1949) *The Concept of Mind*, New York: Barnes & Noble.

Rymer, R. (1993) *Genie: Escape from a Silent Childhood*, London: Michael Joseph.

Rzewuska, M. (2002) 'Drug maintenance treatment compliance and its correlation with the clinical picture and course of schizophrenia', *Prog. Neuropsychopharmacol. Biol. Psychiat.*, 26 (4), pp.811–14.

Sackeim, H.A., Prudic, J., Devanand, D.P., Nobler, M.S., Lisanby, S.H., Peyser, S., Fitzsimons, L., Moody, B.J. and Clark, J. (2000) 'A Prospective, Randomized, Double-blind Comparison of Bilateral and Right Unilateral Electroconvulsive Therapy at Different Stimulus Intensities', *Archives of General Psychiatry*, 57, pp.425–34.

Sackeim, H. A., Roger, F., Haskett, R. F., Mulsant, B.H., Thase, M. E., Mann, J. J., Pettinati, H.M., Greenberg, R. M., Crowe, R. R., Cooper, T. B. and Prudic, J. (2001) 'Continuation pharmacotherapy in the prevention of relapse following electroconvulsive therapy', *The Journal of the American Medical Association*, 285, pp.1299–307.

Sacks, O. (1985) *The man who mistook his wife for a hat and other clinical tales*, New York: Summit.

Sacks, O. 1995 *An Anthropologist On Mars*, London: Picador.

Salkovskis, P.M. and Kirk, J. (1997) 'Obsessive-compulsive disorder', in D.M. Clark and C. Fairburn (eds) *Science and Practice of Cognitive-Behaviour Therapy*, Oxford: Oxford University Press.

Salkovskis, P.M., Thorpe, S.J., Wahl, K., Wroe, A.L. and Forrester, E. (2003) 'Neutralizing increases discomfort associated with obsessional thoughts: An experimental study with obsessional patients', *Journal of Abnormal Psychology*, 112 (4), pp.709–715.

Sample, I. (2009) 'Obesity: Blame the ancestors', *The Guardian*, Thursday 12 February, 2009 available online at: www.guardian.co.uk/science/2009/feb/12/obesity-blame-ancestors (accessed on 19/02/09).

Samuel, J. and Bryant, P. (1984) 'Asking only one question in the conservation experiment', *Journal of Child Psychology and Psychiatry*, 25 (2), pp.315–8.

Santomauro, J. and French, C. C. (in press) 'Terror in the night: The experience of sleep paralysis' *The Psychologist*.

Santrock, J.W. (1975) 'Moral structure: The interrelations of moral behavior, moral judgment, and moral affect', *Journal of Genetic Psychology*, 127 (2), pp.201–13.

Savage, J. and Yancey, C. (2008) 'The effects of media violence exposure on criminal aggression: A meta-analysis', *Criminal Justice and Behavior*, 35, pp.772–91.

Savage-Rumbaugh, E.S. (1988) 'A new look at ape language: comprehension of vocal speech and syntax', *Nebraska Symposium on Motivation*, 35, pp.201–55.

Savage-Rumbaugh, S. and Lewin, R. (1994) *Kanzi: The Ape at the Brink of the Human Mind*, London: Wiley.

Savage-Rumbaugh, E.S. and Fields, W.M. (2000) 'Linguistic, cultural and cognitive capacities of bonobos (*Pan paniscus*)', *Culture and Psychology*, 6, pp.131–53.

Saxe, R. and Wexler, A. (2005) 'Making sense of another mind: the role of the right temporo-parietal junction', *Neuropsychologia*, 43, pp.1391–9.

Saxena, S., Gorbis, E., O'Neill, J., Baker, S.K., Mandelkern, M.A., Maidment, K.M., Chang, S., Salamon, N., Brody, A.L., Schwartz, J.M. and London, E.D. (2008) 'Rapid effects of brief intensive cognitive-behavioural therapy on brain glucose metabolism in obsessive-compulsive disorder', *Molecular Psychiatry*, **14**, pp.197–205.

Scarr, S. and Weinberg, R.A. (1976) 'I.Q. Test Performance of Black Children Adopted by White Families', *American Psychologist*, 31 (10), pp.726–39.

Schachter, S. (1968) 'Obesity and eating', *Science*, 161, pp.751–6.

Schachter, S. and Gross, L. (1968) 'Manipulated time and eating behaviour', *Journal of Personality and Social Psychology*, 10, pp.98–106.

Schachter, S. and Rodin, J. (1974) *Obese Humans and Rats*, Hillsdale, New Jersey: Erlbaum.

Schenck, C.H. and Mahowald, M.W. (2002) 'REM sleep behavior disorder: clinical, developmental, and neuroscience perspectives 16 years after its formal identification in Sleep', *Sleep*, 25, pp.120–38.

Schiappa, E., Allen, M. and Gregg, P.B. (2007) 'Parasocial relationships and television: a meta-analysis of effects', in R.W. Preiss, B.M. Gayle, N. Burrell, M. Allen and J. Bryant (eds) *Mass Media Effects Research: Advances Through Meta-Analysis*, Mahwah, NJ: Lawrence Erlbaum.

Schlenker, B.R., Weigold, M. F. and Hallam, J.R. (1990) 'Self-serving attributions in social context: Effects of self-esteem and social pressure', *Journal of Personality and Social Psychology*, 58, pp.855–863.

Schlinger, H.D. (2003) 'The Myth of Intelligence' *The Psychological Record*, 53 (1), pp.15–33.

Schmidt, H. (1973) 'PK tests with a high-speed random number generator' *Journal of Parapsychology*, 37, 105–118.

Schneider, K. (1959) *Clinical psychopathology*, New York: Grune and Stratton.

Schneier, F.R., Spitzer, R.L., Gibbon, M. and Fyer, A.J. (1991) 'The relationship of social phobia subtypes and avoidant personality', *Comprehensive Psychiatry*, 32(6), pp.496–502.

Schouten, S. A. (1992–1993) 'Psychic healing and complementary medicine' *European Journal of Parapsychology*, 9, 35–91.

Schouten, S. A. (1994) 'An overview of quantitatively evaluated studies with mediums and psychics' *Journal of the American Society for Psychical Research*, 88, 221–254.

Schramm, W., Lyle, J. and Parker, E.B. (1961) *Television in the lives of our children*, Palo Alto, CA: Stanford University Press.

Schwartz, G. E. (2003) 'How not to review mediumship research' *Skeptical Inquirer*, 27(3), 58–61.

Schwartz, G. E. R., Russek, L. G. S., Nelson, L. A. and Barentsen, C. (2001) ,Accuracy and replicability of anomalous after-death communication across highly skilled mediums' *Journal of the Society for Psychical Research*, 65, 1–25.

Schwartz, J. and Begley, S. (2002) *The Mind and the Brain: Neuroplasticity and the Power of Mental Force*, Los Angeles, CA: Regan Books.

Schwartz, J.M., Stoessel, P.W., Baxter, L.R., Martin, K.M. and Phelps, M.E. (1996) 'Systematic changes in cerebral glucose metabolic rate after successful behaviour modification treatment of obsessive-compulsive disorder', *Archives of General Psychiatry*, 53, pp.109–13.

Segal, Z.V. and Ingram, R.E. (1994) 'Mood priming and construct activation in tests of cognitive vulnerability to unipolar depression', *Clinical Psychology Review*, 14(7), pp.663–95.

Segall, M.H., Campbell, D.T. and Herskovits, M.J. (1963) 'Cultural differences in the perception of geometric illusions', *Science*, 193, pp.769–71.

Segall, M.H., Campbell, D.T. and Herskovits, M.J. (1966) *The Influence of Culture on Visual Perception*, Indianapolis: Bobbs-Merrill.

Segall, M.H., Dasen, P.R., Berry, J.W. and Poortinga, Y.H. (1990) *Human Behaviour in Global Perspective: An Introduction to Cross-cultural Psychology*, New York: Pergamon Press, pp.88.

Segrin, C. (2000) 'Social skills deficits associated with depression', *Clinical Psychology Review*, 20, pp.379–403.

Searle, J. (1980) 'Minds, brains and programs', *The Behavioural and Brain Sciences*, 3, pp.417–57.

Sears, D.O. (1986) 'College sophomores in the laboratory: Influences of a narrow data base on psychology's view of human nature', *Journal of Personality and Social Psychology*, 51, pp.513–30.

Segall, M.H., Campbell, D.T. and Herskovits, M.J. (1963) 'Cultural differences in the perception of geometric illusions', *Science*, 193, pp.769–71.

Segall, M.H., Campbell, D.T. and Herskovits, M.J. (1966) *The Influence of Culture on Visual Perception*, Indianapolis: Bobbs-Merrill.

Segall, M.H., Dasen, P.R., Berry, J.W. and Poortinga, Y.H. (1990) *Human Behaviour in Global Perspective: An Introduction to Cross-cultural Psychology*, New York: Pergamon Press, pp.88.

Seligman, M.E.P. (1970) 'On the generality of the laws of learning', *Psychological Review*, 77, pp.406–18.

Seligman, M.E.P. (1971) 'Phobias and preparedness', *Behaviour Therapy*, 2, pp.307–20.

Seligman, M.E.P. (1974) 'Depression and learned helplessness', in R.J. Friedman and M.M. Katz (Eds) *The Psychology of Depression: Contemporary Theory and Research*, Washington, DC: Winston Wiley.

Seligman, M.E.P., Abramson, L.V., Semmel, A. and von Beyer, C. (1979) 'Depressive attributional style', *Journal of Abnormal Psychology*, 88, pp.242–7.

Sellen, D.W. (2001) 'Weaning, complementary feeding, and maternal decision making in a rural East African pastoral population', *Journal of Human Lactation*, 17, pp.233–44.

Selman, R.L. (1980) *The Growth of Interpersonal Understanding*, New York: Academic Press.

Selman, R.L., Watts, C.L. and Schultz, L.H. (eds) (1997) *Fostering Friendship: Pair therapy for treatment and prevention*, New York: Aldine de Gruyter.

Senra, C. and Polaino, A. (1998) 'Assessment of treatment outcome in depressed patients: concordance of methods', *British Journal of Clinical Psychology*, 37, pp.217–27.

Sergent, J. (1984) 'An investigation into component and configural processes underlying face recognition', *British Journal of Psychology*, 75, pp.221–42.

Sergent, J. and Signoret, J.L. (1992) 'Functional and anatomical decomposition of face processing: evidence from prosopagnosia and PET study of normal subjects', in V. Bruce, A. Cowey, A.W. Ellis and D.I. Perrett (eds) *Processing the Facial Image*, Oxford: Clarendon Press.

Seyfarth, R.M. and Cheyney, D.L. (1992) 'Meaning and mind in monkeys', *Scientific American*, 267, pp.122–8.

Shackelford, T.K., Goetz, A.T., Buss, D.M., Euler, H.A. and Hoier, S. (2005) 'When we hurt the ones we love: Predicting violence against women from men's mate retention', *Personal Relationships*, 12, pp.447–63.

Shaffer, H.J. and Korn, D. (2002) 'Gambling and related mental disorders: A public health analysis', *Annual review of Public Health*, 23, pp.171–212.

Shafran, R. (2005) 'Cognitive-behavioural models of OCD', in J.S. Abramowitz and A.C. Houts (eds) *Concepts and controversies in Obsessive-Compulsive Disorder*, New York: Springer Science + Business Media, Inc.

Sharma, A.R., McGue, M.K. and Benson, P.L. (1998) 'The psychological adjustment of United States adopted adolescents and their non-adopted siblings', *Child Development*, 69, pp.791–802.

Sharma, M. (2007) 'Theory of reasoned action & theory of planned behavior in alcohol and drug education', *Journal of Alcohol & Drug Education*, 51, pp.3–7.

Sharkey, K.M. (2001) 'Melatonin administration to phase shift circadian rhythms and promote sleep in human models of night shift work', *Dissertation Abstracts International: Section B – The Sciences and Engineering*, 61, pp.51–78.

Shepherd, R. (1988) 'Belief structure in relation to low-fat milk consumption', *Journal of Human Nutrition and Dietetics*, 1, pp.421–8.

Shepherd, R. and Farleigh, C.A. (1986) 'Attitudes and personality related to salt intake', *Appetite*, 7, pp.343–54.

Shepherd, R. and Stockley, L. (1985) 'Fat consumption and attitudes towards food with high fat content', *Human Nutrition: Applied Nutrition*, 39A, pp.431–42.

Sheridan, L. and Grant, T. (2007) 'Is cyberstalking different?', *Psychology Crime and Law*, 13, pp.627–40.

Sheridan, L. P., Blaauw, E. and Davies, G. M. (2003) 'Stalking: Knowns and Unknowns', *Trauma, Violence and Abuse*, 4(2), pp.148–62.

Sherry, J.L. (2007) 'Violent video games and aggression: why can't we find effects?' in R.W. Preiss, B.M. Gayle, N. Burrell, M. Allen and J. Bryant (eds), *Mass Media Effects Research: Advances Through Meta-Analysis*, Mahwah, NJ: Lawrence Erlbaum.

Shettleworth, S.J. (1998) *Cognition, Evolution, and Behavior*, Oxford: Oxford University Press.

Shkodriani, G.M. and Gibbons, J.L. (1995) 'Individualism and collectivism among university students in Mexico and the United States', *Journal of Social Psychology*, 135, pp.765–72.

Short, R.V. (1987) 'The biological basis for the contraceptive effects of breast feeding', *International Journal of Gynaecology and Obstetrics*, 25 (Supplement), pp.207–17.

Shweder, R.A., Mahapatra, M. and Miller, J.G. (1987) 'Culture and moral development' in J. Kagan and S. Lamb (eds) *The Emergence of Morality in Young Children*, Chicago: University of Chicago Press.

Shweder, R.A., Much, N.C., Mahapatra, M. and Park, L. (1997) 'The "big three" of morality (autonomy, community, divinity) and the "big three" explanations of suffering', in A.M. Brandt and P. Rozin (eds) *Morality and Health*, New York: Routledge, pp.119–69.

Sieber, J.E. and Stanley, B. (1988) 'Ethical and professional dimensions of socially sensitive research', *American Psychologist*, 43 (1), pp.49–55.

Silverman, I. (1971) 'Physical attractiveness and courtship', *Sex Behavior*, pp.22–5.

Silverstone, T. and Kyriakides, M. (1982) 'Clinical pharmacology of appetite', in T. Silverstone (ed.) *Drugs and Appetite*, London: Academic Press, pp.93–123.

Simmel, G. (1971) *On Individuality and Social Forms*, Chicago, IL: University of Chicago Press.

Simon, G.E., Von Korff, M., Saunders, K., Miglioretti, D.L., Crane, P.K., van Belle, G. and Kessler, R.C. (2006) 'Association between obesity and psychiatric disorders in the US adult population', *Archives of General Psychiatry*, 63, pp.824–30.

Simpson, H.B., Liebowitz, M.R. and Foa, E.B. (2004) 'Post-treatment effects of exposure therapy and clomopramine in obsessive-compulsive disorder', *Depression and Anxiety*, 19, pp.225–33.

Simpson, J., Collins, W.A., Tran, S. and Haydon, K. (2007) 'Attachment and the experience and expression of emotion in romantic relationships: A developmental perspective', *Journal of Personality and Social Psychology*, 92 (2), pp.355–67.

Sinclair-de-Zwart, H. (1969) 'Developmental psycholinguistics', in D. Elkind and J.H. Flavell (eds) *Studies in Cognitive Development*, New York: Oxford University Press, pp.315–36.

Singer, P. (1990) *Animal Liberation* (2nd edn), London: Cape.

Singh, S., Ernst, E. (2008) *Trick or Treatment? Alternative Medicine on Trial*, London: Bantam Press.

Sir, A., D'Souza, R.F., Uguz, S. George, T., Vahip, S., Hopwood, M., Martin, A.J., Lam, W. and Burt, T. (2005) 'Randomized trial of sertraline versus venlafaxine XR in major depression: efficacy and discontinuation symptoms', *Journal of Clinical Psychiatry*, 66, pp.1312–20.

Sistrunk, F. and McDavid, J. W. (1971) 'Sex Variable in Conforming Behavior', *Journal of Personality and Social Psychology*, 8, pp.200–7.

Skinner, B.F. (1938) *The Behavior of Organisms: An experimental approach*, Appleton-Century: New York.

Skinner, B. F. (1948) '"Superstition" in the pigeon' *Journal of Experimental Psychology*, 38, 168–172.

Skinner, B.F. (1953) *Science and Human Behavior*, New York: MacMillan.

Skinner, B.F. (1971, 1973) *Beyond Freedom and Dignity*, New York: Knopf

Slaby, R.G. and Frey, K.S. (1975), 'Development of gender constancy and selective attention to same-sex models', *Child Development*, 46, pp.849–56.

Slater, A., Mattock, A. and Brown, E. (1990) 'Size constancy at birth: newborn infants' responses to retinal and real size', *Journal of Experimental Psychology*, 49, pp.314–22.

Slater, M.D. (2003) 'Alienation, aggression, and sensation-seeking as predictors of adolescent use of violent film, computer and website content', *Journal of Communicaion*, 53, pp.105–21.

Slovic, P. (2001) *Smoking: Risk, Perception and Policy*, Thousand Oaks, CA: Sage Publications.

Slavin, R.E. (1987) 'Developmental and motivational perspectives on co-operative learning: a reconciliation', *Child Development*, 58, pp.1161–7.

Slife, B.D. and Williams, R.N. (1995) *What's behind the Research? Discovering Hidden Assumptions in the Behavioural Sciences*, Thousand Oaks: Sage.

Smedslund, J. (1963) 'The concept of correlation in adults' *Scandinavian Journal of Psychology*, 4, 165–173.

Smith, A. and Cooper, S.J. 'Hollywood Schizophrenia', *Student British Medical Journal* Volume 14, pp.346–7

Smith, C. and Lloyd, B.B. (1978) 'Maternal Behaviour and Perceived Sex of Infant', *Child Development*, 49, pp.1263–5.

Smith, E., Nolen-Hoeksema, S., Fredrickson, B. and Loftus, G. (2003) *Atkinson and Hilgard's Introduction to Psychology*, Wadsworth Publishing Company: New York, pp.427.

Smith, M. D. (2003) 'The role of the experimenter in parapsychological research' In J. Alcock, J. Burns and A. Freeman (eds.) *Psi wars: Getting to grips with the paranormal*. Exeter: Imprint Academic. Pp. 69–84.

Smith, P.K. and Daglish, L. (1977) 'Sex differences in parent and infant behaviour in the home', *Child Development*, 48, pp.1250–4.

Smith, P. and Bond, M.H. (1993, 1998 [2nd edn]) *Social Psychology Across Cultures: Analysis and Perspectives*, Harvester Wheatsheaf: New York.

Smith, P.K., Cowie, H. and Blades, M. (2003) *Understanding Children's Development* (5th edn), Oxford: Blackwell Publishing.

Smith, P.K., Smees, R. and Pellegrini, A.D. (2004) 'Play fighting and real fighting', *Aggressive Behavior*, 30, pp.164–73

Smith, S.W., Smith, S.L., Pieper, K.M., Yoo, J.H., Ferris, A.L., Downs, E. and Bowden, B. (2006) 'Altruism on American television: examining the amount of, and context surrounding, acts of helping and sharing', *Journal of Communication*, 56, pp.707–27.

Snarey, J.R. (1985) 'Cross-cultural universality of social-moral development: A critical review of Kohlbergian research', *Psychological Bulletin*, 97, pp.202–32.

Snarey, J.R., Reimer, J. and Kohlberg, I. (1985) 'Development of social-moral reasoning among kibbutz adolescents: A longitudinal cross-sectional study', *Developmental Psychology*, 21, pp.3–17.

Sneddon, L.U., Braithwaite, V.A., Gentle, M.J., Broughton, B. and Knight, P. (2003) 'Trout trauma puts anglers on the hook', *Proceedings from the Royal Society*, April 30.

Snyder, C. R., Shenkel, R. J. and Lowery, C. R. (1977) 'Acceptance of personality interpretations: The "Barnum effect" and beyond' *Journal of Consulting and Clinical Psychology*, 45, 104–114.

Snyder, M. and DeBono, K. (1985) 'Appeals to image and claims about quality: Understanding the psychology of advertising', *Journal of Personality and Social Psychology*, 49, pp.586–97.

Snyder, S.H. (1984) 'Drug and neurotransmitter receptors in the brain', *Science*, 224, pp.22–31.

Soal, S. G. and Goldney, K. M. (1943) 'Experiments in precognitive telepathy' *Proceedings of the Society for Psychical Research*, 47, 21–150.

Soehner, A.M., Kathy, S., Kennedy, K.S. and Monk, T.H. (2007) 'Personality Correlates with Sleep-Wake Variables', *Chronobiology International, 24,* pp.889–903.

Soetens, B., Braet, C., Dejonckheere, P. and Roets, A. (2006) 'When suppression backfires: The ironic effects of suppressing eating-related thoughts', *Journal of Health Psychology*, 11, pp.655–68.

Solley, C.M. and Haig, G. (1958) 'A note to Santa Claus', Menninger Foundation, 18, in C.M. Solley and G. Murphy (eds) (1960) *Development of the Perceptual World,* New York: Basic Books, pp.4–5.

Solyom, L., Beck, P., Solyom, C. and Hugel, R. (1974) 'Some etiological factors in phobic neurosis', *Canadian Psychiatric Association Journal*, 21, pp.109–13.

Sood, S. and Rogers, E. M. (2000) 'Dimensions of parasocial interaction by letter-writers to a popular entertainment-education soap opera in India', *Journal of Broadcasting & Electronic Media, 44,* pp.386–414.

Sosis, R. (2004) 'The adaptive value of religious ritual', *American Scientist*, 92, pp.166–72.

Sosis, R. (2006) 'Religious behaviors, badges, and bans: Signaling theory and the evolution of religion', in P. McNamara (ed.), *Where God and Science Meet: How the brain and evolutionary sciences are revolutionizing our understanding of religion and spirituality*, Westport: Praeger/Greenwood Press.

Sosis, R., Kress, H. and Boster, J. (2005) 'Scars for war: Evaluating alternative explanations for cross-cultural variance in ritual costs', Unpublished manuscript, University of Connecticut, Storrs, CT.

Spanos, N. P. (1996) *Multiple identities and false memories: A sociocognitive perspective*. Washington, DC: American Psychological Association.

Spanos, N. P., Cross, P., Dickson, K. and DuBreuil, S. C. (1993) 'Close encounters: An examination of UFO experiences' *Journal of Abnormal Psychology*, 102, 624–632.

Spanos, N. P., Menary, E., Gabora, N. J., DuBreuil, S. C. and Dewhirst, B. (1991) Secondary identity enactments during hypnotic past-life regression: A sociocognitive perspective' *Journal of Personality and Social Psychology*, 61, 308–320.

Sparks, P. and Shepherd, R. (1992) 'Self-identify and the theory of planned behaviour: Assessing the role of identification with green consumerism', *Social Psychology Quarterly*, 55, pp.1388–99.

Sparks, P., Hedderley, D. and Shepherd, R. (1992) 'An investigation into the relationship between perceived control, attitudes variability and the consumption of two common foods', *European Journal of Social Psychology*, 22, pp.55–71.

Spearman, C. (1923) *The Nature of Intelligence and the Principles of Cognition*, London: Macmillan.

Spence, J.T. and Helmreich, R.L. (1978) 'Masculinity and Femininity: Their psychological dimensions, correlates and antecedents' in P.K. Smith, H. Cowie and M. Blades (eds) *Understanding Children's Development*, Oxford: Blackwell Publishing, p.298.

Spillman, D. (1990) 'Survey of food and vitamin intake responses reported by university students experiencing stress', *Psychological Reports*, 66, pp.499–502.

Spitz, H.H. (1986) *The rising of intelligence: A selected history of attempts to raise retarded intelligence*, Hillsdale, NJ: Lawrence Erlbaum Associates.

Spitzer, L. and Rodin, J. (1981) 'Human eating behavior: A critical review of studies in normal weight and overweight individuals', *Appetite*, 2, pp.293–329.

Spitzer, R.L., Endicott, J. and Robins, E. (1978) 'Research diagnostic criteria: rationale and reliability', *Archives of General Psychiatry*, 35, pp.773–82.

Sprafkin, J.N., Liebert, R.M. and Poulos, R.W. (1975) 'Effects of a prosocial televised example on children's helping', *Journal of Experimental Child Psychology*, 20, pp.119–26.

Sprecher, S., Hatfield, E., Cortese, A., Potapova, E. and Levitskaya, A. (1994) 'Token resistance to sexual intercourse and consent to unwanted sexual intercourse: College students' dating experiences in three countries', *The Journal of Sex Research*, 31, pp.125–32.

Squire, L.R., Ojemann, J.G., Miezin, F.M., Petersen, S.E., Videen, T.O., and Raichle, M.E. (1992) 'Activation of the hippocampus in normal humans: A functional anatomical study of memory', *Proceedings of the National Academy of Science, USA*, 89, pp.1837–41.

Sroufe, L.A. and Fleeson, J. (1986) 'Attachment and the construction of relationships', in W. Hartup and Z. Rubin (eds.) *Relationships and Development*, Hillsdale, N.J.: Earlbaum, pp.51–71.

Stein, M. B., Walker, J.R., Anderson, G., Hazen, A., Ross, C.A., Eldridge, G. and Forde, D. (1996) 'Childhood physical and sexual abuse in patients with anxiety disorders and in a community sample', *American Journal of Psychiatry*, 153(2), pp.275–77.

Steiner, W. (1991) 'Fluoxetine-induced mania in a patient with obsessive-compulsive disorder', *American Journal of Psychiatry*, 148, pp.1403–4.

Stephan, F.K. and Zucker, I. (1972) 'Circadian rhythms in drinking behavior and locomotor activity of rats are eliminated by hypothalamic lesions', *Proceedings of the National Academy of Science, USA*, 69, pp.1583–6.

Steptoe, A., Pollard, T.M. and Wardle, J. (1995) 'Development of a measure of the motives underlying the selection of food: the food choice questionnaire', *Appetite*, 25(3), pp.267–84.

Stern, J.S. (1984) 'Is obesity a disease of inactivity?' in A.J. Stunkard and E. Stellar (eds) *Eating and its Disorders*, New York: Raven Press.

Stern, W.C. and Morgane, P.J. (1974) 'Theoretical view of REM sleep function: maintenance of catecolamine systems in the central nervous system', *Behavioural Biology, 11*, pp.1–32.

Sternberg, R.J. (1985) *Beyond IQ: A triarchic theory of human intelligence*, Cambridge University Press: Cambridge.

Sternberg, R.J. (1988) *The Nature of Creativity: Contemporary Psychological Perspectives*, Cambridge University Press: Cambridge.

Sternberg, R.J. (1996) *Cognitive Psychology* (2nd edn), Harcourt Brace College Publishers.

Sternberg, R.J. (2000) *Handbook of Intelligence*, Cambridge University Press: Cambridge.

Sternberg, R.J. (2002) 'The search for criteria: why study the evolution of intelligence? in R.J. Sternberg and J.C. Kaufman (eds), *The Evolution of Intelligence*, pp. 1–7, Mahwah, NJ: Lawrence Erlbaum.

Sternberg, R.J. and Detterman, D.K. (1986). *What is intelligence?* Norwood, NJ: Ablex.

Sternberg, R.J. and Kaufman, J.C. (1998) 'Human abilities', *Annual Review of Psychology*, 49, pp.479–502.

Stolinsky, S.A, and Stolinsky, D.C. 'Suicide and homicide rates do not covary', *Journal of Trauma* 2000, 48, pp.1168–9.

Stone, A.A. and Brownell, K.D. (1994) 'The stress-eating paradox: Multiple daily measurements in adult males and females', *Psychology and Health*, 9, pp.425–36.

Strack, F., Martin, L.L. and Schwarz, N. (1988) 'Priming and communication: Social determinants of information use in judgments of life satisfaction', *European Journal of Social Psychology*, 18, pp.429–42.

Stroop, J.R. (1935) 'Studies of interference in serial verbal reactions', *Journal of Experimental Psychology*, 18, pp.643–62.

Stuart, S. and O'Hara, M.W. (2002) 'Interpersonal Psychotherapy', In M.A. Reinecke and M.R. Davison (eds) *Comparative treatments for depression*, pp.317–357, New York: Springer.

Stunkard, A.J., Sorenson, T.I.A., Hanis, C., Teasdale, T.W., Chakraborty, R., Schull, W.J. and Schulsinger, F. (1986) 'An adoption study of human obesity', *New England Journal of Medicine*, 314, pp.193–8.

Stumpf, H. and Stanley, J.C. (1996) 'Gender-related differences on the College Board's Advanced Placement and achievement tests', *Journal of Educational Psychology*, 88(2), pp.353–64.

Stunkard, A.J., Harris, J.R., Pedersen, N.L. and McClearn, G.E. (1990) 'A separated twin study of body mass index', *New England Journal of Medicine*, 322, pp.1483–7.

Sutherland, S. (1992) *Irrationality: The enemy within*. London: Constable.

Sutton, S. (1998) 'Predicting and explaining intentions and behaviour: How well are we doing?' *Journal of Applied Social Psychology*, 28, pp.1317–38.

Svartberg, M. and Stiles, T.C. (1991) 'Comparative effects of short-term psychodynamic psychotherapy: A meta-analysis', *Journal of Consulting Clinical Psychology*, 59(5), pp.704–14.

Sykes, G. (1958) *The Society of Captives*, Princeton, N.J.: Princeton University Press.

Takahashi, K. (1990) 'Are the key assumptions of the "strange situation" universal?', *Human Development*, 33, pp.23–30.

Takahashi, T., Sasaki, M., Itoh, H., Yamadera, W., Ozone, M., Obuchi, K., Hayashida, K., Matsanuga, N. and Sano, H. (2002) 'Melatonin alleviates jet lag symptoms caused by an 11-hour eastward flight', *Psychiatry and Clinical Neurosciences*, 56, pp.3001–2.

Takeuchi, S.A. (2006) 'On the matching phenomenon in courtship: A probability matching theory of mate selection', *Marriage and Family Review*, 40 (1), pp.25–51.

Tanaka, J.W. and Farah, M.J. (1993) 'Parts and wholes in face recognition', *Quarterly Journal of Experimental Psychology*, 46A, pp.225–45.

Tataranni, P.A. (2000) 'Mechanisms of weight gain in humans' (Editorial), *European Review for Medical and Pharmacological Sciences*, 4, pp.1–7.

Tataranni, P.A., Harper, I.T., Snitker, S., Del Parigi, A., Vozarova, B., Bunt, J., Bogardus, C. and Ravussin, E. (2003) 'Body weight gain in free-living Pima Indians: Effect of energy intake *vs* expenditure', *International Journal of Obesity*, 27, pp.1578–83.

Tatarsky, A. (2003) 'Harm reduction psychotherapy: Extending the reach of traditional substance use treatment', *Journal of Substance Abuse Treatment*, 25, pp.249–256.

Tavris, C.B. (1992) *The Mismeasure of Woman: Why Women are not the Better Sex, the Inferior Sex or the Opposite Sex*, New York: Touchstone.

Tavris, C. (1993) 'The mismeasure of women', *Feminism and Psychology*, 3(2), pp.149–68.

Tavris, C. and Wade, C. (1995) *Psychology in Perspective*, New York: HarperCollins.

Taylor, E. (1994) 'Physical treatments', In M. Rutter, E. Taylor and L. Hersov (Eds) *Child and Adolescent Psychiatry*, Oxford: Blackwell Scientific Publications.

Taylor, M.C. and Hall, J.A. (1982) 'Psychological androgyny: theories, methods, and conclusions', *Psychological Bulletin*, 92(2), pp.347–66.

Teeson, M., Degenhardt, L. and Hall, W. (2002) *Addictions*, Hove: Psychology Press.

Tennes, K. and Kreye, M. (1985) 'Children's adrenocortical responses to classroom activities and tests in elementary school', *Psychosomatic Medicine*, 47, pp.451–60.

Teuber, H.L. (1968) 'Alteration of perception and memory in man: Perception', in L. Weiskrantz (ed.) *Analysis of Behavioural Change*, New York: Harper and Row, pp.274–328.

Thalbourne, M. A. (1994) 'Belief in the paranormal and its relationship to schizophrenia-relevant measures: A confirmatory study' *British Journal of Clinical Psychology, 33*, 78–80.

Thalbourne, M. A. (1995) 'Science versus showmanship: A history of the Randi hoax' *Journal of the American Society for Psychical Research, 89*, 344–366.

Thalbourne, M. A. (1998) 'Transliminality: Further correlates and a short measure' *Journal of the American Society for Psychical Research, 92*, 402–419.

Thalbourne, M. A., Dunbar, K. A. and Delin, P. S. (1995) ,An investigation into correlates of belief in the paranormal' *Journal of the American Society for Psychical Research, 89*, 215–231.

Thalbourne, M. A. and French, C. C. (1995) 'Paranormal belief, manic-depressiveness, and magical ideation: a replication' *Personality and Individual Differences*, 18, 291–292.

Thalbourne, M. A. & Maltby, J. (2008) 'Transliminality, thin boundaries, Unusual Experiences and temporal lobe lability' *Personality and Individual Differences*, 44, 1617–1623.

Thannickal, T.C., Moore, R.Y., Nienhuis, R., Ramanathan, L., Gulyani, S., Aldrich, M., Cornford, M. and Siegel, J.M. (2000) 'Reduced number of hypocretin neurons in human narcoplepsy', *Neuron*, 27, pp.469–74.

Thapa, S., Short, R. and Potts, M. (1988) 'Breast feeding, birth spacing and their effects on child survival', *Nature*, 335, pp.679–82.

Tharp, R.G. and Gallimore, R. (1988) 'A theory of teaching as assisted performance', in R. Tharp and R. Gallimore (eds) *Rousing Minds to Life: Teaching, learning, and schooling in social context*, Cambridge: Cambridge University Press, pp.27–43.

Thase, M.E., Greenhouse, J.B., Frank, E., Reynolds, C.F., Pilconis, P.A., Hurley, K., Grochocinski, V. and Kupfer, D.J. (1997) 'Treatment of major depression with psychotherapy or psychotherapy-pharmacotherapy combinations', *Archives of General Psychiatry*, 54, pp.1009–15.

Thase, M.E., Jindal, R. and Howland, R.H. (2002) 'Biological aspects of depression', In I. H. Gotlib and C. L. Hammen (eds). *Handbook of depression*, pp.192–218, New York: Guilford Press.

Thibaut, J.W. and Kelley, H.H. (1959) *The Social Psychology of Groups*, New York: Wiley.

Thompson (2008) from the BBC NEWS website: http://news.bbc.co.uk/go/pr/fr/-/1/hi/england/north_yorkshire/7610761.stm

Thompson, J.P., Palmer, R.L. and Petersen, S.A. (1988) 'Is there a metabolic component to counter-regulation?' *International Journal of Eating Disorders*, 7, pp.307–19.

Thompson, P. (1980) 'Margaret Thatcher: a new illusion.' *Perception*, 9, pp.483–4.

Thompson, S.K. (1975) 'Gender labels and early sex role development', *Child Development*, 46, pp.339–47.

Thorgeirsson, T.E., Geller, F., Sulem, P., Rafnar, T., Wiste, A., Magnusson, K.P., Manolescu, A., Thorleifsson, G., Stefansson, H., Ingason, A., Stacey, S.N., Bergthorsson, J.T., Thorlacius, S., Gudmundsson, J., Jonsson, T., Jakobsdottir, M., Saemundsdottir, J., Olafsdottir, O., Gudmundsson, L.J., Bjornsdottir, G., Kristjansson, K., Skuladottir, H., Isaksson, H.J., Gudbjartsson, T., Jones, G.T., Mueller, T., Gottsäter, A., Flex, A., Aben, K.K., de Vegt, F., Mulders, P.F., Isla, D., Vidal, M.J., Asin, L., Saez, B., Murillo, L., Blondal, T., Kolbeinsson, H., Stefansson, J.G., Hansdottir, I., Runarsdottir, V., Pola, R., Lindblad, B., van Rij, A.M., Dieplinger, B., Haltmayer, M., Mayordomo, J.I., Kiemeney, L.A., Matthiasson, S.E., Oskarsson, H., Tyrfingsson, T., Gudbjartsson, D.F., Gulcher, J.R., Jonsson, S., Thorsteinsdottir, U., Kong, A. and Stefansson, K. (2008) 'A variant associated with nicotine dependence, lung cancer and peripheral arterial disease', *Nature*, 452, pp.638–42.

Thorndike, E.L. (1898) *Animal Intelligence: An experimental study of the associative processes*, New York: Teacher's college.

Thorndike, E.L. (1911) *Animal Intelligence: Experimental studies*, New York: Macmillan.

Thornhill, R. and Thornhill, N.W. (1992) 'The evolutionary psychology of men's sexual coercion', *Behavioral and Brain Sciences*, 15, pp.363–75.

Thornhill, R. and Gangestad, S.W. (1993) 'Human facial beauty: Averageness, symmetry and parasite resistance', *Human Nature*, 4, pp.237–69.

Thornhill, R. and Gangestad, S.W. (1999) 'The scent of symmetry: A human sex pheromone that signals fitness?' *Evolution and Human Behavior*, 20, pp.175–201.

Thorpe, S.J. and Salkovskis, P.M. (1997) 'The effect of one-session treatment for spider phobia on attentional bias and beliefs', *British Journal of Clinical Psychology*, 36, pp.225–41.

Thurstone, L.L. (1924) *The Nature of Intelligence*, London: Routledge.

Thurstone, L.L. (1938) *Primary mental abilities*, Chicago: University of Chicago Press.

Tienari, P., Wynne, L.C. and Moring, J. (2000) 'Finnish adoptive family study: sample selection and adoptee DSM-III-R diagnoses', *Acta Psychiatrica Scandinavica*, 101, pp.433–443.

Tienari, P., Sorri, A., Lahti, I. and Naarala, M. (1987) 'Genetic and psychosocial factors in schizophrenia: The Finnish adoptive family study', *Schizophrenia Bulletin*, 13, pp.477–84.

Tilfors, M., Furmark, T. and Marteinsdottir, I. (2001) 'Cerebral blood flow during anticipation of public speaking in social phobia: a PETstudy', *Biological Psychiatry*, 52, pp.1113–19.

Toates, F. (2007) *Biological Psychology*, Harlow: Pearson Education.

Tobacyk, J. J. (2004) 'A revised paranormal belief scale' *International Journal of Transpersonal Studies*, 23, 94–98.

Tobacyk, J. J. and Tobacyk, Z. S. (1992) 'Comparisons of belief-based personality constructs in Polish and American university students: Paranormal beliefs, locus of control, irrational beliefs, and social interest' *Journal of Cross-Cultural Psychology*, 23, 311–325.

Todhunter, E.N. (1973) 'Food habits, food faddism and nutrition', *World Review of Nutrition and Dietetics*, 16, pp.286–317.

Tolnay, S.E. and Beck, E.M. (1995) *A Festival of Violence: An analysis of southern lynching, 1882-1930*, Urbana: University of Illinois Press.

Torgersen, S. (1983) 'Genetic factors in anxiety disorders', *Archives of General Psychiatry*, 40, pp.1085–9.

Torrey, E.F., Rawlings, R. and Waldman, I.N. (1988) 'Schizophrenia births and viral diseases in two states', *Schizophrenia Research*, 1, pp.73–7.

Torrey, E.F., Rawlings, R.R., Ennnis, J.M., Merrill, D.D. and Flores, D.S. (1996) 'Birth seasonality in bipolar disorder, schizophrenia, schizoaffective disorder and stillbirths', *Schizophrenia Research*, 21 (3), pp.141–9.

Townsend, J. (1993) 'Policies to halve smoking deaths', *Addiction*, 88, pp.43–52.

Tremblay, R.E. (2003) 'Why socialization fails? The case of chronic physical aggression', in B.B. Lahey, T.E. Moffitt and A. Caspi (eds), *Causes of Conduct Disorder and Juvenile Delinquency*, New York, NY: Guilford Publications, pp.182–224.

Trenchard, E. and Silverstone, J.T. (1983) 'Naloxone reduces the food intake of human volunteers', *Appetite*, 4, pp.43–50.

Trivers, R. (1972) 'Parental investment and sexual selection', in B. Campbell (ed.) *Sexual Selection and the Descent of Man*, Chicago: Aldine-Atherton, pp.136–79.

Trivers, R.L. (1974) 'Parent–offspring conflict', *American Zoologist*, 14, pp.249–64.

Truzzi, M. (1996) Pseudoscience. In G. Stein (ed.) *The Encyclopedia of the paranormal*. Amherst, NY: Prometheus. Pp. 560–575.

Turing, A.M. (1950) 'Computing machinery and intelligence', *Mind*, 59, pp.433–60.

Turkheimer, E. (2000) 'Three laws of behaviour genetics and what they mean', *Current Directions in Psychological Science*, 9, pp.160–4.

Turkheimer, E., Haley, A., Waldron, M., D'Onofrio, B. and Gottesman, I.I. (2003) 'Socioeconomic status modifies heritability of IQ in young children' *Science*, 14, pp.623–8.

Turkington, D., Sensky,T., Kingdon, D., Scott, J.L., Scott,J., Siddle, R., O'Carroll, M. and Barnes,T.R.E. (2000) 'A Randomized Controlled Trial of Cognitive-Behavioural Therapy for Persistent Symptoms in Schizophrenia Resistant to Medication', *Archives of General Psychiatry*, 57, pp.165–172.

Turnbull, C. (1961) 'Some observations regarding the experiences and behaviour of the Bambuti', *American Journal of Psychology*, 74, pp.153–163.

Twisk, D.A.M. and Stacey, C. (2007) 'Trends in young driver risk and countermeasures in European countries', *Journal of Safety Research*, 38(2), pp.245–57.

Tyler, C.W. (1997) 'Analysis of human receptor density', in V. Lakshminarayanan (ed.) *Basic and Clinical Applications of Vision Science*, Norwell, MA: Kluwer Academic.

Tyler, T.R. and Schuller, R A. (1991) 'Aging and attitude change: Distinguishing the opportunity and the ability to change', *Journal of Personality and Social Psychology*, 61, pp.689–97.

Udry, J.R. (1974) *The Social Context of Marriage* (3rd edn), Philadelphia: J.B. Lippincott.

Unger, R.K. (1979) 'Toward a redefinition of sex and gender', cited in in J. Archer and B. Lloyd (eds) (1992) *Sex and Gender*, Cambridge: Cambridge University Press, p.17.

United Nations Office on Drugs and Crime/World Health Organization (2008) *Principles of Drug Dependence Treatment: Discussion paper*, UN/WHO.

US Department of Health and Human Services (1990) *The Health Benefits of Smoking Cessation: A report of the Surgeon General*, Rockville, MD: USDHHS.

Valentine, E.R. (1992) *Conceptual Issues in Psychology* (2nd edn), London: Routledge.

Valentine, T. (2001) 'Face-space models of face recognition', in M.J. Wenger and J. T. Townsend (eds) *Computational, Geometric and Process Perspectives on Facial Cognition: Contexts and challenges*, Hillsdale, NJ: Lawrence Erlbaum.

Vandenbergh, J. G. (2003) 'Prenatal Hormone Exposure and Sexual Variation', *American Scientist*, 91(3), pp.218–25.

van Goozen, S., Fairchild, G., Snoek, H. and Harold, G. (2007) 'The Evidence for a Neurobiological Model of Childhood Antisocial Behavior', *Psychological Bulletin*, 133, pp.149–82.

van Hasselt, V.B.M., Hull, J.A., Kempton, T. and Bukstein, O.G. (1993) 'Social skills and depression in adolescent substance abusers', *Addictive Behaviors*, 18, pp.9–18.

van IJzendoorn, M.H. and Kroonenberg, P.M. (1988) 'Cross-cultural patterns of attachment: A meta-analysis of the Strange Situation', *Child Development*, 59, pp.147–56.

van Lommel, P., van Wees, R., Meyers, V. and Elfferich, I. (2001) 'Near-death experience in survivors of cardiac arrest: a prospective study in the Netherlands' *Lancet*, 358, 2039–2045.

van Oppen, P., De Haan, E., Van Balkom, A.J.L.M., Spinhoven, P., Hoogduin, K. and Van Dyck, R. (1995) 'Cognitive therapy and exposure in vivo in the treatment of obsessive-compulsive disorder', *Behaviour research and therapy*, 33(4), pp. 379–390.

van Os, J. and Selten, J.P. (1998) 'Prenatal exposure to maternal stress and subsequent schizophrenia: the May 1940 invasion of The Netherlands', *British Journal of Psychiatry*, 172, pp.324–6.

Vaughn, C.E. and Leff, J.P. (1976) 'The influence of family and social factors on the course of psychiatric illness. A comparison of schizophrenia and depressed neurotic patients', *British Journal of Psychiatry*, 129, pp.125–37.

Veijola, J., Puukka, P., Lehtinen, V., Moring, J., Lindholm, T. and Vaisanen, E. (1998) 'Sex differences in the association between childhood experiences and adult depression', *Psychological Medicine*, 28, pp.21–7.

Vendsborg, T.B., Bech, P. and Rafaelson, O.J. (1976) 'Lithium treatment and weight gain', *Acta Psychiatrica Scandinavica*, 53, pp.139–47.

Vidrine, J.I., Simmons, V.N. and Brandon, T.H. (2007) 'Construction of smoking relevant risk perceptions among college students: The influence of need for cognition and message content', *Journal of Applied Social Psychology*, 37, pp.91–114.

Virkkunen, M. (1985) 'Urinary free cortisol secretion in habitually violent offenders', *Acta Psychiatrica Scandinavica*, 72, pp.40–4.

Visser, P.S. and Krosnick, J.A. (1998) 'The development of attitude strength over the life cycle: Surge and decline', *Journal of Personality and Social Psychology*, 75, pp.1389–1410.

Volberg, R.A. (1994) 'The prevalence and demographics of pathological gamblers: Implications for public health', *American Journal of Public Health*, 84, pp.237–241.

Volberg, R.A. (1994) 'Fifteen years of problem gambling prevalence research. What do we know?' *Journal of Gambling Issues*, 10.

Volberg, R.A. (1997) 'Gambling and Problem Gambling in Mississippi', report to the Mississippi Council on Compulsive Gambling, *Social Science Report Series* 97-1. Social Science Research Center, Mississippi State, University.

Volberg, R.A. 1997. 'Gambling and Problem Gambling in Oregon', report to the Oregon Gambling Addiction Treatment Foundation, Northhampton, MA: Gemini Research, Ltd.

Volkow, N.D., Wang, G.J., Fischman, M.W., Foltin, R.W., Fowler, J.S., Abumrad, N.N., Vitkun, S., Logan, J., Gatley, S.J., Pappas, N., Hitzemann, R. and Shea, C.E. (1997) 'Relationship between subjective effects of cocaine and dopamine transporter occupancy', *Nature* 386, pp.827–30.

von Frisch, K. (1967) *The Dance Language and Orientation of Bees*, Cambridge, MA: Harvard University Press.

von Senden, M. (1960) Space and Sight: The Perception of Space and Shape in the Congenitally Blind Before and After Operations, London: Methuen.

Voyer, D., Voyer, S. and Bryden, M.P. (1995) 'Magnitude of sex differences in spatial abilities: A meta-analysis and consideration of critical variables', *Psychological Bulletin*, 117, pp.250–70.

Vygotsky, L.S. (1962) *Thought and Language*, Cambridge, MA: MIT Press [Originally published in Russian in 1934].

Vygotksy, L.S. (1966) 'Genesis of the higher mental functions', in A. Leontyev, A. Luria and A. Smirnoff (eds) *Psychological Research in the USSR*, Vol. 1, Moscow: Progress Publishers, pp.35–45 [This is an abridged translation by D. Myshne of an extensive study by Vygotsky written under the same title in 1930].

Vygotsky, L.S. (1978) *Mind in Society: The development of higher psychological processes*, Cambridge, MA: Harvard University Press [Originally published in Russian in 1930].

Vygotsky, L.S. (1987) 'Thanking and speech', in R.W. Riber and A.S. Carton (eds) *The Collected Works of L.S. Vygotsky, Vol. 1: Problems of general psychology*, New York: Plenum Press..

Vyse, S. A. (1997) *Believing in magic: The psychology of superstition*. New York: Oxford University Press.

Waal, F.B.M. de (1989) *Peacemaking among Primates*, Cambridge Massachusett: Harvard University Press.

Wadden, T.A. (1993) 'Treatment of obesity by moderate and severe caloric restriction: Results of clinical research trials', *Annals of Internal Medicine*, 119 (7), pp.688–93.

Wadden, T.A., Butryn, M.L., Sarwer, D.B., Fabricatore, A.N., Crerand, C.E., Lipschutz, P.E., Faulconbridge, L., Raper, S.E. and Williams, N.N. (2006) 'Comparison of psychosocial status in treatment-seeking women with class 111 *vs* class 1–11 obesity', *Obesity*, 14, (Supp. 2), pp.90S–98S.

Wadeley, A., Birch, A. and Malim, T. (1997) *Perspectives in Psychology* (2nd edn), London: Macmillan.

Wagenaar, W.A. (1988) *Paradoxes of Gambling Behaviour*, London: Erlbaum.

Wahlberg, K.E., Jackson, D. and Haley, H. (2000) 'Gene-environment interaction in vulnerability to schizophrenia: findings from the Finnish Adoptive Family Study of Schizophrenia', American Journal of Psychiatry, 154, pp. 355–62.

Walby, S. and Allen, J. (2004) *Domestic Violence, Sexual Assault and Stalking: Findings from the British Crime Survey*, London: Home Office Research Study 276, Home Office Research, Development and Statistics Directorate.

Walker, L.J. (1989) 'A longitudinal study of moral reasoning', *Child Development*, 60, pp.157–60.

Walker, L.J. (2004) 'Bridging the judgment/action gap in moral functioning', in D.K. Lapsley and D. Narvaez (eds) *Moral Development, Self, and Identity*, Mahwah, NJ: Erlbaum.

Walker, L.J., de Vries, B. and Trevethan, S.D. (1987) 'Moral stages and moral orientations in real-life and hypothetical dilemmas', *Child Development*, 58, pp.842–58.

Walker, M., Langmeyer, L. and Langmeyer, D. (1992) 'Celebrity endorsers: Do you get what you pay for?', *Journal of Consumer Marketing*, 9, pp.69–76.

Walker, M.B. (1992) *The Psychology of Gambling*, Oxford: Pergamon Press.

Walster, E., Aronson, V., Abrahams, D., and Rottmann, L. (1966) 'Importance of physical attractiveness in dating behavior', *Journal of Personality and Social Psychology*, 4, pp.508–16.

Walster, E., Walster, G.W. and Berscheid, E. (1978) *Equity: Theory and research*, Boston: Allyn and Bacon.

Walton, G.E., Bower, N.J.A. and Bower, T.G.R. (1992) 'Recognition of familiar faces by newborns', *Infant Behaviour and Development*, 15, pp.265–9.

Wardle, J. (1980) 'Dietary restraint and binge eating', *Behavioral Analysis and Modification*, 4, pp.201–9.

Wardle, J. and Beales, S. (1988) 'Control and loss of control over eating: An experimental investigation', *Journal of Abnormal Psychology*, 97, pp.35–40.

Wardle, J., Steptoe, A., Oliver, G. and Lipsey, Z. (2000) 'Stress, dietary restraint and food intake', *Journal of Psychosomatic Research*, 48(2), pp.195–202.

Wardle, J., Sanderson, S., Guthrie, C.A., Rapoport, L. and Plomin, R. (2002) 'Parental feeding style and the intergenerational transmission of obesity risk', *Obesity Research*, 10, pp.453–62.

Wargo, E. (2008) 'The many lives of superstition' *Observer*, 21(9), 18–24.

Watson, J.B. (1913) 'Psychology as the behaviourist views it', *Psychological Review*, 20, pp.158–77.

Watson, J.B. and Rayner, R. (1920) 'Conditioned emotional reactions', *Journal of Experimental Psychology*, 3, pp.1–14.

Watson, R.I. Jnr. (1973) 'Investigation into deindividuation using a cross-cultural survey technique', *Journal of Personality and Social Psychology*, 25, pp.342–45.

Watt, C. (1990–1991) 'Psychology and coincidences' *European Journal of Parapsychology*, 8, 66–84.

Webb, W.B. (1974) 'Sleep as an adaptive response', *Perceptual and Motor Skills*, 38, pp.1023–7.

Webb, W.B. (1992) *Sleep, the Gentle Tyrant*, Bolton, MA: Anker.

Weber, R., Ritterfeld, U. and Mathiak, K. (2006) 'Does playing violent video games induce aggression? Empirical evidence of a functional magnetic resonance imaging study', *Media Psychology*, 8, pp.39–60.

Wegner, D.M. (1994) 'Ironic processes of mental control', *Psychological Review*, 101, pp.34–52.

Wegner, D.M., Schneider, D.J., Cater, S.R. and White, T.L. (1987) 'Paradoxical effects of thought suppression', *Journal of Personality and Social Psychology*, 53, pp.5–13.

Wehren, A. and DeLisi, R. (1983) 'The development of gender understanding: judgements and explanations', *Child Development*, 54, pp.1568–78.

Weinberger, D.R. (1987) 'Implications of normal brain development for the pathogenesis of schizophrenia', *Archives of General Psychiatry*, 44, pp.660–669.

Weinraub, M., Clemens, L.P., Sockloff, A., Ethridge, T., Gracely, E. and Myers, B. (1984) 'The development of sex-role stereotypes in the third year: Relationships to gender labelling, gender identity, sex-typed toy preference and family characteristics', *Child Development*, 55, pp.1493–503.

Weissman, M.M., Gershon, E.S., Kidd, K.K., Prussof, B.A., Leckman, J.F., Dibble, E.Hamovit, J., Thompson, W.D., Pauls, D.L., and Guroff, J.J. (1984) 'Psychiatric disorder in the relatives of probands with affective disorders', *Archives of General Pyychiatry*, 41, pp.13–21.

Wellman, H.M. (1990) *The Child's Theory of Mind*, Cambridge, MA: MIT Press.

Wellman, H.M., Cross, D. and Watson, J. (2001) 'Meta-analysis of theory of mind development: The truth about false belief', *Child Development*, 72 (3), pp.655–84.

Wender, P.H., Kety, S.S., Rosenthal, D., Schilsinger, F., Ortmann, J. and Lunde (1986) 'Psychiatric disorders in the biological and adoptive families of adopted individuals with affective disorders', *Archives of General Psychiatry*, 43, pp.923–9.

Wenner, A.M. (1964) 'Sound communication in honey bees'. *Scientific American*, 210, pp. 116–24.

Wenzlaff, R.M. and Wegner, D.M. (2000) 'Thought suppression', *Annual Review of Psychology*, 51, pp.59–91.

Wertsch, J.V. (1985) 'Adult–child interaction as a source of self-regulation in children', in S.R. Yussen (ed.) *The Growth of Reflection in Children*, Madison, Wisconsin: Academic Press, pp.69–97.

West, M.J. and King, A.P. (1988) 'Female visual displays affect the development of male song in the cowbird' *Nature*, 334, pp.244–6.

Whinnery, J. E. (1997) 'Psychophysiologic correlates of unconsciousness and near-death experiences' *Journal of Near-Death Studies*, 18, 231–258Whitson, J. A. and Galinsky, A. D. (2008) Lacking control increases illusory pattern recognition. *Science*, 322, 115–117.

Whiten, A. and Byrne, R.W. (1988) *Machiavellian Intelligence: Social Expertise and the Evolution of Intellect in Monkeys, Apes, and Humans*, Oxford: Clarendon Press.

Whiting, B. and Whiting, J.W.M. (1975) *Children of Six Cultures*, Cambridge, MA: Harvard University Press.

Whiting, B. and Pope Edwards, C. (1988) *Children of Different Worlds: The formation of social behaviour*, Cambridge, Mass: Harvard University Press.

Whiting, J.W. (1966) *Six Cultures Series 1: Field Guide for a Study of Socialization*, New York: Wiley.

Whitson, J.A and Galinsky, A.D. (2008), 'Lacking control increases illusory pattern perception', *Science*, 322 (5898), pp.115–7.

Widyanto, L. and Griffiths, M.D. (2006) Internet addiction: Does it really exist? (Revisited), in J. Gackenbach (ed.), *Psychology and the Internet: Intrapersonal, Interpersonal and Transpersonal Applications* (2nd edn), New York: Academic Press, pp.141–1163.

Wierzbicki, M. (1985) 'Reasoning errors and belief in the paranormal' *Journal of Social Psychology*, 125, 489–494.

Wilde, G.J.S. (1993) 'Effects of mass media communications on health and safety habits: An overview of issues and evidence', *Addiction*, 88, pp.983–996.

Will, K.E., Porter, B.E., Geller, E.S. and DePasquale, J.P. (2005) 'Is television a health and safety hazard? A cross-sectional analysis of at-risk behavior on primetime television', *Journal of Applied Social Psychology*, 35, pp.198–22

Willenbring, M.S., Levine, A.S. and Morley, J.E. (1986) 'Stress-induced eating and food preference in humans: A pilot study', *International Journal of Eating Disorders*, 5, pp.855–64.

Williams, G.C., Grow, V.M., Freedman, Z.R., Ryan, R.M. and Deci, E.L. (1996) 'Motivational predictors of weight loss and weight loss maintenance', *Journal of Personality and Social Psychology*, 70, pp.115–26.

Williams, L. M. and Irwin, H. J. (1991) 'A study of paranormal belief, magical ideation as an index of schizotypy, and cognitive style' *Personality and Individual Differences*, 12, 1339–1348.

Williams, T.M. (1986) 'The Impact of Television: A Natural Experiment in Three Settings', in I. Taylor (ed) *A and AS Level Active Psychology*, Harlow: Pearson Education Limited, p.837.

Wills, C. (1998) *Children of Prometheus: The accelerating pace of human evolution*, Reading MA: Perseus Books.

Wilson, B.J. (2008) 'Media and children's aggression, fear and altruism', *Future of Children*, 18(1), pp.87–118.

Wilson, K. and French, C. C. (2006) 'The relationship between susceptibility to false memories, dissociativity, and paranormal belief and experience' *Personality and Individual Differences*, 41, 1493–1502.

Wilson, M. and Daly, M. (1985) 'Competitiveness, risk-taking and violence: the young male syndrome', *Ethology and Sociobiology*, 6, 59–73.

Wilson, M., Daly, M. and Daniele, A. (1995) 'Familicide: the killing of spouse and children', *Aggressive Behavior*, 21, pp.275–91.

Wilson, S. C., and Barber, T. X. (1983), 'The fantasy prone personality: Implications for understanding imagery, hypnosis, and parapsychological phenomena', in A. A. Sheikh (ed.) *Imagery: Current theory, research, and application*, New York: Wiley. pp.340–87.

Wimmer, H. and Perner, J. (1983) 'Beliefs about beliefs: Representation and constraining function of wrong beliefs in young children's understanding of deception', *Cognition*, 13 (1), pp.103–28.

Winerman, L. (2004) 'A second look at twin studies', *APA Monitor*, 35 (4), p.46.

Winge, E.S. (2003) 'Effects of a smoking prevention simulation on students' smoking attitudes', *American Journal of Health Studies*, 18, pp.173–176.

Wingfield, J.C., Hegner, R.E., Dufty A.M. Jr and Ball, G.F. (1990) 'The "Challenge Hypothesis": theoretical implications for patterns of testosterone secretion, mating systems, and breeding strategies', *American Naturalist*, 136, pp.829–46.

Winslow, D. (2004) 'Rights of passages and group bonding in the Canadian Airborne', *The Hazing Reader*, pp.147–71.

Wise, S. and Rapoport, J. (1989) 'Obsessive compulsive disorder: is it a basal ganglia dysfunction?', in J. Rapoport (ed), *Obsessive Compulsive Disorder in Children and Adolescents*, New York: American Psychiatric Press, pp.327–347.

Wiseman, R. (1997) *Deception and self-deception: Investigating psychics*. Amherst, NY: Prometheus.

Wiseman, R. and Greening, E. (2005) '"It's still bending": Verbal suggestion and alleged psychokinetic ability' *British Journal of Psychology*, 96, 115–127.

Wiseman, R., Greening, E. and Smith, M. (2003) 'Belief in the paranormal and suggestion in the séance room' *British Journal of Psychology*, 94, 285–297.

Wiseman, R. and O'Keeffe, C. (2001) 'Accuracy and replicability of anomalous after-death communication across highly skilled mediums: A critique' *The Paranormal Review*, 19, 3–6

Wiseman, R., Smith, M. D. and Kornbrot, D. (1996) 'Assessing possible sender-to-experimenter acoustic leakage in the PRL autoganzfeld' *Journal of Parapsychology*. 60, 97–128.

Witte, K., Berkowitz, J., Cameron, K. and Lillie, J. (1998) 'Preventing the spread of genital warts: Using fear appeals to promote self-protective behaviors', *Health Education and Behavior*, 25, pp.571–85.

Wober, J.B., Reardon, G. and Fazel, S. (1987) 'Personality Character Aspirations and Patterns of Viewing Among Children', in I. Taylor (ed) *A and AS Level Active Psychology*, Harlow: Pearson Education Limited, p.838.

Wolfgang, M.E. and Ferracuti, E. (1967) *The Subculture of Violence: Towards an Integrated Theory in Criminology*, London: Tavistock Publications.

Wolitzky, D.L. and Eagle, M.N. (1990) 'Psychotherapy', in A.S. Bellack and M. Hersen (eds) *Handbook of Comparative Treatments for Adult Disorders*, New York: Wiley, pp.123–143.

Wolpe, J. (1958) *Psychotherapy by Reciprocal Inhibition*, Stanford, CA: Stanford University Press.

Wong, D.F., Wagner, H.N., Tune, L.E., Dannals, R.F., Pearlson, G.D. and Links, J.M. (1986) 'Positron emission tomography reveals elevated D2 dopamine receptors in drug-naive schizophrenics', *Science*, 234, pp.1558–62.

Wood, D.J. and Middleton, D.J. (1975) 'A study of assisted problem solving', *British Journal of Psychology*, 66, pp.181–91.

Wood, D.J., Bruner, J.S. and Ross, G. (1976) 'The role of tutoring in problem solving', *Journal of Child Psychology and Psychiatry*, 17 (2), pp.89–100.

Wood, S.J., Yucel, M., Velakoulis, D., Phillips, L.J., Yung, A.R., Brewer, W., McGorry, P.D. and Pantelis, C. (2005) 'Hippocampal and anterior cingulated morphology in subjects at ultra-high risk for psychodid: the role of family history of psychotic illness', *Schizophrenia Research*, 75, pp.295–301.

Wood, R.T.A. and Griffiths, M.D. (2004) 'Adolescent lottery and scratchcard players: Do their attitudes influence their gambling behaviour?' *Journal of Adolescence*, 27, pp.467–475.

Wood, W. and Eagly, A.H. (2002) 'A cross-cultural analysis of the behaviour of women and men: Implications for the origins of sex differences', *Psychological Bulletin*, 128, pp.699–727.

Wood, W. and Eagly, A.H. (2007) 'An evolutionary biosocial theory of human mating' in S. Gangestad and J.A. Simpson (eds) *The evolution of mind: Fundamental questions and controversies*, New York: Guilford, pp.383–90.

Woodruff, G. and Premack, D. (1979) 'Intentional communication in the chimpanzee: The development of deception', *Cognition*, 7, pp.333–62.

Woodruff, P.W.R., Wright, I.C., Shuriquie, N., Russouw, H., Rushe, T., Howard, R.J., Graves, M., Bullmore, E.T. and Murray, R.M. (1997) 'Structural brain abnormalities in male schizophrenics reflect fronto-temporal dissociation', *Psychological Medicine*, 27, pp.1257–66.

Woolgar, S. (1988) *Science: The very idea*, London: Routledge.

Worell, J. and Remer, P. (1992) *Feminist Perspectives in Therapy*, Chichester: Wiley.

Workman, L. and Reader, W. (2008) *Evolutionary Psychology: An introduction* (2nd edn) Cambridge: Cambridge University Press, pp.373–7.

Wortman, C.B. and Brehm, J.W. (1975) 'Responses to uncontrollable outcomes: an integration of the reactance theory and the learned helplessness model', in L. Berkowitz (ed) *Advances in Social Psychology*, New York: Academic Press.

Wrangham, R. and Peterson, D. (1996) *Demonic Males: Apes and the origins of human violence*, Boston: Houghton Mifflin.

Xiaohe, X. and Whyte, M.K. (1990) 'Love matches and arranged marriages: A Chinese replication', *Journal of Marriage and the Family*, 52, (3), pp.709–822.

Yalom, I.D., Green, R. and Fisk, N. (1973) 'Prenatal exposure to female hormones: Effect on psychosexual development in boys', in G.C. Davidson and J.M. Neale (eds) *Abnormal Psychology*, New York: John Wiley and Sons, p.383.

Yamagishi, T. (2002) *Big-hearted Japanese: Illusion of Cultural Collectivism*, Tokyo: Nippon Keizai Shinbunsha.

Yang, S.Y. and Sternberg, R.J. (1997) 'Taiwanese Chinese people's conceptions of intelligence' *Intelligence*, 25, pp.21–36.

Yaryura-Tobias, J.E. and Neziroglu, F.A. (1997) *Obsessive-compulsive disorder spectrum,* Washington, DC: American Psychiatric Press.

Yerkes, R.M. and Dodson, J.D. (1908) 'The relation of strength of stimuli to rapidity of habit-formation', *Journal of Comparative Neurology and Psychology*, 18, pp.459–82.

Yin, R.K. (1969) 'Looking at upside-down faces', *Journal of Experimental Psychology*, 81, pp.141–5.

Yonas, A. (1981) 'Infants' responses to optical information for collision', in R.N. Aslin, J.R. Alberts and M.R. Peterson (eds) *Development of Perception: Psychobiological Perspectives,* Vol. 2, *The Visual System,* New York: Academic Press.

Yonas, A. and Owsley, C. (1987) 'Development of visual space perception', in P. Salapatek and L. Cohen (eds) *Handbook of Infant Perception,* Vol. 2, *From Perception to Cognition,* Orlando: Academic Press.

Yonas, A., Farr, M. and O'Connor, A. (2001) 'Seven- but not five-month-old infants extract depth from cast shadows', *Journal of Vision*, 1 (3), p.389a.

Youn, S.F., Faber, R.J. and Shah, D.V. (2000) 'Restricting gambling and the third-person effect', *Psychology and Marketing*, 17, pp.633–649.

Young, A.W., Hay, D.C. and Ellis, A.W. (1985) 'The faces that launched a thousand slips: everyday difficulties and errors in recognising people', *British Journal of Psychology,* 76, pp.495–523.

Young, A.W., Hellawell, D. and Hay, D.C. (1987) 'Configural information in face perception', *Perception*, 10, pp.747–759.

Young, A.W., Newcombe, F., deHaan, E.H.F., Small, M. and Hau, D.C. (1993) 'Face perception after brain injury', *Brain*, 116, pp.941–59.

Young, B. (1990) *Children and Television Advertising*, Oxford: Clarendon.

Young, W.C., Goy, R.W. and Phoenix, C.H. (1964) 'Hormones and sexual behaviour', *Science*, 143, pp. 212–8.

Yum, Y-O. and Hara, K. (2005) 'Computer-mediated relationship development: a cross-cultural comparison', *Journal of Computer-Mediated Communication*, 11 (1).

Zahavi, A. (1975) 'Mate selection – a selection for a handicap', *Journal of Theoretical Biology*, 53, pp.205–14.

Zahavi, A. (1991) 'On the definition of sexual selection, Fisher's model, and the evolution of waste and of signals in general', *Animal Behaviour*, 42, pp.501–3.

Zahn-Waxler, C., Radke-Yarrow, M. and King, R.A. (1979) 'Child rearing and children's prosocial initiations toward victims of distress', *Child Development*, 50 (2), pp.319–30.

Zar, J.H. (1972) 'Significance testing of the Spearman rank correlation coefficient', *Journal of the American Statistical Association*, 67, pp.578–80.

Zeggini, E., Weedon, M.N., Lindgren, C.M. and 23 other colleagues (2007) 'Replication of genome-wide association signals in UK samples reveals risk loci for type 2 diabetes', *Science*, 316 (5829), pp.1336–41 (and *Erratum* in *Science*, 317 (5841), pp.1035–6).

Zerger, S. (2002) *Substance abuse treatment: What works for homeless people? A review of the literature*, Report for the National Health Care for the Homeless Council and HCH Clinicians Network Research Committee.

Zhou, J.N., Hoffman, M.A., Gooren, L. and Swaab, D.F. (1995) 'A sex difference in the human brain and its relation to transsexuality', *Nature*, 378, 6552, pp.68–70.

Ziegler, C.B., Dusek, J.B. and Carter, D.B. (1984) 'Self-concept and sex role orientation: An investigation of multidimensional aspects of personality development in adolescence', *Journal of Early Adolescence*, 14, pp.25–39.

Zielinska, I.E. (1985) 'Verbal and non-verbal sequence in an educational television production: guidelines with attention to developmental cognitive processing styles', Unpublished paper, Concordia University: Montreal.

Zimbardo, P.G. (1973) 'On the ethics of intervention in human psychological research: With special reference to the Stanford prison experiment', *Cognition*, 2, pp.243–56.

Zimbardo, P.G (2007) *The Lucifer Effect: Understanding How Good People Turn Evil*, New York: Random House.

Zimbardo, P.G., Banks, P.G., Haney, C. and Jaffe, D. (1973) 'Pirandellian prison: the mind is a formidable jailor', *New York Times Magazine*, 8 April, pp.38–60.

Zimbardo, P.G., McDermott, M., Janz, J. and Metaal, N. (1995) *Psychology: A European Text*, London: HarperCollins.

Zitrin, C., Klein, D.F. and Werner, M.G. (1978) 'Behaviour therapy, supportive psychotherapy, imipramine and phobias', *Archives of General Psychiatry*, 35, pp.307–16.

Zitzmann, M. (2006) 'Testosterone and the brain', *The Aging Male*, 9(4), pp.195–9.

Zohar, J., Judge, R. and the OCD paroxetine study investigators (1996) 'Paroxetine vs. clomipremine in the treatment of obsessive-compulsive disorder', *British Journal of Psychiatry*, 169, pp.468–74.

Zucker, I. (1976) 'Light, behaviour and biologic rhythms', *Hospital Practice*, 11, pp.83–91.

Zucker, K.J. and Bradley, S.J. (1995) *Gender identity disorder and psychosexual problems in children and adolescents,* New York: Guilford Press.

Zuckerman, M. (1984) 'Sensation seeking: a comparative approach to a human trait', *Behavioural and Brian Sciences*, 7, pp.413–471.

Zung, W.W.K. (1965) 'A self-rating depression scale', *Archives of General Psychiatry*, 12, pp.63–70.

Zusne, L. and Jones, W. H. (1989) *Anomalistic psychology: A study of magical thinking.* 2nd ed. Hillsdale, NJ: Lawrence Erlbaum Associates.

Index